MW01040882

Advanced Torts

Cases and Materials

FOURTH EDITION

Peter B Kutner
HUGH ROFF PROFESSOR OF LAW
THE UNIVERSITY OF OKLAHOMA

Osborne M. Reynolds, Jr.
MAURICE H. MERRILL DISTINGUISHED SCHOLAR
AND PROFESSOR OF LAW EMERITUS
THE UNIVERSITY OF OKLAHOMA

CAROLINA ACADEMIC PRESS
Durham, North Carolina

ISBN 978-1-61163-301-6
LCCN 2012950117

Carolina Academic Press
700 Kent Street
Durham, North Carolina 27701
Telephone (919) 489-7486
Fax (919) 493-5668
www.cap-press.com

Printed in the United States of America

Summary of Contents

Table of Contents

Table of Cases

Preface

The first-year Torts course is a fixture of American legal education. This course is primarily concerned with tort remedies for personal injury and property damage. Most of the torts concerned with intangible harm are never examined. They cannot be, in the hours allotted to the first-year course. Thus, students are never exposed to such major subjects as defamation, the rights of privacy and publicity, harm to family relationships, malicious prosecution, interference with common law civil rights, injurious falsehood, liability for economic loss, interference with contract, misappropriation of trade secrets, unfair competition and other business torts. For these subjects—now the principal "growth areas" of tort liability—one or more courses for upperclass students must be offered.

This book is designed primarily for an Advanced Torts course addressing the subjects mentioned above. It is also appropriate for courses and seminars on economic torts (or business torts), using Chapters 2, 3, 4 and the first section of Chapter 5; defamation and privacy, using Chapters 5 and 6; and the family and tort law, using Chapter 1. None of the casebooks published for the first-year course is suitable for these purposes—hence the need for an Advanced Torts casebook.

The influence of Dean Leon Green, who introduced a casebook on "injuries to relations" in 1940, must be acknowledged. His concept of injuries to relations, which encompasses all the subjects covered in our book, is outlined in the introductory chapter. Some theories of tort liability for economic harm, such as misrepresentation, tortious breach of contract and wrongful discharge from employment, do not involve interference with a "relational interest" and are not addressed in this book. Practical reasons for their exclusion are the impossibility of covering both these torts and a good variety of other "advanced torts" in a single course and the likelihood that they will be addressed in other courses, such as Remedies.

The format of the book is the familiar one of principal cases followed by textual notes. The materials emphasize the facts and decisions of reported cases rather than secondary sources, such as law review commentaries. The principal cases have been substantially edited. Deletions of text, other than citations and footnotes, are indicated by ellipses. Editors' footnotes are followed by "[Ed.]."

Apart from subject-matter, the main respect in which this book differs from other casebooks is the inclusion of cases from outside the United States. They are included for the same reasons as American cases: their roles as legal precedents and value for instructional purposes. In addition, use of non-American cases and treatises makes the point that for many subjects, including Torts, the law is "common," not "American," and cases and literature from other countries with common law legal systems are sources of law and legal analysis for the United States.

This involves more than noting that American law and the law of other places once within the British Empire have foundations in the common law of England, or making references to old, familiar English cases. It means that it is necessary for Americans to undertake research of modern law and literature from common law jurisdictions outside the United States and utilize the results of this research in writing, teaching and practice. It strikes us as strange that practitioners and academics will spare no effort to find some precedent in the lower courts of distant American states but ignore the possibility that there are relevant decisions by such eminent courts as the (English) Court of Appeal, Supreme Court of Canada and High Court of Australia.

We wish to express our appreciation to all of the many persons who assisted and encouraged us in the production of the present edition and previous editions of this book. For the present edition we particularly acknowledge the efforts of the Faculty Support Staff of the University of Oklahoma College of Law; the librarians and personnel of the University of Oklahoma Law Library, the library of the Max Planck Institute for Comparative and International Private Law, and other libraries at which research for the book was conducted; and Keith Sipe, Linda Lacy and staff of Carolina Academic Press.

We thank the Richard-Wagner-Museum, Photofest, the Berkshire Record Office, the Special Collections/Archives of the University Library of the University of Louisiana at Monroe, Professor William M. Roberts of the University of Memphis School of Law, Peppi Marchello of The Good Rats, Theodore G. Gertz, Esq., Carl Ketner, Director of Technology of the University of Oklahoma College of Law, and Professor Darin Fox, Director of the University of Oklahoma Law Library, for providing photographs and images used as illustrations in the book. Specific credits appear with each photograph. Excerpts from the Restatement of Torts are Copyright 1934, 1938, 1939 by The American Law Institute. Excerpts from the Restatement (Second) of Torts are Copyright 1965, 1977, 1979 by The American Law Institute. Excerpts from the Restatement of Unfair Competition are Copyright 1995 by The American Law Institute. Excerpts from the Restatement of the Law Governing Lawyers are Copyright 2000 by The American Law Institute. Reprinted with the permission of The American Law Institute. All rights reserved. Basic Concepts: Persons, Property, Relations, by Leon Green, is Copyright 1938 by the American Bar Association. Reprinted with permission from ABA Journal, The Lawyer's Magazine.

P.B.K.
O.M.R.

Advanced Torts

Introduction

Leon Green, Basic Concepts: Persons, Property, Relations
24 American Bar Association Journal 65 (1938)*

The common law has developed to a very large degree around the interests of person and property. The early common law actions, for example, were devoted primarily to the protection of these interests against physical harms and appropriation. As they have expanded and as the harms to which they may be subjected have become more subtle, the common law too has expanded and grown more subtle. In the meanwhile, through the action on the case and its successor, the code action on the facts, with the assistance of equitable principles, an entirely new group of interests, namely, the interests a person may have in his *relations with other persons*, has been recognized and given protection. But in a society so active and complex it has been difficult to keep distinct these basic concepts of *personality, property and relations*.

The confusion of interests of personality, property and relations is due in part at least to the conflict between law and equity. In the familiar case of *Gee v. Pritchard* (1818) [2 Swans. 403] the court restrained the publication of certain personal letters written by plaintiff to defendant; in *Abernethy v. Hutchinson* (1825) [3 L.J. Ch. 209, Hall & T. W. 28] the court restrained the publication of certain notes taken of plaintiff's oral lectures. In both of these cases the subject matter involved in one sense could be viewed as nothing more than the emotional or intellectual sparks given off by the personalities of the respective plaintiffs. In another sense the conduct of the defendants could be viewed as an interference with plaintiff's relations with other persons. In no legitimate sense could the interests of the plaintiff be viewed as property. The plaintiffs had done nothing to set aside their creations as property. The casual letters and spoken words found their value in their close connection with the personalities of the respective plaintiffs and in their effect upon the relations existing between plaintiffs and other persons. But the chancellors having limited their jurisdiction to property, found it convenient to so characterize these interests in order to give the plaintiffs the protection they deserved. The holdings have been followed in later and analogous cases, but most courts have been sensible enough to recognize that they were not dealing with property interests. . . .

On a parity with both the interests of personality and property are those of relations with other persons — relational interests. When, for example, Jones and Smith by agreement combine their efforts in an enterprise, there is something here identified as a relation brought into existence in addition to the two personalities. That relation incidentally gives each personality power and range beyond that of either. If in their enterprise they combine the resources of lands, chattels and money, they too are bound by the newly created relation. It is as distinct from their persons and property as the latter are distinct from each other. So is the protection that is required for it.

Relational interests are not new to the law. They have long been a very important element in the legal order. But they have never been clearly identified, and the value of the concept and its ramifications have never been appreciated. Relational interests are not infrequently called property interests, and much of the protection which has been extended them by law has been under the guise of protecting property. This, in addition to the long standing conflict between courts of law and equity, has also doubtless been due to the desire to bring them within the peculiar sanctity extended to property under the due process clause and other clauses of our national and state constitutions. But it should not be necessary to invoke the protection of property for these interests. They are entitled to protection for their own sake, for the relational interests of present day society in their aggregate are perhaps as valuable as the aggregate of physical property. Some of them are modern society's substitute for property. They give to property much of its value, and add immeasurably to the power which personalities possess. They demand for their control and protection the projection of law far beyond that required for either person or property.

There are several groups of these relations which are easily recognized. First is the broad group of *family relations*; second, *trade relations*, made up of employment relations on the one hand and general commercial relations on the other; third, *political and professional relations*, yet largely in their formative state; and fourth, *general social relations*.

What are the characteristics of these relations that set them off from the interests of personality and property? Generally, they do not have the attributes of physical things. Their value lies in the fact that one person has an interest in the welfare and conduct of some other person. Normally, hurts to such an interest do not involve physical hurt to the person who has the interest, or to his property, and when they do so result little protection is extended against them. For example, a person may be defamed. The charges against him may react on his physical health, but few courts have allowed any protection for this hurt to the personality. The defamatory hurt is to his standing in the eyes of his business associates, his neighbors, or people generally. His social, family, professional, business, or political relations, or perhaps all of them, may be hurt by such defamatory charges, and it is against such hurts that protection is given. As another example, the title to a person's property is slandered. The loss of its sale may seriously impair his fortune. His property itself is not hurt, but he may have recovery for the hurt done his relation with a particular buyer or to his relation with buyers in general. As a further example, plaintiff may have a contract as the representative of an industry to market its products in a certain locality. A third person induces the industry to breach the contract. Plaintiff suffers no hurt to person or property for which he is given any protection against the third person but for the hurt done his relation which has been destroyed or appropriated he may have recovery against such person....

But it is not the concept of the relational interest *as between the parties to the relation* with which we are concerned in this discussion. It is the relation as it may interfere with or in turn be interfered with by third parties. It is in this particular that relations differ so widely from person and property. *What protection is there to such interests as against the hurts done by third parties? What immunities have those who have such relations against the hurts which they incidentally cause third persons?* These inquiries do not involve the simple two-party situations found in the protection of person and property. They are always three-party situations; a relation which necessarily implies two persons, and a third party who interferes with that relation. It is thus that relational interests demand such different treatment in the protection given under the law.

Let us briefly consider the more important relations. In the group of *family relations*, actions for alienation of affections, criminal conversation, seduction and abduction, physical injury to children, parents and spouses, the wrongful death of some member of a family, failure to deliver death messages and other conduct interfering with the relations between living members of a family and a deceased member, interference with the relations enjoyed by beneficiaries under wills and insurance policies, defamation of one of the spouses, and other like cases, are all the product of the recognition given by law to the interest of one member of the family. Except in rare instances, these interests have not been identified as property interests. They transcend any notion of property. The actions for their protection are relatively new actions and are still little better understood by lawyers than by laymen. Some of them are treated as anomalies, and no one of them has reached a maturity of development.

General social relations have recognition of long standing. These relations have none of the earmarks of either personality or property. They give substance to the thing we call *reputation*. They have not infrequently been thought of as interests of personality, but a person's standing in the eyes of his neighbors, his friends and other people generally is very definitely a relational interest. Their value in some instances has been so great that very able lawyers have been tempted to call them property. But courts of equity in this country have withstood all attempts to invoke their protection in behalf of such relations. Social relations, as is true of other relations, are protected by a very distinctive type of common law known as libel and slander. Practically speaking, they have no other protection. Protection to them, like the protection given the relations of the family group, is relatively new and immature. For several centuries both groups of relations were protected, if at all, by the ecclesiastical courts.

Of growing importance are *political and professional relations*. With the development of democratic society and numerous professional groups, the relational interests created thereby have demanded recognition and protection. The right to vote is one of the earliest political relations to be recognized. It is still relatively young, and the protection afforded it is still inadequate. The protection extended to this group of relations is through the recognition given the common interests of the members of a group. The members of groups of all types — political, professional and otherwise — require freedom of action and communication within the group in order to make the group effective. The recognition of these privileges has given rise to important immunities for the hurts done both outsiders and other members of the group. The recognition of a common interest in the political group, for example, gives a wide immunity to public officials in the performance of their official functions. In the case of judges, legislators, and high executives, immunity for all practical purposes is complete, while in the case of lesser officials it may be quite limited. With respect to non-official groups the immunity is always limited. As an antidote, however, to these privileges and immunities, corresponding privileges and immunities are given critics, who also represent the interests of the public. The idea involved is strikingly similar to the adage that fleas are good for dogs. Public officials, teachers, lawyers, medical men, dramatic and other artists, and in fact all those who touch the public's interests, are legitimate prey of the critic — reporter, columnist, and publisher. Here is involved the difficult subject of freedom of speech and press — the public forum, the newspaper, periodical, radio, and other forms of publication. The protection given relations and interests subject to hurts inflicted through such activities is as yet poorly defined. The interests involved have none of the attributes of property except that they are valuable. They call for peculiar treatment by courts as well as other agencies of government.

But of transcendent importance among relational interests are the *relations of trade* around which is built the structure of our modern order. Trade relations for the most part are based upon express contract, but not entirely so. For example, the relational interests of a business may rest largely in contract, but they may also rest in its good will which is found in the potentialities of future dealings. Likewise, labor relations may rest upon contract, but the great bulk of such relations rests fundamentally upon the needs and customs of industry rather than upon formal contract....

... Society has advanced beyond the state of single personalities and physical property forms; group activities call for something more than barter and sale and even symbolic exchange of property. The answer has been found in the development of relations, and they have given a range to business activities far beyond the range that property could have ever given. They have the advantage of property in their capacity for multiplication and adaptability, as witness the corporate form of organization. They are a distinct form of wealth, and to call them property is to confuse them with other forms of wealth. They require treatment different from that required by property on the part of the people who are dependent upon them, and on the part of the courts and other agencies of government. They are a new type of interest. They tie together modern society and make it possible to utilize the natural resources of property and invention to the end that there may be more activities and a better balanced existence for a constantly growing population. It is the press of these almost infinite relations which is making so many new problems for government and for the legal profession. They can not be subjected to the principles, rules and formulas which have been developed for person and property. They demand treatment peculiar to themselves.

There are many difficult problems in the field of trade relations. Among them are those that arise out of the relations between the owners and managers of industry and those who operate its physical processes. Enormously complex industrial relations are over-simplified by the terms capital and labor, or employer and employee. Having so simplified them, we expect the property law of land and chattels and the tort law of master and servant to work the legal adjustments of their conflicts. When they fail, we think that government has failed. And it has, because the law invoked was not designed for any such usage....

... [The courts'] power to adjust labor disputes is always incidental to something else — incidental to the keeping of the peace, protection of person and property against violence and fraud, or protection against interference with other trade relations. After a century of struggle the limitations upon the means either group can employ to further its ends are by no means definitely outlined. In this mass struggle for economic freedom, we still suffer from ill-timed intrusions of both police and courts....

We have made a beginning too long delayed in the Norris-LaGuardia Act, the Railway Labor Act and the Wagner Act. Although it may take years of painstaking efforts to mold new processes into workable law, when that is done there should be no place left for strikes, pickets, boycotts, sit-downs, lockouts, company unions, detectives, bribery, bombs, rackets, machine guns or the other weapons which have been utilized in the industrial struggle. Government has a definite place in providing adequate protection for the relations of both the capital and labor groups. Instead of constituting the explosion points of the social order, as at present, they should become its most conservative and stabilizing influences.

What is true of industrial relations is true in part of the relations of other classes of traders. The protection and control of those intricate institutions of finance — banks, holding companies, investment and personal trusts, insurance companies — their relations inter sese, as well as their relations with their customers, investors, borrowers, beneficiaries, require law far different from that which concerns chattels and lands. The protection and control of those who produce wealth from agriculture, mines and natural resources of other types with respect to their relations with each other and their relations with their processors and dealers, also demand many new legal forms. The same is true as to those general traders who market, or supply the facilities for marketing the products of industry, invention, agriculture, and mines....

Consider also the matter of fair competition among traders, the protection of consumers against inferior qualities and excessive prices, the regulation of the issuance and sale of securities, the security of unemployed and aged persons, the control of public service companies and other such group interests. The protection the interests here involved require is equally as difficult to provide as is their control. Trade relations present exacting problems for government. Given free reign traders take over government; given unintelligent government, the trade upon which all of us are so dependent may be greatly impaired if not destroyed.

Beginning about half a century ago, government began to do the only thing within its power to meet the demands made upon it by the relations growing out of trade. It fell back upon the administrative agency, the first line defense of Anglo-American government. The list of important national agencies roughly represents the relational interests of trade which I have enumerated: The Federal Reserve Bank, The Interstate Commerce Commission, The Federal Trade Commission, The Securities and Exchange Commission, The National Labor Relations Board, The Boards provided by the Railway Labor Act, The Federal Communications Commission, The Board of Tax Appeals, The Social Security Board, and the more important bureaus of the departments of agriculture and commerce. Many of their counterparts are found in the states....

... As long as human beings are inventive enough to create new forms of wealth and develop new activities, there will be constant necessity for adjusting them to the current order. There are always those who will refuse to recognize intruding legal principles, much as the older members of a club accept its new members with ill grace, or as the established wealthy resent the newly rich, or as classical intellectuals lift an eyebrow at recent pretenders. As the new club member must assume meekness, as the newly rich must go in for culture, and as the recent intellectual must bow down to learning, if recognition is to be readily won, so any new legal interest or new legal principle must disguise itself in an old form before the legal profession will give it recognition. That may be why those who have sought protection for relational interests have done so in the name of property.... But why should the law and lawyers continue to ignore what has become so great a part of everyday life?

Chapter 1

Family Relations

Section 1. Injuries to Family Members

A. Spouse

———

Guy v. Livesey
Court of King's Bench
(1618) Cro. Jac. 501, 79 Eng. Rep. 428,
2 Rolle 51, 81 Eng. Rep. 653

Trespass of assault and battery; for that the defendant did assault, beat, and wound the plaintiff; *necnon* for that he assaulted and beat the wife of the plaintiff, *per quod consortium uxoris suae* for three days *amisit*. The defendant pleaded not guilty; and it was found against him in both ... and the damages given, for that the plaintiff's wife went with the defendant and lived with him in a suspicious manner. And it was now moved in arrest of judgment, that the husband ought not to join the battery of his wife with the battery which was done to himself; and he cannot have an action for the battery of his wife, but ought to join his wife with him in the action; for the damage done to the wife, she ought to have (if she survives her husband); and so the defendant may be twice punished for one and the same battery, if the plaintiff here should recover; for this recovery of the husband shall not bar her of bringing her action, if she survive him. Wherefore if the husband will bring the action, he ought to have joined his wife with him.

But all the Court held, that the action was well brought; for the action is not brought in respect of the harm done to the wife, but it is brought for the particular loss of the husband, for that he lost the company of his wife, which is only a damage and loss to himself, for which he shall have this action, as the master shall have for the loss of his servant's service....

———

Guevin v. Manchester Street Railway
Supreme Court of New Hampshire
78 N.H. 289, 99 A. 298 (1916)

[Mrs. Guevin, while boarding the defendant's electric car, tripped over the protruding fender, which she did not see, fell, and was injured. She brought an action for her injuries, which resulted in verdict for defendant. Her husband then brought suit for loss of his wife's services and society.]

PEASLEE, J....

It is also urged that a nonsuit should have been ordered upon the ground that the husband has now no action for the loss of consortium caused by injuries negligently inflicted upon his wife. It was held otherwise in Booth v. Railway, 73 N.H. 529, 63 Atl. 578; but in view of the facts that one of the authorities then cited by the court has since been overruled (Feneff v. Railroad, 203 Mass. 278, 89 N.E. 436), and that the Connecticut court has followed these later cases, the subject has been re-examined.

Two main reasons are stated in these last cases, and in argument here, for the position taken. It is said that the common-law action for injuries to the husband's right called the consortium was based upon loss of service, and that while other elements might be considered in aggravation of damages, they did not constitute a cause of action; that unless loss of service were shown no recovery could be had....

The action itself was per quod consortium amisit, not per quod servitium. Loss of service as the only basis of legal right was then recognized and discussed in cases for the seduction of a child or servant, but nowhere is such a statement found as to the right of a husband to recover for injuries to his wife. Undoubtedly the term "consortium" included service, but it also included society, comfort, and the sexual rights. In no early case is there a suggestion that any one of these is superior to any other as a basis for legal redress....

But if loss of service is essential the cause of action has not been destroyed since some right to services still remains in the husband. As to this it is urged that the husband's right is not now entitled to protection in this class of cases because the right is merely one to receive services voluntarily rendered, that the wife is not now obliged to work for him; and as he cannot demand her services, neither should he be allowed to complain of being deprived of them. But he had no higher right at common law. While the books abound in statements that the wife's services are the husband's, and that it is her duty to render them to him, he had no legal remedy if she chose to refuse performance of that duty. His legal right as against her was to such service as she chose to perform for him and to the proceeds of such service as she chose to perform for others. This right was based entirely upon an unenforceable obligation upon her part. His right to enforce obedience by personal chastisement had disappeared long before the adoption of the married women's acts.... For her refusal to perform there was no remedy. Notwithstanding this, the husband has always been entitled to recover from third persons whose wrongful acts rendered her less capable of performance....

... [I]t is argued that a new distinction should now be made between the husband's right to recover for intentional and unintentional injuries to his marital rights. It is conceded that some right still exists; but, because the original right has been reduced by the married women's acts, it is held that the right to recover for a negligent injury to it has been taken away....

The married women's acts do not deal with the remedies of which the husband may avail himself. So far as his rights still exist he has all the remedy he ever had....

It is further urged that as to the incidents of consortium other than service the common law gave a remedy for their destruction, but none for their impairment. On its face the proposition seems at variance with the general policy of the law. If a husband is entitled to his wife's affections and to recover compensation from him who steals them, reason and justice seem to require that he should be entitled to damages from one whose illegal efforts in the same direction are partly successful. Indeed it might be a difficult matter to define what was meant by total alienation....

... The husband is entitled to the whole of his wife's marital affection, and to the whole of such society and comfort as her physical state and mental attitude render her capable of affording him. He who steals any substantial part of that affection, or disables her physically or mentally from rendering such aid and comfort, is guilty of an infringement of the husband's rights, and should be required to make compensation....

[It is argued] that if this action is sustained the defendant will be subjected to the payment of double damages. Since she can sue and be sued "as if she were unmarried", it is argued that her damages will be measured without regard to her marital status. This involves a misconception of the true measure of her damages....

... "If she is interfered with in her business transactions, and for that reason unable to earn what she otherwise would have earned, the damage is personal to her." Normile v. Company, 57 W. Va. 132, 49 S.E. 1030. But if she voluntarily performed services for her husband, the impairment of capacity "was his loss, and not that of his wife." Standen v. Railroad, 214 Pa. 189, 200, 63 Atl. 467....

The argument from the assumption that the wife will recover for all loss of capacity to earn money has no force here because the true rule is that she does not so recover. The aggregate amount of the verdicts recovered by the husband and wife on account of loss of her capacity for service is only equal to the total loss of capacity. What she recovers for he does not, and vice versa....

That the damages to this plaintiff could not have been foreseen by the defendant is not a defense. The test in cases for negligence is to inquire whether the resulting damages was "a direct consequence of the defendants' tortious act, without regard to whether the particular damage could or could not have been foreseen by them." Whittemore v. Railroad, 77 N.H. 61, 63, 86 Atl. 824, 825....

Exceptions overruled.

Notes

1. The common law recognized an action in a master whose servant was injured by a third person's tort and thereby rendered unfit to serve the master. See pp. 212–215, infra. From this grew an action in the husband whose wife was injured. The first principal case and Hyde v. Scyssor, (1620) Cro. Jac. 538, 79 Eng. Rep. 462 (K.B.), are among the earliest reported authorities. Were the courts right to accept the analogy between husband and wife and master and servant? When loss of services or consortium was caused by death of the servant or wife, no action arose. Baker v. Bolton, p. 51, infra (wife); Admiralty Commissioners v. S.S. Amerika, [1917] A.C. 38 (H.L.) (servant). This gap in the common law has been filled (partially) by the enactment of wrongful death statutes. See pp. 51–56, infra.

2. The older emphasis was on loss of services, and this was thought indispensable to the husband's action. Cf. Hall v. Hollander, p. 22 , infra (action for injury to child). "Services" came to be interpreted broadly so as to include the wife's general helpfulness, assistance and support. See Marri v. Stamford Street Railroad Co., 84 Conn. 9, 78 A. 582 (1911); Selleck v. City of Janesville, 104 Wis. 570, 80 N.W. 944 (1899). In principle, the damages do not include loss of the injured spouse's contribution to plaintiff's business or

a joint business. That is derived from a business relationship rather than a family relationship. Jones v. Taylor, (1983) 27 Sask. R. 161 (Q.B.). See Redwing v. Moncravie, 131 Cal. App. 569, 21 P.2d 986 (1933). Cf. Burgess v. Florence Nightingale Hospital for Gentlewomen, p. 60, infra (wrongful death). But the distinction may not be observed in practice. See Wheaton v. Guthrie, 89 A.D.2d 809, 453 N.Y.S.2d 480 (1982); Toohey v. Hollier, (1955) 92 C.L.R. 618, 626; McCormick, Law of Damages 332 (1935).

3. Damages now are based substantially on loss of society, companionship and affection, including loss of sexual intercourse. Warner v. Great Atlantic & Pacific Tea Co., Inc., 583 So. 2d 61 (La. App. 1991); All v. John Gerber Co., 36 Tenn. App. 134, 252 S.W.2d 138 (1952); Ballard v. Lumbermens Mutual Casualty Co., 33 Wis. 2d 601, 148 N.W.2d 65 (1967). A commonly stated definition of consortium incorporates the three S's: services, society and sex. See Shreve v. Faris, 144 W. Va. 819, 111 S.E.2d 169 (1959). A wife has no duty in tort law to provide any of these things to her husband. Why should her husband be able to complain of their loss in a suit against a third party?

4. Can a plaintiff recover damages for loss of consortium on an allegation that divorce resulted from the injuries of the other spouse? Prill v. Hampton, 154 Wis. 2d 667, 453 N.W.2d 909 (Ct. App. 1990), review denied, 457 N.W.2d 323 (Wis. 1990), holds that damages are not to be awarded for post-divorce loss of consortium or "wrongful divorce." This followed, the court believed, from the rule that loss of consortium damages were available only to individuals married at the time of injury and from the state's abolition of actions for alienation of affections. Also, it would be difficult to establish the extent to which the failure of the marriage was caused by the injuries and inquiry into other possible causes would expose both former spouses to scrutiny of very personal matters. Accord, Parker v. Dzundza, [1979] Qd. R. 55 (Sup. Ct.), on analogy to the rule that damages for loss of consortium cannot extend beyond the duration of the marriage when defendant has caused the death of a spouse. See also Chizmar v. Mackie, 896 P.2d 196 (Alaska 1995).

5. "Married Women's Acts" granting married women rights to own property, make contracts, keep their own income, etc., were enacted by many jurisdictions in the nineteenth century. In some states, these acts were interpreted as abolishing the husband's action for loss of consortium. See Clark, Law of Domestic Relations in the United States 222–223, 273 (1st ed. 1968). A husband was sometimes permitted to recover actual expenses incurred in caring for his wife. See Erickson v. Buckley, 230 Mass. 467, 120 N.E. 126 (1918). Most courts have held that the husband's action survives the Married Women's Acts. See Birmingham Southern Railway Co. v. Lintner, 141 Ala. 420, 38 So. 363 (1904); Brahan v. Meridian Light & Railway Co., 121 Miss. 269, 83 So. 467 (1919). Under this view, the only change brought about by the acts is that the wife's earnings now belong to her, and any damages for harm to her earning capacity are now recoverable only in her own action. See Gregory v. Oakland Motor Car Co., 181 Mich. 101, 147 N.W. 614 (1914); Hannigan, Damages Recoverable by Husband for Injury to Wife, 16 Colum. L. Rev. 122 (1916); Holbrook, The Change in the Meaning of Consortium, 22 Mich. L. Rev. 1 (1923). Does this mean that a wife's household or child care services still belong to her husband and that when injury prevents a wife from performing these services it is the husband rather than the wife who is to be compensated? If so, does this make any difference to the aggregate liability of the tortfeasor?

6. The action of the injured spouse and the other spouse's action for loss of consortium are separate causes of action. A release of the primary tort action does not defeat a subsequent action for loss of consortium. See Jones v. Elliott, 551 A.2d 62 (Del. 1988); Shepherd v. Consumers Cooperative Association, 384 S.W.2d 635 (Mo. 1964); Annot., Injured Party's Release of Tortfeasors as Barring Spouse's Action for Loss of Consortium,

29 A.L.R.4th 1200 (1984). A judgment of no liability in the primary action may, how-ever, operate to bar the spouse's claim. Sisemore v. Neal, 236 Ark. 574, 367 S.W.2d 417 (1963); Bender v. Peay, 433 N.E.2d 788 (Ind. App. 1982). Contra, Stapleton v. Palmore, 250 Ga. 259, 297 S.E.2d 270 (1982); Kraut v. Cleveland Railway Co., 132 Ohio St. 125, 5 N.E.2d 324 (1936). See Annot., Judgment in Spouse's Action for Personal Injuries as Bind-ing, as Regards Loss of Consortium and Similar Resulting Damage, Upon Other Spouse Not a Party to the Action, 12 A.L.R.3d 933 (1967).

Neuberg v. Bobowicz

Supreme Court of Pennsylvania
401 Pa. 146, 162 A.2d 662 (1960)

EAGEN, Justice.

In a trespass action brought by her husband for injuries and pecuniary losses allegedly sustained by him [in an intersection collision], Mrs. Neuberg has joined as plaintiff and seeks recovery for the resultant loss to her of his "society, services and sexual compan-ionship." ...

... Does a married woman have a cause of action in Pennsylvania for the loss of her husband's consortium caused by the negligent act of a third party? The authorities else-where are many and conflicting....

... In Donoghue v. Consolidated Traction Co., 1902, 201 Pa. 181, 50 A. 952, we said: "There is no natural right in one person for damages for injury to another. At common law the husband had an action for damages for injury to the wife whereby he lost her ser-vices, because he had the right to her services, including her earnings. The right arose from the common-law relation of unity of person, the husband, as to personal property and services, being the person. But marriage is a civil contract, involving rights under the control of the lawmaking power. The legislature may sever the unity of person, and, as to property, the right to separate earnings of the wife, and the damages for personal injury to her, it has already done so to a very great extent. It would be but a step farther in the same direction to take away altogether the husband's action for loss of services of the wife."

... [T]he same question presented here has been ruled on by our lower courts, in only one of which ... was this issue decided favorably to the wife-plaintiff. The ... decision was caused to turn on the theory that "[w]hat is sauce for the gander is sauce for the goose." Even without a painstaking research into the "Game Laws" of this state, we will venture to say that, accepting the analogy, there can be no quarrel with that conclusion as a general proposition. But it is only after an historical inquiry is made into the ancient origins of the gander's sauce, as it were, and as it is applied to the situation at hand, that one can conclude, as we do, that either 1) the sauce was never a proper ingredient of the diet or 2) however indispensable it may have been in decades past, it has no place in that diet today. Be that as it may, it is in our opinion, today more than ever, just that: sauce.

... The roots which at one time, if ever, gave nurture and a legitimate birth to the hus-band's right to assert a claim for loss of consortium have long since wizened and died.... In effect, the woman spouse was her husband's chattel, his property. She owed him du-ties much the same as did a servant his master. If he by injury to her suffered a loss of some feudal service owing to him by her, he and he alone — for she was too inferior a subject to have any such right, much less the privilege to assert it — was allowed to sue to recover, just as he would sue for injuries done to his cattle.... The husband's right to recover on this theory is without present day justification.... "'[H]is action is a fossil from an earlier era. It is one of a group of archaic actions based on the notion that the paterfamilias was alone competent to sue for losses suffered by the family unit.... When to the husband's action, there is now added the wife's action for negligent injuries (which being emancipated she is entitled to bring) there is a danger of duplicating elements of damage. Ingenious efforts must be made to disentangle from the wife's recovery the [constituents] of the husband's cause of action. Indeed, *the emancipation argues for the restriction or abolition of these actions rather than their extension.'*" [Kronenbitter v. Washburn Wire Co., 4 N.Y.2d 524, 176 N.Y.S.2d 354, 151 N.E.2d 898]....

... [W]e feel, as did Lord Porter in Best v. Samuel Fox and Co., Ltd., [1952] A.C. 716, 728 when he said: "Even if it be conceded that the rights of husband and wife (in this respect) ought to be equalized, I agree with the Lord Chief Justice that today a husband's right of action for loss of his wife's consortium is an anomaly and see no good reason for extending it." We cannot assent to the argument that since the status of a married woman is now, in all other respects, so improved as to render her equal with her husband, that this, in itself, establishes her right to a cause of action for loss of consortium.... "[T]o grant the wife a right to so recover does not lift the wife to the status of her husband, but it reduces the husband to the outworn concept of the wife's lowly status. Rather than grant to the wife the right to damages for loss of consortium, the logical solution would be to terminate the husband's claim on the theory that the wife is no longer the servant and chattel." [Mlynek v. Yarnall, 19 Pa. Dist. & Co. R. 2d 333.]

Appellee argues that if we should grant the right to the wife there would follow attempts by others in an intimate relationship to assert similar causes of action. In short, it is contended that if a wife can recover for injuries to her husband, then others—children, dependent members of households, possibly even business partners—should perhaps also be allowed to sue to recover for the inconveniences to which they were put by the injury. Indicative of the efforts made by others to recover on this theory are the following cases.... Recovery was allowed in none.... It would appear, however, that, with few exceptions, the arguments used on behalf of a married person in a consortium suit against the negligent third party could be urged with no less validity in actions against responsible tortfeasors brought by or on behalf of infant children of an injured party.

The fact that recovery is allowed [a wife] for criminal conversation or alienation of affections presents a situation which is not analogous to the matter here at issue.... Said Cohen, L.J., in Best, supra, "In the enticement cases intentional infringement of the rights of the consort is an essential ingredient in the cause of action. The remedy in that case may therefore be treated as a natural extension of the principle.... Moreover, no injustice can be done to the defendant since, ex hypothesi, his action was malicious.... In cases such as the one before us, however, it is impossible to suggest any malice against the wife on the part of the defendant or any intentional interference with her right of consortium.... It seems to me, therefore, that it would be an extension of a line of cases in itself anomalous if we were, in such cases as the present, to recognize a right of action in a wife corresponding to that which the courts have recognized as vested in the husband.... True it is ... that this involves the recognition of a distinction between the respective rights of a husband and wife which is contrary to current opinion; but it has never been held that the wife has any right of servitium from the husband, and an extension of the principle to actions by the wife seems to me to involve real hardship on a defendant who will have already paid damages to the husband, in assessing which, allowance will, I think, have been made for the impairment of his ability to perform his obligation to support his wife." ... [W]e hold that a married woman has no cause of action ... for the loss of her husband's consortium caused by the negligent act of a third party.

[Affirmed. Bok, J., delivered a concurring opinion. Bell, J., concurred in the result.]

MUSMANNO, Justice (dissenting)....

No one can possibly question in enlightened America that the physical and mental companionship of her husband is a right possessed by every married woman. And it is a legal property, not only a moral blessing. It is that kind of property which entitles her to a severance of the marriage contract if he fails to abide by the vows undertaken at the altar rail. This vested prerogative is so firmly established in the married woman that if somebody steals away her husband's affection, society, fellowship and comfort, she may bring an action of alienation of affections against the invader of her personal realm.

If we allow, as we do, a wife to recover against the malefactor who robs from her the love and affection due her from her husband, why should she not be allowed to recover against the person who destroys the husband's capacity to give her the love, affection, and care which constitute the *res litigiosae* of an alienation of affections suit?

The Complaint filed in this case would indicate that the injuries sustained by Israel Neuberg have rendered him incapable to devote to his wife the society and companionship inherent in the marital relationship. It would appear that the disabilities suffered by the husband will deprive the wife of undoubtedly the most precious wealth that a wife could possess, namely, the sacred right to motherhood....

... Are we to understand from the decision rendered by this Court today that a wife may bring an action against any person who steals her pocket book, steps on her foot, or injures her dog, but she may not bring an action for the loss of her most valued privilege? ...

... A woman who has suffered a physical hurt which makes it impossible for her to bear children may recover because of that grave disablement. May she not recover when that disablement is inflicted on her through her husband? ...

... How does the Majority answer the query of how it can take two identical situations and make fish of one and fowl of another? How does it answer the inevitable question which arises: How can it deny sauce to the gander when it ladles it out overflowingly to the goose? The Majority does seek to answer the last question by saying that sauce has no place in the diet of today! It says more; it says that "sauce was never a proper ingredient of the diet."

I respectfully offer the suggestion that the decision of today has made a strange dish of the whole sacred matrimonial relationship. So far as legal recognition is concerned, it has taken all the romance out of married life; it has made of a married couple a simple business partnership. It says in effect that companionship means nothing, love is of no value, society is not recognized, the tender affection between husband and wife has no place in the chronicles of the law....

As a matter of history, the common law recognized woman's right to the consortium of her husband. The only reason she could not sue for the loss of it was the technical barrier presented by the legal fiction that husband and wife were one....

... "The husband owes the same degree of love, affection, felicity, etc., to the wife as she to him. He also owes the material service of support, but above and beyond that he renders other services as his mate's helper in her duties, as advisor and counselor, etc. Under such circumstances it would be a judicial fiat for us to say that a wife may not have an action for loss of consortium due to negligence." [Hitaffer v. Argonne Co., Inc., 87 U.S. App. D.C. 57, 183 F.2d 811, 819.] ...

Notes

1. Until 1950, a wife generally was denied an action for loss of consortium when a third person tortiously injured her husband. See Feneff v. New York Central & Hudson River Railroad Co., 203 Mass. 278, 89 N.E. 436 (1909); Annot., Wife's Right of Action for Loss of Consortium, 23 A.L.R.2d 1378 (1952). Some exceptions were recognized. Recovery was permitted with particular frequency in cases involving wrongful sale of liquor or narcotics to the husband. See Pratt v. Daly, 55 Ariz. 535, 104 P.2d 147 (1940) (liquor sold to husband known to be habitual drunkard); Flandermeyer v. Cooper, 85 Ohio St. 327, 98 N.E. 102 (1912) (continued sale of morphine to husband over protests of wife); Annot., Common Law Right of Action for Damage Sustained by Plaintiff in Consequence of Sale or Gift of Intoxicating Liquor or Habit Forming Drug to Another, 97 A.L.R.3d 528 §§ 5 & 8 (1980). Recovery by the wife occasionally was allowed when there was intentional harm to the husband. See Clark v. Hill, 69 Mo. App. 541 (1897) (husband driven insane). But see Krohn v. Richardson-Merrell, Inc., William S. Merrell Co. Division, 219 Tenn. 37, 406 S.W.2d 166 (1966), cert. denied, 386 U.S. 970 (1967). Courts often allowed a wife to recover medical and/or funeral expenses of her husband when she became liable for them. See Follansbee v. Benzenberg, 122 Cal. App. 2d 466, 265 P.2d 183 (1954); Hansen v. Hayes, 175 Or. 358, 154 P.2d 202 (1944).

2. Hitaffer v. Argonne Co., cited by the dissent in the principal case, was the first American case to allow a wife to recover for loss of consortium when her husband had been injured by negligence. Even after this, a number of cases denied an action to the wife. Most states eventually extended the action to both spouses. See Annot., Wife's Right of Action for Loss of Consortium, 36 A.L.R.3d 900 (1971); Annot., Measure and Elements of Damages in Wife's Action for Loss of Consortium, 74 A.L.R.3d 805 (1976). To afford a husband an action for loss of consortium but refuse an action to a wife now seems a denial of equal protection under the Fourteenth Amendment. See Karczewski v. Baltimore and Ohio Railroad Co., 274 F. Supp. 169 (N.D. Ill. 1967); Clem v. Brown, 3 Ohio Misc. 167, 207 N.E.2d 398 (C.P. 1965). Contra, Miskunas v. Union Carbide Corp., 399 F.2d 847 (7th Cir. 1968), cert. denied, 393 U.S. 1066 (1969).

3. The adoption of an equal rights amendment to the Pennsylvania Constitution required the Pennsylvania Supreme Court to recede from its ruling in Neuberg v. Bobowicz and extend the consortium action to wives or abolish it for husbands. Despite the disapproval of the action expressed in *Neuberg*, the court's decision was to extend it to wives. Hopkins v. Blanco, 457 Pa. 90, 320 A.2d 139 (1974). See also Montgomery v. Stephan, 359 Mich. 33, 101 N.W.2d 227 (1960). In accordance with Best v. Samuel Fox & Co. Ltd., quoted in *Neuberg*, England continued to deny a wife an action for loss of consortium when her husband was negligently injured. In 1982, Parliament abolished the husband's action for loss of his wife's consortium and services (and also the parental action for loss of a child's services). Administration of Justice Act, 1982, c. 53, s. 2. Is this a desirable reform?

———————

Rodriguez v. Bethlehem Steel Corporation

Supreme Court of California
12 Cal. 3d 382, 115 Cal. Rptr. 765, 525 P.2d 669 (1974)

MOSK, Justice.

In this case we are called upon to decide whether California should continue to adhere to the rule that a married person whose spouse has been injured by the negligence of a third party has no cause of action for loss of "consortium," i.e., for loss of conjugal fellowship and sexual relations. (Deshotel v. Atchison, T. & S. F. Ry. Co. (1958), 50 Cal. 2d 664, 328 P.2d 449; West v. City of San Diego (1960), 54 Cal. 2d 469, 6 Cal. Rptr. 289, 353 P.2d 929.) ...

On May 24, 1969, Richard and Mary Anne Rodriguez were married. Both were gainfully employed. In their leisure time they participated in a variety of social and recreational activities. They were saving for the time when they could buy their own home. They wanted children, and planned to raise a large family.

Only 16 months after their marriage, however, their young lives were shattered by a grave accident. While at work, Richard was struck on the head by a falling pipe weighing over 600 pounds. The blow caused severe spinal cord damage which has left him totally paralyzed in both legs, totally paralyzed in his body below the midpoint of the chest, and partially paralyzed in one of his arms.

The effects of Richard's accident on Mary Anne's life have likewise been disastrous. It has transformed her husband from an active partner into a lifelong invalid, confined to home and bedridden for a great deal of the time. Because he needs assistance in virtually every activity of daily living, Mary Anne gave up her job and undertook his care on a 24-hour basis. Each night she must wake in order to turn him from side to side, so as to minimize the occurrence of bedsores. Every morning and evening she must help him wash, dress and undress, and get into and out of his wheelchair. She must help him into and out of the car when a visit to the doctor's office or hospital is required. Because he has lost all bladder and bowel control, she must assist him in the difficult and time-consuming processes of performing those bodily functions by artificial inducement. Many of these activities require her to lift or support his body weight, thus placing a repeated physical strain on her.

Nor is the psychological strain any less. Mary Anne's social and recreational life, evidently, has been severely restricted. She is a constant witness to her husband's pain, mental anguish, and frustration. Because he has lost all capacity for sexual intercourse, that aspect of married life is wholly denied to her: as she explains in her declaration, "To be deeply in love with each other and have no way of physically expressing this love is most difficult physically and mentally." For the same reason she is forever denied the opportunity to have children by him—she is, for all practical purposes, sterilized: again she explains, "I have lost what I consider is the fulfillment of my existence because my husband can't make me pregnant so as to bear children and have a family." The consequences to her are predictable: "These physical and emotional frustrations with no outlet have made me nervous, tense, depressed and have caused me to have trouble sleeping, eating and concentrating." In short, Mary Anne says, "Richard's life has been ruined by this accident. As his partner, my life has been ruined too." ...

... Mary Anne alleged the consequences to her of Richard's injuries, and prayed for general damages in her own right, the reasonable value of the nursing care she furnishes her husband, and compensation for the loss of her earnings and earning capacity. Defendants filed general demurrers to [her] cause of action on the ground that no recovery for any such loss is permitted in California....

To begin with, we delineate the rationale of *Deshotel* and *West*. Clearly it is not the original common law view, which held that a wife could not recover for loss of her husband's services by the act of a third party for the starkly simple reason that she had no independent legal existence of her own and hence had no right to such services in the first place. That rationale was explicitly rejected in *West*, when the court declined to recognize the husband's common law right to recover for loss of his wife's consortium: "his right," we said, "was based upon the wife's subservient position in the marriage relationship whereas, under present-day law, spouses are generally regarded as equals." ...

... At the time of *Deshotel* the majority of the states denied the wife the right to recover for loss of consortium, while that right was recognized in only five jurisdictions. Today those 5 have grown in number to at least 31....

In these circumstances we may fairly conclude that the precedential foundation of *Deshotel* has been not only undermined but destroyed. In its place a new common law rule has arisen, granting either spouse the right to recover for loss of consortium caused by negligent injury to the other spouse....

The second principal rationale of the *Deshotel* opinion was that any departure from the then-settled rule denying the wife recovery for loss of consortium "should be left to legislative action," and defendants in the case at bar echo that plea.... "In effect the contention is a request that courts of law abdicate their responsibility for the upkeep of the common law." [People v. Pierce, 61 Cal. 2d 879, 40 Cal. Rptr. 845, 395 P.2d 893.] ...

... [W]e have judicially abolished long-standing common law tort rules over the specific objection that the question should have been left for legislative action....

... [T]he *Deshotel* court asserted that "Any harm [the wife] sustains occurs *only indirectly* as a consequence of the defendant's wrong to the husband" (italics added). The argument was negated 10 years after *Deshotel* in Dillon v. Legg (1968), 68 Cal. 2d 728, 69 Cal. Rptr. 72, 441 P.2d 912. There the issue was whether a driver who negligently runs over a small child in the street is also liable to the child's mother for emotional shock and resulting physical disorders suffered by the latter when she personally witnessed the occurrence of the accident. Finding such liability, we in effect rejected the argument that the injury to the mother was too "indirect." The critical question, we explained, was foreseeability: "In order to limit the otherwise potential infinite liability which would follow every negligent act, the law of torts holds defendant amenable only for injuries to others which to defendant at the time were reasonably foreseeable." The defendant owes a duty of care to all persons who are foreseeably endangered by his conduct, with respect to all risks which make the conduct unreasonably dangerous. The foreseeable risk need not be of an actual physical impact, but may be of emotional trauma alone. Whether a risk is sufficiently foreseeable to give rise to a duty of care depends on the circumstances of each case, including the relationship of the parties and the nature of the threatened injury....

Applying these rules to the facts alleged, we were of the opinion in *Dillon* that "Surely the negligent driver who causes the death of a young child may reasonably expect that the mother will not be far distant and will upon witnessing the accident suffer emotional trauma." By parity of reasoning, we conclude in the case at bar that one who negligently causes a severely disabling injury to an adult may reasonably expect that the injured person is married and that his or her spouse will be adversely affected by that injury. In our society the likelihood that an injured adult will be a married man or woman is substantial, clearly no less than the likelihood that a small child's mother will personally witness an injury to her offspring. And the probability that the spouse of a severely disabled person will suffer a personal loss by reason of that injury is equally substantial.

... [T]he New York Court of Appeals said in Millington v. Southeastern Elevator Co. (1968), 22 N.Y.2d 498, 293 N.Y.S.2d 305, 308, 239 N.E.2d 897, 899, "Disparagingly described as 'sentimental' or 'parasitic' damages, the mental and emotional anguish caused by seeing a healthy, loving companionable mate turned into a shell of a person is real enough. To describe the loss as 'indirect' is only to evade the issue. The loss of companionship, emotional support, love, felicity and sexual relations are real injuries. The trauma of having to care for a permanent invalid is known to have caused mental illness. There may not be a deterioration in the marital relationship, but it will certainly alter it in a tragic way. Even in the case of a husband the 'sentimental' damages may predominate over the loss of support or material element. Thus to describe these damages as merely parasitic is inaccurate and cruel." ...

The next rationale of the *Deshotel* court was that "the measurement of damage for the loss of such things as companionship and society would involve conjecture since their value would be hard to fix in terms of money." This argument, too, has fared badly in our subsequent decisions. Although loss of consortium may have physical consequences, it is principally a form of mental suffering....

... [U]nder the concept of pain and suffering "a plaintiff may recover not only for physical pain but for fright, nervousness, grief, anxiety, worry, mortification, shock, humiliation, indignity, embarrassment, apprehension, terror or ordeal. Admittedly these terms refer to subjective states, representing a detriment which can be translated into monetary loss only with great difficulty. But the detriment, nevertheless, is a genuine one that requires compensation and the issue generally must be resolved by the 'impartial conscience and judgment of jurors who may be expected to act reasonably, intelligently and in harmony with the evidence.' Indeed, mental suffering frequently constitutes the principal element of tort damages...." [Capelouto v. Kaiser Foundation Hospitals, 7 Cal. 3d 889, 103 Cal. Rptr. 856, 500 P.2d 880.] ...

The third argument ... set forth in *Deshotel* is that if the wife's cause of action were recognized "on the basis of the intimate relationship existing between her and her husband, other persons having a close relationship to the one injured, such as a child or parent, would likely seek to enforce similar claims, and the courts would be faced with the perplexing task of determining where to draw the line with respect to which claims should be upheld." Here again the answer was subsequently given in Dillon v. Legg. In that case it was likewise urged that any cause of action granted to a mother who witnesses her child's injury could also be asserted by other close relatives present at the scene such as siblings or grandparents, thus involving the courts "in the hopeless task of defining the extent of the tortfeasor's liability."

We rejected this argument in *Dillon* on the ground that "the alleged inability to fix definitions for recovery on the different facts of future cases does not justify the denial of recovery on the specific facts of the instant case; in any event, proper guidelines can indicate the extent of liability for such future cases." Those guidelines, as noted hereinabove, are the general principles of negligence law limiting liability to persons and injuries within the scope of the reasonably foreseeable risk....

... [T]he *Deshotel* court expressed the concern that "A judgment obtained by a husband after he is injured by a third person might include compensation for any impairment of his ability to participate in a normal married life, and, if his wife is allowed redress for loss of consortium in a separate action, there would be danger of double recovery." ... [R]ecovery of damages for impairment of "his" ability to participate in a normal married life does not necessarily compensate for the impairment of "her" ability to participate in that life.

It is true the rule against double recovery forecloses the wife from recovering for the loss of her husband's financial support if he is compensated for his loss of earnings and earning power, "because the *source* of the wife's right to support is the husband's earning capacity, for impairment of which *he* is entitled to recover." (Italics in original.) (Kotsiris v. Ling (Ky. 1970), 451 S.W.2d 411, 412.) But there is far more to the marriage relationship than financial support. "The concept of consortium includes not only loss of support or services, it also embraces such elements as love, companionship, affection, society, sexual relations, solace and more." (Millington v. Southeastern Elevator Co. [supra].) As to each, "the interest sought to be protected is personal to the wife" (*ibid.*), so that to compensate her for damage to that interest cannot result in double recovery.

Perhaps the most undeniable proof of the separate and distinct losses of husband and wife is seen when, as in the case at bar, there is impairment or destruction of the sexual life of the couple. "In his personal injury suit it is clear that his damages are predicated upon *his* physical injury which precludes him from copulation, procreation, and an otherwise full enjoyment of his marital state. However, the wife's loss is just as real as it is distinct. She can no longer enjoy *her* legally sanctioned and morally proper privilege of copulation or procreation, and is otherwise deprived of *her* full enjoyment of her marital state. These are *her* rights, not his." (Yonner v. Adams (1961), 53 Del. 229, 167 A.2d 717.)

Nor is the wife's personal loss limited to her sexual rights. As we recognized in *Deshotel*, consortium includes "conjugal society, comfort, affection, and companionship." An important aspect of consortium is thus the *moral* support each spouse gives the other through the triumph and despair of life. A severely disabled husband may well need all the emotional strength he has just to survive the shock of his injury, make the agonizing adjustment to his new and drastically restricted world, and preserve his mental health through the long years of frustration ahead. He will often turn inward, demanding more solace for himself than he can give to others. Accordingly, the spouse of such a man cannot expect him to share the same concern for *her* problems that she experienced before his accident. As several of the cases have put it, she is transformed from a happy wife into a lonely nurse. Yet she is entitled to enjoy the companionship and moral support that marriage provides no less than its sexual side, and in both cases no less than her husband. If she is deprived of either by reason of a negligent injury to her husband, the loss is hers alone. "In the light of the foregoing danger of double recovery is not real for presumably the husband is recovering for his own injuries and she is recovering for injury done to herself by the loss of his companionship. There is no duplication, instead, this is an example of a single tortious act which harms two people by virtue of their relationship to each other." (General Electric Company v. Bush (1972), 88 Nev. 360, 498 P.2d 336.)

… All that is necessary to avoid double recovery "is to insure that each element of the damages is separate and distinct from all the others" and in particular that the wife's recovery does not include any damages for loss of her husband's financial support or other items for which *he* is primarily entitled to be compensated.…

… "As a practical matter, the consortium claim, when asserted at all, will usually be presented together with the negligence claim for the physical injuries, husband and wife joining in the same action. Such joinder is of course permitted and invited by the procedural rules. When, perchance, separate actions have been brought, the defendant (or plaintiffs in the actions) would normally be entitled to have them consolidated for trial. Further, we think the defendant could ordinarily insist, if he considered it to his advantage, that the other spouse be joined in the main negligence action so that a possible claim for loss of consortium should not be outstanding when the negligence claim was disposed of, leaving a possibility of duplicating recoveries." [Diaz v. Eli Lilly and Company, 364 Mass. 153, 302 N.E.2d 555.]

We therefore … declare that in California each spouse has a cause of action for loss of consortium, as defined herein, caused by a negligent or intentional injury to the other spouse by a third party.…

... In view of our holding herein, Mary Anne's prayer for general damages is good and may be supported by proof, if any she has, of loss or impairment of her rights of consortium. Her prayer for the reasonable value of the nursing services she furnishes her husband, however, cannot be maintained. We do not doubt, as Mary Anne says in her declaration, that no hired nurse or attendant could give Richard the same degree of personal devotion, patience, and understanding that she as a wife can give him. But should he prevail in his own cause of action against these defendants, he will be entitled to recover, among his medical expenses, the full cost of whatever home nursing is necessary. To allow Mary Anne also to recover the value of *her* nursing services, however personalized, would therefore constitute double recovery. For the same reason, Mary Anne cannot recover for the loss of her earnings and earning capacity assertedly incurred when she quit her job in order to furnish Richard these same nursing services. To do so would be to allow her to accomplish indirectly that which we have just held she cannot do directly.

[Reversed. McComb, J., dissented on the ground that "any change in the law denying the wife recovery for loss of consortium should be left to legislative action."]

Notes

1. In West v. City of San Diego, cited at the beginning of the principal case, the court denied the husband recovery for loss of the non-economic elements of consortium, after rejecting the action by the wife in the *Deshotel* case. A California statute permitted the husband to recover for loss of services and medical expenses caused by injury to the wife.

2. The insistence of some courts that the consortium action be joined to the other spouse's personal injury claim—in order to reduce the possibility of double recovery and conserve judicial resources—is illustrated by Schreiner v. Fruit, 519 P.2d 462 (Alaska 1974). After her husband had been awarded damages for his injuries, plaintiff instituted an action for loss of consortium. The trial court dismissed the action on the ground that a wife did not have a right of action. On appeal, it was held that wives now had an action for loss of consortium but plaintiff had no action because she had not joined her claim to her husband's. How would a joinder requirement operate when one spouse agrees to a settlement? When a divorce is pending? See Letaksy v. United States, 783 F. Supp. 451 (D. Alaska 1992); Brown v. Metzger, 104 Ill. 2d 30, 470 N.E.2d 302 (1984). See generally Annot., When Must Loss-of-Consortium Claim Be Joined with Underlying Personal Injury Claim, 60 A.L.R.4th 1174 (1988).

3. Occasionally, a tortious act committed against one spouse will result in the latter's having an action other than a consortium claim. In Molien v. Kaiser Foundation Hospitals, 27 Cal. 3d 916, 167 Cal. Rptr. 831, 616 P.2d 813 (1980), it was alleged that defendant negligently diagnosed syphilis in plaintiff's wife. Defendant advised her to tell her husband and have him examined to determine whether he was also infected. Plaintiff's marriage deteriorated, each spouse suspecting the other of contracting syphilis in an extramarital affair and transmitting it, until it was established that neither spouse had the disease. The court held that plaintiff had a cause of action for negligent infliction of emotional distress as well as loss of consortium.

4. A claim for loss of consortium or services probably is maintainable when there is strict tort liability for the personal injury, as well as when personal injury liability is based upon negligence or an intentional tort. See Hammond v. North American As-

bestos Corp., 97 Ill. 2d 195, 454 N.E.2d 210 (1983); Restatement (Second) of Torts § 693 (1977). How should the opinion in the principal case be applied to a strict liability case? Suppose a married person has a tort action for harm that is not physical injury but in which damages for emotional distress and its consequences might be obtained. Can the person's spouse maintain an action for loss of consortium? See Molien v. Kaiser Foundation Hospitals, supra (negligent infliction of emotional distress); Stack v. Marcum, 147 Mich. App. 756, 382 N.W.2d 743 (1985), appeal denied, 426 Mich. 872 (1986) (interference with contract); Maurice v. Snell, 632 So. 2d 393 (La. App. 1994), writ denied, 637 So. 2d 507 (La. 1994) (defamation); Garrison v. Sun Printing & Publishing Association, 207 N.Y. 1, 100 N.E. 430 (1912) (libel); Dunn v. Alabama Oil & Gas Co., 42 Tenn. App. 108, 299 S.W.2d 25 (1956) (false arrest and malicious prosecution); Annot., Necessity of Physical Injury to Support Cause of Action for Loss of Consortium, 16 A.L.R.4th 537 (1982). What if a married person suffers personal injury but has no tort action for it, only an action for breach of contract? See Scarzella v. Saxon, 436 A.2d 358 (D.C. 1981). Cf. Fernandes v. Union Bookbinding Co., 400 Mass. 27, 507 N.E.2d 728 (1987) (breach of product warranty).

5. Consortium is an interest protected against harm caused by third persons. If a wife's negligence results in injury to herself, her husband cannot recover from her for loss of consortium. General Motors Corp. v. Doupnik, 1 F.3d 862 (9th Cir. 1993); Plain v. Plain, 307 Minn. 399, 240 N.W.2d 330 (1976). Is this sound? Does it necessarily follow from the absence of an enforceable obligation to provide consortium to one's spouse?

6. Ultimately, in view of the nature of the defendant's conduct, its effect on the tort victim and spouse, the costs of litigation and liability and the uses to which money recovered will be put, is liability for loss of consortium in its modern form justified? See Kutner, Damages for Injuries to Family Members: Does Reform Mean Abolition?, 1 Torts L.J. 231 (1993).

B. Child or Parent

Hall v. Hollander
Court of King's Bench
(1825) 4 B. & C. 660, 107 Eng. Rep. 1206,
7 Dow. & Ry. K.B. 133, 4 L.J.O.S.K.B. 39

Trespass for driving a carriage against the plaintiff's son and servant, whereby he was injured, and the plaintiff, for a long space of time, to wit, &c., was deprived of the service of his said son and servant, and of all the benefit which would otherwise have accrued to him from such service, and was also forced to expend a large sum of money, to wit, &c., in the cure of his said son and servant. Plea, not guilty.... [T]he plaintiff proved that the defendant drove his carriage against the plaintiff's son, then an infant two years and a half old. The child was much injured, and at first was taken to the Middlesex hospital, where he might have remained without expence to his father, but he was afterwards taken home by his father, who thought he would be better there, and was taken daily to the hospital for advice for some months, at the expiration of which time he was dismissed as cured. The father also hired a servant to attend the child during his illness. Upon this evidence it was objected for the defendant that the child was not competent to perform any service by reason of his tender age, and that as loss of service was the gist of the action, the plaintiff must be nonsuited.... [T]he plaintiff was nonsuited.

Lawes now moved for a new trial, and contended that the plaintiff was entitled to recover without proving any actual service by the child. In this respect the case of a child differs from that of a mere hired servant. In the latter case, loss of actual service must be proved; but in the former, the child being resident with and under the control of the parent, must unavoidably be, in legal acceptation, a servant so as to support an action of this nature. At all events, the plaintiff was entitled to recover the expence which he was put to in obtaining the cure of his son.

BAYLEY J. I am of opinion that the nonsuit in this case was right. It has been contended that the action is maintainable on two grounds; first, for the loss of the services of the child, and, secondly, for the expences incurred by the father, in consequence of the injury sustained by the child. With respect to the first ground, I apprehend that the gist of the action depends upon the capacity of the child to perform acts of service. Here it is manifest that the child was incapable of performing acts of service. The authorities upon this point are all one way. In the cases which have been cited, the child being capable of performing acts of service, and living with the parent, would naturally be called upon to perform some acts of service; and it was, therefore, held, that the service might be presumed, and that evidence of it need not be given. In *Weedon v. Timbrel* (5 T.R. 357), both Lord Kenyon and Ashhurst J. say, that the loss of service is the gist of such an action as the present, and that the plaintiff must give some proof of acts of service, in order to support the allegation in the declaration, although very slight evidence is sufficient.... In this case, too, it was proved that the father did not necessarily incur any expence; if he had done so I am not prepared to say that he could not have recovered upon a declaration describing, as the cause of action, the obligation of the father to incur that expence.

HOLROYD J. It was not established by the evidence at the trial that the father was necessarily put to any expence; the Court are, therefore, not called upon to give any opinion upon his right to recover such expences. It is clear that in cases of taking away a son or daughter, except for taking a son and heir, no action lies, unless a loss of service is sustained. The mere relationship of the parties is not sufficient to constitute a loss of service. The reasoning in all the modern cases shews that some evidence of service is necessary; none could be given in the present case, the nonsuit was, therefore, right.

ABBOTT C.J. It is a principle of the common law that a master may maintain an action for a loss of service, sustained by the tortious act of another, whether the servant be a child or not; and when that foundation of the action has existed, Courts of Justice have allowed all the circumstances of the case to be taken into consideration, with a view to the calculation of the damages. Here we are required to go further, and to hold that the action is maintainable, although no service was or could be performed by the child, and that too upon a declaration alleging the existence of the relation of master and servant, and the loss of the services of such servant. Such a decision would not be warranted by any former case, the nonsuit, therefore, ought not to be disturbed.

Rule refused.

Notes

1. The parent's action for injuries to a minor child was originally considered to be a master's action for injuries to his servant. Loss of services was considered essential to the

cause of action. But most American courts came to sustain the action when the child was too young to render services. See Netherland-American Steam Navigation Co. v. Hollander, 59 F. 417 (2d Cir. 1894); Sebring v. Bell Telephone Co. of Pennsylvania, 275 Pa. 131, 118 A. 729 (1922). Courts now allow recovery of medical expenses without a showing of lost services. See Williams v. Ward, 18 Ohio App. 2d 37, 246 N.E.2d 780 (1969); Trow v. Thomas, 70 Vt. 580, 41 A. 652 (1898). On the division of damages between an injured child's action and the parent's action, see Annots., What Items of Damage on Account of Personal Injury to Infant Belong to Him and What to Parent, 37 A.L.R. 11 (1925); 32 A.L.R.2d 1060 (1953). There are conflicting decisions on the question of whether damages for future medical expenses, to be incurred during the child's minority, may be recovered in the child's action. See Boley v. Knowles, 905 S.W.2d 86 (Mo. 1995); Lopez v. Southwest Community Health Services, 114 N.M. 2, 833 P.2d 1183 (Ct. App. 1992), cert. denied, 113 N.M. 690, 831 P.2d 989 (1992).

2. A court that recognized no parental right to recover the expenses of treating a tortiously injured child surely would find that the child had a right of recovery. Does it really matter whether the claim belongs to the child or the parent? Consider who will control the conduct of the claim and use of the funds obtained, as well as rules of liability that apply to the respective actions. Also consider how a case arising from injury to a minor can be effectively settled. A release signed by a minor is not binding on the minor. Mitchell v. Mitchell, 963 S.W.2d 222 (Ky. App. 1998); Nelson v. Browning, 391 S.W.2d 881 (Mo. 1965). And a release signed by a parent or guardian often is held not binding on the child unless the agreement has been approved by the court. See Pacheco v. Delgardo, 46 Ariz. 401, 52 P.2d 479 (1935); Colfer v. Royal Globe Insurance Co., 214 N.J. Super 374, 519 A.2d 893 (App. Div. 1986). Concern has been expressed that money intended for children may often not reach them. Dixon, Settlement of Minors' Tort Claims, 92 Trusts & Estates 728 (1953). See also Comment, Settling the Personal Injury Claim of a Minor, 38 U. Colo. L. Rev. 377 (1966). A judgment of no liability in the parent's action does not bar a subsequent claim by the child. Whitehead v. General Telephone Co., 20 Ohio St. 2d 108, 254 N.E.2d 10 (1969); Boring v. Miller, 215 Tenn. 394, 386 S.W.2d 521 (1965).

3. The action for loss of a child's services historically belonged to the father, who had the legal right to the child's services. The mother could maintain the action when circumstances made her the head of the household, as when the father had died or abandoned the family. Tornroos v. R.H. White Co., 220 Mass. 336, 107 N.E. 1015 (1915); Furman v. Van Sise, 56 N.Y. 435 (1874); Marks v. City of New York, 101 N.Y.S.2d 105 (Sup. Ct. 1950). Cf. Bunder v. Mains, 139 Me. 231, 28 A.2d 734 (1942) (illegitimate child, for whom no one but mother assumed parental rights or responsibilities). Also, if the father had clearly relinquished his rights to a child's services. McGarr v. National & Providence Worsted Mills, 24 R.I. 447, 53 A. 320 (1902) (mother managed household affairs, received earnings of child, employed physician who treated child). On the relationship between the right to a child's services and the obligation of support, see Flippin v. Jarrell, 301 N.C. 108, 270 S.E.2d 482 (1980); Note, Reciprocity of Rights and Duties Between Parent and Child, 42 Harv. L. Rev. 112 (1928). In the United States, the action now normally goes with custody of the child. Restatement (Second) of Torts § 693, comment e (1977). (There is no action when the child had been completely "emancipated.") Should a court permit one parent to bring an action arising from a child's injury when both parents have custody of the child? See Yordon v. Savage, 279 So. 2d 844 (Fla. 1973).

Borer v. American Airlines, Inc.

Supreme Court of California
19 Cal. 3d 441, 138 Cal. Rptr. 302, 563 P.2d 858 (1977)

TOBRINER, Acting Chief Justice.

In *Rodriguez v. Bethlehem Steel Corp.* [p. 16, supra] we held that a married person whose spouse had been injured by the negligence of a third party may maintain a cause of action for loss of "consortium." We defined loss of "consortium" as the "loss of conjugal fellowship and sexual relations," but ruled that the term included the loss of love, companionship, society, sexual relations, and household services. Our decision carefully avoided resolution of the question whether anyone other than the spouse of a negligently injured person, such as a child or a parent, could maintain a cause of action analogous to that upheld in *Rodriguez*. We face that issue today: the present case presents a claim by nine children for the loss of the services, companionship, affection and guidance of their mother; the companion case of *Baxter v. Superior Court* [p. 30, infra] presents the claim of a mother and father for the loss of the companionship and affection of their 16-year-old son....

... Plaintiffs, the nine children of Patricia Borer, allege that on March 21, 1972, the cover on a lighting fixture at the American Airlines Terminal at Kennedy Airport fell and struck Patricia. Plaintiffs further assert that as a result of the physical injuries sustained by Patricia, each of them has been "deprived of the services, society, companionship, affection, tutelage, direction, guidance, instruction and aid in personality development, all with its accompanying psychological, educational and emotional detriment, by reason of Patricia Borer being unable to carry on her usual duties of a mother." The complaint sets forth causes of action based upon negligence, breach of warranty, and manufacture of a defective product; it names as defendants American Airlines, two companies which manufactured and assembled the lighting fixture, and various fictitious defendants. Each plaintiff seeks damages of $100,000....

Our analysis of plaintiffs' appeal begins with our decision in *Rodriguez v. Bethlehem Steel Corp.* In holding that a spouse has a cause of action for loss of consortium, we considered the proffered argument that such a holding would logically require us to uphold an analogous cause of action in the parent-child context or in even more distant relationships; we rejected that contention....

Rodriguez, thus, does not compel the conclusion that foreseeable injury to a legally recognized relationship necessarily postulates a cause of action; instead it clearly warns that social policy must at some point intervene to delimit liability. Patricia Borer, for example, foreseeably has not only a husband (who has a cause of action under *Rodriguez*) and the children who sue here, but also parents whose right of action depends upon our decision in the companion case of *Baxter v. Superior Court*; foreseeably, likewise, she has brothers, sisters, cousins, inlaws, friends, colleagues, and other acquaintances who will be deprived of her companionship. No one suggests that all such persons possess a right of action for loss of Patricia's consortium; all agree that somewhere a line must be drawn. As stated by Judge Breitel in *Tobin v. Grossman* (1969) 24 N.Y.2d 609, 619, 301 N.Y.S.2d 554, 561, 249 N.E.2d 419, 424; "Every injury has ramifying consequences, like the ripplings of the waters, without end. The problem for the law is to limit the legal consequences of wrongs to a controllable degree."

The decision whether to limit liability for loss of consortium by denying a cause of action in the parent-child context, or to permit that action but deny any claim based upon more remote relationships, is thus a question of policy. As explained by Justice Fleming in *Suter v. Leonard* (1975) 45 Cal. App. 3d 744, 746, 120 Cal. Rptr. 110, 111: "Plaintiff's claim, viewed in the abstract and divorced from its surroundings, carries both logical and sympathetic appeal.... Certain aspects of spousal relationship are similar to those of the parent-child relationship, and there can be little question of the reality of the loss suffered by a child deprived of the society and care of its parent. Nevertheless our decision must take into account considerations in addition to logical symmetry and sympathetic appeal.... [N]ot every loss can be made compensable in money damages, and legal causation must terminate somewhere. In delineating the extent of a tortfeasor's responsibility for damages under the general rule of tort liability, the courts must locate the line between liability and nonliability at some point, a decision which is essentially political."

In the first instance, strong policy reasons argue against extension of liability to loss of consortium of the parent-child relationship. Loss of consortium is an intangible, nonpecuniary loss; monetary compensation will not enable plaintiffs to regain the companionship and guidance of a mother; it will simply establish a fund so that upon reaching adulthood, when plaintiffs will be less in need of maternal guidance, they will be unusually wealthy men and women. To say that plaintiffs have been "compensated" for their loss is superficial; in reality they have suffered a loss for which they can never be compensated; they have obtained, instead, a future benefit essentially unrelated to that loss.

We cannot ignore the social burden of providing damages for loss of parental consortium merely because the money to pay such awards comes initially from the "negligent" defendant or his insurer. Realistically the burden of payment of awards for loss of consortium must be borne by the public generally in increased insurance premiums or, otherwise, in the enhanced danger that accrues from the greater number of people who may choose to go without any insurance. We must also take into account the cost of administration of a system to determine and pay consortium awards; since virtually every serious injury to a parent would engender a claim for loss of consortium on behalf of each of his or her children, the expense of settling or litigating such claims would be sizable.

Plaintiffs point out that courts have permitted recovery of monetary damages for intangible loss in allowing awards for pain and suffering in negligence cases and in sanctioning recovery for loss of marital consortium. The question before us in this case, however, pivots on whether we should recognize a wholly new cause of action, unsupported by statute or precedent; in this context the inadequacy of monetary damages to make whole the loss suffered, considered in light of the social cost of paying such awards, constitutes a strong reason for refusing to recognize the asserted claim. To avoid misunderstanding, we point out that our decision to refuse to recognize a cause of action for parental consortium does not remotely suggest the rejection of recovery for intangible loss; each claim must be judged on its merits, and in many cases the involved statutes, precedents, or policy will induce acceptance of the asserted cause of action.

A second reason for rejecting a cause of action for loss of parental consortium is that, because of its intangible character, damages for such a loss are very difficult to measure. Plaintiffs here have prayed for $100,000 each; yet by what standard could we determine that an award of $10,000 was inadequate, or one of $500,000 excessive? Difficulty in defining and quantifying damages leads in turn to risk of double recovery: to ask the jury, even under carefully drafted instructions, to distinguish the loss to the mother from her inability to care for her children from the loss to the children from the mother's inability to care for them may be asking too much. Thus as observed by the New Jersey Supreme Court in *Russell v. Salem Transportation Co.* (1972) 61 N.J. 502, 507, 295 A.2d 862, 864: "The asserted social need for the disputed cause of action [a child's action for loss of parental consortium] may well be qualified, at least in terms of the family as an economic unit, by the practical consideration recognized by many of the cases on the point that reflection of the consequential disadvantages to children of injured parents is frequently found in jury awards to the parents on their own claims under existing law and practice."

Plaintiffs point out that similar policy arguments could be, and to some extent were, raised in *Rodriguez*, and that our decision to uphold the wife's action for loss of consortium rejected those arguments. We do not, however, read *Rodriguez* as holding that arguments based upon the intangible character of damages and the difficulty of measuring such damages do not merit consideration. Such a holding would imply an indefinite extension of liability for loss of consortium to all foreseeable relationships, a proposition *Rodriguez* plainly repudiates.

Rodriguez, then, holds no more than that in the context of a spousal relationship, the policy arguments against liability do not suffice to justify a holding denying a cause of action. Plaintiffs contend, however, that no adequate ground exists to distinguish a cause of action for loss of spousal consortium from one for loss of parental consortium. We reject the contention for three reasons.

First, as *Rodriguez* pointed out, the spousal action for loss of consortium rests in large part on the "impairment or destruction of the sexual life of the couple." No similar element of damage appears in a child's suit for loss of consortium.

Second, actions by children for loss of parental consortium create problems of multiplication of actions and damages not present in the spousal context. As pointed out by the New Jersey Supreme Court in *Russell v. Salem Transportation Co.*: "If the claim were allowed there would be a substantial accretion of liability against the tortfeasor arising out a single transaction (typically the negligent operation of an automobile). Whereas the assertion of a spouse's demand for loss of consortium involves the joining of only a single companion claim in the action with that of the injured person, the right here debated would entail adding as many companion claims as the injured parent had minor children, each such claim entitled to separate appraisal and award. The defendant's burden would be further enlarged if the claims were founded upon injuries to both parents. Magnification of damage awards to a single family derived from a single accident might well become a serious problem to a particular defendant as well as in terms of the total cost of such enhanced awards to the insured community as a whole."

The instant case illustrates the point. Patricia Borer has nine children, each of whom would possess his own independent right of action for loss of consortium....

Finally, the proposition that a spouse has a cause of action for loss of consortium, but that a child does not, finds overwhelming approval in the decisions of other jurisdictions. Over 30 states, a clear majority of those who have decided the question, now permit a *spousal* suit for loss of consortium. *No* state permits a child to sue for loss of parental consortium. That claim has been presented, at latest count, to 18 jurisdictions, and rejected by all of them....

Plaintiffs place particular emphasis on *Dillon v. Legg* (1968) 68 Cal. 2d 728, 69 Cal. Rptr. 72, 441 P.2d 912, which upheld a cause of action for injuries flowing from a mother's emotional trauma in witnessing the death of her child. We suggested that the cause of action should be sustained whenever the injury was "reasonably foreseeable" and that one factor to be considered was "whether plaintiff and the victim were closely related." Plaintiffs urge that we follow that paradigm for decision of the instant case.

In *Dillon*, however, we carefully limited our ruling to a case in which the plaintiff suffered physical injury. Subsequent decisions, interpreting our holding in *Dillon*, have refused to recognize a cause of action in a case in which the plaintiff suffered no physical injury himself as a result of witnessing the infliction of injury upon a family member. Thus *Dillon* and subsequent authority support our decision in this case to deny a cause of action founded upon purely intangible injury.

We therefore conclude that we should not recognize a cause of action by a child for loss of parental consortium.[3] Plaintiffs contend, however, that such a conclusion would distinguish between the rights of the child in the present context and the rights afforded him in a wrongful death action, without any rational basis for the distinction in contravention of the equal protection of the laws.

Plaintiffs point out that section 377 of the Code of Civil Procedure authorizes an action for wrongful death by the heirs of the victim; judicial decisions interpreting this section permit recovery by children of the value of the deceased's affection and society. Plaintiffs contend that no rational basis supports a ruling that permits the children of a deceased parent to recover the value of lost affection and companionship, but denies the children of a seriously disabled parent a similar cause of action. . . .

We perceive two significant distinctions between the child whose parent is killed and one whose parent is disabled, both of which flow from the fact that in the latter case the living victim retains his or her own cause of action. The first distinction relates to the historical purpose of the wrongful death statutes. By 1846, the date of the enactment of the first wrongful death statute, the common law courts had settled that the heirs of a deceased victim could not bring a cause of action against the tortfeasor. "The result was that it was more profitable for the defendant to kill the plaintiff than to scratch him, and that the most grievous of all injuries left the bereaved family of the victim, who frequently were destitute, without a remedy." (Prosser, Torts (4th ed. 1971) p. 902.) This loophole in the law curtailed the deterrent function of tort recovery, providing to tortfeasors a substantial incentive to finish off their victims. The wrongful death statutes thus met an obvious logical and social need.

Similar policy reasons led the courts to permit the bereaved to recover for the loss of the affection and society of the deceased. As stated in *Krouse v. Graham* [19 Cal. 3d 59, 137 Cal. Rptr. 863, 562 P.2d 1022] "if damages truly were limited to 'pecuniary' loss, recovery frequently would be barred by the heirs' inability to prove such loss. The services of children, elderly parents, or nonworking spouses often do not result in measurable net income to the family unit, yet unquestionably the death of such a person represents a substantial 'injury' to the family." Recovery for loss of affection and society in a wrongful death action thus fulfills a deeply felt social belief that a tortfeasor who negligently kills someone should not escape liability completely, no matter how unproductive his victim.

A suit for loss of consortium of a disabled parent presents a wholly different picture. Here the tortfeasor cannot escape with impunity, for the immediate victim of his tort retains a cause of action for the injuries inflicted. The claim by the child in this setting is not essential to prevent the tortfeasor from totally escaping liability.

Secondly, the wrongful death action serves as the only means by which the family unit can recover compensation for the loss of parental care and services in the case of the

---

3. The considerations which lead us to reject a cause of action for negligent injury to consortium in a parent-child context do not bar an action for intentional interference with parental consortium. An action for intentional interference with consortium, recognized by precedent in California, is a relatively unusual tort that presents no danger of multiplication of claims or damages. The ruling, moreover, may serve to deter child stealing and similar antisocial conduct.

wrongful death of the parent. While the parent lives, however, "the tangible aspects of the child's loss can be compensated in the parent's *own* cause of action. As put by Stainbeck, J., in *Halberg v. Young*, 41 Hawaii 634, 640 ... 'where a parent has been injured by the negligent act of another the parent will recover from the other full damage which he has sustained, including such inability, if any, to properly care for his children, and thus the parent's ability to carry out his duty to support and maintain the child has not, in a legal sense, been destroyed or impaired by the injury to him.'" (*Suter v. Leonard, supra*, 45 Cal. App. 3d 744, 748, 120 Cal. Rptr. 110, 112.)

We conclude that the distinction between the award of damages for loss of affection and society to a child whose parent has been tortiously killed, and the denial of such damages to a child whose parent has been disabled, rests upon a rational basis. Plaintiffs' constitutional argument therefore fails.

In summary, we do not doubt the reality or the magnitude of the injury suffered by plaintiffs. We are keenly aware of the need of children for the love, affection, society and guidance of their parents; any injury which diminishes the ability of a parent to meet these needs is plainly a family tragedy, harming all members of that community. We conclude, however, that taking into account all considerations which bear on this question, including the inadequacy of monetary compensation to alleviate that tragedy, the difficulty of measuring damages, and the danger of imposing extended and disproportionate liability, we should not recognize a nonstatutory cause of action for the loss of parental consortium.

The judgment is affirmed.

MOSK, Justice, dissenting....

Each of the policy arguments which the majority marshal against recognizing the cause of action for loss of consortium in the parent-child relationship was expressly considered and rejected by this court in *Rodriguez v. Bethlehem Steel Corp*....

... [T]he majority claim *Rodriguez* "pointed out" that the spousal action for loss of consortium rests "in large part" on the impairment of the sexual life of the couple. *Rodriguez* "pointed out" no such thing; on the contrary, we there reasoned that the nonsexual loss suffered by a spouse is at least as great as the sexual loss: "Nor is the wife's personal loss limited to her sexual rights.... [C]onsortium includes 'conjugal society, comfort, affection, and companionship.' An important aspect of consortium is thus the *moral* support each spouse gives the other through the triumph and despair of life...."

Precisely the same reasoning can be invoked in the case at bar: a severely disabled mother may well need all her emotional strength to survive the shock of her injury, to adjust to her newly restricted life, and to preserve her mental health through the ensuing years of her frustration; and she will therefore often turn inwards, demanding more solace and comfort from her children than she can give to them in return....

... [P]laintiffs actually ask us to take a smaller, not a larger, step than we took in *Rodriguez*. Inasmuch as adult, emancipated children who are no longer living in the family home could prove little if any damage from loss of parental consortium, I assume the majority are most troubled by the prospect of claims by minor children. Upon reflection, it will be seen that such children inevitably comprise a much more limited class than spouses, for two reasons: not all married persons have children; and of those who do, they are parents of *minor* children for a far shorter period of time than they are spouses. It is therefore not surprising that although more than three-quarters of the adult population is married, almost half of such households—46 percent—have no minor children whatever. It follows that recognition of the cause of action for loss of parental consortium will result in a lesser rather than a greater effect on individual liability and overall insurance costs than our approval of the corresponding action by a spouse in *Rodriguez*....

There is, in short, no valid excuse for denying these children their day in court. Justice, compassion, and respect for our humanitarian values require that the "line" in this matter be drawn elsewhere....

———————

Baxter v. Superior Court of Los Angeles County

Supreme Court of California
19 Cal. 3d 461, 138 Cal. Rptr. 315, 563 P.2d 871 (1977)

TOBRINER, Acting Chief Justice.

Our opinion in *Borer v. American Airlines* [p. 25, *supra*] holds that a child has no cause of action for the negligently caused loss of the affection and society of his parent. The present case presents the related question of whether the parents of an injured child can state a cause of action for the loss of the affection and society of their child. The two cases differ only in that by historical accident the common law permitted a parent to sue for the loss of the earnings and services of his child, but denied a child any cause of action for loss of parental support; relying upon this common law precedent, some states which do not allow a child to sue for loss of parental consortium nevertheless permit the parent, often in the guise of a suit to recover for loss of the child's services, to recover damages for loss of filial affection and society. In California, however, the parent's cause of action has not expanded beyond the ancient right to recover for loss of earnings and services of economic value....

In August of 1970, Andre Baxter, aged 16, entered Huntington Memorial Hospital and was given a general anesthetic in preparation for diagnostic procedures and possible surgery. As a result of the anesthetic, he was rendered unconscious and remained comatose for four months, during which time he underwent fourteen separate neurosurgeries. Upon awakening, it was discovered that he had been reduced to the mental age of three, suffered total blindness and severe impairment of his hearing, and partial paralysis of his right side.

In November of 1974 Andre and his parents filed suit against the hospital and the attending physicians.... [Andre's parents sought damages] for their loss of Andre's "support, comfort, protection, society, and pleasure." ...

Our opinion in *Borer v. American Airlines* explains the policy considerations which impelled us to conclude that a child should not have a cause of action for loss of parental consortium. Those reasons for the most part apply fully to the present issue of a parental claim for loss of filial consortium. The intangible character of the loss, which can never really be compensated by money damages; the difficulty of measuring damages; the dangers of double recovery of multiple claims and of extensive liability—all these considerations apply similarly to both cases. To be sure, the risk of multiple claims and disproportionate awards is slightly less in the present context, since an injured child has only two parents who can sue for loss of consortium, while an injured parent may have many children. That minor difference between the cases, however, plainly does not suffice to justify allowing a parental cause of action while denying a child's claim. Petitioners do not argue to the contrary.

... Although ... no jurisdiction allows a child to recover for loss of parental consortium, the states are divided on the question whether a parent can recover for loss of a child's consortium. Yet none of the decisions upholding a parental cause of action address the question whether the parent's claim can reasonably be distinguished from a child's claim. The majority of decisions that sustain the parental cause of action do so merely by citing the common law right of a parent to recover for loss of a child's services and by treating the child's affection and companionship as among the "services" to which the parent is entitled. The absence of any comparable right of action for the child at common law presumably accounts for the dearth of decisions permitting the child to recover for loss of parental affection and society.

The existence of a common law right to recover for the loss of a child's earnings and services does not, we believe, furnish a sufficient basis to distinguish a parent's suit for loss of consortium from the child's claim denied in *Borer v. American Airlines*. The common law right in question derives from the right of a master to recover for the loss of his servant's services and dates from the period when the labor of the child in his parent's business, or his earnings outside the home, served as an important economic resource of the family. With rare exceptions the parent's right to a child's earnings and services today is of little economic value; it exists less as a significant legal right than as a historical curiosity....

Although the parents' right to their child's earnings and services is established by statute in California (see Civ. Code, § 197), the few decisions enforcing that right grant recovery only for loss of earnings or services of economic value. Expansion of recovery to include damages for loss of affection and society encounters the same arguments invoked in *Borer* in denial of a child's claim for loss of parental consortium. We therefore conclude that a parent has no cause of action in negligence to recover damages for loss of filial consortium.[3] ...

MOSK, Justice, dissenting.

Inasmuch as the majority refuse to recognize the cause of action for loss of filial consortium herein on the same policy grounds that they invoke in denying recovery for loss of parental consortium in the companion case of *Borer v. American Airlines, Inc.*, I dissent for the reasons set forth in my dissenting opinion to the latter.

Hibpshman v. Prudhoe Bay Supply, Inc.

Supreme Court of Alaska
734 P.2d 991 (1987)

RABINOWITZ, Chief Justice.

[Thomas Hibpshman was severely injured while employed on the North Slope. He brought suit against Prudhoe Bay Supply, Inc. and Alaska Explosives, Ltd., alleging negligence in failing to provide premises free from unreasonable defects and hazards. His wife Rebecca asserted a claim for loss of spousal consortium. Their four minor children subsequently asserted a claim against the same defendants for loss of parental consortium. The children appealed from dismissal of this claim.]

Although a majority of the courts which have considered the issue have refused to recognize a child's cause of action based on loss of parental consortium resulting from neg-

---

3. Our decision does not bar a parent's action for intentional interference with the parent-child relationship, a cause of action recognized by California precedent.

ligent injury to a parent, legal commentators have criticized the majority rule, and six of the eleven state supreme courts which have considered the issue since the start of 1980 have endorsed the loss of parental consortium claim....

Prudhoe Bay does not dispute that children of injured parents do themselves suffer an actual injury. When a parent is seriously injured, his or her child suffers a loss of enjoyment, care, guidance, love and protection, and is also deprived of a role model. Even courts that deny the parental consortium cause of action have acknowledged the reality of such emotional and psychological injury to the child, and the Alaska legislature has implicitly done so in allowing recovery by children for loss of consortium under Alaska's wrongful death statute.

Precluding minor children from maintaining a cause of action for loss of parental consortium arising from their parent's injury would, in our view, be inconsistent with the legislature's authorization of such recovery when the parent dies, and with our prior holding ... that a husband or wife may recover damages for loss of consortium when an injured spouse survives. The claim for loss of parental consortium presented in this case is not sufficiently distinguishable from either spousal consortium claims in injury cases or children's consortium claims in death cases to warrant non-recognition....

Prudhoe Bay asserts that permitting claims for parental consortium would augment rather than alleviate any injury to intrafamilial relationships because allowing independent recovery by the child—and thus guarding the child against the possibility that the parents may not spend their financial resources for the child's benefit—disrupts the normal course of parent-child relations in which the parents have full discretion regarding family expenditures. We find this argument meritless. In the circumstances at bar, the possibility of a threat to family harmony is no different from that which arises in other cases involving family litigation, including wrongful death actions. The Alaska legislature has specifically provided for independent recoveries by family members in wrongful death suits, and thus impliedly rejected family harmony as a significant threat. Moreover, we expressly rejected potential intrafamilial conflicts as a ground for denying relief when we abolished both interspousal immunity and parental immunity with respect to the negligent injury of a child....

The parties also dispute whether the difficulty of ascertaining the child's true damages should bar recognition of the parental consortium claim. Prudhoe Bay cites both the speculative nature of the child's intangible damages and the danger of double recovery— that is, for the loss to the parent from his or her inability to care for the children and for the children's loss from the parent's inability to care for them—as militating against recognition of the cause of action.

These arguments are hereby rejected. First, in regard to damage claims for loss of spousal consortium, we have indicated that concern about the purported speculative nature of such claims is overstated and "is inherent in the nature of a jury's assessment of the extent to which an injury may have affected a marital relationship and the somewhat ephemeral nature of the elements of this relational interest." *Rutherford v. State*, 605 P.2d 16, 26 (Alaska 1979). We see no reason to consider the calculation of damages for a child's loss of parental consortium any more speculative or difficult than that necessary in other consortium, wrongful death, emotional distress, or pain and suffering actions. Second, we think that the potential problem of double recovery can be eliminated by recognizing that pecuniary damages such as lost income which would have been used for the benefit of a child or the cost of substitute child care services are damages recoverable by the parent, not the child; the child's damages would thus be limited primarily to an emotional suffering award in most cases. *See* [*Theama v. City of Kenosha*, 117 Wis. 2d 508, 344 N.W.2d 513, 521–522 (1984)] ("The problem may be easily cured by limiting the injured parent's recovery to the child's loss of the parent's pecuniary ability to support the child. Similarly, the child's cause of action can be limited to the loss of the parent's society and companionship.")....

... Prudhoe Bay asserts that recognition of parental consortium should be withheld because the social costs, in particular increased insurance rates and a projected rise in the number of uninsured tortfeasors, outweigh the benefit to the child. We are in agreement with those courts which have concluded that any burden to society is offset by the benefit to the child....

Lastly, Prudhoe Bay argues that recognition of loss of parental consortium will increase the potential for future complex litigation arising from multiple claims which have not been instituted contemporaneously.... [A] practical and fair solution to the problem is to require joinder of the minors' consortium claim with the injured parent's claim whenever feasible.

We hold that minor children have an independent cause of action for loss of parental consortium resulting from injuries tortiously inflicted on their parent by a third person. We further hold that this separate consortium claim must be joined with the injured parent's claim whenever feasible.

[Reversed and remanded.]

Notes

1. It is still the position in numerous states that when a child is injured by a third party, the parent's claim does not include loss of companionship and affection. See Siciliano v. Capital City Shows, Inc., 124 N.H. 719, 475 A.2d 19 (1984); Boucher v. Dixie Medical Center, 850 P.2d 1179 (Utah 1992); Restatement (Second) of Torts § 703 (1977). But there is a growing body of precedent for allowing recovery. See Gallimore v. Children's Hospital Medical Center, 67 Ohio St. 3d 244, 617 N.E.2d 1052 (1993); Shockley v. Prier, 66 Wis. 2d 394, 225 N.W.2d 495 (1975); Annot., Parent's Right to Recover for Loss of Consortium in Connection with Injury to Child, 54 A.L.R.4th 112 (1987). If an action lies for loss of the "consortium" of a minor child, should an action also lie when an adult child is injured? See Howard Frank, M.D., P.C. v. Superior Court, 150 Ariz. 228, 722 P.2d 955 (1986) (action maintainable); Estate of Wells by Jeske v. Mount Sinai Medical Center, 183 Wis. 2d 667, 515 N.W.2d 705 (1994) (action not maintainable).

2. Until Berger v. Weber, 82 Mich. App. 199, 267 N.W.2d 124 (1978), aff'd, 411 Mich. 1, 303 N.W.2d 424 (1981), courts were unanimous in denying a child a cause of action for negligently inflicted injury to a parent. This remains the prevailing view. Mendillo v. Board of Education of the Town of East Haddam, 246 Conn. 456, 717 A.2d 1177 (1998); Garver v. Harrant, 316 Md. 17, 557 A.2d 210 (1989). Contra, Belcher v. Goins, 184 W. Va. 394, 400 S.E.2d 830 (1990); Nulle v. Gillette-Campbell County Joint Powers Fire Board, 797 P.2d 1171 (Wyo. 1990). See Annot., Child's Right of Action for Loss of Support, Training, Parental Attention, or the Like, Against a Third Person Negligently Injuring Parent, 11 A.L.R.4th 549 (1982). It permits no recovery for lost companionship, guidance, services, etc. If a minor child is allowed to recover, will an adult child also have a claim? See Rolf v. Tri State Motor Transit Co., 91 Ohio St. 3d 380, 745 N.E.2d 424 (2001) (yes); Smith v. Vilvarajah, 57 S.W.3d 839 (Ky. App. 2000) (no); Morgan v. Lalumiere, 22 Mass. App. Ct. 262, 493 N.E.2d 206 (1986), review denied, 398 Mass. 1103,

497 N.E.2d 1096 (1986) (disabled adult dependent upon parent permitted action); Annot., Adult Child's Right of Action for Loss of Parental Consortium, 12 A.L.R.6th 241 (2006). Can it be consistent to permit a child's action for injury to a parent but deny a parent damages for loss of consortium when a child is injured? See Roberts v. Williamson, 111 S.W.3d 113 (Tex. 2003). Will a judicial "line" between claims arising from injuries to parents and children and consortium claims for injuries to other blood relations be maintained, or will it be breached in later cases? See Malik v. William Beaumont Hospital, 168 Mich. App. 159, 423 N.W.2d 920 (1988), appeal denied, 431 Mich. 877 (1988), in which a claim was made for a minor child's loss of his adult sister's consortium.

3. How persuasive is the argument that if damages for loss of society or consortium are recoverable in wrongful death actions, they are also recoverable in cases of non-fatal injury? Compare Ferriter v. Daniel O'Connell's Sons, Inc., 381 Mass. 507, 413 N.E.2d 690 (1980) (dependent minor children allowed action for loss of parental society), with Vitro v. Mihelcic, 209 Ill. 2d 76, 806 N.E.2d 632 (2004) (no action for loss of child's society); Norwest v. Presbyterian Intercommunity Hospital, 293 Or. 543, 652 P.2d 318 (1982) (no action for injury to parent). What should be the law in a state that does not compensate such losses in wrongful death actions? Would it be anomalous to grant an action for loss of a parent's or child's companionship because of accidental injury but deny a claim for loss of companionship caused by alienation of affections or other intentional interference with family relationships? See Berger v. Weber, supra. Norman v. Massachusetts Bay Transportation Authority, 403 Mass. 303, 529 N.E.2d 139 (1988), which denied parents damages for loss of a child's consortium after Ferriter v. Daniel O'Connell's Sons, Inc., supra, had given a loss of parental consortium action to minor children, was abrogated by the enactment of Mass. Ann. Laws C. 231 § 85X. Other states also have legislation to create or extend liability for non-fatal injury to a parent or child. E.g., Fla. Stat. Ann. § 768.0415; R.I. Gen. Laws § 9-1-41; Wash. Rev. Code Ann. § 4.24.010.

4. As with a spouse's action for loss of consortium, the child's action for loss of society, etc., can exist, if at all, only against third persons, not against the person whose society is lost. See Clark v. Estate of Rice, 653 N.W.2d 166 (Iowa 2002); Plain v. Plain, 307 Minn. 399, 240 N.W.2d 330 (1976) (woman who negligently injures herself liable to neither husband nor children). Is this an argument against extension of third-party liability?

C. Other Relationships

Hendrix v. General Motors Corporation
California Court of Appeal
146 Cal. App. 3d 296, 193 Cal. Rptr. 922 (1983)

BREINER, Justice, Pro Tem....

Plaintiffs Lebron Mitchell and Sharon Jean Hendrix joined in a complaint against General Motors Corporation, the manufacturer, and Doten Pontiac, the seller, for damages arising out of an automobile accident in which Mitchell was severely injured. Mitchell stated three causes of action for products liability and negligence; in the fourth cause of action, Hendrix alleged loss of consortium. Hendrix alleged that she was "the prospective wife of plaintiff Lebron Mitchell and at all times herein mentioned did reside with Lebron Mitchell." [The trial court dismissed the fourth cause of action on the ground that an action for loss of consortium could not be maintained if the plaintiff was not married to the injured party.] ...

... [T]he Fourth District Court of Appeal concluded that an unmarried cohabitant may state a cause of action for loss of consortium upon a showing that the nonmarital relationship possesses the "characteristics" of a marriage. (*Butcher v. Superior Court* (1983) 139 Cal. App. 3d 58, 188 Cal. Rptr. 503.) For the reasons discussed below, we decline to follow that case, and we adhere to the line of authority which confines recovery for loss of consortium to an injury which occurs within a legal marriage....

... [I]n *Borer v. American Airlines, Inc.* [p. 25, supra] the Supreme Court ... cautioned that [*Rodriguez v. Bethlehem Steel Corp.*] should *not* be read so broadly as to permit a cause of action for loss of consortium whenever there is a "foreseeable injury to a legally recognized relationship...." "Judicial recognition of a cause of action for loss of consortium, we believe, must be narrowly circumscribed." "[S]ocial policy must at some point intervene to delimit liability." "[T]he courts must locate the line between liability and nonliability at some point, a decision which is essentially political."

Absent legislative authority, we think the line must be drawn to exclude a nonmarital cohabitant....

First, we note that at common law a party must have been legally married to the injured person at the time of the injury to assert a claim for loss of consortium. Sound reasons underlie this rule. The cause of action for loss of consortium presupposes that upon entry into a marriage a party is entitled to expect not only financial support or services but also comfort, companionship, sexual relations, and more. An injury to one spouse thus interferes with the other spouse's enjoyment of these benefits. But until marriage, neither party has a legal right to expect any such benefits from the other. Consequently, without marriage, an injury to one of the cohabitants does not interfere with a legally cognizable right of the other.

In California, one cannot sue for breach of a promise to marry. It would be anomalous to permit a person to recover for the loss of consortium yet deny that same person recovery for the loss of those same marital benefits upon the failure to carry out the promise of marriage.

Furthermore, despite what appeared some years ago to be a changing social trend toward cohabitation without marriage, marriage continues to be the foundation of this nation's family life.

We perceive the policy of this state favoring marriage to be based upon the salutary notion that marriage is the basic unit of social order; a policy rooted not only in community mores, but also in the need to define the familial rights and responsibilities of society's members....

The pedestal upon which marriage is placed was well described in *Nieto v. City of Los Angeles* (1982) 138 Cal. App. 3d 464, 188 Cal. Rptr. 31: "Spouses receive special consideration from the state, for marriage is a civil contract 'of so solemn and binding a nature ... that the consent of the parties alone will not constitute marriage ... ; but one to which the consent of the state is also required.' Marriage is accorded this degree of dignity in recognition that '[t]he joining of the man and woman in marriage is at once the most socially productive and individually fulfilling relationship that one can enjoy in the course of a lifetime.' Consonant therewith, the state is most solicitous of the rights of spouses. The state affords similar protection to certain putative relationships in recognition of the good faith in which the innocent party undertook to marry. Unmarried cohabitants receive no similar solicitous statutory protection, nor should they; such would impede the state's substantial interest in promoting and protecting marriage."

This strong public policy would be thwarted if persons could gain marital legal rights without accepting the correlative marital legal responsibilities. Were this court to extend to unmarried persons legal rights heretofore confined to married persons, we would overstep our authority and usurp the authority of the Legislature to set public policy. Only the Legislature responsible to the electorate should have the power to make such a radical change in the fabric of society. To the extent that the *Butcher* opinion advocates that the courts should effect a profound change in public policy because there may be more unmarried cohabitants today than ten years ago we disagree; we would refer that decision to the Legislature, where it properly belongs.

Contrary to popular misconception, *Marvin v. Marvin*, 18 Cal. 3d 660, 134 Cal. Rptr. 815, 557 P.2d 106, did not legitimize the cohabitation of unmarried persons, nor did it open Pandora's box by giving those cohabitants the same causes of action and other benefits as if they were married. *Marvin* did nothing more than establish the right of unmarried cohabitants to enter into valid contractual obligations of support so long as sexual services did not constitute the sole consideration therefor.... [T]here is nothing in *Marvin* which would indicate a result different from that which we reach here.

We also observe that partners who wish social and legal recognition of their relationship consciously elect to marry. It can be argued that the failure of meretricious spouses to assume the responsibility of marital vows and the legal obligation resulting from a formal marriage ceremony evidences a lack of permanent commitment which would render compensation for loss of consortium too speculative to calculate.

Finally, marriage provides a legal touchstone by which the strength of a male-female relationship may be tested. The test articulated in *Butcher* requires the *courts* to decide whether a relationship is "stable and significant." That test strikes us as unworkable and one which places a difficult and unnecessary burden on the judicial branch....

The resolution of the issue in this case does not depend upon an "older morality"; it is not our function in this opinion to either condone or condemn the cohabitation of unmarried persons of any sexual preference....

... [A]n action for loss of consortium cannot be maintained unless the plaintiff was married to the injured person at the time of the accident.

The judgment is affirmed.

Notes

1. Most of the relevant cases hold that there is no action for loss of consortium when injury occurs to one member of an unmarried couple, even if they are engaged or represent themselves as married. See Elden v. Sheldon, 46 Cal. 3d 267, 250 Cal. Rptr. 254, 758 P.2d 582 (1988); Medly v. Strong, 200 Ill. App. 3d 488, 558 N.E.2d 244 (1990); Annot., Action for Loss of Consortium Based on Nonmarital Cohabitation, 40 A.L.R.4th 553 (1985). It is also held that a spouse has no action for loss of marital consortium caused by an injury received before the marriage. Harris v. Sherman, 167 Vt. 613, 708 A.2d 1348 (1998). See Annot., Recovery for Loss of Consortium for Injury Occurring Prior to Marriage, 5 A.L.R.4th 300 (1981). Should there be an exception for injuries not detected until after the marriage ceremony? See Owens-Illinois, Inc. v. Cook, 386 Md. 468, 872 A.2d 969 (2005) (action permitted); Zwicker v. Altamont Emergency Room Physicians Medical Group, 98 Cal. App. 4th 26, 118 Cal. Rptr. 2d 912 (2002) (action denied).

2. If a court is to entertain an action for loss of consortium in a non-marital relationship, what facts are relevant to determine whether the relationship qualifies? Are there any that are critical? See Lozoya v. Sanchez, 133 N.M. 579, 66 P.3d 948 (2003), which extends the loss of consortium action to cohabitants in an "intimate family relationship." In Butcher v. Superior Court, discussed in the principal case, the couple had been "living together as husband and wife" for over eleven years and had two children. In Bulloch v. United States, 487 F. Supp. 1078 (D.N.J. 1980), which also permitted an action, the couple had been married for many years, divorced shortly before the ex-husband was injured, and resumed cohabitation after he was discharged from hospital. What if the couple's relationship is platonic, not sexual? Would a damages claim be accepted when the couple cannot marry each other, as when they are of the same sex or one member is already married? See Bashaway v. Cheney Brothers, Inc., 987 So. 2d 93 (Fla. App. 2008). Should a special rule be created for persons who believe they are married but aren't? Would the process of gathering the relevant facts involve such invasions of privacy as to warrant categorical rejection of unmarried couple consortium actions?

3. In Marvin v. Marvin, it was held that on the basis of express contract, implied contract and equitable grounds, one cohabitant stated a cause of action against the other for division of property and support. Does this have as little bearing on the issue in the principal case as the opinion suggests? Also consider the significance of state law on whether a member of an unmarried couple can be awarded damages for the wrongful death of the other member, whether there can be an action for emotional distress caused by witnessing serious injury to the other member, and whether the survivor of an unmarried couple can obtain statutory benefits, such as workers' compensation payments, that were intended for surviving spouses. See Kiesel v. Peter Kiewit & Sons' Co., 638 F. Supp. 1251 (D. Hawaii 1986); Ledger v. Tippitt, 164 Cal. App. 3d 625, 210 Cal. Rptr. 814 (1985).

4. Statutes in a number of states now permit same-sex and sometimes opposite-sex couples to establish a "civil union" or "domestic partnership." The statutes typically provide that parties to a civil union or domestic partnership shall have legal rights, benefits and protections equivalent to those of spouses. E.g., Cal. Family Code § 297.5; Ill. Comp. Stat. Ann. § 750: 75/20; N.H. Rev. Stat. Ann. § 457-A:6; Ore. Rev. Stat. § 106.340. The legislation in New Jersey and Vermont specifically lists loss of consortium actions as one of the applicable benefits or protections. N.J. Stat. Ann. § 37:1-32; 15 Vt. Stat. Ann. § 1204. Hawaii legislation provides for liability to "reciprocal beneficiaries" of injured persons — a relationship which may be established by any adults prohibited from marrying each other because of gender or family relationship. Haw. Rev. Stat. §§ 572C-4, 663-1.

5. If an adult is a stepparent or otherwise acts as a parent without legally adopting the child, should the adult have an action when the child is injured, or vice versa? See Mendoza v. B.L.H. Electronics, 403 Mass. 437, 530 N.E.2d 349 (1988) (adult stepchild's action for injury to stepparent rejected); Ford Motor Co. v. Miles, 967 S.W.2d 377 (Tex. 1998) (stepparent's action for injury to minor child rejected). Compare Anderson v. Aupperle, 51 Or. 556, 95 P. 330 (1908) (grandmother could bring action for loss of services of granddaughter raised in grandmother's household after father deserted family and mother died). Fernandez v. Walgreen Hastings Co., 126 N.M. 263, 968 P.2d 774 (1998), holds that a grandparent who was "a family caretaker and provider of parental affection" to an injured grandchild may recover for loss of the child's consortium. The child's mother was living in the same household. Does this lend support to the "slippery slope" arguments against allowing any cause of action for loss of a child's or parent's "consortium"?

D. Defenses

Brennan v. Biber
Superior Court of New Jersey, Law Division
93 N.J. Super. 351, 225 A.2d 742 (1966), aff'd,
99 N.J. Super. 247, 239 A.2d 261 (App. Div. 1968)

KOLE, J.C.C. (temporarily assigned).

[A car driven by Biber had an accident with a car driven by John Brennan and carrying his three infant children as passengers. An action was brought against Biber (1) by the three children, to recover for injuries they allegedly sustained; (2) by John Brennan, for his injuries and damage to his vehicle; and (3) by Monica Brennan, the mother of the children, for hospital and medical expenses relating to their injuries and for loss of the children's services, society and companionship. Among the defenses asserted was John Brennan's contributory negligence. The jury returned verdicts against John and Monica Brennan and two of the children. It returned a verdict in favor of the third child. Plaintiffs moved for a new trial.]

... [E]ven if the jury had found that medical expenses were incurred as to all three children — Patrick, Brian and Sean — their mother Monica's claim therefor is barred by her husband John's contributory negligence. It is obvious, from the verdict in favor of Sean for his injuries and against his father John for his own injuries and car damage, that the jury found John guilty of contributory negligence. As I charged the jury, if they found John was contributorily negligent, there could be no recovery by Monica for such expenses, since John in fact paid them. The parent who actually pays or is under the legal obligation to pay medical expenses for the injured child may not recover therefor against the tortfeasor if he himself is guilty of contributory negligence, although he may recover if his spouse and not he is guilty of such negligence....

A father has a duty to pay medical expenses for his children where he is living with his wife and children, even though his wife in fact retained the physician.... The parent whose funds are used to pay, or who is liable to pay, such expenses is the only one entitled to recover therefor.

Accordingly, even though, as claimed, plaintiff mother actually obtained the medical aid for the children or paid therefor from her husband's funds, the legal status of the claim for medical expenses is the same as if the father were the claimant. Since he in fact paid the expenses and was legally obligated to pay them, the claim is his, not his wife's. If he would be barred from recovery thereon, so would she. Such bar to recovery may not be avoided merely by the device of having her sue as plaintiff on the claim. Thus, even if it be assumed that she has standing to sue and recover on the claim, in determining whether recovery may be had thereon it is to be considered as if he were the claimant. Since the jury must have found that he was guilty of contributory negligence, he could not recover for the children's medical expenses; his wife, therefore, is likewise foreclosed from such recovery....

I have concluded ... that a parent in a negligence action may not recover damages for loss of the society and companionship of an injured child....

Assuming, however, that plaintiff Monica Brennan's claim for such loss was a legally proper matter for the jury to consider, was error committed when I charged the following?:[10] " ... if you find that defendants have sustained the burden of proving ... that John Brennan was guilty of contributory negligence ..., [his contributory negligence] would be imputed to his wife because ... both he and his wife are entitled to [the] companionship and society of the children. To permit Monica to recover these damages would, in effect, permit John Brennan to profit by his own wrong. ..."

Plaintiff contends that the charge contravenes the rule established in Savoia v. F.W. Woolworth Co., 88 N.J. Super. 153, 211 A.2d 214 (App. Div. 1965). ... [T]he actual holding of *Savoia* is that the contributory negligence of a wife may not be imputed to her husband so as to bar recovery by *him* of medical expenses actually incurred by him for the injured child.

However, the Appellate Division, in arriving at its decision and by way of *dictum*, did seem to go further than its actual holding by (1) indicating that, since the Married Women's Act, "the wife has been regarded as a separate individual whose negligence is no more to be charged against her husband than in the case of any other person"; (2) relying on out-of-state cases which seem to apply the rule precluding such imputed negligence not only to medical expenses but also to other elements of the parent's *per quod* recovery with respect to an injured child. ...

Because the elements other than medical expenses were not involved, the court did not consider the effect of N.J.S.A. 9:1-1 relating to the parents' right to a child's services and earnings. This statute provides that both parents are "equally entitled to its services and earnings" unless one of them is dead, has abandoned the child or been deprived of custody of the child by a court, in which event "the other is entitled to such services"; and further provides for a joint action by the parents for loss of wages or services against a tortfeasor who injures the child unless one parent is dead, has abandoned the child, been deprived of its custody by a court, or refuses to sue, in which event "the other may sue alone." Thus, where the parents live together with the child they should sue jointly for loss of its wages or services. Nor did the court consider whether a rule similar to that established by this statute should be applied to loss of companionship and society of a child, assuming a cause of action therefor does exist.

I am of the opinion that, notwithstanding the provisions of the Married Women's Act making the wife a separate legal entity with respect to her torts, the effect of N.J.S.A. 9:1-1 is to make her and her husband a unit, while they are living together with their child, with respect to being entitled to the services or earnings of the child and to suing and recovering for the loss thereof against a tortfeasor. The Legislature, in enacting N.J.S.A. 9:1-1, considered that such services and earnings belonged jointly and equally to the parents under such circumstances. In effect, then, with respect to the loss of such services and earnings where the parents and child live together, the statute has decreed that "the husband and wife have a community of interest in the proceeds of a recovery by either." Accordingly, even under the *dictum* of *Savoia*, the contributory negligence of either parent would bar recovery of such loss by the other or by both parents.

If the parents are to be treated in this fashion as a unit with respect to the loss of their child's services and earnings, then certainly the same principle should be applied by the court—even absent statutory authority—with respect to the loss of their child's companionship and society, an even more intangible and indivisible element of the parent-

---

10. The charge related only to the claimed loss of society and companionship, since I had ruled—with consent of counsel—that loss of services could not be recovered under the proofs. Accordingly, the legal propriety of the charge with respect to loss of services and earnings is not here involved, although I believe that logically the same rule should apply thereto.

child relationship. It would appear to be most unrealistic to endeavor to divide that kind of loss and to treat each parent as a separate entity for the purpose of recovering damages for such loss. Hence, if a cause of action does exist in favor of parents for loss of a child's society and companionship, where they are living together with the child, they are entitled to such society and companionship equally as a unit and must sue jointly for the deprivation thereof, and the contributory negligence of either parent is a bar to recover for loss thereof by the other or by both parents.[12]

Accordingly, I hold to be proper the charge I gave that John Brennan's contributory negligence bars Monica Brennan's recovery for loss of the children's companionship and society because "both he and his wife are entitled to [the] companionship and society of the children."[13] ...

The motion for new trial is, accordingly, denied.

––––––––––

Wright v. Standard Oil Company, Inc.
United States Court of Appeals, Fifth Circuit
470 F.2d 1280 (1972), cert. denied, 412 U.S. 938 (1973)

INGRAHAM, Circuit Judge:

[Five-year-old Douglas Wright was visiting relatives with his parents, Albert and Grace Wright. Albert took Douglas across U.S. Highway 45, which was in front of the relatives' home, to a small grocery store. He left Douglas at the store and recrossed the highway to help his brother polish a truck. A few minutes later Douglas attempted to recross the highway alone and was struck by a truck driven by Dennis Tutor. The child's spinal cord was completely transsected and he was left a paraplegic. The Wrights sought damages for loss of their son's services and for past and future medical expenses arising from the accident. Tutor was found negligent because he failed to keep a proper lookout. Grace Wright was not negligent, but Albert was considered contributorily negligent in giving his son an opportunity to cross a dangerous highway alone. The Wrights were found to have suffered damages of $187,104.92, including $115,760 for the value of Mrs. Wright's past and future nursing services. When the Mississippi comparative negligence statute was applied, the trial court concluded that Mr. Wright's negligence had contributed two-thirds to the accident and Tutor's negligence one-third.]

The trial court held that "Albert Wright is the sole owner of the parent's right of action for the consequential damages for the loss of Douglas' services during minority and expenses of his cure." Wright v. Standard Oil Co., 319 F. Supp. 1364, 1374 (N.D. Miss., 1970). On this basis all damages were reduced by the father's two-thirds comparative negligence. The [parents] contend that the trial court erred in this holding and in reducing all damages. The issue is whether a wife, in the parents' action arising from an injury to their minor child, has a legally protected interest independent of her husband....

The district court reasoned that because a father has the primary obligation to support his minor child he is the sole owner of the parents' suit for consequential damages suf-

––––––––––

12. A contrary rule would require the court to charge the jury that it should award one-half of the damages found for such loss to the nonnegligent parent and nothing to the negligent parent....

13. I should further have required that both parents, instead of Monica alone, be joint plaintiffs with respect to this claim for damages. The fact that the father was not joined as plaintiff for this claim does not hide the fact that he is a "real ... party in interest" therein.

fered as a result of the child's injury.... [A]s the sole owner of the right, he is entitled to all the damages. Thus all damages must be reduced by his comparative negligence—a portion of the damages cannot be segregated and remain immune from the application of the comparative negligence standard....

In order to decide whether Mrs. Wright has an independent interest in the parents' right of action, we must identify the elements of damage which comprise it. First is the value of the lost services of the child until majority; second is the medical expense incurred to cure the child's injuries....

Mississippi statutorily established the equality of parents in dealing with their children in section 399 of the Mississippi Code.... "The father and mother are the joint natural guardians of their minor children and are equally charged with their care, nurture, welfare and education, and the care and management of their estates. The father and mother shall have equal powers and rights, and neither parent has any right paramount to the right of the other concerning the custody of the minor or the control of the services or the earnings of such minor, or any other matter affecting the minor...." The district court felt that this statute was not dispositive because "the state Supreme Court has never interpreted it to relieve the father of his primary right and duty [evidently referring to the duty of support], nor has it ever qualified the father's right to sue upon, or waive, the parent's separate cause of action."...

... The statute unequivocally says that parents have an equal right to the services and earnings of their child. We cannot conclude therefore that simply because a father is said to have the primary duty of support, he also has the paramount right to his child's earnings and services. As the district court noted: "In the parent's action the basis for recovering loss of services is the duty of the child to render to its parent such services or earnings as may reasonably be expected...." In Mississippi the parents have an equal expectation to the services and earnings of their child. In other words, a child's duty to his father does not predominate over the child's duty to his mother. To allow a child's father to recover the entire amount of damage attributable to the loss of a child's services would be contrary to the rationale underlying the right of action in addition to violating the express provision of § 399.

We hold that the district court erred in reducing the damages attributable to the loss of the child's earnings by the father's comparative negligence. The mother should be allowed $3000, and the father's $3000 should be reduced by two-thirds.[9]

The second element of damages in a parents' suit arising from injuries to their minor child is for medical expenses caused by the injuries. Of the $181,104.92 of accrued and future medical expenses, $115,760 is derived from the value of actual and prospective nursing services rendered by Mrs. Wright to her son. Mrs. Wright argues that this amount should not have been reduced by her husband's comparative negligence. We agree.

... [C]ourts label the father's duty as "primary," but that characterization was not necessary to the result reached in any of the cases. These cases arose in a divorce or separation setting. When considered in this context, they do little more than hold that a father who sires offspring in the marriage remains liable, in a monetary sense at least, for the

---

9. Our decision does not turn on who is termed the owner of the parents' right of action, and we do not hold that this statute gives the mother a separate cause of action. Nevertheless, this statute, when considered with the Mississippi rule that one spouse's negligence is not imputed to the other, precludes reducing the mother's right to her child's earnings and services by the father's comparative negligence.

support of his offspring notwithstanding his divorce or separation from their mother. We cannot import a deeper meaning than this to these cases. They do not directly support the conclusion that a father should be termed the sole owner of the parents' cause of action....

Moreover, when the attitude of Mississippi toward women is considered with the conclusion that our case does not fit within the mold of cases cited to uphold the obligation to support-sole owner of the cause of action rationale, we cannot deny Mrs. Wright a legally protected interest in the value of her nursing services....

... Mississippi does not regard women as second class citizens. It [has] a policy to treat women with equality and not to relegate them to a secondary status when they get married....

Our decision that Mrs. Wright has a legally protected interest in the damages attributable to the loss of her son's services, as well as in the value of her nursing services, is consistent with the Mississippi rule which does not impute a husband's negligence to his wife merely because of the marriage. It is incongruous to recognize that Mississippi does not impute negligence to Mrs. Wright and then to reduce the damages arising from her nursing services by two-thirds because of her husband's negligence....

As yet, we have not mentioned the $65,344.92 in damages arising from past and future expenses of cure exclusive of the mother's nursing services. The district court reduced these damages by Mr. Wright's comparative negligence. This result also cannot be supported by the obligation to support-sole owner of the cause of action rationale. However, that does not mean that the decision regarding this element of damages is erroneous because it can perhaps be justified on a different basis.

It is clear that a Mississippi woman can enter a contract which does not bind her husband or which binds her separate estate jointly with her husband. But our record is not clear whether Mrs. Wright agreed, either expressly or impliedly, to bind her separate estate for the various medical expenses involved here. Also, the record does not disclose whether the creditors who rendered goods or services to Douglas agreed to look solely to Mrs. Wright for payment. On this record we are reluctant to decide the treatment of this element of damages since we have taken a completely different approach to the issue than did the trial court. We therefore remand for the district court to hear additional evidence relating to this particular element of damages and intimate no view on how the issue should be resolved....

Appellants next assert that the trial court erred in finding the father, Albert Wright, contributorily negligent.... Appellants would have us adopt a rule that a parent who knows that his child is likely to cross a busy highway may abandon his child, go about his business, and rely, both for the safety of his child and for his own safety under the law, on those using the highways to exercise care to avoid running over the child.... Mr. Wright knew the highway was a busy one, that Douglas should not cross it alone, and yet he failed to exercise that degree of care necessary to protect his young son. We realize that even the most careful parent cannot keep an ever-present eye on his child, and our holding does not require this of a parent.[28] A parent is, however, required to exercise reasonable care to protect a child from harm, and under our facts, Mr. Wright did not meet this standard....

[Reversed in part and remanded.]

---

28. We are not faced with a situation where a parent has left a child in a seemingly safe place with the child subsequently wandering on to a busy highway. Nor are we confronted with the plight of a parent who has sent a child out to play in a familiar, though potentially dangerous, environment such

Notes

1. A parent's own contributory negligence is a defense to the claim of that parent arising from injury to the child. See Doyen v. Lamb, 75 S.D. 77, 59 N.W. 550 (1953) (parents prevented from recovering for medical expenses of child); Motsenbocker v. Wyatt, 369 S.W.2d 319 (Tex. 1963) (mother barred by contributory negligence in not supervising child at play); Restatement (Second) of Torts § 704A (1977) (defense when contributory negligence is defense for type of tortious conduct engaged in). The child is not barred by the parent's negligence and may recover for pain and suffering, future loss of income, etc. See Prosser & Keeton, Law of Torts 531–532 (5th ed. 1984). Should a parent be regarded as contributorily negligent for conduct that would not give the child a cause of action against the parent?

2. Most jurisdictions have held that in an action for loss of services, etc., due to negligent injury to a child, one parent's contributory negligence does not bar recovery by the other. See Ward v. Baskin, 94 So. 2d 859 (Fla. 1957); Illingworth v. Madden, 135 Me. 159, 192 A. 273 (1937); Annot., Negligence of One Parent Contributing to Injury or Death of Child as Barring or Reducing Damages Recoverable by Other Parent for Losses Suffered by Other Parent as Result of Injury or Death of Child, 26 A.L.R.4th 396 (1983). Under these authorities, one parent-spouse's negligence will be imputed to the other only when the negligent parent was acting as agent of the other. How should this rule apply to recovery of expenses for treatment and care of the injured child?

3. In actions not arising from injury to a child, the contributory negligence of one spouse generally is not imputed to the other. See Patusco v. Prince Macaroni, Inc., 50 N.J. 365, 235 A.2d 465 (1967) (husband's negligence not defense to wife's claim for medical costs). In earlier times, when the legal identity of husband and wife was accepted doctrine, the imputation regularly occurred. On the modern law, see Sherman v. Korff, 353 Mich. 387, 91 N.W.2d 485 (1958); Ditty v. Farley, 219 Or. 208, 347 P.2d 47 (1959); Restatement (Second) of Torts § 487 (1965). Some states with community property laws have continued to impute one spouse's contributory negligence to the other on the theory that any recovery will belong half to each spouse and, without the imputation, the negligent spouse would profit from his or her own wrongful act. See Note, Community Property—Damages for Husband's Injury—Negligence of Wife, 19 Tulane L. Rev. 456 (1945).

4. If a parent's negligence contributes to a child's injuries, can the effects of a contributory negligence defense be avoided by including a claim for treatment and care expenses in the child's action? See p. 24, supra. Can the "innocent" parent obtain compensation for medical costs, loss of services or loss of "consortium" by bringing suit against the "guilty" parent? Is either form of recovery desirable? It might produce a contribution claim by the third-party tortfeasor against the negligent parent.

5. The contributory negligence of a temporary custodian of an injured child sometimes has been imputed to a parent so as to bar recovery from a negligent third party. The custodian was regarded as the parent's agent, bringing into operation the rule that an agent's negligence is imputed to the principal. See Bellefontaine Railway Co. v. Snyder, 24 Ohio St. 670 (1874); Bamberger v. Citizens' Street Railroad Co., 95 Tenn. 18, 31 S.W. 163 (1895); Annot., Contributory Negligence of Custodian of Child as Affecting Right of Parent to Recover for Its Death or Injury, 23 A.L.R. 655 (1923). Contra, Casas

---

as exists in a crowded tenement neighborhood. Either of the above examples could easily produce a finding of no parental negligence.

v. Maulhardt Buick, Inc., 258 Cal. App. 2d 692, 66 Cal. Rptr. 44 (1968) (no imputation for gratuitous child-minding by relative); Schmidt v. Martin, 212 Kan. 373, 510 P.2d 1244 (1973).

———————

Scott v. Marshall
Supreme Court of British Columbia
(1965) 54 W.W.R. 1, 55 D.L.R.2d 58

AIKINS, J. [Plaintiffs Mr. and Mrs. Scott permitted defendant to drive their car while they rode as passengers. Mrs. Scott was injured in a collision. The court found defendant negligent but not grossly negligent. The British Columbia "guest statute," *Motor-vehicle Act* sec. 71, provided: "No action shall lie against either the owner or the driver of a motor-vehicle ... by a person who is carried as a passenger ... for any injury, loss, or damage sustained by such person ... unless there has been gross negligence on the part of the driver...." Mrs. Scott's claim failed because she did not prove gross negligence.]

The plaintiff, John H. Scott, claims special damages for medical and hospital expenses, the cost of prosthetic appliances for his wife such as traction collars, corsets, etc., and for expenses incurred for household help. The plaintiff, husband, also claims damages for loss of consortium and servitium. In my view, the claim for reimbursement for expenses for household help is properly part of the claim for loss of servitium. As to the claim for special damages and for general damages for loss of consortium and servitium, counsel for the plaintiff, husband, takes the position that this plaintiff should succeed on proof of so-called ordinary negligence only....

The question I think is this: In an action *per quod*, is the cause of action of the plaintiff, husband, plaintiff, father, or plaintiff, master, one which is wholly independent of the cause of action of the wife, child or servant, or is it, on the other hand a derivative action, dependent on the wife, child or servant having a cause of action?

I have reached the conclusion that in Canada the question has been settled by the Supreme Court in *Atty.-Gen. of Can. v. Jackson* [1946] SCR 489. In that case, a soldier on active service in the Canadian army was travelling as a guest passenger in the respondent's motor car. As the result of a collision, the soldier was severely injured. The attorney-general of Canada sued in the supreme court of New Brunswick for damages on the basis of a master-servant relationship existing between the crown and the injured soldier. [The New Brunswick guest statute barred an action by the soldier against the defendant.]

I now quote the judgment of Rand, J: "... [T]he fact that the [soldier] has no right of action ... puts, I think, an end to the controversy.... [¶] The act here, in relation to the servant, is not in law culpable and unless we import into the right given to the master the conception of an independent duty running to him in addition to the duty to the servant—an introduction which, in view of our ignorance of the principle underlying the rule and the comparative modernity of the concept of duty in negligence, I think wholly unwarranted—we must conclude that it is the quality of the act vis-à-vis the servant which determines its significance for purpose of liability to the master. The notion of an act at once innocent and culpable would here be an innovation whatever the theory behind the liability; and I should say that if there is no wrong to the servant the act is innocuous toward the master.[¶] This qualification of the rule has been applied in Ontario where the claim was asserted by a parent for injury to his child, a right based on the same theory of deprivation of service. The United States authorities are uniform in the same view. In these cases the cause of action of the master was held to be dependent upon a right in the servant and to be defeated by the contributory negligence of the latter."

I now quote from the judgment of Kellock, J: "'If A deprives B of his servant's services by a *tort* committed against the servant, B may sue A. In such a case B must prove (i) that A's actions are a tort against the servant; (ii) that B has thereby lost his servant's services.'[¶] Accordingly, if the defendant's conduct does not constitute a *tort against the servant*, the master has no cause of action."...

If the principle enunciated in *Atty.-Gen. of Can. v. Jackson* is to be applied to the facts in the present case, the plaintiff, husband, cannot succeed. The opening portion of sec. 71 of our *Motor-vehicle Act* makes it clear that a person in the position of the plaintiff, wife, in the instant case has no action against a defendant for so-called ordinary negligence. *Qua* the plaintiff, wife, the defendant's conduct was not in law culpable. I have given consideration to the question of whether the law as stated in *Atty.-Gen. of Can. v. Jackson* should not be confined by the facts in that case, that is, confined in its applicability to an action *per quod* brought by a master claiming damages for the loss of services of a servant. I cannot, however, think of any basis upon which, in so far as the principle to be applied is concerned, a father suing *per quod* for damages for loss of services of a child or a husband suing *per quod* for damages for loss of consortium and servitium of a wife, can be distinguished from the case of a master suing *per quod* for the loss of services of a servant....

... I do not wish to leave the impression that I have overlooked the principal authority upon which counsel for the plaintiff relies, *Mallett v. Dunn* [1949] 2 KB 180. In this case, Hilbery, J. held that a husband's cause of action *per quod* was his own and was distinct from his wife's cause of action, with the result that contributory negligence on the part of the wife was held not to defeat the husband's claim at common law or cause any diminution in his damages.

Hilbery, J. proceeded on the conclusion that the husband's cause of action was distinct and separate from that of his wife, so that the cause of action, personal to the husband, would not necessarily be defeated by a defence sufficient to meet the wife's claim on her separate and distinct cause of action. That learned judge drew support for his conclusion from a consideration of the other form of action available to a husband *per quod consortium amisit*, the action for enticement, in which it is no defence to show that the wife left voluntarily, the gist of the action by a husband for enticement lying, not in a wrong done to the wife, but in the wrong done to the husband by the enticer persuading the wife to leave voluntarily....

I have entertained considerable doubt on the question of whether the plaintiff, husband's, claim for special damages, viz., cost of medical treatment, hospitalization, special surgical collars for his wife, etc., should fail together with his claim for damages for loss of consortium and servitium. The husband's action for these expenses does not seem to me to fall strictly within the category of the action *per quod*, but rather to rest on the obligation of the husband to provide necessaries for his wife.... However, on a careful consideration of ... *Atty.-Gen. of Can. v. Jackson* ... I am of the opinion, bearing in mind that the conduct of the defendant towards the plaintiff, wife, was not such as to give her a cause of action, that is, it was not in law culpable *qua* her, that the defendant cannot be held liable to the plaintiff, husband, for the special damages claimed because to so hold would be to treat the defendant's conduct, borrowing the words of Rand, J. as being "at once innocent and culpable," a notion which that learned judge rejects.

For these reasons the action must be dismissed with costs.

Notes

1. Arritt v. Fisher, 286 Mich. 419, 282 N.W. 200 (1938), finding no "actionable wrong" when a guest statute barred an action by the injured spouse, is in accord with the principal case. A guest statute has the same effect upon a parent's action for loss of a child's services. See Shiels v. Audette, 119 Conn. 75, 174 A. 323 (1934). But see Irlbeck v. Pomeroy, 210 N.W.2d 831 (Iowa 1973), discussed in the next principal case. See p. 13, supra, on the effect of a prior judgment for defendant in the injured person's action. It could be expected that when the injured person's assumption of risk or pre-injury release of liability bars a personal injury action, it also bars liability to the victim's spouse or parent. See Byrd v. Matthews, 571 So. 2d 258 (Miss. 1990); Conradt v. Four Star Promotions, Inc., 45 Wash. App. 847, 728 P.2d 617 (1986). But several cases involving race track accidents deny this effect to contractual releases. See Huber v. Hovey, 501 N.W.2d 53 (Iowa 1993); Bowen v. Kil-Kare, Inc., 63 Ohio St. 3d 84, 585 N.E.2d 384 (1992).

2. If a child suffers injury during the course of dangerous employment, the parent may hold the employer liable even if the child cannot, provided the parent has not consented to the employment. See Annot., Act or Omission Which Would Not Support an Action for Damages by Person Injured as Ground of Action by Parent or Spouse for Consequential Damages, 94 A.L.R. 1211 (1935); Restatement (Second) of Torts § 707 (1977). Workers' compensation legislation usually bars family members' claims when it bars a tort action against defendant by the injured worker. See Fritzson v. City of Manhattan, 215 Kan. 810, 528 P.2d 1193 (1974); Lowery v. Wade Hampton Co., 270 S.C. 194, 241 S.E.2d 556 (1978).

3. What if the child marries the tortfeasor and is then barred from suit by a spousal immunity which extends to antenuptial torts? Since the reason for interspousal immunity is to preserve domestic harmony between husband and wife, the parent, under these circumstances, usually has been treated as having an independent cause of action and allowed to sue. See Hudson v. Hudson, 226 Md. 521, 174 A.2d 339 (1961); Annot., Injured Child's Subsequent Marriage to Tortfeasor as Barring Parent's Action for Medical Expense, Loss of Services, and the Like, 91 A.L.R.2d 910 (1963). If a child is immune from tort liability for causing injury to a parent, does the immunity bar a loss of consortium action by the injured parent's spouse?

Handeland v. Brown

Supreme Court of Iowa
216 N.W.2d 574 (1974)

McCORMICK, Justice....

Vincent Handeland is the minor son of plaintiff Ronald D. Handeland. On September 10, 1971, Vincent was operating a borrowed motorcycle in Des Moines. He was injured when he collided at an intersection with an automobile driven by defendant Jane Eileen Brown and owned by defendant Dennis Brown.

Litigation ensued. Vincent, through plaintiff as next friend, brought a negligence action against defendants seeking to recover for his injuries. Plaintiff joined the action individually to assert his rule 8 claim based on Vincent's injuries. Rule 8, R.C.P., provides, "A parent, or the parents, may sue for the expense and actual loss of services, companionship and society resulting from injury to or death of a minor child." Defendants pleaded a defense based on Vincent's alleged contributory negligence in bar of plaintiff's claim as well as Vincent's claim....

The jury returned its verdict for defendants on both claims. Plaintiff alone appealed. The sole issue, squarely presented, is whether trial court erred in instructing the jury a defense of contributory negligence good against Vincent would also be good against plaintiff....

The general rule is stated in § 494, Restatement of Torts, Second: "The plaintiff is barred from recovery for an invasion of his legally protected interest in the health or life of a third person which results from the harm or death of such third person, if the negligence of such third person would have barred his own recovery." ...

Analysis of the cases shows four independent bases relied on by the courts applying the restatement rule: (1) the plaintiff's action is "derivative"; (2) the negligence of the injured party is "imputed" to the plaintiff; (3) the plaintiff receives his cause of action by "assignment" from the injured person; and (4) the rule should be followed because it is well-settled....

I. *The derivative action theory.* Illustrative of cases in the first category is Dudley v. Phillips, 218 Tenn. 648, 405 S.W.2d 468 (1966). There, without saying why, the court held, "[A] cause of action arising in favor of the parent resulting from a tort committed against the child is derivative in nature and such action is subject to the same defenses that are available in the action arising in favor of the child."

We rejected the derivative action rationale as applied to a rule 8 claim in Irlbeck v. Pomeroy, 210 N.W.2d 831, 833 (Iowa 1973) ("Under rule 8 the parent has a cause of action for a legal wrong to himself independent of that of the child."). In Irlbeck we distinguished rule 8 claims from truly derivative actions, such as wrongful death actions, which are brought by one person to redress a wrong done to another rather than himself. A rule 8 claim is brought by a parent to redress a wrong done to himself rather than another.

We cannot use the derivative action shibboleth as a basis for adopting the restatement rule.

II. *The imputed negligence theory.* The imputed negligence rationale had its genesis in a federal case purporting to apply Iowa law, Chicago, B. & Q. R. Co. v. Honey, 63 F. 39 (8 Cir. 1894). It was an action by a husband for medical expense and lost consortium by reason of injuries to his wife. The court held the plaintiff was barred from recovery by his wife's contributory fault because he vouched for her ability to avoid injury by permitting her to go out unattended, and it is thus reasonable to hold him responsible for the manner in which her faculties of self-preservation were exercised. This rule was equated to a rule then extant in Iowa which would impute the wife's contributory negligence to the husband in an action against a third party for damages to a horse and carriage owned by the husband but operated with his consent by the wife....

Another strand of reasoning in the Honey case treated the family relationship itself as a reason for imputing contributory negligence. Permitting recovery where someone in the household was contributorily negligent was considered unjust enrichment of the family treasury. That thinking was rejected by this court long ago....

The reasoning of the Honey case cannot withstand critical analysis. We have implicitly disapproved it; now we explicitly do so. It rests on an archaic and discredited view of familial responsibility. We refuse to accept imputed negligence as a basis for adopting the restatement rule.

III. *The assignment theory....* Basically, the assignment rationale is an effort to explain why the parental action can be called derivative. The Wisconsin court held the parental cause of action for lost services is assigned to the parent by operation of law in return for the parental support obligation. The court said, "The parent takes by operation of law a part of the child's cause of action, and he must take it as the child leaves it." Callies v. Reliance Laundry Co., 188 Wis. 376, 206 N.W. 198 (1925).

This theory has been subjected to devastating and persuasive criticism. The assignment basis is a convenient legal fiction without historical validity....

IV. *The well-settled rule theory....*

... [W]e decline to perpetuate an erroneous doctrine simply to avoid a departure from the past. Kersten Co., Inc. v. Department of Social Services, 207 N.W.2d 117, 121 (Iowa 1973) ("Certainly we should be as willing to correct our own mistakes as we are those of others.").

Similarly, we have no obligation to adopt a rule just because it has generally been adopted elsewhere....

... [W]e have rejected the doctrine that the proximate concurring negligence of a parent will bar either a child's recovery from a third party for his injuries or the other parent's recovery under rule 8 for parental damages caused by injury to the child. We have also rejected the view that one spouse is barred from recovering from a third party for his loss by the proximate concurring negligence of the other spouse. Nor have we accepted the contention that an injured parent should be barred from recovery from a third party by his child's concurring proximate negligence. The restatement is in accord....

If justice is served when family members are permitted to recover damages despite the concurring proximate negligence of another member of the immediate family in all these situations, it is surely as well served by application of the same standard in this rule 8 action.

Negligence law in Iowa includes the principle that the merely concurrent proximate negligence of another is not a bar to recovery from one whose negligence proximately caused the plaintiff's damages....

The eccentricity of the rule in Restatement of Torts, Second, § 494, is most graphically demonstrated by its effect in this case if Vincent had been operating a motorcycle owned by plaintiff. In that event plaintiff's negligence action against defendants for damages to the motorcycle would not have been subject to a defense based on Vincent's contributory negligence. Similarly, if plaintiff had been injured as a passenger on the vehicle his action based on his injuries would not have been subject to that defense. Nor, if Vincent wore clothing owned by his father, would plaintiff's action for its loss have been subject to a defense based on Vincent's contributory negligence. In each of these situations the general principle would be applicable. The merely concurrent negligence of the child would not bar parental redress. By the same logic the father's rule 8 claim should not be subject to a defense predicated on the merely concurrent negligence of the child.

Faced with the choice of following a rule simply because it has generally been followed elsewhere or rejecting it because we believe it is unsound, we choose to reject it. We hold a child's contributory negligence, not the sole proximate cause of his injury, is not a defense to a parental claim under rule 8 for the expense and actual loss of services, companionship and society resulting from injury to or death of the child....

[Reversed and remanded. LeGrand, J., dissented without opinion.]

UHLENHOPP, Justice [with whom Moore, C.J., and Rees, J., joined] (dissenting).

The commentators appear right that most of the legal theories assigned by the courts for denying recovery are not logical. But are the decisions just?

The apparent unanimity of decision denying recovery in this country in spite of the commentators led me to examine a number of cases. The more I did so, the fairer the results appeared in actual practice and the more anomalous any other result seemed. The same was true of the consortium cases....

Suppose, for example, a youth who has had too much to drink is not watchful and falls down on an icy sidewalk. The jury finds the fall was proximately caused by the youth's negligence in not watching and by the city's negligence in not salting the sidewalk. Under those findings and the court's opinion in the present case, the jury must be told that the city is required to pay full damages for the youth's lost services during minority and for his medical expenses. The same would be true even if the youth were 90% to blame. Such a result seems unjust. Application of comparative negligence would most adequately rectify the injustice, but we do not have comparative negligence in these cases.

The city would undoubtedly seek contribution from the negligent youth. The youth would undoubtedly counter that the city cannot have contribution because of the common liability and family immunity rules. Such a result also seems unfair when the youth partly or mainly caused the damage. But if the family immunity rule were abrogated and the city recovered over from the youth for half, the practical effect would be, as to the youth's services which belong to the parent, that the youth would pay his parent for half of them, and, as to the youth's medical expenses which constitute a parental obligation, that the youth would bear half of them. Perhaps the youth would also have to pay for half of the parent's loss of the youth's companionship and society for the period the youth was injured.

It may be said of this that insurance will pay everything anyway. But can we proceed initially on the basis of the fault of the individuals involved and then switch to an insurance basis to reach a result? And what if no insurance exists? ...

I do not think the present case is ruled by Irlbeck v. Pomeroy, 210 N.W.2d 831 (Iowa). There the parent had an otherwise valid cause of action against the third person. The question was whether the guest statute took it away, and we held it did not. We do not have a statute here. Our question is whether the parent has a cause of action in the first place.

I would affirm the judgment.

Notes

1. In most states, a parent's action is barred or, under comparative negligence, reduced by the child's contributory negligence. Hockema v. J.S., 832 N.E.2d 537 (Ind. App. 2005), transfer denied sub nom. Hockema v. Secrest, 855 N.E.2d 998 (Ind. 2006); Callies v. Reliance Laundry Co., 188 Wis. 376, 206 N.W. 198 (1925). Similarly, the spousal action for loss of consortium is barred or reduced by the other spouse's negligence. Lee v. Colorado Department of Health, 718 P.2d 221 (Colo. 1986); Mist v. Westin Hotels, Inc., 69 Hawaii 192, 738 P.2d 85 (1987); Ross v. Cuthbert, 239 Or. 429, 397 P.2d 529 (1964). See Annot., Contributory Negligence of Spouse or Child as Bar to Recovery of Collateral Damages Suffered by Other Spouse or Parent, 21 A.L.R.3d 469 (1968); Annot., Negligence of Spouse or Child as Barring or Reducing Recovery for Loss of Consortium by Other Spouse or

Parent, 25 A.L.R.4th 118 (1983). Some courts are in accord with the principal case. Lantis v. Condon, 95 Cal. App. 3d 152, 157 Cal. Rptr. 22 (1979); Feltch v. General Rental Co., 383 Mass. 603, 421 N.E.2d 67 (1981).

2. In Australia, the contributory negligence of the wife has been held not to bar a husband's action for loss of consortium, unless the wife was acting as agent or servant of the husband at the time of the injury-producing event. Curran v. Young, (1965) 112 C.L.R. 99. This has raised the question of whether the defendant in the husband's suit may join the wife in the action and seek contribution or indemnity from her in case the husband should prevail. In Lawrence v. Slatcher, [1968] V.R. 337 (Sup. Ct.), it was decided that the wife could not be so joined; there could be no contribution unless the plaintiff-husband would have had a cause of action against his wife apart from the spousal relationship. Accord, General Motors Corp. v. Doupnik, 1 F.3d 862 (9th Cir. 1993). Similarly, it has been held that a parent may recover from a third party who negligently injures the parent's child, despite the child's contributory negligence, but the third party has no right to contribution against the child since the parent has no action against the child for necessaries. Howard v. Loney, [1956] Tas. S.R. 57 (Sup. Ct.). Would the court that decided Handeland v. Brown agree? See McIntosh v. Barr, 397 N.W.2d 516 (Iowa 1986). See also Feltch v. General Rental Co., supra (no counterclaim against negligent spouse).

3. In a comparative negligence system, the fault of each party and in various circumstances the fault of third parties who were involved in causing the injury are assessed in terms of percentages totalling 100%. The fault of an injured spouse or child is included in the assessment if the injured person's negligence gives rise to a contributory negligence defense to the claim of the other spouse or parent. If there is no defense, as held in Handeland v. Brown, should the injured person's conduct be included in the allocation of fault? See Schwennen v. Abell, 430 N.W.2d 98 (Iowa 1988), subsequent proceedings, 471 N.W.2d 880 (Iowa 1991).

4. Does the rationale of the principal case warrant the conclusion that the consortium claim should succeed when the injured spouse's illegal conduct is a defense to an otherwise valid tort action? It could be contended that there is no loss of consortium action because the spouse whose injuries arose from illegal conduct has no valid action. Cf. Pappas v. Clark, 494 N.W.2d 245 (Iowa App. 1992) (illegal acquisition and use of drugs a cause of injury).

Section 2. Fatal Injuries to Family Members

Huggins v. Butcher
Court of King's Bench
(1606) 1 Brownl. & Golds. 205, 123 Eng. Rep. 756,
Noy 18, 74 Eng. Rep. 989, Yelv. 89, 80 Eng. Rep. 61

The plaintiff declared that the defendant such a day did assault and beat his wife, of which she died such a day following to his damage 100l. And Serjeant Foster moved that the declaration was not good, because it was brought by the plaintiff for a battery done upon his wife: and this being a personal wrong done unto the woman, is gone by her death: and if the woman had been in life, he could not have brought it alone, but the woman must have joyned in the action; for the damages must be given for the wrong offered to the body of the woman, which was agreed. And Tansfield said, that if one beat the servant of J.S. so that he die of that beating, the master shall not have an action against the other for the battery and loss of service, because the servant dying of the extremity of the beating, it is now become an offence against the Crown, and turned into felony, and this hath drowned the particular offence, and prevails over the wrong done to the master before: and his action by that is gone, which Fenner and Yelverton agreed to.

Baker v. Bolton
Court of King's Bench, Nisi Prius
(1808) 1 Camp. 493, 170 Eng. Rep. 1033

This was an action against the defendants as proprietors of a stage-coach, on the top of which the plaintiff and his late wife were travelling from Portsmouth to London, when it was overturned; whereby the plaintiff himself was much bruised, and his wife was so severely hurt, that she died about a month after in an hospital. The declaration besides other special damage, stated, that "by means of the premises, the plaintiff had wholly lost, and been deprived of the comfort, fellowship, and assistance of his said wife, and had from thence hitherto suffered and undergone great grief, vexation, and anguish of mind."

It appeared that the plaintiff was much attached to his deceased wife; and that, being a publican, she had been of great use to him in conducting his business. — But

Lord Ellenborough said, the jury could only take into consideration the bruises which the plaintiff had himself sustained, and the loss of his wife's society, and the distress of mind he had suffered on her account, from the time of the accident till the moment of her dissolution. In a civil Court, the death of a human being could not be complained of as an injury; and in this case the damages, as to the plaintiff's wife, must stop with the period of her existence.

Verdict for the plaintiff, with £100 damages.

Woolworths Ltd. v. Crotty
High Court of Australia
(1942) 66 C.L.R. 603

LATHAM C.J. This is an appeal from a judgment of the Full Court of the Supreme Court of New South Wales refusing to set aside a verdict for the plaintiff (respondent in this appeal) in an action against the defendant (appellant) under the *Compensation to Relatives Act* 1897–1928 (Lord Campbell's Act) to recover damages for herself and her husband caused by the death of her son. The question which arises upon the appeal is whether Lord Campbell's Act applies in cases where death is brought about by a breach of contract, or whether the Act is limited to cases where death is the result of a tort.

… [T]he plaintiff's daughter bought an electric light globe from the defendant on behalf of her brother. Her brother used the globe. The globe was imperfectly constructed and the result was that the brother was electrocuted and died. The jury found that the defendant company impliedly warranted that the globe was fit for the purpose to which it was subsequently put by the deceased and that it was not reasonably fit for such purpose.... There was no finding of negligence or other breach of duty creating a liability in tort. Thus the verdict depends entirely upon breach of contract and not upon tort....

It will be convenient in the first place to set out the words of sec. 1 of the Act as enacted in Lord Campbell's Act (9 & 10 Vict. c. 93 — 1846) and as reproduced in 11 Vict. No. 32 — 1847 (N.S.W.): — "Whereas no action at law is now maintainable against a person who by his wrongful act neglect or default may have caused the death of another person and it is oftentimes right and expedient that the wrongdoer in such case should be answerable in damages for the injury so caused by him Be it therefore enacted by His Excellency the Governor of New South Wales with the advice and consent of the Legislative Council thereof That whensoever the death of a person shall be caused by a wrongful act neglect or default and the act neglect or default is such as would (if death had not ensued) have entitled the party injured to maintain an action and recover damages in respect thereof then and in every such case the person who would have been liable if death had not ensued shall be liable to an action for damages notwithstanding the death of the person injured and although the death shall have been caused under such circumstances as amount in law to felony." ...

It is necessary first to determine whether and in what cases an action at law was maintainable at the time when the Act was passed against a person who, either by a tort or by a breach of contract, caused the death of another person. The Act was intended to deal with *other* cases, i.e. where no such action was maintainable, but where it was right and expedient that a wrongdoer should be answerable in damages....

Of course, a person who has died cannot bring an action for his own death, simply because he is dead and cannot bring an action for anything, and not by reason of the application of any rule of law. The question can arise only in relation to actions by his personal representatives or by third parties who, in some manner, complain of the death as an injury or damage to them.

It is necessary in this connection to consider two rules of law which have been the subject of much controversy.... The first rule is *actio personalis moritur cum persona* — a personal action dies with the person, whether that person be regarded as a possible plaintiff or as a possible defendant. In this case we are concerned with the position of a possible plaintiff, that is the deceased person, who was a party to the obligation sought to be enforced. The rule has no application to proceedings between persons who are both themselves parties to the alleged obligation for the breach of which a remedy is sought, though the death of a third person may be of significance (under the second rule now to be mentioned) in determining whether any remedy is available in such a case.

The second rule is the rule in *Baker v. Bolton* [p. 51, supra] that "in a civil court the death of a human being cannot be complained of as an injury." ...

... Lord *Wright* [*Rose v. Ford*, [1937] A.C. 826] refers to the rule expressed in the maxim *actio personalis moritur cum persona* as being "the rule preventing the prosecution of a claim in tort for personal injuries where the person who would otherwise be plaintiff or defendant in an action has died." In *Benham v. Gambling* [[1941] A.C. 157] Viscount *Simon* L.C. said that the actual purport of the maxim *actio personalis* &c. was that "under the common law of England it was the general rule that no executor or administrator could sue, or be sued, for any tort committed against or by the deceased in his lifetime." ...

Thus the effect of the maxim *actio personalis* in relation to actions of tort was that the personal representatives of the deceased victim of a tort had no remedy in respect of the pain and suffering, or the death of the deceased, though, by common law exceptions and by statute they had certain rights to recover damages caused to his property by a tort, even though he had died. There was, obviously and admittedly, room for Lord Campbell's Act to operate by giving a remedy of some kind to some persons in relation to damages which were not damages to the estate of the deceased....

... [T]he maxim *actio personalis* "is, or course, not true, generally speaking, of causes of action arising out of contract." [*Benham v. Gambling.*] ...

In the case of personal injuries to a deceased person resulting from an act constituting a breach of contract, there was a limitation upon the damages recoverable. Damages were not recoverable in respect of personal injuries such as personal suffering or death, but only in respect of injury to the personal estate of the deceased.

Thus there were cases of breach of contract causing personal injury in which there was no remedy in damages for certain damages which in fact flowed from the breach where death had resulted. There was accordingly in these cases scope for remedial action by legislation....

The rule [in *Baker v. Bolton*] as stated by Lord *Ellenborough* was that "in a civil court the death of a human being cannot be complained of as an injury." ... [It] applies to prevent an action by ... a third party to recover compensation for loss incurred by him as the result of the death of a person killed by the defendant's tortious act....

Accordingly, in the case of death resulting from breach of contract, the application of the rule in *Baker v. Bolton* was such as to leave room for remedial action by way of legislation.

... The reality and the extent of loss suffered by relatives of a deceased man would be the same whether the act, neglect, or default which caused his death was a tort or a breach of contract. Thus there is no *a priori* reason why Lord Campbell's Act should not be equally applicable in both cases.

Lord Campbell's Act deals only with the case of death, not with personal injuries not resulting in death, or with damages for such personal injury, such as pain and suffering, even where death resulted. It created an entirely new cause of action in the representatives of a deceased person. The action was for the benefit of specified dependants who had suffered pecuniary loss by his death, but who could not complain that the defendant had committed a tort as against them, or that he had broken any contract with them. It was a condition of the right of action that the deceased would have had a right of action, if death had not ensued, to recover damages in respect of the wrongful act, neglect, or default which was the cause of the death. But the right of action given to his executors is quite distinct from any right of action that the deceased would have had. It is a purely statutory creation for the purpose of filling what was regarded as a gap in the law.

... In my opinion breaches of contract are within the mischief with which the Act was intended to deal....

The respondent has quoted authorities to show that, at least up to the date of the passing of Lord Campbell's Act in 1846, actions such as the present (for breach of implied warranty), which would now be regarded as entirely contractual actions, could be brought as actions of tort. Upon this contention an argument has been founded to the effect that, as Lord Campbell's Act admittedly provided a remedy in cases of the tortious causation of death, therefore the Act should be construed as providing a remedy in cases of the contractual, but also tortious, description mentioned. I am unable to attach weight to this argument. Even if accepted, it shows no more than that in some cases of breach of warranty a plaintiff might have declared either in tort or in assumpsit. It does not show that, if a plaintiff chooses to declare as upon a contract, his action is not to be regarded as an action based on contract for the purposes of the application of an Act assumed (for the purposes of this argument) to be dealing only with cases of tort....

In my opinion the language of the Act is capable of being applied to the case of death resulting from breach of contract. The words are very general. "Wrongful act" is a term which in a perfectly natural meaning can be applied to breaches of contract as well as to torts. There is the authority of the House of Lords for saying that a breach of contract is a legal wrong. So also a breach of contract may fall within the heading of neglect or default, as where a party either fails, that is neglects, to perform a contractual duty, or makes default in performing it, either by completely failing to perform it, or by performing it in an insufficient or imperfect manner. The Act is upon its face a remedial measure, and ... should be so construed "as to give the most complete remedy which the phraseology will permit."

For these reasons, I am of opinion that the judgment of the Supreme Court was right. The appeal should be dismissed.

[Rich and McTiernan, JJ., delivered concurring opinions.]

Notes

1. *Actio personalis moritum cum persona.* The origin of the rule that tort actions die with the injured party—and also with the tortfeasor—is obscure. There is conjecture that because a tort remedy developed as an incident to criminal punishment and a wrongdoer could not be punished when dead, his death was also treated as terminating a tort claim against him. As for the death of a plaintiff, the early law developed in cases of homicide, where the Crown executed the defendant and confiscated his property; so nothing was left for tort compensation. See Prosser, Law of Torts 898 (4th ed. 1971); Winfield, Death as Affecting Liability in Tort, 29 Colum. L. Rev. 239 (1929).

2. Statutes enacted in the reign of Edward III allowed actions for loss, damage or conversion of personal property to survive the death of a plaintiff. The action could be brought by his executor or administrator. 4 Edw. III, c. 7; 25 Edw. III, st. 5, c. 5. As thus modified, the common law was received by courts in the United States. Torts involving injury to real property did not survive the death of either party. Browne v. Blick, 7 N.C. 511 (1819) (waste); Sims v. Davis, 70 S.C. 362, 49 S.E. 872 (1904) (trespass). Personal injury actions similarly terminated with the death of either party. Ulvig v. McKennan Hospital, 56 S.D. 509, 229 N.W. 383 (1930); Byrd v. Byrd, 122 W. Va. 115, 7 S.E.2d 507 (1940). Breach of contract actions could survive the death of either party, but this usually did not apply to personal injury claims. See Boor v. Lowery, 103 Ind. 468, 3 N.E. 151 (1885); Tuttle v. Short, 42 Wyo. 1, 288 P. 524 (1930). Survival of tort and other civil claims is surveyed in Evans, Survival of Claims For and Against Executors and Administrators, 19 Ky. L.J. 195 (1931).

3. Statutes have now greatly modified the common law in the area, so that most tort as well as contract actions survive the death of either party. However, survival statutes often contain exceptions—specified torts (such as defamation) and/or specified items of damage (such as injury to reputation, or physical and mental pain and suffering) that do not survive the death of one or either of the parties. See Evans, A Comparative Study of the Statutory Survival of Tort Claims, 29 Mich. L. Rev. 969 (1931); Note, Inadequacies of English and State Survival Legislation, 48 Harv. L. Rev. 1008 (1935). There is some doubt concerning the constitutionality of exceptions in survival legislation, especially where they result in plaintiff's losing an otherwise valid cause of action merely because

the defendant died before judgment could be obtained. See Moyer v. Phillips, 162 Pa. 395, 341 A.2d 441 (1975) (survival statute denied plaintiff equal protection by allowing libel action to abate upon defendant's death); Thompson v. Estate of Petroff, 319 N.W.2d 400 (Minn. 1982) (non-survival of intentional torts denied equal protection; tortfeasor's estate not liable for punitive damages); Annot., Validity of Exception for Specific Kind of Tort Action in Survival Statute, 77 A.L.R.3d 1349 (1977).

4. *Wrongful death actions by survivors.* A common law action for wrongful death might have been tenable at one time. But Baker v. Bolton established that a surviving spouse or relative had no tort action for death. There was some early authority to the contrary in the United States, but the rule in Baker v. Bolton became accepted law. See Malone, The Genesis of Wrongful Death, 17 Stan. L. Rev. 1043 (1965); Smedley, Wrongful Death — Bases of the Common Law Rules, 13 Vand. L. Rev. 605 (1960). A surviving exception is Hawaii, which has long recognized a common law action for death apart from the statutory action it now provides. See Hall v. Kennedy, 27 Hawaii 626 (1923). In Gaudette v. Webb, 362 Mass. 60, 284 N.E.2d 222 (1972), a common law action was created to enable the claimants to avoid the statute of limitations applicable to the state death statute. The Supreme Court accepted a maritime common law action for wrongful death in Moragne v. States Marine Lines, Inc., 398 U.S. 375 (1970). See Annot., Modern Status of Rule Denying a Common Law Recovery for Wrongful Death, 61 A.L.R.3d 906 (1975).

5. During the nineteenth century, the great majority of American states enacted statutes based upon the British Parliament's Lord Campbell's Act. Today, all states have a statutory remedy for fatal injuries. Most provide, as did Lord Campbell's Act, for a single cause of action in which damages are allocated to certain surviving relatives in accordance with the loss suffered by each. Others provide for recovery in a wrongful death action or a survival action of loss to the decedent's estate that results from the death. In some states, both loss to the survivors and loss to the estate can be compensated. See Harper, James & Gray, Law of Torts § 24.2 (3d ed. 2007); Speiser & Rooks, Recovery for Wrongful Death (4th ed. 2005).

6. Attempts by parties to a contract to recover damages for the death of another on an allegation that the death was caused by breach of contract have usually been rejected on the grounds that the common law provided no action for damages caused by death and that the wrongful death statute is the exclusive remedy. See Zostautas v. St. Anthony de Padua Hospital, 23 Ill. 2d 326, 178 N.E.2d 303 (1961) (contract to perform surgery on plaintiff's son); Bloss v. Dr. C.R. Woodson Sanitarium Co., 319 Mo. 1061, 5 S.W.2d 367 (1928) (contract to protect plaintiff's husband from suicide). Contra, Jackson v. Watson & Sons, [1909] 2 K.B. 193 (C.A.) (breach of warranty action for death of wife from food plaintiff purchased). Despite this and the rule that contractual actions for personal injury did not survive death, it has been assumed that wrongful death statutes apply only to death resulting from tortious conduct, not to death caused by a pure breach of contract. See Willey v. Alaska Packers Association, 9 F.2d 937 (N.D. Cal. 1925); Bloss v. Dr. C.R. Woodson Sanitarium Co., supra. As Woolworths Ltd. v. Crotty reflects, some jurisdictions permit wrongful death actions founded upon contract. See Zostautas v. St. Anthony de Padua Hospital, supra; Annot., Action Ex Contractu for Damages Caused by Death, 86 A.L.R.2d 316 (1962).

7. As a consequence of the tort-contract distinction, it was held that a death action could not be based upon breach of warranty, a theory often used in products liability litigation. See Whiteley v. Webb's City, 55 So. 2d 730 (Fla. 1951); DiBelardino v. Lemmon Pharmacal Co., 416 Pa. 580, 208 A.2d 283 (1965). More recent authority tends to treat breach of warranty as sufficiently tortious in nature to support the action. See Dagley v.

Armstrong Rubber Co., 344 F.2d 245 (7th Cir. 1965); Ayala v. Joy Manufacturing Co., 580 F. Supp. 521 (D. Colo. 1984). The same applies to breach of a tort duty arising from a contractual relationship. See Braun v. Riel, 40 S.W.2d 621 (Mo. 1931) (physician-patient).

8. While survival and wrongful death are generally treated as separate matters, they necessarily overlap when the tortfeasor predeceases the victim. In the absence of an express statutory provision, which is found in some jurisdictions, recovery against the tortfeasor's estate might be denied because the tortfeasor was not liable for wrongful death at the date of his demise. What if the tortfeasor dies before the victim sustains the injuries that cause death? Is there an analogy to other situations in which tort liability arises after death? Some cases, for instance, allow recovery to a person defamed by a will, though the will was not published until after its author's death. See Hudak, The Sleeping Tort: Testamentary Libel, 12 Cal. W. L. Rev. 491, 27 Mercer L. Rev. 1147 (1976). Survival also must be addressed when a tortfeasor or beneficiary dies after the victim's death but before judgment is entered in the wrongful death action. See Annot., Effect of Death of Beneficiary, Following Wrongful Death, Upon Damages, 73 A.L.R.4th 441 (1989); Speiser & Rooks, Recovery for Wrongful Death, §§ 3:25–3:31 (4th ed. 2005).

Gaydos v. Domabyl

Supreme Court of Pennsylvania
301 Pa. 523, 152 A. 549 (1930)

KEPHART, J.

Justine Gaydos, a widow, was negligently killed by defendant. She was survived by seven children, whose names and ages are as follows: Stephen, 32; Mary, 30; John, 28; Emma, 25; Joseph, 23; Irene, 17; and Ernest, 14. Stephen, the eldest, was confined in the Mayfield Asylum; Joseph resided away from home; and the five remaining lived at home with their mother. All of the children brought this action for damages and recovered a verdict; from the judgment entered thereon, this appeal is taken. The assignments of error raise a question of the right of any one or all of the children to recover.

At common law there was no right in any one to recover damages for the death of another, but this has been changed by the Act which provides that, "whenever death shall be occasioned by ... negligence, ... the widow of any such deceased, or ... personal representatives may maintain an action for ... damages for the death.... [T]he persons entitled to recover damages for any injuries causing death shall be the husband, widow, children, or parents of the deceased, and no other relatives...."

It was early held that "parents" and "children" were words used to show an intention of indicating a family relation in point of fact as the foundation of the right of action, without regard to age. Family relation, as understood by the act, exists between parent and child when a child receives from a parent services or maintenance or gifts with such reasonable frequency as to lead to an expectation of future enjoyment of these services, maintenance, or gifts.... [T]hose affected by such death need not reside at the same home or under the same roof as the deceased. They may reside elsewhere and still be within the family relation. Before there can be any recovery in damages by one in that relation for the negligent death of another in the same relation, there must be a pecuniary loss.

Pecuniary loss has been defined to be a destruction of a reasonable expectation of pecuniary advantage from the deceased. It is not a matter of guess or conjecture, but must be grounded on reasonably continuous past acts or conduct of the deceased.

The reasonable expectation of pecuniary advantage to one standing in the family relation may be shown in many ways, but more frequently through services, food, clothing, education, entertainment, and gifts bestowed. To be reasonable, the services and gifts must have been rendered with a frequency that begets an anticipation of their continuance; occasional gifts and services are not sufficient on which to ground a pecuniary loss.

As a general rule, pecuniary loss embraces the present worth of deceased's probable earnings during the probable duration of deceased's life, which would have gone for the benefit of the children, parent, husband, or wife, as the case may be, and is broad enough to include the present worth of the value or probable services which would, in the ordinary course of events, be of benefit to one within this class. As stated in Sedgwick on Damages (9th Ed.) vol. 2, § 577: "The probable earnings of the parent which would have enured to the benefit of the child may be recovered and he may also be compensated for the value of the parent's services in the superintendence, attention to, and care of his family, and the education of his children of which they have been deprived by his death." ..."That loss is what the deceased would have probably earned by his intellectual or bodily labor in his business or profession during the residue of his lifetime, and which would have gone for the benefit of his children, taking into consideration his age, ability and disposition to labor, and his habits of living and expenditure." P.R.R. v. Butler [57 Pa. 335]....

Pecuniary loss is not the same measure of damages used in an ordinary negligence case where death does not ensue. In such cases, recovery may be had for medical and other expenses, physical pain and mental distress, loss of time and earning power caused by the injury; but damages in death cases do not include a claim for mental suffering, grief or distress of mind, nor for the loss of the society or companionship, as such, of children or parents. Pecuniary loss does not include loss of the earning power of the deceased as such, nor the value of the deceased's life as such nor as property, as property is generally known....

... If we bear in mind that the basis of calculating pecuniary loss to any one in the class is to ascertain the difference between the value of the benefits claimant legally expected to receive, based on what had been received, and the value of what claimant would have been compelled to contribute or lay out during the balance of the probable life of deceased, reduced to its present worth, we would not be led into any difficulty. Thus, if parents sue for the loss of a minor child, their expectation is the present worth of his earnings or the present worth of the probable value of his services until he reaches the age of 21, less what the parents would be required in the meantime to pay for his maintenance.... Where the action is by the wife for the negligent death of her husband, her compensation is measured by so much of her husband's earnings as would have gone to her benefit, but, as the husband in life must bear his own maintenance and incidental expenses, these items form no part of what would go to the widow, and they must be deducted from his earnings when searching for pecuniary loss. In an action by a husband for the loss of his wife, his pecuniary compensation for the loss is the present value of her services as a wife; from this, however, must be deducted the probable cost of her maintenance which he would have been compelled to pay, as well as other incidental items that he would probably have given her.

In the present case, applying the foregoing general idea, the pecuniary loss to the children is the sum the surviving relatives within the act would have expected to expend for the maintenance (food and clothing) of the deceased for the probable remainder of her life deducted from the gross value of her services, etc. It may be stated that an inheritance through death, or the proceeds of an insurance policy, or sums from other sources, will not relieve or mitigate the liability of a defendant for negligence.

Joseph, an adult, visited home at occasional intervals, and his receipt of services, gifts, or entertainment from his mother was not with such regularity that he could be said to have been pecuniarily damaged by her death.

Stephen was incompetent and in an asylum in Mayfield, Allegheny county. The mother may or may not have owed a duty to maintain him, depending on the circumstances at the time of the parent's death.… The difficulty we encounter is from the failure of the record to show any of the facts necessary on which to predicate a loss. Damages are never presumed; the burden of showing facts which would bring any claimant into the class within the rule that entitles him to recover under the act rests on the one asserting the claim.

Irene and Ernest, two minor children, resided at home. The mother had a right to their earnings until they reached their majority, and she owed a duty to support them for the same period. The law presumes the family relation and pecuniary loss to one under age. Their damage would be the difference between the value of their mother's services, maintenance, and spending money furnished to the minors, and the amount the parent would probably have received from the earnings of the children until 21, and after 21, in view of the relationship here established, their probable contributions to the mother during her life or as long as the family relation was not severed. It is urged that the services of the mother was no more than a housekeeper.… This is not the correct view. Their mother's services consisted of so many indefinable acts of tender solicitude, frugality, industry, usefulness, and attention to her children which only a mother knows how and when to give. These services, in addition to managing the household, buying clothing and food, washing, cooking, and general care and supervision of the house, are certainly more valuable than those of a housekeeper or servant and therefore worth more. Her age, health, expectancy, and diminishing power to serve, all these items are proper for the consideration of the jury.

The adults over age who lived at home contributed all their earnings, and received clothing, food, spending money, and the mother's services; the value of all these, less their contributions to the mother, would be the measure under the rule above. These adult children might reasonably expect to receive from their mother the same shelter, care, attention, and service until her death as each had been given before; now that she is gone, the services cannot be secured altogether from paid help.…

It is necessary to show as nearly as possible what each child paid in to the family; the value of the mother's services as nearly as possible (this is at best a matter of conjecture), and the food, clothing, gifts, and money which she gave them, in an average month or year, and the present worth of the difference, if any, would be the pecuniary loss.…

[Reversed for error in the trial court's charge to the jury.]

Notes

1. Under most modern wrongful death statutes, the action is brought for the benefit of designated surviving relatives of the decedent. Most death acts have been interpreted to provide for awards of damages to beneficiaries based upon the economic benefit each expected to receive from the decedent, with recovery limited to economic ("pecuniary") loss. See Michigan Central Railroad Co. v. Vreeland, 227 U.S. 59 (1913); Pierce v. Conners, 20 Colo. 178, 37 P. 721 (1894). But "pecuniary loss" is interpreted broadly to include loss of such beneficial "services" as a spouse's services in the household. See Annot., Admissibility and Sufficiency of Proof of Value of Housewife's Services, in Wrongful Death Action, 77 A.L.R.3d 1175 (1977). Or the instruction, guidance

and nurture of a parent. See Tilley v. Hudson River Railroad Co., 24 N.Y. 471 (1862), subsequent proceedings, 29 N.Y. 252 (1864). The measure is the reasonable value of the services lost. Loss of an inheritance may also be included in the damages, provided there is proof that the decedent, had he survived, would have accumulated more assets and left them to beneficiaries of the wrongful death action. See Annot., Wrongful Death Damages for Loss of Expectancy of Inheritance from Decedent, 42 A.L.R.5th 465 (1996).

2. In Davies v. Powell Duffryn Associated Collieries, Ltd., [1942] A.C. 601 (H.L.), the general statement was made that any pecuniary benefit accruing to a dependent in consequence of the death must be taken into account. But note that the principal case rejects reduction of damages on account of receipt of an inheritance from the decedent. See also McLaughlin v. United Railroads of San Francisco, 169 Cal. 494, 147 P. 149 (1915). Why? It is well established in the United States that wrongful death damages are not reduced by the amount of insurance proceeds recovered by the beneficiaries. This is sometimes treated as an outgrowth of a general principle that loss to the beneficiaries is based upon the conditions that existed at the time of death. See Annot., Events Between Death and Trial as Bearing Upon Damages to Beneficiary for Wrongful Death, 30 A.L.R. 121 (1924).

3. Are funeral and burial expenses recoverable in a wrongful death action without express statutory authorization? Most U.S. courts treat them as directly attributable to the death and therefore recoverable. A contrary view prevails outside the United States and in a few American jurisdictions. See Speiser & Rooks, Recovery for Wrongful Death §§ 6:48–6:49 (4th ed. 2005). What about the argument that since death is inevitable, the defendant did not actually cause the expenses? See Note, Recovery of Funeral Expenses from the Tortfeasor, 19 Okla. L. Rev. 352 (1966), taking the position that funeral expenses should be recoverable only when parents are suing for the death of a minor child.

4. There has been much litigation over what matters are admissible evidence in establishing the amount recoverable for wrongful death. The decedent's past earnings clearly are relevant in determining how much the decedent would have earned if he had survived, and thus how much pecuniary benefit surviving family members would have received. However, there are some decisions excluding other evidence of the decedent's financial condition, such as wealth or poverty. See Annot., Admissibility in Action for Death of Evidence as to Pecuniary Condition of Deceased, 128 A.L.R. 1084 (1940). There are also various decisions on evidence of the decedent's character traits. E.g., St. Clair v. Eastern Airlines, Inc., 279 F.2d 119 (2d Cir. 1960), cert. denied, 364 U.S. 882 (1960) (excessive drinking and treatment for mental illness relevant; cohabitation with widow prior to divorce from previous spouse not relevant); Sheehan v. Pima County, 135 Ariz. 235, 660 P.2d 486 (Ct. App. 1982) (addition to heroin admissible); Johnson v. Dobrosky, 187 N.J. 594, 902 A.2d 238 (2006) (welfare fraud conviction not admissible). See Admissibility, in Wrongful Death Action for Pecuniary Loss Suffered by Next of Kin, etc., of Evidence as to Decedent's Personal Qualities with Respect to Sobriety or Morality, 99 A.L.R.2d 972 (1965). Should evidence of a criminal conviction or criminal conduct be admitted? See Crenshaw v. McMinds, 456 N.E.2d 433 (Ind. App. 1983); Dobro v. Village of Sloan, 48 A.D.2d 243, 368 N.Y.S.2d 621 (1975), appeal dismissed, 37 N.Y.2d 804, 375 N.Y.S.2d 569, 338 N.E.2d 326 (1975); Maicke v. RDH, Inc., 37 Wash. App. 750, 683 P.2d 227 (1984), review denied, 102 Wash. 2d 1014 (1984). See generally Speiser, Krause & Madole, Recovery for Wrongful Death and Injury §§ 3.8–3.38 (3d ed. 1992).

5. As wrongful death statutes generally specify only family members as beneficiaries, recovery by other parties for loss caused by a death is denied. There is, therefore, no re-

covery for death of an employee or business partner. See Trump Taj Mahal Associates v. Costruzioni Aeronautiche Giovanni Agusta, S.p.A., 761 F. Supp. 1143 (D.N.J. 1991), aff'd, 958 F.2d 365 (3d Cir. 1992), cert. denied, 506 U.S. 826 (1992); In re September 11 Litigation, 760 F. Supp. 2d 433 (S.D.N.Y. 2011); Annot., Employer's Right of Action Against Third Person Tortiously Killing or Injuring Employee, 57 A.L.R.2d 802 §7 (1953); Annot., Right of Professional Corporation to Recover Damages Based on Injury or Death of Attorney or Doctor Associate, 74 A.L.R.3d 1129 (1976). Compare an employer's action for non-fatal injury to an employee, pp. 212–215, infra. What if the deceased spouse and surviving spouse conducted a business together? In Burgess v. Florence Nightingale Hospital for Gentlewomen, [1955] 1 Q.B. 349, plaintiff and his wife had been professional dancing partners. After the wife's death, plaintiff was unable to find another suitable dancing companion. It was held that the benefit in the dancing partnership could not be attributed to the husband-wife relationship and its loss was not compensable in a death action. However, as the spouses had shared their income and expenses, each was, to the extent of such sharing, conferring a benefit on the other that did arise from the husband-wife relationship and loss of this benefit was compensable.

6. The terms "parent" and "child" in death statutes require judicial interpretation. In general, adopting parents are allowed to recover, and natural parents are not, for the death of a child who was legally adopted. Persons merely standing "in loco parentis" cannot recover. See Annot., On Whose Behalf May Action Be Maintained for Wrongful Death of Adopted Child, 56 A.L.R. 1349 (1928). Children who have been legally adopted are normally allowed to recover for the death of the adopting parents, especially if the children are given by statute the same rights as natural children. See McKeown v. Argetsinger, 202 Minn. 595, 279 N.W. 402 (1938). In the absence of a legal adoption, children are usually denied recovery for the death of a stepparent or a relative who had cared for them. See Babb v. Matlock, 340 Ark. 263, 9 S.W.3d 508 (2000); Steed v. Imperial Airlines, 12 Cal. 3d 115, 115 Cal. Rptr. 329, 524 P.2d 801 (1974), appeal dismissed, 420 U.S. 916 (1975); Annot., Action for Death of Stepparent by or for Benefit of Stepchild, 68 A.L.R.3d 1220 (1976). An illegitimate child usually was denied recovery for death of its father but allowed to recover for death of its mother. See Annot., Right of Recovery, Under Wrongful Death Statute, for Benefit of Illegitimate Child or Children of Decedent, 72 A.L.R.2d 1235 (1960). Almost all discrimination in wrongful death law on grounds of legitimacy is now likely to be held unconstitutional, as a denial of equal protection, except conditioning an illegitimate child's claim to damages for the death of a father or a father's claim for the death of a child on some prior judicial determination of paternity or parent-child status. See Annot., Discrimination on Basis of Illegitimacy as Denial of Constitutional Rights, 38 A.L.R.3d 613 (1971).

Selders v. Armentrout

Supreme Court of Nebraska
190 Neb. 275, 207 N.W.2d 686 (1973)

McCOWN, Justice.

This is an action by Earl and Ila Selders to recover damages for the wrongful deaths of three of their minor children. The children were killed in an automobile accident. The jury found the defendants Charles and William Armentrout negligent and returned a verdict against them for the exact amount of the medical and funeral expenses of the three children. The parents have appealed.

The sole issue on this appeal involves the proper elements and measure of damages in a tort action in Nebraska for the wrongful death of a minor child. The court essentially instructed the jury that except for medical and funeral expenses, the damages should be the monetary value of the contributions and services which the parents could reasonably have expected to receive from the children less the reasonable cost to the parents of supporting the children.

The defendants contend that the measure of damages is limited to pecuniary loss and that the instructions to the jury correctly reflect the measure and elements of damage. The plaintiffs assert that the loss of the society, comfort, and companionship of the children are proper and compensable elements of damage, and that evidence of amounts invested or expended for the nurture, education, and maintenance of the children before death is proper....

It would seem clear that the word "pecuniary" as it now appears in the [wrongful death] statute does not refer to the "damages" recoverable but only to the method of apportioning "the avails" or the amount recovered as damages in a wrongful death action [among the surviving relatives].

Although the defendants assert that the measure and elements of damages recoverable in a wrongful death action are by statute limited to pecuniary loss, and this state has sometimes been placed in the category of states having statutes of that kind, the historical background demonstrates the erroneousness of that concept. The case of Ensor v. Compton, 110 Neb. 522, 194 N.W. 458, decided in 1923, ... allowed a recovery by a surviving husband for loss of services and companionship of his wife and said: "In states having a statute similar to our own, it has generally been construed as permitting recovery of damages for loss of service and companionship under special circumstances where the evidence shows they have a money value."

... [A] broadening concept of the measure and elements of damages for the wrongful death of a minor child has been in the development stage for many years.... "It has been recognized that even pecuniary loss may extend beyond mere contributions of food, shelter, money or property; and there is now a decided tendency to find that the society, care and attention of the deceased are 'services' to the survivor with a financial value, which may be compensated. This has been true, for example, not only where a child has been deprived of a parent, ... but also where the parent has lost a child...." Prosser, Law of Torts (4th Ed.), § 127, p. 908.

The original pecuniary loss concept and its restrictive application arose in a day when children during minority were generally regarded as an economic asset to parents. Children went to work on farms and in factories at age 10 and even earlier. This was before the day of child labor laws and long before the day of extended higher education for the general population. A child's earnings and services could be generally established and the financial or pecuniary loss which could be proved became the measure of damages for the wrongful death of a child. Virtually all other damages were disallowed as speculative or as sentimental.

The damages involved in a wrongful death case even today must of necessity deal primarily with a fictitious or speculative future life, as it might have been had the wrongful death not occurred. For that reason, virtually all evidence of future damage is necessarily speculative to a degree. The measure and elements of damage involved in a wrongful death case, however, have been excessively restrictive as applied to a minor child in contrast to an adult. Modern economic reality emphasizes the gulf between the old concepts of a child's economic value and the new facts of modern family life. To limit damages for the death of a child to the monetary value of the services which the next of kin could reasonably have expected to receive during his minority less the reasonable expense of maintaining and educating him stamps almost all modern children as worthless in the eyes of the law. In fact, if the rule was literally followed, the average child would have a negative worth. This court has already held that contributions reasonably to be expected from a minor, not only during his minority but afterwards, may be allowed on evidence justifying a reasonable expectation of pecuniary benefit. Even with that modification, the wrongful death of a child results in no monetary loss, except in the rare case, and the assumption that the traditional measure of damages is compensatory is a pure legal fiction....

In this state, the statute has not limited damages for wrongful death to pecuniary loss but this court has imposed that restriction. For an injury to the marital relationship, the law allows recovery for the loss of the society, comfort, and companionship of a spouse. This court has allowed such a recovery for the wrongful death of a wife. See Ensor v. Compton [supra]. There is no logical reason for treating an injury to the family relationship resulting from the wrongful death of a child more restrictively. It is no more difficult for juries and courts to measure damages for the loss of the life of a child than many other abstract concepts with which they are required to deal. We hold that the measure of damages for the wrongful death of a minor child should be extended to include the loss of the society, comfort, and companionship of the child. To the extent this holding is in conflict with prior decisions of this court, they are overruled....

... [E]vidence of expenses of birth, food, clothing, instruction, nurture, and shelter which have been incurred or were reasonably necessary to rear the child to the age he or she had attained on the date of death are not properly admissible. We conclude that the investment theory of measuring damages by the amounts expended in raising the child is inappropriate and improper.

[Remanded for new trial on issue of damages. Clinton, J., with whom Newton, J., joined, delivered a dissenting opinion.]

WHITE, Chief Justice [with whom Newton, J., joined] (dissenting)....

... [The majority opinion] by judicial fiat is creating a class action on behalf of the next of kin or heirs to recover monetary damages for "society, comfort, and companionship," and permit a jury to translate emotional, conjectural, and speculative sentimental values incapable of having any objective standards applied to them, into an award of money.

With the common assumption by the public and jurors of the presence of liability insurance in damage cases, and with the natural and human elements of sympathy present in the courtroom, it takes no imagination to see the amounts of verdicts that will be returned. In the hands of an imaginative lawyer, marshaling family albums and the testimony of sympathetic friends, and demonstratively organized and staged by a histrionic-minded lawyer, this court will undoubtedly be faced in the future with the almost impossible job of attempting to apply the generalized principles of excessiveness of a verdict to these judgments, which by their nature are an attempt to award money for a purely emotional loss conjectural, speculative in nature, and incapable of measurement or proof by any objective standard or related criteria.

I call attention to the ... outright repeal by judicial fiat of the 1945 statute, which confirmed the court's continued, consistent, and unrepealed interpretation of the measure of damages in a wrongful death case.... ["The avails thereof (from a wrongful death action) shall be paid ... in the proportion that the pecuniary loss suffered by each (heir) bears] to the total pecuniary loss suffered by all such persons." The majority opinion skips with a light fantastic toe over this language and this statute....

... I call attention to the very material distinction that this court has made, and courts generally, between awards for pain and suffering accompanied by physical injury and loss, as distinguished from speculative awards for sentimental value, such as bereavement, comfort, society, and companionship....

Notes

1. The traditional position, established in Blake v. Midland Railway Co., (1852) 16 Jur. 562, 21 L.J.Q.B. 233, 18 L.T.J.S. 330, 18 Q.B. 93, 118 Eng. Rep. 35 (Q.B.), is to allow recovery only for "pecuniary loss," not for loss of the deceased's society, grief, or other non-economic consequences of death. Many courts have continued to apply this rule, except when specifically altered by state legislation. See Miller v. Mayberry, 506 N.E.2d 7 (Ind. 1987); Bell v. Cox, 54 A.D.2d 920, 388 N.Y.S.2d 118 (1976), appeal denied, 41 N.Y.2d 805, 395 N.Y.S.2d 1026, 363 N.E.2d 1386 (1977). But increasing numbers of cases recognize society, companionship, attention, counsel and spousal consortium as compensable values in wrongful death actions. See Elliot v. Willis, 92 Ill. 2d 530, 442 N.E.2d 163 (1982) (death of husband); Green v. Bittner, 85 N.J. 1, 424 A.2d 210 (1980) (child); Sanchez v. Schindler, 651 S.W.2d 249 (Tex. 1983) (child); Jordan v. Baptist Three Rivers Hospital, 984 S.W.2d 593 (Tenn. 1999) (spouse or parent). Statutes in numerous jurisdictions now specifically permit recovery for loss of companionship, society, etc., at least for spouses and possibly also parents or children. Some even allow damages for grief and anguish. Is this desirable? See generally Speiser & Rooks, Recovery for Wrongful Death §§ 6:36–6:42 (4th ed. 2005).

2. When "pecuniary loss" is the measure of recovery, assessing damages for the death of a child can be troubling. The cost of rearing a child now usually exceeds any possible economic benefits to the parents. Nevertheless, large wrongful death awards for children often have been affirmed. Most courts have permitted recovery for expected benefits from the child beyond the age of majority. The lost investment theory, rejected in the principal case, was put forth in Wycko v. Gnodtke, 361 Mich. 331, 105 N.W.2d 118 (1960). It would allow parents or other beneficiaries to recover the amount they had "invested" in the child prior to its death, as well as an amount for loss of companionship. Other courts have been unwilling to accept this. See Fornaro v. Jill Bros. Inc., 42 Misc. 2d 1031, 249 N.Y.S.2d 833 (Sup. Ct. 1964), rev'd, 22 A.D.2d 695, 253 N.Y.S.2d 771 (1964), aff'd, 15 N.Y.2d 819, 257 N.Y.S.2d 938, 205 N.E.2d 862 (1965). If the surviving parents decide to have another child to replace the one they lost, are the costs and disabilities of the later pregnancy compensable? See Kralj v. McGrath, [1986] 1 All E.R. 54 (Q.B.D.). See generally Annot., Measure and Elements of Damages for Personal Injury Resulting in Death of Infant, 14 A.L.R.2d 485 (1950); Annot., Excessiveness and Adequacy of Damages for Personal Injuries Resulting in Death of Minor, 49 A.L.R.4th 1076 (1986).

3. Problems in assessing damages also arise from the death of a person who was retired or quite elderly. See Annot., Excessiveness or Adequacy of Damages Awarded for Personal Injuries Resulting in Death of Retired Persons, 48 A.L.R.4th 229 (1986). If the decedent was in good health and helped family members, a substantial award may be justified. See, e.g., Smith v. McBride, 119 Ga. App. 94, 166 S.E.2d 407 (1969). Life expectancy tables are relevant, but the trier of fact is not bound by them. See Crockett v. United States Fidelity & Guaranty Co., 229 So. 2d 169 (La. App. 1969). Some decisions have refused damages for the death of an elderly person when pecuniary loss was doubtful. E.g., Patison v. Campbell, 337 S.W.2d 72 (Mo. 1960) (no damages awarded daughters for death of seventy-four-year-old mother, despite evidence she made substantial gifts to daughters). Cf. Go-

heen v. General Motors Corp., 263 Or. 145, 502 P.2d 223 (1972) (death of nuns who had taken vows of poverty).

Dubil v. Labate

Supreme Court of New Jersey
52 N.J. 255, 245 A.2d 177 (1968)

PROCTOR, J....

The question before us ... is whether the remarriage of a surviving spouse may be utilized by a defendant in a wrongful death action to mitigate damages.

Of the many American jurisdictions which have considered the question, all but two (Mississippi and Wisconsin) have held that the remarriage of a surviving spouse, or the possibility thereof, does not affect the damages recoverable for the wrongful death of the deceased spouse.

In New Jersey, the measure of damages under the Wrongful Death Act is the "deprivation of a reasonable expectation of a pecuniary advantage which would have resulted by a continuance of the life of the deceased." Carter v. West Jersey & Seashore R.R. Co., 76 N.J.L. 602, 603, 71 A. 253 (E. & A. 1908). The amount of the recovery under this standard is based upon the contributions, reducible to monetary terms, which the decedent reasonably might have been expected to make to the survivors, and is not related to their needs. Clearly, even were a widow to show that her financial needs were greater than the amount her husband formerly provided, she would not be entitled to a recovery greater than the reasonable expectation of pecuniary benefits lost by her husband's death. That a widow is in a better financial position after her husband's death — whether because of insurance benefits, inheritance, or her own earnings — likewise provides no reason, under our statutory scheme, for a diminution of her recovery.

That the receipt of such benefits should not reduce the award long has been recognized in the doctrine that a tortfeasor may not show in mitigation of damages that the plaintiff has received pecuniary advantages from a collateral source. As we recently said in [Patusco v. Prince Macaroni, Inc., 50 N.J. 365, 235 A.2d 465 (1967)] "It should not concern the tortfeasor that someone else is obligated to aid his victim because of a duty assumed by contract or imposed by law.... [A] wrongdoer cannot claim the benefit of the rights his victim may have against others by virtue of contract, employment, or other relation." We conclude that when the "someone else" is a new husband who has assumed, by marital obligation, the duty to support the widow, his contributions are analogous to pecuniary benefits received from insurance, inheritance, employment, or other collateral sources. Just as a widow's receipt of an inheritance from a relative will not decrease the recoverable loss of her deceased husband's potential pecuniary contributions, so her receipt of financial benefits from a new husband — or the possibility thereof — should not be used to reduce her recovery. Accordingly, we hold that the remarriage of a spouse is not a factor to be considered by the jury in their determination of the damages to be awarded for the wrongful death of a deceased spouse.[2] Of course, the same rule applies to the recovery by the dependent children of the deceased....

---

2. A fortiori the mere possibility of remarriage is not to play a role in the jury's determination; in this connection, the conclusion we have reached is even more compelling since an evaluation of the possibility of remarriage would engage the jury in the wildest speculation.

... Though evidence of the plaintiff's remarriage is not relevant to the question of damages, we disagree with the trial court's attempt to suppress any mention of the remarriage. It would be offensive to the integrity of the judicial process if the plaintiff, after taking an oath to be truthful, were permitted to misrepresent her marital status to the jury. Of course, the defendants may not inquire into the details of the remarriage nor may they offer evidence concerning it. However, the desirable exclusion of evidence relating to the remarriage may not be carried to the point of affirmatively misrepresenting the truth to the jury. It seems to us that in the course of the trial of a wrongful death case, it would be virtually impossible to avoid mention of a remarriage without resorting to untruths.[3] (Contrast the situation here with cases where the subject of a defendant's insurance coverage may be kept from the jury without resort to untruths.) Thus, we believe that— while evidence of the details of a remarriage, such as the earnings of the new spouse or the birth of a child, is to be excluded—the mere fact of a plaintiff's remarriage should not be kept from the jury. The trial judge should instruct the jury, at the beginning of the case, that the plaintiff has remarried but that this fact is to play no role in their determination of the pecuniary advantage which would have resulted from a continuance of the life of the deceased.... [W]e have no doubt that the jury, after proper instructions by the court, will be capable of returning a verdict uninfluenced by the plaintiff's remarriage....

Notes

1. Most authority in the United States (but not elsewhere) holds that in an action for the wrongful death of a married person, evidence of the surviving spouse's remarriage is inadmissible on the question of damages. See Wood v. Alves Service Transportation, Inc., 191 Cal. App. 2d 723, 13 Cal. Rptr. 114 (1961); Kimery v. Public Service Co. of Oklahoma, 562 P.2d 858 (Okla. 1977); Wiesel v. Cicerone, 106 R.I. 595, 261 A.2d 889 (1970). A few cases are to the contrary. Nowell v. Universal Electric Co., 792 F.2d 1310 (5th Cir. 1986), cert. denied, 479 U.S. 987 (1986); Jensen v. Heritage Mutual Insurance Co., 23 Wis. 2d 344, 127 N.W.2d 228 (1964). Should remarriage be considered when damages can be obtained for loss of society and companionship as well as pecuniary loss? See Wood v. Detroit Edison Co., 409 Mich. 279, 294 N.W.2d 571 (1980). What if evidence of remarriage is offered to support a claim that the prior marriage would have ended in divorce? See Dixon v. Serodino, Inc., 331 F.2d 668 (6th Cir. 1964) (evidence of remarriage prospect excluded); McGuire v. East Kentucky Beverage Co., 238 S.W.2d 1020 (Ky. 1951) (admissible in conjunction with evidence of difficulties in first marriage, including divorce actions commenced by each spouse); Dixie Motor Coach Corp. v. Shivers, 131 S.W.2d 677 (Tex. Civ. App. 1939) (implied that remarriage admissible for this purpose; surviving spouse's love letters from third person during husband's lifetime held admissible).

2. Where it is error to admit evidence of actual remarriage, it is usually held error to admit evidence of plans for or the possibility of remarriage. See Gallo v. Southern Pacific Co., 43 Cal. App. 2d 339, 110 P.2d 1062 (1941); Dimmey v. Wheeling & Elm Grove Railroad Co., 27 W. Va. 32 (1885). What if a child claims damages for loss of his parent and defendant offers evidence of the surviving parent's remarriage or remarriage prospects? How would a child's adoption after his parents' death affect damages? See Luddy v. State, 50 Misc. 2d 992, 272 N.Y.S.2d 233 (Ct. Cl. 1966), aff'd, 30 A.D.2d 993, 294 N.Y.S.2d 87

---

3. In addition to the problem of a female plaintiff's change of name due to her remarriage, there is the difficulty, in a suit by a surviving husband who has remarried, of examining prospective jurors concerning their possible acquaintance with his new wife.

(1968), aff'd, 25 N.Y.2d 773, 303 N.Y.S.2d 522, 250 N.E.2d 581 (1969); Sheppard v. McAllister, (1987) 60 O.R.2d 309, 40 D.L.R.4th 233 (C.A.); Saint John Regional Hospital v. Comeau, (2001) 244 N.B.R.2d 201 (C.A.) Cf. Hyman & Armstrong, P.S.C. v. Gunderson, 279 S.W.3d 93 (Ky. 2008), cert. dismissed sub nom. Sandoz Pharmaceuticals Corp. v. Gunderson, 557 U.S. 951 (2009) (children cared for by surviving parent's girlfriend). See generally Annot., Remarriage of Surviving Spouse, or Possibility Thereof, as Affecting Action for Wrongful Death of Deceased Spouse, 87 A.L.R.2d 252 (1963); Annot., Remarriage of Surviving Parent as Affecting Action for Wrongful Death of Child, 69 A.L.R.3d 1038 (1976); Annot., Admissibility of Evidence of, or Propriety of Comment as to, Plaintiff Spouse's Remarriage or Possibility Thereof, in Action for Death of Other Spouse, 88 A.L.R.3d 926 (1978).

3. In Roy's Midway Transport Ltd. v. Dickson, (1989) 97 N.B.R.2d 251, sub nom. Dickson v. Roy's Midway Transport Ltd., 60 D.L.R.4th 99 (C.A.), a divorced father assumed custody of his daughter after the death of the child's mother. The mother had been the child's only substantial source of maintenance and support. The court held that damages awarded the child for loss of maintenance and support from her mother were to be calculated without regard to the financial support she was receiving from her father. If parents claim loss of society damages for the death of an infant, should the fact that the parents later had more children be admissible? See Simmons v. University of Chicago Hospitals and Clinics, 162 Ill. 2d 1, 642 N.E.2d 107 (1994).

4. Does a spouse have an action for the demise of the other spouse if the injury causing death took place before the marriage? Usually yes, on the ground that at the time the cause of action accrued—the moment of death—the survivor was a spouse. See Radley v. Le Ray Paper Co., 214 N.Y. 32, 108 N.E. 86 (1915); Annot., Right of Spouse to Maintain Action of Wrongful Death as Affected by Fact that Injury Resulting in Death Occurred Before Marriage, 69 A.L.R.3d 1046 (1976). Could a court properly regard an unmarried couple as spouses for purposes of a wrongful death statute, so as to provide one party a remedy for the death of the other? It is generally held that the survivor is not a beneficiary. See Garcia v. Douglas Aircraft Co., 133 Cal. App. 3d 890, 184 Cal. Rptr. 390 (1982); Cassano v. Durham, 180 N.J. Super. 620, 436 A.2d 118 (Law Div. 1981); Raum v. Restaurant Associates, Inc., 252 A.D.2d 369, 675 N.Y.S.2d 343 (1998), appeal dismissed, 92 N.Y.2d 946, 681 N.Y.S.2d 476, 704 N.E.2d 229 (1998) (same-sex couple who could not marry). Legislation permitting same-sex or opposite-sex couples to enter a "civil union" or "domestic partnership" (see p. 37, supra) generally allows the survivor to claim damages in a wrongful death action on the same basis as a spouse. If wrongful death claims are extended to unmarried partners, should the assessment of damages be the same as in claims by surviving spouses?

Todd v. Sandidge Construction Company

United States Court of Appeals, Fourth Circuit
341 F.2d 75 (1964)

ALBERT V. BRYAN, Circuit Judge:

An unborn child's death as a result of a tortious injury to her mother does not give a cause of action under the wrongful death act of South Carolina, the District Court has held, if the child was not born alive, although the child was viable at the time of injury....

On January 9, 1963 Baby Todd was a live and healthy unborn child of 8 months gestation. While a passenger in an automobile on that day, her mother was violently shaken and suffered serious injury in South Carolina when the front of the car plunged into an opening in a highway left unguarded through the neglect of the defendant-appellee, Sandidge Construction Company. As an immediate result, the child died on January 10, 1963, and was delivered dead....

Appellant and father of the child, Albert J. Todd, qualified in South Carolina as administrator of the estate of Baby Todd and brought this action under the State Act, reading as follows: "Whenever the death of a person shall be caused by a wrongful act, neglect or default of another and the act, neglect or default is such as would, if death had not ensued, have entitled the party injured to maintain an action and recover damages in respect thereof, the person who would have been liable, if death had not ensued, shall be liable to an action for damages, notwithstanding the death of the person injured, although the death shall have been caused under such circumstances as make the killing in law a felony."

The right of an administrator to sue for wrongful death in South Carolina depends upon whether the decedent could have sued for the injury had he survived. We think resolution of the present question hinges on interpretation of the statute in respect to the meaning of "a person".

South Carolina doctrine on the right of action of an unborn child has not been expressly expanded to comprehend the instant circumstances. In West v. McCoy, 233 S.C. 369, 105 S.E.2d 88 (1958), the Court held that an unborn child of 5½ months pregnancy was not a person in being for whose death recovery could be made. There the child was *not viable* at the time of the injury, not did it survive birth. In the first feature the case differs from the present. But in Hall v. Murphy, 236 S.C. 257, 113 S.E.2d 790 (1960) the Supreme Court of South Carolina recognized a right of action for the death of a *viable* child resulting from a prenatal injury to its mother where after a premature birth the child *lived* for 4 hours. The only feature distinguishing that case from ours is the live birth.

... The District Judge felt compelled to that conclusion by the West case. However, we do not believe the State Court intended to raise the bar to the point of disallowing a cause of action to a viable child injured en ventre sa mere when, as here, the injury was the very reason the child did not survive.

To begin with, the Supreme Court of South Carolina has treated an unborn but viable child as a person and personality. Justice Oxner enunciated this concept in Hall ...: "We have no difficulty in concluding that a foetus having reached that period of prenatal maturity *where it is capable of independent life apart from its mother is a person* and if such a child is injured, it may after birth maintain an action for such injuries. A few courts have gone further and held that such an action may be maintained even if the infant had not reached the state of a viable foetus at the time of the injury. This question is not presented and we intimate no opinion thereabout. Our decision is limited to liability for prenatal injuries to a viable child born alive." (Accent added.)

To balance the right of action upon whether the child, fatally injured by the negligence of another, is born dead or alive seems not only an artificial demarcation but unjust as well. To illustrate, if the trauma is severe enough to kill the child, then there could be no recovery; but if less serious, allowing the child to survive, there might be recovery. Again, if the fatality was immediate, the suit could not prevail, but if the death was protracted by a few hours, even minutes, beyond birth, the claim could succeed. Practically, it would mean that the graver the harm the better the chance of immunity. Moreover, it allows the act of the tortfeasor to foreclose his own liability—the life of the action would be in his hands. These results have a sound cogency, quite aside from the general reasons justifying the death statutes, for the argument that those deprived of their own by death should not also be deprived of all recompense by the death.

Once the viable foetus is accorded the status of a person in esse, logic would constitute its wrongful death a cause of action under the South Carolina statute, for "if death had not ensued", to quote the law, the child would have been "entitled ... to maintain an action and recover damages". This is vouched in Hall v. Murphy. The common law attributed an existence to a child prior to birth in respect to property rights.... Semble, if his property may be preserved for him before birth, his life should be entitled to no less protection....

It is suggested that compensation for the loss of the child can be recovered by the mother as part of her reimbursement for physical and mental suffering incident to the still or premature birth. But the South Carolina death statute is of wider purview. It encompasses loss by the parents of the companionship and affection of the child. Pecuniary damages to the mother in her action for injuries to herself would not seem to include this intangible item, and certainly not the father's anguish. The weight to be given to these items, however, is for the trier of the case on the merits, not a factor in the right to maintain the action.

The complaint of the appellant-administrator of Baby Todd stated a cause of action, and it should not have been dismissed as insufficient in law. The action will be remanded for trial.

Reversed and remanded.

HAYNSWORTH, Circuit Judge, (dissenting): ...

This duty of the tortfeasor to pay compensation for the injury he inflicts upon the unborn child who is later born alive seems to me not dependent upon the viability of the child at the time of injury. If, in fact, the child is born alive and if, because of injury, it suffers and occasions extraordinary expense, no logical reason occurs to me why the wrongdoer should escape because the child was not viable when injured, unless the injury occurred so soon after conception that the problem of determining the causal relation between the injury and the child's defect becomes insurmountable.

I recognize, of course, that some courts have either limited recovery cases in which the child was viable or quick at the time of injury, or have announced the rule of recovery in cases in which it happened that the child was viable or quick at the time of injury. Other courts, however, have refused to thus limit the rule.

What in reason then has viability at the time of injury got to do with the problem? The answer, plainly, is nothing....

Conditioning recognition of an unborn child as a live person upon a subsequent live birth, however, stands upon a very different footing. There is solid analogy for it in the common law. There is reason for it. It is consistent with social considerations.

Little can be said in favor of allowance of a cause of action for personal injury to a child *en ventre sa mère*, which thereafter is stillborn for some unrelated reason. When the stillbirth is unrelated to the prenatal injury, the child suffers no economic loss, and it is, at least, highly dubious that it will have endured conscious pain and suffering. The majority here, of course, make no suggestion that a cause of action for personal injury in such circumstances should be recognized or allowed. Yet, and this is where I think they go awry, it is only if an action for personal injury under such circumstances would be allowed that, under their construction of the wrongful death statute, an action for wrongful death would be allowed if the death before birth resulted from the injury rather than from an unrelated cause. Live birth is a prerequisite if we follow the statute's relation of the right to maintain an action for wrongful death to the right to maintain an action for personal injury. There is no right of action for personal injury if the child is stillborn for an unrelated or a related reason, and there is no action for wrongful death if it is stillborn for a related reason. If viability has any usefulness in discovering reasonable answers to the problem, live birth is crucial....

Notes

1. American courts once were unanimous in denying recovery for pre-natal injury, even to a child subsequently born alive. Starting with Bonbrest v. Kotz, 65 F. Supp. 138 (D.D.C. 1946), a cause of action has achieved recognition in practically all jurisdictions. See Annot., Liability for Prenatal Injuries, 40 A.L.R.3d 1222 (1971). A number of opinions have indicated that liability would be limited to cases in which the child was "viable" (capable of independent life, outside the mother's womb) at the time of injury. But this standard presents difficulties in proof, as the time of viability varies from one infant to another. When pressed on the matter, courts have rejected the limitation. See Hornbuckle v. Plantation Pipe Line Co., 212 Ga. 504, 93 S.E.2d 727 (1956); Smith v. Brennan, 31 N.J. 353, 157 A.2d 497 (1960). A child even may be allowed to recover for a tortious act committed prior to its conception. See Renslow v. Mennonite Hospital, 67 Ill. 2d 348, 367 N.E.2d 1250 (1977) (child injured by negligent blood transfusion to mother years before child born); Walker v. Rinck, 604 N.E.2d 591 (Ind. 1992); Annot., Liability for Child's Personal Injuries or Death Resulting from Tort Committed Against Child's Mother Before Child Was Conceived, 91 A.L.R.3d 316 (1979).

2. When an actionable pre-natal injury causes death after a live birth, a wrongful death action can be maintained. Kalafut v. Grover, 239 Va. 278, 389 S.E.2d 681 (1990). The main controversy is over the question presented by the principal case: is there an action for the wrongful death of a stillborn infant? Some courts deny an action. See Giardina v. Bennett, 111 N.J. 412, 545 A.2d 139 (1988); Witty v. American General Capital Distributors, Inc., 727 S.W.2d 503 (Tex. 1987). On what is live birth, see Duncan v. Flynn, 358 So. 2d 178 (Fla. 1978), aff'g 342 So. 2d 123 (Fla. App. 1977). The considerable majority of recent cases grant an action for the death of a stillborn. See Summerfield v. Superior Court, 144 Ariz. 467, 698 P.2d 712 (1985); Amadio v. Levin, 509 Pa. 199, 501 A.2d 1085 (1985); Annot., Right to Maintain Action or to Recover Damages for Death of Unborn Child, 84 A.L.R.3d 411 (1978). Is this wise? Was the term "person" in the wrongful death statute intended to include a fetus? Does extension of the damages recoverable to include loss of companionship provide a rationale for liability? See O'Grady v. Brown, 654 S.W.2d 904 (Mo. 1983).

3. Cases allowing recovery for death of an infant never born alive have stated that liability will be limited to situations in which the fetus was viable at the time of the injury that caused it to be stillborn, and it has been so held. Santana v. Zilog, Inc., 95 F.3d 780 (9th Cir. 1996); Kandel v. White, 339 Md. 432, 663 A.2d 1264 (1995); Wallace v. Wallace, 120 N.H. 675, 421 A.2d 134 (1980). There is now contrary authority. Presley v. Newport Hospital, 117 R.I. 177, 365 A.2d 748 (1976); Farley v. Sartin, 195 W. Va. 671, 466 S.E.2d 522 (1995). Cf. 66 Federal Credit Union v. Tucker, 853 So. 2d 104 (Miss. 2003), holding that the fetus must have been "quick"—i.e. able to move in the womb—but not necessarily viable. Jeter v. Mayo Clinic Arizona, 211 Ariz. 386, 121 P.3d 1256 (Ct. App. 2005), holds that a frozen pre-embryo is not a person within the wrongful death statute. What if a non-viable infant lives briefly after a miscarriage or premature birth? See Gon-

zales v. Mascarenas, 190 P.3d 826 (Colo. App. 2008); Nealis v. Baird, 996 P.2d 438 (Okla. 1999) (action maintainable).

4. Should cases on the right to have an abortion affect the tort rules for death of unborn children? Roe v. Wade, 410 U.S. 113 (1973), held that states cannot prohibit abortion during the first trimester of pregnancy. Because the decision appears not to treat the unborn child as a "person" within constitutional guarantees, at least one court has ruled that an action should not be allowed for death of a child never born alive. Kilmer v. Hicks, 22 Ariz. App. 552, 529 P.2d 706 (1974), disapproved in Summerfield v. Superior Court, supra. See also Byrn v. New York City Health & Hospitals Corp., 31 N.Y.2d 194, 335 N.Y.S.2d 390, 286 N.E.2d 887 (1972), appeal dismissed, 410 U.S. 949 (1973), upholding the validity of New York's liberalized abortion statute and saying there is no requirement that an embryo be recognized as a legal person under state and federal constitutions. Would a statute attaching wrongful death liability to legal abortions survive constitutional scrutiny?

Kelliher v. New York Central & Hudson River Railroad Company

New York Court of Appeals
212 N.Y. 207, 105 N.E. 824 (1914)

The plaintiff in her complaint alleges that her intestate, Daniel Kelliher, was injured through the negligence of the defendant, his employer, on November 22, 1906, and that as a result of such injuries he died February 24, 1912. She was thereafter appointed his administratrix, and on May 20, 1912, about six months after his death, brought this action under section 1902 of the Code of Civil Procedure to recover the damages sustained through his death. The allegations of the complaint charge the defendant with negligence both at common law and under the Employers' Liability Act.

In its answer the defendant set up three separate defenses, numbered "fourth," "fifth," and "sixth," the sufficiency of each of which the plaintiff challenged by demurrer. In the "fourth" defense the defendant alleged, in substance, that the action was barred by the three years' statute of limitations applying to actions for personal injuries based on negligence. The "fifth" denies that the notice required to be served under the Employers' Liability Act was served within the 120 days from the occurrence of the accident as directed by the statute. The "sixth" defense avers that the action was not commenced within one year from the occurrence of the accident as required by the Employers' Liability Act.

WERNER, J....

... [S]ection 1902, Code of Civil Procedure ... provides as follows: "The executor or administrator of a decedent who has left him or her surviving a husband, wife, or next of kin, may maintain an action to recover damages for a wrongful act, neglect or default, by which the decedent's death was caused, against a natural person who, or a corporation which, would have been liable to an action in favor of the decedent by reason thereof if death had not ensued. Such an action must be commenced within two years after the decedent's death."

... [T]his statute gives a cause of action that is new and distinct from the common-law action for damages on account of personal injuries based on negligence. This distinction is the main reliance of counsel for the appellant. He argues that a limitation applicable to actions for personal injuries cannot be construed to apply to an entirely different and separate cause of action arising only when the injured party dies, and in which the damages are "exclusively for the benefit of the decedent's husband or wife, and next of kin." This contention is not without force, for it is supported by authorities in other jurisdictions which have statutory provisions similar to our own. It is to be noted, however, that the right of action provided for in section 1902 is qualified by the condition that the representative action may be brought only where a natural person who, or the corporation which, "would have been liable to an action in favor of the decedent by reason thereof if death had not ensued." We think the framers of the section considered that no action should be maintainable under it unless the decedent, at the time of his death, could have maintained an action. The section has been held to bar an action in favor of the representative where his decedent in his lifetime recovered a judgment for personal injuries, which was afterwards paid; or where there has been a settlement between the injured person and the party charged with negligence; or where the defendant is released from liability by the agreement of the intestate; or where the intestate was guilty of such contributory negligence as would have barred an action by him.

In the case at bar the decedent allowed the three years to expire within which he was permitted to commence an action. His subsequent death could not revive the cause of action based upon his injuries in favor of his representative. By the express language of the statute the wrongdoer is liable to the representative only in a case where he would have been liable to the decedent had death not ensued. In construing the meaning of this language in [Littlewood v. Mayor, etc. of N.Y., 89 N.Y. 24], Judge Rapallo said: "It seems to me very evident that the only defense of which the wrongdoer was intended to be deprived was that afforded him by the death of the party injured, and that it is, to say the least, assumed throughout the act that at the time of such death the defendant was liable."

In a case involving a similar statute the United States Supreme Court said: "As the foundation of the right of action is the original wrongful injury to the decedent, it has been generally held that the new action is a right dependent upon the existence of a right in the decedent immediately before his death to have maintained an action for his wrongful injury." Michigan Cent. R. R. Co. v. Vreeland [227 U.S. 59]....

The conclusion we have reached in sustaining the defense of the three years' statute of limitations is an absolute bar to the maintenance of this action. It will therefore be unnecessary to consider the questions certified as to the sufficiency of the other two defenses....

WILLARD BARTLETT, C.J., dissents on the ground that the sole limitation applicable to such an action is prescribed by section 1902 of the Code of Civil Procedure itself.

Notes

1. How pervasive is the rule, expressed in the principal case, that liability for wrongful death requires liability to the victim at the time of the death? Many courts, fearful of double recovery, have held that a judgment obtained by the decedent prior to his death precludes an action when death results from the injuries for which the judgment was granted. See Simmons First National Bank v. Abbott, 288 Ark. 304, 705 S.W.2d 3 (1986); Varelis v. Northwestern Memorial Hospital, 167 Ill. 2d 449, 657 N.E.2d 997 (1995); Union Bank of California, N.A. v. Copeland Lumber Yards, Inc., 213 Or. App. 308, 160 P.3d 1032 (2007). A judgment against the decedent also has been held to bar the death action. Secrest v. Pacific Electric Railway Co., 60 Cal. App. 2d 746, 141 P.2d 747 (1943); Collins v. Hall, 117 Fla. 282, 157 So. 646 (1934). Decisions are now divided on the ef-

fects of both favorable and adverse judgments. See Smith v. Brown & Williamson Tobacco Corp., 275 S.W.3d 748 (Mo. App. 2008); Annot., Judgment in Favor of, or Adverse to, Person Injured as Barring Action for His Death, 26 A.L.R.4th 1264 (1983). The
injured person cannot recover damages for the losses family members will sustain on
account of the victim's premature death. Natalini v. Little, 278 Kan. 140, 92 P.3d 567
(2004).

2. What if the decedent had settled his claim for injury and given a release? Here, too,
fear of double recovery has led courts to reject a death action. See Schoenrock v. Cigna
Health Plan of Arizona, Inc. (ABC-HMO, Inc.), 148 Ariz. 548, 715 P.2d 1236 (Ct. App.
1985); Haws v. Luethje, 503 P.2d 871 (Okla. 1972). It can be argued that the decedent
may not have appreciated the severity of the injuries and likelihood of death, or the consequences for surviving family members, when negotiating the settlement. A strong minority view permits a death action despite the decedent's release of the tortfeasor. See
Phillips v. Community Tractor Co., 46 Ohio App. 483, 189 N.E. 444 (1933); Rowe v.
Richards, 35 S.D. 201, 151 N.W. 1001 (1915) (reasoning that wrongful death is new action arising at moment of death). What if the tortfeasor obtains a release from the decedent of liability for wrongful death? See Annot., Validity of Release of Prospective Right
to Wrongful Death Action, 92 A.L.R.3d 1232 (1979) (few cases on point).

3. When the decedent obtained a judgment or settlement before his death, courts can
prevent duplicate recovery by controlling the damages awarded for wrongful death. In
Sea-Land Services, Inc., v. Gaudet, 414 U.S. 573 (1976), the court, recognizing a possible overlap between decedent's recovery for loss of future income and dependents' recovery for loss of support, held that the dependents would be estopped from recovering
to the extent the decedent already had recovered. Alfone v. Sarno, 87 N.J. 99, 432 A.2d
857 (1981), holds that no damages are to be awarded in the death action that were or
could have been recovered in the earlier personal injury action. Note that usually there
is an action for personal injuries that survives to the victim's estate as well as a wrongful
death action. On the division of lost future earnings between survival and death actions,
see Annot., Recovery in Action for Benefit of Decedent's Estate, in Jurisdiction Which
Has Both Wrongful Death and Survival Statutes, of Value of Earnings Decedent Would
Have Made After Death, 76 A.L.R.3d 125 (1977) (in death action beneficiaries recover
for earnings decedent would have contributed to their support; division on whether other
earnings lost by premature death recoverable in survival action). Compare Fitch v. Hyde-
Cates, (1982) 150 C.L.R. 482 (loss of earnings capacity during "lost years" compensated
in survival action; inheritance of damages from decedent's estate reduces beneficiaries'
wrongful death recovery).

4. The principal case presented no danger of double recovery because the statute of
limitations had run out on decedent's personal injury action. Russell v. Ingersoll-Rand Co.,
841 S.W.2d 343 (Tex. 1992), is strongly in accord with *Kelliher.* See also Edwards v. Fog-
arty, 962 P.2d 879 (Wyo. 1998); Williams v. Mersey Docks and Harbour Board, [1905] 1
K.B. 804 (C.A.). Other American cases hold that a wrongful death action is not barred
when decedent's claim expired; time runs on the death action only from the date of death.
Western Union Telegraph Co. v. Preston, 254 F. 229 (3d Cir. 1918) (death ten years after
injury); Castorena v. General Electric, 149 Idaho 609, 238 P.3d 209 (2010) (death years
after illness diagnosed); Miller v. Estate of Sperling, 166 N.J. 370, 766 A.2d 738 (2001) (death
two decades after allegedly improper medication). See Annot., Time from Which Statute
of Limitations Begins to Run Against Cause of Action for Wrongful Death, 97 A.L.R.2d
1151 (1964); Annot., Running of Statute of Limitations as Affected by Doctrine of Relation Back of Appointment of Administrator, 3 A.L.R.3d 1234 (1965).

5. What if the decedent failed to meet the procedural requirements of a personal injury action? In Harding v. Lithgow Municipal Council, (1937) 57 C.L.R. 186, a statute required that a month's written notice be given a municipal council before suit could be brought against it. The decedent had died just two days after his injury, without giving such a notice. The court upheld a wrongful death action against the council, saying that while a cause of action must have existed in the deceased at the moment of death, the preliminaries essential to issuance of process need not then have been taken. See also Dyer v. City of Newark, 174 N.J. Super. 297, 416 A.2d 429 (App. Div. 1980) (ninety-day notice of claim requirement satisfied by notice within ninety days of death).

Johnson v. Ottomeier

Supreme Court of Washington
45 Wash. 2d 419, 275 P.2d 723 (1954)

HAMLEY, Justice.

Where a husband murders his wife and then commits suicide, leaving children, does the wife's personal representative have a cause of action against the husband's estate, for the benefit of the children, under the wrongful death act of this state? The trial court said "no." ...

In support of the judgment, respondent reasons: (1) A wife cannot sue her husband for a tort committed against her person during coverture; and (2) this defense is available to the estate of the tort-feasor under the rule that, in an action for wrongful death, the defendant is entitled to the benefit of all defenses he would have had to an action by the deceased had she lived.

In our view, the general exclusionary rule referred to under (2) above has no application to defenses based upon personal disability to sue, as distinguished from defenses which inhere in the tort, or which are based upon decedent's course of conduct after the injury and before death.

Our wrongful death act, in so far as here pertinent, reads as follows: "When the death of a person is caused by the wrongful act, neglect, or default of another, his personal representative may maintain an action for damages against the person causing the death; and although the death was caused under such circumstances as amount, in law, to a felony...." RCW 4.20.010. "Every such action shall be for the benefit of the wife, husband, child or children of the person whose death is so caused...." RCW 4.20.020....

It is true that, in construing this act, we have held that the action may be maintained "where the deceased might have maintained it had he lived." Welch v. Creech, 88 Wash. 429, 435, 153 P. 355, 357. Or, as we stated in Ostheller v. Spokane & Inland Empire R. Co., 107 Wash. 678, 182 P. 630, the action is "dependent upon the right the deceased would have to recover for such injuries up to the instant of his death".

But the language we use in our decisions must always be appraised in the light of the facts of the particular case and the specific issues which were before the court.

The decisions in which we have announced and applied this rule of exclusion fall into two categories. First, there are those cases in which the defense asserted inhered in the tort itself. Welch v. Creech, supra, in which the defense was self-defense; Ostheller v. Spokane & Inland Empire R. Co., supra, in which the defense was that the contributory negligence of the husband of the decedent was attributable to the community; Hart v. Gey-

sel, 159 Wash. 632, 294 P. 570, in which the defense was decedent's consent to engage in
a prize fight; and Ryan v. Poole, 182 Wash. 532, 47 P.2d 981, in which the defense was that
decedent was engaged in unlawful and criminal acts at the time he met his death.

The statutory basis for recognizing defenses of this character is to be found in the word
"wrongful," as used in the statute. If the tort-feasor breached no duty owing to decedent,
or if decedent proximately contributed, through consent, negligence, or unlawful acts,
to his own injury, it is reasonable to say that his death was not wrongful in the contemplation of the statute.

In Upchurch v. Hubbard, 29 Wash. 2d 559, 188 P.2d 82, this court indicated that a
defense based on the host-guest statute would be available in a wrongful death action.
However, it was held that the decedent was not a guest of the tort-feasor at the time of
the accident, and so judgment for the plaintiff was affirmed. The defense there urged is
statutory in character, rather than being based upon common-law principles. It does,
however, pertain to the tort-feasor's duty of care, rather than to any matter of personal
disability. For this reason, Upchurch is properly to be regarded as falling within the category of cases referred to above.

The second category of cases in which this general rule of exclusion has been applied
involves situations in which, after receiving the injuries which later resulted in death, the
decedent pursued a course of conduct which makes it inequitable to recognize a cause of
action for wrongful death. Among such cases are Brodie v. Washington Water Power Co.,
92 Wash. 574, 159 P. 791, where decedent gave an effective release and satisfaction; and
Calhoun v. Washington Venee Co., 170 Wash. 152, 15 P.2d 943, as interpreted in Grant
v. Fisher Flouring Mills Co., 181 Wash. 576, 44 P.2d 193, where the statute of limitations
had run prior to decedent's death....

... [T]he action for wrongful death is derivative only in the sense that it derives from
the wrongful act causing the death, rather than from the person of the deceased. Needless to say, the wife's disability to sue is personal to her, and does not inhere in the tort
itself.

The wife's personal disability necessarily disappears with her death, and hence is not
transferable to the personal representative, who has a new cause of action. Whether, as
in this state, the disability is based upon the supposed unity of husband and wife, or, as
in some states, on the public policy of preserving peace and tranquility in the home, the
reason for the immunity no longer exists when one spouse is dead....

The courts elsewhere are divided on the precise question now before us....

... "By the statute there is given an explicit and independent right of action to recover
the damages peculiarly suffered by the parties named therein. The Legislature has selected
certain relationships to the deceased as determining who those parties are, but the damages to be recovered by them must be pecuniary loss to themselves, it bears no relation
to the damages recoverable by a decedent who sues for the injury while living.... Compensation is being sought, therefore, for the specific wrong to them. Keeping in mind, therefore, the fact that this death statute is an attempt to compensate an independent wrong
to the parties named in the statute, we are confronted with the problem as to whether
we should withhold the right thus given by subjecting it to the incapacity which may have
attended a suit by the daughter because of her relationship to the tort-feasor. There is no
reason why the fortuitous circumstance that the tort-feasor whose act deprived the parent of support, happened to be the husband of the person who was injured by that act,
and who also furnished the support, should be a bar to recovery here. The disability of
the wife to sue is personal. It does not inhere in the tort itself as is the case where she is

guilty of contributory negligence." [Kaczorowski v. Kalkosinski, 321 Pa. 438, 441–442, 184 A. 663, 664.] ...

As before indicated, we do not believe the rule announced in the Ostheller case was intended to extend to the kind of a case we have here....

[Reversed. Hill, J., delivered a dissenting opinion.]

Notes

1. The language of the original English act and many contemporary statutes indicates that the death action exists only when the decedent, if he had lived, would have had an action against the defendant. Most decisions treat a defense that would have been good against the decedent as a good defense in the wrongful death action.

2. When one parent's conduct results in the other parent's death, a wrongful death claim against the surviving parent faces two gauntlets of possible immunity. First, if interspousal immunity still exists in the jurisdiction, there may be no recovery because the decedent, when alive, could not sue the defendant. Second, children of the couple may be denied damages if the jurisdiction continues to recognize parent-child immunity. With both immunities on the decline—and with many jurisdictions holding, in accord with the principal case, that interspousal immunity does not survive the death of one spouse—recovery is increasingly possible. Similar problems arise when one spouse attempts to sue the other for death of the couple's child. Here, too, there is a trend toward permitting recovery. See Speiser & Rooks, Recovery for Wrongful Death §§ 15:23–15:25 (4th ed. 2005).

3. It appears from the principal case that if the decedent would have had no action because of an automobile guest statute, there is no liability for wrongful death. But in Irlbeck v. Pomeroy, 210 N.W.2d 831 (Iowa 1973), it was held that a guest statute did not defeat a wrongful death action. The action was said not to be derivative; it was not brought to redress a wrong done another but to redress the wrong done the plaintiff-beneficiary. It is generally accepted that in wrongful death actions the decedent's assumption of risk or contributory negligence is a defense to the same extent it would have been a defense in a personal injury action by the decedent, had he survived. Under comparative negligence, recovery is reduced by decedent's percentage of fault. See Speiser & Rooks, Recovery for Wrongful Death §§ 15:1, 15:10–15:12 (4th ed. 2005). In Coates v. Newhall Land & Farming, Inc., 191 Cal. App. 3d 1, 236 Cal. Rptr. 181 (1987), plaintiffs' wrongful death action was defeated by the release of liability decedent signed before his fatal injury. Cf. Haigh v. Royal Mail Steam Packet Co. (Ltd.), (1883) 48 J.P. 230, 52 L.J.Q.B. 640, 49 L.T. 802 (C.A.) (shipping company not liable for passenger's death because liability for personal injury excluded by condition in passenger's ticket). Should personal conduct of the decedent defeat wrongful death recovery if an immunity-carrying personal relationship does not?

4. When a beneficiary's negligence is one of the causes of the death, it will usually give rise to a valid contributory negligence defense to that beneficiary's recovery but not affect the entitlements of other beneficiaries. In some states, however, the negligence of one parent is a defense to recovery by the other parent for wrongful death of their child. See Annot., Contributory Negligence of Beneficiary as Affecting Action Under Death or Survival Statute, 2 A.L.R.2d 785 (1948); Annot., Negligence of One Parent Contributing to Injury or Death of Child as Barring or Reducing Damages Recoverable by Other Parent for Losses Suffered by Other Parent as Result of Injury or Death of Child, 26 A.L.R.4th 396 (1983). The contributory negligence defense might apply to a beneficiary who would

not have been liable to a negligence action by the victim—for example, a parent who failed to shield a child from a fatal injury caused by a third person. Cf. Reed v. Witvoet, 311 Ill. App. 3d 735, 724 N.E.2d 553 (2000), holding that the illegal conduct of the deceased's parents in allowing him to work in violation of the child labor law precluded them from recovering damages but did not preclude recovery for the deceased's surviving brother. Can an action be maintained if defendant is also a beneficiary? What if defendant would be the sole beneficiary of the action? See Aetna Casualty and Surety Co. v. Curley, 585 A.2d 640 (R.I. 1991); Annot., Fact that Tortfeasor is Member of Class of Beneficiaries as Affecting Right to Maintain Action for Wrongful Death, 95 A.L.R.2d 585 (1964).

5. In a wrongful death action arising from a traffic accident, surviving family members prove that the victim was providing them with a substantial amount of support. Defendant establishes that most of the victim's income came from criminal activity. What bearing does this have on the wrongful death claim? What if the decedent earned income from an occupation that could be lawful, but decedent's employment, profession or business was unlawful because unlicensed or conducted in a prohibited location? See Burns v. Edman, [1970] 2 Q.B. 541; Beljansky v. Smithwick, [2006] 11 W.W.R. 274, (2006) 275 D.L.R.4th 116 (B.C.C.A.) (career criminal); Foster v. Kerr, [1939] 3 W.W.R. 428 (Alta. Sup. Ct.), modified, [1940] 1 W.W.R. 385, [1940] 2 D.L.R. 47 (Alta. App. Div.) (seller of sweepstake tickets and contraceptives); Lepine v. Demeule, [1973] 3 W.W.R. 732, (1973) 36 D.L.R.3d 388 (N.W.T.C.A.) (bootlegger); LeBagge v. Buses Ltd., [1958] N.Z.L.R. 630 (C.A.) (driver seven days a week instead of lawful six); Santam Insurance Ltd. v. Ferguson, 1985 (4) S.A. 843 (A.D.), rev'g 1985 (1) S.A. 207 (C) (proprietor of unlicensed panelbeating business); Collins v. New York City Health and Hospitals Corp., 201 A.D.2d 447, 607 N.Y.S.2d 387 (1994), rev'g 151 Misc. 2d 266, 575 N.Y.S.2d 227 (Sup. Ct. 1991); Republic Waste Services, Ltd. v. Martinez, 335 S.W.3d 401 (Tex. App. 2011) (illegal immigrant). Cf. Hunter v. Butler [1996] R.T.R. 396 (C.A.) (deceased obtained public assistance payments fraudulently, failing to report income from work).

6. In the principal case, the tortfeasor committed suicide. Suppose a person commits suicide as a result of injuries for which there is tort liability. Is the person who caused the injuries subject to liability for wrongful death? The answer once was "no" on the ground that suicide was not to be considered caused by the injuries. The prevailing rule now is that there can be liability if physical injuries induce insanity or an uncontrollable impulse, as a result of which suicide is attempted or committed, but not if the suicide or attempt is performed with understanding of the nature of the act. This qualification may not be applied to cases of intentional tort. See Tate v. Canonica, 180 Cal. App. 2d 898, 5 Cal. Rptr. 28 (1960); Annot., Liability of One Causing Physical Injuries as a Result of Which Injured Party Attempts or Commits Suicide, 77 A.L.R.3d 311 (1977). Liability for suicide on a wider basis was accepted in Corr v. IBC Vehicles Ltd., [2008] A.C. 884 (H.L.). Can wrongful death liability be premised upon liability to the decedent for a non-physical injury tort, such as defamation or malicious prosecution, when the tort produces emotional distress that leads to suicide? See State ex rel. Richardson v. Edgeworth, 214 So. 2d 579 (Miss. 1968) (abuse of criminal process); Cauverien v. De Metz, 20 Misc. 2d 144, 188 N.Y.S.2d 627 (Sup. Ct. 1959) (conversion of diamond).

7. Consider the impact that resolution of the foregoing issues may have on actions arising from non-fatal injuries to relatives. Should defenses be given the same effects in these actions as they have in wrongful death actions?

Section 3. Interference with Family Relationships

Rose v. Kavanagh

Supreme Court of Newfoundland
(1946) 15 Nfld. L.R. 428

DUNFIELD J. The plaintiff in this case claims damages against the defendant on the ground that the defendant on the 12th day of April, 1945, wrongfully induced and procured the wife of the plaintiff against the will of the plaintiff to depart and remain absent from the house and society of the plaintiff, per quod consortium amisit, and also has since received and harboured her. The defence is a general denial....

The foundation of this law was laid down in the very old case of *Winsmore v. Greenbank*, 125 E.R. 1330, tried before Willes, C.J. in the year 1745. This was the first case of its kind, according to the Lord Chief Justice. English cases on the subject have been uncommon; between 1796 and 1904 there seems not to have been a recorded case; but fortunately we have in *Place v. Searle* (1932) 2 K.B. 497, a modern review of the situation....

... McCardie J. says: "The present form of action rests in substance on the case of Winsmore v. Greenbank, where it was held that a person who 'enticed or persuaded away' a man's wife committed an actionable wrong against the husband. The same rule was applied against a person who 'harboured' a wife after notice that she was absenting herself from the husband without his approval. It is important to remember that in 1745 the position of a wife was wholly different from that which she holds today. Broadly speaking, it was the view of lawyers and of the law in the middle of the eighteenth century that the property of a woman became her husband's on marriage, that her body belonged to him, that he could restrain her liberty at his pleasure, and that he could administer physical correction at his discretion, subject, of course, to the rule of moderation. The law was concisely stated in Bacon's Abridgment in these words: 'The husband hath by law power and dominion over his wife.' ... Today, I suppose, it must be taken to be the law that an action for 'enticement' still lies, although the position of a married woman has undergone a revolutionary change.... By virtue of the Matrimonial Causes Act, 1884, no decree for the restitution of conjugal rights can be enforced by attachment, with the result that neither husband nor wife can force the other to return to conjugal association. The famous decision in Reg. v. Jackson (1891) 1 Q.B. 671 [that it was unlawful for a husband to prevent his wife from leaving his house] was weighty in its significance.... [T]he shackles of servitude fell from the limbs of married women and they were free to come and go at their own will. Their high moral obligation, as wives, remained and their social obligations were unimpaired, but their physical freedom of movement was recognized and established by the law." ...

... [A]s Wright J. indicates in *Smith v. Kaye* (1904) 20 T.L.R. 261, we may have to draw careful distinctions between persuasion of a wife and proper advice to her, having regard to the fact that she is entirely at liberty to leave her husband's house at any time if she pleases. Nevertheless in a proper case, though only with caution and after careful analysis, we may find that a defendant has overstepped the bounds of what is proper and has by his personal attractions and improper persuasion induced a wife to break her marriage contract when she would not otherwise have done so. Nor is it necessary, as [was] pointed out by the Court of Appeal in *Place v. Searle*, that the will of the wife should be overborne by the stronger will of the defendant. "It is quite sufficient," says Scrutton L.J., "to support the action if a wife of equal will with that of the defendant is persuaded to depart from the consortium of the husband"....

The facts in the present case are as follows. Plaintiff and his wife have been married for some thirty-six years and have had fourteen children, of whom nine survive. Defendant has also been married for a long period, and he and his wife have eight children. The defendant was a neighbour of the plaintiff in Clarke's Beach, and it is in evidence that they were on very friendly terms for some fifteen or sixteen years. During this time the defendant seems to have paid considerable attention to the plaintiff's wife, and the evidence is that up to the last two or three years his attentions, which apparently were often quite open and in the view of the family and of the husband, had, in the words of a youthful witness "gone too far". Whether or not quarrels arose entirely out of this or partly out of collateral matters is not clear to my satisfaction, but at any rate it is evident that defendant forced himself on the family to a very considerable extent and was a disturbing factor therein. During the years 1943 to 1945 there were open quarrels and fights between plaintiff and defendant and at least two assaults by the plaintiff upon his wife. Plaintiff had the defendant before the magistrate at Brigus on two or three occasions, one of these occasions being for trespass on the plaintiff's property, and apart from this, twice he procured the magistrate to write letters to the defendant warning him to keep away from the plaintiff's property and his wife. Nevertheless, it is admitted that in the absence of the plaintiff, who was away working in Halifax for some months, the defendant did trespass and enter on the plaintiff's property and pay further attention to his wife, children of the plaintiff testifying that he was there very frequently indeed and that his behaviour was not good, although, not unnaturally, he denies both points. At any rate, by this time the rift between husband and wife had become such that she said that if the trespass action was taken against the defendant she would leave home and not come back. The action was taken and she left home and did not go back but got herself work in St. John's, where she remains. This point was reached on April 12, 1945.

It is in evidence that after that date the defendant was on a number of occasions in the wife's company, both in St. John's and at Foxtrap, at which latter place she was staying with her sister; he went there on one occasion at considerable inconvenience to himself and stayed in the sister's house for a weekend....

The defence is to the effect that the wife had always been unhappy at home, that she had on several occasions gone away from home for a few days because of abuse or ill-treatment by the plaintiff but had been persuaded to go back, that he had shown violence to her privately and publicly, and that his final quarrel over the defendant was the last straw....

... [O]n the basis of the evidence it is quite impossible not to feel that the defendant disturbed, and persistently and with intent disturbed, the relationship of the plaintiff's wife with the plaintiff, notwithstanding all sorts of warning. A child gives evidence that after the trespass case defendant gave the woman some money and told her to go to St. John's and get herself a job, and if she could not do so, to board and that he would support her....

It is admitted that the allegation of "harbouring" can hardly be supported. Defendant did not take her into any establishment of his, or, so far as is known, pay her board. She obtained, and has, a job. I therefore need not consider the question as to how "harbouring" would stand in these days when it is clear that a husband cannot prevent his wife from leaving his house at her will and staying where she pleases....

The question arises in such cases as this whether the wife left because she was persuaded by the defendant or whether she left because conditions had become unendurable and was merely advised in a humanitarian way by the defendant. I have little doubt that whatever may have been the case in the early years of the marriage, as to which I have only her own evidence of continued unhappiness, her situation at home had become very uncomfortable during the last three years. It is admitted that on one occasion the husband struck her across the mouth; it is charged, and in my opinion proved, that he assaulted her on the road at Foxtrap while she was staying with her sister; and it is alleged by her that he chased her though the streets of Clarke's Beach and told her not to be seen in that settlement again. But these conditions may well have arisen out of the relationship between the defendant and the plaintiff's wife, and that may be why the plaintiff, as there is no doubt, went much further than he ought to have done. I feel sure, however, that a jury would find that the defendant's conduct has been reprehensible and that he is largely to blame for what has come about, and I so find. The history of the family is sufficient evidence that relations must have been at least tolerable for over thirty years, and even if they were not all that they might have been, it is possible, and seems likely, that without defendant's backing she might have gone on as she had gone for so many years.

We then come to the question of damages. The principle in these cases is that damages are compensatory not punitive.... The question is what the plaintiff has lost in the way of companionship and service. From the point of view of the household the position is that the youngest child is six years of age and that there are older children; one of them is twenty-four years of age and is married and is looking after the household. In view of the attitude of the wife as to the conditions of her married life, her previous runnings away, and the rough behaviour of the plaintiff during the last three years, I can hardly feel that in the matter of pleasant consortium he had much to lose. I regard this action as dictated much more by personal animosity than by a desire to obtain compensation. I therefore give the plaintiff only nominal damages of one dollar ($1.00), thus recognizing his proper assertion of his rights. Let each party pay his own costs.

Notes

1. Enticement and harboring actions have the same common law origins as actions for injury to a spouse or child: the master's action for loss of a servant's services. That action arose when a master lost services by reason of enticement or harboring of the servant. As with personal injury, enticement and harboring came to be recognized as forms of interference with a spousal or parental relationship that were actionable by the aggrieved husband or father. So, too, with abduction or seduction of a wife or child. (For sexual intercourse with a wife, however, the action of criminal conversation was used.) In many jurisdictions, the parent's action for enticement, harboring, abduction or seduction of a child never discarded its form as a master's action per quod servitium amisit, but the husband's action was a spousal remedy in which loss of consortium constituted a primary element of damages. See Fleming, Law of Torts 737–741 (10th ed. 2011); Prosser & Keeton, Law of Torts 915–928 (5th ed. 1984); Winfield, Tort 521–532 (8th ed. 1967); Brett, Consortium and Servitium — A History and Some Proposals, 29 Aust. L.J. 321, 389, 428 (1955).

2. The action for enticement of a spouse today may be viewed as "a survival from the days when the wife was considered to be the property of her husband." Gottlieb v. Gleiser, [1958] 1 Q.B. 267n, 268n. But it can be defended on the basis that one spouse has a right to the other's consortium and a person who wrongfully interferes with that right by inducing or persuading a spousal separation should incur liability for resulting harm. See Place v. Searle, [1932] 2 K.B. 497 (C.A.). The principal issues in an enticement action are

likely to be whether the spouse left because of defendant's persuasion and the value of the consortium lost by plaintiff as a result. See Spencer v. Relph, [1969] N.Z.L.R. 713 (C.A.).

3. Does the action for harboring have any modern justification? "The reason why harbouring was considered objectionable was because it interfered with the economic process by which a wife, refused food and shelter elsewhere than in the matrimonial home, would eventually be forced to return to it. . . . In a society that is organized on the basis that everyone is in the last resort to be housed and fed by the State, the bottom has dropped out of the action for harbouring." Winchester v. Fleming, [1958] 1 Q.B. 259, 265. If plaintiff's spouse would not have returned to plaintiff, but for the harboring, no damage was caused and an action will fail. See Spencer v. Relph, supra. There is no liability for harboring a wife for motives of "humanity," to protect her from ill-treatment by her husband. Philp v. Squire, (1791) Peake 114, 170 Eng. Rep. 99 (K.B.N.P.). How far this exception extends is uncertain.

4. In the United States, enticement of a spouse long has been overshadowed by the more modern tort of alienation of affections, but it remains part of American tort law. Harboring seems to have disappeared, at least in its common law form. Oakman v. Belden, p. 82, infra, states that a stranger may, without liability, harbor a wife who has left her husband, but he may not persuade her not to return. Would an American court find tortious enticement if one spouse is induced to separate from the other for a purpose other than disruption of the marriage? Cf. Thornburg v. Federal Express Corp., 62 S.W.3d 421 (Mo. App. 2001) (offer of employment in distant location). Restatement (Second) of Torts § 684(2) (1977) recognizes liability when someone, for the purpose of disrupting the marital relation, induces a spouse to separate from the other spouse or not to return after a separation.

Carrieri v. Bush

Supreme Court of Washington
69 Wash. 2d 536, 419 P.2d 132 (1966)

HAMILTON, Judge.

[James Carrieri brought an action for alienation of the affections of his wife. Defendant Bush was the pastor and leader of "an unidentified religious sect." The other defendants were "elders" who, with the pastor, determined and approved the policy and conduct of the order, and their wives. The trial court granted defendants' "challenge to the sufficiency of the evidence" and dismissed the action.]

[According to evidence presented by Carrieri, he and his wife had a "wonderful" married life for four years. They then moved to the area where Bush was starting a church. They decided to attend it. Carrieri soon ceased attendance because of disagreement with Bush's style of preaching. Mrs. Carrieri continued to attend, gradually devoting more and more time to church activities and spending considerable time at the homes of the respondents. There was a change in her attitude toward her husband and children. To Carrieri, she appeared cold and to have no interest in him.]

Respondents transported Mrs. Carrieri to and from her activities with them. One evening, at about 11:30 p.m., when Pastor Bush brought Mrs. Carrieri and the children home from a day's activities, appellant confronted the pastor. In appellant's words, the following exchange took place: "I said, 'Arnold, you know you're causing a lot of dissension in my home by keeping my wife away all the time. I asked you not to come pick her up. I believe we should go to church together.'... [H]is eyes got big and large and ... he said 'No. You're full of the devil.... She does not have to listen to you. You're full of the devil.'... [M]y wife was crying and my children was crying.... He said, 'Inga, we will continue to pick you up.' He said, 'Don't listen to him. I've told you many times before, don't listen to your husband.'"

Thereafter, the marital breach broadened and appellant enlisted the aid of the minister who performed his marriage ceremony in the hope of bringing about a reconciliation. As a result, Mrs. Carrieri determined that, for the sake of her family, she would terminate her association with the sect. She insisted, however, on advising Pastor Bush of her decision. Appellant and his wife then went to the pastor's home to accomplish this mission. After Mrs. Carrieri stated her intentions, the following occurred (according to appellant): "... [Bush] insisted I was full of the devil and my wife could not turn back and leave his group because she took an oath.... And he definitely said that my wife would go to hell with me, and that she would never go to any other church and have any peace in her heart, that if she would go with me she would die. He said, 'There's a curse on Jim and there will be a curse on you.'"

The upshot of this interview was described by appellant as follows: "As we got out I said, 'Well, you can see what kind of man he is.' And to my amazement my wife, with glassy eyes, she was shaking and crying, and she said, 'No, he's right. I can't leave. I can't leave.' That's what my wife said, and our home got all the worse after that. There was just no home left."

Against appellant's wishes, Mrs. Carrieri's participation in the group's activities continued and increased. She attended meetings where it was avowed by the leadership that there were several homes in the church that should be broken up, and that the sooner this took place the better the church would be, accompanied by statements that death would pursue those who did not adhere to the church discipline. On one occasion, Mrs. Carrieri moved out of the family home and respondents concealed her whereabouts for a period of time. On another occasion, appellant testified he overheard the Baxters advising Mrs. Carrieri to divorce him.

Appellant initiated this action for alienation of his wife's affections, and Mrs. Carrieri commenced divorce proceedings. In April, 1964, a divorce was granted, and thereafter appellant's alienation of affections action came to the conclusion heretofore indicated.

... [T]o establish a prima facie cause of action for alienation of affections, a complaining spouse must show (1) an existing marriage relation; (2) a wrongful interference with the relationship by a third person; (3) a loss of affection or consortium; and (4) a causal connection between the third party's conduct and the loss.

Although the tort may be designated as intentional in nature, the alleged tortfeasor's intent or purpose does not have to be established by evidence independent of his conduct. This is so because conduct may infer intent, for, in the eyes of the law, a person intends the natural and probable consequences of his voluntary acts.

To render the conduct wrongful, however, and thus satisfy the second element listed above, it must appear from the evidence that the alleged tortfeasor engaged in some kind of affirmative action, as opposed to inaction, the very design of which was to accomplish an alienation or diversion of the affections of the plaintiff's spouse. It is not necessary that the tortfeasor be motivated by spite or malice, or that adultery or improper relations accompany the alienating conduct. Conduct, without justification or excuse, coupled with a purpose or design to adversely affect the mental attitude of one spouse to the detriment of the other is the keystone of a wrongful interference with a marital relationship.

It is within the context of the defense of justification and excuse that a parent, near relative or one standing in a professional or semiprofessional relationship to a marital partner may be clothed with a qualified privilege to reasonably and in good faith intervene in the domestic affairs of a married couple. This privilege, however, where it appears, may be overcome by evidence that the interference in the marital affairs was prompted by malice or ill will; accompanied by falsehoods; implemented by threats; utilized recklessly; or motivated by an unlawful, immoral or improper purpose. An intermeddling stranger, on the other hand, can claim no privilege to invade the domestic circle. He intervenes at his peril, and bears the burden of otherwise justifying or excusing his action.

The third element of the tort listed above — loss of affection or consortium — concerns itself principally with the diminution, diversion, or alienation of the love, society, companionship, aid, and/or comfort of the alienated spouse. Absent a showing of adulterous conduct, this may ordinarily be demonstrated by substantial evidence of any statement, behavior, conduct, or attitude on the part of the alienated spouse from which a loss or impairment of conjugal attachment can reasonably be inferred. A defense showing of lack of conjugal affection at the time of the alleged alienation goes only to mitigation of damages. Such a showing does not constitute a bar to the action.

The fourth element — causal relationship between the third party's conduct and the loss of affection or consortium — is satisfied by the introduction of substantial evidence that the conduct of the asserted tortfeasor aided in causing the alienation. It is not necessary that it be the sole cause, but merely that it be a causal factor.

Finally, the law recognizes the right of discordant spouses to become reconciled, and one who interferes with that right can be subjected to liability in a suit for alienation of affections. . . .

. . . [O]ne does not, under the guise of exercising religious beliefs, acquire a license to wrongfully interfere with familial relationships. Good faith and reasonable conduct are the necessary touchstones to any qualified privilege that may arise from any invited and religiously directed family counseling, assistance, or advice. Ill will, intimidation, threats, or reckless recommendations of family separation directed toward alienating the spouses, where found to exist, nullify the privilege and project liability.

Thus, where, as here, appellant's evidence, if accepted as true, demonstrates a course of conduct designed to — and which does — alienate the affections of the opposite spouse, a prima facie case of alienation of affections is made out, notwithstanding the acts complained of may have been committed in the guise of religious teachings.

The trial court's order dismissing appellant's case at the conclusion of his evidence is accordingly reversed.

———————

Oakman v. Belden

Supreme Judicial Court of Maine
94 Me. 280, 47 A. 553 (1900)

SAVAGE, J. Action on the case by husband for the alienation of the affections of his wife by her parents, who are the defendants. The plaintiff obtained a verdict.

The plaintiff claims that the defendants unjustifiably interfered in his domestic affairs, and, with intent to break up the harmonious and affectionate relations existing between him and his wife, wrongfully enticed, advised, and persuaded her to leave him, which she did. The defendants, on the other hand, deny that they persuaded their daughter to leave her husband, and they claim, in addition, that such was the daughter's age and condition of health, and such was the plaintiff's cruel and abusive conduct towards her, endangering her health and destroying her peace of mind, they were justified in doing all that the evidence for the plaintiff tends to show that they did, even assuming it to be true. It is admitted that the marriage was clandestine, and against the will of the defendants, and that the wife returned to their home not later than three weeks after the marriage, and has since remained there.

The jury were instructed that if the separation of the plaintiff's wife from him "was the result of the active interference of the parents," if they "put in their oar," and if "the wife would have gone back if it had not been for their interference, either by threats, persuasions, or arguments, ... they have done him a wrong, and he is entitled to compensation for that wrong." To this instruction the defendants except....

Whoever wrongfully interferes in the relations of husband and wife, and entices the wife to leave the husband, is liable to him in damages. While a stranger may, without liability, harbor a wife who has left her husband, he may not persuade her to leave him, or not to return to him. Though she may have just grounds for a separation, yet she may choose to return, and a stranger has no right to intermeddle, and if he does so voluntarily he must answer the consequences. But it is universally conceded that a parent stands on different ground. Though the wife has gone out from the parental home, and has joined her husband "for better, for worse," and though she owes to him marital allegiance, and he possesses the first and the superior right to her affection and comfort and society, it is nevertheless true that the parental relation is not ended, nor has parental affection and duty ended. A husband may be false to his marital obligations, he may be immoral and indecent, he may be grossly cruel and abusive, he may become a confirmed drunkard, his conduct towards her may be such as to endanger health, and entirely destroy peace and comfort, so that she may properly leave him. In such case, to whom shall she fly, if not to her parents? And from whom shall she seek advice, if not from her parents? And such advice may, we think, be enforced by reasonable arguments. A parent may not with hostile, wicked, or malicious intent break up the relations between his daughter and her husband. He may not do this simply because he is displeased with the marriage, or because it was against his will, or because he wishes the marriage relation to continue no longer. But a parent may advise his daughter, in good faith and for her good, to leave her husband, if he, on reasonable grounds, believes that the further continuance of the marriage relation tends to injure her health, or to destroy her peace of mind, so that she would be justified in leaving him. A parent may, in such case, persuade his daughter. He may use proper and reasonable arguments, drawn, it may be, from his greater knowledge and wider experience. Whether the motive was proper or improper is always to be considered. Whether the persuasion or the argument is proper and reasonable, under the conditions presented to the parent's mind, is also always to be considered. It may turn out that the parent acted upon mistaken premises, or upon false information, or his advice and his interference may have been unfortunate; still, we repeat, if he acts in good faith, for the daughter's good, upon reasonable grounds of belief, he is not liable to the husband.

This conclusion is supported by the authorities. Chancellor Kent in Hutcheson v. Peck, 5 Johns. 196, said: "A father's house is always open to his children, and, whether they be married or unmarried, it is still to them a refuge from evil and a consolation in distress. Natural affection establishes and consecrates this asylum.... I should require, therefore, more proof to sustain the action against the father than against a stranger. It ought to appear either that he detains the wife against her will, or that he entices her away from her husband from improper motives." ...

... [T]he jury were told, in substance, that if the separation of plaintiff's wife from him was the result of the active interference of the defendants, either by threats, persuasion, or arguments, then the defendants were liable. This instruction, unqualified as it was, was erroneous, and placed upon the defendants a much more grievous burden of justification than parents in such cases ought to be compelled to bear. ...

Exceptions sustained.

Notes

1. The tort of alienation of affections is an American invention that is not accepted outside the United States as part of the common law. See Kungl v. Schiefer, [1962] S.C.R. 443, (1962) 33 D.L.R.2d 278. How does it differ from enticement? See Mitchell v. Jolly, [1960] O.R. 470, (1960) 25 D.L.R.2d 18 (C.A.). The common law actions for interference with spousal relations, including criminal conversation, could be maintained only by husbands. But American courts have extended these actions and alienation of affections to wives. See Restatement (Second) of Torts §§ 683–685 (1977). This met less resistance than extension of actions for loss of consortium to wives whose husbands had sustained personal injuries. Why?

2. Many judicial statements about alienation of affections are imprecise on the critical question of what is "wrongful" interference with a marital relationship—the type of interference that is a basis of liability when alienation of affections results. It is often stated, as in Carrieri v. Bush, that the defendant's conduct must be intentional and affirmative (active). See Pankratz v. Miller, 401 N.W.2d 543 (S.D. 1987) (not enough that defendant should have known that affair might cause diminution of affections; purpose to cause this required, as in Restatement (Second) of Torts § 683); Fitch v. Valentine, 959 So. 2d 1012 (Miss. 2007), cert. denied, 552 U.S. 1100 (2008) (must be persuasion, enticement or inducement); Archer v. Archer, 31 Tenn. App. 657, 219 S.W.2d 919 (1947) (defendant must be pursuer or enticer of plaintiff's spouse, not pursued by spouse). Must there be a complete loss of affection, or is partial loss sufficient? Is it a tort to persuade a spouse not to have sexual relations with plaintiff? See Plourd v. Jarvis, 99 Me. 161, 58 A. 774 (1904). There is no tort cause of action against the erring spouse. Cluck v. Cluck, 712 S.W.2d 599 (Tex. App. 1986).

3. Should actions for alienation of affections be possible if the spouses were already separated or estranged at the time of the defendant's conduct? Most authority supports this on the ground that defendant may have prevented reconciliation. Separation can be considered in assessing damages. See McNelis v. Bruce, 90 Ariz. 261, 367 P.2d 625 (1961) (spouses had made separation agreement); Ruble v. Ruble, 203 Minn. 399, 281 N.W. 529 (1938). Cf. Clark v. Orr, 127 Fla. 411, 173 So. 155 (1937) (husband had prior affairs known to plaintiff and from "pecuniary standpoint" was almost "total loss"; damages excessive). Compare Adams v. Carrier, 214 Ark. 55, 214 S.W.2d 781 (1948) (no action when wife supposedly deserted plaintiff before meeting defendant); Pankratz v. Miller, supra (wife alienated before relationship with defendant).

4. The spouses' divorce does not prevent the maintenance of an action for alienation of affections, provided the tort preceded it. A marriage is required. There is no action for alienation of the affections of a fiancée. Restatement (Second) of Torts §§ 683, 689, 698 (1977). A suit for inducing breach of promise of marriage would seem possible as

an action for inducing breach of contract (see pp. 123–143, infra), but the weight of American authority rejects such actions. See Harper, James & Gray, Law of Torts § 8.2 (3d ed. 2006).

5. If the elements of liability can be established, what defenses are there? Many alienation of affections actions have been brought against parents or other relatives of the allegedly alienated spouse. Cases such as Oakman v. Belden support recognition of a privilege in such circumstances. Near relatives may provide assistance and advice to the spouse — even persuade the spouse to leave the plaintiff—when this is reasonably believed to advance the spouse's welfare. Conduct actuated by a different purpose or ill will toward plaintiff is outside the privilege. See Poulos v. Poulos, 351 Mass. 603, 222 N.E.2d 887 (1967); Annot., Liability of Parent, Relative, or Person in Loco Parentis in Action by Husband or Wife for Alienation of Affection, 108 A.L.R. 408 (1937); Harper, James & Gray, Law of Torts § 8.4 (3d ed. 2006).

6. Consider the possible differences in the extent of "privilege" allowed to near relatives, distant relatives, friends, professional advisers and members of religious groups. A number of alienation cases involve religious organizations. It has been held that so long as the organization merely publishes or broadcasts its views, it acts within the scope of constitutional protection. Bradesku v. Antion, 21 Ohio App. 2d 67, 255 N.E.2d 265 (1969) (minister wrote wife, in response to her request, telling her his church believed divorced person committed adultery by remarrying). A cause of action might be found if church officials induce family members to cut off all contact with plaintiff. See Bear v. Reformed Mennonite Church, 462 Pa. 330, 341 A.2d 105 (1975), where plaintiff was the object of the defendant church's policy of "shunning." Following plaintiff's excommunication by the church, his wife and children were advised not to speak to him or have social or physical contact with him, on pain of themselves being excommunicated. Cf. Acchione v. Acchione, 376 Pa. 36, 101 A.2d 642 (1954) (husband's family threatened to cut off financial support if couple not married within church; could be alienation of affections if this was aimed at separating husband from wife).

McMillan v. Felsenthal

Texas Court of Civil Appeals
482 S.W.2d 9 (1972), aff'd, 493 S.W.2d 729 (Tex. 1973)

MOORE, Justice.

... [P]laintiff alleged that for many months prior to February 26, 1971, defendant began to visit a lounge owned by him and his wife, where his wife worked as a bartender; that the defendant intentionally set out to seduce and have sexual intercourse with his wife; and that he finally accomplished his purpose during the early morning hours of February 26, 1971, when he took plaintiff's wife to a lakehouse and kept her there until approximately 6:30 a.m. in the morning. Plaintiff further alleged that as a result of the defendant's intentional and wrongful acts, he was deprived of the services, affections, and consortium of his wife, Mary Ann McMillan; that a trespass was committed by the defendant upon the plaintiff's rights to the affection, love, consortium, and exclusive sexual relationship with his wife; that the defendant alienated the affections of the said Mary Ann McMillan; and that defendant's conduct was the controlling cause of the separation between him and his wife and his loss of consortium. His prayer was for actual as well as punitive damages. Defendant denied generally the allegations of the petition. [Defendant moved for summary judgment, contending] that no disputed issue of fact existed upon plaintiff's cause of action for "alienation of affections" because both plaintiff and his wife gave deposition testimony to the effect that the wife's affections had not been alienated. After a hearing the trial court granted a summary judgment in favor of the defendant denying plaintiff any of the relief under any of the allegations in his petition. Plaintiff duly perfected this appeal.

... [H]e contends that the trial court erred in granting defendant a summary judgment because in so doing the trial court refused to recognize that a cause of action for criminal conversation exists under the laws of this State. He further urges that the trial court erred in failing to construe his pleadings as stating a cause of action for criminal conversation and in failing to hold that the evidence raised a disputed issue of material fact upon his alleged cause of action for criminal conversation....

The legal basis of all causes of action arising from situations of this sort springs from the interference with family relations.... With respect to interference with a man's relationship with his wife, the three most common types of interference are (1) enticement or harboring the wife, (2) adultery with the wife, which in its tort aspect usually is called "criminal conversation," and (3) "alienation of affections"....

[Prosser on Torts, 3rd Ed., p. 898] makes the following observations with regard to causes of action of this sort: "Criminal conversation, enticement and alienation of affections still are often treated as separate torts, but there is no good reason for distinguishing them. They represent three forms of interference with aspects of the same relational interest, and of course all three may be present in the same case. When the action is for criminal conversation, proof of enticement or alienation will go to increase the damages, and the converse is likewise true. There is now a decided tendency to confuse the three, or to lump them together, usually under the general name of 'alienation of affections,' without any attempt to distinguish the possible elements of the tort."

Since defendant's motion for summary judgment is leveled only at a cause of action for alienation of affections, it seems that defendant followed the usual tendency of lumping all possible types of interference under the general name of "alienation of affections."

The common law has long furnished an aggrieved husband with a right of action against his wife's adulterer for criminal conversation....

There is a distinction between an action for criminal conversation and an action for alienation of affections. It is possible for a cause of action for either to exist without the other. While an action for alienation of affections and one for criminal conversation are both founded on the injury to the right of consortium, they are generally recognized as essentially different. The gravamen or gist of the action where it is for criminal conversation is the adulterous intercourse, and the alienation of affections thereby resulting is regarded as merely a matter of aggravation, whereas the gravamen in the other case is the alienation of affections with malice or improper motives.

In the present case two primary rights were available to the plaintiff as a basis for a cause of action: one is the right of the plaintiff to the body of his wife, and the other to her mind unpolluted. The interference with the former constitutes a cause of action for criminal conversation while interference with the latter would give rise to a cause of action for alienation of affections. Interference with both, even though by one act, could give rise to two causes of action. It is permissible, however, to allege interference with either as an aggravation of the other.

... [In plaintiff's petition] there seems to be no paragraph specifically on alienation of affections with malice or improper motives. Nowhere in plaintiff's petition did he allege that the defendant had knowledge of the marriage relationship, which, as we understand it, is a necessary allegation in order to state a separate and distinct cause of action for alienation of affections. Since plaintiff did not specifically allege alienation of affections and did not allege defendant's knowledge of the marriage relationship, we do not construe his petition as alleging a separate alternative count for a cause of action for alienation of affection in addition to his cause of action for criminal conversation. For this reason, it occurs to us that plaintiff based his suit only upon his right of action for criminal conversation and that the further charge of alienation of affections was incidental and was to be considered only in aggravation of the damages.

In Vol. 42 C.J.S. Husband and Wife § 698, subsec. b, p.353, it is stated: "To sustain an action for criminal conversation two things must be established: (1) An actual marriage between the spouses. (2) Sexual intercourse between defendant and the guilty spouse during the coverture."

Plaintiff's petition clearly alleged each of the foregoing elements. The evidence offered by the plaintiff shows both the marriage and the illicit relationship. Defendant flatly denied that any illicit relationship occurred. Thus, the record shows a disputed issue of fact upon plaintiff's cause of action for criminal conversation....

... It therefore follows that the defendant was not entitled to a summary judgment upon the cause of action relied on by the plaintiff.

[Reversed and remanded.]

Notes

1. The tort of criminal conversation is notable for its simplicity. It is established by proof of intercourse between plaintiff's spouse and the defendant. No intent to affect the marital relationship is necessary. Not even knowledge of the marriage is required. See Bearbower v. Merry, p. 101, infra; Antonelli v. Xenakis, 363 Pa. 375, 69 A.2d 102 (1949). It makes no difference to liability that plaintiff's own conduct had alienated his spouse. See Browning v. Jones, 52 Ill. App. 597 (1893). Or that plaintiff's spouse, not defendant, was the seducer. See Seiber v. Pettitt, 200 Pa. 58, 49 A. 763 (1901). Prior separation is no bar to the action. Michael v. Dunkle, 84 Ind. 544 (1882); Fennell v. Littlejohn, 240 S.C. 189, 125 S.E.2d 408 (1962) (separation and pending divorce action by plaintiff). Although not bars to liability, such matters bear upon the assessment of damages, especially punitive damages.

2. Plaintiff need not show any loss of services or sexual intercourse. See Rosefield v. Rosefield, 221 Cal. App. 2d 431, 34 Cal. Rptr. 479 (1963); Disch v. Closet, 118 Or. 111, 244 P. 71 (1926). In Wilton v. Webster, (1835) 7 C. & P. 198, 173 Eng. Rep. 87 (K.B.N.P.), plaintiff received large damages although he had no suspicion of his wife's misconduct until she confessed to adultery on her deathbed. Forgiveness ("condonation") is not a defense, but it can affect assessment of damages. See Annot., Condonation or Forgiveness of Spouse as Affecting Liability for Alienation of Affections or Criminal Conversation, 38 A.L.R.2d 1234 (1954).

3. A husband finds that his wife frequently is in the company of or communicating with another man. He goes to court and asks that the other man be enjoined from criminal conversation or alienation of the wife's affections. Under what circumstances would or should such an injunction be granted? See Knighton v. Knighton, 252 Ala. 520, 41 So. 2d 172 (1949); Lyon v. Izen, 131 Ill. App. 2d 594, 268 N.E.2d 436 (1971); Ashby v. Stevenson, 368 S.W.2d 898 (Tex. Civ. App. 1963). Cf. Diamond v. Diamond, 372 Pa. 562, 94

A.2d 569 (1953) (suit to restrain husband, with aid of another defendant, from committing adultery). Would a court enjoin alienation by a spouse's parent or other relative? See Devine v. Devine, 20 N.J. Super. 522, 90 A.2d 126 (Ch. Div. 1952). See generally Moreland, Injunctive Control of Family Relations, 18 Ky. L.J. 207 (1930).

Armstrong v. McDonald
Alabama Court of Appeals
39 Ala. App. 485, 103 So. 2d 818 (1958)

CATES, Judge....

[Defendants persuaded plaintiff's minor son to leave his home with plaintiff in Alabama and go to Maryland as a migrant farm worker. Plaintiff gave no consent to this. While in Maryland, plaintiff's son went swimming and drowned. Plaintiff's action claimed $50,000 damages for deprivation of her son's services and society and for having incurred expense of $700 for the return of her son's body and the funeral. The jury awarded plaintiff damages of $700. Defendants appealed on the grounds that plaintiff had failed to show that her son was taken away for a hazardous occupation and that there was no allegation or proof of negligence by defendants.]

... [Restatement, Torts § 700 states:] "One who, without a privilege to do so, (a) abducts a minor child, or (b) induces it to leave its home with knowledge that the parent has not consented, or (c) with knowledge that it has left its home and that the parent is unwilling that the child should be absent, induces it not to return thereto or prevents it from so doing, is liable to the parent, who is legally entitled to the child's custody."

In 67 C.J.S. Parent and Child § 101, we find: "A parent who has the right to the custody, control, and services of a minor child may maintain an action for damages against anyone who unlawfully entices away or harbors such child"....

... [I]n Restatement, Torts, § 700, comment g, we find: "The parent can recover for the loss of society of his child and for his emotional distress resulting from its abduction or enticement. If there has been a loss of service or if the child, though actually not performing service, was old enough to do so, the parent can recover for the loss of the service which he could have required of the child during the period of its absence. He is also entitled to recover for any reasonable expenses incurred by him in regaining custody of the child and for any reasonable expenses incurred or likely to be incurred in treating or caring for the child if it has suffered illness or other bodily harm as a result of the defendant's tortious conduct."

In Pickle v. Page, 252 N.Y. 474, 169 N.E. 650, the leading case on this doctrine, we find: "An action of trespass for the abduction of a child was originally maintainable by a father where the child abducted was the son and heir and not otherwise. This was 'by reason the marriage of his heir belongs to the father, but not of any other his sons or daughters;' and, although it had been adjudged that the writ of trespass lay 'for a parrot, a popinjay, a thrush, and a dog; the reason thereof is, because the law imputes that the owner hath a property in them,' whereas 'the father hath not any property or interest in the daughter, which the law accounts may be taken from him.' Later it was held that an action of trespass was maintainable by a father per quod servitium amisit where a child old enough to do him service, other than the heir, was abducted.... In [Hall v. Hollander, p. 22, supra] it was said: 'It is clear that in cases of taking a son or daughter, except for taking a son and heir, no action lies, unless a loss of service is sustained...' In the case of an injury inflicted upon a child so immature that it was incapable of rendering service, the parent might have no remedy against the person inflicting the injury.... [¶] ... [W]e find no decisions by the courts of this country holding that, in actions to recover damages for the abduction of a child, the parent must allege and prove, as a condition of his recovery, a loss of the services of the child.... In South Carolina it has been held that the action is maintainable without proof or allegation of loss of service. Kirkpatrick v. Lockhart, 2 Brev., S.C., 276. The court there said: 'The true ground of action is the outrage, and deprivation; the injury the father sustains in the loss of his child; the insult offered to his feelings; the heartrending agony he must suffer in the destruction of his dearest hopes, and the irreparable loss of that comfort, and society, which may be the only solace of his declining age.' In North Carolina the same holding was made in Howell v. Howell, 162 N.C. 283, 78 S.E. 222, the court stating that the theory that such an action was grounded on a loss of service was 'an outworn fiction.'" ...

Hence, we do not consider this a wrongful death action ... : here, the plaintiff complains of the taking away, not of the killing....

The defendants took issue without raising the lack of any averment of negligence by way of demurrer; nor did they request any jury instruction on this theory. Even if we were to concede the wrong complained of required a showing of negligence, we should nevertheless consider the appellants precluded from raising it.

Nor do we think that a show of taking away into a hazardous occupation is necessary for this tort....

Affirmed.

Notes

1. On the basis of the master's action for loss of a servant's services — the action per quod servitium amisit — the common law afforded parents an action for tortious injury to a child. See pp. 22–24, supra. On the same basis, the common law gave parents an action for the abduction, enticement or harboring of a child. Older cases held that loss of services was essential. American courts now are likely to find it sufficient that the plaintiff has a right to the child's services, and there is a trend toward discarding services altogether as an element of liability — especially in abduction cases. See DiRuggiero v. Rodgers, 743 F.2d 1009 (3d Cir. 1984); Khalifa v. Shannon, 404 Md. 107, 945 A.2d 1244 (2008); Prosser & Keeton, Law of Torts 924–926 (5th ed. 1984). Much of the law on "intentional" interference with parent-child relations comes from actions for seduction of a daughter, which have the same common law origins as abduction, enticement and harboring. See pp. 96–100, infra.

2. The basic definitions of enticement and harboring are the same for both spouses and children, but are they to be applied in the same manner? Is a purpose to disrupt the parent-child relationship required for liability? Must defendant induce the child not to return to plaintiff, or is it sufficient that defendant harbors the child with knowledge that plaintiff does not consent? Must defendant be notified of plaintiff's objection, or is it enough that defendant has no reason to believe that the child's parent consents? Is "privilege" to act for the child's welfare the same as in the case of a spouse? See Restatement (Second) of Torts § 700 (1977).

3. Does an action for harboring arise if a child joins a religious order and lives in its establishment without parental consent? See Lough v. Ward, [1945] 2 All E.R. 338 (K.B.D.) (successful action against heads of order). Cf. Murphy v. I.S.K. Con of New England,

Inc., 409 Mass. 842, 571 N.E.2d 340 (1991), cert. denied, 502 U.S. 865 (1991) (action against religious organization for interference with parent-child relationship). What if a child runs away with the circus? See Tavlinsky v. Ringling Bros. Circus Co., 113 Neb. 632, 204 N.W. 388 (1925) (action may lie if circus employed minor without parents' consent, although child sought employment; tort waived if parents received and appropriated child's wages with knowledge of material facts). Cf. Steward v. Gold Medal Shows, 244 Ala. 583, 14 So. 2d 549 (1943) (son induced to accompany travelling show; damages for outrage, mental suffering and deprivation of society as well as loss of services). Is there liability if a minor is persuaded to leave the parental home in order to marry defendant or a third person? See Goodwin v. Thompson, 2 Greene 329 (Iowa 1849) (action not maintainable); Hervey v. Moseley, 7 Gray (73 Mass.) 479 (1856) (no right to recover for loss of service after marriage took place, if lawful).

4. Consider the possibilities of an injunction being issued on the basis of these torts. See Stark v. Hamilton, 149 Ga. 227, 99 S.E. 861 (1919) (defendant induced daughter to abandon parental abode and live with defendant in "state of adultery and fornication"; enjoined from associating and communicating with daughter); Lough v. Ward, supra (heads of religious order enjoined from harboring daughter in abbey).

————————

Plante v. Engel
Supreme Court of New Hampshire
124 N.H. 213, 469 A.2d 1299 (1983)

BATCHELDER, Justice.

[Plaintiff brought suit against the parents of his ex-wife. His declaration alleged that he and his former wife were parents of two minor children. The decree divorcing them, entered by a New Hampshire court, awarded permanent custody of the children to plaintiff. Contrary to the terms of the decree, the former wife moved with the children to Texas without notifying plaintiff. Defendants "were at all times under a duty not to interfere with plaintiff's parental rights or relationship with his children and not to assist [plaintiff's ex-wife] or others in defying a valid and final order of the ... Court; although having knowledge of said court order ... the defendants did aid and abet the [ex-wife] in her efforts to absent herself from the State of New Hampshire with the minor children and move to another location in contravention of the final order of the Court with the intent to deprive the plaintiff of his rightful custody of his minor children."]

The plaintiff argues that recognizing such an action for intentional interference with parental custody is a natural extension of our holding in *Sargent v. Mathewson*, 38 N.H. 54 (1859). In *Sargent*, a father brought an action against a man who had harbored his child and encouraged the child to remain away from him. We let stand a jury verdict for the plaintiff father for the loss of his son's services. In so ruling, we observed: "No question is made that the father, unless he has in some way forfeited or relinquished the right, is entitled to the services and custody of his minor child, and may recover damages against the party who deprives him of this right, by seducing away or harboring the child."

This common-law action for loss of a child's services is distinguishable from an action for loss of custody. In the former action, compensation is sought for the actual pecuniary losses associated with the deprivation of the child's services, while in the latter, compensation is sought primarily for the emotional losses associated with being deprived of the child's care and comfort. An action for interference with custody resembles, in this respect, an action for loss of a spouse's consortium. At common law, no such action for the loss of a child's care, comfort and companionship would lie.

The importance of the parent-child relationship is reflected in its treatment in New Hampshire law. The high place accorded filiation stems not from the material bond whereby services are provided to each other by parent and child but from a recognition that there is a sanctity in the union of parent and child that transcends economics and deserves the utmost respect. Because this relationship is so intimately connected with the parent's person, we hold that where there is an intentional interference with a parent's custody of his or her child, an injured parent is entitled to a remedy that completely compensates him or her.

We see no reason to circumscribe this cause of action either by including only non-parents as defendants, or by excluding them. Accordingly, where a parent has been awarded custody of a child by court decree and the noncustodial parent abducts the child, an action will lie in favor of the custodial parent upon an allegation of damages.

Likewise, we see no reason not to hold liable one who intentionally aids and abets another in interfering with the custodial rights of a parent. This court has held that one may be found liable for damages on a conspiracy theory for combining with another to commit a civil wrong. This rationale has been used by other courts to extend liability for custodial interference.

Certain elements of damages flow directly from an intentional interference with parental custody: recovery of expenses incurred in recovering the child, including legal fees; and compensation for the loss of the child's services and/or his care, comfort and companionship. The trier of fact may award damages for these elements where the plaintiff has sustained his burden of proving them. In addition to the above, the plaintiff has put in a claim for damages for severe emotional distress. We are of the opinion that a claim for the intentional infliction of emotional distress should be treated as a separate cause of action. *See* Restatement (Second) of Torts § 46 (1965).

Reversed and remanded.

Politte v. Politte
Missouri Court of Appeals
727 S.W.2d 198 (1987)

SATZ, Presiding Judge.

In this action, the father of three children sought money damages from the mother, his ex-wife, for interference with his visitation and temporary custody rights. The trial court dismissed the father's petition for failure to state a claim upon which relief can be granted....

In his petition, the father alleges: A dissolution decree was granted in 1975; the mother was awarded custody of the three minor children and the father was awarded temporary custody and visitation rights. In 1980, the mother informed the father she no longer wanted custody. During the next three months, the mother "surreptitiously reassumed custody", and, since that time, the mother has refused to allow the father to exercise his visitation and temporary custody rights. The mother subjected the minor children to an unfit moral atmosphere to the detriment of the welfare of the children, and, as a result the father suffered continuous and extreme emotional distress and suffering. The mother attempted to turn the father's children against him and to poison their relationship with him. As a result of the mother's willful, wanton and malicious actions, the father suffered severe emotional distress and extreme depression, damaging him in the amount of $150,000. The father also sought $50,000 damages for the loss of the society of the children and sought punitive damages in the amount of $50,000.

The tort the father attempts to allege originated as a claim for wrongfully seizing or retaining custody of a child. This claim was based upon the deprivation of the child's services, and, since at early common law the father was the only person entitled to the child's services, only the father could pursue the claim. Upon the father's death, a waiver of his rights, or upon divorce where the mother was awarded custody, the mother was entitled to bring the action.

Under the so-called modern view, the essence of the claim is the interference with the parent's custodial rights, not the loss of the child's services. This view ... is now reflected in [Restatement (Second) of Torts § 700, Causing Minor Child to Leave or not to Return Home]: "One who, with knowledge that the parent does not consent, abducts or otherwise compels or induces a minor child to leave a parent *legally entitled to its custody* or not to return to the parent after it has been left him, is subject to liability to the parent." (emphasis added.) ... [Comment *d*:] "Under the rule stated in this Section, loss of service or impairment of ability to perform service is not a necessary element of a cause of action.... The deprivation to the parent of the society of the child is itself an injury that the law redresses."

Our colleagues in the Southern District recognized that this tort may exist between parents involved in a post-marital conflict.... In [*Kipper v. Vokolek*, 546 S.W.2d 521 (Mo. App. 1977)] the father sought money damages from his ex-wife and her new husband for "unlawfully decoying or enticing away or harboring his two minor daughters...." In affirming the dismissal of the father's petition, the court found the ex-wife had been awarded custody of the two children and also found their custody had not been changed. Therefore, the court concluded, the father "did not plead facts upon which relief could be granted" because he "did not plead facts showing his lawful entitlement to the custody of his daughters at the time the averred tort was committed". Although the court did not expressly define the father's legal relation to his daughters, it clearly implied his visitation rights or right to temporary custody were not significant enough to be protected by this tort.

The father here argues this limitation is neither sound nor logical. This tort, he contends, is designed to protect parental relations generally, not simply the right to permanent custody. Interference with a parent's right to temporary custody or visitation rights, he contends, can cause that parent emotional damage equivalent to the emotional damage caused by interference with permanent custodial rights. Therefore, the father argues, the right to temporary custody and visitation rights should have the same dignity as permanent custodial rights....

... Comment C to § 700 ... states: "When parents are by law jointly entitled to the custody and earnings of the child, no action can be brought against one of the parents who abducts or induces the child to leave the other. When by law only one parent is entitled to the custody and earnings of the child, only that parent can maintain an action under the rule stated in this Section." Clearly, only a custodial parent can sue for custodial interference when he or she possesses superior custody rights to the child. The father cannot rest his claim on § 700 and ignore those Comments explaining the breadth and meaning of § 700....

... [W]e question the need of recognizing the tort claim defined in § 700. The primary goal of this tort is the vindication of one parent against the other, not necessarily the best interests of the child. The interests of the child kept by one parent in violation of a court decree are best served by a prompt return of the child to the parent who the court had determined to be the more qualified custodian. Prompt return of the child can be accomplished by habeas corpus, contempt and, if the facts warrant it, civil actions under the Uniform Child Custody Jurisdiction Acts or the Parental Kidnapping Prevention Act, (18 U.S.C. § 1073; 28 U.S.C. § 1738A; 42 U.S.C. §§ 654, 663, 1305) (1980). Criminal sanctions can be invoked under our "Interference with Custody" statute. § 565.150 RSMo.1978.

Arguably, the economic pressure of a money judgment may persuade the obdurate parent to return the child. But if this incidental benefit is our goal, why preclude the custodial parent from an action for the alienation of a child's affection. *See*, § 699 Restatement (Second) of Torts. Moreover, if society now demands that money damages be granted to a parent for emotional injury caused by interference with parental relations, in general, the amorphous tort of intentional infliction of emotional distress, See § 46 Restatement (Second) of Torts; or the enigmatic action of prima facie tort, *see*, § 870 Restatement (Second) of Torts, are adequate procedural and substantive weapons.

If these weapons are not sufficient for the arsenal of those parents engaged in post-marital warfare, we can, as other jurisdictions have, grant relief under § 700 only to the custodial parent, as intended. We find no reason to extend relief to the non-custodial parent. Disarmament is needed to limit post-marital warfare, not additional armament to increase it.

Judgment affirmed.

Notes

1. The most dramatic development of recent years in the law of tortious interference with family relationships is the appearance of claims for interference with custody and interference with visitation rights. What explains their emergence at this late date? Are these new torts, or merely new applications of the old torts of abduction, enticement and harboring? Cf. Rosefield v. Rosefield, 221 Cal. App. 2d 431, 34 Cal. Rptr. 479 (1963) (action against husband and father-in-law for abducting and harboring child, upheld against father-in-law with no decision as to husband; plaintiff had physical custody of child from birth but no court order); LaGrenade v. Gordon, 46 N.C. App. 329, 264 S.E.2d 757 (1980), appeal dismissed, 300 N.C. 557, 270 S.E.2d 109 (1980) (abduction action against husband and in-laws for taking child and thwarting recovery; spouses had executed agreement providing that plaintiff have custody). If new, do the torts serve a need that could not be met adequately by existing theories of tort liability or other legal mechanisms? Do their advantages outweigh their disadvantages?

2. There now are numerous cases sustaining claims for interference with child custody brought by a parent awarded sole custody by court order. See Stone v. Wall, 734 So. 2d 1038 (Fla. 1999). Generally, a parent without a right of custody is as much subject to liability as a non-parent. See Lloyd v. Loeffler, 694 F.2d 489 (7th Cir. 1982); Wood v. Wood, 338 N.W.2d 123 (Iowa 1983); Annot., Liability of Legal or Natural Parent, or One Who Aids and Abets, for Damages Resulting from Abduction of Own Child, 49 A.L.R.4th 7 (1986). Should a court entertain the action but deny any damages for emotional distress, as in Plante v. Engel? Compare Fenslage v. Dawkins, 629 F.2d 1107 (5th Cir. 1980). What if courts in different states have given conflicting custody orders? See Bennett v. Bennett, 595 F. Supp. 366 (D.D.C. 1984).

3. In Larson v. Dunn, 460 N.W.2d 39 (Minn. 1990), a 4–3 majority refused to establish an action for intentional interference with custodial rights. The majority believed that such an action would intensify intrafamily conflict — it would be a "new weapon" in "intrafamily warfare" — and detrimentally affect the children involved. They would be

placed in the middle of a vigorous and probably vicious lawsuit. Tort liability would not deter abductions, especially when a parent or grandparent believed that the child was in danger of harm. Other remedies were available, including contempt proceedings and tort actions for intentional infliction of emotional distress. See also Zaharias v. Gammill, 844 P.2d 137 (Okla. 1992).

4. Most reported actions for interference with visitation or occasional custody rights have failed, whether brought against the other parent or against a third person. See Hixon v. Buchberger, 306 Md. 72, 507 A.2d 607 (1986); McGrady v. Rosenbaum, 62 Misc. 2d 182, 308 N.Y.S.2d 181 (Sup. Ct. 1970), aff'd, 37 A.D.2d 917, 324 N.Y.S.2d 876 (1971); Cosner v. Ridinger, 882 P.2d 1243 (Wyo. 1994). However, in Khalifa v. Shannon, 404 Md. 107, 945 A.2d 1244 (2008), the court allowed an action for "substantial" interference with parental visitation rights. Is any other remedy adequate for a parent whose child has been concealed for a lengthy period or taken out of the country?

5. An unusual case of interference with parent-child relations is found in Ruffalo v. United States, 590 F. Supp. 706 (W.D. Mo. 1984). A state court order, based on an agreement between plaintiff and her former husband, placed their son in the latter's "possession," although plaintiff had been granted legal custody. Plaintiff retained "reasonable visitation rights" and "possession" for one day on weekends. The father and child disappeared when they were taken into the federal government's Witness Protection Program. The child was included at the request of the father, who had been an informant concerning organized crime. Plaintiff obtained a state court order giving her full custody, but she had no contact with her son for almost four years. Telephone calls and infrequent visitation resumed when plaintiff sued the federal government. The court decided that plaintiff was not entitled to any custody of the child because of the danger to his safety that would result. Only semi-annual visitation and bi-weekly telephone calls were required, more "forced contact" being excessive in view of the unhappy relationship between plaintiff and her son. Damages were awarded against the federal government because of its officials' responsibility for depriving plaintiff over a 4½-year period of the visitation and telephone contact to which plaintiff was entitled.

6. A claim for interference with custody rights might be maintained as one for intentional infliction of emotional distress. See Kajtazi v. Kajtazi, 488 F. Supp. 15 (E.D.N.Y. 1978); Kunz v. Deitch, 660 F. Supp. 679 (N.D. Ill. 1987). But see Friedman v. Friedman, 79 Misc. 2d 646, 361 N.Y.S.2d 108 (Sup. Ct. 1974). Would this work for a parent's complaint against the other parent for interference with visitation? Cf. Pankratz v. Willis, 155 Ariz. 8, 744 P.2d 1182 (Ct. App. 1987) (plaintiff's former wife, with assistance of her parents, disappeared with child; judgment against parents affirmed).

Pyle v. Waechter

Supreme Court of Iowa
202 Iowa 695, 210 N.W. 926 (1926)

VERMILION, J. The petition alleges that the plaintiff is the mother of Donald Waechter, who was born in lawful wedlock and is now about 17 years of age; that for a period of more than 10 years "there has been a continuous, persistent, and concerted effort and conspiracy on the part of the defendants to poison the mind of said son" against plaintiff, and to destroy his natural filial regard, esteem, love and affection for her; that by "words, actions, and influence the defendants have wrongfully, intentionally, and maliciously poisoned the mind of said son" against plaintiff, and have "wholly alienated his natural love and affection, esteem, and regard for her"; and that "said wrongful acts and influence were intended by said defendants to prevent the said son from having anything in common with his mother and to alienate him from her." It is further alleged that as a result of the continuous, persistent, and concerted effort, both positive and negative, on the part of the defendants, the natural filial love, affection, esteem, and regard of the son for his mother have been wholly destroyed and alienated, and his mind so poisoned against her that he now considers and believes he has nothing in common with her, and has not now that proper respect, love, and affection for his mother to which by the law of nature she is entitled, and has now neither love and affection nor proper respect and regard for her.

The demurrer raises the question that the petition does not allege that the plaintiff was deprived of the custody, control, or society of her son, or of his service, and that, therefore, it does not state a cause of action....

The injury complained of may be said to be purely sentimental. The mental anguish, for which alone plaintiff seeks to recover, results, so far as appears from the allegations of the petition, entirely from the alleged mental attitude of the son produced by the alleged wrongful acts of the defendants, and not from any outward manifestation of that attitude toward the plaintiff. There is no allegation that plaintiff was deprived of the services, custody, or control of her son, or of his assistance, association, or companionship. The son may never, under the allegations of the petition, have failed in the performance of any service or duty to which the plaintiff was entitled; he may never have been in the slightest degree remiss in rendering to her every service or attention in the way of companionship or association which the most exacting mother could expect. It is alleged, it is true, that the natural affection of the son for his mother has been destroyed, and that he believes he now has nothing in common with her. Conceding all that could be claimed for this, it is not an allegation that the son has in any respect failed in the actual performance of any natural duty or obligation to the plaintiff....

... [I]f the right of action is not fundamentally grounded upon the right of the parent to the services, custody, and control of the minor, and an action will lie for the mere alienation of the affections of the child, without the loss of either services, companionship or control, we see no sound reason why either the minority of the child, or even the presence of the parental relation, is essential to a right of recovery.

The mental anguish suffered by a parent over the loss of the affections of an adult son or daughter is not different in kind, nor necessarily so in degree, from that suffered in the case of a minor child.... [I]f the alienation of affections alone supports the action, brothers and sisters may recover. Surely no justification could be suggested, in the absence of precedent or controlling legal principle, for so extending the right to recover as for a tort, and the opening of such a Pandora's box of litigation.

... Because damages for mental suffering are recoverable in certain cases it does not follow that in every instance where the act of one is the cause of mental anguish in another an actionable wrong is committed. Where the right to maintain the action exists, the law permits a recovery of all the damages proximately resulting from the wrongful act. But because one entitled to maintain the action may suffer and is allowed to recover for an injury to his feelings, it does not necessarily follow that another, merely because he suffers similarly, may, for that reason alone, maintain an action.... If, as we think is the case, the right of the mother, conceding such right to exist in her, is to the services, custody, control, and companionship of her minor child, without an allegation that she has been deprived of some of these she states no cause of action....

The nearest analogy to the claim made by the appellant is to be found in the right of one spouse to recover for the alienation of the affections of the other. The right of action in that case is based on the loss of the consortium, the conjugal society, and assistance of the spouse. It is a right which exists by virtue of the marriage relation, and is peculiar to it. There is nothing in the principles which underlie such an action, or the rules of law applicable to it, that will justify their application to the claim of a mother to recover for the alienation of the affection of a minor child, where it is not alleged that she was deprived of the services, companionship, care, or custody of the child.

We conclude the demurrer was properly sustained, and the judgment is affirmed.

Notes

1. American common law developed no cause of action for loss of a child's affections, although compensation for this might be awarded if liability existed on another basis. This is still widely accepted, whether the child be a minor or an adult. See Morris v. Bruney, 78 N.C. App. 668, 338 S.E.2d 561 (1986); Bartanus v. Lis, 332 Pa. Super. 48, 480 A.2d 1178 (1984); Annot., Right of Child or Parent to Recover for Alienation of Other's Affections, 60 A.L.R.3d 931 (1974). Cf. Lapides v. Trabbic, 134 Md. App. 51, 758 A.2d 1114 (2000) (no action without physical removal of child from custodial parent). In Hershey v. Hershey, 467 N.W.2d 484 (S.D. 1991), after a divorce in which the mother was awarded custody of the couple's only child, the mother moved to another state and ceased contact with the father. She concealed the child's whereabouts from the father for the next fourteen years, until the child attained the age of majority. The court held that the father stated an action against the mother for alienation of the child's affections.

2. Strode v. Gleason, 9 Wash. App. 13, 510 P.2d 250 (1973), recognized a parental action for "malicious" alienation of the affections of a minor child. Malice was defined as an unjustifiable interference with the parent-child relationship. This was preserved when the court decided to abolish actions for alienation of the affections of a spouse. Wyman v. Wallace, 15 Wash. App. 395, 549 P.2d 71 (1976), rev'd, 91 Wash. 2d 317, 588 P.2d 1133 (1979), reinstated, 94 Wash. 2d 99, 615 P.2d 452 (1980). In the *Borer* and *Baxter* cases, pp. 25–31, supra, which rejected liability for loss of the "consortium" of a parent or child when caused by negligently-inflicted personal injury, the court stated that it was not barring actions for intentional interference with consortium. Are these distinctions justified?

3. Because the right to a child's services was thought to reside in the father, a mother often could not maintain an action for abduction, enticement, harboring or seduction of the child, just as she could not maintain an action for injury to the child. See p. 24, supra. Assuming that mothers and fathers are now entitled to equal rights with respect to interference with parent-child relations, how should the rights of each parent be protected and enforced? Should parental "ownership" of the action be the same as in cases of injuries to children?

Magierowski v. Buckley

Superior Court of New Jersey, Appellate Division
39 N.J. Super. 534, 121 A.2d 749 (1956)

GOLDMANN, S.J.A.D.

The question before us is: Can a father maintain an action for the loss of services of his employed adult daughter, and for punitive damages, by reason of her alleged seduction under a promise of marriage, in view of the provisions of N.J.S. 2A:23-1 et seq., commonly known as the "Heart Balm" Act?

The complaint alleges that plaintiff is the father of Stephanie Magierowski, unmarried and of good repute for chastity, who lived with him and had been employed at a local plant for some 2½ years last past. He charged that shortly after Stephanie became 21, defendant, of age and single, "did, under the promise of marriage," seduce her, and as a result she became pregnant and "was unable to perform her usual tasks and duties, employment, and unable to earn monies as heretofore." The first count sought $25,000 damages for loss of the daughter's services and earnings. By way of second count plaintiff asked $25,000 punitive damages for loss of services, medical and hospital expenses, and for shame, humiliation and nervous shock.

The answer set up by way of separate defenses that N.J.S. 2A:23-1 et seq., was a bar to the action, that plaintiff could not sue for loss of services where the daughter had reached her majority, and further, that she had been emancipated for some period of time. Defendant then moved for an order dismissing the complaint and for summary judgment in his favor, urging the same grounds in support of the motion. The court entered such an order which recited the bar of the cited statute....

An action *ex delicto* did exist at common law in favor of the parent against the seducer.... The law developed as an offshoot of the action for enticing away a servant and depriving the master of his *quasi*-proprietary interest in his services. The wife and minor children were considered, in early common law, as superior servants of the husband and father; loss of their services became the gist of his action. In recent years, however, the emphasis has shifted from services toward recognition of the more intangible elements in the domestic relation, such as companionship and affection....

The law has not always been as ready to protect the relation of parent and child as it has that of husband and wife. It has, perhaps, been most sensitive and given the broadest protection to the parent's interests in permitting the bringing of an action for illicit intercourse with his female child. In the measure that such action redresses injury to family honor, reputation and the feelings involved in the father-child relation, it is somewhat analogous to the husband's action for criminal conversation. Unwilling to permit the woman a right to sue for her own seduction, the common law did what it could to give an action at least to the parent. The result was the action for seduction, supported by nothing more than a fiction which proved to be as embarrassing as it was ingenious.

It is unnecessary to detail every step of the road by which the common law arrived at the final product—an action in the parent for seduction of the daughter, based on loss of services due the parent as master from his daughter as servant....

The father, therefore, was not permitted to bring an action simply for the debauching of his daughter, but if there were loss of services consequent thereon, the action would lie....

The courts of England have persisted in holding fast to the rule that the loss of services is essential to the parent's cause of action; and American courts, generally, have said that loss of services is the gist of the action, without which the action must fail. However, the tendency in this State, as elsewhere, has from the earliest times been to reduce this element of loss of services to a minimum. Any services actually rendered the parent, even of the slightest, such as making a cup of tea, or milking the cows, suffices. If the seduced daughter was a minor and living in her father's home, it was presumed without more that she performed such services; and even where a minor daughter temporarily lived elsewhere, the father could recover if he still had the legal right to command her services at his pleasure—i.e., had not emancipated her from his control, or released his right to her services, or abandoned her. Thus, courts have embraced the idea of constructive service to support the father's action; the mere right to services was enough, though none were rendered in fact.

Not only have American courts been willing to support the fiction of loss of services by recognizing that the right to services without any being performed was sufficient, but the fact of services without the right to them has also been ample to the purpose. This has been the approach where the daughter was of age at the time of her seduction. If she was in a position where the father could command her services, and she rendered them to him, no matter how slight, recovery would lie.

Realistically appraising the lengths to which courts have had to go in order to keep alive and useful the fiction of loss of services, a few jurisdictions logically concluded that the fiction was obsolete and no longer necessary to an action for seduction in the parent.

Technical loss of services once having been established, the parent's action for seduction was recognized (*sub silentio*) for what it really was—an action *ex delicto* for interference with the family relation. As was said in Briggs v. Evans, 27 N.C. 16, 20 (Sup. Ct. 1844), the plaintiff "comes into court as a master; he goes before the jury as a father." The father, suing as a master, has been permitted to recover not only the value of the services lost—often so minor as to be minimal—but damages for medical and other expenses for the care of the daughter, for loss of her society and comfort, for his wounded feelings, or the dishonor brought to himself and his family—with punitive damages imposed....

There can therefore be no question that before 1935 plaintiff could have brought this action for seduction and recovered the damages he now seeks for loss of services and earnings, for medical and other expenses, and for shame and humiliation, upon a showing that his daughter was not emancipated, that he still had the right to command her services, and that he did in fact receive from her a measure of such services....

The abuses attending the so-called "heart balm" actions—alienation of affections, criminal conversation, seduction and breach of promise to marry—have been considered elsewhere. The public had come to look upon "heart balm" suits as devices for extracting large sums of money without proper justification. They were a fruitful source of coercion, extortion and blackmail. Manufactured suits, with their always present threat of publicity, were often used to force a settlement. Thus, an unscrupulous and unprincipled father could threaten to sue, or actually sue, a reputable or wealthy or important member of the community for an alleged act of seduction, timing his action so as to coincide with an important event in the man's life, such as the forthcoming announcement of his engagement, marriage, or his candidacy for public office. If the person charged stood his ground and went to court, he was faced with proof of damages grossly magnified to catch the sympathy of the jury. And juries were generally very liberal in their awards in seduction cases; damages could be and were oppressive, under the guise of punitive or exemplary damages—such as are sought here. As Prosser observes, there is good reason to believe that even genuine actions were "brought, more frequently than not, with purely mercenary or vindictive motives; that it is impossible to compensate for such damage with what has derisively been called 'heart balm'; that people of any decent instincts do not bring an action which merely adds to the family disgrace; and that no preventive purpose is served, since such torts seldom are committed with deliberate plan." [Prosser, Law of Torts 697 (2d ed. 1955).]

In the statement of policy set out in the preamble to L. 1935, c. 279 (now N.J.S. 2A:23-1 et seq.) our Legislature stated: "Whereas, The remedies herein provided for by law for the enforcement of actions based upon alleged alienation of affections, criminal conversation, seduction and breach of contract to marry have been subjected to grave abuses, causing extreme annoyance, embarrassment, humiliation and pecuniary damage to many persons wholly innocent and free of any wrongdoing, who were merely the victims of circumstances, and such remedies having been exercised by unscrupulous persons for their unjust enrichment and such remedies having furnished vehicles for the commission or attempted commission of crime and in many cases have resulted in the perpetration of frauds, it is hereby declared as the public policy of the State of New Jersey that the best interests of the people of the State will be served by the abolition of such remedies." ...

... 17 states, responding to the pressure generated by public opinion and publicity, enacted statutes designed to eliminate, modify or restrict one or more of the "heart balm" actions. Not all of these statutes abolish the civil action for seduction. ...

... The Legislature thus left the punishment of the offending party to rest either in the moral law or in criminal law. N.J.S. 2A:142-1, designates as a high misdemeanor the seduction of a single female of good repute for chastity, by a married man under representation that he is single, or under promise of marriage, she thereby becoming pregnant. And N.J.S. 2A:142-2, designates as a high misdemeanor the seduction of a single female of good repute for chastity and under 21 years of age, by a single man over the age of 18, under a promise of marriage, she thereby becoming pregnant. ...

We consider that the Legislature has effectively ordained that money damages shall not be recovered by the father of an adult girl who has abandoned her virtue and become pregnant. ...

... Our "heart balm" statute was carefully drawn with the evident purpose, in our opinion, to wipe out a cause of action such as the one under consideration, where a father seeks to recover damages for the seduction of his adult daughter under a promise of marriage. ...

The judgment is affirmed.

Notes

1. *Seduction actions.* As the principal case indicates, loss of the daughter's services originally was considered essential to the seduction action. See Tittlebaum v. Boehmcke, 81 N.J.L. 697, 80 A. 323 (1911); Eager v. Grimwood, (1847) 1 Exch. 61, 154 Eng. Rep. 26, 11 J.P. 206, 16 L.J. Ex. 236, 9 L.T.O.S. 200 (Ex.). But a "slight loss of services" (as often would result from pregnancy) has been found sufficient. See Wendt v. Lentz, 197 Wis. 569, 222 N.W. 798 (1929). A number of courts ruled that plaintiff's showing of a right to services sufficed even if there was no evidence of services actually performed by the daughter. See Reutkemeier v. Nolte, 179 Iowa 342, 161 N.W. 290 (1917). A few held that loss of services was no longer necessary. See Breining v. Lippincott, 125 Ark. 77, 187 S.W. 915 (1916); Snider v. Newell, 132 N.C. 614, 44 S.E. 354 (1903). This was established by statute in a number of jurisdictions. See Stoudt v. Shepherd, 73 Mich. 588, 41 N.W. 696 (1899). The loss of services requirement retained importance in regard to the question of who might bring suit for the seduction. It was the person entitled to the daughter's services—usually her father if he was living and had not deserted the family. See p. 24, supra.

2. A parent of an adult daughter, unlike the parent of a minor daughter, was not presumed to have a right to her services. However, if she was providing some services, as normally would be the case when the daughter was living with the parent, the parent

could bring an action for her seduction. See Beaudette v. Gagne, 87 Me. 534, 33 A. 23 (1895); Sutton v. Huffman, 32 N.J.L. 58 (Sup. Ct. 1866). In principle there could be an action if seduction of a son resulted in loss of services. Cf. White v. Nellis, 31 N.Y. 405 (1856), suggesting that a master has an action for seduction of a male servant. But there are no reported cases.

3. Given the seduction action's foundation in loss of services and her own participation in the act, a woman ordinarily had no tort action for her own seduction. An exception often was found when seduction was accomplished by force, duress or overpowering influence or under a promise of marriage. See Breece v. Jett, 556 S.W.2d 696 (Mo. App. 1977); Annot., Promise of Marriage as Condition of Civil Action for Seduction, 21 A.L.R. 303 (1922); Annot., Right of Seduced Female to Maintain Action for Seduction, 121 A.L.R. 1487 (1939). A considerable number of states enacted statutes to permit an action by the seduced female. A few courts came to a similar result without legislation on the ground that the seduced person was the "real party in interest." See Hyatt v. McCoy, 194 N.C. 25, 138 S.E. 405 (1927). See L.N.K. ex rel. Kavanaugh v. St. Mary's Medical Center, 785 N.E.2d 303 (Ind. App. 2003), transfer denied sub nom. Kavanaugh v. St. Mary's Medical Center, 804 N.E.2d 745 (Ind. 2003), for a recent seduction action allowed to both a seduced teenager and her parents.

4. *"Heart balm" statutes.* Many states now have statutes abolishing at least some of the most frequently litigated "heart balm" actions: seduction, breach of promise of marriage, alienation of affections and criminal conversation. See Harper, James & Gray, Law of Torts §8.7 (3d ed. 2006); Cotter, Amatory Torts and Heart Balm Statutes: A State-by-State Survey, 15 Divorce Lit. 219 (2003). On the reasons for the legislation of the 1930s, see Feinsinger, Legislative Attack on "Heart Balm," 33 Mich. L. Rev. 979 (1935); Kane, Heart Balm and Public Policy, 5 Ford. L. Rev. 62 (1936). Would modification of the actions have been preferable to abolition?

5. Where legislation bars a "heart balm" action for damages, an aggrieved spouse still might have a claim. In some jurisdictions, it is possible to obtain an injunction against the offending conduct. See Henley v. Rockett, 243 Ala. 172, 8 So. 2d 852 (1942) (injunction against "another woman," prohibiting her from associating or communicating with plaintiff's husband or otherwise causing him not to provide conjugal companionship, support and affection); Devine v. Devine, 20 N.J. Super. 522, 90 A.2d 126 (Ch. Div. 1952) (heart balm act not bar to suit to enjoin mother-in-law from interfering with marital relations or alienating affections). Would an action of emotional distress succeed? See Slusher v. Oeder, 16 Ohio App. 3d 432, 476 N.E.2d 714 (1984) (husband stated action on allegations that defendant repeatedly telephoned wife to persuade her to have sexual relations with him and had such relations); Weicker v. Weicker, 53 Misc. 2d 570, 279 N.Y.S.2d 852 (Sup. Ct. 1967) (alleged that plaintiff's husband obtained void Mexican divorce and entered bigamous marriage, holding out woman "married" as his wife; action against woman and husband allowed); Quinn v. Walsh, 49 Mass. App. Ct. 696, 732 N.E.2d 330 (2000) (emotional distress action not maintainable against man who openly engaged in extramartial affair with plaintiff's wife and caused end of twenty-year marriage); Koestler v. Pollard, 162 Wis. 2d 797, 471 N.W.2d 7 (1991) (emotional distress action not maintainable by man who assumed he was father of child born to his wife until defendant revealed he was biological father, several years after child's birth); Annot., Action for Intentional Infliction of Emotional Distress Against Paramours, 99 A.L.R.5th 445 (2002).

6. Some cases involving the effects of "heart balm" legislation are actions against a psychiatrist or other professional who provided treatment or counselling to one or both of the spouses. See Richard H. v. Larry D., 198 Cal. App. 3d 591, 243 Cal. Rptr. 807 (1988)

(statute no bar to fraud and negligent infliction of emotional distress actions against psychiatrist for having intercourse with plaintiff's wife while couple were his patients); Figueiredo-Torres v. Nickel, 321 Md. 642, 584 A.2d 69 (1991) (statute did not preclude negligence and emotional distress actions against psychologist who during treatment of plaintiff and wife commenced romantic and sexual relationship with wife, leading to dissolution of marriage); Weaver v. Union Carbide Corp., 180 W. Va. 556, 378 S.E.2d 105 (1989) (spouse not receiving counselling could not maintain action for damages caused by marriage counsellor's sexual involvement with counsellee because claim was essentially one for alienation of affections); R.E.R. v. J.G., 552 N.W.2d 27 (Minn. App. 1996) (plaintiff could not claim damages from minister who had affair with plaintiff's wife after couple sought marital counselling); Bailey v. Faulkner, 940 So. 2d 247 (Ala. 2006) (similar). Would abolition of criminal conversation and seduction actions bar a claim that defendant's sexual activity caused plaintiff to become infected with a disease? See Mussivand v. David, 45 Ohio St. 3d 314, 544 N.E.2d 265 (1989) (negligence action for causing plaintiff to be infected by venereal disease by having sexual relations with plaintiff's spouse). Cf. Kathleen K. v. Robert B., 150 Cal. App. 3d 992, 198 Cal. Rptr. 273 (1984) (action for infecting plaintiff with venereal disease by fraudulent or negligent misrepresentation).

Bearbower v. Merry
Supreme Court of Iowa
266 N.W.2d 128 (1978)

REYNOLDSON, Justice.

The issues in this appeal are whether the tort actions for alienation of affections and for criminal conversation should be abolished....

These torts came to us from the common law. Their viability has not been challenged previously in this jurisdiction.

Of course it is our duty to monitor and interpret the common law, and to abandon antiquated doctrines and concepts....

There is no dispute among members of this court concerning the role of marriage in our social structure. *Board of Dir. of Ind. Sch. Dist. of Waterloo v. Green*, 259 Iowa 1260, 1269, 147 N.W.2d 854, 859 (1967) ("The law looks with favor upon marriage and seeks in all lawful ways to uphold this most vital social institution.")....

... The relevant question is whether a family member's interest in the harmony of her or his home is of sufficient magnitude to warrant judicial protection from those who intentionally would interfere with it.

The reasons usually articulated by those who would abolish the alienation of affection action are thus summarized by H. Clark, Law of Domestic Relations, § 10.2, p. 267 (1968): "The reasons underlying abolition of alienation of affections are many and persuasive. One is the opportunities for blackmail which the action provides, since the mere bringing of the action can ruin the defendant's reputation. Another is that lack of any reasonably definite standards for assessing damages and the possibility of punitive damages makes excessive verdicts likely. Still another is the peculiar light which the whole proceeding throws on the nature of marriage, leaving one with the conviction that the successful plaintiff has engaged in something which looks very much like a forced sale of his spouse's affections. Most significantly of all, the action for alienation is based upon psychological assumptions that are contrary to fact. As has been indicated, viable, contented marriages are not broken up by the vile seducer of the Nineteenth Century melodrama, though this is what the suit for alienation assumes. In fact the break-up is the product of many influences. It is therefore misleading and futile to suppose that the threat of a damage suit can protect the marital relationship. For all these reasons the abolishing statutes reflect a sound public policy and ought to be enacted more widely than they are."

This criticism, of course, proceeds from the wholly unsupported and obviously personal belief of the author that "a marriage is not broken up by outsiders if it is solidly based on the affections of the parties."

One logically could proceed from the equally unsupportable but nonetheless widely held belief that many marriages do not sail their course in unending calm seas and sunny weather. Rather, sometimes the voyage is beset by troublesome but navigable adverse tides and storms. Such occasional stress should not furnish a stranger grounds to wrongfully meddle.

Most marriages are not required to endure the intentional, continuous and often vindictive third-person interference disclosed by our adjudicated decisions. This leaves an inadequate sampling from which to conclude otherwise viable marriages are immune to such abnormal pressures.

We further note the criticisms advanced by *Clark*, supra, are not typical of commentators in this area: "[I]n spite of all of the objections which have been advanced, most of the writers in this field agree that some form of action should be preserved. The purpose of these suits is simply the protection of the home, and in this modern era of increasing instability in family relations, few would discourage any means which might have a more stabilizing effect upon the family." Comment, "Anti-Heart Balm" Legislation Revisited, 56 Nw. L. Rev. 538, 545 (1961). See 1 Harper and James, The Law of Torts, §8.7, p. 629 (1956) ("[I]n the case of alienation, grievous wrongs are suffered and some of life's most important interests ruthlessly invaded. To abolish all remedy in such cases is certainly subject to serious question."); [Prosser, Law of Torts 887–888 (4th ed. 1971)] ("Their [statutes abolishing criminal conversation, seduction, alienation of affections] desirability is another matter. They reverse abruptly the entire tendency of the law to give increased protection to family interests and the sanctity of the home, and undoubtedly they deny relief in many cases of serious and genuine wrong.").

Abolition of the alienation tort in approximately one-third of the states has proceeded by statute except in two instances of judicial intervention. Many of those statutes were the result of notorious breach of promise of marriage cases which received widespread media condemnation in the 1930–1943 period. "[N]ewspaper emphasis has created an illusion of universality as to the evils of unfounded actions, coercive settlements or excessive verdicts which concededly exist in particular cases." Feinsinger, *Legislative Attack on "Heart Balm,"* 33 Mich. L. Rev. 979, 1008–1009 (1935). Thoughtful writers questioned whether justifiable resentment over abuse of the remedy of breach of promise to marry necessitated the wholesale abolition of established rights and remedies....

... Even a shaky marital edifice ought to be permitted to collapse from its own imperfections, if it will, before a third party is authorized to kick out a cornerstone....

In any event, many alienation cases are brought against interfering and harassing near relatives, in which the "damage to reputation" and blackmail arguments have no applicability. Out of some 41 alienation cases reaching this court, 22 were prosecuted against immediate family members of a spouse, absent any allegations of sexual involvement. Seventeen were brought by the wife against one or both of the husband's parents.

Our cases recognize the right of a spouse's parents or adult children to offer advice regarding domestic and marital matters, and presume good faith in the offer. An alienation of affections plaintiff has the burden of proving malice on the part of immediate family members, a burden not imposed as to other defendants in such actions.

Professor Clark's assertions [that] the remedy should be abolished because of a "lack of any reasonably definite standards for assessing damages" will not stand scrutiny. The gravamen of the alienation of affections action is loss of consortium.... We routinely have recognized a jury's ability to measure its value where the loss was caused negligently.

The difficulty of translating damage to intangible rights into money judgments has deterred us not at all in other law areas. [The court had permitted damages to be awarded for invasion of privacy, intentional infliction of emotional harm, emotional distress arising from breach of a funeral service contract, mental pain caused by a physical impact tort and, in a wrongful death case, loss of the companionship and society of a minor child.]

The rationale the destroyed marriage was undoubtedly unstable and therefore no damages for alienation of affections should be permitted goes too far. Of course, mere loss of a spouse's affections does not render defendant liable unless the latter's misconduct was a substantial factor in causing such loss. Defendant is permitted to show a prior deteriorated marital situation in mitigation of damages.

Similarly lacking in substance is Professor Clark's rationale that the opportunity for blackmail justifies abolition of the remedy for alienation. It already has been demonstrated, supra, that in this jurisdiction a large volume of these cases involve no alleged sexual misconduct. They therefore present no risk to "reputation," and consequently, no opportunity for blackmail. There is a palpable inconsistency between this argument and the frequent implication the remedy should be struck down because social mores now condone such extramarital activity. If so, there should be no hazard to a potential defendant's reputation, nor, for that matter, any danger of excessive jury verdicts. There is nothing before this court to show there now is any basis in Iowa for these fears, or that the alleged abuses are occurring in this jurisdiction.

The connection defendant seeks to make between the legislative intent in our no-fault dissolution statute and the necessity to abolish alienation suits is illusory. In view of the resulting flood of dissolution litigation which clogs our courts, it is as logical to conclude the marriage relationship needs more protection from outside interference, not less. A legislature concerned enough to provide for a 60-day compulsory conciliation procedure and a 90-day waiting period might well perceive the desirability of any deterrent to unjustified third-party meddling during those periods in order to permit the parties to work out their differences....

... That some alienation actions may be brought in bad faith (a suggestion not supported by the records in cases which have reached this court) does not provide reason to abolish all such remedies. We would resist such reasoning applied to other types of litigation. After all, "the very purpose of courts is to separate the just from the unjust causes." *Wilder v. Reno*, 43 F. Supp. 727, 729 (M.D. Pa. 1942).

We hold the action for alienation of affections remains consistent with public policy in this jurisdiction and shall be retained.

The action which may be maintained for an isolated instance of criminal conversation presents a different situation....

The tort has been handed down from early common law intact. Defenses which would seem applicable in terms of today's sense of fairness are nonexistent: "At common law and in other jurisdictions where a cause of action [for criminal conversation] is recognized in favor of the husband under these circumstances, consent of the wife is no defense. The fact that the wrongdoer did not know the wife was married but believed her to be single is not a defense. The fact that the wife represented herself as single is not a defense. The fact that the wife was the aggressor is not a defense. The fact that she has been neglected or mistreated by her husband is not a defense. The fact that she and her husband were separated through his fault is not a defense. When the case comes on for trial, moreover, the number of occasions on which the wife has had sexual relations with the defendant and with others is a highly relevant inquiry on the issue of damages." *Felsenthal v. McMillan*, 493 S.W.2d 729, 731 (Tex. 1973) (Steakley, J., dissenting).... [T]he Pennsylvania supreme court observed: "[I]n today's society it is unreasonable to impose upon a defendant such harsh results without affording any real opportunity to interject logically valid defenses on the merits such as the role of the plaintiff's spouse in the adulterous relationship or the quality of the plaintiff's marriage prior to the occurrence of the acts constituting the tort." *Fadgen v. Lenkner*, 469 Pa. 272, 280–281, 365 A.2d 147, 151 (1976).

A fundamental flaw in the criminal conversation remedy, as opposed to alienation of affections remedy, is its insensitive imposition without regard to the viability of the marriage relationship, or to the fact, in a given instance, that relationship may not have been affected adversely. In short, recovery may be allowed where stability of the marriage survives unimpaired.

On the other hand, where a continuous course of adultery has undermined the marital relationship the alienation of affections remedy, left standing, would apply....

The enactment of the new criminal code bears on the continued viability of the tort of criminal conversation. Although it is a common-law tort, the right to maintain a civil action for adultery previously was assured by our statute making adultery a crime. Civil causes of action are available to obtain damages for injuries sustained by reason of crimes in Iowa. However, chapter 702 of the 1975 Code was repealed by the new criminal code. Therefore, no statutory inhibition against eliminating the common-law tort of criminal conversation existed as of January 1, 1978.

We abolish the tort of criminal conversation in Iowa for conduct occurring after January 1, 1978.

But because plaintiff's petition in this case is based on conduct alleged to have occurred prior to that date, we hold trial court was right in overruling defendant's motion to dismiss....

[Affirmed. Rawlings, J., delivered a concurring opinion. Mason, J., delivered a dissenting opinion.]

McCORMICK, Justice [with whom Harris, J., joined] (dissenting in part).

I would abolish the tort of alienation of affections as well as the tort of criminal conversation....

Certainly we should not, as the majority does, endorse decisions of other courts which have recognized the disfavor of heart-balm litigation but are content to leave the issue of eliminating this judge-made doctrine to the legislature. In *Kersten Co., Inc. v. Department of Social Services*, 207 N.W.2d 117 (Iowa 1973), we said we could open the courtroom doors without legislative help. We should have equal confidence in our power to close them....

Although the majority opinion attacks the arguments for abolishing the alienation of affections action which are advanced in H. Clark, Law of Domestic Relations, § 10.2 at

267 (1968), I do not think it responds to Clark's most telling statements: "Still another is the peculiar light which the whole proceeding throws on the nature of marriage, leaving one with the conviction that the successful plaintiff has engaged in something which looks very much like a sale of his wife's affections. Most significantly of all, the action for alienation is based on psychological assumptions that are contrary to fact." ...

When heart-balm torts originated in the English common law they were available only to a husband. They had their basis in property concepts. The husband was said to be superior to his wife and thus to own her affections, companionship and services.... While I agree the broader concept of a right of consortium has validity in the personal injury damages context, I do not believe spousal love is property which is subject to theft or alienation. It is simply a contradiction in terms to say it is. This should be sufficient reason in itself to abolish the alienation tort, but it is not the only reason.

Many authoritative studies have been made of the nature of marriage and the cause, prevention, and cure of marital failure. I have searched among them in vain for any support for the majority's assumption that the existence of the alienation tort is a deterrent to marital breakdown or a device for protecting the family unit....

The disintegration of a marriage is ordinarily as complex a process as is its integration. It seldom occurs overnight. It starts from within. It is not caused by only one factor or through some imperfection of only one of the spouses. Any third person who kicks at the cornerstone of a shaky marriage will not bring it down without active support from one or both of the parties. It is simplistic and unrealistic to suppose the edifice will be held together either so long as or because spouses have the right to obtain vengeance in the form of damage suits against the third person. Although a recovery of damages will punish the third person and sooth the ego while enriching the purse of the plaintiff, it is hardly calculated to be a constructive influence in maintaining or restoring a mature and stable marriage between two individuals with free will and separate identity.

An early reaction to marital failure is the tendency to place all the responsibility for it on someone else. This is a process of self-defense. The fault divorce system provided a mechanism for playing out this fantasy, and the alienation of affections and criminal conversation torts serve the same purpose.

Over the years the public became aware of the hypocrisy, bitterness and emotional stress involved in the fault divorce system, and in 1970 our legislature enacted the dissolution law which eliminated the necessity of proving fault as a basis for terminating a marriage.

The disuse and disfavor of alienation of affections and criminal conversation torts, reflected by the infrequency with which such cases have reached this court in recent years, result from the same considerations. These torts are antithetical to the goal they purport to foster. They are not constructive, but destructive. They do not build, but destroy. They bring out the worst in human nature in the guise of vindicating marital rights. They denigrate human dignity by reducing marital values to monetary terms. They provide a forum for vindictiveness and posturing self-justification.

Moreover, because the very bringing of such cases is sufficient to damage reputations, the threat to file them constitutes a device for the unscrupulous to coerce an unjust payment as the price for avoiding litigation. It does not matter that a jury might ultimately deny the merits of the claim.

Heart-balm actions arise from the same motives and serve no nobler purpose than the stoning of the adulteress condemned in the New Testament or the affixing of the scarlet letter decried by Hawthorne, and they have no more to do with protecting marriage and the family than either of those events.

Notes

1. Some courts have left abolition of heart balm actions to the legislature. Gorder v. Sims, 306 Minn. 275, 237 N.W.2d 67 (1975) (alienation); Kremer v. Black, 201 Neb. 467, 268 N.W.2d 582 (1978) (crim. con.); Felsenthal v. McMillan, 493 S.W.2d 729 (Tex. 1973) (crim. con.). Others, believing that the torts can appropriately be abolished by the courts, have been persuaded to hold that such actions could no longer be maintained. O'Neil v. Schukardt, 112 Idaho 472, 733 P.2d 693 (1986) (alienation); Saunders v. Alford, 607 So. 2d 1214 (Miss. 1992) (crim. con.); Fadgen v. Lenkner, 469 Pa. 272, 365 A.2d 147 (1976) (crim. con.); Norton v. Macfarlane, 818 P.2d 8 (Utah 1991) (crim. con.); Helsel v. Noellsch, 107 S.W.3d 231 (Mo. 2003) (alienation). Bearbower v. Merry's retention of alienation of affections was overruled (5–4) in Fundermann v. Mickelson, 304 N.W.2d 790 (Iowa 1981).

2. A distinct majority of states have now abolished alienation of affections and criminal conversation liability by statute or judicial decision. See Hoye v. Hoye, 824 S.W.2d 422 (Ky. 1992); Veeder v. Kennedy, 589 N.W.2d 610 (S.D. 1999) (decided that alienation not be abolished by judicial decision because codification had given tort statutory foundation in state). Some commentators believe that some form of action for interference with the marital relationship should be retained. See Corbett, A Somewhat Modest Proposal to Prevent Adultery and Save Families: Two Old Torts Looking for a New Career, 33 Ariz. St. L.J. 985 (2001); Note, The Case for Retention of Causes of Action for Intentional Interference with the Marital Relationship, 48 Notre Dame Lawyer 426 (1972). See also Fitch v. Valentine, 959 So. 2d 1012 (Miss. 2007), cert. denied, 552 U.S. 1100 (2008); Nelson v. Jacobsen, 669 P.2d 1207 (Utah 1983) (alienation retained). What are the prospects that a court would abolish alienation of affections but not criminal conversation? That a legislature would do this?

Taylor v. Keefe

Supreme Court of Errors of Connecticut
134 Conn. 156, 56 A.2d 768 (1947)

BROWN, Judge.

This is an action on behalf of a minor son to recover of the defendant for the alienation of his mother's affections. The trial court sustained the defendant's demurrer to the complaint.... The following facts stand admitted upon the demurrer. For many years the plaintiff had been living happily with his mother. In 1943 the defendant by his arts, blandishments and seductions alienated her love and affection and destroyed the happiness of the plaintiff's home. In consequence, the plaintiff has suffered great distress of body and mind and has lost the love, affection and society of his mother. As a further result, he has lost much happiness, has been forced out of the home which he had with his mother, and has been denied her social and moral support, guidance and protection. It is also conceded that the plaintiff's father and mother are divorced and that custody of the plaintiff as a minor child was awarded to the mother.

The sole question for determination is whether a minor child can maintain an action for alienation of affections against one who has alienated from him the affections of his mother.... There appear to be but three reported decisions in which the question has been ruled upon....

... The concrete inquiry is whether, under the present conception of the family relationship, a minor child's natural right to the love and affection of his mother should be accorded by the law the same protection as a husband's or wife's property right of consortium. The nature of the question is well set forth in the editorial comment in 162 American Law Reports 825, where it is pointed out that the underlying problem is, in its last analysis, a sociological rather than a legal one; that a child has an interest in his parents' affection and company which the courts under our system of law have the power to "legalize" by recognizing a right of action for its protection; but that the vital query is whether it is wise for the courts to exercise their power of lawmaking in this particular instance.

Of the two decisions chiefly relied upon by the plaintiff, one is the case of Daily v. Parker, 152 F.2d 174. There, four minor children sued a married woman for enticing their father to leave them and their home and go to live with her and to refuse to contribute further for their maintenance and support. The court held "that a child today has a right enforceable in a court of law, against one who has invaded and taken from said child the support and maintenance of its father, as well as damages for the destruction of other rights which arise out of the family relationship and which have been destroyed or defeated by a wrongdoing third party." ...

In the other case, Johnson v. Luhman, 330 Ill. App. 598, 71 N.E.2d 810, five minor children sued a woman for alienating the affections of their father and depriving them of his support and society, including their rights to his paternal care and to the security of a family life. In upholding the right of action in the plaintiffs, the court cited with approval the reasoning and decision in the Daily case, decided a few months earlier. Referring to the change that has taken place in the conception of the family, it pointed out that under the early common law "The father spoke and acted for the family unit and the individual members thereof had no distinct identity. Hence, it was stated in 3 Blackstone's Commentaries 143 (1765), 'The child hath no property in his father.' It is common knowledge, however, that a transition has taken place in our conception of the family, and in the law which reflects, in a measure, our social standards. The family is now a cooperative enterprise with correlative rights and duties among all members thereof.... The children ... are presently regarded more as responsible individuals than as subservient charges ... they are entitled to both the tangible incidents of family life, such as food, clothing and shelter, and to the intangible, though equally significant elements of affection, moral support, and guidance from both of the parents." The court concluded that the nature of the present-day status of the child, so described, gave rise to a right in the plaintiff warranting the creation of the remedy sought, even though unsupported by binding precedent, since the defendant's conduct had destroyed "the children's family unit ... and deprived them of ... the security afforded by [their father's] affection and presence."

Morrow v. Yannantuono, 152 Misc. 134, 273 N.Y.S. 912, reaches a contrary result. In that case the infant plaintiff sued the male defendant for wrongfully depriving him of the affection, comfort and love of his mother by enticing her away and harboring her.... [I]t has been cogently suggested that, notwithstanding there seems no theoretical reason for denying the relief claimed on the basis of a child's right to the "consortium" of his parents, "numerous practical obstructions ... inhibit application of this reasoning." 83 U. of Pa. L. Rev. 276. Among the difficulties enumerated are (1) possibility of a multiplicity of suits; (2) possibility of extortionary litigation by virtue of the relative tenuousness of the child's relationship; (3) inability to define the point at which the child's right would cease, inasmuch as the status itself hypothesizes mutability, for although a spouse is, barring extraordinary circumstances, always a spouse, the very nature of childhood implies an eventual change to adulthood; and (4) the inability of a jury adequately to cope with the question of damages, particularly because damages thus assessed are apt to overlap, in view of the number and different ages of the children.

These difficulties suggest persuasive reason why as a matter of policy this court should not recognize the validity of the cause of action claimed. Reference to a specific situation may serve to illustrate the practical difficulty of carrying the "family unit" theory to its logical conclusion. Under it, the parent would have the same right of action for the alienation of the affection of the child which the plaintiff here claims for the alienation of that of his parent. Yet the marriage of a child might well give rise to a factual situation which a parent could utilize as the basis of an action against the child's spouse for alienating the child's affections. Such a possibility emphasizes the real distinction between permitting such an action in a case dependent upon the relationship of husband and wife, who have voluntarily created the unit status "for better or for worse" for life, and permitting it in a case dependent upon the relationship of parent and child, where in the course of nature the child is likely to substitute in large part for the family unit of the parents a family unit of his own....

There is no error.

Notes

1. The common law gave a child no action for enticement of a parent, alienation of a parent's affections, criminal conversation with a parent or conduct causing a parent to neglect family duties. A child had no legal (as distinct from moral or social) right to the parent's services or "consortium." Alienation actions have been rejected by most courts in which they have been considered. See Hunt v. Chang, 60 Hawaii 608, 594 P.2d 118 (1979); Henson v. Thomas, 231 N.C. 173, 56 S.E.2d 432 (1949); Annot., Right of Child or Parent to Recover for Alienation of Other's Affections, 60 A.L.R.3d 931 (1974). In addition to the reasons expressed in the principal case, there has been concern with the use of such actions by the child's other parent and the possibility that such a tort would result in children being able to control the associations of their parents. See Zarrella v. Robinson, 492 A.2d 833 (R.I. 1985); Scholberg v. Itnyre, 264 Wis. 211, 58 N.W.2d 698 (1953). A few cases subsequent to Taylor v. Keefe accept an action for enticement of a parent. Rusick v. Hicks, 85 F. Supp. 281 (D. Mich. 1949); Miller v. Monsen, 228 Minn. 400, 37 N.W.2d 543 (1949).

2. When a parent is "alienated" from a child, might the child have an action against the parent? Could the parent or third person concerned incur liability for infliction of emotional distress? See the next principal case and notes following. Cf. Raftery v. Scott, 756 F.2d 335 (4th Cir. 1985); Meikle v. Van Biber, 745 S.W.2d 714 (Mo. App. 1987); Bartanus v. Lis, 332 Pa. Super. 48, 480 A.2d 1178 (1984) (alienation of child from parent). Do statutes intended to abolish actions for alienation of a spouse's affections prevent liability for alienation of a parent's or child's affections? See Bouchard v. Sundberg, 80 Conn. App. 180, 834 A.2d 744 (2003); Rudnick v. Vokaty, 84 Ill. App. 3d 1003, 406 N.E.2d 105 (1980). Michigan has abolished causes of action for "alienation of the affections of any person, animal, or thing capable of feeling affection whatsoever," Mich. Comp. Laws § 600.2901(1).

Burnette v. Wahl

Supreme Court of Oregon
284 Or. 705, 588 P.2d 1105 (1978)

HOLMAN, Justice.

Three identical cases have been consolidated for appeal. Plaintiffs are five minor children aged two to eight who, through their guardian, are bringing actions against their mothers for emotional and psychological injury caused by failure of defendant-mothers to perform their parental duties to plaintiffs. Plaintiffs appeal from orders of dismissal....

The complaints allege that plaintiffs are in the custody of the Children's Services Division of the Department of Human Resources of the State of Oregon and are wards of Klamath County Juvenile Court.

The complaints are substantially identical, each one being in three counts. Among these counts are strewn various allegations of parental failure upon which the causes of action rest. They are: "1. Since [date], defendant intentionally, wilfully, maliciously and with cruel disregard of the consequences failed to provide plaintiff with care, custody, parental nurturance, affection, comfort, companionship, support, regular contact and visitation. 2. She has failed in violation of ORS 109.010 to maintain plaintiff, who, due to ... age and indigency, is poor and unable to work to maintain ... self. 3. She has abandoned plaintiff by deserting the child with intent to abandon ... and with intent to abdicate all responsibility for ... care and raising, in violation of ORS 163.535. 4. She has neglected the plaintiff by negligently leaving ... unattended in or at a place for such period of time as would have been likely to endanger the health or welfare of the plaintiff, in violation of ORS 163.545. 5. She has refused or neglected without lawful excuse to provide support for plaintiff, in violation of ORS 163.555. 6. Defendant has maliciously, intentionally, and with cruel disregard of the consequences, deserted and abandoned her child. 7. Defendant has alienated the affections of the plaintiff in that she has intentionally, wilfully and maliciously abandoned, deserted, neglected and failed to maintain regular contact or visitation, or to provide for the plaintiff and has deprived plaintiff of the love, care, affection and comfort to which plaintiff is entitled." ...

... [T]hese claims of parental failure are different from those tort claims usually made upon behalf of children against parents. The adjudicated cases concern physical or emotional injuries resulting from physical acts inflicted upon children such as beatings and rapes and from automobile accidents. Plaintiffs admit they can cite no cases permitting them to recover from their parents for solely emotional or psychological damage resulting from failure to support, nurture and care for them....

... [T]he legislature has put its mind to the deprivations of which plaintiff children are alleged to be victims and has attempted to remedy such situations by enacting a vast panoply of procedures, both civil and criminal, to insure that children receive proper nurturing, support and physical care. It has never undertaken to establish, however, a cause of action for damages for any emotional injury to the child which may have been caused by a parent's refusal to provide these services. This failure of the legislature to act is significant because this is not a field of recovery which has heretofore been recognized by courts and it would therefore be natural for it to have provided such a remedy if it thought it was wise in view of the social problem it attempts to solve and the statutory provisions it has enacted for that purpose....

There is no doubt but that the statutory provisions previously cited show a strong state policy of requiring the kind of parental nurturing, support and physical care of children which the defendants here are alleged to have denied their children. As previously indicated, it does not follow as a matter of course that it would be wise or judicious to vindicate that policy by a tort action for damages by children against their mothers. The state also has other policies within its statutory plan of which such a cause of action might well be destructive, particularly the policy of reuniting abandoned children with their parents, if possible....

It is recognized by the statutory scheme that in some instances the reestablishment of a biological family is impossible and it therefore provides for a proceeding to terminate parental rights in order that a new family unit for the child may be formed....

It is significant that plaintiffs' complaints do not allege that proceedings for the termination of the defendants' parental rights have taken place. In such circumstances, it would be exceedingly unwise for this court to step in and to initiate a new and heretofore unrecognized cause of action in a field of social planning to which the legislature has devoted a great deal of time and effort in evolving what appears to be an all-encompassing plan. Those persons designated by statute for aiding the plaintiffs in these cases have not yet taken the step for which the plan provides when there is no longer any hope of reestablishing these children in a family unit with their mothers. Tort actions such as the present ones might well be destructive of any plans the social agencies and the juvenile court might have for these children. It is inappropriate for this court to insert a new cause of action into the picture....

... If there is ever a field in which juries and general trial courts are ill equipped to do social engineering, it is in the realm of the emotional relationship between mother and child. It is best we leave such matters to other fields of endeavor. There are certain kinds of relationships which are not proper fodder for tort litigation, and we believe this to be one of them. There are probably as many children who have been damaged in some manner by their parents' failure to meet completely their physical, emotional and psychological needs as there are people. A tort action for damages by emotionally deprived persons against their parents is, in our opinion, not going to solve the social problem in the same manner in which the legislature is attempting to solve it.

In addition to the contention that defendants should be liable for civil damages because of their violation of criminal and regulatory statutes, plaintiffs also contend that defendants are responsible because of the infliction of severe emotional distress by intentional acts. Plaintiffs allege that defendants intentionally deserted and abandoned them; however, they do not contend that defendants deserted them for the purpose of inflicting emotional harm upon them. We recognize that this tort usually also encompasses the infliction of emotional harm under circumstances from which a reasonable person would conclude that harm was almost certain to result. We believe this latter rationale is inapplicable as between parents and children. If it were otherwise, the children of divorced parents would almost always have an action for emotional damage against their parents. Divorce has become a way of life with almost certain emotional trauma of a greater or lesser degree to the children from the legal dissolution of the family and the resultant absence of at least one of the parents and sometimes both.

In addition, plaintiffs contend that the common law tort of alienation of affections is applicable. They argue that because such a cause of action is intended to compensate one spouse for the intentional alienation of the other spouse's affections by a third party, and that because in one case, *Daily v. Parker*, 152 F.2d 174 (7th Cir. 1945), this cause of action has been extended to the children, it should exist against the parent himself. The statement of the argument is its refutation. Also, the tort of alienation of affections has recently been abolished by the legislature.

Plaintiffs generally contend that without respect to previously recognized theories of recovery, we should recognize a new tort of parental desertion. For all the reasons previously given in declining to use recognized theories of recovery, we also decline this invitation.

The judgment of the trial court is affirmed.

TONGUE, Justice, concurring.

Although I agree with much of the dissent and, for that reason, disagree with much of the reasoning of the majority opinion, I concur in the result reached by the majority. The doctrine of intrafamily tort immunity has been previously abandoned by this court with respect to intentional torts resulting in physical injuries. In my opinion, however, it does not follow that the doctrine should also be abandoned with respect to intrafamily torts resulting in "mental and emotional injuries" for reasons stated by the majority, although not in the context of intrafamily tort immunity.

LENT, Justice, concurring in part; dissenting in part....

... "Adequate care of children is not inexpensive. It is just as costly to mend a child emotionally crippled by disorganized family life as it is to cure the crippled leg of a child stricken with polio. For children in need of parents the community will pay the price sooner or later. The high incidence of mental disorders, criminality, or at best economic dependency among adults who as children had lived in the limbo of foster care, is clear evidence of this." [H. Maas and R. Engler, Children in Need of Parents 397 (1959).] ...

In view of the costs, both tangible and intangible to society of caring for these dependent children who have well been termed the "orphans of the living" and the character of defendant's conduct as admitted by the demurrer, I believe defendant should shoulder so much of the financial burden as her resources permit. Further, I would hold that the emotional harm which the demurrer admits plaintiff has suffered is such as the community should conclude is monetarily compensable. As stated in Justice Linde's dissent plaintiff has alleged a cause of action.

LINDE, Justice [with whom Lent, J., joined], dissenting.

... I believe that these allegations, which plead a violation of ORS 163.535, state a claim on which a child so injured may go to trial.[1] ...

Notes

1. See also Hobbs v. Christenson, 198 Cal. App. 3d 189, 243 Cal. Rptr. 633 (1988) (seventeen-year-old child had no tort action for natural father's abandonment after birth and failure ever to provide support, leaving her without adequate financial resources and in bad living conditions); Mroczynski v. McGrath, 34 Ill. 2d 451, 216 N.E.2d 137 (1966) (no tort to son found in father's divorcing mother, leaving state, ceasing to contribute to son's support and disinheriting him). Should no claim for damages arise from abandon-

---

1. ORS 163.535: "(1) A person commits the crime of abandonment of a child if, being a parent, lawful guardian or other person lawfully charged with the care or custody of a child under 15 years of age, he deserts the child in any place with intent to abandon it. (2) Abandonment of a child is a Class C felony."

Since the complaint alleges at least one cause of action, the validity of the other theories of recovery contained in the complaint need not be considered in overruling the demurrer.

ment or neglect that does not cause physical harm? The rejection of a statutory basis for an action by the majority in the principal case has been criticized on the grounds that this basis would help eliminate trivial claims, when desertion has occurred family harmony already is destroyed, and courts have been able to measure the value of emotional nurturing to a minor child in wrongful death and alienation of affections cases, so they should be able to measure it in cases such as this. Comment, Minor Child Has No Cause of Action Against Parent for Emotional Harm Caused by Abandonment, 58 Wash. U. L.Q. 189 (1980). See also Comment, Tort Liability of a Parent to Minor Unemancipated Child for Wilful and Wanton Acts, 41 Marq. L. Rev. 188 (1957) (finding inconsistency in allowing criminal actions against parent while disallowing, often on family harmony grounds, tort action for same conduct).

2. For a long period in the United States, a child had no tort action against its parent because of parent-child immunity. Exceptions gradually were established in numerous jurisdictions, especially for intentional torts. In recent years, many jurisdictions have abrogated the immunity. See Dobbs, Law of Torts 753–757 (2000); Harper, James & Gray, Law of Torts § 8.11 (3d ed. 2006). Could this influence the disposition of tort claims for parental abandonment?

Section 4. Wrongful Birth

Speck v. Finegold

Superior Court of Pennsylvania
268 Pa. Super. 342, 408 A.2d 496 (1979),
modified, 497 Pa. 77, 439 A.2d 110 (1981)

CERCONE, Presiding Judge: …

Frank Speck, Jr. is a victim of the disease known as neurofibromatosis, a crippling disease of the fibrous structures of the nerves. In fact, his two children, Valerie and Lee Ann, are victims of this disease. In Lee Ann it is particularly crippling and disfiguring. Concerned with the possible recurrence of his affliction in a child conceived in the future, Frank and his wife, Dorothy, decided … it would be best if he were made sterile in order to prevent such a consequence. For this reason he went to defendant-physician, Dr. Finegold, a licensed physician and surgeon in urology, for his advice and treatment with respect to a vasectomy procedure.

After examining Mr. Speck, Dr. Finegold represented to him that a vasectomy operation would sterilize him. Pursuant to an oral agreement to that effect reached between the parties on April 28, 1974, Dr. Finegold performed the vasectomy. Following the operation, Dr. Finegold assured Mr. Speck that he was made sterile and that he could engage in sexual relations with his wife without contraceptive devices. (The complaint does not state any specific time had passed before Dr. Finegold made his reassuring statement.) Mr. Speck followed this advice and Mrs. Speck became pregnant. Worried that Mrs. Speck's pregnancy might result in the dreaded consequences they wished to avoid, the Specks then sought advice and treatment by defendant-doctor, Dr. Schwartz, a physician and surgeon practicing in the field of obstetrics and gynecology. Pursuant to an oral agreement, the parents engaged Dr. Schwartz to perform an abortion on Mrs. Speck in order to terminate her pregnancy. On December 27, 1974, Dr. Schwartz performed the abortion procedure and subsequently represented to the Specks that the operation was a success and that Mrs. Speck's pregnancy had been terminated. However, sometime after the operation, Mrs. Speck informed Dr. Schwartz that she felt her pregnancy was continuing. The doctor "again and persistently" assured and represented to the Specks that Mrs. Speck's fetus had been aborted. However, on April 28, 1975, Mrs. Speck gave birth to a premature child, Francine, afflicted with the crippling disease of neurofibromatosis....

Plaintiffs commenced this lawsuit..., seeking damages on behalf of the infant, Francine, for "wrongful life"; on behalf of their daughters, Valerie and Lee Ann, for economic hardship;[6] and in their own right, for the pecuniary expenses they have borne and will in the future bear for the care and treatment of their child, Francine. Plaintiffs' complaint also seeks damages for emotional, mental and physical injuries and expenses suffered by plaintiff-parents as the result of the birth of Francine and damages suffered by Frank Speck, Jr. occasioned by the loss of his wife's services. Additionally, plaintiffs claim damages for their personal expenses, pain and suffering, and emotional distress incident to the alleged negligence in the vasectomy and abortion surgeries.

Plaintiffs allege, inter alia, that Francine's birth was the direct and proximate result of the physicians' acts of negligence, breach of contract and misrepresentation in their incorrect medical advice, in their negligent and unskillful diagnosis, care and treatment and for actions of negligence catalogued as: failure to properly perform the surgeries in the possession, employment and exercise of that degree and skill, learning and care required of them as physicians and specialists in their given fields of medicine; in failing to conduct tests to ascertain the success or failure of the vasectomy and abortion procedures; in failing to inform them of the risks involved; and in representing to the plaintiffs that the operations were successful and for the intended purposes, when, in fact, the doctors knew or should have known that they were not.

The lower court ... held that no relief was cognizable in law which would permit plaintiffs to recover money damages arising out of or related to the life of Francine. The lower court allowed Mr. Speck's claim for damages incident to the vasectomy to stand for trial. It disallowed Mrs. Speck's claim for damages incident to the abortion procedure because she misjoined her counts in the complaint with those of her husband.... The lower court, however, has allowed her to amend that part of the complaint and we agree.

... We hold that the lower court's denial of all damages arising out of the birth of Francine is untenable. According to the lower court, a cloak of inviolability protects doctors and others in the medical profession when their acts of negligence relate to "wrongful birth" cases despite established principles of law which do not protect these same persons in other categories of negligent care. Thus, we do not agree with the lower court in its blanket protection of a tort-feasor in these cases. To agree with the lower court in the instant case would be to allow an infringement of fundamental rights, which infringements are impermissible in other cases involving negligent conduct....

The term "wrongful life" covers a multifaceted concept under which plaintiffs claim factually divergent wrongs in seeking judicial recognition and relief. In this context, the instant case may appropriately be considered to carry three labels: (a) "wrongful conception" wherein Mr. Speck underwent an unsuccessful vasectomy procedure and together with his

---

6. Since the time of the appeal, the claims of plaintiff-parents' daughters, Valerie and Lee Ann, have been withdrawn.

wife seeks damages against Dr. Finegold for the "wrongful birth" of a child arising out of a negligent sterilization procedure. This kind of action, as we will see, meets with mixed reaction by the courts; (b) "wrongful birth" wherein Mr. and Mrs. Speck seek damages against Dr. Schwartz for the birth of a child attributed to a negligent abortion procedure, and a wrongful diagnosis of an existing pregnancy resulting in the deprivation of the mother's choice to terminate the pregnancy within the permissible time period; (c) a "wrongful life" action where an unplanned child seeks recovery for injuries suffered because of the negligent failure to prevent its birth. This kind of action has met with disapproval by the courts.

In reviewing the history of the cases on this subject, we find that the decisions which deny any recovery for "wrongful birth" do so, as did the lower court, primarily on the basis that the sanctity of life precludes a cognizable action in law and/or that it is impossible to measure damages between a child being born, defectively or not, and not being born at all. The courts which point to immeasurability as a reason for denying recovery for both parents and child hold that when a child or his parents claim it would be better if the child had not been born, they make it impossible for damages to be measured.

... [In] an early case, *Shaheen v. Knight*, 6 Lyc. Rptr. 19, 11 Pa. D. & C.2d 41 (1957) (negligent sterilization), ... the court denied damages on grounds of public policy. The court's view was that although sterilization was not against public policy the recovery of damages for the birth of a normal child was foreign to the universal public sentiment of the people. The *Shaheen* court also enlarged on the public policy theme and said, "that it would be unjust for the physician to pay for the 'fun, joy and affection which plaintiff Shaheen will have in the rearing and education of this, defendant's [sic] fifth child.'"

In the instant case, despite the added dimension of a mentally and physically deficient child, the lower court also held that the plaintiffs had set forth no cognizable cause of action in law for damages, because the purpose of life was procreation and the worth and sanctity of the child, regardless of the child's defects, was such that any recovery of money would be against public policy. But the lower court misses the point when it bases its opinion on this premise. The question is not the worth and sanctity of life, but whether the doctors were negligent in their surgical attempts at vasectomy and abortion.

Beside being against public policy, one of the arguments against recovery has been that abortion was against the law.... The last vestige of this public policy view was eliminated in two cases decided by the Supreme Court of the United States. In *Griswold v. Connecticut*, 381 U.S. 479 (1965), the court held that a state statute proscribing the use of contraceptives was an unconstitutional intrusion upon the right of privacy and violated the Fourth and Fifth Amendments to the United States Constitution. In *Roe v. Wade* [410 U.S. 113 (1973)] the Supreme Court held that the constitutional right to privacy includes the woman's decision whether or not to terminate her pregnancy (absolute during first trimester, qualified during last two trimesters)....

Since the *Griswold* and *Roe* cases, however, other public policy grounds are still made the basis for denial of recovery in "wrongful birth" cases. These include, inter alia: (1) the injury is too remote from the negligence; (2) the injury is too wholly out of proportion to the wrongdoer; (3) in retrospect it appears too highly extraordinary that the negligence should have brought about the harm; (4) allowance of recovery would be too unreasonable a burden on defendant; (5) allowance of recovery would open the way for fraudulent claims; (6) allowance for recovery would introduce a field of litigation that had no sensible or just stopping point. Usually one of these reasons sufficed to deny recovery in a "wrongful birth" case. It seems to us that these reasons ignore the judicial processes which daily meet other problems of equal difficulty and complexity with commendable results....

... [T]he first major case holding that parents have a right to recover damages, including the cost of rearing an unplanned child born by reason of negligent sterilization procedures by defendant-physicians, was ... *Custodio v. Bauer* [251 Cal. App. 2d 303, 59 Cal. Rptr. 463 (1967)]. The complaint was predicated on allegations of negligent performance of surgical procedures and medical advice and on breach of contract to successfully abort the plaintiff-wife. The trial court sustained the defendant's demurrer to the complaint and on plaintiffs' appeal the Court of Appeals reversed. The significance of the appellate decision, however, lies not in its holding that the plaintiffs' factual allegations were legally sufficient to state the several causes of action averred. The importance is in its decision on the extent of damages allowable, holding that the plaintiff-parents were entitled to not only costs arising out of the negligent medical procedures but to all costs which reasonably flowed from the negligence. The court in *Custodio* held that even if a woman survives the childbirth unharmed after a failed sterilization, there is still some loss which is compensable if the resultant additional child and change in family status can be measured economically. The court said that the birth of a child may be less than a blessing in an economically deprived family, particularly if the sterilization had been intended to prevent the birth of a physically defective or mentally retarded infant and that child-rearing costs are not remote from the avowed purpose of an operation undertaken for the purpose of avoiding child-bearing. See [also] *Troppi v. Scarf*, 31 Mich. App. 240, 187 N.W.2d 511 (1971), allowing a modified view relating to damages under Section 920, Restatement (Second) of Torts.[20] In *Troppi*, a pharmacist misfilled a prescription for an oral contraceptive; this mistake resulted in Mrs. Troppi's pregnancy and the birth of a healthy child. The court held that damages claimed by the parents were not unduly speculative, but within the scope of the generally applicable rule as to damages in tort actions, namely, that a tort-feasor is liable for all injuries resulting directly from his wrong acts, irrespective of whether they could have been foreseen by him, provided the damages are the legal and natural consequences of the wrong action imputed to the defendant. The *Troppi* court said that the difficulty in determining the amount to be deducted from gross damages under the benefit rule of §920 would not justify "throwing up our hands and denying recovery altogether."

A number of courts have allowed recovery by parents for damages proximately caused by the physician's negligence, including the cost of rearing a healthy child during his minority. These courts have ordinarily required that damages be reduced by any benefits conferred by the child through an application of the "benefit rule," Section 920 Restatement (Second) of Torts. *Sherlock v. Stillwater Clinic*, 260 N.W.2d 169 (Minn. 1977); *Dumer v. St. Michael's Hospital*, 69 Wis. 2d 766, 233 N.W.2d 372 (1975) (failure to diagnose rubella). In *Dumer*, the ... court limited damages attributable to deformities of the child as contrasted to those expenses which would be incurred for a normal child....

The most recent cases agree that the parents have a right in "wrongful birth" cases to claim and recover damages at trial for child-care costs arising out of the physicians' negligence.... In the case of *Karlsons v. Guerinot*, 57 A.D.2d 73, 394 N.Y.S.2d 933 (1977), it

---

20. Section 920 provides: "Where the defendant's tortious conduct has caused harm to the plaintiff or to his property and in so doing has conferred upon the plaintiff a special benefit to the interest which was harmed, the value of the benefit conferred is considered in mitigation of damages, where this is equitable." It was held that the benefits of the unplanned child may be weighed against all elements of claimed damage, including the medical expenses incident to the birth....

was held that parents had a right of recovery in the case of an alleged negligent abortion procedure resulting in the birth of a mongoloid child. Likewise, in *Becker v. Schwartz*, 46 N.Y.2d 401, 413 N.Y.S.2d 895, 386 N.E.2d 807 (1978), the doctor was allegedly negligent for not advising the mother of the risk of Downs Syndrome in children born to women of 35 years of age. Similarly in *Park v. Chessin, id.*, the doctor was charged with negligence for telling the parents that the chance of their conceiving a second child inflicted with polycystic kidney disease was "practically nil." The *Park* case is similar to the instant one, as it relates to the unequivocal assurance of the doctors that their sterilization procedures were successful.

Based on the above discussion, there is no paucity of cases as they apply to Dr. Finegold, the urologist, or to Dr. Schwartz, the obstetrician and gynecologist, which hold that a cognizable cause of action at law exists for recovery of damages on the part of the parents in "wrongful life" cases. It is not contended by plaintiffs that defendant-physicians' treatment of Mr. Speck in the sterilization procedure caused the abnormalities in their infant. But only that had plaintiffs been properly treated and cared for, their child would not have been conceived or born or if they had been sufficiently advised of the possibility of failed sterilization procedures they could have terminated the pregnancy within a prescribed time period by alternative methods of relief. This principle is included in plaintiff-parents' claim for breach of contract and misrepresentation. In the last analysis and evaluation, and irrespective of the category of claims made, we hold plaintiffs' complaint sounds essentially in negligence, tortious breach of contract, and/or medical malpractice. As in any cause of action based on these grounds, a successful plaintiff must demonstrate the existence of a duty, the breach of which may be considered the proximate cause of damages suffered by the injured parties. ...

Once the plaintiff has carried this burden, it is axiomatic that the tort-feasor is liable for all damages which ordinarily and in the natural course of things have resulted from the commission of the tort.

In the instant case, we deny Francine's claim to be made whole. When we examine Francine's claim, we find regardless of whether her claim is based on "wrongful life" or otherwise, there is a failure to state a legally cognizable cause of action even though, admittedly, the defendants' actions of negligence were the proximate cause of her defective birth. Her claims to be whole have two fatal weaknesses. First, there is no precedent in appellate judicial pronouncements that hold a child has a fundamental right to be born as a whole, functional human being. Whether it is better to have never been born at all rather than to have been born with serious mental defects is a mystery more properly left to the philosophers and theologians, a mystery which would lead us into the field of metaphysics, beyond the realm of our understanding or ability to solve. The law cannot assert a knowledge which can resolve this inscrutable and enigmatic issue. Second, it is not a matter of taking into consideration the various and convoluted degrees of the imperfection of life. It is rather the improbability of placing the child in a position she would have occupied if the defendants had not been negligent when to do so would make her nonexistent. The remedy afforded an injured party in negligence is intended to place the injured party in the position he would have occupied but for the negligence of the defendant. Thus, a cause of action brought on behalf of an infant seeking recovery for a "wrongful life" on grounds she should not have been born demands a calculation of damages dependent on a comparison between Hobson's choice of life in an impaired state and non-existence. This the law is incapable of doing.

Finally, we hold that the impossibility of this suit as to Francine comes not so much from the difficulty in measuring the alleged damages as from the fact, unfortunately, that this is not an action cognizable in law. Thus, the recognized principle, not peculiar to traditional tort law alone, that it would be a denial of justice to deny all relief where a wrong is of such a nature as to preclude certain ascertained damages, is inapposite and inapplicable here....

Although we deny Francine's claim, we hold recovery is allowed in the parents' claim in this case. Here there is no dispute the pleadings allege the existence of a duty flowing from the defendant-physicians to themselves, the breach of which resulted in the birth of Francine. The alleged negligence and misrepresentations of both doctors and by the alleged breach of contract by Dr. Finegold has also been adequately pleaded. Unlike Francine's claim based on "wrongful life," plaintiff-parents' causes of action allege in traditional tort language that but for defendants' breach of duty to properly treat and advise plaintiff-parents they would not have been required to undergo the expenditures alleged. In these allegations plaintiff-parents set forth a duty owed to them by the doctors and breached by the doctors with resulting injuries to the plaintiffs.

As to the emotional disturbance and mental stress claimed by plaintiff-parents due to the fact of Francine's birth, we hold these claims must be denied.... Unlike the measurability of pecuniary loss, to which plaintiff-parents are entitled, there is no legal realm of accountability to which they can look for claimed mental and emotional damages arising out of the birth of their child which could factually place them in a more favorable category than parents who generally, in the vicissitudes and vagaries of life, face the everyday potential of pain and suffering in the raising of their children. It is not possible to distinguish the mental and emotional travail which plaintiffs claim here from the pain and suffering of parents who raise a retarded child or whose infant is born blind or mongoloid or falls heir to one of the countless natural diseases or being healthy becomes permanently injured, disfigured or handicapped by reason of accident. The fact the plaintiffs did not want Francine does not alter the sameness in the quality and nature of pain and suffering experienced in the everyday work of parenthood.

... [T]o allow plaintiffs' claim for mental and emotional stress would be to give them a societal advantage not conceivable in other cases of parenthood.

Order of the lower court affirmed in part, reversed in part and remanded for trial....

SPAETH, Judge, concurring and dissenting....

... Appellees did not in any way contribute to Francine's disease. It was a hereditary disease; Francine never had the possibility of being born healthy.... Her only alternatives were either never to be born, or to be born with the disease. In essence, her claim is that appellees, through their negligence, forced upon her the worse of these two alternatives ...

It is the answer to the question of whether Francine suffered an "injury," as the law uses that term, that leads me to the conclusion that she has no cause of action against appellees. As mentioned, in essence she claims that nonexistence—never being born—would have been preferable to existence in her diseased state. But no one is capable of assessing such a claim.... [A]lthough Francine is obviously suffering greatly from her disease, and although her suffering can only cause one sorrow, it is impossible to say that appellees' negligence—assuming it were proved—caused her the sort of "injury" that the law finds compensable.

There is no such impossibility of comprehension, however, impeding the effort of Francine's parents to recover damages in connection with Mr. Speck's vasectomy, Mrs. Speck's abortion, the loss of Mrs. Speck's companionship and services, and for the expenses attributable to the birth and raising of a child, and, more particularly in this case, a child who will need a good deal of special care, training, and medical treatment. The Specks in their complaint alleged that they had decided to have no more children, for two reasons: economic hardship and their fear of the hereditary disease. The birth of Francine represented the realization of both those fears. The birth thus is a direct and foreseeable result of appellees' negligence, and the extent of the damages is similarly direct and foreseeable. I should permit the jury to be instructed, however, that it could reduce these damages by an amount representing the benefit that a child — healthy or unhealthy — would bring to the parents. Restatement of Torts (Second), §920. The majority opinion discusses cases in which the "benefit rule" has been applied, but does not actually say whether it would apply the rule or not....

I disagree with the majority on the Specks' right to recover damages for the emotional distress and physical inconvenience attributable to Francine's birth. As just stated, the Specks have alleged that they did not want another child because of economic hardship and their fear of the hereditary disease. The majority says that many people have children who are unwanted for the same reasons, but with no negligence involved, and that their emotional and mental anguish is identical to that of the Specks. I confess I am puzzled by this reasoning, which ignores the fact that a similar objection could be made in almost any tort case. The right to damages is not defeated by the fact that other persons may suffer them.... If it is proved that appellees were negligent, the emotional distress consequent upon the materialization of exactly the risks that appellants feared would be the direct result of appellees' negligence, and recovery should be permitted....

[Price, J., delivered a concurring and dissenting opinion.]

Notes

1. Both sides appealed the Superior Court's order to the Supreme Court of Pennsylvania, which divided equally on whether there was a claim for wrongful life and held 5–1 that the parents could recover for their emotional distress and physical inconvenience, as well as for the expenses of rearing Francine. 497 Pa. 77, 439 A.2d 110 (1981). In a later case involving a healthy child, allegedly conceived after a negligently performed tubal ligation, a majority of the court held that the mother could recover for medical expenses, lost wages and pain and suffering during the period of pregnancy, delivery and post-natal care. But a differently constituted majority rejected the mother's claim for expenses and emotional distress in raising the child. Mason v. Western Pennsylvania Hospital, 499 Pa. 484, 453 A.2d 974 (1982). Is this consistent with the court's decision in *Speck*?

2. As indicated in the principal case, there are a number of different tort claims described by such terms as "wrongful life" and "wrongful birth." See Dobbs, Law of Torts 791–801 (2000). One situation involves a defendant whose negligence allegedly resulted in the birth of a healthy and normal, but unwanted, child. Damages have been denied on the ground that the addition of a child to a family is a benefit, not an injury. It also has been thought that damages cannot be evaluated satisfactorily. See Boone v. Mullendore, 416 So. 2d 718 (Ala. 1982); Weintraub v. Brown, 98 A.D.2d 339, 470 N.Y.S.2d 634 (1983); McKernan v. Aasheim, 102 Wash. 2d 411, 687 P.2d 850 (1984). In recent years, however, a number of courts have allowed recovery not only for expenses and disability connected with pregnancy and delivery but also for the cost of rearing the child, usually with an offset for benefits to be expected from the child. Liability has been found when defendant negligently performed a sterilization operation. University of Arizona Health Sciences Center v. Superior Court, 136 Ariz. 579, 667 P.2d 1294 (1983); Sherlock v. Stillwater Clinic, 260 N.W.2d 169 (Minn. 1977); Marciniak v. Lundborg, 153 Wis. 2d 59, 450 N.W.2d

243 (1990) (no offset for benefits of having child). See also Clapham v. Yanga, 102 Mich. App. 47, 300 N.W.2d 727 (1980), appeal dismissed, 335 N.W.2d 1 (Mich. 1982) (physician failed to identify fourteen-year-old's symptoms of pregnancy, so abortion not sought; girl's parents, who assumed legal guardianship of child, compensated for costs). This is distinctly a minority view. See Byrd v. Wesley Medical Center, 237 Kan. 215, 699 P.2d 459 (1985); Johnson v. University Hospitals of Cleveland, 44 Ohio St. 3d 49, 540 N.E.2d 1370 (1989); McFarlane v. Tayside Health Board, [2000] 2 A.C. 59 (H.L.) (costs of raising healthy child not recoverable); Annot., Recoverability of Cost of Raising Normal, Healthy Child Born as Result of Physician's Negligence or Breach of Contract or Warranty, 89 A.L.R.4th 632 (1991). Cf. Goodwill v. British Pregnancy Advisory Service, [1996] 1 W.L.R. 1397 (C.A.) (defendants advising man that his vasectomy was successful owed no duty to later sexual partner who became pregnant).

3. In Ladies Center of Clearwater, Inc. v. Reno, 341 So. 2d 543 (Fla. App. 1977), an unwed mother brought suit for an unsuccessful abortion and subsequent birth. The court denied defendants' claim for indemnity or contribution from the child's father, based on his negligent failure to use a contraceptive method. It declared that impregnation by the father was only the "philosophical cause," not the legal proximate cause, of the damage; the only cause of action against the father would be in "bastardy." However, in M. v. Schmid Laboratories, Inc., 178 N.J. Super. 122, 438 A.2d 515 (App. Div. 1981), a contribution claim against the father, alleging negligence in his use of a condom, survived a motion to dismiss. The father and mother of twin girls claimed they were conceived because the condom, sold by defendants, was defective. The court held that damages could not be awarded for the costs of rearing and educating the children even though plaintiffs asserted breach of warranty and strict liability as well as negligence by defendants. There remained, it seems, the potential of recovery for damages attributable to the mother's pregnancy and delivery of the twins.

4. If a woman becomes pregnant after sexual relations with a man who represented that he was sterile, should she be allowed an action against the man for damages attributable to the pregnancy and the birth of the child? Should a man have an action against a sexual partner to recover the costs of child support or emotional distress if defendant falsely represented that she was sterile or practicing birth control? Most of the reported decisions refuse to entertain such actions, even when it is alleged that the representation of sterility was made fraudulently to induce plaintiff to have intercourse with defendant. It is reasoned that to allow such actions to proceed would create an unacceptable invasion of sexual privacy and conflict with the child's right to parental support. See Stephen K. v. Roni L., 105 Cal. App. 3d 640, 164 Cal. Rptr. 618 (1980); C.A.M. v. R.A.W., 237 N.J. Super. 532, 568 A.2d 556 (App. Div. 1990), appeal dismissed, 127 N.J. 285, 604 A.2d 109 (1990); Wallis v. Smith, 130 N.M. 214, 22 P.3d 682 (Ct. App. 2001), cert. denied, 130 N.M. 254, 23 P.3d 929 (2001). But see Barbara A. v. John G., 145 Cal. App. 3d 369, 193 Cal. Rptr. 422 (1983) (battery and deceit actions maintainable for causing pregnancy by fraudulent misrepresentation of sterility); Alice D. v. William M., 113 Misc. 2d 940, 450 N.Y.S.2d 350 (N.Y. City Civ. Ct. 1982) (defendant negligently misrepresented sterility; plaintiff could recover damages for abortion). See Annot., Sexual Partner's Tort Liability to Other Partner for Fraudulent Misrepresentation Regarding Sterility or Use of Birth Control Resulting in Pregnancy, 2 A.L.R.5th 301 (1992).

5. What of the argument that parents who do not want a child can avoid the "damages" by having an abortion or placing the child for adoption? Courts usually reject this argument, finding no duty to mitigate damages by such measures. See Troppi v. Scarf, 31 Mich. App. 240, 187 N.W.2d 511 (1971); Jones v. Malinowski, 299 Md. 257, 473 A.2d

429 (1984). But the parents' ability to decide whether to terminate the pregnancy, release the child for adoption or keep the child has been an influence in some cases, either on the basis that defendants' liability for the cost of raising the child should not depend upon which decision the parents make or on the basis that a decision to keep the child is evidence that the parents believed the benefits of raising the child outweighed the costs. See Sorkin v. Lee, 78 A.D.2d 180, 434 N.Y.S.2d 300 (1980), appeal dismissed, 53 N.Y.2d 797 (1981); Emerson v. Magendantz, 689 A.2d 409 (R.I. 1997). Should parents be able to obtain damages for the costs of maintaining a healthy child when they desired sterilization or abortion to prevent damage to the mother's health or the birth of a defective child? See Hartke v. McKelway, 288 U.S. App. D.C. 139, 707 F.2d 1544 (1983), cert. denied, 464 U.S. 983 (1983) (child's birth not injury to parent).

6. Another type of action for wrongful birth is that in which the child is deformed or otherwise disabled. The parents may sue on allegations that they would have avoided or terminated the pregnancy if defendant had adequately warned them of this risk. Recovery was denied in the past because the damages were not considered measurable. See Gleitman v. Cosgrove, 49 N.J. 22, 227 A.2d 689 (1967) (mother not informed that because she had German measles child would be defective). The trend now is toward allowing recovery, though there is difference of opinion concerning damages. In Becker v. Schwartz and Park v. Chessin, discussed in the principal case, causes of action were held stated against medical practitioners for the extraordinary care and treatment required by the children, but recovery for the parents' psychic harm or emotional distress was denied on the ground that such damages were too speculative. Blake v. Cruz, 108 Idaho 253, 698 P.2d 315 (1984), permitted recovery for emotional injury, offset by "emotional benefits attributable to the birth of the child." See also Keel v. Banach, 624 So. 2d 1022 (Ala. 1993) (recovery for expenses incurred because of child's condition and emotional distress); Smith v. Cote, 128 N.H. 321, 513 A.2d 341 (1986) (extraordinary costs and extraordinary parental care, but not emotional distress, compensable). The emphasis typically is on recovering expenses to be incurred because of the child's disability, but it was held in Robak v. United States, 658 F.2d 471 (7th Cir. 1981), that the costs that would be incurred for a normal child were also recoverable. Atlanta Obstetrics & Gynecology Group v. Abelson, 260 Ga. 711, 398 S.E.2d 557 (1990), and Azzolino v. Dingfelder, 315 N.C. 103, 337 S.E.2d 528 (1985), cert. denied, 479 U.S. 835 (1986), reject these claims entirely.

7. When a disabled child is born after a medical practitioner's negligent failure to warn parents of the danger or terminate the pregnancy, there is also the possibility of the child suing the practitioner. Since the alternative to the child's birth is no live birth, damages are difficult to identify and assess. The argument can be made that life is always preferable to non-life and not an injury. Usually the child has been denied recovery for "wrongful life." See Siemieniec v. Lutheran General Hospital, 117 Ill. 2d 230, 512 N.E.2d 691 (1987) (hemophilia); Kassama v. Magat, 368 Md. 113, 792 A.2d 1102 (2002) (Down's syndrome); Hester v. Dwidevi, 89 Ohio St. 3d 575, 733 N.E.2d 1161 (2000) (spina bifida); Annot., Tort Liability for Wrongfully Causing One to be Born, 83 A.L.R.3d 15 (1978). However, in Curlender v. Bio-Science Laboratories, 106 Cal. App. 3d 811, 165 Cal. Rptr. 477 (1980), a child born with Tay-Sachs disease was held to have an action against medical laboratories which allegedly had been negligent in informing her parents that they were not carriers of the disease. Damages were allowed for expenses she would incur because of the disease and pain and suffering during her shortened life expectancy, but not for loss of a normal life without defects.

8. In Turpin v. Sortini, 31 Cal. 3d 220, 182 Cal. Rptr. 337, 643 P.2d 954 (1982), the court endorsed recovery in wrongful life actions for extraordinary expenses (treatment,

care, training, etc.) caused by the child's condition—in this case, total deafness. But, finding peculiar difficulty in assessing the damages and in determining that the child in fact suffered an injury in being born, pain and suffering and other general damages were denied. Accord, Procanik v. Cillo, 97 N.J. 339, 478 A.2d 755 (1984); Harbeson v. Parke-Davis, Inc., 98 Wash. 2d 460, 656 P.2d 483 (1983). If parents are allowed a wrongful birth claim to recover costs incurred because of the child's disabilities, is there any need to allow the child a wrongful life claim for such costs? See Walker by Pizano v. Mart, 164 Ariz. 37, 790 P.2d 735 (1990); Smith v. Cote, supra (action rejected). What if a defective child is born but defendant's negligence is not related to any risk of a defect? See LaPoint v. Shirley, 409 F. Supp. 118 (W.D. Tex. 1976) (child born with umbilical hernia following tubal ligation; claims of parents and child dismissed, as in case of healthy child).

9. The addition of a child to a family, especially a disabled child, will cause a loss of material support and parental attention to the family's other children. If the parents have an action for wrongful birth, can the children also recover? See Cox v. Stretton, 77 Misc. 2d 155, 352 N.Y.S.2d 834 (Sup. Ct. 1974) (healthy child; no action); Azzolino v. Dingfelder, 71 N.C. App. 289, 322 S.E.2d 567 (1984), rev'd, 315 N.C. 103, 337 S.E.2d 528 (1985), cert. denied, 479 U.S. 835 (1986) (disabled child; no action).

10. A disabled child may come into a family by means of adoption rather than natural parentage. Do adoptive parents of a disabled child have an action against the adoption agency or persons who arranged the adoption if they had been led to believe that the child was healthy? Should tort actions in these circumstances be viewed as a form of wrongful birth claim or as an action for fraudulent or negligent misrepresentation? Infliction of emotional distress may also be alleged. Cases allowing an action for what has been labelled "wrongful adoption" include Roe v. Catholic Charities of the Diocese of Springfield, Illinois, 225 Ill. App. 3d 519, 588 N.E.2d 354 (1992), appeal denied, 146 Ill. 2d 651, 602 N.E.2d 475 (1992); Jackson v. State, 287 Mont. 473, 956 P.2d 35 (1998); Gibbs v. Ernst, 538 Pa. 193, 647 A.2d 882 (1994). See Annot., "Wrongful Adoption" Causes of Action Against Adoption Agencies Where Children Have or Develop Mental or Physical Problems That Are Misrepresented or Not Disclosed to Adoptive Parents, 74 A.L.R.5th 1 (1999); Blair, Getting the Whole Truth and Nothing But the Truth: The Limits of Liability For Wrongful Adoption, 67 Notre Dame L. Rev. 851 (1992).

11. A final situation is that in which a child sues for having been born illegitimate or to a parent incapable of caring for the child. Liability has been uniformly denied. Stills v. Gratton, 55 Cal. App. 3d 698, 127 Cal. Rptr. 652 (1976) (doctors allegedly negligent in ascertaining result of abortion operation); Zepeda v. Zepeda, 41 Ill. App. 2d 240, 190 N.E.2d 849 (1963), cert. denied, 379 U.S. 945 (1963) (defendant alleged to have fraudulently induced plaintiff's mother to have sexual relations on promise of marriage); Cowe v. Forum Group, Inc., 575 N.E.2d 630 (Ind. 1991), rev'g 541 N.E.2d 962 (Ind. App. 1989) (nursing home caring for profoundly retarded persons failed to prevent sexual assault upon resident by another resident, which resulted in conception and birth of plaintiff); Williams v. State, 18 N.Y.2d 481, 276 N.Y.S.2d 885, 223 N.E.2d 343 (1966) (infant conceived in sexual assault upon mentally deficient patient in state hospital; alleged that defendant negligently failed to protect patient).

12. A number of state legislatures have enacted statues barring or limiting wrongful birth and wrongful life actions. These include Me. Rev. Stat. Ann. tit. 24 § 2931; Mich. Comp. Laws § 600.2971; Minn. Stat. Ann. § 145.424; 42 Pa. Cons. Stat. Ann. §§ 8305–8306; S.D. Comp. Laws §§ 21-55-1 to 4; Utah Code Ann. § 78B-3-109. Were their reasons the same as those which have led courts to reject or limit such actions? A California statute, reacting to a suggestion in Curlender v. Bio-Science Laboratories of parental liability for allowing

the birth of a seriously impaired infant, is aimed at preventing wrongful life claims against parents. Cal. Civil Code § 43.6.

13. Courts and commentators have not been consistent in their use of such terms as "wrongful life" and "wrongful birth." "Wrongful birth" may be applied to a suit by parents for the birth and rearing of an unwanted or defective child, "wrongful life" to a suit by a disabled child contending that it should not have been born, and "dissatisfied life" to a suit by a child complaining of the circumstances of its birth or rearing, such as having a mother unable to care for the child. See Morrison, Torts Involving the Unborn: A Limited Cosmology, 31 Baylor L. Rev. 131, 161–163 (1979). Some courts use the term "wrongful pregnancy" or "wrongful conception" to refer to complaints by parents of healthy children, limiting "wrongful birth" to parental claims concerning disabled children. See James G. v. Caserta, 175 W. Va. 406, 332 S.E.2d 872 (1985).

Chapter 2

Economic Relations

Section 1. Interference with Contractual Relations

A. Inducing Breach of Contract

Lumley v. Gye

Court of Queen's Bench
(1853) 2 El. & Bl. 216, 118 Eng. Rep. 749,
17 Jur. 827, 22 L.J.Q.B. 463, 1 W.R. 432

[The renowned Johanna Wagner signed a contract with Lumley, proprietor of Her Majesty's Theatre, to perform in operas at the theatre for a period of three months, during which she was not to sing elsewhere without Lumley's written authorization. Wagner subsequently agreed with Gye, proprietor of the Royal Italian Opera, Covent Garden, to sing there and abandon her agreement with Lumley, who was to pay her less than Gye. Lumley obtained an injunction against Wagner and Gye which restrained them from presenting performances in breach of the negative provision of the Lumley-Wagner contract. Thus Wagner could not sing for Gye; but she did not perform for Lumley. Lumley brought an action for damages against Gye. The first count alleged that Gye, knowing of Lumley's contract with Wagner and wrongfully and maliciously intending to injure him, enticed and procured Wagner to refuse to perform for Lumley and to completely abandon her contract and service thereunder. The second count alleged in similar terms that Gye enticed and procured Wagner to continue to refuse to perform after the injunction until the three month contract period expired. The third count alleged that Wagner was hired to be and had become a "dramatic artiste" at Lumley's theatre and that Gye, knowing this, wrongfully and maliciously enticed and procured Wagner to depart and remain absent from the service and employment of Lumley until the expiration of her engagement. Gye demurred.]

CROMPTON J. . . .

. . . It was said, in support of the demurrer, that it did not appear in the declaration that the relation of master and servant ever subsisted between the plaintiff and Miss Wagner; that Miss Wagner was not averred, especially in the two first counts, to have entered upon the service of the plaintiff; and that the engagement of a theatrical performer, even if the performer has entered upon the duties, is not of such a nature as to make the performer a servant, within the rule of law which gives an action to the master for the wrongful enticing away of his servant. And it was laid down broadly, as a general proposition of law,

JOHANNA WAGNER   Nationalarchiv der Richard-Wagner-Stiftung

that no action will lie for procuring a person to break a contract, although such procuring is with a malicious intention and causes great and immediate injury. And the law as to enticing servants was said to be contrary to the general rule and principle of law, and to be anomalous, and probably to have had its origin from the state of society when serfdom existed, and to be founded upon, or upon the equity of, the Statute of Labourers. It was said that it would be dangerous to hold that an action was maintainable for persuading a third party to break a contract, unless some boundary or limits could be pointed out; and that the remedy for enticing away servants was confined to cases where the relation of master and servant, in a strict sense, subsisted between the parties; and that, in all other cases of contract, the only remedy was against the party breaking the contract.

Whatever may have been the origin or foundation of the law as to enticing of servants, and whether it be, as contended by the plaintiff, an instance and branch of a wider rule, or whether it be, as contended by the defendant, an anomaly and an exception from the general rule of law on such subjects, it must now be considered clear law that a person who wrongfully and maliciously or, which is the same thing, with notice, interrupts the relation subsisting between master and servant by procuring the servant to depart from the master's service, or by harbouring and keeping him as servant after he has quitted it and during the time stipulated for as the period of service, whereby the master is injured, commits a wrongful act for which he is responsible at law. I think that the rule applies wherever the wrongful interruption operates to prevent the service during the time for which the parties have contracted that the service shall continue: and I think that the relation of master and servant subsists, sufficiently for the purpose of such action, during the time for which there is in existence a binding contract of hiring and service between the parties; and I think that it is a fanciful and technical and unjust distinction to say that the not having actually entered into the service, or that the service not actually continuing, can make any difference.... The wrong and injury are surely the same, whether the wrong doer entices away the gardener, who has hired himself for a year, the night before he is to go to his work, or after he has planted the first cabbage on the first morning of his service; and I should be sorry to support a distinction so unjust, and so repugnant to common sense, unless bound to do so by some rule or authority of law plainly shewing that such distinction exists. The proposition of the defendant, that there must be a service actually subsisting, seems to be inconsistent with the authorities that shew these actions to be maintainable for receiving or harbouring servants after they have left the actual service of the master. In *Blake v. Lanyon* (6 T.R. 221) it was held ... that an action will lie for continuing to employ the servant of another after notice, without having enticed him away, and although the defendant had received the servant innocently. It is there said that "a person who contracts with another to do certain work for him is the servant of that other till the work is finished, and no other person can employ such servant to the prejudice of the first master; the very act of giving him employment is affording him the means of keeping him out of his former service." This appears to me to shew that we are to look to the time during which the contract of service exists, and not to the question whether an actual service subsists at the time....

The objection as to the actual employment not having commenced would not apply in the present case to the third count, which states that Miss Wagner had become the artiste of the plaintiff, and that the defendant had induced her to depart from the employment. But it was further said that the engagement, employment or service, in the present case, was not of such a nature as to constitute the relation of master and servant, so as to warrant the application of the usual rule of law giving a remedy in case of enticing away servants. The nature of the injury and of the damage being the same, and the supposed right of action being in strict analogy to the ordinary case of master and servant, I see no reason for confining the case to services or engagements under contracts for services of any particular description; and I think that the remedy, in the absence of any legal reason to the contrary, may well apply to all cases where there is an unlawful and malicious enticing away of any person employed to give his personal labour or service for a given time under the direction of a master or employer who is injured by the wrongful act; more especially when the party is bound to give such personal services exclusively to the master or employer; though I by no means say that the service need be exclusive.... I think that, where a party has contracted to give his personal services for a certain time to another, the parties are in the relation of employer and employed, or master and servant, within the meaning of this rule. And I see no reason for narrowing such a rule; but I should rather, if necessary, apply such a remedy to a case "new in its instance, but" "not new in the reason and principle of it", that is, to a case where the wrong and damage are strictly analogous to the wrong and damage in a well recognised class of cases. In deciding this case on the narrower ground, I wish by no means to be considered as deciding that the larger ground ... is not tenable, or as saying that in no case except that of master and servant is an action maintainable for maliciously inducing another to break a contract to the injury of the person with whom such contract has been made. It does not appear to me to be a sound answer, to say that the act in such cases is the act of the party who breaks the contract; for that reason would apply in the acknowledged case of master and servant. Nor is it an answer, to say that there is a remedy against the contractor, and that the party relies on the contract; for, besides that reason also applying to the case of master and servant, the action on the contract and the action against the malicious wrongdoer may be for a different matter; and the damages occasioned by such malicious injury might be calculated on a very different principle from the amount of the debt which might be the only sum recoverable on the contract....

I think, therefore, that our judgment should be for the plaintiff.

ERLE J.... [A]n action will lie by a master against a person who procures that a servant should unlawfully leave his service.... [This] rests upon the principle that the procurement of the violation of the right is a cause of action, and ... when this principle is applied to a violation of a right arising upon a contract of hiring, the nature of the service contracted for is immaterial.... He who maliciously procures a damage to another by violation of his right ought to be made to indemnify; and that, whether he procures an actionable wrong or a breach of contract....

[Wightman, J., delivered a concurring opinion. Coleridge, J., delivered a dissenting opinion.]

Notes

1. The common law actions for enticement and harboring of a servant trace their ancestry, in major part, to the Statutes of Labourers, enacted in response to the great loss of life in the Plague of the mid-fourteenth century. Finding that labor was in very short supply, that high wages were being demanded and obtained, and that servants were leaving their masters when better terms could be obtained elsewhere, Parliament enacted measures that required persons who did not have land to till or some other form of livelihood to go into service; prohibited departure from service before the term agreed; prohibited receiving or retaining in service a person who had so departed; and limited wages to customary (pre-Plague) amounts. See the dissent of Coleridge, J., in Lumley v. Gye; Jones, *Per Quod Servitium Amisit*, 74 L.Q. Rev. 39 (1958).

2. The idea of an action for procuring breach of contract can be found in cases as early as the sixteenth century. See Baker, Reports of Sir John Spelman, Volume II, 94 Selden Soc'y 253–255 (1978). But the contemporary action stems from Lumley v. Gye. See Waddams, Johanna Wagner and the Rival Opera Houses, 117 L.Q. Rev. 431 (2001), for a valuable examination of the case. Was the court right to establish such an action? Isn't the essential reason the contract was not performed that the person who assumed the contractual obligation chose not to perform? Why add a tort action against a third person to the contract action against the breaching party? In Bowen v. Hall, (1881) 6 Q.B.D. 333 (C.A.), Lumley v. Gye was approved on the basis that to persuade a person to break his contract was a wrongful act, when done for the "indirect purpose" of injuring the plaintiff or benefitting the defendant at plaintiff's expense, and the breach and ensuing injury were natural and probable consequences of the persuasion. Should a third-party beneficiary of the contract be allowed to sue? See Tamposi Associates, Inc. v. Star Market Co., Inc., 119 N.H. 630, 406 A.2d 132 (1974); Willard v. Claborn, 220 Tenn. 501, 419 S.W.2d 168 (1967).

3. Generally it is not a tort to entice a person from the employment of another if no contract is broken. See Triangle Film Corp. v. Artcraft Pictures Corp., 250 F. 981 (2d Cir. 1918); Boston Glass Manufactory v. Binney, 4 Pick. (21 Mass.) 425 (1827) (workmen quit after giving plaintiffs notice that was term of their employment). Liability is possible, but not probable, when the person is an employee at will. See pp. 143–155, infra. Even if there is a breach of an employment contract, should there be liability when the person enticed was not a star soprano or uniquely talented employee, but a person who could be replaced without much difficulty?

4. Not all authority applies to the tort action a measure of damages different from the measure to be applied in an action for breach of the contract, but the prevailing view affords a more expansive recovery. See Dobbs, Law of Torts 1296–1298 (2000). It is debatable whether liability is to extend to all harm "caused in fact" by the tort or be limited to harm that is "proximately" caused or foreseeable. See Rite Aid Corp. v. Lake Shore Investors, 298 Md. 611, 471 A.2d 735 (1984); Restatement (Second) of Torts § 774A (1979). Should the damages include profits or revenues realized by the tortfeasor? See National Merchandising Corp. v. Leyden, 370 Mass. 425, 348 N.E.2d 771 (1976) (unjust enrichment measure appropriate for wilful interference); Annot., Recovery Based On Tortfeasor's Profits in Action for Procuring Breach of Contract, 5 A.L.R.4th 1276 (1981) (majority of cases allow damages based at least in part on profit or revenue realized).

5. Does Lumley v. Gye support the issuance of an injunction against inducement of breach of contract? Should an injunction be granted when plaintiff's object is to retain employment of someone who wants to quit plaintiff? See New England Patriots Football Club, Inc. v. University of Colorado, 592 F.2d 1196 (1st Cir. 1979) (coach induced to leave professional football team and return to college football). Or to prevent the contracting party from replacing plaintiff with someone the contracting party has more confidence in? See Warren v. Mendy, [1989] 1 W.L.R. 853 (C.A.) (boxer broke contract with manager/promoter).

Glamorgan Coal Company, Ltd. v. South Wales Miners' Federation

Court of Appeal
[1903] 2 K.B. 545, aff'd, [1905] A.C. 239 (H.L.)

[Wages paid to coal miners in south Wales varied according to the market price of coal. Concerned that coal dealers were driving down prices, the miners' union declared several "stop-days," i.e., days on which miners would not work, "with a view to regulating the supply according to the demand." The mine owners objected. They claimed damages and an injunction in an action against the union and its officers for "wrongfully and maliciously procuring and inducing" the miners to break their employment contracts. The contracts required a month's notice of termination, which had not been given.]

ROMER L.J. . . . In *Quinn v. Leathem* [[1901] A.C. 495] Lord Macnaghten said [of *Lumley v. Gye*, "the decision was right, not on the ground of malicious intention—that was not, I think, the gist of the action—but on the ground that a] violation of legal right committed knowingly is a cause of action, and it is a violation of legal right to interfere with contractual relations recognised by law if there be no sufficient justification for the interference." And in *Mogul Steamship Co. v. McGregor, Gow & Co.* [p. 167, infra] Bowen L.J. included in what is forbidden "the intentional procurement of a violation of individual rights, contractual or other, assuming always that there is no just cause for it." But although, in my judgment, there is no doubt as to the law, yet I fully recognise that considerable difficulties may arise in applying it to the circumstances of any particular case. When a person has knowingly procured another to break his contract, it may be difficult under the circumstances to say whether or not there was "sufficient justification or just cause" for his act. I think it would be extremely difficult, even if it were possible, to give a complete and satisfactory definition of what is "sufficient justification," and most attempts to do so would probably be mischievous. . . . I respectfully agree with what Bowen L.J. said in the *Mogul Case*, when considering the difficulty that might arise whether there was sufficient justification or not: "The good sense of the tribunal which had to decide would have to analyze the circumstances and to discover on which side of the line each case fell." I will only add that, in analyzing or considering the circumstances, I think that regard might be had to the nature of the contract broken; the position of the parties to the contract; the grounds for the breach; the means employed to procure the breach; the relation of the person procuring the breach to the person who breaks the contract; and I think also to the object of the person in procuring the breach. But, though I deprecate the attempt to define justification, I think it right to express my opinion on certain points in connection with breaches of contract procured where the contract is one of master and servant. In my opinion, a defendant sued for knowingly procuring such a breach is not justified of necessity merely by his shewing that he had no personal animus against the employer, or that it was to the advantage or interest of both the defendant and the workman that the contract should be broken.... [W]hat A. has to justify is his action, not as between him and the workman, but as regards the employer B.... [I]t is to my mind clear that the defendants, the federation, procured the men to break their contracts with the plaintiffs — so that I need not consider how the question would have stood if what the federation had done had been merely to advise the men, or if the men, after taking advice, had arranged between themselves to break their contracts, and the federation had merely notified the men's intentions to the plaintiffs.... And it is not disputed that the federation acted as they did knowingly. So that the only question which remains is one of justification. Now the justification urged is that it was thought, and I will assume for this purpose rightly thought, to be in the interest of the men that they should leave their work in order to keep up the price of coal on which the amount of wages of the men depended. As to this, I can only say that to my mind the ground alleged affords no justification for the conduct of the federation towards the employers; for, as I have already pointed out, the absence on the part of the federation of any malicious intention to injure the employers in itself affords no sufficient justification. But it was said that the federation had a duty towards the men which justified them in doing what they did. For myself I cannot see that they had any duty which in any way compelled them to act, or justified them in acting, as they did towards the plaintiffs. And the fact that the men and the federation, as being interested in or acting for the benefit of the men, were both interested in keeping up prices, and so in breaking the contracts, affords in itself no sufficient justification for the action of the federation as against the plaintiffs, as I have already pointed out. I think, therefore, that the appeal must succeed.

[Stirling, L.J., delivered a concurring opinion. Vaughan Williams, L.J., delivered a dissenting opinion.]

Camden Nominees, Ltd. v. Forcey
Chancery Division
[1940] Ch. 352

[Plaintiffs were landlords of a block of flats. In standard leases they undertook to provide heating, hot water, cleaning of passages and other services. The landlords failed to satisfy tenants' complaints about defaults in providing these services. Tenants organized an association and informed the landlords that rent payments would be withheld temporarily until the landlords fulfilled their obligations under the leases. The landlords brought an action for damages and to restrain leaders of the tenants' association from inducing tenants to breach the lease agreements by withholding rent.]

SIMONDS J. . . .

By the end of the nineteenth century it had been clearly established . . . that it is an actionable wrong without justification to interfere with the contractual rights of another. . . . [N]o corresponding definition was given of what amounts to justification for such interference. . . . *Read v. Friendly Society of Operative Stonemasons* [[1902] 2 K.B. 732] . . . is useful as showing (*a*) that what is otherwise wrong is not made better by an honest belief that it is very much to the advantage of the person committing the wrong, and (*b*) that, where illegal means are used, "just cause" cannot come into the discussion at all. . . .

In *Smithies v. National Association of Operative Plasterers* [[1909] 1 K.B. 310] it was once again sought, but sought in vain, to justify the procurement of breaches of contract of service by workmen. It was there held that a bona fide belief on the part of the union that the employers were intending to evade a settlement of the dispute in accordance with the agreement or even an actual intention on the part of the employers so to do, did not constitute justification for inducing the workmen to break their contract. Again it was recognized that there might be justification, and Buckley L.J. gave the familiar example of inconsistent contracts, but no other example. He added, however, this observation, which bears on the present case: "The contention of the defendants here is: 'We were entitled to induce Forrester to break his contract with you because you had broken your contract, as contained in the National Agreement, with us.' This is setting up that, where there are two independent contracts, the breach of the one by the one party entitles a breach of the other by the other party. This contention, in my opinion, cannot be maintained."

In *Pratt v. British Medical Association* [[1919] 1 K.B. 244] McCardie J. summed up the authorities by saying that malice in the sense of spite or ill-will was not an ingredient of the action; and, secondly, that no justification existed by reason of the fact that the defendants acted either for the advancement of their own trade interests or of the interests of those with whom they were associated.

Thus the law stood when, in 1924, Russell J. decided in *Brimelow v. Casson* [[1924] 1 Ch. 302] that the defendants, though they had procured the breach by certain theatre proprietors of their contracts with the plaintiff, had a sufficient justification for their action. The learned judge . . . said: "These defendants, as it seems to me, owed a duty to their calling and to its members, and, I am tempted to add, to the public, to take all necessary peaceful steps to terminate the payment of this insufficient wage, which in the plaintiff's company had apparently been in fact productive of those results which their past experience had led them to anticipate." . . .

In *De Jetley Marks v. Greenwood* [[1936] 1 All E.R. 863] Porter J. said, with regard to that plea: "The justification must, I think, involve an action taken as a duty, not the mere protection of the defendants' own interests." . . .

. . . [T]he defendants have pleaded that they are justified in their otherwise actionable wrong on two grounds; the first, that they and those whom they would persuade to break their contracts have a common interest in making the landlords perform their obligations; and the second, that there is such a state of affairs here existing, on the one side tenants who are weak and on the other landlords who are strong and take advantage of their strength, that it is justifiable for the defendants to use a weapon which would otherwise be wrongful.

In my judgment, there is no validity in either of these contentions. The defendants owed no duty to their fellow tenants; they sought their co-operation for their own ends, though no doubt a successful campaign would have been for the benefit of all alike. The end which they sought, namely, the performance by the landlords of their obligations, was one which could be reached by process of law. If the landlords broke their contract the law gave the defendants their remedy by way of damages, or in a proper case by way of specific performance. There is neither reason nor authority for the suggestion that in such circumstances a common interest can justify the interference with contractual rights. If A, B, C, and D meet together and agree that in order to persuade or coerce X to a certain course they will each break their contracts with him, that would, I apprehend, be an actionable conspiracy. It would be a strange thing if A, calling together B, C, and D, and urging them to break their contracts could justify that act on the ground of common interest. This contention must, in my judgment, fail.

The second contention was one which appeared to be directed less to my reason than to my emotions. The case was put as something analogous to *Brimelow v. Casson*, in which any step that put an end to an intolerable position might be regarded as justifiable. *Brimelow v. Casson* stands alone, and has been the subject of a good deal of controversy. In a comparable case it would be my duty to follow it, though I would humbly suggest that on the facts stated in the judgment that case might have been simply disposed of by the application of the maxim Ex turpi causa non oritur actio. But, however that may be, there is no real analogy between the two cases. It is a dangerous proposition that inequality in wealth or position justifies a course otherwise actionable, and that tenants may against their landlord adopt measures of self-help because in their judgment the law does not afford them adequate remedy for his default.

… [N]either [*Brimelow v. Casson*] nor any other case supports the view that those who assume the duty of advising the withholding of rent or any other breach of contract can justify their action by protesting that they are performing a public service. Advice which is intended to have persuasive effects is not distinguishable from inducement, and there is no reason to suppose that the giving of such advice is justifiable except by those persons in whom the law recognizes a moral duty to give it.

In the result I hold that the defendants without justification interfered with the plaintiff's contractual rights and it is clear that at the date of the issue of the writ they intended to continue to do so. I must therefore grant an injunction as asked.…

Notes

1. As the *South Wales Miners'* case reflects, it has come to be accepted that the fundamental intent requirement for the tort is intentional procurement of breach of contract, not purpose to cause harm or another form of malice. The action has been utilized most frequently by parties to personal services contracts, but its extension to interference with almost any other type of contract is well-established. See Temperton v. Russell, [1893] 1 Q.B. 715 (C.A.) (supply of building materials by plaintiff); Annot., Liability for Procuring Breach of Contract, 26 A.L.R.2d 1227 (1952). Many interference with contract actions arise from real estate sales and brokerage contracts. See Annots., Right of Real Estate Broker Against Third Person Who Prevented Broker from Earning Commission, or Who Received, or Induced Owner to Pay to Him or Another, Commission Which the Broker Had Earned, 97 A.L.R. 1273 (1935); 146 A.L.R. 1417 (1943); Annot., Liability of Purchaser of Real Estate for Interference with Contract Between Vendor and Another Purchaser, 27 A.L.R.3d 1227 (1969); Annot., Liability of Purchaser of Real Estate for Interference with Contract Between Vendor and Real-Estate Broker, 29 A.L.R.3d 1229 (1970); Annot., Liability of Real-Estate Broker for Interference with Contract Between Vendor and Another Real-Estate Broker, 34 A.L.R.3d 720 (1970). Should this be affected by the availability of an order for specific performance? A number of states have statutes creating a cause of action for or prohibiting interference with certain types of contracts. One example of pro-

hibited interference is inducing a tenant to leave the premises prior to the expiration of the lease. See Annot., Liability for Interference with Lease, 96 A.L.R.3d 862 (1980).

2. A plaintiff is not to succeed without proof that defendant knew of the contract when defendant procured action that breached it. See Tenta v. Guraly, 140 Ind. App. 160, 221 N.E.2d 577 (1966); Stannard v. McCool, 198 Md. 609, 84 A.2d 862 (1951) (successive contracts to convey same land). In principle, a person cannot intentionally procure breach of contract without sufficient knowledge and understanding of the contract's provisions to know that the contract will be broken or that his object involves breach of contract. But some decisions sustain actions on the basis that defendant knew of the contract and therefore had reason to know of the breach of contract. See Bolger v. Danley Lumber Co., Inc., 77 Ill. App. 3d 207, 395 N.E.2d 1066 (1979) (action for inducing vendor of real estate to breach its exclusive listing contract with plaintiff realtors; evidence that defendant's officers saw on property "For Sale" signs with plaintiff's name and telephone number); Williams v. Chittenden Trust Co., 145 Vt. 76, 484 A.2d 911 (1984) (owner of condominium project substituted defendant for plaintiff as architect for project; defendant told that plaintiff designed project and given plaintiff's drawings). Compare Ryan, Elliott and Co., Inc. v. Leggat, McCall & Werner, Inc., 8 Mass. App. Ct. 686, 396 N.E.2d 1009 (1979) (plaintiff's employees employed for term of five years, during which defendant hired them; employees advised defendant that, according to attorney's advice, they were free to leave plaintiff and intended to do so; fixed-term employment contracts rare in business involved).

3. In Emerald Construction Co. Ltd. v. Lowthian, [1966] 1 W.L.R. 691 (C.A.), defendants said they assumed the contract could be terminated on short notice and this lawful termination was all they insisted upon. Lord Denning, M.R., responded: "Even if they did not know of the actual terms of the contract, but had the means of knowledge — which they deliberately disregarded — that would be enough. Like the man who turns a blind eye.... [I]t is unlawful for a third person to procure a breach of contract knowingly, or recklessly, indifferent whether it is a breach or not." Should this be accepted as a general proposition? When it is found (as in *Emerald Construction*) that defendants' intention was to bring the contract to an end whether it was breached or not? What if defendant was aware of the terms of the contract but did not realize that they constituted an obligation inconsistent with what defendant procured — either because of misunderstanding of the terms' effects or belief that the contract was unenforceable? See Robey v. Sun Record Co., Inc., 242 F.2d 684 (5th Cir. 1957), cert. denied, 355 U.S. 816 (1957) (defendant allegedly believed musician's record contract invalid because not approved by union; judgment for plaintiff affirmed); American Cyanamid Co. v. Elizabeth Arden Sales Corp., 331 F. Supp. 597 (S.D.N.Y. 1971) (defendant knew of agreement for purchase of corporation but reasonable to believe it not binding; judgment for defendant); State of Minnesota by Burlington Northern Railroad Co. v. Big Stone-Grant Industrial Development and Transportation, L.L.C., 990 F. Supp. 731 (D. Minn. 1997), aff'd, 131 F.3d 144 (8th Cir. 1997) (defendant liable despite legal opinion that there would not be breach of contract); British Industrial Plastics, Ltd. v. Ferguson, [1938] 4 All E.R. 504 (C.A.), aff'd, [1940] 1 All E.R. 479 (H.L.) (defendants knew that co-defendant obligated not to reveal to them secret manufacturing process of plaintiff, but "in a muddle-headed way" believed this did not apply to process that was patentable; no liability); OBG Ltd. v. Allan, [2008] A.C. 1 (H.L.) (defendant must realize that there would be breach of contract); Restatement (Second) of Torts § 766, comment *i* (1979) (defendant can have necessary intent if knew of contract, even if mistaken about its legal effects). Upon the trial of Lumley v. Gye, subsequent to the decision at p. 123, supra, Lord Campbell, C.J., instructed the jury

that if Gye "bona fide believed" that Lumley's agreement with Wagner had ceased to be binding upon her, scienter was not proved and Gye was entitled to a verdict. The jury resolved this question in favor of Gye, so there was a verdict in his favor even though the agreement was in fact broken in consequence of his inducement. The Times, February 23, 1854, p. 12.

4. *Justification and privilege.* Justification for inducing breach may be found in the relationship between defendant and the party who broke the contract. See Restatement (Second) of Torts § 770 (1979). In Lee v. Silver, 262 App. Div. 149, 28 N.Y.S.2d 333 (1941), aff'd, 287 N.Y. 575, 38 N.E.2d 233 (1941), a mother allegedly induced her daughter, a vocalist, to repudiate her contract with her managers. The court ruled that public policy dictates that parents have an absolute right to advise their minor children, regardless of motive; there could be no liability. Cf. Joel v. Weber, 153 Misc. 2d 549, 581 N.Y.S.2d 579 (Sup. Ct. 1992), in which it was alleged that a musical performer was persuaded by his wife to repudiate the agreement under which plaintiff managed the performer's business and personal affairs. The court decided that spouses were entitled to an immunity from liability for causing the other spouse to alter business relationships. This would enable spouses to freely discuss "all aspects of domestic economics ... without fear of being called to account" for the results. They would not be subject to an inquiry into their motives. Should this be extended to cases in which defendant allegedly acted to protect someone who was not a party to the contract interfered with? In Legris v. Marcotte, 129 Ill. App. 67 (1906), defendant's little girl was enrolled in a convent school. Defendant informed the mother superior that the father of another pupil was rumored to have a contagious "itching disease." This allegedly caused the dismissal of the other pupil from the school. Defendant was held to have been justified in her conduct if she acted without malice. What if an employer induces or assists an employee in breaking a contract with unfavorable terms? See Heywood v. Tillson, 75 Me. 225 (1883).

5. Cases recognize a privilege to advise or procure breach of contract for persons who act as a business advisor for a contracting party or as a professional responsible for the party's interests. See Brown Mackie College v. Graham, 768 F. Supp. 1457 (D. Kan. 1991), aff'd, 981 F.2d 1149 (10th Cir. 1992) (attorney); Spectra Architectural Group Ltd. v. Eldred Sollows Consulting Ltd., (1991) 80 Alta. R. 2d 361, 119 Alta. R. 13 (Sup. Ct. Master) (architectural consultants). In recognizing that a consultant or other advisor was privileged to offer good-faith advice to a client without liability for inducing breach of contract, the court in J.D. Edwards & Co. v. Podany, 168 F.3d 1020 (7th Cir. 1999), stated that the privilege was qualified in two respects. First, it was limited to advice within the scope of the consultant's engagement—what the consultant was engaged to advise on by the client. Second, the privilege was forfeited if the consultant did not give honest advice, but rather gave dishonest advice for his own benefit or out of dislike for the victim. If, however, the advice was honest, a consultant's giving it in order to make money for himself would not be outside the privilege.

Restatement of the Law Governing Lawyers § 57(3) (2000) states that a lawyer who advises or assists a client to make or break a contract, or to enter or not enter a contractual relation, is not liable for interference with contract, or with prospective contractual relations, if the lawyer acts to advance the client's objectives and does not use wrongful means. A lawyer who acts for his own benefit is outside the privilege, but so long as the lawyer acts or advises with the purpose of promoting the client's welfare, it is immaterial that the lawyer hopes to increase his fees or reputation or takes satisfaction in the consequences to the non-client. Ibid., § 57, comment g. In principle, while persuading someone to break a contract is grounds for a tort action, "mere advice" is not. But it can be difficult to distinguish between advice and persuasion. See Carty, An Analysis of the Economic Torts 46–48 (2001). The "privilege" of the advisor protects against liability if persuasion is found.

6. Brimelow v. Casson, discussed in the *Camden Nominees* case, was an action by the manager of a touring pantomime company, the Wu Tut Tut Revue. Defendants, officers of a joint committee of theatrical unions, sought to prevent plaintiff from presenting performances by inducing theatre proprietors to break or refrain from entering contracts with him. Their object was to require plaintiff to pay his chorus girls the minimum wage set by the Actors' Association. Defendants had discovered that plaintiff paid so little that the chorus girls led a "hand-to-mouth existence" and some resorted to prostitution — common effects of failure to pay a theatrical troupe a living wage. Russell, J., was much affected by evidence of an eighteen-year-old "forced by underpayment to continue in sexual association" with a "dwarf" who was also a member of the company. He held that defendants had justification and, therefore, were not liable. Inducing theatre proprietors to deny plaintiff the use of theatres was the only means by which unions could end the underpayment and its evil consequences.

7. Is there a comparable "public interest" justification for interfering with a contract with the object of preventing degradation of the environment or overcharging in government contracts? See Middlesex Concrete Products and Excavating Corp. v. Carteret Industrial Association, 37 N.J. 507, 181 A.2d 774 (1962). What if the object is preventing racial or sexual discrimination? In furtherance of a boycott of the city of Cincinnati, intended to punish the city and obtain redress for grievances over the treatment of blacks and other minorities in the city, leading entertainers were persuaded not to perform in the city. This allegedly included persuading entertainers not to honor existing contracts with the Cincinnati Arts Association, a non-profit organization that operated performing arts venues in Cincinnati. The boycott's organizers had no grievance against the CAA specifically. The CAA sued the boycott organizers for interference with contract and conspiracy. The court held that their conduct was political speech protected by the First Amendment and defendants therefore had justification that barred liability. Cincinnati Arts Association v. Jones, 120 Ohio Misc. 2d 26, 777 N.E.2d 346 (C.P. 2002).

8. Breach of contract by a business is often advised or otherwise caused by an officer, director or employee of the business. This is necessarily the case when the business is a corporation. The officer, director or employee will not be held liable for interference with contract if he acted for the interest of the business and within the scope of his authority or employment. See Swager v. Couri, 77 Ill. 2d 173, 395 N.E.2d 921 (1979); Gruhlke v. Sioux Empire Federal Credit Union, Inc., 756 N.W.2d 399 (S.D. 2008); Said v. Butt, [1920] 3 K.B. 497. What effect should be given to allegations that defendant acted with bad motives or to advance his own career or business interests? See Los Angeles Airways, Inc. v. Davis, 687 F.2d 321 (9th Cir. 1982); Nordling v. Northern States Power Co., 478 N.W.2d 498 (Minn. 1991); Boers v. Payline Systems, Inc., 141 Or. App. 238, 918 P.2d 432 (1996).

9. When a company is wholly owned by one party or a small number of related parties, the company and its owner(s) may be treated as one entity. If so, plaintiff cannot establish third party interference with the contract if the owner interferes. Schoellkopf v. Pledger, 778 S.W.2d 897 (Tex. App. 1989). But see Shapoff v. Scull, 222 Cal. App. 3d 1457, 272 Cal. Rptr. 480 (1990) (owner may be liable if not acting to protect interests of company); Waste Conversion Systems, Inc. v. Greenstone Industries, Inc., 33 S.W.3d 779 (Tenn. 2000) (parent corporation may be liable if acted contrary to subsidiary's economic interests or employed wrongful means). Should a city mayor, council member or agency director be subject to liability for causing breach of a contract the city

had entered? See DeCarlo v. Sullivan, 981 F. Supp. 59 (D. Mass. 1997) (councillor liable for interfering with city employee's contract with improper motives or means); Jolicoeur Furniture Co., Inc. v. Baldelli, 653 A.2d 740 (R.I. 1995), cert. denied, 516 U.S. 964 (1995) (mayor and planning director liable for interfering with sale of land to plaintiffs without justification).

———————

Sweeney v. Smith

United States Circuit Court, Eastern District of Pennsylvania
167 F. 385 (1909), aff'd, 171 F. 645 (3d Cir. 1909),
cert. denied, 215 U.S. 600 (1909)

J.B. McPHERSON, District Judge....

[The bondholders of an insolvent company put their interests in the hands of a committee. The committee made a contract with Sweeney by which he was to acquire a controlling interest in the company's stock and bonds. The contract fixed no time limit for performance and was never carried out. The committee subsequently made a substantially similar contract with defendants. It was carried out. Sweeney brought a bill in equity to recover the profit made by defendants' use of the bonds.] ... [W]hile it may be supposed that the complainant meant to charge that Smith & Co. interfered with the carrying out of his contract of September 12th, and persuaded or induced the committee to break that contract, no such charge appears in the bill. The only complaint is that Smith & Co. had prior knowledge of the complainant's contract when they began the negotiations that resulted in the agreement of January 25th.

Under all the authorities the bill is fatally defective on this point.... The promisor may have excellent reasons for declining to be bound by the earlier contract, and these he need not disclose. If he chooses to take the risk of breaking the first agreement, that is his own affair, which may make him liable on that agreement, but imposes no obligation on the second promisee. It is enough for the second promisee that the agreement is now offered to him without his own procurement or persuasion. If he has done nothing to bring the situation about, the mere fact that he knew of the first contract is no bar to his entering upon the second. Mere knowledge of the first does not make the second an actionable wrong; he is under no legal obligation to insist upon being told why the promisor declines to carry out the first contract, and is not bound to weigh these reasons and decide at his peril whether they are good or bad. Before he can be called to account, some legal ground of liability must appear; he must participate in the breach before he can be held to blame; and the mere knowledge that the promisor intends to break the contract with the first promisee is not wrongful in itself, and does not disable the second promisee from making the subsequent contract. To be blameworthy, he must take some active step to bring about the breach. At the least, he must induce or persuade the promisor to abandon the earlier agreement, and even this he may sometimes do with impunity, unless the decisions in several jurisdictions are to be regarded as erroneous. Take the case of two trade competitors: One makes a contract with a customer; the other, knowing that the contract has been made, persuades the customer by fair and legitimate arguments that his wares are better than his rival's, and thus induces the customer to cancel the contract. In such a situation, I am not aware of any decision that would support a suit against the second merchant, although he has unquestionably interfered actively to supplant his rival....

The demurrer of Smith & Co. is therefore sustained....

Notes

1. Active persuasion or inducement of breach of contract is required for liability. It is not enough that defendant entered into a contract with knowledge of a prior inconsistent one. See Lamport v. 4175 Broadway, Inc., 6 F. Supp. 923 (S.D.N.Y. 1934); Wolf v. Perry, 65 N.M. 457, 339 P.2d 679 (1959). But see Fowler v. Printers II, Inc., 89 Md. App. 448, 598 A.2d 794 (1991), cert. denied, 325 Md. 619, 602 A.2d 710 (1992) (sufficient that defendant employed contracting party in work violative of covenant not to compete). Defendant may be liable if, with knowledge of a prior inconsistent contract, he has taken an active part in holding out an incentive, such as a better price or better terms, to induce a party to the prior contract to make an incompatible agreement. See Cumberland Glass Manufacturing Co. v. De Witt, 120 Md. 381, 87 A. 927 (1913), aff'd, 237 U.S. 447 (1915); Williams v. Chittenden Trust Co., 145 Vt. 76, 484 A.2d 911 (1984). But it is thought that "regular advertising and general solicitation of business" is not a basis of liability. See V. Marangi Carting Corp. v. Judex Enterprises, Inc., 171 Misc. 2d 820, 655 N.Y.S.2d 832 (Sup. Ct. 1997); Restatement (Second) of Torts § 766, comment *m* (1979). Suppose an agreement is negotiated before defendant learns that the other party had entered an inconsistent contract. Is defendant subject to liability for going through with the deal agreed upon?

2. In Amatrudi v. Watson, 19 N.J. Super. 67, 88 A.2d 7 (App. Div. 1952), plaintiff's evidence was that defendant met plaintiff's work crew while they were out on a job. Defendant asked the crew to do some work that afternoon for him. The foreman told defendant to call at plaintiff's office for an estimate. But when defendant replied "Does the boss have to know about it?" the crew agreed to do the work for a payment that they split among themselves. They therefore worked for their own account rather than for plaintiff's during the afternoon. Liability?

3. It has been said that a two-step "but for" approach is employed in determining whether defendant tortiously brought about a breach of contract: (1) Did defendant actively and affirmatively take steps to induce breach? (2) If so, would the contract have been performed absent defendant's interference? Tri-Continental Leasing Co. v. Neidhardt, 540 S.W.2d 210 (Mo. App. 1976) (distributor of laundry equipment actively induced lessee's breach of agreement; evidence that lessee had intended to terminate contract with plaintiff-lessor regardless of anything distributor might have done). Cf. Jones Brothers (Hunstanton) Ltd. v. Stevens, [1955] 1 Q.B. 275 (C.A.) (no liability for employing worker under contract to plaintiff if worker would not in any event have returned to employment with plaintiff).

Wilkinson v. Powe

Supreme Court of Michigan
300 Mich. 275, 1 N.W.2d 539 (1942)

BUSHNELL, Justice.

Plaintiff Jay D. Wilkinson brought this action against defendants Powe and Stinson, individually and doing business as Shamrock Creamery, charging them with wrongfully procuring a breach of plaintiff's contract with certain farmers to haul their milk. [Plaintiff had hauled farmers' milk to creameries for several years. The farmers entered a written agreement with plaintiff covering the year 1937.]

Shortly after the execution of the written agreement, defendant Powe told the Wilkinsons that he wanted to take over the larger route and offered in exchange for the route the trade-in value of plaintiff's old truck, and told plaintiff he would give him a job in the creamery. Plaintiff then informed Powe of the existence of the written contract and refused to give up the route. About three months later Powe informed plaintiff that he would be required to replace the open stake racks on his trucks with insulated bodies because of a municipal ordinance. After plaintiff made this change in his trucks, he was unable to get his trucks into the creamery and the milk had to be handled by hand. This led to friction between the parties.

On May 29, 1937, defendant Powe sent a letter to the farmers doing business with plaintiff, worded as follows: "For reasons which are vital to our business, we the Shamrock Creamery, have decided that on and after June 1st, we will purchase no milk except that which is picked up by our own trucks at the farm. [¶] Nothing on your part has occasioned or made necessary this change, and we are hopeful that you will continue to sell us your milk. Pursuant to the change made, our trucks will call at your place Tuesday afternoon, June 1st, to pick up your milk, if you desire to continue business with us." ...

Wilkinson was unable to find another suitable market for milk after June 10th and was soon forced to abandon his routes. Defendants have since hauled the milk of practically all the farmers formerly under contract with plaintiff.

Plaintiff alleged in his declaration that defendants' object was to prevent him from protecting the farmers on his routes from false, fraudulent, and dishonest practices in the testing, weighing and price paid for milk. This was denied by defendants. They claimed their reason for deciding to haul the milk was that plaintiff failed to deliver the milk on time or in a proper condition, and that the action was taken to protect themselves and their customers by insuring a steady supply of good cream and wholesome milk. The testimony is in conflict on this point; but since the jury found for plaintiff, it must be assumed that they resolved this question against the defendants.

... [T]he trial judge entered a judgment for no cause of action....

The court stated that "the case at bar does not permit of any speculation on the element of falsehood or deceit which would amount to fraud, leaving then only for consideration, whether or not the action of the defendant could be construed factually as the application wrongfully of pressure and force."

[In the trial court's opinion] ... "The jury verdict must be predicated upon a circumstance which does not take into consideration the defendants' right to discontinue its source of supply at any time. To find for the plaintiff is a sympathetic attempt to give legal security to one, who, in a precarious position acted unwisely.... Without their acceptance (defendants) of the product the routes had no value. Lawful action, not unlawful action, then eliminated any value the routes may have had."

If the trial court is to be sustained, the judgment must stand on one of two grounds; first, that, in procuring the breach of contract, defendants were exercising what is often designated as a "superior" or "absolute" right, i.e., to refuse to accept further delivery of milk from plaintiff and, therefore, no justification was necessary; or second, that the injury, if any, was the result of defendants' refusal to accept deliveries of milk from plaintiff, and the breach of contract by the farmers was not the proximate cause of plaintiff's injury.

Morgan v. Andrews, 107 Mich. 33, 64 N.W. 869 ... approves the general proposition ... that: "Merely to persuade a person to break his contract may not be wrongful in law or fact; still, if the persuasion be used for the indirect purpose of injuring the plaintiff, or benefiting the defendant at the expense of the plaintiff, it is a malicious act, which, in law and in fact, is a wrongful act, and therefore an actionable act, if injury issues from it."

A prima facie case is established when plaintiff proves the intentional procurement of a breach of contract, and, upon such proof, it becomes incumbent upon defendant to show justification....

No categorical answer can be made to the question of what will constitute justification, and it is usually held that this question is one for the jury. The language in some of the cases supports defendants' contention that they acted under a "superior" or "absolute" right in refusing to accept further deliveries of milk by plaintiff, and that, under those circumstances, their action requires no justification.

If the defendants in the instant case had merely refused to accept further delivery of milk by plaintiff, they would have been clearly within their legal rights, although this would have resulted in a breach of contract between plaintiff and the farmers. But defendants did more. Their letters ... show active solicitation of a breach of the contract and their refusal to accept delivery of milk was merely another step in bringing about the breach.

Almost analogous facts, so far as the principle is concerned, are found in Knickerbocker Ice Co. v. Gardiner Dairy Co., 107 Md. 556, 69 A. 405. In the Gardiner case, plaintiff Gardiner Company was engaged in the dairy business and required a large quantity of ice during the spring and summer months. In order to meet its requirements it entered into a contract with the Sumwalt Company to deliver not exceeding 20 tons of ice a day until the completion of plaintiff's plant, then in the course of construction, at a price of $5 per ton, delivered. Sumwalt at the time was purchasing ice in large quantities from the defendant, Knickerbocker Ice Company, and when defendant learned of the contract between Gardiner and Sumwalt, it notified Sumwalt that it would refuse to deliver any ice whatever to it unless it refrained from delivering ice to Gardiner. Being compelled by the exigencies of its business to secure ice from Knickerbocker, and alarmed by the threat, Sumwalt breached its contract with Gardiner and advised it that this was done because of the action of Knickerbocker. Gardiner was thereby compelled to purchase ice directly from Knickerbocker at a price considerably greater and on less advantageous terms. The court ... held that: "If the Knickerbocker Company had simply refused to furnish the Sumwalt Company with ice, the Gardiner Company would not for that reason alone have a remedy against the Knickerbocker Company. Such action would not necessarily be unlawful or wrongful, but, if the Knickerbocker Company refused to furnish the Sumwalt Company if it furnished the Gardiner Company, although it knew it was under contract to do so, in order to get the business of the Gardiner Company for itself on it own terms, then it was unlawful to thus interfere with the contract between the Sumwalt Company and the Gardiner Company." ...

Defendants' refusal to accept further deliveries of milk by plaintiff was wrongful in the light of the evidence in the instant case because it was done to accomplish an unlawful purpose, i. e., to bring about a breach of contract. It therefore follows that the problem of proximate cause disappears from consideration in the case. Defendants cannot be heard to say that they should not be held liable for the injury caused plaintiff by their unlawful acts merely because they could have caused the same injury by a lawful act....

[Reversed and remanded for entry of judgment for plaintiff.]

Notes

1. Consider the variables at work in the principal case and the precedents discussed therein, including active procurement of the breach of contract, purpose, "competitive" motives and effects, and defendants' rights of contract and control of property. Which explain

decisions on liability? Is the fact that defendant has no pre-existing contract inconsistent with plaintiff's critical? What if defendant conditions a purchase of property on defendant's or a third person's being the broker for the sale, causing a broker retained by the seller to lose an expected commission? See Katz v. Thompson, 19 Misc. 2d 848, 189 N.Y.S.2d 982 (Co. Ct. 1959), aff'd, 9 A.D.2d 951, 196 N.Y.S.2d 578 (1959), appeal denied, 10 A.D.2d 630, 197 N.Y.S.2d 439 (1960). Will a lender be subject to liability for conditioning credit on measures that secure repayment but also interfere with existing contracts? See Nitzberg v. Zalesky, 370 So. 2d 389 (Fla. App. 1979) (lender required debtor to cut costs, resulting in reduction of employee's pay); Edwin Hill and Partners v. First National Finance Corp. Plc., [1989] 1 W.L.R. 225 (C.A.) (bankers who held mortgage on development property provided additional finance to developer, who was unable to repay loan or secure finance from other sources, on condition that architects be replaced by prestigious firm). On whether union members can lawfully condition their labor on non-performance of certain contracts, see pp. 146–152, infra.

2. Sometimes a person may, by undertaking a particular business, employment or transaction, impliedly consent to a degree of control and possible interference by a third party. In Posluns v. Toronto Stock Exchange, [1964] 2 O.R. 547, (1964) 46 D.L.R.2d 210 (High Ct.), aff'd, [1966] 1 O.R. 285, (1965) 53 D.L.R.2d 193 (C.A.), aff'd, [1968] S.C.R. 330, (1968) 67 D.L.R.2d 165, a stock exchange withdrew permission for plaintiff to serve as a shareholder, director or employee of a member company because he was found to have a conflict of interest. Such action resulted almost inevitably—as the exchange intended— in plaintiff's being discharged by the company. It was held that the agreement between the member company and its employee impliedly gave the exchange a right of control over the employee's conduct, justifying the interference with the contract of employment. Cf. O'Brien v. Western Union Telegraph Co., 62 Wash. 598, 114 P. 441 (1911) (telegraph company leased wires to press association, with condition that association's telegraph operators be satisfactory to company; plaintiff fired by association from job as operator at request of telegraph company).

3. To what extent does competition justify interference with a business rival's contract? It is generally held that a person is not justified in causing a breach of contract simply because he is in competition with one of the parties to that contract and is seeking to further his own economic advantage. See White Plains Coat & Apron Co., Inc. v. Cintas Corp., 8 N.Y.3d 422, 835 N.Y.S.2d 530, 867 N.E.2d 381 (2007) (competitor of plaintiff allegedly induced plaintiff's customers to break exclusive contracts to rent linen products from plaintiff and enter rental agreements with defendant); Imperial Ice Co. v. Rossier, 18 Cal. 2d 33, 112 P.2d 631 (1941) (action stated against ice manufacturers who induced party, who had agreed not to sell ice in certain territory, to violate agreement in order that manufacturers might sell him ice); Fowler v. Printers II, Inc., p. 135, supra (liability for employing former employee of plaintiff in sales work violating her covenant not to compete with plaintiff). Notice the various effects upon competition caused by defendants' interference with contract in the principal and note cases.

4. Interference with a contract is considered justified if defendant is acting to protect a contractual relationship of its own. See Tidal Western Oil Corp. v. Shackelford, 297 S.W. 279 (Tex. Civ. App. 1927) (defendant oil company caused another oil company to stop taking oil from plaintiff under lease by asserting right to oil under prior contract). In Quinlivan v. Brown Oil Co., 96 Mont. 147, 29 P.2d 374 (1934), the lessee of a service station had agreed with the lessor oil company to maintain the price charged at the lessor's other stations. The company was held justified in requiring the lessee to withdraw from a contract which reduced the price. A franchisor may act to protect its relationship with

a franchisee. It might incur liability if its conduct is found to be malicious. See Team Central, Inc. v. Teamco, Inc., 271 N.W.2d 914 (Iowa 1978) (franchisor falsely and maliciously represented that it would buy franchisee's assets and take over operation of its stores and induced third party to abandon plans to purchase franchisee). But in the *Quinlivan* case it is said that certain "absolute rights"—rights incident to ownership of property, rights growing out of contractual relations, and the right to enter or refuse to enter contractual relations—may be exercised without regard to motive. If interference with contract is justified to protect an interest in a contract with a third party, why isn't it justified to protect an interest in a contract with plaintiff, as in Camden Nominees, Ltd. v. Forcey, p. 128, supra?

5. A person may be permitted to act in protection of an existing economic interest, such as an investment or interest in property, despite resulting interference with another person's contract. See Bendix Corp. v. Adams, 610 P.2d 24 (Alaska 1980) (parent corporation's interference with subsidiary's contract); RAN Corp. v. Hudesman, 823 P.2d 646 (Alaska 1991) (lessor's interference with assignment of property by lessee); Meason v. Ralston Purina Co., 56 Ariz. 291, 107 P.2d 224 (1940) (feed seller holding mortgage on flock of turkeys interfered with sale of turkeys); Restatement (Second) of Torts § 769 (1979). Compare Fury Imports, Inc. v. Shakespeare Co., 554 F.2d 1376 (5th Cir. 1977) (foreign company manufactured fishing reels for both plaintiff and defendant; liability for inducing company to cease supplying plaintiff if purpose was to eliminate competitor rather than to preserve defendant's financial interests (shares, debt, continued source of supply) in company). In Knapp v. Penfield, 143 Misc. 132, 256 N.Y.S. 41 (Sup. Ct. 1932), a former Miss America was hired for the lead role in a musical. The play's promoter and the promoter's agent believed she lacked the singing and dancing ability required for the part and brought pressure—eventually including legal action—against the producer to have another performer substituted. As a result, she was discharged from the production. The court held that the interference with the performance contract by the promoter and the agent was a justified act of protecting their investment. Should justification for tort purposes of any broader or narrower than justification for purposes of liability for the breach of contract?

6. What if defendant does not cause an actual repudiation or breach of a contract, but only a modification of the contract's terms to plaintiff's detriment, as when plaintiff is deprived of the right to be the exclusive recipient of a product? See Hannigan v. Sears, Roebuck and Co., 410 F.2d 285 (7th Cir. 1969), cert. denied, 396 U.S. 902 (1969), in which the contract provided that a manufacturer would produce cabinets exclusively for plaintiffs. Defendant acted to have the manufacturer sell cabinets directly to defendant, so that it would not have to buy from plaintiffs, though plaintiffs were to be given a 10% commission on each cabinet sold. A cause of action was found.

United Truck Leasing Corporation v. Geltman

Supreme Judicial Court of Massachusetts
406 Mass. 811, 551 N.E.2d 20 (1990)

WILKINS, Justice....

It is common ground that, in an action for intentional interference with a contract, the plaintiff must prove that (1) he had a contract with a third party, (2) the defendant knowingly induced the third party to break that contract, and (3) the plaintiff was harmed by the defendant's actions. The disputed point is whether the plaintiff must also prove something more, namely, that a defendant's conduct was wrongful or improper in some way. The trial judge recognized that our cases have said that justification for one's conduct is an affirmative defense to be proved by the defendant, but he concluded, relying on principles set forth in the Restatement (Second) of Torts § 767 (1979), that, before the matter of justification need be faced, a plaintiff must prove that what the defendant intentionally did was "wrongful or improper in its means or its ends." ...

Geltman, an officer of the defendant corporation, counsels companies that lease trucks. He educates his customers about the truck leasing business so that they may obtain more favorable leases. He helps in soliciting and critiquing bids from lessors and sometimes negotiates leases. Geltman also attempts to obtain changes in existing leases that will be beneficial to his clients. The plaintiff (United) operates a large truck leasing company in the Commonwealth.

United's claim for intentional interference with a contract is based on its claim that Geltman caused one of his customers (Universal Fixtures) to break its contract with United and to enter into a lease with Flexi-Van, the lessor with whom Universal Fixtures had had a lease prior to its lease with United. It is clear, on the plaintiff's evidence, that Geltman knew of the existing lease between United and Universal Fixtures and recognized the possibility that, if Universal Fixtures signed on with Flexi-Van, United might sue Universal Fixtures for breach of contract. There was evidence that United lost $60,000 because of Universal Fixtures's repudiation of the contract.

United's claim for intentional interference with prospective contractual relations concerns United's inability to obtain a lease with Matthew's Salad House (Matthew's). United had been trying to arrange a lease with Matthew's for about six years. Matthew's retained Geltman to advise it concerning the lease of refrigerated trucks. Geltman did not invite United to bid on the Matthew's account, although there were good reasons why United might have been invited to do so. When asked by a United representative why he had not invited United to bid, Geltman replied that other leasing companies gave him leads for new accounts but that United did not. After learning the amount of its competitor's bid, United did bid on the Matthew's account but was not awarded the account. The trial judge directed a verdict for the defendants....

We start with the observation that malice, in the sense of ill will, has not been a true element of the torts of intentional interference either with a contract or with a prospective contractual relation. Some of our cases have used the word but, in the same breath, have eliminated any requirement of independent proof of malice. See *Keegan v. O'Donnell*, 310 Mass. 346, 350, 37 N.E.2d 995 (1941) ("intentional interference with the plaintiff's business, in the absence of any legal justification, was malicious in law and entitled the plaintiff to damages"); *Anderson v. Moskovitz*, 260 Mass. 523, 526, 157 N.E. 601 (1927) ("Malice is proved if it appears that the defendant with knowledge of the contract intentionally and without justification induced one of the contracting parties to break it"). This formulation of the tort, intentional interference without privilege to do so, is generally consistent with the rule stated in the first Restatement.

More recently, we have expressed the view that a plaintiff must prove, among other things, "the defendant's intentional and malicious interference with" a business relationship or contemplated contract of economic benefit. See *ELM Medical Laboratory, Inc. v. RKO Gen., Inc.*, 403 Mass. 779, 787, 532 N.E.2d 675 (1989)....

In this opinion, we adopt the word "improperly" in place of the word "maliciously." In doing so we agree that more than intentional interference must be established. "Improperly" is the word used in the Restatement (Second) of Torts § 766 (1979)[7] ("intentionally and improperly interferes"). It is the concept the trial judge relied on in directing verdicts in this case. We accept it, as does the Restatement (Second) of Torts, as an element both in the proof of intentional interference with performance of a contract (§ 766) and in the proof of intentional interference with a prospective contractual relationship (§ 766B).

In deciding what conduct is improper, we accept the standard expressed in ... *Top Serv. Body Shop, Inc. v. Allstate Ins. Co.*, 283 Or. 201, 209–210, 582 P.2d 1365 (1978) ("In summary, [a claim of tort liability for intentional interference with contractual or other economic relations] is made out when interference resulting in injury to another is wrongful by some measure beyond the fact of interference itself. Defendant's liability may arise from improper motives or from the use of improper means.... No question of privilege arises unless the interference would be wrongful but for the privilege; it becomes an issue only if the acts charged would be tortious on the part of an unprivileged defendant"); *Leigh Furniture & Carpet Co. v. Isom*, 657 P.2d 293, 304 (Utah 1982) ("improper purpose or by improper means"); *Blake v. Levy*, 191 Conn. 257, 262, 464 A.2d 52 (1983) ("the better reasoned approach requires the plaintiff to plead and prove at least some improper motive or improper means"). In [*Comey v. Hill*, 387 Mass. 11, 19, 438 N.E.2d 811 (1982)] we applied this standard by recognizing liability where the defendant's intentional interference with the plaintiff's employment contract was based on unfair age discrimination, an improper motive.

... The evidence does not warrant a finding that Geltman violated a statute or a rule of common law. There is no evidence that he used threats, misrepresented any facts, defamed anyone, or used any other improper means in relation to either the existing contract or the prospective one. His apparent motives were to benefit his customers and himself financially. There is not enough evidence to warrant a finding that his real motive in these matters was to hurt United.

The judge properly allowed the motion for a directed verdict on the claims we have considered in this appeal.

Judgment of the Superior Court affirmed.

Notes

1. Tort law has long drawn a sharp distinction between intentionally causing a breach of contract and intentionally causing a contract to be lawfully terminated or not entered into. See pp. 143–152, 164–200, infra. Consider the reasons for this and whether it is desirable to apply common principles of liability to all of these situations. Would it be satisfactory to have a common "blackletter" rule but have different standards of what is "improper" interference for each category of case?

2. So far, the influence of the Restatement (Second) reformulation of liability has been seen primarily in cases of interference with prospective contractual relations, e.g. depriving plaintiff of an opportunity to make sales, and cases of inducing termination of contracts. Some cases refer to the presence or absence of improper means or improper

---

7. Section 766 reads as follows: "One who intentionally and improperly interferes with the performance of a contract (except a contract to marry) between another and a third person by inducing or otherwise causing the third person not to perform the contract, is subject to liability to the other for the pecuniary loss resulting to the other from the failure of the third person to perform the contract."

motives in deciding whether causing breach of contract was justified. E.g. National Right To Life Political Action Committee v. Friends of Bryan, 741 F. Supp. 807 (D. Nev. 1990). Potential liability for interference with contract might be limited by requiring some purpose to interfere with the contract or harm plaintiff rather than knowing interference. But this does not have much support in contemporary law. Differentiating liability for interference with existing contracts and liability for interference with prospective economic relations, the Supreme Court of California has held that an element of wrongfulness in defendant's conduct independent of the inducement to breach the contract was not a requirement of liability and that there could be liability without a primary purpose to disrupt the contract. Knowledge that the interference would occur was sufficient. That a legitimate business purpose might constitute justification was, however, recognized. Quelimane Co., Inc. v. Stewart Title Guaranty Co., 19 Cal. 4th 26, 77 Cal. Rptr. 2d 709, 960 P.2d 513 (1998).

3. In Winkler v. V.G. Reed & Sons, Inc., 638 N.E.2d 1228 (Ind. 1994), plaintiff had a fifteen-year contract as general manager of a printing and typesetting company. He was discharged two years into the contract as a result of a transaction in which defendant acquired the assets of the company and assumed its loans but did not assume obligations under existing employment agreements. The company ceased all business activity upon the completion of this transaction. It had been nearly insolvent because its primary lender refused to renew outstanding loans. Evidently, defendant intended to use the company's assets to create a profitable enterprise. The court found justification for interference with plaintiff's employment contract in the interests of the other parties in being able to freely purchase and sell a business in a legitimate transaction having no motive to injure the employees whose contracts were broken. Plaintiff's interests, the court thought, were adequately protected by his remedy for breach of contract. Will this approach be extended to cases in which defendant induces breach of contract by offering a contracting party more favorable terms or conditions than in the contract with plaintiff? See Forehand v. Perlis Realty Co., 198 Ga. App. 165, 400 S.E.2d 644 (1990) (defendant induced tenant of plaintiff's shopping center to move to shopping center owned by defendant, which tenant considered better location for its business; judgment for defendant affirmed); Peoples Security Life Insurance Co. v. Hooks, 322 N.C. 216, 367 S.E.2d 647 (1988) (competitor hired nineteen of plaintiff's employees in violation of their covenants not to compete).

4. Are some contracts so personal in nature that no privilege to interfere should be recognized? This may be true of contracts between physician and patient. See Hammonds v. Aetna Casualty & Surety Co., 237 F. Supp. 96 (N.D. Ohio 1965) (malpractice insurer advised doctor to discontinue treating plaintiff, who was considered potential claimant); National Life & Accident Insurance Co. v. Wallace, 162 Okla. 174, 21 P.2d 492 (1933) (insurance company notified policyholders that it would not pay sickness or accident claims certified by plaintiff as attending physician). But see Waldroup v. Lindman, 28 P.3d 293 (Alaska 2001) (insurer privileged because of direct financial interest). If a family member or friend of the patient believes a physician is not proficient, is it tortious to persuade the patient to discharge the physician? See generally Annot., Liability for Interference with Physician-Patient Relationship, 87 A.L.R.4th 845 (1991).

5. For a critique of interference with contract liability on grounds, inter alia, of its anticompetitive effects and deterrence of economically efficient breaches of contract, see Comment, Intentional Interference with Contract: Market Efficiency and Individual Liberty Considerations, 27 Conn. L. Rev. 279 (1994). See also Remington, Intentional Interference with Contract and the Doctrine of Efficient Breach: Fine Tuning the Notion of the Con-

tract Breacher as Wrongdoer, 47 Buffalo L. Rev. 645 (1999); Woodward, Contractarians, Community, and the Tort of Interference with Contract, 80 Minn. L. Rev. 1103 (1996).

B. Inducing Termination of Contract

Terry v. Dairymen's League Co-Operative Association, Inc.

Supreme Court of New York, Appellate Division
2 A.D.2d 494, 157 N.Y.S.2d 71 (1956)

HALPERN, Justice.

The plaintiff has recovered a substantial judgment for damages upon the theory that the defendant maliciously induced the breach of trucking contracts which had been entered into between the plaintiff and a number of dairy farmers....

The plaintiff was engaged in the business of hauling milk from various dairy farms in the vicinity of Downsville, New York, to the defendant's milk plant at Margaretville, New York. The defendant, as its name indicates, is a co-operative association of dairy farmers. The farmers with whom the plaintiff had contracted for trucking were all members of the defendant association.... [T]he defendant decided to close [its] Downsville plant and to transfer the patronage of the farmers in that area to its Margaretville plant, about 20 miles away. There obviously was not enough business to sustain several truckers and the defendant selected the plaintiff and one Williams as the two truckers who would serve the farmers in the Downsville area and bring their milk to Margaretville. While the defendant had operated its plant at Downsville, the cost of hauling the milk to the plant had been borne wholly by the farmers.... Because of the longer haul to Margaretville, the defendant agreed to contribute ... an additional payment to the truckers. The contract of transportation was in each instance made orally between the farmer and the trucker but, since it was not economically feasible for a trucker to engage in the business of transporting milk unless he had a substantial number of customers along the same route, the farmers had to act cooperatively in arranging for the services of a trucker. The farmers, as members of the defendant, naturally looked to the defendant to make the arrangements for the trucking. As an executive of the defendant testified, the defendant regarded it as part of its responsibility to see to it that suitable trucking service was made available, even though under its contracts with the farmers for the purchase of milk, it was the legal obligation of the farmers to deliver the milk to the plant....

... [S]everal of the dairy farmers on the plaintiff's route ceased to operate, with the result that in 1953 the plaintiff had only 13 customers left. The plaintiff contended that this volume of business did not produce a sufficient income at the rates currently paid. He complained about this from time to time to his farmer customers and to the officials of the defendant. The situation came to a head late in 1953.... [T]he defendant's representatives told him that they could not pay him any more money, and they pointed out that Williams, the other trucker, was willing to continue at the agreed rates.... [T]here is a dispute as to whether the plaintiff gave notice of his intention to quit. The plaintiff denies that he did but the defendant claims that the plaintiff stated unequivocally that, if more money was not forthcoming, he would cease to haul the milk on the following Monday.... [T]he defendant's field representative and its plant manager made arrangements with Williams to take over the plaintiff's route as well as to carry on his own route and they then notified all the farmers whom they were able to find at home, of the change in the arrangements. According to their testimony, they advised the farmers that they were, of course, free to make any trucking arrangements that they wished but that Williams would be available to haul the milk after Monday, if they wished to have him do so. Practically all the farmers whom they interviewed, constituting a majority of the farmers on the plaintiff's route, acquiesced in the change.

Accordingly, on Monday, November 9, after the plaintiff had delivered a truckload of milk at the defendant's plant, the defendant declined to return the empty milk cans to the plaintiff but turned them over to Williams who, in regular course, returned them to the farmers. Thereafter, the farmers continued to ship their milk by Williams' truck, without protest or objection....

It is undisputed that the oral contracts between the plaintiff and the farmers were terminable at will and that the agreement of the defendant to pay a subsidy was also terminable at will. The plaintiff, nevertheless, characterized his action as an action for damages for maliciously inducing the *breach* of the contracts between himself and the farmers. Since the contracts were terminable at will, the discontinuance of the plaintiff's services, however induced, could not constitute a breach of contract. The action must, therefore, be regarded as one for damages for inducing the discontinuance of business relations rather than as one for the inducing of a breach of contract. It is settled that such an action can be maintained only upon a showing that the defendant acted solely out of a malicious desire to injure the plaintiff, without any expectation of furthering its own business interests. The trial court correctly charged the jury: ... "And the action is brought upon the theory that this defendant maliciously and without legal or social justification caused these producers to discontinue the plaintiff's services. If the defendant deprived the plaintiff of his employment by means not in themselves unlawful, by acts not in themselves unlawful, have [sic] any proper purpose to serve, they are not liable for any damage they caused. The genesis which will make a lawful act unlawful must be a malicious one, unmixed with any other, and exclusively directed to injury and damage of another. [¶] In other words it is incumbent upon the plaintiff to establish to your satisfaction that the action of the defendant was without legal or social justification; that their action was not motivated by a proper desire." ...

It is virtually undisputed that the verdict cannot be allowed to stand upon the theory upon which the case was submitted to the jury. It is clear beyond question that the defendant did not act out of "disinterested malevolence", the epigrammatic phrase coined by Justice Holmes in American Bank & Trust Company v. Federal Reserve Bank, 256 U.S. 350, 358....

... The most that could be said, under plaintiff's version of the transaction, was that the defendant had decided, in view of the fact that the volume of business from the Downsville area was falling off and that the plaintiff was demanding a higher rate of pay, that it would be best to concentrate the trucking from that area in the hands of a single trucker who would be able to make a living out of the total volume at the current rates and that it accordingly decided to arrange to have Williams take over all the business. Even upon that hypothesis, the decision by the defendant was a decision taken in the ordinary course of business, designed to serve its interests and those of its farmer members. The defendant was dealing with a highly perishable product and it was important that dependable trucking arrangements should be made, which would not be subject to the constant threat of disruption. In shifting the business to Williams, the defendant merely sought to establish a stable arrangement under which it would be assured that the trucking would continue to be done, free from persistent pressure for increased compensation.

... It is true that economic self-interest does not ordinarily afford a justification for inducing the breach of a contract for a definite term but this rule has no application to the inducing of the termination of a contract which is terminable at will.

... [T]he rules with respect to the scope of the defendant's privilege are wholly different in the two classes of cases. The fact that the contract is terminable at will greatly broadens the scope of the defendant's privilege. The privilege in such a case is substantially the same as the privilege of inducing third persons not to enter into new business relations with the plaintiff. Under the principles of the free enterprise system, that privilege is a very broad one and it is forfeited only when the defendant's action, otherwise lawful, is intended solely to injure the plaintiff without any expectation of social or economic advantage. On the other hand, the furthering of one's business interests does not ordinarily justify the inducing of the breach of a contract for a definite term. Thus, for example, one may not with impunity seek to gain new customers by inducing them to breach their existing contracts with others but, in the free play of competition, one may seek to win for himself the patronage of the customers of others, by inducing them to discontinue their existing business relations, provided that they are terminable at will....

[Reversed. Complaint dismissed.]

Notes

1. The prevailing view is that an action may lie for interference with a contract that is terminable at will. See United States Fidelity & Guaranty Co. v. Millonas, 206 Ala. 147, 89 So. 732 (1921); Bochnowski v. Peoples Federal Savings & Loan Association, 571 N.E.2d 282 (Ind. 1991). This is qualified by holdings, as in the principal case, that interference with a contract at will by otherwise lawful conduct is not actionable unless defendant acted solely, or at least predominantly, out of malice. See also Huskie v. Griffin, 75 N.H. 345, 74 A. 595 (1909); Reinforce, Inc. v. Birney, 308 N.Y. 164, 124 N.E.2d 104 (1954). A reading of many recent cases may justify the conclusion that the required malice is not actual ill will or spite, but only an intent to cause harm without justification, or without a legitimate business purpose. See Annot., Liability for Interference with At Will Business Relationship, 5 A.L.R.4th 9 (1981) (noting that claim is often treated as interference with prospective advantage, considered pp. 164–210, infra).

2. No relief will be granted for interference with a totally invalid contract. See Fairbanks, Morse & Co. v. Texas Electric Service Co., 63 F.2d 702 (5th Cir. 1933), cert. denied, 290 U.S. 655 (1933) (contracts creating monopoly); Carruthers v, Flaum, 365 F. Supp. 2d 448 (S.D.N.Y. 2005) (contracts for development of illegal gambling facilities); Thomas v. Ratiner, 462 So. 2d 1157 (Fla. App. 1984) (retainer illegally solicited by attorney employed by hospital); Cappiello, Hofman & Katz v. Boyle, 87 Cal. App. 4th 1064, 105 Cal. Rptr. 2d 147 (2001) (law firm's contracts with clients illegal because firm was corporation that had failed to register with State Bar). The result may be different if the contract is merely unenforceable. Most authority allows an action for inducing nonperformance of contracts that violate the Statute of Frauds. See Friedman v. Jackson, 266 Cal. App. 2d 517, 72 Cal. Rptr. 129 (1968); Royal Realty Co. v. Levin, 244 Minn. 288, 69 N.W.2d 667 (1955). Cf. United Yacht Brokers, Inc. v. Gillespie, 377 So. 2d 668 (Fla. 1979) (brokerage contract unenforceable against principal without written authorization for transaction). Compare NCH Corp. v. Share Corp., 757 F.2d 1540 (5th Cir. 1985); AMX International, Inc. v. Battelle Energy Alliance, LLC, 744 F. Supp. 2d 1087 (D. Idaho 2010) (no liability for inducing violation of unenforceable employee covenant not to compete). Some decisions permit recovery when the contract is unenforceable due to lack of con-

sideration, mutuality or certainty. See Allen v. Leybourne, 190 So. 2d 825 (Fla. App. 1966); Barlow v. International Harvester Co., 95 Idaho 881, 522 P.2d 1102 (1974); Aalfo Co. v. Kinney, 105 N.J.L. 345, 144 A. 715 (1929). Arguably, this should be treated as interference with prospective advantage, not interference with contract. See Guard-Life Corp. v. S. Parker Hardware Manufacturing Corp., 50 N.Y.2d 183, 428 N.Y.S.2d 628, 406 N.E.2d 445 (1980). The court in PMC, Inc. v. Saban Entertainment, Inc., 45 Cal. App. 4th 579, 52 Cal. Rptr. 2d 877 (1996), held in broad terms that if the contract was not enforceable, the only action is interference with prospective advantage. (The contract in the case was unenforceable because not in writing.) See also OBG Ltd. v. Allan, [2008] A.C. 1 (H.L.), requiring a breach of contract for which the contracting party would be liable. See generally Annot., Liability for Interference with Invalid or Unenforceable Contract, 96 A.L.R.3d 1294 (1980). If a contracting party is under no obligation to perform a contractual undertaking, does it make sense to allow a tort action against the person who persuaded the party not to perform?

3. Not to be overlooked is the question whether there really was a contract at all. This was central to the most celebrated interference with contract case of recent times, Texaco, Inc. v. Pennzoil, Co., 729 S.W.2d 768 (Tex. App. 1987), cert. dismissed, 485 U.S. 994 (1988), cause dismissed, 748 S.W.2d 631 (Tex. App. 1988) (applying New York law, under which existence of contract depended upon whether parties intended to be bound by agreement). Also in issue was whether the defendant (Texaco) had sufficient knowledge of the transaction to know it was a contract. A verdict for ten and a half billion dollars was affirmed except for two of the three billion dollars in exemplary damages. See also ACT, Inc. v. Sylvan Learning Systems, Inc., 296 F.3d 657 (8th Cir. 2002).

Kemp v. Division No. 241, Amalgamated Association of Street & Electric Railway Employees of America

Supreme Court of Illinois
255 Ill. 213, 99 N.E. 389 (1912)

COOKE, J. [with whom Farmer and Vickers, JJ., joined]....

[Several employees of the Chicago Railways Company resigned from their union, objecting to use of membership dues for political purposes. Union officials demanded that the company discharge these employees and threatened a strike by union members if they were not discharged. The members voted to refuse to work with non-union employees. The dissidents refused to withdraw their resignations and sought an injunction restraining the union and its officials from procuring their discharge by the company. The Appellate Court ruled in favor of the dissidents.]

... "That which it is right and lawful for one man to do cannot furnish the foundation for an action in favor of another. Nor can the absence of commendable motive on the part of the party exercising his rights be the legal substitute or equivalent for the thing amiss, which is one of the necessary elements of a wrong." [Cooley, Torts, p. 81.] ...

Every employé has a right to protection in his employment from the wrongful and malicious interference of another resulting in damage to the employé; but, if such interference is but the consequence of the exercise of some legal right by another, it is not wrongful, and cannot, therefore, be made the basis for an action to recover the consequent damages. It is the right of every workman, for any reason which may seem sufficient to him, or for no reason, to quit the service of another, unless bound by contract.... Incident to this constitutional right is the right of every workman to refuse to work with any coemployé who is for any reason objectionable to him, provided his refusal does not violate his contract with his employer; and there is no more foundation for the contention that the employé commits an actionable wrong by informing the employer, before he leaves the service, that he will not work with the objectionable coemployé, and thereby occasioning his discharge, than there would be for the contention that the employé would commit an actionable wrong by quitting the service and afterward stating to the employer his reason therefor, if as a result thereof the employer should choose to discharge the objectionable coemployé.... [H]ad the union employés, as individuals and without any prearranged concert of action, each informed the Railways Company that they would no longer work with appellees because appellees were not members of the union, and had appellees, in consequence thereof, been discharged because the Railways Company chose to retain the services of the union employés, appellees would have had no cause of action against the union employés for thus causing their discharge....

Labor unions have long since been recognized by the courts of this country as a legitimate part of the industrial system of this nation. The ultimate purpose of such organizations is, through combination, to advance the interests of the members by obtaining for them adequate compensation for their labor, and it has been frequently decided by the American courts that the fact that this purpose is sought to be obtained through combination or concerted action of employés does not render the means unlawful....

The purpose of organizing labor unions is to enable those employés who become members to negotiate matters arising between them and their employers through the intermediation of officers and committees of the union and to accomplish their ends through concerted action. If duly authorized by the employés to adjust any controversy arising between them and their employer, the union, its officers, and committees are merely acting as agents of the employés in the matter. If the union employés had the legal right to inform their employer of their refusal to work with appellees, they had the legal right to convey that information to the employer through an agent or agents, and the agent or agents would not commit an actionable wrong thereby nor by reporting back to the union employés the result of the conference with the employer. The demand that appellees be discharged, and the threat that unless the Railways Company complied with the demand the members of the union would call a strike of the employés of the Railways Company, in effect meant no more than the mere statement that the union employés of the Railways Company would no longer work with the nonunion employés, and, if the Railways Company chose to retain in its employ the nonunion men, the union employés would quit the service of the Railways Company.

... The contemplated action of the union employés is not the result of the dictation of any officer or officers of the union or of any person not interested in the employment, but is the voluntary action of the union employés of the Railways Company....

While it cannot be successfully contended that every strike is lawful, it is generally conceded by our courts that workmen may quit in a body, or strike, in order to maintain wages, secure advancement in wages, procure shorter hours of employment, or attain any other legitimate object. An agreement by a combination of individuals to strike or quit work for the purpose of advancing their own interests or the interests of the union of which they are members, and not having for its primary object the purpose of injuring others in their business or employment, is lawful. As to whether the object which this bill discloses was sought to be attained by the members of the union was a lawful one or a valid justification of the threat to strike, the authorities in this country are clearly in conflict....

It does not follow from a consideration of all the material allegations of the bill that the primary object of the union employés, or of the union officers in carrying out the wishes of the members, was to injure appellees. Neither can it be said that any actual malice has been disclosed toward the appellees or an intent to commit a wrongful or harmful act against them. No threats are made, and no violence is threatened....

It is insisted that a strike is lawful only in a case of direct competition, and, as it cannot be said that the union employés are in any sense competing with appellees, their acts cannot be justified. It is true ... that the proposed strike was not to be called for the direct purpose of securing better wages or shorter hours or to prevent a reduction of wages, any one of which would have been a proper object. The motive was more remote than that, but it was kindred to it. The purpose was to strengthen and preserve the organization itself. Without organization, the workmen would be utterly unable to make a successful effort to maintain or increase their wages or to enforce such demands as have been held to be proper....

If it is proper for workmen to organize themselves into such combinations as labor unions, it must necessarily follow that it is proper for them to adopt any proper means to preserve that organization. If the securing of the closed shop is deemed by the members of a labor union of the utmost importance and necessary for the preservation of their organization, through which, alone, they have been enabled to secure better wages and better working conditions, and if to secure that is the primary object of the threat to strike, even though in the successful prosecution of the object of the combination injury may result incidentally to non-union men through the loss of their positions, that object does not become unlawful....

Judgment reversed.

CARTER, J. (specially concurring)....

The authorities are not in accord as to whether the motive with which an act is performed can affect the legality. It has been stated that an act which does not amount to a legal injury cannot be actionable because done with a bad intent. It is clear that there are cases in which wrongful motive has no legal significance. For example, where the plaintiff refuses to leave defendant's house when requested and is forcibly ejected by the defendant. It makes no difference, under such circumstances, that the defendant is gratifying a vindictive spirit in so doing.... The lawfulness of the act which causes damage may depend on whether it is for a justifiable cause, and its justification may be found "sometimes in the circumstances under which it is done, irrespective of motive, sometimes in the motive alone, and sometimes in the circumstances and motive combined." Plant v. Woods, 176 Mass. 492, 57 N.E. 1011....

It is difficult to conceive of a strike without damage to the parties involved in the dispute. The employés intend to deprive the employers of their labor, and prevent them from getting others to take their places. They intentionally inflict harm as a means of compelling the employers to yield to their demands....

Members of a union knowingly inflicting harm upon their employer or a fellow employé, even as a means of benefiting themselves, should be held liable unless the harm comes from what may be called a truly competitive act.... The dispute must be in reference to demands that are real and substantial, relate to the employment, and affect the direct and immediate interests of the persons involved. The damage resulting to the employer or the general public must not be unreasonable as compared with the benefits to the workmen. The rights of the employer and employés, as has been said, are relative, and not absolute. Every absolute right has its limits, and to that extent it is the correlative duty of every person to respect and refrain from obstructing, by force, fraud, intimidation, or other unlawful means, another person's rights....

To hold that a labor organization has a right to strike because the members want the work other people are doing, and cannot be enjoined for so striking, does not seem to differ very materially, in principle, from holding that a labor organization can strike because certain fellow laborers will not join the union. The result of the latter strike, if successful, will be to give the work of the nonunion men to the union men. It would appear, also, to be drawing a very fine distinction to hold that the primary object of a strike in such a case ... was to aid the members of the labor union, while in the case now under consideration the primary object was not to help the members....

... Clearly, in this case the strike was not malevolent—that is, on account of ill-feeling toward the nonunion workmen as individuals or primarily from a desire to injure them—because the union workmen requested and demanded that the nonunion workmen, who had formerly belonged to the union, be required to join the union or else be discharged....

In my judgment union workmen not bound by contract who inform their employer that they will strike unless he discharge nonunion workmen in the same line of employment should be held to be merely dictating the terms of their own employment; that it is not unlawful for members of a labor union to seek by peaceful methods to induce those engaged in the same occupation to become members of such union, and as a means to that end to refuse to allow union laborers to work in the same line of employment in a place where nonunion laborers are employed. The proposed purpose of the strike not being unlawful, it necessarily follows that an injunction should not issue as prayed for in the bill....

CARTWRIGHT, J., DUNN, C.J., and HAND, J. [dissenting]....

The principle involved came before this court in Doremus v. Hennessy, 176 Ill. 608, 52 N.E. 924, 54 N.E. 524.... The plaintiff was conducting a laundry office in the city of Chicago. She had no laundry of her own, but employed persons operating laundries to do her work, who, when the work was done, returned the same to her, and she delivered it to her customers. Her prices were not as high as those fixed by the Chicago Laundrymen's Association, and because she would not be governed by the prices fixed by that association the defendants interfered with her customers and with the laundries that did her work. She brought an action on the case against the parties interfering with her customers and her business and recovered a judgment for $6,000, which was affirmed by this court. It was said: "No persons, individually or by combination, have the right to directly or indirectly interfere with or disturb another in his lawful business or occupation, or to threaten to do so, for the sake of compelling him to do some act, which, in his judgment, his own interest does not require." ... The principle declared was: "Every man has a right, under the law, as between himself and others, to full freedom in disposing of his own labor or capital according to his own will, and any one who invades that right without lawful cause or justification commits a legal wrong, and, if followed by an injury caused in consequence thereof, the one whose right is thus invaded has a legal ground of action for such wrong." ...

The question whether an individual can lawfully, for his own gain, procure the discharge of another from his employment, was settled by this court in London Guarantee Co. v. Horn, 206 Ill. 493, 69 N.E. 526.... Horn was in the employ of Arnold, Schwinn & Co., and while so employed was injured and brought an action against his employers to recover for his injury. Arnold, Schwinn & Co. carried an indemnity policy in the London Guarantee & Accident Company. After a time Horn resumed work for Arnold, Schwinn & Co., when the guarantee company made an offer of settlement of Horn's claim for his injury, which offer was declined, whereupon demand upon Arnold, Schwinn & Co. to discharge Horn was made by the guarantee company, and that company threatened to cancel the guarantee bond held by Arnold, Schwinn & Co. if Horn was not discharged. There was an absolute contract right reserved in the policy to cancel it. The relations between Horn and his employers were satisfactory, but to avoid the cancellation of the policy Horn was discharged. He brought an action against the guarantee company for wrongfully causing his discharge, and recovered, and the recovery was sustained by this court. If the act of the guarantee company in the exercise of its contract right was wrongful and unlawful as an interference with the right of Horn to labor, the act of the union in this case would not be less so....

One circumstance which, under the laws of trade and business, has always been recognized as a sufficient justification for one who seeks his own advantage at the expense of another, is that the parties are in direct competition, and that principle applies to laborers equally to those engaged in trade and business.... The facts of this case will not admit of the application of that doctrine. The only manner in which it is suggested that the appellants are in competition with appellees is that the power and influence of labor organizations depend upon the number of their members, and the threat to procure the discharge of appellees was made for the purpose of strengthening Division 241, and thereby securing a continuance of favorable conditions as against the employer, and good wages....

To justify an act which it is conceded will be an injury and damage to the appellees, and which will not secure better wages, shorter hours of labor, or improved conditions of labor in any other respect, on the mere ground that the object is to strengthen Division 241, is to destroy every vestige of protection against interference with the right of any one to labor who chooses to work independently. A majority may believe, as in this case, that a contribution to the campaign of a political party will strengthen the organization, and there is scarcely any limit to the things that may be so regarded....

... The right of a labor organization to enforce a closed shop for the mere purpose of strengthening the labor organization in future contests with the employer is not competition, and is not of the same character or equal to the right of the individual to dispose of his labor at his own will....

... [T]he judgment of the Appellate Court should be affirmed.

Notes

1. Much of the law on liability for interference with contract or prospective advantage comes from cases involving labor union activity. By the early years of the twentieth century, unions had come to be regarded as lawful organizations rather than criminal conspiracies. Non-violent activity that caused or threatened to cause cessation of business or termination of at-will contracts, as distinct from breach of contract, would not as a general rule result in liability. A union would be liable if it intended only to do harm to an employer, Thacker Coal & Coke Co. v. Burke, 59 W. Va. 253, 53 S.E. 161 (1906). But any objective which tended directly and immediately to benefit the workers was recognized as a legitimate basis for a strike and justification for interference with employment at will. This was true, for instance, of the goal of better wages. Perfect Laundry Co. v. Marsh, 120 N.J. Eq. 508, 186 A. 470 (Ch. 1936). Or shorter hours. Everett Waddey Co. v. Richmond Typographical Union No. 90, 105 Va. 188, 53 S.E. 273 (1906). Or collective bar-

gaining by the employer with the union. International Pocketbook Workers' Union v. Orlove, 158 Md. 496, 148 A. 826 (1930).

2. In a leading case, the prevention of recalcitrant members of a union from working at less than union rates was held insufficient justification for a strike. New England Wood Heel Co. v. Nolan, 268 Mass. 191, 167 N.E. 323 (1929). Courts were divided on the question of whether union efforts to obtain a closed shop justified interference with contract. See Annot., Liability in Damages for Inducing the Discharge of Employee, 29 A.L.R. 532 (1924). In other cases, union members refused to work on material produced or transported by non-union labor or refused to produce for their employer materials to be supplied to non-union businesses. See Annot., Liability of Labor Organization for Inducing Breach of Contract to Furnish or Accept Material, 29 A.L.R. 562 (1924); Annot., Right of Union to Refuse to Work on Materials Produced or Transported by Nonunion Labor, 52 A.L.R. 1144 (1928). Suppose union members refuse work because it involves working with non-union employees of a contractor? See Boylston Housing Corp. v. O'Toole, 321 Mass. 538, 74 N.E.2d 288 (1947) (not liable for refusing to do work necessary to elevator companies' performance of contract to install elevator in plaintiff's building).

3. Union activity is now largely covered by statute. Congress has preempted much of state law, including tort law. See San Diego Building Trades Council v. Garmon, 359 U.S. 236 (1959). Concerning areas still subject to state law, see Prosser, Law of Torts 967–969 (4th ed. 1971); McCoid, State Regulation of Labor-Management Relations: The Impact of Garmon and Landrum-Griffin, 48 Iowa L. Rev. 578 (1963). On the question of when a labor union incurs tort liability for the conduct of its officers and members, see Annot., Liability of Labor Union or its Membership for Torts Committed by Officers, Members, Pickets, or Others, in Connection with Lawful Primary Labor Activities, 36 A.L.R.3d 405 (1971) (union liable when union officers or membership authorized, participated in or ratified tortious acts).

4. Is an employer's customer or supplier liable for inducing the discharge of an employee at will? It has been held that a customer or potential customer acting in good faith will not incur liability for refusing to patronize a business unless an employee is fired. Liability may, however, attach if there is malice or other motive not reasonably related to a legitimate business interest. Cf. Smith v. Ford Motor Co., 289 N.C. 71, 221 S.E.2d 282 (1976) (manufacturer pressured dealer to fire manager active in dealers' alliance); Hill Grocery Co. v. Carroll, 223 Ala. 376, 136 So. 789 (1931) (former employer had worker discharged by threatening to discontinue business with new employer); Thompson v. Rinker Materials of Florida, Inc., 390 F. Supp. 2d 1165 (M.D. Fla. 2005) (driver lost job because defendant, driver's former employer, would not permit driver to make deliveries to its facilities). Compare Lee v. Levi Strauss & Co., 897 S.W.2d 501 (Tex. App. 1995) (plaintiffs discharged because of major contractor's dissatisfaction with their performance). Suppose the customer ends its business relationship with the employer, resulting in an employee's discharge because the employee is no longer needed to serve the customer? See Tennessee Coal, Iron & Railroad Co. v. Kelly, 163 Ala. 348, 50 So. 1008 (1909) (customer not liable, whatever its motives, if it did only what it had right to do — terminate contract by mutual agreement of parties).

5. Is a workers' compensation insurer liable for inducing an employee's discharge by threatening to cancel the employer's policy? See American Surety Co. v. Schottenbauer, 257 F.2d 6 (8th Cir. 1958), in which the insurer's justification — its business interest in avoiding bad insurance risks — was held to be a jury question, and the evidence was found to support a verdict for the discharged employee. There was evidence that the insurer had made false statements to the employer; that the fired employee, though suffering from dis-

ease, had responded to treatment; and that the employer had not been informed that it could obtain workers' compensation insurance elsewhere without additional cost.

6. Have courts been more willing to allow liability in these cases because of the individual worker's need for continuation of employment and the weak position of the worker relative to the power wielded by a labor organization or business? If so, would this be extended to other situations involving a relatively weak party dependent upon the continuation of an at-will relationship? This could be applied to product distributors and franchisees, who are vulnerable to termination of the distributorship or franchise by the manufacturer or franchisor. What other factors would determine liability? See A.S. Rampell, Inc. v. Hyster Co., 3 N.Y.2d 369, 165 N.Y.S.2d 475, 144 N.E.2d 371 (1957).

Adler, Barish, Daniels, Levin and Creskoff v. Epstein

Supreme Court of Pennsylvania
482 Pa. 416, 393 A.2d 1175 (1978),
cert. denied, 442 U.S. 907 (1979)

ROBERTS, Justice....

[Four salaried associates of the Adler Barish law firm decided to leave and form their own partnership. Immediately after their departure, they informed Adler Barish clients on whose cases they had worked that the clients could transfer their legal affairs to the former associates (or any other attorney). One of the former associates, when informed that an Adler Barish client with an open case wished to have him continue to act for the client, would send the client a form letter with which the client could discharge Adler Barish and direct it to hand over the client's file to the former associate. Adler Barish obtained an injunction which permanently restrained the former associates from communicating with clients represented by the firm in active legal matters. (This did not preclude the mailing of a brief professional announcement of the new firm or the representation of clients who voluntarily selected defendants in preference to Adler Barish.) The injunction was reversed by the Superior Court, from which Adler Barish appealed.]

The Code of Professional Responsibility, DR 2-103(A) (as adopted, 1974), provides: "A lawyer shall not recommend employment, as a private practitioner, of himself, his partner, or associate to a non-lawyer who has not sought his advice regarding employment of a lawyer." See also Code of Professional Responsibility, DR 2-104(A). Appellees clearly violated this "proscription against self-recommendation." ...

Ohralik v. Ohio State Bar Association, 436 U.S. 447 (1978), makes plain that ... states may constitutionally impose sanctions upon attorneys engaging in conduct which violates these disciplinary rules, even though the conduct involves "commercial speech." ...

... Section 766 of the Restatement (Second) of Torts (Tent. Draft No. 23, 1977), states ...: "One who intentionally and improperly interferes with the performance of a contract (except a contract to marry) between another and a third person by inducing or otherwise causing the third person not to perform the contract, is subject to liability to the other for the pecuniary loss resulting to the other from the third person's failure to perform the contract." ...

An examination of this case in light of Restatement (Second) of Torts, § 766, reveals that the sole dispute is whether appellees' conduct is "improper." ...

... "What is or is not privileged conduct in a given situation is not susceptible of precise definition. [Harper & James, The Law of Torts] refer in general to interferences which 'are sanctioned by the "rules of the game" which society has adopted', and to 'the area of socially acceptable conduct which the law regards as privileged,' id. at 510, 511, and treat the subject in detail in §§ 6.12 and 6.13." [*Glenn v. Point Park College*, 441 Pa. 474, 482, 272 A.2d 895, 899 (1971).] We are guided, too, by Section 767 of Restatement (Second) of Torts, which focuses on what factors should be considered in determining whether conduct is "improper:" "In determining whether an actor's conduct in intentionally interfering with an existing contract or a prospective contractual relation of another is improper or not, consideration is given to the following factors: (a) The nature of the actor's conduct, (b) The actor's motive, (c) The interest of the other with which the actor's conduct interferes, (d) The interests sought to be advanced by the actor, (e) The proximity or remoteness of the actor's conduct to the interference and (f) The relations between the parties."[17]

We find nothing in the "'rules of the game' which society has adopted" which sanctions appellees' conduct. Indeed, the rules which apply to those who enjoy the privilege of practicing law in the Commonwealth expressly disapprove appellees' method of obtaining clients. We find such a departure from "[r]ecognized ethical codes" "significant in evaluating the nature of [appellees'] conduct." Restatement (Second) of Torts, supra at § 767 comment c. All the reasons underlying our Disciplinary Rules' "proscription against [appellees'] self-recommendation," especially the concern that appellees' contacts too easily could overreach and unduly influence Adler Barish clients with active cases, are relevant here. . . .

It is true that, upon termination of their employment relationship with Adler Barish, appellees were free to engage in their own business venture. See Restatement (Second) of Agency, § 396(a) (1958) ("[u]nless otherwise agreed, after termination of the agency, the agent . . . has no duty not to compete with the principal"). But appellees' right to pursue their own business interests is not absolute. "[u]nless otherwise agreed, after the termination of the agency, the agent . . . has a duty to the principal not to take advantage of a still subsisting confidential relation created during the prior agency relation." Restatement (Second) of Agency, supra at § 396(d).

Appellees' contacts were possible because Adler Barish partners trusted appellees with the high responsibility of developing its clients' cases. From this position of trust and responsibility, appellees were able to gain knowledge of the details, and status, of each case to which appellees had been assigned. In the atmosphere surrounding appellees' departure, appellees' contacts unduly suggested a course of action for Adler Barish clients and unfairly prejudiced Adler Barish. No public interest is served in condoning use of confidential information which has these effects. Clients too easily may suffer in the end. . . .

. . . [T]he court of common pleas correctly determined that Adler Barish is entitled to relief.

[Reversed. Manderino, J., delivered a dissenting opinion.]

Notes

1. It is well-established in American law that when a person intentionally interferes with contractual relations by means that are unlawful in themselves, he is subject to liability even if no breach of contract is caused and defendant is not motivated by a purpose

---

17. Thus, new Restatement (Second) of Torts focuses upon whether conduct is "proper," rather than "privileged." . . .

to cause harm. "Unlawful" means include conduct that is prohibited by statute or un-codified criminal law and conduct that gives rise to a tort action against the actor (not nec-essarily by the person complaining of interference with contract), at least when fault is a basis of liability. Breach of contract, other civil wrongs that do not require fault for lia-bility, fraudulent statements and threats to commit unlawful acts may also constitute un-lawful means. See Top Service Body Shop, Inc. v. Allstate Insurance Co., 283 Or. 201, 582 P.2d 1365 (1978); Leigh Furniture and Carpet Co. v. Isom, 657 P.2d 293 (Utah 1982); Prosser & Keeton, Law of Torts 991–994 (5th ed. 1984). This subject is treated more ex-tensively in the materials on interference with performance of contract, pp. 155–164, infra, and interference with prospective advantage, pp. 164–210, infra, where unlawful means also is a basis of liability. An employee owes a duty of loyalty (fidelity) to his em-ployer until the employment ends. The employer can sue the employee for loss caused by breach of this duty and it can provide the element of unlawful means in an action for in-terference with contract.

2. Restatement (Second) of Torts has no definite rule of liability for interference with contract or prospective advantage by unlawful means. Instead, interference must be "im-proper," with consideration given to the list of factors set forth in § 767. Is this a satisfac-tory basis of liability for interference with contract? The final draft adds to the factors quoted in the *Adler Barish* case "the social interests in protecting the freedom of action of the actor and the contractual interests of the other." In *Adler Barish*, did the Restate-ment approach produce a result different from what would be anticipated under tradi-tional principles of liability? Rule 7.3 of the A.B.A. Model Rules of Professional Conduct permits a lawyer to solicit business from a former client. If this were in force in Pennsyl-vania when the *Adler Barish* case arose, would the result have been different? Concern-ing the preparations an employee may make before leaving the employment, as well as competition with a former employer, see the comments to Restatement (Third) of Agency § 8.04 (2006).

3. In another action against a former associate who had solicited clients of plaintiff's law firm, Fred Siegel Co., L.P.A. v. Arter & Hadden, 85 Ohio St. 3d 171, 707 N.E.2d 853 (1999), the court stated that the standards of the Disciplinary Rules of the Code of Pro-fessional Responsibility were relevant to, but not determinative of, the propriety of the attorney's conduct for purposes of an interference with contract claim. The court noted that the purposes underlying tort law differed from the purposes of attorney disciplinary actions. The interests of clients in receiving information relevant to their decision-making in choosing legal representation were also involved, and Restatement (Second) of Torts § 768 allowed competition that involved causing a third person not to continue a con-tract at will. This was not "improper" interference unless wrongful means were employed or an unlawful restraint of trade was created. Improper use or disclosure of confidential information belonging to plaintiff might be such wrongful means.

4. In an action for interference with a definite contract, there is ordinarily no privilege of competition, see pp. 123–143, supra, but such a privilege is traditionally recognized in the case of a contract terminable at will. See Macklin v. Logan, 334 Md. 287, 639 A.2d 112 (1994); Vincent Horwitz Co. v. Cooper, 352 Pa. 7, 41 A.2d 870 (1945). The privilege of competition generally extends to at-will employment contracts. Thus there is usually no liability for enticing away an employee whose employment is not for a definite term and who is not bound by a covenant not to complete. See Orkin Exterminating Co., Inc. v. Martin Co., 240 Ga. 662, 242 S.E.2d 135 (1978); Annot., Liability for Inducing Employee Not Engaged for Definite Term to Move to Competitor, 24 A.L.R.3d 821 (1969). Under what circumstances can it be tortious to offer alternative employment to employees at

will? According to Albee Homes, Inc. v. Caddie Homes, Inc., 417 Pa. 177, 207 A.2d 768 (1969), it is unlawful to systematically induce employees to leave plaintiff and work for another if the purpose is to cripple plaintiff's business organization. This would occur, for instance, if the employees were lured with the intent of having them disclose plaintiff's trade secrets or "steal" plaintiff's customers. Cf. Reeves v. Hanlon, 33 Cal. 4th 1140, 17 Cal. Rptr. 3d 289, 95 P.3d 513 (2004). If, as was found in the *Albee Homes* case, defendant's motive is to obtain gifted or skilled employees, his conduct is justified and not a basis for liability. What if defendant knows that an employee is critical to plaintiff's business but not to defendant's?

5. Interference with an attorney's contract can occur if an opposing party persuades the client to withdraw or settle a claim. Can this be a tort to the attorney? What if a liability insurance company induces the client to settle and dispense with the attorney's services? In Herron v. State Farm Mutual Insurance Co., 56 Cal. 2d 202, 14 Cal. Rptr. 294, 363 P.2d 310 (1961), the company's interest in settling the claim was found to be insufficient justification for interference with the attorney's expectation of receiving a contingency fee. See also Greenberg v. Panama Transport Co., 185 F. Supp. 320 (D. Mass. 1960), vacated, 290 F.2d 125 (1st Cir. 1961), cert. denied, 368 U.S. 891 (1961) (using misrepresentations, employers induced injured seaman to discharge attorney retained for damages claim against employers and accept optional compensation provided in employment contract); Edwards v. Travelers Insurance of Hartford, Connecticut, 563 F.2d 105 (6th Cir. 1977) (liability insurer fraudulently induced claimant to disavow representation by plaintiff and accept settlement). Should the attorney have a claim if the client, anxious for payment, approaches the insurer on his own and accepts a settlement offer? An action was permitted in Ronald M. Sharrow, Chartered v. State Farm Mutual Automobile Insurance Co., 306 Md. 754, 511 A.2d 492 (1986). See generally Annot., Liability in Tort for Interference with Attorney-Client Relationship, 90 A.L.R.4th 621 (1991).

C. Interference with Performance of Contract

National Phonograph Company, Ltd. v. Edison-Bell Consolidated Phonograph Company, Ltd.

Court of Appeal
[1908] 1 Ch. 335

[Plaintiffs imported phonographs and records. Their "factors" (wholesale traders) and retail dealers were required to sign agreements that they would not supply plaintiffs' products to dealers on plaintiffs' "suspended list." Factors were not to supply products to dealers who had not signed a retailer's agreement. Plaintiffs placed defendants, manufacturers of phonographic products, on the suspended list in order to stop them from selling plaintiffs' products. Two of defendants' agents obtained numerous phonographs from factors at wholesale prices by assuming fictitious names, falsely representing that they were independent dealers, and signing plaintiffs' retailer agreement form. Plaintiffs sought damages and injunctive relief. They claimed that defendants, by carrying plaintiffs' phonographs, made sales of defendants' records and phonographs to customers who otherwise would have purchased plaintiffs' products and, by circumventing plaintiffs' ban of sales to suspended dealers, might dissuade retailers from stocking plaintiffs' products. The trial court held that there was no liability for interference with contractual relations because no damage had been proved and because the factors, being deceived, did not breach their agreements with plaintiffs by selling to a suspended dealer.]

BUCKLEY L.J....

... In *Allen v. Flood* [[1898] A.C. 96] Lord Watson says: "There are, in my opinion, two grounds only upon which a person who procures the act of another can be made legally responsible for its consequences. In the first place, he will incur liability if he knowingly and for his own ends induces that other person to commit an actionable wrong. In the second place, when the act induced is within the right of the immediate actor, and is therefore not wrongful in so far as he is concerned, it may yet be to the detriment of a third party; and in that case, according to the law laid down by the majority in *Lumley v. Gye* [p. 123, supra], the inducer may be held liable if he can be shewn to have procured his object by the use of illegal means directed against that third party." ... [Defendants] argued that an action will not lie unless the defendants' act was intended to damage the plaintiffs. Assuming (contrary as I think to the fact) that it could be maintained in this case that the act of these defendants was not intended to damage these plaintiffs, the proposition is not, I think, one which can be maintained. I find Lord Halsbury, in the *South Wales Miners' Case* [[1905] A.C. 239], saying that if the miners there were sincerely in the belief that their employers would benefit by their collieries being interrupted that was no sort of excuse for breaking a contract when the co-contractor refused to allow the breach.

... The factor was deceived, and, for that reason, an action for breach of contract may not lie against him. He acted innocently, and did not voluntarily commit any breach of his contract. In my judgment this does not differentiate the present case in the respondents' favour from the first proposition found in Lord Watson's words. The defendant company is in no better case because the wrong to the plaintiffs which, in fact, was done was, by reason of the defendants' deceit, done innocently so far as the factor was concerned. Again, if this is not well founded, then, in my judgment, Lord Watson's second proposition at any rate applies. Assuming that the act induced was within the right of the factor in the sense that he, being innocent, did no wrong, and was therefore not wrongful so far as the factor was concerned, yet it was to the detriment of a third party, namely, the plaintiffs. In that case, says Lord Watson, the inducer, that is, the defendants, may be held liable if the defendants can be shown to have procured their object by the use of illegal means directed against the plaintiffs. The deceit which the defendants practised brings them, I think, exactly within these words. Let me now take Lord Macnaghten's words [in *Quinn v. Leathem*, [1901] A.C. 510]. The act which the defendants did was, I think, a violation of a legal right of the plaintiffs, because it interfered with the contractual relations subsisting between the plaintiffs and the factors, and there was no sufficient justification for such interference....

Upon these grounds I think that it was an actionable wrong that the defendants, by deceit, induced the factors to act contrary to the duty which they contractually owed to the plaintiffs, and that this action will lie....

[Lord Alverstone, C.J., and Kennedy, L.J., delivered concurring opinions, finding sufficient evidence of damage, at least of lost record sales, to warrant an injunction. Defendants were enjoined from inducing factors to sell plaintiffs' goods by misrepresenting that the purchaser was not defendants.]

Piedmont Cotton Mills, Inc. v.
H.W. Ivey Construction Company, Inc.

Georgia Court of Appeals
109 Ga. App. 876, 137 S.E.2d 528 (1964)

[The petition alleged that defendants, using a tractor and cable, wilfully and maliciously demolished work on the bridge plaintiff was building as general contractor for the landowner. Plaintiff bore the expense and sought to recover it, with punitive damages. The trial court overruled defendants' demurrers.]

BELL, Presiding Judge.

[Plaintiff, constructing real property with the permission of the landowner, was not in possession of the realty. Consequently, it had no action for trespass or damage to the realty. But this was not fatal to the petition.] ...

As shown by the case of Southern Ry. Co. v. Chambers, 126 Ga. 404, 55 S.E. 37, the tort of the interference with contractual relations is not limited to the procurement of a breach of contract.... The holding in Chambers signifies that one under a duty to render a performance has a property interest in the contract in that he has the right to render the required performance free from unjustified and unprivileged intentional invasions that retard performance or make the performance more difficult or expensive. Interference of that type constitutes an actionable tort which embraces within its scope all intentional invasions of contractual relations, including any act injuring or destroying property and so interfering with the performance itself, regardless of whether breach of contract is induced.

Interference with contractual relations is an *intentional* tort, and if intentional interference is to be required, it presupposes knowledge of the plaintiff's interests or, at least, of facts that would lead a reasonable man to believe in their existence.

However, T.W. Tift's act of going upon the land of General Warehouse 2, Inc. and demolishing the work that had been accomplished on its bridge constitutes conduct unlawful in itself regardless of any specific intent to injure the petitioner in its contractual relations. Under the doctrine that one must be presumed to intend the consequences of his unlawful act, it must be accepted that Tift intended to injure the petitioner in its contractual relations.

It is a question of fact, and thus for the jury, whether the defendant has played a material and substantial part in causing the plaintiff's loss of any benefits of the contract....

[Affirmed.]

Notes

1. What is the basis of liability in these cases? If the basis is intentional interference with a contract by unlawful means, what means are "unlawful"? What intent is required for liability? Note that in Attorney-General for New South Wales v. Perpetual Trustee Co. (Ltd.), [1955] A.C. 457, 483–484 (P.C.), it was said: "If the law had developed in all respects logically, [Lumley v. Gye] would be an authority for saying that, if Miss Wagner had not been maliciously enticed from the service of the plaintiff but had been by battery or otherwise wrongfully prevented from serving him, the plaintiff would have had a good cause of action against the wrongdoer. But it has never been suggested that this is the law. On the contrary, it is fundamental ... that the mere fact that an in-

jury to A. prevents a third party from getting from A. a benefit which he would otherwise have obtained, does not invest the third party with a right of action against the wrongdoer."

2. There may be liability for interference with contract caused by defendant's knowingly false statement. What if a prospective purchaser renounces a sales contract by falsely claiming that the seller's agent made misrepresentations in the course of the negotiations and deprives the agent of the commission expected on the sale? See Glover v. Lee, Higginson Corp., 95 F. Supp. 504 (D. Mass. 1950) (commissioned employee stated cause of action against prospective purchaser for interference with employment contract). Mere mistake is insufficient. In Terry v. Dairymen's League Cooperative Association, Inc., p. 143, supra, there was no liability in the absence of evidence that defendant's agents acted in bad faith in stating that plaintiff was giving up his delivery contracts.

3. Because a third party has claimed a leasehold interest in real estate, a prospective purchaser of the property insists that the purchase agreement permit withdrawal from the purchase if the claim is not released. The third party refuses to execute a release, although its claim is invalid. Can it be held liable to the seller for interference with contract? See Lake Shore Investors v. Rite Aid Corp., 67 Md. App. 743, 509 A.2d 727 (1986).

4. A manufacturer contracts to sell its entire output to a customer. Can the customer hold liable trespassers who invade the manufacturer's plant, stop its machinery, and thus prevent goods from being furnished under the contract? Compare Dale v. Grant, 34 N.J.L. 142 (Sup. Ct. 1870) (no liability), with Aalfo Co. v. Kinney, 105 N.J.L. 345, 144 A. 715 (1929) (liability when stockholders of manufacturer unlawfully took possession of its plant, preventing performance of contract).

5. In Mintuck v. Valley River Band No. 63A, [1976] 4 W.W.R. 543 (Man. Q.B.), aff'd, [1977] 2 W.W.R. 309, (1977) 75 D.L.R.3d 589 (Man. C.A.), plaintiff held a ten-year lease of agricultural lands on an Indian reserve. Members of the Indian band harassed plaintiff and his family and interfered with his farming operations. This was allegedly done with the aim of forcing plaintiff to abandon farming the land, which he eventually did. The trial court found that interference with the lease was tortious as interference with contract by individual band members and the band, which acted in its official capacity. Judgment was affirmed on the basis of liability for the torts of "intimidation" and "unlawful interference with economic interests," as to which see pp. 184–186, 189–190, infra.

6. An auto maker, M, agrees with a tire manufacturer, A, to use A's tires any time M's cars are publicly exhibited. On the night prior to an automobile exhibition, a rival tire manufacturer, B, substitutes its tires for A's on M's cars. Is B liable to A? To M? See G.W.K., Ltd. v. Dunlop Rubber Co., Ltd., (1926) 42 T.L.R. 376 (K.B.D.), appeal dismissed, (1926) 42 T.L.R. 593 (C.A.) (where B aware of agreement between A and M, B could be liable to both parties).

7. Pursuant to a concerted plan to defraud both a debtor and his creditors, defendants obtain the debtor's property for a fraction of its value under the guise of foreclosure sales. Are defendants liable to a creditor prevented in this way from collecting a debt? See Keene Lumber Co. v. Leventhal, 165 F.2d 815 (1st Cir. 1948) (liability; could be no justification when means used were unlawful). Can the creditors of a financially troubled corporation hold liable the corporate directors who, for no consideration, transfer most of the corporation's assets to a "dummy" corporation which the directors control, thereby hindering efforts to collect the debts? See Einhorn v. Westmount Investments Ltd., (1969) 69 W.W.R. 31, 6 D.L.R.3d 71 (Sask. Q.B.), aff'd, (1970) 73 W.W.R. 161, 11 D.L.R.3d 509 (Sask. C.A.) (cause of action stated).

8. Plaintiff contracts with a town to keep a highway in repair for a period of three years. Defendant causes damage to the road during the period, thereby increasing the costs of repair. Is defendant liable? See McNary v. Chamberlain, 34 Conn. 384 (1862) (liability if acts done with intent to injure plaintiff). Suppose defendant wrongfully repossesses the equipment plaintiff intends to use for the road maintenance? See Hickman Construction, Inc. v. South Umpqua State Bank, 109 Or. App. 527, 820 P.2d 838 (1991). Would defendant be liable to the town if it had to pay more to the contractor? Cf. Sunshine Custom Paints & Body, Inc. v. South Douglas Highway Water & Sewer District, 173 P.3d 398 (Wyo. 2007).

9. Restatement (Second) of Torts § 766A (1979) provides: "One who intentionally and improperly interferes with the performance of a contract (except a contract to marry) between another and a third person, by preventing the other from performing the contract or causing his performance to be more expensive or burdensome, is subject to liability to the other for the pecuniary loss resulting to him." This section was applied in Nesler v. Fisher and Co., Inc., 452 N.W.2d 191 (Iowa 1990). Defendant, the owner of real estate leased to county agencies, thwarted plaintiff's plans to renovate and purchase an office building and lease space in it to agencies relocating from defendant's premises. Defendant's actions included pressuring the building inspector to take action against plaintiff's project, suing the county board of supervisors for failure to accept his bid for rental to county agencies, and arranging for an attorney to initiate suit, without charge to the client, over the building's failure to provide adequate handicapped access. (Both suits were dismissed.) The lawsuits, delays and loss of confidence in the project caused by defendant resulted in plaintiff's losing investors and bank finance. Plaintiff had to give up his equity in the building project. The court held that plaintiff stated an action for interference with his performance of the contracts for purchase of the building and lease of space in it to tenants. The suits and building complaints initiated by defendant could be the basis of liability if defendant had an improper motive.

10. Restatement (Second) of Torts § 766 (1979) provides for liability when defendant intentionally and improperly causes someone not to perform a contract with plaintiff. In Price v. Sorrell, 784 P.2d 614 (Wyo. 1989), a majority of the court refused to accept § 766A, although it had adopted § 766. The breach or non-performance of a contract, or the loss of a prospective contractual relation, was considered a "reasonable bright line that reduces the potential for abuse" of the actions for interference with contract or prospective advantage, but § 766A required only that plaintiff's performance of a contract become more expensive or burdensome. This was "too speculative and subject to abuse to provide a meaningful basis for a cause of action."

11. One issue in Nesler v. Fisher and Co., Inc., supra, was a claim of damages for plaintiff's emotional distress. The claim was allowed. Allowance of damages for emotional distress and harm to reputation in an interference with contract action is supported by Restatement (Second) of Torts § 774A(1) (1979). See also Pino v. Protection Maritime Insurance Co., Ltd., 490 F. Supp. 277 (D. Mass. 1980); Trimble v. City and County of Denver, 697 P.2d 716 (Colo. 1985). In one of the few opinions to consider the question at length, the Supreme Court of Oregon decided that damages for emotional distress, injury to reputation and other non-economic loss could be recovered, but only when it should have been expected as a common and predictable result of disrupting the type of relationship interfered with. Mooney v. Johnson Cattle Co., Inc., 291 Or. 709, 634 P.2d 1333 (1981). Should defendant be held liable for interference with contractual relations when emotional distress is the only type of damage claimed or proved? Citing Restatement (Second) of Torts § 47 (1965), which provides that tortious conduct "does not make

the actor liable for an emotional distress which is the only legal consequence of his conduct," the court in Tose v. First Pennsylvania Bank, N.A., 648 F.2d 879 (3d Cir. 1981), cert. denied, 454 U.S. 893 (1981), decided that there was no liability in these circumstances. Contra, Westfield Development Co. v. Rifle Investment Associates, 786 P.2d 1112 (Colo. 1990).

D.C. Thomson & Company Ltd. v. Deakin
Court of Appeal
[1952] Ch. 646

[Workers employed in plaintiffs' printing and publishing business began to strike to oppose plaintiffs' requirement that its employees not join unions. Plaintiffs dismissed them and threatened to dismiss other union members. The union declared plaintiffs "black" and induced members of other unions to lend support by not handling products of or supplies bound for plaintiffs. Bowaters was notified by its loaders and drivers that they might be unwilling to handle paper destined for plaintiffs. Without calling on its employees to handle the paper, Bowaters informed plaintiffs that because of union action it could not supply paper pursuant to its contract with plaintiffs. It thereby breached the contract. Plaintiffs sought injunctions to restrain officials of the unions of plaintiffs' and Bowaters' employees from causing or procuring breaches of contracts between plaintiffs and Bowaters or other suppliers. The trial court held for defendants on the ground that they never directly induced Bowaters to break its contract with plaintiffs. Defendants had only induced Bowaters' employees to refuse to handle supplies, thereby causing Bowaters to breach its contract with plaintiffs.]

EVERSHED M.R. . . .

[Defendants argued] that the tort must still be properly confined to such direct intervention, that is, to cases where the intervener or persuader uses by personal intervention persuasion on the mind of one of the parties to the contract so as to procure that party to break it.

I am unable to agree that any such limitation is logical, rational or part of our law. In such cases where the intervener (if I may call him such) does so directly act upon the mind of a party to the contract as to cause him to break it . . . the intervention itself is thereby considered wrongful.

I cannot think that the result is any different if the intervener, instead of so acting upon the mind of the contracting party himself, by some other act, tortious in itself, prevents the contracting party from performing the bargain. A simple case is where the intervener, for example, physically detains the contracting party so that the contracting party is rendered unable by the detention to perform the contract. . . .

. . . So far I have considered only the case in which the intervener directly acts himself, either by persuasion or by some wrongful act of his own. What is the situation if he attains the same result, indirectly, by bringing his persuasion or procuration to bear upon some third party, commonly a servant of the contracting party, but possibly an independent third person? In my judgment, it is reasonably plain (and the result, as it seems to me, would otherwise be highly illogical and irrational) that, if the act which the third party is persuaded to do is itself an unlawful act or a wrongful act (including in that phrase a breach of contract) and the other elements are present (namely, knowledge and intention to do the damage which is in fact suffered), then the result is the same and the intervener or procurer will be liable for the loss or damage which the injured party sustains....

I have come to the conclusion that the result is otherwise, where the persons induced, being third parties, servants or otherwise, are induced to do acts which are in themselves lawful and involve no breach of contracts on their part with the contracting party....

My instance was of a contract between A and B, whereby A had contracted to sell his house to B at a price beneficial to A. I will assume that it had been disclosed by A to B that there was in fact a public right of way passing close the property, but that B had been informed, correctly, that the use of such right of way had become so slender that it was of little, if any, practical significance. Then let it be supposed that some third party, desiring to cause B to resile from the contract with A and to deprive A of the benefit of the contract, persuaded a number of individuals in the neighborhood to resume the use of the right of way, so that there then passed near the premises a considerable stream of persons, all legitimately using the right of way as such, as a result of which B decided that the amenities of the premises were so damaged that he was no longer willing to continue.

I find it for myself exceedingly difficult to suppose that, the exercise of the right of way by the persons persuaded being lawful, the intervener would be liable according to the principles of the law for having persuaded them to do that lawful thing....

... Let it be supposed that A had made a contract to supply certain goods to B and that the intervener, knowing of the contract and intending to deprive B of its benefit, had proceeded to go into the market and buy up all the goods that he could find of that character, so as to render it impossible for A in fact to perform the contract. Again, I think it is impossible to say, according to the principles of our law, that the intervener in such a case was acting tortiously....

Dealing first with individual contractors, it seems to me that the intervener, assuming in all cases that he knows of the contract and acts with the aim and object of procuring its breach to the damage of B, one of the contracting parties, will be liable not only (1) if he directly intervenes by persuading A to break it, but also (2) if he intervenes by the commission of some act wrongful in itself so as to prevent A from in fact performing his contract; and also (3) if he persuades a third party, for example, a servant of A, to do an act in itself wrongful or not legitimate (as committing a breach of a contract of service with A) so as to render, as was intended, impossible A's performance of his contract with B.

In the case of a company, the approach to or the persuasion of a managing director, or of some person having like authority, may be regarded as being in all respects equivalent to the direct approach of the individual contractor ... ; but, if the approach is made to other servants of the company, the case, in my view, becomes parallel to an approach made not to the contracting party himself, but to some servant of the contracting party, so that the intervener will only be liable if the act which he procures the servant to do is either a breach of contract towards the servant's master or is otherwise tortious in itself....

... [T]here was, on the evidence, no breach of contract by any workmen, since Bowaters, for reasons which I doubt not were prudent, took the line that they would not order any man either to load or to drive paper for the plaintiffs. They accepted the situation as they found it and made no attempt to contrive to get the paper to the plaintiffs by any other means....

... There were, in fact, so far as I can see, no wrongful acts at all on the workmen's part. There is, moreover, no evidence that there was actual knowledge, on the part of any of the persons charged, of the contract or of any contract between Bowaters and the plaintiffs, assuming such contract to have been broken; or at least, if these persons thought that there might be or was some contract, any knowledge of the terms of the contract....

I come to the conclusion that this appeal fails and should be dismissed.

[Jenkins and Morris, L.JJ., delivered concurring opinions.]

Notes

1. This case no longer represents English law, as the House of Lords eventually rejected the whole idea of a tort of interference with contract wider than the Lumley v. Gye tort of inducing breach of contract. OBG Ltd. v. Allan, [2008] A.C. 1 (H.L.). But American law continues to accept intentional interference with a contract as a tort that goes well beyond inducing or procuring breach.

2. The United States Golf Association, a non-profit association of golf courses and clubs, determines the content of the Rules of Golf. The Rules are applied by the U.S.G.A. in the national championships it conducts and are followed in almost all major amateur and professional golf tournaments conducted by other entities. The U.S.G.A. determined that use of a certain golf shoe would violate the rules governing equipment that may be used in the game. It notified other golf associations and the shoe's manufacturer of this decision. As a result, some retail sellers of the shoe returned their stock to the manufacturer and numerous other retailers stopped placing orders. Did the manufacturer have an action against the U.S.G.A.? Would there be an action if a purpose to cause harm to the manufacturer could be established? See Weight-Rite Golf Corp. v. United States Golf Association, 766 F. Supp. 1104 (M.D. Fla. 1991), aff'd, 953 F.2d 651 (11th Cir. 1992).

3. Tortious interference with contract may be found when defendant calls an unlawful strike among the workers of plaintiff's supplier. Quinlivan v. Dail-Overland Co., 274 F. 56 (6th Cir. 1921). When defendant refuses to carry out his contract to supply goods to plaintiff's supplier. Knickerbocker Ice Co. of Baltimore City v. Gardiner Dairy Co. of Baltimore City, 107 Md. 556, 69 A. 405 (1908). When defendant refuses to accept deliveries by plaintiff. Wilkinson v. Powe, p. 135, supra. Or when defendant's breach of his purchase agreement deprives an agent or broker of his commission. Glover v. Lee, Higginson Corp., p. 158, supra; Livermore v. Crane, 26 Wash. 529, 67 P. 221 (1901). How is the principal case different? If defendant's conduct is a breach of contract in itself and defendant knows that plaintiff will suffer loss as a result, is this sufficient for liability? See Windsor Securities, Inc. v. Hartford Life Insurance Co., 986 F.2d 655 (3d Cir. 1993) (no; not wrongful conduct); Winternitz v. Summit Hills Joint Venture, 73 Md. App. 16, 532 A.2d 1089 (1987), cert. denied, 312 Md. 17, 538 A.2d 778 (1988) (breach of contract might suffice, at least in combination with purpose to interfere with second contract).

4. In J.T. Stratford & Son Ltd. v. Lindley, [1965] A.C. 269 (H.L.), plaintiff repaired barges and hired out its own barges. Plaintiff's customers employed members of the watermen's union who regularly picked up and delivered rented and repaired barges. Because plaintiff's subsidiary negotiated an agreement with a rival union, officers of the watermen's union instructed union members not to take barges to plaintiff for repair or return after rental. Finding its business brought to a standstill, plaintiff sought to enjoin

the union embargo. An injunction was granted on the basis that the union officers were, by means of inducing union members to breach their employment contracts, knowingly causing the members' employers to breach their contractual obligation to plaintiff to return rented barges after the job for which they were hired. What if plaintiff's contracts excused late return of the barges if caused by a labor dispute, so there was no actual breach of these contracts? Cf. Merkur Island Shipping Corp. v. Laughton, [1983] 2 A.C. 570 (H.L.). Should procuring breach of a contract to which plaintiff is not a party be a basis of liability?

5. Suppose a term of a contract provides that in limited circumstances one party is excused from performance of an obligation otherwise owed to the other. Defendant, with the object of preventing performance to plaintiff, induces the other contracting party to create the circumstances in which performance is excused. Examples might include: (1) a contract under which plaintiff is appointed as broker and is to receive a commission if a sale of property is arranged within a certain period; defendant induces the property's owner not to enter a sale until this period expires, so that the commission will not be due; (2) a contract under which plaintiff is to receive the entire output of a factory at a fixed price for a certain period of years, subject to early termination if there is a change of ownership in the factory; in order to terminate the contract, the principal owners of the factory are induced to have it sold, or the owners decide on their own to procure sale of the factory to a corporation they control. Liability? See annotations cited p. 135, note 1 (real estate brokers); cases cited p. 168, note 4 (transfer of debtor's assets, to detriment of creditor).

6. A television station has contracts with the national networks under which the station is given the exclusive right to the first run of network and film programs in its community. Since the station can show only one program at a time, it arranges with the networks to film some programs for broadcast at a later time. A community antenna service receives programs of all networks from a large city some distance away, giving subscribing viewers a choice of programs when originally broadcast on the networks. The service's transmissions contain the commercials from the large city, not the local commercials. Since many people receive the antenna service, this hurts the local station's ability to attract sponsors for its broadcasts. Is the antenna service tortiously interfering with the station's contracts with the networks? See Cable Vision, Inc. v. KUTV, Inc., 211 F. Supp. 47 (D. Idaho 1962), rev'd, 335 F.2d 348 (9th Cir. 1964), cert. denied sub nom. Klix Corp. v. Cable Vision, Inc., 379 U.S. 989 (1965) (injunction granted). Compare R.C.A. Corp. v. Pollard, [1983] Ch. 135 (C.A.) (record companies with exclusive contract to market records of Elvis Presley performances had no action against person who marketed "bootleg" recordings of performances); OBG Ltd. v. Allan, [2008] A.C. 1 (H.L.) (magazine published surreptitiously obtained photographs of celebrity wedding, knowing that plaintiff had exclusive right to publish wedding photographs under contract with celebrities).

7. In 1989, the National Hockey League entered an agreement with Coca-Cola Ltd. under which Coca-Cola was designated as the official sponsor of the N.H.L., with the privilege of "associating exclusively with the N.H.L. in the soft-drink category." Diet Coke was designated as the "official Soft Drink of the N.H.L." and Coca-Cola was allowed to use N.H.L. symbols for its promotional programs. Under a separate agreement, another company received from the N.H.L. the right to control and license all advertising during Canadian television broadcasts of N.H.L. games. Some of the advertising time was purchased from the company by Pepsi-Cola Canada Ltd., which began a major promotion of its soft drinks during broadcasts of N.H.L. games. Was this actionable interference with the contractual rights of Coca-Cola or the N.H.L.? See Na-

tional Hockey League v. Pepsi-Cola Canada Ltd., [1992] 6 W.W.R. 216, (1992) 92 D.L.R.4th 349 (B.C. Sup. Ct.), aff'd, [1995] 5 W.W.R. 403, (1995) 122 D.L.R.4th 421 (B.C.C.A.).

Section 2. Interference with Prospective Advantage

A. Interference with Business

―――――――

Walker v. Cronin
Supreme Judicial Court of Massachusetts
107 Mass. 555 (1871)

WELLS, J. The declaration, in its first count, alleges that the defendant did, "unlawfully and without justifiable cause, molest, obstruct and hinder the plaintiffs from carrying on" their business of manufacture and sale of boots and shoes, "with the unlawful purpose of preventing the plaintiffs from carrying on their said business, and wilfully persuaded and induced a large number of persons who were in the employment of the plaintiffs," and others "who were about to enter into" their employment, "to leave and abandon the employment of the plaintiffs, without their consent and against their will;" whereby the plaintiffs lost the services of said persons, and the profits and advantages they would otherwise have made and received therefrom, and were put to large expenses to procure other suitable workmen, and suffered losses in their said business.

This sets forth sufficiently (1) intentional and wilful acts (2) calculated to cause damage to the plaintiffs in their lawful business, (3) done with the unlawful purpose to cause such damage and loss, without right or justifiable cause on the part of the defendant, (which constitutes malice,) and (4) actual damage and loss resulting.

The general principle is announced in Com. Dig. Action on the Case, A.: "In all cases where a man has a temporal loss or damage by the wrong of another, he may have an action upon the case to be repaired in damages." The intentional causing of such loss to another, without justifiable cause, and with the malicious purpose to inflict it, is of itself a wrong....

In the case of *Keeble v. Hickeringill*, as contained in a note to *Carrington v. Taylor*, 11 East, 571, 574, both actions being for damages by reason of frightening wild fowl from the plaintiff's decoy, Chief Justice Holt alludes to actions maintained for scandalous words which are actionable only by reason of being injurious to a man in his profession or trade, and adds: "How much more, when the defendant doth an actual and real damage to another when he is in the very act of receiving profit in his employment. Now there are two sorts of acts for doing damage to a man's employment, for which an action lies; the one is in respect of a man's privilege, the other is in respect of his property." After considering injuries to a man's franchise or privilege, he proceeds: "The other is where a violent or malicious act is done to a man's occupation, profession, or way of getting a livelihood; there an action lies in all cases." From the several reports of this case it is not clear whether the action was maintained on the ground that the wild ducks were frightened out of the plaintiff's decoy, as would appear from 3 Salk. 9, and Holt, 14, 17, 18; or upon the broader one, that they were driven away and prevented from resorting there, as the case is stated in 11 Mod. 74, 130. But the doctrine thus enunciated by Lord Holt covers both aspects of the case; as does his illustration of frightening boys from going to school, whereby loss was occasioned to the master. Of like import is the case of *Tarleton v. McGawley*, Peake, 205, in which Lord Kenyon held that an action would lie for frightening the natives upon the coast of Africa, and thus preventing them from coming to the plaintiff's vessel to trade, whereby he lost the profits of such trade.

There are indeed many authorities which appear to hold that to constitute an actionable wrong there must be a violation of some definite legal right of the plaintiff. But those are cases, for the most part at least, where the defendants were themselves acting in the lawful exercise of some distinct right, which furnished the defence of a justifiable cause for their acts, except so far as they were in violation of a superior right in another.

Thus every one has an equal right to employ workmen in his business or service; and if, by the exercise of this right in such manner as he may see fit, persons are induced to leave their employment elsewhere, no wrong is done to him whose employment they leave, unless a contract exists by which such other person has a legal right to the further continuance of their services. If such a contract exists, one who knowingly and intentionally procures it to be violated may be held liable for the wrong, although he did it for the purpose of promoting his own business.

One may dig upon his own land for water, or any other purpose, although he thereby cuts off the supply of water from his neighbor's well. *Greenleaf v. Francis*, 18 Pick. 117. It is intimated, in this case, that such acts might be actionable if done maliciously. But the rights of the owner of land being absolute therein, and the adjoining proprietor having no legal right to such a supply of water from lands of another, the superior right must prevail. Accordingly it is generally held that no action will lie against one for acts done upon his own land in the exercise of his rights of ownership, whatever the motive, if they merely deprive another of advantages, or cause a loss to him, without violating any legal right; that is, the motive in such case is immaterial.... [But] malicious acts without the justification of any right, that is, acts of a stranger, resulting in like loss or damage, might be actionable; and ... loss of advantages previously enjoyed, although not of vested legal right, might be a ground of damages recoverable against one who caused the loss without superior right or justifiable cause.

Every one has a right to enjoy the fruits and advantages of his own enterprise, industry, skill and credit. He has no right to be protected against competition; but he has a right to be free from malicious and wanton interference, disturbance or annoyance. If disturbance or loss come as a result of competition, or the exercise of like rights by others, it is *damnum absque injuriâ*, unless some superior right by contract or otherwise is interfered with. But if it come from the merely wanton or malicious acts of others, without the justification of competition or the service of any interest or lawful purpose, it then stands upon a different footing, and falls within the principle of the authorities first referred to....

In all these cases, the damage for which the recovery is had is not the loss of the value of actual contracts by reason of their non-fulfillment, but the loss of advantages, either of property or of personal benefit, which, but for such interference, the plaintiff would have been able to attain or enjoy....

... [T]he existence and defeat of rights by contract are not essential to the maintenance of an action for malicious wrong, when the defendant has no pretext of justifiable cause....

The difficulty in such cases is to make certain, by proof, that there has been in fact such loss as entitles the party to reparation; but that difficulty is not encountered in the present stage of this case, where all the facts alleged are admitted by the demurrer. The demurrer also admits the absence of any justifiable cause whatever. This decision is made upon the case thus presented, and does not apply to a case of interference by way of friendly advice, honestly given; nor is it in denial of the right of free expression of opinion. We have no occasion now to consider what would constitute justifiable cause.

The second and third counts recite contracts of the plaintiffs with their workmen for the performance of certain work in the manufacture of boots and shoes; and allege that the defendant, well knowing thereof, with the unlawful purpose of hindering and preventing the plaintiffs from carrying on their business, induced said persons to refuse and neglect to perform their contracts, whereby the plaintiffs suffered great damage in their business....

... [A] legal cause of action is sufficiently stated in each of the three counts of the declaration.

Demurrer overruled.

Notes

1. Early cases of interference with prospective advantage concerned physical interference with plaintiffs' trade. See Keeble v. Hickeringill and Tarleton v. M'Gawley, discussed in the principal case; Garret v. Taylor, (1620) Cro. Jac. 567, 79 Eng. Rep. 485, 2 Rolle 162, 81 Eng. Rep. 726 (K.B.) (defendant verbally threatened workmen with violence if they worked for plaintiff at his stone pit and threatened other persons with violence if they bought from plaintiff). Such conduct will still support an action. See Guillory v. Godfrey, 134 Cal. App. 2d 628, 286 P.2d 474 (1955) (intimidation of prospective customers due to employment of black cook); Roe v. Operation Rescue, 710 F. Supp. 577 (E.D. Pa. 1989), aff'd, 919 F.2d 857 (3d Cir. 1990) (blockades of clinics performing abortions). In these cases, defendants allegedly had and accomplished the purpose of preventing or hindering plaintiff's trade.

2. Suppose that defendant's purpose in the principal case was to induce plaintiffs to pay better wages to employees. Should the court have sustained the action? Suppose the purpose was to induce plaintiffs to provide safer working conditions for employees, bargain with an employees' union, or make better products? What if defendant wanted to drive plaintiffs out of business so that defendant could sell boots and shoes without competition from plaintiffs? Would the persons who were deterred from working for plaintiffs have an action?

3. Consider the following examples:

(a) Defendant maliciously has an employee of a railroad arrested, knowing that his claim against the employee is hopeless and false. The arrest causes loss to the railroad by delaying one of its trains. St. Johnsbury & Lake Champlain Railroad Co. v. Hunt, 55 Vt. 570 (1882) (railroad held to have cause of action).

(b) A blacksmith shoes a horse. Defendant loosens one of the horseshoes and drives a nail into the horse's foot, intending to make the horse's owner believe that the blacksmith's work is of poor quality. As a result, the blacksmith loses the owner's business. Hughes v. McDonough, 43 N.J.L. 459 (Sup. Ct. 1881) (blacksmith held to have cause of action).

(c) To satisfy a debt claim against an Italian pasta manufacturer, a freight forwarder refuses to release containers of the pasta to a U.S. importer and sells the pasta itself. Italverde Trading, Inc. v. Four Bills of Lading, 485 F. Supp. 2d 187 (E.D.N.Y. 2007) (actionable if freight forwarder committed conversion and knowingly interfered with plaintiffs' business relationships with customers).

(d) A dealer orders some stoves for resale. The carrier by mistake delivers the stoves to another dealer, which accepts them, knowing of the error, because stoves are in short supply. The first dealer loses the profit on the sale of the consigned stoves. Newark Hardware & Plumbing Supply Co. v. Stove Manufacturers Corp., 136 N.J.L. 401, 56

A.2d 605 (Sup. Ct. 1948) (dealer held to have cause of action; stove recipient's motive of self-enrichment sufficient to supply element of malice).

(e) Defendant, a regional association of dealers in hardware and farming implements, organizes a subsidiary known as the "Peddlers Association." Its avowed purpose is "competing with the peddlers," especially those selling buggies and wagons, though most of the association's members do not sell buggies or wagons. A manufacturer sells its buggies and wagons through agents. Defendant, through its subsidiary, hires men to follow each of the manufacturer's agents who attempt to conduct business in the region. The men follow the agents throughout the day as they visit prospective customers and interfere with the agent's conversations, usually offering no competitive merchandise. At times they make false statements about the manufacturer and its goods, and discourage and intimidate the agents. Evenson v. Spaulding, 150 F. 517 (9th Cir. 1907) (manufacturer granted injunction against defendant's conduct).

(f) Animal rights activists protest a circus' use of animals in demonstrations outside the entrance to the circus. The demonstrators form lines near patrons entering the circus, waiving placards and shouting "shame" and other slogans. Animal Liberation (Vic.) Inc. v. Gasser, [1991] 1 V.R. 51 (A.D.).

(g) After a dispute with an oil dealer, the owner of a trailer park denies the dealer entry to the park, preventing deliveries to the trailers. Morra v. Hill, 103 N.H. 492, 175 A.2d 824 (1961) (park owner bound to permit persons having business with trailer owners to have access to park, subject to reasonable limitations).

Mogul Steamship Company, Ltd. v. McGregor, Gow, & Company
Court of Appeal
(1889) 23 Q.B.D. 598, aff'd, [1892] A.C. 25 (H.L.)

[Defendants owned ships that carried tea from China to Europe. They organized a conference which acted for the purpose of driving competitors from this trade, so the conference's members could keep the trade for themselves and raise freight charges. Plaintiffs were competing shipowners who lost business as a result of defendants' tactics. The trial court rejected plaintiffs' action for damages and an injunction.]

BOWEN, L.J.... The acts of which the plaintiffs particularly complained were as follows:— First, a circular of May 10, 1885, by which the defendants offered to the local shippers and their agents a benefit by way of rebate if they would not deal with the plaintiffs, which was to be lost if this condition was not fulfilled. Secondly, the sending of special ships to Hankow in order by competition to deprive the plaintiffs' vessels of profitable freight. Thirdly, the offer at Hankow of freights at a level which would not repay a shipowner for his adventure, in order to "smash" freights and frighten the plaintiffs from the field. Fourthly, pressure put on the defendants' own agents to induce them to ship only by the defendants' vessels, and not by those of the plaintiffs. It is to be observed with regard to all these acts of which complaint is made that they were acts that in themselves could not be said to be illegal unless made so by the object with which, or the combination in the course of which, they were done; and that in reality what is complained of is the pursuing of trade competition to a length which the plaintiffs consider oppressive and prejudicial to themselves. We were invited by the plaintiffs' counsel to accept the position from which their argument started—that an action will lie if a man maliciously and wrongfully conducts himself so as to injure another in that other's trade. Obscurity resides in the language used to state this proposition. The terms "maliciously," "wrongfully," and "injure" are words all of which have accurate meanings, well known to the law, but which also have a popular and less precise signification, into which it is necessary to see that the argument does not imperceptibly slide. An intent to "injure" in strictness means more than an intent to harm. It connotes an intent to do wrongful harm. "Maliciously," in like manner, means and implies an intention to do an act which is wrongful, to the detriment of another. The term "wrongful" imports in its turn the infringement of some right. The ambiguous proposition to which we were invited by the plaintiffs' counsel still, therefore, leaves unsolved the question of what, as between the plaintiffs and defendants, are the rights of trade. For the purpose of clearness, I desire, as far as possible, to avoid terms in their popular use so slippery, and to translate them into less fallacious language wherever possible.

The English law, which in its earlier stages began with but an imperfect line of demarcation between torts and breaches of contract, presents us with no scientific analysis of the degree to which the intent to harm, or, in the language of the civil law, the animus vicino nocendi, may enter into or affect the conception of a personal wrong. All personal wrong means the infringement of some personal right. "It is essential to an action in tort," say the Privy Council in *Rogers v. Rajendro Dutt* [13 Moore, P.C. 209] "that the act complained of should under the circumstances be legally wrongful as regards the party complaining; that is, it must prejudicially affect him in some legal right; merely that it will, however directly, do a man harm in his interests, is not enough." What, then, were the rights of the plaintiffs as traders as against the defendants? The plaintiffs had a right to be protected against certain kind of conduct; and we have to consider what conduct would pass this legal line or boundary. Now, intentionally to do that which is calculated in the ordinary course of events to damage, and which does, in fact, damage another in that other person's property or trade, is actionable if done without just cause or excuse. Such intentional action when done without just cause or excuse is what the law calls a malicious wrong. The acts of the defendants which are complained of here were intentional, and were also calculated, no doubt, to do the plaintiffs damage in their trade. But in order to see whether they were wrongful we have still to discuss the question whether they were done without any just cause or excuse. Such just cause or excuse the defendants on their side assert to be found in their own positive right (subject to certain limitations) to carry on their own trade freely in the mode and manner that best suits them, and which they think best calculated to secure their own advantage.

What, then, are the limitations which the law imposes on a trader in the conduct of his business as between himself and other traders? There seem to be no burdens or restrictions in law upon a trader which arise merely from the fact that he is a trader, and which are not equally laid on all other subjects of the Crown. His right to trade freely is a right which the law recognises and encourages, but it is one which places him at no special disadvantage as compared with others. No man, whether trader or not, can, however, justify damaging another in his commercial business by fraud or misrepresentation. Intimidation, obstruction, and molestation are forbidden; so is the intentional procurement of a violation of individual rights, contractual or other, assuming always that there is no just cause for it. The intentional driving away of customers by shew of violence: *Tarleton v. M'Gawley* [Peak, N.P.C. 270]; the obstruction of actors on the stage by preconcerted hissing: *Clifford v. Brandon* [2 Camp. 358]; *Gregory v. Brunswick* [6 Man. & G. 205]; the disturbance of wild fowl in decoys by the firing of guns: *Carrington v. Taylor* [11 East, 571], and *Keeble v. Hickeringill* [11 East, 574, n]; the impeding or threatening servants or workmen: *Garret v. Taylor* [Cro. Jac. 567]; the inducing persons under personal contracts to break their contracts: *Bowen v. Hall* [6 Q.B.D. 333]; *Lumley v. Gye* [2 E. &

B. 216]; all are instances of such forbidden acts. But the defendants have been guilty of none of these acts. They have done nothing more against the plaintiffs than pursue to the bitter end a war of competition waged in the interest of their own trade. To the argument that a competition so pursued ceases to have a just cause or excuse when there is ill-will or a personal intention to harm, it is sufficient to reply ... that there was here no personal intention to do any other or greater harm to the plaintiffs than such as was necessarily involved in the desire to attract to the defendants' ships the entire tea freights of the ports, a portion of which would otherwise have fallen to the plaintiffs' share. I can find no authority for the doctrine that such a commercial motive deprives of "just cause or excuse" acts done in the course of trade which would be to convert into an illegal motive the instinct of self-advancement and self-protection, which is the very incentive to all trade. To say that man is to trade freely, but that he is to stop short at any act which is calculated to harm other tradesmen, and which is designed to attract business to his own shop, would be a strange and impossible counsel of perfection. But we were told that competition ceases to be the lawful exercise of trade, and so to be a lawful excuse for what will harm another, if carried to a length which is not fair or reasonable. The offering of reduced rates by the defendants in the present case is said to have been "unfair." This seems to assume that, apart from fraud, intimidation, molestation, or obstruction, of some other personal right in rem or in personam, there is some natural standard of "fairness" or "reasonableness" (to be determined by the internal consciousness of judges and juries) beyond which competition ought not in law to go. There seems to be no authority, and I think, with submission, that there is no sufficient reason for such a proposition. It would impose a novel fetter upon trade. The defendants, we are told by the plaintiffs' counsel, might lawfully lower rates provided they did not lower them beyond a "fair freight," whatever that may mean. But where is it established that there is any such restriction upon commerce? And what is to be the definition of a "fair freight"? It is said that it ought to be a normal rate of freight, such as is reasonably remunerative to the shipowner. But over what period of time is the average of this reasonable remunerativeness to be calculated? All commercial men with capital are acquainted with the ordinary expedient of sowing one year a crop of apparently unfruitful prices, in order by driving competition away to reap a fuller harvest of profit in the future; and until the present argument at the bar it may be doubted whether shipowners or merchants were ever deemed to be bound by law to conform to some imaginary "normal" standard of freights or prices, or the Law Courts had a right to say to them in respect of their competitive tariffs, "Thus far shalt thou go and no further." To attempt to limit English competition in this way would probably be as hopeless an endeavour as the experiment of King Canute. But on ordinary principles of law no such fetter on freedom of trade can in my opinion be warranted. A man is bound not to use his property so as to infringe upon another's right. Sic utere tuo ut alienum non laedas. If engaged in actions which may involve danger to others, he ought, speaking generally, to take reasonable care to avoid endangering them. But there is surely no doctrine of law which compels him to use his property in a way that judges and juries may consider reasonable. If there is no such fetter upon the use of property known to the English law, why should there be any such a fetter upon trade?

It is urged, however, on the part of the plaintiffs, that even if the acts complained of would not be wrongful had they been committed by a single individual, they become actionable when they are the result of concerted action among several. In other words, the plaintiffs, it is contended, have been injured by an illegal conspiracy. Of the general proposition, that certain kinds of conduct not criminal in any one individual may become criminal if done by combination among several, there can be no doubt. The distinction is based on sound reason, for a combination may make oppressive or dangerous that which if it proceeded only from a single person would be otherwise, and the very fact of the combination may shew that the object is simply to do harm, and not to exercise one's own just rights. In the application of this undoubted principle it is necessary to be very careful not to press the doctrine of illegal conspiracy beyond that which is necessary for the protection of individuals or of the public; and it may be observed in passing that as a rule it is the damage wrongfully done, and not the conspiracy, that is the gist of actions on the case for conspiracy. But what is the definition of an illegal combination? It is an agreement by one or more to do an unlawful act, or to do a lawful act by unlawful means; and the question to be solved is whether there has been any such agreement here. Have the defendants combined to do an unlawful act? Have they combined to do a lawful act by unlawful means? A moment's consideration will be sufficient to shew that this new inquiry only drives us back to the circle of definitions and legal propositions which I have already traversed in the previous part of this judgment. The unlawful act agreed to, if any, between the defendants must have been the intentional doing of some act to the detriment of the plaintiffs' business without just cause or excuse. Whether there was any such justification or excuse for the defendants is the old question over again, which, so far as regards an individual trader, has been already solved. The only differentia that can exist must arise, if at all, out of the fact that the acts done are the joint acts of several capitalists, and not of one capitalist only. The next point is whether the means adopted were unlawful. The means adopted were competition carried to a bitter end. Whether such means were unlawful is in like manner nothing but the old discussion which I have gone through, and which is now revised under a second head of inquiry, except so far as a combination of capitalists differentiates the case of acts jointly done by them from similar acts done by a single man of capital. But I find it impossible myself to acquiesce in the view that the English law places any such restriction on the combination of capital as would be involved in the recognition of such a distinction. If so, one rich capitalist may innocently carry competition to a length which would become unlawful in the case of a syndicate with a joint capital no larger than his own, and one individual merchant may lawfully do that which a firm or a partnership may not. What limits, on such a theory, would be imposed by law on the competitive action of a joint-stock company limited, is a problem which might well puzzle a casuist. The truth is, that the combination of capital for purposes of trade and competition is a very different thing from such a combination of several persons against one, with a view to harm him, as falls under the head of an indictable conspiracy. There is no just cause or excuse in the latter class of cases. There is such a just cause or excuse in the former. There are cases in which the very fact of a combination is evidence of a design to do that which is hurtful without just cause — is evidence — to use a technical expression — of malice. But it is perfectly legitimate, as it seems to me, to combine capital for all the mere purposes of trade for which capital may, apart from combination, be legitimately used in trade. To limit combinations of capital, when used for purposes of competition, in the manner proposed by the argument of the plaintiffs, would, in the present day, be impossible — would be only another method of attempting to set boundaries to the tides. Legal puzzles which might well distract a theorist may easily be conceived of imaginary conflicts between the selfishness of a group of individuals and the obvious well-being of other members of the community. Would it be an indictable conspiracy to agree to drink up all the water from a common spring in a time of drought; to buy up by preconcerted action all the provisions in a market or district in times of scarcity; to combine to purchase all the shares of a company against a coming settling-day; or to agree to give away articles of trade gratis in order to withdraw custom from a trader? May two itinerant match-vendors combine to sell matches below their value in order by competition to drive a third match-vendor from the street? In cases like these, where the elements of intimidation, molestation, or the other kinds of illegality to which I have alluded are not present, the question must be decided by the application of the test I have indicated. Assume that what is done is intentional, and that it is calculated to do harm to others. Then comes the question, Was it done with or without "just cause or excuse"? If it was bona fide in the use of a man's own property, in the exercise of a man's own trade, such legal justification would, I think, exist not the less because what was done might seem to others to be selfish or unreasonable. But such legal justification would not exist when the act was merely done with the intention of causing temporal harm, without reference to one's own lawful gain, or the lawful enjoyment of one's own rights. The good sense of the tribunal which had to decide would have to analyse the circumstances and to discover on which side of the line each case fell. But if the real object were to enjoy what was one's own, or to acquire for one's self some advantage in one's property or trade, and what was done was done honestly, peaceably, and without any of the illegal acts above referred to, it could not, in my opinion, properly be said that it was done without just cause or excuse. One may with advantage borrow for the benefit of traders what was said by Erle, J., in *Reg. v. Rowlands* [17 Q.B. 671, at p. 687, n], of workmen and of masters: "The intention of the law is at present to allow either of them to follow the dictates of their own will, with respect to their own actions, and their own property; and either, I believe, has a right to study to promote his own advantage, or to combine with others to promote their mutual advantage."

Lastly, we are asked to hold the defendants' Conference or association illegal, as being in restraint of trade. The term "illegal" here is a misleading one. Contracts, as they are called, in restraint of trade, are not, in my opinion, illegal in any sense, except that the law will not enforce them. It does not prohibit the making of such contracts; it merely declines, after they have been made, to recognise their validity. The law considers the disadvantage so imposed upon the contract a sufficient shelter to the public.... No action at common law will lie or ever has lain against any individual or individuals for entering into a contract merely because it is in restraint of trade.... If indeed it could be plainly proved that the mere formation of "conferences," "trusts," or "associations" such as these were always necessarily injurious to the public—a view which involves, perhaps, the disputable assumption that, in a country of free trade, and one which is not under the iron regime of statutory monopolies, such confederations can ever be really successful—and if the evil of them were not sufficiently dealt with by the common law rule, which held such agreements to be void as distinct from holding them to be criminal, there might be some reason for thinking that the common law ought to discover within its arsenal of sound common-sense principles some further remedy commensurate with the mischief. Neither of these assumptions are, to my mind, at all evident, nor is it the province of judges to mould and stretch the law of conspiracy in order to keep pace with the calculations of political economy. If peaceable and honest combinations of capital for purposes of trade competition are to be struck at, it must, I think, be by legislation, for I do not see that they are under the ban of the common law.

... [C]ompetition, however severe and egotistical, if unattended by circumstances of dishonesty, intimidation, molestation, or such illegalities as I have above referred to, gives rise to no cause of action at common law. I myself should deem it to be a misfortune if we were to attempt to prescribe to the business world how honest and peaceable trade was to be carried on in a case where no such illegal elements as I have mentioned exist, or were to adopt some standard of judicial "reasonableness," or of "normal" prices, or "fair freights," to which commercial adventurers, otherwise innocent, were bound to conform.

In my opinion, accordingly, this appeal ought to be dismissed with costs.

[Fry, L.J., delivered a concurring opinion. Lord Esher, M.R., delivered a dissenting opinion.]

Notes

1. Courts have long found no liability in "competition." The Schoolmaster Case, (1410) Y.B. 11 Hen. IV, f. 47, pl. 21 (C.P.), holds that the owner of an established school could not recover damages when a new school attracted prospective pupils from him. Generally, a business is free to attract prospective customers away from its competitors without incurring liability unless it violates a statutory prohibition or engages in unlawful conduct. See Passaic Print Works v. Ely & Walker Dry-Goods Co., 105 F. 163 (8th Cir. 1900); Lough v. Outerbridge, 143 N.Y. 271, 38 N.E. 292 (1893); Restatement (Second) of Torts § 768 (1979). But there may be some qualifications to this. See generally Annot., Liability of Third Party for Interference with Prospective Contractual Relationship Between Two Other Parties, 6 A.L.R.4th 195 (1981). See also Speakers of Sport, Inc. v. Pro-Serv, Inc., p. 197, infra, and the notes following the case.

2. Is a monopoly sufficiently harmful to the public interest that the purpose to establish it should be considered unlawful or wrongful? According to the famous Case of Monopolies, (1602) 11 Co. Rep. 84 b, 77 Eng. Rep. 1260, sub nom. Darcy v. Allen, Moore K.B. 671, 72 Eng. Rep. 830, Noy 173, 74 Eng. Rep. 1131 (Q.B.), in which the court held void a royal grant of a monopoly in playing cards, monopolies are bad because they not only damage persons in the same trade but also always raise prices, diminish the quality of the commodity sold, and impoverish and idle workers. Is this correct?

3. In the United States, some older decisions denied relief to a business injured by a contract or combination in restraint of trade. See Palmer v. Atlantic Ice & Coal Corp., 178 Ga. 405, 173 S.E. 424 (1934) (retail ice dealer injured by defendants' contract for purchase of all ice produced by only manufacturer in area). Relief, however, usually was granted when there was a conspiracy to monopolize directed particularly against the complainant. See Brown v. Jacobs Pharmacy Co., 115 Ga. 429, 41 S.E. 553 (1902). The trend is now to recognize that an unlawful restraint of trade can give rise to a private cause of action for any party injured. See Grillo v. Board of Realtors of Plainfield Area, 91 N.J. Super. 202, 219 A.2d 635 (Ch. Div. 1966); Annot., Right of One Not a Party to a Combination or Contract in Restraint of Trade to Maintain a Suit to Enjoin the Same or to Recover Damages He Suffers by Reason Thereof, 92 A.L.R. 185 (1934). Much of the conduct in the *Mogul Steamship* case, and in the note cases involving concerted activities by businesses or inducements not to deal with competitors, is now prohibited by and actionable under antitrust law, thus providing a statutory remedy and an "unlawful means" basis for a tort action. See Restatement (Second) of Torts § 768, comment *f* (1979).

4. What if plaintiffs in the *Mogul Steamship* case, instead of seeking relief from the conference's activities, sought to participate in those activities? Courts sometimes have compelled real estate multiple listing services to allow participation by non-members. See Grillo v. Board of Realtors of Plainfield Area, supra. Compare Grempler v. Multiple Listing Bureau of Harford County, Inc., 258 Md. 419, 266 A.2d 1 (1970) (realtor barred from participating in county multiple listing bureau because her main office was outside county could not maintain action against bureau; reasonable limitation). See Validity, Construction, and Effect of Real-Estate Brokers' Multiple-Listing Agreement, 45 A.L.R.3d 190

(1972), noting that some cases hold multiple listing services to be illegal combinations in restraint of trade when they unreasonably exclude licensed brokers in area.

5. Will relief be granted a worker who is prevented from obtaining employment when he is "blacklisted" by a labor union? See Annot., Rights and Remedies of Workmen Blacklisted by Labor Union, 46 A.L.R.2d 1124 (1956). What about a physician who is denied access to local hospitals? See Willis v. Santa Ana Community Health Association, 58 Cal. 2d 806, 26 Cal. Rptr. 640, 376 P.2d 568 (1962) (action stated against health association, its directors and administrators for interference with physician's practice); Margolin v. Morton F. Plant Hospital Association, Inc., 342 So. 2d 1090 (Fla. App. 1977) (action stated by surgeon against officers and anesthesiologists of hospital for refusing to provide anesthesia services); Annot., Liability in Tort for Interference with Physician's Contract or Relationship with Hospital, 7 A.L.R.4th 572 (1981).

J.F. Parkinson Company v. Building Trades Council of Santa Clara County

Supreme Court of California
154 Cal. 581, 98 P. 1027 (1908)

BEATTY, C.J. [with whom Lorigan, J., joined. The county Building Trades Council, an association of labor unions, adopted a rule that members of its affiliated unions would not work on the same job or in the same shop with non-union men and would not handle or use material supplied by a dealer whom the council had declared "unfair" because of his employment of non-union labor. Plaintiff, a lumber yard proprietor, refused to discharge an employee who refused to join a union. Pursuant to its rule, the council declared plaintiff "unfair." Upon notification of this, plaintiff's union employees quit work and, in order to avoid walkouts by their union employees, contractors ceased purchasing materials from plaintiff. After a temporary shutdown, plaintiff's mill reopened with non-union labor. The trial court enjoined the council, its affiliated unions and their members "from boycotting plaintiff—that is to say, from coercing others against their will to withdraw from plaintiff their beneficial business intercourse, through or by threats that, unless those others do so, the defendants will cause directly and indirectly, loss to them...." Defendants appealed.] ...

Can it be said ... that the defendants entered into a conspiracy for the purpose of compelling the plaintiff, by coercion and intimidation, to subject its business to their control? Can it be said that they entered into a conspiracy at all? A combination there certainly was, but it had no reference to the plaintiff except as the business of the plaintiff put it into the general class (employers of labor) who would necessarily be affected by the enforcement of the regulations of the unions. Their object was to secure higher wages, shorter hours, and more favorable conditions generally than employers of labor might be willing to concede, and just so far as they might be successful in accomplishing this object it may be assumed that employers, as a class, the plaintiff included, would incur a corresponding loss. But assuming all this, would that constitute the combination a conspiracy? A conspiracy is a combination of two or more persons to accomplish by concerted action a criminal or unlawful purpose, or a lawful purpose by criminal or unlawful means....

... [I]t is clear that the avowed object of these organizations—the several unions of working men and the council in which they were combined—was in no sense unlawful, and the discussion may be confined to the question whether the means proposed for its attainment were unlawful, a question as to which there is a wide divergence of view.... In one of the more recent [boycotting cases] (National Protective Association v. Cumming, 170 N.Y. 315, 63 N.E. 369) the seven justices of the Court of Appeals were divided, four to three, as to the lawfulness of the avowed object of the defendants, and as to the means employed by them against the plaintiff. Chief Justice Parker— three of his associates concurring—held both object and means to have been lawful, while Justice Vann, with the concurrence of the other two justices, condemned the means employed by the defendants to accomplish their purpose, not because the acts of defendants were otherwise unlawful, but because they were rendered unlawful by the selfish and censurable motive which inspired them. "The object of the defendants," he concluded, "was not to get higher wages, shorter hours, or better terms for themselves, but to prevent others from following their lawful calling." This conclusion was based upon evidence which showed clearly enough what appears as clearly in this case— that the immediate object of the defendants was to exclude the competition of men outside of their unions. This purpose Judge Vann considered so selfish, and its accomplishment so opposed to public policy and common right as to infect acts otherwise entirely lawful with the taint of illegality. The opposing opinion of the Chief Justice—the majority opinion—seems to be rested partly upon the ground that, in order to secure employment on more favorable terms for themselves, individuals have an absolute right to combine for the purpose of preventing the employment and competition of others, and partly upon the further and independent ground that, whether such right is absolute or not, every man is clearly privileged to stop work with or without reason whenever he can do so without violating his contract, and that no one can question his motive, since a bad motive does not convert an act otherwise lawful into a ground of action. This last proposition embodies the rule of decision which was approved by this court in the case of Boyson v. Thorn, 98 Cal. 578, 33 Pac. 492.... [This case and the opinions of the majority in Allen v. Flood, [1898] A.C. 1 (H.L.), were interpreted as establishing that, "An act lawful in itself is not converted by a malicious or bad motive into an unlawful act so as to make the doer of the act liable to a civil action." Plaintiff's argument that Quinn v. Leathem, [1901] A.C. 495 (H.L.), repudiated Allen v. Flood was rejected.]

... The general objects of the union and the council being lawful, if they used no unlawful means for their attainment, the motives which inspired their action in this case are irrelevant to the question of conspiracy and immaterial as affecting the cause of action.

... In case of a peaceable and ordinary strike, without breach of contract, and conducted without violence, threats, or intimidation, this court would not inquire into the motives of the strikers. Their acts being entirely lawful, their motives would be held immaterial. [Applying even the dissenting opinion in National Protective Association v. Cumming, where it was said that workers had the right to strike "provided the object is not to gratify malice or inflict injury upon others, but to secure better terms of employment for themselves," there is no liability in this case.] The rule that their members could not work with nonunion men, or handle material supplied by an employer of nonunion men, was adopted before any difference had arisen between them and the plaintiff or its manager. It was a rule which they supposed would benefit them, and that was its sole purpose. Whatever others may think of the policy or justice of such a rule that is a matter outside the province of the courts, and as with regard to other questions of economic or political aspect, the remedy, if a remedy is needed, must be found by the Legislature....

... Was it unlawful to send the written notices to the contractors employing union labor that the plaintiff had been declared unfair, and that union men could not work for it or handle material supplied by it till further notice? There are authorities on both sides of this question, but I think those which would answer it in the negative have the better reason. The contractors were working in harmony with the union (as indeed the plaintiff had previously done), and fair dealing required that the council, representing and acting for the unions, should protect such contractors from any loss they might incur if left in ignorance of the action it had taken. If they had not sent the notices some of those contractors who felt constrained to stop dealing with plaintiff when informed that it had been declared unfair might have purchased material which they could not have used, and it is only upon the assumption that such purchases would have been made that the plaintiff can base a claim that it was damaged by the notices.... Nor was there anything unlawful in the presentation to the plaintiff of an agreement embodying the conditions upon which union men would consent to reenter its service and handle the output of its mill and shops. Conceding that the conditions of the proposed contract were intolerable, the right to propose them stood upon the same plane as the right to reject them, and no right of the plaintiff was infringed unless it can be held that men who are free to work or not to work, with or without reason, are breaking the law in proposing unreasonable terms as a condition of entering the employment of another. If this were so, why would it not equally follow that an employer would be breaking the law by proposing to men seeking employment conditions of service which they might consider intolerable, or a court deem unreasonable? ...

... We do not question the doctrine of Quinn v. Leathem.... Any injury to a lawful business, whether the result of a conspiracy or not, is prima facie actionable, but may be defended upon the ground that it was merely the result of a lawful effort of the defendants to promote their own welfare. To defeat this plea of justification the plaintiff may offer evidence that the acts of the defendants were inspired by express malice, and were done for the purpose of injuring plaintiff, and not to benefit themselves. The principle is the same which permits proof of express malice to defeat the plea of privilege in libel, or the defense of probable cause in actions for malicious prosecution or false imprisonment. In such cases as Quinn v. Leathem a verdict for the plaintiff imports a finding by the jury that the injurious acts of the defendants, which standing by themselves are actionable, have not been justified, or, in other words, that they were done to injure the plaintiff and not to benefit the defendants, or that the means employed were unlawful. In Quinn v. Leathem the verdict was supported on both grounds. There was proof of express malice, and of unlawful means employed to injure plaintiff's business. In this case there was overwhelming proof that the council, when the occasion arose, simply put in force a rule long before adopted for their own benefit, and not directed against the plaintiff or any particular person. Nor did the council, the unions, or their members generally use any unlawful means to injure the plaintiff....

[Reversed. Angellotti, J., (with whom Henshaw and Melvin, JJ., joined) delivered a concurring opinion.]

SLOSS, J. I concur in the judgment....

Upon a consideration of the authorities, I think the sounder rule is that one who is under no contract relation to another may freely and without question withdraw from business relations with that other. This includes the right to cease to deal, not only with one person but with others; not only with the individual who may be pursuing a course deemed detrimental to another who opposes it, but with all who by their patronage aid in the maintenance of the objectionable policies. In other words, if the defendants violated no right of the Parkinson Company by refusing to work for it, they violated none by refusing to work for contractors who used material bought of Parkinson. Such refusal, as is shown in the opinion of the Chief Justice, and as is stated in the testimony of plaintiff's manager and principal witness, was the "sum total of the interference" which was practiced or threatened. An agreement by shipowners, in order to secure a carrying trade exclusively for themselves, that agents of members should be prohibited upon pain of dismissal from acting in the interest of competing shipowners; a combination of retailers binding the members to refuse to purchase of wholesalers who should sell to nonmembers of the combination; an agreement of contractors to withdraw their patronage from wholesalers selling to a contractor who had conceded the demands of his employés for an eight-hour day; a threat by a railroad company to discharge any employé who should deal with the plaintiff; a threat by an employer that he would discharge any laborer who rented plaintiff's house—have been held to give no right of action to the individuals affected. The defendants in each case were held to be acting within their absolute legal right in entering or refusing to enter into business relations with persons to whom they were not bound by contract. I see no reason why workmen have not the same absolute right to dispose of their labor as they see fit. So long as they abstain from breach of contract, violence, duress, menace, fraud, misrepresentation, or other unlawful means, they may lawfully inflict such damage as results from the withholding of their labor or patronage.... The terms "intimidation" and "coercion," so frequently used in the discussion of this question, seem to me to have no application to such acts as were here committed. One cannot be said to be "intimidated" or "coerced" in the sense of unlawful compulsion by being induced to forego business relations with A., rather than lose the benefit of more profitable relations with B. It is equally beside the question to speak of "threats" where that which is threatened is only what the party has a legal right to do. It may be that the combination of great numbers of men, as of great amounts of capital, has placed in the hands of a few persons an immense power, and one which, in the interest of the general welfare, ought to be limited and controlled. But if there be, in such combinations, evils which should be redressed, the remedy is to be sought, as to some extent it has been sought, by legislation....

SHAW, J. I dissent....

... The class to which the conduct of the defendant belongs, if it can be characterized as illegal, is that of undue influence.... It is not necessary, in order to constitute such undue influence or coercion, that there should be any sort of physical violence done or threatened, or that there should be any act done or threatened, which in itself, and apart from its effect in controlling the action of the person coerced, would be unlawful. It is sufficient if the acts threatened, although lawful, were of such a character that, if done, they would cause loss or injury to the person threatened of so serious a nature that the mere threat prevents him from exercising his own will in the matter, and causes him, against his will, to act injuriously to the person intended to be injured.

These principles are established by a great number of decisions of the courts of this country and England. One of the latest of these is Quinn v. Leathem, in the House of Lords. Leathem, a butcher, was employing nonunion men. Quinn and others, members of a union, threatened Leathem that, if he did not discharge these men, they would stop his custom and call out his union men. He refused to discharge the objectionable men, and thereupon, by threats to a customer named Munce that they would also call out his men if he did not cease dealing with Leathem, they forced Munce to comply with their demand and cease buying of Leathem, to his injury. One Dickie, a workman, was by similar means compelled to quit Leathem's service. The question was whether or not there was sufficient evidence to sustain a verdict for the plaintiff for damages. [The verdict was sustained.] ...

... [W]hile men have a right to strike, they have no right by that means to coerce their employers so as to compel them to act to the injury of a third person. The fact that they were to strike in such numbers gave them a power over the threatened customers of plaintiff, which constituted undue influence over them, or coercion or intimidation, as most of the authorities usually express it, and this coercion, exercised for the purpose of injuring a third person, is an unlawful act, and makes the resulting injury an unlawful injury, which may be enjoined if only threatened, and which, if committed, may be redressed by an action for damages. . . .

Notes

1. Whether actions which persons are free to take individually may become tortious or illegal when taken by persons acting in concert has long been a controversial question. In addition to trade combination cases, such as *Mogul Steamship*, p. 167, supra, the problem often has been presented in connection with labor disputes. See Kales, Coercive and Competitive Methods in Trade and Labor Disputes, 8 Corn. L.Q. 128 (1922). Many early cases and a few later ones adopted the position that the collective nature of an action does not render it unlawful or support liability when the same action can be taken lawfully by individual members of the group. See Bohn Manufacturing Co. v. Hollis, 54 Minn. 223, 55 N.W. 1119 (1893); John D. Park & Sons Co. v. National Wholesale Druggists' Association, 175 N.Y. 1, 67 N.E. 136 (1903); McNeill v. Hall, 220 N.C. 73, 16 S.E.2d 456 (1941). Most modern cases in the United States recognize that concerted action almost inevitably raises possibilities of intimidation and coercion not presented by individual conduct. Accordingly, group refusals to deal with a person or business may be found tortious unless strong justification is shown. See Martell v. White, note 4, infra; Louis Kamm, Inc. v. Flink, 113 N.J.L. 582, 175 A. 62 (1934); Keviczky v. Lorber, 290 N.Y. 297, 49 N.E.2d 146 (1943).

2. Labor organizations were likely to be held liable for coercive action unless the action was against the party or parties with whom there was a labor dispute and had the purpose of achieving a goal reasonably related to employment conditions. In Pickett v. Walsh, 192 Mass. 572, 78 N.E. 753 (1906), it was held that union bricklayers and masons employed by a contractor on certain buildings could not strike because the contractor was working on another building on which some jobs were being performed by non-union employees of the building owners. However, it was lawful to strike over the contractor's refusal to hire them for additional jobs in the projects on which they were already working. Unions' secondary boycotts—boycotts of third parties in order to compel them not to deal with an employer—have found little acceptance. See Hellerstein, Secondary Boycotts in Labor Disputes, 47 Yale L.J. 341 (1938); Smith, Coercion of Third Parties in Labor Disputes—The Secondary Boycott, 1 La. L. Rev. 277 (1939). Cf. Auburn Draying Co. v. Wardell, 227 N.Y. 1, 124 N.E. 97 (1919) (union enjoined from threatening employer's customers with labor trouble if they did not withdraw patronage). What if a union instructs its members not to work for plaintiff because plaintiff previously had taken action adverse to the union? See Reinforce, Inc. v. Birney, 308 N.Y. 164, 124 N.E.2d 104 (1954). See generally Annots., The Boycott as a Weapon in Industrial Disputes, 6 A.L.R. 909 (1920); 16 A.L.R. 230 (1922); 27 A.L.R. 651 (1923); 32 A.L.R. 779 (1924); 116 A.L.R. 484 (1938).

3. The common law limitation that union actions must relate to conditions of employment is illustrated by Opera on Tour, Inc. v. Weber, 285 N.Y. 348, 34 N.E.2d 349 (1941). Officers of the musicians' union induced members of the stagehands' union to strike in support of the musicians' demand that live musicians rather than mechanical means be used to produce orchestral accompaniment to opera performances. The court held this not a lawful labor objective. See also Hopkins v. Oxley Stave Co., 83 F. 912 (8th Cir.

1897) (members of two labor organizations combined to compel manufacturer of casks and barrels to discontinue use of machines for hooping these products and return to hand-hooping; held an unlawful conspiracy to deprive employer of right to manage business as it thought best); Annot., Elimination or Reduction of Use of Machinery or Mechanical Devices in Order to Maintain or Increase Employment as a Proper Labor Objective, 136 A.L.R. 282 (1942) (noting division of opinion). The law on strikes, boycotts, picketing and other union activities has been altered considerably by legislation. See p. 151, supra.

4. Business associations have often exerted pressure upon non-members. In Martell v. White, 185 Mass. 255, 69 N.E. 1085 (1904), a city association of granite manufacturers adopted a by-law requiring any member having business with a non-member manufacturer to pay a fine to the association. Plaintiff, a non-member who had quarried granite and sold it in the city, found his business ruined. The court held that coercion by fines was an illegal method of business competition, for which the participants could be held liable in damages. In Klingel's Pharmacy of Baltimore City v. Sharp & Dohme, 104 Md. 218, 64 A. 1029 (1906), retail and wholesale druggists formed an association to maintain a maximum price schedule. They refused to sell to plaintiff, a retailer who did not join the combination, and coerced other druggists not to sell to plaintiff. Again, the coercive group action, together with intimidation of others, was held to exceed the bounds of permissible competition. Cf. Farmers' & Merchants' Bank of Catlettsburg, Kentucky v. Federal Reserve Bank of Cleveland, Ohio, 286 F. 610 (E.D. Ky. 1922), applying American Bank & Trust Co. v. Federal Reserve Bank of Atlanta, Georgia, 256 U.S. 350 (1921), and ruling that a Federal Reserve Bank could not accumulate checks drawn on a state bank and then demand cash payment over the counter in order to induce the bank to abandon its practice of charging for the payment of checks sent by mail. (But see the later proceedings in the *American Bank* case, 262 U.S. 643 (1923), holding it within the statutory powers of the Federal Reserve Bank to collect the checks of state banks and present them for immediate payment.)

5. Coercion of businesses is sometimes practiced by ethnic, religious and analogous organizations attempting, for instance, to influence the employment policies of a business. When do their tactics become actionable? See National Association for the Advancement of Colored People v. Overstreet, 221 Ga. 16, 142 S.E.2d 816 (1965), cert. dismissed, 348 U.S. 118 (1966), in which plaintiff allegedly had beaten a fourteen-year-old black employee. In protest, defendants, trying to induce a boycott of plaintiff's business, engaged in mass picketing of plaintiff's store and reportedly harassed and intimidated customers and employees. Plaintiff's complaint was held to state a cause of action for an injunction and damages. In A.S. Beck Shoe Corp. v. Johnson, 153 Misc. 363, 274 N.Y.S. 946 (Sup. Ct. 1934), the court ruled that picketing, even if free from violence or misrepresentation, could be enjoined if the purpose did not justify the means. Defendants' purpose here—to compel a business to employ a certain percentage of black workers in place of white persons—was held not to justify direct damage to the picketed business.

6. Most cases involving group actions taken in support of demands not connected with labor matters uphold the right of groups to picket and boycott businesses so long as there is no violence, physical threat or intimidation. See Annot., Nonlabor Picketing or Boycott, 93 A.L.R.2d 1284 (1964). Potential liability is constrained by the First Amendment. See National Association for the Advancement of Colored People v. Claiborne Hardware Co., 458 U.S. 886 (1982) (black citizens' boycott of white merchants in support of numerous demands, mostly addressed to local government officials); Caruso v. Local Union No. 690 of International Brotherhood of Teamsters, Chauffeurs, Warehousemen and Helpers of America, 100 Wash. 2d 243, 670 P.2d 240 (1983) (union's "do not patronize" messages, containing misstatements, aimed at merchant involved in dispute about parking of trucks driven

by union members). What about residents of an area picketing to rid their neighborhood of a supposed nuisance? See 1621, Inc. v. Wilson, 402 Pa. 94, 166 A.2d 271 (1961) (picketing intended to eliminate taproom, in fact a nuisance, from neighborhood; injunction refused). Consumers picketing a business establishment to protest poor service or high prices? See Pebble Brook, Inc. v. Smith, 140 N.J. Super. 273, 356 A.2d 48 (Ch. Div. 1976) (dissatisfied home buyers picketing and distributing literature at new development after suing developer for alleged substandard construction of homes); Stansbury v. Beckstrom, 491 S.W.2d 947 (Tex. Civ. App. 1973) (picketing physician's office to protest fees constitutionally protected); Annot., Consumer Picketing to Protest Products, Prices, or Services, 62 A.L.R.3d 227 (1975). Secondary boycotts have met much the same disfavor in these situations as they have in labor disputes. See Southern Christian Leadership Conference, Inc. v. A.G. Corp., 241 So. 2d 619 (Miss. 1970) (loosely organized group boycotted white merchants; defendants had no complaint individually against plaintiff, a grocer; unlawful conspiracy found). But see Environmental Planning and Information Council of Western El Dorado County, Inc. v. Superior Court, 36 Cal. 3d 188, 203 Cal. Rptr. 127, 680 P.2d 1086 (1984) (under common law, influenced by First Amendment principles, environmental organization not liable for suggesting boycott of businesses advertising in plaintiff's "prodevelopment" newspaper).

7. What of groups that scrutinize publications, films, etc., and take action against those they consider immoral or otherwise objectionable? Courts are reluctant to interfere in the internal affairs of religious and other groups and are likely to take a "hands off" attitude when such groups forbid or advise their members not to read certain publications or attend certain events. See Kuryer Publishing Co. v. Messmer, 162 Wis. 565, 156 N.W. 948 (1916) (Catholic bishops forbade communicants from reading or subscribing to plaintiff's newspaper; held to be within church's right of discipline). Nevertheless, a continued course of threatening prosecution, designed to curb the circulation of certain publications, may be enjoined. See American Mercury, Inc. v. Chase, 13 F.2d 224 (D. Mass. 1926) (organization scrutinized publications and advised large distributors of those they considered unlawful, expressly or impliedly threatening legal action if publications distributed; reputable dealers hesitant to take risk of prosecution). Under what circumstances could groups be held liable for ordering or advising their members or others to stop smoking cigarettes, using pesticides, or doing business with a country that violates human rights? Would organization of a secondary boycott in aid of such causes be restrained? See Top Service Body Shop, Inc. v. Allstate Insurance Co., 283 Or. 201, 205 n.3, 582 P.2d 1365, 1368 n.3 (1978).

8. Sometimes improper pressure against a business is exerted not by a group but by a single individual, particularly one who is in a position of leadership or influence. In Hutton v. Watters, 132 Tenn. 527, 179 S.W. 134 (1915), defendant was president of a school near which plaintiff operated a boarding house. Defendant had a disagreement with a student boarding there and asked plaintiff to eject him. She refused. Thereafter, defendant allegedly attempted to destroy plaintiff's business by deterring newly arrived students from going to plaintiff's house and threatening students who boarded there. The court held that there was a cause of action if defendant was motivated by malice; no privilege of competition could exist since the parties were not in competition. What if an employer forbids employees' dealing or associating with a third person? Deon v. Kirby Lumber Co., 162 La. 671, 111 So. 55 (1926), holds that an employer can induce its employees to discontinue trading with rival establishments, even by threatening to fire them, but can be liable if it maliciously prohibits employees from associating socially with the owner of a rival. See Annot., Liability of Employer Forbidding Employees to Trade or Associate with Another, 52 A.L.R. 1028 (1928).

Dunshee v. Standard Oil Company

Supreme Court of Iowa
152 Iowa 618, 132 N.W. 371 (1911)

WEAVER, J. During all the period covered by this controversy, the Standard Oil Company has been a wholesale dealer in oil at the city of Des Moines. In the year 1893 the Crystal Oil Company (plaintiff's assignor), a local corporation, entered the retail trade in oil, selling its goods from tank wagons hauled about the streets, and delivered to its customers at their homes. Its business grew from year to year until, in 1898, it employed from four to eight wagons, covering the territory of the city very generally. During the period mentioned, the Crystal Company purchased its supplies from the defendant, but in 1898 it for some reason began to make purchases from other wholesale dealers. Trouble at once ensued. [The Crystal Company refused to yield to the Standard's insistence that it wanted "all or none" of Crystal's trade.] The defendant, which, up to that time, had abstained from the retail trade, proceeded to equip itself with tank wagons, teams, and drivers substantially equal in number to those of the Crystal Company, and began active solicitation for the patronage of the "ultimate consumer." At the end of some months of strife, the Crystal Company abandoned the contest and quit the business at a loss, claiming to have been driven out by the tactics of its rival. The plaintiff, as assignee of said company, brings this action for damages, alleging a conspiracy between the Standard Oil Company and its managers, agents, and employes to ruin the business of said Crystal Company, and setting forth alleged wrongful acts done in pursuance of such conspiracy by which said company's business was destroyed. [Defendants appealed from a judgment for plaintiff.] ...

... [T]he case as made by the plaintiff tends strongly to show that defendant installed its scheme of retail distribution of oil in the city of Des Moines not for the purpose of establishing a retail trade, but as a mere temporary expedient to drive out the Crystal Company, and that, this being accomplished and having the field to itself, it withdrew its wagons and drivers, and gave its whole attention to its wholesale business. [There was little or no attempt to build up a retail trade with the public generally rather than to take away trade from Crystal. The Standard instructed its drivers to give special attention to places displaying Crystal's "green cards," which signified customers who wanted a distributor to stop and furnish oil. The Standard's drivers would try to get to customers displaying green cards and make a sale in advance of Crystal's wagons. Some drivers permitted buyers to think that the drivers were agents of Crystal. Sometimes the Standard's drivers removed Crystal's green cards. The drivers did business ostensibly as independent dealers driving their own wagons, but actually they were under the management of an agent of the Standard and the Standard furnished the wagons and paid all expenses.].... [T]he record as a whole is sufficient to justify the inference that the real end sought to be accomplished was to bar or exclude from the retail trade one who would not give the Standard Company, as a wholesale dealer, its exclusive patronage....

As we understand appellants' contention, it is that their conduct did not transgress the bounds of legitimate competition, and that so long as they kept within this limitation the question of the alleged malice or motive inspiring their acts is wholly immaterial.... Many authorities may be found holding without apparent qualification or exception, that the law takes no account whatever of motives as constituting an element of civil wrong. In other words, if a man do a thing which is otherwise lawful, the fact that he does it maliciously and for the express purpose of injuring his neighbor affords the latter no remedy at law.... If this be the correct view of the law, a man may excavate the earth near the boundary of his own land for the mere purpose of seeing the foundation of the house of his neighbor slide into the pit thus prepared for it; he may dig through his own soil to the subterranean sources of his neighbor's spring or well and divert the water into a ditch, where it will serve no purpose of use or profit to himself or any one else; if a banker or merchant, he may punish the blacksmith who refuses to patronize him by temporarily establishing a shop on the next lot and hiring men to shoe horses without money and without price, until he has driven the offending smith to come to his terms or to go out of business; and if a farmer, dependent upon a subterranean supply of water for the irrigation of his soil or watering of his live stock, he may contrive to ruin his competing neighbor by wasting the surplus not reasonably required for his own use. The laws of competition in business are harsh enough at best; but if the rule here suggested were to be carried to its logical and seemingly unavoidable extreme there is no practical limit to the wrongs which may be justified upon the theory that "it is business." Fortunately, we think, there has for many years been a distinct and growing tendency of the courts to look beneath the letter of the law and give some effect to its beneficent spirit, thereby preventing the perversion of the rules intended for the protection of human rights into engines of oppression and wrong. It is doubtless true that under many circumstances an act is legally right and defensible without regard to the motive which induces or characterizes it; but there is abundance of authority for saying that this is by no means the universal rule, and that an act which is legally right when done without malice may become legally wrong when done maliciously, wantonly, or without reasonable cause....

... [W]e may concede to the appellants the undoubted right to establish a retail oil business in Des Moines, to employ agents and drivers, and send them out over the same routes and make sales to the same people with whom the Crystal Oil Company was dealing; but in so doing it was bound to conduct such business with reasonable regard and consideration for the equal right of the Crystal Company to continue supplying oil to such of its customers as desired to remain with it. If, however, there was no real purpose or desire to establish a competing business, but under the guise or pretense of competition, to accomplish a malicious purpose to ruin the Crystal Company or drive it out of business, intending themselves to retire therefrom when their end had been secured, then they can claim no immunity under the rules of law which recognize and protect competition between dealers in the same line of business seeking in good faith the patronage of the same people. And if, under such pretense of competition, defendants maliciously interfered with the business of the Crystal Oil Company in the manner charged, and injury to the latter was thereby inflicted, a right of action exists for the recovery of damages. It may be conceded that authorities are not wanting to sustain the position that, even though the Standard Oil Company had no intention of becoming a retail dealer in oil in Des Moines, but entered the business of selling oil in this manner temporarily, for the sole purpose of driving the Crystal Company out, it is a matter into which the courts will not inquire; but we think such precedents are out of harmony with fundamental principles of justice, which, as we have said, underlie the law, as well as out of harmony with the later and better-considered cases. True the Standard Company, as a wholesale dealer, would violate no law in offering its product for sale at retail at half price in the territory supplied by the Crystal Company, but such fact, if proven, would have a distinct bearing upon the reasonableness of its methods employed in diverting trade from said company, as well as upon the charge that in interfering between the Crystal Company and its customers the Standard Company was actuated by malice or spirit of wanton assault upon the business of another, who had given it offense.

... Sufficiently analogous in fact to illustrate the principle is Tuttle v. Buck, 107 Minn. 145, 119 N.W. 946. There the plaintiff had an established and profitable business as a barber, and defendant, a banker, owned a building which he wished plaintiff to occupy with his shop. This being declined, it was alleged that defendant sought to punish the plaintiff by injuring his trade and driving him out of business. To that end defendant employed other barbers to occupy the shop and entice away the plaintiff's patrons, whom he personally and persistently solicited to no longer employ plaintiff's services, and by these other wrongful means did in fact injure plaintiff's business, all of which was done with the sole design of injuring the plaintiff, and not for the purpose of serving any legitimate interest of defendant himself. This was held on appeal to state a good cause of action.... [T]he court says: "It is not at all correct to say that the motive with which an act is done is immaterial, providing the act itself is not unlawful.... To call such conduct competition is a perversion of terms. It is simply the application of force without legal justification, which in its moral quality may be no better than highway robbery." ... No man entering or carrying on business has any right to demand protection against fair competition, and if he cannot meet it and succeed he must expect to fail, and for losses and injuries resulting the law affords him no remedy. But if competition be "war," in which "everything is fair," or if it be so regarded by those who participate therein, certainly the law will not give that doctrine its sanction. It follows of necessity that the trial court did not err in refusing to direct a verdict in defendants' favor.

[Errors were found in other respects, including a jury instruction which treated displays of green cards by the Crystal Company's customers as definite orders for oil rather than notices that they wished to buy oil. Defendants interfered with potential sales, not existing contracts. However, malicious interference with customers' invitations to sell, such as removal of the green cards, was actionable. Reversed and remanded.]

Notes

1. Is there liability if defendant establishes a business with the purpose of driving plaintiff out of the same trade? Older cases state broadly that motive is immaterial when an act is itself lawful. See Katz v. Kapper, 7 Cal. App. 2d 1, 44 P.2d 1060 (1935), in which the parties were rival wholesalers of fish. It was alleged that defendants, with the sole intention of putting plaintiff out of business, threatened to ruin plaintiff's customers if they continued to buy from plaintiff and opened a retail store that undersold plaintiff and his customers. The prevailing position now is that there may be liability when a business is established only for the purpose of driving out another; if defendant is shown to have "mixed" motives, some of which are justifiable, there is no liability. Compare Tuttle v. Buck, discussed in the principal case, with Beardsley v. Kilmer, 236 N.Y. 80, 140 N.E. 203 (1923), aff'g 200 App. Div. 378, 193 N.Y.S. 285 (1922). There, plaintiff in his newspaper had accused defendants of manufacturing "quack medicines" and of marketing "Swamp Rot" and "Rump Swat." (The real name of defendants' drug was "Swamp Root.") Defendants responded by establishing their own newspaper, partly out of a desire for revenge and partly to protect themselves from plaintiff's attacks and operate a legitimate and profitable business. Plaintiff was denied relief. See Annot., Purpose in Starting Business to Injure Another as Ground of Action by Latter, 27 A.L.R. 1417 (1923). Isn't the principal case one of mixed motives?

2. Dunshee v. Standard Oil Co. indicates that the privilege of competition does not extend to a defendant whose purpose is not to acquire business diverted from plaintiff, but to gratify ill will. See Peek v. Northern Pacific Railroad Co., 51 Mont. 295, 152 P. 421 (1915). Should there be liability when defendant cuts prices out of spite? See Memphis Steam Laundry-Cleaners v. Lindsey, 192 Miss. 224, 5 So. 2d 227 (1941) (liable on evidence

that defendant's dominant purpose was to destroy or injure plaintiff). What if prices are cut for the purpose of driving competitors out of the market, as in Bartholomew County Beverage Co., Inc. v. Barco Beverage Corp., Inc., 524 N.E.2d 353 (Ind. App. 1988)? Should a person who causes plaintiff economic loss through operation of a competing business be required to justify his conduct or motives in a lawsuit? How often does competition actuated by malice with no otherwise tortious conduct occur? Restatement of Unfair Competition § 1, comment *c* (1995), takes the position that there should be no liability for harm caused merely by engaging in a business or trade, irrespective a motive.

3. Can the exercise of a contractual right, such as a right to delivery of goods or repayment of a debt, at a bad time for the other contracting party be the basis of an action that alleges purpose to cause the party harm? Should it be? See Uptown Heights Associates Limited Partnership v. Seafirst Corp., 320 Or. 638, 891 P.2d 639 (1995) (bank initiated mortgage foreclosure, knowing this would prevent mortgagee selling property for amount exceeding loan balance). What if the contractual right was acquired by assignment for this purpose? See American Bank & Trust Co. v. Federal Reserve Bank of Atlanta, Georgia, 256 U.S. 350 (1921) (dismissal of plaintiffs' complaint reversed). Could a company whose business is selling products or component parts prevail on an allegation that defendant changed its specifications for the products or components with intent to cause plaintiff harm? See Weight Rite Golf Corp. v. United States Golf Association, p. 162, supra. Suppose defendant simply refuses to provide plaintiff with supplies, services, credit, insurance or advertising facilities that plaintiff cannot obtain from another source? The traditional position is that individual refusals to deal with another are not actionable, irrespective of motive, but will this always be accepted? See Great Atlantic & Pacific Tea Co. v. Cream of Wheat Co., 227 F. 46 (2d Cir. 1915); Restatement of Torts § 762 (1939); p. 196, note 4, infra.

Clark v. Crown Drug Company

Supreme Court of Missouri
348 Mo. 91, 152 S.W.2d 145 (1941)

DOUGLAS, Judge.

Plaintiff, a tavern keeper, [obtained] an injunction to restrain the defendant drug store from taking orders over the telephone for intoxicating liquor and then delivering the liquor so ordered by messenger and collecting the purchase price on delivery. Plaintiff claims that such sales are prohibited by our liquor control act and therefore constitute illegal competition with his lawful business to his damage....

Ordinarily a court of equity has no authority to enjoin the commission of a crime. But in cases of injury to property or rights of a pecuniary nature or in cases involving a public nuisance, this rule does not prevent a court of equity from exercising its jurisdiction....

We will assume, only for the sake of argument but not decide, that the telephone sales violated the law and hence were criminal. Such being the case the jurisdiction of the trial court as a court of equity must arise from the fact that plaintiff's property rights have been damaged. But the evidence fails to show any damage whatsoever has been in fact suffered by plaintiff because of defendant's telephone sales. The record is devoid of proof as to any loss of patronage or profit by plaintiff as a result of such sales. It must be borne in mind that the parties are continuingly engaged in lawful competition as to over-the-counter package sales. Should defendant, without any license, make sales by the drink as plaintiff and other tavern proprietors only are permitted to do, then perhaps we might find that the tavern proprietors suffered damage from the proof alone of the unlawful sales although the decisions on this point are divided. But in the situation as we find it we cannot presume that plaintiff was damaged on the mere showing that defendant made some of its sales by telephone. Since plaintiff has failed to show that his rights have been damaged in any way he has no standing in a court of equity merely to enjoin the commission of a crime. A court of equity has no such authority where no civil or property rights are concerned. To proceed under such circumstances would be to usurp the functions of a criminal court without following the appropriate rules incidental to criminal procedure....

There is another class of cases where the invasion or threatened invasion of a franchise without legal sanction is a sufficient ground for injunctive relief. And this is so although the owner of the franchise may not be entitled to any protection as against the granting of a similar franchise to another.

In Frost v. Corporation Comm., 278 U.S. 515, the United States Supreme Court held that a franchise to carry on a public service constitutes a property right and is an exclusive right as against an attempt by another to invade the field without first obtaining a valid permit. "The injury threatened by such an invasion is the impairment of the owner's business, for which there is no adequate remedy at law." This rule, however, does not justify injunctive relief against an unlicensed or unlawful competitor in a calling not clothed with a public interest or charged with a public use.... A license to sell liquor is not a contract or franchise in any such sense....

Under the facts of this case plaintiff has proved no right to equitable relief and no injunction should have been granted. The decree is reversed.

Notes

1. It is generally said that in an action to enjoin a competitor's illegal conduct, plaintiff must show that the conduct has caused plaintiff "special damage," injured its property rights, or harmed a public interest worthy of protection. Why? Compare Massachusetts Society of Optometrists v. Hatfield, 340 Mass. 581, 165 N.E.2d 394 (1960) (registered optometrists not entitled, without proof of special damage, to injunction against practice of optometry by unregistered persons), with Oklahoma Utilities Co. v. City of Hominy, 2 F. Supp. 849 (D. Okla. 1933) (grantee of public utility franchise has property rights therein; can enjoin illegal competition), and Feiler v. New Jersey Dental Association, 191 N.J. Super. 426, 467 A.2d 276 (Ch. Div. 1983), aff'd, 199 N.J. Super. 363, 489 A.2d 1161 (App. Div. 1984), cert. denied, 99 N.J. 162, 491 A.2d 673 (1984) (without proof of loss of particular patients to defendant, association of most of state's dentists granted injunction against dentist whose five "dental centers" required little or no payment from patients and fraudulently billed insurance carriers). Cf. Glover v. Malloska, 238 Mich. 216, 213 N.W. 107 (1927) (loss of customers due to competitor's conducting illegal lottery was injury to property rights of pecuniary nature, entitling plaintiff to injunction); R.C.A. Corp. v. Pollard, [1983] Ch. 135 (C.A.) (record companies with exclusive contract to market records of performances had no action against person who, in violation of criminal law, marketed "bootleg" recordings of performances). See Annot., Right to Enjoin Business Competitor from Unlicensed or Otherwise Illegal Acts or Practices, 90 A.L.R.2d 7 (1963).

2. Does knowingly causing economic loss to a noncompetitor by illegal conduct provide a basis of tort liability? A typical example is the harm caused by illegal strikes, such

as work stoppages by public employees, to businesses that depend upon services or supplies provided by the workers. Also, a business may know that certain conduct, prohibited by criminal law or civil statute, is injurious to another business. Courts have been reluctant to find a cause of action in either illegal labor action or illegal business conduct. Why? In Lonrho Ltd. v. Shell Petroleum Co. Ltd. (No. 2), [1982] A.C. 173 (H.L.), British oil companies allegedly violated the United Kingdom law that prohibited the supply of oil to Rhodesia. The law was a response to the unilateral declaration of independence ("U.D.I.") by the Rhodesian government in 1965. Because of this and like measures by other countries, plaintiffs' pipeline from a port in Mozambique to defendants' oil refinery in Rhodesia lay idle for many years. Plaintiffs claimed that defendants' assurances before U.D.I. of a supply of oil and maintenance of the supply after U.D.I. influenced the declaration of independence and prolonged the period of disuse of plaintiffs' pipeline, thus causing loss of revenue. The House of Lords held that plaintiffs had no action in tort. Among other reasons, the law violated had not been brought into force for the benefit or protection of a particular class of persons that included plaintiffs.

3. An example involving unions is City and County of San Francisco v. United Association of Journeymen and Apprentices of the Plumbing and Pipefitting Industry of the United States and Canada, Local 38, 42 Cal. 3d 810, 230 Cal. Rtpr. 856, 726 P.2d 538 (1986). It was held that a city had no action for damages for an illegal two-week strike by city employees belonging to building trades unions. (No action for interference with contract was asserted.) Another example is Burns Jackson Miller Summit & Spitzer v. Lindner, 59 N.Y.2d 314, 464 N.Y.S.2d 712, 451 N.E.2d 459 (1983), in which two law firms sued unions engaged in an illegal public transit strike. The New York Court of Appeals held the law firms had no action for public nuisance, because they had not suffered harm of a kind different from that suffered by the general public, and no action for interference with business, because the interference was an "incidental" result of defendants' conduct and such a cause of action was not recognized in the state's otherwise comprehensive plan for governance of public employer-employee relations.

4. What if defendant's conduct is a civil wrong to a third person? See the *Mogul Steamship* case, p. 167, supra. In Ashley v. Harrison, (1793) 1 Esp. 48, 170 Eng. Rep. 276, Peake 256, 170 Eng. Rep. 148 (K.B.N.P.), defendant, allegedly with intent to injure a director of musical performances, libelled a leading singer, "in consequence of which she was prevented from singing, from an apprehension of being hissed and ill-treated." The court non-suited the director's action as "too remote, and impossible to be connected with the cause assigned for it." OBG Ltd. v. Allan, [2008] A.C. 1 (H.L.), recognizes the tort of intentionally causing loss by unlawful means and equates unlawful means with acts against a third party that are actionable by that party (or would be actionable if the party had suffered loss). But that tort would apply only when the unlawful means interfered with the third party's freedom to deal with the plaintiff. Compare Van Camp Chocolates Ltd. v. Auslebrooks Ltd., [1984] 1 N.Z.L.R. 354 (C.A.), in which plaintiff alleged that its business was damaged by wrongful use of confidential information imparted to defendant by plaintiff's licensor. The court refrained from deciding whether misuse of confidential information in breach of a duty to a third party would constitute unlawful means, but it noted the argument that a remedy for a party in plaintiff's position should be found in extension of breach of confidence principles rather than the "circuitous route" of the tort of "unlawful interference with business interests."

5. What intent requirement applies? Korea Supply Co. v. Lockheed Martin Corp., 29 Cal. 4th 1134, 131 Cal. Rptr. 2d 29, 63 P.3d 937 (2003), held that the intent required for liability can be shown by establishing that defendant knew that interference with plain-

tiff's economic advantage was substantially certain to result from defendant's action. It was not necessary to show that defendant had a specific intent, purpose or design to interfere with plaintiff's advantage. Under Della Penna v. Toyota Motor Sales, U.S.A., Inc., 11 Cal. 4th 376, 45 Cal. Rptr. 2d 436, 902 P.2d 740 (1995), defendant's action must have been "independently wrongful" for a reason other than the interference itself or an improper motive. OBG Ltd. v. Allan, supra, adopts the position that while there must be an intention to cause economic loss, that loss did not have to be an end in itself. A defendant could be liable when causing the loss was only a means to achieve another end, such as economic gain, and it was not required that the unlawful conduct be aimed or directed at plaintiff. Compare Burke & Thomas, Inc. v. International Organization of Masters, Mates & Pilots, p. 189, infra.

K & K Management, Inc. v. Lee

Maryland Court of Appeals
316 Md. 137, 557 A.2d 965 (1989)

RODOWSKY, Judge.

[Defendants, owners of a motel, entered a contract under which plaintiffs (the Lees) were to operate the motel's restaurant and have a profit-sharing lease for five years. Defendants voiced various complaints about the operation of the restaurant and after two years decided to terminate the arrangement. Defendants had the right to terminate the agreement immediately if plaintiffs created a liability or other obligation for defendants. If the operation of the restaurant did not meet defendants' general operating standards, the agreement could be terminated on thirty days' notice. On the ground, which could be found pretextual, that plaintiffs' dismissal of a waitress caused defendants to incur a liability, defendants declared they were terminating the agreement immediately, changed the locks to the restaurant doors so plaintiffs could not enter, and prevented plaintiffs from removing equipment and furniture purchased with the receipts of the restaurant. Defendants began to operate the motel restaurant themselves, unprofitably. At trial, plaintiffs were successful on causes of action for breach of contract, conversion and interference with business. Judgments were entered on jury verdicts totalling almost a million dollars. The Court of Appeals affirmed the judgment for breach of contract, interpreting the jury's verdict to mean that neither immediate termination nor termination on thirty days' notice was justified. It also affirmed liability for conversion of plaintiffs' property but held that punitive damages should not have been awarded because it was not shown that defendants acted with actual malice. Defendants had claimed ownership of the property under an interpretation of the parties' agreement.]

The merits concerning the legal sufficiency of appellees' case for malicious interference with business present a question of fundamental legal analysis. Appellants' position accepts as its premise that K & K breached its contract with the Lees for which K & K is responsible for actual damages, including consequential damages. Appellants submit that even the intentional breach of a contract by the promisor cannot give rise to a cause of action in the promisee for malicious interference. Appellants argue that the effect of a breach of the primary contract, including the breach's incidental effects on business relationships of the promisee with third parties to the primary contract, is remedied at law exclusively by the contract damages suffered by the promisee.

Appellees disclaim undermining the rule that a contract breacher generally does not commit a tort by "interfering" with the breacher's own promised performance. The Lees assert that they enjoyed advantageous economic relationships at the time of the restaurant closing with their customers and with their suppliers. The Lees say that K & K and the Kirbys [K & K's owners] maliciously interfered with those relationships....

Tortious interference with business relationships arises only out of the relationships between three parties, the parties to a contract or other economic relationship (P and T) and the interferer (D)....

... [Restatement (Second) of Torts] Section 766B's rule subjects D to liability to P where D "intentionally and improperly interferes with [P's] prospective contractual relation ... whether the interference consists of (a) inducing or otherwise causing [T] not to enter into or continue the prospective relation or (b) preventing [P] from acquiring or continuing the prospective relation."

A two party situation is entirely different. If D interferes with D's own contract with P, D does not, on that ground alone, commit tortious interference, and P's remedy is for breach of the contract between P and D. This Court has "never permitted recovery for the tort of intentional interference with a contract when both the defendant and the plaintiff were parties to the contract." *Wilmington Trust Co. v. Clark*, 289 Md. 313, 329, 424 A.2d 744, 754 (1981)....

In this case the Lees seek to skirt the settled rule described above by contending that this is a case of tortious interference by D with business relations between P and T where T is comprised of the customers and suppliers of the Seoul Restaurant at Harbor City Inn....

With respect to suppliers, there was no evidence of any particular contract with any particular supplier with which the appellants interfered.... Further, the evidence is uncontradicted that the Lees did not suffer any impairment of their ability to obtain credit from suppliers when the Lees went back into the food service business after having been locked out by the appellants....

We shall assume that the Lees' arrangements with customers who had made reservations were existing contracts. Nevertheless the Lees did not attempt to prove actual loss resulting from any specific contract. The Lees did, however, show actual loss resulting from their business relations with prospective customers by proving, as part of the consequential damages resulting from breach of the Agreement, the loss of profit to the Lees from general restaurant operations projected over the balance of the life of the Agreement and its two extensions....

At oral argument, the Lees emphasized that appellants' interference was intentional, in the tort sense of "intentional." Under the Restatement, D's preventing P from continuing a prospective relation is intentional if D "desires to bring it about or if he knows that the interference is certain or substantially certain to occur as a result of his action." § 766B, comment *d*. Here the officers of K & K knew that the Seoul Restaurant was a meeting place for Korean organizations. We shall assume, *arguendo*, that the evidence supports a finding that the closing would be substantially certain to prevent the Lees from honoring arrangements with one or more Korean organizations.

But acts have multiple effects. D's breach of contract with P can interfere with P's business relations with T. Whether that effect is tortious interference with the P-T relationship depends in large measure on whether D's purpose or motive in breaching the D-P contract is to interfere with the P-T relationship. The Restatement analysis of the tort distinguishes purpose from intent. Even if the officers of K & K could be found to have tortious intent based on the assumed substantial certainty of interference with Korean customers, there is no tort because the evidence is uncontradicted that appellants' purpose or motive in closing the restaurant was not directed at the Lees' relations with their customers....

This is not to say that acts which constitute a breach of contract between P and D can never be the basis of malicious interference by D with business relations between P and T. Unlike appellants' breach of the Agreement, the breach or threatened breach of the P-D contract may be the instrument selected by D for the purpose of interfering with the P-T contract....

... The Lees cannot claim that the guests at the motel or the persons working in the neighborhood were their customers whom the appellants sought to appropriate by breaking the lease. The patronage of those classes of customers primarily depended on location, and the Lees' rights to the location depended on the Agreement. Any claim of tortious interference with the Lees' business relations with those customers is indistinguishable from the breach of the Agreement and has been compensated by damages measured by lost profits for the life of the Agreement. The Lees additionally had a personal following of Korean customers and, indeed, tried their case with emphasis on that business relationship. But no reasonable person could conclude on the evidence in this case that the appellants' purpose in closing the Seoul Restaurant was to attempt to obtain for themselves the future business of the Korean customers. The Lees' loss of that business (as it developed, a temporary loss) was an incidental effect of appellants' breach of the Agreement and not the object or purpose of the breach....

From the premise that the tort of interference with economic relations will be recognized if D's means of interference with the P-T relation are sufficiently improper, the Lees argue that appellants' conduct should be labeled "egregious" and that the tort should be found to have been committed here. One defect we find in the argument is that it seeks to apply to an essentially two party situation law relevant to a three party situation. The degree of impropriety of the means employed by D in breaching a P-D contract should not convert an incidental interference with a P-T relationship, foreseeably resulting from the breach, into an interference having the purpose or object of interfering with P's relationship with T. Secondarily, the means employed here were neither illegal nor tortious....

Here appellants retook possession of the restaurant premises by changing the locks without notice.[12] But K & K owns the premises. The Lees' rights either to occupy the premises or to receive notice of termination rested on the Agreement. Appellants' action was unlawful exclusively in the sense that it was a breach of contract....

If breach of the P-D contract were treated as an improper means which overrides the lack of motive to interfere in the incidental relations between P and T, then the interference tort becomes boundless and only rarely would the breach of a commercial contract fail to be a tort as well....

For the foregoing reasons the trial court erred in denying appellants' motion for judgment on the claim for malicious interference....

[Adkins, J., (with whom Cole, J., joined) delivered an opinion dissenting from the disallowance of punitive damages in the conversion action and the disposition of the interference with business action. The dissent concluded that there was sufficient evidence of actual malice to support punitive damages and that the judgment for plaintiffs in the interference action should be affirmed. Defendants had employed tortious means—con-

---

12. The incidental interference with the Lees' relationship with the Korean customers was effected by the lockout and not by the conversion of certain equipment or utensils. Even if the Agreement had clearly specified that equipment purchased through the business accounts was the Lees' property and the Lees had been permitted to remove it, the Seoul Restaurant would nevertheless have remained closed.

version of plaintiffs' restaurant equipment and furniture. This had, the dissent found, substantially interfered with plaintiffs' ability to re-establish their restaurant in another location. It therefore interfered with plaintiffs' relations with established customers. Also, there was evidence from which the jury could find that defendants' conduct was "calculated to enhance injury to the Lees." The mere breach of defendant's contract with a plaintiff might not supply grounds for a tortious interference action, but an action would lie if the breach was attended by improper conduct.]

Notes

1. Authority outside the United States holds that breach of contract constitutes unlawful means for purposes of an action for interference with business relations as well as an action for interference with contract. See Fleming, Law of Torts 784–787 (10th ed. 2011). Also that inducing breach is unlawful means. See J.T. Stratford & Son Ltd. v. Lindley, p. 162, supra. Of the American cases, Buxbom v. Smith, 23 Cal. 2d 535, 145 P.2d 305 (1944), found tort liability for interference with business when breach of contract with plaintiff was utilized to facilitate defendant's hiring of plaintiff's employees. In Cherberg v. People National Bank of Washington, 88 Wash. 2d 595, 564 P.2d 1137 (1977), tenants sued their landlord for interference with their business allegedly caused by the landlord's wilful refusal to perform duties owed the tenants under a commercial lease. The court held that liability for intentional interference with "business expectancies" could be imposed if the landlord's motive was "not the economic viability of [its] investment ... but rather was economic considerations outside the scope of the parties' obligations under their existing agreement," such as removal of the tenants. See also Leigh Furniture and Carpet Co. v. Isom, 657 P.2d 293 (Utah 1982) (breach of contract with plaintiff wrongful means if done with purpose to injure). Compare Burke & Thomas, Inc. v. International Organization of Masters, Mates & Pilots, West Coast and Pacific Region Inland Division, Branch 6, 92 Wash. 2d 762, 600 P.2d 1282 (1979) (in violation of collective bargaining agreement, union called strike of members working on ferry system, causing loss to island resorts and area residents; no liability in absence of object to interfere with private businesses).

2. In Pizza Management, Inc. v. Pizza Hut, Inc., 737 F. Supp. 1154 (D. Kan. 1990), tortious interference with prospective advantage was among the numerous claims brought against Pizza Hut, Inc. by a corporation that held Pizza Hut franchises and the corporation's principal owner. It was alleged that defendants prevented plaintiffs from making a public offering of the corporation's stock, which would have enabled plaintiffs to raise capital and purchase additional franchise territories, by wrongfully refusing to give consent to the offering. This violated defendants' duty under agreements with plaintiffs not to withhold consent to transfers of interest unreasonably. The court concluded that a party's breach of contract could serve as the predicate of an action for interference with prospective advantage, but plaintiff would also have to allege that the breach was committed with the motive of interfering with prospective business relationships between plaintiff and third parties. Furthermore, under Kansas law, plaintiffs could not maintain a tort action without alleging injuries beyond those asserted in their breach of contract claim, which encompassed damages directly resulting from defendants' failure to consent to the public offering. Plaintiffs failed to do this, so their claim of tortious interference was dismissed. On claims of tortious interference by contracting parties generally, see Dobbs, Law of Torts 1272–1274 (2000).

3. It is widely accepted that a threat to use unlawful means as well as employment of unlawful means is a basis of liability. (Outside the United States this is called tortious "intimidation.") If unlawful means for this purpose includes breach of contract, the result is that

threats to break a contract can give rise to liability to the person intentionally injured thereby. Rookes v. Barnard, [1964] A.C. 1129 (H.L.). This could be someone with whom the threatened person has business relations. (In Rookes v. Barnard, plaintiff was an employee whom a union had fired by threatening the employer with a walkout.) Or it could be the threatened person himself. See Carty, An Analysis of the Economic Torts 107–121 (2d ed. 2010).

4. *Conspiracy*. When plaintiff has been injured by unlawful means, it may be contended that there is a cause of action for conspiracy, which is discussed in the *Mogul Steamship* and *Parkinson* cases, supra. Whether this adds to the tort liability that otherwise would exist is not clear, despite the number of cases in which conspiracy has been alleged. When unlawful means are employed, a conspiracy action can be maintained if an intent to cause injury to plaintiff can be shown. Defendants can be liable even if their primary purpose is to further or protect their own legitimate interests, not to harm plaintiff's interests. Lonrho Plc. v. Fayed, [1992] 1 A.C. 448 (H.L.); Canada Cement LaFarge Ltd. v. British Columbia Lightweight Aggregate Ltd., [1983] 1 S.C.R. 452, (1983) 145 D.L.R.3d 385. When unlawful means are not employed, injury to plaintiff (not advancement of defendants' interests) may have to be the predominant purpose of defendants' agreement for economic loss to be actionable on the basis of civil conspiracy. See Lonrho Ltd. v. Shell Petroleum Co. Ltd. (No. 2), p. 185, supra; Robitaille v. Morse, 283 Mass. 27, 186 N.E. 78 (1933). See generally Carty, An Analysis of the Economic Torts 122–154 (2d ed. 2010); Fleming, Law of Torts 789–795 (10th ed. 2011); Note, Civil Conspiracy: A Substantive Tort?, 59 Boston U. L. Rev. 921 (1979).

Top Service Body Shop, Inc. v. Allstate Insurance Company
Supreme Court of Oregon
283 Or. 201, 582 P.2d 1365 (1978)

LINDE, Justice.

Plaintiff, the operator of an automobile body repair shop in Coos Bay, Oregon, sued defendant insurance company for general and punitive damages for injuries alleged to result from defendant's wrongful practices in directing insurance claimants to have repairs made at body shops other than plaintiff's. [The trial court entered judgment for defendant notwithstanding the jury's verdict for plaintiff.] ...

Either the pursuit of an improper objective of harming plaintiff or the use of wrongful means that in fact cause injury to plaintiff's contractual or business relationships may give rise to a tort claim for those injuries. However, efforts to consolidate both recognized and unsettled lines of development into a general theory of "tortious interference" have brought to the surface the difficulties of defining the elements of so general a tort without sweeping within its terms a wide variety of socially very different conduct.... The main problem is what weight to give to the defendant's objective in interfering with plaintiff's contract or with plaintiff's prospective business relations. If the focus in defining the tort is on defendant's wrongful motive or use of wrongful means, this element will likely be a necessary part of plaintiff's case. If the tort is defined primarily as an invasion of plaintiff's protected interests, defendant's reasons are likely to be treated as questions of justification or privilege. Section 766 of the first *Restatement of Torts* read: "Except as stated in section 698, one who, without a privilege to do so, induces or otherwise purposely causes a third person not to (a) perform a contract with another, or (b) enter into or continue a business relation with another is liable to the other for the harm caused thereby." The term "purposely" meant that a defendant must not only have expected, or "intended," his conduct to interfere with plaintiff's contract or business relationship but that this interference must have been at least one purpose of defendant's act. Reasons that would excuse such an interference were then stated as "privileges" in sections 767–774.

In preparing the *Restatement (Second) of Torts* in 1969, the then Reporter, Dean William Prosser, proposed to change "purposely" to "intentionally" with respect to any interference with an existing contract that was not justified by a privilege. He would have retained "purposely" with respect to interference with future contractual relations. However, the change to liability based simply on unprivileged intent was not accepted even with respect to inducing or causing breaches of existing contracts.... As the *Restatement* now stands, [interference with existing or prospective contracts] would give rise to liability if it is both intentional and affirmatively improper (replacing reliance on lack of "privilege" in the definition of the tort), and a purpose to harm the injured party would be one factor making the interference improper. *Restatement (Second) of Torts* §§ 766–767 (Tent. Draft No. 23, 1977).[8]

[*Nees v. Hocks*, 272 Or. 210, 536 P.2d 512 (1975)] rejected the concept that every intentional infliction of harm is prima facie a tort unless justified. Finding that this concept was no longer needed to escape the rigidity of the common-law forms of pleading, the court concluded that it created as many difficulties as it solved. However, the court found that the plaintiff had effectively pleaded and proved that her discharge by defendant was tortious by reason of an improper motive.

We conclude that the approach of *Nees v. Hocks* is equally appropriate to claims of tort liability for intentional interference with contractual or other economic relations. In summary, such a claim is made out when interference resulting in injury to another is wrongful by some measure beyond the fact of the interference itself. Defendant's liability may arise from improper motives or from the use of improper means. They may be wrongful by reason of a statute or other regulation, or a recognized rule of common law, or perhaps an established standard of a trade or profession. No question of privilege arises unless the interference would be wrongful but for the privilege; it becomes an issue only if the acts charged would be tortious on the part of an unprivileged defendant. Even a recognized privilege may be overcome when the means used by defendant are not justified by the reason for recognizing the privilege. To this extent we agree with the analysis of the second *Restatement*.

In the present case, Top Service pleaded both improper motives and improper means of interference. It alleged that Allstate sought to and did induce Top Service's patrons not to have Top Service repair their automobiles, making false statements about the quality of plaintiff's workmanship and threats about withdrawing insurance coverage or subjecting the settlement of claims to possible arbitration. It also alleges that this was done "with the sole design of injuring Plaintiff and destroying his business," and in an endeavor

---

8. [§ 767 Comment *d*]: " ... The interference with the other's prospective contractual relation is intentional if the actor desires to bring it about or if he knows that the interference is certain or substantially certain to occur as a result of his action. [¶] The interference, however, must also be improper. The factors to be considered in determining whether an interference is improper are stated in § 767. One of them is the actor's motive and another is the interest sought to be advanced by him. Together these factors mean that the actor's purpose is of substantial significance. If he had no desire to effectuate the interference by his action but knew that it would be a mere incidental result of conduct he was engaging in for another purpose, the interference may be found to be not improper. Other factors come into play here, however, particularly the nature of the actor's conduct. If the means used are innately wrongful, predatory in character, a purpose to produce the interference may not be necessary. On the other hand, if the sole purpose of the actor is to vent his ill will, the interference may be improper although the means are less blameworthy...."

to "compel Plaintiff to abandon the same." If proved, along with damages and causation, these allegations satisfy the elements of the tort we have reviewed above....

... But the record will not support an inference that Allstate had any design or purpose to inflict injury on Top Service as such, even short of the "sole design" to put Top Service out of business that the complaint alleged.

Taken most favorably to plaintiff, as is proper after a verdict for plaintiff, the evidence showed that Allstate has a practice of designating certain repair shops in the locality as "competitive shops" to which it prefers to send insurance claimants for whose repairs Allstate is obligated; that Top Service at one time was a "drive-in" shop for Allstate, where claimants would be directed for an estimate by an Allstate insurance adjuster; that after a dispute Top Service's owner decided that it would not continue as a drive-in shop for Allstate; and that thereafter Allstate adjusters would actively discourage claimants under its insurance policies from taking work to be paid for by Allstate to Top Service, sending them instead to other shops on its preferred list. As specific bases for an inference of destructive purpose, Top Service lists two occasions when Allstate adjusters disparaged the quality of Top Service's work (apart from its relative cost), although Allstate personnel had generally considered Top Service a high quality shop; Allstate's willingness to disappoint its own insured who preferred Top Service; one occasion when Allstate took its option to "total" a car, *i. e.* to pay off its value, when the insured wanted it repaired at Top Service; and finally Allstate's resort to "improper and unlawful means" to direct business away from Top Service to other shops. Without setting forth here the excerpts of the record cited by plaintiff, we agree with the trial court that these acts were wholly consistent with Allstate's pursuit of its own business purposes as it saw them and did not suffice to support an inference of the alleged improper purpose to injure Top Service. The court's ruling on this point was not error....

... [T]he case was submitted to the jury solely on the theory of liability for purposely seeking to harm plaintiff's business. Even if defendant might also have been liable on an alternative theory of tortious interference by improper means, we cannot reinstate the verdict on that theory, which was not presented to the jury....

[Affirmed.]

Pleas v. City of Seattle

Supreme Court of Washington
112 Wash. 2d 794, 774 P.2d 1158 (1989)

UTTER, Justice.

[Parkridge, a general partnership, bought property in Seattle with the intent of constructing a high-rise apartment complex on it. Existing zoning regulations permitted this use of the land. Because of opposition to a high-rise complex by residents of the neighborhood and organizations formed by them, the City of Seattle required an environmental impact statement, which was inconsistent with the city's normal procedures, long delayed the issuance of permits for demolition of the existing structures on the property and building the apartment complex, and downzoned the property to single family residential use. Parkridge obtained a court ruling that the rezoning was void, as arbitrary and capricious, and the city's refusal to process Parkridge's application for a building permit was improper. Subsequently, it commenced an action against the city seeking damages for intentional interference with business expectancy. The demolition and building permits, which had been applied for in the winter of 1973–1974, were not granted until 1983. Trial was held following construction of the apartment building to a modified design in 1984. The court determined that Parkridge had been damaged in the amount of $969,468 by lost profits, loss of favorable financing, increased construction costs due to inflation, the costs of the first environmental impact statement, which the city required to be replaced as outdated, attorneys' fees, and other items. Parkridge appealed from the Washington Court of Appeals' decision that it had presented insufficient evidence to prove that the city's interference with its business was improper.]

... The theory underlying this tort was aptly summarized by the appellate court of Illinois: " ... the law draws a line beyond which no member of the community may go in intentionally intermeddling with the business affairs of others; that if acts of which complaint is made do not rest on some legitimate interest, or if there is sharp dealing or overreaching or other conduct below the behavior of fair men similarly situated, the ensuing loss should be redressed...." *Rock Falls v. Chicago Title & Trust Co.*, 13 Ill. App. 3d 359, 300 N.E.2d 331, 333 (1973).

In *King v. Seattle*, 84 Wash. 2d 239, 525 P.2d 228 (1974), this court recognized that the tort of interference with prospective economic expectancy ... may apply to the actions of a municipality denying a building permit. In that case, the court found that the City's intentional and wrongful refusal to issue street and building permits constituted intentional interference with Kings' business expectancy in developing their property. *King* is not alone in applying the tort of intentional interference against a municipality. *See Rock Falls* (finding a cause of action for tortious interference with business expectancy against municipality when it wrongfully withheld various permits requested by developer).

Under [*Calbom v. Knudtzon*, 65 Wash. 2d 157, 396 P.2d 148 (1964)] liability is based simply on the intentional interference with a known business expectancy. Any justification or privilege the defendant might have is treated as an affirmative defense which a defendant must prove. This is the general approach of the first Restatement and of most courts.

The authors of the second Restatement of Torts modified this approach in favor of one that defines the tort as involving "improper" as well as intentional interference. Restatement (Second) of Torts, §§ 766, 766B (1979). Factors to be weighted in determining the impropriety of the defendant's interference are discussed in § 767, and are similar to the factors used to determine a defendant's privilege or justification under the first Restatement.

This change was made in response to a concern articulated by many courts and commentators that the prima facie tort approach in which every intentional infliction of harm is prima facie tortious unless justified. This approach required too little of the plaintiff insofar as it let the major issue in the controversy—the wrongfulness of the defendant's conduct—to be resolved by asserting an affirmative defense.

Although its authors declined to take a clear position on the matter, the revised language of the second Restatement can be interpreted to require the plaintiff to show in the first instance that the defendant's interference was improper.... [T]he Court of Appeals expressly adopted the second Restatement and held that Parkridge had not met its burden of proving that the City acted improperly.

While we agree with the general thrust of § 766B, we disagree with the interpretation given this provision of the second Restatement by the Court of Appeals, particularly regarding the burden of persuasion problem. Far from announcing a new rule as the Court of Appeals suggests, the authors of the second Restatement acknowledge that " ... there is little consensus on who has the burden of raising the issue of whether the interference was improper or not and subsequently of proving that issue.... Instead of laying down a categoric rule for one position or the other, therefore, it seems appropriate to draw a more particularized line depending upon whether the precise matter goes more specifically to the culpability of the actor's conduct in general or to its justification under the specific facts." § 767, Comment k....

We believe that the right balance has been struck by [*Top Service Body Shop v. Allstate Insurance Co.*, p. 190, supra].... Thus, a cause of action for tortious interference arises from either the defendant's pursuit of an improper objective of harming the plaintiff or the use of wrongful means that in fact cause injury to plaintiff's contractual or business relationships....

... Implicit in our previous cases dealing with tortious interference has been some showing that the interference complained of be "wrongful" in some way or that [defendant] had a "duty of non-interference." Thus, in *King* we found that the City was under a "duty to act fairly and reasonably in its dealings with the plaintiffs" and that this duty was breached when the City wrongfully refused to grant a building permit. However, matters of privilege or justification continue to be affirmative defenses to be raised by the defendant.

In the present case, Parkridge alleges both improper motives and improper means of interference. The improper motives arise from the City officials' apparent desire to gain the favor of a politically active and potentially influential group opposing the Parkridge project. The improper means arise from the City's actions in refusing to grant necessary permits and arbitrarily delaying this project. As we stated in *King*, the City's arbitrary and capricious actions can be considered evidence of tortious interference with a business expectancy.

There is ample evidence to support the trial court's finding that the City's actions in this decade-long episode were sufficiently improper or wrongful so as to support a claim for tortious interference even under our new formulation of this tort. Parkridge was required to show that the City's conduct was not only intentional but wrongful, and it has done so; the burden then shifted to the City to show that its conduct was either privileged or justified. The City has failed to produce persuasive evidence that its conduct comes under either category....

The Court of Appeals also stated that the City's motive carries little weight in this case because City officials acted for the primary purpose of political gain, not for the purpose of interfering with Parkridge's prospective business opportunities. "The City's motive was to curry favor with the voters who lived on Capitol Hill." Insofar as the City officials could gain political favor with this group only by directly interfering with Parkridge's business expectancies, this conclusion is curious. The second Restatement does not say that interference must be the actor's primary motive before liability will attach. To the contrary, the authors suggest that the plaintiff be required to show only that "the actor was motivated, in whole or in part, by a desire to interfere.... The desire to interfere with the other's contractual relations need not, however, be the sole motive." Restatement (Second) of Torts § 767, Comment d.

The second Restatement further states that impropriety may be more easily found if the means of interference was wrongful, even if the actor had no specific purpose to interfere. The efforts made by employees in the Mayor's Office and building department to block Parkridge's legitimate construction project were an improper means of interference. There is ample evidence in the record to support the finding of the trial court that the City singled out Parkridge's project and applied its land use regulations in such a manner to block any apartment development on the property.

There is no rational basis for the argument that allowing a cause of action for tortious interference against a municipality for actions involved here would have a "chilling effect" on public officials who must exercise discretion in reviewing permits for controversial projects. The only "chilling effect" we envision is against public officials exercising their official powers in a blatantly biased manner to gain favor with a certain community group.

Nor do we accept the suggestion of the Court of Appeals that the City's actions in this instance were simply part of the "political process." Municipal liability for the flagrant abuse of power by officials who intentionally interfere with the development rights of property owners cannot be avoided simply by labeling such actions "political."

… Parkridge presented sufficient evidence to support its claim for tortious interference….

[Reversed. Dore, Acting Chief Justice, delivered a dissenting opinion.]

Notes

1. The proposition that "every intentional infliction of harm is prima facie a tort unless justified" can be traced to the statement of Bowen, L.J., in the *Mogul Steamship* case, p. 167, supra, that "intentionally to do that which is calculated in the ordinary course of events to damage, and which does, in fact, damage another in that other person's property or trade, is actionable if done without just cause or excuse." In Aikens v. Wisconsin, 195 U.S. 194 (1904), Holmes, J., interpreted this to mean that "*prima facie*, the intentional infliction of temporal damage is a cause of action, which … requires a justification if the defendant is to escape." He went on to elaborate that justification may depend upon defendant's motives or the end for which the act was done. That there is such a prima facie tort, outside recognized categories of tort liability, has been accepted in New York. But this has been limited by rules that conduct falling within specific tort categories is not actionable as prima facie tort and that "disinterested malevolence" must be defendants' sole motivation. (The issue in *Aikens* was whether a Wisconsin statute punishing persons who combined for the purpose of injuring another in his trade or business violated the Fourteenth Amendment. The statute's constitutionality was sustained on an interpretation that limited its application to persons who did harm "malevolently for the sake of the harm as an end in itself, and not merely as a means to some further end legitimately desired.") The prima facie tort theory has been accepted in a few other states, such as Missouri, but in most states there is no established action for "prima facie tort." See Annot., Prima Facie Tort, 16 A.L.R.3d 1191 (1967); Bieg, Prima Facie Tort Comes to New Mexico: A Summary of Prima Facie Tort Law, 21 N.M. L. Rev. 327 (1991); Vandevelde, The Modern Prima Facie Tort Doctrine, 79 Ky. L.J. 519 (1991).

2. An alternative approach is to find a cause of action when plaintiff can establish not only that harm was intentionally (in the sense of knowingly) caused, but also that defendant's conduct was "wrongful" or "improper" for some other reason. In *Top Service Body Shop* this was the basis of a rule that liability for intentional interference with economic relations could arise in the presence of improper motives (specifically, purpose to inflict injury) or improper means. This was followed in Leigh Furniture and Carpet Co. v. Isom, 657 P.2d 293 (Utah 1982), which requires for the first alternative that the improper purpose predominate. Improper means were found in defendant's initiation of groundless lawsuits against plaintiff and defendant's deliberate breach of contract with purpose to inflict injury. See also Della Penna v. Toyota Motor Sales, U.S.A., Inc., p. 186, supra, which advocates "a sharpened distinction" between interference with prospective economic relations and interference with existing contracts. Restatement (Second) of

Torts §870 (1979) provides, "One who intentionally causes injury to another is subject to liability to the other for that injury, if his conduct is generally culpable and not justifiable under the circumstances...." Is this a reformulation of the prima facie tort theory or is it closer to the approach of the *Top Service* case?

3. Does the statement in *Top Service Body Shop* that defendant's means may be wrongful by reason of a statute or other regulation permit recovery for diversion of customers caused by a competitor's illegal practices, as claimed in Clark v. Crown Drug Co. (p. 190)? In Klinger v. Morrow County Grain Growers, Inc., 102 Or. App. 375, 794 P.2d 811 (1990), review denied, 310 Or. 422, 799 P.2d 151 (1990), the operator of a retail gasoline station brought an interference with business action, seeking damages and injunctive relief, against the proprietor of a business that allowed self-service pumping of gasoline, which was illegal in Oregon. The court held plaintiff had no cause of action. The statute violated had the purpose of safety, not the purpose of protecting business interests or competition. The *Top Service* opinion was not to be read as permitting an action when defendant violated a statute which had no connection to the business or economic relationships alleged to have been damaged. The statement in *Top Service* that means may be wrongful by reason "an established standard of a trade or profession" was applied in Volt Services Group v. Adecco Employment Services, Inc., 178 Or. App. 121, 35 P.3d 329 (2001), review denied, 333 Or. 567, 42 P.3d 1246 (2002) (industry's voluntary code of ethics).

4. Plaintiff wants to sell his business as a common carrier. Defendant, an important customer, wants to buy the business at a low price. It informs prospective purchasers that it will cancel its contract with the carrier if the business is sold. Because of defendant's conduct, no one else will purchase the carrier. Defendant ultimately buys it at a low price. Can plaintiff obtain damages? See Lowell v. Mother's Cake & Cookie Co., 79 Cal. App. 3d 13, 144 Cal. Rptr. 664 (1978) (cause of action stated, since defendant's purpose was to discourage potential buyers and parties, being in entirely different lines of business, were not competitors).

5. Plaintiff applies to a building association for a loan in order to purchase property. The loan is to be secured by a mortgage on the property. After the loan application is made, the building association buys the property itself. Has it committed any tort? See Goldman v. Harford Road Building Association, 150 Md. 677, 133 A. 843 (1926) (no fraud, breach of fiduciary relation or other tort shown). But see Djowharzadeh v. City National Bank and Trust Co. of Norman, p. 328, infra.

6. A newspaper regularly conducts puzzle contests, publishing puzzles and awarding prizes for correct solutions. Professional puzzle solvers, who offer solutions to prospective contestants, are sued by the newspaper, which alleges that their activities tend to destroy the effectiveness of the contests, to discourage contestants who have not subscribed to the professionals' services, and to induce breaches of the contest rules. What result? See Philadelphia Record Co. v. Leopold, 40 F. Supp. 346 (S.D.N.Y. 1941) (unlawful interference with newspaper's business found).

7. An American company, formerly selling a large amount of equipment in a foreign country, finds that its sales there have dropped almost to zero. It discovers the reason: another American company, a competitor, is paying large bribes to people in that country. Is the competitor liable in tort? Would distinctions be drawn between bribes to purchase the competitor's equipment, bribes to speed up the importation of its equipment, and bribes to slow down the handling of plaintiff's equipment?

8. An insurance company may have a near monopoly of a type of insurance needed in certain businesses or occupations. Is it tortious for the insurer to deny coverage of per-

sons who have filed claims against it in the past? To charge high premiums for coverage of these persons? See Pino v. Trans-Atlantic Marine, Inc., 358 Mass. 498, 265 N.E.2d 583 (1970), and Pino v. Protection Maritime Insurance Co., Ltd., 599 F.2d 10 (1st Cir. 1979), cert. denied, 444 U.S. 900 (1979) (insurers of about 75% of port's fishing vessels enjoined from denying coverage and from charging higher premiums for insurance of fishermen who had pursued personal injury insurance claims). What if the only newspaper in an area refuses to publish advertisements for plaintiff's business? For this, there has been no tort liability, a publisher being under no obligation to accept advertisements from all who apply. See Annot., Right of Publisher of Newspaper or Magazine, in Absence of Contractual Obligation, to Refuse Publication of Advertisement, 18 A.L.R.3d 1286 (1968).

Speakers of Sport, Inc. v. ProServ, Inc.

United States Court of Appeals, Seventh Circuit
178 F.3d 862 (1999)

POSNER, Chief Judge.

The plaintiff, Speakers of Sport, appeals from the grant of summary judgment to the defendant, ProServ, in a diversity suit in which one sports agency has charged another with tortious interference with a business relationship and related violations of Illinois law.... Ivan Rodriguez, a highly successful catcher with the Texas Rangers baseball team, in 1991 signed the first of several one-year contracts making Speakers his agent. ProServ wanted to expand its representation of baseball players and to this end invited Rodriguez to its office in Washington and there promised that it would get him between $2 and $4 million in endorsements if he signed with ProServ—which he did, terminating his contract (which was terminable at will) with Speakers. This was in 1995. ProServ failed to obtain significant endorsement for Rodriguez and after just one year he switched to another agent who the following year landed him a five-year $42 million contract with the Rangers. Speakers brought this suit a few months later, charging that the promise of endorsements that ProServ had made to Rodriguez was fraudulent and had induced him to terminate his contract with Speakers....

... [I]nducing the termination of a contract, even when the termination is not a breach because the contract is terminable at will, can still be actionable under the tort law of Illinois, either as an interference with prospective economic advantage, or as an interference with the contract at will itself. Nothing turns on the difference in characterization....

There would be few more effective inhibitors of the competitive process than making it a tort for an agent to promise the client of another agent to do better by him—which is pretty much what this case comes down to. It is true that Speakers argues only that the competitor may not make a promise that he knows he cannot fulfill, may not, that is, compete by fraud. Because the competitor's privilege does not include a right to get business from a competitor by means of fraud, it is hard to quarrel with this position in the abstract, but the practicalities are different. If the argument were accepted and the new agent made a promise that was not fulfilled, the old agent would have a shot at convincing a jury that the new agent had known from the start that he couldn't deliver on the promise. Once a case gets to the jury, all bets are off. The practical consequence of Speakers' approach, therefore, would be that a sports agent who lured away the client of another agent with a promise to do better by him would be running a grave legal risk.

This threat to the competitive process is blocked by the principle of Illinois law that promissory fraud is not actionable unless it is part of a scheme to defraud, that is, unless it is one element of a pattern of fraudulent acts [a rule rejected in most states].…

… The only reasonable meaning to attach to ProServ's so-called promise is that ProServ would try to get as many endorsements as possible for Rodriguez and that it was optimistic that it could get him at least $2 million worth of them. So understood, the "promise" was not a promise at all. But even if it was a promise (or a warranty), it cannot be the basis for a finding of fraud because it was not part of a scheme to defraud evidenced by more than the allegedly fraudulent promise itself.

It can be argued, however, that competition can be tortious even if it does not involve an actionable fraud (which in Illinois would not include a fraudulent promise) or other independently tortious act, such as defamation, or trademark or patent infringement, or a theft of a trade secret; that competitors should not be allowed to use "unfair" tactics; and that a promise known by the promisor when made to be unfulfillable is such a tactic, especially when used on a relatively unsophisticated, albeit very well to do, baseball player. Considerable support for this view can be found in the case law. But the Illinois courts have not as yet embraced the doctrine, and we are not alone in thinking it pernicious. The doctrine's conception of wrongful competition is vague — "wrongful by reason of … an established standard of a trade or profession," *Yoakum v. Hartford Fire Ins. Co.* [129 Idaho 171, 923 P.2d 416 (1996)], or "a violation of recognized ethical rules or established customs or practices in the business community," *RTL Distributing, Inc. v. Double S Batteries, Inc.* [545 N.W.2d 587 (Iowa App. 1996)], or "improper because they [the challenged competitive tactics] violate an established standard of a trade or profession, or involve unethical conduct, … sharp dealing [or] overreaching." *Duggin v. Adams* [234 Va. 221, 360 S.E.2d 832 (1987)]. Worse, the established standards of a trade or profession in regard to competition, and its ideas of unethical competitive conduct, are likely to reflect a desire to limit competition for reasons related to the self-interest of the trade or profession rather than to the welfare of its customers or clients. We agree with Professor Perlman that the tort of interference with business relationships should be confined to cases in which the defendant employed unlawful means to stiff a competitor, Harvey S. Perlman, "Interference With Contract and Other Economic Expectancies: A Clash of Tort and Contract Doctrine," 49 *U. Chi. L. Rev.* 61 (1982), and we are reassured by the conclusion of his careful analysis that the case law is generally consistent with this position as a matter of outcomes as distinct from articulation.

Invoking the concept of "wrongful by reason of … an established standard of a trade or profession," Speakers points to a rule of major league baseball forbidding players' agents to compete by means of misrepresentations. The rule is designed to protect the players, rather than their agents, so that even if it established a norm enforceable by law Speakers would not be entitled to invoke it; it is not a rule designed for Speakers' protection. In any event its violation would not be the kind of "wrongful" conduct that should trigger the tort of intentional interference; it would not be a violation of law.

[The court found no violation by ProServ of the Illinois Consumer Fraud and Deceptive Business Practices Act.]

We add that even if Speakers could establish liability under either the common law of torts or the deceptive practices act, its suit would fail because it cannot possibly establish, as it seeks to do, a damages entitlement (the only relief it seeks) to the agent's fee on Rodriguez's $42 million contract. That contract was negotiated years after he left Speakers, and by another agent. Since Rodriguez had only a year-to-year contract with Speakers—terminable at will, moreover—and since obviously he was dissatisfied with Speakers at least to the extent of switching to ProServ and then when he became disillusioned with ProServ of *not* returning to Speakers' fold, the likelihood that Speakers would have retained him had ProServ not lured him away is too slight to ground an award of such damages....

Affirmed.

Notes

1. A number of recent cases do not accept that liability attaches only when illegal or independently tortious means were employed. See Scutti Enterprises, LLC v. Park Place Entertainment Corp., 322 F.3d 211 (2d Cir. 2003); Stella Foods, Inc. v. Superior Court (Cacique, Inc.), 60 Cal. App. 4th 299, 70 Cal. Rptr. 2d 91 (1998); Maximus, Inc. v. Lockheed Information Management Systems Co., Inc., 254 Va. 408, 493 S.E.2d 375 (1997). But there seems to be growing support for the position adopted in the *Speakers of Sport* case. See Trade 'N Post, L.L.C. v. World Duty Free Americas, Inc., 628 N.W.2d 707 (N.D. 2001); Wal-Mart Stores, Inc. v. Sturges, 52 S.W.3d 711 (Tex. 2001). Cf. OBG Ltd. v. Allan., p. 185, supra. The majority opinion in the *Wal-Mart* case, which included an extensive history and analysis of tortious interference liability, criticized the lack of clear standards and "misassociation" of interference with prospective advantage with interference with contract. "Justification" and "privilege" were said to be useful concepts for interference with contract, but not for interference with prospective business relations. For the latter, the court decided, liability would require proof that defendant's conduct was illegal or independently actionable under tort law. Conduct that was merely "sharp" or unfair would not suffice.

2. Another possibility is for a court to decide that unlawful or independently actionable conduct is required when defendant acted as a competitor of plaintiff, leaving open the rule to be applied when they were not in competition. See DP-Tek, Inc. v. AT & T Global Information Solutions Co., 100 F.3d 828 (10th Cir. 1996); Brokerage Concepts, Inc. v. U.S. Healthcare, Inc., 140 F.3d 494 (3d Cir. 1998) (distinguishing application of pressure to third party in market where parties did not compete from competition). This stems from the distinction between "improper" interference, under the Restatement (Second) of Torts general rule for tortious interference liability, and employment of "wrongful means," under the Restatement's specific rule for a competitor who deprives another of a prospective contractual relation or causes termination of a contract terminable at will. Restatement (Second) of Torts § 768 (1979).

3. *Tortious interference claims as alternatives to other tort actions.* The law of injurious falsehood (pp. 239–263, infra) applies to false statements directed at persons in plaintiff's market that cause economic harm. Should an action for interference for prospective advantage be entertained in this situation? This was one of a number of theories asserted in an author's suit against *The New York Times* for failure to include his novel in the newspaper's "best seller" list, Blatty v. New York Times Co., 175 Cal. App. 3d 571, 221 Cal. Rptr. 236 (1985), rev'd, 42 Cal. 3d 1033, 232 Cal. Rptr. 542, 728 P.2d 1177 (1986), cert. denied, 485 U.S. 934 (1988). This allegedly diminished the sales of the book and the amounts at which paperback and film rights could be sold. The Court of Appeal decided that the complaint, which alleged defendant's knowledge of the influence of the best seller list on book sales, knowing misrepresentation that the list was an objective and accurate compilation of book stores sales, and purpose to deprive plaintiff, stated a cause of action. The California Supreme Court held that the claim was barred on First Amendment

grounds because the best seller list was not "of and concerning" the author or his novel—
i.e. no specific reference to either was made. Should the suit in Gold v. Los Angeles Democratic League, 49 Cal. App. 3d 365, 122 Cal. Rtpr. 732 (1975), have met the same fate?
The court sustained a complaint for "interference with perspective [sic] employment" by
a candidate for the office of city controller. He was the endorsed candidate of the local Democratic Central Committee. Defendants (another organization of Democrats and its
chairman), immediately before the election, mailed to voters a pamphlet urging them to
"Vote Democratic" but listing plaintiff's opponent, a Republican, as the candidate for
city controller. Allegedly, this cost plaintiff the election.

4. When the alleged wrongful conduct by defendant was a defamatory statement about
plaintiff, courts have applied the various First Amendment limitations on defamation liability (see pp. 626–684, infra) to actions for interference with business. See Beverly Hills
Foodland, Inc. v. United Food and Commercial Workers Union, Local 655, 39 F.3d 191
(8th Cir. 1994) (statements in labor dispute protected against defamation liability also
protected against liability for tortious interference); Jefferson County School District No.
R-1 v. Moody's Investor's Services, Inc., 175 F.3d 848 (10th Cir. 1999) (statement must
contain factual assertion capable of being proved false); Medical Laboratory Management Consultants v. American Broadcasting Companies, Inc., 306 F.3d 806 (9th Cir.
2002) (plaintiff must demonstrate statements' falsity and defendants' fault); Lakeshore
Community Hospital, Inc. v. Perry, 212 Mich. App. 396, 538 N.W.2d 24 (1995) (when
plaintiff is public figure, must prove that defendant made factual statement with knowledge or reckless disregard of falsity). Cf. A & B-Abell Elevator Co., Inc. v. Columbus/
Central Ohio Building & Construction Trades Council, 73 Ohio St. 3d 1, 651 N.E.2d
1283 (1995) (statements protected by qualified privilege for defamation liability have
same protection in tortious interference action).

5. Under Restatement (Second) of Torts § 772(a) (1979), defendant's giving truthful information to a third person is not "improper" interference with plaintiff's economic relationships. Thus there is no liability for causing interference by a true statement. This is
accepted in Kutcher v. Zimmerman, 87 Hawaii 394, 957 P.2d 1076 (Ct. App. 1998); Wal-
nut Street Associates, Inc. v. Brokerage Concepts, Inc., 610 Pa. 371, 20 A.3d 468 (2011);
Tiernan v. Charleston Area Medical Center, Inc., 203 W. Va. 135, 506 S.E.2d 578 (1998).
Cf. Wabash Railroad Co. v. Young, 162 Ind. 102, 69 N.E. 1003 (1904) (plaintiff allegedly
denied employment with other railroads because of statements that he was "labor agitator"). Other cases, however, treat truth as a factor to be considered in deciding whether
the interference was improper. See Kachmar v. SunGard Data Systems, Inc., 109 F.3d 173
(3d Cir. 1997); Pratt v. Prodata, Inc., 885 P.2d 786 (Utah 1994).

6. A merchant erroneously reports to credit agencies that a customer has failed to pay
bills for purchases when they were due. As a result of the negative information about his
credit history, the customer's application for a loan or credit card is refused. Does the
customer have an action for tortious interference against the merchant? If so, what intent
or fault must be proved? See Bell v. May Department Stores Co., 6 S.W.3d 871 (Mo. 1999),
which recognizes an action for "intentional interference with credit expectancy." Can the
initiation of a meritless lawsuit against plaintiff, which may in limited circumstances give
rise to an action for malicious prosecution, be the basis of a tortious interference action?
See Nesler v. Fisher and Co., Inc., 452 N.W.2d 191 (Iowa 1990); Mantia v. Hanson, 190
Or. App. 412, 79 P.3d 404 (2003). If someone prevents the sale of property by making a
false claim to the property or an interest in it, the normal remedy if any is an action for
slander of title (see pp. 239–242, infra). Should an action for interference with prospective advantage be an alternative remedy?

B. Interference with Other Expectations

Harmon v. Harmon
Supreme Judicial Court of Maine
404 A.2d 1020 (1979)

NICHOLS, Justice....

... [T]he Plaintiff, Richard Harmon, asserted that the Defendants, Harold C. Harmon and Virginia S. Harmon (who are the Plaintiff's brother and brother's wife) had by fraud and undue influence induced the Plaintiff's mother, Josephine F. Harmon, while she was 87 years old and in ill health, to transfer to the Defendants valuable property. By her 1976 will and by her more recent statements the mother had indicated her intention that the Plaintiff son should receive at least a one-half interest in this property. Thus, this transfer effectively disinherited the Plaintiff son. The mother, it appears, is still living....

[The trial court dismissed Plaintiff's complaint.] Thus, the issue before us is whether, prior to the mother's death, a son and expectant legatee can maintain an action in tort against a third party for wrongful interference with an intended legacy to the son....

... [I]t has become a settled rule in the United States that the expectancy of future contractual relations, such as the prospect of obtaining employment or employees, or the opportunity of obtaining customers, will be protected by the law from wrongful interference....

If the law protects a person from interference with an opportunity to receive a benefit by entering into contractual relations in the future, the same protection should be accorded to a person's opportunity to receive a benefit as a prospective legatee. The uncertainty attendant upon the expectancy is equivalent. Neither the employee nor the prospective legatee has any enforceable right to his likely benefit....

Recognition of such a cause of action was made in the *Restatement of Torts* § 870 (1939) which declares the imposition of liability for the intended consequences of any tortious act. Comment (b), Illustration 2, is enlightening: "A, who is zealous in the cause of labor, is about to make a gift to B, a college when C, for the purpose of preventing the gift, falsely represents that the president of B is opposed to collective bargaining. As a result, A refuses to make the gift which otherwise he would have made. B is entitled to maintain an action of tort against C."

The parallel between our present factual setting and this illustration is striking indeed. The prospective donor could elect to rescind or affirm the transaction at any time. Furthermore, he was under no obligation to make a gift and had not yet completed it....

Likewise, the expectancy of a beneficiary in the proceeds of an insurance policy upon the life of another is an interest which the courts are ready to protect against the wrongful interference of a third person.

Such liability in tort is recognized notwithstanding that clearly the beneficiary's interest includes no vested right, but is a "mere" expectancy. The issue is not whether the interest is vested or expectant; rather the issue is whether it is legally protected so that intentional and wrongful interference causing damage to the plaintiff gives rise to liability in tort.

We conclude that where a person can prove that, but for the tortious interference of another, he would in all likelihood have received a gift or a specific profit from a transaction, he is entitled to recover for the damages thereby done to him. We apply this rule to the case before us where allegedly the Defendant son and his wife have tortiously interfered with the Plaintiff son's expectation that under his mother's will he would receive a substantial portion of her estate....

In early cases several courts denied any remedy for tortious interference with one's expectancy of benefit from an ancestor or a testator. Our holding, however, in [*Cyr v. Cote*, 396 A.2d 1013 (1979)] put our Court in step with those courts which in recent years have developed a considerable body of precedent for the proposition that when, following the death of an ancestor or testator, one establishes that the fraud or undue influence of another has interfered with his expectancy of benefit from that ancestor or testator, he is entitled to relief. Sometimes the remedy has been to impose a constructive trust or to set aside the transfer; at other times damages have been found to be an appropriate remedy.

In the case before us, we go one step further than we did in *Cyr*. Here we recognize that one may proceed to enforce this liability, grounded in tort, before the death of the prospective testatrix occurs, even as we have seen that the victim of tortious interference with a contract of employment or with a policy of life insurance has been permitted to proceed.

There are several considerations which strongly favor according the Plaintiff brother an early day in court, notwithstanding the ambulatory nature of the mother's will and voidable nature of a trust arrangement. These include (a) the availability of witnesses to the allegedly tortious acts while their memories are relatively fresh, (b) the present availability of relevant exhibits, and (c) especially the prospect that the court may gain the testimony of the parties' aged mother, which testimony may determine the outcome here....

It should be noted that the claim of the Plaintiff son is to a loss of his expectancy, not to a loss of the actual property of his mother....

Order of dismissal vacated.

Notes

1. When a testamentary instrument or a part thereof is intentionally destroyed without the testator's permission, there is a strong case for recovery by a legatee who is thereby disinherited. See In re Estate of Legeas, 210 Cal. App. 3d 385, 258 Cal. Rptr. 858 (1989); Creek v. Laski, 248 Mich. 425, 227 N.W. 817 (1929). Occasionally it has been held that the only remedy lies in probate court. See Thayer v. Kitchen, 200 Mass. 322, 86 N.E. 952 (1909). Should it matter whether the destruction occurs prior to or after the testator's death? What if property is destroyed in order to prevent its inheritance by plaintiff? Cf. Yates v. Joyce, p. 208, infra (defendant demolished property to prevent its being taken to satisfy judgment debt assigned to plaintiff).

2. There is more difficulty when, as in the principal case, the action concerns alleged fraud or undue influence on the testator, such as pressure to amend or revoke a will, not to make a will at all, or to make inter vivos transfers of property. It might be held that only the testator or the party succeeding to the rights of the testator has an action to set aside a conveyance or recover damages. See Holt v. Holt, 232 N.C. 497, 61 S.E.2d 448 (1950). One could take the position that any prospective legacies are merely matters of hope and speculation and that no right to them can exist prior to the testator's death. See Cunningham v. Edward, 52 Ohio App. 61, 3 N.E.2d 58 (1936) (due to husband's threats, wife never made will; husband inherited all her property; not liable to wife's sister). The modern tendency is to approach this as a subject of proof and hold that there can be liability for wrongfully interfering with the prospect of an inheritance. See Firestone v. Galbreath,

25 F.3d 323 (6th Cir. 1994); Doughty v. Morris, 117 N.M. 284, 871 P.2d 380 (Ct. App. 1994). This may be qualified by denying the action while the testator or donor is still living. Labonte v. Giordano, 426 Mass. 319, 687 N.E.2d 1253 (1997). Or by requiring a showing that plaintiff could not obtain an adequate remedy in the probate court. See Graham v. Manche, 974 S.W.2d 580 (Mo. App. 1998); Wilson v. Fritschy, 132 N.M. 785, 55 P.3d 997 (Ct. App. 2002). See generally Dobbs, Law of Torts 1279–1280 (2000).

3. Finding a close analogy between expectancies of an inheritance and expectancies within the tort of interference with prospective advantage, the Supreme Court of Oregon extended the tort to intentional interference with a prospective inheritance and applied the elements of liability established in the *Top Service Body Shop* case (p. 190, supra). Allen v. Hall, 328 Or. 276, 974 P.2d 199 (1999). The court rejected arguments by defendants that this would interfere with the statutory scheme which regulated disputes over disposition of property under a will and conflict with the rule that a decedent's testamentary intent is to be ascertained only from what is expressed in the will. While controlling in a will contest, the rule did not have to be followed in a tort action.

4. Analogous questions arise when there is wrongful interference with life insurance benefitting plaintiff or an inter vivos gift. See Mitchell v. Langley, 143 Ga. 827, 85 S.E. 1050 (1915) (action stated for inducing by fraudulent statements substitution of defendant for plaintiff as beneficiary of decedent's benefit society certificate); Hammons v. Eisert, 745 S.W.2d 253 (Mo. App. 1988) (liability for undue influence inducing now-deceased settlor to revoke trust in which plaintiff was beneficiary); Ross v. Wright, 286 Mass. 269, 190 N.E. 514 (1934) (clerk of business trust refused to transfer shares as requested by owner, who was thereafter unable to make gift because of mortal illness; clerk owed duty only to trust; not liable to potential donor). For a colorful case of interference with plaintiff's prospects of receiving millions from her much older husband, in which the trial court found destruction and alteration of documents, fraud and perjury, see In re Marshall, 275 B.R. 5 (C.D. Cal. 2002), vacated, 392 F.3d 1118 (9th Cir. 2004), rev'd sub nom. Marshall v. Marshall, 547 U.S. 293 (2006). (The Supreme Court held that the case did not fall within the probate exception to federal court jurisdiction.) See generally Restatement (Second) of Torts § 774B (1979); Annot., Liability in Damages for Interference with Expected Inheritance or Gift, 22 A.L.R.4th 1229 (1983); Johnson, Tortious Interference with Expectancy of Inheritance or Gift—Suggestions for Resort to the Tort, 39 U. Toledo L. Rev. 769 (2008).

5. Another disappointed expectation is failing to win a contest. Courts have not been inclined to grant relief. In Harrison v. Jones, 52 Ga. App. 852, 184 S.E. 889 (1936), an unsuccessful contestant in a newspaper subscription contest sued the first prize winner, alleging that a number of the winner's subscriptions were not bona fide—they were unauthorized by and unknown to the supposed subscribers—and, but for this fraud, plaintiff would have won. The court declared that the contest judges had absolute power to determine the winner and that the fraud, if any, was perpetrated on them, not plaintiff. In contest cases, courts tend to find insufficient proof that plaintiff would, but for defendant's misconduct, have received the anticipated prize or benefits. See also Phillips v. Pantages Theatre Co., 163 Wash. 303, 300 P. 1048 (1931) (contestant not permitted to enter final contest after winning preliminary); Collatz v. Fox Wisconsin Amusement Corp., 239 Wis. 156, 300 N.W. 162 (1941) (defendant allegedly breached rules of its contest). Cf. Smitha v. Gentry, 20 Ky. L. Rptr. 171, 45 S.W. 515 (1898) (plaintiffs planned to capture murder suspect and receive reward; defendant learned suspect's whereabouts by impersonating constable, arrested suspect and received reward). Compare Restatement (Second) of Torts § 912, comment *f* (1979). See generally Annot., Recovery in Tort for Wrongful In-

terference with Chance to Win Game, Sporting Event, or Contest, 85 A.L.R.4th 1048 (1991).

6. In Youst v. Longo, 43 Cal. 3d 64, 233 Cal. Rptr. 294, 729 P.2d 728 (1987), the owner of a horse entered in a harness race sued the driver of another horse on allegations that defendant drove his horse into the path of plaintiff's horse and struck plaintiff's horse with a whip. This allegedly caused plaintiff's horse to break stride and finish the race in sixth place (moved to fifth when defendant's horse was disqualified) rather than in a better position. Plaintiff sought to recover the purse amount for the position in which his horse would have finished but for defendant's interference, less the $5000 purse he received. The court affirmed dismissal of the action. A "threshold requirement" of liability for interference with prospective advantage was that it be reasonably probable the economic advantage would have been realized but for the interference. In most sporting events, including horse races, the probability that a competitor would have won the contest or a prize, but for the interference, was too speculative to be a basis of tort liability. Plaintiff's complaint therefore failed to meet the threshold requirement of probable advantage. Furthermore, as a matter of public policy, it would be undesirable to entertain actions for prospective economic loss between competitors in a sporting contest. Supervision of horse racing and other sports by regulatory agencies had proved to be a relatively successful and generally accepted method of dealing with competitors' misconduct. The prospect of tort liability and intensive litigation scrutiny of participants' conduct could, the court feared, seriously harm competitive sports.

Goff v. Harold Ives Trucking Company, Inc.

Supreme Court of Arkansas
342 Ark. 143, 27 S.W.3d 387 (2000)

TOM GLAZE, Justice.

[Lisa Goff was injured in a collision with a tractor-trailer driven by an employee of the Harold Ives Trucking Company. She and her husband sued Ives in federal court. They requested production of the truck driver's logs for the driver involved in the accident. These showed how long the driver had been on the road. Federal law required the logs to be kept for six months. However, Ives had lost or destroyed the logs, so they were never produced. Ives subsequently admitted negligence liability for the accident, so in the trial the jury determined only the amount of damages. The Goffs then commenced an action against Ives in state court for "spoliation of evidence," alleging that the destruction of the logs had deprived them of "relevant and central" information and interfered with their opportunity to recover damages in the previous action. Punitive damages were demanded. Ives moved for dismissal of the complaint on the grounds that Arkansas did not recognize the tort of spoliation of evidence and the Goffs had won their negligence action. The trial court dismissed the complaint.]

Spoliation is defined as "the intentional destruction of evidence and when it is established, [the] fact finder may draw [an] inference that [the] evidence destroyed was unfavorable to [the] party responsible for its spoliation." *Black's Law Dictionary* 1401 (6th ed. 1990). Our research reflects that few jurisdictions have acknowledged spoliation as an independent tort. In those few states which have recognized the tort, several courts have likened the harm arising from the destruction of evidence to that suffered by plaintiffs in cases involving intentional interference with prospective economic advantage. This reasoning was first employed in *Smith v. Superior Court*, 151 Cal. App. 3d 491, 198 Cal. Rptr. 829 (1984).... [The court] held that a prospective civil action in a products liability case was a valuable probable expectancy to the plaintiff, and as such, the court could and should protect that interest from the kind of interference posed by the destruction of evidence necessary to prove such a claim. Several other jurisdictions adopted this approach to the tort. *See Bondu v. Gurvich*, 473 So. 2d 1307 (Fla. App. 1985); *Hazen v. Municipality of Anchorage*, 718 P.2d 456 (Alaska 1986); *Hirsch v. General Motors Corp.*, 266 N.J. Super. 222, 628 A.2d 1108 (1993) (New Jersey recognizes intentional spoliation of evidence as a tort, but not negligent spoliation of evidence); *Holmes v. Amerex Rent-A-Car*, 180 F.3d 294 (D.C. Cir. 1999) (holding that negligent or reckless spoliation of evidence is an independent and actionable tort); *Smith v. Howard Johnson Co.*, 67 Ohio St. 3d 28, 615 N.E.2d 1037 (1993) (holding without explanation that a "cause of action exists in tort for interference with or destruction of evidence"); and *Coleman v. Eddy Potash*, 120 N.M. 645, 905 P.2d 185 (1995).

These states, however, represent what we have determined to be the minority view. We find it instructive that California, the first state to adopt spoliation as an independent tort, has changed course and, more recently, that state's highest court has held specifically that the tort would no longer be recognized. *Cedars-Sinai Medical Center v. Superior Court*, 18 Cal. 4th 1, 74 Cal. Rptr. 2d 248, 954 P.2d 511 (1998). In rejecting the logic of the *Smith* case, the California Supreme Court noted that while "[n]o one doubts that the intentional destruction of evidence should be condemned, ... [t]hat alone, however, is not enough to justify creating tort liability for such conduct."

The California Supreme Court based its decision on a number of public policy concerns, noting primarily the "strong policy favoring use of nontort remedies rather than derivative tort causes of action to punish and correct litigation misconduct and the prohibition against attacking adjudications on the ground that evidence was falsified or destroyed." Chief among these nontort remedies is the evidentiary inference, often quoted in its Latin form, "*omnia praesumuntur contra spoliatorem*," meaning "all things are presumed against a spoliator." This inference ... allows a fact-finder to infer from the destruction of evidence that whatever was contained in that evidence was unfavorable to the party that destroyed it....

In addition to this evidentiary inference or presumption, the California Supreme Court noted the "broad range of [discovery] sanctions for conduct that amounts to a misuse of the discovery process." In California, these sanctions include "monetary sanctions, contempt sanctions, issue sanctions..., evidentiary sanctions..., and terminating sanctions that include striking part or all of the pleadings, dismissing part or all of the action, or granting a default judgment against the offending party." Arkansas has similar sanctions.... [Counsel for the Goffs did not seek discovery sanctions.]

The California court also discussed the two following nontort remedies for the spoliation of evidence: the fact that lawyers may be subject to disciplinary proceedings for participating in the destruction or suppression of evidence (and thus would take steps to see to it that their clients do not engage in such behavior), and the existence of criminal penalties for spoliation....

Besides the existence of the foregoing nontort remedies are several strong policy concerns that weigh against the recognition or adoption of spoliation as a new tort. We are concerned, as was the California Supreme Court, with the speculative nature of damages in a case such as this. The question goes not only to the amount of damages caused by the destruction of evidence, but also to the very *existence* of injury. The California court discussed this problem in its *Cedars-Sinai* decision as follows: "In such cases, even if the jury infers from the act of spoliation that the spoliated evidence was somehow unfavorable to the spoliator, there will typically be no way of telling what precisely the evidence would have shown and how much it would have weighed in the spoliation victim's favor. Without knowing the content and weight of the spoliated evidence, it would be impossible for the jury to meaningfully assess what role the missing evidence would have played in the determination of the underlying action. The jury could only speculate as to what the nature of the spoliated evidence was and what effect it might have had on the outcome of the underlying litigation."

We agree with the California court's analysis. In the present case, the Goffs' complaint is devoid of any suggestion as to what the missing logs contained. Although the complaint states that the destruction of the logs deprived the Goffs of relevant evidence concerning their negligence action, it does not allege that the logs would have shown that the driver of the truck that struck Mrs. Goff had been on the road for more hours than federal law permits. Therefore, even if the Goffs had been permitted to present their spoliation claim to a jury, there would have been no way for that jury to tell what the logs would have shown and what injury, if any, the Goffs had suffered as a result of the logs' destruction. We also find it telling that the Goffs *won* their underlying negligence action in the federal district court. In such a situation, whether any additional damages could have been proven is certainly open to question.

... [R]ecognition of the tort is not, as the Goffs suggest, a "growing trend" in this country. The majority of jurisdictions which have considered it have either expressly rejected the cause of action or have declined to reach the question on the facts presented [citing cases from fourteen states].

We join those jurisdictions that have expressly declined to recognize the tort of intentional spoliation of evidence. As discussed above, we believe that there are sufficient other avenues, short of creating a new cause of action, that serve to remedy the situation for a plaintiff. Most significant, an aggrieved party can request that a jury be instructed to draw a negative inference against the spoliator. Additionally, and as discussed earlier, the plaintiff can ask for discovery sanctions or seek to have a criminal prosecution initiated against the party who destroyed relevant evidence. In short, we do not find it necessary to create a new tort out of whole cloth in order to provide a party with a remedy. The following language of the Texas Supreme Court succinctly addresses our own position on the subject: "This Court treads cautiously when deciding whether to recognize a new tort. While the law must adjust to meet society's changing needs, we must balance that adjustment against boundless claims in an already crowded judicial system. We are especially averse to creating a tort that would only lead to duplicative litigation, encouraging inefficient relitigation of issues better handled within the context of the core cause of action. We thus decline to recognize evidence spoliation as an independent tort.... [The] traditional response to the problem of evidence spoliation *properly frames the alleged wrong as an evidentiary concept, not a separate cause of action.*" *Trevino v. Ortega*, 969 S.W.2d 950, 951–52 (emphasis added).

Because we find it unnecessary and unwise to recognize first-party spoliation of evidence as an independent tort in Arkansas, we affirm the decision of the trial court.

Notes

1. A spoliation claim may be made when evidence vital to a liability or damages claim or a defense has been destroyed or lost. Most of the cases cited in *Goff* arose from loss of

the allegedly defective product or part needed for a product liability action, or loss of medical or hospital records which could prove that a patient was injured by the negligence of a physician or hospital personnel. However, Hazen v. Municipality of Anchorage was an action alleging a prosecutor's intentional alteration of a tape recording made when plaintiff was arrested, removing exculpatory evidence. Other cases involve various allegations that evidence necessary to prove a defendant's negligence had been destroyed, as in *Goff*. E.g., Torres v. El Paso Electric Co., 127 N.M. 729, 987 P.2d 386 (1999). If an action for intentional spoliation is accepted, what must plaintiff allege and prove?

2. The spoliation tort survives in some jurisdictions where it had been accepted earlier. See Hibbits v. Sides, 34 P.3d 327 (Alaska 2001); Torres v. El Paso Electric Co., supra (requiring intent to disrupt or defeat plaintiff's lawsuit). But the trend is adverse to recognition of such a cause of action. See Fletcher v. Dorchester Mutual Insurance Co., 437 Mass. 544, 773 N.E.2d 420 (2002); Dowdle Butane Gas Co., Inc. v. Moore, 831 So. 2d 1124 (Miss. 2002); Burns v. National Bank of New Zealand Ltd., [2004] 3 N.Z.L.R. 289 (C.A.). Contra, Rizzuto v. Davidson Ladders, Inc., 280 Conn. 225, 905 A.2d 1165 (2006); Hannah v. Heeter, 213 W. Va. 704, 584 S.E.2d 560 (2003). In jurisdictions where a spoliation action is possible, it has been denied to plaintiffs who were aware of the spoliation at some time prior to the trial of the underlying action. See rsc The Quality Measurement Co. v. IPSOS-ASI, Inc., 196 F. Supp. 2d 609 (S.D. Ohio 2002), aff'd, 56 Fed. Appx. 639 (6th Cir. 2003). Compare Davis v. Wal-Mart Stores, Inc., 93 Ohio St. 3d 488, 756 N.E.2d 657 (2001), clarification denied, 94 Ohio St. 3d 1407, 759 N.E.2d 785 (2001). The California Supreme Court's decision in Cedars-Sinai Medical Center v. Superior Court, which is discussed in the principal case, limited its rejection of spoliation actions to cases in which plaintiff knew or should have known of the alleged spoliation before the trial or other decision on the merits of the underlying action.

3. In specifying that "first-party" spoliation is not to be recognized as a tort in Arkansas, the *Goff* case leaves open the possibility that a spoliation action against a "third party"— one who was not a party to the cause of action for which the lost evidence was to be used—might be entertained. Adverse inferences, litigation sanctions and most other alternatives to a tort action would usually have no application to a third party. Furthermore, viable claims of intentional spoliation by a non-litigant might not be so numerous as to engage concerns about burdening the legal system with additional lawsuits. See Hibbits v. Sides, supra; Oliver v. Stimson Lumber Co., 297 Mont. 336, 993 P.2d 11 (1999). The California Supreme Court, however, has extended to third-party spoliation its decision not to allow an action for first-party spoliation. Temple Community Hospital v. Superior Court, 20 Cal. 4th 464, 84 Cal. Rptr. 2d 852, 976 P.2d 223 (1999). The Supreme Court of Arkansas did the same in Downen v. Redd, 367 Ark. 551, 242 S.W.3d 273 (2006), adopting the California court's reasoning that "The doubtful benefit of the proposed tort remedy is outweighed by the prospect of a spiral of litigation giving rise to verdicts based upon speculation [and] it would be anomalous for a nonparty to be liable in damages, including punitive damages, for conduct that would not give rise to tort liability if committed by a party." On the intentional spoliation tort generally, see Annot., Intentional Spoliation of Evidence, Interfering with Prospective Civil Action, as Actionable, 70 A.L.R.4th 984 (1989); Dobbs, Law of Torts 1280–1282 (2000).

4. Could it be a tort to intentionally interfere with plaintiff's recovery of damages *after* plaintiff has been awarded judgment in a lawsuit? In Folmar & Associates LLP v. Holberg, 776 So. 2d 112 (Ala. 2000), the court rejected a claim for intentionally depriving plaintiff of amounts due under a divorce judgment, framed as a claim for interference with a contractual or business relationship. But it was held in Sharum v. Sharum, 101 Okla. 273, 225 P. 682 (1924), that a child could maintain an action against a third party for mali-

cious interference that prevented the child's receiving court-ordered support from his father. Cf. Yates v. Joyce, 11 Johnson 136 (N.Y. Sup. Ct. 1814) (plaintiff had action when defendant demolished property to prevent its being taken in satisfaction of judgment debt assigned to plaintiff).

————————

Trautwein v. Harbourt

Superior Court of New Jersey, Appellate Division
40 N.J. Super. 247, 123 A.2d 30 (1956),
cert. denied, 22 N.J. 220, 125 A.2d 233 (1956)

CONFORD, J.A.D....

[Plaintiffs formed a new chapter of the Order of the Eastern Star under a temporary "dispensation." Some had transferred from other chapters. The Order's statewide governing body defeated a motion to grant a charter to this chapter. This had the effect of severing the chapter and its members from the Order. Plaintiffs sought damages from certain officials of the Order for wilfully and maliciously conspiring to destroy the reputations of plaintiffs as members of the Order, to prevent the new chapter from obtaining a charter, and to make each plaintiff an "outcast" from the Order. The trial court granted summary judgment for defendants.]

The gravamen of plaintiffs' argument is that defendants' activities caused them to be expelled from and made "outcasts" of a fraternal order in which they were members. Defendants, on the other hand, contend there was but a denial of membership in a voluntary, private, fraternal organization. The resolution of this issue is our first concern, since the law accords important rights and status to members of voluntary organizations not extended to mere aspirants to membership therein. One wrongfully expelled from such an organization may be restored to membership by mandamus. Or he may bring an action for damages. On the other hand, there is no "abstract right to be admitted" to membership in a voluntary association, and a court will not compel the admission of a person to membership in such an organization who has not been elected according to its rules and by-laws. The general rule is that there is no legal remedy for exclusion of such an individual from admission into a voluntary association, no matter how arbitrary or unjust the exclusion....

[The court held that as the Order's constitution and by-laws made plaintiffs' membership in the Order contingent upon the grant of a charter to the new chapter and gave the statewide governing body the unqualified power to deny a charter, denial of the charter was an exclusion of plaintiffs from admission to the Order, not expulsion of plaintiffs or the chapter from the Order. This was not an expulsion even as to plaintiffs who had transferred from other chapters.]

We come, then, to the question as to whether concerted activity of members of a strictly fraternal organization designed to exclude aspirants from admission thereto is actionable where such activity is confined within the organization but is actuated in substantial degree by motives legally classifiable under the head of malice....

We have no difficulty with the theoretical concept, expressed in various ways by modern jurisprudents, that intentional, willful or malicious harms of any kind are actionable unless justified. Nor can there be reasonable quarrel with the general idea that in assaying the range of interests requiring protection the law should recognize the "demand involved in social life in civilized society that all individuals shall have fair or reasonable ... opportunities—political, physical, cultural, social and economic." Pound, "A Survey of

Social Interests," 57 Harv. L. Rev. 1, 36 (1943); and see Green, "Relational Interests," 29 Ill. L. Rev. 460, 1041 (1943), 30 Ill. L. Rev. 1, 314 (1935), passim. The rub comes on the point of "justification." As particularly applied to the cause *sub judice*, it cannot be doubted that, in a sense, the intended consequence of defendants' actions was the exclusion of the plaintiffs from entry into the Order.... This may be conceded to have constituted the infliction upon plaintiffs of an injury in respect of an interest for which the law has concern. If maliciously done by a stranger to the order, there might well be an action. But in the case of the present defendants, was it not done "in the exercise of an equal or superior right," and therefore justifiable in a legal sense, whatever one's views as to the underlying social ethics? ...

We have seen that voluntary associations generally have the unquestionable right to exclude from membership on any basis whatever. Fraternal association implies a degree of social intimacy but one step removed from that of the family. So long as this form of social organism remains as deeply embedded in our culture as it is now, the law must respect it and its ordinary concomitants, chief among which is selectivity of membership. Clearly to be implied from the absolutism over admission residing in the organization as an entity is the derivative right of individual members to be heard within the organization on their objections to an applicant and to persuade other members toward their views. To qualify that right by the peril of liability for punitive damages at the suit of an excluded applicant who can convince a jury that the objecting member was motivated by ill will, spite, or prejudice, would be, in our judgment, substantially to impair commonly accepted concepts as to freedom of selectivity in social and fraternal organizations, and, perhaps, in the long run, to foment and exacerbate rather than relieve the kinds of social stresses which lie beneath the present controversy. There is here apparent a clear "counter-policy" to the general policy of redressing the intentional infliction of harm. Past unsavory experiences of a member with an applicant may be at once the source of ill will motivating the activity against admission and also a thoroughly justifiable reason for such activity. Other motives may be less justifiable but hardly capable of reliable segregation from good ones by a jury. We do not yet live in the age of the literal brotherhood of man. The "blackball" continues to hold its place in our fraternal life. While courts may be expected continually to tug in the direction of a higher ethic, yet, absent legislation, they will wisely wait for new standards of conduct to be invested "in the minds of the multitude with the sanction of moral obligation" before they invest them with the sanction of the law. Cf. Cardozo, "The Paradoxes of Legal Science" (1928), p. 18....

We hold that what the defendants here did, in the aspect challenged by plaintiffs, was in the exercise of a primary right of the defendants; a right to act, individually and jointly, for the exclusion from the order of the proposed chapter for any reasons which they deemed warranted such action; and that in exercising such right their motives were immaterial....

[Affirmed.]

Notes

1. Most authority agrees with the principal case that there is no right to recover for non-admission to a social or fraternal organization. See Grand Lodge Order Hermann's Sons of Texas v. Schuetze, 36 Tex. Civ. App. 539, 83 S.W. 241 (1904); Ross v. Ebert, 275 Wis. 523, 82 N.W.2d 315 (1957) (union denying plaintiffs admission because of race); Annot., Right to Damages for Exclusion from Membership in Social or Fraternal Orga-

nization, 59 A.L.R.2d 1290 (1958). Does this bar actions against persons outside the organization? Is this subject affected by recent legislation that prohibits discrimination by certain private clubs?

2. The contrast between exclusion and expulsion is illustrated by a case in the same court as Trautwein v. Harbourt: Zelenka v. Benevolent and Protective Order of Elks of United States, 124 N.J. Super. 379, 324 A.2d 35 (App. Div. 1974), cert. denied, 66 N.J. 317, 331 A.2d 17 (1974). Plaintiff was expelled from the Elks, after a hearing, for violating an Elks statute prohibiting the circulation of a writing on the organization's affairs without first submitting it to the Grand Exalted Ruler for approval. Plaintiff had submitted for publication in a daily newspaper a statement calling for abolition of the rule restricting Elks membership to white persons. The court held that the statute plaintiff violated was contrary to the public policy of "free discussion of issues of ... broad public interest." Plaintiff, therefore, could not be expelled for its violation and was entitled to an order for his restoration to membership. Compare Aspell v. American Contract Bridge League of Memphis, Tennessee, 122 Ariz. 399, 595 P.2d 191 (Ct. App. 1979) (no tort action for suspension from American Contract Bridge League; suggests contract action if rules for disciplinary action breached). See generally Annot., Suspension or Expulsion from Social Club or Similar Society and the Remedies Therefor, 20 A.L.R.2d 344 (1951).

3. What if a person is ousted from a religious or other group and leaders of the group tell its members to avoid business or social contact with that person? See Bear v. Reformed Mennonite Church, 462 Pa. 330, 341 A.2d 105 (1975) (excommunicated member of church alleged that his business and family were in collapse because of church's practice of "shunning"; held that this might constitute actionable interference with family and business relationships; First Amendment right of free exercise of religion not bar to judicial action). Compare Paul v. Watchtower Bible and Tract Society of New York, Inc., 819 F.2d 875 (9th Cir. 1987), cert. denied, 484 U.S. 926 (1987) (First Amendment barred action for governing body's direction that Jehovah's Witnesses shun former members of church).

Section 3. Unintentional Interference

Connecticut Mutual Life Insurance Company v.
New York and New Haven Railroad Company

Supreme Court of Errors of Connecticut
25 Conn. 265 (1856)

STORRS, J. The defendants, a railroad company, are charged with having negligently occasioned the death of one Dr. Beach, by which event the plaintiffs, a life insurance company, have been compelled to pay to his representatives, the amount of an insurance effected upon his life; of which amount a recovery is sought in this action. A plea in bar sets forth a payment to the administratrix of the deceased of the damages for which the defendant's negligence had rendered them legally liable, and also a discharge by her. This plea and demurrer thereto require no examination, as they are immaterial in the view which we take of the declaration....

We have no inclination to abrogate the common law doctrine, that the death of a human being, whatever may be its consequences in a pecuniary or in any other aspect, is not an actionable injury....

... The single question is, whether a plaintiff can successfully claim a legal injury to himself from another, because the latter has injured a third person in such a manner that the plaintiffs' contract liabilities are thereby affected. An individual slanders a merchant and ruins his business; is the wrong doer liable to all the persons, who, in the consequence of their relations by contract to the bankrupt, can be clearly shown to have been damnified by the bankruptcy? Can a fire insurance company, who have been subjected to loss by the burning of a building, resort to the responsible author of the injury, who had no design of affecting their interest, in their own name and right? Such are the complications of human affairs, so endless and far-reaching the mutual promises of man to man, in business and in matters of money and property, that rarely is a death produced by a human agency, which does not affect the pecuniary interest of those to whom the deceased was bound by contract. To open the door of legal redress to wrongs received through the mere voluntary and factitious relation of a contractor with the immediate subject of the injury, would be to encourage collusion and extravagant contracts between men, by which the death of either through the involuntary default of others, might be made a source of splendid profits to the other, and would also invite a system of litigation more portentious than our jurisprudence has yet known. So self-evident is the principle that an injury thus suffered is indirectly brought home to the party seeking compensation for it, that courts have rarely been called upon to promulgate such a doctrine. The case, however, of *Anthony v. Slaid*, 11 Metc., 290, referred to at the bar, is in point. A contractor for the support of paupers had been subject to extra expense by means of a beating which one of those paupers had received, and he sought from the assailant a recovery of the expenditure. But the court held that the damage was remote and indirect; having been sustained not by means of any natural or legal relation between the plaintiff and the party injured, but by means of the special contract by which he had undertaken to support the town paupers.

... [W]hen an agreement is entered into, neither party contemplates the requirements from the other, of a duty towards all the persons to whom he may have a relation by numberless private contracts, and who may therefore be affected by the breach of the others' undertakings. We can not find that any public law charged the present defendants with any duty to the plaintiffs regarding Dr. Beach's life; nor can we see that Dr. Beach exacted, either expressly or by reasonable intendment, any obligation from the defendants towards the insurers of his life, when he contracted for his transportation to New York. Had the life of Dr. Beach been taken with intent to injure the plaintiffs through their contract liability, a different question would arise, inasmuch as every man owes a duty to every other not intentionally to injure him.

We decide, that in the absence of any privity of contract between the plaintiffs and defendants, and of any direct obligation of the latter to the former growing out of the contract or relation between the insured and the defendants, the loss of the plaintiffs, although due to the acts of the railroad company, being brought home to the insurers only through the artificial relation of contractors with the party who was the immediate subject of the wrong done by the railroad company, was a remote and indirect consequence of the misconduct of the defendants, and not actionable....

The cases in which insurers have been permitted to recover against the authors of their losses, are not in contravention of these principles. They have recovered, not by color of their own legal right, but under a general doctrine of equity jurisprudence, commonly known as the doctrine of subrogation, applicable to all cases, wherein a party, who has indemnified another in pursuance of his obligation so to do, succeeds to, and is entitled to a cession of, all the means of redress held by the party indemnified against the party who has occasioned the loss.

Judgment for defendants.

_____

Morton v. Merrillville Toyota, Inc.
Indiana Court of Appeals
562 N.E.2d 781 (1990)

STATON, Judge.

[Michael Marino was operating a car owned by his employer, Merrillville Toyota, when the car collided with a tractor-trailer operated by Morton. Marino was injured and unable to resume his normal employment duties. Merrillville Toyota sued Morton and his employer, seeking compensation for loss of Marino's services and resulting loss of profits as well as damage to its automobile. The trial court denied defendants' motion to dismiss the loss of services claim.]

Our review of the legal sufficiency of Merrillville Toyota's complaint takes us back to the genesis of our American legal system. Although the United States became politically emancipated from Great Britain in the late eighteenth century, it did not divorce itself culturally from the mother country. Among the cultural baggage retained by our infant nation was the English common law system. The basis of our present system of jurisprudence, the Anglo-Saxon common law consisted of principles and rules of law which arose and were perpetuated in the judgments and decrees of the English courts, and which were founded upon usages and customs of antiquity. One such rule of law gave rise to an action *per quod servitium amisit*. Literally, "whereby he lost the service," Blackstone described the cause of action as follows: "A master also may bring an action against any man for beating or maiming his servant; but in such a case he must assign, as a special reason for so doing, his own damage by the loss of his service; and the loss must be proved upon the trial." 1 W. Blackstone, *Commentaries on the Laws of England* 429 (9th ed. 1783).

The action *per quod servitium amisit* was borrowed by the English from the early Roman law. The Roman *actio iniuriarum* seeking recovery for injury to members of a household could only be brought by the head of the household — the *paterfamilias*. The Roman view of the household was broad, and included relatives, dependents, and slaves, all of which were closely identified with the *paterfamilias*. In incorporating this notion into the common law, the English allowed both a direct action for injury to a servant or another under the master's power, as well as an indirect action for the consequential loss of his services. Sayre, *Inducing Breach of Contract*, 36 Harvard L. Rev. 663 (1923). Thus, the action gained acceptance in the time when the master had a proprietary interest in the servant, acquired through the hiring of the servant and purchased through the payment of his wages.

Consistent with its rationale, the action was limited to injury to domestic servants. Such servants were a part of the master's household, and thus enjoyed a quasi-familial relationship with the master. While the domestic servant had an expectation that he would be cared for by the master, the master had a corresponding property interest in the servant, and if the servant was injured, the master could reasonably expect compensation for his trouble. [*Inland Revenue Commissioners v. Hambrook*, [1956] 2 Q.B. 641.]

Over time, the makeup of society changed, and the English courts found that the rationale underlying the action *per quod servitium amisit* was no longer viable. The modern employment relation in England, as in the United States, does not depend upon status but arises out of a contract between the "master" and the "servant". In 1956 the English Court of Appeal in *Inland Revenue Comm'rs v. Hambrook, supra*, stated: "Now, having traced the history of this action, I think it should be confined today (as it was in the eighteenth century) to the realm of domestic servants where a member of the master's household is injured: for that is the only realm to which it can in reason be applied. It does not lie, therefore, at the instance of governments, limited companies, or other employers who keep no household." Thus, if the action *per quod servitium amisit* ever allowed recovery by an employer for an injury to non-domestic employees, such an action has now been expressly repudiated in the English common law by the *Inland* decision.

... Some early American courts extended the action to allow recovery for negligent injury even to non-household employees. However, like their English counterparts, courts in this country began to note that the rationale for the action for negligent injury to a servant or employee no longer rang true in today's society. The number of states which recognize the action has been gradually decreasing, with many courts noting the trend toward non-recognition of the action and the repudiation of the action in the country of its origin....

Even if the cause of action is not recognized under Indiana law, Merrillville Toyota argues that we should adopt it in order to prevent defendants from escaping liability for economic injuries which proximately result from their tortious conduct. In support of this argument, Merrillville Toyota argues vigorously that its claim is analogous to rights conferred in other areas of Indiana law, including the right of recovery for loss of consortium....

... [W]e note that the right to recover for loss of consortium is dependent upon a familial relationship, which is not present here. In addition, the Indiana Supreme Court has recently expressed an unwillingness to extend this action even to other members of the immediate family of the injured individual, limiting the right to recover strictly to spouses....

Merrillville Toyota finally contends that employers may suffer a cognizable loss of profits when their employee is injured by a negligent third party, and rather than place the cost upon the shoulders of the employer, it should be borne by the tortfeasor whose negligence caused the loss. It argues that placing the burden of the loss upon the employers who exist in a competitive environment will result in the costs being passed on to the consumer through higher prices.

Merrillville Toyota fails to recognize the probable countervailing effect upon society. Permitting employers to recover for loss of profits for negligent injury to their employees would result in a multiplicity of actions out of the same tortious act. The overwhelming majority of people in today's society are employed, and thus for nearly every injury another possible claim and another possible party would become a factor in the average lawsuit. Disputes would arise surrounding the alleged failure to mitigate damages through employment of an underqualified individual or payment of excessive wages. Expert testimony of an economist would be required in an attempt to pin down the probable future profit rates of the corporation and how those had been affected by the loss of the employee. Expert medical testimony would be required to establish how long the employee would be absent from work, if he would be able to return, and how his future productivity would be affected by the injury.

Thus, already overloaded court dockets and burgeoning litigation costs would be augmented by the recognition of the action, all to prevent any loss of profits from being passed on to consumers. Will this result in a benefit to society at large? We think not. Most judgments, as well as litigation costs, will be paid by insurance companies. Insurance companies will pass on these costs to their insured in the form of higher insurance premiums. Consequently, society would bear both the cost of the economic injury and the cost of litigating the injury. Overcrowded dockets would further burden society, costing more tax dollars and causing extended delay of pending litigation.

In summary, the rationale underlying the action for loss of services of a negligently injured employee is outmoded, the policy reasons for adopting it are dubious, and its basis in Indiana law is nonexistent. We are disinclined to adopt a cause of action which has been rejected by every modern court which has addressed it, including that of the country of its origin.

We conclude that the trial court should have granted Morton's motion to dismiss Merrillville Toyota's claim for loss of Marino's services due to the negligence of a third party. Accordingly, we reverse and remand to the trial court with instructions that the motion to dismiss be granted.

Notes

1. In the twentieth century employees' salaries, which reflected the value of their services, rose from their formerly low levels, and employers began to provide continuance of wages and coverage of medical expenses to injured employees. As a consequence, financial loss resulting from injury to an employee could be much larger than in earlier times. In a few states, unrepealed nineteenth century codifications of common law provide statutory authority for a "master" to claim damages on account of injury to a "servant." Cal. Civil Code §49; Mont. Code Ann. §27-1-516; 76 Okla. Stat. §8. But it was decided in I.J. Weinrot and Son, Inc. v. Jackson, 40 Cal. 3d 327, 220 Cal. Rptr. 103, 708 P.2d 682 (1985), that this allowed recovery only for injuries to servants who were members of a master's household. It could not be used by a corporate employer. Modern American cases generally reject any negligence claim for loss resulting from injury to an employee. See Anderson Plasterers v. Meinecke, 543 N.W.2d 612 (Iowa 1996); Cravens/Pocock Insurance Agency, Inc. v. John F. Beasley Construction Co., Inc., 766 S.W.2d 309 (Tex. App. 1989); Hartridge v. State Farm Mutual Automobile Insurance Co., 86 Wis. 2d 1, 271 N.W.2d 598 (1978); Annot., Employer's Right of Action for Loss of Services or the Like Against Third Person Tortiously Killing or Injuring Employee, 4 A.L.R.4th 504 (1981). The master's action for loss of a servant's services has been abolished by statute in England. Administration of Justice Act, 1982, c. 53, s. 2. See generally Fleming, Law of Torts 204–206, 769–773 (10th ed. 2011); Prosser & Keeton, Law of Torts 997–1000 (5th ed. 1984).

2. Refusal to permit recovery by the employer may be based upon a conclusion that the employer's loss was too indirect or remote from defendant's negligence. Chelsea Moving & Trucking Co. v. Ross Towboat Co., 280 Mass. 282, 182 N.E. 477 (1932); Nemo Foundations, Inc. v. New River Co., 155 W. Va. 149, 181 S.E.2d 687 (1971). Or that plaintiff and the injured party did not have a relationship of master and servant. Attorney-General for New South Wales v. Perpetual Trustee Co. (Ltd.), [1955] A.C. 457 (P.C.) (government's action for injury to police constable). Cf. United States v. Standard Oil Co., 332 U.S. 301 (1947) (United States could not recover expenses incurred because of injury to soldier); Annot., Right of Professional Corporation to Recover Damages Based on Injury or Death of Attorney or Doctor Associate, 74 A.L.R.3d 1129 (1976) (no American authority for action by professional corporation whose member was injured by de-

fendant's negligence). Should a distinction be drawn between accidental and intentional injuries? Between injuries suffered on the job and injuries suffered during nonemployment activities?

3. The action *per quod servitium amisit* was examined at length in Commissioner for Railways (New South Wales) v. Scott, (1959) 102 C.L.R. 392. A 4–3 majority rejected the decision in Inland Revenue Commissioners v. Hambrook, [1956] 2 Q.B. 641 (C.A.), that the action lies only in cases of injuries to domestic or menial servants. Apart from precedent contrary to this limitation there was the difficulty of determining whether an employee was "domestic" or "menial" for this purpose. It was held that injury sustained in a level crossing accident by a locomotive driver for the state railways, which caused him to cease work for a short period, gave rise to an action by his employer. Judges differed on whether the action *per quod* was out of harmony with contemporary social and economic conditions and whether it was more anomalous to permit the action to employers generally than to restrict it to employers of domestic or menial servants. If a remedy is to be allowed in such a case, why deny it to a person for whom the injured party is a partner or independent contractor, an employee who has lost employment through injury to his employer, an insurance company that must make payments under a casualty or health policy, or a government that pays for the injured person's medical care or a pension? A statute now gives the United States government the right to recover from tortfeasors the value of medical treatment and care furnished by the government to injured persons. 42 U.S.C. § 2651.

4. If a "master" or employer has an action, what should be the measure of damages? Can a defendant be subject to double liability for the same loss? Recovery can be limited to such direct damages as the amount paid in wages to substitutes employed to perform the services that the injured party would have performed. See Genereux v. Peterson Howell & Heather (Canada) Ltd., [1973] 2 O.R. 558, (1972) 34 D.L.R.2d 614 (C.A.) (solicitor could recover for loss of services of law clerk, but not loss of profit). The action is for damage due to loss of services, which is not necessarily the same as the value of the services lost or payments for which the employer receives no services in return. See Interstate Telephone & Telegraph Co. v. Public Service Electric Co., 86 N.J.L. 26, 90 A. 1062 (Sup. Ct. 1914) (worker's compensation payments to injured worker not recoverable); John Holland (Constructions) Pty. Ltd. v. Jordin (No. 2), (1985) 36 N.T.R. 1, 79 F.L.R. 210 (Sup. Ct.); Attorney-General v. Wilson and Horton Ltd., [1973] 2 N.Z.L.R. 238 (C.A.) (payment of wage to employee unable to work not showing of recoverable damages). But see The King v. Richardson [1948] S.C.R. 57, [1948] 2 D.L.R. 305 (recovery could be based on employee's remuneration, continued while unable to work; cost of medical and hospital treatment also recoverable).

5. How is the employer's action affected by a defense applicable to the injured employee's action against defendant, such as contributory negligence? Such defenses probably have the same effects as in an action for loss of the services or consortium of an injured family member, treated at pp. 38–50, supra. See Restatement (Second) of Torts § 494 (1965).

Berg v. General Motors Corporation

Supreme Court of Washington
87 Wash. 2d 584, 555 P.2d 818 (1976)

WRIGHT, Associate Justice.

[Plaintiff, a commercial fisherman, purchased a General Motors engine for his new boat from a retail dealer. This engine and replacement engines broke down during the fishing season. Plaintiff sued General Motors and the dealer for damages based in part on the anticipated value of the fish which could have been caught during the period his boat was laid up. The action against General Motors was dismissed on the grounds that it was not liable for breach of warranty, in the absence of privity with plaintiff, and the negligence of a manufacturer in failing to inform its dealer of known facts (here, clutch use prohibitions) and in failing to use due care in repairing or manufacturing its product would not support recovery for lost fishing production or diminution in value of a fishing vessel.]

When products liability cases are based on negligence or strict liability, some jurisdictions have held that pecuniary loss alone is not recoverable. There are two often-cited rationales for this result.... In *Seely v. White Motor Co.*, 63 Cal. 2d 9, 45 Cal. Rptr. 17, 403 P.2d 145 (1965), Justice Traynor established the pattern followed by many courts in suits where only lost profits were pled as damages and a theory other than warranty or misrepresentation was the remedy for recovery: "The distinction that the law has drawn between tort recovery for physical injuries and warranty recovery for economic loss is not arbitrary and does not rest on the 'luck' of one plaintiff in having an accident causing physical injury. The distinction rests, rather, on an understanding of the nature of the responsibility a manufacturer must undertake in distributing his products. He can appropriately be held liable for physical injuries caused by defects by requiring his goods to match a standard of safety defined in terms of conditions that create unreasonable risks of harm. He cannot be held for the level of performance of his products in the consumer's business unless he agrees that the product was designed to meet the consumer's demands. A consumer should not be charged at the will of the manufacturer with bearing the risk of physical injury when he buys a product on the market. He can, however, be fairly charged with the risk that the product will not match his economic expectations unless the manufacturer agrees that it will. *Even in actions for negligence, a manufacturer's liability is limited to damages for physical injuries and there is no recovery for economic loss alone.*" (Italics supplied.)

The second rationale for denying lost-profit damages in nonwarranty actions is the belief that a malfunctioning product, generating solely a loss of income, violates only a contractual expectation. Only toward the injured person, or owner of injured property, is there liability in tort. In *Trans World Airlines, Inc. v. Curtiss-Wright, Corp.* [1 Misc. 2d 477, 148 N.Y.S.2d 284 (1955)] it was held that latent defects in aircraft engines, which caused injury only to the engines themselves, were not actionable in negligence.... "If the ultimate user were allowed to sue the manufacturer in negligence merely because an article with latent defects turned out to be bad when used in 'regular service' without any accident occurring, there would be nothing left of the citadel of privity and not much scope for the law of warranty.... Manufacturers would be subject to indiscriminate lawsuits by persons having no contractual relations with them, persons who could thereby escape the limitations, if any, agreed upon in their contract of purchase. Damages for inferior quality, per se, should better be left to suits between vendors and purchasers since they depend on the terms of the bargain between them." The case of *Santor v. A & M Karagheusian, Inc.*, 44 N.J. 52, 207 A.2d 305 (1965), departed from the rule that a commercially worthless product could not be the subject of a lawsuit against a manufacturer with which there was no privity of contract. The rationale for modifying that rule was based on avoidance of circuity of litigation where the same result (*i.e.*, manufacturer's liability) would be reached. The court in *Santor* justified its decision with ... [a quotation from *Randy Knitwear Inc. v. American Cyanamid Co.*, 11 N.Y.2d 5, 226 N.Y.S.2d 363, 181 N.E.2d 399]: "[I]f the consumer or ultimate business user sues and recovers, for breach of warranty, from his immediate seller and if the latter, in turn, sues and recovers against his supplier in recoupment of his damages and costs, eventually, after several separate actions by those in the chain of distribution, the manufacturer may finally be obliged 'to shoulder the responsibility which should have been his in the first instance.'.... [T]his circuity of action is 'an expensive, time consuming and wasteful process, and it may be interrupted by insolvency, lack of jurisdiction, disclaimers, or the statute of limitations.'" ...

... We find no compelling reasons for denying lost profits, per se, in negligence actions, whether against immediate or remote sellers.... First, we do not see any increased hazard of a manufacturer being subjected to indiscriminate lawsuits where a plaintiff is permitted to recover lost profits against that remote manufacturer. Under warranty liability, the manufacturer eventually is obliged "'to shoulder the responsibility which should have been his in the first instance.'" Negligence actions usually avoid multiple suits. Second, ... [a] distinction that would allow recovery if the product in question destroyed the property of another, yet would deny recovery were the same product merely to disintegrate, is a specious one. The proper functioning of equipment owned by a plaintiff, from which that person plans to derive income is of great concern to him. To suggest that a breakdown in production is not serious is naive. Third, we do not agree with the suggestion that unless the manufacturer knows and "consents" to the use being made of its product, it would be unfair to charge such manufacturer with commercially poor performance. "Foreseeability" and a duty to the complaining party must be proved. The scope of the duty owed is measured by the foreseeability of the risk, and whether the danger created by that risk is sufficiently large to embrace the specific harm alleged to have occurred. A manufacturer intending and foreseeing that its product would eventually be purchased by persons operating commercial ventures, owes such persons the duty not to impair that purchaser's commercial operations by a faulty product. The negligent manufacture of such an article sold, poses the foreseeable risk that the output of the entire enterprise would be diminished or even temporarily halted. The specie of harm generated by such work stoppage (lost profits) is well within the zone of danger created and foreseen by the negligent act.... [Fourth], we conclude that no substantive basis exists for denying lost profits against the remote manufacturer, at least in negligence. The only basis for such a rule exists in the historical development of products liability law, which at an early date relied on implied contract to sidestep the very burdensome proof required to charge a remote manufacturer in negligence. Courts are anxious to find some legal theory sufficient to protect the public interest. Implied warranty was the convenient legal device selected to accomplish this purpose. However, this theory has frequently suffered the stricture of "privity". Eventually, these two theories contributed to the formation of a third theory of recovery, which has elements of contract and of tort, *i.e.*, strict liability. Each theory has a historical basis and should have its identity kept intact. "Privity" as a limitation, only inheres in warranty. "Foreseeability" as a limitation, only inheres in negligence. "Personal or property damage" as a limitation only inheres in strict liability. We conclude that there is nothing in the tort of negligence which prevents lost profits from being a specie of recompensable harm which is actionable against the remote manufacturer....

[Dismissal of the negligence cause of action vacated.]

Notes

1. As the opinion in Berg v. General Motors Corp. reflects, there is considerable authority denying recovery in negligence for purely economic loss caused by a defective product. The rationale of Superwood Corp. v. Siempelkamp Corp., 311 N.W.2d 159 (Minn. 1981), is that liability for economic losses arising from commercial transactions is gov-

erned by provisions of the Uniform Commercial Code. The provisions would be "emasculated" if their limitations of liability could be circumvented by tort actions. What if the purchaser has incurred costs to repair a product that endangers persons or property? Recovery of these costs was denied in Rivtow Marine Ltd. v. Washington Iron Works, [1974] S.C.R. 1189, (1973) 40 D.L.R.3d 530, even though the court found that defendants had assumed and violated a duty to warn of known defects and therefore were liable for revenue lost, during a busy period, while plaintiff had the defects repaired. See also National Crane Corp. v. Ohio Steel Tube Co., 213 Neb. 782, 332 N.W.2d 39 (1983). In Winnipeg Condominium Corp. v. Bird Construction Co. Ltd., [1995] 1 S.C.R. 85, (1995) 121 D.L.R.4th 193, the court allowed the second owner of a building to sue the construction contractor for the costs of eliminating a defect that was a substantial danger to persons and property, effectively overruling this aspect of *Rivtow Marine*.

2. In the principal case, the court, when referring to circuitry of actions, seems to have thought that holding the manufacturer liable in negligence would have the same effect on the manufacturer as plaintiff suing the seller and the seller claiming indemnity from the manufacturer. But this would not be the case when the manufacturer had disclaimed warranties. The seller would not have an action against the manufacturer if the relevant warranty was effectively disclaimed by the manufacturer. If the manufacturer did disclaim warranties in the sale to the seller, would this bar a negligence action? What if the manufacturer disclaimed warranties to ultimate purchasers?

3. Would the decision in *Berg* support a negligence claim by a homeowner against a contractor or builder-vendor for the cost of repairing construction defects, or impairment of the value of the home? In Stuart v. Coldwell Banker Commercial Group, Inc., 109 Wash. 2d 406, 745 P.2d 1284 (1987), tort claims by the occupants of a condominium complex against the builder-vendor were rejected. The court in Aas v. Superior Court, 24 Cal. 4th 627, 101 Cal. Rptr. 2d 718, 12 P.3d 1125 (2000), applied the distinction between property damage and economic loss in ruling against homeowners' tort claims against the buildings' contractor and subcontractor, which alleged many defects in construction. In Casa Clara Condominium Association, Inc. v. Charley Toppino and Sons, Inc., 620 So. 2d 1244 (Fla. 1993), the court rejected a negligence action by homeowners against the supplier of concrete used in construction, which cracked and broke off after the dwellings were occupied. The court considered the home-sellers' duty to disclose defects and the warranties protecting buyers, together with the buyers' ability to inspect houses for defects and bargain over price, sufficient protections "when compared with the mischief that could be caused by allowing tort recovery for purely economic losses." Cf. 2314 Lincoln Park West Condominium Association v. Mann, Gin, Ebel & Frazier, Ltd., 136 Ill. 2d 302, 555 N.E.2d 346 (1990) (condominium owners could not bring negligence actions against architects to recover costs of repairs). However, the court in Council of Co-Owners Atlantis Condominium, Inc. v. Whiting-Turner Contracting Co., 308 Md. 18, 517 A.2d 336 (1986), held that a condominium association and unit owners could bring negligence actions against the general contractor, architects and developer for construction deficiencies that were safety hazards but had not caused injuries. A.C. Excavating v. Yacht Club II Homeowners Association, Inc., 114 P.3d 862 (Colo. 2005), allowed homeowners to bring negligence actions against subcontractors to recover losses caused by construction defects. See also Bryan v. Maloney, (1995) 182 C.L.R. 609, allowing the third owner of a house to recover the cost of remedial work needed because of the builder's negligence.

4. A few cases extend strict product liability to economic losses such as repair costs or loss of a product's value. See Blagg v. Fred Hunt Co., Inc., 272 Ark. 185, 612 S.W.2d 321 (1981) (defective carpet causing odor and fumes). However, the prevailing rule is to reject any strict tort liability for economic loss and limit remedies to liability under commercial law, including breach of warranty, and possibly liability for misrepresentation. See State Farm Mutual Automobile Insurance Co. v. Ford Motor Co., 225 Wis. 2d 305, 592 N.W.2d 201 (1999). One reason is that a product causing only economic loss may not be considered "unreasonably dangerous." See Two Rivers Co. v. Curtiss Breeding Service, 624 F.2d 1242 (5th Cir. 1980), cert. denied, 450 U.S. 920 (1981) (cattle breeder purchased semen of bull which carried genetic abnormality); Brown v. Western Farmers Association, 268 Or. 470, 521 P.2d 537 (1974) (feed for plaintiff's chickens allegedly caused bad-tasting eggs, resulting in loss of profits). However, the main reasons are the existence of the Uniform Commercial Code and policy arguments against tort liability for economic loss. Seely v. White Motor Co., discussed in the principal case, is often quoted in this regard. See generally Annot., Privity of Contract as Essential in Action Against Remote Manufacturer or Distributor for Defects in Goods Not Causing Injury to Person or to Other Property, 16 A.L.R.3d 683 (1967).

5. In Daanen & Janssen, Inc. v. Cedarapids, Inc., 216 Wis. 2d 395, 573 N.W.2d 842 (1998), and State Farm Mutual Automobile Insurance Co. v. Ford Motor Co., 225 Wis. 2d 305, 592 N.W.2d 201 (1999), the Supreme Court of Wisconsin identified three policies that supported the "economic loss doctrine." First, the doctrine maintained the distinction between tort law, which is "rooted in the concept of protecting society as a whole from physical harm to person or property," and contract law, which is based on "obligations imposed by bargain" and protects "the expectancy interest of parties to private bargained-for agreements." Contract law most appropriately enforced the duties that parties imposed upon themselves by entering into contracts. Parties can protect themselves by bargaining. Second, the doctrine protected parties' freedom to allocate economic risk by contract. There would be no such freedom if tort recovery for economic loss were allowed. Third, the doctrine encouraged "the party best situated" to assume, allocate or insure against economic risk. In the court's opinion, this was usually the purchaser because purchasers had knowledge of how and where the product would be used and their needs and expectations. They were in a better position than manufacturers to assess and plan for economic loss caused by a defect.

6. If the harm caused by a product's defect is damage to that product, should this be considered consequential property damage (for which recovery is allowed under strict tort, negligence and warranty) or economic loss? Compare Thompson v. Nebraska Mobile Homes Corp., 198 Mont. 461, 647 P.2d 334 (1982) (strict liability for damage to mobile home); John R. Dudley Construction, Inc. v. Drott Manufacturing Co., 66 A.D.2d 368, 412 N.Y.S.2d 512 (1979) (strict liability if defective bolts caused crane to collapse), with Bocre Leasing Corp. v. General Motors Corp. (Allison Gas Turbine Division), 84 N.Y.2d 685, 621 N.Y.S.2d 497, 645 N.E.2d 1195 (1995) (no negligence or strict liability for damage to helicopter in forced landing caused by part failure); Mid Continent Aircraft Corp. v. Curry County Spraying Service, Inc., 572 S.W.2d 308 (Tex. 1978) (airplane destroyed in crash caused by defect; said to be—at least as between commercial seller and commercial buyer—only economic loss, governed by Uniform Commercial Code). The Supreme Court's admiralty law decision in East River Steamship Corp. v. Transamerica Delaval, Inc., 476 U.S. 858 (1986), that loss resulting from damage to the product is an economic loss for which there is no negligence or strict liability, has influenced land-based law on this point.

7. Some of the cases distinguish damage caused by a "sudden and calamitous occurrence" (an "accident") from a product's deterioration or internal disintegration. Pennsylvania Glass Sand Corp. v. Caterpillar Tractor Co., 652 F.2d 1165 (3d Cir. 1981) (strict liability for fire damage to front-end loader); Vulcan Materials Co., Inc. v. Driltech, Inc., 251 Ga. 383, 306 S.E.2d 253 (1983) (drilling machine burst into flames). Contra, REM Coal Co., Inc. v. Clark Equipment Co., 386 Pa. Super, 401, 563 A.2d 128 (1989); Trans States Airlines v. Pratt & Whitney Canada, Inc., 177 Ill. 2d 21, 682 N.E.2d 45 (1997); Lincoln General Insurance Co. v. Detroit Diesel Corp., 293 S.W.3d 487 (Tenn. 2009). Other cases emphasize the presence or absence of danger to persons or other property. Russell v. Ford Motor Co., 281 Or. 587, 575 P.2d 1383 (1978) (strict liability for damage to truck when defective axle caused driver to lose control); Northern Power & Engineering Corp. v. Caterpillar Tractor Co., 623 P.2d 324 (Alaska 1981) (no strict liability for damage to engine which seized because of failure of shutdown system); Pratt & Whitney Canada, Inc. v. Sheehan, 852 P.2d 1173 (Alaska 1993) (strict liability for damage to aircraft in forced landing caused by engine failure). The *Trans States Airlines* case, supra, quotes with approval the statement in Prosser & Keeton, Law of Torts 709 (5th ed. 1984), that "the risk of harm to the product itself due to the condition of the product would seem to be a type of risk that the parties to a purchase and sale contract should be allowed to allocate pursuant to the terms of the contract.... Therefore, contract law and the rules pertaining to contract restrictions on warranty liability should control rather than the rules and principles of tort law." See generally Annot., Strict Products Liability: Recovery for Damage to Product Alone, 72 A.L.R.4th 12 (1989).

Dunlop Tire and Rubber Corporation v. FMC Corporation
Supreme Court of New York, Appellate Division
53 A.D.2d 150, 385 N.Y.S.2d 971 (1976)

SIMONS, Justice.

Defendant manufactures chemicals in Tonawanda, New York. On March 1, 1973 an explosion occurred in its plant, casting stones and debris on plaintiff's tire factory nearby and also damaging it by concussion. In addition, plaintiff claims that it sustained substantial damage because the explosion destroyed towers and distribution lines owned by Niagara Mohawk Power Corporation which supplied electrical energy to its factory, thereby causing a loss of power and a 24-hour shutdown of plaintiff's production facilities. The towers and distribution lines passed in front of defendant's plant on Sawyer Avenue en route from Niagara Mohawk's generating station to serve plaintiff's plant and other customers east of plaintiff. The amended complaint includes causes of action based upon negligence, trespass, nuisance and strict liability in tort. Defendant's motion to dismiss is addressed to the negligence cause of action....

... The pleadings establish that plaintiff was within the zone of foreseeable danger from negligent acts of defendant (see *Palsgraf v. Long Is. R.R. Co.*, 248 N.Y. 339, 162 N.E. 99). Plaintiff's property was located near defendant's property in a highly industrialized section of the town, the two separated only by railroad tracks, and the explosion (which was not the first explosion experienced by defendant in its chemical operations) occurred at a point less than 1200 feet from plaintiff's buildings. Given the nature of defendant's business and the relationship of the two parties, it is apparent that the amended complaint states facts entitling plaintiff to recover for damage due to flying debris and concussion from the blast if a jury determines that defendant failed to exercise reasonable care considering the risk that could be anticipated.

The circumstance which makes this case unique, however, is that the damages claimed by plaintiff stem not so much from the direct invasion of plaintiff's premises as from the interruption of power caused by destruction of Niagara Mohawk's transmission lines. The amended complaint alleges that "the explosion and fire created a substantial interference with the right and ability of plaintiff to carry on the production of tires at its place of business"....

Plaintiff's claim may be conveniently divided into damages representing lost profits sustained during the 24-hour shutdown resulting from the loss of energy ($170,000) and physical damage to the property which resulted both from the blast and from the loss of energy ($16,445). It is the claim for damages sustained when the electrical power failed, principally those for lost profits (anticipated sales less cost of production and selling) to which the parties address themselves on this appeal. Defendant contends that plaintiff may not maintain a cause of action to recover for negligent interference with its contract to obtain electrical power from Niagara Mohawk and that any duty imposed on defendant to prevent injury to the power lines was owed to Niagara Mohawk, the owner of the property, not plaintiff, a consumer of the electrical energy. The few cases in New York which have considered claims based upon negligent interference with contract have so held....

We think that rule inapplicable in the present case because plaintiff's claim is not vicarious or derivative, nor is it founded upon some unfilled contract expectancy from Niagara Mohawk acting as a conduit. Plaintiff's rights arise from an independent duty of care owed to it by defendant. It was a duty defendant owed to a known plaintiff to protect it against a predictable risk. Eliminate the duty owed to Niagara Mohawk and defendant's duty to plaintiff remained, for plaintiff was within the area of apparent danger created by any lack of care on defendant's part.

... Plaintiff's physical damage, losses in materials or equipment and cost of clean-up resulting from flying debris and concussion, are compensable under familiar principles of law and to the extent that similar damages were sustained and are proved, which were caused by the interruption of electrical service, they are also compensable.

There remains for consideration plaintiff's claim for lost profits. Logically, if damage from the loss of power was foreseeable, then the interruption of production was also foreseeable and the lost profits resulting from the interruption should be compensable, if proved and if, indeed, lost profits are recoverable at all in a tort action. However, while there is some limited authority that lost profits may be recovered, such damages are subject to the general rule of certainty which requires that plaintiff prove the extent of the damage and the causal relationship between defendant's negligence and the damage.

... A stoppage in production, however, does not necessarily result in lost profits and the damage which a manufacturer may sustain from a 24-hour shutdown in production as a result of an interruption of electrical power may well be too remote and speculative to be compensated.

There are cases in which compensation for lost profits has been permitted, primarily those involving the sale of time or services. One example is the tortious interference with a hotel owner's use of rented hotel space. The night having passed, the owner's lost profit can never be recovered. So too, profits may be considered in some cases because they reflect the value of lost time or diminished earning capacity to an injured party or they are parasitic to personal or property injury claims. Undoubtedly, there are other situations which may be analyzed, but these are sufficient to illustrate the distinction between a delay in the production of tires which if not produced and sold today will be produced and sold tomorrow. The profit which might have been earned during the period of shutdown usually will not be compensable for tort purposes because of the difficulty of demonstrating that it has been lost.

[Order denying the motion to dismiss affirmed.]

Beck v. FMC Corporation

Supreme Court of New York, Appellate Division
53 A.D.2d 118, 385 N.Y.S.2d 956 (1976), aff'd,
42 N.Y.2d 1027, 398 N.Y.S.2d 1011, 369 N.E.2d 10 (1977)

PER CURIAM....

The explosion at the FMC plant [see Dunlop Tire and Rubber Corp. v. FMC Corp., p. 220, supra] disrupted Niagara Mohawk's electrical power service to a Chevrolet plant located approximately one and a half miles away. The Chevrolet plant was unable to operate without electricity and its management neither employed nor paid its hourly employees on the date of the explosion.

Plaintiffs are more than 600 hourly employees of Chevrolet, together with their respective unions. They claim to represent approximately 8,500 similarly situated individuals and seek judgment in the amount of $340,000 for lost wages. Defendants moved to dismiss the complaint for failure to state a cause of action and for failure to qualify as a class action. This appeal is taken from Special Term's denial of those motions....

... Plaintiffs do not allege any affirmative act of negligence, but rely solely on the failure of Niagara Mohawk to maintain and perpetuate electrical service. Under such circumstances, we are bound to conclude that Niagara Mohawk owed no duty to plaintiffs for a negligent failure to furnish electricity to their employer. A contrary determination would unduly extend the liability of this defendant to an indefinite number of potential beneficiaries....

The same rationale applies to plaintiffs' causes of action against defendant FMC based upon common law negligence....

FMC urges that what plaintiffs seek is recovery for an alleged interference with a contract right of employment and that in such circumstances recovery can be had only where there is a showing of an intentional disturbance of the employment relationship....

While we recognize that the extent of one's duty is determined by the risk reasonably to be perceived (*Palsgraf v. Long Island R.R. Co.*, 248 N.Y. 339, 162 N.E. 99), the foreseeability factor is not determinative of the issue. It is argued that FMC should have foreseen the ultimate damage to plaintiffs. "If foreseeability be the sole test, then once liability is extended the logic of the principle would not and could not remain confined." (*Tobin v. Grossman*, 24 N.Y.2d p. 616, 301 N.Y.S.2d p. 559, 249 N.E.2d p. 423.) It would extend endlessly, like the rippling of the waters, far beyond the zone of danger of the explosion, to all who suffered injury or economic loss caused by the absence of electric power.

Judicial sanction of the causes of action pleaded here would make it nearly impossible to guard against unlimited or unduly burdensome liability and avoid arbitrary distinctions in defining the areas of liability....

[Order reversed and complaint dismissed.]

J'Aire Corporation v. Gregory

Supreme Court of California
24 Cal. 3d 799, 157 Cal. Rptr. 407, 598 P.2d 60 (1979)

BIRD, Chief Justice....

... Appellant, J'Aire Corporation, operates a restaurant at the Sonoma County Airport in premises leased from the County of Sonoma. Under the terms of the lease the county was to provide heat and air conditioning. In 1975 the county entered into a contract with respondent for improvements to the restaurant premises, including renovation of the heating and air conditioning systems and installation of insulation.

As the contract did not specify any date for completion of the work, appellant alleged the work was to have been completed within a reasonable time as defined by custom and usage. Despite requests that respondent complete the construction promptly, the work was not completed within a reasonable time. Because the restaurant could not operate during part of the construction and was without heat and air conditioning for a longer period, appellant suffered loss of business and resulting loss of profits.

[The trial court sustained a demurrer to plaintiff's action for damages, based upon negligence in not completing the work within a reasonable time.] ...

This court has held that a plaintiff's interest in prospective economic advantage may be protected against injury occasioned by negligent as well as intentional conduct. For example, economic losses such as lost earnings or profits are recoverable as part of general damages in a suit for personal injury based on negligence. Where negligent conduct causes injury to real or personal property, the plaintiff may recover damages for profits lost during the time necessary to repair or replace the property.

Even when only injury to prospective economic advantage is claimed, recovery is not foreclosed. Where a special relationship exists between the parties, a plaintiff may recover for loss of expected economic advantage through the negligent performance of a contract although the parties were not in contractual privity. *Biakanja v. Irving* (1958) 49 Cal. 2d 647, 320 P.2d 16, held that intended beneficiaries of wills could sue to recover legacies lost through the negligent preparation of the will.

... [T]he court determined that defendants owed plaintiffs a duty of care by applying criteria set forth in *Biakanja v. Irving*. Those criteria are (1) the extent to which the transaction was intended to affect the plaintiff, (2) the foreseeability of harm to the plaintiff, (3) the degree of certainty that the plaintiff suffered injury, (4) the closeness of the connection between the defendant's conduct and the injury suffered, (5) the moral blame attached to the defendant's conduct and (6) the policy of preventing future harm.

Applying these criteria to the facts as pleaded, it is evident that a duty was owed by respondent to appellant in the present case. (1) The contract entered into between respondent and the county was for the renovation of the premises in which appellant maintained its business. The contract could not have been performed without impinging on that business. Thus respondent's performance was intended to, and did, directly affect appellant.

(2) Accordingly, it was clearly foreseeable that any significant delay in completing the construction would adversely affect appellant's business beyond the normal disruption associated with such construction. Appellant alleges this fact was repeatedly drawn to respondent's attention. (3) Further, appellant's complaint leaves no doubt that appellant suffered harm since it was unable to operate its business for one month and suffered additional loss of business while the premises were without heat and air conditioning. (4) Appellant has also alleged that delays occasioned by the respondent's conduct were closely connected to, indeed directly caused its injury. (5) In addition, respondent's lack of diligence in the present case was particularly blameworthy since it continued after the probability of damage was drawn directly to respondent's attention. (6) Finally, public policy supports finding a duty of care in the present case. The wilful failure or refusal of a contractor to prosecute a construction project with diligence, where another is injured as a result, has been made grounds for disciplining a licensed contractor. (Bus. & Prof. Code, § 7119.) Although this section does not provide a basis for imposing liability where the delay in completing construction is due merely to negligence, it does indicate the seriousness with which the Legislature views unnecessary delays in the completion of construction.

In light of these factors, this court finds that respondent had a duty to complete construction in a manner that would have avoided unnecessary injury to appellant's business, even though the construction contract was with the owner of a building rather than with appellant, the tenant. It is settled that a contractor owes a duty to avoid injury to the person or property of third parties. As appellant points out, injury to a tenant's business can often result in greater hardship than damage to a tenant's person or property. Where the risk of harm is foreseeable, as it was in the present case, an injury to the plaintiff's economic interests should not go uncompensated merely because it was unaccompanied by any injury to his person or property....

Respondent cites *Fifield Manor v. Finston* (1960) 54 Cal. 2d 632, 7 Cal. Rptr. 377, 354 P.2d 1073 for the proposition that recovery may not be had for negligent loss of prospective economic advantage. *Fifield* concerned the parallel tort of interference with contractual relations. There a nonprofit retirement home that had contracted with Ross to provide him with lifetime medical care sued a driver who negligently struck and killed Ross. The plaintiff argued it had become liable under the contract for Ross' medical bills and sought recovery from the driver, on both a theory of direct liability and one of subrogation. Recovery was denied.

The critical factor of foreseeability distinguishes *Fifield* from the present case. Although it was reasonably foreseeable that defendant's negligence might cause injury to Ross, it was less foreseeable that it would injure the retirement home's economic interest. Defendant had not entered into any relationship or undertaken any activity where negligence on his part was reasonably likely to affect plaintiff adversely. Thus, the nexus between the defendant's conduct and the risk of the injury that occurred to the plaintiff was too tenuous to support the imposition of a duty owing to the retirement home. In contrast, the nexus in the present case between the injury that occurred and respondent's conduct is extremely close. *Fifield* does not entirely foreclose recovery for negligent interference with prospective economic advantage....

However, the factors enumerated in *Biakanja* and applied in subsequent cases place a limit on recovery by focusing judicial attention on the foreseeability of the injury and the nexus between the defendant's conduct and the plaintiff's injury. These factors and ordinary principles of tort law such as proximate cause are fully adequate to limit recovery without the drastic consequence of an absolute rule which bars recovery in all such cases. Following these principles, recovery for negligent interference with prospective economic advantage will be limited to instances where the risk of harm is foreseeable and is closely connected with the defendant's conduct, where damages are not wholly speculative and the injury is not part of the plaintiff's ordinary business risk....

[Reversed. Clark and Richardson, JJ., concurred in the judgment.]

Notes

1. Various rationales appear in cases conforming to the traditional rule against recovery for economic loss caused by negligent interference with contract or prospective advantage. In jurisdictions where there no longer is a flat rule against recovery, these rationales remain viable as criteria of liability. It was observed in Just's, Inc. v. Arrington Construction Co., Inc., 99 Idaho 462, 583 P.2d 997 (1978), that "some courts have simply ruled that the defendant owes no duty to plaintiffs seeking compensation for such purely economic losses. Other courts have reached the same result by applying the doctrine of proximate cause. Still other courts have found such economic losses to be too remote to permit recovery. Courts have also denied recovery of purely economic losses on the ground that they were too speculative.... Though the rule has been expressed in different ways, the common underlying pragmatic consideration is that a contrary rule, which would allow compensation for losses of economic advantage caused by the defendant's negligence, would impose too heavy and unpredictable a burden on the defendant's conduct."

Restatement (Second) of Torts § 766C, comment a (1979), states: "The explanation usually given by the courts, when one is given at all, is that the harm is too 'remote' for negligence liability and that the defendant's conduct is not the 'proximate cause.' In most of the cases in which recovery has been denied, the defendant has had no knowledge of the contract or prospective relation and no reason to foresee any harm to the plaintiff's interests; and the decision sometimes has been explained under the rule as to unforeseeable plaintiffs.... It seems more likely, however, that it is the character of the contract or prospective interest itself that has led the courts to refuse to give it protection against negligent interference. They apparently have been influenced by the extremely variable nature of the relations, the fear of an undue burden upon the defendant's freedom of action, the probable disproportion between the large damages that might be recovered and the extent of the defendant's fault, and perhaps in some cases the difficulty of determining whether the interference has in fact resulted from the negligent conduct."

2. The leading cases supporting the rule against negligence liability for economic loss include Cattle v. Stockton Waterworks Co., (1875) L.R. 10 Q.B. 453 (leak from defendant's waterworks delayed plaintiff's construction of tunnel for landowner and caused monetary loss); Byrd v. English, 117 Ga. 191, 43 S.E. 419 (1903) (construction contractors broke power company wires supplying electricity to plaintiff's printing works, interrupting business for several hours); Thompson v. Seaboard Air Line Railway, 165 N.C. 377, 81 S.E. 315 (1914) (sparks from railway engine caused fire which destroyed timber that plaintiff had contract to saw; plaintiff lost expected profit); Robins Dry Dock & Repair Co. v. Flint, 275 U.S. 303 (1927) (damage to ship plaintiffs had chartered, causing loss of use of ship for two weeks); Rickards v. Sun Oil Co., 23 N.J. Misc. 89, 41 A.2d 267 (Sup. Ct. 1945) (defendant's barge destroyed drawbridge, cutting off all road access to island where plaintiffs' businesses were located); and Stevenson v. East Ohio Gas Co., 47 Ohio L. Abs. 586, 73 N.E.2d 200 (Ct. App. 1946) (gas explosion and danger of further explosions near plaintiff's place of work prevented plaintiff from working for eight days, causing loss of wages). State of Louisiana ex rel. Guste v. M/V Testbank, 752 F.2d 1019

(5th Cir. 1985), cert. denied sub nom. White v. M/V Testbank, 477 U.S. 903 (1986), in which the consequences of a ship collision seriously impacted many marine and land-based enterprises in the region, is an important modern decision. Aikens v. Debow, 208 W. Va. 486, 541 S.E.2d 576 (2000), in which a motel and restaurant lost business when an accident caused a nearby bridge to be closed for nineteen days, is a recent successor to this line of cases.

3. When plaintiff is linked to defendant by a chain of separate contracts, application of the rule against recovery for economic loss may be defended on the grounds that defendant had no detailed knowledge of plaintiff's circumstances and could not predict the consequences that any negligence might cause to plaintiff, whereas plaintiff would have been aware of its exposure to economic loss and could secure protection against loss through a term in the contract or some other means, such as insurance or back-up equipment. For example, in J'Aire Corp. v. Gregory, plaintiff might have negotiated protection against interruption of its business with the lessor of the building, or secured a lower rent in return for accepting the risk. In Beck v. FMC Corp., workers at the Chevrolet plant might have bargained with their employer for continuance of wages during unplanned shutdowns. It might also be thought incongruous for a defendant to be liable in tort for loss of profits when liability for breach of contract would not ordinarily extend to such consequential losses.

These views are articulated in Judge Posner's opinion for the court in Rardin v. T & D Machine Handling, Inc., 890 F.2d 24 (7th Cir. 1989). In *Rardin*, the seller of a printing press hired a contractor to dismantle the press and load it onto a truck that was to take the press to the purchaser. The cost of this was built into the price paid by the purchaser to the seller. Due to the contractor's negligence, the press was damaged. Under the contract, the seller was liable to the purchaser for physical damage to the press caused by the contractor, but not for profits lost because of the delay before the press could be made operational. These, the purchaser sought to recover from the contractor in a negligence action. The court affirmed dismissal of the action. Judge Posner posed a hypothetical in which plaintiff missed an important business meeting because his watch, taken to a retail store for repair and sent by the store to a watchmaker, was inaccurate on account of the watchmaker's negligence. He also referred to EVRA Corp. v. Swiss Bank Corp., 673 F.2d 951 (7th Cir. 1982), cert. denied, 459 U.S. 1017 (1982), in which plaintiff lost a contract because the correspondent bank of plaintiff's bank negligently failed to deposit a payment. Are these situations analogous to those presented in the *J'Aire* case?

4. How would this reasoning apply to a case in which defendant broke a water main, leaving residential and business premises without running water for several days? See Quest Diagnostics, Inc. v. MCI WorldCom, Inc., 254 Mich. App. 372, 656 N.W.2d 858 (2002), appeal denied, 469 Mich. 975, 671 N.W.2d 886 (2003). A case in which oil spilled from a large tank and migrated to an area where a sewer was being constructed, causing a long and expensive delay for the construction contractor? Garweth Corp. v. Boston Edison Co., 415 Mass. 303, 613 N.E.2d 92 (1993). Or a case in which defendant's negligence caused the spread of an agricultural pest or livestock disease, causing plaintiff no physical damage but preventing or greatly limiting plaintiff's ability to sell his produce, meat or livestock? See Perre v. Apand Pty. Ltd., (1999) 198 C.L.R. 180 (plaintiffs' most profitable market for potatoes barred sale because of outbreak of potato disease on land near plaintiffs'). Compare Weller & Co. v. Foot and Mouth Disease Research Institute, [1966] 1 Q.B. 569 (cattle auctioneers lost business when cattle markets closed because of foot and mouth disease in vicinity).

5. When property damage occurs as a direct result of an interruption in the supply of electricity or other vital service, a party whose negligence was responsible for the interruption can be held liable for the damage and consequential losses. See A.J. Decoster Co.

v. Westinghouse Electric Corp., 333 Md. 245, 634 A.2d 1330 (1994) (140,000 chickens suffocated when power supply for ventilation system interrupted); S.C.M. (United Kingdom) Ltd. v. W.J. Whittall and Son Ltd., [1971] 1 Q.B. 337 (C.A.) (molten material solidified and damaged machinery when power cut). Most authority denies recovery for loss of production capacity caused by interruption of utility supply. E.g., Byrd v. English, p. 225, supra. In Spartan Ṣteel & Alloys Ltd. v. Martin & Co. (Contractors) Ltd., [1973] Q.B. 27 (C.A.), the court denied recovery for profits lost when the interruption of electricity for 14½ hours prevented melting of metal in a factory, although recovery was allowed for damage to melted material that was in the furnace when the power went off and loss of profit on the material. Lord Denning, M.R., observed that most people do not take legal action when their electricity supply is cut off; they just try to make up the loss by doing more work the next day. He believed this attitude should be encouraged. If a power outage causes loss of material in a computer, is this property damage or pure economic loss? See Seaboard Life Insurance Co. v. Babich, [1995] 10 W.W.R. 756 (B.C. Sup. Ct.) (loss of computer data not property damage). Cf. Transport Corp. of America, Inc. v. International Business Machines Corp., Inc., 30 F.3d 953 (8th Cir. 1994) (loss of computer data economic loss for purposes of action against sellers of computer system). What if "contamination" of food products or agricultural land by genetically modified varieties prevents sale of the food to organic food markets or countries that ban imports of genetically modified food? See Sample v. Monsanto Co., 283 F. Supp. 2d 1088 (E.D. Mo. 2003); In re Genetically Modified Rice Litigation, 666 F. Supp. 2d 1004 (E.D. Mo. 2009).

6. In Caltex Oil (Australia) Pty. Ltd. v. The Dredge "Willemstad," (1976) 136 C.L.R. 529, a dredge fractured a pipeline connecting an oil refinery with an oil terminal. An action was allowed the owner of the terminal for loss caused by interruption of the oil supply. Several of the judges emphasized that the owners of the dredge knew the pipeline led from the refinery to the terminal and, therefore, should have had plaintiff in mind as a party who would suffer economic loss if the pipeline were broken. Cf. Canadian National Railway Co. v. Norsk Pacific Steamship Co. Ltd., [1992] 1 S.C.R. 1021, (1992) 91 D.L.R.4th 289, involving damage to a bridge primarily used, but not owned, by a railway with tracks and land on both sides of the river the bridge crossed. A leading American case upholding an action for negligently caused economic loss is People Express Airlines, Inc. v. Consolidated Rail Corp., 100 N.J. 246, 495 A.2d 107 (1985). A railroad tank car was punctured when it was coupled with another car. This caused a fire with a risk of explosion, as the tank car contained a highly volatile substance. Municipal authorities evacuated the area within a one mile radius of the fire. This included the airport terminal where plaintiff's operations were based. Because the terminal could not be used for twelve hours, flights were cancelled and telephone calls for reservations were not answered. The court held that a duty of care to avoid the risk of economic damages is owed to "particular plaintiffs or plaintiffs comprising an identifiable class with respect to whom defendant knows or has reason to know are likely to suffer such damages." An "identifiable" class was one that was "particularly" foreseeable, not "simply" foreseeable. "Particular" foreseeability was also to be a test of proximate or legal cause in such cases. Recoverable damages were those "reasonably to be anticipated" by defendant as risks to "identifiable" plaintiffs. If *People Express* is followed, should an employer's claim for loss caused by injury to an employee be entertained? See Mattingly v. Sheldon Jackson College, 743 P.2d 356 (Alaska 1987); Champion Well Service, Inc. v. NL Industries, 769 P.2d 382 (Wyo. 1989).

7. A building contractor often becomes liable for liquidated damages and may incur other costs if a project is not completed by a set date. If this is the fault of a supplier who has not furnished goods on schedule to one of the subcontractors, can the contractor hold that supplier liable for the resultant costs? It has been held that this states a cause of action. Chameleon

Engineering Corp. v. Air Dynamics, Inc., 101 Cal. App. 3d 418, 161 Cal. Rptr. 463 (1980). The same result is found in contractors' actions to recover costs incurred because of the negligence of an architect or engineer. A.R. Moyer, Inc. v. Graham, 285 So. 2d 397 (Fla. 1973); Forte Brothers, Inc. v. National Amusements, Inc., 525 A.2d 1301 (R.I. 1987); Tommy L. Griffin Plumbing & Heating Co. v. Jordan, Jones & Goulding, Inc., 320 S.C. 49, 463 S.E.2d 85 (1995). But in Berschauer/Phillips Construction Co. v. Seattle School District No. 1, 124 Wash. 2d 816, 881 P.2d 986 (1994), it was held that a general contractor could not maintain a tort action for monetary loss against the architect, structural engineer and field inspector of a construction project. See also BRW, Inc. v. Dufficy & Sons, Inc., 99 P.3d 66 (Colo. 2004), rejecting a subcontractor's tort action against a project engineer and construction inspector. See generally Annot., Tort Liability of Project Architect or Engineer for Economic Damages Suffered by Contractor or Subcontractor, 61 A.L.R.6th 445 (2011).

8. Does J'Aire Corp. v. Gregory affect liability for economic loss caused by product defects, discussed pp. 215–220, supra? In Ales-Peratis Foods International, Inc. v. American Can Co., 164 Cal. App. 3d 277, 209 Cal. Rptr. 917 (1985), plaintiff sued to recover losses incurred because 119,200 cans manufactured by defendant, which plaintiff purchased from a supplier for use in canning abalone, were unusable. On the basis of the *J'Aire* case, the court held that plaintiff stated a negligence action. Plaintiff alleged that defendant sold the cans to the supplier with knowledge that they were to meet plaintiff's requirements for cans suitable for packing abalone and the ability to foresee the loss of a sales contract and profits resulting from the supply of defective cans.

9. Suppose an oil spill or chemical discharge diminishes or contaminates marine life. Can commercial fishermen who regularly work in the affected area recover lost profits? In Union Oil Co. v. Oppen, 501 F.2d 558 (9th Cir. 1974), the court held that an oil company with offshore drilling operations had a duty not to negligently harm sea life and could be liable for loss of profits. In Pruitt v. Allied Chemical Corp., 523 F. Supp. 975 (E.D. Va. 1981), potential recovery was extended beyond seafood harvesters to marina owners and proprietors of boat, tackle and bait shops at the edge of the contaminated waters, but not to businesses deprived of supplies of seafood. Compare French Knit Sales Pty. Ltd. v. N. Gold & Sons Pty. Ltd., [1972] 2 N.S.W.L.R. 132 (C.A.). Defendant's negligence in allowing water to escape damaged the inventory of plaintiff's supplier. Plaintiff, temporarily deprived of a supply of goods, lost profits. The court denied recovery. In Margarine Union G.m.b.H. v. Cambay Prince Steamship Co. Ltd., [1969] 1 Q.B. 219, due to defendants' negligence in failing to fumigate their vessel, copra being shipped to plaintiffs was damaged by giant cockroaches. Plaintiffs were denied recovery on the ground that English law recognized no duty of care toward a party who had neither ownership nor entitlement to possession of the goods when they were damaged. See Leigh and Sillavan Ltd. v. Aliakmon Shipping Co. Ltd., [1986] A.C. 785 (H.L.). Cf. Stromer v. Yuba City, 225 Cal. App. 2d 286, 37 Cal. Rptr. 240 (1964) (destruction of prune trees in orchard, causing prospective buyer to cancel purchase of orchard and real estate broker to lose commission).

10. A nuisance action is another possibility in cases such as *Union Oil* and *Pruitt*. See Burgess v. M/V Tamano, 370 F. Supp. 247 (D. Me. 1973) (liability in public nuisance when oil discharge in coastal waters caused "particular damage" to such plaintiffs as commercial fishermen). But see Hickey v. Electric Reduction Co. of Canada Ltd., (1971) 2 Nfld. & P.E.I.R. 246, 21 D.L.R.3d 368 (Nfld. Sup. Ct.) (fishermen did not suffer particular damage from pollution of bay; economic loss too remote to be recoverable). In Stop & Shop Companies, Inc. v. Fisher, 387 Mass. 889, 444 N.E.2d 368 (1983), defendants' barge struck a street bridge adjacent to plaintiff's supermarket and retail store. Defendants allegedly were negligent. During the two months the bridge was closed for

repairs, there was a substantial decline in the number of customers patronizing the stores. Plaintiff was held to have an action in public nuisance if it suffered "substantial impairment of access" and "special pecuniary loss" different from that of other persons. Compare Nebraska Innkeepers, Inc. v. Pittsburgh-Des Moines Corp., 345 N.W.2d 124 (Iowa 1984) ("special damages" required for public nuisance not shown by operators of retail business near closed bridge; negligence action also rejected); 532 Madison Avenue Gourmet Foods, Inc. v. Finlandia Center, Inc., 96 N.Y.2d 280, 727 N.Y.S.2d 49, 750 N.E.2d 1097 (2001) (building collapses in midtown Manhattan caused closure of nearby streets for some weeks and temporary evacuation of nearby buildings; court rejected public nuisance and negligence claims of retail businesses and other firms in affected areas).

11. A municipality or other governmental body may incur substantial costs when it rescues victims of an accident, cleans up debris, fights a fire or evacuates persons who are endangered. May these costs be recovered from a person whose negligence caused the accident or peril? What if defendant conducted an abnormally dangerous activity? It is usually held that there is no liability. See City of Flagstaff v. Atchison, Topeka and Santa Fe Railway Co., 719 F.2d 322 (9th Cir. 1983) (evacuation because of derailment of tank cars containing liquified petroleum gas); District of Columbia v. Air Florida, Inc., 243 U.S. App. D.C. 1, 750 F.2d 1077 (1984) (airplane crash); Town of Freetown v. New Bedford Wholesale Tire, Inc., 384 Mass. 60, 423 N.E.2d 997 (1981) (fire); City of Bridgeton v. B.P. Oil, Inc., 146 N.J. Super. 169, 369 A.2d 49 (Law Div. 1976) (oil spill from leaks in tanks); Annot., Construction and Application of "Municipal Cost Recovery Rule," or "Free Public Services Doctrine," 32 A.L.R.6th 261 (2008); Note, Tortfeasor Liability for Disaster Response Costs: Accounting for the True Cost of Accidents, 55 Ford. L. Rev. 1001 (1987). Cf. County of San Luis Obispo v. Abalone Alliance, 178 Cal. App. 3d 848, 223 Cal. Rptr. 846 (1986) (defendants organized illegal blockade to prevent operation of nuclear power plant; county could not recover costs of deploying law enforcement personnel). Should liability be imposed? In Attorney General for Ontario v. Fatehi, [1984] 2 S.C.R. 536, (1984) 15 D.L.R.4th 132, rev'g (1981) 34 O.R.2d 129, 127 D.L.R.3d 603 (C.A.), it was necessary to remove debris and gasoline spilled onto a highway as a result of a traffic collision. The costs were held recoverable on the basis that this was an instance of damage to plaintiff's property, not pure economic loss.

12. Should there be special rules for liability for economic loss caused by negligence? Or should liability be governed by the general principles of negligence law applied to claims for personal injury and property damage? The House of Lords appeared to embrace the latter position in Junior Books Ltd. v. Veitchi Co. Ltd., [1983] 1 A.C. 520 (H.L.) (claim for cost of replacing floor against subcontractors who installed floor in factory being built for plaintiffs). Subsequent cases indicate that liability for economic loss in Britain remains subject to special regulation and might attach only in relatively limited circumstances. See, finding no liability, Candlewood Navigation Corp. Ltd. v. Mitsui O.S.K. Lines Ltd., [1986] A.C. 1 (P.C.) (damage to vessel under time charter to plaintiffs); Muirhead v. Industrial Tank Specialties Ltd., [1986] Q.B. 507 (C.A.) (defective pumps manufactured by defendant installed with plaintiff's lobster tanks, leading to death of lobsters, loss of anticipated profit on their sale, additional labor costs, replacement of pumps); Murphy v. Brentwood District Council, [1991] 1 A.C. 398 (H.L.) (house built on defective foundation, plans for which had been negligently approved by local government; after foundation cracked and house damaged, homeowner sought recovery of amount by which defects diminished house's value, which was less than cost of repairing defects). In other nations, negligence liability for economic loss is expanding. See Bernstein, Economic Loss (2d ed. 1998); Feldthusen, Economic Negligence: The Recovery of Pure Eco-

nomic Loss (6th ed. 2012). On the American case law, see Feinman, Economic Negligence: Liability of Professionals and Businesses to Third Parties for Economic Loss (1995).

Pelham v. Griesheimer

Appellate Court of Illinois
93 Ill. App. 3d 751, 417 N.E.2d 882 (1981),
aff'd, 92 Ill. 2d 13, 440 N.E.2d 96 (1982)

REINHARD, Justice:

[Plaintiffs' mother retained defendant, an attorney, to obtain a divorce from plaintiffs' father. Plaintiffs were minors at the time. The divorce decree required the father to "maintain all four of his children as the prime beneficiaries in his life insurance policies." He had a $10,000 life insurance policy provided by his employer. The father remarried and named his new wife as the beneficiary of this policy. Upon his death, she received the proceeds of the policy. Plaintiffs sued defendant for $10,000, alleging that defendant owed plaintiffs a duty to exercise a reasonable degree of professional care and that defendant breached that duty by failing to notify (or advise plaintiffs' mother to notify) the father's employer or the life insurance company that the divorce decree required plaintiffs to be named as the beneficiaries of the policy, and by failing to advise plaintiffs that they had not been so named. The trial court dismissed the complaint.]

... While courts in several other states have held that attorneys may be liable for professional negligence to persons other than their clients, the cases so holding are distinguishable factually from the case at bar and typically have involved will-drafting situations where intended beneficiaries are damaged by an attorney's failure to fulfill the testamentary directions of his client....

... [I]n *Heyer v. Flaig* (1969), 70 Cal. 2d 223, 74 Cal. Rptr. 225, 449 P.2d 161, a negligence action was brought by the daughters of a deceased client against her attorney for failing to fulfill the testamentary directions of his client. The court held that the attorney owed a duty of reasonable care to the intended beneficiaries of the testatrix-client ... : "We impose this duty because of the relationship between the attorney and the intended beneficiary; public policy requires that the attorney exercise his position of trust and superior knowledge responsibly so as not to affect adversely persons whose rights and interests are certain and foreseeable." ...

While the injury which befell plaintiffs was reasonably likely and foreseeable given allegations of defendant's failure to take steps to insure compliance with the insurance provision of the divorce decree, and while the burden of guarding against the injury is not oppressive, we feel that placing that burden on defendant, and other attorneys in this state, would lead to undesirable consequences, not the least of which would be potential conflicts of interest between an attorney and his client and less than vigorous representation of the client. In *Berlin v. Nathan* [p. 710, infra] the court expressed similar fears in holding that it would be contrary to public policy to rule that an attorney has a duty to an intended defendant not to file a "weak" lawsuit against him.

In dissolution proceedings, the legal rights of several parties often are affected, i. e., a husband, a wife and one or more children, and it is not uncommon that one or more of those parties may lack the benefit of legal counsel. In that type of situation, there is already an ever-present danger that a conflict of interest will arise. Were we to conclude that an attorney representing one of the spouses (or conceivably opposing attorneys representing each spouse) also owes a duty of reasonable care to the minor children of the parties despite a lack of privity of contract, we only would serve to increase the likelihood of such a conflict as, for example, between a minor's right to support versus that spouse's interest in the property and maintenance.... [C]ourts always have possessed inherent equitable power as well as statutory authority to appoint a guardian *ad litem* for minors. Under such provisions, the rights of minor children of the parties can be protected, thus avoiding the fate which befell plaintiffs, without compromising the undivided loyalty of a spouse's attorney. While it is unfortunate that a guardian *ad litem* was not appointed to protect plaintiffs' interests when they were minors, practical realities often preclude such appointment.

Finally, we would point out that the line of out-of-state cases extending an attorney's duty to non-clients appears to be limited to a narrow range of factual situations wherein the client's sole purpose in retaining an attorney is to benefit directly some third party or parties, such as intended beneficiaries under a will. Such is not the factual situation in the present case. Clearly, plaintiffs' mother retained defendant for the primary purpose of representing her own interests in a divorce proceeding. Any intention of plaintiffs' mother to confer benefits on plaintiffs could be described as incidental or collateral. Under the facts as pleaded, we hold that there is no duty owed by the attorney to his client's children; hence no cause of action accrues to them....

AFFIRMED.

Notes

1. At one time, a negligent attorney, accountant or other professional would not be held liable to persons not in privity of contract with the professional — i.e. non-clients. The privity requirement has been relaxed in recent decades. Following Biakanja v. Irving, 49 Cal. 2d 647, 320 P.2d 16 (1958), some courts have, in order to determine whether a professional is liable, weighed such factors as the extent to which the transaction was intended to affect plaintiff, the foreseeability of harm to plaintiff, the "degree of certainty" that plaintiff suffered injury, the closeness of the connection between defendant's conduct and the injury suffered, the moral blame attached to defendant's conduct, and the policy of preventing future harm. See Annot., What Constitutes Negligence Sufficient to Render Attorney Liable to Person Other Than Immediate Client, 61 A.L.R.4th 464 (1988); Annot., Attorney's Liability, to One Other Than Immediate Client, for Negligence in Connection with Legal Duties, 61 A.L.R.4th 615 (1988); Symposium, The Lawyer's Duties and Liabilities to Third Parties, 37 S. Tex. L. Rev. 957 (1996). In affirming the Appellate Court's judgment in the principal case, the Supreme Court of Illinois laid down that to recover in tort, "plaintiffs must allege and prove facts demonstrating that they are in the nature of third-party intended beneficiaries of the relationship between the client and the attorney.... [T]o establish a duty owed by the defendant attorney ... the nonclient must allege and prove that the intent of the client to benefit the nonclient ... was the primary or direct purpose of the transaction or relationship." Why require this for attorney malpractice but not malpractice by most other professionals?

2. Some contemporary cases deny actions to persons who were deprived of an inheritance by an attorney's improper preparation of a will — one of the most common situations of alleged professional negligence resulting in harm to a "third person." See Barcelo v. Elliott, 923 S.W.2d 575 (Tex. 1996) (will with invalid trust); Noble v. Bruce, 349 Md. 730, 709 A.2d 1264 (1998) (avoidable taxes reducing inheritance); Robinson v. Benton, 842 So. 2d 631 (Ala. 2002) (failure to destroy will as testator requested). However, an intended beneficiary is allowed a cause of action in most of the more recent decisions. See Biakanja

v. Irving, supra (notary public liable when will invalid because notary failed to direct proper attestation); Heyer v. Flaig, 70 Cal. 2d 223, 47 Cal. Rptr. 225, 449 P.2d 161 (1969) (attorney knew testatrix intended to leave estate to daughters; will lacked adequate provision for subsequent marriage by testatrix and attorney failed to advise testatrix to change her will after marriage); Hale v. Groce, 304 Or. 281, 744 P.2d 1289 (1987) (attorney did not include in will or related trust bequest client allegedly intended for plaintiff); Leak-Gilbert v. Fahle, 55 P.3d 1054 (Okla. 2002) (bequest invalid because not made clear that omission of other family members was intentional); White v. Jones, [1995] 2 A.C. 207 (H.L.) (failure to prepare will before client died); Annot., Liability of One Drawing an Invalid Will, 65 A.L.R.2d 1363 (1959). Cf. Pizel v. Zuspann, 247 Kan. 54, 795 P.2d 42 (1990), modified, 247 Kan. 699, 803 P.2d 205 (1990) (inter vivos trust invalid). Is this desirable? The courts in Krawczyk v. Stingle, 208 Conn. 239, 543 A.2d 733 (1988), and Rydde v. Morris, 381 S.C. 643, 675 S.E.2d 431 (2009), concluded that allowing intended beneficiaries to sue for an attorney's alleged negligence in failure to arrange execution of the documents before the decedent's death would create conflicts of interest. Were they correct?

3. The will or trust instrument's failure to clearly designate plaintiff as the intended beneficiary may result in a decision that the attorney owed plaintiff no duty of care. See Ventura County Humane Society for the Prevention of Cruelty to Children and Animals, Inc. v. Holloway, 40 Cal. App. 3d 897, 115 Cal. Rptr. 464 (1974) (will with residuary clause ambiguously designating one of intended beneficiaries; potential beneficiaries sued for cost of ensuing litigation, delay and compromise of claims). Espinosa v. Sparber, Shevin, Shapo, Rosen and Heilbronner, 612 So. 2d 1378 (Fla. 1993), holds that an intent to leave plaintiff a testamentary disposition must be expressed in the will; extrinsic evidence offered to show an intent to provide for plaintiff would not be admitted. Accord, Beauchamp v. Kemmeter, 240 Wis. 2d. 733, 625 N.W.2d 297 (Ct. App. 2000), review denied, 242 Wis. 2d 546, 629 N.W.2d 785 (2001). Contra, Simpson v. Calivas, 139 N.H. 1, 650 A.2d 318 (1994). Should a court entertain an action by a beneficiary who claims that an attorney's negligence led to a will contest, in which plaintiff prevailed, and that the costs of defending the contest depleted the estate? This type of claim was accepted in Rathblott v. Levin, 697 F. Supp. 817 (D.N.J. 1988). Of course, for liability to exist, defendant must have failed to exercise reasonable professional skill and care. See Lucas v. Hamm, 56 Cal. 2d 583, 15 Cal. Rptr. 821, 364 P.2d 685 (1961) (attorney not negligent in failing to understand rule against perpetuities).

4. In Burger v. Pond, 224 Cal. App. 3d 597, 273 Cal. Rptr. 709 (1990), an attorney had represented the husband in a divorce case. He allegedly was aware that the husband intended to marry a certain person and begin a family with her as soon as the first marriage was dissolved. A divorce was granted, the second marriage took place, and a child was born to the couple. The divorce was then set aside, allegedly because of the attorney's negligence in handling it. The attorney was sued by both the husband and the second wife, who sought damages for emotional distress and humiliation attributable to her marriage being declared invalid and her child illegitimate. The court held she was owed no duty by the attorney and could not maintain an action against him. What if a child is unable to claim support from an attorney's former client because the attorney negligently failed to perfect adoption of the child by the client? See Metzker v. Slocum, 272 Or. 313, 537 P.2d 74 (1975) (attorney not liable to child). In view of these decisions, is there any basis to a claim by the spouse of a client represented in a personal injury matter that the attorney owed a duty to advise the spouse of the spouse's right to claim damages for loss of consortium? Such an action was allowed in Jordan v. Lipsig, Sullivan, Mollen & Liapakis, P.C., 689 F. Supp. 192 (S.D.N.Y. 1988), and Meighan v. Shore, 34 Cal. App. 4th 1025, 40 Cal. Rptr. 2d 744 (1995).

5. The opinion in Metzker v. Slocum, supra, states that cases permitting recovery by a person not in privity with the attorney involved (a) an action by an intended beneficiary of a will who lost an inheritance; (b) an action by a purchaser of real estate who relied upon the seller's attorney's negligent approval of a faulty title, where the seller was obligated to furnish an approved title; or (c) an action by a creditor who had placed an account with a collection agency and suffered loss when the agency's attorney negligently failed to pursue court proceedings. Category (b) involves negligent misrepresentation, as such title opinions are provided for the purchaser's use. See Restatement (Second) of Torts § 552 (1977). Other claims by participants in a transaction in which the attorney represented someone else usually have failed. See St. Paul Title Co. v. Meier, 181 Cal. App. 3d 948, 226 Cal. Rptr. 538 (1986) (escrow agent in real estate sale sued purchaser's attorney, claiming escrow instructions confusing); Flaherty v. Weinberg, 303 Md. 116, 492 A.2d 618 (1985) (home purchasers sued mortgage lender's attorney for loss caused by error in description of property boundaries; different if attorneys' hiring intended to benefit purchasers as well as lenders).

6. *Harm caused by legal process.* Does the defendant in a groundless suit have a negligence action against the attorney who filed the action? See Berlin v. Nathan, p. 710, infra; Norton v. Hines, 49 Cal. App. 3d 917, 123 Cal. Rptr. 237 (1975) (might be action for malicious prosecution, but not for negligence; adverse party is not intended beneficiary of attorney's client and there is public policy of encouraging free access to courts); Friedman v. Dozorc, 412 Mich. 1, 312 N.W.2d 585 (1981) (physician had no negligence action against attorneys who filed medical malpractice action; duty to adversary would create "unacceptable conflict of interest"); Elguzouli-Daf v. Commissioner of Police of the Metropolis, [1995] Q.B. 335 (C.A.) (prosecutors owed no duty to person jailed on pending criminal charge that could not be proved); Annot., Medical Malpractice Countersuits, 84 A.L.R.3d 555 (1978). What if an attorney causes garnishment of plaintiff's funds, in order to enforce a client's judgment, when he should have known that the garnishment was invalid? See Allied Financial Services, Inc. v. Easley, 676 F.2d 422 (10th Cir. 1982) (no action). Should there be liability for negligent procurement of a warrant to search plaintiff's home? Simpson v. Attorney-General, [1994] 3 N.Z.L.R. 667 (C.A.), holds that there is no action for this.

7. *Identity theft.* Another situation in which professional or business negligence causes loss to a non-client is "identity theft." If an imposter establishes an account in plaintiff's name with a merchant, credit card issuer or financial services business, can the business be sued for a lack of due care in allowing the account to be opened? If a thief is able to make charges to or withdrawals from plaintiff's account, or open an account in plaintiff's name, by gaining access to non-public information held by a commercial enterprise, such as plaintiff's account number or password or Social Security number, can the company be sued for negligently releasing or failing to secure the information? In Patrick v. Union State Bank, 681 So. 2d 1364 (Ala. 1996), the court held that a bank was under a duty of care to the person in whose name and with whose identification the account was opened. (Plaintiff was arrested and jailed because of the worthless checks written by the imposter.) See also Wolfe v. MBNA America Bank, 485 F. Supp. 2d 874 (W.D. Tenn. 2007) (bank issued credit card in plaintiff's name on application sent by someone else). However, Polzer v. TRW, Inc., 256 A.D.2d 248, 682 N.Y.S.2d 194 (1998), and Huggins v. Citibank, N.A., 355 S.C. 329, 585 S.E.2d 275 (2003), rejected negligence actions against banks issuing credit cards in plaintiffs' names to imposters. Should courts allow such actions, or should they leave any redress for identity theft to legislative action?

8. *Spoliation of evidence.* Defendant comes into possession of evidence vital to the success of an action that plaintiff will bring to recover damages for personal injuries, such as medical records or the allegedly defective part of a product. Through defendant's negligence,

the evidence is destroyed or lost. Does plaintiff have an action for this? The trend of recent cases is to reject actions for "negligent spoliation of evidence." See Lips v. Scottsdale Healthcare Corp., 224 Ariz. 266, 229 P.3d 1008 (2010); Fletcher v. Dorchester Mutual Insurance Co., 437 Mass. 544, 773 N.E.2d 420 (2002); Ortega v. City of New York, 9 N.Y.3d 69, 845 N.Y.S.2d 773, 876 N.E.2d 1189 (2007). This parallels and is influenced by the recent trend to reject actions for intentional spoliation, which is discussed at pp. 204–208, supra. There are, however, cases accepting actions for negligent spoliation. Holmes v. Amerex Rent-A-Car, 710 A.2d 846 (D.C. 1998); Oliver v. Stimson Lumber Co., 297 Mont. 336, 993 P.2d 11 (1999). And there are some other cases holding that a party may come under a duty to preserve evidence and be held liable for negligent loss or destruction of the evidence, especially if defendant has voluntarily undertaken such a duty. Smith v. Atkinson, 771 So. 2d 429 (Ala. 2000); Boyd v. Travelers Insurance Co., 166 Ill. 2d 188, 652 N.E.2d 267 (1995); Gilleski v. Community Medical Center, 336 N.J. Super. 646, 765 A.2d 1103 (App. Div. 2001). If an action lies against third parties for negligent spoliation of evidence, should an action also be available for spoliation by the party the evidence was to be used against? See Martino v. Wal-Mart Stores, Inc., 908 So. 2d 342 (Fla. 2005); Hannah v. Heeter, 213 W. Va. 704, 584 S.E.2d 560 (2003). How would plaintiff prove causation of loss? See generally Annot., Negligent Spoliation of Evidence, Interfering with Prospective Civil Action, As Actionable, 101 A.L.R.5th 61 (2002).

Stinson v. Physicians Immediate Care, Limited

Appellate Court of Illinois
269 Ill. App. 3d 659, 646 N.E.2d 930 (1995)

Justice GEIGER delivered the opinion of the court:

[Plaintiff's employer required him to have a drug-screening test performed at defendant's facility. Defendant reported to the employer that plaintiff's urine specimen tested positive for cocaine. Plaintiff's action alleged that the test result or report of the result was false, that this was due to negligence on the part of defendant's employees, and that he was dismissed from his employment as a consequence. In a second count, plaintiff brought a class action on behalf of all persons similarly situated. The trial court dismissed the complaint.]

We now turn to the core issue of this appeal: whether, as a matter of law, the defendant owed a duty to the plaintiff.... Whether a duty exists is a question of law which depends on whether the parties stood in such a relationship to one another that the law imposes an obligation on the defendant to act reasonably for the protection of the plaintiff. "In considering whether a duty exists in a particular case, a court must weigh the foreseeability of the injury, the likelihood of the injury, the magnitude of the burden of guarding against it and the consequences of placing that burden on the defendant." [*Gouge v. Central Illinois Public Service Co.* (1991), 144 Ill. 2d 535, 542, 582 N.E.2d 108.]

... In arguing that count I sets forth only a duty to the plaintiff's employer, the defendant confuses concepts of contract and tort law. There need not be a contract between the plaintiff and the defendant for the defendant to owe a tort duty. For example, in *McLane v. Russell* (1989), 131 Ill. 2d 509, 546 N.E.2d 499, the supreme court ruled that, in an attorney malpractice case, an attorney may owe a duty to a third party if the nonclient can show that he was the intended beneficiary of the attorney-client relationship.

In a case very similar to the present one, *Lewis v. Aluminum Co. of America* (La. Ct. App. 1991), 588 So. 2d 167, cited by neither party, an employee sued a drug-testing laboratory for falsely reporting to his employer that he had failed the drug test. The court found that the drug-testing laboratory owed a duty to the plaintiff, pointing out that the plaintiff was known to the defendant, and, when the defendant analyzed the plaintiff's specimen, it knew that negligent testing could wrongfully identify the plaintiff as a drug user. The defendant also was aware that, if the test results it submitted to the plaintiff's employer were inaccurate, the plaintiff's reputation and employment opportunities would be harmed....

Here, the injury, that the plaintiff would be terminated from his employment, is not only foreseeable, but also is a virtual certainty in the event of a positive drug test result. In addition, the likelihood of injury is great; the plaintiff allegedly lost his job and was hindered in his efforts to find other employment because of the false positive drug test report. The first two factors favor imposing a duty. We now consider the two remaining factors, the magnitude of guarding against the injury and the consequences of placing that burden upon the defendant.

"'[D]uty' is not sacrosanct in itself, but is only an expression of the sum total of those considerations of policy which lead the law to say that the plaintiff is entitled to protection." W. Keeton, Prosser & Keeton on Torts § 53, at 358 (5th ed. 1984). The risk of harm in our society to an individual because of a false-positive drug test is so significant that failure to find protection under our law would be a step backwards for the protection of the individual. "As information services become more prevalent in our economy and society, the information providers [, such as drug-tested laboratories,] should be held accountable for the information they provide. Such information should be complete and not misleading. Credit-reporting agencies have long been held to the exercise of due care in securing and distributing information concerning the financial standing of individuals, firms, and corporations." (*Doe v. SmithKline Beecham Corp.* (Tex. App. 1993), 855 S.W.2d 248, 255–56.) We agree ... that public policy requires the imposition of a duty here. The drug-testing laboratory is in the best position to guard against the injury, as it is solely responsible for the performance of the testing and the quality control procedures. In addition, the laboratory, which is paid to perform the tests, is better able to bear the burden financially than the individual wrongly maligned by a false positive report. We therefore hold that a drug-testing laboratory owes a duty of reasonable care to persons whose specimens it tests for employers or prospective employers....

[The court reversed the trial court's dismissal of the individual and class actions and remanded the case.]

Notes

1. Is there liability if a negligent misstatement causes economic loss to someone other than a person to whom the statement was directed? The principal case is one of several in which defendant conducted drug tests on an employee and reported a positive result to the employer. In some of the cases, the court held that the employee was owed a duty of care and could bring a negligence action. Sharpe v. St. Luke's Hospital, 573 Pa. 90, 821 A.2d 1215 (2003); Duncan v. Afton, Inc., 991 P.2d 739 (Wyo. 1999). Compare SmithKline Beecham Corp. v. Doe, 903 S.W.2d 347 (Tex. 1995), holding that a laboratory owed no duty to a person being drug-tested as a condition of initial employment to warn her that eating poppy seeds before the test could cause the test to falsely indicate the use of opiates. (This reversed the Texas Court of Appeals decision cited in the *Stinson* opinion.) The court in Willis v. Roche Biomedical Laboratories, Inc., 61 F.3d 313 (5th Cir. 1995), extrapolated from the *Doe* case that a laboratory owed an employee no duty to use reasonable care in performing drug testing required by the employer.

2. There are also cases in which plaintiff was discharged from employment because defendant reported that plaintiff failed a polygraph test. Lawson v. Howmet Aluminum Corp., 449 N.E.2d 1172 (Ind. App. 1983), held that the polygraph examiner, although hired by the employer, owed a duty of care to the employee. Hall v. United Parcel Service of America, Inc., 76 N.Y.2d 27, 556 N.Y.S.2d 21, 555 N.E.2d 273 (1990), amendment denied, 76 N.Y.2d 846, 560 N.Y.S.2d 131, 559 N.E.2d 1290 (1990), held that there was no negligence liability in this situation. Recognizing that the validity of lie detector tests was open to serious question and that substantial harm might result from their misuse, the court decided that this was a problem more appropriately resolved by legislation than by the creation of a new tort cause of action. It noted the enactment of the Employee Polygraph Protection Act, 29 U.S.C. §§ 2001 et seq., as well as limited state legislation. Does consistency require courts to make the same decision on duty and negligence liability for both drug tests and polygraph tests? The court in Calbillo v. Cavender Oldsmobile, Inc., 288 F.3d 721 (5th Cir. 2002), thought there was little difference between the two types of cases. Having held previously that a laboratory owed no duty in performing drug testing, the court held that a polygraph examiner hired by an employer to conduct polygraph examinations of employees owed no duty to the employees. In Santiago v. Greyhound Lines, Inc., 956 F. Supp. 144 (N.D.N.Y. 1997), however, the court reasoned that regulation of polygraph testing by state and federal statutes, which included private remedies, had weighed against a common law cause of action for negligence in conducting polygraph examinations and a different conclusion should apply to drug testing, for which no similar statutory regulation and remedies existed. See generally Annot., Employee's Action in Tort Against Party Administering Polygraph, Drug, or Similar Test at Request of Actual or Prospective Employer, 89 A.L.R.4th 527 (1991).

3. Would there be a cause of action if a physical examination was a condition of employment and the physician negligently reported that plaintiff was medically unfit for the position? See Armstrong v. Morgan, 545 S.W.2d 45 (Tex. Civ. App. 1976) (doctor owed plaintiff "a duty not to injure him physically or otherwise"); Felton v. Schaeffer, 229 Cal. App. 3d 229, 279 Cal. Rptr. 713 (1991) (no duty in examination where plaintiff did not seek medical treatment or advice). Cf. Rand v. Miller, 185 W. Va. 705, 408 S.E.2d 655 (1991) (physician evaluating employment applicant's medical records owed no duty). Should an action lie if defendant conducts knowledge or aptitude tests for job applicants and plaintiff claims he received a low score, causing loss of prospective employment, because of defendant's negligence?

4. In a number of cases, plaintiffs have sued on claims they lost insurance or workers' compensation payments they deserved because a physician or claims investigator made an erroneous report to the insurer or workers' compensation agency. The courts appear to be unanimous in holding that a physician is not liable to a negligence action on such claims. See Hafner v. Beck, 185 Ariz. 389, 916 P.2d 1105 (Ct. App. 1995); Martinez v. Lewis, 969 P.2d 213 (Colo. 1998). However, they are split on the potential liability of claims investigators and insurance adjusters. See Morvay v. Hanover Insurance Companies, 127 N.H. 723, 506 A.2d 333 (1986); Brown v. State Farm Fire and Casualty Co., 58 P.3d 217 (Okla. Civ. App. 2002) (investigator owed duty to insured); Sanchez v. Lindsey Morden Claims Services, Inc., 72 Cal. App. 4th 249, 84 Cal. Rptr. 2d 799 (1999); Hamill v. Pawtucket Mutual Insurance Co., 179 Vt. 250, 892 A.2d 226 (2005) (no duty).

5. In Spring v. Guardian Assurance Plc., [1993] I.C.R. 412, [1993] 2 All E.R. 273 (C.A.), rev'd, [1995] 2 A.C. 296 (H.L.), plaintiff had lost his position in a firm which sold insurance. Insurance companies considering appointment of plaintiff as a representative requested a reference from his former employer. The former employer gave such a neg-

ative reference that plaintiff was refused appointment. He sued his former employer for negligence and injurious falsehood. Finding that the persons responsible for the reference stated inaccurate allegations without taking reasonable care in ascertaining their truth, the trial court upheld plaintiff's negligence action. The injurious falsehood action failed because the persons responsible for the reference had not acted with malice. Because a qualified privilege attached to the giving of references, plaintiff's failure to show malice would also defeat a defamation claim. The Court of Appeal, reasoning that liability for giving a damaging reference was governed by the rules of defamation and injurious falsehood and that to recognize a duty of care would bypass the limits of liability established by those rules, held that a negligence action was not maintainable. The House of Lords held that because of the employer-employee relationship, the dependence of employees on references furnished by former and present employers, and the clear foreseeability of economic loss if an inaccurate reference is given because of a want of care, the subject of an employment reference is owed a duty of care. A majority found no conflict between this conclusion and the law of defamation and injurious falsehood, especially because these torts did not involve a concept of a duty of care, on which negligence liability was founded. Extension of a remedy for damage caused by negligence in giving employment references was thought beneficial. Plaintiff's negligence action was thus sustained.

6. The proposition that a negligence action can be maintained in circumstances where the law of defamation or injurious falsehood would apply has received a mixed reception in other jurisdictions. See the cases discussed in Dinyer-Fraser v. Laurentian Bank, (2005) 40 B.C.L.R.4th 39 (Sup. Ct.). American cases tend to reject negligence actions for harm to reputation and its consequences. See Note, Negligent Injury to Reputation: Defamation Priority and the Economic Loss Rule, 48 Ariz. L. Rev. 1103 (2006).

7. Additional negligence actions for harm allegedly caused by a false statement include an action against a bank for stating to another bank that plaintiff failed to repay a loan when due, causing plaintiff to be denied credit. Graney Development Corp. v. Taksen, 66 A.D.2d 1008, 411 N.Y.S.2d 756 (1978), aff'g 92 Misc. 2d 764, 400 N.Y.S.2d 717 (Sup. Ct. 1978) (no negligence action; bank protected by qualified privilege). An action by a corporation's former business manager, dismissed as a result of statements in a report by an accountant retained to audit corporate records. Demetracopoulos v. Wilson, 138 N.H. 371, 640 A.2d 279 (1994) (accountant owed plaintiff no duty as report prepared for benefit and guidance of corporation's board, not plaintiff). Cf. Rodriguez v. ECRI Shared Services, 984 F. Supp. 1363 (D. Kan. 1997) (hospital stopped using plaintiff's radiology services after report from consultant). An action against a pharmacy for telling third parties that the prescription medicine plaintiff purchased was for treatment of venereal disease. Evans v. Rite Aid Corp., 324 S.C. 269, 478 S.E.2d 846 (1996) (no action for "negligent falsehood"). An action against the publisher of an encyclopedia of chemicals and drugs for misrepresenting the toxicity of a chemical utilized in plaintiff's product, causing a loss of sales. Demuth Development Corp. v. Merck & Co., Inc., 432 F. Supp. 990 (E.D.N.Y. 1977) (no cause of action). And an action by the South Carolina State Ports Authority against consultants commissioned by the Georgia Ports Authority to prepare a report comparing the ports of Savannah, Georgia and Charleston, South Carolina. The report was highly favorable to Savannah's port and Charleston allegedly lost traffic as a result. South Carolina State Ports Authority v. Booz-Allen & Hamilton, Inc., 289 S.C. 373, 346 S.E.2d 324 (1986) (when consultant undertakes to objectively analyze attributes of commercial competitors for purpose of giving one market advantage over other, duty of care owed to competitor who is criticized; no duty owed to pilots and longshoremen in Charleston).

Chapter 3

Marketplace Falsehoods

Section 1. Injurious Falsehood

Fen v. Dixe

Court of King's Bench
(1639) W. Jones 444, 82 Eng. Rep. 233,
March N.R. 59, 82 Eng. Rep. 411, 1 Rolle Abr. 58

[Action on the case for words. Thomas Fen declared that he was a brewer, and defendant, in a conversation with another person, said, "I will give my mare a peck of malt, and give her water after it, and she shall piss as good beer as Thomas Fen breweth," whereby plaintiff lost several customers to his damage. Porter moved in arrest of judgment for plaintiff that an action could not be maintained on these words. The Attorney General argued that an action could be maintained, because it is a scandal to plaintiff in his trade; no averment that he had lost any particular customer is necessary.]

Brampston, Jones & Barkeley, that the words without allegation of particular loss were not a good action, and the words in themselves could not be any scandal, and on this judgment was stayed.* And Barkeley said, that the words are only comparative, and altogether impossible also. And he said, that it had been adjudged, that where one says of a lawyer, that he had as much law as a monkey, that the words were not actionable; because he hath as much law, and more also. But if he had said, that he hath no more law than a monkey, those words were actionable....

Hatchard v. Mège

Queen's Bench Division
(1887) 18 Q.B.D. 771

[The original plaintiff's statement of claim made the following allegations: Plaintiff was a wine merchant and importer, a dealer in a brand of champagne introduced by him and known as "Delmonico" champagne, and the registered proprietor of a trade-mark in it. Defendants wrote and published "of and concerning the plaintiff and his said trade as a wine merchant and importer the following false and malicious libel ... 'Caution: Del-

---

* The account of the case to this point is a translation of the report in W. Jones. The remainder is from March N.R. [Ed.]

monico Champagne. Messrs. Delbeck & Co., finding that wine stated to be Delmonico Champagne is being advertised for sale in Great Britain, hereby give notice that such wine cannot be the wine it is represented to be, as no champagne shipped under that name can be genuine unless it has their names on their labels. Messrs. Delbeck & Co. further give notice that if such wine be shipped from France they will take proceedings to stop such shipments, and such other proceedings in England as they may be advised,' thereby meaning that the plaintiff had no right to use his said registered trade-mark or brand for champagne imported or sold by him, and that in using such trade-mark or brand he was acting fraudulently, and endeavouring to pass off an inferior champagne as being of the manufacture of Messrs. Delbeck & Co., and that the champagne imported and sold by the plaintiff was not genuine wine, and that no person other than the defendants had the right to use the word 'Delmonico' as a trade-mark or brand, or part of a trademark or brand, or champagne in the United Kingdom. [¶] In consequence of the publication of the libel aforesaid, the plaintiff has been greatly injured in his credit and reputation, and in his said trade and business of a wine merchant and importer and dealer in champagne." After the close of the pleadings the original plaintiff died, and an order was made by the master that the action should be carried on in the name of his executrix. A nonsuit was entered on the ground that the action came to an end on the death of the original plaintiff.]

DAY, J....

... [T]he statement of claim may be subdivided into two separate and distinct claims. The first is for ordinary defamation, either independently of the plaintiff's trade, affecting his character by charging him with being a dishonest man, or defamation of him in his trade by charging him with being a dishonest wine-merchant. That claim would not survive, for it is nothing more than a claim in respect of a libel on an individual. But this publication may be construed to mean that the plaintiff had no right to use his trade-mark. This is not properly a libel, but is rather in the nature of slander of title, which is well defined in Odgers on Libel and Slander: "... [T]here is a branch of the law (generally known by the inappropriate but convenient name—slander of title) which permits an action to be brought against any one who maliciously decries the plaintiff's goods or some other thing belonging to him, and thereby produces special damage to the plaintiff. This is obviously no part of the law of defamation, for the plaintiff's reputation remains uninjured; it is really an action on the case for maliciously acting in such a way as to inflict loss upon the plaintiff...."

It appears, therefore, that the first and last parts of the innuendo in the present case suggest slander of title. As appears from the passage I have read, an action for slander of title is not an action for libel, but is rather in the nature of an action on the case for maliciously injuring a person in respect of his estate by asserting that he has no title to it. The action differs from an action for libel in this, that malice is not implied from the fact of publication, but must be proved, and that the falsehood of the statement complained of, and the existence of special damage, must also be proved in order to entitle the plaintiff to recover. The question whether the publication is false and malicious is for the jury. Here, I think, special damage is alleged by the statement of claim, and if the plaintiff could have shewn injury to the sale of the wine which he sold under his trade-mark, he would have been entitled to recover, and that is a cause of action which survives.

For these reasons I am of opinion that the nonsuit was right so far as it related to the claim in respect of a personal libel, but was wrong as to the claim in respect of so much of the publication as impugned the plaintiff's right to sell under his trade-mark or brand....

[Wills, J., delivered a concurring opinion.]

Notes

1. The common law developed an action—known as "slander of title"—to protect persons against aspersions upon their title to land, which hindered them in selling or leasing the land. The action was extended to cases involving chattels, where it was called "slander of goods." In the nineteenth century, liability extended to disparagement of the quality of property, and English courts declared that an action could exist whenever damaging untruths were spoken or published about a business. See Riding v. Smith, (1876) 1 Ex. D. 91. The tort is now comprehensively styled "injurious falsehood" (in England "malicious falsehood"). See Carty, An Analysis of the Economic Torts 200–203 (2d ed. 2010); Prosser & Keeton, Law of Torts 962–964 (5th ed. 1984). Is Fen v. Dixe an early injurious falsehood case or just an unsuccessful action for personal slander?

2. There remains considerable lack of uniformity in terminology. In the law of defamation "slander" connotes oral communication and "libel" a writing, but this distinction is not observed for injurious falsehood. False communications regarding the quality of goods or services are often called "disparagement," "product disparagement," "trade libel" or "slander of goods." Some authorities use "injurious falsehood" to mean only product disparagement, differentiating "slander of title." See System Operations, Inc. v. Scientific Games Development Corp., 555 F.2d 1131, 1138 n.6 (3d Cir. 1977). Why might such an action survive death when a defamation claim does not?

3. Slander of title extends beyond aspersions upon plaintiff's title or interest and adverse claims to assertions or recording of liens, mortgages, contracts and other encumbrances. Would it be slander of title to dispute plaintiff's claim to be heir of an estate? See Annot., Recording of Instrument Purporting to Affect Title as Slander of Title, 39 A.L.R.2d 840 (1955); Restatement (Second) of Torts § 629, comments *c, d* (1977). Compare Hatchard v. Mège to a case in which defendant gave notice that plaintiff unlawfully appropriated defendant's business name, or that plaintiff was selling items that infringed defendant's patent or copyright. Would it be accurate to label plaintiff's action as "slander of title"? Would the result be the same as in Hatchard v. Mège? See Andrew v. Deshler, 43 N.J.L. 16 (Sup. Ct. 1881) (patent); Dicks v. Brooks, (1880) 15 Ch. D. 22 (C.A.) (copyright).

4. Plaintiff deals exclusively in kosher meat. Defendant falsely publishes a statement that plaintiff sells defendant's brand of bacon. Actionable? See Braun v. Armour & Co., 254 N.Y. 514, 173 N.E. 845 (1930). What if defendant falsely states that plaintiff, a successful radio personality, is unable to draw an adequate listening audience and incapable of earning good ratings for his program? See Menefee v. Columbia Broadcasting System, Inc., 458 Pa. 46, 329 A.2d 216 (1974) (actionable as "untruthful disparagement"). An artist claims to have painted the first portrait of Vice President Harry S Truman (who subsequently had become president) and to have benefitted from his right to reproduce the portrait. Defendant publishes a different portrait and claims it is the first portrait of Truman. "Injurious falsehood"? See Pendleton v. Time, Inc., 339 Ill. App. 188, 89 N.E.2d 435 (1949) (cause of action stated).

5. To be actionable, the false statement must have been communicated to someone other than plaintiff. Arnold v. Producers' Oil Co., 196 S.W. 735 (Tex. Civ. App. 1917); Barquin v. Hall Oil Co., 28 Wyo. 164, 201 P. 352 (1921), reh'g denied, 28 Wyo. 164, 202 P. 1107 (1922). The principles of defamation law's "publication" requirement are applied. See Belcher v. Little, 315 N.W.2d 734 (Iowa 1982); Restatement (Second) of Torts § 630 (1977). Also, the falsehood must have caused the harm of which plaintiff complains. Is the necessary causal link shown if, for instance, plaintiff purchased goods and defendant

falsely asserted a lien on the goods, inducing the seller not to deliver them to plaintiff? See Green v. Button, (1835) 2 C.M. & R. 707, 150 Eng. Rep. 299, 1 Gale 349, 5 L.J. Ex. 81, Tyr. & Gr. 118 (Ex.) (judgment for plaintiff). In Western Technologies, Inc. v. Sverdrup & Parcel, Inc., 154 Ariz. 1, 739 P.2d 1318 (Ct. App. 1986), plaintiff stated a case in alleging that defendants' false assignment of blame to plaintiff in a report on the cause of cracks in a stadium led the stadium's owner to bring suit against plaintiff. Compare Ajello v. Worsley, [1898] 1 Ch. 274, in which defendant advertised at low prices pianos manufactured by plaintiffs. In fact, plaintiffs had refused to supply defendant because of his failure to charge retail trade prices. It was held that the cause of any damage to plaintiffs was the offer for sale at wholesale prices, not the false statement that defendant had plaintiffs' pianos in stock. Plaintiffs' action was dismissed.

Young v. Macrae

Court of Queen's Bench
(1862) 3 B. & S. 264, 122 Eng. Rep. 100,
9 Jur. N.S. 538, 27 J.P. 132, 32 L.J.Q.B. 6,
7 L.T. 354, 1 New Rep. 52, 11 W.R. 63

[Plaintiffs were manufacturers and sellers of Young's paraffin oil. Defendant sold American oil produced by the Portland Kerosine Company. Plaintiffs declared that defendant, with intent to injure plaintiffs, falsely and maliciously libelled them by distributing circulars which contained a report comparing the two oils: "Professor Muspratt's Report— I certify that I have carefully tested the [American] oil, and that I find it a colourless and somewhat aromatic liquid, while Young's Scotch has a reddish brown tinge, is much thicker, and has a more disagreeable odour than it. I further certify, that in burning the two oils comparatively in the ordinary ls. lamp, I found the power of the light produced by the American equals 4¼ wax candles. The sample of Young's burned under the same conditions in the same lamp, yields, while the lamp remains well filled, a light of nearly the same power as the American; but a feebler one after the oil has burned down to one-half. The difference at this stage I found to amount to nearly the light of one such candle, or say twenty-five per cent. in favour of the Portland Kerosine Company's oil. (Signed) Sheridan Muspratt, M.D., F.R.S., M.R.I.A., &c., &c., Professor of Chemistry." It was alleged that, as a result of this publication, plaintiffs' business was injured, sales of Young's oil had declined, and certain persons who had been buying Young's oil were induced to buy the American oil instead. Defendant demurred.]

COCKBURN, C.J. I think that our judgment must be in favour of the defendant upon this demurrer. I am very far from saying that if a trader maliciously, and falsely to his own knowledge, publishes matter disparaging an article manufactured or sold by another, even if he makes no reflection upon the character, trade or profession of that other, and if special damage followed, that there would not be an actionable libel, for a most grievous wrong might be done in that way, and the person injured ought to have a remedy by an action. But it is not necessary to determine that in the present case, for this declaration does not allege facts which are necessary to support such an action. The defendant is alleged to have falsely and maliciously published a disparaging comparison between the oil manufactured by the plaintiffs and that which he was advertising; but that allegation may mean merely that the part of the circular which relates to the American oil was false, and that it was not so good as represented; it is not averred that the defendant falsely represented that the oil of the plaintiffs had a reddish brown tinge, was much thicker,

and that it had a more disagreeable odour. If that had been falsely represented, and special damage had ensued, an action might have been maintained; but the averment in this
declaration may mean only that the representation of the defendant as to the oil manufactured by himself being colourless was untrue. Upon the whole, it seems to me that the
action is not maintainable.

WIGHTMAN, J. I am of the same opinion, though not without some doubt. I think
that the circular amounts only to a comparison between the oil of the plaintiffs and that
of some one else, and not to a representation that the oil of the plaintiffs was bad. It may
be true that it is inferior to that which is manufactured by the defendant, and yet it may
be very good. It is said that where, as in this case, special damage ensues, an action will
lie; but here as it seems to me, it is only alleged that in consequence of the comparison
between the different oils certain persons have dealt with the defendant instead of with
the plaintiffs. I do not think that the action is maintainable.

[Blackburn, J., delivered a concurring opinion.]

[Counsel for plaintiffs requested leave to amend.] COCKBURN, C.J. You can bring
another action, and perhaps get another professor to make a report in favour of your oil.

White v. Mellin
House of Lords
[1895] A.C. 154

[The proprietor of Mellin's infants' food sought an injunction and damages from a
retailer who was proprietor of a competing food, Vance's. Defendant was selling plaintiff's product with a label attached to the wrapper: "Notice. The public are recommended to try Dr. Vance's prepared food for infants and invalids, it being far more
nutritious and healthful than any other preparation yet offered." The price and defendant's name were included. Romer, J., dismissed the action, but the Court of Appeal
ordered a new trial.]

LORD HERSCHELL L.C....

... I am not satisfied that it has been shewn that by means of this advertisement the
defendant falsely disparaged the plaintiff's goods. But, my Lords, assuming that he did
so, the Court of Appeal regarded it as requisite for the maintenance of the action that
something further should be proved, and that is that the disparaging statement has caused
injury to or is calculated to injure the plaintiff.... [T]he advertisement is of a very common description, puffing, it may be, extremely and in an exaggerated fashion, these particular goods, Vance's food. That advertisement was outside the wrapper; inside was found
an advertisement of Mellin's food, in which Mellin's food was stated to be recommended
by the faculty as best for infants and invalids. Why is it to be supposed that any one buying this bottle at the chemist's would be led to believe that Mellin's food which he had bought
was not a good article or not as good an article as another, merely because a person who
obviously was seeking to push a rival article said that his article was better? My Lords,
why should people give such a special weight to this anonymous puff of Vance's food,
obviously the work of some one who wanted to sell it, as that it should lead him to determine to buy it instead of Mellin's food ...? I confess I do not wonder that the plaintiff
did not insist that he had sustained injury by what the defendant had done. There is an
entire absence of any evidence that the statement complained of either had injured or
was calculated to injure the plaintiff....

[Counsel for plaintiff] ... said that if this were an action for damages that might be a well-founded objection to it, but that it is not an action for damages but a claim for an injunction, and that although it may be that to support an action for damages it would be necessary to allege and prove special damage, that is not necessary where an injunction is claimed—that it is enough if a false statement is made and is likely to be repeated....

My Lords, obviously to call for the exercise of that power it would be necessary to shew that there was an actionable wrong well laid, and if the statement only shewed a part of that which was necessary to make up a cause of action—that is to say, if special damage was necessary to the maintenance of the action, and that special damage was not shewn—a tort in the eye of the law would not be disclosed ... and no injunction would be granted. I think, therefore, for these reasons, that the plaintiff would not be entitled to an injunction, any more than he would be entitled to maintain an action unless he established all that was necessary to make out that a tort had been committed....

But, my Lords, I cannot help saying that I entertain very grave doubts whether any action could be maintained for an alleged disparagement of another's goods, merely on the allegation that the goods sold by the party who is alleged to have disparaged his competitor's goods are better either generally or in this or that particular respect than his competitors' are. Of course, I put aside the question (it is not necessary to consider it) whether where a person intending to injure another, and not in the exercise of his own trade and vaunting his own goods, has maliciously and falsely disparaged the goods of another, an action will lie; I am dealing with the class of cases which is now before us, where the only disparagement consists in vaunting the superiority of the defendant's own goods. In *Evans v. Harlow* [5 Q.B. 624] Lord Denman expressed himself thus: "The gist of the complaint is the defendant's telling the world that the lubricators sold by the plaintiff were not good for their purpose, but wasted the tallow. A tradesman offering goods for sale exposes himself to observations of this kind, and it is not by averring them to be 'false, scandalous, malicious and defamatory' that the plaintiff can found a charge of libel upon them. To decide so would open a very wide door to litigation, and might expose every man who said his goods were better than another's to the risk of an action." My Lords, those observations seem to me to be replete with good sense....

[Counsel] sought to distinguish the present case by saying that all that Lord Denman referred to was one tradesman saying that his goods were better than his rival's. That, he said, is a matter of opinion, but whether they are more healthful and more nutritious is a question of fact. My Lords, I do not think it is possible to draw such a distinction. The allegation of a tradesman that his goods are better than his neighbour's very often involves only the consideration whether they possess one or two qualities superior to the other. Of course "better" means better as regards the purpose for which they are intended, and the question of better or worse in many cases depends simply upon one or two or three issues of fact. If an action will not lie because a man says that his goods are better than his neighbour's, it seems to me impossible to say that it will lie because he says that they are better in this or that or the other respect. Just consider what a door would be opened if this were permitted. That this sort of puffing advertisement is in use is notorious; and we see rival cures advertised for particular ailments. The Court would then be bound to inquire, in an action brought, whether this ointment or this pill better cured the disease which it was alleged to cure—whether a particular article of food was in this respect or that better than another. Indeed, the Courts of law would be turned into a machinery for advertising rival productions by obtaining a judicial determination which of the two was the better....

... [T]he judgment of Romer J. was right and ought to be restored....

LORD SHAND:

... I should be quite content with the ground of judgment which Romer J. expressed in dismissing the case after the evidence of the plaintiff had been led. The learned judge then said: "No doubt, on the evidence on the plaintiff's side, so far as that goes, it does tend to shew that his food is the best, at any rate for infants under six month old"; and he goes on to say: "But, as I have said, no person on seeing what the defendant has done would have read this statement put upon the plaintiff's cases as being anything more than a rival puff. Of course it is always very annoying to a man who has a good article to find a person who is puffing a rival article stating that the rival article is really the best, and it is still more annoying to find that statement put upon the goods of the man who complains. But, however annoying the form of the advertisement of the defendant may be to the plaintiff, I come to the conclusion that what has been done by the defendant has not amounted in any true sense to a trade libel as against the plaintiff, and that the plaintiff has no legal remedy in respect of it." It appears to me that in order to constitute a libel of the class here complained of there must be a statement in disparagement of the plaintiff's goods, and that the statement must be false and injurious. But, then, I do not think that disparagement in a popular sense would be enough for the plaintiff's case. It is a disparagement of one man's goods to say that they are inferior to the goods of another; but such a statement cannot, I think, be the ground of a claim of damages or a claim for injunction such as the plaintiff here asked. If there had been in this case an imputation of intentional misrepresentation for the purpose of misleading purchasers, or a statement that Mellin's food was positively injurious, or that it contained deleterious ingredients, and would be hurtful if it were used, I think there would have been a good ground of action; and if the authorities have not settled the law otherwise, I should even say that an averment of special damage ought not to be necessary. But when all that is done is making a comparison between the plaintiff's goods and the goods of the person issuing the advertisement, and the statement made is that the plaintiff's goods are inferior in quality or inferior, it may be, in some special qualities, I think this cannot be regarded as a disparagement of which the law will take cognizance....

[Lords Watson, Macnaghten and Morris delivered concurring speeches. Appeal allowed.]

De Beers Abrasive Products Ltd. v.
International General Electric Company of New York Ltd.

Chancery Division
[1975] 1 W.L.R. 972

WALTON J. [The first plaintiff was the manufacturer of Debdust, a natural diamond abrasive marketed principally for use in cutting concrete. The third plaintiff marketed Debdust in the United Kingdom, purchasing its supplies from the second plaintiff, which purchased the manufacturer's entire output. The defendants were the manufacturer and marketer of a competing abrasive, MBS-70, made from synthetic diamonds. As part of a sales drive, the manufacturer of MBS-70 circulated a pamphlet entitled "Tech-Data/1."]

... The crucial part of the [pamphlet] reads as follows: "MBS-70 Debdust performance comparison. In 1972, Debdust natural diamond was introduced to the market and since that time has been promoted as a premium quality abrasive for cutting cured concrete. Since its introduction, we have received many requests for information about Debdust and how it compares to man-made MBS-70 diamond in the more demanding sawing applications. This bulletin presents highlights of the application laboratory's comparative studies of these two diamond abrasives. In these studies, the performance of MBS-70 diamond was compared to that of Debdust cutting both cured concrete and granite workpieces. In the cured concrete evaluations, blades from four different manufacturers were used to compare the performance of 25/35 MBS-70 to that of 20/30 Debdust. In the tests on granite, 40/50 MBS-70 was compared to 40/50 Debdust under two sets of sawing conditions, in blades supplied by two separate manufacturers. Results of both the concrete and the granite sawing evaluations show that MBS-70 consistently outperformed Debdust in terms of blade life. This superior MBS-70 wear performance was observed in all cases regardless of differences in blade manufacturer, diamond size tested, work material, or sawing parameters. In the concrete tests, the blades containing 25/35 MBS-70 cut faster and more freely, and with one exception required less horsepower. Cutting Barre Granite, blades containing 40/50 Debdust required less horsepower than blades with 40/50 MBS-70, in all but one case. However in each instance where Debdust required less horsepower, the MBS-70 blades completely overshadowed the wear performance of Debdust by providing from 2.4 to 16.9 times the blade life. In these four cases, the breakdown of Debdust crystals was so rapid that less power was required in the system." That letterpress is followed by four block graphical representations of the blade performances.

Naturally incensed by this unfavourable comparison of Debdust with MBS-70, the plaintiffs issued a writ [seeking damages and an injunction against further publication of the statements in the pamphlet. Plaintiffs alleged that "Tech-Data/1" was false and misleading in representing that proper scientific tests were carried out on the abrasives and that its contents reflected a scientific and objective evaluation of the results of such tests, as well as in its statements about Debdust. Defendants moved to strike plaintiffs' statement of claim.]

[Mr. Walton, for the defendants] has urged upon me that the contents of Tech-Data/1 are, in substance, no more than a glorified statement that MBS-70 is superior to Debdust, and that every trader is entitled, as of right, to claim that his product is the best product of that kind in the world, far superior to any of his rivals' products, without thereby committing any wrong of any description in respect of which he is answerable to his rivals, even if, as a matter of sheer fact, his claims are complete nonsense....

Mr. Dillon, for the plaintiffs, on the other hand accepts that a mere puff by any trader of his own products is not actionable, but says that the matter becomes quite different if the trader descends to particularise precisely why his product is better than his rival's or his rival's is worse than his; and, he says fairly read, what Tech-Data/1 in the present case is doing is to say in substance not merely that MBS-70 is superior to Debdust, but that Debdust is not proper for its purpose.

What precisely is the law on this point? It is a blinding glimpse of the obvious to say that there must be a dividing line between statements that are actionable and those which are not; and the sole question upon a dry point of law such as we are discussing here is: where does that line lie? On the one hand, it appears to me that the law is that any trader is entitled to puff his own goods, even though such puff must, as a matter of pure logic, involve the denigration of his rival's goods. Thus in the well known case of the three adjoining tailors who put notices in their respective windows reading: "The best tailor in the world," "The best tailor in this town," and "The best tailor in this street," none of the three committed an actionable wrong.

This is, I think, a proposition which extends to a much wider field than the slander of goods; for example, I think it extends to other vague commendatory statements about goods or services on offer.... [I]n the kind of situation where one expects, as a matter of ordinary common experience, a person to use a certain amount of hyperbole in the description of goods, property or services, the courts will do what any ordinary reasonable man would do, namely, take it with a large pinch of salt.

Where, however, the situation is not that the trader is puffing his own goods, but turns to denigrate those of his rival, then, in my opinion, the situation is not so clear cut. Obviously the statement: "My goods are better than X's" is only a more dramatic presentation of what is implicit in the statement: "My goods are the best in the world." Accordingly, I do not think such a statement would be actionable. At the other end of the scale, if what is said is: "My goods are better than X's, because X's are absolute rubbish," then it is established by dicta of Lord Shand in the House of Lords in *White v. Mellin* [1895] A.C. 154, 171, which were accepted by Mr. Walton as stating the law, the statement would be actionable.

Between these two kinds of statements there is obviously still an extremely wide field; and it appears to me that, in order to draw the line, one must apply this test, namely, whether a reasonable man would take the claim being made as being a serious claim or not.

A possible alternative test is to ask whether the defendant has pointed to a specific allegation of some defect or demerit in the plaintiff's goods. This is, I think, the test favoured by the editors of the last few editions of *Salmond on Torts*. My difficulty in accepting this test is simply that I feel that there might conceivably be such an allegation which, for some reason—perhaps the light-hearted way in which it was expressed or perhaps, on the contrary, the extremely vituperative way in which it was expressed—was nevertheless not one which any reasonable man would take seriously. Mr. Walton furnished a very good example: if the makers of an amphibious car were to advertise that their car floated while a Rolls-Royce car would not, although this would be a specific enough criticism of the Rolls, nobody would take it seriously.

Per contra, in the present case to say that the Debdust is no use for cutting granite would clearly be taken as a reflection on its cutting power in general, even although it is not put forward as a suitable medium for that purpose. Moreover, the principle I favour can be applied universally to all cases where what is in substance urged is that the language must not be taken literally. I think that, as the law now stands, the cases are probably fully consistent with the adoption of either test, and that whichever is adopted would make no difference to the outcome of the present motion.

... [Under section 3 of the Defamation Act, 1952, no averment of special damage] is now necessary in a claim for slander of goods or injurious falsehood or whatever label one chooses to place upon this particular tort....

... [C]an I be so certain that nobody would have taken the results of Tech-Data/1 seriously that I should grant the relief sought by the defendants and strike out the statement of claim? I do not feel able to do so in any way at all. It appears to me that, where the interested parties are presented with what purports to be a proper scientific test, properly carried out by the "application laboratory"—whatever that is—they must be intended by the persons who furnished them with this information to take it all very seriously indeed. Such a report framed as the present report is framed cannot be dismissed in any way as a mere idle puff. If may well be of course that that is all in fact it is; but, if so, then the defendants have only themselves to blame for having dressed up a stupid old moke as a thoroughbred Arabian stallion.

If traders take the time and trouble to dress up their advertising material in this manner, then I think they must stand by it; and, if it contains, as in the case here, statements in disparagement of the plaintiffs' goods and if, further, on investigation those statements prove to be false and the plaintiff can show malice, the precise constituents of which for present purposes I think it is better not to investigate, it appears to me that they must answer for it.

Mr. Walton in substance submitted that such a conclusion would mean that the courts would be used as a forum for advertising the plaintiffs' wares by means of a judicial decision that their goods were better than the defendants'. Nothing, I think, is further from the truth. All the courts will decide is whether a specific statement, which may of course be express or implied, made concerning the plaintiffs' goods or services is or is not untrue. This appears to me to be a task which the courts are well fitted to perform; which they have on numerous occasions in the past performed; and which they will continue to perform as and when necessary....

Motion dismissed with costs.

Notes

1. Various attempts have been made to frame a test for distinguishing actionable from non-actionable disparagement of goods and businesses. Did the court in the *De Beers* case select the best test? In Testing Systems, Inc. v. Magnaflux Corp., 251 F. Supp. 286 (E.D. Pa. 1966), defendant allegedly published a false report that the government tested plaintiff's product and found it about 40% as effective as defendant's competing product. The court stated that an unfavorable comparison of products is not ordinarily actionable. But a distinction was drawn between saying that one's product is, in general, better than another's and asserting that the other's is only 40% as effective as one's own. The former, arguably, merely expresses an opinion, the truth or falsity of which is impossible to ascertain. The latter is an assertion of fact, not subject to the same frailties of proof, which implies that the party making the statement is fortified with substantive facts. The latter, therefore, might form the basis of a claim for injurious falsehood.

2. Does a company or organization that tests products run the risk of liability if test results are advertised? What about an organization that reports in a non-advertising medium its conclusions from tests or comparisons of products and services? An author who reports on and assigns ratings to hotels or restaurants? See Bose Corp. v. Consumers Union of United States, Inc., p. 259, infra; Mayfair Farms, Inc. v. Socony Mobil Oil Co., Inc., 68 N.J. Super. 188, 172 A.2d 26 (Ch. Div. 1961). It appears that there can be liability if defendant falsely states that plaintiff has fewer sales or a smaller audience than a competitor. See Brunson Communications, Inc. v. Arbitron, Inc., 266 F. Supp. 2d 377 (E.D. Pa. 2003) (viewers of television stations); Integrated Information Pte. Ltd. v. CD-Biz Directories Pte. Ltd., [2000] 3 Sing. L.R. 457 (High Ct.) (circulation of directories).

3. In contrast to the common law of injurious falsehood, statutes prohibiting and providing remedies for false advertising have addressed primarily defendants' false representations about their own products and services. 1988 amendments to section 43(a) of the federal Lanham Act, 15 U.S.C. § 1125(a), extended its coverage to misrepresentations about the goods, services and commercial activities of another person. Any false or misleading representation of fact in "commercial advertising or promotion" about the "the nature, characteristics, qualities, or geographic origin" of goods, services or commercial activities is actionable. Injunctive relief and other remedies beyond payment of compensatory damages are available for violation of section 43(a). The Federal Trade Commission has adopted a policy encouraging advertising which names or refers to competitors. Its Policy Statement on Comparative Advertising, 16 C.F.R. § 14.15, declares that truth-

ful comparative advertising should not be restrained because it is a source of important information to consumers, assisting them to make rational purchase decisions, it encourages product improvement and innovation, and it can lead to lower prices.

4. *Absence of specific reference to plaintiff.* Does plaintiff have an action if defendant's comparative advertising never mentions plaintiff or its product? Unitel Communications Inc. v. Bell Canada, (1994) 56 C.P.R.3d 232 (Ont. Gen. Div.), involved a television commercial for Bell Canada. In the commercial, a woman receives a telephone call offering a long distance service. The woman is told about a plan in which she would have to sign up her friends. The carrier serves only major centers and it is implied that there is no repair service. The woman ends the conversation by saying that she will stay with Bell. Unitel brought suit against Bell, saying that because it offered a plan involving signing up friends, the caller in the commercial would be identified as a representative of Unitel. It alleged that the commercial falsely represented that Unitel served only major centers and had no repair service. The evidence indicated that there was no consensus among people seeing the commercial on the identity of its target. Instead, there was confusion about the target's identity or a belief that the representation was generic. Saying that "the key to a claim for injurious falsehood is identity," the court rejected Unitel's motion for an interim injunction against the commercial. Compare DSG Retail Ltd. v. Comet Group Plc., [2002] F.S.R. 899 (Q.B.D.), in which defendant's assertion in its advertising that its prices were lower than competitors' "10% off promotions and £10 price-cuts" was found to be clearly directed at plaintiff and knowingly false. The court continued an injunction against displaying the advertising, except at stores where the ticketed prices were in fact lower than plaintiff's promotional prices.

5. In Blatty v. New York Times Co., 175 Cal. App. 3d 571, 221 Cal. Rptr. 236 (1985), rev'd, 42 Cal. 3d 1033, 232 Cal. Rptr. 542, 728 P.2d 1177 (1986), cert. denied, 485 U.S. 934 (1988), an author sued *The New York Times* for failure to include his novel in the newspaper's "best seller" list. This allegedly diminished the sales of the book and the amounts at which paperback and film rights could be sold. The Court of Appeal found no "trade libel" because "Silence is not libel." Drawing on New York Times Co. v. Sullivan, 376 U.S. 254 (1964), and other decisions in defamation cases, the Supreme Court of California held that the claim was barred on First Amendment grounds because the best seller list was not "of and concerning" the author or his novel—no specific reference to either was made. Should this apply to deliberate omission of a painting from what is supposed to be an authoritative complete listing of a famous artist's work? See Thome v. Alexander & Louisa Calder Foundation, 70 A.D.3d 88, 890 N.Y.S.2d 16 (2009), appeal denied, 15 N.Y.3d 703, 906 N.Y.S.2d 817, 933 N.E.2d 216 (2010).

6. On whether there must be a specific reference to the plaintiff or the plaintiff's goods or property, see also Marathon Mutual Ltd. v. Waters, [2010] E.M.L.R. 63 (Q.B.D.), holding that an injurious falsehood action could be brought by the company that managed the insurance fund the defendants disparaged; Keith v. Laurel County Fiscal Court, 254 S.W.3d 842 (Ky. App. 2008), holding that a landowner had no action for loss resulting from false statements about adjacent property; and Auvil v. CBS "60 Minutes," 800 F. Supp. 928 (E.D. Wash. 1992), a class action disparagement claim by nearly 5000 Washington apple growers affected by a broadcast on the use of an alleged carcinogen in the apple industry. In view of the other requirements of injurious falsehood liability, is there any need for a stringent "reference to plaintiff" or "of and concerning" requirement?

7. *Agricultural product disparagement statutes.* The *Auvil* case, in which it was alleged that growers and others dependent upon apple production lost up to $75,000,000 because of the safety controversy ignited by the broadcast, demonstrated that the common

law would probably provide no remedy for economic losses caused by disparagement of a product sold by many people, particularly losses sustained on account of false or unverifiable statements in mass media about the safety of a food product. This led to efforts in numerous states to establish a statutory remedy. More than a dozen states enacted statutes creating a cause of action for damages resulting from false disparagement of an agricultural product or perishable product. The statutes differ considerably in their provisions, especially on the level of culpability required for liability. This ranges from knowing falsehood to an absence of any fault requirement. Most but not all of the agricultural product disparagement statutes limit claims to producers or growers. Whether the statutes can be applied without violating the First Amendment is questionable.

The one sustained effort to date to establish liability under an agricultural product disparagement statute is an action brought by several Texas cattle ranchers on account of statements in a broadcast of the Oprah Winfrey television program. During a segment on the subject of "dangerous food," a guest on the program asserted that there was a risk of "mad cow disease" occurring in the United States. Winfrey responded by saying "It has just stopped me cold from eating another burger." Immediately following the broadcast, which reached an audience of many millions of viewers, sales and prices in cattle markets plummeted. The effects of what was called the "Oprah Crash" in the markets lasted for over two months. It was ultimately decided that defendants were not liable under the Texas perishable products disparagement act because the act required knowledge that the information was false and plaintiffs failed to establish knowing falsehood on the part of any of the defendants. Also, the trial court considered plaintiffs' live cattle not to be a "perishable food product" within the Texas statute. This left plaintiffs with only a common law claim for disparagement, which required that the statement be "of and concerning" a plaintiff's specific business. The jury decided that it was not, so Winfrey and the other defendants prevailed on all the claims against them. Texas Beef Group v. Winfrey, 201 F.3d 680 (5th Cir. 2000), aff'g 11 F. Supp. 2d 858 (N.D. Tex. 1998).

See generally Smolla, Law of Defamation §§ 16:1–16:4 (2d ed. 1999); Symposium, Limitations on Commercial Speech: The Evolution of Agricultural Disparagement Statutes, 10 DePaul Bus. L.J. 169 (1998); Comment, Mad Cows, Offended Emus, and Old Eggs: Perishable Product Disparagement Laws and Free Speech, 73 Wash. L. Rev. 1019 (1998); Note, Agricultural Disparagement Statutes: Tainted Beef, Tainted Speech, and Tainted Law, 9 Ford. Intel. Prop. Media & Ent. L.J. 981 (1999).

National Refining Company v. Benzo Gas Motor Fuel Company

United States Circuit Court of Appeals, Eighth Circuit
20 F.2d 763 (1927), cert. denied, 275 U.S. 570 (1927)

BOOTH, Circuit Judge.

[Plaintiff was the only producer in Kansas City of a product known as Benzo Gas, a mixture of gasoline and benzol (a substance distilled from bituminous coal). This was sold as a fuel for motor vehicles at a few filling stations that plaintiff owned and about seventy other filling stations in the Kansas City area. In this and certain other parts of the United States, mixtures of gasoline and benzol were in common use. Defendant was in the business of selling petroleum products, including a brand of gasoline. It operated in many states and had some twenty or thirty filling stations in Kansas City, including one across the street from a Benzo Gas station. As part of an "educational campaign," defendant had a leaflet (150,000 copies of which were printed) distributed at defendant's filling stations, including those in Kansas City. Plaintiff claimed that the following portions of the leaflet were libellous:

> A mixture of benzol and gasoline or a mixture of benzol and kerosene oil is not a proper fuel for an automobile, tractor or truck for the reason that when benzol is ignited by the electric spark, it explodes instantaneously. The entire power of the explosion being instantaneous, it is delivered on one spot of all the bearings in the motor and acts the same as if a sledge hammer were taken and a severe blow delivered on one spot at the rate of from twelve hundred to three thousand sledge hammer blows per minute. The result is that the bearings become egg-shaped, resulting in repairs in the form of new bearings....
>
> Benzol, or a mixture of benzol and gasoline, or a mixture of benzol and kerosene, causes corrosion and pitting of the cylinders and valves, likewise overheats the engine, causing the valves to become exceedingly hot, necessitating frequent grinding of the valves in order to get proper compression due to the corroding and warping. These mixtures, used in cold weather, cause trouble in the gasoline running from the supply tank to the carburetor. Unmixed benzol starts to flake and congeal at 40 temperature, and if mixed with kerosene oil or gasoline, forms flakes in the small delivery pipe to the carburetor, often causing it to plug up....
>
> No engineer has designed a motor for burning anything other than gasoline. Therefore, why go contrary and use other fuels for which the motor was not designed?
>
> Dopes advertised to increase the efficiency of gasoline, to prevent the formation of carbon and other claims are nothing but dopes and should not be used. They are harmful to the motor. They do not increase the efficiency of good gasoline, and even when used with mixtures of gasoline and kerosene or low grade gasolines, they are more harmful than the material used. You can take several different acids and introduce them in a motor, and they will eat the surface of the iron until it is clean and bright, but they are destroying the motor.

Plaintiff's evidence tended to prove that the statements were untrue. The jury returned a verdict of $1 actual damages and $10,000 punitive damages.]

... [T]he legal principles constituting the law of libel are the same whether corporations or individuals are involved. But there are recognized distinctions between the application of those principles to individuals and their application to corporations, growing largely out of the differences between natural and artificial persons. For example, a corporation is incapable of committing certain acts, especially some crimes, which an individual would be capable of committing; and again, a corporation has no merely personal reputation in the sense that an individual has. Libels against a corporation are, therefore, confined to attacks which injure the property, the credit, the business of the corporation.

[The court rejected defendant's contention that the leaflet's statements did not constitute a libel against plaintiff because neither plaintiff nor plaintiff's product (Benzo Gas) was mentioned in the leaflet. It was not necessary that the party be named in the article claimed to be libellous. There was substantial evidence that persons who received the leaflet understood that plaintiff's product was aimed at. The court then addressed defendant's contention that the leaflet was not libellous per se because it disparaged only the product or property of plaintiff, not plaintiff itself.] ...

... [I]n the English courts three different classes or grades of defamatory statements in reference to the goods or products of tradesmen are recognized: (1) Those where, though the alleged libelous statement is made in reference to goods or product, there are also included libelous words in reference to the vendor or producer, which impute to him, in connection with the goods or product, fraud, deceit, dishonesty, or reprehensible business methods. (2) Those where the alleged libelous statement is made merely as to the quality of the goods or product of another. In these cases special damage must be alleged and proved, or no recovery can be had.... (3) Those where the alleged libelous statements amount to no more than assertions by one tradesman that his goods are superior to those of his rival. Here no recovery can be had, though the statements are false and malicious, and though special damage is alleged.

These same distinctions of classes or grades are recognized in the decisions of American courts.

In Larsen v. Brooklyn Daily Eagle, 165 App. Div. 4, 150 N.Y.S. 464, the alleged libelous article stated that a child ate some of plaintiff's ice cream, was shortly thereafter seized with convulsions, and died; that it was believed the ice cream was responsible; that four other children had been taken ill after eating ice cream in the same place; that the ice cream was made by plaintiff. On demurrer it was held that the statements were libelous per se. The court said that the published article was more than an attack upon the goods or product — it was a reflection upon the honesty and integrity of the manufacturer....

In Erick Bowman Remedy Co. v. Jensen Salsbery Laboratories [17 F.2d 255] the complaint alleged that plaintiff was a manufacturer and seller of a medical preparation for stock, and had built up a profitable business; that defendant was engaged in the manufacture and sale of live stock remedies and also published a trade journal; that defendant published in its journal, what purported to be an analysis of plaintiff's medical preparation, ending with the statement: "'Sample is brown sugar and bran.'" Following this were the statements: "'This analysis corresponds in all respects to the analysis of samples of this product sent to our laboratory, which only goes to prove that P.T. Barnum's statement 50 years ago can be applied even at the present time. We understand that the Farm Bureau of North Dakota is going to put on a publicity campaign to protect the live stock owners against expenditures for such products. This is one piece of work that the Farm Bureau can handle in an effective way.'"

The complaint further alleged: "That by the publication of said words and article, the defendant intended to assert and to be understood as asserting and by the readers of said journal and publication was in fact understood as asserting that the said remedy manufactured and sold by this plaintiff was worthless, and would not cure the disease of abortion among cows and sows, and that the said remedy was a fraud and a humbug, and that this plaintiff was knowingly engaged in the business of cheating and defrauding the public and all persons who bought said remedy for the purpose for which it was manufactured and sold, and that the Farm Bureau of North Dakota was going to engage in a publicity campaign to expose said fraud and to protect live stock owners against buying such worthless products as plaintiff was manufacturing and selling, and by so doing the said Farm Bureau would be doing a good service to all those who might be victimized by buying plaintiff's said remedy. [¶] That the said article published by the defendant is misleading, false, defamatory and malicious, and by means of said publication the plaintiff has been greatly injured in its good name and business reputation, and has suffered great loss in its business and credit."

On the trial, following the opening statement of counsel, the case was dismissed, on the ground that neither the complaint nor counsel's statement set out any cause of action.

The grounds of the dismissal were that the article was not libelous per se, and that special damage was not alleged. The judgment of dismissal was affirmed by this court....

Johnson v. Hitchcock, 15 Johns. (N.Y.) 185, was an action for damages for representing that plaintiff's ferry was not as good as a rival ferry. It was held no action would lie. This case falls into the third class....

The result of the above-cited cases appears to be that, where the publication on its face is directed against the goods or product of a corporate vendor or manufacturer, it will not be held libelous per se as to the corporation, unless by fair construction and without the aid of extrinsic evidence it imputes to the corporation, fraud, deceit, dishonesty, or reprehensible conduct in its business in relation to said goods or product.

Viewed in the light of the principles announced in the foregoing cases, into what class does the case at bar fall? Not into the third, because, plainly, the statements were not confined to disparaging comparison between the product of plaintiff and that of defendant. After careful consideration we have concluded that it falls into the second class....

There is a striking similarity between the facts in the Erick Bowman Company Case and the case at bar. In both the publication was made by one manufacturer and seller of a product against another manufacturer and seller of products in a similar line of business. In both publications the main attack was against the product manufactured and sold. In neither publication was it stated that plaintiff was engaged in the manufacture or sale of the product.

There are differences, but they are not vital. In the Erick Bowman Company Case the statement indicated that the product was harmless, and merely a worthless humbug, but it was not stated that plaintiff knew that it was a worthless humbug. In the case at bar the statements indicate that the product attacked was harmful in its use; but it was not stated that plaintiff knew that such was the case, nor that the character of the product was such that plaintiff must have known that it would produce harm ...

... [W]e find nothing in them which reflects on the honesty or integrity of plaintiff; nothing that imputes to it fraud or deception; nothing which indicates reprehensible methods in the conduct of its business. We think the article was not libelous per se, and was not actionable unless special damage was alleged and proven. Neither of these requisites was met....

The motion for a directed verdict in favor of defendant should have been sustained. The judgment must be reversed....

[Lewis, Circuit Judge, delivered a dissenting opinion.]

Notes

1. There are several important differences in the elements of injurious falsehood and defamation: (1) In injurious falsehood, it must be proved that plaintiff sustained special damage — economic harm — as a result of the falsehood. This is unnecessary in most defamation cases, including those in which defamation pertains to plaintiff's trade, business or profession. (2) In injurious falsehood, plaintiff must show the falsity of the assertion. In defamation, the burden is on defendant to prove truth as an affirmative defense. (This has been modified by the interpretation of the United States Constitution as requiring plaintiff to carry the burden of proof in certain defamation cases. See pp. 670–674, infra.) (3) In injurious falsehood, unlike defamation, plaintiff must show that the statement was made with "malice." See Fleming, Law of Torts 795–800 (10th ed.

2011). Should statements harmful to business and statements harmful to reputation be treated differently? Will a plaintiff always prefer to have the claim treated as one for defamation? On whether advertising that disparages the quality or value of others' products is actionable as defamation or injurious falsehood, see Annot., Actionable Nature of Advertising Impugning Quality or Worth of Merchandise or Products, 42 A.L.R.4th 318 (1985); Annot., Defamation of Manufacturer, Regarding Product, Other Than Through Statement Charging Breach or Nonperformance of Contract, 104 A.L.R.5th 523 (2002).

2. Libel and slander actions can be brought not only by natural persons, but also by corporations and other business and non-business entities. See pp. 504–512, infra. Consider whether the following statements are actionable as defamation:

(a) "He has rotten goods in his shop." Burnet v. Wells, (1700) 12 Mod. 420, 88 Eng. Rep. 1423 (K.B.).

(b) A certain brand of ukulele is worthless, no one should be deceived into buying it, and those who sell it ought to be jailed. Tex Smith, The Harmonica Man, Inc. v. Godfrey, 198 Misc. 1006, 102 N.Y.S.2d 251 (Sup. Ct. 1951).

(c) A machine sold to doctors for use in treatment of patients is "rank misrepresentation" and has not been "clinically proven." Diapulse Corp. of America v. Birtcher Corp., 362 F.2d 736 (2d Cir. 1966), stay denied, 87 S. Ct. 6 (1966), cert. dismissed, 385 U.S. 801 (1966).

(d) A sleep-aid product is full of habit-forming drugs; it will make a person "feel like a run-down hound dog" and lose weight. Harwood Pharmacal Co., Inc. v. National Broadcasting Co., Inc., 9 N.Y.2d 460, 214 N.Y.S.2d 725, 174 N.E.2d 602 (1961).

(e) A manufacturer has weak financial backing, is "going to be in trouble," and will not be in business long, leaving buyers with "orphan machines on their hands." Maytag Co. v. Meadows Manufacturing Co., 45 F.2d 299 (7th Cir. 1930), cert. denied, 283 U.S. 843 (1931).

(f) Numerous rapes occur in or near an amusement park. Fairyland Amusement Co. v. Metromedia, Inc., 413 F. Supp. 1290 (W.D. Mo. 1976).

(g) A restaurant is a good place to meet sellers of cocaine. El Meson Espanol v. NYM Corp., 521 F.2d 737 (2d Cir. 1975).

3. *Injunctions.* Is a plaintiff who establishes a prima facie case of injurious falsehood entitled to an injunction against its repetition? Some courts will grant injunctions against injurious falsehoods as they will for other economic torts. Other courts, however, apply the rule against injunctions that applies to defamation. This is supported by the constitutional doctrine of no prior restraint of speech and by the recently increased constitutional protection for commercial speech. Still other courts will permit injunctions in particular circumstances, as when other torts are present or substantial and irreparable injury otherwise would be suffered. When a dissatisfied purchaser of an automobile drove it around town with a white elephant and "Hudson" painted on it, seeking to induce a Hudson dealer to give him another car, an injunction issued. Carter v. Knapp Motor Co., 243 Ala. 600, 11 So. 2d 383 (1943). See also Menard v. Houle, p. 257, infra. Was this correct? If disparagement of a business is defamatory, false and well-publicized, should an injunction be issued in order to protect the business from harm or denied under the rule against enjoining defamatory statements? What if defendant has a web site that targets plaintiff's business? Cf. Willing v. Mazzocone, 482 Pa. 377, 393 A.2d 1155 (1978), rev'g 246 Pa. Super. 98, 369 A.2d 829 (1976) (demonstration with sandwich board proclaiming

that law firm "stole money from me and sold me out to the insurance company" could not be enjoined). See generally Annot., Injunction Against Acts or Conduct, in Street or Vicinity, Tending to Disparage Plaintiff's Business or His Merchandise, 144 A.L.R. 1181 (1943); Annot., Injunction as Remedy in Case of Trade Libel, 148 A.L.R. 853 (1944); Dobbs, Law of Remedies §6.8(3) (2d ed. 1993); Prosser & Keeton, Law of Torts 976–977 (5th ed. 1984).

Annbar Associates v. American Express Company
Missouri Court of Appeals
565 S.W.2d 701 (1978)

ROBERT R. WELBORN, Special Judge Presiding.

[For several months, the Muehlebach Hotel in Kansas City accepted American Express credit cards for purchases at the hotel and was part of the American Express Reservations "Space Bank" system, which made reservations at member hotels and motels for persons calling a toll-free telephone number. The hotel then decided, because of the costs involved, to terminate both its agreement with the American Express Company for acceptance of credit cards and its agreement with American Express Reservations (a subsidiary of the American Express Company). On February 1, 1973, the hotel gave written notice of this to American Express and immediately stopped accepting American Express credit cards. However, the hotel's reservations personnel, who were not told of the termination of the reservations agreement, continued to receive and accept reservations from the American Express system. American Express Reservation's bills to the hotel for these reservations were not paid. On May 30, American Express Reservations notified the hotel that because of its delinquency in payments, its participation in the Space Bank was being terminated. In September, the hotel discovered that people calling American Express Reservations were being told that rooms at the Muehlebach Hotel were "sold out" or "not available." This was confirmed by making test calls to the reservations system, seeking accommodation at the hotel when rooms were in fact available.]

[The owners of the hotel brought suit against American Express and American Express Reservations, alleging that the hotel had been deprived of substantial business because persons seeking accommodation were told that it was not available. At the trial, there was evidence that the computer system American Express Reservations began to use in February 1973 displayed "Not Available" to operators taking telephone calls whenever "a hotel closed out to the system for any reason." The prior computer system displayed a distinct message for hotels not in the Space Bank system, but the new system did not. (After the suit was filed, a response of "Not available on system" was added.) When the response "Not Available" appeared, operators would say "I'm sorry that hotel is not available." Callers might interpret this to mean that the hotel had no rooms to sell. Records of the computer system showed that between May 23 and October 21, 1973, there were availability checks for 487 room nights and attempted sales for 336 room nights at the Muehlebach Hotel. Plaintiffs abandoned a claim that defendants conspired against them after the hotel terminated the credit card and reservation system contracts. They maintained, however, that the American Express Company was jointly liable with American Express Reservations because it loaded the "Not Available" response into the computer system. The jury awarded $25,000 compensatory damages and, against each defendant, $100,000 punitive damages.]

[Restatement (Second) of Torts § 623A] states the general principle of liability in this area as follows: "One who publishes a false statement harmful to the interests of another is subject to liability for pecuniary loss resulting to the other if (a) he intends for publication of the statement to result in harm to interests of the other having a pecuniary value, or either recognizes or should recognize that it is likely to do so, and (b) he knows that the statement is false or acts in reckless disregard of its truth or falsity." ...

... The tort of injurious falsehood involves, at least, legal malice. As [Prosser on Torts (4th ed.) pp. 921–922 (1971)] expresses it: "There is liability when the defendant acts for a spite motive, and out of a desire to do harm for its own sake; and equally so when he acts for the purpose of doing harm to the interests of the plaintiff in a manner in which he is not privileged so to interfere. There is also liability when the defendant knows that what he says is false, regardless of whether he has an ill motive or intends to affect the plaintiff at all. The deliberate liar must take the risk that his statement will prove to be economically damaging to others; and there is something like the 'scienter' found in an action of deceit. Any of these three is sufficient to constitute 'malice' and support the action. But in the absence of any of the three there is no liability, where the defendant has made his utterance in good faith, even though he may have been negligent in failing to ascertain the facts before he made it."

In this case, respondents produced no evidence of a spite motive, made clear by the abandonment of a conspiracy theory. They produced no evidence of purposeful harm to respondents by appellants. Therefore, the respondents were entitled to succeed in this case only if appellants knew that the "not available" response was false or if appellants acted in "reckless disregard" of the truth or falsity of the "not available" response.

[The trial court's instructions failed to submit this issue to the jury. For this error, the judgment had to be reversed. Absent proof of one defendant's responsibility for the acts of the other, it was necessary to require a finding against each defendant of the requisite elements of liability.]

Reversed and remanded.

Notes

1. Until the late nineteenth century, at the outset of an injurious falsehood case a plaintiff needed only to prove defendant's intention to disparage. Then, if defendant established a prima facie case of privilege, such as protection of his own interest, plaintiff, in order to succeed, had to rebut the privilege by showing malice. Today, it is widely accepted that malice is an essential element of all injurious falsehood actions—the most difficult and controversial element. Malice has been said variously to mean ill will or spite, an intent to injure, or lack of an honest belief in the truth of the statement. See Spring v. Guardian Assurance Plc., [1993] I.C.R. 412, [1993] 2 All E.R. 273 (C.A.), rev'd, [1995] 2 A.C. 296 (H.L.); Harper, James & Gray, Law of Torts § 6.1A (3d ed. 2006); Sack, Defamation: Libel, Slander, and Related Problems, § 13.1.4[E] (4th ed. 2010). In Shapiro v. La Morta (1923) 130 L.T. 622 (C.A.), defendants falsely advertised a professional singer as engaged at their music hall during a particular week. The singer claimed that as a result she lost another opportunity to perform. It was held that she could not recover because defendants believed that the announcements were correct. Cf. Balden v. Shorter, [1933] Ch. 427 (no action for detrimental statements carelessly made without intent to injure).

2. A landlord wants a tenant to quit the premises. In order to make this more likely, the landlord's secretary makes false statements to the tenant's suppliers and others to the

effect that the tenant has quit the premises or is no longer available, causing manufacturers to cut off the tenant's supply of goods. Liability? See Joyce v. Motor Surveys Ltd., [1948] Ch. 252 (malice found). A purchaser is dissatisfied with his car's steering apparatus and asks the dealer to install another. The dealer refuses, finding the apparatus to be in good condition. The purchaser then covers the car with writing stating that the car is "no good" and attaches to it lemons and papers identifying the dealer. He drives the car around town and exhibits it near the dealer's place of business. Does the dealer have an action? See Menard v. Houle, 298 Mass. 546, 11 N.E.2d 436 (1937) (injunction and nominal damages granted). A newspaper reports that a house is haunted. Crowds congregate around the house and damage it. A planned sale of the house falls through. Is the newspaper liable to the house's owner? See Nagy v. Manitoba Free Press Co., (1907) 16 Man. R. 619, 5 W.L.R. 453 (C.A.), aff'd, (1907) 39 S.C.R. 340 (reporter and sub-editor responsible for publication were educated men and must have known report was false; malice presumed from "reckless publication"). Cf. Cromarty v. Prentice-Hall, Inc., 72 A.D.2d 782, 421 N.Y.S.2d 603 (1979) (book reporting visitation of plaintiffs' house by occult phenomena).

3. Some cases, especially cases of slander of title, exhibit a holdover of the old relationship between the malice requirement and the assertion of privilege. E.g., Fischer v. Bar Harbor Banking and Trust Co., 857 F.2d 4 (1st Cir. 1988), cert. denied, 489 U.S. 1018 (1989) (rival claimant to property has "conditional privilege" to assert claim by lien or otherwise). However, it has been asserted that the malice requirement is necessary in slander of title actions because a person claiming an interest in property would otherwise not be able to litigate the claim without fear of being held liable in damages. Ward v. Mid-West & Gulf Co., 97 Okla. 252, 223 P. 170 (1923). Similarly, recording a document which casts a cloud on another person's interest in property is not actionable if the recording party reasonably believes, or at least in good faith believes, he has a valid claim to the property. See Annot., Recording of Instrument Purporting to Affect Title as Slander of Title, 39 A.L.R.2d 840 (1955). What if a person claiming real property fails to secure an expert opinion on the claim's validity or verify the land's boundaries? See Horning v. Hardy, 36 Md. App. 419, 373 A.2d 1273 (1977) (not "reckless disregard of truth" so did not defeat "conditional privilege" to make claim). See generally Annot., Malice as Element of Action for Slander of Title, 129 A.L.R. 179 (1940). It seems to be accepted that the privileges of the law of defamation apply also to injurious falsehood. See Harper, James & Gray, Law of Torts § 6.3 (3d ed. 2006). An example is the decision in Western Technologies, Inc. v. Sverdrup & Parcel, Inc., p. 242, supra, that defendants' report was absolutely privileged because it was commissioned by the stadium's owner in contemplation of litigation over the cracks in the structure.

Granada Biosciences, Inc. v. Forbes, Inc.

Texas Court of Appeals
49 S.W.3d 610 (2001), rev'd,
124 S.W.3d 167 (Tex. 2003)

MAURICE AMIDEI, Justice.

[*Forbes* magazine published an article that referred to Granada Biosciences, Inc. (GBI) and Granada Foods Corporation (GFC), two companies in the Granada organization whose stock was publicly traded. The article contained a number of negative statements about the organization, GBI and GFC, including that GBI had failed to disclose guarantees of loans to officers, that a Granada employee had backdated documents at the direction of a superior, that a well-known near-billionaire was suing Granada, and that both GBI and GFC were "broke." GBI and GFC sued Forbes, Inc., the magazine's publisher, for business disparagement.]

While the parties agree that "malice" is an essential element of a business disparagement claim, they are sharply divided on how to apply this element. Forbes contends that because GBI and GFC are public figures suing a media defendant, they must prove that the publication was made with "actual malice." "Actual malice" is defined as "knowledge that [the statement] was false or with reckless disregard of whether it was false or not." [*New York Times Co. v. Sullivan*, 376 U.S. 254, 280 (1964).] "Reckless disregard" means that the publisher "in fact entertained serious doubts as to the truth of his publication." *St. Amant v. Thompson*, 390 U.S. 727, 731 (1968).... Thus, proof of actual malice requires sufficient evidence to permit the conclusion that, at the time of publication, the defendant either knew the statement was false or entertained serious doubts as to the truth of the publication.

GBI and GFC argue, however, that the standard of "actual malice" applied in defamation cases is inapplicable here. Instead, they claim that the proper definition of "malice" in a suit for business disparagement comes from the Texas Supreme Court in [*Hurlbut v. Gulf Atlantic Life Insurance Co.*, 749 S.W.2d 762, 766 (Tex. 1987)]: "[T]he defendant in an action for business disparagement or injurious falsehood is subject to liability 'only if he knew of the falsity or acted with reckless disregard concerning it, or if he acted with ill will or intended to interfere in the economic interest of the plaintiff in an unprivileged fashion.'" (quoting RESTATEMENT (SECOND) OF TORTS § 623A cmt. g (1977)). Thus, GBI and GFC contend that, in any suit involving a claim for business disparagement, the element of malice may be proven in one of four ways: (1) the defendant knew of the falsity of the publication; *or* (2) the defendant acted with reckless disregard concerning the falsity of the publication; *or* (3) the defendant acted with ill will; *or* (4) the defendant intended to interfere in the economic interest of the plaintiff in an unprivileged fashion.

At the outset, we note that the plaintiff in *Hurlbut* was a private individual. GBI and GFC nevertheless argue that the *Hurlbut* court's enunciation of the standard for imposing liability in a business disparagement suit should be applied regardless of the plaintiff's status. We disagree.

The United States Supreme Court's requirement of "actual malice" was not developed for the purpose of distinguishing claims for defamation from other torts. In *New York Times*, the Court was faced with the conflict between the protections afforded by the First and Fourteenth Amendments and a state's power to award damages for defamatory statements. The Court concluded that when the plaintiff is a public official, the constitutional guarantee of freedom of expression prohibits that plaintiff from recovering damages unless the defamatory statement was made with actual malice. This requirement was later expanded to apply to public figures as well. *See Gertz v. Robert Welch, Inc.*, 418 U.S. 323 (1974). The plaintiff's evidence must be clear and convincing to support a recovery.

In *Hustler Magazine v. Falwell*, 485 U.S. 46 (1988), the Supreme Court applied this same First Amendment limitation to a claim for intentional infliction of emotional distress....

GBI and GFC nonetheless contend that defamation and business disparagement are two separate torts, protecting different interests, and thus have different elements of proof. *See Hurlbut*, 749 S.W.2d at 766 (noting that defamation protects personal reputation, whereas business disparagement protects economic interests). While this is undoubtedly true, GBI and GFC fail to provide any explanation why this difference would prevent a court from applying the constitutional protections set forth by *New York Times* and its progeny. Although defamation and business disparagement may be designed to protect different interests, both causes of action seek to impose liability for injuries caused by "publications to third parties of a false statement affecting the plaintiff." *Id.* There can be no dispute, therefore, that the same conflict recognized by the Supreme Court in New York Times — the conflict between constitutionally-protected free expression and a state's power to award damages based on a defendant's statements — is present in business disparagement claims as well as defamation.

Furthermore, the court in *Hurlbut* expressly noted that the differences between the two torts historically resulted in "[m]ore stringent requirements" on plaintiffs who allege business disparagement. Under GBI and GFC's theory, the differences between the two torts, which were designed to make it *more difficult* to recover for business disparagement, would in fact make business disparagement claims *easier* to prove in those cases where the First Amendment is implicated. We decline to adopt such an interpretation.

We therefore hold that, when the plaintiff in a business disparagement cause of action is a public official or public figure, that plaintiff has the burden of proving by clear and convincing evidence that the disparaging words were published with knowledge that they were false or with reckless disregard as to whether or not they were true.

[The court found that there was a material issue of fact concerning whether Forbes acted with "actual malice" in publishing the article, as well as the other facts bearing on liability for disparagement. The trial court's grant of summary judgment to Forbes was therefore reversed. The further appeal to the Supreme Court of Texas concerned only whether plaintiffs produced evidence of "actual malice." The court held that there was no evidence that Forbes published the statements about GBI and GFC with "actual malice," so Forbes prevailed.]

Notes

1. Under New York Times Co. v. Sullivan, 376 U.S. 254 (1964), it is a First Amendment requirement that "malice" be proved in order to hold a defendant liable for defamation of a "public official." This requirement was extended to defamation actions by a "public figure" in Curtis Publishing Co. v. Butts, 388 U.S. 130 (1967). "Malice" is defined for this purpose as knowledge of falsity or reckless disregard of truth. Plaintiffs in injurious falsehood cases (other than slander of title) typically are business proprietors or corporations. See pp. 646–657, infra, on whether they would be classified as "public figures." "Malice" does not have to be shown if the defamatory statement did not pertain to the plaintiff's role as public figure or public official.

2. Because of concern that it would be held unconstitutional to impose liability for injurious falsehood in the absence of knowing falsehood or reckless disregard of truth, the Restatement (Second) provision quoted in the *Annbar Associates* case, p. 255, supra, took no position on whether defendant's ill will or intent to interfere with plaintiff's interests is a sufficient basis of liability for injurious falsehood. See caveats to Restatement (Second) of Torts §623A (1977). In Bose Corp. v. Consumers Union of United States, Inc., 508 F. Supp. 1249 (D. Mass. 1981), subsequent proceedings, 529 F. Supp. 357 (D. Mass. 1981), rev'd, 692 F.2d 189 (1st Cir. 1982), aff'd, 466 U.S. 485 (1984), it was held that the "malice" required for defamation actions brought by a public figure was also a requirement of liability in an injurious falsehood action brought by a public figure. See also Blatty v. New York Times Co., p. 249, supra.

3. In litigation arising from "a comparative advertising war" between the Philadelphia region's largest health care insurer and a 600,000-member health maintenance organization, U.S. Healthcare, Inc. v. Blue Cross of Greater Philadelphia, 898 F.2d 914 (3d Cir. 1990),

cert. denied sub nom. Independent Blue Cross v. U.S. Healthcare, Inc., 498 U.S. 816 (1990), the court held that "commercial speech" was not subject to the rule of Curtis Publishing Co. v. Butts, supra. For purposes of liability for commercial speech, plaintiff was not to be treated as a public figure even it was a public figure in other contexts. A defendant could be held liable for disparagement and defamation without proof of knowing falsehood or reckless disregard of truth. The court reasoned that commercial speech was not susceptible to being "chilled" by the prospect of liability and therefore did not require the protection given non-commercial speech. Determination of whether speech was "commercial" would depend upon whether it was an advertisement, whether it referred to a specific product or service, and whether it had an economic motivation.

4. In Procter & Gamble Co. v. Amway Corp., 242 F.3d 539 (5th Cir. 2001), cert. denied, 534 U.S. 945 (2001), the court agreed with the decision in *U.S. Healthcare* that the "actual malice" requirement does not apply to injurious falsehood and related claims arising from "commercial speech." The court reasoned that as commercial speech received less First Amendment protection from government regulation than non-commercial speech, it should also receive less protection from private suits, which were not much more likely than government regulation to infringe on First Amendment values. Whether defendants' speech was commercial depended upon whether the primary motivation for it was economic. Procter & Gamble was suing because distributors for Amway, a major competitor, spread rumors of Procter & Gamble's having links to Satanism. Such rumors had long bedevilled the company and allegedly damaged its business by causing a loss of customers.

5. Jefferson County School District No. R-1 v. Moody's Investor's Services, Inc., 175 F.3d 848 (10th Cir, 1999), is another case in which First Amendment limitations on defamation liability were applied to an injurious falsehood action. Applying Milkovich v. Lorain Journal Co., p. 678, infra, the court held that Moody's was not liable for an evaluation of bonds issued by a school district because the evaluation did not contain or imply a provably false assertion of fact.

Teilhaber Manufacturing Company v. Unarco Materials Storage
Colorado Court of Appeals
791 P.2d 1164 (1989), cert. denied, 803 P.2d 517 (Colo. 1991)

Opinion by Judge METZGER....

[Teilhaber and Unarco were competitors in the production of industrial storage racks. Unarco provided its employees and distributors a report of what was said to be tests of a Teilhaber product. Teilhaber was awarded $1,763,131 for disparagement by statements in this report. The court found the requisite element of falsity in the tested product being a "hybrid" of components from Teilhaber and another company rather than a product furnished by Teilhaber.]

Unarco next contends that the trial court erroneously admitted evidence concerning general business damages, in violation of the general rule that only special damages may be recovered in a product disparagement action....

In a product disparagement action, the plaintiff must always prove special damages. He is required to establish a pecuniary loss that has been realized or liquidated, as in the case of specific lost sales. If a plaintiff cannot show special damages, no cause of action is established. To make the required showing, a plaintiff usually must identify those persons who refuse to purchase his product because of the disparagement.

Strict imposition of this requirement has led to many difficulties. Formerly, it was nearly always held that it was not enough to show a general decline in business following the publication of the falsehood. This was so, even if there was evidence eliminating other causes for the decline. Thus, a plaintiff was required to identify the particular purchasers who refrained from dealing with him and had to specify the transactions of which he claims to have been deprived. But, if there was wide dissemination of the disparagement to persons unknown, this was obviously impossible.

Accordingly, the current tendency rejects such an arbitrary rule. It is guided by the principles set out in *Ratcliffe v. Evans*, [1892] 2 Q.B. 524 (C.A.)], one of the first opinions to reject the strict approach. There, the court observed: "As much certainty and particularity must be insisted on, both in pleading and proof of damages, as is reasonable, having regard to the circumstances and to the nature of the acts themselves by which the damage is done. To insist upon less would be to relax old and intelligible principles. To insist upon more would be the vainest pedantry."

Currently, the plaintiff is required to be particular only if it is reasonable to expect him to be so. If it is not a practical possibility to show specific losses, damages may then be proved by evidence similar to that used to prove lost profits resulting from a breach of contract. Consequently, if a plaintiff can present sufficient evidence, using detailed statistical and expert proof, to exclude the possibility that other factors caused the loss of general business, recovery is allowed.

Teilhaber presented evidence that identification of end users of its product was impossible because product sales were made only through independent distributors, over whom Teilhaber had no control. This explanation was sufficient to satisfy application of the current approach. The evidence concerning damages consisted of extensive and complex statistical and expert evaluations of the industry, the market, and Teilhaber's business pattern. This evidence provides ample support for the jury's verdict, and we must, therefore, uphold it on appeal ...

[Affirmed.]

Notes

1. The special damages requirement has been one of the principal obstacles for plaintiffs in injurious falsehood cases. See, e.g., Barquin v. Hall Oil Co., 28 Wyo. 164, 201 P. 352 (1921), reh'g denied, 28 Wyo. 164, 202 P. 1107 (1922). What must be pleaded and proved? Loss of a sale to an identifiable intending purchaser is a classic example of special damage. See Ideal Savings Loan & Building Association of Newport v. Blumberg, 295 Ky. 858, 175 S.W.2d 1015 (1943). So is loss of trade from particular prospective customers. See Write v. Coules, 4 Cal. App. 343, 87 P. 809 (1906). Some of the more recent decisions hold that specific prospective customers need not be identified; other proof of loss of sales is sufficient. See Prosser & Keeton, Law of Torts 970–973 (5th ed. 1984). Should slander of title be distinguished from other falsehoods in this respect? See Annot., What Constitutes Special Damage in Action for Slander of Title, 4 A.L.R.4th 532 (1981). What if plaintiff complains of disparagement of a single item? See Kirby v. Wildenstein, 784 F. Supp. 1112 (S.D.N.Y. 1992) (valuable painting).

2. In Annbar Associates v. American Express Co., p. 255, supra, plaintiffs presented two theories of damage. One was a loss of profits of about $200,000 on the basis that occupancy for the period in which defendants told callers that rooms in plaintiffs' hotel were not available was 12,830 room nights below the same period in the proceeding year. The

Court of Appeals, noting the jury's evident rejection of this theory, said that the evidence of damage on this theory was "too speculative to admit of a calculation" and should not have been received. The second theory was based on the records from defendants' computer system showing 823 room nights for which reservations had been requested or enquired about. Plaintiffs' hotel manager computed a $27,375 loss of profits, consisting of 90% of the lost rent for 823 nights and profits on food and beverage sales based on the percentage which such sales bore to room rentals for the year 1973 and the rate of profit on these sales. He justified the high rate of profit on room rentals by saying that no additional hotel staff would be required. The court held that this evidence sufficed to meet plaintiffs' burden of proof.

3. When defendant has not impaired plaintiff's ability to sell or lease his property or reduced the price plaintiff could obtain, but plaintiff has been caused expense in establishing his title or right to dispose of the property, does this expense constitute special damage? See Paidar v. Hughes, 615 N.W.2d 276 (Minn. 2000); Lau v. Pugh, 299 S.W.3d 740 (Mo. App. 2009) (attorney fees and other expenses incurred to clear disparaged title were special damages); Restatement (Second) of Torts § 633(1)(b) (1977). It appears that recovery of consequential damages is strictly controlled. For instance, loss of the advantageous use of the money that plaintiff would have received, but for the falsehood, is not compensable. See Restatement (Second) of Torts § 633, comment *i* (1977). Mental distress, even if immediately resulting from disparagement, is not considered because it does not constitute harm to a pecuniary interest. See Ebersole v. Fields, 181 Ala. 421, 62 So. 73 (1913). As stated in the *De Beers* case, p. 245, supra, the special damage requirement has been abolished in England for most injurious falsehood actions. Defamation Act, 1952, 15 & 16 Geo. 6 & 1 Eliz. 2, c. 66, s. 3. Is this desirable?

4. Injurious falsehood is generally described as a false statement that is calculated to injure a person's trade, business or other pecuniary interest. See Riding v. Smith, (1876) 1 Ex. D. 91; Fleming, Law of Torts 796–797 (10th ed. 2011). Must a plaintiff convince the court that defendant's statement has a tendency to cause or likelihood of causing such an injury, as well as that special damages have been sustained? With respect to both elements, consider the examples in note 2, p. 262, and also the following:

(a) A statement that plaintiff is employed by defendant. Balden v. Shorter, [1933] Ch. 427 (plaintiff lost commission). Cf. Shapiro v. La Morta, (1923) 130 L.T. 622 (C.A.) (music hall advertised performance by plaintiff).

(b) A landlord's notification to telephone callers and the Post Office that a business tenant has moved away. Joyce v. Motor Surveys Ltd., [1948] Ch. 252. Cf. Ratcliffe v. Evans, [1892] 2 Q.B. 524 (C.A.) (plaintiff's business had ceased to exist).

(c) A report that a competitor's product has higher sales than plaintiff's. Integrated Information Pte. Ltd. v. CD-Biz Directories Pte. Ltd., [2000] 3 Sing. L.R. 457 (High Ct.). Cf. Brunson Communications, Inc. v. Arbitron, Inc., 266 F. Supp. 2d 377 (E.D. Pa. 2003) (viewers of television stations); Advance Music Corp. v. American Tobacco Co., 268 App. Div. 707, 53 N.Y.S.2d 337 (1945), rev'd, 296 N.Y. 79, 70 N.E.2d 401 (1946) (popularity of songs); Menefee v. Columbia Broadcasting System, Inc., 458 Pa. 46, 329 A.2d 216 (1974) (popularity of radio personality).

(d) A statement that the product or service of plaintiff's competitor is the only one of its kind. Dale System, Inc. v. Time, Inc., 116 F. Supp. 527 (D. Conn. 1953); Quinby & Co. v. Funston, 13 Misc. 2d 134, 177 N.Y.S.2d 736 (Sup. Ct. 1958). Cf. Jarrahdale Timber Co. (Ltd.) v. Temperley and Co., (1894) 11 T.L.R. 119 (Q.B.D.) (only importer).

(e) Statements that aerosol products are damaging to the earth's ozone layer. Ruder & Finn Inc. v. Seaboard Surety Co., 52 N.Y.2d 663, 439 N.Y.S.2d 858, 422 N.E.2d 518 (1981).

(f) A statement that plaintiff's wife committed adultery on the premises where plaintiff's grocery and residence were located. Riding v. Smith, supra.

(g) A statement that a condom manufacturer which tells pharmacists it sells only to them also supplies various retail stores and vending machines. Youngs Drug Products Corp. v. Dean Rubber Manufacturing Co., 362 F.2d 129 (7th Cir. 1966).

(h) A statement that the proprietor of a service station and rooming house primarily patronized by truck drivers was giving Interstate Commerce Commission officials the names of truck drivers who violated I.C.C. rules on working hours. Connelly v. McKay, 176 Misc. 685, 28 N.Y.S.2d 327 (Sup. Ct. 1941). Cf. Rose v. Borenstein, 119 N.Y.S.2d 288 (N.Y. City Ct. 1953) (statements that person who worked in diamond industry informed French customs authorities of defendants' illegal possession of industrial diamonds).

(i) A telephone directory yellow pages advertisement for plaintiff, intended to read "Get it in gear" but proclaiming "Get it in rear." Southern Bell Telephone and Telegraph Co. v. Coastal Transmission Service, Inc., 167 Ga. App. 611, 307 S.E.2d 83 (1983).

5. Defendant falsely asserts that plaintiff is his wife, causing plaintiff's fiancé to back out of the proposed marriage. Is this injurious falsehood? See Shepherd v. Wakeman, (1662) 1 Keble 255, 269, 308, 326, 459, 83 Eng. Rep. 931, 939, 963, 974, 1052, 1 Lev. 53, 83 Eng. Rep. 293, 1 Sid. 79, 82 Eng. Rep. 982 (K.B.) (after many motions, plaintiff obtained judgment). What if an employer makes false statements to tax authorities regarding wages paid an employee, causing the employee to be subjected to governmental investigation and possible criminal prosecution? In Gale v. Ryan, 263 App. Div. 76, 31 N.Y.S.2d 732 (1941), it was held that the employee, alleging the statements to have been made intentionally and maliciously, stated a cause of action. Could an action be maintained if defendant falsely stated that a prison inmate is an informer, resulting in actual or threatened violence from other inmates? Cf. Burrascano v. Levi, 452 F. Supp. 1066 (D. Md. 1978), aff'd, 612 F.2d 1306 (4th Cir. 1979) (no defamation action).

Section 2. Passing Off (Unfair Competition)

"'Unfair competition' is the most comprehensive doctrine of trader's law, now covering practically every type of trade competition case. The term itself gives no hint of what is 'unfair' and is thus only a general label for the types of practices which have been held by the courts in specific cases to be 'unfair.' Hence it takes place alongside the other expansive tort doctrines—trespass, deceit, nuisance and negligence—as a concept under which tort law for the protection of traders can develop case by case through the litigation process without undue doctrinal embarrassment. Its virtue is that it focuses attention on the *facts* of the particular case, leaving judgment unfettered to be articulated by the refinement of doctrine appropriate to the facts.

"The types of cases labeled 'unfair' usually have specific doctrinal tags such as palming off, infringement of trade name, disparagement, filching of trade secrets and trade lists, plagiarism or lotteries. Many smack of deceit, fraud, libel, violation of statutes, while others involve nothing more than a simple appropriation of trade values. New cases which are not easily identified by some specific tag are indiscriminatingly lumped together as 'unfair competition.' Moreover, now that the Federal Trade Commission has specified nearly all condemned trade practices, the resort to any one of them by a competitor may be designated 'unfair competition.' In the area of advertising and the marketing of artistic and literary products and performances, and attendant services, hurtful practices have developed which do not readily fall under the general doctrine or any one of the more specific doctrines. Difficult to pinpoint doctrinally, these practices, too, are termed 'unfair competition.'

"Perhaps the most important and useful of the doctrines developed in this class of cases is based on *International News Serv. v. Associated Press*." Green, Protection of Trade Relations Under Tort Law, 47 Va. L. Rev. 559, 565–566 (1961).

Much of this area is addressed by the Restatement of Unfair Competition (1995), which draws on both common law and legislation.

A. Products

Fischer v. Blank

Supreme Court of New York
64 Hun 635, 19 N.Y.S. 65 (1892),
modified, 138 N.Y. 244, 33 N.E. 1040 (1893)

ANDREWS, J. This action is brought to restrain the defendant from an alleged infringement of plaintiffs' wrappers, labels, and packages used in the sale of tea, and of their alleged trade name of "Black Package Tea," and for an accounting of profits. The special term found that about February, 1888, the plaintiffs were dealers in teas, and, for the purpose of identifying their tea, adopted a black wrapper, upon which appeared a number of peculiar labels, and a certain style of package containing such tea; that at the same time they adopted as a designation of such tea the term "Black Package Tea;" that since the year 1888 their tea has been known and identified in the market as "Black Package Tea," and that there has existed a large and increasing demand for the same; that the plaintiffs' "Black Package Tea" was and is consumed chiefly by ignorant and illiterate people, and is to a large extent sold by retail dealers whose places of business are in cellars and dark stores, and where the exact appearance of the article was and is not likely to be readily observed; that plaintiffs' tea is of a superior quality, and of that particular kind known to Russians as "Russian Caravan Tea;" that, after plaintiffs placed their "Black Package Tea" upon the market, and a demand for the same had been created, the defendant made use of, to inclose tea not of plaintiffs' selection and importation, a black wrapper, with labels upon the same, and that such wrapper and labels are imitations of those of the plaintiffs, and are so nearly like those of the plaintiffs that there is danger of the defendant's wrapper being mistaken for that of the plaintiffs; that the packages containing the defendant's tea are of the same size and shape as those which contain the defendant's tea, and that the defendant's packages are so nearly like those of the plaintiffs that there is danger of the one being mistaken for the other; that the defendant's tea has been handed out and sold when plaintiffs' "Black Package Tea" has been asked for; that the defendant's packages of tea were by the defendant caused to be devised and arranged so as to resemble plaintiffs' packages, with the intent, and to the end, that defendant's tea might be sold in lieu of the plaintiffs'.

... The law is well settled that, where a defendant is endeavoring by such means to palm off his goods upon the public as the goods of another, a court of equity will restrain him. "A tradesman, to bring his privilege of using a particular mark under the protection of a court of equity, need not prove that it has been copied in every particular. It would be sufficient to show that the devices employed bear such a resemblance to his as to be calculated to mislead the public generally, who are purchasers of the article bearing the device, and make it pass with them for his article. Hence where, on ordinary observation, the labels used by two parties would not be apt to be distinguished the one from the other, the size, form, shape, vignette, coloring, and marking being so nearly identical as to make them easily pass for the same, and the only difference discernible on considerable scrutiny being in the name of the warrantor stamped upon them, in letters so small as not readily to attract attention, an injunction was granted.... [T]he fact that he puts his own name on the wrappers, etc., as the manufacturer of the article, will not prevent it from being an infringement on plaintiff's trade-mark.... Where a person, by a combination of elements and symbols, has produced a wrapper to inclose and designate an article manufactured by him, under which it has gone into use, he cannot be interfered with or despoiled of his lawful business by the adoption of a label by another similar in color, size, border, ornamentation, symbol, and colored ink, and so closely an imitation that the careless or unobservant purchaser may be readily misled. Such practices are deceptive, and have their origin in and promote dishonorable competition. In order to justify the intervention of a court of equity, it is sufficient that the imitation is so close that a crafty vendor may palm off on the buyer the article manufactured by the latter as that of the former. It is no answer to an application for an injunction that in certain particulars the label of the defendant differs from that of the plaintiff, so long as the imitation in other respects is so close that the general appearance is the same, and purchasers have been and are likely to be deceived." Cod. Trade-Marks [§§ 353, 378, 392, 497].... [T]he plaintiffs were entitled to the injunction and to the other relief granted by the special term.

... [Affirmed.]

Notes

1. The Court of Appeals modified the injunction to make it clear that defendant was not barred entirely from using the name "Black Package Tea," the same form of package as plaintiffs', or the same colors and labelling devices (disks and diamonds containing printed information). The name was "simply descriptive of the color of the package," and package form, color and labelling devices could not be appropriated to plaintiffs' exclusive use. "But when all, or a number of them, are combined in a single package, and so arranged and exhibited that when they strike the eye of the intending purchaser, possessed of ordinary intelligence and judgment, the false impression is likely to be produced that the goods of the plaintiffs are offered, it is the province of equity to interfere for the protection of the purchasing public, as well as of the plaintiffs, and for the suppression of unfair and dishonest competition. The true test, we think, is whether the resemblance is such that it is calculated to deceive, and does in fact deceive, the ordinary buyer, making his purchases under the ordinary conditions which prevail in the conduct of the particular traffic to which the controversy relates."

2. The principal concern of the common law has been the "passing off" of one's product, service or business as that of another. This may occur because of simulation of plaintiff's trademark or trade name. Such practices are often given the label "unfair competition." In modern cases, the emphasis is on the injury suffered by the complaining party and

(secondarily) the public from confusion caused by defendants' practices. See Annot., Actual Competition as Necessary Element of Trademark Infringement or Unfair Competition, 148 A.L.R. 12 (1944); Annot., Trade Dress Simulation of Cosmetic Products as Unfair Competition, 86 A.L.R.3d 505 (1978) ("trade dress" may be entitled to protection when it is distinctive, distinguishing source of product from other sources, and consumer identifies it with particular source). Compare the law pertaining to "dilution," pp. 294–299, infra, which emphasizes diminishment of the value of plaintiff's mark or name by defendant's use of it. Most complaints in the United States arising from marketing a product or service with a name, symbol, design, container, etc. that resembles plaintiff's now rely on federal and state trademark legislation, especially the Lanham Act, 15 U.S.C. §§ 1051 et seq. Common law claims, however, are not preempted, and they are frequently joined to claims of statutory liability.

3. The primary remedy for passing off is injunctive relief. As an equitable remedy, an injunction is available without proof of defendant's intent to cause deception or to harm plaintiff's business. The older view is that intent is necessary for liability to pay damages. See Restatement of Torts § 745 (1938). More modern authority allows recovery for damages or an accounting of profits without proof of defendant's wrongful intent. See Gillette U.K. Ltd. v. Edenwest Ltd., [1994] R.P.C. 279 (Ch. D.); Restatement of Unfair Competition § 4, comment *d* (1995); Prosser & Keeton, Law of Torts 1016 (5th ed. 1984).

4. In William Edge & Sons, Ltd. v. William Niccolls & Sons, Ltd., [1911] A.C. 693 (H.L.), plaintiffs had long sold laundry blue in a calico bag with a wooden stick attached to it. The bag bore no name. Defendants began selling laundry blue in a similar bag, with a similar stick, but with their own name on a label attached to the bag. Plaintiffs prevailed because retail purchasers identified products with this "get up" as the product made by plaintiffs. In Reckitt & Colman Products Ltd. v. Borden Inc., [1990] 1 W.L.R. 491 (H.L.), plaintiffs were the proprietors of Jif brand lemon juice. Jif was sold in the United Kingdom in plastic squeeze containers having the shape, size and color of natural lemons. For many years, Jif was the only lemon juice sold in a plastic container that looked like a lemon. Then Bordens began to sell its ReaLemon brand juice in a similar container. In litigation brought against Bordens, the trial judge found that a buyer of lemon juice who read the label attached to the Bordens product would know at once that the container did not contain Jif. But the judge also found that the ordinary shopper would not pay any attention to the label. Because consumers associated plastic lemons with Jif and would not read the label attached to ReaLemon, many people would purchase ReaLemon in the belief it was Jif. The judge awarded plaintiffs a permanent injunction. The House of Lords held that on the trial judge's findings passing off had been established and plaintiffs were entitled to the relief that had been granted. Note that the product confusion found in casual purchases may be absent when purchase is a more serious decision or the buyers are sophisticated (or have the guidance of sophisticated advisers). See McGregor-Doniger Inc. v. Drizzle Inc., 599 F.2d 1126 (2d Cir. 1979) (expensive coats; no confusion among requisite "appreciable number" of consumers); Hodgkinson & Corby Ltd. v. Wards Mobility Services Ltd., [1994] 1 W.L.R. 1564 (Ch. D.) (cushions for wheelchairs).

5. Consider the potential for liability in the sale of lower-priced "private label" products whose packaging and coloring resemble those of the leading brands. For example, drug stores and other retailers have sold medicinal mouthwash that is amber in color, like Listerine, and comes in a "bar-bell" shaped bottle, similar to the Listerine bottle. Listerine's manufacturer brought suit against one retail chain in Warner Lambert Co. v. McCrory's Corp., 718 F. Supp. 389 (D.N.J. 1989). The court thought that defendant sufficiently distinguished its product from plaintiff's to make consumer confusion of the

products unlikely. One point of distinction was the large price differential between the two products. Could defendant prevail on the ground that its use of the same color and bottle shape serves a legitimate informational function by indicating that its mouthwash is of the same type as plaintiff's? Cf. SK&F Co. v. Premo Pharmaceutical Laboratories, Inc., 625 F.2d 1055 (3d Cir. 1980) (imitation of drug capsule's color pattern by generic equivalent). In Tas-T-Nut Co. v. Variety Nut & Date Co., 245 F.2d 3 (6th Cir. 1957), defendant, a seller of packaged nuts, imitated a competitor's packaging and color combinations that indicated different varieties of nut meats. The court held that conspicuous placement of defendant's trade name on the packages did not preclude a remedy for sale of packages deceptively similar to plaintiff's. See Mills, Own Label Products and the "Lookalike" Phenomenon: A Lack of Trade Dress and Unfair Competition Protection?, 17 E.I.P.R. 116 (1995).

6. Can there be liability because features of plaintiff's advertising are copied or imitated? See Annots., Right to Protection Against Appropriation of Advertising Matter or Methods, 17 A.L.R. 760 (1922); 30 A.L.R. 615 (1924). In Cadbury-Schweppes Pty. Ltd. v. Pub Squash Co. Pty. Ltd., [1981] 1 W.L.R. 193 (P.C.), plaintiffs had begun to sell a new canned lemon drink. It was advertised extensively on radio and television. The next year, defendant launched a similar drink, using a name and advertising slogans allegedly based on the theme and slogans of plaintiffs' advertising. Claiming that this caused sales of plaintiffs' drink to decline, plaintiffs sought an injunction and damages. The court accepted that the tort of passing off was wide enough to encompass descriptive material such as slogans and visual images used in advertising. However, to prevail a plaintiff had to show that defendant misled the market into thinking that defendant's product was a product of the plaintiff. That had not been shown here. A number of cases hold that use of a deceptively similar advertising slogan may be enjoined if the slogan has acquired a "secondary meaning" — that is, become identified in the public mind with plaintiff as the source of the advertised goods or services. See Boston Shoe Shop v. McBroom Shoe Shop, 196 Ala. 262, 72 So. 102 (1916) ("We Fix Em Quick" and "We Fix Em Quicker"); Charles S. Cash, Inc. v. Steinbook, 220 App. Div. 569, 222 N.Y.S. 61 (Sup. Ct. 1927), aff'd, 247 N.Y. 531, 161 N.E. 170 (1928) ("Every good nut that grows" and "Every fine nut that grows"); Annot., Rights and Remedies With Respect to Another's Use of a Deceptively Similar Advertising Slogan, 2 A.L.R.3d 748 (1965). Cf. Telstra Corp. Ltd. v. Royal & Sun Alliance Insurance Ltd., (2003) 57 I.P.R. 453 (Fed. Ct. Aust.) (use of advertising character formerly used by plaintiff).

7. Is there liability if a book is given a title similar to that of an existing book on the same subject? See Oxford Book Co. v. College Entrance Book Co., 98 F.2d 688 (2d Cir. 1938) (*Visualized American History and Visualized Units in American History*); Litwin v. Maddox, 7 Misc. 2d 750, 164 N.Y.S.2d 489 (Sup. Ct. 1957) (adventure novel and book of garden-inspired poetry and prose, both entitled *The Green Kingdom*); McGraw-Hill Book Co., Inc. v. Random House, Inc., 32 Misc. 2d 704, 225 N.Y.S.2d 646 (Sup. Ct. 1962) (*PT 109: John F. Kennedy in World War II* and *John F. Kennedy and PT-109*); Lyle Stuart, Inc., v. Pinnacle Books, 171 U.S.P.Q. 444 (N.Y. Sup. Ct. 1971) (*The Sensual Male and The Sensuous Man*). Cf. Avon Periodicals, Inc. v. Ziff-Davis Publishing Co., 27 Misc. 2d 160, 113 N.Y.S.2d 737 (Sup. Ct. 1952), modified, 282 App. Div. 200, 122 N.Y.S.2d 92 (1953) (two series of comics entitled *Eerie*, with similar size, cover, format). What if the title of a radio or television program resembles the title of a program on a competing station? See Eirinberg v. CBS Inc., 521 F. Supp. 450 (N.D. Ill. 1981) (*Your Dollar's Worth and Your Dollars;* merely descriptive and no secondary meaning/identification with plaintiff shown); South Australian Telecasters Ltd. v. Southern Television Corp. Ltd., [1970] S.A.S.R. 207 (Sup. Ct.) (*New Faces* de-

scriptive of talent quest programs and confusion improbable). Could there be liability if the title of a film is the same as the title of a play which had a different plot and little success in its production? See Jackson v. Universal International Pictures, 36 Cal. 2d 116, 222 P.2d 433 (1950) (judgment for playright affirmed; title acquired secondary meaning because of publicity and attendance during play's short run). Plaintiff's title or trademark might be deliberately copied, but in such a manner that confusion among the public is unlikely. See Intermedia Media Films, Inc. v. Lucas Entertainment, Inc., 703 F. Supp. 2d 456 (S.D.N.Y. 2010) (Fellini film *La Dolce Vita* and pornographic *La Dolce Vita*); Jordache Enterprises, Inc. v. Hogg Wyld, Ltd., 828 F.2d 1482 (10th Cir. 1987) (action by manufacturer of Jordache blue jeans against sellers of "Lardashe" jeans for large women).

Havana Cigar and Tobacco Factories, Ltd. v. Oddenino
Court of Appeal
[1924] 1 Ch. 179

[Plaintiffs were manufacturers of Havana cigars. They had sold cigars under the "Corona" brand for many years. Cigars typically were sold under both a brand name and a size name, which indicated the size and shape of the cigar—e.g., "Corona Exceptionales." About thirty years before this case arose, plaintiffs introduced a new size of cigar, "Coronas." These became known as "Corona Coronas." Other manufacturers sold similar cigars under their own brand names and the "Corona" size name—e.g., "Partagas Coronas." Plaintiffs sought to restrict their competitors' use of the name "Corona" and filling of orders for "Coronas." They arranged for "four gentlemen" to dine at a London restaurant and ask the waiter for "some cigars—Coronas." In response to this "trap order," the waiter brought cigars which the gentlemen recognized as "Partagas Coronas." The cigars had no labels, but they were wrapped with a ribbon showing both brand and, much more prominently, size names. Plaintiffs sued the restaurant's proprietor for "passing off." They sought an injunction restraining the proprietor from offering or supplying cigars not of plaintiffs' manufacture in response to orders for "Corona" cigars or "by the use of any words consisting of or containing the word 'Corona' as a brand name." The trial court found that the words "Corona cigar" originally meant and to a majority of persons still meant only cigars of plaintiffs' manufacture. Thus, a majority of customers requesting a "Corona" would expect plaintiffs'. However, due to long usage of "Corona" as a size name attached to cigars by other companies, to many people the term referred only to the type of cigar, not the brand. These persons would expect only a cigar of the "Corona" size and shape in response to a request for a "Corona." The court granted an injunction restraining defendant from selling or supplying cigars not of plaintiffs' Corona brand in response to an order for "Coronas" or "a Corona," unless it was first clearly ascertained that the customer did not require cigars of the Corona brand. Defendant appealed.]

SARGANT L.J. We are not here concerned with the particular facts as to the supply by the defendant through his waiters of cigars on the occasion which was the starting point of this action. We have to deal with the general question clearly raised by the pleadings—namely, whether the defendant (and as a consequence other retailers in the like position) are entitled in response to a demand for Corona cigars to make a practice of supplying without more cigars which are not of the Corona brand but are of a size and shape known as Corona. Or, in other words, can he sell as "Coronas" cigars which are not of the Corona brand? ...

Russell J. has found that the majority of customers who ask for a Corona or a Corona cigar desire and intend to be furnished with a cigar of the Corona brand, and not merely with a cigar of Corona dimensions. It follows, therefore, that the practice contended for by the appellant would result in more than half of these customers receiving, without any explanation, an article different from that which they in fact required and intended to demand. Did every customer asking for a Corona cigar desire to receive a cigar of the Corona brand, it is clear that the defendant's practice would amount to a passing off of the clearest and most elementary kind in every case. Is a new complexion put on the matter in the case of the majority, who are in fact similarly deceived, because there are a minority of customers who obtain what they require?

The defendant asserts that all the difference is made by the ambiguity of the terms of the demand, and that, the request being ambiguous, he is entitled to determine the ambiguity in his own favour and supply a class of article which is either the only class in his stock or will yield him a larger profit than he would obtain from the supply of a cigar of the Corona brand. And he is supported in this contention by the rival makers of cigars not of that brand, who naturally desire the largest market for their wares. But to my mind this contention is contrary to the plain rules of ordinary morality. It cannot, in my judgment, be legitimate to adopt a practice which deliberately takes advantage of an ambiguity of language, and will in the result and to the knowledge of the vendor deceive a majority of his customers. Such a practice is not merely inconsistent with that higher standard of honour or ethics which would be adopted by a specially conscientious trader, but directly violates those ordinary everyday principles of honest trading which the Courts have consistently endeavoured to enforce. The fact that it may be impossible to predicate for certain of any particular customer that he is deceived is quite immaterial in view of the certainty that a majority of customers will in fact be so deceived, and that the resultant loss to them and to the owners of the Corona brand will be as great as if each victim had been definitely and separately ascertained.

It has however been strenuously contended on behalf of the appellant that these general considerations do not apply to a trade mark consisting of a word or words. It is asserted that in the case of a "word" mark the plaintiff cannot succeed unless he can establish that the word or words in question, when used in the market in which the transaction takes place, denote solely and exclusively the goods of the plaintiff and are inapplicable to the goods supplied by the defendant, or indeed apparently to any other goods than the plaintiff's. And this assertion is said to be supported by three cases of the highest authority....

... In the present case the plaintiffs have selected as their word-mark a word which is a foreign word and has no reference to the nature or quality of their goods. But in each of the three cases referred to the words forming the trade mark were words taken from the common stock of the English language, and were directly descriptive of the nature and characteristics of their goods. And, therefore, an extraordinarily heavy onus was cast on the plaintiffs to establish that, when the defendant's goods were described in terms which, according to the ordinary use of the English language, were as applicable to his goods as to the plaintiffs', these terms would not convey their ordinary descriptive meaning but would be understood as signifying simply and solely the plaintiffs' goods....

But beyond this I am not satisfied that, even in the case of trade marks consisting of descriptive words, these three cases establish that the plaintiff can never succeed unless he can show that the words are universally and exclusively used in the market with reference to his goods....

... [Mellish L.J. in *Ford v. Foster*, L.R. 7 Ch. 611, said] "[W]hat is the test by which a decision is to be arrived at whether a word which was originally a trade mark has become publici juris? I think the test must be, whether the use of it by other persons is still calculated to deceive the public, whether it may still have the effect of inducing the public to buy goods not made by the original owner of the trade mark as if they were his goods. If the mark has come to be so public and in such universal use that nobody can be deceived by the use of it, and can be induced from the use of it to believe that he is buying the goods of the original trader, it appears to me, however hard to some extent it may appear on the trader, yet practically, as the right to a trade mark is simply a right to prevent the trader from being cheated by other persons' goods being sold as his goods through the fraudulent use of the trade mark, the right to the trade mark must be gone." Or, in other words, where the originally exclusive denotation of an ordinary non-descriptive word-mark such as "Eureka" or "Corona" has been extended so as to include some goods which are not of the plaintiff's make, the onus is precisely the opposite of that which is contended for by the appellant here. It is for the defendant who is supplying or offering goods under the word-mark to show that it has entirely lost its original meaning and that no purchaser can be deceived by its use. How completely the defendant has failed to discharge his onus here is shown by the unquestioned findings of the learned judge.

In my opinion the judgment of Russell J. is perfectly right, and the plaintiffs are entitled to an injunction. For myself I should have preferred to grant an injunction in a wider and simpler form—namely, to prevent the defendant from selling or offering for sale under the name "Corona" cigars which are not of the plaintiffs' make. Such an injunction would not prevent the defendant in answer to a request for Coronas from supplying with proper explanation cigars of another brand. But as the plaintiffs are content with the more limited form of injunction that has been granted, and as this form prohibits the specific form of passing off which is insisted on by the defendant, and has been supported by the rival manufacturers, I agree that the order of this Court should be merely that the order appealed from should be slightly varied as suggested by Warrington L.J. [to add the words, "or unless it be made clear by word of mouth or otherwise that the cigar supplied [is] of a brand other than the plaintiffs' brand."]

[Pollock, M.R., and Warrington, L.J., delivered concurring opinions.]

Notes

1. In this litigation, the restaurant proprietor represented the interests of manufacturers of "Corona" cigars other than plaintiffs. They paid the restaurateur's costs. What is the effect of this case on those manufacturers? What if it were found that considerably less than a majority of cigar smokers expected to receive only a Corona brand cigar in response to a request for a "Corona"?

2. In Coca-Cola Co. v. Dorris, 311 F. Supp. 287 (E.D. Ark. 1970), defendant operated a restaurant which did not sell Coca-Cola. Signs to this effect were posted on the premises. Waitresses, attendants, etc. were instructed to inform customers that only defendant's own cola was served. Nevertheless, many customers ordered "Coke" and were served defendant's cola without being told that Coca-Cola was unavailable. The court required defendant to advise each customer who requested "Coke" that it was not available and provide an opportunity for acceptance or rejection of a substitute product. Was Coca-Cola entitled to this protection? Suppose a bar serves a mixture of rum and another cola in response to orders for "rum and Coke"? If there is a well-known nickname for a prod-

uct, can use of the nickname be limited? See Volkswagenwerk AG v. Hoffman, 489 F. Supp. 678 (D.S.C. 1980) (defendant's car repair business "The Bug House"). Cf. Volkswagenwerk Aktiengesellschaft v. The Bug Hospital, Inc., 208 U.S.P.Q. 887 (D. Mass. 1979), in which the Volkswagen Company, having registered the term "bug" as a service mark with the U.S. Patent Office, succeeded in enjoining its use by an auto repair business ("Bug Hospital") and a used car business ("Bug House").

3. Product trademarks often are used by members of the public to refer to products of the same general type. Examples include "Baggies" for plastic bags, "Jell-O" for gelatin desserts, "Kleenex" for facial tissues, "Q-tips" for cotton swabs, "Scotch tape" for cellophane tape, "Styrofoam" for plastic foam, "Vaseline" for petroleum jelly, "Dictaphone" for dictating equipment, and "Xerox machine" for photocopy machine. Manufacturers of such products strive to prevent "generic" use of the names, which could lead to a judicial determination that the name has become descriptive, no longer identifying the products of a single manufacturer. This was the fate of such brand names as Aspirin, Cellophane, Kerosene, Linoleum and Mimeograph, which now can freely be used in the United States. See Restatement of Unfair Competition § 15, comment *c* (1995); Kiesel, Protecting a Good Name is a Never-Ending Fight, 71 A.B.A.J. No. 3, 62 (1985).

4. Is a manufacturer legally responsible if its retail dealers palm off its products as those of another manufacturer? See Philadelphia Dairy Products, Inc. v. Quaker City Ice Cream Co., 306 Pa. 164, 159 A. 3 (1932) (manufacturer not enjoined from selling products to dealers even though dealers committing fraud upon customers). Cf. Cadbury Ltd. v. Ulmer GmbH, [1988] F.S.R. 385 (Ch. D.) (defendant's chocolate bar, which had same appearance as plaintiff's, inserted into ice cream by retailers who displayed plaintiff's advertising). Compare William R. Warner & Co. v. Eli Lilly & Co., 265 U.S. 526 (1924) (defendant's agents promoted sales to retailers by suggesting substitution of defendant's preparation for plaintiff's more expensive product); Ciba-Geigy Corp. v. Bolar Pharmaceutical Co., Inc., 747 F.2d 844 (3d Cir. 1984) (imitation of appearance of plaintiff's prescription drug facilitated substitution of defendant's product by pharmacists).

5. One who purchases a product generally has the right to advertise its use or availability for sale. The product's brand name can be used in the advertising. See Sweezy v. McBrair, 89 Hun 155, 35 N.Y.S. 11 (Sup. Ct. 1895), aff'd, 157 N.Y. 710, 53 N.E. 1132 (1899) (dentist not liable for advertising his use of plaintiff's anesthetic for extraction of teeth); Winchester Repeating Arms Co. v. Butler Bros., 128 F. 976 (N.D. Ill. 1904) (mail order business permitted to advertise sale of plaintiff's rifles even when not held in stock); Dodge Bros. v. East, 8 F.2d 872 (E.D.N.Y. 1925) (business specializing in sale of second-hand Dodge cars and repair of Dodges permitted to use name Dodge; not permitted to use distinct typography used by Dodge in its advertising of new cars or term "Dodge Dealer" as this deceived public into believing that defendant had business association with Dodge); Ty Inc. v. Perryman, 306 F.3d 509 (7th Cir. 2002), cert. denied, 538 U.S. 971 (2003) (www.bargainbeanies.com could be used for web site of seller of second-hand "Beanie Babies," which plaintiff manufactured and sold new). The product's producer might have an action if the product when sold by defendant was not in the same condition as when sold by plaintiff and there is an element of "passing off." See Champion Spark Plug Co. v. Sanders, 331 U.S. 125 (1947) (defendants reconditioned plaintiff's spark plugs, which displayed manufacturer's trademark; court required that word "used" or "repaired" be distinctly stamped on each plug and that containers and advertising state that defendants reconditioned plugs); Morris Motors Ltd. v. Lilley, [1959] 1 W.L.R. 1184 (Ch. D.) (defendant enjoined from advertis-

ing as new car that had been sold by plaintiff's authorized dealer and resold to defendant); Adolph Coors Co. v. A. Genderson & Sons, Inc., 486 F. Supp. 131 (D. Colo. 1980) (defendant enjoined from unauthorized distribution of plaintiff's beer; beer distributed by defendant deteriorated because brewer's quality control procedures not adhered to); Wilts United Dairies, Ltd. v. Thomas Robinson Sons & Co., Ltd., [1958] R.P.C. 94 (C.A.) (plaintiffs limited time between canning of its condensed milk and retail sale to six months; wholesalers liable for selling cans without disclosure that they were much older).

6. In Gilliam v. American Broadcasting Companies, Inc., 538 F.2d 14 (2d Cir. 1976), plaintiffs were the writers and performers of the British Broadcasting Corporation television program *Monty Python's Flying Circus*. They retained common law copyright in their scripts and, by agreement with the BBC, retained considerable control. Only minor changes could be made without consultation. An American television network, ABC, acquired a license from the BBC to broadcast some of the *Monty Python* programs. Without consulting plaintiffs, ABC substantially edited the programs. The network claimed the changes were necessary because the programs in their original form were obscene under U.S. law. It was decided that ABC could not, without infringing plaintiffs' rights, broadcast a *Monty Python* program in altered form.

7. When a company sells a product in different countries under the same brand but with some difference in product composition or warranties, can importing the product from one country to another result in liability? See Dial Corp. v. Manghnani Investment Corp., 659 F. Supp. 1230 (D. Conn. 1987) (company selling Dial Soap of American manufacture granted relief against importation of Dial Soap made in Cyprus under license from plaintiff); Consumers Distributing Co. Ltd. v. Seiko Time Canada Ltd., [1984] 1 S.C.R. 583, (1984) 10 D.L.R.4th 161 (advertising and sale of imported Seiko watches without warranty and after-sale service of authorized dealers not passing off). Cf. Societe Des Produits Nestle, S.A. v. Casa Helvetia, Inc., 982 F.2d 633 (1st Cir. 1992) (defendant commenced import of Venezuelan-made Perugina chocolates into Puerto Rico, where plaintiff's distributor had long sold Perugina chocolates manufactured in Italy).

Kellogg Company v. National Biscuit Company

Supreme Court of the United States
305 U.S. 111 (1938)

Mr. Justice BRANDEIS delivered the opinion of the Court.

This suit was brought ... by National Biscuit Company against Kellogg Company to enjoin alleged unfair competition by the manufacture and sale of the breakfast food commonly known as shredded wheat. The competition was alleged to be unfair mainly because Kellogg Company uses, like the plaintiff, the name shredded wheat and, like the plaintiff, produces its biscuit in pillow-shaped form.

Shredded wheat is a product composed of whole wheat which has been boiled, partially dried, then drawn or pressed out into thin shreds and baked. The shredded wheat biscuit generally known is pillow-shaped in form. It was introduced in 1893 by Henry D. Perky....

In 1935, the District Court dismissed the bill. It found that the name "Shredded Wheat" is a term describing alike the product of the plaintiff and of the defendant; and that no passing off or deception had been shown. It held that upon the expiration of the Perky patent ... the name of the patented article passed into the public domain.... [The Circuit Court of Appeals directed that Kellogg Company be enjoined: "(1) from the use of the name 'Shredded Wheat' as its trade name, (2) from advertising or offering for sale its product in the form and shape of plaintiff's biscuit, and (3) from doing either."]

First. The plaintiff has no exclusive right to the use of the term "Shredded Wheat" as a trade name. For that is the generic term of the article, which describes it with a fair degree of accuracy; and is the term by which the biscuit in pillow-shaped form is generally known by the public. Since the term is generic, the original maker of the product acquired no exclusive right to use it. As Kellogg Company had the right to make the article, it had, also, the right to use the term by which the public knows it ...

Moreover, the name "Shredded Wheat", as well as the product, the process and the machinery employed in making it, has been dedicated to the public. The basic patent for the product and for the process of making it, and many other patents for special machinery to be used in making the article, issued to Perky. In those patents the term "shredded" is repeatedly used as descriptive of the product. The basic patent expired October 15, 1912; the others soon after. Since during the life of the patents "Shredded Wheat" was the general designation of the patented product, there passed to the public upon the expiration of the patent, not only the right to make the article as it was made during the patent period, but also the right to apply thereto the name by which it had become known. As was said in Singer Mfg. Co. v. June Mfg. Co., 163 U.S. 169, 185: " ... To say otherwise would be to hold that, although the public had acquired the device covered by the patent, yet the owner of the patent or the manufacturer of the patented thing had retained the designated name which was essentially necessary to vest the public with the full enjoyment of that which had become theirs by the disappearance of the monopoly."

It is contended that the plaintiff has the exclusive right to the name "Shredded Wheat", because those words acquired the "secondary meaning" of shredded wheat made at Niagara Falls by the plaintiff's predecessor. There is no basis here for applying the doctrine of secondary meaning. The evidence shows only that due to the long period in which the plaintiff or its predecessor was the only manufacturer of the product, many people have come to associate the product, and as a consequence the name by which the product is generally known, with the plaintiff's factory at Niagara Falls. But to establish a trade name in the term "shredded wheat" the plaintiff must show more than a subordinate meaning which applies to it. It must show that the primary significance of the term in the minds of the consuming public is not the product but the producer. This it has not done. The showing which it has made does not entitle it to the exclusive use of the term shredded wheat but merely entitles it to require that the defendant use reasonable care to inform the public of the source of its product....

Second. The plaintiff has not the exclusive right to sell shredded wheat in the form of a pillow-shaped biscuit—the form in which the article became known to the public. That is the form in which shredded wheat was made under the basic patent. The patented machines used were designed to produce only the pillow-shaped biscuits. And a design patent was taken out to cover the pillow-shaped form. Hence, upon expiration of the patents the form, as well as the name, was dedicated to the public....

Where an article may be manufactured by all, a particular manufacturer can no more assert exclusive rights in a form in which the public has become accustomed to see the article and which, in the minds of the public, is primarily associated with the article rather

THE START OF A PERFECT DAY

Thanks to Mother

There goes Father, ready to plough through his morning's work, feeling like a million dollars. There go the children, red cheeked, full of health and energy, happy, carefree — their minds and bodies alert to get everything school has to offer in education and fun too!

Who is responsible for this happy family on its way to do things?

Just Mother.

Mother who knew that the *right breakfast* was half the battle!

Mother who took the trouble to find out what would give them the most nourishment, what would be easiest for them to digest, what would build their bodies and give them energy and health to meet the day's work.

So Mother started the day right for them with delicious, crisp, nut-brown Shredded Wheat and milk, with fruit on the side, and everybody's happy.

So easy and so *right!* Why not try it tomorrow morning?

A Product of NATIONAL BISCUIT COMPANY

"Uneeda Bakers"

Please be sure to get this package with the picture of Niagara Falls and the N. B. C. Uneeda Seal

Good for you because

1. **SHREDDED WHEAT** brings you all the *healthful qualities* of whole wheat: bran to keep you regular and aid your digestion; mineral salts to build bone; proteins to build tissue; Vitamin B for growth and resistance to disease; carbohydrates for energy.

2. **SHREDDED WHEAT** is *so nourishing* that *one* Shredded Wheat Biscuit gives you the same amount of nourishment as you get in a bowl of home-cooked hot cereal (8 rounded tablespoonfuls).

3. **SHREDDED WHEAT** is *easy to digest*—never lies heavy on your stomach. The shape of its fibers lets the digestive juices do their work in the shortest possible time. Every Shredded Wheat Biscuit has been double cooked, boiled and baked.

4. **SHREDDED WHEAT** *tastes good!* It keeps its chewy crispness no matter how much you drench it with milk or cream. It mixes with things. Grand with fruit. Delicious under poached egg. Many eat it hot instead of toast, with butter. You never get tired of it.

5. **SHREDDED WHEAT** *saves trouble* and it *saves money.* Comes in handy, attractive biscuit form ready to serve.

Eat **SHREDDED WHEAT** *for breakfast*

IT KEEPS YOU GOING TILL LUNCH

PICTORIAL REVIEW August 1934   *Refuse substitutes; buy the advertised brand every time!*

3

ADVERTISEMENT FOR SHREDDED WHEAT (1934)

than a particular producer, than it can in the case of a name with similar connections in the public mind. Kellogg Company was free to use the pillow-shaped form, subject only to the obligation to identify its product lest it be mistaken for that of the plaintiff.

Third. The question remains whether Kellogg Company in exercising its right to use the name "Shredded Wheat" and the pillow-shaped biscuit, is doing so fairly. Fairness requires that it be done in a manner which reasonably distinguishes its product from that of plaintiff.

Each company sells its biscuits only in cartons. The standard Kellogg carton contains fifteen biscuits; the plaintiff's twelve. The Kellogg cartons are distinctive. They do not resemble those used by the plaintiff either in size, form, or color. And the difference in the labels is striking. The Kellogg cartons bear in bold script the names "Kellogg's Whole Wheat Biscuit" or "Kellogg's Shredded Whole Wheat Biscuit" so sized and spaced as to strike the eye as being a Kellogg product. It is true that on some of its cartons it had a picture of two shredded wheat biscuits in a bowl of milk which was quite similar to one of the plaintiff's registered trade-marks. But the name Kellogg was so prominent on all of the defendant's cartons as to minimize the possibility of confusion.

Some hotels, restaurants, and lunchrooms serve biscuits, not in cartons, and guests so served may conceivably suppose that a Kellogg biscuit served is one of the plaintiff's make. But no person familiar with plaintiff's product would be misled. The Kellogg biscuit is about two-thirds the size of plaintiff's; and differs from it in appearance. Moreover, the field in which deception could be practiced is negligibly small. Only 2½ per cent of the Kellogg biscuits are sold to hotels, restaurants and lunchrooms. Of those so sold 98 per cent are sold in individual cartons containing two biscuits. These cartons are distinctive and bear prominently the Kellogg name. To put upon the individual biscuit some mark which would identify it as the Kellogg product is not commercially possible. Relatively few biscuits will be removed from the individual cartons before they reach the consumer. The obligation resting upon Kellogg Company is not to insure that every purchaser will know it to be the maker but to use every reasonable means to prevent confusion.

It is urged that all possibility of deception or confusion would be removed if Kellogg Company should refrain from using the name "Shredded Wheat" and adopt some form other than the pillow-shape. But the name and form are integral parts of the goodwill of the article. To share fully in the goodwill, it must use the name and the pillow-shape. And in the goodwill Kellogg Company is as free to share as the plaintiff. Moreover, the pillow-shape must be used for another reason. The evidence is persuasive that this form is functional—that the cost of the biscuit would be increased and its high quality lessened if some other form were substituted for the pillow-shape.

Kellogg Company is undoubtedly sharing in the goodwill of the article known as "Shredded Wheat"; and thus is sharing in a market which was created by the skill and judgment of plaintiff's predecessor and has been widely extended by vast expenditures in advertising persistently made. But that is not unfair. Sharing in the goodwill of an article unprotected by patent or trade-mark is the exercise of a right possessed by all—and in the free exercise of which the consuming public is deeply interested. There is no evidence of passing off or deception on the part of the Kellogg Company; and it has taken every reasonable precaution to prevent confusion or the practice of deception in the sale of its product.

Fourth. By its "clarifying" decree, the Circuit Court of Appeals enjoined Kellogg Company from using the picture of the two shredded wheat biscuits in the bowl only in connection with an injunction against manufacturing the pillow-shaped biscuits and the use of the term shredded wheat, on the grounds of unfair competition. The use of this picture was not enjoined on the independent ground of trade-mark infringement. Since the National Biscuit Company did not petition for certiorari, the question whether use of the picture is a violation of that trade-mark although Kellogg Company is free to use the name and the pillow-shaped biscuit is not here for review.

Decrees reversed with direction to dismiss the bill.

Mr. Justice McREYNOLDS and Mr. Justice BUTLER are of opinion that the decree of the Circuit Court of Appeals is correct and should be affirmed. To them it seems sufficiently clear that the Kellogg Company is fraudulently seeking to appropriate to itself the benefits of a goodwill built up at great cost by the respondent and its predecessors.

Notes

1. Whether a trade dress or name or term is entitled to protection against imitation is often put in terms of whether it has acquired "secondary meaning," i.e. come to represent a particular product or producer in the mind of the public. See Annot., Doctrine of Secondary Meaning in the Law of Trademarks and of Unfair Competition, 150 A.L.R. 1067 (1944); Schechter & Thomas, Intellectual Property 587–589 (2003). What evidence is relevant to this question? One list of factors to be considered includes the period of time plaintiff's product has been on the market, the volume of sales, the nature and extent of advertising, and efforts to promote a conscious connection in the public mind between the product and its source. Squeezit Corp. v. Plastic Dispensers, Inc., 31 N.J. Super, 217, 106 A.2d 322 (App. Div. 1954) (secondary meaning not found in plastic tomato-shaped catsup and mustard dispensers, colored red or yellow with green leaves and stems on top). Association or identification of a term with plaintiff or plaintiff's product is not secondary meaning unless the term is understood to signify one entity's product or business. See Gordon v. Warner Bros. Pictures, Inc., 269 Cal. App. 2d 31, 74 Cal. Rptr. 499 (1969) (defendants produced film entitled *The FBI Story;* plaintiffs had written novel with same title). In accord with the principal case is Canadian Shredded Wheat Co. Ltd. v. Kellogg Co. of Canada Ltd., [1936] O.R. 281, [1936] 2 D.L.R. 492 (High Ct.), aff'd, [1936] O.R. 613, [1936] 4 D.L.R. 760 (C.A.), aff'd, [1938] 1 All E.R. 618 (P.C.), in which it was held that neither the words "shredded wheat" nor the pillow shape of the biscuit had acquired a secondary meaning entitled to protection against use by others. The Privy Council commented that once it was established that the name of the product—shredded wheat—was also descriptive of it, the action for passing off by use of these words must fail.

2. Whether a term is descriptive and whether a term or trade dress has a secondary meaning is determined by its meaning to prospective purchasers. In Blisscraft of Hollywood v. United Plastics Co., 294 F.2d 694 (2d Cir. 1961), plaintiff sold pitchers made of polyethylene as "Poly Pitchers." Persons in the trade understood "poly" to mean polyethylene, but to the retail public it was a name for plaintiff's product rather than descriptive. Defendant was held liable for selling its own pitchers with a "Poly Pitcher" label. In Bayer Co. v. United Drug Co., 272 F. 505 (S.D.N.Y. 1921), on a finding that "Aspirin" meant a type of product to the general public but the product of a specific manufacturer to physicians and druggists, defendant was enjoined from using the term in sales to the latter groups but not on packages for retail sale. If a medical product is available only on a doctor's prescription, does the possibility that the patient may be confused about the product's source have any bearing on liability? See Ciba-Geigy Canada Ltd. v. Apotex Inc., [1992] 3 S.C.R. 120, (1992) 95 D.L.R.4th 385. When the term or trade dress used by the plaintiff is so distinctive that use of a similar term or trade dress by defendant is likely to mislead potential customers, plaintiff may not be required to prove a secondary meaning. See Perfect Fit Industries, Inc. v. Acme Quilting Co., Inc., 618 F.2d 950 (2d Cir. 1980).

3. In litigation between rival sellers of "cheese head" hats in Wisconsin, plaintiff claimed that defendants were liable on the basis of "unfair competition." The court concluded that because the configuration (shape) of the hat was the essence of the product and why it was valued by consumers, plaintiff's hat was protected from sale of defendants' similar hat only if its configuration had acquired secondary meaning. It had to be shown that "a product feature's primary significance to consumers is as an identifier of source as op-

posed to an element which contributes to the inherent appeal of the product." This had not been shown, so defendants were not liable. Foamation, Inc. v. Wedeward Enterprises, Inc., 970 F. Supp. 676 (E.D. Wis. 1997).

4. Can the color of a product acquire legally protected secondary meaning? See Norwich Pharmacal Co. v. Sterling Drug, Inc. 271 F.2d 569 (2d Cir. 1959), where plaintiff unsuccessfully sought an injunction against a competitor's copying the pink color of plaintiff's remedy for upset stomachs. The court recognized the possibility of injunctive relief if secondary meaning were shown, but stated that a color cannot ordinarily become anyone's exclusive property. Proof of deliberate copying did not shift the burden of proof to defendant. Cf. Qualitex Co. v. Jacobson Products Co., Inc., 514 U.S. 159 (1995); Christian Louboutin S.A. v. Yves Saint Laurent America Holding, Inc., 696 F.3d 206 (2d Cir. 2012) (color may sometimes qualify as trademark if it identifies source of goods without serving utilitarian or aesthetic functions). Is the distinctive sound produced by a musical group protected against imitation? See Shaw v. Time-Life Records, 38 N.Y.2d 201, 379 N.Y.S.2d 390, 341 N.E.2d 817 (1975) (no property rights in band's "sound"; if musical arrangements of bandleader in public domain, another person could copy them, provided recordings not palmed off as bandleader's own).

5. The American law of unfair competition was much affected by Sears, Roebuck & Co. v. Stiffel Co., 376 U.S. 225 (1964), and Compco Corp. v. Day-Brite Lighting, Inc., 376 U.S. 234 (1964). Sears involved "pole lamps," which were a great commercial success. Soon after Stiffel put its pole lamps on the market, Sears brought out a nearly identical lamp, which it sold more cheaply. There was evidence that identifying tags were not attached to the Sears lamps, although labels appeared on the cartons in which they were delivered to customers; that customers had asked Stiffel whether its lamps differed from those sold by Sears; and that a few customers who had bought Stiffel lamps complained to Stiffel that Sears was selling the same kind of lamp at a much lower price. The district court found a likelihood of confusion between the two lamps—it had, in fact, occurred. It enjoined Sears from selling lamps "identical to or confusingly similar to" Stiffel's. The Supreme Court reversed, holding that when an article is not patentable under federal law, state law cannot prohibit the copying of the article or award damages for copying. Unpatented articles were in the public domain and could be freely copied. The court reasoned that if a state could use its law of unfair competition to forbid copying, this would result in perpetual protection for articles too lacking in novelty to merit a patent, which could be granted only for a limited period of time. States could require labelling and other precautions and could protect trademarks and distinctive package dress, in order to prevent deception as to the source of the goods. But the inability of the public to "tell two identical articles apart" did not permit an injunction against copying or damages for it.

6. These points were reiterated in Compco, whose facts were similar to those of Sears. The court specified that neither the fact that the article's configuration has a secondary meaning identifying its maker nor the fact that the copied design is "nonfunctional" could provide a valid basis for liability under state law for the acts of copying and selling the copied article. Bonito Boats, Inc v. Thunder Craft Boats, Inc., 489 U.S. 141 (1989), which is discussed in more detail at p. 355, infra, reinforced the Sears-Compco holding on the application of state law to copying of unpatented articles. At the same time, it made clear that states could grant protections, including "regulations on the circumstances in which ... designs are used" as well as protection of trademarks and distinctive package dress, in order to prevent consumer confusion about the source of articles in the marketplace.

B. Business Names

Zimmerman v. B. & C. Motel Corporation

Supreme Court of Pennsylvania
401 Pa. 278, 163 A.2d 884 (1960)

BOK, Justice.

[Plaintiff Zimmerman owned and operated two large motels, each located at a Pennsylvania Turnpike exit near Harrisburg. Both had undergone name changes, but all designations contained the word "Holiday." Plaintiff was the first in the state to use that word for a motel. His motels were now known as "Holiday West" and "Holiday East." West was opened in 1953, East in 1957. In 1958, defendant opened "Holiday Inn," a motel located near a Pennsylvania Turnpike Extension exit in the Allentown area, about eighty miles from Harrisburg. Two years earlier, defendant had signed a license agreement with Holiday Inns of America, Inc., a corporation then operating motels in Memphis but intending to establish a national chain. Plaintiff and defendant both catered to persons travelling by car. Plaintiff maintained road signs, along the Pennsylvania Turnpike and other highways, within a fifty mile radius of his motels. He also advertised extensively in trade publications. Defendant maintained billboards on the Turnpike Extension, but not near plaintiff's locations. Plaintiff sought to enjoin defendant's use of the name "Holiday Inn." The trial court dismissed the complaint.]

The complaint being one of unfair competition, the question is whether the parties are competing in the same market, and, if they are, whether plaintiff has a position that he can defend against invaders.

There come to mind at once the many National, Grand, Palace, Congress, Station, Railroad, Ambassador, and Mayflower Hotels that dot the nation, and it is likely that the public does not confuse them because the effective distinction is one of locality. The same hospitality is not necessarily expected in the Congress Hotel in Portland, Maine, as in the Congress Hotel in St. Louis, Missouri. The plaintiff suggests that it is different with modern turnpikes and long-distance driving, and founds his case on long-haul competition only: to the traveler from Arizona to Maine, he mentions as example, the distance between Harrisburg and Allentown is negligible and the competition for his patronage real. Plaintiff does not suggest the presence of local competition as the basis for relief.

We agree with the plaintiff that proof of fraudulent intent in the defendant is not essential nor is proof of financial loss or damaged reputation, or proof of actual deception, tendency to deceive being enough in a proper case.

Here our agreement with the plaintiff ceases.

We are not dealing with a trade mark or a trade name, like Kool-Vent (Kool Vent Metal Awning Corp of America v. Price, 1951, 368 Pa. 528, 84 A.2d 296) ... where we must determine whether there is sufficient similarity in the competing sign to amount to unfairness. Here we have a straight English word, holiday, and to decide whether its repetition by a competitor is unfair we must apply a different rule.

There is no question of what this rule is. It is set forth in the Kool Vent case: "Descriptive, geographical and generic words, as well as words of common or general usage belong to the public and are not capable of exclusive appropriation by anyone. This general principle is subject to the limitation or exception that if a trade-name or trade-mark or other word or words have acquired, in the trade and in the minds of the purchasing public, a special or so-called secondary meaning, i.e., have come to mean that the article is the product of a certain manufacturer or of a particular individual or corporation, such trade-name or trade-mark or word or words will be protected against infringement...."

It is obvious that a secondary meaning cannot appear unless there is evidence of it, and there is none before us except a charge of $5.00 sent once by a utility company to plaintiff by mistake. As the court below indicated, one swallow does not make a summer. Since plaintiff began suit five years after opening Holiday West, it is interesting to note that in Quaker State Oil Refining Co. v. Steinberg, 1937, 325 Pa. 273, 189 A. 473, 476, five years of marketing and national advertising was held not enough to associate the plaintiff's name with his product....

We reject plaintiff's contention that he can pre-empt the word "Holiday" in Pennsylvania against all comers or that he can use it and expect protection from the courts because he might in future be harmed through use of it by someone else. Only evidence of a secondary meaning could aid him. To credit his argument, anyone could corner common English words simply by using them, and that has never been the law. The words do not confer meaning on the enterprise: the enterprise must confer meaning on the words.

Beyond this, we agree with the court below that the parties are not operating in the same market. The motels in question are too far apart for realistic competition, and we note that the letters and telegrams offered by the plaintiff as addressed to him are all but one addressed to "Holiday Inn", which rather puts him unfairly in competition with defendant if the evidence is to be credited at all. As for the mythical motorist from Arizona, he can be reduced to absurdity by starting him from Alaska and asserting that all Holiday motels on the Eastern seaboard are in competition for him....

We approve the lower court's leaving the case without prejudice, in case the parties extend their facilities in this rapidly expanding industry.

[Affirmed. Bell, J., dissented.]

Notes

1. In Niger Chemists Ltd. v. Nigeria Chemists, [1961] All Nigeria L.R. 171 (High Ct.), plaintiff had carried on business for some years under the name "Niger Chemists," with branches in several towns of Eastern Nigeria. Defendant established a firm carrying on exactly the same business under the name "Nigeria Chemists," located on the same street as one of plaintiff's shops. Plaintiff sought to prevent use of this name. In granting this relief, the court held (1) plaintiff need not show intent to deceive or actual deception but only that the name used by defendant was so similar as to be likely to cause confusion in the mind of the public; (2) defendant could not be restrained from using ordinary English words which were simply descriptive of his trade or of the articles he sold, but could be restrained from using a confusion-creating term descriptive of defendant; and (3) use of the official and geographical name of the country could be restrained when this would likely cause confusion. Plaintiff's managing director said he continually received bills, receipts, etc. intended for defendant. A literate person might well mistake one of these firms for the other, the court concluded. Certainly illiterates, as many of the potential customers were, could make such a mistake. Would the names "Coalgate Abstract Company" and "Coal County Abstract Company" cause confusion in an American town? See Coalgate Abstract Co. v. Coal County Abstract Co., 180 Okla. 8, 67 P.2d 37 (1937). Would

adoption of the name "University Orthopedics" for an entity providing orthopedic and sports medicine services lead the public to believe that it is affiliated with a university that is located in the same town and has a unit that also provides orthopedic and sports medicine services? See Pennsylvania State University v. University Orthopedics, Ltd., 706 A.2d 863 (Pa. Super. Ct. 1998).

2. Courts distinguish between terms that are "arbitrary" or "fanciful" and terms that are "generic" or "descriptive." Specific proof of "secondary meaning" is required for the latter. A geographic term is "descriptive" if it indicates the business' location or trade area or the origin of its products. See Manor of Burlingame, Inc. v. SHCC, Inc., 22 Kan. App. 2d 437, 916 P.2d 733 (1996) ("Santa Fe Trail"; considered arbitrary); Pennsylvania State University v. University Orthopedics, Ltd., supra ("University"; considered generic); Restatement of Unfair Competition § 14 (1995). Widely used arbitrary names may lack the particular association with plaintiff's business in the public mind needed for liability. See Annots., Protection of Business or Trading Corporation Against Use of Same or Similar Name by Another Corporation, 66 A.L.R. 948 (1930); 115 A.L.R. 1241 (1938) (listing examples including "federal," "fidelity," "metalcraft" and "united").

3. How widespread must the confusion be among the public or potential customers? See President and Trustees of Colby College v. Colby College-New Hampshire, 508 F.2d 804 (1st Cir. 1975) (sufficient "secondary meaning" when "significant quantity of the consuming public" understands name to refer exclusively to party); Neutrogena Corp. v. Golden Ltd., [1996] R.P.C. 473 (C.A.) (deception of "substantial number" of customers or potential customers of plaintiff). Should relief be granted if the names of the parties are very similar but potential customers are too sophisticated to be confused about the parties' identity, or the nature of the transactions in the particular business makes confusion unlikely? See Powder River Oil Co. v. Powder River Petroleum Corp., 830 P.2d 403 (Wyo. 1992), in which the potential for confusion among suppliers, service companies and others who might do business with the parties was considered a basis of liability. Sufficient, also, was confusion in the initial stages of discussing a transaction, creating interest in doing business with defendant when otherwise there would be none ("initial interest confusion").

4. When a term used in a business name merely indicates the type of merchandise sold or service provided, that term ordinarily cannot be exclusively appropriated by the first user. See Choynski v. Cohen, 39 Cal. 501 (1870) (plaintiff operated "Antiquarian Book Store"; defendant opened "Antiquarian Book and Variety Store" in same city); Restatement of Unfair Competition § 15 (1995). Can a business that specializes in the sale or repair of a brand-name product include the brand in the business' name or advertising without incurring liability to the proprietor of the brand? See Dodge Bros. v. East, p. 271, supra; Volkswagenwerk Aktiengesellschaft v. Church, 411 F.2d 350 (9th Cir. 1969) (permissible to advertise as "Independent Volkswagen Porsche Service"; defendant's business adequately distinguished from Volkswagen's franchised dealers and repairers); Volkswagenwerk Aktiengesellschaft v. The Bug Hospital, Inc., p. 271, supra.

5. Some cases involve simulation of the physical appearance of a business or particular physical features. Relief has been available upon a showing of likelihood of confusion. In Yellow Cab Co. v. Creasman, 185 N.C. 551, 117 S.E. 787 (1923), in which a successful taxicab business used vehicles of a particular color and design, a rival was enjoined from using similar vehicles in order to mislead the public. Cf. Fuddruckers, Inc. v. Doc's B.R. Others, Inc., 826 F.2d 837 (9th Cir. 1987) (restaurants' similar designs and service features); Fotomat Corp. v. Cochran, 437 F. Supp. 1231 (D. Kan. 1977) (similar small buildings for drive-through photo processing). See Annots., Right to Protection Against Simulation of Physical Appearance or Arrangement of Place of Business, or Vehicle, 17 A.L.R. 784

(1922); 28 A.L.R. 114 (1924); Annot., Unfair Competition by Imitation in Sign or Design of Business Place, 86 A.L.R.3d 884 (1978) (noting that many cases require sign or design to have acquired secondary meaning signifying particular business before it can be protected against imitation).

6. If plaintiff's advertising features the telephone number of plaintiff's business, is there a cause of action against a competitor that advertises or uses a similar number? What if the number consists of a word identifying the parties' trade? In Dial-a-Mattress Franchise Corp. v. Page, 880 F.2d 675 (2d Cir. 1989), a retail mattress dealer had the local exchange number that spelled "MATTRES(S)" and used the slogan "Dial-a-Mattress." Defendant acquired and promoted the number "1-800-MATTRESS." The court affirmed an order prohibiting the connection of calls to this 800 number from plaintiff's metropolitan area. In Dranoff-Perlstein Associates v. Sklar, 967 F.2d 852 (3d Cir. 1992), where the parties were personal injury attorneys advertising the local numbers "INJURY-1" and "INJURY-9," the court was of the opinion that a number descriptive of the service or product offered should be considered "generic" and not protected from use by another. Accordingly, it refused to follow *Dial-a-Mattress*. However, the court allowed plaintiff an opportunity to obtain relief by showing that confusion between the suffixes 1 and 9 was likely.

Saskatoon Star Phoenix Group Inc. v. Noton

Saskatchewan Court of Queen's Bench
(2001) 206 Sask. R. 106, [2001] 9 W.W.R. 63

LAING J:

The plaintiff requests an assessment of damages and an order for permanent injunctive relief with respect to its claim of "passing off"....

The plaintiff carries on the business of publishing The StarPhoenix, a Saskatoon daily newspaper. The newspaper is the largest daily in Saskatchewan and is widely distributed throughout the province. The name StarPhoenix has been associated with the paper for decades.

The plaintiff maintains an internet website with the domain name and address "www.thestarphoenix.com". The main page of the website contains the current day's lead news stories from The StarPhoenix along with advertising paid for by the plaintiff's customers. This main page is the first page that members of the public see when they search for The StarPhoenix on the Internet.

Sometime between July and November 2000, the defendant created an Internet website with the domain name and address "http://saskatoonstarphoenix.com" (hereinafter referred to as the "Noton StarPhoenix site"). The defendant set up the main page of the Noton StarPhoenix site to look exactly the same as the plaintiff's main page except:

(a) He substituted his own advertising for the plaintiff's top banner advertising;

(b) The bottom of his page states "Noton Inc. now offers FREE Internet Access & FREE Website Hosting CLICK HERE";

(c) His page contains a scrolling message in the bottom bar of the browser that "saskatoonstarphoenix.com is designed, hosted and marketed by Noton Inc."

A member of the public who is viewing the Noton StarPhoenix site does not see all of the advertising placed by the plaintiff for viewing on its site, and instead, sees advertising placed by the defendant.

The Noton StarPhoenix site was set up to be located by members of the public when they conducted an internet search for the plaintiff's site by establishing "metatags" (which are used as key words to locate search results) for the website that contained repeated variations of "StarPhoenix", "Saskatoon StarPhoenix", "newspaper", and combinations of the same. In the case of a member of the public who is looking for the plaintiff's website in relation to The StarPhoenix, that person is likely to enter as search words exactly the words that the defendant has established as his metatags. . . .

The plaintiff asserts and it is accepted, that in choosing the domain name he did, and in using the metatags he has chosen, the defendant was trying to attract members of the public who were looking for the plaintiff's website.

The defendant also maintains a website for "Noton Inc." At that site the defendant advertises the sale of domain names. Included among the domain names he offers for sale are:

(a) http://thestarphoenix.com

(b) http://starphoenix.com

He also maintains a website for "http://shoppingonlinemadeeasy.com". On this website listed under "courtesy links" is "The StarPhoenix". When a person clicks on this courtesy link, he or she is taken to the Noton StarPhoenix site. . . .

[The defendant refused The StarPhoenix's demand that he discontinue his StarPhoenix website.] However, he did offer to sell the "StarPhoenix" domain names to the plaintiff and indicated this was the sole reason for his having registered the domain names in the first place; namely, to sell them back to the persons who would have a business interest in retaining their name on the Web. . . .

. . . The Supreme Court of Canada in *Ciba-Geigy Canada Ltd. v. Apotex Inc.*, [1992] 3 S.C.R. 120 . . . concluded: "The three necessary components of a passing-off action are thus: the existence of goodwill, deception of the public due to a misrepresentation and actual or potential damage to the plaintiff."

The plaintiff has established that it is the owner of the goodwill associated with the name StarPhoenix. It has also established that certain members of the public were deceived into believing that the Noton StarPhoenix site was the plaintiff's site. With respect to actual or potential damage the plaintiff admits that it cannot point to any direct pecuniary loss as a result of the defendant's activities in the form of cancelled subscriptions or lost advertising revenue, but does claim actual and potential loss of reputation for being unable to control its own website and advertising. . . . The plaintiff has established all three necessary components. . . .

. . . [C]onsidering the short period of time the passing off occurred, and what I perceive to be minimal damage to the plaintiff's goodwill and reputation, I conclude a general damage award of $5,000.00 is appropriate.

. . . I do not consider this an appropriate case for punitive damages.

. . . [The defendant] is 22 years old, and he obtained the idea to register domain names approximately one year ago while travelling in Europe with a friend. Up until the interim injunction was issued he considered domain names a commodity which anyone could register and thereafter sell back to any person who wished to use such registered name. Newspaper articles indicate he was not alone in this belief. One such article indicates Celine Dion recently obtained a United Nations World Intellectual Property Organizational Panel ruling restoring to her the right to use her name as a domain name. There was very little, if any, precedent to guide would be entrepreneurs of domain names prior to this and other recent decisions.

The defendant's use of the plaintiff's website material to pass off his Noton StarPhoenix site as that of the plaintiff's is in a different category than his registration and sale of domain names. It is difficult to imagine that he thought this activity was legal, and yet, tied in as it was to his overall scheme of selling back registered domain names this activity was not "so malicious, oppressive and high handed that it offended this court's sense of decency" (*per* Cory J. in *Hill v. Church of Scientology of Toronto*, [1995] 2 S.C.R. 1130). Punitive damages may be appropriate in the future if, after several decisions such as this, the defendant or others persist in the activity.

The plaintiff is entitled to an order restraining and enjoining the defendant from:

(a) Using the internet domain names:

- http://saskatoonstarphoenix.com
- http://thestarphoenix.com
- http://starphoenix.com

(b) Using the name "Star Phoenix" or any variation thereof.

(c) Directing public attention to his internet websites in such a way as to cause or be likely to cause the public to think the defendant's website is the plaintiff's website.

The plaintiff also requests that the defendant be ordered to transfer to the plaintiff registration of the three domain sites referred to above. Its point is that without such an order the defendant would be free to sell the names to a third party whose use of the names would be beyond the control of the plaintiff. Given the fact the defendant admits that he is in the business of selling domain names, there is merit to this request. Therefore, it is ordered that the defendant transfer to the plaintiff registration of the three domain site names referred to above within 30 days....

Notes

1. For an analogous case, see Law Society of British Columbia v. Canada Domain Name Exchange Corp., (2004) 32 B.C.L.R.4th 129, 243 D.L.R.4th 746 (Sup. Ct.), aff'd, (2005) 46 B.C.L.R.4th 36, 259 D.L.R.4th 171 (C.A.) (defendant registered lawsocietyofbc.ca). In the United States, the "Anticybersquatting Consumer Protection Act," 15 U.S.C. § 1125(d), and other provisions of the trademark laws provide a statutory remedy in some but by no means all instances in which a domain name appropriates the trade name of a business or individual, or causes confusion with an existing trade name or web site. The Anticybersquatting Act creates a cause of action for the owner of a trademark when someone, with a "bad faith intent to profit" from the mark, registers, traffics in or uses a domain name with an identical or confusingly similar mark. The act contains an elaborate but not exclusive definition of "bad faith intent." Because of the difficulty of identifying the persons responsible for "cybersquatting" or "cyberpiracy" and obtaining personal jurisdiction over them (especially when they are in a foreign country), the act authorizes an in rem action against the domain name complained of in the judicial district in which the domain name registry, or the registrar or authority that registered or assigned the domain name, is located. The in rem action's remedies are forfeiture, cancellation or transfer of the domain name.

2. Another Internet-related issue is whether there is liability if defendant uses plaintiff's business or product name as a search engine "keyword": when Internet users type the name in a search engine such as Google, defendant's advertising or web site is dis-

played. The court in Morningware, Inc. v. Healthware Home Products, Inc., 673 F. Supp. 2d 630 (N.D. Ill. 2009), held there was a cause of action for this on statutory grounds. "Initial interest confusion" was a basis of liability, even though the confusion is brief and ends before any sale.

Zimmerman v. Holiday Inns of America, Inc.

Supreme Court of Pennsylvania
438 Pa. 528, 266 A.2d 87 (1970),
cert. denied, 400 U.S. 992 (1971)

O'BRIEN, Justice.

[After the litigation in Zimmerman v. B. & C. Motel Corporation, p. 278, supra, the Holiday Inns of America chain established fourteen "Holiday Inns" in Pennsylvania in addition to the Allentown location. Zimmerman brought an action to enjoin the chain from using the name "Holiday Inn" in motels, hotels and restaurants within a corridor adjacent to the Pennsylvania Turnpike, for its entire length, and within a one hundred mile radius of Harrisburg. Defendant counterclaimed to restrain the use of "Holiday Inn" in plaintiff's new downtown Harrisburg motel, the "Holiday Inn Town." The trial court enjoined defendant's use of "Holiday Inn" within "greater Harrisburg" (the area within twenty-two miles of the city center) and rejected the counterclaim. On appeal, Zimmerman sought protection within a larger area and the chain sought reversal or limitation of the injunction to a smaller area.]

… In order to prove that he is entitled to relief from the courts in the form of an injunction to protect his use of the name "Holiday," from a competing use by the defendants, Zimmerman must prove that he has a legal right to exclusive use of the word "Holiday," that the defendant Holiday Inn is using a name or mark confusingly similar to Zimmerman's name or mark, and that defendants' use of the name is likely to cause confusion in Zimmerman's competitive area.…

… The chancellor found that although Zimmerman had failed to prove that he had acquired a secondary meaning in "Holiday" throughout the state of Pennsylvania, he had established a secondary meaning in the word "Holiday" in the greater Harrisburg area.

The record amply supports this finding. Greater Harrisburg is the only area in which Zimmerman has rendered motel and restaurant services under the name "Holiday." Zimmerman has done extensive advertising of his Holiday motels, but most of this advertising was confined to the Harrisburg area. The witnesses, whose testimony carried the most weight with the chancellor in establishing that Zimmerman had achieved a secondary meaning for his use of the word "Holiday," were people whose business brought them frequently to Harrisburg, such as George Bloom, former Secretary of the Commonwealth of Pennsylvania and now Chairman of the Public Utility Commission, and George M. Leader, former Governor of the State, both of whom testified that the generally accepted meaning of the word "Holiday" when used in relation to a motel or motor hotel among all people in government in Harrisburg with whom they had come in contact was one of Zimmerman's motels.

However, the chancellor did not find the testimony persuasive on the question of establishing a secondary meaning for Zimmerman's use of Holiday anywhere in Pennsylvania outside of Harrisburg. There was ample evidence in this case concerning extensive use of the word "Holiday" for motels and restaurants in Pennsylvania which were not connected with either Zimmerman or the Holiday Inn System. In addition, although many of Zimmerman's witnesses testified that they had seen "Holiday Inns" operated by the defendant system and they testified that they believed that the motels of both plaintiffs and defendants were all part of the same system, there was often no indication that Zimmerman's use of the name "Holiday" had acquired a secondary meaning lost in the minds of these witnesses, before these witnesses had seen or heard of the motels of the defendant system. Moreover, the witnesses chosen by Zimmerman's counsel to give testimony were not chosen at random or by any scientific method. Only thirty witnesses were brought in, seven from the Philadelphia area, twenty-two from the Pittsburgh area and one from Harrisburg. There was no indication that they were representative of the estimated 5 to 8 million people who live along the Pennsylvania Turnpike. There was no indication of the total number of people who use the Pennsylvania Turnpike, and the geographic source for these travelers. Surely they do not all stem from within Pennsylvania. In view of the extensive advertising done by the defendant system, many of these travelers have probably heard of the defendant system's motels first rather than Zimmerman's motels in Harrisburg....

The defendant Holiday Inn Systems also contends that there is no confusion because their Holiday Inn sign does not conflict with Zimmerman's Holiday sign. The chancellor found that there was conflict because Holiday was the key word. We agree with the chancellor. Many witnesses testified that they did not remember whether the word "Holiday" was followed by the word "Inn" on either Zimmerman's or the defendants' motel. There were many instances of confusion in marking and in registration of guests. Moreover, various advertising done by the defendant Holiday Inns of America System clearly indicated that they, too, considered "Holiday" the key word.

Zimmerman's argument that the area described by the court order, a twenty-two mile radius from the center of Harrisburg, does not mark the full scope of his motel trading area is not relevant. We agree that a motel's trading area, in these days of high speed traffic, covers a wide range. However, Zimmerman is entitled to protection only where his use of the name has acquired secondary meaning, not in all parts of his trading area....

One more issue remains. The wording of the final decree prohibits the Holiday Inn system from "encroaching" on the area defined within a twenty-two mile radius of Harrisburg. Zimmerman contends that the word "encroaching" should include advertising as well as actual operation of motels. We disagree. As we have already said, Zimmerman is only entitled to protection within the zone of a circle with a radius of twenty-two miles of Harrisburg. If we barred the Holiday Inn System from advertising within that twenty-two mile radius, we would, in effect, be enlarging Zimmerman's zone of protection by diminishing the effective market area of the Holiday Inns which are outside that zone. This we will not do.

[Affirmed. Cohen, J., dissented.]

Notes

1. The traditional rule for common law trademarks and unfair competition actions generally has been that a business' name will be protected only in areas in which the business is operating. It has been said that there can be no unfair competition unless there is some competition between plaintiff and defendant. See Annot., Right to Protection Against Use of Trademark or Tradename Beyond the Territory in Which Plaintiff Operates, 36 A.L.R. 922 (1925). Occasionally, a denial of relief is qualified, as when a court states that the first user of the name is not entitled to protection outside its area of operation unless

the later user is taking benefit of the other's reputation or trying to forestall the other's expansion. See Hanover Star Milling Co. v. Metcalf, 240 U.S. 403 (1916).

2. What if a company enjoys international fame and plans eventually to serve the location in which the alleged infringement occurs? See Maison Prunier v. Prunier's Restaurant & Cafe, Inc., 159 Misc. 551, 288 N.Y.S. 529 (Sup. Ct. 1936) (famous restaurant in France contemplated opening in New York at expedient time; could enjoin use of same name for restaurants in New York); Orkin Exterminating Co. Inc. v. Pestco Co. of Canada Ltd., (1985) 50 O.R.2d 726, 19 D.L.R.4th 90 (C.A.) (American pest control company granted injunction against use of same name by pest control company in Canada; plaintiff well-known in Canada through advertising reaching Canada and Canadians in United States, some of whom used plaintiff's services for American property); Pick-'N-Pay Stores Ltd. v. Pick-'N-Pay Superette (Pvt.) Ltd., 1973 (1) R.L.R. 244, 1973 (3) S.A. 564 (Rhod. Gen. Div.), aff'd, 1974 (1) S.A. 597 (Rhod. App. Div.) (plaintiff developed chain of supermarkets in South Africa and planned to expand into Rhodesia, where it was already known; defendant established supermarket in Rhodesia using same name and logo as plaintiff; no action because plaintiff had never used name and logo in trade in Rhodesia); ConAgra Inc. v. McCain Foods (Aust.) Pty. Ltd., (1992) 33 F.C.R. 302, 106 A.L.R. 465 (Full Ct.) (plaintiff need not have existing business activities or customers within jurisdiction, but business or product must have reputation among substantial number of persons who would be potential customers if plaintiff commenced business there). Cf. Pepsico Inc. v. United Tobacco Co. Ltd., 1988 (2) S.A. 334 (W) (plaintiffs' potato chips introduced to representatives of major retail chains in South Africa but sales to consumers had not commenced; held to have acquired sufficient reputation to be protected against defendant's sale through small retail stores of potato chips with same brand name). Hotel Cipriani Srl v. Cipriani (Grovernor Street) Ltd., [2010] R.P.C. 485 (C.A.), requires for passing off liability that plaintiff have a significant number of customers within the jurisdiction but not that plaintiff provide goods or services there.

3. Does the proprietor of a business that has been closed have a right to restrain the use of the business' name by another? A name can be protected when it has not been abandoned. Closure of the business is not necessarily abandonment of the name. It is said that abandonment depends upon the proprietor's intent. However, abandonment can be inferred from a long period of disuse of the name. Compare Gold Seal Associates, Inc. v. Gold Seal Associates, Inc., 56 F.2d 452 (S.D.N.Y. 1932) (cessation of business for more than year, with some efforts to revive it), and Bank of Tomah v. Warren, 94 Wis. 151, 68 N.W. 549 (1896) (suspension of bank operations after failure), with Sayles Biltmore Bleacheries Inc. v. Narragansett Wiping Supply Co., 86 R.I. 99, 134 A.2d 57 (1957) (defendant opened "Lorraine Mill Outlet" in mill buildings formerly used by Lorraine Manufacturing Co., which had gone out of manufacturing business and left state), and Pink v. J.A. Sharwood and Co. Ltd. (No. 2), (1913) 109 L.T. 594 (Ch. D.) (business closed and assets sold because of proprietor's mental incapacity; suit three years after manufacturing ceased). Holding that the use of a name by others could be restrained after a business' closure so long as good will attached to the business or its name, the court in Ad-Lib Club Ltd. v. Granville, [1971] 2 All E.R. 300 (Ch. D.), enjoined the use of the same name by a nightclub nearly five years after plaintiff's nightclub closed. See generally Annot., Abandonment of Trademark or Tradename, 3 A.L.R.2d 1226 (1949); Restatement of Unfair Competition § 30 (1995).

4. *Use of personal name.* Can a defendant be restrained from doing business under a personal or family name? At one time, the generalization could be made that a person had a right to the honest use of his family name in conducting his own business despite the harm that might result to others also using that name. More recent cases reflect attempts

to balance against this the right of a business not to have its customers lured away by another's misleading use of a similar name. Sometimes both rights have been protected by allowing an individual to use his name in his business, but under conditions that will prevent confusion with a prior user. See Parker-Knoll, Ltd. v. Knoll International, Ltd., [1962] R.P.C. 265 (H.L.) (plaintiffs registered trademark Parker-Knoll; defendants enjoined from using their full name, Knoll-International, unless they clearly distinguished their goods from plaintiffs'). See generally Annots., Right, in Absence of Self-Imposed Restraint, to Use One's Own Name for Business Purposes to Detriment of Another Using the Same or a Similar Name, 47 A.L.R. 1189 (1927); 44 A.L.R.2d 1156 (1955).

5. A distinction has been drawn between the right of a person to use his name in a personal business and use of a personal name in or by a corporation, which can freely choose its trading name. See Great Atlantic & Pacific Tea Co. v. A. & P. Radio Stores, 20 F. Supp. 703 (E.D. Pa. 1937); Asprey and Garrard Ltd. v. WRA (Guns) Ltd., [2002] F.S.R. 487 (C.A.). But it has been pointed out that people are not compelled to use their own names for their businesses. Modern cases tend to speak less of a right to use one's own name and more of intent to deceive and likelihood of confusion. See Annot., Use of "Family Name" by Corporation as Unfair Competition, 72 A.L.R.3d 8 (1976). What if a family member wishes to compete with the family business, using his own name? In David B. Findlay, Inc. v. Findlay, 18 N.Y.2d 12, 271 N.Y.S.2d 652, 218 N.E.2d 531 (1966), amended, 18 N.Y.2d 676, 273 N.Y.S.2d 422, 219 N.E.2d 872 (1966), cert. denied, 385 U.S. 930 (1966), plaintiff had an established reputation as an art dealer in New York City, operating under the names "Findlay Galleries" and "Findlay's on 57th St." He specialized in French impressionist and post-impressionist paintings. Next door, his brother opened the "Wally Findlay Galleries," which specialized in the same types of paintings. An injunction against the brother's use of the family name was upheld (4–3) on the basis that one can be enjoined from using a name, even one's own, if its use in a particular vicinity causes confusion. See also Joseph Scott Co. v. Scott Swimming Pools, Inc., 764 F.2d 62 (2d Cir. 1985); Cunetto House of Pasta v. Tuma, 689 S.W.2d 690 (Mo. App. 1985).

6. Persons practicing a profession generally do so under their own names, either individually or as part of firm names. So do many people performing personal services. Would a court enjoin this if confusion resulted? In Suisman, Shapiro, Wool, Brennan, Gray & Greenberg P.C. v. Suisman, 80 U.S.P.Q.2d 1072 (D. Conn. 2006), lawyers named Suisman and Shapiro, who had left the "Suisman Shapiro" law firm, were enjoined from using "Suisman & Shapiro" for the name of their new firm. In Cockrell v. Davis, 198 Miss. 660, 23 So. 2d 256 (1945), the owner of a swing band performed under his given name— Jimmie Davis, dropping his surname. He thereby capitalized on the fame of "Hill Billy" band leader Jimmie Davis. The famous Jimmie Davis (who had been elected governor of Louisiana) was granted an injunction.

Oklahoma District Council of the Assemblies of God of the State of Oklahoma, Inc. v. New Hope Assembly of God Church of Norman, Oklahoma, Inc.

Supreme Court of Oklahoma
597 P.2d 1211 (1979)

IRWIN, Vice Chief Justice.

... New Hope Assembly of God Church of Norman (New Hope), appealed from a summary judgment permanently enjoining it from using the term "Assembly of God" in its name. The litigation arose after the General Council of the Assemblies of God, Inc. and the Oklahoma District Council of the Assemblies of God of the State of Oklahoma, Inc., (District), withdrew recognition of New Hope as an affiliated member and New Hope continued to use its previously adopted name....

... [T]he First Amendment to the United States Constitution guarantees, inter alia, religious freedom and separation of church and state, and clearly prohibits civil courts from deciding whether religious doctrines have or have not been followed as a basis for resolving a dispute between religious institutions. However, the issue presented here does not involve a controversy over a religious doctrine or a doctrinal dispute. The question presented is whether District is entitled to an injunction enjoining New Hope from using the term "Assembly of God" in its name. This question must be resolved upon neutral, non-religious grounds.

New Hope contends that the term "Assembly of God", as it appears in its name, is a generic or descriptive term having no specific relationship to any body or group but having a wide and broad application to those people who assemble to do God's work as they see it. New Hope argues that no entity is entitled to exclusive use of the name or term because it is generic or descriptive.

District admits that the term "Assembly of God" is generic or descriptive in origin but contends it has acquired a secondary meaning and it is entitled to protection. District argues that by usage of the term, it has acquired a secondary meaning, i. e. it stands for churches affiliated with District and its parent organization. District asserts that it is entitled to protection under the rules relating to unfair competition....

... [In *Purcell v. Summers*, 4 Cir., 145 F.2d 979 (1944), the court said:] "[P]rinciples ordinarily applied in the case of business and trading corporations are equally applicable in the case of churches and other religious and charitable organizations; for, while such organizations exist for the worship of almighty God and for the purpose of benefiting mankind and not for purposes of profit, they are nevertheless dependent upon the contributions of their members for means to carry on their work, and anything which tends to divert membership or gifts of members from them injures them with respect to their financial condition in the same way that a business corporation is injured by diversion of trade or custom.... [¶] 'It is well established that [a] benevolent, fraternal, or social organization will be protected in the use of its name by injunction restraining another organization from using the same or another name so similar as to be misleading.' The reasons underlying the rule are thus stated in Nims on Unfair Competition and Trademarks (3d Ed.) §86: 'The fact that a corporation is [an] eleemosynary or charitable one and has no goods to sell, and does not make money, does not take it out of the protection of the law of unfair competition. Distinct identity is just as important to such a company, oftentimes, as it is to a commercial company. Its financial credit—its ability to raise funds, its general reputation, the credit of those managing it and supporting it, are all at stake if its name is filched away by some other organization, and the two become confused in the minds of the public.'" ...

In *National Board of YWCA v. YWCA of Charleston, S.C.*, 335 F. Supp. 615 (1971), the Court said the National Board, by the long and continued use of the name "Young Women's Christian Association", had acquired a secondary meaning to the name, and having acquired a secondary meaning, the name was entitled to protection even though it may have been at one time merely descriptive....

If District has established a secondary meaning in the term "Assembly of God", and confusion will likely result if New Hope uses the term in its name, District is entitled to the injunctive relief requested....

The trial court did not find that a "secondary meaning" had been established. According to its journal entry the order was based on "[t]aking judicial notice of the correct usage of grammar, 'Assemblies of God' is found to be a correct denomination of a group constituting more than one 'Assembly of God.'" Also, the trial court determined that "an obvious qualification of the name, such as 'Holiness Assembly of God', 'Southern Assembly of God' or the like might constitute a different situation not posed by this defendant (New Hope) whose name indicates the 'Assembly of God' church in the New Hope community of the city of Norman, Oklahoma." There is no evidence in the record that New Hope derived its name from a community or that there is a community of New Hope in the city of Norman.

The record will simply not support the trial court's order sustaining District's Motion for Summary Judgment based on the theory that District had established a secondary meaning in the term "Assembly of God". Neither will the record support a sustaining of New Hope's Motion for Summary Judgment. Therefore, the judgment granting District summary judgment is reversed, and the trial court did not err in overruling New Hope's Motion for Summary Judgment.

Notes

1. Compare Christian Science Board of Directors of First Church of Christ, Scientist v. Evans, 105 N.J. 297, 520 A.2d 1347 (1987) ("Christian Science Church" a generic term for church that practices Christian Science religion; could be used by church that separated from "Mother Church"); New Thought Church v. Chapin, 159 App. Div. 723, 144 N.Y.S. 1026 (1913) (incorporated church organization had no exclusive right to words "new thought" and "church" either singly or in combination; words generic and in common use). If the law of unfair competition is applied to religious bodies, can courts avoid involvement in doctrinal controversies?

2. The right of non-profit organizations to bring suit under the law of unfair competition is widely recognized. See Annot., Right of Charitable or Religious Association or Corporation to Protection Against Use of Same or Similar Name by Another, 37 A.L.R.3d 277 (1971). Does this provide a good basis for adjudicating disputes between rival community or charitable organizations? See Girls Clubs of America, Inc. v. Boys Club of America, Inc., 683 F. Supp. 50 (S.D.N.Y. 1988), aff'd, 859 F.2d 148 (2d Cir. 1988) (action by Girls Clubs to prevent Boys Clubs changing name to Boys and Girls Clubs); British Diabetic Association v. Diabetic Society Ltd., [1995] 4 All E.R. 812 (Ch. D.). Golden Slipper Square Club v. Golden Slipper Restaurant & Catering, Inc., 371 Pa. 92, 88 A.2d 734 (1952), exemplifies an action against a commercial business which adopted a name used by a non-profit organization.

3. A benevolent or fraternal organization can claim protection of its name, ritual and insignia. See Order of Owls v. Owls Club of McKees Rocks, 99 F. Supp. 555 (W.D. Pa. 1951); Annot., Right of Benevolent or Fraternal Society or Organization to Protection Against Use of Same or Similar Name, Insignia, or Ritual by Another Organization, 76 A.L.R.2d 1396 (1961). Should this extend to a union label, which shows that goods were made by union members? Compare Hetterman Bros. & Co. v. Powers, 102 Ky. 133, 43 S.W. 180 (1897) (protected), with Weener v. Brayton, 152 Mass. 101, 25 N.E. 46 (1890) (not protected). See Annot., Rights in Union Label, Shop Card, or Other Insignia Denoting Union Shop or Workmanship, 42 A.L.R.2d 709 (1955).

4. Does a political party have a common law right to prevent use of the same name by another party? In Kean v. McGivan, [1982] F.S.R. 119 (C.A.), injunctive relief was re-

fused on the ground that the law of passing off had no application where there was no commercial activity. But the court in Tomei v. Finley, 512 F. Supp. 695 (N.D. Ill. 1981), granted Republicans a preliminary injunction against use of the initials "REP" by candidates in township elections sponsored by Democrats. (The Democrats had formed a local party whose acronym was REP.) In another case, an authorized U.S. section of a Dominican Republic political party obtained an injunction against use of the party's name and insignia by an unauthorized section. Partido Revolucionario Domincano (PRD) Seccional Metropolitana de Washington-DC, Maryland y Virginia v. Partido Revolucionario Dominicano, Seccional de Maryland y Virginia, 312 F. Supp. 2d 1 (D.D.C. 2004). Cf. Burge v. Haycock, [2002] R.P.C. 28 (C.A.), a passing off action brought by a large membership organization that sought to influence government policy but did not have any candidates in elections. A candidate in a town council election was enjoined from representing himself as being a member of or having any connection with the organization.

C. Non-Competitors

Philadelphia Storage Battery Company v. Mindlin
Supreme Court of New York
163 Misc. 52, 296 N.Y.S. 176 (1937)

SHIENTAG, Justice.

Plaintiff, a manufacturer of radio sets, storage batteries, and associated products, seeks an injunction pendente lite restraining defendant from using its nationally celebrated brand "Philco" in connection with the sale of razor blades. Plaintiff has never manufactured or sold razor blades and, so far as appears from the papers, has no present intention of entering that field of endeavor. Defendant offers no explanation for its adoption of a mark which has been so widely and successfully exploited in other fields by plaintiff. The motion thus presents for determination the interesting question as to whether the use of a famous brand on a noncompeting product constitutes an actionable infringement of a common-law trade-mark....

The tendency of the courts, at an earlier time, was to confine the protection of a trade-mark to the product on which, and the territory in which, it had been used.... "Courts generally have come to recognize that actual competition in a product is not essential to relief under the doctrine of unfair competition." [Maison Prunier v. Prunier's Restaurant & Cafe, Inc., 159 Misc. 551, 288 N.Y.S. 529, 533.] ... To paraphrase the much-quoted and classic dictum of Denison, J., the word "unfair" rather than "competition" should be underscored in any judicial definition of unfair competition. Vogue Co. v. Thompson-Hudson Co. (C.C.A.) 300 F. 509, 512.

But is every commercial use of a mark previously adopted by another necessarily unfair? There is no difficulty in so stigmatizing a use which results in a diversion of the plaintiff's custom and the deception of the public. "The whole Law and the Prophets on the subject," says Learned Hand, J., is "that one merchant shall not divert customers from another by representing what he sells as emanating from the second." Yale Electric Corporation v. Robertson (C.C.A.) 26 F.(2d) 972, 973. But diversion of trade is not the only injury which may be caused by the second use. The normal potential expansion of the plaintiff's business may be forestalled. His reputation may be tarnished by the use of his mark upon an inferior product. A false impression of a trade connection between the parties may be created, possibly subjecting the plaintiff to liability or to the embarrassments of litigation, or causing injury to his credit and financial standing.

The second use may generate confusion of source or of identities, without, however, engendering any immediate pecuniary loss to plaintiff. To postpone the granting of relief until actual injury could be proved would be to deprive the equitable remedy of its most valuable trait—the dispensation of preventive justice. Similarly, to condition relief on a demonstration of inferiority of product would be to convert the court into a laboratory for the testing of rival products and claims. Cf. White v. Mellin, L.R. [1895] A.C. 154. The second user is hardly a fit guardian of the good will symbolized by the plaintiff's mark. The court may properly presume that the confusion of source will be injurious and therefore wield its injunctive powers with despatch to prevent the infliction of harm. A merchant's "mark is his authentic seal; by it he vouches for the goods which bear it; it carries his name for good or ill. If another uses it, he borrows the owner's reputation, whose quality no longer lies within his own control. This is an injury, even though the borrower does not tarnish it, or divert any sales by its use; for a reputation, like a face, is a symbol of its possessor and creator, and another can use it only as a mask." Learned Hand, J., in Yale Electric Corporation v. Robertson, 26 F.(2d) 972, at page 974. Where confusion of source is probable, an injunction should be forthcoming, whether the infringing use is upon a competing or noncompeting product. A mark, it has been pointed out, is more than a symbol of existing good will or a mere commercial signature; it has a creative function; it serves as a "silent salesman" to attract custom. The dilution of its selling powers and "the whittling away of its uniqueness" by use on noncompeting products constitutes a real injury for which there should be redress. Schechter, Rational Basis of Trademark Protection, 40 Harvard Law Review, 813; Fog and Fiction in Trademark Protection, 36 Columbia Law Review, 60....

The element of the possibility of confusion at source has been stressed in various decisions. The ambit of protection is constantly being widened. The adoption of "Kodak" for cameras precludes its use on bicycles [Eastman Photo. Materials Co. v. Griffiths Cycle Corporation, 15 Robb, Pat. Cas. 105]; "Rolls-Royce," the name of an automobile, may not be appropriated for radio tubes [Wall v. Rolls-Royce of America (C.C.A.) 4 F.(2d) 333]; "Times" as a brand for bicycles may be restrained by the proprietor of a newspaper bearing that name [Walton v. Ashton, L.R. (1902) 2 Ch. 282]; "Waterman" as a mark for razor blades may be interdicted at the suit of the fountain pen company [Waterman Co. v. Gordon (C.C.A.) 72 F.(2d) 272]; the use of "Dunhill," the famous brand for smokers' supplies, on shirts constitutes an infringement [Alfred Dunhill of London v. Dunhill Shirt Shop (D.C.) 3 F. Supp. 487]; the same mark may not be used on liniment and soap [Omega Oil Co. v. Weschler, 35 Misc. 441, 71 N.Y.S. 983, affirmed 68 App. Div. 638, 74 N.Y.S. 1140]; automobiles and tires [Hudson Motor Car Co. v. Hudson Tire Co. (D.C.) 21 F.(2d) 453]; food products and oleomargarine [Del Monte Special Food Co. v. California Packing Corporation (C.C.A.) 34 F.(2d) 774]; upon electrical appliances and spark plugs [Duro Co. v. Duro Co. (C.C.A.) 27 F.(2d) 339]; upon cooking utensils and wash boilers [Aluminum Cooking Utensil Co. v. Sargoy Bros. & Co. (D.C.) 276 F. 447]; or upon mineral oil and figs [Standard Oil Co. v. California Peach & Fig Growers (D.C.) 28 F.(2d) 283].

Confusion of source is inevitable in the present case. "Philco" has been widely advertised in various media—newspapers, magazines, billboards, radio programs—and is well known as a brand for radio sets and accessories. It will hardly be contended that defendant was ignorant of this extensive prior use. His adoption of the mark cannot be charged to coincidence. It is obvious that he is seeking to trade upon plaintiff's reputation. It is not material that there has been no direct representation of trade connection with plaintiff or that the aggravating circumstances present in some of the other cases are absent here. The very use of the brand is sufficient to induce a mistake of identities and therefore an injunction should issue....

There may be situations in which protection should not be projected beyond the field of the plaintiff's exploitation of his mark. Defendant's use may be entirely too remote to occasion any conceivable injury; the mark may be so nondescript as to render further dilution of its selling power improbable; defendant may have used the mark for many years and developed a good will of his own before any conflict occurs; there may be an honest commercial need for the use of the term by defendant. The law, particularly in this field, is still in a formative stage and its frontiers are yet to be defined....

The motion for an injunction pendente lite is granted....

Notes

1. Should a business be protected against use of the same name in a different type of business and a different area? See Tiffany & Co. v. Tiffany Productions, Inc., 147 Misc. 679, 264 N.Y.S. 459 (Sup. Ct. 1932), aff'd, 237 App. Div. 801, 260 N.Y.S. 821 (1932), aff'd, 262 N.Y. 482, 188 N.E. 30 (1933) (nationally famed New York City jewelry store protected against use of name by motion picture production company; otherwise, plaintiff's identity and name's hold on public mind would gradually be whittled away). Should the result depend on the extent of plaintiff's renown or the distinctiveness of its name? In Caesars World, Inc. v. Caesar's Palace, 490 F. Supp. 818 (D.N.J. 1980), a New Jersey beauty salon used the same name as a Nevada resort hotel. The court reasoned that since plaintiff's name was well-known in the marketplace and was unique, arbitrary and nondescriptive, it was a "strong" mark, entitled to more protection than a "weak" one. An injunction was granted.

2. In which of the following cases should an injunction have been granted?

(a) Plaintiff sells flour bearing a distinctive trademark. Defendant begins selling syrup with an identical trademark. Aunt Jemima Mills Co. v. Rigney & Co., 234 F. 804 (E.D.N.Y. 1916), rev'd, 247 F. 407 (2d Cir. 1917), cert. denied, 245 U.S. 672 (1918) (lower court refused injunction on ground that flour and syrup not in competition; reversed on appeal; defendant's adoption of trademark intended either to obtain benefit of flour advertising or forestall expansion of plaintiff's trade).

(b) A store sells and services radio and television sets under the name of its proprietor. A nationally known radio and television personality, who has endorsed particular brands of television sets, has the same name. Sullivan v. Ed Sullivan Radio & T.V., Inc., 1 A.D.2d 609, 152 N.Y.S.2d 227 (1956) (personality granted injunction pendente lite).

(c) The business of plaintiff, known as the "TAB," is taking off-course bets on races. Defendant publishes under the name "TAB" a weekly newspaper devoted to tips on races. The newspaper contains a disclaimer of any connection with plaintiff, but plaintiff has evidence that a number of people believe a connection exists. Totalizator Agency Board v. Turf News Pty. Ltd., [1967] V.R. 605 (Sup. Ct.) (plaintiff sustained burden of showing probability of deception and damage; plaintiff could be injured in reputation if public thought it connected with defendant; publishers of such periodicals had poor standing with public).

(d) A men's clothing store uses the same name as a magazine that specializes in articles about men's fashion. Esquire, Inc. v. Maira, 101 F. Supp. 398 (M.D. Pa. 1951) (defendant's use of name likely to generate belief that store had been approved, endorsed or sponsored by magazine or that clothes sold there had been advertised or mentioned in magazine; injunction granted). Cf. Triangle Publications, Inc. v. Rohrlich, 167 F.2d 969 (2d Cir. 1948) (owner of trademark "Seventeen," used as title of magazine for young women, granted injunction against sale of "Miss Seventeen" girdles); Time, Inc. v. Life Television Corp., 123 F. Supp. 470 (D. Minn. 1954) (name and mark of "*Life*" magazine used on television sets; enjoined).

(e) The British Medical Association, a non-profit organization representing the British medical profession, finds that defendant operates "B.M.A." drug stores, sells medical remedies labelled "B.M.A." and guarantees that reproductions of patent medicines are prepared according to the analyses of the British Medical Association. The medical association is often referred to by the public as the "B.M.A." and has published in books analyses of proprietary medicines in order to warn the public against useless, harmful and overpriced remedies. British Medical Association v. Marsh, (1931) 48 R.P.C. 565 (Ch. D.) (injunction granted to medical association; public would conclude that association was connected with defendant's shops; defendant's conduct would injure association's "business" by causing people to leave it or abstain from joining).

(f) A motel in South Carolina uses the name of its proprietor, which is also the name of a well-known brand of Scotch whiskey. John Walker & Sons, Ltd. v. Bethea, 305 F. Supp. 1302 (D.S.C. 1969) (injunction granted; some of public might believe there was common source or some connection). .

(g) Polaraid, a business which installs refrigeration and heating systems, is sued by Polaroid, the well-known manufacturer of optical devices and photographic equipment. Polaroid Corp. v. Polaraid, Inc., 319 F.2d 830 (7th Cir. 1963) (injunction granted).

(h) A labor union distributes to employees a brochure critical of the company for which they work. The cover, which displays the company's logo and does not identify the brochure's author, can give the impression that the brochure is published by the company. Persons who read through the brochure will know it is not from the company. Canada Safeway Ltd. v. Manitoba Food & Commercial Workers, Local 832, [1983] 5 W.W.R. 327 (Man. C.A.), rev'g [1983] 5 W.W.R. 321 (Man. Q.B.) (company granted injunction).

3. If defendant sells a product that is a parody of plaintiff's product, or publishes a parody of plaintiff's business or advertising, it may be restrained from doing this if some members of the public will think that plaintiff produced or authorized the parody. They may fail to realize that it is a parody. See Schieffelin & Co. v. Jack Co. of Boca, Inc., 850 F. Supp. 232 (S.D.N.Y. 1994) ("Dom Popingnon" popcorn sold in champagne bottles with labels resembling labels of Dom Pérignon champagne); Anheuser-Busch, Inc. v. Balducci Publications, 28 F.3d 769 (8th Cir. 1994), cert. denied, 513 U.S. 1112 (1995) (parody advertisement in humor magazine for "Michelob Oily" beer); Mutual of Omaha Insurance Co., v. Novak, 836 F.2d 397 (8th Cir. 1987), cert. denied, 488 U.S. 933 (1988) (defendant sold T-shirts, caps, coffee mugs and other items with emaciated version of plaintiff's "Indian Head" logo and words "Mutual of Omaha Nuclear Holocaust Insurance"); Coca-Cola Co. v. Gemini Rising, Inc., 346 F. Supp. 1183 (E.D.N.Y. 1972) (posters reproducing Coca-Cola's distinctive script and slogan "Enjoy Coca-Cola," changed to "Enjoy Cocaine"). Compare (finding no likelihood of confusion) Tommy Hilfiger Licensing, Inc. v. Nature Labs, LLC., 221 F. Supp. 2d 410 (S.D.N.Y. 2002) (perfumes for pets whose names parodied famous-brand perfumes for humans); General Mills, Inc. v. Henry Regnery Co. 421 F. Supp. 359 (N.D. Ill. 1976) (action by seller of "Betty Crocker" food prod-

ucts and publications against publisher of cookbook entitled *Morey Amsterdam's Betty Cooker's Crock Book for Drunks*); American Family Life Insurance Co. v. Hagan, 266 F. Supp. 2d 682 (N.D. Ohio 2002) (gubernatorial candidate's political commercials based on quacking duck in insurance company's television commercials); American Express Co. v. Vibra Approved Laboratories Corp., 10 U.S.P.Q.2d 2006 (S.D.N.Y. 1989) (sale of condoms inside cards resembling American Express credit cards, bearing variant of American Express slogan "Don't leave home without it."). See also cases on pp. 297–298, infra.

4. The standard of liability in Restatement of Unfair Competition § 4 (1995) is that defendant, in connection with the marketing of goods or services, "makes a representation likely to deceive or mislead prospective purchasers by causing the mistaken belief that the [defendant's] business is the business of the [plaintiff], or that the [defendant] is the agent, affiliate, or associate of the [plaintiff], or that the goods or services that the [defendant] markets are produced, sponsored, or approved by the [plaintiff]." Section 43(a) of the Lanham Act, 15 U.S.C. § 1125(a), now provides for civil liability when a person's use of "any word, term, name, symbol, or device, or any combination thereof, or any false designation of origin … or false or misleading representation of fact, … is likely to cause [confusion, mistake or deception] as to the affiliation, connection, or association of such person with another person, or as to the origin, sponsorship, or approval of his or her goods, services, or commercial activities by another person."

Cue Publishing Company, Inc. v. Colgate-Palmolive Company
Supreme Court of New York
45 Misc. 2d 161, 256 N.Y.S.2d 239 (1965),
aff'd, 23 A.D.2d 829, 259 N.Y.S.2d 377 (1965)

THOMAS A. AURELIO, Justice.

[In 1934, plaintiff began publication of Cue Magazine, a weekly guide to dining, theatre, radio and television programs, sports and other events and attractions in New York City and surrounding suburbs. The magazine "exert[ed] its greatest influence upon the well-educated upper middle classes" of metropolitan New York. One of its promotional activities was the Cue "seal of approval" for restaurants, night clubs and resorts. A guide called "Cue's New York" was published in 1963 and distributed nationally. Defendant was a large company selling soaps, toothpaste and other toiletries throughout the nation. From 1939 to 1946 it sold "Cue" liquid dentrifice and in 1953 it test-marketed "Cue" shampoo. Around 1960 it began development of "Cue" toothpaste. When defendant had test-marketed the toothpaste and prepared to launch an extensive national advertising campaign, plaintiff sought an injunction under New York's "anti-dilution" statute, General Business Law § 368-d. This provided: "Likelihood of injury to business reputation or of dilution of the distinctive quality of a mark or trade name shall be a ground for injunctive relief in cases of infringement of a mark registered or not registered or in cases of unfair competition, notwithstanding the absence of competition between the parties or the absence of confusion as to the source of goods or services."]

Plaintiff's claim for relief is essentially based upon three grounds: (1) dilution, (2) tarnishment and (3) confusion. These will be discussed in inverse order.

As to confusion: It is generally true under the laws of trade-marks and unfair competition that where there is the likelihood of confusion as to source or sponsorship of a product there may be a basis for injunctive relief. However, the existence of a general resemblance between trade-marks is not always sufficient to show infringement and the fact of similarity in and of itself is not sufficient to warrant equitable interference. The test is whether there is likelihood of confusion or deception.

... Plaintiff has neither shown any actual confusion or mistake on the part of the public arising from the simultaneous use of the mark "Cue" in their respective businesses nor is the Court sufficiently satisfied or convinced that there will be a likelihood of such confusion or mistake on the part of the general public which would entitle plaintiff to the injunctive relief herein sought. Although plaintiff attempted to show possible confusion as a result of a test survey of "Cue" toothpaste and "Cue" magazine, the Court was not favorably impressed with the methodology used for the survey or the reliability of the results obtained thereby.

As to tarnishment: Plaintiff contends that Colgate's advertising and promotion of the decay-preventive qualities of "Cue" toothpaste will create a variety of oral hygiene connotations for the name "Cue" (including therapeutic diet control) which are grossly inconsistent with and repugnant to plaintiff's development and use of the name as a symbol of fine dining and other forms of pleasurable leisure-time activity; that the tarnishment of plaintiff's name by creation of such unpleasant and inappropriate connotations results in a distinct form of injury to plaintiff's mark and/or trade name.

In the opinion of this court such a claim by plaintiff is fantastic, far-fetched and entirely without merit. It is unsupported by the evidence, and there is no analogy between the circumstances here involved and the authorities cited by plaintiff in its brief.

With respect to the latter, this Court is not yet ready to apply the same connotation of the mark "Cue" to such world-famous names as Tiffany, Yale (as applied to the trademark for locks), Rolls-Royce, Bullova, Philco or the slogan of Budweiser Beer, "Where there's life — there's Bud". The Court will take judicial notice of the fact that the foregoing marks have existed for a great number of years and that actually millions of dollars have been invested in good will and advertising to the point where a mere mention of the name will immediately cause an association of its product. Cue Magazine has not yet achieved the pleasure of such fame....

Several of plaintiff's witnesses who were restaurateurs gave testimony on the subject of continuing with their advertising in Cue Magazine if an intense campaign were begun for "Cue" toothpaste. The consensus of opinion resolved itself: if circulation and business would not be hurt, advertising would continue. Consequently, it is my opinion that plaintiff's name will in no way suffer any tarnishment as a result of the intensive and extensive advertising campaign to introduce "Cue" as a toothpaste.

As to dilution: ... Plaintiff contends that Colgate's advertising campaign for "Cue" toothpaste will not merely "dilute" but "inundate" and "obliterate" its name and trademark to the point where the name and mark "Cue" will spontaneously and instantly be associated with toothpaste.

The dilution doctrine protects the good will built up for a trade-mark from dilution by another's mark. "Its underlying rationale is that the gradual diminution or whittling away of the value of a trade-mark, resulting from extensive use by another of a mark identical or similar to that of the senior user, constitutes an invasion of the senior user's property right in his trademark and gives rise to an actionable wrong. The wrong, under this theory, is not dependent upon a showing of competitive relationship of the products or likelihood of confusion" (G. B. Kent & Sons v. P. Lorillard & Co., 114 F. Supp. 621, 630–631). While the right has been recognized the doctrine has been sparingly applied.... It would appear [that] some measure of confusion must be present....

... Plaintiff has urged the point that its mark "Cue" has achieved such "distinctive quality" that its use by another as a trade-mark will do it great injury. The evidence has failed to establish that "Cue" has acquired such secondary meaning so that the general public will associate it only with plaintiff's magazine. By that I do not mean to imply that it has not achieved a certain degree of recognition in its field. However, as a common, simple dictionary word, plaintiff is not entitled to a monopoly of the mark....

I am further convinced that defendant's "Cue" toothpaste is so dissimilar, unlike, alien and foreign to plaintiff's business that there will be no confusion in the public market and there will be no dilution, within the meaning of section 368-d of the General Business Law, of its trade-mark "Cue—the complete entertainment guide". Under these circumstances, if plaintiff were to be granted the relief which it seeks, it would be tantamount to giving it "Cue" as against the whole world.

I am also satisfied that the status, standing and stature of the defendant corporation do not lend themselves to such reliance upon the efforts of the plaintiff for the upbuilding of the trade-mark "Cue", as would suggest that this defendant now seeks to "cash in" on the good will attained by the plaintiff....

Accordingly, both plaintiff and defendant may use the word "Cue" as a trade-mark for its goods—plaintiff on its magazine; defendant on its toothpaste—without infringement of the rights of the other, and the complaint of the plaintiff is dismissed....

Notes

1. In affirming the trial court's judgment, the Appellate Division said that injunctive relief under the anti-dilution statute was not warranted because, while there might be some dilution, the evidence did not establish "a sufficient likelihood of injury of the distinctive quality of plaintiff's trade mark." Also, injunctive relief would be inequitable because plaintiff knew of defendant's use of the name "Cue" for liquid dentrifice in 1939 and for toothpaste as early as 1961, but did not object until 1964, after defendant had incurred much expense in market preparation.

2. Judge Kozinski's opinion for the court in Mattel, Inc. v. MCA Records, Inc., 296 F.3d 894 (9th Cir. 2002), cert. denied, 537 U.S. 1171 (2003), gives the following explanation of dilution: "'Dilution' refers to the 'whittling away of the value of a trademark' when it's used to identify different products.... For example, Tylenol snowboards, Netscape sex shops and Harry Potter dry cleaners would all weaken the 'commercial magnetism' of these marks and diminish their ability to evoke their original associations. These uses dilute the selling power of these trademarks by blurring their 'uniqueness and singularity,' and/or by tarnishing them with negative associations. [¶] By contrast to trademark infringement, the injury from dilution usually occurs when consumers *aren't* confused about the source of the product. Even if no one suspects that the maker of analgesics has entered into the snowboard business, the Tylenol mark will now bring to mind two products, not one. Whereas trademark law targets 'interference with the source signaling function' of trademarks, dilution protects owners 'from an appropriation of or free riding on' the substantial investment that they have made in their marks."

3. The name of the noted Tiffany jewelry store, located in New York City, is adopted by a restaurant and lounge in Boston. Should this be enjoined? See Tiffany & Co. v. Boston Club, Inc., 231 F. Supp. 836 (D. Mass. 1964) (jewelry store entitled to injunction; defendant's assumption of its name had tendency to subject plaintiff's good will and reputation to hazards of defendant's business). A law firm, expanding nationwide with the use of extensive advertising, takes its name from the surname of its founding partner, which happens also to be the name of a major hotel chain. Is this to be restrained? Of what

significance is it that the chain's hotel rooms have moderate to high prices and the law firm's mission is to provide basic legal services at low prices to persons of moderate means? See Hyatt Corp. v. Hyatt Legal Services, 736 F.2d 1153 (7th Cir. 1984), cert. denied, 469 U.S. 1019 (1984), on remand, 610 F. Supp. 381 (N.D. Ill. 1985) (law firm required to add founder's first initial). Is there dilution of the famous "Dairy Queen" trade name if a film about beauty contest participants in rural "dairy country" is called *Dairy Queens*? See American Dairy Queen Corp. v. New Line Productions, Inc., 35 F. Supp. 2d 727 (D. Minn. 1998) (preliminary injunction against use of name).

4. How "distinctive" must a mark or trade name be? In Allied Maintenance Corp. v. Allied Mechanical Trades, Inc., 42 N.Y.2d 538, 399 N.Y.S.2d 628, 369 N.E.2d 1162 (1977), a 4–3 majority decided that "Allied Maintenance" was too weak to be protected because "allied" was a common word found in the names of many businesses. The public would not associate the word particularly with plaintiff. What if plaintiff's name is strong in a particular trade or market but not well-known to the general public? This was a major factor in the Second Circuit's decision not to hold the manufacturer of the Lexus luxury car liable to the proprietor of the computerized legal research service Lexis, marketed to attorneys and accountants. The court also believed that in commercial advertising, there would be "no substantial similarity" between the two marks. Mead Data Central, Inc. v. Toyota Motor Sales, U.S.A., Inc., 575 F.2d 1026 (2d Cir. 1989). See also Parenting Unlimited Inc. v. Columbia Pictures Television Inc., 743 F. Supp. 221 (S.D.N.Y. 1990) (proprietor of *Baby Talk* magazine, published for expectant parents and parents of infants, denied injunction against use of *Baby Talk* as title of television "sitcom").

5. "Kodak" is a coined word that for decades has been a famous brand name with great selling power. It is frequently given as an example of a trade name that cannot be used without incurring liability under an unfair competition or dilution theory to the company which has long used the name to sell products and services. But is there a likelihood of injury when "Kodak" or another very famous name is used by a small business in a completely different trade? One example is inclusion of "Dior" in the names of two small cleaning establishments. Christian Dior, S.A.R.L. v. Miss Dior of Flatbush, Inc., 173 U.S.P.Q. 416 (E.D.N.Y. 1972). See also Caesars World, Inc. v. Caesar's Palace, p. 292, supra. In Eastman Kodak Co. v. Rakow, 739 F. Supp. 116 (W.D.N.Y. 1989), the Eastman Kodak Company obtained an injunction forbidding the use of "Kodak" by a stand-up comedian who had adopted it as his stage name!

6. The McDonald's Corporation has brought suit against businesses using words beginning with "Mc." These words may have been adopted because of the McDonald's-related association of "Mc" with fast service and consistent products. Should these actions succeed? Should the outcome depend upon whether defendant sells food? Caters to travellers? Operates through franchisees? See McDonald's Corp. v. McBagel's, Inc., 649 F. Supp. 1268 (S.D.N.Y. 1986) (small-town bagel bakery called "McBagel's"); Quality Inns International, Inc. v. McDonald's Corp., 695 F. Supp. 198 (D. Md. 1988) (chain of economy hotels called "McSleep Inn"); McDonald's Corp. v. Druck and Gerner, DDS., P.C., 814 F. Supp. 1127 (N.D.N.Y. 1993) ("McDental" dentists' office).

7. Should plaintiff be granted relief if defendant's use of plaintiff's trademark or name might cause ridicule or offense, or otherwise tarnish plaintiff's image? In Dallas Cowboys Cheerleaders, Inc. v. Pussycat Cinema, Ltd., 467 F. Supp. 366 (S.D.N.Y. 1979), aff'd, 604 F.2d 200 (2d Cir. 1979), the Dallas Cowboys Cheerleaders, an organization of cheerleaders for a professional football team, sued the producer and distributor of a pornographic film, *Debbie Does Dallas*. In the film, the main character, Debbie, is chosen to become a cheerleader in Dallas. The film clearly conveys, the court found, that Debbie is to join the Dallas Cowboys Cheerleaders. To finance travel to Dallas, Debbie and her girl friends

(who decide to accompany her) offer sexual services to local businessmen. In the culminating episode, Debbie engages in a number of minutely depicted sex acts, portions of her cheerleader uniform being in view throughout. The uniform closely resembled plaintiffs'. The film's advertising referred to the star, who never had been a Dallas Cowboys cheerleader, as an "ex Dallas Cowgirl Cheerleader." In enjoining the distribution, exhibition and advertising of the film, the court decided that the film wilfully misappropriated plaintiff's trade names and marks and that if such activities were allowed to continue, there would be a whittling down or dilution of the reputation and good will associated with the name and marks. Dilution was described as an "infection" which if allowed to spread would destroy the advertising value of a mark. Confusion of source was unnecessary to a dilution action, but the use of the Dallas Cheerleaders marks was found to suggest that the film was sponsored by plaintiff or that plaintiff's cheerleaders were performing in it.

8. The Court of Appeals' rejection of defendants' First Amendment arguments in the *Debbie Does Dallas* case was criticized in L.L. Bean, Inc. v. Drake Publishers, Inc., 811 F.2d 26 (1st Cir. 1987), appeal dismissed, 483 U.S. 1013 (1987), which held it unconstitutional to enjoin publication and distribution of an "erotic" magazine's parody of plaintiff's catalogue. Compare Pillsbury Co. v. Milky Way Productions, 215 U.S.P.Q. 124 (N.D. Ga. 1981), where plaintiff was a food company whose advertising featured the characters "Popping Fresh" and "Poppie Fresh." They were portrayed in defendant's pornographic magazine engaging in intercourse and oral sex. The offending picture included plaintiff's barrelhead trademark and its jingle. Plaintiff contended the picture was so placed as to suggest it was an actual advertisement by plaintiff. There was no likelihood of confusion, but actionable dilution was found. Complaints about parodies of non-profit organizations failed in Girl Scouts of the United States of America v. Personality Posters Manufacturing Co., 304 F. Supp. 1228 (S.D.N.Y. 1969) (poster portraying pregnant Girl Scout with Girl Scout motto "Be Prepared"), and in University of Notre Dame Du Lac v. Twentieth Century-Fox Film Corp., 22 A.D.2d 452, 256 N.Y.S.2d 301 (1965), aff'd, 15 N.Y.2d 940, 259 N.Y.S.2d 832, 207 N.E.2d 508 (1965) (novel and film farce about football game between plaintiff's team and team of fictional Arab country). Should use of a non-commercial organization's name or symbols be treated differently from use of a commercial party's? Can a non-commercial entity suffer actionable "dilution"?

9. Suppose a business not in competition with plaintiff employs a variant of plaintiff's advertising slogan? Does it matter what is being advertised? In Chemical Corp. of America v. Anheuser-Busch, Inc., 306 F.2d 433 (5th Cir. 1962), plaintiff manufactured Budweiser Beer and used the slogan "Where there's life ... there's Bud." Defendant, in its advertising for a combined floor wax and insecticide, adopted the slogan, "Where there's life ... there's bugs." The court granted an injunction, cautioning that plaintiff's protection extended only to the entire slogan, not to every slogan containing the phrase "Where there's life." Another Budweiser slogan is "This Bud's for you." Can it be used by a florist? See Anheuser-Busch, Inc. v. Florists Association of Greater Cleveland, Inc., 603 F. Supp. 35 (N.D. Ohio 1984). The proprietors of the Ringling Bros.-Barnum & Bailey Circus, known as "The Greatest Show on Earth," obtained a preliminary injunction prohibiting a car dealership from using the slogan "The Greatest Used Car Show on Earth." Ringling Bros.-Barnum & Bailey Combined Shows, Inc. v. Celozzi-Ettelson Chevrolet, Inc., 855 F.2d 480 (7th Cir. 1988). Compare Ringling Bros.-Barnum & Bailey Combined Shows, Inc. v. B.E. Windows Corp., 937 F. Supp. 204 (S.D.N.Y. 1996), denying a preliminary injunction against naming a bar at the top of the World Trade Center "The Greatest Bar on Earth."

10. Does the dilution theory provide an action if plaintiff's business or product name is used in a competitor's comparative advertising? See Diversified Marketing, Inc. v. Estee

Lauder, Inc., 705 F. Supp. 128 (S.D.N.Y. 1988). In Eveready Battery Co., Inc. v. Adolph Coors Co., 765 F. Supp. 440 (N.D. Ill. 1991), the court found no dilution in a television commercial that parodied the advertising of a non-competing product.

11. A good illustration of the use of an anti-dilution statute to prevent dilution of the advertising value of plaintiff's name, as distinct from tarnishment or confusion, is Wedgwood Homes, Inc. v. Lund, 294 Or. 493, 659 P.2d 377 (1983). Plaintiffs (Wedgwood Homes) developed residential real estate. Defendant maintained apartment complexes for retired persons: Wedgwood Downs and Wedgwood Place. The court rejected defendant's arguments that the statute was intended to protect only nationally famous names (plaintiff was well-known only in the county where it did business) and that only "coined" words were protected. More than thirty states have anti-dilution statutes. See Restatement of Unfair Competition § 25 (1995), and the history and critique of dilution liability in Martino, Trademark Dilution (1996).

12. A federal dilution statute came into force in 1996. 15 U.S.C. § 1125(c). As expanded in 2006, the federal statute provides a remedy for the owner of "a famous mark that is distinctive" when there is "use of a mark or trade name in commerce that is likely to cause dilution by blurring or ... tarnishment of the famous mark." A mark is "famous" if "it is widely recognized by the general consuming public of the United States as a designation of the source of goods or services of the mark's owner." Relief is limited to an injunction unless the defendant "willfully intended" to trade on recognition of the famous mark or harm its reputation. The statute explicitly excludes noncommercial use of a mark, news reporting and commentary, and "any fair use" of the mark, including for purposes of commentary, criticism or parody or for comparison of goods or services. However, "fair use" does not extend to using plaintiff's mark as a "designation of source" for defendant's own goods or services. See Starbucks Corp. v. Wolfe's Borough Coffee, Inc., 588 F.3d 97 (2d Cir. 2009).

Wyatt Earp Enterprises, Inc. v. Sackman, Inc.

United States District Court, Southern District of New York
157 F. Supp. 621 (1958)

EDELSTEIN, District Judge....

Plaintiff is a producer of motion pictures for television and is the proprietor of a very successful series entitled "The Life and Legend of Wyatt Earp", nationally and internationally televised over the facilities of the American Broadcasting Company [weekly for over two years]. The defendant has been in the business of manufacturing children's playsuits for many years, and, after the commencement of the "Wyatt Earp" television program by the plaintiff, entered into a license agreement with it purporting to grant the right to defendant to use "the name and likeness of Hugh O'Brian in the characterization of Wyatt Earp", O'Brian being the star of the program, portraying the title character. The agreement was not renewed by the plaintiff upon its expiration, another manufacturer having been licensed in place of defendant. The defendant has, after the expiration of its rights under the agreement, continued to manufacture and market children's playsuits under the name, mark and symbol of "Wyatt Earp", although without using the name and likeness of Hugh O'Brian and without specific reference to "ABC-TV".

The plaintiff seeks to enjoin the defendant's use of the name, mark and symbol "Wyatt Earp" on its playsuits on the ground that, by plaintiff's efforts, the name has come to have a secondary meaning indicative of origin, relationship and association with the television program; and that the public is likely to attribute the use of the name "Wyatt Earp" by the defendant to the plaintiff as a source of sponsorship and buy defendant's merchandise in this erroneous belief. The defendant denies the possibility of secondary meaning attaching to the name, arguing that it belonged to a living person out of the nation's history, and hence has become a part of the public domain not subject to commercial monopolization by anyone. Such a contention, I believe, overstates the law.... [T]he plaintiff has a cognizable interest in preventing the likelihood of consumer confusion, and it is such an interest as the law will protect against an opposing interest no greater than that of all persons in the use of the names in history. It is true that where a symbol is not fanciful but merely descriptive, the plaintiff bears a very heavy burden of proving confusion is likely. Or it may be that a nonfanciful, real name is such a part of the national fabric that all have a measurable interest in its use, to the extent that it acquires no secondary meaning extending into a defendant's field so as to cause a likelihood of confusion.... If the plaintiff can show that it is likely to succeed, at trial, in proving that it invested the name of Wyatt Earp with a commercial significance and good will that is attributable to itself and that is likely to be appropriated by the defendant by way of consumer-confusion, it will be entitled to the relief it seeks.

HUGH O'BRIAN AS WYATT EARP   Photofest

... [T]he name of Wyatt Earp has been battered into the public consciousness by the tele-vision program to an extent far beyond any fame or notoriety ever previously attached to the marshal's name.... By reason of the popularity of the production, enormous publicity has been generated in other media of mass communication. Popularly known as the "Wyatt Earp Program", it has from its inception been among the most popular television enter-tainments in the nation, viewed weekly on millions of television receivers by additional mil-lions of persons. As an indication of the public acceptance of the program, there has been a great and increasing nation-wide demand for articles and products sponsored by the plain-tiff and bearing the name, mark and symbol of "Wyatt Earp". It has been asserted without denial or other comment that goods and merchandise marketed under the name of "Wyatt Earp" were unheard of prior to the first telecast of the show. The finding is nearly inescapable that the commercial value now enjoyed by the name is attributable almost entirely to the pro-gram. The plaintiff, as a result, has entered into the business of licensing merchandise rights in connection with the program under agreements controlling the nature and quality of the goods licensed so as to maintain high standards and to preserve the integrity of its good will. Under these agreements the royalties to be received for the year 1957 will exceed $100,000. The merchandise so promoted, in no way unique aside from its program identi-fication, obviously sells much more readily than the same merchandise would sell without the program identification, as borne out by the fact that manufacturers pay and seek to pay substantial sums of money for the privilege of sponsorship, by way of licensing agreements. It can be found preliminarily, therefore, that the name and characterization of "Wyatt Earp" as televised by the plaintiff has become identified in the mind of the consumer public with merchandise upon which the name has been imprinted; that this identification and good will has extended to the field of children's playsuits sold and distributed under the name, mark and symbol "Wyatt Earp"; and the defendant is merchandising "Wyatt Earp" playsuits be-cause of a popular demand for merchandise identified with the program and the plaintiff.

... Defendant's present outfit ... appears to bear a striking resemblance to the outfit it previously made under license and to the one made by the present licensee; and these cos-tumes, approximating the one worn by the television "Wyatt Earp", indeed seem to be markedly different from other "western" costumes. The defendant continues to mark on its boxes the name "Wyatt Earp" together with the legend "official outfit". Moreover, in its catalogue, the Wyatt Earp outfit is advertised in a context with three "TV personality" western outfits, all of them being characterized as "official", but with the "TV personal-ity" designation omitted from the Wyatt Earp display. The text and layout are presented in such a manner as to convey the impression of an identification of defendant's Wyatt Earp playsuit with the Wyatt Earp television program. Indeed, it is so difficult to understand how any other impression could be conveyed that the finding of an intent to convey an erroneous notion of association with the program is highly probable. Unless the word "official" is passed over as sheer gibberish, the idea of sponsorship is inescapably implied.

The "critical question" in a case of secondary meaning "always is whether the public is moved in any degree to buy the article because of its source and what are the features by which it distinguishes that source." Charles D. Briddell, Inc. v. Alglobe Trading Corp., 2 Cir., 194 F.2d 416, 419.... [T]he likelihood of consumer-confusion is the test of secondary meaning. I find that, for the purposes of preliminary injunctive relief, plaintiff has met the burden of proving the likelihood of consumer-confusion. The public is moved to buy merchandise because of an identification with the name "Wyatt Earp" as developed by the plaintiff's television program. The defendant's use of the name created a likelihood that the public would believe, erroneously, that its playsuits were licensed or sponsored by the plaintiff, to the injury of the plaintiff's good will and to the hazard of its reputation. There is a high probability that, upon the trial of the issues, plaintiff will be able to establish that the name, mark and symbol "Wyatt Earp" has acquired a secondary meaning in the minds of the public as identified and associated with the television program and the plaintiff, and extending into the field of children's playsuits.

It is true that the plaintiff and defendant are not direct competitors in the same field of endeavor. The plaintiff does not manufacture children's playsuits. But where secondary meaning and consumer-confusion are established, use of a trade name even upon non-competing goods may be enjoined. See Triangle Publications v. Rohrlich, 2 Cir., 167 F.2d 969, 972, 973. And as held by the Court of Appeals in that case, the same principle applies to the situation of confusion about sponsorship. "In either case, the wrong of the defendant consisted in imposing upon the plaintiff a risk that the defendant's goods would be associated by the public with the plaintiff, and it can make no difference whether that association is based upon attributing defendant's goods to plaintiff or to a sponsorship by the latter when it has been determined that plaintiff had a right to protection of its trade name." Furthermore, in the case at bar, it would seem that something more than mere sponsorship is involved, something that very closely approaches direct competition. The plaintiff does not manufacture children's playsuits, but it licenses another to do so on a royalty basis. Any customers purchasing from the defendant on the strength of the "Wyatt Earp" name are customers diverted from plaintiff's licensee, to its direct pecuniary injury, in addition to any danger to its reputation.

While there is little doubt that the violation of plaintiff's rights by a diversion of purchasers to the defendant could readily be compensated for in a judgment for money damages, it also appears that a denial of preliminary injunctive relief would work irreparable and serious injury to the plaintiff by jeopardizing the entire licensing system it has built at great effort and expense. On a balance of the harms, the plaintiff stands to suffer much greater injury by a denial of injunctive relief than any which can befall defendant by granting such relief. Accordingly, the motion for a preliminary injunction will be granted....

Notes

1. To what extent does the person who creates a character or uses it in a popular work of entertainment or literature have control over use of the character in merchandising? Does liability for unlicensed use depend upon actual competition between the parties? Competition with a licensee of plaintiff? Potential licensing of what defendant is doing without a license? When can plaintiff demonstrate both secondary meaning and a likelihood of damage if defendant is not restrained? Should the public persona of an entertainer or other celebrity be considered a "character" if it appears in merchandise without the celebrity's consent? If so, are the principles of liability the same as for wholly fictional characters?

2. Some decisions, especially of courts outside the United States, have found no liability for passing off because the parties had no "common field of activity." See McCulloch v. Lewis A. May (Produce Distributors) Ltd., [1947] 2 All E.R. 845 (Ch. D.) (plaintiff a radio personality featured on "Children's Hour" program, in which he was known as "Uncle Mac"; defendants began distributing cereal called "Uncle Mac's Puffed Wheat," with cartons proclaiming "Uncle Mac loves children—and children love Uncle Mac"); Lyngstad v. Anabas Products Ltd., [1977] F.S.R. 62 (Ch. D.) (defendants manufactured badges, T-shirt transfers, pillow slips, etc. bearing pictures of rock group, which did not license such products; no showing that public would believe that plaintiffs associated with or approved defendants' goods). A "common field of activity" is no longer required. See

Irvine v. Talksport Ltd., [2002] 1 W.L.R. 2355 (Ch. D.), rev'd, [2003] 1 W.L.R. 1576, [2003] 2 All E.R. 881 (C.A.). Cf. Hirsch v. S.C. Johnson & Son, Inc., 90 Wis. 2d 379, 280 N.W.2d 129 (1979) (plaintiff a football player nicknamed "Crazylegs"; seller of Crazylegs shaving gel for women liable for trade name infringement if use of name on product caused confusion as to approval or sponsorship by plaintiff).

3. In Children's Television Workshop, Inc. v. Woolworths (N.S.W). Ltd., [1981] 1 N.S.W.L.R. 273 (Sup. Ct.), plaintiffs produced a television program featuring the "Muppets" puppet characters. Defendants sold toys resembling the Muppets. Evidence showed that the public believed these were being sold under some license from or arrangement with plaintiffs. Plaintiffs planned to grant such licenses. The court enjoined defendants' sale of Muppet toys, finding a common field of business activity. In Paramount Pictures Corp. v. Howley, (1991) 5 O.R.3d 573, 39 C.P.R.3d 419 (Gen. Div.), amended, (1992) 39 C.P.R.3d 419n (Ont. Gen. Div.), defendant sold sportswear with crocodiles and features taken from or suggested by the film *Crocodile Dundee* and its star, Paul Hogan. The name Crocodile Dundee was also used. Suit was brought by the company which had exclusive rights to distribution of *Crocodile Dundee* in the United States and Canada. It hoped to earn revenue by its own licensing of Crocodile Dundee merchandise, as it had with other films, but defendant's products were on the market long before plaintiff granted licenses. The court thought it unlikely that consumers or stores purchased defendant's merchandise because of confusion with any of plaintiff's products or reliance upon any reputation that plaintiff had for clothing. Nevertheless, if found actionable passing off on the basis that both parties were in the business of licensing the use of clothing with images and characters, stores would purchase defendant's clothing on the assumption that defendant had obtained a license from plaintiff, and plaintiff's licensing business would be injured. Should a court enjoin sale of a non-competing product because a portion of the public erroneously believes that the product is marketed or approved by the plaintiff? See Anheuser-Busch, Inc. v. VIP Products, LLC, 666 F. Supp. 2d 974 (E.D. Mo. 2008) (producer of Budweiser beer granted preliminary injunction against marketing of "Buttwiper" dog toy).

4. If plaintiff produces a television program which features a distinctive car, will there be liability if someone sells a toy model of the car without a license from plaintiff? See Warner Bros. Inc. v. Gay Toys, Inc. 724 F.2d 327 (2d Cir. 1983) (consumers' identification of toy with television series, motivating purchase, sufficient for liability; need not believe that plaintiff sponsored or authorized toy). What about an amusement park ride inspired by plaintiff's film? In Paramount Pictures Corp. v. Dorney Park Coaster Co., 698 F. Supp. 1274 (E.D. Pa. 1988), suit was brought by the producer and distributor of the film *Top Gun*. The film was a portrayal of fighter pilot trainees at a naval air station in California. "Top Gun" was a nickname for the California training facility. The film included scenes of aerial "dog fights" between instructors and students. Eighteen months after the release of *Top Gun*, which was quite successful, defendant sold to an amusement park a ride called "Top Gun." During the ride, the occupants of each car, using a control stick and video monitor, would attempt to "shoot down" other cars. Plaintiff's licensing program for *Top Gun* included video games for arcades and homes but not amusement park equipment. A preliminary injunction was granted. What if defendant makes a film whose plot uses a story or song written or produced by plaintiff?

5. In Bi-Rite Enterprises, Inc. v. Button Master, 555 F. Supp. 1188 (S.D.N.Y. 1983), rock groups and individual performers sued businesses that sold buttons bearing plaintiffs' likenesses and logos. A company that the performers licensed to sell such buttons was also a plaintiff. The court held that in the absence of consumer confusion about source or sponsorship, there was no action for unfair competition. Unfair competition law did

not protect marks that were exploited only for their functional value and not to confuse the public. It therefore did not restrict the sale of marks to consumers (here, the performers' fans) who desired a mark because of its intrinsic value to them rather than because it was a designation of origin. The court decided, however, that the groups, individual performers and, when the performers had granted it an exclusive license to market buttons bearing their marks, the plaintiff button company could maintain actions for violation of the performers' "right of publicity," and defendants' unlicensed marketing of the buttons was a violation. Compare Hutchence v. South Seas Bubble Co. Pty. Ltd., (1986) 64 A.L.R. 330 (Fed. Ct. Gen. Div.) (sellers of T-shirts displaying name or album titles of rock group did not avoid passing off liability by selling goods with notice that they were "genuine bootleg products" not authorized by performers). On whether it is actionable to *perform* a personality or character created by plaintiff, see pp. 361–373, infra. The right of publicity is addressed in Chapter 5.

6. A young women's fraternal organization alleges that a jeweler is selling jewelry bearing the organization's insignia. Is this actionable? See International Order of Job's Daughters v. Lindeburg & Co., 633 F.2d 912 (9th Cir. 1980), cert. denied, 452 U.S. 941 (1981) (no relief; manufacturer using organizations' emblem as functional part of design of certain jewelry; no showing that anyone misled about origin, sponsorship or endorsement). National Football League member clubs grant an exclusive license for the reproduction and sale of their jerseys. Defendant, who is not licensed, begins manufacturing and selling replicas of the jerseys. Should this be enjoined? See National Football League Properties, Inc. v. Wichita Falls Sportswear, Inc., 532 F. Supp. 651 (W.D. Wash. 1982) (injunction justified; defendant's activities created likelihood of confusion as to source).

7. The Rock and Roll Hall of Fame in Cleveland has a very distinctive building, designed by one of the world's leading architects. A professional photographer took a photograph of the building against a colorful sunset and created a poster that was sold for $40 to $50. "Rock N' Roll Hall of Fame Cleveland" and (in smaller print) the photographer's name and production company appeared below the photograph on the poster. Did sale of the poster infringe the legal rights of the Hall of Fame, which also sold a poster containing a photograph of the building as well as postcards of the building? See Rock and Roll Hall of Fame and Museum, Inc. v. Gentile Productions, 134 F.3d 749 (6th Cir. 1998), on remand, 71 F. Supp. 2d 755 (N.D. Ohio 1999).

Section 3. False Advertising

Mosler Safe Company v. Ely-Norris Safe Company

Supreme Court of the United States
273 U.S. 132 (1927)

Mr. Justice HOLMES delivered the opinion of the Court.

This is a bill in equity brought by a corporation of New Jersey against a corporation of New York alleging unfair competition. It was treated below as a suit by the only manufacturer of safes containing an explosion chamber for protection against burglars. It seeks an injunction against selling safes with a metal band around the door in the place where the plaintiff put the chamber, or falsely representing that the defendant's safes contain an explosion chamber. The plaintiff admitted that the defendant's safes bore the defendant's name and address and that the defendant never gave any customer reason to believe that its safes were of the plaintiff's make.... The Circuit Court of Appeals held that if, as it took it to be alleged, the plaintiff had the monopoly of explosion chambers and the defendant falsely represented that its safes had such chambers, the plaintiff had a good case....

... The bill alleges that the plaintiff has a patent for an explosion chamber "as described and claimed in said letters patent"; and it has the exclusive right to make and sell "safes containing such an explosion chamber"; that no other safes containing "such an explosion chamber" could be got in the United States before the defendant, as it is alleged, infringed the plaintiff's patent, for which alleged infringement a suit is pending. It then is alleged that the defendant is making and selling safes with a metal band around the door at substantially the same location as the explosion chamber of plaintiff's safes, and has represented to the public "that the said metal band was employed to cover or close an explosion chamber" by reason of which "the public has been led to purchase defendant's said safes as and for safes containing an explosion chamber, such as is manufactured and sold by the plaintiff herein." It is alleged further that sometimes the defendant's safes have no explosion chamber under the band but are bought by those who want safes with a chamber and so the defendant has deprived the plaintiff of sales, competed unfairly and damaged the plaintiff's reputation. The plaintiff relies upon its patent suit for relief in respect of the sales of safes alleged to infringe its rights. It complains here only of false representations as to safes that do not infringe but that are sold as having explosion chambers although in fact they do not.

It is consistent with every allegation in the bill and the defendant in argument asserted it to be a fact, that there are other safes with explosion chambers beside that for which the plaintiff has a patent. The defendant is charged only with representing that its safes had "an" explosion chamber, which, so far as appears, it had a perfect right to do if the representation was true. If on the other hand the representation was false as it is alleged sometimes to have been, there is nothing to show that customers had they known the facts would have gone to the plaintiff rather than to other competitors in the market, or to lay a foundation for the claim for a loss of sales....

Decree reversed.

Notes

1. In American Washboard Co. v. Saginaw Manufacturing Co., 103 F. 281 (6th Cir. 1900), the sole manufacturer of washboards with aluminum rubbing surfaces was denied an injunction against defendant's misrepresenting its zinc washboards as aluminum, aluminum being the superior material. The court believed that a private right of action arose from deception of the public only when defendant induced the public to purchase goods in the belief that they were plaintiff's. It expressed concern over the "Pandora's box of litigation" that would ensue if other alleged falsehoods in attaching names to goods gave rise to an action. This case and the principal case are the leading American authorities on whether an action can be maintained against a competitor which allegedly deprives plaintiff of custom by misrepresentations about its own products or services.

2. The Supreme Court's decision in *Mosler Safe* leaves upon the possibility that relief can be obtained on a showing that defendant's false statements necessarily divert sales

from plaintiff. This could be the case when the statements concern parts or accessories needed to operate equipment and there is no other supplier. See Electronics Corp. of America v. Honeywell, Inc., 428 F.2d 191 (1st Cir. 1970) (defendant sold replacement component for system made by plaintiff with misrepresentations about cost and ease of installation). But the difficulty of making such a showing supports the conclusion that apart from the theories of liability addressed in the first two sections of this chapter and any statutory remedies, false advertising does not give rise to an action. Why not allow at least injunctive relief? If there are some circumstances in which an action can be maintained, must defendant know of the falsity of the advertising? Lack reasonable grounds for the statements made?

3. The subject of false and misleading advertising is now governed by an extensive body of federal and state legislation which provides for both private remedies and administrative action. Every state has enacted some version of the Uniform Deceptive Trade Practices Act or other "unfair trade practices" legislation. Section 43(a) of the Lanham Act, 15 U.S.C. § 1125(a), provides that "any person who believes that he or she is or is likely to be damaged" can bring an action for misrepresentations in "commercial advertising or promotion" about the "nature, characteristics, qualities, or geographic origin of his or her or another person's goods, services, or commercial activities." The provision applies to "all commerce which may lawfully be regulated by Congress." 15 U.S.C. § 1127.

4. *"Extended passing off" liability.* Concerning the possibilities of finding a non-statutory cause of action, the major development of recent years has been the extension of passing off liability by courts outside the United States to some false descriptions of goods sold in competition with plaintiffs'. See Naresh, Passing-off, Goodwill and False Advertising: New Wine in Old Bottles, 45 Camb. L.J. 97 (1986). This originated in an action brought by the producers of champagne from the Champagne district of France against the sellers of "Spanish champagne," a champagne-like beverage produced in Spain. The court found that this use of "champagne" was likely to mislead a substantial portion of the public into believing defendants' product was champagne. It enjoined the "passing off" of Spanish wine as champagne. J. Bollinger v. Costa Brava Wine Co. Ltd. (No. 2), [1961] 1 W.L.R. 277 (Ch. D.). Similarly, sellers of the purely Scottish product were allowed an action for the sale as "Scotch whisky" of a beverage containing spirit not distilled in Scotland. John Walker & Sons Ltd. v. Henry Ost & Co. Ltd., [1970] 1 W.L.R. 917 (Ch. D.). In the champagne litigation, it was necessary to find that "champagne" was widely understood to mean wine grown in a particular region of France, not merely a type of wine. Compare Wineworths Group Ltd. v. Comite Interprofessionel du Vin de Champagne. [1992] 2 N.Z.L.R. 327 (C.A.) (successful passing off action for sale in New Zealand of Australian sparkling wine labelled as champagne or Australian champagne), with Institut National des Appellations d'Origine des Vins et Eaux-de-Vie v. Andres Wines Ltd., (1987) 60 O.R.2d 316, 40 D.L.R.4th 239 (High Ct.), aff'd, (1990) 74 O.R.2d 203, 71 D.L.R.4th 575 (C.A.) (Canadian champagne distinct product not confused with French champagne). Is "Swiss cheese" understood to mean cheese made in Switzerland? See Schweizerishe Kaeseunion Bern v. Saul Starck, Inc., 162 Misc. 485, 293 N.Y.S. 816 (Sup. Ct. 1937) ("imported Swiss cheese").

5. There is some older American precedent finding an action when defendant falsely labels its product with a geographic term signifying particular qualities possessed by the genuine product. See Newman v. Alvord, 51 N.Y. 189 (1872) (cement from stone quarried near Syracuse labelled "Akron Cement," taking advantage of good reputation of cement from stone quarried near Akron, New York); California Fruit Canners' Association v. Myer, 104 F. 82 (C.C.D. Md. 1899) (suit by California canners of pears grown in state, alleging

defendants labelled as California pears fruit grown and canned elsewhere); Pillsbury-Washburn Flour Mills Co., v. Eagle, 86 F. 608 (7th Cir. 1898), cert. denied, 173 U.S. 703 (1899) (Minneapolis millers sought injunction against advertising flour from mills in Milwaukee as Minneapolis flour); Douglas v. Newark Cheese Co., 153 Misc. 85, 274 N.Y.S. 406 (Sup. Ct. 1934) (defendants sold as "Roquefort" cheese not from Roquefort district of France). Contra, New York & Rosendale Co. v. Coplay Cement Co., 44 F. 277 (C.C.E.D. Pa. 1890), reh'g denied, 45 F. 212 (C.C.E.D. Pa. 1891) ("Rosendale Cement").

6. In Erven Warnink Besloten Vennootschap v. J. Townsend & Sons (Hull) Ltd., [1979] A.C. 731 (H.L.), plaintiffs had long manufactured in the Netherlands a liquor called "advocaat." It was exported to Britain, where it became quite popular. As required by regulations in the Netherlands, the ingredients were the spirit brandewijn, egg yolks and sugar. Defendants began marketing in Britain a beverage called "Keeling's Old English Advocaat," composed of dried egg powder mixed with Cyprus sherry. This resembled what was known in Britain as an "egg-flip." It could not be shown that this had been mistaken for Dutch advocaat, but the new drink did capture a substantial part of plaintiffs' English market. The House of Lords held that a product having a particular character because of its ingredients and having gained a public reputation under a descriptive name should be protected from deceptive use of that name by competitors even though the ingredients did not come from a particular locality and the good will attaching to the use of the name was shared by a number of traders. Though there was no passing off in its classic form, it was thought that the law of passing off should be extended to this situation. The name "advocaat" denoted in England a distinct and recognizable species of beverage. Defendants' product had no natural association with the word "advocaat" and its use could cause damage to plaintiffs both directly through loss of sales and indirectly through debasement of the term "advocaat." The possibility of further extension of the "extended" passing off theory to other misrepresentations in defendant's advertising or marketing practices is addressed in Bristol Conservatories Ltd. v. Conservatories Custom Built Ltd., p. 352, infra.

Chapter 4

Intangible Assets

Section 1. Trade Secrets and Confidential Information

Wilson Certified Foods, Inc. v. Fairbury Food Products, Inc.
United States District Court, District of Nebraska
370 F. Supp. 1081 (1974)

SCHATZ, District Judge....

[Wilson Certified Foods, Inc., a manufacturer of food products, developed a process for manufacturing cooked bacon particles known as "Bits-O-Bacon." Bits-O-Bacon was produced in Wilson's Omaha plant. Arden Schacht was foreman of the department in which this work was done. In 1971, Schacht left Wilson and became president of Fairbury Foods, Inc. Subsequently, Fairbury began producing a cooked bacon particle similar to Wilson's. Wilson brought suit against Schacht, Fairbury Foods, Inc., Fairbury's current president, and a corporation which distributed Fairbury's products, asserting that by applying his knowledge of Wilson's process in his work at Fairbury, Schacht unlawfully appropriated a Wilson trade secret. There was no claim that Schacht took from Wilson any written material.]

... "[I]n Sandlin v. Johnson, 141 F.2d 660 (8th Cir. 1944), this Court recognized and approved the general rule that a trade secret consists of any formula, pattern, device or compilation of information which is used in one's business and which gives him an opportunity to obtain an advantage over competitors who do not know or use it. [Restatement, Torts, § 757, comment *b.*] ... The essential elements of a cause of action for appropriation of a trade secret are (1) existence of a trade secret, [*] (2) acquisition of the secret as a result of a confidential relationship, and (3) unauthorized use of the secret." [E.W. Bliss Company v. Struthers-Dunn, Inc., 408 F.2d 1108 (8th Cir. 1969).]

[Six factors are] set forth in Restatements, Torts, § 757, as the basis for determining the existence of a trade secret....

---

* "The threshold issue in every case is not whether there was a confidential relationship or a breach of contract or some other kind of misappropriation, but whether, in fact, there was a trade secret to be misappropriated." 2 R. Callman, *The Law of Unfair Competition, Trade-marks and Monopolies*, Sec. 51.1 at 348 (3d Ed. 1968).

I. THE EXTENT TO WHICH THE PROCESS IS KNOWN OUTSIDE THE PLAINTIFF'S BUSINESS.

The defendants' principal contention here is that the plaintiff's process is essentially a form of dry-rendering, a technique well known throughout the cooked food industry. The only expert witness called to testify in this trial stated that Wilson's process was indeed no more than dry-rendering.... Plaintiff argues that its system is not dry-rendering because the purposes of the two processes are different. The goal in dry-rendering is to remove useful fat from animal tissue with the residue, known as tankage, then used for animal feed. It is the fat which is primarily desired. On the other hand, in the plaintiff's Bits-O-Bacon process, the desired end product is not fat, but edible meat. Even though the goals or desired end products of these two processes may be different, it is apparent to the Court that the manner in which these results are reached is basically the same....

... [T]here are many factors such as starting temperatures and amount of raw material, amount of vacuum pressure, and time of cooking, which interrelate in the cooking and no fixed formula as to these factors was and is used by Wilson.

As to the equipment used in Wilson's process, there is no indication that any of the items are unique or that Wilson's adaptations of them to its bacon-cooking process is novel.

Therefore, because the basic process used by Wilson is dry-rendering and because no significant adaptations of that process have been made by Wilson, this Court finds that the process used by Wilson is one of general knowledge outside Wilson's business.

II. THE EXTENT TO WHICH THE PROCESS IS KNOWN BY EMPLOYEES OF THE PLAINTIFF AND BY OTHER PERSONS IN THE PLAINTIFF'S BUSINESS....

It is unclear exactly how many of Wilson's employees were familiar with the Bits-O-Bacon process from the time of its development until Mr. Schacht's departure in May, 1971. Mr. Schacht was at one time in charge of as many as seventy people on both the second and sixth floors, although not all of these were working on Bits-O-Bacon. By May of 1971, there were at least eight to ten full-time equipment operators for the Bits-O-Bacon process. But the individuals engaged in the process varied on a given day because work in Wilson's plant was allocated on the basis of seniority, and employees with greater seniority had first choice as to the particular jobs they wished to perform. There is no evidence that there was any special training required for or skill involved in becoming an operator. Nor did Wilson make significant efforts to restrict knowledge of the Bits-O-Bacon process to any certain employees within the Wilson operation.

These factors weigh heavily in the Court's finding and concluding that the Bits-O-Bacon process was relatively well-known within the Wilson operation.

III. THE EXTENT OF THE MEASURES TAKEN BY THE PLAINTIFF TO GUARD THE SECRECY OF THE PROCESS.

All of the actions which are relevant to this lawsuit took place at Wilson's Omaha Plant. This plant has a general security system whereby all persons desiring entry to the plant are questioned by a guard concerning their identification and purpose for visiting. Visitors are then issued passes and are accompanied by a Wilson employee at all times while within the plant. Bits-O-Bacon is produced solely on the sixth floor. There is only one entrance to this floor and all persons entering must pass in front of the foremen's office from which they can be seen through a glass window. The Court finds, however, that these measures constitute nothing more than general plant security of a type which is often present in manufacturing operations.

Mr. Schacht signed two agreements wherein he promised not to disclose any confidential information belonging to Wilson. The first of these is a part of the general employment form which all persons applying for work at Wilson must sign. The second is an agreement executed by all Wilson supervisory and managerial personnel. The Court does not find these two agreements to be significant or controlling in this case. Neither agreement mentions the Bits-O-Bacon process in any respect and it is undisputed that forms of this type were signed by untold numbers of Wilson employees over the years, most of whom were never involved in the Bits-O-Bacon operation. Moreover, Mr. Schacht would not be legally permitted to disclose any valid trade secrets of Wilson even in the absence of these agreements, so their presence cannot aid Wilson in proving that a trade secret did exist.

There are a number of other facts which the Court finds are relevant in determining the extent of the secrecy Wilson maintained concerning its Bits-O-Bacon process: 1) A copy of the Plant Operating Instructions for the Bits-O-Bacon operation was kept unlocked in Mr. Schacht's desk, and access to Mr. Schacht's office was not restricted. 2) A Bits-O-Bacon information sheet, which gave a general description of the manufacturing process, was distributed to Wilson's sales brokers. 3) Signs on the sixth floor restricting access to the Bits-O-Bacon production area were maintained with great irregularity. 4) The operators of the Bits-O-Bacon process were not cautioned that the process was confidential. 5) Approximately ten to twelve tours of college students were conducted through the Bits-O-Bacon production area each year and viewed the entire procedure.

While each of these elements, individually, may not indicate a lack of secrecy by Wilson, the total combines to lead this Court to conclude that Wilson clearly has not made significant efforts to guard and maintain the secrecy of its Bits-O-Bacon process.

IV. THE VALUE OF THE INFORMATION TO THE PLAINTIFF AND TO ITS COMPETITORS.

There has been a paucity of evidence introduced on this issue, and the Court recognizes the difficulty of proof in this area. The evidence does show that Fairbury Foods has made a substantial profit from its cooked bacon particles operation and the Court infers that it has also been a profitable venture for Wilson. There is also evidence that four or five other well-known companies are producing cooked bacon particles. Some of these products have been introduced in evidence, and based upon the testimony and the Court's own observation, the Court finds that there is no substantial difference between the various products. In short, there is no evidence to indicate that the process used by Wilson gives it an advantage of any kind over the other producers and the Court concludes that the value of the particular process used by Wilson is not significant.

V. THE AMOUNT OF EFFORT OR MONEY EXPENDED BY THE PLAINTIFF TO DEVELOP ITS PROCESS.

The best evidence on this issue would have been the research and development records kept by Wilson while the Bits-O-Bacon process was being worked on and formulated. Unfortunately, however, these records and any copies thereof, were lost and mislaid. One of the originators of the Wilson process, Mr. James J. Kohout, testified that according to his recollection, it took the equivalent of two full men a period of approximately one to one and a half years to develop the process which, when broken down, amounted to approximately 4,000 man hours spent on development and 1,000 man hours spent on testing. This testimony is sharply controverted by witnesses produced by the defendants as to the length of time and expense necessary to formulate such a process.... There was also some evidence that Wilson spent some time and effort in getting government label approval for its product. However, the proof introduced by Wilson on this particular issue was not strong or convincing and in the absence of the best evidence, must weigh against the plaintiff.

VI. THE EASE OR DIFFICULTY WITH WHICH THE PROCESS COULD BE PROPERLY ACQUIRED OR DUPLICATED.

All the testimony relevant to this issue was offered by the defendants. Doctor Walter Urbain, the only expert to testify, stated that he felt he could duplicate the Wilson process, with or without the help of the information sheet Wilson gave its brokers, in less than a week.

Mr. William B. Phalen, a chemist and former employee of Cudahy Packing Co., testified that in 1962, he developed a satisfactory cooked bacon particle product after eight to ten hours of work at Cudahy. Although the amount of material produced by Mr. Phalen was considerably less than is produced by Wilson, the basic process is the same. Considering the testimony of Doctor Urbain and Mr. Phalen, and also the literature which is available on dry-rendering, the Court concludes that duplicating the Wilson process would not be a difficult problem for any person familiar with meat processing in general.

One last important consideration which does not fall within the six points discussed above is the contribution of the defendant Schacht to the Wilson process upon which the plaintiff strongly relies to establish a case of wrongful acquisition of a trade secret. While Mr. Schacht took no part in the research and development of the Bits-O-Bacon theory, he conducted the first large-scale production. He was the foreman of the department in which Bits-O-Bacon was produced at all times from that first large-scale production until his departure in 1971. He made several suggestions for improving the process....

... In [Cudahy Co. v. American Laboratories, Inc., 313 F. Supp. 1339, 1345 (D. Neb. 1970)] the Court stated: "It is uncontradicted that Mr. Phalen contributed substantially to the materials contained in these instructions. He was also the man in charge of the plant. He was responsible for much of the process. To deny him the right to practice his trade by attempting to establish the general experience and knowledge of the employer as a trade secret when actually the employees' knowledge and experience in his trade is a substantial contribution to this general process is not the type of situation within the contemplation of the law guarding the disclosure of trade secrets. Any knowledge and experience of this nature desired to be protected is more properly the subject matter of a covenant not to compete. There is none present in this case." *See also* Metal Lubricants Co. v. Engineered Lubricants Co., 411 F.2d 426 (8th Cir. 1969), where the Court stated, at page 429: "As noted by the Missouri Supreme Court, we are dealing with two conflicting public policies. One policy seeks to protect a business from unfair competition. The other policy favors free competition in the economic sphere.... '"It is necessary that there be a balancing of the equities between these two rights, for if the former is carried to its extreme it will deprive a man of his right to earn a living; while conversely, the latter right if unchecked, would probably make a mockery of the fiduciary concept, with its concomitants of loyalty and fair play." ... "Were we to measure the sentiment of the law by both English and American decisions in order to determine whether it favors protecting a businessman from certain forms of competition or protecting an individual in his unrestricted pursuit of a livelihood, the balance would heavily favor the latter."'" National Rejectors, Inc. v. Trieman, 409 S.W.2d 1 (Mo. 1966).

With this last consideration in mind, and giving due weight to each of the factors considered above, the Court concludes that Wilson has not met its burden in proving that the Bits-O-Bacon process is a trade secret.... [J]udgment is entered for the defendants.

Notes

1. The law of trade secrets was addressed in the first Restatement of Torts §§ 757–760 (1939), but not in the Restatement (Second). It is now included in Restatement of Unfair Competition §§ 39–45 (1995). Most states have established a statutory framework for their trade secrets law by enactment of a version of the Uniform Trade Secrets Act. See Samuels & Johnson, The Uniform Trade Secrets Act: The States' Response, 24 Creighton L. Rev. 49 (1990); Symposium, 33 Hamline L. Rev. 375 (2010).

2. There have been numerous attempts to define "trade secret." One of the most quoted definitions is in Restatement of Torts § 757, comment *b* (1939): "A trade secret may consist of any formula, pattern, device, or compilation of information which is used in one's business, and which gives him an opportunity to obtain an advantage over competitors who do not know or use it. It may be a formula for a chemical compound, a process of manufacturing, treating or preserving materials, a pattern for a machine or other device, or a list of customers.... A trade secret is a process or device for continuous use in the operation of a business." The comment goes on to state that a trade secret generally relates to the production of goods, but it may instead relate to the sale of goods or to other business operations. Compare the definition of "trade secret" in Uniform Trade Secrets Act § 1(4): "information, including a formula, pattern, compilation, program, device, method, technique, or process, that: (i) derives independent economic value, actual or potential, from not being generally known to, and not being readily ascertainable by proper means by, other persons who can obtain economic value from its disclosure or use, and (ii) is the subject of efforts that are reasonable under the circumstances to maintain its secrecy." Restatement of Unfair Competition § 39 (1995) states simply that "A trade secret is any information that can be used in the operation of a business or other enterprise and that is sufficiently valuable and secret to afford an actual or potential economic advantage over others." See generally Annot., What is "Trade Secret" So As to Render Actionable Under State Law Its Use or Disclosure by Former Employee, 59 A.L.R.4th 641 (1988).

3. A "trade secret" need not be so original or novel as to be patentable. Neither must it be totally beyond the capacity of others to discover without improper conduct. A process for making a product that can be obtained by analysis of the product or other research — but only with considerable difficulty, expense or consumption of time — can be a trade secret. Thus, the plaintiff in Tabor v. Hoffman, 118 N.Y. 30, 23 N.E. 12 (1889), was held to have a trade secret in patterns used to manufacture a pump although the pump had long been sold to the public. If information or an idea is well-known or readily discoverable, it is not a secret. See Restatement of Unfair Competition § 39, comment *f* (1995), and the several opinions in Cataphote Corp. v. Hudson, 422 F.2d 1290 (5th Cir. 1970), on remand, 316 F. Supp. 1122 (S.D. Miss. 1970), aff'd, 444 F.2d 1313 (5th Cir. 1971), where a gas-fired furnace for making glass beads was found to incorporate techniques known to the trade and therefore not to involve trade secrets. A plaintiff may have a secret in the combination or interaction of non-secret components. See Integrated Cash Management Services, Inc. v. Digital Transactions, Inc., 920 F.2d 171 (2d Cir. 1990); Graves & Macgillivray, Combination Trade Secrets and the Logic of Intellectual Property, 20 Santa Clara Computer & High Tech. L.J. 261 (2004).

4. What degree of secrecy must surround a "trade secret"? The requirement of secrecy is not absolute. Informing persons who are necessary to the utilization of the secret does not ordinarily release the secret. To avoid divestiture, however, those who are told the secret must be bound to confidence. This obligation of confidence may arise from an express contractual restriction or by implication from the relationship between the parties,

such as agency, partnership, joint venture, license or employment. See pp. 321–325, infra. For example, in Dior v. Milton, 9 Misc. 2d 425, 155 N.Y.S.2d 443 (Sup. Ct. 1956), aff'd, 2 A.D.2d 878, 156 N.Y.S.2d 996 (1956), fashion designers showed their new creations to invited individuals, including some members of the press. Defendants operated a "sketch service" that reproduced plaintiffs' original designs and sold them to subscribers. In rejecting defendants' contention that plaintiffs had no cause of action, the court emphasized that the persons allowed to be present at the showings were aware of and agreed to the condition that they not divulge details of the designs or make copies without plaintiffs' specific authorization. See generally Annot., Disclosure of Trade Secret as Abandonment of Secrecy, 92 A.L.R.3d 138 (1979).

5. A manufacturer may be required by law to disclose secret processes to a government agency. Kitch, The Law and Economics of Rights in Valuable Information, 9 J. Legal Stud. 683, 693–695 (1980), notes that "freedom of information" laws may work great changes as to what is protectable as a trade secret; if information is in government files and the government makes those files accessible to others, the trade secret right will disappear. Is it an obstacle to trade secret protection that plaintiff will have to reveal the information to a court in order to gain relief? Courts have been willing to preserve secrecy by receiving evidence in camera, limiting the persons to whom disclosure is made during judicial proceedings, and curtailing discovery. See Puritan-Bennett Corp. v. Pruitt, 142 F.R.D. 306 (S.D. Iowa 1992). Cf. Application of Sarkar, 575 F.2d 870 (Cust. & Pat. App. 1978), an appeal from denial of a patent. The court granted applicant's motion to seal the record and hold oral argument in camera in order to keep the invention secret, so that trade secret protection might be preserved even if the patent appeal failed. Uniform Trade Secrets Act § 5 requires courts to preserve the secrecy of an alleged trade secret by reasonable means.

Aetna Building Maintenance Company, Inc. v. West

Supreme Court of California
39 Cal. 2d 198, 246 P.2d 11 (1952)

EDMONDS, Justice.

For about three years, James A. West was employed by Aetna Building Maintenance Company, Inc., as a salesman and supervisor. After he left that employment and engaged in the same business, Aetna sued him for damages assertedly resulting from unfair competition....

The complaint alleges that, during his employment, West became familiar with the details of its business, including customer lists; the extent and type of service required by its customers; the use of certain procedures, material and equipment; the net costs of performing service for each customer and the charges made for it. Aetna claims that with this information, which, it asserts, constitutes trade secrets, West solicited some of its customers to transfer their patronage to him and obtained contracts to do work for them....

There is evidence showing that West had told three out of about 50 to 75 establishments with which he had worked for Aetna that he had gone into business for himself. He notified one of them of his intentions before leaving Aetna. The other two were informed of his plans after they learned that he had left Aetna. He visited one firm three times without invitation, but "he did not solicit business." Estimates for maintenance service were submitted to two firms upon their invitations. His estimates were similar to the contracts which these firms had entered into with Aetna. In one instance, Aetna's contract had been cancelled before any negotiations were begun with West.

Samuel S. Zagel, president of Aetna, testified that West, as Aetna's supervisor, had been advised of the price received for each job and understood the amount of time and material allotted to it. He taught West how to estimate and sell a job, and trained him in the technique of window cleaning. The information given West, he said, was vital to the successful estimation of a contract in such manner as to avoid loss....

West stated that he was not given the amount of the charges made to the customers of Aetna, nor the cost of doing the work. However, he was informed of their service requirements. At the time he left Aetna, he returned to it the list of customers which he had been using. While with Aetna, he kept a personal memorandum book containing notations of calls to be made in accordance with Joseph Zagel's instructions. He did not return this book to Aetna. He admitted that, as to two of the Aetna customers, whom he contacted after he went into business for himself, he understood the type of service required because of his experience with them and his general background of knowledge regarding the work to be performed. In one instance, he remembered the amount paid by the client....

Upon this evidence, the trial court found that West commenced a competing business and solicited and secured the maintenance business of three Aetna customers, whose names, addresses and requirements he learned while employed by Aetna. These acts were intended to, and did, damage Aetna's business. Unless restrained, West could continue to divert Aetna's customers, to its irreparable damage....

In accordance with these findings, judgment was entered against West for $1,467. In addition, he was "permanently enjoined and restrained from soliciting, diverting, or taking away, directly or indirectly, any customers of the plaintiff ... and ... from performing janitorial or window cleaning service for any customer of the plaintiff whom defendant has persuaded to terminate his contract with plaintiff...." He also was restrained from divulging any confidential information pertaining to Aetna's customers....

In the absence of an enforceable contract containing negative covenants to the contrary, equity will not enjoin a former employee from soliciting business from his former employer's customers, provided his competition is fairly and legally conducted....

West had the right to advise Aetna's customers that he was severing his business relations with it and engaging in business for himself....

... West was entitled to accept business from Aetna's former customers and such acceptance, by itself, did not constitute solicitation.

However, even in the absence of solicitation, Aetna is entitled to protection against West's use, or disclosure in competition with it, of trade secrets given to him only for the purpose of carrying on his employer's business....

The facts of this case do not justify the application of principles governing the rights of the parties in connection with retail delivery routes.... [T]o obtain relief against a former employee it must be shown: (1) The information was confidential and not readily accessible to competitors; (2) The former employee solicited the customers of his former employer with intent to injure him; (3) The former employee sought out certain preferred customers whose trade is particularly profitable and whose identities are not generally known to the trade; (4) The business is such that a customer will ordinarily patronize only one concern; (5) The established business relationship between the customer and the former employer would normally continue unless interfered with.

These factors are here absent. Prospective customers are commonly known to the trade or may easily be discovered through business directories or by observation. There is no evidence that West sought out preferred customers. In any event, the evidence produced by Aetna is to the effect that there are no preferred customers in the trade. Accounts are sold upon the open market at flat rates without regard to either their duration or profitableness. The evidence shows that the business is highly competitive and patronage depends upon efficiency of service rather than personal relationship. Contracts are of brief duration and cancellations are frequent. Under such trade conditions, equity will not enjoin the solicitation of the former employer's customers.

Equitable protection may be invoked against the subsequent use by a former employee of knowledge of the "'peculiar likes and fancies and other characteristics'" of the former employer's customers where such knowledge will aid him in securing and retaining their business. This rule applies where friendly contact with customers is important to solicitors, a circumstance typical of the so-called "trade route" cases. It has also been applied to situations involving a knowledge of the customer's desire for specialized information, his preference for certain products, and his buying habits. However, where, as here, superiority of product or service, rather than personal relationships or a secret specialty, is the basis for patronage, a knowledge of the customer's requirements is not sufficient reason for an injunction. Under circumstances of open competition, such knowledge is readily available to all in the trade. ...

According to Aetna, its procedure for estimating the price of a new contract, was a trade secret. However, no evidence was introduced tending to prove that Aetna had developed a secret, or even improved, system of making estimates. The very most which is shown by the evidence is that Aetna utilized a highly efficient system designed to meet competition and avoid losses. Of necessity, any competitor in the business must consider all of the factors which entered into Aetna's computations. ...

The evidence upon the question of whether West had access to Aetna's cost records is conflicting. The trier of fact could have believed that West, during his employment, acquired knowledge of costs of doing business and took it with him. ...

The evidence clearly shows that the janitorial business does not depend upon patrons whose work can be done at an exceptionally low cost. Under these circumstances, the records in West's possession could have no value to him unless he desired to do janitorial work for less than Aetna's contract prices for the same service. But in the only two transactions shown in evidence where West submitted bids to Aetna's customers, his estimates were higher than the amounts which Aetna was receiving. He charged $5 more for identical service in one case. On the other bid, he offered janitorial service only for $13.50 less than Aetna charged for both janitor and window cleaning service. Such evidence is insufficient to support the finding that West used and intended to use Aetna's confidential cost data in unfair competition with it.

The judgment is reversed.

CARTER, Justice [with whom Shenk, J., joined, dissenting]. ...

... In Scavengers' Protective Ass'n v. Serv-U-Garbage Co., 218 Cal. 568, 24 P.2d 489, the issue was whether a former employee of a corporation engaged in the garbage collection business could be prevented from soliciting customers of his former employer. This court held that he could, stressing the fact that some of the customers were preferred because they discarded material that could be salvaged and sold as junk. This is similar to the nature of the conditions, the premises of the persons desiring janitorial service, varying with each customer. As in that case, the case at bar involves customers who could be found from directories, as nearly everyone had garbage disposal service, but each customer had his peculiarities.

The trial court had adequate justification for concluding that defendant employee had acquired the names of his employer's customers, the particular needs of each, what each complained of in respect to the service supplied by plaintiff, the idiosyncrasies of each, the particular needs for each job and the itemized cost thereof from actual experience while in the employ of plaintiff.... Defendant acquired that knowledge in the course of his employment and information which was more than a part of his learning of the work generally. Having acquired that knowledge and information while in the employ of plaintiff, he sought to apply it to plaintiff's detriment by inducing plaintiff's customers to forsake plaintiff and employ him to do that which plaintiff had apparently been doing to the mutual benefit and satisfaction of plaintiff and its customers before defendant interfered....

Notes

1. There is a great variety of information that may be protected as a trade secret — not only manufacturing methods, formulae, technical elements of designs and computer programs, but also marketing and pricing techniques, the identities and details of customers, and compilations of information. See Restatement of Unfair Competition § 39, comment *d* (1995). Should an employer be permitted to claim as confidential information the prices of its purchases and sales and resulting profit margins? See Applied Industrial Materials Corp. v. Brantjes, 891 F. Supp. 432 (N.D. Ill. 1994) (not secret because other party to sale free to divulge price).

2. In Leo Silfen, Inc. v. Cream, 29 N.Y.2d 387, 328 N.Y.S.2d 423, 278 N.E.2d 636 (1977), plaintiffs sold building maintenance supplies to industrial and commercial users. The customers were necessarily known to all in the trade as likely or actual users of such supplies and were themselves engaged in business at advertised locations. Defendant, a former employee of plaintiffs', solicited forty-seven out of eleven hundred customers on a list which plaintiffs had prepared from their confidential files. He was not shown to have stolen, copied or memorized any information. Were plaintiffs entitled to an injunction or damages? Cf. Suburban Gas of Grand Junction, Inc. v. Bockelman, 157 Colo. 78, 401 P.2d 268 (1965) (former employee solicited customers of propane gas business; injunction denied; propane tanks usually visible so identity of potential customers readily known); Spring Steels, Inc. v. Molloy, 400 Pa. 354, 162 A.2d 370 (1960) (use of customer lists by former employees; no breach of confidence found). In American Credit Indemnity Co. v. Sacks, 213 Cal. App. 3d 622, 262 Cal. Rptr. 92 (1989), a former employee of an insurance company was enjoined from solicitation of the company's policyholders, including policyholders whose business the employee had obtained for the company. Solicitation was distinguished from announcement of the establishment of an independent business. The identity of policyholders for credit insurance, which relatively few businesses having accounts receivable purchased, was considered a trade secret of the insurance company. If knowledge of customer or client identities is the plaintiff's trade secret, it can be protected from use by a former employee even if the employee used only memorized knowledge rather than a written record of customers. See Al Minor & Associates, Inc. v. Martin, 117 Ohio St. 3d 58, 881 N.E.2d 850 (2008).

3. In numerous cases in which a business' employee has learned of special processes used in manufacturing operations, courts have enjoined the employee from disclosing or using the processes after he has left that business' employ. Courts also issue injunc-

tions when a former employee discloses or uses confidential information gained during the employment. See Annot., Implied Obligation of Employee Not to Use Trade Secrets or Confidential Information for His Own Benefit or That of Third Persons After Leaving the Employment, 165 A.L.R. 1453 (1946); Annot., Employee's Duty, in Absence of Express Contract, Not to Disclose or Use in New Employment Special Skills or Techniques Acquired in Earlier Employment, 30 A.L.R.3d 631 (1970). Suppose a chemist develops certain formulas, using skills his employment helped him to acquire but not any appreciable volume of information obtained from his employer. Is he free to disclose his formulas to and use them in behalf of a subsequent employer? See Wexler v. Greenberg, 399 Pa. 569, 160 A.2d 430 (1960) (chemist had unqualified privilege to use information which formed part of technical knowledge and skill acquired in former employment). According to FSS Travel & Leisure Systems Ltd. v. Johnson, [1998] I.R.L.R. 382, [1999] F.S.R. 505 (C.A.), the critical question is whether the former employee has trade secrets which can fairly be regarded as the former employer's property, as distinct from the skill, experience, know-how and general knowledge which can fairly be regarded as the employee's property. See Restatement of Unfair Competition §42, comment *d* (1995).

4. Employment carries with it a duty of loyalty. So long as the employment relationship continues, an employee may not solicit business from the employer's customers for himself or another business, including one to be formed by the employee after his departure from the employment. However, an employee may, prior to resignation, prepare for competition which is to commence after the resignation and solicit fellow employees to join him in it. The duty of loyalty ends at the termination of the employment, but any duty to maintain the confidentiality of confidential information belonging to the employer continues. See Cudahy Co. v. American Laboratories, Inc., 313 F. Supp. 1339 (D. Neb. 1970); Restatement (Third) of Agency §§8.04–8.05 (2006).

5. The primary protection of an employer against future competition from an employee to whom the employer has imparted knowledge or skills is not tort law but contract. The contract may take the form of an agreement by the employee not to disclose or use, subsequent to his employment, any confidential information he had acquired. This type of agreement leaves the employee free to work for a competing firm and is difficult to enforce. A covenant against competition is likely to be more effective, but to be enforceable its terms must be reasonable. According to Restatement (Second) of Contracts §188 (1981), a promise to refrain from competition is unreasonable if it grants the promisee more protection than needed to protect its legitimate interests or if the promisee's need is outweighed by hardship to the promisor and likely injury to the public. A test of reasonableness is generally applied to determine the permissible duration and territorial scope of a covenant against competition and the type of occupation or business a party may be prohibited from engaging in. See Annot., Enforceability of Restrictive Covenant, Ancillary to Employment Contract, as Affected by Duration of Restriction, 41 A.L.R.2d 15 (1955); Annot., Enforceability of Restrictive Covenant, Ancillary to Employment Contract, as Affected by Territorial Extent of Restriction, 43 A.L.R.2d 94 (1955). In determining whether an employee's covenant not to compete is reasonable, a court will consider whether the employer was trying to protect confidential information and whether the restraint is reasonably related to protection of this information. See Water Services, Inc. v. Tesco Chemicals, Inc., 410 F.2d 163 (5th Cir. 1969); Purchasing Associates, Inc. v. Weitz, 13 N.Y.2d 267, 246 N.Y.S.2d 600, 196 N.E.2d 245 (1963). In some jurisdictions, the enforceability of restraints of competition is limited by statute. See Annot., Statutes Prohibiting Restraint on Profession, Trade, or Business as Applicable to Restrictions in Employment or Agency Contracts, 3 A.L.R.2d 522 (1949).

Bayer Corporation v. Roche Molecular Systems, Inc.

United States District Court, Northern District of California
72 F. Supp. 2d 1111 (1999)

ALSUP, District Judge....

[Bayer and Roche were competing producers of products used to measure Human Immunodeficiency Virus (HIV) in blood samples. Pete Betzelos left his position as Bayer's "HIV Marketing Manager" and began work in a similar position with Roche. Claiming that Betzelos would use or disclose Bayer's trade secrets in his new position, Bayer sought a preliminary injunction that would, inter alia, bar Betzelos' employment by Roche in marketing HIV products competing with Bayer's. Betzelos' contract with Roche provided that he would not disclose or use any trade secret belonging to Bayer. After the litigation commenced, Betzelos gave a further undertaking not to use any confidential or proprietary information belonging to Bayer in the performance of his position with Roche.]

The Court finds it likely that Bayer will prove all the elements of its trade-secrets case but one: actual or threatened use or disclosure....

This brings us to Bayer's theory of inevitable disclosure. Invoking this concept, Bayer argues that the disclosure of its trade secrets is unavoidable because Mr. Betzelos inevitably will use them in his new position with Roche. Citing *PepsiCo v. Redmond*, 54 F.3d 1262 (7th Cir. 1995), Bayer claims that a plaintiff may prove a claim of threatened misappropriation of a trade secret by demonstrating that a former employee's new employment will inevitably lead him to rely on plaintiff's trade secret.

In that case, PepsiCo sought a preliminary injunction against its former employee William Redmond and its competitor Quaker Oats Company to prevent him from working for Quaker. Because of his relatively high-level position at PepsiCo, Redmond had access to trade secrets and confidential information. PepsiCo alleged that Redmond's new position at Quaker posed a threat of misappropriation of PepsiCo's trade secrets. Applying Illinois trade-secrets law, the district court agreed and granted a six-month injunction against Redmond's employment with Quaker. The Seventh Circuit affirmed, finding (1) that Redmond possessed knowledge of specific PepsiCo trade secrets and not just "general skills and knowledge," (2) that armed with this knowledge and because his responsibilities at Quaker would parallel those at PepsiCo, Redmond would be able to anticipate PepsiCo's business moves, and (3) Redmond's "lack of forthrightness ... and out and out lies" demonstrated a "lack of candor ... and a willingness to misuse [PepsiCo's] trade secrets."

... Although Redmond and Quaker argued that they did not intend to use any of PepsiCo's trade secrets and offered as proof an agreement signed by Redmond and Quaker to that effect, the district court rejected the argument.

The *PepsiCo* decision has given new life to the theory of inevitable disclosure. Previously, courts had recognized the theory, but were reluctant to apply it because of strong public policies in favor of employee mobility. One commentator contends that 21 states (not including California) now allow plaintiffs to show liability for trade-secrets misappropriation under the theory. The theory allows plaintiff employers to demonstrate threatened misappropriation without evidence of an employee's intent to disclose trade secrets....

A decision from the Southern District of Texas has identified the following factors for determining whether a trade secret will be "inevitably disclosed": "(1) Is the new employer a competitor? (2) What is the scope of the defendant's new job? (3) Has the employee been less than candid about his new position? (4) Has plaintiff clearly identified the trade secrets which are at risk? (5) Has actual trade secret misappropriation already occurred? (6) Did the employee sign a nondisclosure and/or non-competition agreement? (7) Does the new employer have a policy against use of others' trade secrets? (8) Is it possible to 'sanitize' the employee's new position?" *Maxxim Medical v. Michelson*, 51 F. Supp. 2d 773, 786 (S.D. Tex. 1999)....

... California public policy favors employee mobility and freedom. California Business and Professions Code Section 16600 provides that "every contract by which anyone is restrained from engaging in a lawful profession, trade, or business of any kind is to that extent void." Reading this language broadly, California courts generally do not enforce covenants not to compete. Nor do they generally enforce covenants that seek to avoid the policy by penalizing former employees who compete with their former employers. In the words of the California Supreme Court: "Equity will to the fullest extent protect the property rights of employers in their trade secrets and otherwise, but public policy and natural justice require that equity should also be solicitous for the right inherent in all people, not fettered by negative covenants upon their part to the contrary, to follow any of the common occupations of life. Every individual possesses as a form of property, the right to pursue any calling, business or profession he may choose. A former employee has the right to engage in a competitive business for himself and to enter into competition with his former employer, even for the business of those who had formerly been the customers of his former employer, provided such competition is fairly and legally conducted." *Continental Car-Na-Var Corp. v. Moseley*, 24 Cal. 2d 104, 110, 148 P.2d 9 (1944). To the extent that the theory of inevitable disclosure creates a de facto covenant not to compete without a nontrivial showing of actual or threatened use or disclosure, it is inconsistent with California policy and case law.

In sum, the Court holds that California trade-secrets law does not recognize the theory of inevitable disclosure; indeed, such a rule would run counter to the strong public policy in California favoring employee mobility. A trade-secrets plaintiff must show an actual use or an actual threat. Once a nontrivial violation is shown, however, a court may consider all of the factors considered by the jurisdictions allowing the theory in determining the possible extent of the irreparable injury. In other words, once the employee violates the trade-secrets law in a nontrivial way, the employee forfeits the benefit of the protective policy in California. For example, that a high-level employee takes a virtually identical job at the number one competitor in a fiercely competitive industry would be a factor militating in favor of a broader injunction once sufficient evidence of a nontrivial violation is shown. In the present case, however, sufficient evidence of such a nontrivial violation has not been shown.

... Here, Bayer and Roche both face hardship. Should the Court decline to enjoin Mr. Betzelos from working on Roche products that compete with Bayer products, and Roche subsequently uses Bayer's trade secrets, the value of those secrets will be lost to Bayer, and damages will not repair the loss. That hardship has, however, diminished with time, for the trade secrets have lost currency. If, on the other hand, the Court enjoins Mr. Betzelos from working on Roche's HIV Amplicor products, Roche would have to start over looking for a person to fill Mr. Betzelos' position. Not only would Roche face an immediate void, but his successor, when found, would need to spend time getting up to speed. Regarding whether Roche should be enjoined from continuing to employ Mr. Betzelos, the balance of hardships does not tip sharply in favor of Bayer. Nonetheless, the balance of the hardships certainly supports the minimum relief outlined below, namely an order (1) to Mr. Betzelos directing him to honor his undertaking to the Court (quoted earlier) not to use or disclose Bayer's confidential and/or proprietary information and (2) to Mr. Betzelos and Roche to stand for the periodic examinations in discovery imposed below....

... Should the discovery reveal evidence of use or disclosure of Bayer's confidential or proprietary information, Bayer may renew its motion for a preliminary injunction....

Notes

1. As stated in the principal case, the "inevitable disclosure" theory has now been accepted, at least in principle, in quite a number of cases. However, it is rejected in some recent opinions. See Annot., Applicability of Inevitable Disclosure Doctrine Barring Employment of Competitor's Former Employee, 36 A.L.R.6th 537 (2008). What would be the best resolution of this issue? See Rowe, When Trade Secrets Become Shackles: Fairness and the Inevitable Disclosure Doctrine, 7 Tulane J. Tech. & Intel. Prop. 167 (2005); Comment, The Inevitable Disaster of Inevitable Disclosure, 67 U. Cinc. L. Rev. 809 (1999). In PepsiCo, Inc. v. Redmond, the trade secrets plaintiff sought to protect were marketing, distribution and pricing strategies. Might these be differentiated from confidential information and industrial processes?

2. In Christopher M's Hand Poured Fudge, Inc. v. Hennon, 699 A.2d 1272 (Pa. Super. Ct. 1997), appeal denied, 553 Pa. 686, 717 A.2d 1026 (1998), a former employee of plaintiff's gourmet fudge business had launched a competing business, utilizing plaintiff's secret recipe and other trade secrets. A lower court enjoined defendant from manufacturing or selling fudge entirely. This was affirmed, over defendant's objection that the injunction was too wide, on the basis that a defendant could be enjoined from manufacturing the type of product in which the trade secret is utilized when the secret is "inextricably connected" to defendant's manufacture of the product. In these circumstances, defendant could not be relied upon to "unlearn" or abandon the misappropriated technology.

Forest Laboratories, Inc. v. Formulations, Inc.

United States District Court, Eastern District of Wisconsin
299 F. Supp. 202 (1969), aff'd sub nom.

Forest Laboratories, Inc. v. Pillsbury Company

United States Court of Appeals, Seventh Circuit
452 F.2d 621 (1971)

MYRON L. GORDON, District Judge.

The plaintiff is a manufacturer and packager of food and drug items. It claims to have developed a successful process for packaging effervescent sweetener tablets so that their shelf life is lengthy. The production and sale of effervescent sweetener tablets is limited to a small group of companies; of the approximately 1000 tablet manufacturers in the United States, only a few produce this type of tablet.

Tidy House Corporation, the defendant's predecessor, had been interested in marketing an effervescent sweetener tablet. Prior to 1957, Tidy House had engaged several firms to manufacture tablets for this purpose. However, Tidy House experienced difficulties with each of these sources of supply, and in 1958 Tidy House learned that the plaintiff manufactured such tablets. In December, 1958, Tidy House sent its technical director, Mr. Egan, and his co-employee, Mr. Steinhauser, to observe the plaintiff's operation in New York. During that visit Mr. Lowey, the president of the plaintiff, claims to have disclosed to Mr. Egan what are alleged to be Forest Laboratories' trade secrets for packaging. Shortly thereafter, the plaintiff began to supply Tidy House with tablets in bulk; Tidy House packaged the tablets for the consumer.

In 1960, the Tidy House assets were purchased by the Pillsbury Company, and the plaintiff continued to supply the tablets to what became known as the Tidy House division of Pillsbury. This relationship continued until January, 1964, when Pillsbury engaged Formulations, Inc. as a new source of supply. Subsequently, the plaintiff brought this action, alleging that Pillsbury was using its confidential packaging secrets....

[The court found that several steps in the packaging process were trade secrets. These steps were not well-known in the industry; only a handful of plaintiff's employees knew of the packaging operations; these employees were bound by secrecy agreements and packaging information was closely guarded; the information was of significant value to plaintiff since technical problems had prevented more than a few companies from packaging effervescent tablets; there was evidence that development and testing the packaging process took a long period of time; it was possible for others to duplicate the process but possessing it gave plaintiff a substantial advantage over competitors who did not possess it.]

The second issue presented is whether *these* trade secrets were given by Mr. Lowey to the defendant under circumstances which reveal that a confidential relationship existed between them. At the outset, Pillsbury argues that even if a confidential relationship as to these secrets was established with Tidy House, Pillsbury would not be bound unless it had actual notice of these facts. It bases its argument on §758, Restatement of Torts. That section deals with situations in which a distinct third party receives confidential information without being aware of its secret nature; but that section does not apply to the situation at hand. In this case, Pillsbury purchased all the assets of Tidy House.... Most employees remained the same. In my opinion, Pillsbury, as successor, was bound by any confidential disclosure made to Tidy House. If Tidy House had notice that these secrets were confidentially disclosed, that knowledge does not end when the Tidy House personnel become Pillsbury employees. It does not matter, therefore, whether any member of the Pillsbury management actually received notice that the packaging information was a confidential trade secret.

The testimony on whether this information was given to Tidy House in confidence is contradictory. It is my conclusion, however, that the plaintiff has established that there was a confidential disclosure to Tidy House employees in 1958.

When early arrangements were made with Tidy House, which was looking for a new supplier of effervescent sweetener tablets, Mr. Lowey sent the plaintiff's manufacturing formula to Mr. Sherrard, Tidy House's purchasing agent. The letter which conveyed this information said that the formula was to be kept confidential. [T]he letter also stated that "we agree with you that details on packaging, etc. should be taken up later". In December, 1958, Mr. Egan, the Tidy House technical director, and Mr. Steinhauser, Mr. Egan's associate, [visited] the plaintiff's facilities in New York. During that meeting, Mr. Lowey told Mr. Egan that Forest Laboratories did not want to package the tablets for the consumer because of a lack of space. Mr. Egan testified that he asked Mr. Lowey to give him "some advice as to the conditions under which this packaging should be carried on", because Tidy House had not previously packaged tablets. Both Mr. Lowey and Mr. Egan testified that Mr. Lowey agreed to furnish the packaging techniques in confidence. [B]oth men also testified that all of the trade secrets were communicated orally to Mr. Egan, who took notes at such meeting....

The defendant asserts that Mr. Lowey never formally reasserted after the 1958 meeting that the packaging techniques were trade secrets. While this may be true, the parties appear to have clearly *understood* that this was the case.... Mr. Lowey testified that since a confidential relationship had been established in 1958, and since he was dealing with Tidy House employees or people who were under contract with them, he felt no need to reiterate what was already an established fact. I do not believe that Mr. Lowey was careless in his dealings with the defendant.

... "The question is simply whether in the circumstances B knows or should know that the information is [the plaintiff's] trade secret and that its disclosure is made in confidence." Restatement of Torts, § 757, comment on cl. (b) at 14....

[Pillsbury was found to have used plaintiff's secret packaging process after plaintiff was discharged as supplier of the tablets, although Pillsbury's specifications differed in some details from plaintiff's specifications. Having been given trade secrets in confidence, Pillsbury violated that confidence and made improper use of the trade secrets by using the packaging process after plaintiff's discharge.]

While the plaintiff has requested an injunction to prevent further use of the trade secret by the defendant, it is my opinion that such an injunction should not issue where, as here, the trade secret process has now been made public by the declarations made in the plaintiff's patent. Damages will suffice to compensate the plaintiff for its injury....

[Pillsbury's new supplier of tablets, Formulations, Inc., was also a defendant. It was dismissed from the case because it did not have notice of plaintiff's trade secret. Pillsbury appealed to the Court of Appeals.]

CUMMINGS, Circuit Judge....

Pillsbury purchased the assets of Tidy House Corporation on June 1, 1960. The district court found that the trade secret had been divulged by Forest to Tidy House on a confidential basis and that as Tidy House's successor, Pillsbury was bound by the confidential disclosure to Tidy House. On the state of this record we cannot sustain the district court's conclusion. The well settled rule of American jurisdictions, including Wisconsin, is that a corporation which purchases the assets of another corporation does not, by reason of succeeding to the ownership of property, assume the obligations of the transferor corporation. Exceptions to this rule exist where (a) the purchasing corporation expressly or impliedly agrees to assume the liabilities of the seller, (b) the transaction amounts to a consolidation or merger of the two companies, (c) the purchasing corporation is merely a continuation of the selling corporation, or (d) the transaction is entered into fraudulently to escape liability.

[This case did not come within the exceptions.] [W]e are not convinced that Pillsbury subjected itself to the obligation of secrecy as Tidy House's "successor." Moreover, the knowledge of Tidy House's employees cannot properly be imputed to Pillsbury just because they went to work for Pillsbury.

Section 757(b) of the Restatement of Torts provides: "One who discloses or uses another's trade secret, without a privilege to do so, is liable to the other if ... (b) his disclosure or use constitutes a breach of confidence reposed in him by the other in disclosing the secret to him...." Since Pillsbury does not stand in the shoes of Tidy House, plaintiff's confidant, Pillsbury's use of the secret does not come within the confines of § 757(b).

... [T]he evidence shows that Pillsbury acquired actual knowledge of the confidentiality of the disclosure made by Forest to Tidy House. Thus Mr. Richard Egan, a former employee of Tidy House and of Pillsbury, and considered by the trial judge to be a credible witness, testified that he communicated the trade secret to [persons] employed by Pillsbury at a meeting in the middle of 1962. He also told them that the Forest process had been received in confidence by Tidy House.

Section 758(b) of the Restatement states: "One who learns another's trade secret from a third person without notice that it is secret and that the third person's disclosure is a breach of his duty to the other, or who learns the secret through a mistake without notice of the secrecy and the mistake, ... is liable to the other for a disclosure or use of the secret after the receipt of such notice unless prior thereto he has in good faith paid value for the secret or has so changed his position that to subject him to liability would be inequitable." Thus under § 758(b) of the Restatement of Torts, Pillsbury would be liable for its use of the secret after receipt of the notice unless prior thereto it had in good faith paid value for the secret. To satisfy this exception, Pillsbury argues that it purchased the trade secret when it acquired Tidy House's assets, and that Mr. Egan's communications did not occur until well after the acquisition. However, the record does not show that Pillsbury paid anything specifically for the trade secret. For all that appears on the record, Pillsbury's purchase of Tidy House assets at most involved only the purchase of its packaging facilities as part of the existing marketing structure, which included plaintiff as supplier. Nothing has been brought to our attention which would show that Pillsbury actually gave value for Tidy House's tempering expertise with a view toward independently exploiting that know-how for its intrinsic value. Comment (e) to § 758(b) of the Restatement states that "not every change of position prevents the recipient of a trade secret from being subjected to the duty not to disclose or use the secret after notice. The issue is whether the imposition of the duty would be inequitable under the circumstances." The mere possibility that some arbitrary portion of the purchase price could *ex post facto* be ascribed to the potential of the trade secret for Pillsbury's later independent use does not demonstrate a change of position which it would be inequitable not to protect under the circumstances. The purpose of Restatement § 758(b) is to protect bona fide purchasers and reasonable reliance, but it may operate harshly on those who have expended substantial sums in development of their trade secrets. For this reason, we require a specific showing that Pillsbury in good faith paid value for Forest's trade secret at that time, and since there is a dearth of such proof, under § 758(b) of the Restatement, it remained liable to Forest for using the trade secret after the receipt of notice.

... Both parties agree that the "reasonable royalty" method of computing damages was properly invoked. According to that method, the primary inquiry in fixing a reasonable royalty is "what the parties would have agreed upon, if both were reasonably trying to reach an agreement." Egry Register Co. v. Standard Register Co., 23 F.2d 438, 443 (6th Cir. 1928)....

... Pillsbury concludes the $75,000 award is too speculative and uncertain to stand.... The basis for an award of damages should be as explicit as the method of calculating the damages permits, but the reasonable royalty method used in this case is not amenable to a completely mathematical articulation. Here the master considered the factors of Forest's loss of profits, its profits prior to 1964, and its claimed cost of development, and to these factors he assigned values supported by ample evidence. But the master also correctly considered other factors not susceptible of precise valuation, such as Forest's ability to continue in the tablet-producing business, the nature of the trade secret, its utility, and advantages and extent of use. And, of course, the commercial posture of the parties must have entered into the master's picture. Because of the type of factors considered and the necessarily judgmental process involved in constructing a hypothetical business agreement, we cannot fault any lack of specificity in arriving at what must necessarily be a reasonable approximation....

[Affirmed except as to award of attorneys' fees to plaintiff.]

Notes

1. *Recipients of trade secrets and other confidential information.* A number of trade secret cases involve defendants which gained information from a company during negotiations for possible purchase of the company. Consider: Plaintiffs manufacture freight containers. They reveal the design to defendant, a potential purchaser of the business. Defendant does not make the purchase but uses the design. Smith v. Dravo Corp., 203 F.2d 369 (7th Cir. 1953) (plaintiffs entitled to have defendant enjoined from using information, to recover lost investment, and to receive profits realized by defendant from use of design). During negotiations for possible sale of his business, plaintiff reveals to defendant, a prospective purchaser, information about the extent of plaintiff's advertising and of orders by several customers. Defendant makes no promise not to use the information and could secure the names of likely customers through alternative means. Heyman v. AR. Winarick, Inc., 325 F.2d 584 (2d Cir. 1963) (express agreement not necessary to create confidential relationship precluding use of all information not generally known; evidence did not establish that information was used). Cf. Phillips v. Frey, 20 F.3d 623 (5th Cir. 1994) (secret disclosed to persons representing interest in purchasing plaintiffs' business protectable without express request that it be held in confidence). See Annot., Implied Obligation Not to Use Trade Secrets or Similar Confidential Information Disclosed During Unsuccessful Negotiations for Sale, License, or the Like, 9 A.L.R.3d 665 (1966). See also p. 341, note 3.

2. What are the obligations and potential liabilities of persons who come into possession of a trade secret or other confidential information? If they owed no obligation of confidence to the proprietor of the secret, should they be subject to liability for using or disclosing the information? If a company obtains and uses information about an industrial process knowing that the provider of the information was breaching an obligation of confidence or had acquired the information by wrongful means, the company can be held liable to the proprietor of the information. This is embodied in Restatement of Torts § 758 (1939), quoted in the principal case. On what basis is this rule applicable to Pillsbury, whose Tidy House division was given details of the tablet packaging process by Forest Laboratories? The Restatement and Uniform Trade Secrets Act § 1 treat as misappropriation the use or disclosure of a trade secret by a person who has notice that his knowledge of the trade secret is the result of someone's breach of duty or a mistake. See also Restatement of Unfair Competition § 40(b) (1995). How broadly should this be applied? In B.C. Ziegler and Co. v. Ehren, 141 Wis. 2d 19, 414 N.W.2d 48 (Ct. App. 1987), a securities underwriter's confidential customer lists, which were supposed to be shredded or burned after use, were instead included in scrap paper delivered to a scrap dealer. One of the dealer's employees, who happened to be a former securities salesman, recognized the value of the lists and sold them to a securities broker. The employee was enjoined from further use or disclosure of the information in the lists and the documents were ordered destroyed.

3. The outer limits of the original proprietor's rights against subsequent recipients of confidential information were tested in a series of cases involving the memoirs of a British intelligence officer, entitled *Spycatcher*. The British government claimed, and it was generally accepted, that publication of the book constituted a breach of the officer's obligation of confidence to the government. The government sought injunctions not only against the officer and the Australian publisher of his book, but also against a British newspaper which serialized portions of the book and other newspapers which reported the allegations in the book and the details that had come out in the litigation about it. The House of Lords considered the newspaper which serialized *Spycatcher* in breach of a duty of confidence and held it liable to account to the British government for the profits it received. The other newspapers were found to have committed no actionable breach of confidence because what they published was not damaging to the public interest. None of the newspapers was enjoined from future publication of the contents of *Spycatcher* because the information in the book was by this time well-known and no further damage to the public interest could be caused. Damage to the public interest was specified as a requirement for the grant to a government of an order against publication of information imparted in confidence. Attorney-General v. Guardian Newspapers Ltd. (No. 2), [1990] 1 A.C. 109 (H.L.). See also Lord Advocate v. The Scotsman Publications Ltd., [1990] 1 A.C. 812 (H.L.), involving an attempt to ban media publication of information in a book privately published by a former member of the British intelligence service. Compare G v. Day, [1982] 1 N.S.W.L.R. 24 (Sup. Ct.), in which plaintiff had given information to the police and a government commission on the condition that his identify as the source of the information not be revealed. Fearing for his safety, plaintiff sought an injunction restraining publication of his identity and address in a newspaper. The injunction was granted.

4. In Bartnicki v. Vopper, 532 U.S. 514 (2001), discussed infra at p. 472, the Supreme Court held that when defendants disclosed material knowing or having reason to know that it was obtained by others through illegal interception of an electronic communication, but the material disclosed was a matter of public concern, the First Amendment barred liability. (A concurring opinion stressed the presence of a matter of "unusual public concern.") Consider whether this has any application to actions against recipients of trade secrets. Could this depend upon whether the information fits or does not fit within traditional definitions of a protectable trade secret, which emphasize the economic value of the information as a secret? In Ford Motor Co. v. Lane, 67 F. Supp. 2d 745 (E.D. Mich. 1999), the court held that publication of plaintiff's trade secrets and other internal documents on defendant's web site could not be restrained because of the prohibition of "prior restraints" on publication derived from the First Amendment. But in DVD Copy Control Association, Inc. v. Bunner, 31 Cal. 4th 864, 4 Cal. Rptr. 3d 69, 75 P.3d 1 (2003), the court decided that it was not a violation of the First Amendment to enjoin publication of a trade secret on a web site when the publisher knew or had reason to know that the information came from someone who acquired it unlawfully. The court even denied that a preliminary injunction was a prior restraint — because it was granted against a defendant who had already unlawfully communicated the secret and "content neutral" because it was grounded in a purpose to protect plaintiff's trade secret rather than a governmental purpose to suppress communication with a particular content.

5. *Remedies*. A considerable variety of remedies — based on tort, contract, trust or restitution principles — is available when wrongful use of a trade secret harms its proprietor. The principal remedies are damages, restitution and injunctions. See Dobbs, Law of Remedies § 10.5(3) (2d ed. 1993). Uniform Trade Secrets Act §§ 2–4 provide guidelines for damages and injunctive relief. Damages can be awarded for both actual loss and

unjust enrichment. Alternatively, the "reasonable royalty" measure of damages can be used. There can be exemplary damages, not exceeding twice the compensatory, and recovery of attorneys' fees in cases of "willful and malicious" misappropriation. A victim of trade secret misappropriation is entitled to damages "except to the extent that a material and prejudicial change of position prior to acquiring knowledge or reason to know of misappropriation renders a monetary recovery inequitable." See also Restatement of Unfair Competition §§ 44–45 (1995); Annot., Proper Measure and Elements of Damages for Misappropriation of Trade Secret, 11 A.L.R.4th 12 (1982).

6. The theory of restitution—allowing plaintiff to recover defendant's gain from improper use of confidential information—has been important in much trade secret litigation. In Servo Corp. of America v. General Electric Co., 337 F.2d 716 (4th Cir. 1964), cert. denied, 383 U.S. 934 (1966), Servo had developed a hotbox detector, which it disclosed to Southern Railway in order that the device could be tested on the railway's lines. Southern disclosed the device to General Electric, which knew it had been received by Southern in confidence. General Electric proceeded to develop a similar device. Although Servo's patents on its detector were invalid, Servo was held to have an action against General Electric for unjust enrichment. It could recover the reasonable value of the data acquired and utilized by General Electric in competition with Servo. See generally Palmer, Law of Restitution § 2.8 (1978).

7. There has been considerable disagreement about the proper duration of an injunction against use of a trade secret and its continuance beyond the time that the information becomes public knowledge. See Jamieson, Just Deserts: A Model to Harmonize Trade Secret Injunctions, 72 Neb. L. Rev. 515 (1993). Compare Shellmar Products Co. v. Allen-Qualley Co., 87 F.2d 104 (7th Cir. 1936), cert. denied, 301 U.S. 695 (1937) (permanent injunction not modified despite public disclosure of secret in patent issued to third party), with Conmar Products Corp. v. Universal Slide Fastener Co., 172 F.2d 150 (2d Cir. 1949) (injunction cannot issue or continue after information disclosed in patent). Cf. Reddi-Wip, Inc. v. Lemay Valve Co., 354 S.W.2d 913 (Mo. App. 1962) (confidential relation arose when parties cooperated on development of product; information obtained in relationship could be exploited after it had become public). Uniform Trade Secrets Act § 2(a) provides that upon application to the court, an injunction shall be terminated when the trade secret has ceased to exist, but the injunction may be continued for an additional period of time to eliminate commercial advantage that otherwise would be derived from the misappropriation.

8. May a misappropriator's use of a trade secret be permanently enjoined if plaintiff's competitors have had an opportunity to duplicate the secret through studying plaintiff's product? See Curtiss-Wright Corp. v. Edel-Brown Tool & Die Co., Inc., 381 Mass. 1, 407 N.E.2d 319 (1980); Annot., Propriety of Permanently Enjoining One Guilty of Unauthorized Use of Trade Secret from Engaging in Sale or Manufacture of Device in Question, 38 A.L.R.3d 572 (1971) (permanent injunction may be issued). Should a permanent injunction against the marketing of a product be granted if defendant's own effort or talent, as well as wrongful use of a trade secret, played a substantial role in the product's development? See M. Bryce & Associates, Inc. v. Gladstone, 107 Wis. 2d 241, 319 N.W.2d 907 (Ct. App. 1982); Restatement of Torts § 757, comment c (1939).

Djowharzadeh v. City National Bank and Trust Company of Norman

Oklahoma Court of Appeals
646 P.2d 616 (1982)

BOYDSTON, Presiding Judge.

[Action for damages against a bank and its loan officer. According to the complaint, plaintiff, a customer of the bank, learned that the owner of a duplex was offering it for sale at a price much below market value. The duplex had been placed with a realtor, but it was not "officially" listed, advertised for sale or publicly known to be for sale. Plaintiff decided to purchase the duplex. The realtor agreed to "hold" it, giving plaintiff time to borrow the down payment. The next day, plaintiff applied at the bank for a loan of the down payment, fully disclosing the proposed purchase to the loan officer. The officer, who realized that the duplex was worth as much as $20,000 more than the asking price, said he would consult the bank's loan committee. The next day, he rejected the loan on the ground that the bank did not make "100% loans." Within five days, the wives of the bank's president and senior vice president purchased the property for $500 over the asking price. Both wives were bank stockholders and one was a bank employee. One gave a deposition stating that she learned of the duplex from the loan officer at a cocktail party; he did not give her its location; she "looked it up" at the courthouse and made telephone calls, reaching the owner on the second call and then submitting a written offer to the realtor.]

Defendants pled several defenses, but the gist of their position is that a bank owes no confidential duty to its customers. Bank further argues that if a wrongful disclosure was made, it was outside the scope of the employee's duty and therefore Loan Officer is personally and solely liable for Customer's damages. Trial judge agreed, sustaining both defendants' motion for summary judgment....

The relationship created when a prospective borrower applies for a loan from a bank is a very special one. It has not yet ripened into a contract—because it has not yet crossed the threshold of formal agreement. Neither is it fiducial—because it is by nature an arm's length transaction. It does, however, impose special duties on each party which go beyond mere matters of courtesy.

Customer has the duty to fairly and fully disclose his assets, personal credit history and circumstances, intimate intra-family situations, past conduct, future plans and a myriad of other sometimes highly personal information. Details concerning the purpose of the loan—for reasons amply demonstrated by the facts of this case—are no less private to the applicant. In fact, most of the information which is routinely demanded by and candidly disclosed to a bank by its customer is so critically personal that it would not even be shared with the customer's own minister.

This intimate, private information is not furnished to any bank official lightly, nor, strictly speaking, voluntarily. Rather, the borrower is compelled to disclose the information. The delicately balanced relationship thus temporarily created is not, in ordinary cases, one composed of equals because of the inordinate power of the bank. The precarious position of the borrower and the relatively superior position of the bank mandates there be a counterbalancing special duty imposed on the part of the bank.

Banks exist and operate almost solely by using public funds and are invested with enormous public trust. Their financial power within the community amounts to a virtual financial monopoly in the field of money lending. The legislature has carefully defined their corporate charge within finite limits in direct proportion to their power.

One goal of this system is to assure that banks do not compete financially with their customers, but rather serve public financial needs fairly and evenly. Implicit in this policy of fair dealing and evenhandedness is a requirement that banks not use their favored position to the detriment of their customers, either directly or indirectly.

If it were otherwise, banks would quickly become pervasive financial webs, serving only their owners, managers and friends by trapping all the best investments being innocently funnelled by the public through their loan departments. Such a policy would soon destroy their public usefulness and benefit neither the public nor, ultimately, the banking industry.

... [*Peterson v. Idaho First Nat'l Bank*, 83 Idaho 578, 367 P.2d 284 (1961), cited] with approval the following language now found at 10 Am. Jur. 2d Banks § 332 (1963): "[I]t is an implied term of the contract between a banker and his customer that the banker will not divulge to third persons, without the consent of the customer, express or implied, either the state of the customer's account or any of his transactions with the bank, or any information relating to the customer acquired through the keeping of his account, unless the banker is compelled to do so by order of a court...." The court went further: "It is inconceivable that a bank would at any time consider itself at liberty to disclose the intimate details of its depositors' accounts. Inviolate secrecy is one of the inherent and fundamental precepts of the relationship of the bank and its customers or depositors...."

We hold, under these circumstances, Bank's relationship to a loan applicant implicitly imposes the duty to keep the contents of loan applications confidential....

We next turn to whether Bank can properly be excused on the ground Loan Officer's disclosure was outside the scope of his employment.

The record clearly shows confidential information was given to Loan Officer whose specific duty was to collect and keep such information. Damages caused by his carelessness in its handling are directly chargeable to the bank.

Customer's cause of action is, with these special facts, properly framed in terms of tortious conduct. It could have as properly been pled in terms *ex contractu*. He alleges that Bank has a duty of confidentiality which it breached, causing him financial damage. Indeed it appears that Bank's stockholders, officers and directors benefited directly and indirectly from the transaction. He has offered proof that his damages resulted from deliberate conduct because Bank not only breached its duty, but it has no official policy recognizing this basic customer safeguard, and may, in fact, have a contrary policy requiring employees to inform insiders of prime investment opportunities. These facts, if proven, are sufficient to raise jury issues both as to actual and punitive damages.

Summary judgment is reversed....

Notes

1. In Pigg v. Robertson, 549 S.W.2d 597 (Mo. App. 1977), defendant was conducting an operational audit on a bank. He sat in the bank president's office during the president's absence and advised bank customers and employees. Plaintiff came to the bank to arrange a loan for the purchase of a farm and was referred to defendant by one of the tellers. Defendant denied the loan request, telling plaintiff to return later to talk to the president. Defendant was interested in purchasing the property himself but did not disclose

this. He proceeded to purchase the farm, which he sold seven months later for a profit. Plaintiff claimed damages or a constructive trust for breach of a confidential relationship. What result?

2. In Pre-Cam Exploration & Development Ltd. v. McTavish, (1965) 53 W.W.R. 662, 55 D.L.R.2d 69 (Sask. C.A.), rev'd, [1966] S.C.R. 551, (1966) 57 D.L.R.2d 557, plaintiffs hired defendant, an employee of a mining engineering firm, to conduct exploration work. Plaintiffs had already recorded fifteen mineral claims and wanted, with defendant's help, to stake any additional claims necessary to bring an entire area under their control. In the course of his work, defendant discovered a zone northeast of plaintiffs' stakings that gave promise of being profitable. He secretly staked this in his own right. Was he in breach of a fiduciary duty? The lower court denied relief, finding no fraud and concluding that defendant was under no duty to plaintiffs as to the area outside the fifteen claims. The Supreme Court of Canada reversed, holding that, in view of defendant's duty to help plaintiffs secure the entire area for themselves, defendant was a trustee of the new claims he had staked and could be compelled to transfer them to plaintiffs.

3. A good summary of situations that may involve a "confidential relationship" is found in McManis, Intellectual Property and Unfair Competition 364–367 (6th ed. 2009), which lists the relations between a business and its employees, between partners in a business, between a corporation and its officers and directors, and between a business and some other commercial or noncommercial party, including a prospective purchaser of the business. It is pointed out that not every trade relation is a confidential one. In employment and the unsolicited submission of ideas, for instance, there must be additional circumstances from which the confidential relationship can be inferred—as when an employee was hired specifically to develop the information that constitutes the alleged trade secret. In addition, confidential relations may be created by express contract. There may be an express promise not to disclose or use information or ideas.

4. To what extent may an employee use or reveal what he has learned about his employer's income and expenses? In Bents Brewery Co., Ltd. v. Hogan, [1945] 2 All E.R. 470 (K.B.D.), the individuals involved were employed by brewery companies to manage "licensed houses" dispensing the breweries' products. The union to which the managers belonged sent them a questionnaire concerning the terms of their employment and the income and expenses of the houses they managed. The breweries sought a declaratory judgment that the union was not entitled to the requested information. The court held that information concerning weekly sales and wages could not be revealed, since this could only be acquired by the managers in the course of, and as a result of, their employment. The managers were free, however, to disclose matters relating solely to the terms and conditions of their own employment. See also Byrd's Lawn & Landscaping, Inc. v. Smith, 142 N.C. App. 371, 542 S.E.2d 689 (2001), holding that the cost history of a landscape and lawn maintenance business was a trade secret, and Norbrook Laboratories Ltd. v. King, [1983] N.I. 306, 325–328 (C.A.), in which the court found it a breach of confidence for a discharged accountant to tell striking workers about a bonus paid to an employee and a government grant paid to the employer.

5. Does the law of trade secrets provide a basis for a cause of action when plaintiff seeks to protect information for reasons other than its commercial value? In American law, with its emphasis on the use of information in business and deriving economic value from secrecy, the answer seems to be "no." Accordingly, in Religious Technology Center v. Wollersheim, 796 F.2d 1076 (9th Cir. 1986), cert. denied, 479 U.S. 1103 (1987), the court denied an injunction to a church seeking to prevent a splinter group from using and disseminating materials used to bring adherents to a "higher spiritual existence." The

alleged harm was not commercial, but rather religious harm that would be suffered by adherents through premature and unsupervised exposure to the materials at issue. Compare Foster v. Mountford, (1976) 14 A.L.R. 71, 29 F.L.R. 233 (N.T. Sup. Ct.), in which, at the request of a council representing Australian Aborigines, the court granted an ex parte injunction against the distribution of an anthropologist's book that revealed sacred sites, objects and ceremonies, disclosed to the anthropologist in confidence. In Aboriginal tradition, these matters were not to be revealed to women and uninitiated males.

6. In English law, which was followed in Foster v. Mountford, the emphasis has been on the confidentiality of the information. A remedy is available if the information is confidential, in the sense that it is not accessible to the public; if it was originally disclosed in circumstances imposing an obligation of confidence upon the recipient; and if this obligation has been breached, at least when this is detrimental to the complainant. See Coco v. A.N. Clark (Engineers) Ltd., [1968] F.S.R. 415, [1969] R.P.C. 41 (Ch. D.); Gurry, Breach of Confidence 3–6 (1984). Is the *Djowharzadeh* case essentially different from this? British courts have applied breach of confidence principles to non-commercial information in the *Spycatcher* cases, p. 326, supra. A case involving publication of a prominent politician's diaries, which included details of discussions in the Cabinet, Attorney-General v. Jonathan Cape Ltd., [1976] 1 Q.B. 752. And a number of cases involving disclosure of sensitive personal information. See pp. 470–473, infra, where there are also analogous American decisions.

7. Snepp v. United States, 444 U.S. 507 (1980), originated in circumstances close to those of *Spycatcher*. A former employee of the Central Intelligence Agency had agreed not to publish information about the C.I.A. without its permission, but he published a book without having submitted it to the C.I.A. for review. He was held to have breached a fiduciary obligation. All proceeds from the book were impressed with a constructive trust for the benefit of the government. The court considered immaterial that the book may not have contained classified information. The British government received advice that publication of *Spycatcher* could not be restrained in the United States. Was this correct?

8. Are cases such as *Djowharzadeh* and the cases mentioned in the last four notes governed by the Uniform Trade Secrets Act, in jurisdictions that have adopted the act? This depends in part on whether plaintiff's claim for relief is based upon "misappropriation of a trade secret," as defined in the act. The act's preemption provision, §7, originally displaced all state law pertaining to civil liability for trade secret misappropriation, but it has been amended to provide that contractual remedies (whether or not based upon misappropriation of a trade secret) are not affected by the act. The preemption provision might or might not be interpreted to include confidential information that does not fit the act's definition of a trade secret. See BlueEarth Biofuels, LLC v. Hawaiian Electric Co., Inc., 123 Hawaii 314, 235 P.3d 310 (2010).

E.I. duPont deNemours & Company, Inc. v. Christopher
United States Court of Appeals, Fifth Circuit
431 F.2d 1012 (1970), cert. denied, 400 U.S. 1024 (1971)

GOLDBERG, Circuit Judge:

This is a case of industrial espionage in which an airplane is the cloak and a camera the dagger. The defendants-appellants, Rolfe and Gary Christopher, are photographers in Beaumont, Texas. The Christophers were hired by an unknown third party to take aerial photographs of new construction at the Beaumont plant of E.I. duPont deNemours & Company, Inc. Sixteen photographs of the DuPont facility were taken from the air on March 19, 1969, and these photographs were later developed and delivered to the third party.

DuPont employees apparently noticed the airplane on March 19 and immediately began an investigation to determine why the craft was circling over the plant. By that afternoon the investigation had disclosed that the craft was involved in a photographic expedition and that the Christophers were the photographers. DuPont contacted the Christophers that same afternoon and asked them to reveal the name of the person or corporation requesting the photographs. The Christophers refused to disclose this information, giving as their reason the client's desire to remain anonymous.

Having reached a dead end in the investigation, DuPont subsequently filed suit against the Christophers, alleging that the Christophers had wrongfully obtained photographs revealing DuPont's trade secrets which they then sold to the undisclosed third party. DuPont contended that it had developed a highly secret but unpatented process for producing methanol, a process which gave DuPont a competitive advantage over other producers. This process, DuPont alleged, was a trade secret developed after much expensive and time-consuming research, and a secret which the company had taken special precautions to safeguard. The area photographed by the Christophers was the plant designed to produce methanol by this secret process, and because the plant was still under construction parts of the process were exposed to view from directly above the construction area. Photographs of that area, DuPont alleged, would enable a skilled person to deduce the secret process for making methanol. DuPont thus contended that the Christophers had wrongfully appropriated DuPont trade secrets by taking the photographs and delivering them to the undisclosed third party. In its suit DuPont asked for damages to cover the loss it had already sustained as a result of the wrongful disclosure of the trade secret and sought temporary and permanent injunctions prohibiting any further circulation of the photographs already taken and prohibiting any additional photographing of the methanol plant.

[The trial court held that DuPont's complaint stated a cause of action and ordered defendants to divulge the name of their client. Defendants took an interlocutory appeal.]

... The Christophers argued both at trial and before this court that they committed no "actionable wrong" in photographing the DuPont facility and passing these photographs on to their client because they conducted all of their activities in public airspace, violated no government aviation standard, did not breach any confidential relation, and did not engage in any fraudulent or illegal conduct. In short, the Christophers argue that for an appropriation of trade secrets to be wrongful there must be a trespass, other illegal conduct, or breach of a confidential relationship. We disagree.

... [I]n Hyde Corporation v. Huffines, 1958, 158 Tex. 566, 314 S.W.2d 763, the Texas Supreme Court specifically adopted the rule found in the Restatement of Torts which provides: "One who discloses or uses another's trade secret, without a privilege to do so, is liable to the other if (a) he discovered the secret by improper means, or (b) his disclosure or use constitutes a breach of confidence reposed in him by the other in disclosing the secret to him...." Restatement of Torts § 757 (1939). Thus, although the previous cases have dealt with a breach of a confidential relationship, a trespass, or other illegal conduct, the rule is much broader than the cases heretofore encountered. Not limiting itself to specific wrongs, Texas adopted subsection (a) of the Restatement which recognizes a cause of action for the discovery of a trade secret by any "improper" means....

The question remaining, therefore, is whether aerial photography of plant construction is an improper means of obtaining another's trade secret. We conclude that it is and that the Texas courts would so hold. The Supreme Court of that state has declared that "the undoubted tendency of the law has been to recognize and enforce higher standards of commercial morality in the business world." Hyde Corporation v. Huffines, *supra*. That court has quoted with approval articles indicating that the *proper* means of gaining possession of a competitor's secret process is "through inspection and analysis" of the product in order to create a duplicate. Later another Texas court explained: "The means by which the discovery is made may be obvious, and the experimentation leading from known factors to presently unknown results may be simple and lying in the public domain. But these facts do not destroy the value of the discovery and will not advantage a competitor who by unfair means obtains the knowledge *without paying the price expended by the discoverer.*" Brown v. Fowler, Tex. Civ. App. 1958, 316 S.W.2d 111, 114, writ ref'd n.r.e. (emphasis added).

We think, therefore, that the Texas rule is clear. One may use his competitor's secret process if he discovers the process by reverse engineering applied to the finished product; one may use a competitor's process if he discovers it by his own independent research; but one may not avoid these labors by taking the process from the discoverer without his permission at a time when he is taking reasonable precautions to maintain its secrecy. To obtain knowledge of a process without spending the time and money to discover it independently is *improper* unless the holder voluntarily discloses it or fails to take reasonable precautions to ensure its secrecy.

In the instant case the Christophers deliberately flew over the DuPont plant to get pictures of a process which DuPont had attempted to keep secret. The Christophers delivered their pictures to a third party who was certainly aware of the means by which they had been acquired and who may be planning to use the information contained therein to manufacture methanol by the DuPont process. The third party has a right to use this process only if he obtains this knowledge through his own research efforts, but thus far all information indicates that the third party has gained this knowledge solely by taking it from DuPont at a time when DuPont was making reasonable efforts to preserve its secrecy. In such a situation DuPont has a valid cause of action to prohibit the Christophers from improperly discovering its trade secret and to prohibit the undisclosed third party from using the improperly obtained information.

We note that this view is in perfect accord with the position taken by the authors of the Restatement. In commenting on improper means of discovery the savants of the Restatement said: "f. *Improper means of discovery.* The discovery of another's trade secret by improper means subjects the actor to liability independently of the harm to the interest in the secret. Thus, if one uses physical force to take a secret formula from another's pocket, or breaks into another's office to steal the formula, his conduct is wrongful and subjects him to liability apart from the rule stated in this Section. Such conduct is also an improper means of procuring the secret under this rule. But means may be improper under this rule even though they do not cause any other harm than that to the interest in the trade secret. Examples of such means are fraudulent misrepresentations to induce disclosure, tapping of telephone wires, eavesdropping or other espionage. A complete catalogue of improper means is not possible. In general they are means which fall below the generally accepted standards of commercial morality and reasonable conduct." Restatement of Torts § 757, comment f at 10 (1939).

In taking this position we realize that industrial espionage of the sort here perpetrated has become a popular sport in some segments of our industrial community. However, our devotion to free wheeling industrial competition must not force us into accepting the law of the jungle as the standard of morality expected in our commercial relations. Our tolerance of the espionage game must cease when the protections required to prevent another's spying cost so much that the spirit of inventiveness is dampened. Commercial privacy must be protected from espionage which could not have been reasonably anticipated or prevented. We do not mean to imply, however, that everything not in plain view is within the protected vale, nor that all information obtained through every extra optical extension is forbidden. Indeed, for our industrial competition to remain healthy there must be breathing room for observing a competing industrialist. A competitor can and must shop his competition for pricing and examine his products for quality, components, and methods of manufacture. Perhaps ordinary fences and roofs must be built to shut out incursive eyes, but we need not require the discoverer of a trade secret to guard against the unanticipated, the undetectable, or the unpreventable methods of espionage now available.

In the instant case DuPont was in the midst of constructing a plant. Although after construction the finished plant would have protected much of the process from view, during the period of construction the trade secret was exposed to view from the air. To require DuPont to put a roof over the unfinished plant to guard its secret would impose an enormous expense to prevent nothing more than a school boy's trick. We introduce here no new or radical ethic since our ethos has never given moral sanction to piracy. The market place must not deviate far from our mores. We should not require a person or corporation to take unreasonable precautions to prevent another from doing that which he ought not do in the first place. Reasonable precautions against predatory eyes we may require, but an impenetrable fortress is an unreasonable requirement, and we are not disposed to burden industrial inventors with such a duty in order to protect the fruits of their efforts. "Improper" will always be a word of many nuances, determined by time, place, and circumstances. We therefore need not proclaim a catalogue of commercial improprieties. Clearly, however, one of its commandments does say "thou shall not appropriate a trade secret through deviousness under circumstances in which countervailing defenses are not reasonably available." . . .

[Affirmed.]

Notes

1. *Acquiring trade secrets by improper means.* Restatement of Torts § 759 (1939) provides for liability when, for the purpose of advancing a rival business interest, a person procures information about another's business by improper means. Comment *c* lists some "improper means": theft, trespass, bribing or otherwise inducing employees or others to reveal information in breach of duty, fraudulent misrepresentation, threats of harm by unlawful conduct, wiretapping, and inducing one's own employees or agents to become employees of another business for purposes of espionage. Under Uniform Trade Secrets Act § 1(1), improper means include "theft, bribery, misrepresentation, breach or inducement of a breach of a duty to maintain secrecy, or espionage through electronic or other means." Compare Restatement of Unfair Competition § 43 (1995) (improper means include theft, fraud, unauthorized interruption of communications, inducement of or knowing participation in breach of confidence, and other means "either wrongful in themselves or wrongful under the circumstances of the case").

2. Plaintiffs are orchardists who grow a special type of nectarine. They are the sole suppliers in their market. It is impossible to repeat the cross-breeding program followed

by plaintiffs to produce this fruit except by grafting to root stock plaintiffs' budwood cuttings, which plaintiffs will not sell. Defendants, who operate an orchard in the same vicinity, steal budwood cuttings from plaintiffs' orchard and carry out the grafting process necessary to produce the special nectarines. Can they enjoy the fruits of their labors without liability to plaintiffs? See Franklin v. Giddins, [1978] Qd. R. 72 (Sup. Ct.) (since means of acquiring business advantage had been stolen, defendants must deliver to plaintiffs for destruction all productive budwood).

3. *Preemption by federal law.* Recall the *Sears* and *Compco* cases, p. 277, supra, which held that when a product is not patentable under federal law, there cannot be an injunction or award of damages under state law for copying it. May a state protect trade secrets that are not patentable, or should this be considered another subject of federal preemption? In Kewanee Oil Co. v. Bicron Corp., 416 U.S. 470 (1974), the Supreme Court decided against preemption. The invention involved was ineligible for patent protection because it had been in public use more than a year. The court discussed three categories of trade secrets: (1) clearly unpatentable matters, for which the patent alternative is unavailable and trade secret law would encourage inventions and their exploitation; (2) doubtfully patentable matters, for which the risk and cost of eventual patent invalidity might lead an inventor not to seek patent protection regardless of the existence of trade secret law; if trade secret protection were eliminated, this would encourage patent applications for doubtfully patentable inventions, with harmful effects for patent policy and society; and (3) clearly patentable matters, for which trade secret law would not deter patent applications. The court believed that trade secret law provided weaker protection than patent law, which forbids any unlicensed use of the invention for a specified number of years. It therefore found no reason to eliminate state laws protecting trade secrets. Even if it had, would any sufficient reason for exclusion of state law be found in a case like the *duPont* case?

4. Influenced by the Supreme Court's decision on the federal preemption issue in the *Bonito Boats* case, p. 355, infra, the court in Acuson Corp. v. Aloka Co., Ltd., 209 Cal. App. 3d 425, 257 Cal. Rptr. 368 (1989), held that trade secret law does not provide protection against use of trade secrets acquired by lengthy and expensive reverse engineering of a product sold on the open market. The court also decided that when plaintiff's product was publicly available for sale, a competitor's concealment of its identity when purchasing the product did not constitute a basis of trade secret liability. If a patent has been issued on a process or other invention, does the protection of trade secret law remain available? See Forest Laboratories, Inc. v. Formulations, Inc. p. 321, supra (once patent issued, essential element of secrecy gone and information protected by patent dedicated to public; better rule is that use of trade secret prior to issuance of patent remains actionable).

5. Another preemption issue arises from the Copyright Act of 1976, 17 U.S.C. §§ 101 et seq. Under the old law, only published works were within the Copyright Act, but the 1976 act includes unpublished documents as well. See pp. 342–343, infra. If a trade secret is reduced to writing, does the proprietor still have a state law remedy for misappropriation of the secret? Or must an action be brought under the federal act, which preempts state law? Does placing a copyright notice on the document affect this? Would a federal copyright claim provide compensation for loss of the economic value of the information as a trade secret, or only for loss of the economic rewards of publishing the information? In principle, the preemption question depends upon whether state trade secret law grants rights "equivalent to any of the exclusive rights within the general scope of" copyright rights. 17 U.S.C. § 301. If so, state law is preempted. The prevailing view is that trade secret law is not preempted, as it is based upon violation of confidence, not copy-

ing; the substance of the information, not the expression of it; and loss of the information's value as a secret, not infringement of the right to reproduce it. See Balboa Insurance Co. v. Trans Global Equities, 218 Cal. App. 3d 1327, 267 Cal. Rptr. 787 (1990), cert. denied sub nom. Collateral Protection Insurance Services v. Balboa Insurance Co., 498 U.S. 940 (1990); M. Bryce & Associates, Inc. v. Gladstone, 107 Wis. 2d 241, 319 N.W.2d 907 (Ct. App. 1982). But see Videotronics, Inc. v. Bend Electronics, 564 F. Supp. 1471 (D. Nev. 1983) (state law claim for misappropriation of computer program preempted). See generally Comment, Federal Copyright Protection and State Trade Secret Protection: The Case for Partial Preemption, 33 Am. U.L. Rev. 667 (1984).

Section 2. Literary, Artistic and Commercial Creations

A. Common Law Copyright

Palmer v. De Witt
New York Court of Appeals
47 N.Y. 532 (1872)

[The author of a drama assigned to plaintiff the exclusive right of printing, publishing and producing it in the United States. The drama was subsequently presented in theatres by plaintiff or with his permission. Defendant obtained the script of the drama, complete with division of scenes, stage directions, etc., and sold copies of it. Plaintiff sought an injunction restraining defendant from printing, publishing, selling or offering for sale the drama, and an accounting of profits.]

ALLEN, J. Whatever rights the plaintiff has in the drama, which is the subject of the controversy, exist at common law independent of any statute either of the State or the United States. The protection he seeks is of property, and a right of property which is well established and recognized wherever the common law prevails, and not of a franchise or privilege conferred by statute....

... The author of a literary work or composition has, by law, a right to the first publication of it. He has a right to determine whether it shall be published at all, and if published, when, where, by whom, and in what form. This exclusive right is confined to the first publication. When once published it is dedicated to the public, and the author has not, at common law, any exclusive right to multiply copies of it, or to control the subsequent issues of copies by others. The right of an author or proprietor of a literary work to multiply copies of it to the exclusion of others is the creature of statute. This is the right secured by the "copyright" laws of the different governments. It is said by Yates, J., in *Millar v. Taylor*, 4 Burr. 2303, 2379, "that it is certain that every man has a right to keep his own sentiments if he pleases; he certainly has a right to judge whether he will make them public, or commit them only to the sight of his friends. In that State the manuscript is, in every sense, his peculiar property, and no man can take it from him, or make any use of it which he has not authorized, without being guilty of a violation of his property" ...

... "Every new and innocent product of mental labor which has been embodied in writing, or some other material form, being the exclusive property of its author, the law securing it to him as such, and restraining every other person from infringing his right. Whether the ideas thus unpublished take the shape of written manuscripts of literary, dramatic or musical compositions, or whether they are the designs for works of ornament or utility planned by the mind of an artist, they are equally inviolable while they remain unpublished, and the author possesses an absolute right to publish them or not as he thinks fit (and if he does not desire to publish them), to hinder their publication, either in whole or in part, by any one else." Shortt on the Law of Literature, 48. ...

The assignability of a copyright before publication is not questioned. The right of sale and transfer is one of the inseparable incidents of property, and the property in a manuscript may be transferred and upon the death of the owner goes to the personal representatives or next of kin of the owner, as other personal property. A literary man realizes the product of his labor either by the sale of his manuscript or the publication and sale of his works. ...

So far as is disclosed by the case, the drama remained in manuscript until printed by the defendant, and there is no claim that it has been published by the author or the plaintiff, or with their assent, except by its public performance on the stage, and if it has not by that act become *publici juris*, it still remains the private property of the author or his assignee, who alone have the exclusive right to it and may prevent its publication. When a literary work is exhibited for a particular purpose, or to a limited number of persons, it will not be construed as a general gift or authority for any purpose of profit or publication by others. An author retains his right in his manuscript until he relinquishes it by contract or some unequivocal act indicating an intent to dedicate it to the public. An unqualified publication by printing and offering for sale is such a dedication. The rights of an author of a drama in his composition are twofold. He is entitled to the profit arising from its performance, and also from the sale of the manuscript, or the printing and publishing it. Lectures and plays are not, by their public delivery or performance in the presence of all who choose to attend, so dedicated to the public that they can be printed and published without the author's permission. It does not give to the hearer any title to the manuscript or a copy of it, or a right to the use of a copy. The manuscript and the right of the author therein are still within the protection of the law, the same as if they had never been communicated to the public in any form. The permission to act a play at a public theater does not amount to an abandonment by the author of his title to it, or to a dedication of it to the public. ... The printing and selling copies of the drama by the defendant was a violation of the legal and equitable rights of the plaintiff, as the sole proprietor of the right to print and publish the work within the United States; and the plaintiff was entitled upon the case made, to the relief demanded. ...

Notes

1. The common law recognizes a property right in unpublished writings and artistic creations. It exists apart from any right in the paper or other material on which the writing or artwork is placed. An early case finding this so-called "common law copyright" is Prince Albert v. Strange, (1848) 2 De G. & Sm. 652, 64 Eng. Rep. 293 (Ch.), aff'd, (1849) 1 H. & Tw. 1, 47 Eng. Rep. 1302, 13 Jur. 109, 18 L.J. Ch. 120, 12 L.T.O.S. 441, 1 Mac. & G. 25, 41 Eng. Rep. 1171 (L.C.), involving etchings made as a hobby by Prince Albert and Queen Victoria. A workman had been entrusted with copperplates for the purpose of making impressions of the etchings for the Queen and Prince. He took impressions for

himself and sold them to defendant, who published a catalogue of them. It was held that Prince Albert, as owner of an unpublished artistic or literary creation, was entitled to an injunction restraining publication of the etchings and to a decree ordering destruction of the impressions.

2. In the nineteenth century, most authority on common law copyright focused upon literature and letters. In Gee v. Pritchard, (1818) 2 Swan. 403, 36 Eng. Rep. 670 (L.C.), plaintiff had written letters to defendant. Defendant returned them to plaintiff but made copies, which he proposed to publish. The court enjoined publication. Folsom v. Marsh, 9 Fed. Cas. 342 (No. 4,901) (C.C.D. Mass. 1841), involving correspondence by George Washington, held that the author of any letter, whether personal or business, possesses the exclusive copyright therein and no one else, including the addressee, has a right to publish it. See also Baker v. Libbie, 210 Mass. 599, 97 N.E. 109 (1912) (no requirement that letters have literary merit; executor of letters' writer granted injunction against publication; recipient had title to papers and could transfer them); Annot., Copyright Protection for Private Letters, 87 A.L.R. Fed. 871 (1988). Compare Pushman v. New York Graphic Society, Inc., 287 N.Y. 302, 39 N.E.2d 249 (1942) (artist's unconditional sale of painting carried with it transfer of common law copyright and right to reproduce).

3. Warren & Brandeis, The Right to Privacy, 4 Harv. L. Rev. 193, 198–199 (1890), concluded that the existence of common law copyright did not depend upon the particular method of expression adopted — words, signs, painting, sculpture or music. Is it a violation of common law copyright to imitate plaintiff's presentation of a drama, or choreography, or musical or comedy style, without much use of plaintiff's script? See Murray v. Rose, 30 N.Y.S.2d 6 (Sup. Ct. 1941) (imitation of dance performance; no liability); Miller v. Universal Pictures Co., Inc., 11 A.D.2d 47, 201 N.Y.S.2d 632 (1960), modified, 13 A.D.2d 473, 214 N.Y.S.2d 645 (1961), aff'd, 10 N.Y.2d 972, 224 N.Y.S.2d 662, 180 N.E.2d 248 (1961) (no property right in famous band leader's "sound"). Compare Lombardo v. Doyle, Dane & Bernbach, Inc. p. 408, infra (imitation of Guy Lombardo in commercial actionable on basis that there was deception of public); Chaplin v. Amador, 93 Cal. App. 358, 269 P. 544 (1928) (imitation of Charlie Chaplin; remedy based on right to be protected against public deception, not an exclusive right to role, mannerisms, garb, etc.). But see Waring v. WDAS Broadcasting Station, 327 Pa. 433, 194 A. 631 (1937), finding that a conductor had common law rights in his orchestra's rendition of popular music. Direct reproduction or dissemination of a performance by recording or broadcasting has usually been addressed by the misappropriation doctrine. See pp. 359–361, infra.

4. In Columbia Broadcasting System, Inc. v. Documentaries Unlimited, Inc., 42 Misc. 2d 723, 248 N.Y.S.2d 809 (Sup. Ct. 1964), a noted radio announcer had announced the assassination of President Kennedy over a national television network. His announcement was subsequently included, without his consent or that of the network, in a commercially distributed phonograph record on the life of Kennedy. It was held that the announcer and the network were entitled to an injunction and damages. The announcer's voice and style of speaking were said to be the foundation and source of his employment and income and a form of art expression. Does an acrobat who performs as a "human cannonball" have a common law copyright in his performance? In Zacchini v. Scripps-Howard Broadcasting Co., 47 Ohio St. 2d 224, 351 N.E.2d 454 (1976), rev'd, 433 U.S. 562 (1977), the court found no copyright because no writing or intellectual property was involved and there was nothing original in the act. Cf. Dane v. M. & H. Co., 136 U.S.P.Q. 426 (N.Y. Sup. Ct. 1963), aff'd, 21 A.D.2d 751, 251 N.Y.S.2d 901 (1964), appeal denied, 14 N.Y.2d 487, 253 N.Y.S.2d 1025, 202 N.E.2d 156 (1964), where a choreographic performance,

telling a story about and satirizing strip teasers, was held not subject to common law copyright. It did not "promote the progress of science or the useful arts."

5. Can a person claim common law copyright in thoughts and other material communicated orally to an interviewer? Generally the answer has been no. See Falwell v. Penthouse International, Ltd., 521 F. Supp. 1204 (W.D. Va. 1981) (expression of opinions too general and abstract to be literary or intellectual creation that could enjoy protection of copyright); Estate of Hemingway v. Random House, Inc., 53 Misc. 2d 462, 279 N.Y.S.2d 51 (Sup. Ct. 1967), aff'd, 29 A.D.2d 633, 285 N.Y.S.2d 568 (1967), aff'd, 23 N.Y.2d 341, 296 N.Y.S.2d 771, 244 N.E.2d 250 (1968) (lower court held that participation by Ernest Hemingway in spontaneous conversations could not be considered literary work subject to common law copyright; Court of Appeals held that any reservation by Hemingway of common law copyright in interviews was negatived because Hemingway never suggested to interviewer that remarks were to be regarded as literary creations). Compare Jenkins v. News Syndicate Co., 128 Misc. 284, 219 N.Y.S. 196 (Sup. Ct. 1926), in which plaintiff gave a newspaper publisher an oral synopsis of proposed articles during negotiations with the publisher. When plaintiff subsequently refused to write the articles, the newspaper published a purported interview with plaintiff that substantially reproduced the material in the synopsis. See Annot., Common-Law Copyright in the Spoken Word, 32 A.L.R.3d 618 (1970).

National Institute, Inc., for the Improvement of Memory v. Nutt

United States District Court, District of Connecticut
28 F.2d 132 (1928), aff'd, 31 F.2d 236 (2d Cir. 1929)

BURROWS, District Judge.

[Plaintiff's president, Renick, conducted a business in memory training, beginning in 1921. He delivered lectures on this subject to audiences or classes which paid admission. He did not copyright the lectures under federal law until 1925. Later, Renick assigned the copyright to plaintiff. Plaintiff claimed that defendant, a former employee also engaged in memory training, infringed the copyright. Defendant attacked the validity of the copyright by claiming that the lectures' contents had been "dedicated to the public" by their presentation to audiences.]

The claim of dedication is not well founded. The record shows that these lectures were not delivered to the general public, but only to paying audiences or classes. In the case of Werckmeister v. American Lithographic Co., 134 F. 321, the court said: "Publication of a subject of copyright is effected by its communication or dedication to the public. Such a publication is what is known as a 'general publication.' There may be also a 'limited publication.' The use of the word 'publication' in these two senses is unfortunate, and has led to much confusion. A limited publication of a subject of copyright is one which communicates a knowledge of its contents under conditions expressly or impliedly precluding its dedication to the public."

The court continued: "On this capacity for public representation, as distinguished from the publication of other literary productions, the courts have founded the rule that such public exhibition is not a general publication. By admission to such exhibition the general public acquire no right to reproduce the composition, either by taking notes or by the exercise of the memory. The spectator is entitled to the enjoyment of the exhibition, but there is no implication of abandonment by the author of his title, or of surrender of the rights attached to his creation. The spectator, in paying for his ticket of admission, has not paid for any right to get possession of the play for subsequent representation. The same rule applies to lectures orally delivered. In such cases, even where the hearers were allowed to make copies for their personal use, such license was limited to such individuals for the purpose of their own information, and they could not publish for profit that which they had not obtained the right of selling." ...

In the case of Bobbs-Merrill Co. v. Straus (C.C.A.) 147 F. 15, the court said: "The owner of the common-law copyright has a perpetual right of property and the exclusive right of first general publication, and may, prior thereto, enjoy the benefit of a restricted publication without forfeiture of the right of general publication. Thus, he may communicate the contents of his work under restrictions without forfeiture of the right. This communication of contents under restriction, known as a restricted or limited publication, is illustrated by lectures to classes of students, dramatic performances before a select audience, exhibitions of paintings in private galleries, private circulation of copies of manuscript, etc."

... [N]either Renick nor the plaintiff, by delivering these lectures to paid audiences or classes, abandoned or dedicated them to the public....

The defendant further claims that the plaintiff's copyrighted lectures did not originate anything new; that they consist of wholesale appropriations from other authors and lectures on this subject. It is apparent, from an examination of the exhibits, that Renick obtained the foundation of his lectures from other sources, and especially from the Roth memory course, and occasionally used, to illustrate a principle, a story occurring in Roth and other works on this subject. But this does not necessarily take the plaintiff's lectures out of the realm of originality. The principle laid down in Emerson v. Davies et al. (C.C. Mass. 1845), Fed. Cas. No. 4,436, that *any new and original plan, arrangement or combination of materials would entitle an author to a valid copyright therein, whether the materials themselves be new or old*, would seem to apply in this case....

... [W]hosoever, *by his own skill, labor, and judgment*, writes a new work, may have a copyright therein, unless it be directly copied or evasively imitated from another....

The claim of the defendant that there has been no infringement of copyright is not borne out by the evidence. The unusual similarity disclosed by a comparison of the two lecture courses would seem to call for some explanation by the defendant, if he did not imitate the plaintiff's lectures; but neither the defendant nor any other person has testified in this regard. The defendant has seen fit to rest his case, in so far as lack of infringement is concerned, entirely upon a comparison of the two lectures. A comparison, however, shows that the plaintiff's lectures have been appropriated, not only as to the substantial and material parts, but also the general method of treatment, as well as the illustrations, stories, and phraseology.

It seems to me that the value of the plaintiff's property has been diminished by the defendant, and that the plaintiff is thereby injured in violation of the rule stated in [West Publishing Co. v. Edward Thompson Co. (C.C.) 169 F. 833, 854] "That to constitute an invasion of copyright it is not necessary that the whole of a work should be copied, nor even a large portion of it, in form or substance, but that, *if so much is taken that the value of the original is sensibly diminished, or the labors of the original author are substantially, to an injurious extent, appropriated by another, that is sufficient to constitute an infringement*."

[Plaintiff granted an injunction against infringement, an accounting, and damages.]

Notes

1. In Williams v. Weisser, 273 Cal. App. 2d 726, 78 Cal. Rptr. 542 (1969), defendant paid a U.C.L.A. student to attend a class and take notes, which defendant then copied

and sold. The court found that the professor teaching the class owned a copyright in his lectures which was not divested by their being orally delivered. An injunction and damages were awarded. Cf. Nicols v. Pitman, (1884) 26 Ch. D. 374 (author who delivered public lecture at college on "The Dog as the Friend of Man" could enjoin unauthorized publication of nearly verbatim account of lecture); Public Affairs Associates, Inc. v. Rickover, 268 F. Supp. 444 (D.D.C. 1967) (vice admiral of U.S. Navy had copyright in speeches not written or delivered as part of official duties); New Jersey State Dental Society v. Dentacure Co., 57 N.J. Eq. 593, 41 A. 672 (Ch. 1898), aff'd, 58 N.J. Eq. 582, 43 A. 1098 (1899) (report of committee of dental society, in nature of original essay, was read at society's annual meeting; held to be exclusive property of society that could not be reproduced without its permission). See generally Annot., Literary Property in Lectures, 38 A.L.R.3d 779 (1971).

2. Dr. Martin Luther King, Jr. delivered his famous "I Have a Dream" speech before a very large public audience. Advance texts of the speech were distributed to the press. It was broadcast on national radio and television. Was there a general publication? Dr. King's estate claimed infringement of copyright by a historical documentary series that included about 60% of the speech. In the U.S. Court of Appeals, one judge took the position that performance of a work without distribution of a tangible copy is not a publication, regardless of the size of the audience or widespread dissemination of the work through the media. A second judge accepted that performance of a work without distribution of tangible copies was not a "general publication" but allowed that general publication might occur if the work was exhibited or displayed in such a manner as to permit unrestricted copying by the general public. Factual issues on this point, precluding summary judgment, were found. This judge asserted that distribution of copies of the speech to the news media to obtain press coverage was only a limited publication. The third judge agreed with the district court that there had been general publication of Dr. King's speech on account of its widespread dissemination to very large live and broadcast audiences and encouragement of media coverage, with no express or implied limitation being placed on reproduction of the contents of the speech or use of film footage of the speech. Estate of Martin Luther King, Jr., Inc. v. CBS, Inc., 194 F.3d 1211 (11th Cir. 1999), rev'g 13 F. Supp. 2d 1347 (N.D. Ga. 1998). See also King v. Mister Maestro, Inc., 224 F. Supp. 101 (S.D.N.Y. 1963), in which defendants were selling records of the speech. Would the court have sustained an action complaining of rebroadcast of the speech or publication of a transcript as "news"?

3. As held in Palmer v. De Witt, p. 336, supra, the performance of a dramatic or musical composition does not constitute a general publication of the composition. See Ferris v. Frohman, 223 U.S. 424 (1912) (dramatic work); McCarthy & Fisher, Inc. v. White, 259 F. 364 (S.D.N.Y. 1919) (musical composition). In Glazer v. Hoffman, 153 Fla. 836, 16 So. 2d 53 (1943), however, a magician's public performance was said to constitute a dedication to the public of the trick performed. See generally Selvin, Should Performance Dedicate?, 42 Calif. L. Rev. 40 (1954). The court in Capitol Records, Inc. v. Naxos of America, Inc., 4 N.Y.3d 540, 797 N.Y.S.2d 352, 830 N.E.2d 250 (2005), concluded that while distribution of a written work to the public ended common law copyright in the work, public sale of a sound recording did not end common law copyright in the recording—because it was not possible to obtain statutory copyright protection for a recording (until 1972).

4. Does an owner of property have a right to enjoin publication of pictures and reproductions of the property? Or is common law copyright limited to protection of authors, creators and their assignees? In Lawrence v. Ylla, 184 Misc. 807, 55 N.Y.S.2d 343

(Sup. Ct. 1945), plaintiff employed a photographer to take photographs of her dog. The photographer sold one of the photographs for use in advertisements. Plaintiff successfully brought proceedings to have publication of the pictures enjoined. The court distinguished Prince Albert v. Strange, p. 337, supra, and held that all rights in this situation were contractual. Since the photographs were taken at the request of the dog's owner, who paid the photographer, all property in the photographs was in the owner. Otherwise, it would have been in the photographer.

5. If a property owner could claim common law copyright, would putting the property in a place where it could be freely seen by the public be "general publication"? See Masterson v. McCroskie, 194 Colo. 460, 573 P.2d 547 (1978) (construction of house in public view is publication of general design obtainable by observation, but not of construction plans). Would the creator or owner of a work of art relinquish a claim to common law copyright by allowing the work to be displayed in a public place? See Letter Edged in Black Press, Inc. v. Public Building Commission of Chicago, 320 F. Supp. 1303 (N.D. Ill. 1970), involving the Picasso sculpture installed in Chicago's Civic Center Plaza and the model for the sculpture, which had been displayed in an art museum. In Morton v. Raphael, 334 Ill. App. 399, 79 N.E.2d 522 (1948), it was held that an artist did not retain common law copyright in murals painted on the walls of a public room in a hotel.

6. What constitutes infringement of a common law copyright? See Annot., Literary and Artistic Rights for Purposes of, and Their Infringement by or in Connection with, Motion Pictures, Radio, and Television, 23 A.L.R.2d 244 (1952). In Fendler v. Morosco, 253 N.Y. 281, 171 N.E. 56 (1930), plaintiff claimed that defendant had substantially copied her unpublished play. Both plays involved a story about an American man who went to Hawaii to work and fell in love with a Hawaiian girl. Ruling that there could be no liability for appropriation of general ideas, themes or basic plot lines, the court found that the materials that were closely similar throughout the two works—story themes, atmosphere, etc.—were too general to be protectable. Literary property might be claimed in a particular combination of ideas or in the form in which ideas were embodied, but not in the ideas themselves. What would constitute infringement of common law copyright in a work of art or performance?

7. *Common law and federal law.* Since 1790, federal statutory protection has been granted to creators of various kinds of literary and artistic products. Under the 1909 Copyright Act, copyright was available for books, periodicals, maps, prints, musical compositions, photographs and reproductions of works of art. It was the exclusive source of protection for works that had been "published." Statutory and common law copyright co-existed. Statutory copyright was limited to a certain number of years. Common law copyright was perpetual, so long as no "publication" occurred. See Boorstyn, Copyright §§ 1.02–1.05 (2d ed. 1994). A new Copyright Act was enacted in 1976. 17 U.S.C. §§ 101 et seq. Protection now attaches under federal law at the point at which a "work of authorship" is "fixed in a tangible medium of expression." This is subject to statutory requirements for retention and enforcement of copyright rights. See Gorman, An Overview of the Copyright Act of 1976, 126 U. Pa. L. Rev. 856 (1978); Symposium: The Copyright Act of 1976, 24 U.C.L.A. L. Rev. 951 (1977).

8. Common law copyright, under state law, still operates with respect to works "not fixed in any tangible medium of expression." 17 U.S.C. § 301(b). Live performances and speeches are principal examples of works not "fixed" unless they are recorded with the author's authority. (Sound and visual recordings of a performance are now within the scope of federal copyright law, as are scripts and scores used in a performance.) Nimmer, Copyright §§ 1.08[C][2], 2.02 (1978). If there is a work "fixed in a tangible medium of ex-

pression," can common law copyright exist, or does the 1976 Copyright Act preempt the field? The act expressly preempts any state law that grants rights equivalent to copyright in works capable of federal copyright protection, but it expressly permits state protection of any subject-matter not covered by the act and rights not equivalent to those specified in the act. 17 U.S.C. § 301. Trade secret and privacy rights are examples of rights usually regarded as not equivalent to copyright rights and therefore not preempted. See pp. 335–336, supra, p. 407, infra. Titles of literary and artistic works are not copyrightable under federal law. States are free, therefore, to protect titles from copying if they choose to do so. See generally Brown, Unification: A Cheerful Requiem for Common Law Copyright, 24 U.C.L.A. L. Rev. 1070 (1977).

9. The requirement of originality applies to both common law and federal copyright. The federal statute protects a compilation or derivative work so long as it has enough originality to constitute a substantially new work of authorship. The copyright law's minimal requirement of originality is to be contrasted with the more stringent requirement of novelty for a patent. See Alfred Bell & Co. v. Catalda Fine Arts, 191 F.2d 99 (2d Cir. 1951) (originality found when "author" makes contribution beyond a trivial variation); Nimmer, Copyright §§ 2.01, 2.02, 3.03 (1978).

10. While the 1976 Copyright Act preempts much of the law of common law copyright, it is necessary to understand common law copyright in order to understand other common law doctrines, especially those considered in the remaining portion of this chapter.

B. Misappropriation

International News Service v. Associated Press

Supreme Court of the United States
248 U.S. 215 (1918)

Mr. Justice PITNEY delivered the opinion of the court.

The parties are competitors in the gathering and distribution of news and its publication for profit in newspapers throughout the United States. The Associated Press, which was complainant in the District Court, is a co-operative organization, ... its members being individuals who are either proprietors or representatives for about 950 daily newspapers published in all parts of the United States.... Complainant gathers in all parts of the world, by means of various instrumentalities of its own, by exchange with its members, and by other appropriate means, news and intelligence of current and recent events of interest to newspaper readers and distributes it daily to its members for publication in their newspapers. The cost of the service, amounting approximately to $3,500,000 per annum, is assessed upon the members and becomes a part of their costs of operation, to be recouped, presumably with profit, through the publication of their several newspapers. Under complainant's by-laws each member agrees upon assuming membership that news received through complainant's service is received exclusively for publication in a particular newspaper, language, and place specified in the certificate of membership, that no other use of it shall be permitted, and that no member shall furnish or permit any one in his employ or connected with his newspaper to furnish any of complainant's news in advance of publication to any person not a member. And each member is required to gather the local news of his district and supply it to the Associated Press and to no one else.

Defendant is a corporation ... whose business is the gathering and selling of news to its customers and clients, consisting of newspapers published throughout the United States, under contracts by which they pay certain amounts at stated times for defendant's service. It has widespread news-gathering agencies; the cost of its operations amounts, it is said, to more than $2,000,000 per annum; and it serves about 400 newspapers located in the various cities of the United States and abroad, a few of which are represented, also, in the membership of the Associated Press....

[Complainant filed a bill to restrain defendant from, inter alia, copying news from bulletin boards and early editions of complainant's newspapers and selling this, either bodily or after rewriting it, to defendant's customers. The Circuit Court of Appeals remanded the case with directions that defendant be enjoined from taking or using complainant's news "until its commercial value as news to the complainant and all of its members has passed away."]

... Complainant's news matter is not copyrighted. It is said that it could not, in practice, be copyrighted, because of the large number of dispatches that are sent daily; and, according to complainant's contention, news is not within the operation of the copyright act. Defendant, while apparently conceding this, nevertheless invokes the analogies of the law of literary property and copyright, insisting as its principal contention that, assuming complainant has a right of property in its news, it can be maintained (unless the copyright act be complied with) only by being kept secret and confidential, and that upon the publication with complainant's consent of uncopyrighted news of any of complainant's members in a newspaper or upon a bulletin board, the right of property is lost, and the subsequent use of the news by the public or by defendant for any purpose whatever becomes lawful....

In considering the general question of property in news matter, it is necessary to recognize its dual character, distinguishing between the substance of the information and the particular form or collocation of words in which the writer has communicated it. [Federal copyright may be secured for news articles in newspapers, but there is no exclusive right to report the news therein.]

We need spend no time, however, upon the general question of property in news matter at common law, or the application of the copyright act, since it seems to us the case must turn upon the question of unfair competition in business. And, in our opinion, this does not depend upon any general right of property analogous to the common-law right of the proprietor of an unpublished work to prevent its publication without his consent; nor is it foreclosed by showing that the benefits of the copyright act have been waived. We are dealing here not with restrictions upon publication but with the very facilities and processes of publication. The peculiar value of news is in the spreading of it while it is fresh; and it is evident that a valuable property interest in the news, as news, cannot be maintained by keeping it secret. Besides, except for matters improperly disclosed, or published in breach of trust or confidence, or in violation of law, none of which is involved in this branch of the case, the news of current events may be regarded as common property. What we are concerned with is the business of making it known to the world, in which both parties to the present suit are engaged. That business consists in maintaining a prompt, sure, steady, and reliable service designed to place the daily events of the world at the breakfast table of the millions at a price that, while of trifling moment to each reader, is sufficient in the aggregate to afford compensation for the cost of gathering and distributing it, with the added profit so necessary as an incentive to effective action in the commercial world. The service thus performed for newspaper readers is not only innocent but extremely useful in itself, and indubitably constitutes a legitimate business. The parties are competitors in this field; and, on fundamental principles, applicable here as elsewhere, when the rights or privileges of the one are liable to conflict with those of the other, each party is under a duty so to conduct its own business as not unnecessarily or unfairly to injure that of the other....

In order to sustain the jurisdiction of equity over the controversy, we need not affirm any general and absolute property in the news as such. The rule that a court of equity concerns itself only in the protection of property rights treats any civil right of a pecuniary nature as a property right; and the right to acquire property by honest labor or the conduct of a lawful business is as much entitled to protection as the right to guard property already acquired. It is this right that furnishes the basis of the jurisdiction in the ordinary case of unfair competition....

Not only do the acquisition and transmission of news require elaborate organization and a large expenditure of money, skill, and effort; not only has it an exchange value to the gatherer, dependent chiefly upon its novelty and freshness, the regularity of the service, its reputed reliability and thoroughness, and its adaptability to the public needs; but also, as is evident, the news has an exchange value to one who can misappropriate it.

The peculiar features of the case arise from the fact that, while novelty and freshness form so important an element in the success of the business, the very processes of distribution and publication necessarily occupy a good deal of time. Complainant's service, as well as defendant's, is a daily service to daily newspapers; most of the foreign news reaches this country at the Atlantic seaboard, principally at the city of New York, and because of this, and of time differentials due to the earth's rotation, the distribution of news matter throughout the country is principally from east to west; and, since in speed the telegraph and telephone easily outstrip the rotation of the earth, it is a simple matter for defendant to take complainant's news from bulletins or early editions of complainant's members in the eastern cities and at the mere cost of telegraphic transmission cause it to be published in western papers issued at least as early as those served by complainant. Besides this, and irrespective of time differentials, irregularities in telegraphic transmission on different lines, and the normal consumption of time in printing and distributing the newspaper, result in permitting pirated news to be placed in the hands of defendant's readers sometimes simultaneously with the service of competing Associated Press papers, occasionally even earlier.

Defendant insists that when, with the sanction and approval of complainant, and as the result of the use of its news for the very purpose for which it is distributed, a portion of complainant's members communicate it to the general public by posting it upon bulletin boards so that all may read, or by issuing it to newspapers and distributing it indiscriminately, complainant no longer has the right to control the use to be made of it; that when it thus reaches the light of day it becomes the common possession of all to whom it is accessible; and that any purchaser of a newspaper has the right to communicate the intelligence which it contains to anybody and for any purpose, even for the purpose of selling it for profit to newspapers published for profit in competition with complainant's members.

The fault in the reasoning lies in applying as a test the right of the complainant as against the public, instead of considering the rights of complainant and defendant, competitors in business, as between themselves. The right of the purchaser of a single newspaper to spread knowledge of its contents gratuitously, for any legitimate purpose not unreasonably interfering with complainant's right to make merchandise of it, may be admitted; but to transmit that news for commercial use, in competition with complainant—

which is what defendant has done and seeks to justify—is a very different matter. In doing this defendant, by its very act, admits that it is taking material that has been acquired by complainant as the result of organization and the expenditure of labor, skill, and money, and which is salable by complainant for money, and that defendant in appropriating it and selling it as its own is endeavoring to reap where it has not sown, and by disposing of it to newspapers that are competitors of complainant's members is appropriating to itself the harvest of those who have sown. Stripped of all disguises, the process amounts to an unauthorized interference with the normal operation of complainant's legitimate business precisely at the point where the profit is to be reaped, in order to divert a material portion of the profit from those who have earned it to those who have not; with special advantage to defendant in the competition because of the fact that it is not burdened with any part of the expense of gathering the news. The transaction speaks for itself and a court of equity ought not to hesitate long in characterizing it as unfair competition in business.

The underlying principle is much the same as that which lies at the base of the equitable theory of consideration in the law of trusts—that he who has fairly paid the price should have the beneficial use of the property. It is no answer to say that complainant spends its money for that which is too fugitive or evanescent to be the subject of property. That might, and for the purposes of the discussion we are assuming that it would furnish an answer in a common-law controversy. But in a court of equity, where the question is one of unfair competition, if that which complainant has acquired fairly at substantial cost may be sold fairly at substantial profit, a competitor who is misappropriating it for the purpose of disposing of it to his own profit and to the disadvantage of complainant cannot be heard to say that it is too fugitive or evanescent to be regarded as property. It has all the attributes of property necessary for determining that a misappropriation of it by a competitor is unfair competition because contrary to good conscience.

The contention that the news is abandoned to the public for all purposes when published in the first newspaper is untenable. Abandonment is a question of intent, and the entire organization of the Associated Press negatives such a purpose. The cost of the service would be prohibitive if the reward were to be so limited. No single newspaper, no small group of newspapers, could sustain the expenditure. Indeed, it is one of the most obvious results of defendant's theory that, by permitting indiscriminate publication by anybody and everybody for purposes of profit in competition with the news-gatherer, it would render publication profitless, or so little profitable as in effect to cut off the service by rendering the cost prohibitive in comparison with the return. The practical needs and requirements of the business are reflected in complainant's by-laws which have been referred to. Their effect is that publication by each member must be deemed not by any means an abandonment of the news to the world for any and all purposes, but a publication for limited purposes; for the benefit of the readers of the bulletin or the newspaper as such; not for the purpose of making merchandise of it as news, with the result of depriving complainant's other members of their reasonable opportunity to obtain just returns for their expenditures.

It is to be observed that the view we adopt does not result in giving to complainant the right to monopolize either the gathering or the distribution of the news, or, without complying with the copyright act, to prevent the reproduction of its news articles, but only postpones participation by complainant's competitor in the processes of distribution and reproduction of news that it has not gathered, and only to the extent necessary to prevent that competitor from reaping the fruits of complainant's efforts and expenditure, to the partial exclusion of complainant....

Affirmed.

Mr. Justice HOLMES [with whom Mr. Justice McKenna joined], dissenting.

When an uncopyrighted combination of words is published there is no general right to forbid other people repeating them — in other words there is no property in the combination or in the thoughts or facts that the words express. Property, a creation of law, does not arise from value, although exchangeable — a matter of fact. Many exchangeable values may be destroyed intentionally without compensation. Property depends upon exclusion by law from interference, and a person is not excluded from using any combination of words merely because some one has used it before, even if it took labor and genius to make it. If a given person is to be prohibited from making the use of words that his neighbors are free to make some other ground must be found. One such ground is vaguely expressed in the phrase unfair trade. This means that the words are repeated by a competitor in business in such a way as to convey a misrepresentation that materially injures the person who first used them, by appropriating credit of some kind which the first user has earned. The ordinary case is a representation by device, appearance, or other indirection that the defendant's goods come from the plaintiff. But the only reason why it is actionable to make such a representation is that it tends to give the defendant an advantage in his competition with the plaintiff and that it is thought undesirable that an advantage should be gained in that way. Apart from that the defendant may use such unpatented devices and uncopyrighted combinations of words as he likes....

Fresh news is got only by enterprise and expense. To produce such news as it is produced by the defendant represents by implication that it has been acquired by the defendant's enterprise and at its expense.... If the plaintiff produces the news at the same time that the defendant does, the defendant's presentation impliedly denies to the plaintiff the credit of collecting the facts and assumes that credit to the defendant. If the plaintiff is later in Western cities it naturally will be supposed to have obtained its information from the defendant. The falsehood is a little more subtle, the injury, a little more indirect, than in ordinary cases of unfair trade, but I think that the principle that condemns the one condemns the other.... [T]he defendant should be enjoined from publishing news obtained from the Associated Press for ___ hours after publication by the plaintiff unless it gives express credit to the Associated Press....

Mr. Justice BRANDEIS, dissenting....

... The creations which are recognized as property by the common law are literary, dramatic, musical, and other artistic creations; and these have also protection under the copyright statutes. The inventions and discoveries upon which this attribute of property is conferred only by statute, are the few comprised within the patent law. There are also many other cases in which courts interfere to prevent curtailment of plaintiff's enjoyment of incorporeal productions; and in which the right to relief is often called a property right, but is such only in a special sense. In those cases, the plaintiff has no absolute right to the protection of his production; he has merely the qualified right to be protected as against the defendant's acts, because of the special relation in which the latter stands or the wrongful method or means employed in acquiring the knowledge or the manner in which it is used. Protection of this character is afforded where the suit is based upon breach of contract or of trust or upon unfair competition....

... To appropriate and use for profit, knowledge and ideas produced by other men, without making compensation or even acknowledgment, may be inconsistent with a finer sense of propriety; but, with the exceptions indicated above, the law has heretofore sanctioned the practice. Thus it was held that one may ordinarily make and sell anything in any form, may copy with exactness that which another has produced, or may otherwise use his ideas without his consent and without the payment of compensation, and yet not inflict a legal injury; and that ordinarily one is at perfect liberty to find out, if he can by lawful means, trade secrets of another, however valuable, and then use the knowledge so acquired gainfully, although it cost the original owner much in effort and in money to collect or produce.

Such taking and gainful use of a product of another which, for reasons of public policy, the law has refused to endow with the attributes of property, does not become unlawful because the product happens to have been taken from a rival and is used in competition with him. The unfairness in competition which hitherto has been recognized by the law as a basis for relief, lay in the manner or means of conducting the business; and the manner or means held legally unfair, involves either fraud or force or the doing of acts otherwise prohibited by law....

That competition is not unfair in a legal sense, merely because the profits gained are unearned, even if made at the expense of a rival, is shown by many cases besides those referred to above. He who follows the pioneer into a new market, or who engages in the manufacturer of an article newly introduced by another, seeks profits due largely to the labor and expense of the first adventurer; but the law sanctions, indeed encourages, the pursuit....

The means by which the International News Service obtains news gathered by the Associated Press is also clearly unobjectionable. It is taken from papers bought in the open market or from bulletins publicly posted....

... [T]he defendant and its subscribers, unlike members of the Associated Press, were under no contractual obligation to disclose the source of the news; and there is no rule of law requiring acknowledgment to be made where uncopyrighted matter is reproduced. The International News Service is said to mislead its subscribers into believing that the news transmitted was originally gathered by it and that they in turn mislead their readers. There is, in fact, no representation by either of any kind....

Nor is the use made by the International News Service of the information taken from papers or bulletins of Associated Press members legally objectionable by reason of the purpose for which it was employed. The acts here complained of were not done for the purpose of injuring the business of the Associated Press. Their purpose was not even to divert its trade, or to put it at a disadvantage by lessening defendant's necessary expenses. The purpose was merely to supply subscribers of the International News Service promptly with all available news....

... The unwritten law possesses capacity for growth; and has often satisfied new demands for justice by invoking analogies or by expanding a rule or principle. This process has been in the main wisely applied and should not be discontinued. Where the problem is relatively simple, as it is apt to be when private interests only are involved, it generally proves adequate. But with the increasing complexity of society, the public interest tends to become omnipresent; and the problems presented by new demands for justice cease to be simple. Then the creation or recognition by courts of a new private right may work serious injury to the general public, unless the boundaries of the right are definitely established and wisely guarded. In order to reconcile the new private right with the public interest, it may be necessary to prescribe limitations and rules for its enjoyment; and also to provide administrative machinery for enforcing the rules. It is largely for this reason that, in the effort to meet the many new demands for justice incident to a rapidly changing civilization, resort to legislation has latterly been had with increasing frequency.

The rule for which the plaintiff contends would effect an important extension of property rights and a corresponding curtailment of the free use of knowledge and of ideas; and the facts of this case admonish us of the danger involved in recognizing such a property right in news, without imposing upon news-gatherers corresponding obligations....

Courts are ill-equipped to make the investigations which should precede a determination of the limitations which should be set upon any property right in news or of the circumstances under which news gathered by a private agency should be deemed affected with a public interest. Courts would be powerless to prescribe the detailed regulations essential to full enjoyment of the rights conferred or to introduce the machinery required for enforcement of such regulations. Considerations such as these should lead us to decline to establish a new rule of law in the effort to redress a newly disclosed wrong, although the propriety of some remedy appears to be clear.

Notes

1. International News Service's copying of news from Associated Press and other news services followed the British government's banning INS from the Official Press Bureau and all facilities for transmission of news from Great Britain. Because of World War I, news transmission from Britain was censored by the government. Stories published in American newspapers and attributed to an INS correspondent in London reported that the British Navy had admitted "overwhelming defeat" by the Germans in the Battle of Jutland. The Home Secretary stated that no such news accounts had been sent from Britain; they must have been composed in the New York offices of INS. This alleged "garbling" of news stories was given as the reason for the ban of INS. INS, however, claimed that it was because INS "did not print the kind of news that the English desired to have printed." See Kitch & Perlman, Intellectual Property and Unfair Competition 20–21 (5th ed. 1998).

2. A news agency supplies news reports to its member newspapers. A radio station takes reports from a member newspaper and broadcasts them. Is this distinguishable from the misappropriation in the *INS* case? In Associated Press v. KVOS, Inc., 9 F. Supp. 279 (W.D. Wash. 1934), rev'd, 80 F.2d 575 (9th Cir. 1935), rev'd, 299 U.S. 269 (1936), the district court denied relief to the agency. It concluded that once news had been printed in newspapers and distributed, it belonged to the public, including radio stations, for all purposes except sale by a rival news agency. The fact that the radio station competed with newspapers in advertising did not make the station and the newspapers rivals for profits in the dissemination of news. The Court of Appeals found misappropriation of the news agency's "quasi-property interest" in the news it had gathered. The court believed that the public had an interest in protecting news agencies against impairment of their efficiency by reduction of their business income—which would result if a radio station, with its more rapid means of distributing news, were allowed to appropriate the agencies' reports. The station was enjoined from broadcasting any news gathered by plaintiff "for the period following its publication in [plaintiff's] newspapers during which the broadcasting of the pirated news to KVOS' most remote auditors may damage [plaintiff's] papers' business of procuring or maintaining their subscriptions and advertising." See also Pottstown Daily News Publishing Co. v. Pottstown Broadcasting Co., 411 Pa. 383, 192 A.2d 657 (1963) (unfair competition for radio station to use in its news broadcasts articles on local news gathered and published by area newspaper).

3. When a news-gathering agency makes stock market quotations available to its customers via ticker tape, is it misappropriation if another company copies the quotations

and supplies them to its own patrons? See National Telegraph News Co. v. Western Union Telegraph Co., 119 F. 294 (7th Cir. 1902) (copying enjoined; "unfair competition"). If a trade newspaper collects news relating to the engineering and building construction trades and provides this information to persons in that line of work, can it enjoin a competing publication from copying and publishing its news items? See Gilmore v. Sammons, 269 S.W. 861 (Tex. Civ. App. 1925) ("unfair interference with business"). Compare Benjamin T. Crump Co., Inc. v. J.L. Lindsay, Inc., 130 Va. 144, 107 S.E. 679 (1921) (many pages of defendant's catalogue were photographic copies of plaintiff's catalogue; parties competitors, selling goods purchased from same manufacturers; suit dismissed). Many Internet sites now reproduce news and information from other sources. Is misappropriation a viable remedy for this? Would it depend on whether the information is valuable only for a limited period ("hot news")? On whether the information is provided for free or only as a paid-for service? See Note, Hot News Misappropriation in the Internet Age, 9 J. Telecomm. & High Tech L. 313 (2011).

4. Misappropriation liability usually has been limited to situations analogous to that in *INS*, in which defendant's conduct was likely to destroy or greatly impair plaintiff's primary opportunity to market its goods or services. Most efforts to expand *INS* into a general unjust enrichment principle barring any "free ride" on a competitor's creation of products or services have been unsuccessful. When defendant's "free-riding" diverts some profits from plaintiff but does not threaten the viability of plaintiff's primary services or products, misappropriation claims usually fail. Relief may be granted against appropriation of plaintiff's creation without material change, but is not likely when defendant has incurred substantial expenditures and produced something different of value to society. See National Basketball Association v. Motorola, Inc., p. 356, infra; Malone, Torts: Injuries to Family, Social and Trade Relations 307–312 (1979); Rahl, The Right to "Appropriate" Trade Values, 23 Ohio St. L.J. 56 (1962). The case law is reviewed in Sease, Misappropriation Is Seventy-Five Years Old; Should We Bury It or Revive It?, 70 N.D. L. Rev. 781 (1994). Most courts outside the United States do not accept the misappropriation doctrine or a general action for "unfair competition." See Moorgate Tobacco Co. Ltd. v. Philip Morris Ltd. (No. 2), (1984) 156 C.L.R. 414; L'Oreal S.A. v. Bellure N.V., [2008] R.P.C. 196 (C.A.). But see Schultz v. Butt, 1986 (3) S.A. 667 (A.D.) (applied in South African law).

5. If a lottery makes use of the schedules and scores of a football league's teams, is this misappropriation of the league's property? See National Football League v. Governor of State of Delaware, 435 F. Supp. 1372 (D. Del. 1977) (no, but lottery required to make disclaimer of association with league on all its tickets, to avoid impression that league sponsored lottery). In United States Golf Association v. St. Andrews Systems, Data Max, Inc., 749 F.2d 1028 (3d Cir. 1984), defendant was sued for marketing a computer system for the calculation of golfers' "handicaps." The system used the mathematical formula for handicaps prescribed by the United States Golf Association, the "governing body" for amateur golf. The court held that the association had no action for misappropriation. It emphasized that defendant was not in direct competition with the association and, therefore, would not interfere with the association's incentive to maintain and update the handicap formula.

6. The United States Golf Association was successful in later litigation involving unauthorized commercial use of its handicapping system. Defendant in this case included the USGA's handicap formulas in a computer software program sold to golfers, something which required only the purchase for $5 of a copy of the formulas from USGA and twenty to thirty hours of work on the software. Misappropriation was found because of USGA's investment of much time, skill and expense in developing the formulas, defendant's appropri-

ation of the formulas at little cost, and injury to USGA. Direct competition between the parties was not required. Injury was found because use of the formulas other than by authorized golf associations and clubs threatened the integrity of USGA's handicapping system, which depended on peer review, and could damage USGA's reputation and viability. *United States Golf Association v. Arroyo Software Corp.*, 40 U.S.P.Q.2d 1840 (Cal. Super. Ct. 1996), aff'd, 69 Cal. App. 4th 607, 81 Cal. Rptr. 2d 708 (1999). See also *Board of Trade of City of Chicago v. Dow Jones & Co., Inc.*, 98 Ill. 2d 109, 456 N.E.2d 84 (1983), holding (4–3) that the Chicago Board of Trade's offering stock index futures contracts utilizing the Dow Jones Industrial Average was a misappropriation of Dow Jones' index and averages.

7. Can a defendant commit misappropriation by its advertising? What if the advertising copies an advertising campaign developed and presented by plaintiff with great cost, effort and ingenuity? Substantially reduces the impact of plaintiff's advertising by flooding the market with similar advertising? Reduces the value of plaintiff's advertising by associating it with defendant's less attractive product or service? Harms plaintiff's ability to market or license related products and services? Courts have not been inclined to find liability for misappropriation but sometimes have found a cause of action for passing off or analogous unfair competition. See *Cadbury-Schweppes Pty. Ltd. v. Pub Squash Co. Pty. Ltd.*, [1981] 1 W.L.R. 193 (P.C.) (use of rival soft drink's advertising themes and slogans); *Sea Harvest Corp. (Pty.) Ltd. v. Irvin & Johnson Ltd.*, 1985 (2) S.A. 355 (C) (defendant called its fish product "prime cuts" following plaintiff's successful advertising campaign for its "prime cuts" of fish); *Chemical Corp. of America v. Anheuser-Busch, Inc.* 306 F.2d 433 (5th Cir. 1963) (plaintiff a brewer with well-known slogan "Where there's life . . . there's Bud"; defendant selling insecticidal floor wax under slogan "Where there's life . . . there's bugs"); *Samuelson v. Producers' Distributing Co., Ltd.*, [1932] 1 Ch. 201 (C.A.) (defendant used favorable notices of plaintiff's theatrical sketch to market defendant's film, which featured same comedian; this gave impression that film was of sketch, to detriment of plaintiff's exclusive right to make film of sketch).

8. A corporation is formed to carry on for its member stores a system of customer identification and credit, using small tin plates which the corporation issues. Its members share the expense of operating the system in proportion to their use of it. Defendant is not a member of the corporation but permits and encourages use in its store of the tin plates. This results in considerable savings of time and of clerical and bookkeeping costs. Does the corporation have any cause of action? See *Hartford Charga-Plate Associates v. Youth Centre-Cinderella Stores, Inc.*, 215 F.2d 668 (2d Cir. 1954) (having relinquished its plates to customers, plaintiff cannot burden plates with "servitude" binding on strangers; no passing off or damage to plaintiff's business reputation found).

9. Someone publishes a set of solutions to the problems contained in a textbook used by students. Do the creators of the textbook have an action? See *Addison-Wesley Publishing Co. v. Brown*, 207 F. Supp. 678 (E.D.N.Y. 1962) (publishers and authors of college physics text granted preliminary injunction; solutions would destroy usefulness of text). What if defendant sells answers for plaintiff's newspaper contest? See *Philadelphia Record Co. v. Leopold*, 40 F. Supp. 346 (S.D.N.Y. 1941) ("unlawful interference" with plaintiff's business). Does a manufacturer commit misappropriation by using in advertising product ratings published by an organization that tests products? See *Consumers Union of United States, Inc. v. Hobart Manufacturing Co.*, 189 F. Supp. 275 (S.D.N.Y. 1960) (plaintiff claimed that subscribers would lose confidence in plaintiff's impartiality if ratings used in advertising).

10. *Reverse passing off.* In Capital Films Corp. v. Charles Fries Productions, Inc., 628 F.2d 387 (5th Cir. 1980), the owner of a film released in 1964 brought suit against a production company and television network because of the production and broadcast in 1977 of a film with the same title and subject-matter. Vacating a summary judgment for defendants, the court held that an unfair competition action did not require that plaintiff show the public would be confused into believing that the network was broadcasting plaintiff's film. It would be unfair competition for defendants to create "reverse confusion," i.e. to confuse the public as to the source of the 1964 film. In Bajpayee v. Rothermich, 53 Ohio App. 2d 117, 372 N.E.2d 817 (1977), plaintiff was employed as a biochemist in charge of a medical research laboratory. Defendant was an official of the foundation that owned the laboratory. Plaintiff had set forth some of his medical discoveries in an unpublished abstract. He claimed no common law copyright in the abstract. By contract, all property interest was in his employer. At a meeting of a professional medical group, defendant presented plaintiff's discoveries as his own. Did these allegations state a cause of action for unfair competition, misappropriation or other tort? The court found an action for "prima facie tort," violating "the right of the author to be recognized for his work product."

11. On the actionability of "reverse passing off," see Summit Machine Tool Manufacturing Corp. v. Victor CNC Systems, Inc., 7 F.3d 1434 (9th Cir. 1993); Annot., Reverse Confusion Doctrine Under State Trademark Law, 114 A.L.R.5th 129 (2003). Restatement of Unfair Competition § 5 (1995) supports such claims. Extending further the "extended passing off" theory developed in the "Spanish Champagne" and "Advocaat" cases, pp. 306–307, supra, the court in Bristol Conservatories Ltd. v. Conservatories Custom Built Ltd., [1989] R.P.C. 455 (C.A.), held that a company which designed and constructed conservatories had a cause of action against a competitor whose salesmen showed prospective customers photographs of plaintiff's work and represented them as samples of defendant's work. Mastro Plastics Corp. v. Emenee Industries, Inc., 16 A.D.2d 420, 228 N.Y.S.2d 514 (1962), aff'd, 12 N.Y.2d 826, 236 N.Y.S.2d 347, 187 N.E.2d 360 (1962), rejected an unfair competition claim against a competitor that used plaintiff's products, with the trademark removed, as trade samples and used photographs of plaintiff's products, with the trademark obscured, for advertising and promotion. It noted that defendant was free to make and market an exact copy of plaintiff's product. In United Merchants and Manufacturers v. Bromley Fabrics, 3 Misc. 2d 179, 148 N.Y.S.2d 22 (Sup. Ct. 1955), the court held that there was no cause of action for defendant's use of plaintiff's fabrics as sample pieces for sale of its own fabrics, provided defendant did not represent that the pieces were manufactured by defendant.

––––––––––

Cheney Brothers v. Doris Silk Corporation

United States Circuit Court of Appeals, Second Circuit
35 F.2d 279 (1929), cert. denied, 281 U.S. 728 (1930)

L. HAND, Circuit Judge.

The plaintiff, a corporation, is a manufacturer of silks, which puts out each season many new patterns, designed to attract purchasers by their novelty and beauty. Most of these fail in that purpose, so that not much more than a fifth catch the public fancy. Moreover, they have only a short life, for the most part no more than a single season of eight or nine months. It is in practice impossible, and it would be very onerous if it were not, to secure design patents upon all of these; it would also be impossible to know in advance which would sell well, and patent only those. Besides, it is probable that for the most part they have no such originality as would support a design patent. Again, it is impossible to copyright them under the Copyright Act, or at least so the authorities of the Copyright Office hold. So it is easy for any one to copy such as prove successful, and the plaintiff, which is put to much ingenuity and expense in fabricating them, finds itself without protection of any sort for its pains.

Taking advantage of this situation, the defendant copied one of the popular designs in the season beginning in October, 1928, and undercut the plaintiff's price. This is the injury of which it complains....

The plaintiff asks for protection only during the season, and needs no more, for the designs are all ephemeral. It seeks in this way to disguise the extent of the proposed innovation, and to persuade us that, if we interfere only a little, the solecism, if there be one, may be pardonable. But the reasoning which would justify any interposition at all demands that it cover the whole extent of the injury. A man whose designs come to harvest in two years, or in five, has prima facie as good right to protection as one who deals only in annuals. Nor could we consistently stop at designs; processes, machines, and secrets have an equal claim. The upshot must be that, whenever any one has contrived any of these, others may be forbidden to copy it. That is not the law. In the absence of some recognized right at common law, or under the statutes—and the plaintiff claims neither—a man's property is limited to the chattels which embody his invention. Others may imitate these at their pleasure....

Of the cases on which the plaintiff relies, the chief is International News Service v. Associated Press, 248 U.S. 215. Although that concerned another subject-matter—printed news dispatches—we agree that, if it meant to lay down a general doctrine, it would cover this case; at least, the language of the majority opinion goes so far. We do not believe that it did. While it is of course true that law ordinarily speaks in general terms, there are cases where the occasion is at once the justification for, and the limit of, what is decided. This appears to us such an instance; we think that no more was covered than situations substantially similar to those then at bar. The difficulties of understanding it otherwise are insuperable. We are to suppose that the court meant to create a sort of common-law patent or copyright for reasons of justice. Either would flagrantly conflict with the scheme which Congress has for more than a century devised to cover the subject-matter....

True, it would seem as though the plaintiff had suffered a grievance for which there should be a remedy, perhaps by an amendment of the Copyright Law, assuming that this does not already cover the case, which is not urged here. It seems a lame answer in such a case to turn the injured party out of court, but there are larger issues at stake than his redress. Judges have only a limited power to amend the law; when the subject has been confided to a Legislature, they must stand aside, even though there be an hiatus in completed justice. An omission in such cases must be taken to have been as deliberate as though it were express, certainly after long-standing action on the subject-matter. Indeed, we are not in any position to pass upon the questions involved, as Brandeis, J., observed in International News Service v. Associated Press. We must judge upon records prepared by litigants, which do not contain all that may be relevant to the issues, for they cannot disclose the conditions of this industry, or of the others which may be involved....

The order [denying an injunction pendente lite] is affirmed, and, as the bill cannot in any event succeed, it may be dismissed, if the defendant so desires.

Notes

1. Suppose that dresses designed and sold by a famous couturier are copied by another designer. Copies are sold with the statement that they are copies of the models designed by the couturier. Does the latter have a remedy? In Societe Comptoir De L'Industrie Cotonniere, Establissements Boussac v. Alexander's Department Stores, Inc., 190 F. Supp. 594 (S.D.N.Y. 1961), aff'd, 299 F.2d 33 (2d Cir. 1962), the answer was "no": once the dresses were sold, they were in the public domain. The law did not prevent a rival's truthfully denominating his goods as a copy of the design. Unfair competition required either deception or appropriation of plaintiff's property, which was not shown. Cf. Smith v. Chanel, Inc., 402 F.2d 562 (9th Cir. 1968) (defendants could advertise their perfume as duplicate of plaintiffs').

2. Through costly advertising and other publicity, certain symbols become identified in the public mind with the member clubs of a professional football league. These marks are affixed to merchandise manufactured by the league's licensees. Defendant, who is not a licensee, begins to make and sell cloth emblems that duplicate the league's symbols. Can the league or its licensees have this restrained? See National Football League Properties, Inc. v. Consumer Enterprises, Inc., 26 Ill. App. 3d 814, 327 N.E.2d 242 (1975), cert. denied, 423 U.S. 1018 (1976) (member clubs' licensing agent had property rights entitled to protection; probability of ultimate success shown, based on unfair competition and deceptive practices).

3. Plaintiff and defendant both manufacture electrical devices, plugs and receptacles. Defendant adopts the same size and shape that plaintiff uses for parts of the electrical contact devices, thus making its parts interchangeable with plaintiff's. Is this actionable? See Harvey Hubbell, Inc. v. General Electric Co., 262 F. 155 (S.D.N.Y. 1919) (no; in absence of patent protection, no monopoly had ever been given over proportions and measurements of manufactured items). Cf. New England Telephone & Telegraph Co. v. National Merchandising Corp., 335 Mass. 658, 141 N.E.2d 702 (1957) (telephone company not entitled to injunction against merchandising corporation's free distribution of plastic covers to fit over company's directories, in absence of passing off or deception). But see Meyer v. Hurwitz, 5 F.2d 370 (E.D. Pa. 1925), in which plaintiff manufactured uncopyrighted picture post cards, sold through coin-operated vending machines distributed by plaintiff. Businesses that purchased the machines did not contract to use plaintiff's cards exclusively. The court decided that defendant could be restrained from selling those businesses similar cards at lower prices for placement in plaintiff's machines.

4. If copyright on a work expires and the work passes into the public domain, can its contents be freely photographed, reproduced and sold by anyone, or might this be enjoined as misappropriation? In Grove Press, Inc. v. Collectors Publication, Inc., 264 F. Supp. 603 (C.D. Calif. 1967), plaintiff, a publisher, had incurred considerable expense in setting a book's type and engraving the plates. Defendants photographed and reproduced plaintiff's edition through an offset lithography process. It was decided that the words could be copied by anyone but that it would be unjust to allow defendants to appropriate the value and benefit of plaintiff's expenditures. The court enjoined preparation and sale of reproductions of plaintiff's edition. Defendants remained free to publish an edition they set in type themselves, even though they used plaintiff's edition for the text. In E.P. Dutton & Co. v. Cupples, 117 App. Div. 172, 102 N.Y.S. 309 (1907), plaintiff published a series of books, each of which contained an uncopyrightable poem or hymn, illustrated with illuminated capitals and type adapted from ancient missals and with color pictures prepared by plaintiff's artists or copied from well-known paintings. Defendant was re-

strained from selling a nearly identical series photographically reproduced from plaintiff's books, the court finding a strong probability of deception of the public. Relief from copying sometimes has been denied when there was no copyright in force and no intent to deceive purchasers. See Black v. Ehrich, 44 F. 793 (C.C.S.D.N.Y. 1891) (no injunction against publication and sale of encyclopedia with same name and contents as that published by plaintiff); Hebrew Publishing Co. v. Scharfstein, 288 N.Y. 374, 43 N.E.2d 449 (1942) (defendant not restrained from photographing and selling books originally published by plaintiff; no copyright infringement, passing off, fraud or interference with business or good will of plaintiff; no appropriation of plaintiff's ingenuity or artistic competence); Flamingo Telefilm Sales, Inc. v. United Artists Corp., 22 A.D.2d 778, 254 N.Y.S.2d 36 (1964) (if film was in public domain, it could be duplicated and broadcast on television).

5. Numerous cases have found no cause of action for the mere imitation or copying of products. E.g., Hawley Products Co. v. United States Trunk Co., 259 F.2d 69 (1st Cir. 1958) (luggage); Neely v. Boland Manufacturing Co., 170 F. Supp. 773 (D. Minn. 1958) (garment bag). In a case involving alleged copying of type fonts, the court stated that no unfair competition claim based solely on copying of a tangible product had ever been recognized in New York. Leonard Storch Enterprises, Inc. v. Mergenthaler Linotype Co., 208 U.S.P.Q. 58 (E.D.N.Y. 1980). Under the *Sears-Compco* decisions of the Supreme Court, p. 277, supra, state law cannot be applied to forbid or create liability for copying that is permitted by the federal patent and copyright laws. Whether preemption of state law extends to all prohibition of product simulation is a point of contention. See Symposium, Product Simulation: A Right or Wrong?, 64 Colum. L. Rev. 1178 (1964). Despite the statement in *Compco* that neither the fact that the article's configuration had a secondary meaning nor that fact that the copied design was non-functional provided a basis for liability under state law for copying, the court in Duo-Tint Bulb & Battery Co., Inc. v. Moline Supply Co., 46 Ill. App. 3d 145, 360 N.E.2d 798 (1977), concluded that it was still possible to forbid copying of an "arbitrary embellishment" or other non-functional design feature.

6. Can plaintiffs who make claims under a state misappropriation doctrine avoid federal preemption on the argument that appropriation is to be distinguished form copying? See Note, The "Copying-Misappropriation" Distinction: A False Step in the Development of the *Sears-Compco* Pre-emption Doctrine, 71 Colum. L. Rev. 1444 (1971), which advocates a case-by-case analysis of whether state action would interfere with federal policy. In Bonito Boats, Inc. v. Thunder Craft Boats, Inc., 489 U.S. 141 (1989), a manufacturer of recreational boats fitted with an unpatented hull brought suit under a Florida statute that prohibited the duplication of boat hulls by direct molding from another person's hull and the sale of hulls so duplicated. The Supreme Court held that the statute was preempted. For articles within the scope of federal patent legislation but not protected by it, state law could not grant an equitable or monetary remedy even for the direct use of plaintiff's product in defendant's manufacturing process. It fell within the *Sears-Compco* prohibition on state law liability for copying. In Schultz v. Butt, 1986 (3) S.A. 667 (A.D.), an injunction was granted on the basis of common law against manufacture and sale of boats with hulls made from a mold of one of plaintiff's hulls. The court's decision was founded in large measure on the *INS* case. Under the opinion in *Bonito Boats*, a common law claim as well as one brought under a state statute would be preempted in the United States.

7. When defendant has copied or imitated copyrightable material, as in *INS* itself, a misappropriation action is preempted by the 1976 Copyright Act unless the wrong and the remedy can be distinguished from copying and rights granted by the act. See Barclays Capital Inc. v. Theflyonthewall.com, Inc., 650 F.3d 876 (2d Cir. 2011); Schuchart & As-

sociates, Professional Engineers, Inc. v. Solo Serve Corp., 540 F. Supp. 928 (W.D. Tex. 1982); Nimmer, Copyright § 1.01[B] (1978). The court in National Basketball Association v. Motorola, Inc. 105 F.3d 841 (2d Cir. 1997), concluded that a claim of misappropriation of "hot news" was not preempted when it contained certain "extra elements" that went beyond copyright infringements: (1) the factual information was highly time-sensitive; (2) defendant's use of the information was "free-riding" on plaintiff's costly efforts to generate or collect the information; and (3) the "free-riding" threatened the existence of plaintiff's service or product. Using information from reporters who watched NBA games on television or listened to radio broadcasts, Motorola was transmitting details of games in progress to specialized pagers and a web site. The web site also included player and team statistics. NBA intended to support a similar pager product in the future. The broadcasts, although not the games themselves, were within federal copyright law and use of factual information culled from the broadcasts was not an infringement of NBA's copyright in the broadcasts.

8. In Fred Wehrenberg Circuit of Theatres, Inc. v. Moviefone, Inc., 73 F. Supp. 2d 1044 (E.D. Mo. 1999), defendant was a company which provided, through an automated telephone system and Internet web site, listings of films shown in movie theatres. Defendant collected information on theatre schedules for this purpose. It earned revenue by including advertisements by other companies, including publicity for films, in the telephone system and web site. Plaintiff was the operator of numerous movie theatres whose schedules were included, sometimes inaccurately, in defendant's telephone system and web site. Plaintiff had its own web site containing information about its theatres and schedules of films shown there. It earned revenue from a few companies in exchange for displaying schedule information. It also had an automated telephone system and ticketing system through which patrons could purchase tickets. Defendant sold theatre tickets through an automated telephone system and its web site in some areas, but not where plaintiff operated theatres. On these facts, could plaintiff prevail in a misappropriation action?

9. In Goldstein v. California, 412 U.S. 546 (1973), the Supreme Court held that a state was free to protect subject-matter — in this instance, musical recordings — that Congress had left "unattended." It seems that preemption will now be found only if a state attempts to regulate a field of activity that Congress expressed an intention to leave without protection, rather than a field Congress merely left unattended, or if a conflict is found with the scheme established in the federal legislation. See, e.g., Synercom Technology, Inc. v. University Computing Co., 474 F. Supp. 37 (N.D. Tex. 1979) (application of state misappropriation law to limit use of plaintiff's computer-input format would create conflict with federal patent and copyright laws).

Intermountain Broadcasting & Television Corporation v. Idaho Microwave, Inc.

United States District Court, District of Idaho
196 F. Supp. 315 (1961)

SWEIGERT, District Judge....

[Defendants operated a community antenna television service in Twin Falls, Idaho. The service carried the Twin Falls station, KLIX, and two Boise stations. When defendants took steps to add three Salt Lake City stations to the service, these stations brought suit to prevent this. Because Twin Falls was not included in the national television net-works' circuits, KLIX had arrangements with plaintiffs to pick up their broadcasts of net-work programs for rebroadcast on KLIX. KLIX paid an agreed hourly sum for use of plaintiffs' signals.]

Pointing out the elements of cost, labor and skill, which are necessary to arrange and broadcast television programs over their facilities, plaintiffs assert that the announced and threatened practice of defendants amounts to a misappropriation of the fruits of plaintiffs' money, skill and labor, and is "unfair competition" and "unjust enrichment" within the mean-ing of International News Service v. Associated Press, 1918, 248 U.S. 215....

Those courts which have followed and applied the doctrine of International News Service have done so in identical fact situations, or in cases where there was manifest unjust en-richment, for example, where rights in private enterprises or events for which the investor had granted exclusive TV or Radio licenses were involved — unique situations in which the primary purpose of an investor to charge the public for the privilege of watching an event, would be frustrated or defeated through exhibition by others than itself or its exclusive licensee.

No such exclusive license rights are relied upon by plaintiffs on these pending motions. The existence of possible exclusive license with respect to particular programs is not suf-ficiently documented to justify a determination of that point by summary judgment....

A cautious approach to recognition of novel rights protectible upon the theory of un-fair competition is especially wise when the unjust practice complained of occurs in a field over which the Congress has already assumed a control sufficient to enable it, if it so chooses, to regulate the practice one way or another in the public interest....

... [T]here has been a plenary exercise by Congress of the power to occupy and regu-late the field of television.

In Sec. 325(a) of the [Federal Communications] Act, the Congress has already dealt with a practice substantially similar to the practice of defendants in the pending cases by providing that no broadcasting station shall rebroadcast the programs, or any part thereof, of another broadcasting station without the express authority of the originating station.

... [T]his section of the Act, as presently written, does not apply to the practice of these defendants for the sole reason, however, that the practice of defendants does not tech-nically constitute "rebroadcasting" within the meaning of the Act....

[The Federal Communications Commission had not been given jurisdiction over com-munity antenna systems, although it did grant permits for microwave facilities used to bring in signals, such as those intended to be used in this case.]

... Associated Press and International News Service were identical businesses engaged in the keenest competition to supply news to their respective members for sale to the public, a competitive factor which the majority opinion considered in its discussion of misappropriation.

In the pending cases the plaintiffs and the defendants are not engaged in the same kind of business. They operate in different ways for different purposes.

Plaintiffs are in the business of selling their broadcasting time and facilities to the spon-sors to whom they look for their profits. They do not and cannot charge the public for their broadcasts which are beamed directly, indiscriminately and without charge through the air to any and all reception sets of the public as may be equipped to receive them.

Defendants, on the other hand, have nothing to do with sponsors, program content or arrangement. They sell community antenna service to a segment of the public for which the plaintiff's programs were intended but which is not able, because of location or topographical condition, to receive them without rebroadcast or other relay service by community antennae. Any profit to defendants must come from the public for this service.

The practice of International News Service interfered with the primary purpose of Associated Press and its members in the sale of its gathered news, first or fresh, to the paying public, while in the pending cases the practice of defendants does not interfere with any such primary purpose of plaintiffs....

In the International News Service case the Court recognized that no one should be permitted to reap the fruits of another's expenditure of money and skill. Assuming that plaintiffs' expenditure of money and skill for its purposes is fairly comparable with the gathering, writing and editing of news releases by the widespread personnel and facilities of Associated Press, there is, however, a basic difference in the two situations which must be borne in mind in connection with the question whether defendants' practice here is an unfair misappropriation of the fruits of plaintiffs' expense and skill....

... [D]efendants' practice does not amount to interference at the point where plaintiffs' profit is to be made. Certainly, defendants' practice does not interfere with plaintiffs' profits derived from sponsors. On the contrary, the practice may enhance plaintiffs' possibilities of profit in that field by extending the reception of plaintiffs' programs.

... Defendants here make no claim, either expressly or impliedly, to their service subscribers of having themselves produced the programs which are relayed. On the contrary, defendants relay the programs as program broadcasts of the plaintiffs and so identified....

The real, and it seems to the Court, the only claimed interference here involved is interference by defendants with plaintiffs' asserted right to charge for any rebroadcast or other relay of their broadcasts—a purpose which is, not only subordinate to, but inconsistent with plaintiffs' primary purpose and function as a broadcasting station....

Plaintiffs allege that KLIX, the local Twin Falls station, will not continue to pay plaintiffs for their rebroadcast consents if the defendants are also permitted to pick up plaintiffs' broadcasts for microwave relay to Twin Falls receiving sets, and that plaintiffs' income from that source will be reduced or cut off.

This argument, however, begs the very question here involved, namely, whether plaintiffs, apart from statutory or common law copyright or exclusive license rights, have a property right, quasi or otherwise, in their broadcasts, as such, sufficient to support a requirement of consent before either rebroadcast by KLIX, Twin Falls or microwave relay by defendants.

Such a property right cannot be established or inferred from the mere fact that plaintiffs may have successfully asserted it with KLIX-TV, Twin Falls.

The Twin Falls Station, which is a broadcaster and, therefore, a re-broadcaster, within the meaning of Sec. 153(o), is required by Sec. 325(a) to obtain plaintiffs' consent before rebroadcast of the programs and, presumably, is willing to pay to get that consent.

But, the statutory requirement of consent before rebroadcast is not based upon, or intended to recognize any property right of the originating station in its broadcast signal as such. It was designed only as a means for safeguarding the interests of such persons as might have property rights in program content which would be protectible under established law, as, for example, statutory or common law copyright or exclusive license arrangements protectible under the doctrine of unfair competition....

... [I]ndividual owners of receiving sets in the Twin Falls area, or groups of such owners, could, without infringing on any rights of plaintiffs, construct their own antenna of sufficient height, location and design to pick up the plaintiffs' broadcasts and bring them to their home receiving sets. The fact that owners, unable or unwilling to undertake the difficulties and expense of such construction, prefer to use the similar antenna service provided by defendants does not change the essential situation....

[Plaintiffs' motions for summary judgment denied.]

Plaintiffs, upon further presentation, may make a case for protection under copyright law, statutory or common law, with respect to any programs which they themselves creatively produce or for protection under the doctrine of unfair competition with respect to any exclusive license arrangements which have heretofore been recognized as ground for invoking that doctrine....

Notes

1. The community antenna operators in the principal case subsequently brought an antitrust action against the Twin Falls station, KLIX. KLIX counterclaimed, asserting exclusive contractual rights to the first run of certain programs in the Twin Falls area and claiming that the activities of the community antenna operators in picking up the programs broadcast by the Salt Lake City stations for simultaneous distribution to the Twin Falls subscribers constituted unfair competition. KLIX sought a preliminary injunction. The district court enjoined the antenna service's "reproducing" of the programs. The Court of Appeals reversed, relying upon the *Sears-Compco* policy of promoting free access to matter in the public domain. Cable Vision, Inc. v. KUTV, Inc., 211 F. Supp. 47 (D. Idaho 1962), rev'd, 335 F.2d 348 (9th Cir. 1964), cert. denied, 379 U.S. 989 (1965). It appears that a misappropriation claim would be successful if defendant picked up and disseminated television or radio programs that plaintiff was transmitting to subscribers who paid for the service. See KMLA Broadcasting Corp. v. Twentieth Century Cigarette Vendors Corp., 264 F. Supp. 35 (C.D. Cal. 1967); American Television and Communications Corp. v. Manning, 651 P.2d 440 (Colo. App. 1982).

2. A radio broadcasting company has the exclusive right, by contract with the commissioner of baseball, to broadcast a play-by-play account of the World Series. The Muzak Corporation, a commercial enterprise that supplies music, news, etc., to its customers, picks up the radio broadcast of the Series by means of a conventional radio receiver in its studio and transmits the sounds through leased telephone lines and its distribution system to its customers. Is the broadcasting company entitled to an injunction? See Mutual Broadcasting System, Inc. v. Muzak Corp., 177 Misc. 489, 30 N.Y.S.2d 419 (Sup. Ct. 1941) (temporary injunction granted).

3. Unable to obtain permission to broadcast descriptions of horse races from plaintiff's track, defendant has a platform erected on a nearby building. From there, races are observed by an announcer, whose descriptions of races are broadcast by defendant's radio station. Allegedly, attendance at plaintiff's track declines as a result. Should an injunction issue? Victoria Park Racing & Recreation Grounds Co. Ltd. v. Taylor, (1937) 58 C.L.R. 479, holds that no legal right is infringed in these circumstances. See also Loeb v. Turner, 257 S.W.2d 800 (Tex. Civ. App. 1953), where a Texas radio station had its agent listen to the broadcast of races by an Arizona station and telephone the details to the Texas station, which broadcast a re-creation of each race. But in Pittsburgh Athletic Co. v. KQV Broadcasting Co., 24 F. Supp. 490 (W.D. Pa. 1938), where the owner of a baseball team by con-

tract gave certain advertisers the exclusive right to broadcast the team's games, it was held that unauthorized broadcasting of descriptions of the games, using paid observers stationed outside the ball park, interfered with a property right of the advertisers and amounted to unfair competition. Cf. Twentieth Century Sporting Club, Inc. v. Transradio Press Service, Inc., 165 Misc. 71, 300 N.Y.S. 159 (Sup. Ct. 1937) (company with exclusive broadcast rights to prize fight, granted by promoter, could enjoin news service and its agents from supplying information on progress of fight to various radio stations, utilizing plaintiffs' broadcast).

4. Do the sponsors of an event to which an admission fee is charged have the right to limit publication of photographs of the event? Compare Sports and General Press Agency, Ltd. v. "Our Dogs" Publishing Co., Ltd., [1916] 2 K.B. 880 (promoters of dog show purported to assign sole photographic rights but placed no notice, on admission tickets or otherwise, forbidding others to take pictures; defendants published their photographs in journal; held for defendants), with New York World's Fair 1964–65 Corp. v. Colourpictures Publishers, Inc., 2 A.D.2d 896, 251 N.Y.S.2d 885 (1964) (manufacturers of post cards and other souvenirs not permitted to photograph any unique building, structure or object within World's Fair grounds without permission of sponsoring corporation).

5. In Ettore v. Philco Television Broadcasting Corp., 229 F.2d 481 (3d Cir. 1956), cert. denied, 351 U.S. 926 (1956), plaintiff had participated in a boxing match held in 1936. Motion pictures of the match were taken. Plaintiff had a contract under which he was to receive 20% of the proceeds from the sale of motion picture rights. Commercial television did not then exist. Thirteen years later, defendant televised the motion pictures in a commercial program without plaintiff's consent. He claimed damages. The court supported the claim. It believed that when a performer performs for hire, curtailment without consideration of his right to control his performance is a wrong to him. Furthermore, fairness required the court to treat the absence of an unknown medium (television) as equivalent to a reservation against use of the performer's work product in a known medium.

6. If a noted performer, such as Elvis Presley, willingly participates in a news conference, does either the performer or the record company granted exclusive contract rights to his "performances" have rights in the conference? See Current Audio, Inc. v. RCA Corp., 71 Misc. 2d 831, 337 N.Y.S.2d 949 (Sup. Ct. 1972) (since non-artistic use of singer's speaking voice was involved, company had no rights; performer who willingly participated in news conference had no property rights superseding right of free dissemination). Compare Columbia Broadcasting System, Inc. v. Documentaries Unlimited, Inc., p. 338, supra, where a radio announcer, suing on the basis of common law copyright, was granted an injunction and damages because his announcement of President Kennedy's assassination was included in a phonograph record.

7. Plaintiff originates a magical trick. He performs it in public many times. The public comes to associate the trick with plaintiff's name. Defendant makes a film using the same title as plaintiff uses for his act, producing the same illusion, and attempting to explain the manner in which the illusion is produced. Does plaintiff have any remedy? See Goldin v. Clarion Photoplays, Inc., 202 App. Div. 1, 195 N.Y.S. 455 (1922), in which plaintiff established he was originator of the illusion "Sawing a Woman in Half." Defendant was found to have depreciated the value of plaintiff's act. Plaintiff was granted an injunction pendente lite.

8. A number of cases established record or tape "piracy" (the sale of records or tapes made by duplicating someone else's record or tape) as a situation in which the misappropriation doctrine could be utilized. See Capitol Records, Inc. v. Erickson, 2 Cal. App.

3d 526, 82 Cal. Rptr. 798 (1969); Columbia Broadcasting System, Inc. v. Custom Recording Co., 258 S.C. 465, 189 S.E.2d 305 (1972), cert. denied, 409 U.S. 1007 (1972); Mercury Record Productions, Inc. v. Economic Consultants, Inc., 64 Wis. 2d 163, 218 N.W.2d 705 (1974), appeal dismissed, 420 U.S. 914 (1975); Annot., Unfair Competition by Direct Reproduction of Literary, Artistic, or Musical Property, 40 A.L.R.3d 566 (1971). At the time these cases arose, federal law did not provide for copyrights in sound recordings. In Goldstein v. California, p. 356, supra, the Supreme Court held that state laws prohibiting piracy of sound recordings were valid. State controls on and remedies for such copying—under the misappropriation doctrine as well as common law copyright—now seem to have been excluded by the extension of statutory copyright to recordings and other "works of authorship fixed in any tangible medium of expression." 17 U.S.C. § 102. See Nimmer, Copyright § 1.01 [B] (1978). Even live performances may not be protected from unauthorized exploitation by state misappropriation law when the performances have been recorded and thus "fixed." See Baltimore Orioles, Inc. v. Major League Baseball Players Association, 805 F.2d 663 (7th Cir. 1986), cert. denied, 480 U.S. 941 (1987).

C. Characters and Characterizations

Booth v. Colgate-Palmolive Company

United States District Court, Southern District of New York
362 F. Supp. 343 (1973)

BONSAL, District Judge....

Plaintiff Shirley Booth is a well-known comedy and dramatic actress who has performed on the legitimate stage, in motion pictures, and on television. From 1961 to 1966, she played the title role of "Hazel" in a popular television comedy series.... The series was based on the adventures of a copyrighted cartoon character named Hazel, with the permission of Ted Key, the character's creator and copyright holder, who was given credit during the broadcasts. Since 1967, television and audio tape recordings of the series have been presented throughout the United States and in other countries.

Defendant Bates is an advertising agency which produced radio and television commercials promoting [defendant] Colgate's laundry detergent "Burst". These commercials, first broadcast on January 16, 1971, used the name and likeness of the copyrighted cartoon character Hazel pursuant to a written license agreement with Key, the creator and copyright holder, dated June 22, 1970. The voice of Hazel in the commercials was performed by Ruth Holden. Neither she nor the plaintiff was named or identified during the commercials....

Plaintiff relies on three arguments to support her first cause of action under the New York State common law of unfair competition. Plaintiff's first argument is that star performers such as herself have a property right in their performances, which property right permits the protection of those performances against both direct misappropriation, such as for example the unauthorized tape recording of a vocal performance, as well as against indirect misappropriation, such as the imitation of a performer's timing, inflection, tone, or general performing style. Plaintiff, Shirley Booth, has devoted many years to training as an actress and has attained stardom. She contends that she endowed the role of Hazel with her own unique and creative artistic interpretation, and that the "modern liberalized and considerably expanded doctrines of the New York law of unfair competition" protect her against imitation of her voice in defendants' commercials.

... [D]efendants concede that "Ruth Holden's voice as used in the Burst commercials constituted an 'imitation' of the 'normal speaking voice'... of Shirley Booth as plaintiff used it and it was heard in the 'Hazel' situation comedy series." ...

[In Metropolitan Opera Association, Inc. v. Wagner-Nichols Recorder Corp., 199 Misc. 786, 101 N.Y.S.2d 483 (Sup. Ct. 1950), aff'd, 279 App. Div. 632, 107 N.Y.S.2d 795 (1951), involving defendants' sale of records made by recording broadcasts of Metropolitan Opera performances, an injunction was granted the Opera] on the basis that the rights plaintiff had granted to the broadcasting company and [another] recording company were contractual, exclusive rights and that defendants' conduct constituted a direct misappropriation of plaintiff's property rights. Similarly, in [Dior v. Milton, 9 Misc. 2d 425, 155 N.Y.S.2d 443 (Sup. Ct.), aff'd, 2 A.D.2d 878, 156 N.Y.S.2d 996 (1956)], which involved the copying of plaintiff's fashion designs, the court emphasized the fact that the defendants had been permitted to see the designs on the express condition that they would not make or divulge any reproduction of any of the designs. Here, in contrast, there was neither use of an actual recording of plaintiff's voice in defendants' commercials nor any express condition to viewers of the Hazel television serious analogous to that set forth in *Dior*.

Moreover, the argument that New York law protects a performer from imitators is undercut by the Supreme Court decisions in Sears, Roebuck & Co. v. Stiffel Co., 376 U.S. 225 (1964), and Compco Corp. v. Day-Brite Lighting, Inc., 376 U.S. 234 (1964). *Sears* and *Compco*, both involving invalid design patents, held that the states are preempted from protecting, under state unfair competition law, designs that Congress has not chosen to protect by means of the federal patent laws. The Court's reasoning, however, was not based upon peculiarities of patent law. Rather, the Court spoke in broad and general terms about the purpose of patent and copyright laws and about the need for national uniformity: "[B]ecause of the federal patent laws a State may not, when the article is unpatented and *uncopyrighted*, prohibit the copying of the article itself or award damages for such copying." (Emphasis added.) ...

Moreover, there are persuasive reasons of public policy for refusing to recognize a performer's right of protection against imitators. The policing of a performance or the creation of a performer in playing a role would present very difficult, if not impossible, problems of supervision for a court of equity. In addition, the recognition of a performer's right in a copyrighted work would impose undue restraints on the potential market of the copyright proprietor since a prospective licensee would have to gain permission from each of possibly many performers who might have rights in the underlying work before he could safely use it. Such a right could also conflict with the Constitutional policy of permitting exclusive use of patented and copyrighted works for only a limited period of time. Finally, the vesting of a monopoly in the performer and the prevention of others from imitating his postures, gestures, voices, sounds, or mannerisms may impede, rather than "promote the Progress of ... useful Arts." U.S. Const., art. I, §8.

For the foregoing reasons, the court finds that the imitation by defendants of plaintiff's voice without more, does not constitute unfair competition under New York law.

Plaintiff's second theory to support her claim of unfair competition is that the defendants infringed plaintiff's "rights of publicity" in her name, appearance, likeness, signature or personality....

Under [the] cases, however, the plaintiff must show that her name or a likeness was used by defendants. Since the commercials in issue here are anonymous and do not use plaintiff's name or likeness in any way to identify her as the source of the voice of Hazel, this court finds that plaintiff cannot show an infringement of her rights to publicity.

Plaintiff's third theory to support her claim of unfair competition is based on her contention that the Hazel television series has been so closely connected with the voice she used in playing the part of Hazel that her voice has acquired a "secondary meaning." She contends that defendants, by "concealing the identity of the performer who imitated [her] voice," were attempting to deceive the public into thinking that the plaintiff endorsed Burst, in effect that defendants' acts constituted the tort of "free-ride" unfair competition under New York law. Plaintiff argues that defendants used two "clues" to plaintiff's identity in the commercials in order to bolster the association of Colgate's laundry detergent with Shirley Booth in the mind of the public: 1) the references of the anonymous performer in the commercials to herself as "Hazel," and 2) the word "Burst" itself as a "quickly recognizable symbol of the limitless 'bursts' of energy" with which Shirley Booth portrayed the television series character. . . .

In the present case, the plaintiff has not shown either that what she seeks to protect from imitation — her voice — functions as a trademark or trade name entitling it to protection, or that her voice was ever used in connection with any product or service in competition with a product or service of defendants. Moreover, in contrast to the cases cited by the plaintiff, in the present case defendants had a right to use the name and character of Hazel pursuant to the license agreement. And the name of its product, Burst, which name has been a registered trademark of Colgate's since 1956, cannot be said to identify or refer to the plaintiff. Accordingly, the strong federal policy emphasized in *Sears* and *Compco* permitting imitation prevails here over plaintiff's interest in protecting whatever secondary meaning may be attached to her voice as that of the television series' Hazel. . . .

Plaintiff contends that the defendants' commercials constitute a libel per se inasmuch as they deceive the public into thinking that "of necessity, Shirley Booth has been reduced to using and selling her talents for anonymous radio and television commercials and advertising announcements, and that her talents have deteriorated and are less valuable." . . .

. . . The commercials she contends are libelous do not refer to her nor mention her name. Even if it could be found that, due to a "secondary meaning," the public would associate her either with the cartoon character Hazel or merely with the name "Hazel," it cannot be said that performing the "voice over" in television and radio commercials would have a tendency directly to injure plaintiff in her business, profession, or trade. There is no allegation that the voice was performed in an inferior manner in the commercials. A star performer's endorsement of a commercial product is a common occurrence and does not indicate either a diminution of professional reputation nor a loss of professional talent, though plaintiff herself might prefer to avoid such engagements. Accordingly, plaintiff's cause of action based on the theory that defendants' commercials constitute libel per se is not tenable.

For the foregoing reasons, defendants' motion for summary judgment dismissing the complaint is granted. . . .

Notes

1. In Gardella v. Log Cabin Products Co., 89 F.2d 891 (2d Cir. 1937), defendant was the proprietor of Aunt Jemima Pancake Flour — a leading brand for many years. Some of

its promotions included public appearances of women portraying Aunt Jemima. Independently, plaintiff, a singer and actress, acquired fame in portraying Aunt Jemima in numerous stage and radio performances over a seventeen-year period. Defendant's advertising agency sought to have plaintiff portray Aunt Jemima in radio promotions for its flour. When negotiations ceased because of inability to agree on plaintiff's compensation, two other persons were engaged to perform as Aunt Jemima, one reading the dialogue and the other doing the singing. The court, implying that the public would associate the radio character with the "pancake" Aunt Jemima rather than with plaintiff's "theatrical" Aunt Jemima, held there was no liability in the absence of proof of deception, i.e. that the public were led to confuse defendant's radio character with plaintiff.

2. In Lahr v. Adell Chemical Co., 300 F.2d 256 (1st Cir. 1962), a television commercial for a household cleaner featured a cartoon duck, whose voice and vocal delivery imitated the well-known entertainer Bert Lahr. Lahr's complaint was held to state a cause of action for unfair competition because the imitation enhanced the value of the commercial by causing the audience to believe they were hearing Lahr and because it might reduce the demand for Lahr's own services. The court also found sufficient allegations that the commercial defamed Lahr by giving the impression that he had been "reduced to making anonymous television commercials." Compare Sinatra v. Goodyear Tire & Rubber Co., 435 F.2d 711 (9th Cir. 1970), cert. denied, 402 U.S. 906 (1971), where a tire company in its radio and television commercials used the music and lyrics (somewhat revised) of a song that Nancy Sinatra had made popular. The court found no unfair competition, noting that plaintiff did not claim her sound was uniquely personal.

3. Midler v. Ford Motor Co., 849 F.2d 460 (9th Cir. 1988), involved a series of television commercials that featured songs of the previous decade. When the singers who had popularized the songs declined to participate in the commercials, "sound alikes" were employed to sing the numbers. An imitation of Bette Midler's distinctive voice led some people to believe that she herself was singing the commercial. She was held to have a cause of action for "an appropriation of the attributes of one's identity"—essentially the type of "right of publicity" claim that failed in the principal case. Nancy Sinatra's case was distinguished on the grounds that the basis of her complaint was unfair competition and she was complaining of the use of the song. What if the voice of a well-known person who is not in "show business" is imitated in a commercial?

4. Can an actor or singer be restrained from giving a dramatic or musical performance that is an imitation of a famous performer's act? Consider:

(a) Estate of Presley v. Russen, 513 F. Supp. 1339 (D.N.J. 1981). A performer developed a stage show patterned on that of the late Elvis Presley, imitating his appearance and singing style. The court issued an injunction in favor of Presley's estate. It found a likelihood of confusion among the public concerning the estate's sponsorship of or association with defendant's show. The court believed that the show had an informational and entertainment element but was designed primarily as a commercial exploitation of the deceased singer's legend and contributed nothing of substantial value to society.

(b) Chaplin v. Amador, 93 Cal. App. 358, 269 P. 544 (1928). Defendant, using the name "Charles Aplin," made a film in which he imitated the dress and mannerisms made famous on the screen by Charlie Chaplin. Chaplin was granted an injunction against imitation likely to deceive the public into thinking that Chaplin was in a film. Cf. Lugosi v. Universal Pictures, 25 Cal. 3d 813, 160 Cal. Rptr. 323, 603 P.2d 425 (1979), where the court said that the tie-up of a performer's name, face and/or likeness with a characterization creates a tangible and saleable product, much as property is created by one who organizes a business. Thus, the actor Bela Lugosi created a right of value in his motion picture portrayals of Count Dracula and could have protected this right against invasion by others. But the court would protect this right only during Lugosi's lifetime.

(c) Groucho Marx Productions, Inc. v. Day and Night Co., Inc., p. 419, infra. Defendants imitated in a theatrical production the humor and comedy style of the Marx Brothers. This was enjoined by the district court, which found that defendants had gone beyond merely building on the original Marx Brothers act and had duplicated as faithfully as possible their performances, though in a new situation with original lines. Since this was mere imitation, not parody, the First Amendment did not preclude relief. The Court of Appeals reversed on the ground that the Marx Brothers' "right of publicity" did not, under California law, survive their death.

5. Was Shirley Booth free to use the Hazel voice herself in commercials? To portray Hazel, in commercials or otherwise? See Lone Ranger, Inc. v. Cox, p. 369, infra, in which the company owning the *Lone Ranger* radio program was granted relief on the basis of "unfair competition" against live performances as "The Lone Ranger" by an actor who had portrayed the Lone Ranger in a film, and KGB, Inc. v. Giannoulas, 101 Cal. App. 3d 323, 161 Cal. Rptr. 583 (1980), vacated, 104 Cal. App. 3d 844, 164 Cal. Rptr. 571 (1980), in which radio station KGB failed in its attempt to have a man who performed as the "KGB Chicken" enjoined from continuing to perform in a chicken suit after he left the station's employ. (He was, however, enjoined from appearing in the distinct "KGB Chicken" costume.)

Columbia Broadcasting System, Inc. v. DeCosta

United States Court of Appeals, First Circuit
377 F.2d 315 (1967), cert. denied, 389 U.S. 1007 (1967)

COFFIN, Circuit Judge.

This is an appeal by defendants from jury verdicts in the total amount of $150,000 awarded plaintiff on his claim that he created, and the defendants misappropriated, the character of Paladin, the protagonist of the CBS television series entitled "Have Gun Will Travel".

The story of this case — more bizarre than most television serial installments — is one of "coincidence" run riot. The plaintiff, of Portuguese parents, is a Rhode Island mechanic whose formal education ceased after the fourth grade. During the Depression, having tired of factory work, he hopped a freight for the West, lived in hobo jungles, and eventually became a range hand on a Texas ranch. After two years of riding and roping he returned to Rhode Island to work as a mechanic and later received training as a motor machinist in the Coast Guard. But he retained his passion for all things western. In 1947 he began to participate in rodeos, horse shows, horse auctions, and parades.

From the beginning plaintiff indulged a penchant for costume. He was already equipped with a moustache. He soon settled on a black shirt, black pants, and a flat-crowned black hat. He had acquired a St. Mary's medal at a parade and affixed this to his hat. He adopted the name Paladin after an onlooker of Italian descent had hurled an epithet at him containing the word "Paladino". On looking up the word Paladin in a dictionary he found it meant "champion of Knights" and was content that people began so to call him. One day when he had donned his costume in preparation for a horse show, and was about to mount his horse, one of a group waiting for him shouted "Have Gun Will Travel", a cry immediately picked up by the children present.

The finishing touches were a chess knight, bought for fifteen cents at an auction, which plaintiff thought was a good symbol, and which he used on a business card along with the words "Have", "Gun", "Will", "Travel", and "Wire Paladin, N. Court St., Cranston, R.I.", hand-printed with separate rubber stamps; a silver copy of the chess piece on his holster; and an antique derringer strapped under his arm. So accoutered, he would appear in parades, the openings and finales of rodeos, auctions, horse shows, and a pony ring he once operated. From time to time at rodeos he would stage a western gunfight, featuring his quick draw and the timely use of his hidden derringer. He would pass out photographs of himself and cards — printed versions soon replacing the rubber-stamped ones. Hospitals, drug stores, barber shops, sports shops, diners — all were the repositories of his cards, some 250,000 of them. Children clamored for the cards, and clustered about him to the extent that he was likened to the Pied Piper and Gene Autry. This was perhaps one of the purest promotions ever staged, for plaintiff did not seek anything but the entertainment of others. He sold no product, services, or institution, charged no fees, and exploited only himself.

Ten years after he had begun to live his avocational role of Paladin, he and his friends saw the first CBS television production of "Have Gun Will Travel", starring moustachioed Richard Boone, who played the part of an elegant knight errant of the Old West, always on the side of Good — for a fee. The television Paladin also wore a black costume, a flat-crowned black hat bearing an oval silver decoration, and a silver chess knight on his holster, and announced himself with a card featuring a chess piece virtually — if not absolutely — identical with the plaintiff's and the words "HAVE GUN WILL TRAVEL, WIRE PALADIN, SAN FRANCISCO". The series was notably successful; it appeared in 225 first-run episodes in the United States, was licensed in foreign countries, and by the time of trial had grossed in excess of fourteen million dollars.

The writers and network executives responsible for the series testified in detail that the television Paladin was a spontaneous creation, developed in total ignorance of the attributes of his Rhode Island predecessor. The writers, Herb Meadow and Sam Rolfe, testified that the germ of the idea was the title, "Have Gun Will Travel", which Meadow had evolved from mulling over a familiar theatrical advertising phrase, "Have tux, will travel". The character was originally conceived as a denizen of contemporary New York, but was changed to a western hero because the network hoped to cast Randolph Scott in the role. The name "Paladin" resulted from a thesaurus search for words meaning "knight" or "hero" or "champion". The chess piece symbol was inspired by Meadow's observation, while teaching his son the game, that the knight's movements were uniquely erratic and unpredictable. In the pilot script for the series, Paladin used a hidden derringer because it was a convenient way to extricate him from the obligatory dangerous situation.

The show's original producer, Julian Claman, testified that after Randolph Scott and other "fairly well known" actors were found to be unavailable he selected Richard Boone to be tested for the role of Paladin. Boone appeared for the test with a moustache, for reasons unknown, and was outfitted in a black suit because it was the only available costume that fitted. The hat, bearing a silver "conche", was selected by Claman because it looked appropriate. The card, which had been described in Meadow and Rolfe's original prospectus, was realized by the CBS art department from a rough sketch by Claman. The "shocking similarity" to DeCosta's cards was pure coincidence. Boone's test was successful, and Claman, reluctant to change any element of a winning combination, decided to keep card, costume, and moustache intact for the pilot film. He also decided to add the silver chess knight to Paladin's holster because it produced a distinct article that would be marketable if the series succeeded.

Meadow, Rolfe, Claman, and the other witnesses for the defendants all testified that they had never seen DeCosta or any of his cards. The jury obviously disbelieved at least this much of their testimony, and we think it clear that they were amply justified. Thus, the plaintiff has had the satisfaction of proving the defendants pirates. But we are drawn to conclude that that proof alone is not enough to entitle him to a share of the plunder. Our Paladin is not the first creator to see the fruits of his creation harvested by another, without effective remedy; and although his case is undeniably hard, to affirm the judgments below would, we think, allow a hard case to make some intolerably bad law.

In the first place, it is by no means clear that such state law of intellectual property as we have found supports relief on these facts. Several cases have been cited around the general proposition that it is an actionable wrong to appropriate and exploit the product of another's creative effort; but all seem to involve distinguishable wrongs of at least equal or even superior significance. Most rest on the tort of "passing off": appropriation not of the creation but of the value attached to it by public association (the so-called "secondary meaning"), by misleading the public into thinking that the defendant's offering is the product of the plaintiff's established skill....

Plaintiff argues that he has established "secondary meaning" through testimony of some witnesses that they thought he was the Paladin on television and evidence that most people knew him only as Paladin, not as Victor DeCosta. Whether or not this assertion is true, it is here irrelevant, for the issue was not submitted to the jury. The complaint alleged three causes of action: misappropriation, trade and/or service mark infringement, and unfair competition by "passing off" the television Paladin as the plaintiff. Only the first was tried, the court reserving judgment on defendant's motions to dismiss the other two....

... [T]he leading case affording a remedy for mere copying, International News Serv. v. Associated Press, 1918, 248 U.S. 215, is no longer authoritative for a least two reasons: it was decided as a matter of general federal law before the decision in Erie R. R. v. Tompkins, 1938, 304 U.S. 64; and, as it prohibited the copying of published written matter that had not been copyrighted..., it has clearly been overruled by the Supreme Court's recent decisions in Sears, Roebuck & Co. v. Stiffel Co., 1964, 376 U.S. 225, and Compco Corp. v. Day-Brite Lighting, Inc., 1964, 376 U.S. 234. While this normally would not prevent the state court from adopting the reasoning of *INS* in fashioning a rule of state law, we think it important to consider the scope of state power in this area in view of *Sears* and *Compco*.

It is true that *Sears* and *Compco* both deal with copying of articles covered by invalid design patents. But the opinions refer throughout to both copyright and patent; and in *Compco* the Court took pains to articulate the broad scope of its decisions: "Today we have held ... that when an article is unprotected by a patent or a copyright, state law may not forbid others to copy that article. To forbid copying would interfere with the federal policy, found in Art. I, § 8, cl. 8, of the Constitution and in the implementing federal statutes, of allowing free access to copy whatever the federal patent and copyright laws leave in the public domain." ...

Does the language in *Compco*, "whatever the federal patent and copyright laws leave in the public domain", refer to creations that Congress has deliberately chosen not to protect or more broadly to those it has simply not protected, whether by choice or by chance? In the case of patents the two questions are coterminous, for Congress has deliberately chosen not to protect inventions lacking the element of originality, and an invention is thus either patentable or unprotectible. In the case of "writings" there is no such universal test of qualification. But Congress has established a procedural scheme of protection by notice and registration. The necessary implication of this approach, we conclude, is that, absent compliance with the scheme, the federal policy favoring free dissemination of intellectual creations prevails. Thus, if a "writing" is within the scope of the constitutional clause, and Congress has not protected it, whether deliberately or by unexplained omission, it can be freely copied....

[The court considered and rejected the argument that a character is inherently uncopyrightable, either because it is not a "writing" in the sense used in the copyright clause of the Constitution (or, "what is the same thing," that it is not an "article" in the sense used in *Sears* and *Compco*), or because it would be impracticable to incorporate into the copyright system a procedure for registering characters. "[I]n view of the federal policy of encouraging intellectual creation by granting a limited monopoly at best, we think it sensible to say that the constitutional clause extends to any concrete, describable manifestation of intellectual creation; and to the extent that a creation may be ineffable, we think it ineligible for protection against copying *simpliciter* under either state or federal law." Plaintiff also contended that his creation was protected under copyright law as an unpublished work.]

Here, plaintiff's "performance" consisted of two components: appearing in public and passing out cards and photographs. No other "action" was involved, except an occasional "quick draw" demonstration at a rodeo. So far as his costume and menacing appearance were concerned, it was fully conveyed on the cards bearing his photograph—which also contained the chess piece, the slogan, and the name "Paladin". The cards were passed out in great quantities over the years to all who would have them. So far as any action accompanying his personal appearance is concerned, whether it be simply riding a horse, or staging a quick-draw gun fight, these are hallowed shelf items in the tradition of the early West. In any event, the theme and plots of defendant's television series could not be said to have derived from anything created by plaintiff which was not revealed by his cards.

The cards were unquestionably "writings" within the meaning of the copyright clause, and arguably were copyrightable under the statute. The consequence is that the plaintiff's character-creation was published, and that this case falls squarely under the rule of *Sears* and *Compco*. Not having copyrighted the cards, the plaintiff cannot preclude others from copying them. We accordingly reverse.

Notes

1. The case again came before the First Circuit in DeCosta v. Columbia Broadcasting System, Inc., 520 F.2d 499 (1st Cir. 1975), cert. denied, 423 U.S. 1073 (1976). The court admitted that in light of Goldstein v. California, p. 356, supra, the principal case's interpretation of "the preemptive reach of the Copyright Clause" was "over-inclusive." However, plaintiff's claim of misappropriation had been disposed of. There remained the claims of trade and service mark infringement and unfair competition, which supported plaintiff's demand for an accounting of defendants' profits from the television series. Six witnesses testified that on first viewing the television series they thought that plaintiff portrayed the principal character. The court found this insufficient to establish a likelihood of confusion between plaintiff's creation and defendants' series. Plaintiff's enterprise was localized while defendants' was nationwide; plaintiff's performances were "simple happenings" while defendants presented "an elegant hired gun on manifold missions";

plaintiff's "customers" were those attending rodeos, parades, etc., while defendants' purchasers were program sponsors "responsive" to a nationwide audience. The court emphasized that there was no deception of the public because defendants did not pass off their "Paladin" or their program as creations of plaintiff. A later effort by DeCosta to obtain legal relief failed in DeCosta v. Viacom International, Inc., 981 F.2d 602 (1st Cir. 1992), cert. denied, 509 U.S. 923 (1993).

2. In Hines v. Winnick, [1947] Ch. 708, plaintiff conducted and played in an orchestra, whose performances were broadcast by a radio network under the name "Dr. Crock and his Crackpots." He built up a considerable public reputation for the broadcasts. The program's producer claimed the right to employ another person as "Dr. Crock." It was held that the name had become part of plaintiff's stock-in-trade and that he was entitled to an injunction restraining defendant from presenting any other musical act under the same designation. Compare West v. Lind, 186 Cal. App. 2d 563, 9 Cal. Rptr. 288 (1960). Plaintiff had been billed throughout her show-business career as "Mae West as Diamond Lil" or "Mae West and her own Revue," but never as "Diamond Lil." Defendant began making stage appearances as "Diamond Lil." The court denied an injunction, finding no evidence that anyone who saw defendant's billings was deceived and expected to see plaintiff.

3. A journalist writes a newspaper column under a *nom de plume*, which in time becomes well-known to readers of the paper. The journalist then leaves the newspaper. Can he prevent it from continuing the column under the same *nom de plume*? According to Sykes v. John Fairfax & Sons Ltd., p. 408, infra, an author may establish an exclusive right in the name of a fictional character if he has invented and used the name and if the name has become associated in readers' minds with a particular author, even though the readers may be unaware of the author's true identity. The journalist in this case was found to have such a right.

Lone Ranger, Inc. v. Cox
United States Circuit Court of Appeals, Fourth Circuit
124 F.2d 650 (1942)

PARKER, Circuit Judge.

This is an action for damages and for injunction based upon alleged infringement of copyright and unfair competition. The plaintiff is the Lone Ranger, Inc., a Michigan corporation, which since the year 1933 has been broadcasting over the radio copyrighted dramatic serial stories featuring the heroic exploits of a mythical western cowboy, "The Lone Ranger", who rides about masked and on a white horse, called "Silver", championing the cause of the oppressed and redressing the wrongs of the community. Plaintiff has licensed a comic strip, entitled "The Lone Ranger", appearing in a number of newspapers and has licensed the use of the name, "The Lone Ranger", as a trademark to vendors of various articles. The radio programs of plaintiff are broadcast from one hundred or more radio stations, are very popular and appeal particularly to children. A "Lone Ranger" safety club, promoted in connection with the programs, has attained a membership of between three and four million young people.

The defendant Powell is a motion picture actor, who in 1937 played the part of Allan King as the "Lone Ranger" in a motion picture produced under license from plaintiff. He has been appearing [in a small circus operated by the defendant Cox] in which he takes the part of the "Lone Ranger", riding masked on a white horse and giving the cry "Hi, yo

WALLACE BROS. CIRCUS ADVERTISEMENT FOR LEE POWELL AS LONE RANGER

Silver" or "Hi, yo, Silver, away!", which is the distinctive call of the "Lone Ranger" to his horse in each of plaintiff's radio programs. He is advertised by the circus as the original "Lone Ranger" or the "Lone Ranger" in person. The words "talking picture" or "of talking picture fame" are prefixed or added to the words "Lone Ranger" in the advertisements, but these qualifying words are in smaller lettering than "Lone Ranger", which is given great prominence. In some, the call to the horse, "Hi, yo, Silver" is prominently displayed. Newspaper advertisements are addressed particularly to children and stress that the "Lone Ranger" is appearing in person. In all, the effect of the advertisements is to create the impression that the original "Lone Ranger", made famous by the radio programs, is appearing with the circus—a result more easily achieved because the public interested is composed very largely of children.

The plaintiff did not produce its copyrights in evidence, relying upon the principles of unfair competition. Its contention is that the advertising and appearances of Powell are unfair in that they are an attempt on his part to appropriate to himself a portion of the good will which plaintiff has built up in connection with its radio programs, and in that the inevitable effect of this infringement upon its rights is to destroy the element of mystery surrounding the character of the "Lone Ranger" as presented by its programs and show him to be a very commonplace person in whom the young people have no further interest, once he has been seen....

The answer of the defendants denies any representation that Powell had had anything to do with the radio programs. They claim the right to advertise Powell as the actor who had played the part of the "Lone Ranger" in the motion picture of that name.... [The court below denied relief.]

... [W]e think that plaintiff, under the principles of unfair competition, was entitled to relief. Under the name or title of "The Lone Ranger", plaintiff had built up a radio feature of great value. The exploits of this mythical character, as portrayed in the radio programs, had become of great interest to countless young people throughout the country and were a source of large revenue to plaintiff. Defendants were attempting to avail themselves of the good will created by the broadcasting of the radio programs and the advertising connected therewith, including the "Lone Ranger" safety clubs. Their conduct in advertising Powell as the "Original Lone Ranger" was manifestly calculated and intended to lead the public to believe that he was the "Lone Ranger" of the radio programs and to attract to the circus those who were interested in the programs and particularly the young people who were members of the safety clubs. The fact that the advertisements contained a reference to the talking picture did little, if anything, to minimize the deception of the children to whom they were primarily addressed, and this deception was accentuated by use of the call "Hi, yo, Silver" in some of the advertisements and in Powell's act in the circus. The defendants were in the business of furnishing entertainment, just as was plaintiff, and there can be no doubt but that they were attempting to pass off their show as being identified with the radio programs of plaintiff, or at least as being connected in some manner therewith, and thus to benefit from the good will which had been built up by plaintiff through its broadcasts and advertising....

And we are not impressed by the argument that defendants are protected in what they have done because of Powell's connection with the motion pictures licensed by plaintiff. The contention that the advertisement is true is not correct. Powell is not the "Lone Ranger" at all. He is merely a moving picture actor who took the part of the "Lone Ranger" in a motion picture play of that name produced long after the "Lone Ranger" of radio had become widely known. The only reason that defendant's desire to call him the "talking picture Lone Ranger" or the "Lone Ranger of talking picture fame", with "Lone Ranger" emphasized and the qualifying words in smaller lettering, is to attract the patronage of those who will confuse him in some way with the "Lone Ranger" of the radio programs; and the principle is applicable that, not only must one tell the truth, but he must tell it in a truthful way, i. e. so as not to deceive the public. Thus, one may not use even his own name or the name of the town in which he does business as descriptive of his goods, if the effect will be to mislead the public to the prejudice of a competitor.... If it is desired to advertise Powell as the man who played the part of Allan King as the "Lone Ranger" in the motion picture of that name, this should be allowed; but any advertisement that he is the "Lone Ranger" must be avoided, as must any other language tending to imply connection with the "Lone Ranger" of plaintiff's radio programs or any form of advertising which will lead the public to believe that there is such connection.

For the reasons stated, we think that plaintiff was entitled to relief....

Reversed.

Notes

1. See also Lone Ranger, Inc. v. Currey, 79 F. Supp. 190 (M.D. Pa. 1948) (defendants enjoined from any use of name "Lone Ranger" and imitation of any of "distinctive and dominant characteristics" of *Lone Ranger* program, including Ranger's garb, white horse "Silver," Indian companion "Tonto" and call "Hi Yo Silver"). Suppose the public is not led to believe that plaintiff is responsible for defendant's performance or creation. Should a court restrain the unlicensed exploitation of a character plaintiff created by actors or producers? By authors or pictorial artists? In the principal case, the lower court found no trademark infringement or unfair competition—defendants did not lead the public to believe that Powell was the radio Lone Ranger or that entertainment was being offered by plaintiff—and no basis in copyright law for granting the owner of copyright in a radio serial a monopoly on the characters or ideas in the serial. Lone Ranger, Inc. v. Cox, 39 F. Supp. 487 (W.D.S.C. 1941).

2. Does the author of a popular novel or story about a fictional character have an action when a film or radio program about the character is produced without the author's permission? See Prouty v. National Broadcasting Co., 26 F. Supp. 265 (D. Mass. 1939) (*Stella Dallas* radio broadcasts based upon novel of same name; author held to have cause of action for unfair competition against broadcasting company, notwithstanding absence of competition between them). What if the character's name is used but the theme or plot is different? See Patten v. Superior Talking Pictures, Inc. 8 F. Supp. 196 (S.D.N.Y. 1934) (name "Frank Merriwell" had become associated in public mind exclusively with work of author of numerous Frank Merriwell stories; author protected by law of unfair competition from unauthorized use of name in films). But see Atlas Manufacturing Co. v. Street & Smith, 204 F. 398 (8th Cir. 1913), cert. denied, 231 U.S. 755 (1913), appeal dismissed, 231 U.S. 348 (1913), cert. denied, 232 U.S. 724 (1914) (publishers of stories featuring detective "Nick Carter" not entitled to prevent use of name in title and story of motion picture). Cf. Warner Bros. Pictures, Inc. v. Columbia Broadcasting System, Inc., 102 F. Supp. 141 (S.D. Cal. 1951), aff'd, 216 F.2d 945 (9th Cir. 1954), cert. denied, 348 U.S. 971 (1955) (owner of rights to *Maltese Falcon* could not restrain broadcasts of other Dashiell Hammett stories featuring detective "Sam Spade").

3. Plaintiff creates characters who become well-known through a popular comic strip. Another cartoonist adopts the same names for his characters. Liability? See Fisher v. Star Co., 231 N.Y. 414, 132 N.E. 133 (1919), cert. denied, 257 U.S. 654 (1921) (creator of "Mutt" and "Jeff" entitled to injunction restraining publication of cartoons using those names). Could the holders of the copyrights in the "Superman" comic book and cartoon character prevent the publication or broadcast of stories about a man with similar superhuman powers? In Warner Bros. Inc. v. American Broadcasting Companies, Inc., 720 F.2d 231 (2d Cir. 1983), the court held that because of the differences between the two characters there was no copyright infringement or unfair competition, even if some viewers might think that plaintiffs produced or authorized defendants' television series, and there was no action under the state anti-dilution statute. But in DC Comics Inc. v. Unlimited Monkey Business, Inc., 598 F. Supp. 110 (N.D. Ga. 1984), the publisher of "Superman" and "Wonder Woman" comic books was granted an injunction against companies in the business of delivering "singing telegrams." The telegrams were delivered by persons portraying characters that were "take-offs" on plaintiff's—"Super Stud" and "Wonder Wench"—and had similar costumes and slogans.

4. The law is not clear on whether characters in works of fiction are eligible in their own right for federal copyright protection and whether state law may protect characters ap-

pearing in copyrightable works. See Nimmer, Copyright §§ 1.01, 2.12 (1978). Cartoon characters are protectable under the federal statute, and it has been suggested that if rendered in three-dimensional form they might even be eligible for protection under a design patent. Copyrightable or patentable characters can be protected against deceptive imitation under the common law so long as this does not grant a right equivalent to copyright. Thus, a state can require labelling even if it cannot forbid copying. McManis, Intellectual Property and Unfair Competition 146–147 (6th ed. 2009).

5. Fictional characters may be exploited in the marketing of products and services. See Wyatt Earp Enterprises, Inc. v. Sackman, Inc., p. 299, supra, concerning common law remedies for unlicensed "character merchandising."

D. Ideas

Educational Sales Programs, Inc. v. Dreyfus Corporation
Supreme Court of New York
65 Misc. 2d 412, 317 N.Y.S.2d 840 (1970)

EDWARD J. GREENFIELD, Justice....

Defendant Dreyfus Sales Corporation is the marketing and distributing organization for the Dreyfus Fund, one of the largest and most successful mutual funds in the world. Defendant Harvey I. Epstein is president of the sales corporation. Plaintiff is a corporation engaged in the business of sales training and promotion. It was headed by Herbert Abelow, a man of extensive experience in the sale of mutual funds, and a friend of Mr. Epstein.

In the fall of 1969, at a trade convention, Abelow approached Mr. Epstein to tell him about an exceptional idea he had, which he asked to be kept confidential. He also requested that if they didn't reach an agreement on it, Dreyfus was not to use it. Epstein assured him that because of their long-standing relationship there was no cause for worry, and if Dreyfus didn't use his idea, Abelow was free to take it to anyone else. Abelow thereupon disclosed his idea, which was to make tape players and monthly tape cassettes containing educational and promotional material available free of charge to independent mutual fund salesmen, with the players, cassettes and contents to be purchased from plaintiff.

Defendant had previously experimented with video and reel tapes for communication and education of its sales force, but what appealed to Epstein in Abelow's idea was going directly to the independent fund salesman via tape cassettes. He indicated, however, that it would be too costly to supply the players and cassettes free of charge to salesmen. During the course of negotiations the plan was changed, to sell the program—players and one cassette a month on a technical aspect of fund sales—for $60 a year, with defendant bearing the cost of the players and the cassettes in part, and having the responsibility for advertising and promoting the program.

There were disagreements over the prices plaintiff was asking for the hardware, the use of defendant's mailing list, and other matters, and although many memos were exchanged, no written agreement was consummated. Defendant decided not to buy the tapes and cassettes from plaintiff corporation, but asked Abelow to work with it individually as a consultant on the program content. This suggestion was rejected, and all further contact between the parties was broken off in November of 1969.

In January, 1970 Abelow received a flyer in the mail announcing the "Dreyfus Portable Sales Seminar", the very name he had helped formulate, offering fund salesmen a free tape player and 12 monthly tapes cassettes to "increase product knowledge" and "tell about proven sales techniques" for a total price of $60. Admittedly, in December of 1969, after negotiations with plaintiff had been terminated, Dreyfus proceeded with a tape cassette program of its own, purchasing the players and cassettes elsewhere, preparing the program content, and placing the promotional program advertising in publications going to the trade.

Plaintiff thereupon brought this action alleging that defendant, by wrongfully misappropriating plaintiff's idea had breached its agreement of confidentiality, had been unjustly enriched, had breached its oral agreement to carry out the specifics of plaintiff's suggested program at a guaranteed minimum price, and was guilty of fraud. By way of relief, plaintiff sought an injunction against defendant's program, an accounting, and money damages.

The cause of action for fraud was dismissed during trial, and on the cause of action for breach of contract the issue of whether or not there was a meeting of the minds on the details of marketing and promoting the tape cassette program was submitted to the jury for a special verdict. The jury by its negative answer, found that despite all the negotiations no agreement between the parties had ever materialized. There remain for disposition the causes of action for breach of confidence and unjust enrichment which were expressly reserved for decision by the court.

The first cause of action alleges that plaintiff has been damaged because defendant's breach of its promise of confidentiality has prevented plaintiff from selling its "novel and unique program" to others. The second cause of action alleges that defendant has been unjustly enriched by the wrongful misappropriation of plaintiff's unique and novel idea. Both causes of action turn on whether plaintiff's idea was indeed novel, unique, and original. If it was not, it had no value as property, and would not suffice either as consideration for a promise of confidentiality, or as a basis for finding defendant was unjustly enriched.

There can be no question but that after the rupture of negotiations between the parties, defendant proceeded on its own with a program that was similar in many respects. It was offering players and 12 monthly tape cassettes to independent mutual funds salesmen under the name of "Dreyfus Portable Sales Seminar" at a price of $60, and the program content covered essentially the same topics as those suggested by plaintiff. While the use of tapes for education and sales training was known to the industry, and defendant had experimented itself on a limited basis, unquestionably it was the impetus of plaintiff's suggestion which galvanized it into action. While there are points of difference as to the way the program was promoted, the genesis of the defendant's ultimate actions was the proposal by plaintiff.

Defendant acted on plaintiff's idea. Plaintiff sues for the theft of that idea. Does the use of that idea create the legal obligation of compensation? An idea is impalpable, intangible, incorporeal, yet it may be a stolen gem of great value, or mere dross of no value at all, depending on its novelty and uniqueness. Its utility is not the test. An idea may be regarded as useful, and worth putting into execution, even though the imparting of it gives no claim for recovery to its originator. Thus in Soule v. Bon Ami Co., 201 App. Div. 794, 195 N.Y.S. 574, affd. 235 N.Y. 609, 139 N.E. 754, plaintiff promised to tell defendant a method to increase its profits. The revelation that it should raise its prices was held not to entitle plaintiff to compensation. Similarly, in Lueddecke v. Chevrolet Motor Co., 8 Cir., 70 F.2d 345, the suggestion that the way to correct an improperly balanced car was to relocate some of the weightier components, though adopted, gave rise to no recovery; and in Anderson v. Distler, 173 Misc. 261, 17 N.Y.S.2d 674, where plaintiff offered to reveal a matter of great value, and then suggested defendant pay the premiums and not allow his elderly father-in-law's insurance policies to lapse, which defendant did to his great financial advantage, plaintiff's claim for compensation was disallowed. Not every "good idea" is a legally protectible idea. A sensible suggestion must have more to it than good sense to be compensable. Its adoption may be the occasion for gratitude or the voluntary bestowal of tangible reward, but that does not of itself call into play legal compulsion.

Nothing is bestowed if the facts of a "secret" imparted in confidence are already the subject of general knowledge. Under those circumstances the promise of compensation or confidentiality, even though undoubtedly made, is without consideration.... An agreement premised on the disclosure of a secret is a blind deal. When the purveyor of that secret exacts a promise of confidentiality, he knows what he is dealing with, but the recipient is in the dark. The enforcibility of such a threshold agreement—a promise in exchange for a revelation—turns on the value of the disclosure.... [W]hile the confidence cannot be denied, its worth as property can be. If the idea is of such a nature that it cannot be appropriated by a party, it cannot be misappropriated by another. One cannot be forever barred from using a worthwhile but unoriginal idea merely because it was once asked to be treated in confidence.

Was plaintiff's idea here of such originality as to be deemed property of a value sufficient to constitute consideration for a promise not to use it without compensation? Was it so uniquely plaintiff's creation that its use without payment can be labelled as the theft of an idea? The fact that the basic idea was simple—using tape for sales training and indoctrination—does not negate its value, for truly great ideas, like the wheel or the safety pin, can be stunning in their simplicity. Taking a page from the patent law dealing with the property right in inventions, the idea need not reflect the "flash of genius", but it must show genuine novelty and invention, and not a merely clever or useful adaptation of existing knowledge. Improvement of standard technique or quality, the judicious use of existing means, or the mixture of known ingredients in somewhat different proportions— all the variations on a basic theme—partake more of the nature of elaboration and renovation than of innovation.

Concededly, there was nothing new in the idea of using tape or tape cassettes to carry a sales message or a wealth of repeatable information. It had been done in many fields, and even in the mutual funds field, though no prior efforts quite fit the bill. Nor was there anything unique about putting the material, which was not only educational but promotional and self-laudatory, directly into the hands of the independent salesmen. While plaintiff insisted that was the truly unique aspect of its plan—bypassing the middle-men, the broker-dealer organizations—and that was one aspect the defendant found attractive— putting the sales message on a convenient tape cassette and offering it at an attractive price not for immediate profit but for long-range institutional advertising, was no more than a clever sales "gimmick", useful, appealing, but hardly of dazzling originality. The topics to be covered, the content, the media for promotion, and the marketing plan (six-month trial subscriptions, a cassette a month with player "free", quantity discounts, etc.) were natural outgrowths of existing factual patterns, with no element of novelty....

If there be no novelty, neither the promise of the protected secret nor the claim of theft and unjust enrichment can stand.... The fact that the parties had extended negotiations does not fortify plaintiff's claim of the value of its idea. The details of presentation and marketing changed considerably from September to November. Clearly it was quite malleable and not in such fixed and concrete form as to indicate a protectible idea. "Ideas not reduced to concrete form are not protected." O'Brien v. RKO Radio Pictures, Inc., D.C., 68 F. Supp. 13, 14....

There is no evidence defendant was appreciably and unjustly enriched, nor that plaintiff was deprived of the chance of promoting its program with anyone else.... Judgment for defendant.

Hamilton National Bank v. Belt

United States Court of Appeals, District of Columbia Circuit
93 U.S. App. D.C. 168, 210 F.2d 706 (1953)

FAHY, Circuit Judge.

The appellee, Lloyd K. Belt, sued the appellant, Hamilton National Bank, for damages incurred by reason of the Bank's appropriation of a type of radio program which he claimed to have originated and made known to the Bank. The jury returned a money verdict for Mr. Belt and the Bank appeals from the ensuing judgment.

Expressly reserving the right to negotiate with any school, radio station, or sponsor, as well as all other rights, Mr. Belt by letter of October 21, 1948, to the Assistant Superintendent of Public Schools set forth a plan to select student talent by holding auditions in the high schools and with talent thus selected to put on half-hour weekly broadcasts. Each show would be presented first to the student body as an assembly, recorded, and the recording broadcast in the evening. A school atmosphere would be retained by referring to the show as a class, to the acts as class assignments, and to the action as class recitations. A different school would be featured each week. The program would include several pieces by the glee club in addition to the talent. The actual content of each show, with the exception of the glee club and an orchestra, could not be predicted until selection of the talent. Such selection, together with production and presentation of the show, would be subject at all times to supervision and approval by the school authorities. If desired, Mr. Belt would conduct the auditions, production and presentation with such assistance as would be available. There would be a minimum of conversation and introductions, the time being devoted principally to a "fast moving, first rate, entertaining show", and there would be no commercial "spots", though the sponsoring firm would be accorded a brief acknowledgment of its sponsorship at the beginning and end of the broadcast.

This plan was proposed by Mr. Belt to several Washington business establishments. They were not interested in sponsoring it. He then presented it to the Bank, which was interested. A contract between the Bank and Mr. Belt was entered into November 1, 1948. Mr. Belt was to be paid $25 a week and was to make the necessary arrangements with the schools for auditions and transcriptions. Should the Board of Directors of the Bank approve transcribed programs and put them on the air a revised agreement covering the duties and compensation of Mr. Belt would be made.

The school authorities did not at first give the necessary approval. Pursuant to the terms of their agreement the Bank thereupon canceled its contract with Mr. Belt, later paying him $50 in full settlement of a controversy over two weeks compensation. In March, 1949, the Board of Education advised the Bank of its willingness to approve such a program. The bank then, with the assistance of someone other than Mr. Belt, carried the plan forward with periodical broadcasts [costing $43,000] for over a year....

... [A] person has such a property right in his own idea as enables him to recover damages for its appropriation or use by another when the idea is original, concrete, useful, and is disclosed in circumstances which, reasonably construed, clearly indicate that compensation is contemplated if it is accepted and used.

That the idea must be new and novel, or, as sometimes termed, original, is clear.... It is not disputed that the issue of novelty is for the jury if the evidence raises a question of fact in that regard. Appellant does contend there was not sufficient evidence of originality to go to the jury....

In addition to being new, novel or original, an idea to be legally protected must also be concrete. The law shies away from according protection to vagueness, and must do so especially in the realm of ideas with the obvious dangers of a contrary rule. An abstract idea, in any event when not the subject of a contract, is so unattached as to be deemed legally without the quality of individual identity or property. Protection of ideas at all, in contrast with inventions, literary productions and trade secrets, the law with respect to which we do not now consider, must be careful to avoid attributing to individual ownership that which is in reality common property; and it would be unwise to place a burden upon communication of ideas by requiring compensation for their adoption and use. But the dangers suggested are sufficiently avoided to warrant the law in placing an idea among protected property rights when it is definite and concrete, new and novel, has usefulness and is disclosed for commercial purposes in circumstances which the parties ought reasonably to construe as contemplating compensation for its use....

If the idea had been merely to broadcast programs of selected student talent it would have been too general and abstract, and perhaps would also have lacked newness and novelty. On the other hand, had the plan been accompanied with a script for each broadcast it would have been sufficiently concrete. Some opinions indicate that such detailing is essential. See O'Brien v. RKO Radio Pictures, D.C.S.D.N.Y., 68 F. Supp. 13, 14, where it is said: "It is the means of expressing these ideas rather than the ideas themselves which warrant protection." See also, Bowen v. Yankee Network, D.C.Mass., 46 F. Supp. 62, 63, where it is stated: "Such a right can only exist in the arrangement and combination of the ideas, i.e., in the form, sequence, and manner in which the composition expresses the ideas, not the ideas themselves." We think, however, that in the field of radio broadcasting concreteness may lie between the boundaries of mere generality on the one hand and, on the other, a full script containing the words to be uttered and delineating the action to be portrayed. Where the plan is for a series of broadcasts the contents of which depend upon selection of talent at different times, a detailed program cannot be presented at the preliminary stages of negotiation. This should not in and of itself deprive the originator of a property right in his plan.

As we have seen, in addition to the utilization of student talent selected for each broadcast from a different high school, the show was to be presented and recorded as a student assembly, retaining the atmosphere of a school by referring to the show as a class, to the acts as assignments and to the action as recitations. There was to be a rendition of several pieces by the school glee club, a minimum of conversation and introductions, a brief acknowledgment of sponsorship at the beginning and end of the broadcasts, and no provision for commercial "spots". And a very important element in the plan was the co-operation and participation of the school authorities through the use of school buildings and facilities and the assistance of faculty members. These details, when added to the basic general idea which, alone, would be too abstract, give sufficient concreteness....

In view of our conclusion that the plan was concrete it is unnecessary to express an opinion as to what protection, if any, should be afforded an abstract idea. Some jurisdictions deny protection in the absence of a contract entered into prior to disclosure and expressly reserving rights in the originator....

A remaining problem is whether the plan, assuming originality, concreteness, and usefulness, the latter of course uncontested because of the use actually made of it, was disclosed to the Bank in circumstances which contemplated compensation for its use. Factually this question is answered by pointing out that when the plan was first disclosed to the Bank it was made the subject of a contract between the parties. This contract, it is true, was largely for Mr. Belt's own personal services, but it nevertheless also placed the disclosure in circumstances indicating that compensation was expected for its use. While the contract itself, as we have said, was terminated, this did not erase the fact of disclosure in those circumstances. Nor did the idea become public property on disclosure to the Bank[10]

....

Affirmed.

Notes

1. Novelty (or originality) and concreteness are usually, but not always, required of claims to rights in an idea. Did the following ideas merit legal protection?

(a) The idea of a film built around the history of the Palace Theatre in New York and the vaudeville performers who appeared there. O'Brien v. RKO Radio Pictures, Inc., 68 F. Supp. 13 (S.D.N.Y. 1946) (too abstract).

(b) A plan for a radio program involving a musical broadcast from a different large city each week, using local musicians in each city. Bowen v. Yankee Network, Inc., 46 F. Supp. 62 (D. Mass. 1942) (mere idea in which there was no property right; lacked necessary concrete form).

(c) An idea for a radio program presenting dramas which then, depending upon audience response, might be used as the basis of motion pictures. Stanley v. Columbia Broadcasting System, Inc., 35 Cal. 2d 653, 221 P.2d 73 (1950) (action on implied contract; jury question of originality).

(d) A proposal for a television comedy series about a black middle class family, starring Bill Cosby. Murray v. National Broadcasting Co., 844 F.2d 988 (2d Cir. 1988), cert. denied, 488 U.S. 955 (1988) (not novel).

(e) An idea for radio broadcasts of flight arrival and departure information. Official Airlines Schedule Information Service, Inc. v. Eastern Air Lines, Inc., 333 F.2d 672 (5th Cir. 1964) (no liability when defendant airline, having refused to participate in joint airline broadcasts proposed by plaintiff, began broadcasts limited to information on its own flights; plaintiffs' broadcasts preceded defendant's).

(f) A hotel employee's idea that the hotel construct a recreational vehicle park. Smith v. Recrion Corp., 91 Nev. 666, 541 P.2d 663 (1975) (not sufficiently concrete and novel for quasi-contractual liability).

---

10. The previous efforts of Mr. Belt to enlist the interest of other commercial concerns, in like circumstances of expectation of compensation, did not take this case out of the rule stated, nor did these firms themselves place the idea in the public realm. The Bank obtained the idea from Mr. Belt.

2. A leading case rejecting a contractual claim because the idea lacked novelty is Masline v. New York, New Haven & Hartford Railroad Co., 95 Conn. 702, 112 A. 639 (1921). Plaintiff, a railroad brakeman and baggagemaster, allegedly made an agreement with a vice president of the line to impart valuable information in return for 5% of the amounts the railroad would receive by using it. The information was advice to sell advertising space on stations, cars, rights of way and fences. The court considered that the information had no value to the railroad because it was common knowledge.

3. By invitation, an advertising agency submits to a beer manufacturer various ideas for an advertising campaign, including the slogan "The Beer of the Century." The beer company does not hire that agency for the advertising campaign, but uses the slogan. Is the agency entitled to recover the value of its services? See How J. Ryan & Associates, Inc. v. Century Brewing Association, 185 Wash. 600, 55 P.2d 1053 (1936) (yes; recovery based on value of services to manufacturer, not on momentary act of conceiving idea). What if an advertising idea is unsolicited and submitted with a request for compensation? See Liggett & Meyer Tobacco Co., Inc. v. Meyer, 101 Ind. App. 420, 194 N.E. 206 (1935) (scheme for billboard advertising of cigarettes featuring one man extending package of cigarettes to another, who declines with statement that he smokes advertised brand; creator held to have property right in scheme and to be entitled to compensation). In another case of an unsolicited idea submitted to a tobacco company, Thomas v. R.J. Reynolds Tobacco Co., 350 Pa. 262, 38 A.2d 61 (1944), the idea was use of a letter by plaintiff stating his conviction that the company's brand was the best and most economical. Plaintiff told the company that it was at liberty to use the letter for advertising purposes, provided it compensated him for his idea and "test" of various brands of cigarettes. It was held that the idea was not sufficiently novel to constitute a property right and plaintiff could not recover, in the absence of express agreement for payment, for the company's use of portions of his idea. See generally Annots., Rights and Remedies as Between Originator of Uncopyrighted Advertising Plan or Slogan, or His Assignee, and Another Who Uses or Infringes the Same, 104 A.L.R. 1357 (1936); 157 A.L.R. 1436 (1945).

4. In Blaustein v. Burton, 9 Cal. App. 3d 161, 88 Cal. Rptr. 319 (1970), plaintiff alleged that he conceived the idea of producing a film of Shakespeare's The Taming of the Shrew, to be directed by Franco Zeffirelli, with Richard Burton and Elizabeth Taylor as the stars. Damages were claimed from Zeffirelli, Burton and Taylor. The court reversed a summary judgment in favor of Burton and Taylor. It held that this idea could be protected by contract even if not novel. If plaintiff had disclosed the idea to defendants on condition that if they used it, plaintiff would be engaged as producer or else receive the compensation he would have earned as producer, defendants became obligated to pay plaintiff the compensation upon using the idea. The court took note of the usual practice in the motion picture industry. Proposed projects would be submitted to agents of major stars, who screened the proposals and submitted some of them to the stars. The agent then pursued the matter if the actor was interested. Unlike the situation in other industries, the agent could not commit the actor without the actor's approval.

5. While the novelty of the idea continues to be required for claims of "misappropriation" or unjust enrichment, it has not been required in a number of cases when plaintiff alleged an express or implied-in-fact contractual agreement concerning defendant's use of the idea. See Wrench LLC v. Taco Bell Corp., 256 F.3d 446 (6th Cir. 2001), cert. denied, 534 U.S. 1114 (2002), involving defendant's alleged use of a cartoon character created by plaintiffs, and Reeves v. Alyeska Pipeline Service Co., 926 P.2d 1130 (Alaska 1996), involving plaintiff's idea for a visitor center at a turnout overlooking the Trans-Alaska Pipeline. Nadel v. Play-By-Play Toys & Novelties, Inc,. 208 F.3d 368 (2d Cir. 2000), in-

terpreted New York law to require for contract-based claims only "novelty to the buyer" rather than novelty or originality generally. One of the leading cases on this subject is Desny v. Wilder, 46 Cal. 2d 715, 299 P.2d 257 (1956). Plaintiff had revealed an idea for a motion picture to a producer's secretary. The secretary allegedly said that plaintiff would be paid if the story was used. The court accepted that in the entertainment field, a producer may agree in advance that he will pay for the service of conveying ideas that he can put to profitable use. Where an idea has been conveyed with the expectation of compensation if the idea is used, a producer might promise compensation and thereby create a valid obligation. But the law would not imply a promise to pay for an idea in the mere conveyance of the idea, even if it was valuable and later used for profit. There was no property in abstract ideas, but they could be made the subject of a valid contract. The court reversed a summary judgment for defendant, finding factual issues concerning whether plaintiff had submitted his idea on condition he be paid if the story was used and whether material from plaintiff's synopsis actually had been used.

Richter v. Westab, Inc.

United States Court of Appeals, Sixth Circuit
529 F.2d 896 (1976)

WEICK, Circuit Judge....

Plaintiffs were partners in the firm of Richter & Mracky Design Associates, which created and developed designs for products and marketing concepts. In 1964 Mark Seitman, an employee of Richter & Mracky, observed that the school supplies industry was characterized by drabness and a lack of attractiveness in the various product lines. He believed that a school supply firm could improve its sales by using on notebook covers and binders fashion designs and fabrics which matched clothing being advertised in young women's fashion magazines; that such fashion-oriented supplies could be matched as a package so that the fashion-conscious buyer could purchase all items from one company; and that these lines of school supplies could be advertised in fashion magazines rather than in trade journals as had been the practice with school supplies in the past.

Seitman solicited Westab and arranged a meeting for February 10, 1965, with its officers. Westab was the largest manufacturer of school supplies in the country. At this meeting Seitman presented his concept, which resulted in authorization for Richter & Mracky to produce tentative designs and samples for presentation to Westab sales officials. During the meeting a Westab officer suggested that the notebook binders in the fashion line have interchangeable covers, and Richter & Mracky was also authorized to develop this idea.

After the meeting Seitman discussed with Edgar Stovall, Vice-President of Westab, the matter of compensation which included a royalty of five percent of Westab's sale price, to be paid on specific designs submitted by Richter & Mracky and used by Westab. It did not include royalties on the mere concept of fashion design.

During the summer of 1965 Richter & Mracky worked to perfect interchangeable binder covers and to produce fashion designs which it named "Fashion Goes To School." Samples were submitted to Westab. The interchangeable covers became loose when the notebook was opened, and were not practical.... None of the designs was acceptable to Westab, and the project was rejected in October 1965 when Westab marketing officials balked at the projected retail price of $4.95 for the package. Westab then paid Richter & Mracky for shop expenses and asked that the work product not be given to competitors....

In 1965 Westab's research and marketing personnel independently developed a package of school supplies with matching plaid covers, packed together in a transparent shrink wrapper, and called "Campus Mates". This package was a success. In 1967 Westab introduced paisley-patterned binder covers. In 1968 more paisley patterns and stripe patterns were introduced in the "Girl Talk" line, promoted by advertisements in the magazine *Seventeen*. In 1969 Westab coordinated binder fabrics with fashion trends in "The Wet Look" and "The Leather Look" lines. In 1970 the fashion binder lines were promoted in fashion magazines as clothing accessories: "Think of a notebook as something you wear"; "Westab's got notebook ensembles to go along with all those sharp new clothes you've just bought this fall." These fashion lines generated sales revenues in excess of $4.6 million in the years 1966–1969.

In 1969 Seitman first noticed that Westab's marketing strategy resembled the concept which he had presented to Westab in 1965. In 1971 the present suit was brought to recover five percent royalties on all sales by Westab of fashion-coordinated school supplies.

[Plaintiffs sought to recover on the basis of breach of express contract. The district court found no breach; the contract required plaintiffs to submit specific designs and to be paid royalties only for defendants' use of designs so submitted. The court granted judgment for defendants.]

An alternate theory of recovery claimed was that an implied contract arises to pay for use of a trade secret when the secret is divulged as part of a confidential relationship. Even if this principle is a correct statement of Ohio law it cannot create an implied contract in Ohio because the fashion coordinating concept is not a trade secret as defined in [Restatement of Torts, § 757, comment *b*.]

This definition does not include a marketing concept or a new product idea. Trade secret law is designed to protect a continuing competitive advantage, which a company enjoys due to confidential information it possesses, from destruction due to disclosure by a departed former employee. A marketing concept does not by confidentiality create a continuing competitive advantage because once it is implemented it is exposed for the world to see and for competitors to legally imitate.

This conclusion is even more compelling because Richter & Mracky is asking for compensation to cover periods when fashion binders were widely sold on the market by Westab's competitors as well as by Westab. Even if Westab had been paying Richter & Mracky to use the concept, it would have ceased being a trade secret upon introduction of the products, and Richter & Mracky thereafter would have no legal right to the concept.

Any competitive advantage to be gained from use of this concept would last only until a competitor could place similar items on the market. Richter & Mracky would have no remedy against Westab's competitors for their use of the concept....

We must recognize that firms which sell ideas as their product should be able to protect their right to ask for and to receive compensation for their products just as any other business can. These firms have traditionally been protected by patent and copyright laws. However, intangible concepts which are being sold by many consultants today cannot be protected by patent or copyright statutes.

Richter & Mracky suggests that legal protection is sometimes given to advertising slogans, marketing concepts, and television program concepts. This is true, but such relief is not found under the law of trade secrets. The logical means to protect a marketing concept is a tort action for conversion of intellectual property, or a quasi-contract action for wrongful appropriation of intellectual property....

If an idea cannot meet the requirements of patent or copyright laws which entitle it to protection, the states can not render such requirements nugatory by affording such ideas protection under state law. *Sears, Roebuck & Co. v. Stiffel Co.*, 376 U.S. 225, 231 (1964)....

With respect to ideas which are colorably patentable the law seems clear that states are limited in their ability to protect items not meeting patent criteria. However, with respect to literary property the failure to meet the criteria for copyright protection does not necessarily preclude protection under state common law. This is particularly true of unfinished program concepts presented to the broadcast media. The reason for this toleration of state law copyrighting is that the federal copyright statutes antedate the development of modern marketing concepts and the broadcast media. The need for legal protection of unfinished marketing and broadcast program concepts has not been met by amendment of the copyright laws, so the common law has once again served to meet new legal problems by finding protection for such concepts....

Common law copyright protection has been held in other jurisdictions to protect not only polished manuscripts but also advertising slogans. However, when protection is to be afforded to a concept rather than to a specific expression, the concept must be both novel and concrete.

The idea of fashion-coordinated designs on binder covers does not appear to meet the test of novelty required in *Stevens v. Continental Can Co.*, 308 F.2d 100 (6th Cir. 1962). There the plaintiff's concept was to place a wood grain design on paper plates and cups. We held that even if wood grain patterns had never been used before on paper plates and cups the idea was not novel because the wood grain design was not novel. The idea of using a design on a particular item is abstract. The design to be used is concrete; but if the design to be used is not novel then no legal protection is available.

In the case at bar Richter & Mracky suggested that Westab apply to their school supplies designs already seen on clothing fashions. Since the designs to be used were not originated by Richter & Mracky, the suggestion lacks novelty according to *Stevens, supra*, and the idea that the designs be placed on binders, standing alone, also lacks concreteness.

While there is authority in other jurisdictions for permitting recovery on an implied contract theory for use of an idea which is neither novel nor concrete in the legal sense, *Blaustein v. Burton*, 9 Cal. App. 3d 161, 88 Cal. Rptr. 319 (1970), an implied contract theory is inappropriate here because an express contract has been found to exist.

The law does not favor the protection of abstract ideas as the property of the originator. An idea should be free for all to use at least until someone is able to translate such idea into a sufficiently useful form that it may be patented or copyrighted. Thus competition in the use of ideas is a social good, hastening the process of invention.

When a design firm suggests that a particular product be decorated with thematic designs, this act of suggesting should not establish an exclusive right to exploit the idea. Perhaps the design firm will not be sufficiently competent to produce good designs based upon the concept. A concept is of little use until solidified into a concrete application. The idea of fashion designs is useless unless good designs are obtained. If the design firm is incapable of producing good designs the public should not be denied the benefit of the idea if another designer could produce good designs. Thus the principle denying legal protection to abstract ideas has important social interests behind it.

In spite of this policy, firms which specialize in selling abstract concepts may protect their work product by contract. If Richter & Mracky had made a contract with Westab which required Westab to pay a royalty on all fashion binders sold by Westab, the contract would have been enforceable in the courts. Likewise, if the parties had made an agreement in advance of the meeting that any sale arising from the use of concepts presented at the meeting would require royalty payments to Richter & Mracky, the facts here would probably require a judgment for plaintiffs.

We doubt that Westab would ever enter into such a contract, preferring to hear the presentation or to see the proposed designs, before agreeing to a contract for their use. Such action would merely reflect the fact that an abstract idea has little commercial value until translated into a specific utilization....

Denying the existence of a legal interest in abstract ideas disclosed in confidence will not as a practical matter impede the flow of ideas between companies. In this case Richter & Mracky never intended to sell its concept of fashion binders; it intended to sell designs to the school supplies industry. The disclosure of the concept was made in soliciting a contract to design binder covers. This disclosure would have occurred regardless of the legal status of the idea disclosed.

We do not find in the circumstances of this case any basis under which Richter & Mracky, or its members, would be entitled to compensation for use by Westab of the fashion design concept.

Affirmed.

Notes

1. Plaintiff writes an unsolicited letter to (among many others) a law school dean, disclosing his idea for a foreign tax service and attempting to secure the dean's participation in the venture. No contract is ever made and plaintiff is advised that the dean is not interested. The dean and his law school subsequently use plaintiff's idea in preparing a system of reports to the United Nations on foreign tax systems. Is plaintiff entitled to any relief for "conversion" of his idea? See J. Irizarry y Puente v. President and Fellows of Harvard College, 248 F.2d 799 (1st Cir. 1957), cert. denied, 356 U.S. 947 (1958) (even if idea novel and concrete, which it was not, gratuitous and unsolicited disclosure imposed no duty not to use idea). Cf. Haskins v. Ryan, 71 N.J. Eq. 575, 64 A. 436 (Ch. 1906), where plaintiff made a study of an industry, formulating a plan for combining most of the companies into a single company, and laid this before a capitalist, seeking his cooperation and financial aid. The capitalist indicated his probable willingness but then used the information furnished by plaintiff to get control of the industry for himself. The court concluded that the plan was a mere idea which the originator was incapable of applying to his own use, not protectable property.

2. An employer offers awards for suggestions submitted by employees and used by the employer. An employee suggests that certain components of circuit breakers be made from heavy gauge steel rather than cast aluminum. The employer purports to reject the idea but subsequently uses it in the business, achieving considerable savings. Has the employer incurred liability to the employee? See Schott v. Westinghouse Electric Corp., 436 Pa. 279, 259 A.2d 443 (1969) (employee has claim in quantum meruit for unjust enrichment). Could there be liability if the suggestion was unsolicited? In Galanis v. Procter and Gamble Corp., 153 F. Supp. 34 (S.D.N.Y. 1957), plaintiff submitted an unsolicited idea to a soap manufacturer for a granulated soap containing pulverized bluing. Later, the manufacturer began to sell this type of product. The court held that despite the lack of any property or contract rights in her idea, plaintiff could recover on the basis of unjust enrichment upon proof that the idea was novel, concrete and actually appropriated by the manufacturer in developing its product.

3. Ideas for products, equipment or methods of operation are often developed by a company's employees or customers and revealed to the company in hopes of reward. In Materese v. Moore-McCormack Lines, Inc., 158 F.2d 631 (2d Cir. 1946), plaintiff, an immigrant of little education who had long worked around the docks of New York, formulated an idea for a device to assist in the loading and unloading of ships. He revealed the idea to an agent of a shipping company, for which plaintiff was then working as a part-time stevedore. The agent allegedly promised plaintiff one-third of any savings the company realized by using the device. Plaintiff was given the full-time job of supervising construction of such devices, but he never received compensation based upon the company's savings and was eventually fired. In an action against the shipping company, plaintiff's contractual claim failed for want of the agent's authority, but it was held that he was entitled to damages on the basis of unjust enrichment. The court referred to the relationship between the parties before and after disclosure of the idea, the agent's promise of compensation, plaintiff's eventual acquisition of a patent on his device, and defendant's use of the device.

4. In Lueddecke v. Chevrolet Motor Co., 70 F.2d 345 (8th Cir. 1934), plaintiff's unsolicited letter to a car manufacturer stated that the car had a design defect (not identified) which would greatly reduce sales of the car. He offered to reveal, for compensation, an inexpensive means of correcting the defect. The manufacturer responded that if plaintiff's design change was of sufficient interest, a mutually satisfactory agreement might be made, and requested drawings and a description. Plaintiff did not provide drawings but described his idea in some detail—adding spring leaves or shifting items in the car in a way that would prevent the body sagging on one side, which caused the fender to rub against a tire. The manufacturer replied that the redesign was "not advisable" but allegedly implemented plaintiff's ideas. The court ruled that plaintiff was not entitled to compensation because the idea was not novel and the manufacturer had neither invited its submission nor offered to pay for it.

5. Women Golfer, Inc. v. Meredith Corp., 792 F. Supp. 211 (S.D.N.Y. 1992), illustrates that a defendant will not be held liable simply because it profited from a good idea learned in communications with plaintiff. Plaintiff's owners had identified what they perceived as a void in the consumer magazine market: there was no major magazine targeted solely at women golfers. They developed a proposal to establish a magazine called "Woman Golfer." They presented this proposal at a meeting with defendant's senior vice president. He was interested in the proposal, but the ultimate outcome of the meeting was defendant's purchase of a small-circulation magazine for women golfers. Allegedly, he first heard of this magazine's existence when it was mentioned by one of plaintiff's owners during the meeting. The court dismissed the complaint on the grounds that the proposal to establish a women's golf magazine lacked novelty and originality and plaintiff had failed to show that defendants utilized any novel and original ideas within the proposal. Plaintiff's assertion that standard practice in the publishing industry was to treat all proposals as confidential was mentioned but not discussed.

6. Keep in mind the variety of theories under which ideas have been given some protection—express contract, implied-in-fact contract, quasi-contract (or unjust enrichment or restitution), property rights (including common law copyright), misappropriation, protection of trade secrets, and protection of confidences. A number of factors have been considered—the novelty or originality of the idea, its concreteness, its utility, any prior relationship of the parties, industry practice, and the confidentiality surrounding revelation of the idea. See generally Barrett, The "Law of Ideas" Reconsidered, 71 J. Pat. & Tmk. Off. Soc'y 691 (1989); Nimmer, The Law of Ideas, 27 S. Cal. L. Rev. 119 (1954).

7. *Preemption by federal law.* How does the federal preemption doctrine of *Sears* and *Compco* affect litigation over ideas? In Aronson v. Quick Point Pencil Co., 440 U.S. 257 (1979), a patent applicant agreed that a manufacturer could produce and sell the item which was the subject of his patent application—a keyholder—in exchange for specified royalties, with the royalties to be reduced by 50% if the patent was not obtained within five years. The patent was refused. The manufacturer claimed that the agreement was unenforceable as inconsistent with the federal patent laws or the federal policy against withdrawing ideas from the public domain. The court rejected this argument. It noted that commercial agreements were traditionally the domain of state law and state law was not displaced merely because the agreement related to intellectual property which might or might not be patentable. Enforcement of this agreement did not withdraw any idea from the public domain since the idea had not been in the public domain prior to the agreement concerning its manufacture, and enforcement would not prevent anyone from copying the keyholder. It would merely require the manufacturer to pay the consideration it promised. There was, in the court's opinion, no interference with patent law's objectives of fostering and rewarding invention, promoting disclosure of inventions, stimulating further innovation, and assuring that ideas in the public domain remain there. See also Kewanee Oil Co. v. Bicron Corp., 416 U.S. 470 (1974) (state protection of trade secrets not preempted).

8. Section 102(b) of the 1976 Copyright Act states: "In no case does copyright protection for an original work of authorship extend to any idea, procedure, process, system, method of operation, concept, principle, or discovery, regardless of the form in which it is described, explained, illustrated, or embodied in such work." Accordingly, in principle there is no preemption of a common law claim to an idea. See Dunlap v. G&L Holding Group, Inc., 381 F.3d 1285 (11th Cir. 2004). However, courts have decided that intangible uncopyrightable ideas embodied in writings and other copyrightable material are within the "subject matter of copyright." See United States ex rel. Berge v. Board of Trustees of the University of Alabama, 104 F.3d 1453 (4th Cir. 1997), cert. denied, 522 U.S. 916 (1997); Wrench LLC v. Taco Bell Corp., 256 F.3d 446 (6th Cir. 2001), cert. denied, 534 U.S. 1114 (2002). If so, state law-based claims will be preempted unless the court finds a basis of liability that is not equivalent to claims under copyright law, which protects a creator's exclusive rights to reproduce, distribute and display publicly the copyrighted work. See Montz v. Pilgrim Films & Television, Inc,. 649 F.3d 975 (9th Cir. 2011), cert. denied, ___ U.S. ___ (2011) (breach of confidence claim for disclosure of ideas and claim of implied-in-fact contract requiring compensation if ideas used for television program not preempted; unjust enrichment claim would be preempted; dissent believed all claims preempted as equivalent to infringement of copyright); Katz Dochtermann & Epstein Inc. v. Home Box Office, 50 U.S.P.Q.2d 1957 (S.D. Ill. 1999) (advertising agency's misappropriation claim preempted; claim of implied-in-fact contract to pay for use of idea separate from violation of copyright in written material presented by agency, so not preempted); Fischer v. Viacom International, Inc., 115 F. Supp. 2d 535 (D. Md. 2000) (claim of implied-in-fact contract to compensate plaintiff if ideas for animated television program used was equivalent to creator's exclusive rights under Copyright Act, so preempted; valid breach of confidence claim generally not preempted); Selby v. New Line Cinema Corp., 96 F. Supp. 2d 1053 (C.D. Cal. 2000) (claim of implied-in-fact contract to compensate plaintiff and give him screen credit if ideas used to produce film preempted because alleged contract did not prohibit conduct beyond what was prohibited by Copyright Act). See generally Nimmer, Copyright § 19D.03 (1978).

Chapter 5

Publicity and Privacy

Section 1. Appropriation of Name, Likeness or Identity

Hinish v. Meier & Frank Company, Inc.

Supreme Court of Oregon
166 Or. 482, 113 P.2d 438 (1941)

LUSK, Justice.

[Plaintiff brought an action to recover damages for "invasion of the plaintiff's right of privacy" against Meier & Frank (a general merchant) and the manager of its optical department. The complaint stated that defendants, without plaintiff's knowledge or consent, signed his name and address to a telegram which they sent to the governor of Oregon. The telegram urged the governor to veto a bill that would prevent Meier & Frank from continuing to sell optical glasses to the public. The telegram allegedly jeopardized plaintiff's position as a civil service employee, to whom political activity was prohibited, and caused him mental anguish.]

The case presents to this court for the first time the question whether there is such a thing in this state as a legal right of privacy, for breach of which an action for damages will lie. This right, first brought forcefully to the attention of the profession in the year 1890 by an article in the Harvard Law Review by Louis D. Brandeis (later Mr. Justice Brandeis) and Samuel D. Warren ("The Right to Privacy", 4 Harv. L. Rev. 193), is said to be one that inheres in an "inviolate personality".…

Where this right has been invaded, as for example, by using the name or photograph of a person without his authority, for advertising or commercial purposes, or by parading a person's intimate, private affairs before the public gaze, unjustifiably and against his will, some of the courts of this country have thought that no legal redress could be granted, largely because the right was unknown to the common law, and to recognize it would be judicial legislation.…

The Court of Appeals of New York refused to recognize the existence of a legal right of privacy in the leading case of Roberson v. Rochester Folding Box Co., 171 N.Y. 538, 64 N.E. 442. The plaintiff was a young woman whose picture had been appropriated for advertising purposes by a milling company. Twenty-five thousand likenesses of the plaintiff, printed as a part of an advertisement of the defendants' product, had been "conspicuously posted and displayed in stores, warehouses, saloons, and other public places". The court divided four to three on the question whether the complaint for an injunction and damages stated a cause of action. The opinion of the majority, written by Chief Judge Parker, while based primarily on the inability of the court to find authority or precedent for granting the relief sought, since, as it was said, no property right was involved, does not, as it seems to us, properly evaluate the enormity of the wrong done to the plaintiff. "Such publicity", it was said, "which some find agreeable, is to plaintiff very distasteful, and thus, because of defendants' impertinence in using her picture, without her consent, for their own business purposes, she has been caused to suffer mental distress where others would have appreciated the compliment to their beauty implied in the selection of the picture for such purposes...."

But, to Judge Gray, who dissented with two of his associates, the proposition seemed "an inconceivable one that these defendants may, unauthorizedly, use the likeness of this young woman upon their advertisement as a method of attracting widespread public attention to their wares, and that she must submit to the mortifying notoriety, without right to invoke the exercise of the preventive power of a court of equity." And, referring to decisions protecting a writer's or lecturer's right to a literary property in a letter or a lecture against its unauthorized publication, he said that he thought the plaintiff had the same property in the right to be protected against the use of her portraiture for the defendants' commercial purposes, and that: "Any other principle of decision, in my opinion, is as repugnant to equity as it is shocking to reason."

In the similar case of Pavesich v. New England Life Ins. Co., 122 Ga. 190, 50 S.E. 68, the court reached a conclusion contrary to that of the New York court....

... In Flake v. Greensboro News Co., 212 N.C. 780, 195 S.E. 55, it was held to be a tort to use the likeness of the plaintiff in connection with and as a part of an advertisement without the plaintiff's consent. The court approved the reasoning of [*Pavesich* and the dissent in *Roberson*] but expressly limited the decision to the facts of the case before it, saying: "So far as we have been able to ascertain, no court has yet held that it constitutes a tort for a newspaper to publish an image of an individual when such publication is not libelous, except when such publication involves the breach of a trust, the violation of a contract, or when the photograph is used in connection with some commercial enterprise, and we are presently called upon to decide only the right of an individual to prohibit the unauthorized use of an image of her features and figure in connection with and as part of an advertisement." ...

In Jones v. Herald Post Co., 230 Ky. 227, 18 S.W.2d 972, the defendant published in its newspaper a picture of the plaintiff in connection with an account of the tragic death of her husband. The court, while recognizing the right of privacy, held that it was not applicable in the circumstances of the case because the plaintiff had become an actor in an occurrence of public or general interest. She had emerged from her seclusion.... "The right of privacy may be defined as the right to live one's life in seclusion, without being subjected to unwarranted and undesired publicity. In short, it is the right to be let alone." ...

There are precedents dealing with the right of privacy, but in another guise.... The writer of a private letter is protected against its unjustified publication. In Prince Albert v. Strange, 1849, 1 Mac. & G. 25, 41 Eng. Rep. 1171, 2 DeG. & Sm. 652, 64 Eng. Rep. 293, the defendant was enjoined not only from exhibiting copies of etchings which he had taken from plates unlawfully obtained, but also from selling descriptive catalogues of such etchings. It is a legal wrong for a photographer, employed to take a patron's picture, to make additional copies and use them for his own purposes without authorization. The case of the photograph is put on the ground of breach of confidence or of implied condition of the contract; the others on a property in the letter or etchings. As to the letter, it is beside the mark whether it has great literary value or none at all....

There is a good deal to be said for the view that in these cases invasion of privacy was the wrong, though breach of contract, of confidence or a property right was the peg upon which the decision was hung....

As to names, it is the general rule (although, as we have observed, there is authority to the contrary) that a person has no such exclusive right to the use of his own name as to prevent the assumption of its use by another. But it is different when one's own name is used in such a way as to amount to unfair competition. In connection with questions of that kind, a man's name is said to be his own property.

By analogy to this principle, there ought to be little difficulty today in deciding a question such as that involved in the Roberson case in favor of the one asserting the exclusive right to the use of his own picture as against appropriation by another for the purpose of advertising his wares; for selling one's likeness to be so used is today a business in itself. Faces, some faces, at any rate, have a recognized commercial value. The face of the plaintiff in the Roberson case must have had such value, else the defendants would not have gone to the trouble and expense of reproducing and distributing broadcast her likeness. If it was of value to the defendants, why not to her, even though she preferred not to capitalize upon it? ...

But we deem it unnecessary to search for a right of property, or a contract, or a relation of confidence. The question is whether a right of privacy, distinct and of itself and not incidental to some other long recognized right, is to be accepted by the courts and a violation of the right held actionable. We are called upon, as Mr. Justice Holmes says somewhere, "to exercise the sovereign prerogative of choice" between the view that the courts for want of a precedent are impotent to grant redress for injury resulting from conduct which universal opinion in a state of civilized society would unhesitatingly condemn as indecent and outrageous, and the view that the common law, with its capacity for growth and expansion and its adaptability to the needs and requirements of changing conditions, contains within itself the resources of principle upon which relief in such a case can be founded....

Our consideration of the subject leads us to the conclusion that natural justice and the needs of the society in which we live should prevail over objections based upon the novelty of the asserted cause of action. It is time that fictions be abandoned and the real character of the injury be frankly avowed. When Brandeis and Warren wrote in 1890, it was the unseemly intrusions of a portion of the press into the privacy of the home that was emphasized as the main source of evil; since then motion pictures and the radio have been perfected and have taken their places among our great industries, while instantaneous photography today accomplishes miracles scarcely dreamed of fifty years ago. Thus, the potentialities for this character of wrong are now greatly multiplied. A decision against the right of privacy would be nothing less than an invitation to those so inclined who control these instrumentalities of communication, information and education, to put them to base uses, with complete immunity, and without regard to the hurt done to the sensibilities of individuals whose private affairs might be exploited, whether out of malice or for selfish purposes.

We should not be deterred by fear of being accused of judicial legislation. Much of our law is judge-made, and there are those who think that it is the best law. Cardozo, "The Growth of the Law", p. 133. The common law's capacity to discover and apply remedies for acknowledged wrongs without waiting on legislation is one of its cardinal virtues....

... That there are difficulties may be conceded. They arise especially in that class of cases where the complaint is founded on unwanted publicity and are well illustrated by the recent case of Sidis v. F-R Publishing Corp., 2 Cir., 113 F.2d 806 [p. 459, infra].... In such cases, other interests, such, for example, as the freedom of the press, are involved, and the courts must needs proceed cautiously. We are not embarrassed by questions of that kind here....

It remains only to say that the complaint plainly states a cause of action for breach of the plaintiff's right of privacy. If the facts are as alleged, the defendants appropriated to themselves for their own purposes, without the plaintiff's consent and against his will, his name, his personality and whatever influence he may have possessed, and injected them into a political controversy in which, as far as appears, he had no interest. This they had no legal right to do, and on account of their wrong the plaintiff is entitled to recover nominal damages at least, and any additional damages for injury to his feelings that he may be able to prove, besides punitive damages if there was actual malice. He is not entitled to damages, however, on the theory that the defendants' acts endangered his position or his retirement rights as an employee of the government, since, although it possibly would have been a violation of the United States Civil Service Rules for the plaintiff to have sent the telegram himself, he did not in fact do so, and it cannot be assumed that he would have been penalized for misconduct of which he was not guilty....

[The trial court's judgment, sustaining a demurrer to the complaint, was reversed.]

Notes

1. Pavesich v. New England Life Insurance Co., 122 Ga. 190, 50 S.E. 68 (1905), is the first major case recognizing a common law right of privacy. An insurance company published a newspaper advertisement containing a recognizable picture of plaintiff. Above his likeness were the words "Do it now. The man who did." Next to this was the picture of an ill-dressed and sickly man, with the caption "Do it while you can. The man who didn't." The advertisement went on to quote plaintiff as saying, "In my healthy and productive period of life I bought insurance in the New England Mutual Life Insurance Co., of Boston, Mass., and to-day my family is protected and I am drawing an annual dividend on my paid-up policies." Plaintiff had not consented to use of his picture, did not have a policy with defendant, and never made the statement attributed to him. Believing that personal liberty included a right of privacy, the court held that publication of a person's picture without his consent as part of a business advertisement is a violation of the right and gives rise to liability without proof of special damage. See generally Annot., Invasion of Privacy by Use of Plaintiff's Name or Likeness in Advertising, 23 A.L.R.3d 865 (1969).

2. It is now generally accepted in the United States that there is a cause of action for use of a person's name or likeness in commercial advertising without consent. See generally Annot., Invasion of Privacy by Use of Plaintiff's Name or Likeness in Advertising, 23 A.L.R.3d 865 (1969). In response to the *Roberson* decision, the New York legislature enacted in 1903 a statute providing that "Any person whose name, portrait or picture is used within this state for advertising purposes or for the purposes of trade without ... written consent ... may maintain an equitable action ... against the person, firm or corporation so using his name, portrait or picture, to prevent and restrain the use thereof; and may also sue and recover damages for any injuries sustained by reason of such use, and if the defendant shall have knowingly used such person's name, portrait, or picture in such manner as is forbidden or declared to be unlawful by this act, the jury, in its discretion, may award exemplary damages." (Now in N.Y. Civil Rights Law §51.) Several

other states have similar statutes, including Neb. Rev. Stat. §§ 20-201 to 211; 21 Okla. Stat. §§ 839.1–839.3; R.I. Gen. Laws §§ 9-1-28, 9-1-28.1; Va. Code § 8.01-40; Wis. Stat. Ann. § 995.50. The many cases involving the New York statute are considered consistent with the common law of privacy developed in other states. See Prosser & Keeton, Law of Torts 850–851 (5th ed. 1984). However, the courts of a state with a privacy statute may conclude that there is no common law remedy for invasions of privacy not covered by the statute, such as non-commercial appropriation of name or likeness or publication of private facts. See Wojtowicz v. Delacorte Press, 58 A.D.2d 45, 395 N.Y.S.2d 205 (1977), aff'd, 43 N.Y.2d 858, 403 N.Y.S.2d 218, 374 N.E.2d 129 (1978) (no non-statutory right of privacy in New York). Contra, McCormack v. Oklahoma Publishing Co., 613 P.2d 737 (Okla. 1980) (all categories of invasion of privacy actionable under Oklahoma law).

3. To be liable, must defendant know that plaintiff's name or likeness is being used without consent? What if defendant publishes plaintiff's picture in an advertisement by mistake? In Flake v. Greensboro News Co., 212 N.C. 780, 195 S.E. 55 (1938), a newspaper published an advertisement which had the leading lady of a travelling vaudeville show say that a "sylph-like figure" could be kept by eating a certain brand of bread. The advertisement described the performer as "an exotic red-haired Venus" and contained a photograph. The photograph used was not of this performer but of plaintiff, a radio entertainer, in a bathing suit. Upon discovery of its mistake, the newspaper ceased using the incorrect picture and publicly apologized to plaintiff. It was held that plaintiff was entitled to nominal damages from the newspaper for violation of her right to privacy.

4. Would there be liability if a name used in an advertisement is thought to be fictitious but turns out to be that of a real person? In Kerby v. Hal Roach Studios, Inc., 53 Cal. App. 2d 207, 127 P.2d 577 (1942), a handwritten letter was signed with the name of the leading female character of a film and sent to a thousand men in Los Angeles. The recipients were invited to rendezvous with that character at a theatre where the film was being shown. Plaintiff had the same name as the character—the only person of that name listed in the local telephone and city directories. This was held to be an invasion of plaintiff's privacy. In Hooker v. Columbia Pictures Industries, Inc. 551 F. Supp. 1060 (N.D. Ill. 1982), a noted woodcarver, who specialized in portrayals of ducks and other wildlife, brought suit because the principal character in a television program—a policeman— and the program itself had the same name as plaintiff. The court found no liability because the producers and broadcasters of the program had not appropriated for their benefit the value of plaintiff's name.

5. Is there liability if an advertisement included a picture of plaintiff, but plaintiff's likeness was not a distinctive or prominent element of the advertising? In D'Andrea v. Safla-Demetrious, 972 F. Supp. 154 (E.D.N.Y. 1997), aff'd, 146 F.3d 64 (2d Cir. 1998), a former medical resident of a hospital sued because his photograph was included in an informational brochure for prospective candidates on the hospital's residency and internship programs. The brochure was sixteen pages in length and included the pictures of over forty other people. The court held that this was within the "incidental" uses of a person's picture or name to which no liability attached.

6. In Cox v. Hatch, 761 P.2d 556 (Utah 1988), plaintiffs were United States Postal Service workers who had been photographed, with their consent, with a Republican senator who visited their place of employment when he was running for re-election. They sued for use of one of the photographs in political literature distributed by one of the senator's campaign committees. The literature contained several photographs of the senator with workers and was aimed at union members. The court held that plaintiffs had no action because their photograph was not used for the purpose of ap-

propriating any value that plaintiffs' names or likenesses had. A political endorsement by an unknown member of the general public had no intrinsic value. It did not matter which workers' pictures were used. The use of plaintiffs' photograph was "incidental." Is this consistent with the opinion in *Hinish*? Compare Shamsky v. Garan, Inc., 167 Misc. 2d 149, 632 N.Y.S.2d 930 (Sup. Ct. 1995), in which defendants sold a shirt displaying a reproduction of a team photograph of the New York Mets — the winners of the 1969 World Series. The court held defendants liable to the team members in the photograph.

7. Suppose a model who looks like a famous celebrity is employed to appear in a magazine advertisement. Does the celebrity have an action? Does this depend upon whether readers will think the person in the advertisement is the celebrity? See Onassis v. Christian Dior-New York, Inc., 122 Misc. 2d 603, 472 N.Y.S.2d 254 (Sup. Ct. 1984), aff'd, 110 A.D.2d 1095, 488 N.Y.S.2d 943 (1985) (Jacqueline Kennedy Onassis granted injunction against publication of advertisement containing photograph of "lookalike" model). In Allen v. National Video, Inc., 610 F. Supp. 612 (S.D.N.Y. 1985), advertising for a video rental chain used a person who looked like Woody Allen. The court concluded that the advertisement would not be found to contain Allen's "portrait or picture" unless most persons would think the photograph actually was his; but there was sufficient likelihood of confusion for an injunction under the Lanham Act. Compare Young v. Greneker Studios, 175 Misc. 1027, 26 N.Y.S.2d 357 (Sup. Ct. 1941) (sale of mannequins in plaintiff's likeness actionable).

8. Does an action arise if a deceased person's name or likeness is used in an advertisement? If so, who is a proper plaintiff and whose consent is necessary to prevent liability? See Atkinson v. John E. Doherty & Co., 121 Mich. 372, 80 N.W. 285 (1899), involving a cigar whose label carried the name and likeness of a well-known lawyer and politician. In an action by his widow, the court held that use of the name and picture of a deceased person would not be restrained. See Annot., Right to Publicize or Commercially Exploit Deceased Person's Name or Likeness as Inheritable, 10 A.L.R.4th 1192 (1981).

9. Is the decision in the principal case a logical extension of the decisions in cases involving advertising? Would an action lie if a person's signature was forged to a tax return? See Schlessman v. Schlessman, 50 Ohio App. 2d 179, 361 N.E.2d 1347 (1975), where plaintiff sued her mother-in-law, alleging forgery of plaintiff's name to an income tax return filed by plaintiff's husband. This was held an invasion of privacy when done without authorization and under circumstances indicating that authorization would be denied. In Steding v. Battistoni, 3 Conn. Cir. 76, 208 A.2d 559 (1964), plaintiff recovered damages because, without his consent, he was named as a plaintiff in a suit concerning obstruction of a road. Should these cases have been addressed as injurious falsehood rather than as invasion of privacy? See also Moore v. Big Picture Co., 828 F.2d 270 (5th Cir. 1987), finding a privacy action in defendant's including the name of a person then working for another company in a proposed staffing chart used in defendant's bid for a government contract.

10. Would falsely claiming to be a person's wife or child and assuming the person's surname be grounds for this type of tort action? See Baumann v. Baumann, 250 N.Y. 382, 165 N.E. 819 (1929); Bartholomew v. Workman, 197 Okla. 267, 169 P.2d 1012 (1946) (not ground for injunctive relief); Vanderbilt v. Mitchell, 72 N.J. Eq. 910, 67 A. 97 (1907) (property rights provided basis for equitable relief; otherwise would grant relief on basis of *Pavesich* and dissent in *Roberson*).

Minnifield v. Ashcraft

Alabama Court of Civil Appeals
903 So. 2d 818 (2004)

YATES, Presiding Judge....

... Minnifield sued Ashcraft and Skin Worx, Inc., alleging invasion of privacy arising out of photographs of a tattoo on Minnifield's upper right breast that Ashcraft submitted, without Minnifield's permission, to "Dark Skin Art," a national tattoo magazine. Minnifield alleged that the publication of the photographs embarrassed, degraded, and demeaned her, causing her mental anguish and emotional distress.... The trial court entered a summary judgment in favor of Ashcraft and Skin Worx. Minnifield appeals....

Viewing the evidence in a light most favorable to Minnifield, as we are required to do, the evidence indicates that after Ashcraft completed Minnifield's tattoo he asked her if he could photograph the tattoo for his portfolio. One photograph showed Minnifield pointing to her tattoo. Minnifield's face is clearly identifiable in the photograph. The other photograph was a close-up of the tattoo. According to Minnifield, Ashcraft told her that the photographs would stay in his office. Minnifield believed that Ashcraft would not show the photographs to anyone else.

Minnifield testified that her cousin's roommate saw the photographs in the magazine and recognized Minnifield. Minnifield also testified that she was approached by a stranger while she was swimming and her tattoo was exposed and that the man stated that he had seen her tattoo in a magazine. Minnifield stated that she believed that the publication of the photographs was degrading because, she said, the other photographs in the tattoo magazine were not tasteful and she felt like she was being stereotyped with the other people featured in the magazine.

Our supreme court has stated: "It is generally accepted that invasion of privacy consists of four limited and distinct wrongs: (1) intruding into the plaintiff's physical solitude or seclusion; (2) giving publicity to private information about the plaintiff that violates ordinary decency; (3) putting the plaintiff in a false, but not necessarily defamatory, position in the public eye; or (4) appropriating some element of the plaintiff's personality for a commercial use." *Butler v. Town of Argo*, 871 So. 2d 1, 12 (Ala. 2003).... Each of these categories of invasion of privacy (intrusion into seclusion, public disclosure of private information, putting a person in a false light, and appropriation of an element of a person's personality for commercial use) has distinct elements, and each category establishes a separate privacy interest that may be invaded....

Of the four categories of invasion of privacy, Minnifield asserts a commercial-appropriation claim (i.e., that Ashcraft and Skin Worx used her likeness without her authorization to obtain some commercial benefit and that she was damaged as a result)....

With regard to commercial appropriation, our supreme court has stated: "*Restatement (Second) of Torts*, §652C, states that liability for this wrong arises when one's name or likeness is 'appropriated' by another to the other's 'use or benefit.' Comment d to this section states, in part: 'No one has the right to object merely because his name or his appearance is brought before the public, since neither is in any way a private matter and both are open to public observation. It is only when the publicity is given for the purpose of appropriating to the defendant's benefit the commercial or other values associated with the name or the likeness that the right of privacy is invaded.'" *Schifano v. Greene County Greyhound Park, Inc.*, 624 So. 2d 178, 181 (Ala. 1993). In *Schifano*, patrons of a dog-racing park were photographed as they sat in a section of the park that can be reserved by interested groups. The park printed the photograph in an advertising brochure. The patrons in the photograph were not identified by name.... The court held that there was no unique quality or value in the patrons' likenesses that would result in commercial profit to the park simply from using a photograph that included them—unidentified and seated in a group. The court noted that the patrons had failed to rebut the evidence indicating that the photograph was taken in full view of, and only a few feet away from, them and, therefore, that the patrons had failed to present a genuine issue of material fact regarding their consent.

There is a "legitimate public interest" exception to the right of privacy. In *Smith v. Doss*, 251 Ala. 250, 37 So. 2d 118 (1948), the right to privacy was defined in part as "'the right of a person to be free from unwarranted publicity' or 'the unwarranted appropriation or exploitation of one's personality, the publicizing of one's private affairs with which the public has no legitimate concern.'" However, the *Smith* court held that the broadcast of matters of "legitimate public interest" is not prohibited by the right to privacy because of the interest of the public in being informed....

In the present case, Minnifield is clearly identifiable in one of the photographs. When Ashcraft submitted the photographs of Minnifield to the magazine, the caption beside the photographs listed his name and Skin Worx. Certainly, it is reasonable to infer that Ashcraft and his business entity, Skin Worx, sought a commercial benefit from the photographs being published in the magazine. Ashcraft's submission of the photographs to the magazine for publication did not pertain to a legitimate newsworthy public interest. Therefore, the publication of the photographs is not protected under the legitimate-public-interest exception.

The damage that Minnifield claims flows from the publication of the photographs is a result of injuries to her feelings rather than from an injury to an economic interest in her property right in her likeness. The United States Court of Appeals for the Eleventh Circuit, applying Alabama law, has questioned the interest sought to be protected under our commercial-appropriation invasion-of-privacy tort and whether injuries to psychological interests are compensable under the commercial-appropriation category of invasion of privacy. See *Allison v. Vintage Sports Plaques*, 136 F.3d 1443 (11th Cir. 1998)....

"Although the Alabama Supreme Court has addressed the tort of commercial appropriation only twice and thus has provided us with little guidance in determining the contours of the cause of action, we read Alabama law to permit a cause of action for invasion of privacy when the defendant appropriates without consent the 'plaintiff's name or likeness to advertise the defendant's business or product, or for some other similar commercial purpose.' *Kyser-Smith*, 873 F. Supp. at 1525. The plaintiff must demonstrate that there is a 'unique quality or value in [his] likeness[]' that if appropriated, would result in 'commercial profit' to the defendant. *Schifano*, 624 So. 2d at 181; cf. *Montana v. San Jose Mercury News, Inc.*, 34 Cal. App. 4th 790, 793, 40 Cal. Rptr. 2d 639, 640 (1995) ('A cause of action for common law misappropriation of a plaintiff's name or likeness may be pled by alleging: (1) the defendant's use of the plaintiff's identity; (2) the appropriation of plaintiff's name or likeness to defendant's advantage, commercially or otherwise; (3) lack of consent; and (4) resulting injury.')" [*Allison*,] 136 F.3d at 1446–47.

We cannot say that Alabama's commercial-appropriation invasion-of-privacy tort bases liability solely on commercial rather than psychological interests.... For a private person, psychological interests would likely be the main concern resulting from the appropriation of his or her likeness, even if only their family members or close friends were to recognize their likeness....

... This is not to say that a celebrity's personal interests cannot serve as a basis for a commercial-appropriation claim or that a noncelebrity's economic interests cannot serve as a basis for recovery....

Accordingly, the summary judgment entered in favor of the defendants, Ashcraft and Skin Worx, is reversed, and the cause is remanded for further proceedings.

[The other judges of the court concurred in the result.]

Notes

1. The division of invasion of privacy liability into four distinct categories was devised by Prosser, Privacy, 48 Calif. L. Rev. 383 (1960), and adopted in Restatement (Second) of Torts §§ 652A–652E (1977), for which Prosser served as reporter.

2. In Joe Dickerson & Associates, LLC v. Dittmar, 34 P.3d 995 (Colo. 2001), plaintiff sued a private investigation firm on account of an article in a free newsletter the firm distributed to financial institutions, law firms, law enforcement agencies and others. The article related that the firm had been retained to investigate plaintiff and discovered that plaintiff had taken and cashed bearer bonds belonging to a client of her employer; further investigation by the firm revealed the falsity of plaintiff's claim that she was given the bonds as a gift, and she was convicted of theft of the bonds. A photograph of plaintiff accompanied the article. The court decided that plaintiff stated a cause of action for appropriation of her name and likeness. Distinguishing claims for appropriation of the commercial value of a person's identity from claims for injury to personal feelings caused by commercial use of a person's identity, the court rejected defendant's argument that it was not liable because plaintiff presented no evidence that her name and likeness had commercial value. As plaintiff's claim was for mental suffering rather than commercial damages, proof that plaintiff's name or likeness had commercial value would not be required. However, the court held that the use of plaintiff's name and picture in this instance was privileged under the First Amendment because the article was a newsworthy and "predominantly noncommercial" account of plaintiff's crime and conviction. As such, it could be published without liability not only in a newspaper but also by a publication produced by defendant for a profit motive. Compare Morse v. Studin, 283 A.D.2d 622, 725 N.Y.S.2d 93 (2001), holding a plastic surgeon liable for including "before and after" photographs of a patient in a newsletter that was found to be a solicitation for patronage.

3. A real estate broker negotiates the sale of a large house. After the purchasers move into it, an advertisement for the broker features the sale of the house. The house's appointments, its address, the purchase price and the purchasers' names are mentioned. Has the privacy of the purchasers been violated? Cf. Bisbee v. John C. Conover Agency, Inc., 186 N.J. Super. 335, 452 A.2d 689 (App. Div. 1982). An advertisement for dog food identifies plaintiff, a blind girl, as the prospective donee of a seeing-eye dog. It contains a photograph of her. This is done without plaintiff's consent and she has no need for the dog, having already acquired one. Claiming to have suffered humiliation and mental anguish, plaintiff sues the manufacturer of the dog food. Has she a cause of action? See Eick v. Perk Dog Food Co., 347 Ill. App. 293, 106 N.E.2d 742 (1952) (yes). If she accepted the dog, could the donation be publicized without obtaining her consent? Cf. Canessa v. J.I. Kislak, Inc., 97 N.J. Super. 327, 235 A.2d 62 (Law Div. 1967) (defendant reprinted newspaper article on large family that for years could not find housing until defendant's real estate salesman assisted family in purchasing home).

4. Is it an invasion of privacy for a magazine to sell its subscription list to direct mail advertisers without the subscribers' consent? The court in Shibley v. Time, Inc., 45 Ohio App. 2d 69, 341 N.E.2d 337 (1975), found no invasion of privacy, even assuming that buyers of the lists were able to draw conclusions about the financial position, social habits and personality of the listed subscribers. The right of privacy did not extend to the mailbox. Should a credit card company be liable for selling to merchants the names and addresses of cardholders with particular spending habits? See Dwyer v. American Express Co., 273 Ill. App. 3d 742, 652 N.E.2d 1351 (1995), appeal denied, 165 Ill. 2d 549, 662 N.E.2d 423 (1996), which reasons that the name of an individual cardholder has little or no value other than the value given to it by the credit card company in identifying and aggregating cardholders' spending traits. Cf. Remsburg v. Docusearch, Inc., 149 N.H. 148, 816 A.2d 1001 (2003) (sale of personal information by investigator not appropriation because value not derived from person's commercial or social standing). See generally Annot., Invasion of Privacy by Sale or Rental of List of Customers, Subscribers, or the Like, to One Who Will Use It for Advertising Purposes, 82 A.L.R.3d 772 (1978).

5. Plaintiff leads an expedition to the Arctic. The expenses of the expedition are to be borne in part by a news service which films the expedition and hopes to recoup some of the expenses through distribution of the film. Defendant also takes motion pictures of the expedition, planning to sell them in competition with the films of the news service. Is this actionable? See Smith v. Suratt, 7 Alaska 416 (1926) (injunction denied; expedition was of public nature and interest and its members were public characters). If a magazine offers for sale a photograph that has been published in the magazine, does it violate the privacy of the person or persons in the photograph? See Mendonsa v. Time Inc., 678 F. Supp. 967 (D.R.I. 1988) (famous "kissing sailor" photograph taken at end of World War II). What if photographs of plaintiff are sold by defendant *to* the news media? See Holmes v. Underwood & Underwood, Inc., 225 App. Div. 360, 233 N.Y.S. 153 (1929); Barrows v. Rozansky, 111 A.D.2d 105, 489 N.Y.S.2d 481 (1985). In Li Yau-wai v. Genesis Films Ltd., [1987] H.K.L.R. 711 (High Ct.), plaintiff's photograph was used in a ribald film to depict the late husband of one of the film's main characters. Would this be actionable under American law?

6. Most of the major informational and entertainment media are commercial in nature, and in many the informational or entertainment content appears adjacent to or in between commercial advertising. Is there an actionable invasion of privacy if the content of such a publication makes more than "incidental" use of someone's name, likeness or identity? Claims of "commercial appropriation" in these circumstances are usually rejected. See Jenkins v. Dell Publishing Co., 251 F.2d 447 (3d Cir. 1958), cert. denied, 357 U.S. 921 (1958) (magazine article); Dempsey v. National Enquirer, 702 F. Supp. 934 (D. Me. 1989) (tabloid newspaper article); Brooks v. American Broadcasting Companies, Inc., 737 F. Supp. 431 (N.D. Ohio 1990), vacated, 932 F.2d 495 (6th Cir. 1991) (television broadcast); Gautier v. Pro-Football, Inc., 304 N.Y. 354, 107 N.E.2d 485 (1952) (television broadcast).

7. In Finger v. Omni Publications International, Ltd., 77 N.Y.2d 138, 564 N.Y.S.2d 1014, 566 N.E.2d 141 (1990), a magazine used a photograph of a large family (two adults and their six children) to illustrate a story reporting that research at the University of Pennsylvania indicated that *in vitro* fertilization rates may be enhanced by exposing sperm to high concentrations of caffeine. The caption beneath the photograph read "Want a big family? Maybe your sperm needs a cup of Java in the morning...." The family in the photograph had no involvement with *in vitro* fertilization or the research at the University of Pennsylvania. The New York privacy statute had been interpreted to include the use of a

person's picture to illustrate an article when the illustration had "no real relationship" to the article. Otherwise, putting aside cases in which an article was "an advertisement in disguise," there was no liability under the statute for publications concerning newsworthy events or matters of public interest. Interpreting the magazine article to relate to fertility in general rather than only to caffeine-enhanced *in vitro* fertilization, the court found a "real relationship" between the family in the photograph and the theme of the article. The family members' action against the magazine's publisher was therefore dismissed.

8. Advertising for a book, film, broadcast or issue of a magazine or newspaper frequently includes the name or picture of persons who are depicted or written about. Is there liability if the persons concerned have not given their consent to the advertising? It is generally held that this is a permissible use of a person's name or likeness. See Groden v. Random House, Inc., 61 F.3d 1045 (2d Cir. 1995); Almeida v. Amazon.com, Inc., 456 F.3d 1316 (11th Cir. 2006); Lawrence v. A.S. Abell Co., 299 Md. 697, 475 A.2d 448 (1984); Leddy v. Narragansett Television, L.P., 843 A.2d 481 (R.I. 2004); Stern v. Delphi Internet Services Corp., 165 Misc. 2d 21, 626 N.Y.S.2d 694 (Sup. Ct. 1995) (radio celebrity's name and photograph used in print media advertisements for defendant's on-line computer service, which included "bulletin board" on celebrity's candidacy for governor of state). It is, however, actionable to use a person's name or likeness in advertising when the work being advertised actually does not involve the person at all. See Lerman v. Chuckleberry Publishing, Inc., 496 F. Supp. 1105 (S.D.N.Y. 1980) (pornographic magazine falsely stated in text and on cover that celebrity was in photograph in magazine); Tellado v. Time-Life Books, Inc., 643 F. Supp. 904 (D.N.J. 1986) (photograph of plaintiff used in advertising for book series, although not included in books).

9. It also appears to be actionable for commercial advertising to reproduce the text of a news article that includes plaintiff's name or photograph. See Fanelle v. Lojack Corp., 29 Media L. Rptr. 1513 (E.D. Pa. 2000) (manufacturer of anti-theft device used newspaper article about police raid on car theft operation, in which plaintiff was arrested, in its promotional literature; police had recovered stolen car and then gathered evidence for raid because car was equipped with device); Flores v. Mosler Safe Co., 7 N.Y.2d 276, 196 N.Y.S.2d 975, 164 N.E.2d 853 (1959) (advertisement for fire-proof safes used newspaper article, with "eye-catching" photograph, on building fire accidentally started by plaintiff and another man). Cf. Reilly v. Rapperswill Corp., 50 A.D.2d 342, 377 N.Y.S.2d 488 (1975) (television news report on insulation products used in film distributed by insulation manufacturer; action brought by television journalists seen in film).

10. Liability for the other three categories of invasion of privacy is limited by a requirement that the invasion be "highly offensive to a reasonable person." Restatement (Second) of Torts §§ 652B, 652D, 652E (1977). Does this factor have any bearing on liability for appropriation of a person's name, likeness or identity? In Bitsie v. Walston, 85 N.M. 655, 515 P.2d 659 (Ct. App. 1973), cert. denied, 85 N.M. 639, 515 P.2d 643 (1973), an artist had photographed an eighteen-month-old Navajo Indian child with the consent of her father. The artist prepared from the photograph a sketch printed on note cards sold to raise funds for a cerebral palsy association. A photograph of the sketch appeared in a newspaper story publicizing the sale of the cards. The court decided that the child had no action against the artist, charity or newspaper. It applied a rule that there is liability only for conduct that a defendant should have realized would offend "persons of ordinary sensibilities." There was evidence that publication of plaintiff's likeness in connection with an ailment was offensive to New Mexico's traditional Navajos, who believed that this "wished her harm." The majority of the court would not equate offense to a group holding a traditional belief with offense to "persons of ordinary sensibilities," which

encompassed the state community as a whole. "Ordinary sensibilities" is rejected as a criterion of liability in Canessa v. J.I. Kislak, Inc., supra.

Uhlaender v. Henricksen
United States District Court, District of Minnesota
316 F. Supp. 1277 (1970)

NEVILLE, District Judge.

Presented to the court is the question as to whether some several hundred Major League Baseball Players, appearing in this action by one such individual player and by an unincorporated association of major league baseball players have a proprietary or property interest in their names, sporting activities and accomplishments so as to enable them to enjoin the use thereof for commercial purposes by private entrepreneurs engaged in the manufacture of parlor or table games which employ and use their names and sports accomplishments....

Defendants manufacture and sell games called "Negamco's Major League Baseball" and "Big League Manager Baseball." These employ the names and professional statistical information such as batting, fielding, earned run and other averages of some 500 to 700 major league baseball players, identified by team, uniform number, playing position and otherwise....

It is clear to the court that the use of the baseball players' names and statistical information is intended to and does make defendants' games more salable to the public than otherwise would be the case. Counsel for plaintiff Association of Major League Baseball Players, an unincorporated association, testified that the association was formed in 1966 to represent the major league baseball players' common interest and that this association is authorized by all but a handful of major league baseball players to act for them in marketing and licensing the use of group names or for group endorsement purposes. The association does not represent players insofar as they desire to make or have made individual product or other endorsements. The Association now represents over 850 major league baseball players and to date it has issued some 27 different licensing contracts or agreements for group licenses, including four or five other parlor game manufacturers, calling for payments of 5% of gross sales with a minimum royalty of $2,500 per year. These agreements generated over $400,000 income in 1969 all of which is distributed equally, and not according to prominence or excellence in accomplishments, to the various player members. As far back as January, 1967 the plaintiff association wrote defendants notifying them that they were exploiting a claimed property right and offering to enter into a licensing agreement. Defendants have consistently refused to do so....

Defendants do not deny that they are using the names as alleged. They assert, however, (1) that there is nothing offensive nor demeaning about the way the names are used ... (2) that the names and statistics concerning sports achievements used in the game are readily available to anyone at Major League offices on inquiry, are published with some regularity in the newspapers and news media and are thus in the public domain; (3) baseball players seek and are anxious for publicity which defendants' games tend to further....

The defendants insist upon characterizing this action as one involving an alleged invasion of the right of privacy. The complaint however does not predicate its claim for relief upon any assertion of a right to be let alone. Instead, plaintiffs claim "misappropriation and use for commercial profit of the names of professional major league baseball players without the payment of royalties." ...

Although misappropriation of one's name, likeness or personality for commercial use has been considered as one species of the general tort of invasion of privacy, many authorities suggest that misappropriation is a distinctly independent tort. The reasoning behind this approach is that Prosser's [other three categories of invasion of privacy] involve the incidence of specific personal harm (i. e., injury to feelings), while [this category] is generally considered to involve a pecuniary loss, an interference with *property*....

However misappropriation is classified, recent cases illustrate that there may be substantive importance in distinguishing it from torts involving invasion of the plaintiff's "right to be let alone." In O'Brien v. Pabst Sales Co., 124 F.2d 167 (5th Cir. 1941), cert. denied 315 U.S. 823 (1942), a famous football player alleged that the defendant had used his photograph for certain commercial purposes without his consent. The complaint claimed damages for invasion of privacy. While the Court recognized the existence at common law of such an action, it affirmed the trial court's directed verdict for defendant because plaintiff had failed to establish direct injury to his personal feelings. The court went on to state that its decision on that claim would not affect: "The right of a person to recover on quantum meruit, for the use of his name in advertising. That was not the case pleaded and attempted to be brought. The case was not for the value of plaintiff's name in advertising a product but for damages by way of injury to him in using his name in advertising beer."

In Canessa v. J.I. Kislak, Inc. [97 N.J. Super. 327, 235 A.2d 62 (1967)] plaintiffs sued defendants to recover damages for the unauthorized appropriation by defendant of their pictures, names, and elements of their personalities and private lives in connection with the defendant's republication for commercial purposes of a news article in which they had appeared. The court stated, *inter alia*, "Plaintiffs' names and likenesses belong to them. As such they are property. They are things of value."

A logical extension of the concept that misappropriation of one's name or public personality is a compensable trespass to property has been the recognition of the so-called "right of publicity." It has been held that the exclusive licensee of the right to exploit a celebrity's name, likeness or personality has a proprietary interest (a "right of publicity"), assignable in gross to the extent permitted under the original licensing agreement with the celebrity.

Since the authorities recognize a cause of action for misappropriation of a name, likeness or personality that is not dependent upon an invasion of privacy in the technical sense, the only issue before the court is whether the plaintiffs' names and published statistics can be considered property subject to legal protection from unauthorized use.

A history of the successful licensing of such names and statistics by the plaintiff association to other game manufacturers obviously does not establish that plaintiffs have any such legal right....

In Haelan Laboratories, Inc. v. Topps Chewing Gum, 202 F.2d 866 (2nd Cir. 1953), cert. denied 346 U.S. 816 (1953), defendant Topps induced baseball players to grant it a license to distribute picture cards of the players with its product, an act which violated an exclusive licensing agreement in existence between the plaintiff and the same players for the commercial use of their pictures. In this action between the competing licensees, the dispositive issue was whether this licensed right to use the players' likenesses was a proprietary interest subject to legal protection. In reversing the trial court's dismissal of the complaint for failure to state a claim, the Second Circuit held specifically that "a man has a right in the publicity value of his photograph."

Sharman v. C. Schmidt & Sons, Inc., 216 F. Supp. 401 (E.D. Pa. 1963), involved a suit by a well-known professional basketball player to enjoin the allegedly unauthorized use of his picture in connection with the distribution of defendant's product. The court ruled against plaintiff's claims of defamation and invasion of privacy on the basis of its interpretation of a release executed pursuant to a contract licensing Sharman's photograph to certain agencies, but stated that "a sports figure can complain when his name or likeness is used to advertise a product.... Public figures in the celebrity category have a valuable property right in their name and image." Thus, as in O'Brien v. Pabst Sales Co., *supra*, a court ruling against a "public personality" plaintiff who sued on the inappropriate theory expressly recognized that such a person has a property right in the commercial value of his name, likeness, and public personality....

It is this court's view that a celebrity has a legitimate proprietary interest in his public personality. A celebrity must be considered to have invested his years of practice and competition in a public personality which eventually may reach marketable status. That identity, embodied in his name, likeness, statistics and other personal characteristics, is the fruit of his labors and is a type of property.

Defendants' contention has no merit that by the publication in the news media and because of the ready availability to anyone of the names and statistical information concerning the players, such information is in the public domain and the players thus have waived their rights to relief in this case. Such argument may or may not have some weight against a right of privacy claim, but in an appropriation action such as in the case at bar the names and statistics are valuable only because of their past public disclosure, publicity and circulation. A name is commercially valuable as an endorsement of a product or for use for financial gain only because the public recognizes it and attributes good will and feats of skill or accomplishments of one sort or another to that personality. To hold that such publicity destroys a right to sue for appropriation of a name or likeness would negate any and all causes of action, for only by disclosure and public acceptance does the name of the celebrity have any value at all to make its unauthorized use enjoinable.

It seems clear to the court that a celebrity's property interest in his name and likeness is unique, and therefore there is no serious question as to the propriety of injunctive relief. Defendants have violated plaintiffs' rights by the unauthorized appropriation of their names and statistics for commercial use. The remedy at law, considering particularly the difficulty in determining and measuring damages, past or future, is inadequate....

Notes

1. Does a cause of action for "invasion of privacy" properly lie in favor of a person who courts publicity? A person who agrees to use of his name or photograph in advertisements? If so, should damages be awarded for interference with the person's ability to market his fame to best advantage, or should damages be limited to the embarrassment and emotional distress for which a private person is compensated? Can a solid basis of liability be found in a source other than the "right to privacy"? If one accepts that it is tortious to appropriate a celebrity's name or likeness for use in advertising or product packaging, is it also tortious to appropriate a celebrity's name or likeness for use in a product or service?

2. Short biographies and playing charts of twenty-three famous golfers are included in a game. Should the game's manufacturer be liable to the golfers? See Palmer v. Schonhorn Enterprises, Inc., 96 N.J. Super. 72, 232 A.2d 458 (Ch. Div. 1967) (invasion of golfers'

privacy found; defendant capitalizing on fruits of plaintiffs' labors in commercial project other than dissemination of news or information). In Rosemont Enterprises, Inc. v. Urban Systems, Inc., 72 Misc. 2d 788, 340 N.Y.S.2d 144 (Sup. Ct. 1973), modified, 42 A.D.2d 544, 345 N.Y.S.2d 17 (1973), defendants marketed and distributed an "adult educational career" game entitled "The Howard Hughes Game." It was based upon the biographical data of the famous but reclusive billionaire Howard Hughes. The court denied defendants' motion for summary judgment, finding a violation of the New York privacy statute.

3. If the baseball players in *Uhlaender* had licensed the use of their names and statistics in a game, without including advertising in the license, would they have an action for use of their names and playing histories in advertising for the game? Would baseball players who licensed the production of trading cards with their names, photographs and statistics have an action if the cards were reproduced in advertising for the sale of the cards when new, or for sale by subsequent owners? What if such cards or licensed photographs are incorporated into other products, such as framed plaques, not included in the license? Allison v. Vintage Sports Plaques, 136 F.3d 1443 (11th Cir. 1998), holds that the right of publicity is limited by the "first-sale doctrine" applied to intellectual property rights. Once an item is sold with the consent of the right's holder, the holder has no right to control the distribution or disposition of the item. The recipient is free to sell the item without liability for infringement of the right of publicity. See also Diavoco, Going Once, Going Twice, Sold: The First Sale Doctrine Defense in Right of Publicity Actions, 12 U. Miami Ent. & Sports L. Rev. 57 (1995). Would there be an action if players' names or photographs were used to advertise a package tour that included tickets to games in which the players were expected to participate? Cf. Carson v. National Bank of Commerce Trust and Savings, 501 F.2d 1082 (8th Cir. 1974) (tour to Las Vegas that included nightclub performance by Johnny Carson).

4. Publishers, broadcasters and web site proprietors may enhance their revenues by inviting their audiences to participate in polls and surveys. Participation sometimes involves payment. If the subject of a poll is the popularity of an entertainment celebrity, is there a tortious appropriation of the celebrity's personality? See New Kids on the Block v. News America Publishing, Inc., 745 F. Supp. 1540 (C.D. Cal. 1990), aff'd, 971 F.2d 302 (9th Cir. 1992) (no liability for fee-generating telephone poll on celebrities' popularity because connected to news gathering and reporting). A land developer decides to name a street after a local or national celebrity, to both honor the celebrity and cater to the desire of some people to live on a street with a famous name. If the celebrity has not consented to this, is there any action against the developer? If not, can businesses on the street freely use the street's name as part of their businesses' names?

5. The freedom to use a person's name or picture in advertising a publication, broadcast or film involving the person has been applied to the right of publicity as well as appropriation of name or likeness claims (see p. 397, supra). In Page v. Something Weird Video, 960 F. Supp. 1438 (C.D. Cal. 1996), the court held there was no liability for using the name and likeness of an actress in advertising sales of cassettes of two films in which the actress starred and defendants' film series as a whole. There can, however, be liability when the advertising makes a false association between what is being advertised and plaintiff. The actor Clint Eastwood recovered damages for publication in *The National Enquirer* of what purported to be an "exclusive interview" article, when actually he had never spoken to the *Enquirer*. Eastwood v. National Enquirer, Inc., 123 F.3d 1249 (9th Cir. 1997). In Cher v. Forum International, Ltd., 692 F.2d 634 (9th Cir. 1982), cert. denied, 462 U.S. 1120 (1983), advertising for a magazine which published an interview with the entertainer Cher falsely stated that she had told the magazine

things she would not tell a rival publication. The magazine's advertisements also asked people to join Cher as well as hundreds of thousands of others in reading the magazine. The advertisements were held to appropriate Cher's right of publicity and entitle her to compensatory and punitive damages. Because of the falsity element and plaintiffs' public figure status, proof of defendant's knowledge or reckless disregard of the falsity may be required, by analogy to the constitutional rule for defamation and "false light" actions. Cf. Lerman v. Flynt Distributing Co., Inc., 745 F.2d 123 (2d Cir. 1984), cert. denied, 471 U.S. 1054 (1985) (false statements that nude photographs in magazine were of plaintiff).

6. Should an otherwise sustainable claim for using plaintiff's name or likeness in advertising fail if the text of the advertisement accurately reports an actual connection between plaintiff and the product or service being advertised? In Nature's Way Products, Inc. v. Nature-Pharma, Inc., 736 F. Supp. 245 (D. Utah 1990), defendants had purchased an herbal products business founded by Dr. John Christopher, a well-known author and lecturer on herbal medicine. Dr. Christopher then formed a new corporation, which purportedly held his trademarks and formulas. A second company claimed to have purchased from Dr. Christopher exclusive rights to use Dr. Christopher's name and endorsement in the selling of herb products. These two entities sued defendants for stating in their advertising that Dr. Christopher was the founder of their business, that they sold herbal products based on formulas developed by him, and other uses of his name. The court held that plaintiffs stated a cause of action for violation of Dr. Christopher's right of publicity. Defendants were subject to liability for use of "historical information" to market a product that did not incorporate the information itself, as would a book or article dealing with the life of Dr. Christopher. See also Town & Country Properties, Inc. v. Riggins, 249 Va. 387, 457 S.E.2d 356 (1995) (not violation of First Amendment to hold real estate broker liable for advertising house as former home of sports celebrity).

7. Does a critic have a cause of action if for commercial purposes he is quoted in praise of a book, play, film or work of art? Does this depend upon whether the quotation truly represents the critic's opinion? In the case of a book, could a distinction be drawn between quotations in the book's preface, on its jacket, or in separate advertising? In Thompson v. G.P. Putnam's Sons, 40 Misc. 2d 608, 243 N.Y.S.2d 652 (Sup. Ct. 1963), a literary critic sued a publisher because the introductory note to *Memoirs of a Woman of Pleasure* quoted him out of context and thereby implied that he thought the work had literary merit. His actual opinion was that the *Memoirs* were "tediously and bewilderingly pornographic." The suit survived a motion to dismiss. Compare Groden v. Random House, Inc., 61 F.3d 1045 (2d Cir. 1995), in which a photograph of plaintiff and a quotation from his book were included in advertising for a book that criticized plaintiff's theories, and Rand v. Hearst Corp., 31 A.D.2d 406, 298 N.Y.S.2d 405 (1969), aff'd, 26 N.Y.2d 806, 309 N.Y.S.2d 348, 257 N.E.2d 895 (1970), in which a book publisher used a reviewer's statement that the "underlying drive" and "mystique analysis" of the author were the same as those of plaintiff, a much more famous writer.

8. The organizers of a new political party, nominating candidates for state office, use a presidential candidate's name as part of their party's name without the candidate's consent. Can he prevent this? See State ex rel. La Follette v. Hinkle, 131 Wash. 86, 229 P. 317 (1924) (unauthorized use of person's name presumed to damage him; writ issued to strike presidential candidate's name from state party name on ballot). Cf. State ex rel. La Follette v. Hinkle, 131 Wash. 695, 229 P. 320 (1924) (unauthorized use of presidential candidate's name by party nominating presidential electors). Would it be tortious to use a statement by a candidate or other contemporary political leader in commercial advertising?

Carson v. Here's Johnny Portable Toilets, Inc.

United States Court of Appeals, Sixth Circuit
698 F.2d 831 (1983)

BAILEY BROWN, Senior Circuit Judge....

Appellant, John W. Carson (Carson), is the host and star of "The Tonight Show," a well-known television program broadcast five nights a week by the National Broadcasting Company. Carson also appears as an entertainer in night clubs and theaters around the country. From the time he began hosting "The Tonight Show" in 1962, he has been introduced on the show each night with the phrase "Here's Johnny." This method of introduction was first used for Carson in 1957 when he hosted a daily television program for the American Broadcasting Company. The phrase "Here's Johnny" is generally associated with Carson by a substantial segment of the television viewing public. In 1967, Carson first authorized use of this phrase by an outside business venture, permitting it to be used by a chain of restaurants called "Here's Johnny Restaurants."

Appellant Johnny Carson Apparel, Inc. (Apparel), formed in 1970, manufactures and markets men's clothing to retail stores. Carson, the president of Apparel and owner of 20% of its stock, has licensed Apparel to use his name and picture, which appear on virtually all of Apparel's products and promotional material. Apparel has also used, with Carson's consent, the phrase "Here's Johnny" on labels for clothing and in advertising campaigns. In 1977, Apparel granted a license to Marcy Laboratories to use "Here's Johnny" as the name of a line of men's toiletries. The phrase "Here's Johnny" has never been registered by appellants as a trademark or service mark.

Appellee, Here's Johnny Portable Toilets, Inc., is a Michigan corporation engaged in the business of renting and selling "Here's Johnny" portable toilets. Appellee's founder was aware at the time he formed the corporation that "Here's Johnny" was the introductory slogan for Carson on "The Tonight Show." He indicated that he coupled the phrase with a second one, "The World's Foremost Commodian," to make "a good play on a phrase."

Shortly after appellee went into business in 1976, appellants brought this action alleging unfair competition, trademark infringement under federal and state law, and invasion of privacy and publicity rights. They sought damages and an injunction prohibiting appellee's further use of the phrase "Here's Johnny" as a corporate name or in connection with the sale or rental of its portable toilets.

... The [district] court ordered the dismissal of the appellants' complaint. On the unfair competition claim, the court concluded that the appellants had failed to satisfy the "likelihood of confusion" test....

... Although the appellee had intended to capitalize on the phrase popularized by Carson, the court concluded that appellee had not intended to deceive the public into believing Carson was connected with the product. The court noted that there was little evidence of actual confusion and no evidence that appellee's use of the phrase had damaged appellants. For these reasons, the court determined that appellee's use of the phrase "Here's Johnny" did not present a likelihood of confusion, mistake, or deception.

... The general concept underlying the likelihood of confusion is that the public believe that "the mark's owner *sponsored or otherwise approved* the use of the trademark." *Warner Bros., Inc. v. Gay Toys, Inc.,* 658 F.2d 76, 79 (2d Cir. 1981) (emphasis added).

The facts as found by the district court do not implicate such likelihood of confusion, and we affirm the district court on this issue....

We do not believe that Carson's claim that his right of privacy has been invaded is supported by the law or the facts. Apparently, the gist of this claim is that Carson is embarrassed by and considers it odious to be associated with the appellee's product. Clearly, the association does not appeal to Carson's sense of humor. But the facts here presented do not, it appears to us, amount to an invasion of any of the interests protected by the right of privacy. In any event, our disposition of the claim of an invasion of the right of publicity makes it unnecessary for us to accept or reject the claim of an invasion of the right of privacy....

The district court dismissed appellant's claim based on the right of publicity because appellee does not use Carson's name or likeness. It held that it "would not be prudent to allow recovery for a right of publicity claim which does not more specifically identify Johnny Carson." We believe that, on the contrary, the district court's conception of the right of publicity is too narrow. The right of publicity ... is that a celebrity has a protected pecuniary interest in the commercial exploitation of his identity. If the celebrity's identity is commercially exploited, there has been an invasion of his right whether or not his "name or likeness" is used. Carson's identity may be exploited even if his name, John W. Carson, or his picture is not used....

[Defendant's owner selected the name "Here's Johnny" because of its identification with Carson.]

... [A]ppellants are entitled to judgment. The proof showed without question that appellee had appropriated Carson's identity in connection with its corporate name and its product....

... [A] celebrity's legal right of publicity is invaded whenever his identity is intentionally appropriated for commercial purposes.... It is not fatal to appellant's claim that appellee did not use his "name." Indeed, there would have been no violation of his right of publicity even if appellee had used his name, such as "J. William Carson Portable Toilet" or the "John William Carson Portable Toilet" or the "J.W. Carson Portable Toilet." The reason is that, though literally using appellant's "name," the appellee would not have appropriated Carson's identity as a celebrity. Here there was an appropriation of Carson's identity without using his "name."

... Carson's achievement has made him a celebrity which means that his identity has a pecuniary value which the right of publicity should vindicate. Vindication of the right will tend to encourage achievement in Carson's chosen field. Vindication of the right will also tend to prevent unjust enrichment by persons such as appellee who seek commercially to exploit the identity of celebrities without their consent....

[Vacated and remanded. Kennedy, Circuit Judge, delivered a dissenting opinion. The court subsequently affirmed a judgment awarding damages and enjoining defendant from using the phrase "Here's Johnny" anywhere in the United States. 810 F.2d 104 (1987).]

Landham v. Lewis Galoob Toys, Inc.
United States Court of Appeals, Sixth Circuit
227 F.3d 619 (2000)

BATCHELDER, Circuit Judge.

Landham is a fringe actor who has played supporting roles in several motion pictures, including *48 Hours*, *Action Jackson*, and *Maximum Force*. as well as several unrated, pornographic films. This suit concerns the role of "Billy, the Native American Tracker," that Landham portrayed in Fox's 1987 action film *Predator*.... In 1995, Fox licensed to Galoob the rights to produce and market a line of its "Micro Machines" toys based on *Predator*. One of these three sets of toys contained a "Billy" action figure. Because the toy is only 1.5 inches tall and has no eyes or mouth, it bears no personal resemblance to Landham. Moreover, Eric Shank, the Galoob employee who designed the toy, purposely avoided any such resemblance. Nonetheless, Landham argues that the toy violates his right of publicity under Kentucky law and amounts to a false endorsement under the Lanham Act. The district court disagreed, finding insufficient evidence to suggest that consumers would associate the toy with Landham....

Before addressing the substance of Landham's claim, we must address Galoob's jurisdictional objection that Landham's claim is preempted by the federal Copyright Act merely because the claim involves a copyrighted work—in this case, *Predator*....

Landham's claim is not preempted by the Copyright Act. The Supreme Court has recognized that rights of publicity are generally consistent with the Copyright Act. *See* [*Zacchini v. Scripps-Howard Broadcasting Co.*, p. 421, *infra*]. As long as a plaintiff states a claim of invasion of personal, state-law rights that are distinct from copyright protections, the claim will not be preempted. Unlike the baseball player-plaintiffs in *Baltimore Orioles, Inc. v. Major League Baseball Players Assoc.*, 805 F.2d 663 (7th Cir. 1986), Landham is not claiming the right of publicity in order to gain rights in the telecast of his performance, or to contest Fox's right to create derivative works from its copyrighted work in general. Rather, he claims that the toy evokes his personal identity—an inchoate "idea" which is not amenable to copyright protection—to his emotional and financial detriment. Regardless of the merits of this claim, it does assert a right separate from those protected by the Copyright Act. *See* [*Wendt v. Host Int'l, Inc.*, 125 F.3d 806, 809 (9th Cir. 1997)] (claim that animatronic robots "look like" plaintiff and thereby evoke his identity in violation of his right of publicity is not preempted); *cf. Midler v. Ford Motor Co.*, 849 F.2d 460, 462 (9th Cir. 1988) (distinctive sound of celebrity's voice is not protected by copyright)....

The right of publicity is designed to reserve to a celebrity the personal right to exploit the commercial value of his own identity.... Landham correctly argues that he need not be a national celebrity to prevail. But in order to assert the right of publicity, a plaintiff must demonstrate that there is value in associating an item of commerce with his identity....

To succeed, then, Landham must show that a merchant would gain significant commercial value by associating an article of commerce with him. He presented no such evidence to the district court. Landham argues vigorously on appeal that Galoob's use of Landham's identity is itself sufficient evidence of commercial value. But this argument assumes that by identifying its toy as "Billy," Galoob has evoked Landham's identity in the public mind.

Although the right began as a protection for a celebrity's "name and likeness," *i.e.*, physical features, it is now generally understood to cover anything that suggests the plaintiff's personal identity....

What is not as clear, however, is the point at which the identity of a fictional character becomes so synonymous with the identity of the actor playing the role that the actor may challenge the character's exploitation. If the use of a fictional character also evokes the identity of the actor who played that character, he may challenge that use regardless of the fact that the actor's personal notoriety was gained exclusively through playing that role. *See Wendt*, 125 F.3d at 811 (reversing summary judgment against two actors from the TV series *Cheers* who challenged the use of animatronic bar patrons modeled after their characters in *Cheers*-themed airport bars); [*McFarland v. Miller*, 14 F.3d 912 (3d Cir. 1994)] at 920 (reversing summary judgment against George McFarland, who played "Spanky" in *Our Gang*, in suit against owner of the restaurant "Spanky McFarland's"). Courts have generally been careful, however, to draw the line between the character's identity and the actor's, siding with plaintiffs only when it is shown that the two personalities are inseparable in the public's mind. *See* [*Lugosi v. Universal Pictures*, 25 Cal. 3d 813, 160 Cal. Rptr. 323, 603 P.2d 425 (1979)] at 432 (Mosk, J., concurring) (explaining that actors have no inherent right in their roles, although those who play themselves or characters of their own creation may).... [A]lthough exploitation of a fictional character may, in some circumstances, be a means of evoking the actor's identity as well, the focus of any right of publicity analysis must always be on the actor's own persona and not the character's.

One case that may be read to depart significantly from this rule, and one upon which Landham heavily relies, is *White v. Samsung Electronics America, Inc.*, 971 F.2d 1395 (9th Cir. 1982). There, an advertiser humorously evoked a futuristic version of the game show *Wheel of Fortune* through an animatronic replica of its hostess, Vanna White. The robot bore no facial resemblance to White, but it was adorned with a blond wig, jewelry and clothing similar to White's typical ensemble, and in her familiar pose turning the game board's letters. Although none of these factors individually suggested White, the court found that, taken together, they clearly evoked her identity. The dissenting judge argued that the majority had confused White, the person, with her TV role, and that the only element of the commercial that was unique to her was the *Wheel of Fortune* set, which was not part of her personal identity. *See id.* at 1404–05 (Alarcon, J., dissenting). Three other judges on the circuit agreed.... *White v. Samsung Elecs. Am., Inc.*, 989 F.2d 1512 (9th Cir. 1993) (Kozinki, J., dissenting from denial of rehearing en banc). The judges warned of the dangers of overextending intellectual property laws, noting that it is impossible to evoke a movie or TV show without evoking the identities of its actors to some extent....

We decline Landham's invitation to extend *White* to this case. First, the holding is factually distinguishable, as White used her own name in her television role, and also produced evidence that her identity was invoked and had commercial value. More importantly, we share, as we think the Kentucky courts would, Judge Kozinsky's unwillingness to give every individual who appears before a television or movie camera, by occupation or happenstance, the right as a matter of law to compensation for every subtle nuance that may be taken by someone as invoking his identity without first being required to prove significant commercial value and identifiability. Such a holding would upset the careful balance that courts have gradually constructed between the right of publicity and the First Amendment and federal intellectual property laws, undermining the right's viability....

In sum, Landham has not demonstrated — either through direct evidence or by virtue of Galoob's use of the "Billy" character — that his persona has "significant commercial value" or that the "Billy" toy invokes his own persona, as distinct from that of the fictional character. For these reasons, we affirm the district court's grant of summary judgment to Defendants on this claim.

[The court also affirmed grant of summary judgment on the Lanham Act claim, saying that "Our findings on the right of publicity issue dictate the outcome of this claim as well." Landham had offered no evidence that he had recognition among the toy-buying public. Consequently, there was no showing that the consuming public was likely to be confused about whether Landham endorsed Galoob's "Billy" toy.]

Notes

1. *Preemption of state law by federal copyright law.* Under 17 U.S.C. § 301, a person cannot claim under state law "rights that are equivalent to any of the exclusive rights within the general scope of copyright." Federal law applies when, with the authority of the "author," a work is "fixed" in "a tangible medium of expression." This applies to a wide variety of literary, dramatic and artistic works and visual and sound recordings. 17 U.S.C. §§ 101–102. Exclusive copyright rights include reproduction of the copyrighted work, distribution of copies, public display or performance of the work, and preparation of derivative works. 17 U.S.C. § 106. Therefore, if plaintiff's privacy or publicity complaint involves reproduction or imitation of something that was "fixed" with plaintiff's consent, as in a photograph or recording, an argument of preemption seems apposite, provided the complaint can be equated with an assertion of copyright rights. However, the tort claims have generally survived preemption arguments when the claims did not conflict with the rights of a copyright holder. See, e.g., Brown v. Ames, 201 F.3d 654 (5th Cir. 2000), cert. denied sub nom. Collectibles, Inc. v. Brown, 531 U.S. 925 (2000); Downing v. Abercrombie & Fitch, 265 F.3d 994 (9th Cir. 2001); KNB Enterprises v. Matthews, 78 Cal. App. 4th 362, 92 Cal. Rptr. 2d 713 (2000). Restatement of Unfair Competition § 46, comment *i* (1995), asserts that the subject matter of the right of publicity generally lies outside the scope of copyright because copyright does not extend to a person's name, likeness, voice or other identifying characteristics. Should preemption be avoided by differentiating protection of likeness or identity from protection of the tangible embodiments of a celebrity's likeness or identity? Or by differentiating celebrity value from the rewards of copying or exhibiting creative endeavors?

2. In the *Carson* case, the court drew support for its decision from Hirsch v. S.C. Johnson & Son, Inc., 90 Wis. 2d 379, 280 N.W.2d 129 (1979), and Motschenbacher v. R.J. Reynolds Tobacco Co., 498 F.2d 821 (9th Cir. 1974). In the former, defendant used the name "Crazylegs" for a women's shaving gel. This led to a suit by "Crazylegs" Hirsch, who was known by this nickname in his successful sports career. The court held that Hirsch had a cause of action for appropriation of his name. It also sustained an action for "tradename infringement," finding ample evidence of likely confusion about plaintiff's sponsorship of the product. In *Motschenbacher*, a television commercial used a picture of the car of a noted racing driver. The car's distinctive decorations were included but alterations were made and there was no recognizable likeness of the driver. The court found that the driver and his car could be identified and found a cause of action for appropriation of the driver's "identity."

3. In Booth v. Colgate-Palmolive Co., p. 361, supra, a well-known actress portrayed in a television series a character created in a cartoon strip. This character was subsequently used in a television commercial cartoon, with a voice that imitated plaintiff's. Did this infringe plaintiff's right of privacy or publicity? The court thought not. As the commercial was anonymous and did not use plaintiff's name or likeness or identify her as the source of the voice, rights in her name, likeness, personality, etc. were not infringed. However, in Midler v. Ford Motor Co., 849 F.2d 460 (9th Cir. 1988), a celebrated singer whose distinctive voice and rendition of a popular song were imitated in a television commercial was held to have a cause of action for "appropriation of the attributes of one's identity." See also Waits v. Frito-Lay, Inc., 978 F.2d 1093 (9th Cir. 1992), cert. denied, 506 U.S. 1080 (1993) (imitation of singer's voice in radio commercial).

4. Compare Lombardo v. Doyle, Dane & Bernbach, Inc., 58 A.D.2d 620, 396 N.Y.S.2d 661 (1977). Over a forty-year period the band leader Guy Lombardo had developed a reputation as "Mr. New Year's Eve." A car manufacturer's television commercial portrayed a New Year's Eve party with a band leader whose gestures, musical beat and choice of music imitated Lombardo's. (Defendant planned to have Lombardo himself perform in the commercial but substituted an actor when negotiations with Lombardo fell through.) It was held (3–2) that Lombardo did not have an action under the New York privacy statute. His name or picture had not been used. However, he could maintain suit on the basis of the "common-law property right in one's public personality." This would be violated by an unfair imitation that caused deception of the public. The common law right identified by the court appears to be a right under the law of passing off (unfair competition). When there is commercial use of an attribute other than name or likeness, is there any reason to grant a remedy that is not afforded by the law of unfair competition? When a name or likeness is used in commerce, an action derived from the law of passing off as well as an action derived from the right of privacy may lie — provided that use of plaintiff's name or likeness represents a connection with the product or service being marketed and thereby causes or will cause damage. See pp. 263–304, supra.

5. Does a person who writes under a *nom de plume* or the name of a character he has created have an exclusive right to use that name? See Sykes v. John Fairfax & Sons Ltd., [1977] 1 N.S.W.L.R. 415 (Sup. Ct.) where a journalist who wrote a newspaper's investment column invented "Pierpont" as the purported author of the column. A dispute about the right to this name arose when the journalist ceased working for the newspaper's publisher. The court stated that an exclusive right in the journalist probably could be recognized only if he established both that he was the inventor and user of the name and that he had acquired a reputation in it — that is, that the name was associated in the minds of readers with a particular author, though they might be unaware of his true identity. Here, the journalist was found to have met both requirements. Cf. Bi-Rite Enterprises, Inc. v. Button Master, p. 303, supra (unauthorized sale of buttons bearing names and logos of rock groups violated group members' right of publicity).

6. If a picture is taken of someone's real or personal property and is published without explicitly identifying the owner, can this be invasion of the owner's privacy? In addition to Motschenbacher v. R.J. Reynolds Tobacco Co., supra, see Rawls v. Conde Nast Publications, Inc., 446 F.2d 313 (5th Cir. 1971), cert. denied, 404 U.S. 1038 (1972) (advertisement with picture of interior of plaintiff's house); Bayer v. Ralston Purina Co., 484 S.W.2d 473 (Mo. 1972) (advertisement with picture of plaintiff's registered Appaloosa horse). See generally Annot., Invasion of Privacy by Use of a Picture of Plaintiff's Property for Advertising Purposes, 87 A.L.R.3d 1279 (1978) (use of photograph of person's property generally not invasion of privacy unless there is something unique about property, apparent from photograph, that identifies owner).

7. Suppose a photograph taken of plaintiff is used in an advertisement, but plaintiff's face is not shown and few, if any, persons other than plaintiff and defendant identify plaintiff as the person photographed. Is there a cause of action? What must be proved? See Cohen v. Herbal Concepts, Inc., 63 N.Y.2d 379, 482 N.Y.S.2d 457, 472 N.E.2d 307 (1984).

8. Under Restatement of Unfair Competition § 46 (1995), the right of publicity is violated when one "appropriates the commercial value of a person's identity by using without consent the person's name, likeness, or other indicia of identity for purposes of trade"; intent to infringe the right of publicity is not required for liability, but it is relevant to whether a monetary remedy will be granted.

Memphis Development Foundation v. Factors Etc., Inc.

United States Court of Appeals, Sixth Circuit
616 F.2d 956 (1980), cert. denied, 449 U.S. 953 (1980)

MERRITT, Circuit Judge.

This appeal raises the interesting question: Who is the heir of fame? The famous have an exclusive legal right during life to control and profit from the commercial use of their name and personality. We are called upon in this diversity case to determine whether, under Tennessee law, the exclusive right to publicity survives a celebrity's death....

[In exchange for royalties, the singer Elvis Presley conveyed to Boxcar Enterprises the exclusive right to exploit the commercial value of his name and likeness. Presley's manager was the majority shareholder of Boxcar. Presley and Boxcar's president were the mi-

ELVIS PRESLEY STATUE   William M. Roberts

nority shareholders. Two days after Presley's death, Boxcar sold to Factors Etc. a license to use this right. Presley's father agreed to the sale on behalf of Presley's estate. The Memphis Development Foundation, a non-profit corporation, laid plans to erect a large bronze statue of Presley in Memphis. Public contributions were solicited to pay for the statue. Donors of $25 or more received an eight-inch pewter replica of the proposed statue from the Foundation. Factors Etc. claimed that the Foundation was selling the statues for $25 apiece and infringing its rights as assignee of Presley's "right of publicity." The district court held that Factors Etc. had an exclusive right to exploit Presley's name and likeness. It issued an injunction which allowed the Foundation to build the Presley memorial but prohibited the Foundation from manufacturing, selling or distributing any statuette bearing the image or likeness of Presley or utilizing commercially the name, image, photograph or likeness of Presley.]

Recently, a few cases have characterized the right of publicity as property which may be passed on to heirs or assigns. In addition, a recent law journal article advocates recognition of such a right after death where a person has exploited his fame during life by assigning it to an agent or otherwise entering into a contract for its use. The theory is that the law should recognize that "the possibility of providing for one's heirs may have a motivational effect during one's life." Assignment during life is the touchstone because "if no contract has been created, the identification of ... harm is ... difficult" and evidently "such concerns were not a substantial motivation." The article thus distinguishes between "the unrealized potential ability of a person to profit from his attributes," an interest insufficient to establish an inheritable right, and the conscious exploitation of the right during life, the continuation of which after death fulfills "the social policy of encouraging individual creativity." Felcher & Rubin, *Privacy, Publicity, and the Portrayal of Real People by the Media*, 88 Yale L.J. 1577, 1618–19 (1979)....

Recognition of a post-mortem right of publicity would vindicate two possible interests: the encouragement of effort and creativity, and the hopes and expectations of the decedent and those with whom he contracts that they are creating a valuable capital asset. Although fame and stardom may be ends in themselves, they are normally by-products of one's activities and personal attributes, as well as luck and promotion. The basic motivations are the desire to achieve success or excellence in a chosen field, the desire to contribute to the happiness or improvement of one's fellows and the desire to receive the psychic and financial awards of achievement. As John Rawls has written, such needs come from the deep psychological fact that the individuals want the respect and good will of other persons and "enjoy the exercise of their realized capacities (their innate or trained abilities), and this enjoyment increases the more the capacity is realized, or the greater its complexity." ... *A Theory of Justice* 426–27 (1971).

Fame is an incident of the strong motivations that Rawls describes. The desire to exploit fame for the commercial advantage of one's heirs is by contrast a weak principle of motivation. It seems apparent that making the right of publicity inheritable would not significantly inspire the creative endeavors of individuals in our society.

On the other hand, there are strong reasons for declining to recognize the inheritability of the right. A whole set of practical problems of judicial line-drawing would arise should the courts recognize such an inheritable right. How long would the "property" interest last? In perpetuity? For a term of years? Is the right of publicity taxable? At what point does the right collide with the right of free expression guaranteed by the first amendment? Does the right apply to elected officials and military heroes whose fame was gained on the public payroll, as well as to movie stars, singers and athletes? Does the right cover posters or engraved likenesses of, for example, Farah Fawcett Majors or Mahatma Gandhi, kitchen utensils ("Revere Ware"), insurance ("John Hancock"), electric utilities ("Edison"), a football stadium ("RFK"), a pastry ("Napoleon"), or the innumerable urban subdivisions and apartment complexes named after famous people? Our legal system normally does not pass on to heirs other similar personal attributes even though the attributes may be shared during life by others or have some commercial value. Titles, offices and reputation are not inheritable. Neither are trust or distrust and friendship or enmity descendible. An employment contract during life does not create the right for heirs to take over the job. Fame falls in the same category as reputation; it is an attribute from which others may benefit but may not own.

The law of defamation, designed to protect against the destruction of reputation including the loss of earning capacity associated with it, provides an analogy. There is no right of action for defamation after death. The two interests that support the inheritability of the right of publicity, namely, the "effort and creativity" and the "hopes and expectations" of the decedent, would also support an action for libel or slander for destruction of name and reputation after death. Neither of these reasons, however, is sufficient to overcome the common law policy terminating the action for defamation upon death.

Fame often is fortuitous and fleeting. It always depends on the participation of the public in the creation of an image. It usually depends on the communication of information about the famous person by the media. The intangible and shifting nature of fame and celebrity status, the presence of widespread public and press participation in its creation, the unusual psychic rewards and income that often flow from it during life and the fact that it may be created by bad as well as good conduct combine to create serious reservations about making fame the permanent right of a few individuals to the exclusion of the general public. Heretofore, the law has always thought that leaving a good name to one's children is sufficient reward in itself for the individual, whether famous or not. Commercialization of this virtue after death in the hands of heirs is contrary to our legal tradition and somehow seems contrary to the moral presuppositions of our culture.

There is no indication that changing the traditional common law rule against allowing heirs the exclusive control of the commercial use of their ancestor's name will increase the efficiency or productivity of our economic system. It does not seem reasonable to expect that such a change would enlarge the stock or quality of the goods, services, artistic creativity, information, invention or entertainment available. Nor will it enhance the fairness of our political and economic system. It seems fairer and more efficient for the commercial, aesthetic, and political use of the name, memory and image of the famous to be open to all rather than to be monopolized by a few. An equal distribution of the opportunity to use the name of the dead seems preferable. The memory, name and pictures of famous individuals should be regarded as a common asset to be shared, an economic opportunity available in the free market system.

These same considerations also apply to the Presley assigns' more narrow argument based on the fact that Presley entered into contracts during his life for the commercial use of his image. It is true that the assignment of the right of publicity during life shows that Presley was aware of the value of the asset and intended to use it. The assignment also suggests that he intended to convert a mere opportunity or potential for profit into a tangible possession and consciously worked to create the asset with, perhaps, the hope of devising it.

The question is whether the specific identification and use of the opportunity during life is sufficient to convert it into an inheritable property right after death. We do not think that whatever minimal benefit to society may result from the added motivation and extra creativity supposedly encouraged by allowing a person to pass on his fame for the commercial use of his heirs or assigns outweighs the considerations discussed above.

[Reversed and remanded.]

Notes

1. There have been conflicting decisions on whether the right of publicity survives a person's death and passes to his heirs or assignees. The Second Circuit held that the right was descendible and Factors Etc. could obtain an injunction against the sale of an Elvis Presley "memorial poster." Factors Etc., Inc. v. Pro Arts, Inc., 579 F.2d 215 (2d Cir. 1978), cert. denied, 440 U.S. 908 (1979). The court subsequently ruled that the case was governed by Tennessee law and conformed to the decision in the principal case. 652 F.2d 278 (2d Cir. 1981), cert. denied, 456 U.S. 927 (1982). Some authority holds that the right of publicity survives when it was exploited by the decedent during his lifetime. Whether this means that the decedent must have used his fame to market goods or services other than those that made him a celebrity is in dispute. In Groucho Marx Productions, Inc. v. Day and Night Co., Inc., p. 419, infra, the district court, applying New York law, held that Groucho, Chico and Harpo Marx met the exploitation requirement through appearances in and promotions of their performances as the Marx Brothers characters. The Court of Appeals held that the applicable law was that of California, under which the right of publicity was either not descendible at all or descendible only in connection with "particular commercial situations — products and services" that a celebrity promoted with his name or likeness during his lifetime. Compare Hicks v. Casablanca Records, p. 413, infra (Agatha Christie exploited name by use in connection with her literary works and derivative plays and films), and Acme Circus Operating Co., Inc. v. Kuperstock, 711 F.2d 1538 (11th Cir. 1983) (under California law, Clyde Beatty's right of publicity survived with respect to Clyde Beatty Circus). Some authority holds that the right of publicity survives whether or not the decedent commercially exploited it during his lifetime. See Martin Luther King, Jr., Center for Social Change, Inc. v. American Heritage Products, Inc., 250 Ga. 135, 296 S.E.2d 697 (1982) (defendants created and sold busts of deceased civil rights leader; heirs had action to prevent this). See generally Annot., Right to Deceased Person's Name or Likeness as Inheritable, 10 A.L.R.4th 1192 (1981).

2. One of the leading cases involved the actor Bela Lugosi. He played the title role in the 1931 film *Dracula* and was identified with Count Dracula for the rest of his life. Following Lugosi's death, the company that produced the film granted licenses to various commercial firms to make use of the Dracula character. The firms were authorized to use the likeness of Dracula, as portrayed by Lugosi, in such products as masks, model figures, T-shirts, games, soap, pencil sharpeners and beverage stirrers. Lugosi had never granted or authorized any license of this type. He had not used his name or likeness as Dracula in connection with any product or business. Lugosi's widow and son sought damages and an injunction. The Supreme Court of California adopted the position that the general right to control exploitation of one's name or likeness did not survive death. Accordingly, the action failed. Bird, C.J., in a lengthy dissent, advanced the view that the right to control exploitation of a name or likeness survived even when there was no commercial exploitation during the person's lifetime, but it should be terminated after a defined period of years. Lugosi v. Universal Pictures, 25 Cal. 3d 813, 160 Cal. Rptr. 323, 603 P.2d 425 (1979).

3. Schuyler v. Curtis, 27 Abb. N.C. 387, 15 N.Y.S. 787 (Sup. Ct. 1891), aff'd, 64 Hun 594, 19 N.Y.S. 264 (Sup. Ct. 1892), subsequent proceedings, 147 N.Y. 434, 42 N.E. 22

(1895), involved a Mrs. Schuyler, who had worked tirelessly for many philanthropic causes but kept out of the public eye. Fourteen years after her death, a group proposed to erect a statue of her entitled "Typical Philanthropist," to be placed at an exposition next to the statue of a woman designated as the "Typical Reformer" (Susan B. Anthony, whose activities Mrs. Schuyler did not approve). Neither Mrs. Schuyler nor her family ever consented to the statue. Members of the family sought an injunction. The first court favored an injunction because Mrs. Schuyler had not become a "public character" during her lifetime. The second court asserted that the action could be maintained even if she was a public character. The New York Court of Appeals ordered dismissal of the complaint. It declared that Mrs. Schuyler's aversion to publicity died with her and erection of the statue furnished no reasonable ground for distress in her relatives. This case arose before general acceptance of an enforceable right of privacy. What should be the position if a similar case arose today?

4. If a film exploits the life of a person after the person's death, should his family have an action for invasion of the deceased person's privacy or their own? See Maritote v. Desilu Productions, Inc., 345 F.2d 418 (7th Cir. 1965), cert. denied, 382 U.S. 883 (1965) (television series *The Untouchables* used name of Al Capone in dramatizations of fictional events; action by Capone's widow and son dismissed); James v. Screen Gems, Inc., 174 Cal. App. 2d 650, 344 P.2d 799 (1959) (allegedly falsified film about deceased son of famous outlaw; son's widow, who was not portrayed in film, could not recover).

5. A Tennessee state court has decided that the right of publicity is descendible. State ex rel. Elvis Presley International Memorial Foundation v. Crowell, 733 S.W.2d 89 (Tenn. App. 1987). It reasoned that this promotes several policies "deeply ingrained in Tennessee's jurisprudence": recognition of the individual's right of testamentary disposition, protection of the decedent's investment in creating capital assets that he expects will benefit heirs and assigns after death, maintenance of the value of contract rights, prevention of deception of the public concerning sponsorship and approval of goods or services, and the unjust enrichment principle that "one may not reap when another has sown nor gather where another has strewn." A considerable number of states have now enacted statutes providing for a survivable right of publicity or privacy. E.g., Cal. Civil Code § 3344.1; Fla. Stat. Ann. § 540.08; Ind. Stat. Ann. §§ 32-36-1-1 et seq.; Nev. Rev. Stat. §§ 597.770–597.810; 12 Okla. Stat. § 1448; Tex. Prop. Code Ann. §§ 26.001–26.015.

6. A corporation or other entity cannot maintain an action for commercial appropriation of its name or identity because the action, as a branch of the law of privacy, serves only to protect natural persons. Felsher v. University of Evansville, 755 N.E.2d 589 (Ind. 2001). Does the same rule apply to an action for violation of the right of publicity? See Bear Foot, Inc. v. Chandler, 965 S.W.2d 386 (Mo. App. 1998) (corporation has no right of publicity of its own; whether corporation could maintain action as assignee not decided).

Hicks v. Casablanca Records

United States District Court, Southern District of New York
464 F. Supp. 426 (1978)

PIERCE, District Judge.

Plaintiffs, the heir and assignees of the late Agatha Christie, seek an order enjoining the defendant movie producers, Casablanca Records, Filmworks, First Artists and Warner Brothers (hereinafter referred to as the "movie case") from distributing or showing the motion picture "Agatha". Plaintiffs, in a related case, similarly seek an order enjoining defendant publisher, Ballantine Books (hereinafter referred to as the "book case") from distributing or making the book *Agatha* available to the public....

Plaintiffs' decedent and assignor was the late Dame Agatha Christie, one of the best known mystery writers in modern times. Her career spanned five decades until her death in 1976, and culminated in the production of scores of mystery novels, not the least famous of which are *Murder on the Orient Express* and the short story, "Witness for the Prosecution." Although Mrs. Christie attempted to shun publicity with respect to her personal life, professionally, she cultivated the name "Agatha Christie" in such a way as to make it almost synonymous with mystery novels. Thus, during her life, she agreed to the use of her name in connection with various motion pictures and plays based on her works. Upon her death, the rights in her works descended to plaintiff, Rosalind Christie Hicks, Mrs. Christie's sole legatee, and plaintiffs, Agatha Christie, Ltd. and William Collins Sons & Co., Ltd., her assignees.

In the winter of 1977, defendants in the movie case began the filming of a movie entitled, "Agatha" which, like the book in the related case, presents a fictionalized account of a true incident which occurred during the life of Mrs. Christie. The book [also entitled "Agatha"] is scheduled for distribution shortly....

It appears that on or about December 4, 1926, Mrs. Christie, then married to Colonel Archibald Christie, disappeared from her home in England. This disappearance was widely-publicized and, although a major effort was launched to find her, everyone was at a loss to explain her disappearance. However, eleven days after she was reported missing, Mrs. Christie reappeared, but her true whereabouts and the reasons for her disappearance are, to this day, a mystery.

In view of the death of Mrs. Christie, the public may never know the facts surrounding this incident, but should the defendants prevail herein, the public will have a fictionalized account of this disappearance as set forth in the movie and in the book. In each instance, Mrs. Christie is portrayed as an emotionally unstable woman, who, during her eleven-day disappearance, engages in a sinister plot to murder her husband's mistress, in an attempt to regain the alienated affections of her husband. Given this portrayal of their decedent and assignor, plaintiffs, mindful of the personal nature of defamation and privacy actions, bring the instant actions alleging ... infringement of the right of publicity.

... [In *Factors Etc., Inc. et al. v. Pro Arts, Inc. et al.*, 579 F.2d 215 (2d Cir. 1978)] the Court found that the right of publicity, i. e., the right in the publicity value of one's name or likeness, is a valid property right which is transferable and capable of surviving the death of the owner. However, the Court went on to state that this interest survives only if it is found that the owner "exploited" the right during his or her lifetime. While the *Factors* opinion does not define "exploitation", it would appear that a party claiming the right must establish that the decedent acted in such a way as to evidence his or her own recognition of the extrinsic commercial value of his or her name or likeness, and manifested that recognition in some overt manner, *e. g.*, making an *inter vivos* transfer of the rights in the name, or posing for bubble gum cards.

In applying the *Factors* analysis to the cases at bar, this Court finds for purposes of the present motions that plaintiffs have established that Mrs. Christie assigned rights to her literary works to plaintiff, Agatha Christie Ltd., and also bequeathed similar rights by testamentary disposition. The Court notes that this evidence, when considered together with evidence of contracts entered into by Mrs. Christie for the use of her name during

BERKSHIRE CONSTABULARY, WOKINGHAM DIVISION.

9th. December 1926.

MISSING

From her home "Styles" Sunningdale in this Division.

Mrs. Agatha Mary Clarissa CHRISTIE

(WIFE OF COLONEL A. CHRISTIE)

AGE 35 YEARS, HEIGHT 5 ft. 7 ins., HAIR RED (Shingled), NATURAL TEETH, EYES GREY, COMPLEXION FAIR, WELL BUILT.

DRESSED—Grey Stockingette Skirt, Green Jumper, Grey and dark Grey Cardigan, small Green Velour Hat, may have hand bag containing £5 to £10. Left home in 4 seater Morris Cowley car at 9.45 p.m. on 3rd. December leaving note saying she was going for a drive. The next morning the car was found abandoned at Newlands Corner, Albury, Surrey.

Should this lady be seen or any information regarding her be obtained please communicate to any Police Station, or to

CHARLES GODDARD, Superintendent,

Telephone No. 11 Wokingham. **WOKINGHAM.**

PRINTED AT THE "BERKSHIRE GAZETTE" OFFICES, PEACH STREET, WOKINGHAM.

AGATHA CHRISTIE MISSING POSTER   Berkshire Record Office her lifetime in connection with movies and plays based on her books, sufficiently establishes "exploitation". Thus, it seems clear as it pertains to the present motions that her right of publicity survived her death and was properly transferred to the plaintiffs as her heirs and assignees.

However, unlike the *Factors* case, our inquiry here does not end upon this finding that plaintiffs possess valid property rights. Here, the Court is faced with the novel and rather complex question of "whether the right of publicity attaches where the name or likeness is used in connection with a book or movie?" The question is novel in view of the fact that more so than posters, bubble gum cards, or some other such "merchandise", books and movies are vehicles through which ideas and opinions are disseminated and, as such, have enjoyed certain constitutional protections, not generally accorded "merchandise." It is complex because this Court is unaware of any other cases presenting a similar fact pattern or similar constitutional question with respect to this issue of the right of publicity.... [J]udicial interpretations with respect to the limits of the right of privacy could be helpful in determining the limitations, if any, to be placed on the right of publicity.

The New York privacy statute, Civil Rights Law § 51, provides in pertinent part: "Any person whose name, portrait or picture is used within this state for advertising purposes or for the purposes of trade without the written consent first obtained ... may maintain an equitable action...." In interpreting this provision, the New York State Supreme Court, Appellate Division, has held that: "engrafted upon [the statute are] certain privileged uses or exemptions ... [*i. e.*] matters of news, history, biography, and other factual subjects of public interest despite the necessary references to the names, portraits, identities, or histories of living persons." *Spahn v. Julian Messner, Inc.*, 23 A.D.2d 216, 219, 260 N.Y.S.2d 451, 453 (1st Dep't 1965). This Court finds that the same privileges and exemptions "engrafted" upon the privacy statute are engrafted upon the right of publicity.

In addressing defendants' argument that the book *Agatha* is a biography protected under *Spahn*, this Court, while noting that the affidavit of the author of the book details her investigation with respect to the "facts" surrounding the disappearance, finds the book to be fiction, not biography. Indeed, defendant Ballantine Books' use of the word "novel" on the cover of the book, as well as the notable absence of any cited source or reference material therein, belie its contention that the book is a biography. Moreover, the only "facts" contained in the book appear to be the names of Mrs. Christie, her husband, her daughter, and Ms. Neeley; and that Mrs. Christie disappeared for eleven days. The remainder is mainly conjecture, surmise, and fiction. Accordingly, the Court finds that the defendants in both cases cannot avail themselves of the biography privilege in connection with the book or movie. Further since the book and the movie treat these few scant facts about the disappearance of Mrs. Christie as mere appendages to the main body of their fictional accounts, neither can be considered privileged as "fair comment" or as "newsworthy"; or historical.

Thus, finding none of the *Spahn* privileges available to the defendants herein, the Court must next inquire as to whether the movie or the novel, as fictionalizations, are entitled to any constitutional protection. In so doing, it is noted that other courts, in addressing the scope of first amendment protections of speech, have engaged in a balancing test between society's interest in the speech for which protection is sought and the societal, commercial or governmental interests seeking to restrain such speech. And unless there appears to be some countervailing legal or policy reason, courts have found the exercise of the right of speech to be protected.... Here, this Court is of the opinion that the interests in the speech sought to be protected, *i. e.*, the movie and the novel, should be protected and that there are no countervailing legal or policy grounds against such protection.

... The *Spahn* case, like the book case here, involved the distribution of a book which was presented by the defendant as being a biography of the well-known baseball player Warren Spahn. However, presented in the book were deliberate falsifications of events represented to be true, manufactured dialogue, and erroneous statistical data. Defendant argued that his material was presented in an effort to make the book more attractive to youngsters. Plaintiff sued on the ground that the book constituted a violation of his right of privacy under §51. The New York Court of Appeals agreed, stating: "We hold in conformity with our policy of construing sections 50 and 51 so as to fully protect free speech, that, before recovery by a public figure may be had for an unauthorized presentation of his life it must be shown, in addition to the other requirements of the statute, that the presentation is infected with *material and substantial falsification ... or with a reckless disregard for the truth." Spahn v. Julian Messner, Inc.*, 21 N.Y.2d 124, 127, 286 N.Y.S.2d 832, 834, 233 N.E.2d 840, 842 (1967) (emphasis supplied).

[*University of Notre Dame Du Lac v. Twentieth Century-Fox Film Corp.*, 22 A.D.2d 452, 256 N.Y.S.2d 301 (1965), *aff'd*, 15 N.Y.2d 940, 259 N.Y.S.2d 832, 207 N.E.2d 508 (1965)] involved the distribution of a movie, entitled, "John Golfarb, Please Come Home" which satirized modern-day events, people, and institutions, including a football team, identified as that of Notre Dame. Notre Dame University and its president, Father Hesburg, brought suit against the defendant pursuant to the New York Civil Rights Act and the common law on unfair competition. The Appellate Division, in denying the relief requested, stated: ... "Defendants argue that injunctive relief would violate the First Amendment, but that is an issue we do not reach. It is permissible to express praise or derision of a college's athletic activities in a journal of news or opinion. If such a journal, a novel and a photoplay are on a parity in law as media of expression, extension of the doctrine of unfair competition to interdict praise or derision by means of the novel or photoplay would seem without justification. Social cost may properly be considered in these matters ... and the granting of an injunction in this case would outlaw large areas heretofore deemed permissible subject matter for literature and the arts...."

In applying the holdings of these two cases to those at bar, it would appear that the later decided *Spahn* case—which curiously did not cite *Notre Dame*—would dictate the result herein. However, upon closer scrutiny of *Spahn*, this court is of the opinion that the *Spahn* holding should be and was intended to be limited to its facts, and that the result here should follow the holding in the *Notre Dame* case.... [T]he Court in *Spahn* stressed the fact that the lower court had found that the defendant had engaged in deliberate falsifications of the circumstances surrounding the life of plaintiff and that such falsifications, which the reader might accept as true, were capable of presenting plaintiff in a false light. Thus, the Court of Appeals in *Spahn* balanced the plaintiff's privacy rights against the first amendment protection of fictionalization *qua* falsification and, after finding there to be no such protection, held for the plaintiff. Conversely, in the *Notre Dame* case, the Appellate Division, as affirmed by the New York Court of Appeals, found that the defendant had not represented the events in the movie to be true and that a viewer of the film would certainly know that the circumstances involved therein were fictitious; thus, the finding for the defendants.

It is clear from the review of these two cases that the absence or presence of deliberate falsifications or an attempt by a defendant to present the disputed events as true, determines whether the scales in this balancing process, shall tip in favor of or against protection of the speech at issue. Since the cases at bar are more factually similar to the *Notre Dame* case, *i. e.*, there were no deliberate falsifications alleged by plaintiffs, and the reader of the novel in the book case by the presence of the word "novel" would know that the work was fictitious, this Court finds that the first amendment protection usually accorded novels and movies outweighs whatever publicity rights plaintiffs may possess and for this reason their complaints must be dismissed.

Accordingly, the Court finds that the right of publicity does not attach here, where a fictionalized account of an event in the life of a public figure is depicted in a novel or a movie, and in such novel or movie it is evident to the public that the events so depicted are fictitious....

Notes

1. In the *Spahn* case, discussed in the *Hicks* opinion, the plaintiff—the famous baseball pitcher Warren Spahn—ultimately prevailed. The New York Court of Appeals held that an action would lie for a biography published, without the subject's permission, in an intentionally fictionalized manner—with imaginary incidents, manufactured dialogue, and a manipulated chronology—so as to appeal to juvenile readers. It was no justification that the literary technique used was customary in children's books or that the dialogue was assertedly based upon probable facts, the author's research having consisted mainly of using newspaper and magazine clippings. However, because plaintiff was a public figure, it was necessary to establish defendant's knowledge of falsity or reckless disregard of the truth. Also, the presentation had to be "infected with material and substantial falsification." Compare Matthews v. Wozencraft, 15 F.3d 432 (5th Cir. 1994) (no liability to public figure for novel fictionalizing events in "public domain"); Restatement of Unfair Competition § 47, comment *c* (1995) (when work contains substantial falsifications, liability should be determined by law of defamation and false light privacy).

2. In Guglielmi v. Spelling-Goldberg Productions, 25 Cal. 3d 860, 160 Cal. Rptr. 352, 603 P.2d 454 (1979), a nephew of the film star Rudolph Valentino sued on account of the film *Legend of Valentino: A Romantic Fiction*. The nephew claimed that the film, which was advertised with Valentino's name and likeness, was a fictionalized portrayal of Valentino's life. The action failed on the ground that Valentino's right of publicity died with him. Bird, C.J., concurred on the ground that a work of fiction was not an actionable infringement of the right of publicity. For works of fiction, as for works of fact, the value of free expression outweighed the "proprietary interests" protected by the right of publicity. Concern for freedom of expression and the fact that the title was related to the film's plot led the court in Rogers v. Grimaldi, 875 F.2d 994 (2d Cir. 1989), to reject a claim that the film *Ginger and Fred*, a story about a dance couple who imitated Ginger Rogers and Fred Astaire, violated Ginger Rogers' right of publicity.

3. Should fictionalized biographies be actionable when the fictionalization is not readily apparent to the readers or audience? When the readers or audience might erroneously conclude that the work has been authorized by its subject? See the dissent from dismissal of the complaint in the *Notre Dame* case, University of Notre Dame Du Lac v. Twentieth Century-Fox Film Corp., 15 N.Y.2d 940, 259 N.Y.S.2d 832, 207 N.E.2d 508 (1965). Can "docudramas" be made without the consent of the persons portrayed in them? See Taylor v. National Broadcasting Co. Inc., 22 Media L. Rptr. 2433 (Cal. Super. Ct. 1994) (television mini-series about life of Elizabeth Taylor; preliminary injunction against use of her name and image denied; "expressive" rather than "commercial" speech and therefore protected against "prior restraint"); Manson, The Television Docudrama and the Right of Publicity, 7 Comm. & L. No. 1, 41 (1985). What if a living public figure is made a prominent character in a novel that mixes fact and fiction? See Marcinkus v. NAL Publishing Inc., 138 Misc. 2d 256, 522 N.Y.S.2d 1009 (Sup. Ct. 1987).

4. Beginning with Haelan Laboratories, Inc. v. Topps Chewing Gum, Inc., 202 F.2d 866 (2d Cir. 1953), cert. denied, 346 U.S. 816 (1953), courts identified in New York law a common law right of publicity independent of New York's statutory right of privacy. It was this common law right that was assignable and survived death. In Stephano v. News Group Publications, Inc., 64 N.Y.2d 174, 485 N.Y.S.2d 220, 474 N.E.2d 580 (1984), the New York Court of Appeals held that the right of publicity was "encompassed under the Civil Rights Law as an aspect of the right of privacy." Plaintiff could not claim an independent common law right.

Groucho Marx Productions, Inc. v. Day and Night Company, Inc.

United States District Court, Southern District of New York
523 F. Supp. 485 (1981), rev'd, 689 F.2d 317 (2d Cir. 1982)

CONNER, District Judge.

[Plaintiffs sued the producers of a musical play that had a successful run on Broadway, *A Day in Hollywood/A Night in the Ukraine*. The producers brought the play's authors into the litigation as third-party defendants. The second ("Ukraine") half of the play portrayed the way the Marx Brothers would have dramatized Chekhov's novel *The Bear*. Though the names of the Marx Brothers were not used, the script called for the three principal performers to reproduce the appearance and comedy style made memorable by Groucho, Chico and Harpo Marx. Plaintiffs sought damages "in the nature of a license fee" on the ground that exhibition of the play violated their "exclusive rights of publicity relating to the commercialization of the characters of Groucho, Chico and Harpo." One plaintiff, the widow of Adolph "Harpo" Marx, claimed the right of publicity in relation to "Harpo" on the basis that she was the trustee of the residuary trust under his will. The other plaintiff, Groucho Marx Productions, claimed the right of publicity in relation to "Groucho" on the basis that Julius "Groucho" Marx had assigned to it "all right, title and interest in the name, likeness and style of the character Groucho, both as an individual and as a member of the Marx Brothers." This plaintiff's claims in relation to "Chico" were based upon a similar assignment by the widow of Leo "Chico" Marx as the residuary beneficiary of his will.*]

[The court decided that New York law recognized a right of publicity that survived a celebrity's death if it was exploited during his lifetime. The exploitation requirement was interpreted to mean action by the celebrity that demonstrated an intent to capitalize on the commercial value of his name and likeness. It did not require commercial "tie-ups" outside the celebrity's major activity, such as the endorsement of products or services. The requirement was satisfied in the present case because "the Marx Brothers' fame arose as a direct result of their efforts to develop instantly recognizable and popular stage characters, having no relation to their real personalities.... Every appearance, contract and advertisement involving the Marx Brothers signified recognition by the performers of the commercial value of the unique characters they portrayed." Also, Julius Marx had demonstrated recognition of and intent to capitalize on the value of the character Groucho by

---

* This statement of facts is taken in part from the Court of Appeals' opinion. [Ed.]

Chico, Harpo and Groucho Marx   Photofest

making an *inter vivos* transfer of his rights and by including a disposition of his rights in his will.]

Defendants contend that the first amendment protects dramatic performances of literary works and therefore plaintiffs' claim of infringement of the right of publicity must fail. Unquestionably, first amendment interests must be considered in defining the scope of the right.... Although "entertainment ... enjoys First Amendment protection," the purpose or function of such entertainment must be scrutinized in determining the scope of the right of publicity.

As a general rule, if the defendants' works are designed primarily to promote the dissemination of thoughts, ideas or information through news or fictionalization, the right of publicity gives way to protected expression. If, however, the defendants' use of the celebrity's name or likeness is largely for commercial purposes, such as the sale of merchandise, the right of publicity prevails....

... [L]iterary works, including fictionalizations, are entitled to protection. By analogy to copyright law and the fair use doctrine, parody, burlesque, satire and critical review might be immune from the right of publicity because of their contribution as entertainment and as a form of literary criticism. In contrast to an imitator, who usurps a work for commercial gain without contributing substantially to the work, a commentator, parodist or satirist makes use of another's attributes in order to create a larger presentation.

Defendants contend that the play is a parody of the Marx Brothers' performance and cite reviews of the play terming it a "spoof," "compendium" and "parody." Defendants also rely on the affidavit of Richard Vosburgh, author of the play and a third-party defendant here, stating that his intention was to write a satiric comment on Hollywood movies using a parody of the Marx Brothers movies as one of the literary devices.

Applying the principles discussed above to the present case, I find as a matter of law that the defendants' production of the play is not protected expression.... Although entertainment can merit first amendment protection, entertainment that merely imitates "even if skillfully and accurately carried out, does not really have its own creative component and does not have a significant value as pure entertainment." *Estate of Elvis Presley v. Russen*, 513 F. Supp. at 1359.

Although literary commentary may have been the intent of the playwright, any such intent was substantially overshadowed in the play itself by the wholesale appropriation of the Marx Brothers characters. Under the fair use doctrine in copyright law, a parodist is entitled to "conjure up" the original—a concept that allows the artist considerable leeway in building upon the original. Here, defendants have gone beyond merely building on the original to the point of duplicating as faithfully as possible the performances of the Marx Brothers, albeit in a new situation with original lines. The Marx Brothers themselves were a parody on life; the play does not present a parody on their parody but instead successfully reproduced the Marx Brothers' own style of humor. Although the playwright may have intended to comment "about 1930's Hollywood, its techniques, its stars and its excesses," the content of the relevant portion of the play attempts to accomplish that objective exactly as would the Marx Brothers themselves....

... The play at issue is not biographical nor can it be viewed as an attempt to convey information about the Marx Brothers themselves or about the development of their characters.

For all the reasons stated, the Court finds that defendants' production of the play is not protected and has infringed the plaintiffs' rights of publicity in the Marx Brothers characters.

[The court granted partial summary judgment in plaintiffs' favor. The Court of Appeals reversed on the ground that the applicable law was that of California, not New York, and under California law the right of publicity was either not descendible at all or descendible only in connection with "particular commercial situations—products and services" that a celebrity promoted with his name or likeness during his lifetime. See pp. 409–413, supra.]

Notes

1. In the principal case, the court heavily relied upon Estate of Presley v. Russen, 513 F. Supp. 1339 (D.N.J. 1981), in which Elvis Presley's estate sought to stop a production that featured an entertainer who imitated Presley's stage shows. The court concluded that the production was an exploitation of Presley's likeness that violated the right of publicity surviving in Presley's estate. It enjoined the use of various names, pictures and symbols related to Presley, but not the production itself. Also relied upon was the Supreme Court's decision in Zacchini v. Scripps-Howard Broadcasting Co., 433 U.S. 562 (1977), rev'g 47 Ohio St. 2d 224, 351 N.E.2d 454 (1976). A television station broadcast on a news program plaintiff's performance as a "human cannonball" at a county fair. Plaintiff had objected to the filming of his performances. He claimed damages on the ground of appropriation of his name and likeness. The Ohio court held the station had a privilege to

televise the performance as a matter of legitimate public interest. The Supreme Court reversed (5–4), holding that, while the media might have a privilege under state law, the First Amendment did not immunize broadcasters from liability for economic harm caused by showing the entirety of a performance on television. The court in *Presley* believed that a live performance by an imitator was similar to a film of a performance. Both appropriated the activity by which the original performer acquired his reputation.

2. In Sharkey v. National Broadcasting Co., 93 F. Supp. 986 (S.D.N.Y. 1950), plaintiff was a former heavyweight boxing champion who "engaged professionally in various activities in the fields of sports and entertainment." Without his consent, a television network broadcast on its program *Greatest Fights of the Century* a film of one of the fights in which plaintiff participated. This was held to give him a claim for damages under the New York statute. Plaintiff had claimed the use of his name and picture made them less valuable in his present professional activities. But see Man v. Warner Bros., Inc., 317 F. Supp. 50 (S.D.N.Y. 1970), in which a professional musician had performed before 400,000 people at the Woodstock Festival. Defendant included forty-five seconds of that performance in its widely exhibited film about the festival. It was held that the musician's voluntary appearance at the event made him newsworthy and deprived him of the right to complain that showing a film of the performance invaded his privacy. The court also reasoned that the brevity of the film segment devoted to him made any harm "*de minimis*." See generally Annot., Invasion of Privacy by Use of Plaintiff's Name or Likeness for Non-advertising Purposes, 30 A.L.R.3d 203 (1970); Annot., Invasion of Privacy by Radio or Television, 56 A.L.R.3d 386 (1974).

3. In Cardtoons, L.C. v. Major League Baseball Players Association, 95 F.3d 959 (10th Cir. 1996), the alleged violation of the right of publicity was the marketing of trading cards with caricatures of major league baseball players and parody text. The cards' humorous depictions and commentary on the players and their careers were held to be entitled to First Amendment protection. The court referred to the valuable role played by parodies, including parodies of celebrities, as social commentary, entertainment and a form of self-expression. In resolving this issue, the court could find no principled distinction between "speech" and "merchandise." Applying the rule of Comedy III Productions, Inc. v. Gary Saderup, Inc. (p. 426, infra) that there is a First Amendment-based defense to liability when a work contained "significant transformative elements," a court decided that the musicians Johnny and Edgar Winter could not prevail when they sued the publishers of a comic book series depicting the fictional characters "Johnny and Edgar Autumn." That defendants were trading on plaintiffs' likenesses and reputations to generate interest in the comic books and increase sales was said to be irrelevant to whether there was constitutional protection. Winter v. DC Comics, 30 Cal. 4th 881, 134 Cal. Rptr. 2d 634, 69 P.3d 473 (2003). However, in another case involving a comic book character based on a celebrity (the professional hockey player Tony Twist), the court rejected the proposition that there was First Amendment protection whenever there were "significant transformative elements" with "expressive" content. If use of plaintiff's identity was "predominantly a ploy to sell comic books and related products" rather than artistic or literary expression, "free speech must give way to the right of publicity." Doe v. TCI Cablevision, 110 S.W.3d 363 (Mo. 2003), cert. denied sub nom. McFarlane v. Twist, 540 U.S. 1106 (2004), subsequent proceedings sub nom. Doe v. McFarlane, 207 S.W.3d 52 (Mo. App. 2006) ($15,000,000 verdict for plaintiff affirmed). Would there be liability if a humorous greeting card uses the persona or likeness of a prominent celebrity? See Hilton v. Hallmark Cards, 599 F.3d 894 (9th Cir. 2009).

C.B.C. Distribution and Marketing, Inc. v.
Major League Baseball Advanced Media, L.P.

United States Court of Appeals, Eighth Circuit
505 F.3d 818 (2007), cert. denied, 553 U.S. 1090 (2008)

ARNOLD, Circuit Judge....

CBC sells fantasy sport products via its Internet website, e-mail, mail, and the telephone. Its fantasy baseball products incorporate the names along with performance and biographical data of actual major league players. Before the commencement of the major league baseball season each spring, participants form their fantasy baseball teams by "drafting" players from various major league baseball teams. Participants compete against other fantasy baseball "owners" who have also drafted their own teams. A participant's success, and his or her team's success, depends on the actual performance of the fantasy team's players on their respective actual teams during the course of the major league baseball season. Participants in CBC's fantasy baseball games pay fees to play and additional fees to trade players during the course of the season.

From 1995 through the end of 2004, CBC licensed its use of the names of and information about major league players from the [Major League] Baseball Players Association pursuant to license agreements that it entered into with the association in 1995 and 2002. The 2002 agreement, which superseded in its entirely the 1995 agreement, licensed to CBC "the names, nicknames, likenesses, signatures, pictures, playing records, and/or biographical data of each player" (the "Rights") to be used in association with CBC's fantasy baseball products.

In 2005, after the 2002 agreement expired, the Players Association licensed to Advanced Media, with some exceptions, the exclusive right to use baseball players' names and performance information "for exploitation via all interactive media." Advanced Media began providing fantasy baseball games on its website, MLB.com, the official website of major league baseball. It offered CBC, in exchange for a commission, a license to promote the MLB.com fantasy baseball games on CBC's website but did not offer CBC a license to continue to offer its own baseball products. This conduct by Advanced Media prompted CBC to file the present suit, alleging that it had "a reasonable apprehension that it will be sued by Advanced Media if it continues to operate its fantasy baseball games."

The district court granted summary judgment to CBC. It held that CBC was not infringing any state-law rights of publicity that belonged to major league baseball players. The court reasoned that CBC's fantasy baseball products did not use the names of major league baseball players as symbols of their identities and with an intent to obtain a commercial advantage, as required to establish an infringement of a publicity right under Missouri law (which all parties concede applies here). The district court further held that even if CBC were infringing the players' rights of publicity, the first amendment preempted those rights....

... In Missouri, "the elements of a right of publicity action include: (1) That defendant used plaintiff's name as a symbol of his identity (2) without consent (3) and with the intent to obtain a commercial advantage." *Doe v. TCI Cablevision*, 110 S.W.3d 363, 369 (Mo. 2003), *cert. denied*, 540 U.S. 1106 (2004). The parties all agree that CBC's continued use of the players' names and playing information after the expiration of the 2002 agreement was without consent. The district court concluded, however, that the evidence was insufficient to make out the other two elements of the claim....

Here, we entertain no doubt that the players' names that CBC used are understood by it and its fantasy baseball subscribers as referring to actual major league baseball players.... We think that by reasoning that "identity," rather than "mere use of a name," "is a critical element of the right of publicity," the district court did not understand that when a name alone is sufficient to establish identity, the defendant's use of that name satisfies the plaintiff's burden to show that a name was used as a symbol of identity.

It is true that with respect to the "commercial advantage" element of a cause of action for violating publicity rights, CBC's use does not fit neatly into the more traditional categories of commercial advantage, namely, using individuals' names for advertising and merchandising purposes in a way that states or intimates that the individuals are endorsing a product. But the Restatement, which the Missouri Supreme Court has recognized as authority in this kind of case, also says that a name is used for commercial advantage when it is used "in connection with services rendered by the user" and that the plaintiff need not show that "prospective purchasers are likely to believe" that he or she endorsed the product or service. Restatement (Third) of Unfair Competition § 47 & cmt. a. We note, moreover, that in Missouri, "the commercial advantage element of the right of publicity focuses on the defendant's intent or purpose to obtain a commercial benefit from use of the plaintiff's identity." *Doe*, 110 S.W.3d at 370–71. Because we think that it is clear that CBC uses baseball players' identities in its fantasy baseball products for purposes of profit, we believe that their identities are being used for commercial advantage and that the players therefore offered sufficient evidence to make out a cause of action for violation of their rights under Missouri law.

CBC argues that the first amendment nonetheless trumps the right-of-publicity action that Missouri law provides. Though this dispute is between private parties, the state action necessary for first amendment protection exists because the right-of-publicity claim exists only insofar as the courts enforce state-created obligations that were "never explicitly assumed" by CBC. *See Cohen v. Cowles Media Co.*, 501 U.S. 663, 668 (1991).

The Supreme Court has directed that state law rights of publicity must be balanced against first amendment considerations, *see Zacchini v. Scripps-Howard Broad.*, 433 U.S. 562 (1977), and here we conclude that the former must give way to the latter. First, the information used in CBC's fantasy baseball games is all readily available in the public domain, and it would be strange law that a person would not have a first amendment right to use information that is available to everyone. It is true that CBC's use of the information is meant to provide entertainment, but "[s]peech that entertains, like speech that informs, is protected by the First Amendment because '[t]he line between the informing and the entertaining is too elusive for the protection of that basic right.'" *Cardtoons, L.C. v. Major League Baseball Players Ass'n*, 95 F.3d 959, 969 (10th Cir. 1996). We also find no merit in the argument that CBC's use of players' names and information in its fantasy baseball games is not speech at all. We have held that "the pictures, graphic design, concept art, sounds, music, stories, and narrative present in video games" is speech entitled to first amendment protection. *See Interactive Digital Software Ass'n v. St. Louis County, Mo.*, 329 F.3d 954, 957 (8th Cir. 2003). Similarly, here CBC uses the "names, nicknames, likenesses, signatures, pictures, playing records, and/ or biographical data of each player" in an interactive form in connection with its fantasy baseball products. This use is no less expressive than the use that was at issue in *Interactive Digital*.

Courts have also recognized the public value of information about the game of baseball and its players, referring to baseball as "the national pastime." *Cardtoons*, 95 F.3d at

972. A California court, in a case where Major League Baseball was itself defending its use of players' names, likenesses, and information against the players' asserted rights of publicity, observed, "Major league baseball is followed by millions of people across this country on a daily basis.... The public has an enduring fascination in the records set by former players and in memorable moments from previous games.... The records and statistics remain of interest to the public because they provide context that allows fans to better appreciate (or depreciate) today's performances." *Gionfriddo v. Major League Baseball*, 94 Cal. App. 4th 400, 411, 114 Cal. Rptr. 2d 307 (2001). The Court in *Gionfriddo* concluded that the "recitation and discussion of factual data concerning the athletic performance of [players on Major League Baseball's website] command a substantial public interest, and, therefore, is a form of expression due substantial constitutional protection." We find these views persuasive.

In addition, the facts in this case barely, if at all, implicate the interests that states typically intend to vindicate by providing rights of publicity to individuals. Economic interests that states seek to promote include the right of an individual to reap the rewards of his or her endeavors and an individual's right to earn a living. Other motives for creating a publicity right are the desire to provide incentives to encourage a person's productive activities and to protect consumers from misleading advertising. But major league baseball players are rewarded, and handsomely, too, for their participation in games and can earn additional large sums from endorsements and sponsorship arrangements. Nor is there any danger here that consumers will be misled, because the fantasy baseball games depend on the inclusion of all players and thus cannot create a false impression that some particular player with "star power" is endorsing CBC's products.

Then there are so-called non-monetary interests that publicity rights are sometimes thought to advance. These include protecting natural rights, rewarding celebrity labors, and avoiding emotional harm. We do not see that any of these interests are especially relevant here, where baseball players are rewarded separately for their labors, and where any emotional harm would most likely be caused by a player's actual performance, in which case media coverage would cause the same harm. We also note that some courts have indicated that the right of publicity is intended to promote only economic interests and that noneconomic interests are more directly served by so-called rights of privacy. For instance, although the court in *Cardtoons*, 95 F.3d at 975–76, conducted a separate discussion of noneconomic interests when weighing the countervailing rights, it ultimately concluded that the non-economic justifications for the right of publicity were unpersuasive as compared with the interest in freedom of expression. "Publicity rights ... are meant to protect against the loss of financial gain, not mental anguish." We see merit in this approach.

[W]e hold that CBC's first amendment rights in offering its fantasy baseball products supersede the players' rights of publicity....

[Affirmed. Colloton, Circuit Judge, dissented on a different issue.]

Notes

1. *Distinction between literary or artistic works and products.* The cases on fictionalized biographies (pp. 413–418, supra) make it clear that non-fictionalized biographies in literary form are not actionable as appropriations of name or likeness. However, factual biographical material in product form, such as in games, has usually been found to be a basis

of liability for appropriation or infringement of the right of publicity. See pp. 398–402 supra. Is this sound?

2. If a distinction between literary and product material is made, could the decision in Ann-Margret v. High Society Magazine, Inc., 498 F. Supp. 401 (S.D.N.Y. 1980), have been wrong? Plaintiff was an actress who agreed "in light of the script necessities" to appear semi-nude in one scene of a film. A magazine devoted to "revealing" photographs of well-known women published photographs of plaintiff, including one from the nude scene. The court found no violation of the New York statute or plaintiff's right of publicity. See also Paulsen v. Personality Posters, Inc., 59 Misc. 2d 444, 299 N.Y.S.2d 501 (Sup. Ct. 1968) (unauthorized campaign-type poster of comedian who was waging mock campaign for President; "privileged by virtue of its public interest character"); Bosley v. Wildwett.com, 310 F. Supp. 2d 914 (N.D. Ohio 2004), stay granted, 32 Media L. Rptr. 1641 (6th Cir. 2004) (sale of videos showing television anchorwoman removing her clothing in nightclub's "wet t-shirt contest"; preliminary injunction stayed on appeal to avoid unconstitutional prior restraint). Montana v. San Jose Mercury News, Inc., 34 Cal. App. 4th 790, 40 Cal. Rptr. 2d 639 (1995) (newspaper pages featuring photographs and drawing of football star in game reproduced and sold as posters by newspaper; no liability because posters portrayed newsworthy matters and newspaper had right to promote itself by reproducing its articles and photographs). Compare Titan Sports, Inc. v. Comics World Corp., 870 F.2d 85 (2d Cir. 1989), rev'g 690 F. Supp. 1315 (S.D.N.Y. 1988) (oversized photographs of professional wrestlers folded and stapled inside magazines; publications, which had such titles as "Wrestling All-Stars Poster Magazine" and "Wrestling All Stars Giant Pin-Ups," also contained text about each wrestler featured in photographs; summary judgment for defendants reversed); Toffoloni v. LFP Publishing Group LLC, 572 F.3d 1201 (11th Cir. 2009), cert. denied, ___ U.S. ___ (2010), subsequent proceedings, 38 Media L. Rptr. 2589 (N.D. Ga. 2010), vacated, 40 Media L. Rptr. 1681 (11th Cir. 2012) (*Hustler* magazine's publication of nude photographs of murdered female wrestler actionable because not newsworthy).

3. Display and sale of an original work of art that embodies a person's likeness is not an infringement of the right of publicity. But does this allow sale and advertising of copies of the work or of products that incorporate copies? Can art be satisfactorily distinguished from products or from commercial exploitation of a person's celebrity value? See Simeonov v. Tiegs, 159 Misc. 2d 54, 602 N.Y.S.2d 1014 (N.Y. City Civ. Ct. 1993) (no liability for sale of ten copies of sculpture of model); Young v. Greneker Studios, 175 Misc. 1027, 26 N.Y.S.2d 357 (Sup. Ct. 1941) (sale of mannequins in plaintiff's likeness actionable under New York statute); Hoepker v. Kruger, 200 F. Supp. 2d 340 (S.D.N.Y. 2002) (museum not liable for displaying and advertising art work based on photographic image of plaintiff, for reproduction of work in book, or for museum shop's sale of post cards and gift items such as T-shirts and refrigerator magnets, showing copies of work; sale of gift items considered sale of art rather than sale of plaintiff's image).

4. *First Amendment limitations.* In Comedy III Productions, Inc. v. Gary Saderup, Inc., 25 Cal. 4th 387, 106 Cal. Rptr. 2d 126, 21 P.3d 797 (2001), cert. denied, 534 U.S. 1078 (2002), an artist made a drawing of "The Three Stooges" and sold lithographs and T-shirts depicting this drawing. The drawing itself, as an artistic work that did not advertise or endorse a product, was considered "noncommercial speech" entitled to First Amendment protection from liability. But it was held constitutional to allow a celebrity's heirs and assigns control of the merchandising of the celebrity's image and apply this to "depictions of celebrities amounting to little more than the appropriation of the celebrity's economic value." First Amendment protection would attach only when a work contained

"significant transformative elements" so that it was primarily defendant's own expression rather than the celebrity's likeness, or when the value of the work came principally from a source other than the fame of the celebrity, such as the skill and reputation of the artist. In the instant case, the marketability and economic value of the artist's work came primarily from the fame of the celebrities depicted and the work was not transformative. The artist's goal was to create literal, conventional depictions of the Three Stooges so as to exploit their fame. The lithographs and T-shirts were therefore actionable infringements of the right of publicity. Compare ETW Corp. v. Jireh Publishing, Inc., 332 F.3d 915 (6th Cir. 2003), in which defendants published prints of a painting commemorating Tiger Woods' victory at the Masters golf tournament. In the foreground of the painting were views of Woods in different poses. The court believed that the work contained "significant transformative elements" that made it especially worthy of First Amendment protection and also less likely to interfere with the economic interest protected by Woods' right of publicity. It was a "collage of images" that described a historic event in sports history and conveyed a message about the significance of Woods' achievement. See also Hart v. Electronic Arts, Inc., 808 F. Supp. 2d 757 (D.N.J. 2011) (interactive college football video game using alterable images of actual players sufficiently transformative for First Amendment protection).

5. While First Amendment arguments against liability for invasion of privacy or publicity rights are frequently raised, the Constitution so far has not had much effect upon liability for use of a person's name or likeness in advertising products or services. See Town & Country Properties, Inc. v. Riggins, 249 Va. 387, 457 S.E.2d 356 (1995) (realtor's advertising house as former home of prominent football player); Dryer v. National Football League, 689 F. Supp. 2d 1113 (D. Minn. 2010) (images and names of players in football league promotional videos distinguished from use in fantasy sports products). Will this remain the position? Can the contents of promotional newsletters, magazines and videos be denied First Amendment protection because the publications are intended primarily to increase sales of products or services? Why doesn't the First Amendment protect truthful use in advertising of a person's activities or statements—which may show why the product or service being promoted should be purchased—or the fact that a person actually used the advertised product or service?

Section 2. Intrusion

Froelich v. Werbin

Supreme Court of Kansas
219 Kan. 461, 548 P.2d 482 (1976)

PRAGER, Justice....

In *Froelich v. Adair* [213 Kan. 357, 516 P.2d 993] we set forth briefly the factual circumstances claimed by plaintiff as the basis for invasion of his privacy. They are as follows: Burneta Adair's former husband, Tom Hamilton, had previously sued her seeking to recover a million dollars for defamation because she had stated he was homosexual and William Froelich was his lover. Truth is a defense to an action for defamation and Mrs. Adair was interested in obtaining evidence from William Froelich as to the truth of her statements. Syd Werbin, deputy sheriff and a friend of Mrs. Adair, informed her that Froelich had become ill and was at St. Francis Hospital. Mrs. Adair then became alarmed that he might not be able to testify in the defamation action. She had previously obtained hair from her former husband's bed and under clothing and had it analyzed, and she suggested in her conversation with Werbin it would be a good idea to get samples of Froelich's hair for analysis and comparison. Werbin paid an orderly who obtained combings from Froelich's hairbrush and a discarded adhesive bandage to which Froelich's hair was attached. Werbin passed these on to Mrs. Adair and she had them analyzed. During a deposition session with Hamilton's attorneys, she let it be known she had the samples of Froelich's hair obtained from his hospital room. Although he had not been aware of the taking of his hair samples at the time they were taken, when he later learned of the intrusion he claimed he was emotionally upset over the alleged invasion of his privacy and brought suit against both Mrs. Adair and Syd Werbin in separate actions. [This appeal concerned the action against Werbin.] ...

... If an invasion of privacy is to be made from the evidence it must, of necessity, be based upon some unreasonable intrusion upon Froelich's seclusion as defined in Restatement, Second, Torts § 652B ... : "One who intentionally intrudes, physically or otherwise, upon the solitude or seclusion of another, or his private affairs or concerns, is subject to liability to the other for invasion of his privacy, if the intrusion would be highly offensive to a reasonable man."

... [T]he only evidence of an intruding act in the record now before us is contained in the deposition testimony of the defendant ...: "He recalled Mrs. Adair's statement that 'she sure would like to have a sample of his hair, and what for I didn't know, and I just said that if possible I would see what I could do, but I said I didn't know.' ... He recalled a time when he took Froelich to the lockup ward at St. Francis Hospital and on one occasion when he was at the hospital he talked to an orderly ... named Dan Marlett. He asked Marlett if Froelich was still in the hospital and when he was told yes he asked if there was anyway that he could arrange to obtain a sample of his hair. A few days later, the witness recalled, Marlett said that he had obtained a sample of Froelich's hair and Marlett said that he had gotten some of the hair off a brush lying on a stand or dresser and some from a bandaid which a nurse had laid down. The defendant then gave $5 to Marlett and testified that he was not reimbursed by Mrs. Adair when he delivered the hair to her. He told her he didn't want the money, that he was doing it as a favor to her...."

We have concluded that on the basis of the evidentiary record before us the plaintiff Froelich failed as a matter of law to establish an invasion of his right of privacy. There is no evidence in the record to show physical intrusion into a privately secluded place which Froelich had secured for himself. The plaintiff introduced no evidence that the hair was taken from *plaintiff Froelich's hospital room*. There was no evidence that the hair was taken from the person of the plaintiff. In fact, both court and counsel throughout the trial assumed that the hair was taken from a piece of adhesive tape which had been thrown into a trash container in a utility room. Plaintiff offered no evidence to establish that the plaintiff's state of mind was disturbed at the time the hair was obtained by the orderly. The evidence was undisputed that the plaintiff did not know that the hair had been obtained by Marlett until three or four months later....

In comment (*d*) of § 652B of the Restatement it is stated that there is no liability for intrusion upon seclusion unless interference with the plaintiff's seclusion is a substantial one, of a kind that would be highly offensive to the ordinary reasonable man, as the result of conduct to which the reasonable man would strongly object. In our judgment the trial court was correct in holding that the plaintiff's evidence failed to establish a wrongful intrusion of such a nature as to outrage or cause mental suffering, shame or humiliation to a person of ordinary sensibilities. Here the undisputed evidence showed that the plaintiff's hair was obtained by the hospital orderly in an unobtrusive manner....

[Affirmed.]

Notes

1. Liability for invasion of privacy by "intrusion" was first established in cases involving devices used to listen to private conversations. Invasion of privacy can easily be found when a listening device has been installed at a person's home. See Roach v. Harper, 143 W. Va. 869, 105 S.E.2d 564 (1958) (landlord installed device in tenant's apartment and listened to conversations). It has been stated that whenever a telephone line is tapped, the privacy of those talking over the line is invaded. Rhodes v. Graham, 238 Ky. 225, 37 S.W.2d 46 (1931) (overruling demurrer to complaint that defendants tapped telephone wires running into plaintiff's home). What if a party to a telephone conversation records it without the consent of the other party? See Smith v. Cincinnati Post & Times-Star, 475 F.2d 740 (6th Cir. 1973); Chaplin v. National Broadcasting Co., Inc., 15 F.R.D. 134 (S.D.N.Y. 1953). Cf. Kemp v. Block, 607 F. Supp. 1262 (D. Nev. 1985) (no action for defendant's recording plaintiff's argument with supervisor because occurred in area of employer's premises where there was no reasonable expectation of privacy).

2. Installation of a hidden camera in a person's home is another example of conduct actionable as intrusion, as in In re Marriage of Tigges, 758 N.W.2d 824 (Iowa 2008), and Miller v. Brooks, 123 N.C. App. 20, 472 S.E.2d 350 (1996), review denied, 345 N.C. 344, 483 S.E.2d 172 (1997). (In both, a suspicious spouse used the device to record the other spouse's activities in the bedroom.) What if a homeowner uses a camera to secretly film guests? See Lewis v. LeGrow, 258 Mich. App. 175, 670 N.W.2d 675 (2003) (video camera in defendant's bedroom recorded sex with girlfriends; held actionable notwithstanding plaintiffs' consent to defendant's participation in what was recorded). Is there a cause of action if plaintiff can prove that a camera or eavesdropping device was installed but cannot prove that anything was recorded or overheard? See Hamberger v. Eastman, 106 N.H. 107, 206 A.2d 239 (1964) (landlord's installation of listening and recording device adjacent to tenants' bedroom). Cf. Harkey v. Abate, 131 Mich. App. 177, 346 N.W.2d 74 (1983) (installation of see-through panels in ceiling of staking rink restroom; no proof that defendant observed plaintiffs there required); Koeppel v. Speirs, 808 N.W.2d 177 (Iowa 2011) (installation of camera in office bathroom actionable if camera could have operated when plaintiff used bathroom; viewing of images not required). But see LeCrone v. Ohio Bell Telephone Co., 120 Ohio App. 129, 201 N.E.2d 533 (1963) (after spouses' separation, telephone company installed in husband's residence extension telephone on wife's line); Marks v. Bell Telephone Co. of Pennsylvania, 460 Pa. 73, 331 A.2d 424 (1975) (system recording all telephone calls to and from police department).

3. When there is intrusion of this type, the dispositive issue may be whether defendant had justification. If a company believes that a person is fraudulently asserting a personal injury claim against it, does this justify the company's installing a listening device in that person's hospital room in order to overhear the patient's conversations with family members, nurses and physicians? See McDaniel v. Atlanta Coca-Cola Bottling Co., 60 Ga. App. 92, 2 S.E.2d 810 (1939) (no justification even though plaintiff had authorized company's attorneys to make any necessary investigation of plaintiff's claim). Cf. Pinkerton National Detective Agency, Inc. v. Stevens, 108 Ga. App. 159, 132 S.E.2d 119 (1963) (detective agency hired by insurance company allegedly shadowed plaintiff constantly, in

manner calculated to frighten plaintiff and give impression that plaintiff was engaged in some wrongful activity). If plaintiff is receiving telephone service at the rate for residential service rather than the higher rate charged businesses, is the telephone company justified in monitoring conversations in order to determine whether calls are being made for business purposes? See Schmukler v. Ohio-Bell Telephone Co., 66 Ohio L. Abs. 213, 116 N.E.2d 819 (C.P. 1953) (no liability where company had reasonable grounds, due to large number of calls, to believe that telephone was used for business). If store employees have reason to believe that criminal activity may be occurring in a customer restroom, are they justified in viewing the interior of a restroom stall through a crack in the ceiling? See Elmore v. Atlantic Zayre, Inc., 178 Ga. App. 25, 341 S.E.2d 905 (1986) (intrusion justified). Cf. Hernandez v. Hillsides, Inc., 47 Cal. 4th 272, 97 Cal. Rptr. 3d 274, 211 P.3d 1063 (2009) (not highly offensive to install hidden cameras in two-person business office to find person who was using computer there at night to view pornographic web sites).

4. The hair samples in Froelich v. Werbin were collected for use as defense evidence. Was this "justification" (or a basis for "privilege")? Or did this strengthen plaintiff's case because of the harm that use of the samples could cause? The court in the earlier proceedings, Froelich v. Adair, 213 Kan. 357, 516 P.2d 993 (1973), believed that privileges found in other branches of privacy law and defamation had no application to intrusion, in which liability is not based upon communication. The court also stated that the "precise motives" were unimportant. Compare Saldana v. Kelsey-Hayes Co., 178 Mich. App. 230, 443 N.W.2d 382 (1989), appeal denied, 435 Mich. 857 (1990). To investigate an employee's claim that injuries were suffered in an accident, his employer engaged a firm whose activities included observation, through an open window, of plaintiff in his home. The observations were made by eyesight and use of a high-powered camera lens. The court concluded that the employee pleaded intrusions that could be found objectionable to a reasonable person. However, a majority sustained the entry of summary judgment for defendants on the ground that the intrusions were not into matters which plaintiff had a right to keep private from the employer. The employer had a legitimate right to investigate suspicions that plaintiff's claim of a work-related disability was false and to investigate matters that were a potential source of liability. See also Shulman v. Group W Productions, Inc., p. 439, infra, which states that the motives or justification of the intrusion are pertinent to the offensiveness element of liability.

5. For reasons of "security" a federal agency has personal letters sent to and from the Soviet Union opened and photocopied. Some letters are chosen by criteria established by the agency. Others are selected at random. Is this a tort against the correspondents? See Birnbaum v. United States, 588 F.2d 319 (2d Cir. 1978) (damages awarded for mental anguish). Is it a tort to open and read mail delivered to a business office but marked "personal"? See Vernars v. Young, 539 F.2d 966 (3d Cir. 1976). Cf. Roth v. Farner-Bocken Co., 667 N.W.2d 651 (S.D. 2003) (supervisor read contents of envelope and distributed photocopies, realizing envelope contained material from law firm for plaintiff personally). "Hacking" to access files stored on a personal computer or personal e-mails may be actionable as intrusion. See Coalition for an Airline Passengers' Bill of Rights v. Delta Air Lines, Inc., 693 F. Supp. 2d 667 (S.D. Tex. 2010); Annot., Invasion of Privacy by Using or Obtaining E-Mail or Computer Files, 68 A.L.R.6th 331 (2011). However, employers accessing files in employees' workplace computers, or messages sent on the employer's e-mail system, may avoid liability on the ground that the employee lacked a reasonable expectation of privacy in these circumstances, or perhaps that this is not highly offensive. See Smyth v. Pillsbury Co., 914 F. Supp. 97 (E.D. Pa. 1996); Hilderman v. Enea TekSci, Inc., 551 F. Supp. 2d 1183 (S.D. Cal. 2008).

6. *Non-surreptitious conduct.* Almost daily, for a period of several years, a woman unwilling to accept a married man's termination of a brief affair with her maintains "visual

contact" by going to his home and office and following him when he travels to work, to lunch, back home, out for dinner, or to his children's school. She also has numerous letters, cards and gifts delivered to him. Although she keeps her distance from him and remains on public property, the man is upset and fearful for his safety and that of his family. Does he have an action? See Kramer v. Downey, 680 S.W.2d 524 (Tex. App. 1984) (damages and injunctive relief affirmed). Cf. Galella v. Onassis, 353 F. Supp. 196 (S.D.N.Y. 1972), modified, 487 F.2d 986 (2d Cir. 1973), subsequent proceedings, 533 F. Supp. 1076 (S.D.N.Y. 1982) (photographer ordered to keep distance from Jacqueline Kennedy Onassis and her children); Wolfson v. Lewis, 924 F. Supp. 1413 (E.D. Pa. 1996) (preliminary injunction barring television reporters from "harassing, hounding, following, intruding, frightening, terrorizing or ambushing" plaintiffs or their children). Could there be liability for taking photographs of a person in a private location when the person has objected? See Estate of Berthiaume v. Pratt, 365 A.2d 792 (Me. 1976) (dying patient objected to doctor taking photographs for medical records; directed verdict for doctor reversed).

7. If a person is repeatedly harassed by telephone calls—for instance, by a creditor—is there an action for invasion of privacy? In Rugg v. McCarty, 173 Colo. 170, 476 P.2d 753 (1970), this was held to state a claim for relief based upon either invasion of privacy or intentional infliction of mental anguish. See also Donnel v. Lara, 703 S.W.2d 257 (Tex. App. 1985) (frequent telephone calls at night); Irvine v. Akron Beacon Journal, 147 Ohio App. 3d 428, 770 N.E.2d 1105 (2002), appeal denied, 96 Ohio St. 3d 1491, 774 N.E.2d 765 (2002) (numerous "hang-up" calls generated by automatic telemarketing system). But see Kelly v. Franco, 72 Ill. App. 3d 642, 391 N.E.2d 54 (1979), where plaintiff alleged that defendant called his residence on many occasions and hung up when the telephone was answered. The court held that this was insufficient for an intrusion action and lacked the outrageous character necessary to an action for intentional infliction of emotional distress. Another possible tort theory is private nuisance. In Motherwell v. Motherwell, [1976] 6 W.W.R. 550, (1976) 73 D.L.R.3d 62 (Alta. App. Div.), defendant continually harassed plaintiffs with telephone calls containing false accusations and derogatory statements. The court recognized "invasion of privacy by abuse of the telephone system" as a new variety of nuisance. See also Khorasandjian v. Bush, [1993] Q.B. 727 (C.A.).

8. What if defendant causes plaintiff to be inundated with calls by other persons? See Harms v. Miami Daily News, Inc., 127 So. 2d 715 (Fla. App. 1961) (newspaper article said that readers could hear "sexy telephone voice" by calling telephone number and asking for "Louise"; number belonged to business office in which plaintiff answered telephone); Jeppson v. United Television, Inc., 580 P.2d 1087 (Utah 1978) (plaintiffs received numerous abusive telephone calls at home after *Dialing for Dollars* television program broadcast their number and name). Cf. Vescovo v. New Way Enterprises, Ltd., 60 Cal. App. 3d 582, 130 Cal. Rptr. 86 (1976) (newspaper published sexual contact advertisement containing woman's first name and street address, resulting in letters to woman with lewd solicitations and in numerous people coming to or driving by home; actions for invasion of privacy and emotional distress brought by woman, husband and minor child).

9. A cancer patient partially disrobes in an oncologist's office so her breasts can be examined by the oncologist. A man, introduced to the patient as "a person looking at the doctor's work," is present in the room. He is actually a drug company salesman participating in his employer's "mentor program," which has sales representatives observe oncologists in their work with patients. Could either the salesman or the doctor be found liable to the patient for intrusion upon seclusion? See Sanchez-Scott v. Alza Pharmaceuticals, 86 Cal. App. 4th 365, 103 Cal. Rptr. 2d 410 (2001). Cf. Knight v. Penobscot Bay

Medical Center, 420 A.2d 915 (Me. 1980) (delivery of child in hospital observed by nurse's husband, dressed in "hospital attire"); Shulman v. Group W Productions, Inc., supra (television cameraman in rescue helicopter taking accident victims to hospital).

10. Can the intrusion tort provide a remedy when someone uses deception or misrepresentation to obtain sensitive personal information about the plaintiff—for example, pretending to have a professional relationship with the plaintiff, or a need to obtain medical history in order to provide treatment or insurance benefits to plaintiff? Taus v. Loftus, 40 Cal. 4th 683, 54 Cal. Rptr. 3d 775, 151 P.3d 1185 (2007), allows an action if the plaintiff had a reasonable expectation of privacy and the defendant's conduct was sufficiently egregious to be highly offensive.

———————

Creel v. I.C.E. & Associates, Inc.
Indiana Court of Appeals
771 N.E.2d 1276 (2002)

BAKER, Judge.

[Myra Creel was seriously injured in a motor vehicle collision. She sought long-term disability benefits under a Fortis Benefits insurance plan provided by her employer. Fortis made some payments to Myra but then decided that she was no longer eligible and discontinued payments. Myra appealed this decision. As part of its administrative review, Fortis commissioned I.C.E., a licensed private detective agency, to conduct surveillance and videotape Myra's activities. The purpose of the surveillance was to confirm Myra's unemployment and ascertain whether her activities were consistent with her medical diagnosis and disability determination. Fortis instructed I.C.E. to videotape Myra's activities during services at the church where her husband, Claude, was the pastor. On two occasions an I.C.E. investigator, Renner, came to the church and presented himself as a worshipper at scheduled church services. The services were open to the public. When greeted by Claude Creel, Renner indicated that he was in the area visiting family or friends. Renner wore a sling on his arm that concealed a video camera. During the church service, Renner covertly videotaped Myra as she played piano at the stage in front of the congregation. He also taped Claude as he presided over the service. Fortis subsequently rejected Myra's appeal from the denial of disability benefits. Myra and Claude learned about the videotaping when they inquired about the basis for this decision. They sued I.C.E. for invasion of privacy and infliction of emotional distress. The trial court granted summary judgment to I.C.E.]

The Creels first contend that the trial court erred in granting I.C.E.'s motion for summary judgment on their invasion of privacy claim because a question of material fact exists regarding whether their emotional and physical seclusion and solitude was violated by I.C.E.'s covert videotaping of them during the church worship services. The Creels assert that a "Church sanctuary is unlike any other public place [because it] is a place where people go to seek peace of mind, solitude and physical seclusion from the world's problems as they seek an intimate relationship with the God of their choice." Accordingly, they argue that they "had a reasonable expectation of privacy, solitude, or seclusion within the bounds of their Church worship service" which was invaded by I.C.E....

Indiana courts have narrowly construed the tort of invasion of privacy by seclusion. In [*Cullison v. Medley*, 570 N.E.2d 27 (Ind. 1991)] our supreme court stated that the tort of invasion of privacy by intrusion requires intrusion into the plaintiff's private "physical" space. There have been no cases in Indiana in which a claim of intrusion was proven without physical contact or invasion of the plaintiff's physical space such as the plaintiff's home. *See, e.g., … Cullison* (concluding that, while invasion of the plaintiff's home could constitute a claim for invasion of privacy, harassment of the plaintiff in a restaurant or on the public street outside his home could not).

More recently, in [*Branham v. Celadon Trucking Servs., Inc.*, 744 N.E.2d 514 (Ind. Ct. App. 2001)], this court was confronted with the question of whether intrusion into a person's emotional solace was sufficient to establish the tort of invasion of privacy. In that case, employees of the defendant posed and then took a photograph of a sleeping plaintiff in a sexually suggestive pose in the employee break room. We declined to address whether emotional intrusion would suffice after determining that under either analysis — physical intrusion or emotional intrusion — the plaintiff's claim failed. We rejected the plaintiff's claim of physical intrusion, because other employees were in the lunchroom when the plaintiff fell asleep and the employees used the break room to eat their lunches. We also rejected the plaintiff's claim of emotional intrusion because he was "asleep when the picture was posed and taken [and t]herefore he could not have suffered any emotional disturbance from it."

Similarly, here, it is undisputed that the Creels were unaware of the videotaping as it occurred, and, therefore, they could not have suffered any emotional disturbance from being filmed. Thus, even if intrusion upon one's emotional privacy would suffice to establish the tort of invasion of privacy by intrusion, we would not find such intrusion in this instance.

With respect to whether I.C.E. intruded on the Creel's physical solitude and seclusion by videotaping them during the church service, we note that they were neither alone nor secluded when the videotaping occurred. Renner, the I.C.E. investigator, videotaped the Creels at scheduled church services that were open to the general public. There were no signs posted indicating that only church members or invitees could attend the services or stating that services could not be videotaped or could only be videotaped with church permission. Using a hidden camera, Renner videotaped Myra as she played the piano on stage in full view of the entire congregation of approximately 140 people. Similarly, he videotaped pastor Claude as he presided over the services, led prayer and share time, preached sermons, and gave benediction to the large gathering of worshipers. At no time did Renner have physical contact with Myra or Pastor Claude. While the Creels object to the covert videotaping, it simply captured activity that was open to the public, observed by many, and which Renner or any other of the church attendees could have testified to witnessing at trial.

Moreover, it is undisputed that Renner confined his videotaped surveillance to areas of the church that were open to the public. Specifically, he videotaped as he entered the church, sat in a pew as part of the congregation, and exited the building. At no time did he film into any closed area or area not visible from the church entrance, aisles, or pews where he sat during the service. Under these circumstances, we conclude as a matter of law that the Creels had no reasonable expectation of privacy in their activities. Thus, the trial court did not err in determining that no genuine issue of material fact existed on this issue, and in granting summary judgment in I.C.E.'s favor on the Creels invasion of privacy claim.

[The court affirmed summary judgment on the claim for infliction of emotional distress because I.C.E.'s conduct "did not rise to the level of outrage necessary to support a claim."]

Medical Laboratory Management Consultants v. American Broadcasting Companies, Inc.
United States Court of Appeals, Ninth Circuit
306 F.3d 806 (2002)

HUG, Circuit Judge.

[ABC's "investigative journalism" program, *PrimeTime Live*, included a segment, entitled *Rush to Read*, on medical laboratories that analyzed pap smears. It reported on pressure placed on lab technicians to process pap smear slides quickly, which caused errors in testing. The segment included footage surreptitiously videotaped at the premises of Medical Lab. A representative of ABC had obtained a meeting with Medical Lab's owner, Devaraj, by posing as someone who wanted to start a pap smear laboratory. Devaraji agreed to the meeting because he thought it might result in some business for Medical Lab. His visitor came to the meeting with two others: ABC representatives who posed as a business manager and a computer expert. One had a camera hidden in his wig, which recorded the entire visit. Devaraj spoke to the three in a conference room and then took them on a tour of the lab. They conversed generally about the pap smear testing industry, Medical Lab, and the first visitor's supposed plans to open her own laboratory. After the broadcast of *Rush To Read*, Devaraj and Medical Lab brought suit on several grounds, including intrusion upon seclusion. The district court disposed of Medical Lab's claim by ruling that a corporation had no action for invasion of privacy.]

Courts have interpreted [Restatement (Second) of Torts] §652B to require a plaintiff to prove (1) an intentional intrusion into a private place, conversation, or matter (2) in a manner highly offensive to a reasonable person. To prevail on the first prong, the plaintiff must show (a) an actual, subjective expectation of seclusion or solitude in the place, conversation, or matter, and (b) that the expectation was objectively reasonable.

Devaraj identifies his subjective expectation of privacy as an expectation of privacy in the location of his conversation with the undercover ABC representatives, an expectation of privacy in the contents of the conversation, and an expectation that the ABC representatives were not videotaping the conversation for broadcast to the general public....

Devaraj contends that he had a subjective expectation of privacy in Medical Lab's administrative offices where he conducted his meeting with the ABC representatives and gave them a tour. Medical Lab was a semi-public place of business. Although the laboratory portion of Medical Lab was open to the public, Medical Lab's administrative offices were open only to employees and invited individuals. Devaraj, however, extended such an invitation to the three ABC representatives, who were strangers to Devaraj. Devaraj's only knowledge of the three was based upon Gordon's statements that she was a cytotechnologist interested in starting her own laboratory, and upon statements that the other two ABC representatives would be involved in the computer and business administration aspects of Gordon's laboratory.

Devaraj's willingness to invite these strangers into the administrative offices for a meeting and then on a tour of the premises indicates that Devaraj did not have an objectively reasonable expectation of solitude or seclusion in the parts of Medical Lab that he showed the ABC representatives....

Devaraj also claims that he had an expectation of privacy in the contents of his conversation with the ABC representatives, particularly in the contents of the conversation that transpired in the conference room. To support this expectation, Devaraj asserts that the conversation involved his private affairs and took place mostly behind closed doors in a conference room that he typically used for private conversation.

The transcript of the recorded conversation between Devaraj and the ABC representatives belies Devaraj's contention that he disclosed private matters in the conversation. Devaraj did not reveal any information about his personal life or affairs, but only generally discussed Medical Lab's business operations, the pap smear testing industry, and Gordon's supposed plans to open her own laboratory. This information was, at most, company confidential, not private to Devaraj himself. Privacy is personal to individuals and does not encompass any corporate interest. This common-sense notion that privacy is an aspect of one's personal life is reflected in the law. *See* Rest. (2d) Torts § 652I (indicating that "[t]he right protected by the action for invasion of privacy is a personal right, peculiar to the individual whose privacy is invaded" and that "[a] corporation, partnership or unincorporated association has no personal right of privacy"). Because Devaraj's conversation with the ABC representatives did not involve his private and personal affairs, Devaraj did not have an objectively reasonable expectation of privacy in the contents of the conversation.

Lastly, Devaraj argues that he expected that the three undercover ABC representatives were not surreptitiously videotaping his dealings with them for broadcast to the general public. Devaraj's argument implicates the privacy interest that the California Supreme Court has termed the "expectation of limited privacy," which is an expectation of privacy against the electronic recording of a communication even though the speaker lacks an expectation of complete privacy in the communication. [*Sanders v. American Broadcasting Companies*, 20 Cal. 4th 907, 85 Cal. Rptr. 2d 909, 978 P.2d 67 (1999).] The notion of limited privacy recognizes that although an individual may be visible or audible to some limited group of persons, the individual may nonetheless expect to remain secluded from other persons and particularly from the public at large. *See id.* (holding that an employee engaged in personal conversation with a coworker in an office to which the general public did not have unfettered access could enjoy a limited, but legitimate, expectation that his conversation would not be secretly videotaped by an undercover television reporter, even though the conversation may not have been completely private from other coworkers); [*Shulman v. Group W Productions, Inc.*, 18 Cal. 4th 200, 74 Cal. Rptr. 2d 843, 955 P.2d 469 (1998)] (holding that an injured accident victim could reasonably expect that communications with a rescue nurse that were inaudible to the general public, but possibly overheard by others involved in the rescue, would not be electronically transmitted and recorded by a television producer)....

Devaraj undeniably held the subjective expectation that the ABC representatives were not secretly videotaping his conversation with them for television broadcast. Devaraj's ignorance of the covert videotaping was essential to ABC's operation of undercover, investigative journalism. Thus, although Devaraj lacked an expectation of complete privacy in his conversation with three strangers during a business meeting, he could have reasonably expected that the conversation would be confined to them for the most part, and not widely exposed to the public at large. In imparting information to strangers, one inevitably risks its secondhand repetition. However, as the California Supreme Court has observed [in *Sanders*], there is "a substantial distinction ... between the secondhand repetition of the contents of a conversation and its simultaneous dissemination to an unannounced second auditor, whether that auditor be a person or a mechanical device." The question before us then is whether Arizona law would recognize as objectively reasonable Devaraj's subjective expectation that his conversation with the ABC representatives would not be broadly disseminated to others, in other words, whether Arizona law would extend legal protection to such an expectation.

Exercising our best judgment, we conclude that, under Arizona law, Devaraj could not have reasonably expected privacy against the ABC representatives' secret videotaping of his communications with them. We conclude that the Arizona Supreme Court would not recognize as broad an interest in limited privacy as the California Supreme Court has done. In reaching this conclusion, we find significant the differences between the California and Arizona law in the area of electronic eavesdropping. The California Supreme Court's holding in *Shulman*—that an injured accident victim could reasonably expect that her conversation with a rescue nurse was not being electronically amplified and recorded through a small microphone worn by the nurse—relied upon California's Invasion of Privacy Act, which prohibits the electronic recording of any "confidential communication" without the consent of all parties to the communication. Under California law, a "confidential communication" includes "any communication carried on in circumstances as may reasonably indicate that any party to the communication desires it to be confined to the parties thereto." Cal. Penal Code § 632(c).

By comparison, Arizona law offers more limited protection against the electronic interception of oral communications. In Arizona, any person present at a conversation may record the conversation without obtaining the consent of the other parties to the conversation. Arizona law thus reflects a policy decision by the state that the secret recording of a private conversation by a party to that conversation does not violate another party's right to privacy. Under Arizona law, then, Devaraj could have no reasonable expectation that the ABC representatives were not surreptitiously videotaping his communications with them.

However, even if we assume that the Arizona Supreme Court would embrace an interest in limited privacy as broad as that articulated by the California Supreme Court, we still conclude that as a matter of law Devaraj's privacy expectation was not reasonable. The expectation of limited privacy in a communication—namely the expectation that a communication shared with, or possibly overheard by, a limited group of persons will nonetheless remain relatively private and secluded from the public at large—is reasonable only to the extent that the communication conveys information private and personal to the declarant. *Shulman* and *Sanders*, the two California Supreme Court opinions addressing the interest in limited privacy, are illustrative of this point....

Shulman involved a patient's conversation with a provider of medical care in the course of emergency treatment at an accident scene. The patient's communications with the rescue nurse were intensely private and personal....

In *Sanders*, the recorded conversation between two coworkers was also of a private and personal nature. The plaintiff "discussed his personal aspirations and beliefs and gave [the defendant] a psychic reading." The California Supreme Court held that given that the workplace where this conversation took place was not generally open to the public, the plaintiff could have a reasonable expectation of privacy against a television reporter's covert videotaping of the conversation even though the plaintiff lacked a reasonable expectation of complete privacy because he was visible and audible to other coworkers....

The California Supreme Court distinguishes between "internal" and "external" workplace communications in assessing the likely reasonableness of any expectation of limited privacy. Unlike the "internal" conversation between coworkers in *Sanders*, an "external" conversation between a workplace insider, such as a proprietor, and a workplace outsider, like a customer, is more probably business-related and thus not sufficiently private and personal in character to make any privacy expectation reasonable....

The case currently before us involves the covert videotaping of "external" workplace communications.... Devaraj, in his capacity as Medical Lab's founder and co-owner, invited three strangers whom he regarded as potential business partners, but also possible competitors, to the Medical Lab offices where they discussed business, not personal matters. As already discussed, Devaraj held no objectively reasonable expectation of privacy in the parts of Medical Lab that he showed the undercover ABC representatives. The videotaping therefore did not intrude upon any private place of his. Devaraj's subjective expectation of privacy in the contents of his conversation with the ABC representatives, which was wholly business-related and did not implicate Devaraj's private and personal affairs, was also not objectively reasonable. Thus, the videotaping did not invade any conversation or matter that was private to Devaraj. In short, Devaraj presented himself to the three strangers from ABC as no more than a public face and voice for Medical Lab. Given that Devaraj cannot assert a privacy right on behalf of Medical Lab, Devaraj could have no reasonable expectation of limited privacy in a workplace interaction with three strangers that was purely professional and touched upon nothing private and personal to Devaraj himself.

We conclude that while Devaraj may have maintained a subjective expectation of privacy over the location of his conversations with the undercover ABC representatives, an expectation of privacy in the contents of the conversation, and an expectation ... against the ABC's secret videotaping of his communication for future broadcast to the general public, these expectations were not objectively reasonable.

Even if we assume that, under Arizona law, the ABC representatives' secret videotaping intruded upon Devaraj's reasonable expectation of privacy, the intrusion was not sufficiently offensive to state a claim for intrusion upon seclusion....

Any intrusion by the ABC representatives was *de minimis* and thus not highly offensive to a reasonable person. The covert videotaping of a business conversation among strangers in business offices does not rise to the level of an exceptional prying into another's private affairs, which the Restatement's illustrations indicate is required for "offensiveness." In addition, any offensiveness of the alleged intrusion is mitigated by the public interest in the news gathered for *Rush To Read*....

The district court properly granted Defendants' summary judgment motion on Devaraj's claim of intrusion upon his seclusion....[7]

[Affirmed.]

Notes

1. Tagouma v. Investigative Consultant Services, Inc., 4 A.3d 170 (Pa. Super. Ct. 2010), like the *Creel* case, involved an investigator filming a claimant for disability benefits at a

---

7. We do not reach the district court's alternative holding that Devaraj failed to state a claim for intrusion upon his seclusion because he identified no damages from the alleged intrusion apart from those resulting from the publication of *Rush To Read*.

place of worship. However, the investigator remained outside the building and filmed the plaintiff through a window, using "vision-enhanced" equipment, while the plaintiff was praying in a mosque. The court believed there was no reasonable expectation of privacy because the plaintiff was in a public place and visible through the window.

2. Is there any invasion of privacy by intrusion if the occupant of a jail cell is filmed? The majority in DeBlasio v. Pignoli, 918 A.2d 822 (Pa. Cmwlth. 2007), appeal denied, 598 Pa. 770, 956 A.2d 437 (2008), believed the occupant of a jail cell has no reasonable expectation of privacy and therefore no cause of action. But the court in Huskey v. National Broadcasting Co., Inc., 632 F. Supp. 1282 (N.D. Ill. 1986), thought that a prisoner's visibility to prison personnel and inmates did not mean that there was no expectation of privacy with respect to others. It held that a prison inmate stated an intrusion claim over being filmed in an exercise cage by a television news crew.

3. Having experienced theft, vandalism and sabotage at a large distribution center, and suspecting the use and sale of drugs there, K Mart engaged a security firm to perform undercover investigative and security work at the center. This included two detectives posing as employees. They provided detailed written reports on their observations and on conversations with employees they participated in or overheard, including information on employees' personal and family matters, future employment plans, and complaints about K Mart. The personal and family matters reported on included medical problems, domestic violence, impending divorces, children's criminal conduct, romantic interests and sexual activities. Employees claimed the undercover investigations and reports were an actionable intrusion. Holding that it was error to grant K Mart summary judgment on this claim, the court in Johnson v. K Mart Corp., 311 Ill. App. 3d 573, 723 N.E.2d 1192 (2000), concluded that plaintiffs had a reasonable expectation that their conversations with "co-workers" would remain private, at least to the extent that intimate life details would not be published to their employer. The disclosures were not truly voluntary because of the deception of placing detectives posing as employees in the workplace, soliciting highly personal information about employees.

4. Intrusive or covert methods of obtaining material for television broadcasts have become prominent in litigation of intrusion claims. Desnick v. Capital Cities/ABC, Inc., 851 F. Supp. 303 (N.D. Ill. 1994), rev'd sub nom. Desnick v. American Broadcasting Companies, Inc., 44 F.3d 1345 (7th Cir. 1995), is one of several important cases involving ABC's *PrimeTime Live* program. For a segment on an eye clinic that supposedly performed unnecessary surgery for financial gain, the producer employed people to go to the clinic in the guise of patients accompanied by a relative or friend, who was actually a person secretly taping the clinic's doctors with the "patient." The federal district court and Court of Appeals rejected the doctors' invasion of privacy claims against ABC. For the district court, the most important factors were that there was no intrusion into the privacy of a patient and that the harm plaintiffs alleged they suffered resulted from the broadcast rather than the intrusion. For the Court of Appeals, apparently the most important factors were that the clinic's offices were open to anyone expressing a desire for ophthalmic services and that the doctors were taped in professional communications with strangers, not personal communications. Both courts noted that there was no violation of doctor-patient privilege because the "patient" consented to the surreptitious taping. Judge Posner's opinion for the Court of Appeals is notable for its discussion of whether the clinic had an action for trespass, because its consent to the entry of ABC's employees onto the premises was gained by fraud, and conclusion that no trespass or fraud action could be maintained.

5. In Dietemann v. Time, Inc., 449 F.2d 245 (9th Cir. 1971), plaintiff was a person with no medical training who practiced in his home what was found to be "simple quackery." Two employees of *Life* magazine went to plaintiff's home and gained entrance by pretending a need for treatment. One employee photographed plaintiff with a hidden camera while he was examining the other. The latter had a radio transmitter in her purse which transmitted her conversation with plaintiff to a car parked outside the house, which was occupied by another employee of *Life* and a person from the office of the local district attorney. *Life* published the surreptitiously taken photograph and information derived from the transmitted conversation in an article depicting plaintiff as a quack. It was held that there was an actionable invasion of privacy. The fact that this was done for the purpose of gathering news did not insulate the magazine's publisher from liability, including damages for harm done by publication.

6. Can there be liability if a television crew openly or secretly tapes victims at the scene of a crime, accident or fire? The court's opinion in Shulman v. Group W Productions, Inc., 18 Cal. 4th 200, 74 Cal. Rptr. 2d 843, 955 P.2d 469 (1998), which is discussed in the *Medical Laboratory* case, states that the cameraman's presence and filming at the accident scene was not an intrusion, and that plaintiffs could not have had a reasonable expectation that members of the media would be excluded or prevented from photographing the scene. However, plaintiffs could have had a reasonable expectation of privacy in conversations with a nurse participating in the rescue that were overheard only by means of a microphone worn by the nurse. On "intrusion" by the media generally, see Annot., Intrusion by News-Gathering Entity as Invasion of Right of Privacy, 69 A.L.R.4th 1059 (1989).

7. Is there a remedy if a news columnist receives copies of documents and publishes information contained therein, knowing that the documents were obtained illegally? In Pearson v. Dodd, 133 U.S. App. D.C. 279, 410 F.2d 701 (1969), cert. denied, 395 U.S. 947 (1969), former employees removed documents from a senator's office at night, photocopied them, returned them undamaged before office operations resumed in the morning, and turned the copies over to newspaper columnists. The columnists were aware of how the copies had been obtained. The court held that they had committed no tort in receiving the copies and that publication of information in the documents, which was not an invasion of privacy in itself because it related to plaintiff's conduct as a senator, did not make the act of receiving copies tortious. Could the senator have succeeded on another theory?

8. The district courts in the *Medical Laboratory* and *Desnick* cases, supra, held that a corporation cannot maintain an action for intrusion. But in Socialist Workers Party v. Attorney General of United States, 642 F. Supp. 1357 (S.D.N.Y. 1986), the court held that an association—in this case, a political organization—had a right of action. Damages were assessed for surreptitious entries and burglaries into the organization's offices, removal and copying of private documents, and the use of informers (who became members of the organization) to obtain private information, including personal information about the organization's members. In E.I. duPont deNemours & Co., Inc. v. Christopher, p. 331, supra, the duPont Company was constructing a plant designed to produce methanol by a secret process. During the construction, parts of the process were exposed to view from above. Defendants, acting for clients whose identity they would not reveal, took aerial photographs of the plant. These photographs would enable a skilled person to deduce duPont's secret process. Should this have been actionable as an invasion of privacy?

Section 3. Disclosure of Private Facts

A. Publication of Private Facts

Meetze v. Associated Press
Supreme Court of South Carolina
230 S.C. 330, 95 S.E.2d 606 (1956)

OXNER, Justice....

Plaintiffs Troyce Brindel Meetze and Lewie Herman Meetze are approximately 12 and 20 years of age, respectively. They were married on March 13, 1955. On March 13, 1956, a son was born to this couple at a hospital in Columbia. Two days later the Associated Press caused to be published in The State, a Columbia newspaper, the following article: "A chubby, blonde 12-year-old mother of a day-old healthy baby boy greeted visitors cheerfully yesterday, but declined to have her picture taken or talk generally with reporters. Her young husband, Lewis Herman Meetze, a West Columbia construction company worker whose age could not be learned, also declined to see newsmen or let his wife talk with outsiders after an Associated Press reporter talked to her briefly. Mrs. Meetze, in the brief visit she granted the news service reporter, was cheerful but uncommunicative. She had just concluded a nursing visit from her young son. At her orders, the baby was placed in the obstetrical ward nursery at a point where he cannot be seen by outsiders through the viewing window. Occupying a choice private room, she would say only that she had read The State lying on her bed. 'I just don't want any publicity,' she said pleasantly. She agreed to reconsider the matter in a later talk with her husband, but both stood by her original decision, hospital attendants said. The hospital said the six pound, 14-ounce baby was 'fine and healthy.' He was seen as he was carried by a nurse from the room to the nursery and his appearance bore out the hospital judgment. Mrs. Meetze's family — her father is listed as Oliver Brindeis from Georgia, but from what place could not be learned." [Paragraphing omitted.]

In both the complaint by Mrs. Meetze and that by her husband it was alleged that the Associated Press, despite the wishes and requests of the plaintiff, spitefully and maliciously caused said article to be published not only in the Columbia State but in numerous other newspapers and thereby exposed the plaintiff "to an unwanted public light" and "public gaze", and made the plaintiff "an object of scorn and ridicule" because of the youth of the mother at the time of the birth of the child. It was further alleged in each complaint that the plaintiff suffered "extreme embarrassment, humiliation, mental anguish, mental agony, wounded feelings and loss of privacy."...

The "right of privacy" has been defined as the right of an individual to be let alone, to live a life of seclusion, to be free from unwarranted publicity. 77 C.J.S., Right of Privacy, § 1. "The unwarranted appropriation or exploitation of one's personality, the publicizing of one's private affairs with which the public has no legitimate concern, or the wrongful intrusion into one's private activities, in such manner as to outrage or cause mental suffering, shame, or humiliation to a person of ordinary sensibilities." 41 Am. Jur., Privacy, Section 2. "A person who unreasonably and seriously interferes with another's interests in not having his affairs known to others or his likeness exhibited to the public is liable to the other." 4 Restatement, Torts, Section 867....

The right of privacy is not an absolute right. Some limitations are essential for the protection of the right of freedom of speech and of the press and the interests of the public in having a free dissemination of news and information. None of these rights are without qualification. Courts have encountered considerable difficulty in seeking to balance these conflicting interests. In almost every case involving assertion of a right of privacy, the court is called upon to resolve a conflict between the rights of the individual on the one hand and the interests of society on the other.

One of the primary limitations placed on the right of privacy is that it does not prohibit the publication of matter which is of legitimate public or general interest. "At some point, the public interest in obtaining information becomes dominant over the individual's desire for privacy. It has been said that the truth may be spoken, written, or printed about all matters of a public nature, as well as matters of a private nature in which the public has a legitimate interest. However, the phrase 'public or general interest', in this connection does not mean mere curiosity." 41 Am. Jur., Privacy, Section 14. And we may add that newsworthiness is not necessarily the test. As stated in Sidis v. F-R Publishing Corp., 2 Cir., 113 F.2d 806, 809, "Revelations may be so intimate and so unwarranted in view of the victim's position as to outrage the community's notions of decency."

A person may by his acts, achievements or mode of life become a public character and lose to some extent the right of privacy that otherwise would be his. There are times when one, whether willingly or not, becomes an actor in an occurrence of public or general interest. When this takes place, he emerges from his seclusion and the publication of his connection with such occurrence is not an invasion of his right of privacy....

It is equally well settled that the right of privacy protects only the ordinary sensibilities of an individual and not supersensitiveness. In 41 Am. Jur., Privacy, Section 12, it is said: "The right of privacy is relative to the customs of the time and place, and it is determined by the norm of the ordinary man. The protection afforded by the law to this right must be restricted to 'ordinary sensibilities', and cannot extend to supersensitiveness or agoraphobia. In order to constitute an invasion of the right of privacy, an act must be of such a nature as a reasonable man can see might and probably would cause mental distress and injury to anyone possessed of ordinary feelings and intelligence, situated in like circumstances as the complainant; and this question is to some extent one of law."

After careful consideration of the allegations of the complaint in the light of the foregoing principles, we are constrained to hold that the facts in this article do not show an unwarranted invasion of the right of privacy. It is rather unusual for a twelve year old girl to give birth to a child. It is a biological occurrence which would naturally excite public interest. Moreover, it was an event which the law required to be entered as a public record.... In Metter v. Los Angeles Examiner, 35 Cal. App. 2d 304, 95 P.2d 491, 495, the Court said: "Manifestly an individual cannot claim a right to privacy with regard to that which cannot, from the very nature of things and by operation of the law, remain private."

There is perhaps another reason why the facts do not show a wrongful invasion of the right of privacy. It would be going pretty far to say that the article complained of was reasonably calculated to embarrass or humiliate the plaintiffs or cause mental distress. Although Mrs. Meetze was only eleven years old when she married, the marriage was not void.

The fact that plaintiffs charged actual malice in the publication does not, as their counsel seem to think, have any material bearing on the question. A publication which otherwise does not violate the right of privacy is not rendered violative of such right because it was made maliciously....

In conclusion, we desire to say that there is some justification for the complaint made by plaintiffs as to the conduct of this newspaper reporter. He visited the mother's room on the day following the birth of the child. It would seem he could have waited a reasonable time before seeking to interview her. He was obviously an unwelcome visitor and a source of great annoyance. We regret that we cannot give legal recognition to Mrs. Meetze's desire to avoid publicity but the courts do not sit as censors of the manners of the Press.

The order sustaining the demurrer in each case is affirmed.

Notes

1. Consider whether an action for invasion of privacy arises in the following situations:

(a) Without their consent, a husband and wife are photographed in an affectionate pose at a confectionery they operate in a market. They are in view of persons in the market and numerous people are nearby. The photograph is published in a magazine article on the subject of love. Gill v. Hearst Publishing Co., 40 Cal. 2d 224, 253 P.2d 441 (1953) (incident photographed was in public domain; husband and wife could not assert right of privacy unless they showed something more than publication of picture, such as unfavorable reflection on them in article).

(b) As a woman is leaving a fun house at a county fair, her skirt is blown in the air by one of the fun house machines. A newspaper takes and publishes a photograph of this incident. Daily Times Democrat v. Graham, 276 Ala. 380, 162 So. 2d 474 (1964) (invasion of privacy, even though picture taken in public place; plaintiff's status changed to one embarrassing to person of reasonable sensitivity). Compare McNamara v. Freedom Newspapers, Inc. 802 S.W.2d 901 (Tex. App. 1991) (newspaper not subject to liability for publishing embarrassing photograph of player in high school soccer game).

(c) Plaintiff's home, which is visible from a public street, is photographed for a newspaper's series of pictures of local scenes. When published, the photograph bears the caption "One of Crowley's stately homes, a bit weatherworn and unkempt, stands in the shadow of a spreading oak." The house is indeed in need of repairs. Jaubert v. Crowley Post-Signal, Inc., 375 So. 2d 1386 (La. 1979) (no right to privacy attached since property in public view).

(d) Plaintiff is a psychic, predicting future events in the lives of her clients. She obtains new clients only through recommendations by existing clients. A newspaper publishes an article on her practice as a psychic. Buller v. Pulitzer Publishing Co., 684 S.W.2d 473 (Mo. App. 1984) (action for invasion of privacy stated).

(e) A hospital which conducts an *in vitro* fertilization program invites couples who have participated in the program to a social function and meeting celebrating the program's fifth anniversary. The hospital assures the invitees that there will be no publicity or "public exposure" of persons attending the gathering. Nevertheless, a television film crew is present and films plaintiffs (a husband and wife pregnant with triplets conceived through *in vitro* fertilization) despite their efforts to avoid being filmed or interviewed at the function. Plaintiffs are recognized when the film is broadcast on the evening news. Y.G. v. Jewish Hospital of St. Louis, 795 S.W.2d 488 (Mo. App. 1990) (dismissal reversed).

(f) Plaintiff agrees to appear on a live television program in which he will be identified as an AIDS patient. The television station assures plaintiff that his image will be electronically distorted, so he will not be recognizable to the television audience. The distortion is inadequate during part of the broadcast. That plaintiff had AIDS was already known to his family, a number of friends, medical personnel, and members of an AIDS support group in which he participated. Multimedia WMAZ, Inc. v. Kubach, 212 Ga. App. 707, 443 S.E.2d 491 (1994).

(g) The story of a real-life bank robber is told in a motion picture and books. The robber's wife and children are depicted — the wife as an unpleasant person who may have contributed to her husband's problems — without using their real names or likenesses. Wojtowicz v. Delacorte Press, 58 A.D.2d 45, 395 N.Y.S.2d 205 (1977), aff'd, 43 N.Y.2d 858, 403 N.Y.S.2d 218, 374 N.E.2d 129 (1978) (not within New York statute).

(h) A woman tells the audience of a nationally syndicated television program: Her husband raped her daughter by a previous marriage when the daughter was eleven years old. The daughter became pregnant as a result and gave birth to a son. The boy was raised as the adopted child of the woman and her husband and learned the truth about his origins when he was fifteen. Until then, the woman had continued to live with her husband because of economic need. The subject of the program is pregnancies resulting from incest or rape. Anonsen v. Donahue, 857 S.W.2d 700 (Tex. App. 1993), cert. denied, 511 U.S. 1128 (1994).

Gilbert v. Medical Economics Company

United States Court of Appeals, Tenth Circuit
665 F.2d 305 (1981)

McKAY, Circuit Judge.

... [D]efendants published in the periodical *Medical Economics* an article entitled "Who Let This Doctor In The O.R.? The Story Of A Fatal Breakdown In Medical Policing." The article ... outlines two incidents of alleged medical malpractice in which patients of plaintiff, an anesthesiologist, suffered fatal or severely disabling injuries in the operating room as a result of plaintiff's acts of alleged malpractice. The article indicates that in the case of the disabling injuries, plaintiff's insurer settled the ensuing malpractice action for $900,000. It notes further that in the case of the fatal injury, the patient's family was attempting to reach a settlement. Following a description of these incidents, the article suggests that they occurred because of "a collapse of self-policing by physicians and of disciplinary action by hospitals and regulatory agencies." To show the substantiality of this inadequate policing of medical personnel, the article discusses plaintiff's history of psychiatric and related personal problems. The article suggests (1) that there was a causal relationship between plaintiff's personal problems and the acts of alleged malpractice, (2) that plaintiff's lack of capacity to engage responsibly in the practice of medicine was or should have been known to the policing agents of the medical profession, and (3) that more intensive policing of medical personnel is needed. The article identified plaintiff by name and included her photograph.

... Defendants moved for summary judgment on the ground that the article contained only truthful factual statements or opinions relating to newsworthy matters and therefore was protected by the first amendment. Plaintiff conceded that no issues of fact were involved. She urged summary judgment on the theory that although the general theme of the article was newsworthy and therefore privileged, the defendants nevertheless had tortiously invaded her privacy by including in the article her name, photograph, and certain private facts about her life that were not privileged.

In granting summary judgment for the defendants, the trial court agreed that the general subject of the article was indeed newsworthy insofar as it dealt with the competency of licensed professionals. The court noted that the public has a legitimate concern with the fitness of professionals to hold the public trust that a professional license bestows. It further noted that the area of legitimate public concern extends far enough to encompass accounts of factors in the life of a licensed professional that may impair that person's ability to perform competently. The court concluded that, where the general contents of an article are newsworthy, editors must be allowed a measure of discretion to determine how an article should be written and what details should be included. To question whether defendants should have omitted certain details from this particular article, the court believed, would amount to "editorial second-guessing" rather than legal analysis. The court therefore held that the entire article was protected by the first amendment....

The first amendment sometimes protects what would otherwise be an actionable invasion of privacy where a publication by the media is involved. This constitutional privilege clearly applies to the public disclosure of private facts, the invasion of privacy tort alleged in this action. The privilege extends to public figures, as well as to those private individuals "who have not sought publicity or consented to it, but through their own conduct or otherwise have become a legitimate subject of public interest." Restatement (Second) of Torts §652D, comment *f* (1977). This privilege is not absolute, however, and as in other areas involving the media, the right of the individual to keep information private must be balanced against the right of the press to disseminate newsworthy information to the public. In attempting to strike an acceptable balance between these competing interests, liability may be imposed for publicizing matters concerning the private life of another "if the matter publicized is of a kind that (a) would be highly offensive to a reasonable person, and (b) is not of legitimate concern to the public." Restatement (Second) of Torts §652D (1977). As comment *h* points out, not all matters are of legitimate public interest: "The line is to be drawn when the publicity ceases to be the giving of information to which the public is entitled, and becomes a morbid and sensational prying into private lives for its own sake with which a reasonable member of the public, with decent standards, would say that he had no concern." Thus, dissemination of nonnewsworthy private facts is not protected by the first amendment. The privilege does immunize the reporting of private facts, however, when discussed in connection with "matters of the kind customarily regarded as 'news.'" Comment *g*. Any information disseminated "for purposes of education, amusement or enlightenment, when the public may reasonably be expected to have a legitimate interest in what is published," is also protected by the privilege. Comment *j*. Thus, it is clear from the foregoing that the first amendment protects the publication of private facts that are "newsworthy," that is, of legitimate concern to the public. In our view, this standard properly restricts liability for public disclosure of private facts to the extreme case, thereby providing the breathing space needed by the press to properly exercise effective editorial judgment. This standard provides a privilege for truthful publications that ceases to operate only when an editor abuses his broad discretion to publish matters that are of legitimate public interest.

... In *Virgil v. Time, Inc.*, 527 F.2d 1122 (9th Cir. 1975) ... the Ninth Circuit pointed out that "[t]he fact that [people] engage in an activity in which the public can be said to have a general interest does not render every aspect of their lives subject to public disclosure." Because each member of our society at some time engages in an activity that fairly could be characterized as a matter of legitimate public concern, to permit that activity to open the door to the exposure of any truthful secret about that person would render meaningless the tort of public disclosure of private facts. The first amendment does not require such a result. Therefore, to properly balance freedom of the press against the right of privacy, every private fact disclosed in an otherwise truthful, newsworthy publication must have some substantial relevance to a matter of legitimate public interest. When these conditions are satisfied, the facts in the publication and inferences reasonably drawn therefrom fall within the ambit of first amendment protection and are privileged.

Plaintiff maintains that the publishing of her photograph, name, and private facts about her psychiatric history and marital life adds nothing to the concededly newsworthy topic of policing failures in the medical profession. Plaintiff argues that any relationship between her psychiatric history and marital life and the incidents of alleged malpractice is purely speculative, that this information was not of legitimate public interest, and that defendants unjustifiably "appointed themselves judge, jury and executioner of [plaintiff]."

With respect to the publication of plaintiff's photograph and name, we find that these truthful representations are substantially relevant to a newsworthy topic because they strengthen the impact and credibility of the article. They obviate any impression that the problems raised in the article are remote or hypothetical, thus providing an aura of immediacy and even urgency that might not exist had plaintiff's name and photograph been suppressed. Similarly, we find the publication of plaintiff's psychiatric and marital problems to be substantially relevant to the newsworthy topic. While it is true that these subjects would fall outside the first amendment privilege in the absence of either independent newsworthiness or any substantial nexus with a newsworthy topic, here they are connected to the newsworthy topic by the rational inference that plaintiff's personal problems were the underlying cause of the acts of alleged malpractice.

Plaintiff claims that the drawing of such inferences is not within the protected scope of editorial discretion unless a public tribunal first declares such an inference to be legally established. We conclude, however, that a rule forbidding editors from drawing inferences from truthful newsworthy facts would result in a far too restrictive and wholly unjustifiable construction of the first amendment privilege. If the press is to have the generous breathing space that courts have afforded it thus far, editors must have freedom to make reasonable judgments and to draw one inference where others also reasonably could be drawn. This is precisely the editorial discretion contemplated by the privilege. Because the inferences of causation drawn in this case are not, as a matter of law, so purely conjectural that no reasonable editor could draw them other than through guesswork and speculation, we hold that defendants did not abuse their editorial discretion in this case.

Since we have concluded that the inference of causation properly could be drawn in the exercise of reasonable editorial discretion, we find that plaintiff's name, photograph, and psychiatric and marital problems, are substantially relevant to the newsworthy topic of policing the medical profession. If plaintiff's psychiatric and marital problems plausibly contributed to her commission of medical malpractice, then the publication of these facts together with her name and photograph serves the legitimate public interest of warning potential future patients, as well as surgeons and hospitals, of the risks they might encounter in being treated by or in employing the plaintiff. This is particularly crucial where, as here, potential patients and colleagues may not otherwise receive notice of these risks. Clearly, under these circumstances the public has a very strong and immediate legitimate interest, and the first amendment protects the media's right to reveal this information.

… Although application of the newsworthiness standard to undisputed facts may well present a jury question in some cases, here objective and reasonable minds cannot differ in finding the article in question to be privileged in its entirety, thus precluding liability for public disclosure of private facts.[1] …

[Affirmed.]

Notes

1. In Shulman v. Group W Productions, Inc., 18 Cal. 4th 200, 74 Cal. Rptr. 2d 843, 955 P.2d 469 (1998), a mother and her son had been injured in a traffic accident. The mother was pinned under the car and injured very seriously. A rescue helicopter came to the scene and took the accident victims to a hospital. In addition to the pilot, a medic and a flight nurse, the helicopter carried a video camera operator. The camera operator was employed by two production companies to tape material for a television program. He videotaped the rescue of the mother and son at the scene of the accident, the mother and the flight nurse during the flight to the hospital, and the removal of the mother from the helicopter into the hospital. To obtain a sound recording for the television program, the nurse wore a wireless microphone that picked up her conversations with the mother and the other rescue personnel. What the mother said as well as her appearance and conduct from the time she was pinned under the car to the time she was brought inside the hospital was recorded. The tape was edited to create a nine-minute segment on emergency rescues that was broadcast several months after the accident.

The mother and son sued the producers of the television program and others, claiming that the taping was an invasion of privacy by intrusion and that the broadcast was an actionable publication of private facts. The Supreme Court of California held that there was a triable case of intrusion for invading the plaintiffs' privacy while inside the rescue helicopter and for transmitting and recording the mother's conversations with the rescue personnel by use of the microphone worn by the flight nurse. (As to this, see the opinion in Medical Laboratory Management Consultants v. American Broadcasting Companies, Inc., p. 434, supra.) The private facts claim, however, was rejected. The material broadcast was held to be newsworthy: the mother's appearance and words as well as the subject of automobile accidents and victims' rescue and treatment were of legitimate public concern. One reason was the connection between the mother's injuries and statements and the work of the flight nurse, which was a focus of the broadcast. That the broadcast could have been edited to exclude some of the words and images of the accident victims and still excite viewer interest was not determinative.

The majority opinion contains an extensive analysis of the law on "newsworthiness," which is considered to be both a common law and constitutional limit of tort liability. According to the opinion, when a private individual became involved in a matter of public interest, newsworthiness was to be determined by assessing whether or not there was a logical relationship, or nexus, between the events or activities that brought the person into the public eye and the particular facts discussed, with consideration also of whether

---

1. The Colorado Supreme Court has held in a libel action that the question of whether a publication is newsworthy is a question of law for the court. In *Virgil v. Time, Inc.*… the Ninth Circuit … approved an approach that permits the jury, in some circumstances, to determine the newsworthiness according to the mores of the community. The court in *Virgil* recognized, however, that it is the judge who must decide whether a jury question is presented.…

there was a revelation of intensely personal or intimate matters whose "intrusiveness" was greatly disproportionate to its relevance.

2. Consider whether a newspaper or magazine should be held liable for publishing the following:

(a) An article on teenage pregnancies, which focuses on an unmarried teenage mother, identifies the youth who fathered her child. Hawkins v. Multimedia, Inc., 288 S.C. 569, 344 S.E.2d 145 (1986), cert. denied, 479 U.S. 1012 (1986) (jury to determine whether this was matter of public interest).

(b) An article on a public school special education class for retarded children includes the names and photographs of children in the class. Deaton v. Delta Democrat Publishing Co., 326 So. 2d 471 (Miss. 1976) (public school instruction for retarded children is matter of public interest but fact that child has limited mental capabilities is private, notwithstanding enrollment in public school).

(c) A newspaper reports that a man held in jail after his arrest for violent crimes was raped by another inmate. Doe v. Berkeley Publishers, 329 S.C. 412, 496 S.E.2d 636 (1998), cert. denied, 525 U.S. 963 (1998) (publication of person's connection with occurrence of public or general interest, such as violent crime between jail inmates, not invasion of right of privacy; lower court erred in separating plaintiff's identity from event).

(d) A magazine story on coaches who sexually molest youths playing team sports includes a Little League team manager's pleading guilty to lewd acts with five children. A photograph of the team the manager coached accompanies the article, thus showing the public the group that includes the children the manager molested. M.G. v. Time Warner, Inc., 89 Cal. App. 4th 623, 107 Cal. Rptr. 2d 504 (2001) (plaintiffs' membership on manager's Little League team could be found a private fact and not newsworthy).

(e) An article on a "county home" identifies plaintiff as one of the persons involuntarily sterilized there. Howard v. Des Moines Register and Tribune Co., 283 N.W.2d 289 (Iowa 1979), cert. denied, 445 U.S. 904 (1980) (plaintiff's identity newsworthy; contributed to impact and credibility of article).

(f) A newspaper reports that plaintiff has a serious disease which might be communicated to other persons, when actually there is no risk that plaintiff will spread the disease. Cf. X v. Y, [1988] 2 All E.R. 648 (Q.B.D.) (doctors who continued practice after contracting AIDS).

3. In Lee v. Calhoun, 948 F.2d 1162 (10th Cir. 1991), cert. denied sub nom. Lee v. Baptist Medical Center of Oklahoma, Inc., 504 U.S. 973 (1992), plaintiff had agreed to the performance of an appendectomy by defendant. The surgery revealed that plaintiff suffered from a perforated bowel rather than appendicitis. Defendant therefore performed a colostomy. Plaintiff subsequently filed suit against defendant, claiming that defendant misdiagnosed plaintiff's condition and failed to obtain consent for the surgical procedure that was performed. The suit claimed damages in the amount of $38,000,000. On the day after plaintiff's action was filed, defendant was interviewed by a newspaper reporter. Defendant said that plaintiff needed emergency surgery because he had a perforated colon and was infected by the AIDS virus. There was a pre-operation diagnosis of appendicitis because plaintiff had not related that he was an AIDS carrier, which would indicate that more esoteric infections should be considered. After this appeared in the newspaper, plaintiff amended his original complaint to include invasion of privacy. The court held

that plaintiff had no cause of action because of his medical malpractice suit. Medical malpractice and a $38,000,000 claim were matters of legitimate public interest. Plaintiff had become a "public figure" because the suit attracted the attention of the news media. Defendant's comments pertained to his defense of the suit and were privileged by analogy to the defamation law privilege to make a statement in defense of one's own reputation.

4. A documentary film is made about a state correctional institution for the insane. It includes scenes in which identifiable inmates are shown naked or suffering from insanity. Is there an actionable invasion of the privacy of the inmates and institution employees seen in the film? The court in Cullen v. Grove Press, Inc., 276 F. Supp. 727 (S.D.N.Y. 1967), denied an injunction against the distribution and exhibition of the film *Titicut Follies* because of the legitimate public interest in conditions at such an institution. However, in Commonwealth v. Wiseman, 356 Mass. 251, 249 N.E.2d 610 (1969), cert. denied, 398 U.S. 960 (1970), state authorities obtained an injunction against public exhibition of the film except to specialized or professional groups having a serious interest in rehabilitation. The court discussed the state's duty to protect inmates from invasions of privacy and the filmmaker's failure to comply with a contractual condition to obtain valid releases from all persons portrayed. In 1991 a Massachusetts judge, concluding that the passage of time had diminished the privacy concern, lifted the injunction. See Benson & Anderson, The Freeing of *Titicut Follies*, 30 Free Speech Yrbk. 40 (1992).

5. There is generally no liability for reporting or broadcasting a person's arrest, even for a minor offense. An arrest is considered a matter of public concern. See Best v. Berard, 776 F. Supp. 2d 752 (N.D. Ill. 2011). Would it be different if embarrassing details are revealed? In Taylor v. K.T.V.B., Inc., 96 Idaho 202, 525 P.2d 984 (1974), plaintiff, while nude, had threatened his housekeeper's sister with a shotgun and was ultimately arrested. A television station's cameraman filmed the arrest. This film, including plaintiff in the nude, was shown on the station's news program the following evening. The court held that the station was immune from liability for invasion of privacy unless it had acted with "malice," i.e., "for the purpose of embarrassing or humiliating the arrestee, or with reckless disregard as to whether that disclosure will result in such embarrassment or humiliation." What if the victim of a crime is so photographed? See Cape Publications, Inc. v. Bridges, 423 So. 2d 426 (Fla. App. 1982), review denied, 431 So. 2d 988 (Fla. 1983), cert. denied, 464 U.S. 893 (1983) (plaintiff kidnapped by husband and forced to disrobe; newspaper not liable for publishing photograph when plaintiff rescued by police). Cf. Anderson v. Suiters, 499 F.3d 1228 (10th Cir. 2007) (television station broadcast excerpts of videotape of rape of plaintiff by estranged husband; no liability because of public interest in prosecution of husband for sexual assaults on multiple victims).

6. In Jacova v. Southern Radio and Television Co., 83 So. 2d 34 (Fla. 1955), plaintiff had stopped at a cigar store to buy a newspaper. A gambling raid took place while he was there. This was photographed and shown on television. Plaintiff was seen standing near the cigarette counter, talking to two police officers. It was not clear from the telecast that plaintiff was only a bystander. The court denied his claim for invasion of privacy, stating that if a person, even unwillingly, becomes an actor in an occurrence of public interest, he emerges from his seclusion and his photograph can be published in an account of the occurrence.

7. A prostitute is tried for murder and acquitted. She then marries and leads an exemplary life. Eight years after her "rehabilitation" defendants produce a film about her life, using her maiden name in the film and its advertising. Many of her friends then learn of her past. Does she have an action? See Melvin v. Reid, 112 Cal. App. 285, 297 P. 91 (1931) (use of name violated state-law right to pursue and obtain happiness; plaintiff's reputa-

tion and social standing should not be destroyed for defendants' private gain). Cf. Briscoe v. Reader's Digest Association, 4 Cal. 3d 529, 93 Cal. Rptr. 866, 483 P.2d 34 (1971) (article in national magazine mentioned as typical truck hijacking one eleven years earlier by "beginner" who afterwards led law-abiding life; jury could find identification of plaintiff grossly offensive and not newsworthy; state had compelling interest in rehabilitating criminals).

8. Some cases treat facts as newsworthy irrespective of the passage of time. See Barbieri v. News-Journal Co., 56 Del. 67, 189 A.2d 773 (1963) (when legislator was to introduce bill to make whipping mandatory punishment for certain crimes, newspapers mentioned that plaintiff had dubious distinction of being last person whipped in state); Rawlins v. Hutchinson Publishing Co., 218 Kan. 295, 543 P.2d 988 (1975) (newspaper's "Looking Backward" column reported news from ten, twenty-five and fifty years ago; included suspension and discharge of policeman ten years earlier for annoying woman); Roshto v. Hebert, 439 So. 2d 428 (La. 1983) (newspaper reprinted pages from past; page from twenty-five years earlier had article about plaintiffs receiving prison sentence for cattle theft).

The Florida Star v. B.J.F.

Supreme Court of the United States
491 U.S. 524 (1989)

Justice MARSHALL delivered the opinion of the Court....

The Florida Star is a weekly newspaper which serves the community of Jacksonville, Florida, and which has an average circulation of approximately 18,000 copies. A regular feature of the newspaper is its "Police Reports" section. That section, typically two to three pages in length, contains brief articles describing local criminal incidents under police investigation.

On October 20, 1983, appellee B.J.F. reported to the Duval County, Florida, Sheriff's Department (the Department) that she had been robbed and sexually assaulted by an unknown assailant. The Department prepared a report on the incident which identified B.J.F. by her full name. The Department then placed the report in its press room. The Department does not restrict access either to the press room or to the reports made available therein.

A Florida Star reporter-trainee sent to the press room copied the police report verbatim, including B.J.F.'s full name, on a blank duplicate of the Department's forms. A Florida Star reporter then prepared a one-paragraph article about the crime, derived entirely from the trainee's copy of the police report. The article included B.J.F.'s full name. It appeared in the "Robberies" subsection of the "Police Reports" section on October 29, 1983, one of fifty-four police blotter stories in that day's edition. The article read: "[B.J.F.] reported on Thursday, October 20, she was crossing Brentwood Park, which is in the 500 block of Golfair Boulevard, enroute to her bus stop, when an unknown black man ran up behind the lady and placed a knife to her neck and told her not to yell. The suspect then undressed the lady and had sexual intercourse with her before fleeing the scene with her 60 cents, Timex watch and gold necklace. Patrol efforts have been suspended concerning this incident because of a lack of evidence." In printing B.J.F.'s full name, The Florida Star violated its internal policy of not publishing the names of sexual offense victims.

On September 26, 1984, B.J.F. filed suit in the Circuit Court of Duval County against the Department and The Florida Star, alleging that these parties negligently violated [Fla. Stat. §794.03, providing: "No person shall print, publish, or broadcast ... in any instrument of mass communication the name, address, or other identifying fact or information of the victim of any sexual offense within this chapter. An offense under this section shall constitute a misdemeanor...."] Before trial, the Department settled with B.J.F. for $2,500. The Florida Star moved to dismiss, claiming, *inter alia*, that imposing civil sanctions on the newspaper pursuant to §794.03 violated the First Amendment. The trial judge rejected the motion.

At the ensuing day-long trial, B.J.F. testified that she had suffered emotional distress from the publication of her name. She stated that she had heard about the article from fellow workers and acquaintances; that her mother had received several threatening phone calls from a man who stated that he would rape B.J.F. again; and that these events had forced B.J.F. to change her phone number and residence, to seek police protection, and to obtain mental health counseling. In defense, The Florida Star put forth evidence indicating that the newspaper had learned B.J.F.'s name from the incident report released by the Department, and that the newspaper's violation of its internal rule against publishing the names of sexual offense victims was inadvertent.

... At the close of newspaper's defense, the judge granted B.J.F.'s motion for a directed verdict on the issue of negligence, finding the newspaper *per se* negligent based upon its violation of §794.03. This ruling left the jury to consider only the questions of causation and damages. The judge instructed the jury that it could award B.J.F. punitive damages if it found that the newspaper had "acted with reckless indifference to the rights of others." The jury awarded B.J.F. $75,000 in compensatory damages and $25,000 in punitive damages.... [The Florida Star appealed to the Supreme Court after an unsuccessful appeal to the Florida District Court of Appeal.]

The parties to this case frame their contentions in light of a trilogy of cases which have presented, in different contexts, the conflict between truthful reporting and state-protected privacy interests. In *Cox Broadcasting Corp. v. Cohn*, 420 U.S. 469 (1975), we found unconstitutional a civil damages award entered against a television station for broadcasting the name of a rape-murder victim which the station had obtained from courthouse records. In *Oklahoma Publishing Co. v. District Court*, 430 U.S. 308 (1977), we found unconstitutional a state court's pretrial order enjoining the media from publishing the name or photograph of an 11-year-boy in connection with a juvenile proceeding involving that child which reporters had attended. Finally, in *Smith v. Daily Mail Publishing Co.*, 443 U.S. 97 (1979), we found unconstitutional the indictment of two newspapers for violating a state statute forbidding newspapers to publish, without written approval of the juvenile court, the name of any youth charged as a juvenile offender. The papers had learned about a shooting by monitoring a police band radio frequency, and had obtained the name of the alleged juvenile assailant from witnesses, the police, and a local prosecutor.

Appellant takes the position that this case is indistinguishable from *Cox Broadcasting*. Alternatively, it urges that our decisions in the above trilogy, and in other cases in which we have held that the right of the press to publish truth overcame asserted interests other than personal privacy, can be distilled to yield a broad First Amendment principle that the press may never be punished, civilly or criminally, for publishing the truth. Appellee counters that the privacy trilogy is inapposite, because in each case the private information already appeared on a "public record," and because the privacy interests at stake were far less profound than in the present case. In the alternative, appellee urges that *Cox Broadcasting* be overruled and replaced with a categorical rule that publication of the name of a rape victim never enjoys constitutional protection.

We conclude that imposing damages on appellant for publishing B.J.F.'s name violates the First Amendment, although not for either of the reasons appellant urges. Despite the strong resemblance this case bears to *Cox Broadcasting*, that case cannot fairly be read as controlling here. The name of the rape victim in that case was obtained from courthouse records that were open to public inspection, a fact which Justice WHITE's opinion for the Court repeatedly noted. Significantly, one of the reasons we gave in *Cox Broadcasting* for invalidating the challenged damages award was the important role the press plays in subjecting trials to public scrutiny and thereby helping guarantee their fairness. That role is not directly compromised where, as here, the information in question comes from a police report prepared and disseminated at a time at which not only had no adversarial criminal proceedings begun, but no suspect had been identified.

Nor need we accept appellant's invitation to hold broadly that truthful publication may never be punished consistent with the First Amendment. Our cases have carefully eschewed reaching this ultimate question.... We continue to believe that the sensitivity and significance of the interests presented in clashes between First Amendment and privacy rights counsel relying on limited principles that sweep no more broadly than the appropriate context of the instant case.

In our view, this case is appropriately analyzed with reference to such a limited First Amendment principle. It is the one, in fact, which we articulated in *Daily Mail* in our synthesis of prior cases involving attempts to punish truthful publication: "[I]f a newspaper lawfully obtains truthful information about a matter of public significance then state officials may not constitutionally punish publication of the information, absent a need to further a state interest of the highest order." According the press the ample protection provided by that principle is supported by at least three separate considerations, in addition to, of course, the overarching "'public interest, secured by the Constitution, in the dissemination of truth.'" *Cox Broadcasting, supra....*

First, because the *Daily Mail* formulation only protects the publication of information which a newspaper has "lawfully obtain[ed]," the government retains ample means of safeguarding significant interests upon which publication may impinge, including protecting a rape victim's anonymity. To the extent sensitive information rests in private hands, the government may under some circumstances forbid its nonconsensual acquisition, thereby bringing outside of the *Daily Mail* principle the publication of any information so acquired. To the extent sensitive information is in the government's custody, it has even greater power to forestall or mitigate the injury caused by its release. The government may classify certain information, establish and enforce procedures ensuring its redacted release, and extend a damages remedy against the government or its officials where the government's mishandling of sensitive information leads to its dissemination. Where information is entrusted to the government, a less drastic means that punishing truthful publication almost always exists for guarding against the dissemination of private facts....

A second consideration undergirding the *Daily Mail* principle is the fact that punishing the press for its dissemination of information which is already publicly available is relatively unlikely to advance the interests in the service of which the State seeks to act. It is not, of course, always the case that information lawfully acquired by the press is known, or accessible, to others. But where the government has made certain information publicly available, it is highly anomalous to sanction persons other than the source of its release....

A third and final consideration is the "timidity and self-censorship" which may result from allowing the media to be punished for publishing certain truthful information. *Cox Broadcasting* noted this concern with overdeterrence in the context of information made public through official court records, but the fear of excessive media self-suppression is applicable as well to other information released, without qualification, by the government. A contrary rule, depriving protection to those who rely on the government's implied representations of the lawfulness of dissemination, would force upon the media the onerous obligation of sifting through government press releases, reports, and pronouncements to prune out material arguably unlawful for publication. This situation could inhere even where the newspaper's sole object was to reproduce, with no substantial change, the government's rendition of the event in question.

Applied to the instant case, the *Daily Mail* principle clearly commands reversal. The first inquiry is whether the newspaper "lawfully obtain[ed] truthful information about a matter of public significance." [The information in appellant's article was accurate. Appellant's obtaining B.J.F.'s name from the Sheriff's Department was not unlawful. The article involved a matter of "paramount public import": the commission and investigation of a violent crime which had been reported to the authorities.]

The second inquiry is whether imposing liability on appellant pursuant to § 794.03 serves "a need to further a state interest of the highest order." Appellee argues that a rule punishing publication furthers three closely related interests: the privacy of victims of sexual offenses; the physical safety of such victims, who may be targeted for retaliation if their names become known to their assailants; and the goal of encouraging victims of such crimes to report these offenses without fear of exposure.

At a time in which we are daily reminded of the tragic reality of rape, it is undeniable that these are highly significant interests, a fact underscored by the Florida Legislature's explicit attempt to protect these interests by enacting a criminal statute prohibiting much dissemination of victim identities. We accordingly do not rule out the possibility that, in a proper case, imposing civil sanctions for publication of the name of a rape victim might be so overwhelmingly necessary to advance these interests as to satisfy the *Daily Mail* standard. For three independent reasons, however, imposing liability for publication under the circumstances of this case is too precipitous a means of advancing these interests to convince us that there is a "need" within the meaning of the *Daily Mail* formulation for Florida to take this extreme step....

First is the manner in which appellant obtained the identifying information in question. As we have noted, where the government itself provides information to the media, it is most appropriate to assume that the government had, but failed to utilize, far more limited means of guarding against dissemination than the extreme step of punishing truthful speech. That assumption is richly borne out in this case. B.J.F.'s identity would never have come to light were it not for the erroneous, if inadvertent, inclusion by the Department of her full name in an incident report made available in a press room open to the public....

A second problem with Florida's imposition of liability for publication is the broad sweep of the negligence *per se* standard applied under the civil cause of action implied from § 794.03. Unlike claims based on the common law tort of invasion of privacy, see Restatement (Second) of Torts § 652D (1977), civil actions based on § 794.03 require no case-by-case findings that the disclosure of a fact about a person's private life was one that a reasonable person would find highly offensive. On the contrary, under the *per se* theory of negligence adopted by the courts below, liability follows automatically from publication. This is so regardless of whether the identity of the victim is already known throughout the community; whether the victim has voluntarily called public attention to the offense; or whether the identity of the victim has otherwise become a reasonable subject of public concern—because, perhaps, questions have arisen whether the victim fabricated an assault by a particular person. Nor is there a scienter requirement of any kind under § 794.03, engendering the perverse result that truthful publications challenged pursuant to this cause of action are less protected by the First Amendment than even the least protected defamatory falsehoods....

Third, and finally, the facial underinclusiveness of § 794.03 raises serious doubts about whether Florida is, in fact, serving, with this statute, the significant interests which appellee invokes in support of affirmance. Section 794.03 prohibits the publication of identifying information only if this information appears in an "instrument of mass communication," a term the statute does not define. Section 794.03 does not prohibit the spread by other means of the identities of victims of sexual offenses. An individual who maliciously spreads word of the identity of a rape victim is thus not covered, despite the fact that the communication of such information to persons who live near, or work with, the victim may have consequences equally devastating as the exposure of her name to large numbers of strangers....

[Reversed. Scalia, J., delivered a concurring opinion, agreeing with the ground for reversal stated in the last quoted paragraph of the majority opinion.]

Justice WHITE, with whom THE CHIEF JUSTICE and Justice O'CONNOR join, dissenting....

... Florida has done precisely what we suggested, in *Cox Broadcasting*, that States wishing to protect the privacy rights of rape victims might do: "respond [to the challenge] by means which *avoid* public documentation or other exposure of private information." By amending its public records statute to exempt rape victims names from disclosure, and forbidding its officials from releasing such information, the State has taken virtually every step imaginable to prevent what happened here. This case presents a far cry, then, from *Cox Broadcasting* or *Oklahoma Publishing*, where the State asked the news media not to publish information it had made generally available to the public: here, the State is not asking the media to do the State's job in the first instance. Unfortunately, as this case illustrates, mistakes happen: even when States take measures to "avoid" disclosure, sometimes rape victim's names are found out....

... There is no public interest in publishing the names, addresses, and phone numbers of persons who are the victims of crime—and no public interest in immunizing the press from liability in the rare cases where a State's efforts to protect a victim's privacy have failed....

... Permitting liability under a negligence *per se* theory does not mean that defendants will be held liable without a showing of negligence, but rather, that the standard of care has been set by the legislature, instead of the courts. The Court says that negligence *per se* permits a plaintiff to hold a defendant liable without a showing that the disclosure was "of a fact about a person's private life ... that a reasonable person would find highly offensive." But the point here is that the legislature—reflecting popular sentiment—has determined that disclosure of the fact that a person was raped is categorically a revelation that reasonable people find offensive. And as for the Court's suggestion that the Florida courts' theory permits liability without regard for whether the victim's identity is already known, or whether she herself had made it known—these are facts that would surely enter into the calculation of damages in such a case. In any event, none of these mitigating factors was present here.…

… [C]ases which have struck down laws that limit or burden the press due to their underinclusiveness have involved situations where a legislature has singled out one segment of the news media or press for adverse treatment, or singled out the press for adverse treatment when compared to other similarly situated enterprises. Here, the Florida law evenhandedly covers all "instrument[s] of mass communication" no matter their form, media, content, nature or purpose. It excludes neighborhood gossips because presumably the Florida Legislature has determined that neighborhood gossips do not pose the danger and intrusion to rape victims that "instrument[s] of mass communication" do. Simply put: Florida wanted to prevent the widespread distribution of rape victims' names, and therefore enacted a statute tailored almost as precisely as possible to achieving that end.…

… By holding that only "a state interest of the highest order" permits the State to penalize the publication of truthful information, and by holding that protecting a rape victim's right to privacy is not among those state interests of the highest order, the Court accepts appellant's invitation to obliterate one of the most noteworthy legal inventions of the 20th-Century: the tort of the publication of private facts. Even if the Court's opinion does not say as much today, such obliteration will follow inevitably from the Court's conclusion here. If the First Amendment prohibits wholly private persons (such as B.J.F.) from recovering for the publication of the fact that she was raped, I doubt that there remain any "private facts" which persons may assume will not be published in the newspapers, or broadcast on television.…

Notes

1. To what extent does First Amendment freedom of the press protect publishers from liability for disclosure of private facts? Can it be constitutional to impose liability for publishing true information? Would liability be consistent with Philadelphia Newspapers, Inc. v. Hepps, p. 670, infra, which requires that plaintiff prove the statement's falsity when bringing a defamation action for a statement on a matter of public concern? On what may remain of the private facts tort, see Comment, The Tort that Refuses to Go Away: The Subtle Reemergence of Public Disclosure of Private Facts, 36 San Diego L. Rev. 489 (1999).

2. Shortly before the decision in the principal case, the court in Ross v. Midwest Communications, Inc., 870 F.2d 271 (5th Cir. 1989), cert. denied, 493 U.S. 935 (1989), addressed a case in which a rape victim's identity was disclosed in a television documentary. The documentary was intended to prove that a man was innocent of two rapes for which he had been convicted. It supported this conclusion by showing similarities between one of the two rapes and the rape of plaintiff, who had said at a police lineup that the subject of the documentary was not her assailant. Could a court entertain an invasion of privacy action in these circumstances?

3. In Times Mirror Co. v. Superior Court, 198 Cal. App. 3d 1420, 244 Cal. Rptr. 556 (1988), stay denied, 488 U.S. 1036 (1989), cert. dismissed, 489 U.S. 1094 (1989), an invasion of privacy action was brought by a woman who was identified by a newspaper as the discoverer of her murdered roommate's body. She had seen the apparent murderer in the apartment and could identify him. He was still at large. The court upheld denial of

defendants' motions for summary judgment, primarily because of the personal and public interest in protecting the safety of witnesses to violent crime.

4. In McNutt v. New Mexico State Tribune Co., 88 N.M. 162, 538 P.2d 804 (Ct. App. 1975), cert. denied, 88 N.M. 318, 540 P.2d 248 (1975), police officers had been in a gun battle with two members of a group known as the Black Berets, who were trying to steal dynamite from a highway construction site. The two were killed. In an account of the incident, a newspaper published the names and addresses of the officers involved. Thereafter, anonymous threats were made against the officers and their families. Their invasion of privacy suit failed. The court believed that identification of the participants in a newsworthy event is an essential part of the story. Identification by name and address was usual practice. Cf. Alvarado v. KOB, L.L.C., 493 F.3d 1210 (10th Cir. 2007) (identification of plaintiffs as undercover police officers, with names and home addresses, in connection with story on alleged misconduct). Might another theory of liability apply? In Hyde v. City of Columbia, 637 S.W.2d 251 (Mo. App. 1982), cert. denied sub nom. Tribune Publishing Co. v. Hyde, 459 U.S. 1226 (1983), plaintiff was the victim of an abduction. A newspaper published her name and address while her assailant was still at large. She then was terrorized another seven times by the same person. The court held that an action for negligence was stated against the newspaper. Plaintiff's name and address were thought to be of trivial public concern when weighed against the risk to her from publication. See also Remsburg v. Docusearch, Inc., 149 N.H. 148, 816 A.2d 1001 (2003) (because of foreseeable risks of stalking and identity theft, information broker owes duty of care in disclosing someone's personal information to client; information provided by broker had enabled murderer to find victim).

5. Can media defendants incur liability to members of the victim's family for what they publish in connection with a murder or other violent crime? See Jenkins v. Dell Publishing Co., 251 F.2d 447 (3d Cir. 1958), cert. denied, 357 U.S. 921 (1958) (widow and children of man killed by youth gang could not recover from magazine that published account illustrated by photograph of plaintiffs); Bremmer v. Journal-Tribune Publishing Co., 247 Iowa 817, 76 N.W.2d 762 (1956) (newspaper not liable to parents for publishing photograph of mutilated and decomposed body of eight-year-old son; legitimate public interest in discovery of body); Armstrong v. H & C Communications, Inc., 575 So. 2d 280 (Fla. App. 1991) (television evening news showed recently-identified skull of child murdered several years earlier; no liability because of legitimate public interest in facts related to crime, including possession of child's remains by police and investigation after remains discovered). Cf. Justice v. Belo Broadcasting Corp., 472 F. Supp. 145 (N.D. Tex. 1979) (no liability to murder victim's parents for broadcasting report, alleged to be false, that victim had homosexual relationship with another victim). What if the family member was a suicide or died in an accident? See Metter v. Los Angeles Examiner, 35 Cal. App. 2d 304, 95 P.2d 491 (1939) (plaintiff's wife jumped to her death from Los Angeles office building); Kelley v. Post Publishing Co., 327 Mass. 275, 98 N.E.2d 286 (1951) (picture of mutilated body of daughter killed in automobile accident). A few cases find a privacy cause of action when police or personnel of a medical examiner's office show corpse photographs to others. Catsouras v. Department of California Highway Patrol, 181 Cal. App. 4th 856, 104 Cal. Rptr. 3d 352 (2010); Reid v. Pierce County, 136 Wash. 2d 195, 961 P.2d 333 (1998). See generally Annot., Invasion of Privacy by Publication Dealing with One Other Than Plaintiff, 18 A.L.R.3d 873 (1968).

6. Mentioning that a person had committed or had been arrested for a crime many years earlier might be found to be an offensive invasion of privacy and not newsworthy. See Briscoe v. Reader's Digest Association, p. 449, supra; Conklin v. Sloss, 86 Cal. App.

3d 241, 150 Cal. Rptr. 121 (1978) (local newspaper listed plaintiff's being charged with crime in "Twenty Years Ago Today" column). But under the Supreme Court's decisions from Cox Broadcasting Corp. v. Cohn to *Florida Star*, there can be no liability for accurately publishing facts about "a matter of public significance" that are in open public records or lawfully obtained from the government. This appears to exclude almost all potential for invasion of privacy as a remedy for harm caused by reporting that a person had once been convicted, jailed, charged or arrested. See Gates v. Discovery Communications, Inc., 34 Cal. 4th 679, 21 Cal. Rptr. 3d 663, 101 P.3d 552 (2004), cert. denied, 546 U.S. 828 (2005) (2001 television program about 1988 murder included plaintiff's involvement; he had pled guilty to being accessory after the fact); Montesano v. Donrey Media Group, 99 Nev. 644, 668 P.2d 1081 (1983), cert. denied, 466 U.S. 959 (1984) (1978 newspaper article on police officers who lost their lives in line of duty included death of policeman in 1955 hit-and-run accident for which plaintiff was adjudicated as juvenile delinquent).

7. For similar reasons, as well as the reasoning that a fact in an open public record should not be considered private, courts have concluded that the media cannot be held liable for publication of other highly sensitive information taken from records of judicial proceedings and other records that were open or available to the public. In Howard v. Des Moines Register and Tribune Co., p. 447, supra, this was one of the grounds for deciding that a newspaper was not liable for reporting that plaintiff had been involuntarily sterilized. In Uranga v. Federated Publications, Inc., 138 Idaho 550, 67 P.3d 29 (2003), cert. denied, 540 U.S. 940 (2003), it was held that there was no liability for publishing an unsworn statement, made forty years earlier, which said that plaintiff had a homosexual affair with his cousin. The statement was reproduced from court records and had been given to police during a large-scale investigation of homosexual conduct that was the subject of the newspaper's story.

Diaz v. Oakland Tribune, Inc.

California Court of Appeal
139 Cal. App. 3d 118, 188 Cal. Rptr. 762 (1983)

BARRY-DEAL, Associate Justice.

[Plaintiff, born a male, underwent a "sex change" operation at the age of twenty-seven. Soon thereafter, plaintiff enrolled at a community college. Plaintiff looked and behaved as a woman and was accepted as such. The sex change was kept secret from all but plaintiff's immediate family and closest friends. In 1977, plaintiff was elected as president of the college's student body (the first woman to hold that office) and selected as the student body's representative to the community college district board of trustees (the governing board of five colleges including plaintiff's). These events were publicized in the college newspaper and community college district bulletin. While student body president, plaintiff became embroiled in a controversy in which plaintiff charged college administrators with misuse of student funds. Shortly after the controversy arose, Sidney Jones, a columnist for the Oakland Tribune, was informed by several confidential sources that plaintiff had been a man. After verifying this information, Jones put into his column the following item: "More Education Stuff: The students at the College of Alameda will be surprised to learn their student body president, Toni Diaz, is no lady but is in fact a man whose real name is Antonio.[¶] Now I realize, that in these times, such a matter is no big deal, but I suspect his female classmates in P.E. 97 may wish to make other showering arrangements." Plaintiff recently had been mentioned in the Oakland Tribune and another daily newspaper in connection with the student funds controversy. Publication of the column forced plaintiff to reveal the sex change and caused much emotional trauma, with attendant physical consequences. Plaintiff sued Jones and the Tribune for invasion of privacy. The trial court entered judgment on a jury's award of substantial compensatory and punitive damages against both defendants.]

As discerned from the decisions of our courts, the public disclosure tort contains the following elements: (1) public disclosure (2) of a private fact (3) which would be offensive and objectionable to the reasonable person and (4) which is not of legitimate public concern....

The trial court instructed the jury on plaintiff's burden of proof as follows: "In this action, the plaintiff has the burden of establishing by a preponderance of the evidence all of the facts necessary to prove the following issues: One, that the defendants publicly disclosed a fact concerning plaintiff; Two, that before defendants' publication appeared, the fact was private and not public; Three, that the fact was one which would be highly offensive to a reasonable person of ordinary sensibilities; Four, that the defendants disclosed the fact with knowledge that it was highly offensive or with reckless disregard of whether it was highly offensive or not; Five, that the disclosure was a proximate cause of injury or damage to her; and Six, the nature and extent of the injuries claimed to have been so suffered, the elements of her damage, and the amounts thereof."

As originally proffered by defendants, this instruction also required plaintiff to prove that the article was not newsworthy. The trial court struck this element from the instruction and, instead, directed the jury that *defendants* had the burden of proving newsworthiness in order to prevail in this action.

... While a publisher may *defend* itself against a public disclosure cause of action by proving that the matter was newsworthy, it is misleading to assert that said defendant has the burden of proving newsworthiness to be free from tort liability.... Of course, defendants may rebut plaintiff's showing with evidence that the matter was newsworthy. However, to assert, as plaintiff does, that defendants have the burden of proving newsworthiness is error....

... [T]o place the burden of proving newsworthiness on the defendants in order to defend against the action would have a chilling effect on their freedom of expression....

... [W]hether the fact of Diaz's sexual identity was newsworthy is measured along a sliding scale of competing interests: the individual's right to keep private facts from the public's gaze versus the public's right to know. In an effort to reconcile these competing interests, our courts have settled on a three-part test for determining whether matter published is newsworthy: "'[1] the social value of the facts published, [2] the depth of the article's intrusion into ostensibly private affairs, and [3] the extent to which the party voluntarily acceded to a position of public notoriety.'" [*Briscoe v. Reader's Digest Association, Inc.*, 4 Cal. 3d 529, 93 Cal. Rptr. 866, 483 P.2d 34 (1971).] ...

Next, defendants urge that, as the first female student body president of the College, Diaz was a public figure, and the fact of her sexual identity was a newsworthy item as a matter of law. We disagree.

It is well settled that persons who voluntarily seek public office or willingly become involved in public affairs waive their right to privacy of matters connected with their public conduct. The reason behind this rule is that the public should be afforded every opportunity of learning about any facet which may affect that person's fitness for office.

However, the extent to which Diaz voluntarily acceded to a position of public notoriety and the degree to which she opened her private life are questions of fact. As student body president, Diaz was a public figure for some purposes. However, ... we cannot state that the fact of her gender was newsworthy per se.

Contrary to defendants' claim, we find little if any connection between the information disclosed and Diaz's fitness for office. The fact that she is a transsexual does not adversely reflect on her honesty or judgment.

Nor does the fact that she was the first woman student body president, in itself, warrant that her entire private life be open to public inspection. The public arena entered by Diaz is concededly small. Public figures more celebrated than she are entitled to keep some information of their domestic activities and sexual relations private.

Nor is there merit to defendants' claim that the changing roles of women in society make this story newsworthy. This assertion rings hollow. The tenor of the article was by no means an attempt to enlighten the public on a contemporary social issue. Rather, as Jones himself admitted, the article was directed to the students at the College about their newly elected president. Moreover, Jones' attempt at humor at Diaz's expense removes all pretense that the article was meant to educate the reading public. The social utility of the information must be viewed in context, and not based upon some arguably meritorious and unintended purpose....

Defendants next urge that the award of punitive damages was improper, since there was insufficient evidence to support a finding of malice on the part of either defendant....

Here Jones knew that Diaz would certainly suffer severe emotional distress from the publicity alone. Nevertheless, he added to the indignity by making Diaz the brunt of a joke. The defendants' knowledge of the extent and severity of plaintiff's injuries is relevant to a finding of malice. The jury could reasonably have inferred from these facts that Jones acted with the intent to outrage or humiliate Diaz or that he published the article with a conscious disregard of her rights....

[Reversed for error in jury instructions. Feinberg, Associate Justice, delivered a concurring opinion.]

Notes

1. Consider whether media publication of the following items, related to a public figure, gives rise to a cause of action for invasion of privacy:

(a) The scholastic standing of a member of a university's basketball team, which might affect his continued eligibility for the team. Bilney v. Evening Star Newspaper Co., 43 Md. App. 560, 406 A.2d 652 (1979).

(b) The diagnosis that a person prominent in professional sports has AIDS or is HIV-positive — as in the case of tennis star Arthur Ashe (1992).

(c) The homosexuality of a man who prevented a would-be assassin from shooting the President of the United States. Sipple v. Chronicle Publishing Co., 154 Cal. App. 3d 1040, 201 Cal. Rptr. 665 (1984).

(d) The delinquency of children, mentioned in a newspaper editorial opposing the election of their mother to the city council. The editorial opines that she is needed at home to take care of the children. Kapellas v. Kofman, 1 Cal. 3d 20, 81 Cal. Rptr. 360, 459 P.2d 912 (1969).

(e) A man's brief marriage, about the time he was a high school senior, to a girl who subsequently became a motion picture actress — recounted in a magazine article eighteen years after the event. Carlisle v. Fawcett Publications, Inc., 201 Cal. App. 2d 733, 20 Cal. Rptr. 405 (1962) (marriage and later annulment were matters of public record; no invasion of privacy unless revelation of intimate details, tending to outrage public decency, shown).

(f) The home address in Los Angeles of a popular actress. Carafano v. Metro-splash.com, Inc., 207 F. Supp. 2d 1055 (C.D. Cal. 2002), aff'd, 339 F.3d 1119 (9th Cir. 2003).

(g) The life of a one-time child prodigy, a mathematical genius who as a child and teenager was the object of considerable public attention. He then suffered a breakdown. Thereafter, he avoided publicity and worked as an obscure clerk. Many years after his days in the limelight, his past history and present circumstances are described in a magazine article. Sidis v. F-R Publishing Corp., 113 F.2d 806 (2d Cir. 1940) (no liability; since plaintiff was once celebrity, his subsequent history and whether he fulfilled early promise remained matters of legitimate public concern).

2. An article on body surfing at a California beach features a "daredevil" surfer prominent at the beach. Can the publisher be held liable for revealing incidents in the surfer's life that occurred some time in the past, including his putting out cigarettes in his mouth and diving off stairs to impress women, hurting himself in order to obtain unemployment payments and go surfing, participating in juvenile gang fights and eating insects? See Virgil v. Sports Illustrated, 424 F. Supp. 1286 (S.D. Cal. 1976), applying Virgil v. Time, Inc., 527 F.2d 1122 (9th Cir. 1975), cert. denied, 425 U.S. 998 (1976) (facts included to explain plaintiff's daring and dangerous style of body surfing, not morbid or sensational; therefore newsworthy and not highly offensive).

3. In Cohen v. Marx, 94 Cal. App. 2d 704, 211 P.2d 320 (1949), plaintiff was a former professional boxer who used the name "Canvasback Cohen." He retired after six years of losses. Ten years later, Groucho Marx said on his radio program, "I once managed a prizefighter, Canvasback Cohen. I brought him out here, he got knocked out, and I made him walk back to Cleveland." Cohen was not amused. He sued Marx—and once again lost. Having sought publicity as a professional boxer, he relinquished his right to privacy on matters pertaining to that activity. He could not, in the court's opinion, rescind this "waiver" at some later time and hold others liable for commenting upon acts that had taken place when he was in the public eye.

Norris v. King

Louisiana Court of Appeal
355 So. 2d 21 (1978), cert. denied, 439 U.S. 995 (1978)

FORET, Judge....

Plaintiff, Michael Norris, was arrested for the theft of money taken from a Coke machine located in a washateria in the City of Alexandria which is owned by defendant, Brian King. On November 5, 1974, Michael Norris pled guilty to the charge for theft in the Alexandria City Court. For the commission of the theft, Norris was given a $100.00 fine, a suspended jail sentence, and was placed on probation for a period of one year.

During the above mentioned theft, photographs were taken of Norris and an alleged accomplice by means of a hidden security camera located in the washateria. Subsequent to the guilty plea entered by Norris, defendant, Brian King, erected in his washateria a bulletin board upon which he posted two photographs of Michael Norris and one photograph of his alleged accomplice taken during the commission of the theft. Posted at the top of the bulletin board was the following printed heading:

CAUGHT IN THE ACT!

THESE ARE ACTUAL PHOTOGRAPHS TAKEN BY HIDDEN CAMERAS OF A THEFT IN PROGRESS.

Immediately below this heading was a typewritten caption which read:

ANY THIEVES OR VANDALS OPERATING ON THIS PRIVATE PROPERTY SHOULD REMEMBER TO SMILE … THEY'LL BE ON CANDID CAMERA!

Immediately below this caption were two typewritten captions printed on cut out arrows each of which pointed to one of the photographs taken of Norris and which read:

HMMMM … HERE WE HAVE MICHAEL NORRIS OF RT. 1 BOX 556, PINEVILLE, LOUISIANA. MICHAEL IS CAREFUL—HE WANTS TO BE SURE NO ONE IS WATCHING!

WOW … MICHAEL IS SWIFT—IF HE RUNS FAST ENOUGH WHILE HOLD-ING THE MONEY BOX WITH BOTH HANDS—MAYBE HE WON'T GET CAUGHT.

Immediately following the above two captions was another caption which stated:

TOO BAD … MICHAEL ISN'T FASTER THAN OUR CAMERAS! AND MICHAEL ISN'T FASTER THAN THE POLICE! MICHAEL PAYS THE COURT $105.00. MICHAEL GETS 91 DAYS IN JAIL (suspended). MICHAEL MUST REPORT TO A PROBATION OFFICER FOR 1 YEAR. MICHAEL NOW HAS A POLICE RECORD.

[Below this caption was a photograph of the alleged accomplice, with a caption that gave his name and address and stated:]

THE POLICE SAY MARVIN WAS WITH MICHAEL NORRIS DURING THE ABOVE THEFT. WAS MARVIN A LOOKOUT? WHAT WILL THE JUDGE SAY? WHEN WILL HIS TRIAL BE HELD? WHAT WILL HAPPEN TO MARVIN?

Norris brought suit against Brian King alleging that the publication of the photographs and captions referring to the theft and subsequent guilty plea caused him considerable humiliation and embarrassment and constituted undue harassment. The trial court rendered judgment in favor of Norris in the amount of $500.00 and permanently enjoined the defendant, Brian King, from further publicizing in any manner the arrest and conviction of Michael Norris.

The trial judge stated that the issue facing the Court was whether the actions of Brian King constituted an unlawful invasion of the "Right of Privacy" of the plaintiff, Michael Norris. He further stated that the award was to compensate the plaintiff both for the improper use of his name and picture on the bulletin board and for any over-zealous attempts to collect for the damages resulting from the theft....

Defendant denies that he displayed the pictures to pressure the plaintiff into making restitution. We find difficulty in reconciling that contention of the defendant with the fact that he delayed six or seven months before posting the pictures in his place of business. When questioned on cross-examination as to why he could not have omitted the name and address of the plaintiff, and/or have blacked out the identifiable facial features of the plaintiff, defendant replied that the desired effect of the publication would have been lost, because they would not appear as authentic, and therefore be of less benefit to the defendant....

Defendant cites several United States Supreme Court decisions for his contention that the conduct did not constitute an invasion of privacy and that the ruling of the trial court violated defendant's Constitutionally-guaranteed freedoms of speech and press.... [These] involve publication by either the news media, or by some other organization acting in the public interest. This case involves a publication by one individual, involving information concerning another individual.... The whole purpose and aim of the news media is to bring forth information to the public, to apprise the public of the events transpiring from day to day. That responsibility, duty, and purpose are not shared by the ordinary individual....

The facts of this case illustrate the repeated harassment by defendant King of plaintiff and his family. That harassment was unreasonable, and seriously interfered with plaintiff's privacy. Accordingly, the invasion is actionable. Instead of pursuing restitution in a civil proceeding, defendant King instead chose to telephone plaintiff and his mother and make threats to plaintiff, the mother, and the integrity of the entire family. When these threats did not produce the results which he sought, defendant finally chose to display the photographs of plaintiff in a manner most ridiculing to plaintiff, and to announce to the world that plaintiff had been convicted of a crime, in a manner motivated by reasons which would continuously enure to defendant's benefit (and to plaintiff's detriment) by aiding defendant in safeguarding his property from theft, etc.

We are unable to discern any public interest to be served by defendant's actions such as to bring him within the protection of the rights of free speech and press. Any such right[s] that he might have had were lost to him when his motives evolved into continued punishment and harassment of the plaintiff; and his selfish motive of protection of his property became the main motivation for his continued publication of plaintiff's picture and the information pertinent thereto.

It appears obvious, from the record, that one of the defendant's motives in displaying plaintiff's picture in defendant's washateria was to coerce payment of that which defendant claims that plaintiff took from him....

A creditor may employ any reasonable, non-coercive methods in an attempt to collect that which is owed to him. However, when he oversteps the bounds of propriety and takes unreasonable, coercive action, he has committed tortious conduct for which the law provides a remedy....

AFFIRMED.

HOOD, Judge (dissenting)....

I think my colleagues erred in concluding, contrary to the findings of the trial court, that King made threats against the plaintiff. The evidence establishes, I think, that defendant erected the bulletin board displays solely to deter further thefts in his washateria, and not to coerce anyone into paying a debt. The evidence shows that it effectively accomplished that purpose. Even if we accept my colleagues' holding that *one* of the defendant's motives was to coerce payment, they cannot deny that his principal motive was to reduce the number of thefts which were being committed, for his own protection and that of his customers. I think that that is a reasonable and justifiable reason for the display....

In the instant suit the publicizing of Norris' name occurred shortly after the theft was committed. It was publicized only in defendant's place of business where that offense and many others had occurred. It demonstrated to would-be-thieves and to customers, the probable victims, that offenders would be caught and punished. And, it effectively reduced thefts....

... [T]he majority has gone much too far in allowing the judicially-created right of privacy to prevail over the constitutionally guaranteed right of freedom of speech.

I realize that defendant should not be permitted to leave the display up indefinitely, because eventually it would cease to serve the purpose intended and the continued maintenance of it would constitute an abuse of the latter's right of freedom of speech. For that reason I would concur in that part of the trial court judgment which enjoins him from continuing to publicize plaintiff's conviction. I believe, however, that the display was justified and that it was maintained for only a reasonable length of time. For that reason, I cannot agree with that part of the trial court judgment which condemns defendant, who was the victim of the crime, to pay damages to the person who committed that crime, solely because defendant informed his other customers of the fact that the theft had been committed....

Notes

1. Non-media defendants may not have a claim to First Amendment freedom of the press, but they clearly have a claim to that amendment's freedom of speech. Should tort liability for publishing truthful facts be any wider for non-media defendants than for media defendants?

2. Defendants receive information that plaintiffs will have abortions at a clinic. Defendants go to the clinic at the time they believe plaintiffs will arrive and demonstrate with signs displaying plaintiffs' names, that they are about to have abortions, and messages imploring them not to "kill their babies." Can defendants be held liable? See Doe v. Mills, 212 Mich. App. 73, 536 N.W.2d 824 (1995), appeal denied, 452 Mich. 869, 552 N.W.2d 168 (1996) (dismissal reversed).

3. There are few reported cases in which, in furtherance of a private purpose, widespread publicity has been given to "private facts." One is Brents v. Morgan, 221 Ky. 765, 299 S.W. 967 (1927). A local veterinarian owed money to the proprietor of a garage. The latter placed a notice in a window of his garage, facing a main street, stating "Dr. W.R. Morgan owes an account here of $49.67. And if promises would pay an account this account would have been settled long ago." The veterinarian was held to state a good claim for damages. See also Biederman's of Springfield, Inc. v. Wright, p. 466, infra; Mason v. Williams Discount Center, Inc., 639 S.W.2d 836 (Mo. App. 1982) (plaintiffs' names on "no checks" list posted at store checkout in view of customers). It seems that in incidents of this nature, the matter is usually given insufficient publicity for defendants to be held liable for invasion of privacy. See the next principal case and the notes following.

4. In Young v. Jackson, 572 So. 2d 378 (Miss. 1990), suit was brought by an employee of a nuclear power station. She alleged that after fainting on the job and being taken to the hospital, she was told by another employee that the employer's "safety man" and the Nuclear Regulatory Commission needed to know what type of surgery she had had two months earlier. On the promise that no one else would be told, plaintiff disclosed that she had a hysterectomy. Rumors spread among the power station that plaintiff had been injured by radiation. In order to squelch the rumors and calm employees' fears for their own safety, a supervisor called together the people who worked under him and told them that plaintiff's hospitalization had nothing to do with radiation exposure; she had passed out because of the after-effects of a hysterectomy. The court held that ordinarily public disclosure of a woman's hysterectomy would be actionable, but in this case it was privileged as an effort to allay the workers' fears of radiation exposure. See also Zinda v.

Louisiana Pacific Corp., 149 Wis. 2d 913, 440 N.W.2d 548 (1989), in which a factory newsletter's "comings and goings" column reported that an employee was terminated for falsification of employment forms.

5. In Smith v. Calvary Christian Church, 462 Mich. 679, 614 N.W.2d 590 (2000), it was held that a pastor and his church were not liable for announcing during a service that plaintiff formerly visited prostitutes because plaintiff had consented to accepting discipline imposed by the church, which included detailing a person's sins before the congregation. Compare Guinn v. Church of Christ of Collinsville, 775 P.2d 766 (Okla. 1989), holding that church elders could be liable for disclosures about plaintiff's private life after, but not before, plaintiff withdrew from membership in the church.

B. Disclosure Without Publicity

Swinton Creek Nursery v. Edisto Farm Credit, ACA

Supreme Court of South Carolina
334 S.C. 469, 514 S.E.2d 126 (1999)

TOAL, Justice....

[Plaintiff borrowed money from defendant to expand his nursery business. He defaulted on the loan payments and undertook to liquidate the assets of the business in order to pay off the debt. Plaintiff found a buyer who agreed to pay $97,500 for the assets. The buyer then applied to defendant for a loan. Defendant's loan officer sent the buyer a letter which questioned the buyer's capacity to repay the loan and included the statement that "the operation you are purchasing has been under financial duress." The buyer then told plaintiff that he would be unable to obtain the money for the purchase. Eventually plaintiff sold the business' assets to the buyer for $20,000 less than originally agreed. Plaintiff sued defendant for disclosure of his financial problems, including the letter to the buyer. The jury found defendant liable for invasion of privacy, but the Court of Appeals ruled that there should have been a directed verdict for defendant on this and other claims.]

Though never directly addressed by this Court, our Court of Appeals has consistently held that publicity, as opposed to mere publication, is what is required to give rise to a cause of action for this branch of invasion of privacy; communication to a single individual or to a small group of people will not give rise to an invasion of privacy claim.[10] By defining "publicity" in this manner, our Court of Appeals is in line with the majority of other jurisdictions. Many of these courts have borrowed directly from the Restatement (Second) of Torts [§ 652D, comment *a*], which contains the following discussion of "publicity:" "The form of invasion of the right of privacy covered in this Section depends upon publicity given to the private life of the individual. 'Publicity,' as it is used in

---

10. One commentator has suggested that this requirement ensures that public communications comply with minimum standards of civility, while liberating private communications from the threat of legal enforcement of such restraints. Robert C. Post, *The Social Foundations of Privacy: Community and Self In the Common Law Tort*, 77 Cal. L. Rev. 957 (1989).

this Section, differs from 'publication,' as that term is used in sec. 577 in connection with liability for defamation. 'Publication,' in that sense, is a word of art, which includes any communication by the defendant to a third person. 'Publicity,' on the other hand, means that the matter is made public, by communicating it to the public at large, or to so many persons that the matter must be regarded as substantially certain to become one of public knowledge. The difference is not one of the means of communication, which may be oral, written or by any other means. It is one of a communication that reaches, or is sure to reach, the public. [¶] Thus it is not an invasion of the right of privacy, within the rule stated in this Section, to communicate a fact concerning the plaintiff's private life to a single person or even to a small group of persons. On the other hand, any publication in a newspaper or a magazine, even of small circulation, or in a handbill distributed to a large number of persons, or any broadcast over the radio, or statement made in an address to a large audience, is sufficient to give publicity within the meaning of the term as it is used in this Section. The distinction, in other words, is one between private and public communication."

[At the trial, plaintiff testified that numerous people had questioned him about the letter. Another witness testified that "word on the street" was that plaintiff was having problems with a bank. The trial court ruled that there was enough to make a jury issue on how the information "got out."]

In their article, *The Right to Privacy*, Warren and Brandeis were primarily concerned with new mechanical devices that would catapult once private gossip into the public domain. They clearly did not advocate abolishing entirely *personal* correspondences, whether written or oral. As originally conceived by Warren and Brandeis, public disclosure of private facts requires disclosure akin to publications in mass-media. In the instant case, there is no evidence that EFC published the contents of the letter to anyone other than Buyer. The letter was sent only to Buyer in an attempt to address his loan application. We find no evidence to support a claim for public disclosure of private facts.

[Plaintiff] nevertheless argues that EFC should be liable for "sparking the flame" of publicity. In other words, even if EFC published the statement to only one person, if the information eventually became public, EFC should be held accountable. However, such an approach would effectively eviscerate the requirement that the *defendant* be the one to have publicized the private information. If this approach were adopted, almost any form of gossip would be actionable, regardless of the discretion taken in its initial communication. We therefore affirm the Court of Appeals on this issue....

... [Plaintiff] argues that a plaintiff need not prove publicity in an invasion of privacy claim if there is a breach of contract, trust, or other confidential relationship. We disagree.

... [T]hough the facts of a case may give rise to a breach of contract or confidentiality claim, that does not excuse the requirement that the private information be "publicized" in order to maintain an invasion of privacy claim....

Although related in policy, breach of confidentiality and invasion of privacy are not so closely connected in law that the presence of the former obviates proof of "publicity" in the latter. Warren and Brandeis envisaged a privacy right that would occupy ground not already covered by contract and confidentiality theories. In this sense, if a plaintiff has a claim for breach of contract or confidentiality, there is no justification for reviving an otherwise invalid invasion of privacy claim....

[Affirmed as to the invasion of privacy claim, but reversed on a defamation claim arising out of the same facts.]

Notes

1. Why is "publicity" a requirement of liability? Should it be? Consider whether there is sufficient publicity in the following cases:

(a) In an effort to obtain payment of debts owed by customers, a retail store contacts employers and relatives of the customers, sometimes discussing the debts. In each instance, between two and four persons are contacted. Vogel v. W.T. Grant Co., 458 Pa. 124, 327 A.2d 133 (1974) (not sufficient for liability).

(b) To compile a record of accidents and injuries at truck terminals, the safety director of a trucking company faxes to sixteen terminals (located in six states) a list containing the names and social security numbers of 204 employees of the company. Bodah v. Lakeville Motor Express, Inc., 663 N.W.2d 550 (Minn. 2003), rev'g 649 N.W.2d 859 (Minn. App. 2002) (not substantially certain to become public knowledge; required publicity therefore absent; lower court would have allowed action if employees exposed to significant risk of misuse of social security numbers).

(c) A woman who had a sexual relationship with plaintiff prior to his present marriage writes letters, saying "what a bastard" plaintiff is, to plaintiff, his wife, their former spouses, their parents, neighbors, the parents' neighbors, and the president and faculty members of the university that plaintiff attends. Kinsey v. Macur, 107 Cal. App. 3d 265, 165 Cal. Rptr. 608 (1980) (sufficient publicity).

(d) Plaintiff's husband taps her telephone and learns that she is having an affair with a co-worker. The husband gives this information to the chief operating officer of the plant where plaintiff, her husband and the co-worker are all employed. This officer conveys the information to five other management employees of the company. Plaintiff and the co-worker whom she was dating are fired. Beard v. Akzona, Inc., 517 F. Supp. 128 (E.D. Tenn. 1981) (insufficient publicity). Cf. Doe v. Methodist Hospital, 690 N.E.2d 681 (Ind. 1997) (communication of plaintiff's HIV-positive status to small number of co-employees); Jones v. U.S. Child Support Recovery, 961 F. Supp. 1518 (D. Utah 1997) (company attempting to collect child support from plaintiff sent "wanted" posters referring to her as "dead beat parent" to plaintiff's employer and family members).

(e) A report on plaintiff sent to an insurance company is one of 35,000,000 reports on individuals that defendant provides in a year to insurers, lenders, merchants, employers and other businesses. There is no evidence that the report has been sent anywhere else, but it could be included in future reports about plaintiff requested by other businesses. Tureen v. Equifax, Inc., 571 F.2d 411 (8th Cir. 1978) (no liability).

(f) Defendant provides the private facts to a newspaper reporter, leading to publication of the facts in the newspaper. Bean v. Gutierrez, 980 A.2d 1090 (D.C. 2009).

(g) A newspaper publishes private facts about plaintiff, but because her name is not used and some facts are altered, only a small number of the newspaper's readers connect the newspaper's article with plaintiff. Harris v. Easton Publishing Co., 335 Pa. Super. 141, 483 A.2d 1377 (1984).

2. Is there sufficient publicity if personal information is included in a publicly available web site? In Yath v. Fairview Clinics, N.P., 767 N.W.2d 34 (Minn. App. 2009), sensitive medical information about the plaintiff reached someone who posted it on an Internet web page. The web page was removed in a day or two. It may have been seen by only a few people. Quoting the Restatement's statements that "'Publicity'... means that the matter is made public, by communicating it to the public at large, or to so many per-

sons that the matter must be regarded as substantially certain to become one of public knowledge." and "The distinction ... is one between private and public communication." (Restatement (Second) of Torts § 652D, comment *a* (1977)), the court concluded that the publicity element of liability was satisfied by any communication to the public. It held a publicly accessible web page to be a medium that delivered information directly to the public and therefore satisfied the publicity requirement. The number of actual viewers was irrelevant. A concurring opinion criticized the decision as overbroad, treating all Internet sites alike although some are not intended to disseminate information to a large number of people or actually viewed by a large number.

3. In Beaumont v. Brown, 65 Mich. App. 455, 237 N.W.2d 501 (1975), rev'd, 401 Mich. 80, 257 N.W.2d 522 (1977), plaintiff had appealed his dismissal from a state agency. In connection with the appeal, the agency's personnel director wrote to the employee's commanding officer in the Army. The letter asked about the employee's absences from work for military duty and made numerous negative statements about his conduct, including that he had been extremely disloyal and insubordinate. The letter was seen by support personnel of the sender and the recipient. It also was "leaked" to a few other persons. Plaintiff sued the personnel director and the head of his agency. The lower court held that the publicity requirement was not satisfied and ordered summary judgment for defendants. The Supreme Court of Michigan held there was a genuine issue of fact on whether there was public disclosure because the letter had passed through many hands in the army bureaucracy and was included in the Civil Service Commission transcript of the dismissal case. The court commented that the derogatory remarks made in the letter seemed to assure that it would be circulated within the Army. The court also said that "An invasion of a plaintiff's right to privacy is important if it exposes private facts to a public whose knowledge of those facts would be embarrassing to the plaintiff. Such a public might be ... a particular public such as fellow employees, club members, church members, family, or neighbors...." On this basis, the court in Miller v. Motorola, Inc., 202 Ill. App. 3d 976, 560 N.E.2d 900 (1990), held it sufficient to allege that the fact of plaintiff's mastectomy surgery had been disclosed to her co-employees.

4. Can liability arise from oral statements? In Biederman's of Springfield, Inc. v. Wright, 322 S.W.2d 892 (Mo. 1959), a store employee allegedly went to the cafe where plaintiff worked as a waitress, followed her around the cafe, stated in a loud voice that plaintiff and her husband owed the store money and had refused to pay their bill, called plaintiff and her husband "deadbeats," and threatened to have both of them fired from their jobs. The court found a cause of action for invasion of privacy. Compare Gautier v. General Telephone Co., 234 Cal. App. 2d 302, 44 Cal. Rptr. 404 (1965), where a telephone company told certain persons that plaintiffs' telephone had been disconnected. This led those persons to conclude that plaintiffs had not paid their telephone bill. The court held that the telephone company was not liable because of the oral nature of the communications; the right of privacy could only be violated by printed or other permanent publications or reproductions. Why should the oral nature of the communication preclude liability? A reason sometimes given is that the chance of serious damage from oral assertions is slight. Some courts might, therefore, permit recovery when there is proof of serious harm. See Carr v. Watkins, 227 Md. 578, 177 A.2d 841 (1962) (loss of job). See generally Annot., Invasion of Right of Privacy by Merely Oral Declarations, 19 A.L.R.3d 1318 (1968).

5. If disclosure is not sufficiently public, some other theory of liability might succeed. There may be an intrusion type of invasion of privacy. See pp. 427–439, supra. Or breach of confidence. See pp. 467–473, infra. In Porten v. University of San Francisco, 64 Cal. App. 3d 825, 134 Cal. Rptr. 839 (1976), a university disclosed to the State Scholarship

and Loan Commission the grades that a student earned at another school. The student allegedly had been assured by the university that these grades would not be revealed without his consent. The court ruled that there was no public disclosure since the communication had not been to the general public or a large number of persons. But there was a prima facie case of violation of the state constitutional right to privacy.

McCormick v. England

South Carolina Court of Appeals
328 S.C. 627, 494 S.E.2d 431 (1997)

ANDERSON, Judge: ...

Dr. England was the family physician for McCormick, her former husband, and their children. McCormick and her husband became involved in a divorce action in which custody of the children was at issue. In support of his Motion for Emergency Relief and a Restraining Order, McCormick's husband submitted two letters to the family court regarding McCormick's emotional status. One letter was from a licensed social worker, defendant Michael Meyers, who alleged that McCormick had a severe drinking problem which caused her to be a danger to herself and to her family. The other letter was prepared by Dr. England and was addressed "To Whom It May Concern." In his letter, Dr. England diagnosed McCormick as suffering from "major depression and alcoholism, acute and chronic." Further, Dr. England stated the children had experienced school difficulties due to the family discord caused by McCormick's drinking. He stated it was his medical opinion that McCormick was "a danger to herself and to her family with her substance abuse and major depressive symptoms," and concluded that she required hospitalization. There is no indication in the record that the letter was prepared under court order.

McCormick brought this action for negligence, libel, invasion of privacy, outrage, breach of confidence, and civil conspiracy against Dr. England and Meyers. She alleged in her fifth cause of action for breach of confidence that Dr. England and Meyers had breached "a duty of non-disclosure of confidential communications with the plaintiff concerning her mental health conditions" by publishing and disseminating these confidential communications to the public "in direct contravention of South Carolina statutory law." Specifically, McCormick alleged a duty of confidentiality existed pursuant to S.C. Code Ann. § 19-11-95 (Supp. 1996), entitled "Confidences of patients of mental illness or emotional conditions."

Dr. England filed a motion to strike the fifth cause of action for breach of confidence on the basis the facts alleged failed to constitute a cause of action. At the hearing on the motion, McCormick additionally relied on the Physicians' Patient Records Act, S.C. Code Ann. §§ 44-115-10 to -150 (Supp. 1996), which prohibits the disclosure of medical records without the patient's consent.

The judge granted the motion to strike the breach of confidence action as to Dr. England, stating, "It is well known that South Carolina does not recognize the physician patient-privilege at common law." The judge found there was no statutory duty of confidentiality alleged that was applicable to Dr. England. The judge noted that, under its terms, § 19-11-95 applies only to licensed psychologists, counselors, family therapists, social workers, and registered nurses. Therefore, the statute did not apply to Dr. England. Further, since the letter did not disclose any medical records as such, the judge found the "duty of confidentiality" imposed by the Records Act was also inapplicable. Finally, the judge found that, in any event, there was no breach of confidence resulting from Dr. England's disclosures because "the letter was written out of necessity and for the express purpose of protecting others as well as [McCormick] herself due to her mental and emotional condition at that time." ...

McCormick argues the trial court erred in finding South Carolina does not recognize the common law tort of breach of confidence as applied to the physician-patient relationship. We agree....

... Although many states have statutorily created a "physician-patient testimonial privilege," South Carolina has not enacted a similar statute and does not recognize the physician-patient privilege. However, the absence of a testimonial privilege prohibiting certain in-court disclosures is not determinative of our issue because this evidentiary privilege is distinguishable from a duty of confidentiality. As our Supreme Court recently observed in *South Carolina State Board of Medical Examiners v. Hedgepath*, 325 S.C. 166, 480 S.E.2d 724 (1997): "The terms 'privilege' and 'confidences' are not synonymous, and a professional's duty to maintain his client's confidences is independent of the issue whether he can be legally compelled to reveal some or all of those confidences, that is, whether those communications are privileged." ....

[In *Hedgepath* the] court held that a physician commits misconduct when he reveals a patient's confidences where the revelation is neither compelled by law (i.e. by subpoena or statute) nor consented to by the patient....

... A majority of the jurisdictions faced with the issue have recognized a cause of action against a physician for the unauthorized disclosure of confidential information unless the disclosure is compelled by law or is in the patient's interest or the public interest....

In the absence of express litigation, courts have found the basis for a right of action for wrongful disclosure in four main sources: (1) state physician licensing statutes, (2) evidentiary rules and privileged communication statutes which prohibit a physician from testifying in judicial proceedings, (3) common law principles of trust, and (4) the Hippocratic Oath and principles of medical ethics which proscribe the revelation of patient confidences. The jurisdictions that recognize the duty of confidentiality have relied on various theories for the cause of action, including invasion of privacy, breach of implied contract, medical malpractice, and breach of fiduciary duty or a duty of confidentiality....

In *Hague v. Williams*, 37 N.J. 328, 181 A.2d 345 (1962), the Supreme Court of New Jersey stated that, ordinarily, a physician receives information relating to a patient's health in a confidential capacity and should not disclose such information without the patient's consent except where the public interest or the private interest of the patient so demands.... The court explained the importance of the physician-patient duty of confidentiality: "A patient should be entitled to freely disclose his symptoms and condition to his doctor in order to receive proper treatment without fear that those facts may become public property. Only thus can the purpose of the relationship be fulfilled." ...

We find the reasoning of the cases from other jurisdictions persuasive on this issue and today we join the majority and hold that an actionable tort[7] lies for a physician's

7. "[T]he duty of confidentiality, where it exists, generally arises out of broadly applicable societal norms and public policy concerning the kinds of relationship at issue. It does not arise out of specific agreement or particularized circumstances. Moreover, the object of the law when this duty is violated is compensation for the resulting injuries, not fulfillment of expectation. Therefore, liability should be grounded in tort law." Alan B. Vickery, Note, *Breach of Confidence: An Emerging Tort*, [82 Colum. L. Rev. 1426 (1982)] at 1451.

breach of the duty to maintain the confidences of his or her patient in the absence of a compelling public interest or other justification for the disclosure.

... [T]he existence of a cause of action for invasion of privacy should not preclude our recognition of an independent tort for a physician's breach of confidence because the actions are distinguishable....

... [A]n invasion of privacy claim narrowly proscribes the conduct to that which is "highly offensive" and "likely to cause serious mental injury." This standard is not consistent with the duty attaching to a confidential relationship because it focuses on the *content*, rather than the *source of information*. The unauthorized revelation of confidential medical information should be protected without regard to the degree of its offensiveness....

Further, the requirement of "publicity" is a limitation which would preclude many cases involving a breach of confidentiality. Publicity involves disclosures to the public, not just an individual or a small group. However, where the information disclosed is received in confidence, "one can imagine many cases where the greatest injury results from disclosure to a single person, such as a spouse, or to a small group, such as an insurance company resisting a claim. A confidential relationship is breached if unauthorized disclosure is made to only one person not a party to the confidence, but the right of privacy does not cover such a case." ... "Privacy is a right against the public at large. Its doctrinal limits narrowly circumscribe the zone of proscribed conduct in order to prevent hindrance of public expression. In contrast, a right to confidentiality exists against a specific person, who, by virtue of his relationship to the confider, has notice of the duty to preserve the secrecy of clearly identifiable information. Privacy's doctrinal limits are thus unnecessary in breach-of-confidence situations, and should not bar recovery to plaintiffs deserving of a remedy." [Alan B. Vickery, Note, *Breach of Confidence: An Emerging Tort, supra.*]

Although many jurisdictions recognize a cause of action for breach of the duty of confidentiality, they do not hold that this duty is absolute. Public policy requires that where it is reasonably necessary to protect the interest of the patient or others, a physician may breach the duty to maintain patient confidentiality. The Utah Supreme Court explained, "Where life, safety, well-being or other important interest is in jeopardy, one having information which could protect against the hazard, may have a conditional privilege to reveal information for such a purpose...." *Berry v. Moench*, 8 Utah 2d 191, 331 P.2d 814, 817–18 (1958)....

... Because this claim for breach of confidence was decided on a motion to strike, the record is incomplete on whether the disclosure was necessary for the protection of the children and we make no comment in this regard. On remand, the could should consider whether under the circumstances Dr. England's disclosures were privileged....

[Reversed and remanded.]

Notes

1. An employer provides health insurance for employees and their families. An employee's wife is hospitalized. Her treatment—"acute and chronic alcoholism detoxification"—is stated on an insurance claim form sent by her treating physician to the employer. This disclosure may have been inadvertent. Liability? See Prince v. St. Francis-St. George Hospital, Inc., 20 Ohio App. 3d 4, 484 N.E.2d 265 (1985). A psychiatrist writes a book that reveals information learned in sessions with former patients. Does this give a nonconsenting patient a cause of action? Should the remedy include an injunction? See Doe

v. Roe, 93 Misc. 2d 201, 400 N.Y.S.2d 668 (Sup. Ct. 1977) (doctor impliedly covenants to keep in confidence all of patient's disclosures about physical or mental condition; patient entitled to injunction against further circulation of book, although treatment by psychiatrist had ended years earlier and book had educational purpose).

2. What if a psychiatrist reveals information only to a patient's spouse? See MacDonald v. Clinger, 84 A.D.2d 482, 446 N.Y.S.2d 801 (1982) (information should not be disclosed without patient's authorization unless there is danger to patient, spouse or other person). Compare Mikel v. Abrams, 541 F. Supp. 591 (W.D. Mo. 1982), aff'd, 716 F.2d 907 (8th Cir. 1983) (details of patient's psychological condition disclosed to wife; wife had been present, with patient's consent, during discussions of treatment). A mother gives up her baby for adoption immediately after birth. The child later wants to learn who is her natural mother. If the doctor who delivered the baby helps the child learn the mother's identity, is the doctor liable to the mother? See Humphers v. First Interstate Bank of Oregon, 298 Or. 706, 696 P.2d 527 (1985).

3. If a duty of medical confidentiality is recognized, when will the interests of the patient or other persons warrant exceptions? If the obligation of confidence is an understanding that is an implied term of a doctor-patient contract, should any exception be found? See Horne v. Patton, 291 Ala. 701, 287 So. 2d 824 (1973) (disclosure of employee's nervous condition to employer); Morris v. Consolidation Coal Co., 191 W. Va. 426, 446 S.E.2d 648 (1994) (plaintiff claimed workers' compensation for injury; physician communicated with representative of plaintiff's employer); Simonsen v. Swenson, 104 Neb. 224, 177 N.W. 831 (1920) (doctor warned hotel proprietor that guest had contagious disease); Chizmar v. Mackie, 896 P.2d 196 (Alaska 1995) (doctor informed husband that wife had tested positive for HIV/AIDS); Bryson v. Tillinghast, 749 P.2d 110 (Okla. 1988) (learning that police were looking for rapist with injuries inflicted by victim, doctor told police that patient had such injuries). On liability of a physician for disclosure of confidential information generally, see Annot., Physician's Tort Liability for Unauthorized Disclosure of Confidential Information About Patient, 48 A.L.R.4th 668 (1986).

4. Can someone who is not a health care professional be liable for disclosing confidential medical information that was received as a result of a breach of medical confidence? Is it a tort to induce a breach of medical confidence? See Alberts v. Devine, 395 Mass. 59, 479 N.E.2d 113 (1985), cert. denied sub nom. Carroll v. Alberts, 474 U.S. 1013 (1985) (minister's action against superiors for inducing his psychiatrist to violate duty of confidence and communicating information to church committees and reporters); X v. Y, [1988] 2 All E.R. 648 (Q.B.D.) (employees of health authority supplied newspaper reporter with information from hospital records identifying two doctors who continued practice after contracting AIDS; newspaper enjoined from publishing doctors' identities and other information from confidential hospital records).

5. Recognizing a cause of action for disclosure of non-public medical information acquired within a physician-patient relationship, the court in Biddle v. Warren General Hospital, 86 Ohio St. 3d 395, 715 N.E.2d 518 (1999), held that hospital patients had a tort action for the hospital's disclosure of patient registration forms to its law firm. The disclosure was intended to identify patients eligible for Supplemental Security Income (Social Security) coverage, which would pay unpaid medical bills. The court also held that the patients had an action against the law firm for inducing unauthorized, unprivileged disclosure of non-public medical information. The court found no privilege applicable to the case. It rejected the argument that the hospital could freely disclose information to its law firm, which would be expected to keep it confidential. The court concluded that the facts did not support a privilege claim based on the interests of the patients or the hospital's interest in debt collection.

6. Consider whether there can be liability on the basis of breach of confidence in the following situations:

(a) A pharmacist tells someone that a customer has obtained a certain prescription medication. Fanean v. Rite Aid Corp., 984 A.2d 812 (Del. Super. Ct. 2009); Evans v. Rite Aid Corp., 324 S.C. 269, 478 S.E.2d 846 (1996). Cf. Anonymous v. CVS Corp., 188 Misc. 2d 616, 728 N.Y.S.2d 333 (Sup. Ct. 2001).

(b) Plaintiff's application for life insurance authorizes release of confidential medical information to the insurance company. The company transmits this to an information exchange bureau used by seven hundred member life insurance companies. Senogles v. Security Benefit Life Insurance Co., 217 Kan. 438, 536 P.2d 1358 (1975).

(c) An employee is seriously injured on the job. Without his permission, his employer uses a color photograph of his wound as a "shocker" to remind other employees of the possible consequences of an industrial accident. The employee is identified by name in the photograph. Lambert v. Dow Chemical Co., 215 So. 2d 673 (La. App. 1968).

(d) A member of the clergy discloses the contents of a confidential conversation with a parishioner. Lightman v. Flaum, 97 N.Y.2d 128, 736 N.Y.S.2d 300, 761 N.E.2d 1027 (2001), cert. denied, 535 U.S. 1096 (2002).

(e) A clerk in a government department tells her brother about the pregnancy of an unmarried woman who has applied for a government maternity benefit in her office. The woman had kept her pregnancy a secret and the pregnancy soon ended in a miscarriage. O'Neill v. Department of Health and Social Services (No. 2), [1986] N.I. 290 (Q.B.D.).

(f) An airline tells a caller that an individual has made reservations for a certain flight. Carr v. City of New Orleans, 622 So. 2d 819 (La. App. 1993), writ denied, 629 So. 2d 404 (La. 1993) (disclosed to law enforcement personnel).

(g) A mother tells her son's teacher "in strict confidence" that the boy has a progressively disabling and eventually fatal disease that he is not yet aware of. The teacher discloses this to the boy's classmates, who then tell the boy he has a fatal disease and ask him when he will die. Wynne v. Orcutt Union School District, 17 Cal. App. 3d 1108, 95 Cal. Rptr. 458 (1971).

(h) After being assured that his identity as a source of the information will not be revealed, a private citizen gives police and other government officials information pertinent to an investigation the officials are conducting. His identity is leaked to the press. G v. Day, [1982] 1 N.S.W.L.R. 24 (Sup. Ct.) (newspaper enjoined from publishing identity). Cf. X v. Attorney-General, [1997] 2 N.Z.L.R. 623 (Sup. Ct.) (identity of undercover police officer confirmed by police inspector).

(i) A husband obtains a divorce from his wife on the ground of her adultery. The husband intends to give a newspaper, for publication, information he obtained during the marriage about his ex-wife's private life, personal affairs and conduct. Duchess of Argyll v. Duke of Argyll, [1967] Ch. 302 (communication of information by husband enjoined; law's policy is to preserve confidence and mutual trust between husband and wife; ex-wife's adultery did not entitle husband to publish confidences of married life). Compare Lennon v. News Group Newspapers Ltd., [1978] F.S.R. 573 (C.A.) (ex-Beatle John Lennon refused injunction against publication of article by former wife; not breach of confidence because both had put their relationship in "public domain" by previous revelations).

7. Is it a tort, on the basis of breach of confidence, to gain access to the contents of plaintiff's confidential communications with a professional by electronic eavesdropping or going into the professional's files? See Madden v. Creative Services, Inc., 84 N.Y.2d 738, 622 N.Y.S.2d 478, 646 N.E.2d 780 (1995) (defendants intruded into files of plaintiff's attorney). Cf. Francome v. Mirror Group Newspapers Ltd., [1984] 1 W.L.R. 892 (C.A.) (electronic eavesdropping on telephone conversations). Would there be liability for using confidential documents if they were sent to the user by mistake? See English & American Insurance Co. Ltd. v. Herbert Smith, [1988] F.S.R. 232 (Ch. D.) (solicitors received documents intended for solicitors for other side in pending litigation; use of information enjoined).

8. It has been recognized as an implied term of the contract between a bank and its customer that the bank will not, without the customer's consent, divulge to third persons the state of the customer's account or any information concerning the customer acquired through the bank's handling of the account—unless compelled by court order, a public duty, or the need for self-protection. Thus, a breach of confidence has been found when a bank customer endorsed a check over to another party and the bank, learning that the other party was a bookmaker, revealed this to third persons. Tournier v. National Provincial and Union Bank of England, [1924] 1 K.B. 461 (C.A.). What if a bank tells a customer's employer that some of the customer's checks have been returned for insufficient funds? See Peterson v. Idaho First National Bank, 83 Idaho 578, 367 P.2d 284 (1961) (breach of implied contract not to disclose information concerning account). Suppose a bank suspects that a customer is involved in a criminal activity, because of his deposit of numerous bills with sequential serial numbers, and reports this to the police? See Suburban Trust Co. v. Waller, 44 Md. App. 335, 408 A.2d 758 (1979) (disclosure wrongful in absence of consent by customer or court order; resulted in filing of mistaken robbery charge against customer). Is it wrongful to tell a creditor that the debtor has money on deposit at the bank? See Milohnich v. First National Bank of Miami Springs, 224 So. 2d 759 (Fla. App. 1969) (creditors sued to enjoin paying out funds on deposit). Banks appear to owe no duty of confidence to borrowers concerning the making and repayment of loans. See Hopewell Enterprises, Inc. v. Trustmark National Bank, 680 So. 2d 812 (Miss. 1996); Schoneweis v. Dando, 231 Neb. 180, 435 N.W.2d 666 (1989). Compare Djowharzadeh v. City National Bank and Trust Co. of Norman, p. 328, supra.

9. Cohen v. Cowles Media Co., 479 N.W.2d 387 (Minn. 1992), held newspapers liable on the basis of promissory estoppel for publishing the identity of the source of a news story in violation of promises given the source by the newspapers' reporters. This followed a 5–4 decision by the United States Supreme Court that liability would not violate the First Amendment despite the newsworthiness of the information. Cohen v. Cowles Media Co., 501 U.S. 663 (1991). The Supreme Court emphasized that the promissory estoppel doctrine was a law of general application that did not single out the press. What if a private individual violates a promise to keep personal information confidential by revealing it to a reporter? See Stephens v. Avery, [1988] Ch. 449 (plaintiff had discussed personal matters with close friend, including fact that plaintiff had lesbian relationship with woman killed by her husband; friend communicated this to newspaper, which published it in connection with husband's trial for homicide; held that information was subject to duty of confidence enforceable against ex-friend and newspaper).

10. Bartnicki v. Vopper, 532 U.S. 514 (2001), might affect considerably the extent to which the recipient of information obtained through another party's breach of confidence can be held liable. The case involved a statutory damages claim by persons whose cellular telephone conversation had been illegally intercepted and recorded. A tape of the

conversation was given to a private citizen, who delivered it to a local radio station commentator. He played the tape on his program. Another station broadcast the tape and local newspapers published its contents. All of the parties came within statutory provisions making it unlawful to disclose the contents of a communication knowing or having reason to know the contents were obtained through illegal interception of the communication. The Supreme Court held (6–3) that the First Amendment precluded the application of the statutes in the circumstances of the case. Four justices concluded that the First Amendment barred liability because what defendants disclosed was a matter of public concern and defendants did not act unlawfully in receiving it. Two other justices decided the case on the more narrow ground that as the conversation broadcast included a threat of physical harm to others and the parties to the conversation were "limited public figures," a "matter of unusual public concern" was involved and the parties had little or no legitimate interest in maintaining the privacy of the conversation.

11. Note that breach of confidence theories of liability do more than avoid the requirement of publicity applied to invasion of privacy actions. They afford a remedy in places, such as New York and Great Britain, that have no common law invasion of privacy action. See generally Gilles, Promises Betrayed: Breach of Confidence as a Remedy for Invasions of Privacy, 43 Buffalo L. Rev. 1 (1995); Richards & Solove, Privacy's Other Path: Recovering the Law of Confidentiality, 96 Georgetown L.J. 123 (2007).

Section 4. False Light

Leverton v. Curtis Publishing Company

United States Court of Appeals, Third Circuit
192 F.2d 974 (1951)

GOODRICH, Circuit Judge....

[Plaintiff, when a child of ten, was involved in a street accident in Birmingham, Alabama. A car nearly ran over her. A newspaper photographer who happened to be at the scene took a dramatic photograph of the child being lifted to her feet by a bystander. The photograph appeared in a Birmingham newspaper the next day. Twenty months later it was used as an illustration for a magazine article on traffic accidents, emphasizing pedestrian carelessness, entitled "They Ask To Be Killed." The print was purchased by the magazine's publisher from a supplier of illustration material. Plaintiff claimed that the publication of her picture violated her right of privacy.] ...

The general criterion for liability, as stated in the Restatement, is that "liability exists only if the defendant's conduct was such that he should have realized that it would be offensive to persons of ordinary sensibilities." This is just the criterion which the trial judge submitted in leaving this case to the jury....

... It is agreed on all sides that the original publication of the picture of this traffic accident was not actionable. If it invaded the right of the plaintiff to stay out of public attention, it was a privileged invasion, her interest in being left alone being overbalanced by the general public interest in being informed. As we see the questions in this case, they are two. (1) Is the privilege involved in the original publication lost by the lapse of time between the date of the original publication immediately following the accident and the reappearance of the plaintiff's picture in the Saturday Evening Post twenty months later? (2) The second question is whether, if the privilege has not been lost by lapse of time, it is lost by the using of the plaintiff's picture, not in connection with a news story, but as an illustration heading an article on pedestrian traffic accidents? ...

It could be easily agreed that the plaintiff in this case, because she was once involved in an automobile accident does not continue throughout her life to have her goings and comings made the subject of newspaper stories. That, however, is a long way from saying that the occasion of her once becoming a subject of public interest cannot be brought again to public attention later on. Suppose the same newspaper which printed the plaintiff's photograph the day after her accident printed a resume sometime later of traffic accidents and supplied pictures dealing with them, including this one, which photographers on its staff had compiled. We cannot think that their publication under those circumstances would subject the publisher to liability....

We conclude that the immunity from liability for the original publication was not lost through lapse of time when the same picture was again published.

Now to the second point. The first publication of the plaintiff's photograph was purely news. The second publication was a sort of dramatic setting for the discussion of a traffic problem by Mr. Wittels [the article's author]. Does that much of a change in the purpose of the publication lose the privilege? ...

... [W]e think this particular publication was an actionable invasion of plaintiff's right of privacy. Granted that she was "newsworthy" with regard to her traffic accident. Assume, also, that she continued to be newsworthy with regard to that particular accident for an indefinite time afterward. This use of her picture had nothing at all to do with her accident. It related to the general subject of traffic accidents and pedestrian carelessness. Yet the facts, so far as we know them in this case, show that the little girl, herself, was at the time of her accident not careless and the motorist was. The picture is used in connection with several headings tending to say that this plaintiff narrowly escaped death because she was careless of her own safety. That is not libelous; a count for defamation was dropped out in the course of the trial. But we are not talking now about liability for defamation. We are talking about the privilege to invade her interest in being left alone.

The heading of the article was called "They Ask To Be Killed". Underneath the picture of the little girl was the heading "Safety education in schools has reduced child accidents measurably, but unpredictable darting through traffic still takes a sobering toll." In a box beside the title appears the following: "Do you invite massacre by your own carelessness? Here's how thousands have committed suicide by scorning laws that were passed to keep them alive." The sum total of all this is that this particular plaintiff, the legitimate subject for publicity for one particular accident, now becomes a pictorial, frightful example of pedestrian carelessness. This, we think, exceeds the bounds of privilege.

An analogous case, though admittedly not right in point, is Mau v. Rio Grande Oil, Inc., D.C.N.D. Cal. 1939, 28 F. Supp. 845. There a man who was a holdup victim had his unhappy experience translated into a radio program with garnishment and embellishment appropriate for that form of entertainment. The news account of the holdup was, of course, comparable to a news account of a traffic accident. But when his account came to be the basis for public entertainment, the Court considered the bounds of privilege exceeded. We think the same is true here.

[Judgment awarding plaintiff $5000 damages affirmed.]

Notes

1. A number of cases find a cause of action for invasion of privacy in the inappropriate use of a photograph as an illustration. See Peay v. Curtis Publishing Co., 78 F. Supp. 305 (D.D.C. 1948) (photograph of Washington, D.C. taxi driver illustrating article depicting Washington taxi drivers as ill-mannered, contemptuous of patrons and dishonest); Gill v. Curtis Publishing Co., 38 Cal. 2d 273, 239 P.2d 630 (1952) (in article concerning love and its relation to divorce, photograph of embracing couple, actually happily married, with caption about "love at first sight" being "bad risk"). In Quezada by De Lamota v. Daily News, 125 Misc. 2d 302, 479 N.Y.S.2d 682 (N.Y. Civ. Ct. 1984), modified, 130 Misc. 2d 842, 501 N.Y.S.2d 971 (Sup. Ct. 1986), a drawing based on a photograph of plaintiffs was used to illustrate an article about juvenile crime. Plaintiffs claimed that the drawing was virtually identical to the photograph and they were recognized as the boys in the drawing. Defendant claimed that the artist substantially altered the boys' appearance in order to avoid legal problems.

2. In Martinez v. Democrat-Herald Publishing Co., Inc., 64 Or. App. 690, 669 P.2d 818 (1983), review denied, 296 Or. 120, 672 P.2d 1193 (1983), a newspaper story on drug use in a junior high school was accompanied by photographs of what were said to be "apparent drug transactions" between students. In a suit by one of the students photographed, defendants were permitted to present evidence of this student's use of marijuana. Was this correct? Should plaintiff have an action if an advertisement containing his name was supposed to be illustrated with his picture, but someone else's picture is used by mistake? See Barr v. Southern Bell Telephone and Telegraph Co., 13 N.C. App. 388, 185 S.E.2d 714 (1972).

3. A fictionalized account of a public event may lead to liability if it portrays the participants in a misleading light. See Garner v. Triangle Publications, Inc., 97 F. Supp. 546 (S.D.N.Y. 1951), where plaintiffs had been convicted of murder. Their convictions were eventually reversed, but meanwhile defendants' magazines published articles, with lurid titles, about the alleged murder and plaintiffs' relations with one another. It was held that liability depended upon whether the articles were factual reports or fictional accounts. Cf. Varnish v. Best Medium Publishing Co. Inc., 405 F.2d 608 (2d Cir. 1968), cert. denied, 394 U.S. 987 (1969). An article concerning the suicide of plaintiff's wife portrayed her as a happy person. It indicated that her husband was insensitive and lacking in understanding toward her. The husband alleged in an action against the publisher that the wife had been a depressed, despondent person; she and plaintiff had had a difficult life, but plaintiff had done all he could for her. The evidence was held sufficient to support a finding that the article presented a false and distorted picture of plaintiff's relationship with his wife.

4. In Leopold v. Levin, 45 Ill. 2d 434, 259 N.E.2d 250 (1970), plaintiff had been a defendant in a famous murder case, the "Leopold-Loeb case." Three decades after plaintiff's prosecution, in which he pled guilty, a novel based on the case was published. Soon thereafter, a film based on the novel was produced. Plaintiff's name was not used in the novel or film, but advertising for the novel and film represented them as fictionalized accounts of the Leopold-Loeb case. Plaintiff's invasion of privacy claim against the author and distributors of the novel and producer, distributor and exhibitors of the film failed. One reason was that the fictionalized aspects of the book and motion picture were "reasonably comparable to, or conceivable from facts of record from which they were drawn."

5. In Hinish v. Meier & Frank Co., Inc., p. 387, supra, a store manager signed plaintiff's name to a telegram urging the governor to veto a bill. The court decided that plaintiff, a civil service employee of the government prohibited by law from engaging in political

activity, had an invasion of privacy action on the basis of appropriation of his name and personality. Might he have had an action by reason of the false representation that he supported veto of the bill or that he was engaged in political activity? Are there other cases in which invasion of privacy by "appropriation" was found but false representation would be a better basis of liability?

6. This theory of liability has the same requirement of "publicity" as liability for disclosure of private facts. When the element of publicity is absent, defendant is not liable. See Polin v. Dun & Bradstreet, Inc., 768 F.2d 1204 (10th Cir. 1985) (sending credit report to seventeen subscribers not publicity); Moore v. Big Picture Co., 828 F.2d 270 (5th Cir. 1987); Pace v. Bristol Hospital, 964 F. Supp. 628 (D. Conn. 1997). It is also limited to individuals and thus denied to such entities as corporations. Restatement (Second) of Torts § 652I (1977). Is this desirable?

Uhl v. Columbia Broadcasting Systems, Inc.

United States District Court, Western District of Pennsylvania
476 F. Supp. 1134 (1979)

WEBER, Chief Judge

The season when ordinarily kind hearted business men fill up their pockets with cartridges,

And go prowling around the woods in search of caribous and partridges.

O. Nash

...

This was a diversity action for invasion of privacy under the rule of Sec. 652E of the Restatement of Torts (Second).* It did not include a claim for defamation which, by a quirk of Pennsylvania procedural law then in effect, was time barred.... The jury found for plaintiff and awarded nominal damages of one dollar. Defendant moves for Judgment N.O.V.

The action arose out of the CBS special TV broadcast called "The Guns of Autumn." This TV special ran on the nationwide network for 1½ hours of prime time. In format, development, dramatic arrangement, and commentary (like the chorus which supplies the continuity in the classic Greek drama) it was a splendid piece of "show biz", and evoked a storm of adverse comment throughout the country. Although plaintiff belatedly attempted to raise a second false light invasion of privacy claim by reason of the inclusion of his picture in the entire production, which generally portrayed bad hunting practices, he was limited at trial by his pleading to the specific segment which he had pleaded as depicting him in a false light....

The short segment giving rise to the cause of action was of about a minute's duration, showing some frames of wild geese walking in a cleared patch of ground at the edge of a cornfield, an immediate switch to frames showing close-up views of some hunters (including plaintiff) in a blind fashioned from cornstocks rising and shooting in a generally

---

* "One who gives publicity to a matter concerning another that places the other before the public in a false light is subject to liability to the other for invasion of his privacy, if (a) the false light in which the other was placed would be highly offensive to a reasonable person, and (b) the actor had knowledge of or acted in reckless disregard as to the falsity of the publicized matter and the false light in which the other would be placed." [Ed.]

horizontal direction, then an immediate switch to the plaintiff walking in the cleared cornfield and picking up a dead goose. The plaintiff argued that the inference of the immediate juxtaposition of these scenes made him appear in the false light of a hunter who engaged in the very unsportsmanlike and unethical act of shooting a goose on the ground. The jury heard the testimony of the plaintiff and his companion that the spliced together segments of film did not accurately portray the events, that they did not shoot the geese walking in the clearing despite the urging of the CBS camera crew to do so, and that the downed goose was shot in the air as it approached the clearing....

The first point raised in Defendant's Motion for Judgment N.O.V. is that as a matter of law the film on which the claim is based is not capable of conveying the false light meaning which plaintiff ascribes to it; i.e. that it portrayed plaintiff as having shot a goose that was on the ground when he shot it. The issue of falsity was submitted to the jury. The court and jury saw three scenes in short and quick sequence, a long shot of geese walking on the ground, a close up of the plaintiff shooting, a long shot of plaintiff walking in the field and picking up a dead goose. The implication is clear. The falsity of the portrayal was shown by plaintiff's testimony that these were separate shots of separate incidents divided by time intervals, and the editing of the film to provide this sequence to fit within the time frame of the broadcast was evident not only for this incident, but for the whole segment dealing with the Pymatuning waterfowl propagation area where the film passed from the pre-dawn darkness, to sunrise, to mid-morning in a few minutes.

The defendant complains that even if this message was conveyed to the viewer it would not be highly offensive to a reasonable person, and that therefore the matter should not have been submitted to the jury. This essential element of the cause of action under Sec. 652E was given to the jury in the instructions. Regardless of what a cameraman from Brooklyn or a lawyer from New York might think, or even what a Pennsylvania trial judge who is not a hunter might think, it appears from the testimony at trial that in wide reaches of America west of the Hudson where the flights of wild geese darken the noonday sky this is a rather nasty thing to say about a hunter, even if you smile when saying it. This was so testified by witnesses and supported by documentary evidence. It is clearly a fact question for a jury to say what the reaction of a reasonable man might be....

The most strongly pressed of defendant's arguments is the failure of plaintiff to present evidence to defeat defendant's constitutional privilege under the First Amendment.

We will accept the premise that the rule of *New York Times v. Sullivan*, 376 U.S. 254 (1964), applies to this case, under the extension of that rule to matters of public concern, which include news, information, education and entertainment. While this requires proof of malice in the sense of scienter, that defendant had knowledge of the falsity or acted in reckless disregard of the truth or falsity of the matters presented, defendant also argues that such evidence requires proof of the subjective state of mind of defendant's agents, a subjective test, by clear and convincing evidence.... [The court rejected this argument.]

In *Cantrell v. Forest City Publishing Co.*, 419 U.S. 245 (1974), the Court upheld a finding of malice in an invasion of privacy case on a showing that the writer's account gave an impression of a face-to-face interview with the plaintiff, which had not occurred. The Court found these pseudo-factual recitals of matters occurring during the interview to be "calculated falsehoods" sufficient to support a finding of knowing or reckless untruth. In the present case the testimony of the plaintiff and his companion as to the sequence of the events in the blind, compared to the obviously edited film version clearly demonstrate that the film version was not true and that the employees who spliced the segments of film together did so to produce the effect of shock they were seeking. Plaintiff and his witness testified that the portrayal was not accurate, yet the resulting pictorial episode produced an illustration of unsportsmanlike behavior to illustrate defendant's message. This is similar to the situation in *Leverton v. Curtis Publishing Co.* [p. 473, supra]....

While punitive or exemplary damages were claimed in this action, the court refused plaintiff's request for a charge on this claim.... In so doing we were following the distinction between the definition of "actual malice" as established in *New York Times v. Sullivan*, and the common law standard of malice generally required to support an award of punitive damages.... *Sullivan's* malice is "'with knowledge that [a defamatory statement] was false or with reckless disregard of whether it was false or not.' As so defined, of course, 'actual malice' is a term of art, created to provide a convenient shorthand expression for a standard of liability that must be established before a State may constitutionally permit public officials to recover for libel in actions brought against publishers.... In a false-light case, common-law malice — frequently expressed either in terms of personal ill will toward the plaintiff or reckless or wanton disregard of the plaintiff's rights — would focus on the defendant's attitude toward the plaintiff's privacy, not toward the truth or falsity of the material published." [*Cantrell*, at 251–252.] ...

[Motion denied.]

Notes

1. A picture in a sociology textbook shows a white policeman prodding a black man with his night stick. The caption identifies the social status of an offender as the most significant determinant of arrest, conviction and penalty and asks whether the police officer would have acted in the same manner if the "offender" were a well-dressed white person. Does the policeman have a "false light" action? See Cibenko v. Worth Publishers, Inc., 510 F. Supp. 761 (D.N.J. 1981) (no; picture and caption incapable of conveying highly offensive meaning or innuendo).

2. A magazine publishes a picture of plaintiff wearing his "mummer's" costume in the Philadelphia Mummers Parade. The caption below the photograph includes the statement, "A New Year's tribute here to all the ostriches who gave their tails to make the world free for closet transvestites from South Philly to get themselves stinking drunk." Plaintiff claims this portrays him as a closet transvestite and a drunk. The magazine says that no reasonable person could so interpret the publication. Liability? See Martin v. Municipal Publications, 510 F. Supp. 255 (E.D. Pa. 1981) (jury question on whether plaintiff placed in false light highly offensive to reasonable person).

3. Plaintiff performs an aquatic act at an amusement park with "Ralph, the Diving Pig." The amusement park's public relations director supplies a publicity photograph of plaintiff and Ralph to what the director thinks is a fashion magazine. In reality, the magazine is highly pornographic. It publishes the photograph with an innocuous caption. Has the pig's partner been placed in a false light? See Braun v. Flynt, 726 F.2d 245 (5th Cir. 1984), reh'g denied, 731 F.2d 1205 (5th Cir. 1984), cert. denied sub nom. Chic Magazine, Inc. v. Braun, 469 U.S. 883 (1984) (verdict for plaintiff upheld). What if plaintiff has agreed to be photographed nude but not to publication of the photographs in a magazine? See Wood v. Hustler Magazine, Inc., 736 F.2d 1084 (5th Cir. 1984), cert. denied, 469 U.S. 1107 (1985). Cf. Douglass v. Hustler Magazine, Inc., 769 F.2d 1128 (7th Cir. 1985) (plaintiff agreed to publication of nude photographs in *Playboy* but not *Hustler*). Is there false light if readers of defendant's publication recognize that the reference to plaintiff is fictionalized or a fantasy? See Dworkin v. Hustler Magazine, Inc., 668 F. Supp.

1408 (C.D. Cal. 1987), aff'd 867 F.2d 1188 (9th Cir. 1989), cert. denied, 493 U.S. 812 (1989). Cf. Byrd v. Hustler Magazine, Inc., 433 So. 2d 593 (Fla. App. 1983), review denied, 443 So. 2d 979 (Fla. 1984) (caption said photograph was altered).

4. In Peoples Bank and Trust Co. of Mountain Home v. Globe International Publishing, Inc., 978 F.2d 1065 (8th Cir. 1992), aff'g 786 F. Supp. 791 (W.D. Ark. 1992), a supermarket tabloid had reported that a woman in Australia quit her job delivering newspapers at the age of 101 because an extramarital affair with a millionaire customer left her pregnant. To illustrate this fictitious story and a cover headline ("Pregnancy Forces Granny To Quit Work At Age 101"), the tabloid used file photographs of a ninety-five-year-old Arkansas woman who delivered newspapers. The court upheld an award of $850,000 in punitive damages to this woman, rejecting the publisher's argument that the story was so patently fictional that it could not be reasonably interpreted to contain actual facts about plaintiff. Even if the assertion of pregnancy could not be believed, other aspects of the story, including the extramarital affair and ceasing newspaper deliveries, were capable of belief. Compare the disposition of the libel claim in Pring v. Penthouse International, Ltd., p. 528, infra.

5. If a group is pictured in a false light, may individual members recover? In Michigan United Conservation Clubs v. CBS News, 485 F. Supp. 893 (W.D. Mich. 1980), aff'd, 665 F.2d 110 (6th Cir. 1981), a Michigan organization of hunters and several of its members sued the television network for the same broadcast involved in the principal case, alleging it portrayed Michigan hunters as cruel, selfish and unfeeling. The court held that when a group is portrayed in a false light, a member can maintain an action only if the group is so small that publicity reasonably can be understood as referring to that individual member, or if the circumstances surrounding the publicity support the conclusion that there is particular reference to the individual. Since the group in this case (Michigan sport hunters) had over one million members, a claim could not be maintained by individual members or on their behalf. Compare Peay v. Curtis Publishing Co., 78 F. Supp. 305 (D.D.C. 1948) (article about Washington taxi drivers illustrated by photograph of plaintiff; plaintiff could maintain privacy action).

6. In Time, Inc. v. Hill, 385 U.S. 374 (1967), plaintiffs had been held hostage in their home by escaped convicts. The event was made the subject of a novel, and later a play, both of which added fictional incidents of violence and verbal sexual insult. A magazine transported the play's actors to the home where the incident had occurred, photographed them there performing scenes from the play, and published the pictures together with text indicating that the play was a reenactment of plaintiffs' actual experience. The state courts found a cause of action under the New York privacy statute. The Supreme Court held that the First Amendment required that liability under the statute for "false reports of matters of public interest" be conditioned upon proof of "actual malice," i.e. knowing or reckless falsity in publication. This is the requirement earlier applied to defamation actions by public officials. New York Times Co. v. Sullivan, 376 U.S. 254 (1964).

7. In defamation law, Gertz v. Robert Welch, Inc., 418 U.S. 323 (1974), confined the "actual malice" requirement to cases in which a public official or "public figure" was defamed. It did not suffice that a matter of public or general interest was involved. In other cases, liability required only "fault," which has been interpreted to mean lack of reasonable prudence (negligence). Then came Cantrell v. Forest City Publishing Co., 419 U.S. 245 (1974), involving an article about the family of a man killed in a bridge disaster. The article, published about nine months after the tragedy, emphasized the family's poverty and contained several inaccuracies. "Most conspicuously," although the victim's widow was not present during the reporter's visit to her home, he wrote that she would not talk about what had happened and wore "the same mask of non-expression she wore at the funeral."

The widow and her children sued. The trial court allowed the case to go to the jury on a false light theory. The jury returned a verdict in plaintiffs' favor. The Supreme Court held the record sufficient to support a finding of false light through knowing or reckless untruth and ordered entry of judgment on the jury's verdict.

8. Does "actual malice" remain a requirement of "false light" even for plaintiffs who were not public figures? See Dodrill v. Arkansas Democrat Co., 265 Ark. 628, 590 S.W.2d 840 (1979), cert. denied, 444 U.S. 1076 (1981). Plaintiff's name was not on a list furnished to a newspaper of persons who had passed the bar examination. The newspaper published an article stating that plaintiff had failed the exam. Plaintiff alleged that he had in fact passed but his name was omitted due to an investigation into his character and he was subsequently certified for admission. In plaintiff's false light suit against the newspaper the court ruled that plaintiff, even if a private figure, was required to show knowing falsity or reckless disregard. This was not proved. The court concluded that Time, Inc. v. Hill was unaffected by the subsequent defamation cases. In Lovgren v. Citizens First National Bank of Princeton, 126 Ill. 2d 411, 534 N.E.2d 987 (1989), and Colbert v. World Publishing Co., 747 P.2d 286 (Okla. 1987), the court retained knowledge or reckless disregard of falsity as a state law requirement. Compare Crump v. Beckley Newspapers, Inc., 173 W. Va. 699, 320 S.E.2d 70 (1983), in which the photograph of a female coal miner was used to illustrate an article that discussed harassment of women working in mines. The court held that a negligence standard of liability applied to false light claims, as well as defamation claims, involving private individuals. Accord, Wood v. Hustler Magazine, Inc., supra (negligence in ascertaining that there was consent to publication of nude photograph and caption).

Cain v. Hearst Corporation

Supreme Court of Texas
878 S.W.2d 577 (1994)

Justice GONZALEZ delivered the opinion of the Court....

Clyde Cain is a prison inmate in the Texas Department of Corrections serving a life sentence for murder. He sued the Hearst Corporation, d/b/a the Houston Chronicle Publishing Company, claiming that a newspaper article invaded his privacy by placing him in a false light. The article, which appeared in the Chronicle on June 30, 1991, referred to Cain as a burglar, thief, pimp, and killer. In recounting Cain's criminal record the article, in summary, states that: "Cain is believed to have killed as many as eight people; Cain killed one of his lawyers in 1973 and married the lawyer's widow a few months later; Cain killed a 67 year old man in 1977; in 1983 he 'bought' a prostitute from a friend to help finance his activities; Cain persuaded the prostitute to marry a trailer park owner named Anderson, so that Cain could kill Anderson and share the prostitute's inheritance from Anderson; when the prostitute balked, Cain threatened to kill her 5 year old daughter and 'deliver her daughter's head in a wastepaper basket'; the prostitute married Anderson 3 days later, and on January 5, 1985 Cain killed Anderson." Cain's sole complaint is that the article printed false information that he was a member of the "Dixie Mafia" and that he had killed as many as eight people. Cain asserted that these statements put him in a false light with the public. Suit was filed in state court one and one-half years after the article was published.

[The action was removed to a federal district court. The court dismissed the action on the grounds that plaintiff's action "lies in libel" and the one-year limitation period for the action had expired. The Court of Appeals certified to the Supreme Court of Texas the questions whether Texas recognized the tort of false light invasion of privacy and which statute of limitations governed that action.]

If we were to recognize a false light tort in Texas, it would largely duplicate several existing causes of action, particularly defamation.... [L]ike false light, defamatory statements must be false in order to be actionable. The false light tort also overlaps with some of the other, better recognized, privacy torts ...

Furthermore, the elements of damages that have been recognized in false light actions are similar to those awarded for defamation. The principal element of actual damages for false light claims is typically mental anguish, but physical illness and harm to the plaintiff's commercial interests have also been recognized. These are essentially the types of damages sought in defamation actions. Thus many, if not all, of the injuries redressed by the false light tort are also redressed by defamation.

The false light cases considered by Texas courts of appeals, were all brought, or could have been brought, under another legal theory. See ... *Mitre v. Brooks Fashion Stores, Inc.*, 840 S.W.2d 612, 622 (Tex. App.—Corpus Christi 1992, writ denied) (holding that defendant's publication was actionable as both a false light invasion of privacy and a defamation); *Boyles v. Kerr*, 806 S.W.2d 255 (Tex. App.—Texarkana 1991) *rev'd* 855 S.W.2d 593, 594, 603 (Tex. 1993) (false light action could have been brought as intentional infliction of emotional distress).... [W]e see no reason to recognize a cause of action for false light invasion of privacy when recovery for that tort is substantially duplicated by torts already established in this State.

As discussed above, the false light tort bears remarkable similarities to defamation. However, the torts are not wholly identical for two reasons: (1) defamation actions are subject to a number of procedural requirements, to which invasion of privacy actions are not subject, and (2) certain publications not actionable under a defamation theory might be actionable under false light. Far from persuading us that these distinctions justify a separate tort, we believe they demonstrate that adopting a false light tort in this State would unacceptably derogate constitutional free speech rights under both the Texas and the United States Constitution.

Actions for defamation in Texas are subject to numerous procedural and substantive hurdles. [The court referred to the privileges of the law of defamation; statutory provisions for mitigation of damages by apology, retraction or correction and for protection of broadcasters from liability for transmitting third parties' broadcasts; requirements that special damages be proved; and provisions for posting of bonds in defamation actions.]

These technical restrictions serve to safeguard the freedom of speech. Every defamation action that the law permits necessarily inhibits free speech.... Thus, the defamation action has been narrowly tailored to limit free speech as little as possible.

Courts in many jurisdictions have preserved their protection of speech by holding false light actions to the same strictures as defamation actions.... Permitting plaintiffs to bring actions for false light without the limits established for defamation actions may inhibit free speech beyond the permissible range. On the other hand, no useful purpose would be served by the separate tort if these restrictions are imposed. As the court observed in *Renwick v. News & Observer Publishing Co.*, 310 N.C. 312, 312 S.E.2d 405, cert. denied, 469 U.S. 858 (1984): "Given the First Amendment limitations placed upon defamation actions by [*New York Times v.*] *Sullivan* and upon false light invasion of privacy actions by [*Time, Inc. v.*] *Hill*, we think that such additional remedies as we *might* be required to make available to plaintiffs should we recognize false light invasion of privacy claims are not sufficient to justify the recognition in this jurisdiction of such inherently constitutionally suspect claims for relief." ...

In theory, the false light action may provide a remedy for certain non-defamatory speech against which there may be no other remedy in tort law.... This rationale, however, does not persuade us to recognize the false light tort.

It is questionable whether a remedy for non-defamatory speech should exist at all. In *Time, Inc. v. Hill*, 385 U.S. 374 (1967), the Supreme Court plurality viewed with disfavor the restriction of nondefamatory statements by the New York privacy statute: "We create a grave risk of serious impairment of the indispensable service of a free press in a free society if we saddle the press with the impossible burden of verifying to a certainty the facts associated in news articles with a person's name, picture or portrait, particularly as related to *non-defamatory* matter."

... The class of speech restricted by defamation is only that which defames. False light may be brought against any untruth to which the subject of the speech takes umbrage. Editors for the media may guard against defamation by being alert to facts which tend to diminish reputation; under false light, any fact in the story, no matter how seemingly innocuous, may prove to be the basis for liability.

The Restatement adds an element not associated with defamation, the requirement that the statement places the subject in a false light "highly offensive" to the reasonable person. The distinction fails to draw reasonably clear lines between lawful and unlawful conduct, however. "A law forbidding or requiring conduct in terms so vague that men of common intelligence must necessarily guess at its meaning and differ as to its application violates due process." *Baggett v. Bullitt*, 377 U.S. 360 (1964); *see also Hustler Magazine v. Falwell*, 485 U.S. 46 (1988) (classification of speech as "outrageous" for suits for intentional infliction of emotional distress does not provide a meaningful standard, and would allow jury to impose damages on the basis of the jurors' tastes or views).

Thus, the uncertainty of not knowing what speech may subject the speaker or writer to liability would have an unacceptable chilling effect on freedom of speech....

On balance, the marginal benefit to be achieved by permitting recovery against non-defamatory speech not addressed by any existing tort is outweighed by the probable chilling effect on speech and, in some cases, on freedom of the press, that would result from recognition of the false light tort. For the reasons expressed in this opinion, we expressly decline to recognize the tort of false light.

Justice HIGHTOWER, joined by Justice DOGGETT, Justice GAMMAGE and Justice SPECTOR, dissenting....

... The court argues first that false light largely duplicates defamation and second that false light unduly increases the tensions between tort and free speech law. Not only do these arguments strain against each other, but they simply are not persuasive....

First, the court rightly notes ... that there are communications which, based on their content, are not defamatory but may be false light violations of privacy because they are highly offensive. For example, an article which falsely reports that an individual suffers from a serious disease such as cancer would not be defamatory but could comprise a cause of action for false light.

Second, the torts protect different interests. Defamation preserves individuals' reputation interests, but false light invasion of privacy, as the other branches of the right of privacy, safeguards individuals' sensitivities about what people know and believe about them.

The need for protection of individual sensitivity already has been recognized by this court: "[T]he increased complexity and intensity of modern civilization and the development of man's spiritual sensibilities have rendered man more sensitive to publicity and have increased his need of privacy, while the great technological improvements in the means of communication have more and more subjected the intimacies of his private life to exploitation by those who pander to commercialism and to prurient and idle curiosity. A legally enforceable right of privacy is deemed to be a proper protection against this type of encroachment upon the personality of the individual." *Billings v. Atkinson*, 489 S.W.2d 858, 860 (Tex. 1973).

That, in some cases, both torts allow mental anguish damages does not detract from these differing protections. For example, mental anguish damages are available in suits for medical malpractice, certain violations of the Deceptive Trade Practices Act, or personal injury, but that does not mean that the torts duplicate each other or the interests they serve....

The court's only explanation of why it will tolerate no overlap in this arena is that free speech rights are implicated because the procedures attending defamation are lacking. Rather than assess and weigh the interests at stake in each right and add any procedures necessary to effectuate an even balance of the rights, the court simply concludes that false light invasion of privacy and free speech cannot coexist.

The court questions the constitutional viability of false light invasion of privacy in a cursory and unsatisfactory analysis. For example, the court fails to address the United States Supreme Court's acceptance of false light invasion of privacy so long as the plaintiff proves that the defendant acted with actual malice—that is, with knowledge of the falsity or in reckless disregard for the truth. *Time, Inc. v. Hill*, 385 U.S. 374 (1967)....

... That recognizing a right of privacy involves perplexing questions to determine where it ends and the rights of others and of the public begin is a poor excuse for not recognizing the right of privacy. Cases may arise near the border marking the right of privacy and the right of another individual or of the public, but this is true of many other individual rights recognized by the law. Our justice system allows us to remain confident that with "honest and fearless trial judges to pass in the first instance upon the question of law as to the existence of the right in each case, whose decisions are subject to review by the court of last resort, and with fair and impartial juries to pass upon the questions of fact involved, and assess the damages in the event of a recovery, whose verdict is, under our law, in all cases subject to supervision and scrutiny by the trial judge, within the limits of a legal discretion, there need be no more fear that the right of privacy will be the occasion of unjustifiable litigation, oppression, or wrong than that the existence of many other rights in the law would bring about such results." [*Pavesich v. New England Life Ins. Co.*, 122 Ga. 190, 50 S.E. 68, 72 (1905).]

Notes

1. Does the Restatement (Second) provision on false light, quoted in Uhl v. Columbia Broadcasting Systems, Inc., p. 476, supra, accurately reflect the older cases involving misleading use of plaintiff's photograph or name? Is the false light form of invasion of privacy really a necessary part of tort law, or could an adequate remedy for damaging falsehoods be found in defamation or injurious falsehood or liability for infliction of emotional distress? Renwick v. News and Observer Publishing Co., 310 N.C. 312, 312 S.E.2d 405 (1984), cert. denied, 469 U.S. 858 (1984), preceded Cain v. Hearst Corp. in refusing to recognize the false light action because it often would overlap rights of recovery for libel or slander and because, to the extent this tort would allow recovery beyond that permit-

ted by the law of defamation, it would add to tension between the First Amendment and the law of torts. The court stated that the false light action reduced judicial efficiency by requiring courts to consider two claims for substantially the same relief. The court was influenced by its perception that the conditions which led Warren and Brandeis to argue for a separate tort of invasion of privacy, such as prevalent "yellow journalism," had subsided considerably. See also Denver Publishing Co. v. Bueno, 54 P.3d 893 (Colo. 2002); Jews for Jesus, Inc. v. Rapp, 997 So. 2d 1098 (Fla. 2008); Lake v. Wal-Mart Stores, Inc., 582 N.W.2d 231 (Minn. 1998); Zimmerman, False Light Invasion of Privacy: The Light That Failed, 64 N.Y.U. L. Rev. 364 (1989).

2. When both false light and defamation actions are available, what advantages will be derived from use of the false light theory? Should plaintiffs be permitted to avoid restrictions on defamation actions by asserting an action for false light? See Fellows v. National Enquirer, Inc., 42 Cal. 3d 234, 228 Cal. Rptr. 215, 721 P.2d 97 (1986) (special damages requirement); Sullivan v. Pulitzer Broadcasting Co., 709 S.W.2d 475 (Mo. 1986) (statute of limitations); Colbert v. World Publishing Co., 747 P.2d 286 (Okla. 1987) (statute of limitations).

3. Most state courts have accepted the Restatement (Second) false light tort when a decision on the issue was necessary. In Welling v. Weinfeld, 113 Ohio St. 3d 464, 866 N.E.2d 1051 (2007), the court decided in favor of the tort because "Without false light, the right to privacy is not whole, as it is not fully protected by defamation laws." A privacy action had already been recognized when true private details of a person's life were published. "The right to privacy naturally extends to the ability to control false statements made about oneself." See also West v. Media General Convergence, Inc., 53 S.W.3d 640 (Tenn. 2001). The *Welling* opinion contends that legal protection is necessary because "thanks to the accessibility of the Internet," barriers to generating publicity are slight, ethical standards regarding the "acceptability of certain discourse" have been lowered, and the ability to do harm has increased.

4. The number of reported cases addressing false light and related invasion of privacy theories is now quite large. See Annot., False Light Invasion of Privacy—Cognizability and Elements, 57 A.L.R.4th 22 (1987); Annot., False Light Invasion of Privacy—Defenses and Remedies, 57 A.L.R.4th 244 (1987); Annot., False Light Invasion of Privacy—Accusation or Innuendo as to Criminal Acts, 58 A.L.R.4th 902 (1987); Annot., False Light Invasion of Privacy—Neutral or Laudatory Depiction of Subject, 59 A.L.R.4th 502 (1988); Annot., False Light Invasion of Privacy—Disparaging but Noncriminal Depiction, 60 A.L.R.4th 51 (1988). See also Kelso, False Light Privacy: A Requiem, 32 Santa Clara L. Rev. 783 (1992).

Section 5. Review

Anderson v. Fisher Broadcasting Companies, Inc.
Supreme Court of Oregon
300 Or. 452, 712 P.2d 803 (1986)

LINDE, Justice.

A television cameraman for defendant broadcasting company photographed the scene of an automobile accident in which plaintiff was injured. Plaintiff was recognizable and was shown bleeding and in pain while receiving emergency medical treatment. Defendant did not use the video taped pictures or report the accident on its regular news program. Some time later, without seeking plaintiff's consent, defendant used a brief excerpt showing plaintiff to illustrate promotional spots advertising a special news report about a new system for dispatching emergency medical help.

Plaintiff sued for general damages for mental anguish alleging that defendant "violated plaintiff's right to privacy" by "appropriating to defendant's own use and advantage" the pictures its photographer had taken of plaintiff and by "publicizing" his picture in a condition "offensive to a reasonable person" and not of legitimate public concern. In defense, the broadcaster asserted that its use of plaintiff's picture occurred in advertising another news program, that this use was constitutionally privileged and that the undisputed facts gave rise to no common-law claim. The trial court gave summary judgment for defendant, holding that the pictures were "newsworthy," that they remained so despite not being promptly published, and that they did not lose their newsworthiness when used only to advertise another newsworthy broadcast.

The Court of Appeals held that there was an issue of fact whether the film showing plaintiff's injured condition was newsworthy, because it was not used to report plaintiff's accident itself but only to draw viewers for a different program in which the accident was not mentioned. The court did not discuss the parties' other legal theories beyond rejecting defendant's First Amendment claim. 72 Or. App. 539, 696 P.2d 1124 (1985).

In this court, defendant again stressed its constitutional claims along with its common-law arguments, understandably so in defending against a tort claim for wrongful publicity to which media of mass communication are peculiarly vulnerable. The constitutional issues are significant....[1] The First Amendment status of tort claims such as those asserted here is unsettled.

... But we shall not decide this case on constitutional grounds when it is unnecessary to do so, and when a premature decision would foreclose legislative consideration....

Generally, Oregon decisions have not allowed recovery for injury to a stranger's feelings as such, unless the infliction of psychic distress was the object of defendant's conduct or the conduct violated some legal duty apart from causing the distress. In the absence of some other duty or relationship of the defendant to plaintiff, it does not suffice for tort liability that defendant's offensive conduct is an intentional act. The conduct must be designed to cause severe mental or emotional distress, whether for its own sake or as a means to some other end, and it must qualify as extraordinary conduct that a reasonable jury could find to be beyond the farthest reach of socially tolerable behavior. Here the use of plaintiff's picture, of course, was intentional, but there is no claim or evidence that the broadcaster wished to distress plaintiff. Plaintiff does not charge defendant with the tortious intentional infliction of severe emotional distress. The duty defendant is said to have violated is a duty not to invade plaintiff's "privacy" in the two ways stated above, by "appropriating" and by "publicizing" his picture.

---

1. Article 1, section 8 of the Oregon Constitution, provides: "No law shall be passed restraining the free expression of opinion, or restricting the right to speak, write, or print freely on any subject whatever; but every person shall be responsible for the abuse of this right."

Article 1, section 10, of the Oregon Constitution, provides: "No court shall be secret, but justice shall be administered, openly and without purchase, completely and without delay, and every man shall have remedy by due course of law for injury done him in his person, property, or reputation."

"Privacy" denotes a personal or cultural value placed on seclusion or personal control over access to places or things, thoughts or acts. "Privacy" also can be used to label one or more legally recognized interests, and this court has so used the term in several cases since *Hinish* [p. 387, supra]. But like the older word "property," which it partially overlaps, "privacy" has been a difficult legal concept to delimit. Lawyers and theorists debate the nature of the interests that privacy law means to protect, the criteria of wrongful invasions of those interests, and the matching of remedies to the identified interests....

The common-law tort claim based solely on publicizing private facts that are true but not newsworthy has met critical response. *See, e.g.,* Zimmerman, *Requiem for a Heavyweight: A Farewell to Warren and Brandeis's Privacy Tort*, 68 Cornell L. Rev. 291 (1983), reviewing part of the extensive literature. Such a tort was not part of the "common law of England" adopted by Oregon in 1843, and after study it was rejected in England, the home of the common law, in favor of alternative theories.[7] Criticism has not implied a lack of sympathy with the feelings of persons whose past or present lives are brought to public attention against their own wishes; but the obstacles to defining when publicity as such is tortious, without more, are formidable.

What is "private" so as to make its publication offensive likely differs among communities, between generations, and among ethnic, religious, or other social groups, as well as among individuals. Likewise, one reader's or viewer's "news" is another's tedium or trivia. The editorial judgment of what is "newsworthy" is not so readily submitted to the *ad hoc* review of a jury as the Court of Appeals believed. It is not properly a community standard. Even when some editors themselves vie to tailor "news" to satisfy popular tastes, others may believe that the community should see or hear facts or ideas that the majority finds uninteresting or offensive.

If the tort is defined to protect a plaintiff's interest in nondisclosure only against widespread publicity, as in the Restatement's § 652D, it singles out the print, film, and broadcast media for legal restraints that will not be applied to gossipmongers in neighborhood taverns or card parties, to letter writers or telephone tattlers. Finally, a successful tort action may serve to rectify a defamatory, appropriative, or "false light" publication, but in the pure "private facts" tort even success sacrifices rather than protects the plaintiff's interest in the privacy of the wrongfully publicized facts, for litigation only breeds renewed and often wider publicity, this time unquestionably privileged.[10] Writing in 1979, Professor Dorsey D. Ellis, Jr., found that there had been no reported case in which a plaintiff successfully recovered damages for truthful disclosure by the press since the United States Supreme Court reversed a New York judgment in *Time, Inc. v. Hill*, 385 U.S. 374 (1967), and he concluded that the tort's "very existence is in doubt, at least outside the law reviews." Ellis, *Damages and the Privacy Tort: Sketching a Legal Profile*, 64 Iowa L. Rev. 1111, 1133 (1979).

Discussion of the tort often assumes that what the plaintiff objects to is the reporting of past or present "facts" or "information" by traditional forms of written publication. The classic illustration is *Sidis v. F-R Pub. Corporation*, 113 F.2d 806 (2nd Cir.), *cert. den.* 311 U.S. 711 (1940), in which the New Yorker magazine was absolved from tort liability for publishing the story of a one-time child prodigy who had long lived a life of some-

---

7. *See* Report of the Committee on Privacy (HMSO 1972) Cmnd. 5012....

10. Even assuming that the more logical remedy against wrongfully publicizing private facts is to enjoin the defendant's publication, despite the so-called "presumption" against prior restraints, media reporting of the facts pleaded and presented in the legal proceedings undercut the effectiveness of that remedy.

what eccentric obscurity. Arguably, the widespread dissemination of a person's picture, which television has made the essence of much otherwise unremarkable as well as of traditional "news," sacrifices the pictured person's privacy in a sense distinct from disclosure of factual information.

Claims to a right to prevent unconsented use of one's likeness in fact long antedate the advent of television. The first decisions respectively rejecting and accepting a "privacy" basis for such claims, *Roberson v. Rochester Folding Box Co.*, 171 N.Y. 538, 64 N.E. 442 (1902), and *Pavesich v. New England Life Ins. Co.*, 122 Ga. 190, 50 S.E. 68 (1905), involved commercial use of plaintiff's pictures. Sensitivity about reproduction of one's likeness is not a 19th century refinement of western civilization, as is sometimes supposed; many cultures have feared the magical power conferred by possession of a person's image....

Doubtless in many instances a picture not only is worth a thousand words to a publisher but words would be worth nothing at all. The respective editors would not likely have thought it worthwhile to publish a written report that Mrs. Graham had her dress blown by air jets at an amusement part, *see Daily Times Democrat v. Graham*, 276 Ala. 380, 162 So. 2d 474 (1964), or that Mr. and Mrs. Gill showed affection characteristic of "love at first sight," *see Gill v. Curtis Pub. Co.*, 38 Cal. 2d 273, 239 P.2d 630 (1952). Some filmed or broadcast scenes compare to verbal reports in dramatic impact about as hearing music compares to reading a score, and the emotional reaction of the person who is depicted rather than described may likewise be greater. In *Commonwealth v. Wiseman*, 356 Mass. 251, 249 N.E.2d 610, *cert. den.* 398 U.S. 960 (1969), Massachusetts courts restricted the showing of a film of the conditions and treatment of mental patients in a state institution, a subject whose obvious public importance would have prevented censorship of written documentation.

Nonetheless, the difference between undesired publicity by word or by picture seems to concern only the degree of the subject's psychic discomfort rather than the nature of the interest claimed to be invaded. Perhaps the present plaintiff would not have felt offended if KATU-TV had verbally described his bloodied and disheveled condition rather than showing it. But neither the courts nor the commentators have made a distinction in principle between one woman's objections to a book based on her experiences, *Cason v. Baskin*, 155 Fla. 198, 20 So. 2d 243 (1944), and another's to a motion picture, *Melvin v. Reid*, 112 Cal. App. 285, 297 P. 91 (1931), and we perceive none.

A distinction has been perceived, however, between publicizing a person's name, image, or other identifying facts for some intrinsic interest or for purposes of advertising someone's products or services. As already noted, the early decisions for and against such claims based on "privacy," *Pavesich v. New England Life Ins. Co., supra*, and *Roberson v. Rochester Folding Box Co., supra*, involved commercial use of plaintiff's pictures to advertise, respectively, life insurance and a brand of flour. When the New York Court of Appeals declined to hold that defendants' unconsented use of a young woman's pictures to advertise flour was an invasion of a right to privacy under existing law, the New York legislature by statute provided for damages as well as injunctive relief against using "the name, portrait or picture" of any person "for advertising purposes, or for the purposes of trade without the written consent first obtained." Many of the reported "privacy" cases are interpretations of this and similar statutes, which necessarily require courts to decide what is an "advertising purpose" or a "purpose of trade." Some courts have reached comparable decisions without statutes.

Plaintiff in the present case concedes that KATU-TV would not be liable to him if it had included his picture in the ordinary news coverage of a traffic accident. He contends that the broadcaster became liable because instead it used the footage to draw audience attention to a later broadcast concerning emergency medical services, in which plaintiff's picture was not included. Does the distinction between "commercial" and "noncommercial" use of a person's name, likeness, or life history rest on a difference in the interest invaded by the publication or in the character of the publisher's motives and purposes? The reason should bear on the remedy.

When actors, athletes or other performers object, not to a loss of anonymity, but to unauthorized exploitation of their valuable public identities, the remedy should reflect the wrongful appropriation of a "right to publicity" that has economic value to the plaintiff as well as to the defendant, rather than damages for psychic distress at a loss of "privacy." When a person who neither has nor wants a marketable public identity demands damages for unauthorized publicity, such a person may claim injury to a noneconomic rather than an economic interest in his or her privacy; but it is not always obvious, as it is not in this case, why the loss of privacy is different when it occurs in a "commercial" rather than a "noncommercial" form of publication. If the plaintiff can show no psychic injury at all, for instance an infant whose picture has been used in an advertisement for baby food rather than in a magazine or television report on child care, the answer must be that the advertiser, but not the reporter, has unjustly enriched himself by appropriating something for which he is expected to pay, an answer that begs the question.

Our system relies for freedom of information, ideas, and entertainment, high or low, primarily on privately owned media of communication, operating at private cost and seeking private profit. Books, newspapers, films, and broadcasts are produced and distributed at private cost and for private profit, that is to say, "commercially," and the use of materials from the lives of living persons in such publications can enrich authors, photographers, and publishers just as their use in advertisements.... This predictably causes problems in applying a test such as New York's "advertising" or "purposes of trade".... Publication of an accident victims's photograph is not appropriation for commercial use simply because the medium itself is operated for profit. *Leverton v. Curtis Publishing Co.* [p. 473, supra].

There is another reason why an unauthorized use of a person's name or image to sell goods or services can be a tortious appropriation when the same use in the content of material published to be sold is not. The use may make it appear that the person has consented to endorse the advertised product, with or without being paid to do so. When that impression is in fact false, the appropriation of the person's identity places the person in a false light much as the unauthorized use of Mr. Hinish's name in the political telegram did in *Hinish v. Meier & Frank Co., supra.* Such an inference is most likely to be drawn about professional performers, who are widely known to be paid for endorsing products in print and television advertisements and even for using their sponsors' sports clothes and equipment in their work....

This theory is not available, however, to a person whose image, with no established public familiarity, appears in a commercial context only incidentally, perhaps as one of several persons in a public scene, or otherwise under circumstances that plainly are not presented so as to convey any endorsement by that person....

In the present case, plaintiff does not claim that KATU-TV's promotional spots portrayed him as an accident victim in a manner implying that he endorsed its forthcoming program about emergency medical services, and the record on summary judgment suggests no such inference. His claim is not for the economic value of such an endorsement, or for any gain unjustly realized by the broadcaster from appropriating a photograph belonging to plaintiff. The videotape was made at the accident scene by defendant's cameraman, and the identity of the accident victim was immaterial. Rather, plaintiff claims damages for mental distress from its publication. Without a showing that plaintiff's picture was either obtained or broadcast in a manner or for a purpose wrongful beyond the unconsented publication itself, that claim fails.

To summarize, we conclude that in Oregon the truthful presentation of facts concerning a person, even facts that a reasonable person would wish to keep private and that are not "newsworthy," does not give rise to common-law tort liability for damages for mental or emotional distress, unless the manner or purpose of defendant's conduct is wrongful in some respect apart from causing the plaintiff's hurt feelings. For instance, a defendant might incur liability for purposely inflicting emotional distress by publishing private information in a socially intolerable way; or the publicized information might be wrongfully obtained by conversion, bribery, false pretenses, or trespassory intrusion, or published by a photographer who has been paid for what the subject reasonably expects to be the exclusive use of a picture; or when a defendant disregards a duty of confidentiality or other statutory duty, or exploits a distinctive economic value of an individual's identity or image beyond that of other similar persons for purposes of associating it with a commercial product or service, although this court has not decided all such issues. And, of course, the distressing report or presentation of a person's private affairs might not be truthful. Because plaintiff has shown no such wrongful element in defendants' conduct, we have no occasion to anticipate constitutional questions in the event the legislature were to enter this field of tort law.

The decision of the Court of Appeals is reversed, and the judgment of the circuit court is reinstated.

Notes

1. The Supreme Court of North Carolina, which in Renwick v. News and Observer Publishing Co., p. 483, supra, rejected liability for false light invasion of privacy, decided in Hall v. Post, 323 N.C. 259, 372 S.E.2d 711 (1988), that it would not entertain an action for publication of "private facts." The court considered the private facts tort "constitutionally suspect" under the First Amendment. Even if it survived constitutional scrutiny, it would "add to the existing tensions between the First Amendment and the law of torts." Furthermore, it would be of little practical value because it was unlikely that a defendant would be found liable on this theory without also coming within the action for intentional infliction of emotional distress.

2. Putting aside jurisdictions in which the right to privacy is considered a creation of statute, only a few recent judicial decisions exhibit unwillingness to accept the four categories of invasion of privacy specified by Prosser and the Restatement (Second). There is, however, a body of law review literature criticizing the Prosser/Restatement approach and other aspects of privacy law. Among the most prominent articles are Kalven, Privacy in Tort Law—Were Warren and Brandeis Wrong?, 31 Law & Contemp. Probs. 326 (1966), and Bloustein, Privacy As An Aspect of Human Dignity: An Answer to Dean Prosser, 39 N.Y.U. L. Rev. 962 (1964). Kalven concluded that Warren and Brandeis—and Prosser— were wrong; there should be no tort action for invasion of privacy other than a remedy to prevent unjust enrichment when defendant appropriated "some aspect of the plaintiff that would have market value and for which he would normally pay." Bloustein, believing that all invasion of privacy cases involved a single interest in preserving human dignity and individuality, attacked Prosser's division of invasion of privacy into four different

torts. See also Felcher & Rubin, Privacy, Publicity, and the Portrayal of Real People by the Media, 88 Yale L.J. 1577 (1979); Comment, An Integrative Alternative for America's Privacy Torts, 38 Golden Gate U. L. Rev. 71 (2007); Symposium: Toward a Resolution of the Expanding Conflict between the Press and Privacy Interests, 64 Iowa L. Rev. 1061 (1979); Symposium, Prosser's *Privacy* at 50: A Symposium on Privacy in the 21st Century, 98 Calif. L. Rev. 1711 (2010).

Chapter 6

Defamation

Section 1. Defamatory Communications

A. Defamatory Meanings

Denny v. Mertz

Supreme Court of Wisconsin
84 Wis. 2d 654, 267 N.W.2d 304 (1978)

DAY, Justice....

[Plaintiff Denny was employed by Koehring Company in 1954. In 1969, when he was senior staff attorney, he resigned to go into the private practice of law. Defendant Mertz was employed by Koehring in various executive positions until December 1975, when he was terminated as chief executive officer. Mertz attributed the termination to recent shareholder controversies that focused on senior management. Various shareholders, including Denny, had been openly critical to Koehring's board of directors about Mertz's performance as chief executive. In January 1976, Business Week magazine published an article, entitled "Top Management Ferment At Koehring," about the change in management of the company. Among other things, the article stated that "Mertz now claims he was the target of a 'harassment campaign' by the dissidents, who include the company's largest individual shareholder, a former chairman deposed by Mertz 16 months ago, and a former general counsel.... [¶] Also about that time, William Denny, general counsel of Koehring until Mertz fired him in 1969, began to question many of Koehring's management decisions. He even sued the company twice to get minutes of meetings and other information...." The rest of the article stated how a group of Koehring minority shareholders, including Denny, tried to force Mertz's resignation. The article related Mertz's actions as Koehring chief executive and implied that he was responsible for low management morale and the company's poor performance in recent years.]

[Denny brought a libel action against Mertz and the publisher of Business Week, McGraw-Hill. Denny alleged that Mertz defamed him by telling the Business Week interviewer that he (Mertz) fired Denny. McGraw-Hill allegedly defamed Denny by stating in Business Week that Denny had been fired. Damage to his reputation in the amount of $500,000 was claimed. Mertz and McGraw-Hill appealed from the trial judge's denial of their motions to dismiss the complaint.]

... [In *Lathan v. Journal Co.,* 30 Wis. 2d 146, 140 N.W.2d 417 (1966), we stated:]

Defamation has been defined as: "that which tends to injure 'reputation' in the popular sense; to diminish the esteem, respect, goodwill or confidence in which the plaintiff is held, or to excite adverse, derogatory or unpleasant feelings or opinions against him." Prosser [Law of Torts (3d ed.)] page 756.

In *Scofield v. Milwaukee Free Press Co.* (1905), 126 Wis. 81, 105 N.W. 227, we held that for a newspaper article to be libelous it " … need only tend to degrade or disgrace the plaintiff generally, or to subject him to public distrust, ridicule, or contempt in the community…."

The Restatement, sec. 559, provides that: "A communication is defamatory if it tends so to harm the reputation of another as to lower him in the estimation of the community or to deter third persons from associating or dealing with him."

[In *Schaefer v. State Bar*, 77 Wis. 2d 120, 252 N.W.2d 343 (1977), we stated:] "If the alleged communication is capable of a defamatory meaning, the demurrer must be overruled; and if the language is of such a character that it is capable of a non-defamatory meaning as well as a defamatory meaning, then a jury question is presented whether such communication was understood in fact in a defamatory sense by the persons to whom it was published. If the communication cannot reasonably be considered defamatory or to be so understood, the demurrer must be sustained."

The words alleged to be libelous "are to be construed and taken in their plain and popular sense…." *Pandow v. Eichstad*, 90 Wis. 298, 63 N.W. 284 (1895).

Words or elements in an article may not be considered in isolation, but must be viewed in the context of the whole article to determine if they are defamatory.

Mr. Mertz and McGraw-Hill argue that "firing" is a neutral term and no defamatory meaning can be concluded. However, in previous cases this court has determined that a fact question arose in libel cases where more than one meaning for a word was possible. In *Lathan v. Journal Co.,* Reverend Lathan, the pastor of a large Baptist church in Milwaukee, sued for libel because of a newspaper article that implied that he was responsible for the non-appearance of the Rev. Martin Luther King, Jr. at a fund raising rally in Milwaukee. This court stated that, "A newspaper article that could reasonably be construed to reflect on his [Rev. Lathan's] administrative ability might well have tended to lower him in the esteem of the community."

In *Wozniak v. Local 1111 of U.E.*, 57 Wis. 2d 725, 205 N.W.2d 369 (1973) the defendant union circulated leaflets to plaintiff's neighbors. The leaflets referred to plaintiff as a scab. On motions before and after verdict the union contended that "scab" was capable of only one meaning. On appeal, this court held that a jury question was presented. That question was whether the use of the word "scab" communicated to the neighbors the idea that plaintiff was a scoundrel, or merely the idea that plaintiff had chosen not to participate in the strike….

The defendants contend that the statement that plaintiff was fired could carry no bad connotations that would harm plaintiff's reputation in the community…. The *Business Week* article gave no reasons for the firing. It does not say that the firing was for incompetence or cause or for any particular reason at all.

The defendants also argue that the article as a whole tends to vindicate the plaintiff. The article is much more critical of defendant Mertz than it is of the plaintiff. The plaintiff is mentioned as a member of a group of dissidents who questioned Mertz's bad management decisions and who were successful in a rare example of corporate democracy. The major portion of the article certainly does not defame plaintiff, but there is nothing in the article to suggest that the plaintiff was fired for questioning Mertz's decisions. Such a conclusion might be implied from the article, but then again it might not.

The parties agree that to fire means to discharge from employment peremptorily or summarily. Both the statement that plaintiff was fired and the article as a whole could be understood by reasonable people in a defamatory sense. Reasonable people could conclude that a person's being fired would tend to injure their reputation in the popular sense or to diminish the respect or esteem that people have for him. Whether the article would actually have that effect is a question for the jury. We only hold that this complaint is not legally insufficient to state a claim.

Order affirmed.

Notes

1. The legal history of defamation long predates its entry into tort law. As related in Lovell, The "Reception" of Defamation By the Common Law, 15 Vand. L. Rev. 1051 (1962), early English canon law afforded a person aggrieved by defamation the opportunity to seek vindication of his character in the local courts. If proof by compurgation or ordeal went in his favor, he would be entitled to a public apology from the person who made the false allegation. Under the laws of Alfred the Great (compiled about the year 880), "public slander" was to be "compensated with no lighter penalty than the cutting off of [the slanderer's] tongue, with the proviso that it be redeemed at no cheaper rate than it is valued in proportion to the *wergild*" (the value of the person's life). Both the Church and the monarch sought to maintain public order by providing an alternative to acts of revenge or efforts to preserve "honor" by use of arms, but this was ineffectual.

William the Conqueror placed the administration of the remedy for defamation in ecclesiastical courts, which developed a more sophisticated jurisprudence. Canon law considered defamation to be a sin. It demanded penance of the sinner, not compensation to the injured person. Thus, when a person was found guilty of defamation, he was to acknowledge his "false witness" and beg the pardon of the victim. Then, he received absolution. Canon law treated as defamatory only allegations of a crime cognizable by it. The statement had to be made to a third party, i.e. "published." Truth was a defense, as one did not commit the sin of false witness by making a true defamatory allegation.

Concern about criticism of government policies, as well as duels that were used to settle defamation grievances, led to the use of criminal law to suppress defamation of high officials and the nobility. It fell to the Court of Star Chamber to administer this "libel" law. The Star Chamber was principally concerned with handwritten and (after the development of the printing press) printed defamation of a seditious (political) nature. But its work also extended to non-political defamation, and it could order the defamer to pay the aggrieved party substantial damages, the amount depending upon the degree of insult. The possibility of receiving payment and the absence of defenses, including truth, naturally encouraged defamed persons to turn from the ecclesiastical courts to the Star Chamber for redress.

It was not until the sixteenth century that common law courts began to exercise jurisdiction over defamation—primarily over oral slanders, since a remedy for written libels could be obtained through the Star Chamber. A slander would be within the cognizance of the common law courts, it was declared, if the plaintiff had been accused of a crime indictable at common law and if it was pleaded and proved that temporal damages resulted. Soon, other types of slander were accepted as a foundation for a civil action. Slanders became actionable by way of an action on the case when damages were alleged and proved. Slander actions became so numerous that courts attempted to deter them by such means as the "mitior sensus" doctrine, discussed in note 3. However, the damages requirements of the action on the case were relaxed for types of slander that in modern law are known as "slander per se." See pp. 533–542, infra.

The abolition of the Star Chamber in 1641 required that cases of libel henceforth be brought before the courts of common law, the ecclesiastical courts now being moribund. Rather than develop a single body of law for both written and oral defamation, the courts sharpened the division between the two, applying to written defamation doctrines derived from the Star Chamber with no requirement of "special damage" in civil actions. In part this was motivated by a continuing desire to suppress seditious libel. For oral defamation, the pre-existing rules of slander liability were applied. Today, the tort rules for libel and slander are the same in many respects, including the position of truth as an absolute bar to liability. But they differ in some important particulars, and the division of defamation into libel and slander remains a feature of contemporary law. This is considered further in pp. 533–542, infra.

Privileges and other important elements of modern defamation law had not been delineated when the common law was brought to what is now the United States. Americans tended to enforce defamation law less rigorously than their English counterparts, perhaps because of the "rough-and-tumble" atmosphere of American society, less certainty that not bringing suit would be taken as an admission of the defamatory statement's truth, and the greater opportunities to overcome damage to reputation through social or geographic mobility. See Chafee, Government and Mass Communications 106–107 (1947), and the trial judge's remarks in Lewis v. Williams, 105 S.C. 165, 89 S.E. 647 (1916). But the American law of libel and slander remained generally consistent with the defamation law of other common law countries until 1964, when the Supreme Court of the United States decided that the First Amendment to the Constitution required that liability for defamation of a public official be severely restricted. Since then, a series of Supreme Court decisions and numerous cases from other courts have interpreted the First Amendment to place substantial restrictions upon liability for defamation and the damages recoverable. See pp. 626–684, infra. The right to have a jury determine the factual issues bearing upon liability, such as whether defendant's statement conveyed a defamatory meaning, also has constitutional dimensions in the United States. But it should be noted that foreign jurisdictions, such as England, which have largely abolished trial by jury in other types of civil cases, have preserved it in cases of libel and slander. Why do this?

2. In Parmiter v. Coupland, (1840) 6 M. & W. 105, 151 Eng. Rep. 340, 4 Jur. 701, 9 L.J. Ex. 202 (Ex.), Baron Parke stated that "A publication, without justification or excuse, which is calculated to injure the reputation of another, by exposing him to hatred, contempt, or ridicule, is a libel." This is the basis of an oft-stated definition of defamation as a communication "which tends to hold the plaintiff up to hatred, contempt or ridicule, or cause him to be shunned or avoided." See Prosser & Keeton, Law of Torts 773 (5th ed. 1984). Sometimes the definition is expanded, as in Kimmerle v. New York Evening Journal, Inc., 262 N.Y. 99, 186 N.E. 217 (1933): "words which tend to expose one to public hatred, shame, obloquy, contumely, odium, contempt, ridicule, aversion, ostracism, degradation, or disgrace, or to induce an evil opinion of one in the minds of right-thinking persons, and to deprive one of their confidence and friendly intercourse in society." Most modern authorities in the United States are in accord with the wider, more generally stated, definitions of Prosser and the Restatement, quoted in the principal case. See Dobbs,

Law of Torts 1126–1134 (2000), and Prosser & Keeton, Law of Torts 773–778 (5th ed. 1984), for detail on what meanings are defamatory.

3. At one time, courts applied the rule that if more than one meaning could possibly be attributed to allegedly slanderous words, the words were to be construed "in mitiori sensu" — in the more favorable or lenient sense, the one not defamatory or the one less injurious. See Spencer Bower, Actionable Defamation 302–305 (2d ed. 1923). Thus, in Miles v. Jacob, (1614) Hob. 6, 80 Eng. Rep. 156, sub. nom. Jacob v. Mills, Cro. Jac. 343, 79 Eng. Rep. 293 (Ex. Ch.), an accusation that plaintiff had poisoned a person was held not to support an action, for it did not appear in the words that plaintiff had poisoned the victim willingly or that the victim was dead at the time the words were spoken. See also Holt v. Astgrigg, (1608) Cro. Jac. 184, 79 Eng. Rep. 161 (K.B.), in which defendant allegedly said that plaintiff "struck his cook on the head with a cleaver, and cleaved his head; the one part lay on the one shoulder, and another part on the other." The court granted defendant judgment, for "notwithstanding such wounding, the party may yet be living; and it is then but a trespass." The mitior sensus doctrine was not applied to libel. It has now been almost universally discarded. See MacLeod v. Tribune Publishing Co., 52 Cal. 2d 536, 343 P.2d 36 (1959). Instead, plaintiff's action is subject to the test of whether the words are reasonably susceptible of any defamatory meaning. Defamation can occur by implication as well as by direct statement. See Annot., Libel and Slander: Defamation by Question, 53 A.L.R.4th 450 (1987); Spiegel, Defamation by Implication — In the Confidential Manner, 29 S. Cal. L. Rev. 306 (1965).

4. Not all personal criticisms or embarrassments are defamatory. In Cowan v. Time Inc., 41 Misc. 2d 198, 245 N.Y.S.2d 723 (Sup. Ct. 1963), a picture of plaintiff at the tiller of a small boat, in which there were four other persons, was published above the caption "Rub-a-dub dub, too many in a tub." It accompanied an article entitled "Some Idiots Afloat." The court held that plaintiff was at most charged with a single act of carelessness and the words were not subject to any reasonable interpretation that would make them defamatory. See also Twiggar v. Ossining Printing & Publishing Co., 161 App. Div. 718, 146 N.Y.S. 529 (1914), appeal dismissed, 220 N.Y. 716, 116 N.E. 1080 (1917) (distinguishing between imputation of professional's ignorance or want of skill in particular instance and imputation of general unskillfulness or ignorance in calling); Tracy v. New York Magazine, 3 Media L. Rptr. 2294 (N.Y. Sup. Ct. 1978) (not defamatory to report that only distinction of plaintiff's career as New York City mounted policeman was to fall asleep in railroad boxcar and wake up, with his horse, in Schenectady). Suppose it is said that a person is "heartily detested" by his professional colleagues? See Murphy v. LaMarsh, [1971] 2 W.W.R. 196, (1970) 18 D.L.R.3d 208 (B.C.C.A.). A statement that a person does not pay his debts is likely not defamatory when the person does not conduct a business and there is no implication that he refuses to discharge valid obligations. See Annot., Libel: Imputing Credit Unworthiness to Nontrader, 99 A.L.R.2d 700 (1965). On the possibility of a defamation claim for a statement that plaintiff breached a contract, see Annot., Libel and Slander: Charging One with Breach or Nonperformance of Contract, 45 A.L.R.5th 739 (1997).

5. Words of abuse directed at plaintiff, even if rude and vulgar, do not suffice for liability. They often are not taken literally and not considered to cause any harm. Cf. Weinberg v. Pollock, 19 Media L. Rptr. 1442 (Conn. Super. Ct. 1991) (mother not defamed by calling her son "a bastard" in connection with his conviction for murder); Sack, Defamation: Libel, Slander, and Related Problems § 2.4.7 (4th ed. 2010). "Mr. Justice Maule once tried an action in which damages were claimed for a slander which consisted of a statement that the plaintiff was a b_____ i.e. a person addicted to unnatural habits. He charged the jury as follows: 'The word is horrible and is said to impute that the plaintiff

habitually committed a detestable crime which is not fit to be mentioned among Christians. The defendant says that the word was mere vulgar abuse and did not convey a charge of a crime, and if that is proved, the defendant is entitled to the verdict. Vulgar abuse is not actionable at Law. Now, gentlemen, you must say whether the word imputed a crime to the defendant or not. It is for you to say. And in considering your verdict you will remember that it has been proved before you that on the same occasion the defendant used the same word about a clothes-horse, a black beetle, and a piece of toasted cheese.'" The jury's verdict was for the defendant. Gilbert, Oxford Book of Legal Anecdotes 225 (1986). Cf. Morrissette v. Beatte, 66 R.I. 73, 17 A.2d 464 (1941) (similar case; directed verdict for defendant). To attribute to plaintiff the use of vulgar or otherwise offensive language can support a defamation action. See Spence v. Funk, 396 A.2d 967 (Del. 1978); Southern Bell Telephone and Telegraph Co. v. Coastal Transmission Service, Inc., 167 Ga. App. 611, 307 S.E.2d 83 (1983); Schrottman v. Barnicle, 386 Mass. 627, 437 N.E.2d 205 (1982); Mount Cook Group Ltd. v. Johnstone Motors Ltd., [1990] 2 N.Z.L.R.488 (High Ct.); Muller v. S.A. Associated Newspapers Ltd., 1972 (2) S.A. 589 (C).

6. It is usually considered defamatory to state that a person has been arrested or indicted for a serious crime, without implying that he is guilty. See Oklahoma Publishing Co. v. Givens, 67 F.2d 62 (10th Cir. 1933) (report that plaintiff held in jail on forgery charges); Freeman v. Schwenker, 73 S.W.2d 609 (Tex. Civ. App. 1934) (statement that bank officers indicted in connection with bank shortage); Annot., Libel and Slander: Statement or Publication that Plaintiff Has Been Indicted or Is Under Indictment, 52 A.L.R.2d 1178 (1957); Annot., Actionability of False Newspaper Report That Plaintiff Has Been Arrested, 93 A.L.R.3d 625 (1979). Should it also be considered defamatory to state that a person is a suspect in a serious crime, or should be a suspect? See Hatfill v. New York Times Co., 416 F.3d 320 (4th Cir. 2005), reh'g denied (with dissent), 427 F.3d 253 (4th Cir. 2005), cert. denied, 547 U.S. 1040 (2006); Lewis v. Daily Telegraph Ltd., [1964] A.C. 234 (H.L.) (report of investigation or suspicion of fraud defamatory, but does not mean that plaintiffs guilty of fraud). Is it defamatory to state that a person is party to a pending divorce action? See Gersten v. Newark Morning Ledger Co., 52 N.J. Super. 152, 145 A.2d 56 (Law Div. 1958) (libelled both named person and wife; divorce grounds in state were adultery, extreme cruelty, desertion).

7. Can allegations of illness or other misfortune be defamatory? For example, could one incur liability for reporting that plaintiff has a fatal disease? See Chuy v. Philadelphia Eagles Football Club, 595 F.2d 1265 (3d Cir. 1979) (said that professional football player had blood disease; not defamatory since disease not contagious or associated with socially repugnant conduct, and player's career was over when article published). That plaintiff has attempted suicide numerous times? See Wandt v. Hearst's Chicago American, 129 Wis. 419, 109 N.W. 70 (1900) (stated that plaintiff a "suicide fiend"; defamatory). That plaintiff has a mental illness? See Annot., Libel and Slander: Actionability of Imputing to Private Person Mental Disorder or Incapacity, or Impairment of Mental Faculties, 23 A.L.R.3d 652 (1969); Markin, Still Crazy After All These Years: The Enduring Defamatory Power of Mental Disorder, 29 Law & Psych. Rev. 155 (2005) (generally defamatory). That plaintiff is ugly? See Murray v. Schlosser, 41 Conn. Supp. 362, 574 A.2d 1339 (Super. Ct. 1990) (radio disc jockeys' selection of "dog of the week" from bridal photographs in newspaper). What about a statement describing plaintiff as impoverished? See Katapodis v. Brooklyn Spectator, Inc., 287 N.Y. 17, 38 N.E.2d 112 (1941) (parents said to be "in dire financial straits" and unable to afford private burial for their child; could be defamatory). But see Sousa v. Davenport, 3 Mass. App. Ct. 715, 323 N.E.2d 910 (1975) (poverty and unemployment). See generally Annot., Libel and Slander: Imputation of Poverty, 137 A.L.R. 913 (1942).

8. With the principal case, compare Skopp v. First Federal Savings of Wilmette, 189 Ill. App. 3d 440, 545 N.E.2d 356 (1989) (statement that plaintiff terminated "for cause" conveyed only that he did not leave employment voluntarily); Nichols v. Item Publishers, Inc., 309 N.Y. 596, 132 N.E.2d 860 (1956) ("removal" of church pastor not defamatory); Morris v. Sanders Universal Products, [1954] 1 W.L.R. 67 (C.A.) ("dismissed from our employ" capable of defamatory meaning). In Coulson v. Rapport Uitgewers (Edms.) Bpk., 1979 (3) S.A. 286 (A.D.), a newspaper had reported that plaintiff was "summarily dismissed" as editor of another newspaper. The court held that such a report did not imply misconduct on plaintiff's part. Summary dismissal might occur on grounds to which no unfavorable connotation attached, or without any lawful ground at all. Plaintiff, therefore, had not been defamed. What if defendant said that plaintiff was demoted? Cf. Gowin v. Hazen Memorial Hospital Association, 349 N.W.2d 4 (N.D. 1984). See generally Annot., Libel and Slander: Publication of Notice of Cessation of Relationship of Principal and Agent or Employer and Employee, or of Business or Professional Relationship, 138 A.L.R. 671 (1942).

Hepburn v. TCN Channel Nine Pty. Ltd.
New South Wales Court of Appeal
[1983] 2 N.S.W.L.R. 682

[Plaintiff, a medical practitioner and medical superintendent of the "Preterm Family Planning Clinic," sued on account of statements made in a television program broadcast by defendant. Plaintiff pleaded that the statements carried imputations that "(a) The plaintiff unlawfully procures miscarriages. (b) The plaintiff unlawfully procures miscarriages for financial gain. (c) The plaintiff is an abortionist. (d) The plaintiff in her medical practice advocates and performs abortions on request regardless of reasons. (e) The plaintiff regards financial gain to herself as an important and necessary matter when considering whether to terminate pregnancies." The Court of Appeal held that the imputations "are capable of bearing a meaning defamatory of the plaintiff and capable of being supported by the material published."]

GLASS JA.... Much of the argument on appeal was devoted to imputation (c) viz that the plaintiff was an abortionist. It was incumbent on the plaintiff, so the argument ran, to define the precise sense in which the term was used, the sense complained of was that she performed illegal abortions and, when the imputation was so narrowed, it coincided with imputation (a) and was therefore objectionable for duplication.

I see no reason why the plaintiff should be compelled to define the sense in which the defendant employed a general expression. If the plaintiff is castigated as a criminal, criminality is predicated of him in all its amplitude. He is not faced with the need to choose between the lower end of the range which will moderate his damages and the upper end which, in the context of the publication, the jury may not accept. The defendant is expected to know what his language conveyed and that, in adopting an epithet with a spread of meanings, he will be understood as imputing them all.

The term abortionist applied to a medical practitioner can impute that she terminates pregnancies with or without lawful authority. The defendant may be able to persuade the jury that the contextual framework limited the meaning to lawful conduct. But even if it did, I am of opinion that the jury could, acting reasonably, treat as defamatory the imputation that pregnancies were lawfully terminated by the plaintiff.

There is no need to document the existence in the community of a deep factional divide on the issue of abortion. The pro-abortion lobby approves the existing grounds for lawful termination of pregnancies and seeks to have them extended. The anti-abortion lobby contends that all abortion is morally wrong and that no abortion should be lawful. So the description of the plaintiff as a lawful abortionist will excite both approbation and disapprobation in different sections of the community. How does the law of defamation accommodate these discrepant social attitudes? There is a body of English authority which suggests that the standard of opinion is that of "right thinking people generally". The corollary to this proposition was that an imputation of conduct which disparaged the plaintiff only in the eyes of a limited class was not defamatory. In the United States, on the other hand, an imputation can be defamatory if it injures a man in the eyes of "a considerable and respectable class in the community" though it be only a minority, *Peck v. Tribune* Co. 214 US 185, at 190 (1909), in which Holmes J said "liability is not a question of a majority vote".

In *Slatyer v Daily Telegraph Newspaper Co Ltd* (1908) 6 CLR 1, at 7, Griffith CJ, disapproved of the use of the term "right thinking" reader unless it were to be equated with a reader of fair average intelligence. I take this to be a rejection of the notion that a moral consensus exists upon what constitutes creditable or discreditable behavior. It has been argued in this country that principle requires that regard should be paid to actual community attitudes, right or wrong, "The Criterion of Defamation" G L Fricke (1958) 32 ALJ 7. In the absence of any binding pronouncement of the High Court I would hold the view that it is proper for the law of defamation to recognize that there are many subjects in a pluralist society upon which contradictory attitudes exist—e.g. uranium mining and State aid for private schools to name two others—and that it would be futile for the judges to arbitrate between them. As Fleming says, by adopting the standard of the "right thinking" man the question becomes not what people actually think but what they should think, *Law of Torts*, 5th ed (1977), at 530.

It is defamatory to describe a person in terms which to the general public are innocuous, if they diminish him in the eyes of those aware of special facts, provided publication is made to those persons. Consistency in my view requires that a man can justly complain that words, which lower him in the estimation of an appreciable and reputable section of the community, were published to members of it, even though those same words might exalt him to the level of a hero in other quarters. Where a television programme has been beamed to a large audience it can be presumed, without special proof, that its viewers will include some who advocate the "right to life" and abhor the destruction of foetuses, whatever the circumstances. In the estimation of such persons the plaintiff can claim to have been disparaged even if abortionist meant lawful abortionist. If it also meant unlawful abortionist, she can also claim to have been denigrated in the eyes of a different but substantial section of the viewers who support the existing law but do not want it extended. Of course, I omit from consideration the question whether the imputation in either of its aspects can be justified so far as concerns this particular plaintiff. For these reasons I would allow the submission of imputation (c) to the jury.

[Hutley and Priestley, JJ.A., delivered concurring opinions.]

Notes

1. U.S. cases echo the English rule that a communication is defamatory when plaintiff is defamed in the estimation of the community in general, represented by "right-thinking" persons. E.g., Kimmerle v. New York Evening Journal, Inc., p. 494, supra. But there is now wide acceptance of the position of Peck v. Tribune Co., referred to in the principal case,

that a statement is defamatory if it would hurt plaintiff in the estimation of an "important and respectable part of the community." See Eldredge, Law of Defamation 31–36 (1978); Sack, Defamation: Libel, Slander, and Related Problems §§ 2.4.3, 2.4.4 (4th ed. 2010). Restatement (Second) of Torts § 559, comment *e* (1977), distinguishes between a communication that prejudices plaintiff in the eyes of a "substantial and respectable minority" of the community and one that would be derogatory in the view of only a single individual or very small group. Also, there is no defamation when the communication reaches individuals "with views sufficiently peculiar to regard as derogatory what the vast majority of persons regard as innocent." The *Peck* case involved use of plaintiff's picture in an advertisement for whiskey. Cf. Tolley v. J.S. Fry and Sons, Ltd., [1931] A.C. 333 (H.L.), in which an advertisement for chocolates included a caricature of an amateur golfer, thereby calling into question his amateur status. Would it be defamatory to say of a Jehovah's Witness that he accepted a blood transfusion? See Eldredge, Law of Defamation 35–36 (1978). To include a kosher meat dealer in a list of stores that sell a brand of bacon? See Braun v. Armour & Co., 254 N.Y. 514, 173 N.E. 845 (1930). To call a black person an "Uncle Tom"? See Moore v. P.W. Publishing Co., 3 Ohio St. 2d 183, 209 N.E.2d 412 (1965), cert. denied, 382 U.S. 978 (1966). Compare Weiner v. Time & Life Inc., 133 Misc. 2d 622, 507 N.Y.S.2d 784 (Sup. Ct. 1986) ("community" standard in action against national magazine not that of plaintiff's small Orthodox community). What if plaintiff was called a German during one of the wars with Germany? See Richter v. Mack, 1917 A.D. 201 (not defamatory). Is it defamatory to say that someone is an atheist?

2. "Respectable" would exclude persons who may be substantial in numbers but whose views are so anti-social that it is not proper for the courts to recognize them—for example, criminals, in the case of a statement that a former gang member bungled holdups, or has reformed and is no longer to be trusted. Restatement (Second) of Torts § 559, comment *e* (1977). Should a court for this reason now refuse to follow the precedents, mostly from southern states, treating as defamatory references to a white person as black? See Smolla, Law of Defamation § 4:5 (2d ed. 1999). It is usually held that an imputation of homosexuality is defamatory. See Annot., Imputation of Homosexuality as Defamation, 7 A.L.R.6th 135 (2005). But this was rejected in Albright v. Morton, 321 F. Supp. 2d 130 (D. Mass. 2004), aff'd sub nom. Amrak Productions, Inc. v. Morton, 410 F.3d 69 (1st Cir. 2005). The court believed that identifying a person as homosexual would not now discredit him in any "considerable and respectable class of the community" and that to find this defamatory would validate the view that homosexuals were immoral and legitimize prejudice against them. What is the best position on this issue? See generally Lidsky, Defamation, Reputation, and the Myth of Community, 71 Wash. L. Rev. 1 (1996).

3. Whether it is defamatory to refer to a person as an "informer" is addressed in a number of cases. Most conclude that it is not. See Saunders v. Board of Directors, WHYY-TV (Channel 12), 382 A.2d 257 (Del. Super. Ct. 1978) ("F.B.I. informant"); Connelly v. McKay, 176 Misc. 685, 28 N.Y.S.2d 327 (Sup. Ct. 1941) (proprietor of service station and rooming house primarily patronized by truck drivers said to be informing authorities of truckers' violations of Interstate Commerce Commission regulations); Rose v. Borenstein, 119 N.Y.S.2d 288 (N.Y. City Ct. 1953) (plaintiff said to have informed French customs authorities that defendants were in illegal possession of diamonds); Prinsloo v. S.A. Associated Newspapers Ltd., 1959 (2) S.A. 693 (W) (allegation that student was doing espionage work on university campus for South African Police). But see Westby v. Madison Newspapers, Inc., 81 Wis. 2d 1, 259 N.W.2d 691 (1977) (could be defamatory to report that plaintiffs spied on their political-activist neighbors as paid informants for government agency); Graham v. Roy, (1851) 13 D. 634 (Scot. Ct. Sess.) (circulation of re-

port that plaintiff informed excise officers about distiller for purpose of obtaining half share of penalties assessed). Byrne v. Deane, [1937] 1 K.B. 818 (C.A.), arose from a poem placed on the wall of a golf club. The poem was subject to the interpretation that plaintiff furnished information that led to a raid on the club in which illegal gambling machines were removed. It was held that the words were incapable of a defamatory meaning; saying that a person put in motion the proper machinery for suppressing crime could not be defamatory. In Burrascano v. Levi, 452 F. Supp. 1066 (D. Md. 1978), aff'd, 612 F.2d 1306 (4th Cir. 1979), the court decided that a newspaper's statement that a prison inmate would be given a new identity through the government's witness protection program was not libellous, though it allegedly resulted in his being shunned by other inmates and danger to his safety. Cf. Michtavi v. New York Daily News, 587 F.3d 551 (2d Cir. 2009) (not defamatory to report that inmate planned to cooperate with prosecutors).

4. It has been held that it is not defamatory to attribute political views to which many persons in the community are strongly opposed. Steinman v. Di Roberts, 23 A.D.2d 693, 257 N.Y.S.2d 695 (1965), aff'd, 17 N.Y.2d 512, 267 N.Y.S.2d 512, 214 N.E.2d 789 (1966) ("liberal"); Rawlins v. McKee, 327 S.W.2d 633 (Tex. Civ. App. 1959) ("radical" "leftwinger" "backed and financed by … labor bosses"). Cf. Chicago, Rock Island & Pacific Railway Co. v. Medley, 55 Okla. 145, 155 P. 211 (1916) ("labor agitator"). Is this because the possession of political views cannot reasonably be regarded as discreditable, or because to entertain such actions would have the courts of a democracy decide which political philosophies are acceptable and which are not? The question of whether it is defamatory to associate a person with Communism has been affected by changing community views about the threat posed to the United States by the Soviet Union. See Harper, James & Gray, Law of Torts § 5.1 (3d ed. 2006). During the "Cold War" period following World War II, the prevailing view was that this is defamatory. See Utah State Farm Bureau Federation v. National Farmers Union Service Corp., 198 F.2d 20 (10th Cir. 1952); Herrmann v. Newark Morning Ledger Co., 48 N.J. Super. 420, 138 A.2d 61 (App. Div. 1958), on reh'g, 49 N.J. Super. 551, 140 A.2d 529 (App. Div. 1958). In Grant v. Reader's Digest Association, Inc., 151 F.2d 733 (2d Cir. 1945), cert. denied, 326 U.S. 797 (1946), the court found actionable a statement that a lawyer was a legislative representative for a state Communist Party, even though it might cause only "wrong-thinking" people to have adverse feelings about plaintiff. Cf. MacLeod v. Tribune Publishing Co., 52 Cal. 2d 536, 343 P.2d 36 (1959) (libellous to say of candidate for public office that he was endorsed by newspaper recognized as mouthpiece for Communist Party). But see National Association of Government Employees, Inc. v. Central Broadcasting Corp., 379 Mass. 220, 396 N.E.2d 996 (1979) (charge of Communism against labor union merely "pejorative rhetoric"). What if the imputation is right-wing extremism? See Washburn v. Wright, 261 Cal. App. 2d 789, 68 Cal. Rptr. 224 (1968) ("extremist" and allegation of John Birch Society membership not defamatory). See generally Annot., Libel and Slander: Imputation of Subversive or Otherwise Objectionable Political or Social Principles, 33 A.L.R.2d 1196 (1954).

5. Imputing "unchastity" is a classic form of defamation. See pp. 533–542, infra. And it has been held that to say a person is illegitimate is actionable. See Shelby v. Sun Printing and Publishing Association, 38 Hun 474 (N.Y. Sup. Ct. 1886), aff'd, 109 N.Y. 611, 15 N.E. 895 (1888); Annot., Libel and Slander: Charging One with Being a Bastard or Illegitimate, 53 A.L.R. 548 (1928). Should changing community attitudes on these subjects and their relevance to social standing lead to the conclusion that such remarks are no longer defamatory? Would a court still hold, as in Van Wiginton v. Pulitzer Publishing Co., 218 F. 795 (8th Cir. 1914), that it is defamatory to portray a person as the child of a convicted murderer? Cf. Rose v. Daily Mirror, Inc., 284 N.Y. 335, 31 N.E.2d 182 (1940) (plaintiffs reported to be widow and children of notorious murderer); Hamilton

v. UPI, 9 Media L. Rptr. 2453 (S.D. Iowa 1983) (plaintiff reported to be husband of business proprietor charged with indecent exposure). What about a gossip column insinuating a rift between husband and wife? See Lyman v. New England Newspaper Publishing Co., 286 Mass. 258, 190 N.E. 542 (1934).

Burton v. Crowell Publishing Company
United States Circuit Court of Appeals, Second Circuit
82 F.2d 154 (1936)

L. HAND, Circuit Judge.

This appeal arises upon a judgment dismissing a complaint for libel upon the pleadings. The complaint alleged that the defendant had published an advertise-ment ... made up of text and photographs; that one of the photographs was "susceptible of being regarded as representing plaintiff as guilty of indecent exposure and as being a person physically deformed and mentally perverted"; that some of the text, read with the offending photograph, was "susceptible of being regarded as falsely representing plaintiff as an utterer of salacious and obscene language"; and finally that "by reason of the premises plaintiff has been subjected to frequent and conspicuous ridicule, scandal, reproach, scorn, and indignity." The advertisement was of "Camel" cigarettes; the plaintiff was a widely known gentleman steeple-chaser, and the text quoted him as declaring that "Camel" cigarettes "restored" him after "a crowded business day." Two photographs were inserted; the larger, a picture of the plaintiff in riding shirt and breeches, seated apparently outside a paddock with a cigarette in one hand and a cap and whip in the other. This contained the legend, "Get a lift with a Camel"; neither it, nor the photograph, is charged as part of the libel, except as the legend may be read upon the other and offending photograph. That represented him coming from a race to be weighed in; he is carrying his saddle in front of him with his right hand under the pommel and his left under the cantle; the line of the seat is about twelve inches below his waist. Over the pommel hangs a stirrup; over the seat at his middle a white girth falls loosely in such a way that it seems to be attached to the plaintiff and not to the saddle. So regarded, the photograph becomes grotesque, monstrous, and obscene; and the legends, which without undue violence can be made to match, reinforce the ribald interpretation. That is the libel. The answer alleged that the plaintiff had posed for the photographs and been paid for their use as an advertisement; a reply, that they had never been shown to the plaintiff after they were taken. On this showing the judge held that the advertisement did not hold the plaintiff up to the hatred, ridicule, or contempt of fair-minded people, and that in any event he consented to its use and might not complain.

We dismiss at once so much of the complaint as alleged that the advertisement might be read to say that the plaintiff was deformed, or that he had indecently exposed himself, or was making obscene jokes by means of the legends. Nobody could be fatuous enough to believe any of these things; everybody would at once see that it was the camera, and the camera alone, that had made the unfortunate mistake. If the advertisement is a libel, it is such in spite of the fact that it asserts nothing whatever about the plaintiff, even by the remotest implications. It does not profess to depict him as he is; it does not exaggerate any part of his person so as to suggest that he is deformed; it is patently an optical illusion, and carries its correction on its face as much as though it were a verbal utterance which expressly declared that it was false. It would be hard for words so guarded to carry any sting, but the same is not true of caricatures, and this is an example; for, notwithstanding all we have just said, it exposed the plaintiff to overwhelming ridicule. The contrast between the drawn and serious face and the accompanying fantastic and lewd deformity was so extravagant that, though utterly unfair, it in fact made of the plaintiff a preposterously ridiculous spectacle; and the obvious mistake only added to the amusement. Had such a picture been deliberately produced, surely every right-minded person would agree that he would have had a genuine grievance; and the effect is the same whether it is deliberate or not. Such a caricature affects a man's reputation, if by that is meant his position in the minds of others; the association so established may be beyond repair; he may become known indefinitely as the absurd victim of this unhappy mischance. Literally, therefore, the injury falls within the accepted rubric; it exposes the sufferer to "ridicule" and "contempt." ...

The defendant answers that every libel must affect the plaintiff's character; but if by "character" is meant those moral qualities which the word ordinarily includes, the statement is certainly untrue, for there are many libels which do not affect the reputation of the victim in any such way. Thus, it is a libel to say that a man is insane; or that he has negro blood if he professes to be white; or is too educated to earn his living; or is desperately poor; or that he is a eunuch; or that he has an infectious disease, even though not venereal; or that he is illegitimate; or that his near relatives have committed a crime; or that he was mistaken for Jack Ketch; or that a woman was served with process in her bathtub. It is indeed not true that all ridicule, or all disagreeable comment, is actionable; a man must not be too thin-skinned or a self-important prig; but this advertisement was more than what only a morbid person would not laugh off; the mortification, however ill-deserved, was a very substantial grievance.

A more plausible challenge is that a libel must be something that can be true or false, since truth is always a defense. It would follow that if, as we agree, the picture was a mistake on its face and declared nothing about the plaintiff, it was not a libel. We have been able to find very little on the point. In Dunlop v. Dunlop Rubber Co. (1920) 1 Irish Ch. & Ld. Com. 280, 290–292, the picture represented the plaintiff in foppish clothes, and the opinion seems to rely merely upon the contempt which that alone might have aroused, but those who saw it might have taken it to imply that the plaintiff was in fact a fop. In Zbyszko v. New York American, 228 App. Div. 277, 239 N.Y.S. 411, however, though the decision certainly went far, nobody could possibly have read the picture as asserting anything which was in fact untrue; it was the mere association of the plaintiff with a gorilla that was thought to lower him in others' esteem. Nevertheless, although the question is almost tabula rasa, it seems to us that in principle there should be no doubt. The gravamen of the wrong in defamation is not so much the injury to reputation, measured by the opinions of others, as the feelings, that is, the repulsion or the light esteem, which those opinions engender. We are sensitive to the charge of murder only because our fellows deprecate it in most forms; but a head-hunter, or an aboriginal American Indian, or a gangster, would regard such an accusation as a distinction, and during the Great War an "ace," a man who had killed five others, was held in high regard. Usually it is difficult to arouse feelings without expressing an opinion, or asserting a fact; and the common law has so much regard for truth that it excuses the utterance of anything that is true. But it is a non sequitur to argue that whenever truth is not a defense, there can be no libel; that would invert the proper approach to the whole subject.... The only reason why the law makes truth a defense is not because a libel must be false, but because the utterance of truth is in all circumstances an interest paramount to reputation; it is like a privileged communication, which is privileged only because the law prefers it conditionally to reputation. When there is no such countervailing interest, there is no excuse; and that is the situation here. In conclusion therefore we hold that because the picture taken with the legends was calculated to expose the plaintiff to more than trivial ridicule, it was prima facie actionable; that the fact that it did not assume to state a fact or an opinion is irrelevant; and that in consequence the publication is actionable.

Finally, the plaintiff's consent to the use of the photographs for which he posed as an advertisement was not a consent to the use of the offending photograph; he had no reason to anticipate that the lens would so distort his appearance. If the defendant wished to fix him with responsibility for whatever the camera might turn out, the result should have been shown him before publication. Possibly any one who chooses to stir such a controversy in a court cannot have been very sensitive originally, but that is a consideration for the jury, which, if ever justified, is justified in actions for defamation.

Judgment reversed; cause remanded for trial.

Notes

1. "Ridicule" is included in the traditional defamation formula of a publication that holds a person up to "hatred, contempt or ridicule." In most of the relevant cases, the ridicule implied a defect in plaintiff's conduct or character. One example is Francis Mezzara's Case, 2 N.Y. City Hall Recorder 113 (Ct. Gen. Sess. 1817), a criminal libel case in which an artist had added to his portrait of the complainant a pair of ass' ears. Another example is Villers v. Monsley, (1769) 2 Wils. K.B. 403, 95 Eng. Rep. 886 (C.P.). There, defendant had composed doggerel verse which suggested that plaintiff stank and had "the itch." See also Farnsworth v. Hyde, 266 Or. 236, 512 P.2d 1003 (1973) (book portraying plaintiff as very lazy man with wife who did most of work on farm). In Powers v. Durgin-Snow Publishing Co., 154 Me. 108, 144 A.2d 294 (1958), a newspaper column stated that a thirty-five-year-old man—"a classic example of typical yankee thrift"—was building his own coffin, in order to save the cost of a casket, and planning to dig his own grave. Was this libellous?

2. When a publication imputes nothing "wrong" to plaintiff, is there any good reason why a defamation action should be permitted? How can plaintiff's reputation have been harmed? Eldredge, Law of Defamation 39 (1978), relates that when the *Burton* case was before the Second Circuit, there was a meeting in New York of the American Law Institute's Reporter for Torts and his advisers, one of whom was Learned Hand. During luncheon at the Harvard Club Judge Hand pulled the advertisement out of his briefcase and without any comment passed it around the table. The persons who saw the advertisement burst into roars of laughter. "That settles it," said Judge Hand. "It's defamatory." Cf. Mazatti v. Acme Products, Ltd., [1930] 3 W.W.R. 43, [1930] 4 D.L.R. 601 (Man. K.B.), involving an advertisement for a patent medicine. The advertisement contained a supposed recommendation by plaintiff, saying that the medicine cured him of a variety of ailments including dizzy spells and constipation.

3. Zbyszko v. New York American, Inc., 228 App. Div. 277, 239 N.Y.S. 411 (1930), to which the principal case refers, arose from an article on the scientific theory of evolution. It was illustrated with the picture of a gorilla and a picture of plaintiff in a wrestling pose, captioned "Stanislaus Zbyszko, the Wrestler, Not Fundamentally Different from the Gorilla in Physique." Was *Burton* a stronger or a weaker case for liability? In Berkoff v. Burchill, [1996] 4 All E.R. 1008 (C.A.), a 2–1 majority accepted a libel action for a newspaper column that said plaintiff was hideous-looking. Compare Byrd v. Hustler Magazine, Inc., 433 So. 2d 593 (Fla. App. 1983), review denied, 443 So. 2d 979 (Fla. 1984), in which, to make a point about advertising by tobacco companies, defendant altered a cigarette advertisement for which plaintiff posed. The alteration gave the impression that

plaintiff was making a rude gesture, but defendant's magazine made it clear that the advertisement had been altered. The court ordered entry of judgment for defendant.

4. Is it defamatory to publish a false obituary notice? See Decker v. Princeton Packet, Inc., 116 N.J. 418, 561 A.2d 1122 (1989); Cardiff v. Brooklyn Eagle, Inc., 190 Misc. 730, 75 N.Y.S.2d 222 (Sup. Ct. 1947) (notice that plaintiff had died and was "lying in state" at address of his bar and grill; not defamatory as did not injure plaintiff's reputation). Cf. Lemmer v. The Tribune, 50 Mont. 559, 148 P. 338 (1915) (report that plaintiff died of morphine overdose). What about a false or premature wedding announcement? See Emerson v. Grimsby Times and Telegraph Co., Ltd., (1926) 42 T.L.R. 238 (C.A.) (full account of ceremony composed and published on day prior to wedding, with statement that couple now on honeymoon; plaintiff ridiculed when at business on day of wedding; action dismissed); Kirman v. Sun Printing & Publishing Co., 99 App. Div. 367, 91 N.Y.S. 193 (1904) (allegedly false article about wedding at which, when it was realized that bridegroom would not appear, bride fell screaming to floor and guests rushed to get food before it was put away).

5. Is a photograph of a person in the nude defamatory? See McCabe v. Village Voice, Inc., 550 F. Supp. 525 (E.D. Pa. 1982) (not libellous if not obscene or suggestive; might indicate plaintiff is supportive of avant garde photography, but that is not defamatory). What if it is used in a parody? See Vitale v. National Lampoon, Inc., 449 F. Supp. 442 (E.D. Pa. 1978). Some types of pictorial representations are likely to be found defamatory—for example, the inclusion of plaintiff's likeness in a wax museum depicting notorious crimes. See Monson v. Tussauds Ltd., [1894] 1 Q.B. 671 (C.A.) (plaintiff had been tried for murder in Scotland, with verdict of "not proven"; portrayed with gun in hand, not far from "Chamber of Horrors").

———————

Derbyshire County Council v. Times Newspapers Ltd.

House of Lords
[1993] A.C. 534

LORD KEITH OF KINKEL. My Lords, this appeal raises, as a preliminary issue in an action of damages for libel, the question whether a local authority is entitled to maintain an action in libel for words which reflect on it in its governmental and administrative functions. That is the way the preliminary point of law was expressed in the order of the master, but it has opened out into an investigation of whether a local authority can sue for libel at all.

Balcombe L.J., giving the leading judgment in the Court of Appeal, summarised the facts thus: " … In two issues of 'The Sunday Times' newspaper on 17 and 24 September 1989 there appeared articles concerning share deals involving the superannuation fund of the Derbyshire County Council. The articles in the issue of 17 September were headed 'Revealed: Socialist tycoon's deals with a Labour [Party] chief' and 'Bizarre deals of a council leader and the media tycoon:' that in the issue of 24 September was headed 'Council share deals under scrutiny.' The council leader was Mr. David Melvyn Bookbinder; the 'media tycoon' was Mr. Owen Oyston…. [These articles] question the propriety of certain investments made by the council of moneys in its superannuation fund, with Mr. Bookbinder as the prime mover, in three deals with Mr. Oyston or companies controlled by him…."

Following the publication actions of damages for libel were brought against the publishers of "The Sunday Times," its editor and the two journalists who wrote the articles, by Derbyshire County Council, Mr. Bookbinder and Mr. Oyston. Mr. Oyston's action was settled by an apology and payment of damages and costs. The statements of claims in this action by the plaintiff and in that by Mr. Bookbinder are for all practical purposes in identical terms. That of the plaintiff asserts in paragraph 6 that there were written and published "of and concerning the council and of and concerning the council in the way of its discharge of its responsibility for the investment and control of the superannuation fund" the words contained in the article of 17 September, and paragraph 8 makes a similar assertion in relation to the article of 24 September. Paragraph 9 states: "By reason of the words published on 17 September 1989 and the words and graph published on 24 September 1989 the plaintiff council has been injured in its credit and reputation and has been brought into public scandal, odium and contempt, and has suffered loss and damage."

No special damage is pleaded....

[The council appealed from the Court of Appeal's decision that it could not maintain a libel action.]

There are only two reported cases in which an English local authority has sued for libel. The first is *Manchester Corporation v. Williams* [1891] 1 Q.B. 94; 63 L.T. 805. The defendant had written a letter to a newspaper alleging that "in the case of two, if not three, departments of our Manchester City Council, bribery and corruption have existed, and done their nefarious work." A Divisional Court consisting of Day J. and Lawrance J. held that the statement of claim disclosed no cause of action. The judgment of Day J. in the Queen's Bench report is in these terms: "This is an action brought by a municipal corporation to recover damages for what is alleged to be a libel on the corporation itself, as distinguished from its individual members or officials. The libel complained of consists of a charge of bribery and corruption. The question is whether such an action will lie. I think it will not. It is altogether unprecedented, and there is no principle on which it could be founded. The limits of a corporation's right of action for libel are those suggested by Pollock C.B. in the case which has been referred to. A corporation may sue for a libel affecting property, not for one merely affecting personal reputation. The present case falls within the latter class. There must, therefore, be judgment for the defendant." ...

Metropolitan Saloon Omnibus Co. Ltd. v. Hawkins (1859) 4 H. & N. 87 was an action by a company ... in respect of a libel imputing to it insolvency, mismanagement and dishonest carrying on of its affairs. The Court of the Exchequer held the action to be maintainable. Pollock C.B., in the passage referred to by Day J., said, at p. 90: "That a corporation at common law can sue in respect of a libel there is no doubt. It would be monstrous if a corporation could maintain no action for slander of title through which they lost a great deal of money. It could not sue in respect of an imputation of murder, or incest, or adultery, because it could not commit those crimes. Nor could it sue in respect of a charge of corruption, for a corporation cannot be guilty of corruption, although the individuals composing it may. But it would be very odd if a corporation had no means of protecting itself against wrong; and if its property is injured by slander it has no means of redress except by action. Therefore it appears to me clear that a corporation at common law may maintain an action for a libel by which its property is injured."

In *South Hetton Coal Co. Ltd. v. North-Eastern News Association Ltd.* [1894] 1 Q.B. 133 a newspaper had published an article alleging that the houses in which the company accommodated its colliers were in a highly insanitary state. The Court of Appeal held that the company was entitled to maintain an action for libel without proof of special damage, in respect that the libel was calculated to injure the company's reputation in the way of its business. Lord Esher M.R. said, at p. 138: "... I have come to the conclusion that the law of libel is one and the same as to all plaintiffs; and that, in every action of libel, whether the statement complained of is, or is not, a libel, depends on the same question—viz., whether the jury are of opinion that what has been published with regard to the plaintiff would tend in the minds of people of ordinary sense to bring the plaintiff into contempt, hatred, or ridicule, or to injure his character. The question is really the same by whomsoever the action is brought—whether by a person, a firm, or a company. But though the law is the same, the application of it is, no doubt, different with regard to different kinds of plaintiffs. There are statements which, with regard to some plaintiffs, would undoubtedly constitute a libel, but which, if published of another kind of plaintiffs, would not have the same effect."

He went on to say that certain statements might have the same effect, whether made with regard to a person, or a firm, or a company, for example statements with regard to conduct of a business, and having elaborated on the question whether or not a particular statement might reflect on the manner of conduct of a business, continued: "With regard to a firm or a company, it is impossible to lay down an exhaustive rule as to what would be a libel on them. But the same rule is applicable to a statement made with regard to them. Statements may be made with regard to their mode of carrying on business, such as to lead people of ordinary sense to the opinion that they conduct their business badly and inefficiently. If so, the law will be the same in their case as in that of an individual, and the statement will be libellous. Then, if the case be one of libel—whether on a person, a firm, or a company—the law is that the damages are at large. It is not necessary to prove any particular damage; the jury may give such damages as they think fit, having regard to the conduct of the parties respectively, and all the circumstances of the case." In *National Union of General and Municipal Workers v. Gillian* [1946] K.B. 81 the Court of Appeal held that a trade union could, in general, maintain an action in tort, and that an action for libel was no exception to that rule. No detailed consideration was given to the nature of the statements in respect of which the action might lie, though Scott L.J. referred to the disintegration of a trade union which might result from a libel, and Uthwatt J. said that he saw no reason why a non-trading corporation should not have the same rights as a trading corporation as respects imputations on the conduct by it of its activities.

The second case involving proceedings by a local authority is *Bognor Regis Urban District Council v. Campion* [1972] 2 Q.B. 169, a decision of Browne J. Mr. Campion had distributed at a meeting of a ratepayers' association a leaflet savagely attacking the council, which sued him for libel. At the trial Mr. Campion conducted his own case without the assistance of solicitors or counsel. Browne J. found in favour of the council and awarded it damages of £2,000. At p. 173, he stated his intention to apply a principle to be found in *National Union of General and Municipal Workers v. Gillian*, from which he quoted extensively in the following pages. He continued: "Just as a trading company has a trading reputation which it is entitled to protect by bringing an action for defamation, so in my view the plaintiffs as a local government corporation have a 'governing' reputation which they are equally entitled to protect in the same way—of course, bearing in mind the vital distinction between defamation of the corporation as such and defamation of its individual officers or members. I entirely accept the statement made in *Gatley on Libel and Slander*, 6th ed. (1967), p. 409, para. 890: 'A corporation or company cannot maintain an action of libel or slander for any words which reflect, not upon itself, but solely upon its individual officers or members.' Then there is a quotation: 'To merely attack or challenge the rectitude of the officers or members of a corporation, and hold them or either of them up to scorn, hatred, contempt, or obloquy for acts done in their official capacity, or which would render them liable to criminal prosecution, does not give the corporation a right of action for libel.' I stress the words 'solely' and 'merely' in those passages...."

Browne J. then proceeded to consider *Manchester Corporation v. Williams*, and after quoting from the judgment of Day J. in the Law Times Report, 63 L.T. 805, 806–807, said: "Day J. seems to put his judgment on two grounds; first, that a corporation may sue for a libel affecting property and not for one merely affecting personal reputation. If this was ever right, it has in my view been overruled by *South Hetton Coal Co. v. North-Eastern News Association Ltd.* (where substantially this argument was used by the defendants) and by *National Union of General and Municipal Workers v. Gillian* (where the *Manchester Corporation* case was cited). The other ground seems to have been that a corporation cannot be guilty of corruption and therefore it cannot be defamatory to say or write that it has been guilty of corruption. This was based on the obiter dictum of Pollock C.B. in *Metropolitan Saloon Omnibus Co. v. Hawkins* and was repeated later by Lopes L.J. in *South Hetton Coal Co. v. North-Eastern News Association Ltd.* The *Manchester Corporation* case is severely criticised in *Spencer Bower on Actionable Defamation* (1908), pp. 279 and 280; in *Fraser on Libel and Slander*, 7th ed. (1936), pp. 89 and 90; and by Oliver J. in *Willis v. Brooks* [1947] 1 All E.R. 191 where he said that after reading the *National Union of General and Municipal Workers* case he agreed with the editors of *Fraser*, who say: 'It is respectfully submitted that the above statement of the law by Day J ... is unsound in principle and would not be upheld in the Court of Appeal.' ..."

It is to be observed that Browne J. did not give any consideration to the question whether a local authority, or any other body exercising governmental functions, might not be in a special position as regards the right to take proceedings for defamation. The authorities cited above clearly establish that a trading corporation is entitled to sue in respect of defamatory matters which can be seen as having a tendency to damage it in the way of its business. Examples are those that go to credit such as might deter banks from lending to it, or to the conditions experienced by its employees, which might impede the recruitment of the best qualified workers, or make people reluctant to deal with it. The *South Hetton Coal Co.* case would appear to be an instance of the latter kind, and not, as suggested by Browne J., an authority for the view that a trading corporation can sue for something that does not affect it adversely in the way of its business. The trade union cases are understandable upon the view that defamatory matter may adversely affect the union's ability to keep its members or attract new ones or to maintain a convincing attitude towards employers. Likewise in the case of a charitable organisation the effect may be to discourage subscribers or otherwise impair its ability to carry on its charitable objects. Similar considerations can no doubt be advanced in connection with the position of a local authority. Defamatory statements might make it more difficult to borrow or to attract suitable staff and thus affect adversely the efficient carrying out of its functions.

There are, however, features of a local authority which may be regarded as distinguishing it from other types of corporation, whether trading or non-trading. The most important of these features is that it is a governmental body. Further, it is a democratically elected body, the electoral process nowadays being conducted almost exclusively on party political lines. It is of the highest public importance that a democratically elected governmental body, or indeed any governmental body, should be open to uninhibited public criticism. The threat of a civil action for defamation must inevitably have an inhibiting effect on freedom of speech. In *City of Chicago v. Tribune Co.* (1923) 139 N.E. 86 the Supreme Court of Illinois held that the city could not maintain an action of damages for libel. Thompson C.J. said, at p. 90: "The fundamental right of freedom of speech is involved in this litigation, and not merely the right of liberty of the press. If this action can be maintained against a newspaper it can be maintained against every private citizen who ventures to criticise the ministers who are temporarily conducting the affairs of his government. Where any person by speech or writing seeks to persuade others to violate existing law or to overthrow by force or other unlawful means the existing government, he may be punished ... but all other utterances or publications against the government must be considered absolutely privileged. While in the early history of the struggle for freedom of speech the restrictions were enforced by criminal prosecutions, it is clear that a civil action is as great, if not a greater, restriction than a criminal prosecution. If the right to criticise the government is a privilege which, with the exceptions above enumerated, cannot be restricted, then all civil as well as criminal actions are forbidden. A despotic or corrupt government can more easily stifle opposition by a series of civil actions than by criminal prosecutions...."

After giving a number of reasons for this, he said: "It follows, therefore, that every citizen has a right to criticise an inefficient or corrupt government without fear of civil as well as criminal prosecution. This absolute privilege is founded on the principle that it is advantageous for the public interest that the citizen should not be in any way fettered in his statements, and where the public service or due administration of justice is involved he shall have the right to speak his mind freely."

These propositions were endorsed by the Supreme Court of the United States in *New York Times Co. v. Sullivan* (1964) 376 U.S. 254, 277. While these decisions were related most directly to the provisions of the American Constitution concerned with securing freedom of speech, the public interest considerations which underlaid them are no less valid in this country. What has been described as "the chilling effect" induced by the threat of civil actions for libel is very important. Quite often the facts which would justify a defamatory publication are known to be true, but admissible evidence capable of proving those facts is not available. This may prevent the publication of matters which it is very desirable to make public....

It is of some significance to observe that a number of departments of central government in the United Kingdom are statutorily created corporations, including the Secretaries of State for Defence, Education and Science, Energy, Environment and Social Services. If a local authority can sue for libel there would appear to be no reason in logic for holding that any of these departments (apart from two which are made corporations only for the purpose of holding land) was not also entitled to sue. But as is shown by the decision in *Attorney-General v. Guardian Newspapers Ltd.* (No. 2) [p. 326, supra], a case concerned with confidentiality, there are rights available to private citizens which institutions of central government are not in a position to exercise unless they can show that it is the public interest to do so. The same applies, in my opinion, to local authorities. In both cases I regard it as right for this House to lay down that not only is there no public interest favouring the right of organs of government, whether central or local, to sue for libel, but that it is contrary to the public interest that they should have it. It is contrary to the public interest because to admit such actions would place an undesirable fetter on freedom of speech. In *Die Spoorbond v. South African Railways*, 1946 A.D. 999 the Supreme Court of South Africa held that the South African Railways and Harbours, a governmental department of the Union of South Africa, was not entitled to maintain an action for defamation in respect of a publication alleged to have injured its reputation as the authority responsible for running the railways. Schreiner J.A. said, at pp. 1012–1013: "I am prepared to assume, for the purposes of the present argument, that the Crown may, at least in so far as it takes part in trading in competition with its subjects, enjoy a reputation, damage to which could be calculated in money. On that assumption there is certainly force in the contention that it would be unfair to deny to the Crown the weapon, an action for damages for defamation, which is most feared by calumniators. Nevertheless it seems to me that considerations of fairness and convenience are, on balance, distinctly against the recognition of a right in the Crown to sue the subject in a defamation action to protect that reputation. The normal means by which the Crown protects itself against attacks upon its management of the country's affairs is political action and not litigation, and it would, I think, be unfortunate if that practice were altered. At present certain kinds of criticism of those who manage the state's affairs may lead to criminal prosecutions, while if the criticism consists of defamatory utterances against individual servants of the state actions for defamation will lie at their suit. But subject to the risk of these sanctions and to the possible further risk ... of being sued by the Crown for injurious falsehood, any subject is free to express his opinion upon the management of the country's affairs without fear of legal consequences. I have no doubt that it would involve a serious interference with the free expression of opinion hitherto enjoyed in this country if the wealth of the state, derived from the state's subjects, could be used to launch against those subjects actions for defamation because they have, falsely and unfairly it may be, criticised or condemned the management of the country. Such actions could not, I think, be confined to those brought by the railways administration for criticism of the running of the railways. Quite a number of government departments ... indulge in some form of trading on a greater or a lesser scale. Moreover, the government, when it raises loans, is interested in the good or bad reputation that it may enjoy among possible subscribers to such loans. It would be difficult to assign any limits to the Crown's right to sue for defamation once its right in any case were recognised."

These observations may properly be regarded as no less applicable to a local authority than to a department of central government. In the same case Watermeyer C.J. observed that the reputation of the Crown might fairly be regarded as distinct from that of the group of individuals temporarily responsible for the management of the railways on its behalf. In the case of a local authority temporarily under the control of one political party or another it is difficult to say that the local authority as such has any reputation of its own. Reputation in the eyes of the public is more likely to attach itself to the controlling political party, and with a change in that party the reputation itself will change. A publication attacking the activities of the authority will necessarily be an attack on the body of councillors which represents the controlling party, or on the executives who carry on the day to day management of its affairs. If the individual reputation of any of these is wrongly impaired by the publication any of these can himself bring proceedings for defamation. Further, it is open to the controlling body to defend itself by public utterances and in debate in the council chamber.

The conclusion must be, in my opinion, that under the common law of England a local authority does not have the right to maintain an action of damages for defamation. That was the conclusion reached by the Court of Appeal, which did so principally by reference to article 10 of the European Convention for the Protection of Human Rights and Fundamental Freedoms (1953).... Article 10 is in these terms: "1. Everyone has the right to freedom of expression. This right shall include freedom to hold opinions and to receive and impart information and ideas without interference by public authority and regardless of frontiers.... 2. The exercise of these freedoms, since it carries with it duties and responsibilities, may be subject to such formalities, conditions, restrictions or penalties as are prescribed by law and are necessary in a democratic society, in the interests of national security, territorial integrity or public safety, for the prevention of disorder or crime, for the protection of health or morals, for the protection of the reputation or rights of others, for preventing the disclosure of information received in confidence, or for maintaining the authority and impartiality of the judiciary."

... The Court of Appeal approached the matter upon the basis that the law of England was uncertain upon the issue lying at the heart of the case, having regard in particular to the conflicting decisions in *Manchester Corporation v. Williams* and *Bognor Regis Urban District Council v. Campion* and to the absence of any relevant decision in the Court of Appeal or in this House. In that situation it was appropriate to have regard to the Convention. Balcombe L.J ... concluded, having carried out the balancing exercise requisite for purposes of article 10 of the Convention, that there was no pressing social need that a corporate public authority should have the right to sue in defamation for the protection of its reputation. That must certainly be true considering that in the past hundred years there are only two known instances of a defamation action by a local authority. He considered that the right to sue for malicious falsehood gave such a body all the protection which was necessary.... All three Lords Justices also alluded to the consideration that the publication of defamatory matter concerning a local authority was likely to reflect also on individual councillors or officers, and that the prospect of actions for libel at their instance also afforded some protection to the local authority....

... I would dismiss the appeal. It follows that *Bognor Regis Urban District Council v. Campion* was wrongly decided and should be overruled.

Appeal dismissed with costs.

Notes

1. It has long been accepted that a business corporation can have an action for defamation. It has a reputation that can be injured. An action for libel or slander can be maintained when the statement has the tendency to deter persons from dealing with the corporation or otherwise to prejudice it in the conduct of business. See Dupont Engineering Co. v. Nashville Banner Publishing Co., 13 F.2d 186 (M.D. Tenn. 1925); Restatement (Second) of Torts § 561(a) (1977). Whether particular criticisms of a business, its products or its services are defamatory is treated at pp. 250–255. supra. If not defamatory, they may be actionable as injurious falsehood. Should a corporation be allowed to maintain a defamation action without proof of actual financial loss? See Jameel v. Wall Street Journal Europe Sprl, [2007] 1 A.C. 359 (H.L.).

2. National Refining Co. v. Benzo Gas Motor Fuel Co., p. 250, supra, categorizes as defamatory statements concerning goods or products which impute to the vendor or producer fraud, deceit, dishonesty or reprehensible business methods. This omits the important category of statements adversely reflecting upon a business proprietor's solvency or creditworthiness. El Meson Espanol v. NYM Corp., 521 F.2d 737 (2d Cir. 1975), states that a corporation can be protected only against statements affecting its credit or property. What is meant by "property"? Is it defamatory to report that a corporation provides very poor working or living conditions for its employees? See Di Giorgio Fruit Corp. v. American Federation of Labor and Congress of Industrial Organizations, 215 Cal. App. 2d 560, 30 Cal. Rptr. 350 (1963). See generally Annots., Action by Corporation for Libel or Slander, 52 A.L.R. 1199 (1928); 86 A.L.R. 442 (1933).

3. In some circumstances, statements directed at an officer or employee of a corporation also defame the corporation. In Neiman-Marcus Co. v. Lait, 107 F. Supp. 96 (S.D.N.Y. 1952), a book said that a department store's president "may not know" that some of the store's models were "call girls—the top babes in town." It was also reported that saleswomen

were available at a cheaper price and that most of the male sales staff were "fairies." The company that owned the store claimed damages for libel and survived a motion to dismiss, the court deciding that a corporation could be defamed and damaged by a report that it employs "seriously undesirable personnel." It is also possible for statements directed at a corporation to defame its officers or principal stockholders. This is especially likely in the case of a small, closely held corporation or a corporation that has the same name as the individual complaining of defamation. See Brayton v. Crowell-Collier Publishing Co., 205 F.2d 644 (2d Cir. 1953); Schiavone Construction Co. v. Time, Inc., 619 F. Supp. 684 (D.N.J. 1985).

4. It is generally accepted that a non-profit corporation may have an action for defamation. See New York Society for the Suppression of Vice v. MacFadden Publications, Inc., 260 N.Y. 167, 183 N.E. 284 (1932); Restatement (Second) of Torts § 561(b) (1977). Also a partnership or an unincorporated association, whether profit or non-profit. See Restatement (Second) of Torts § 562 (1977). In the case of a partnership, it cannot be assumed that because a partnership is composed of the individual partners, defamation of the partnership defames the partners or vice versa. See Annot., Parties Plaintiff to Actions Based on Libel or Slander of a Firm or Its Members, 52 A.L.R. 912 (1928). Cf. Gilbert v. Crystal Foundation Lodge, 80 Ga. 284, 4 S.E. 905 (1887) ("the venereal disease was not a partnership malady; that was individual property"). But see Cohn v. Am-Law, 5 Media L. Rptr. 2367 (N.Y. Sup. Ct. 1980) (libel of lawyer in professional capacity also libel of firm). The principal rationale for allowing an action to a non-profit corporation or association is that defamation can interfere with its receipt of financial support. On what basis does a labor union have standing to maintain a defamation action?

5. Drawing upon the *Derbyshire County Council* case, the court in Goldsmith v. Bhoyrul, [1998] Q.B. 459, concluded that a political party could not maintain a defamation action. The court believed it was in the public interest that free speech and criticism respecting political parties, as well as elected governmental bodies, not be fettered by defamation actions or threats of actions. Contra, Argus Printing and Publishing Co. Ltd. v. Inkatha Freedom Party, 1992 (3) S.A. 579 (A.D.). What about an action for defamation of a religious group? See Church of Scientology of California v. Siegelman, 475 F. Supp. 950 (S.D.N.Y. 1979), rearg. denied, 481 F. Supp. 866 (S.D.N.Y. 1979); Gorman v. Swaggart, 524 So. 2d 915 (La. App. 1988), cert. denied, 530 So. 2d 571–575 (La. 1988), cert. denied sub nom. Treeby v. Gorman, 489 U.S. 1017 (1989); Anderson v. Church of Scientology Inc., [1981] W.A.R. 279 (Full Ct.), rev'g [1980] W.A.R. 71 (Sup. Ct.).

6. On the question of whether a defamation action can be maintained by a governmental body, City of Prince George v. British Columbia Television System, [1979] 2 W.W.R. 404, (1979) 95 D.L.R.3d 577 (B.C.C.A.), decides that the way in which a municipality legislates, administers its legislation and conducts its activities creates a municipal reputation that can be the subject of a defamation nation. Cf. Windsor Roman Catholic Separate School Board v. Southam Inc., (1984) 46 O.R.2d 231, 9 D.L.R.4th 284 (High Ct.) (school board). In Ballina Shire Council v. Ringland, (1994) 33 N.S.W.L.R. 680 (C.A.), the *Derbyshire County Council* case was followed as to defamation liability, but the majority permitted an action for injurious falsehood. American cases reject defamation actions by governments and government agencies. City of Chicago v. Tribune Co., 307 Ill. 595, 139 N.E. 86 (1923) (defendant published articles alleging that city was "broke" and headed for bankruptcy; held that city could not recover for defamation even if publications malicious and harmful to city's "proprietary" enterprises); State v. Time, Inc., 249 So. 2d 328 (La. App. 1971) (state of Louisiana had no action and could not bring action on behalf of its citizens); College Savings Bank v. Florida Prepaid Postsecondary Education Expense

Board, 919 F. Supp. 756 (D.N.J. 1996) (government agency that operated college tuition savings program could not sue for defamation, or injurious falsehood, despite its "proprietary" functions). The First Amendment may be interpreted to prevent defamation actions by governmental entities. See Port Arthur Independent School District v. Klein & Associates Political Relations, 70 S.W.3d 349 (Tex. App. 2002) (school district suing over report about alleged fight at high school prom); Cox Enterprises, Inc. v. Carroll City/County Hospital Authority, 247 Ga. 39, 273 S.E.2d 841 (1981) (guarantee of free speech held to preclude defamation actions based on criticism of government, including criticism of hospital authority that lacked power to tax but had such attributes of sovereignty as power of eminent domain). See generally Annot., Right of Governmental Entity to Maintain Action for Defamation, 45 A.L.R.3d 1315 (1972).

7. Any living person may be defamed, even a small child. An example would be referring to an infant as illegitimate. No action lies for defamation of the dead, but when it reflects upon persons still living they can have a cause of action. There are some statutes that make defamation of the dead a crime. They have been held not to provide a civil remedy. See Flynn v. Higham, 149 Cal. App. 3d 677, 197 Cal. Rptr. 145 (1983); Gugliuzza v. K.C.M.C., Inc., 606 So. 2d 790 (La. 1992); Restatement (Second) of Torts §560 (1977); Dobbs, Law of Torts 1139–1140 (2000). Would it be desirable to create a civil remedy? See Armstrong, Nothing but Good of the Dead?, 18 A.B.A.J. 229 (1932); Note, Dead but Not Forgotten: Proposals for Imposing Liability for Defamation of the Dead, 67 Tex. L. Rev. 1525 (1989).

———

Cassidy v. Daily Mirror Newspapers, Ltd.

Court of Appeal
[1929] 2 K.B. 331

SCRUTTON L.J. The facts in this case are simple. A man named Cassidy, who for some reason also called himself Corrigan and described himself as a General in the Mexican Army, was married to a lady who also called herself Mrs. Cassidy or Mrs. Corrigan. Her husband occasionally came and stayed with her at her flat, and her acquaintances met him. Cassidy achieved some notoriety in racing circles and in indiscriminate relations with women, and at a race meeting he posed, in company with a lady, to a racing photographer, to whom he said he was engaged to marry the lady and the photographer might announce it. The photographer, without any further inquiry, sent the photograph to the Daily Mirror with an inscription: "Mr. M. Corrigan, the race horse owner, and Miss X"—I omit the name—"whose engagement has been announced," and the Daily Mirror published the photograph and inscription. This paper was read by the female acquaintances of Mrs. Cassidy or Mrs. Corrigan, who gave evidence that they understood from it that that lady was not married to Mr. M. Corrigan and had no legal right to take his name, and that they formed a bad opinion of her in consequence. Mrs. Cassidy accordingly brought an action for libel against the newspaper setting out these words with an innuendo, meaning thereby that the plaintiff was an immoral woman who had cohabited with Corrigan without being married to him.

At the trial counsel for the defendants objected that the words were not capable of a defamatory meaning. McCardie J. held that they were; the jury found that they did reasonably bear a defamatory meaning and awarded the plaintiff 500l. damages. The damages were high, but the plaintiff called considerable evidence of damage to social reputation....

The real questions involved were: (1.) Was the alleged libel capable of a defamatory meaning? (2.) As the defendants did not know the facts which caused the friends of Mrs. Cassidy to whom they published the words to draw defamatory inferences from them about the plaintiff, were they liable for those inferences?

Now the alleged libel does not mention the plaintiff, but I think it is clear that words published about A may indirectly be defamatory of B. For instance, "A is illegitimate." To persons who know the parents those words may be defamatory of the parents. Or again, "A has given way to drink; it is unfortunately hereditary"; to persons who know A's parents these words may be defamatory. Or "A holds a D. Litt. degree of the University at X, the only one awarded." To persons who know B, who habitually describes himself (and rightly so) as "D. Litt. of X," these words may be capable of a defamatory meaning. Similarly, to say that A is a single man or a bachelor may be capable of a defamatory meaning if published to persons who know a lady who passes as Mrs. A and whom A visits.... It was argued that the words were not capable of the meaning that Corrigan was a single man, for they might mean that Corrigan was intending to seduce a woman under promise of marriage, or that he was divorced and could marry. On this I would remark that it would be so unusual for a seducer publicly to make his untrue representations, that the jury might well reject this meaning. Also, that I do not agree with some dicta to the effect that if words are capable of several meanings, some defamatory and some innocent, they should not be left to the jury. I agree with the view expressed arguendo by Sir Montague Smith in the case of *Simmons v. Mitchell* [(1880) 6 App. Cas. 156]: "The judge must decide if the words are reasonably capable of two meanings; if he so decide, the jury must determine which of the two meanings was intended;" and by "intended" I understand that a man is liable for the reasonable inferences to be drawn from the words he used, whether he foresaw them or not, and that if he scatters two-edged and ambiguous statements broadcast, without knowing or making inquiry about facts material to the statements he makes and the inferences which may be drawn from them, he must be liable to persons who, knowing those facts, draw reasonable inferences from the words he publishes....

In my view the words published were capable of the meaning "Corrigan is a single man," and were published to people who knew the plaintiff professed to be married to Corrigan; it was for the jury to say whether those people could reasonably draw the inference that the so-called Mrs. Corrigan was in fact living in immoral co-habitation with Corrigan, and I do not think their finding should be interfered with.

But the second point taken was that the defendants could not be liable for the inference drawn, because they did not know the facts which enabled some persons to whom the libel was published, to draw an inference defamatory of the plaintiff. This was rested on some dicta of Brett L.J. in [*Capital and Counties Bank v. Henty*, (1880) 5 C.P.D. 514] that the evidence which made apparently innocent statements defamatory must be, "known both to the person who wrote the document and to the persons to whom it was published." This, I think, was originally obiter, and, since the decision in *E. Hulton & Co. v. Jones* [[1910] A.C. 20], is no longer law. The statement in the judgment of Farwell L.J. [[1909] 2 K.B. 444, 478] in that case is: "The rule is well settled that the true intention of the writer of any document, whether it be contract, will, or libel, is that which is apparent from the natural and ordinary interpretation of the written words; and this, when applied to the description of an individual, means the interpretation that would be reasonably put upon those words by persons who know the plaintiff and the circumstances." ... This judgment was approved by Lord Gorell and Lord Atkinson in the House of Lords, and supported by Lord Shaw, who says: "... Sufficient expression is given to the same principles by Abbott C.J. in *Bourke v. Warren* [(1826) 2 C. & P. 307] ... in which that learned judge says: 'The question for your consideration is whether you think the libel designates the plaintiff in such a way as to let those who knew him understand that he was the person meant. It is not necessary that all the world should understand the libel; it is sufficient if those who know the plaintiff can make out that he is the person meant.' I think it is out of the question to suggest that that means 'meant in the mind of the writer' or of the publisher; it must mean 'meant by the words employed.' ..." In my view, since *E. Hulton & Co. v. Jones*, it is impossible for the person publishing a statement which, to those who know certain facts, is capable of a defamatory meaning in regard to A, to defend himself by saying: "I never heard of A and did not mean to injure him." If he publishes words reasonably capable of being read as relating directly or indirectly to A and, to those who know the facts about A, capable of a defamatory meaning, he must take the consequences of the defamatory inferences reasonably drawn from his words.

It is said that this decision would seriously interfere with the reasonable conduct of newspapers. I do not agree. If publishers of newspapers, who have no more rights than private persons, publish statements which may be defamatory of other people, without inquiry as to their truth, in order to make their paper attractive, they must take the consequences, if on subsequent inquiry, their statements are found to be untrue or capable of defamatory and unjustifiable inferences. No one could contend that "M. Corrigan, General in the Mexican Army," was "a source in whom we have full confidence." To publish statements first and inquire into their truth afterwards, may seem attractive and up to date. Only to publish after inquiry may be slow, but at any rate it would lead to accuracy and reliability.

In my opinion the appeal should be dismissed with costs.

[Russell, L.J., delivered a concurring opinion.]

GREER L.J. [dissenting] ... Both the picture and the words are in themselves unobjectionable. They contain in their ordinary signification no defamatory statement about anybody, and it was necessary for the success of the plaintiff in the action that she should establish by innuendo that by the picture and the words the defendants said something which was defamatory of her. She therefore pleaded ... an extended meaning, to the effect that the said Kettering Edward Cassidy, otherwise known as M. Corrigan, was not a man bound in lawful wedlock to the plaintiff, and that the plaintiff was not lawfully married to her husband, and that the plaintiff was living in adultery with him, and that she was a dissolute and immoral woman, and was a despicable person who had imposed upon her friends and acquaintances, and upon such members of the public as knew her, by pretending to be a respectable married woman, whereas she had been living in concubinage with the said Kettering Edward Cassidy, otherwise known as M. Corrigan, for many years.

In order to succeed in her action the plaintiff was bound to show that, reasonably interpreted, the words used in the newspaper were intended to convey the meaning set out in the innuendo, the intention being judged not by what was in the mind of the writer, but what appears from the words he has used. In my judgment it was not enough for her to show that people who knew her jumped to the conclusion that she was living with Corrigan as his mistress. She was bound to show that, reasonably interpreted, the words of the alleged libel contained an allegation to that effect. She called as her witnesses three ladies who knew her as the wife of Cassidy and knew that her husband was the man who owned racehorses under the name of Corrigan. Each of these ladies knew that her husband, as they admitted in their evidence, was a blackguard who had treated her badly and had been unfaithful to her. They knew that she was living apart from Cassidy, but had seen him on several occasions visiting the shop where she was employed, and when they saw the paragraph in the Daily Mirror they appear to have jumped to the conclusion that she was a dishonest woman who had been deceiving them and had been living in concubinage with the scoundrel who occasionally visited her at the shop where she was employed....

In my judgment this appeal ought to succeed. I think so for two reasons. First, it is not sufficient to establish liability for a witness to prove that by reason of some fact to which the libel refers he draws an unfavourable inference against the plaintiff. That is not sufficient to justify a verdict that the words in question are libellous. The jury must be satisfied by evidence that, on a reasonable interpretation of the words used, the innuendo is proved to be an implicit part of the statement made by the defendants.... The language of the alleged libel refers to the fact of the announcement of Mr. Corrigan's engagement, and some persons, that is to say the ladies who gave evidence, have chosen, not by reason of the language of the alleged libel, but by reason of a fact to which it refers, to draw an unfavourable inference against Mrs. Corrigan; but none of the three has stated that she interpreted the words as containing an allegation that Mrs. Corrigan was not the wife of Corrigan, and if they had done so I should myself have come to the conclusion that they put upon the words an interpretation which they could not reasonably bear....

The other reason why I think the decision of the learned judge was wrong is that in my view, notwithstanding the case of *E. Hulton & Co. v. Jones,* the law still is as it was laid down by Brett L.J. in *Henty*'s case. If extrinsic facts are relied upon for the purpose of converting that which would otherwise be an innocent statement of fact into a defamatory libel, the extrinsic facts must be known both to the person who framed the alleged libel and to the persons to whom it was published....

... I think one must apply the words of Brett L.J. in the sense of that which they "knew or ought to have known." If it could be said in this case that those responsible for the publication in question knew or ought to have known that Corrigan was a man who had a wife living at the time, or was a man with whom there was a lady living and claiming to be his wife, it may be that the question whether the words were or were not defamatory ought to have been left to the jury; but there was no evidence from which it is reasonable to conclude that they knew or ought to have known that he was a married man. They were surely entitled to suppose that, as he said he was engaged to marry the lady in question, he was not in fact a married man, unless they knew to the contrary.

One or two illustrations may be given which indicate the danger of carrying the law of libel as far as it is argued in this case it should be carried. It is written of A.B. that he is ill-mannered and uneducated. It turns out, though the writer did not know it, that A.B. was in fact brought up by his uncle. Could it be said that the uncle could succeed in an action alleging that the words meant that he had badly brought up and educated A.B.? A writer might state that A.B. is an ignoramus. Unknown to the writer, A.B. may have spent five years under the tuition of X.Y. at Eton. Could X.Y. allege that this was a libel upon him, the writer having been ignorant, and having no reason to suppose, that A.B. had been at Eton? Take another case. A being under the mistaken impression that he saw Mr. B walking away from a theatre with Miss C, says next morning to an acquaintance: "I saw B and C leaving the theatre together last night." Unknown to A, but to the knowledge of his acquaintance, C had been murdered by the man with whom she left the theatre. Could A be successfully sued by B for saying he had murdered C? If the case against the present defendants was rightly left to the jury, A could be so sued. To me it seems quite certain that it would be the duty of the judge to rule that the words were incapable of being so interpreted.

The decision of the House of Lords in *E. Hulton & Co. v. Jones*, which was very much relied upon by the respondents, does not, in my opinion, afford sufficient authority for deciding the present case in favour of the plaintiff. In that case the words complained of appeared in form to relate to an existing individual who was named. The words, if applied to an existing person, were clearly defamatory, and the House of Lords, affirming the Court of Appeal, held that the mere fact that the writer did not intend to injure the plaintiff afforded no defence to the action. It seems clear that the writer took the risk of making defamatory statements about an individual by name when he ought to have known that it was possible that there might be a person bearing that name who would be understood to be meant by the words which were used. Lord Loreburn in giving judgment pointed out that a person charged with libel cannot defend himself by showing that he intended in his own breast not to defame, or that he intended not to defame the plaintiff, if in fact he did both, and that his remedy was to abstain from using defamatory words. In the present case no defamatory words were used about anybody, and the defendants are, in my judgment, entitled to succeed, not because in his own mind the writer did not intend to defame, but because in fact he has not used language which reasonable persons either have or could have interpreted as defamatory of the plaintiff. . . .

Notes

1. Despite the references to "intention" in the principal case, it is clear that no intention to defame plaintiff—or anyone—was required for liability. One could incur liability without any intent to cause harm to reputation, to include a defamatory meaning or any other specific meaning in one's statement, to refer to plaintiff, or to utter falsehood. This was established by not only the *Cassidy* case but also other British and American cases, early in the twentieth century, that involved "innocent" defamation—cases in which defendant was unaware that the matter published carried a defamatory meaning, that it would be understood as referring to plaintiff or (with publication of what purported to be fiction) to any actual person, or that it was false, at least insofar as plaintiff was concerned.

Strict liability was not always the rule. The early law apparently did impose liability without fault, but in the seventeenth century it came to be required that plaintiff plead and prove defendant's intent to defame and malice. This is attributed to the criminal libel requirement of malicious intent and ecclesiastical law's concern with the moral sin of slander. Then, while the pleading of malice remained a requirement, it evolved into a formality. In 1825, it was decided that malice would be implied from the publication of a false defamatory statement. Bromage v. Prosser, (1825) 4 B. & C. 247, 107 Eng. Rep. 1051, 1 C. & P. 673, 171 Eng. Rep. 1362, 6 Dow. & Ry. K.B. 296, 3 L.J.O.S.K.B. 203 (K.B.). Since that time, malice, if considered an element of defamation liability at all, has been a mere formality or fiction. No malice need be shown to make out a prima facie case of liability. (Malice does, however, play an important role in the law of qualified privilege and as a basis for awarding punitive damages. In this regard, it is termed "actual malice" or "malice in fact," to distinguish it from the "implied malice" or "malice in law" found in Bromage v. Prosser.)

The one respect in which common law defamation liability is not strict is the requirement of publication. Defendant must have published the defamatory material to a person other than plaintiff. Usually, this has meant intentional communication to a third person. However, the publication requirement has been watered down to encompass communication by means defendant should have anticipated would publish the material to a third person. See pp. 542–546, infra. This requirement may explain why defamation is not usually classified as a strict liability tort. See generally Fleming, Law of Torts 629–632 (10th ed. 2011); Prosser, Law of Torts 766–776 (4th ed. 1971); Prosser, Wade & Schwartz, Cases and Materials on Torts 905–907 (12th ed. 2010).

2. In order to make out a prima facie case of libel or slander, plaintiff must in substance prove that defendant published a statement that defamed plaintiff. More precisely, it must be shown that defendant communicated to a third person a statement or other expression that conveyed a defamatory meaning about plaintiff. When the statement has a defamatory meaning "on its face" and refers to a named person, plaintiff need show only that he is the person named. But when the statement is not defamatory on its face or does not identify the person referred to, plaintiff must show the "extrinsic facts" which would cause persons to draw a defamatory meaning from the statement or conclude that it referred to plaintiff. Plaintiff's reputation could only be damaged if the statement reached persons aware of the extrinsic facts, so this also must be shown.

Courts developed strict requirements for pleading the elements of a defamation case— the defamatory words or conduct, publication, the defamatory meaning(s) conveyed, that the matter "concerned" plaintiff, the pertinent extrinsic facts, and (where necessary to liability) "special damages." These requirements have been relaxed to some degree, but they still have much force. See Wyse, The Complaint in Libel and Slander: A Dilemma for Plaintiff, 33 Chi.-Kent L. Rev. 313 (1955). The pleading addressed to alleging that the statement was understood as referring to plaintiff is known as the "colloquium." The pleading of extrinsic facts to show that the statement had a defamatory meaning is called the "inducement." An alleged defamatory meaning is known as an "innuendo." It is common to apply the term "innuendo" to any defamatory meaning other than the one explicitly stated in the published matter. But a distinction is drawn between a "true" innuendo—one drawn only in conjunction with extrinsic facts—and meanings that can be drawn from the statement without knowledge of extrinsic facts.

If defendant uttered to X the words "He burned down his own barn," the "inducement" would plead the facts known to X that gave this statement a defamatory connotation concerning plaintiff—for example, defendant pointed toward plaintiff when speaking and plaintiff had insured his barn. The "colloquium" would be the allegation (using the fact that defendant pointed toward plaintiff) that the words were understood to refer to plaintiff. The "innuendos" would be that plaintiff committed arson and sought to defraud his insurance company. Prosser, Wade & Schwartz, Cases and Materials on Torts 861 (8th ed. 1988). If the extrinsic facts (known to X) actually were that an invading army was advancing toward plaintiff's farm, defendant's words would be laudatory rather than defamatory. Extrinsic facts may give a defamatory meaning to a statement wholly innocent on its face—for example, "Mrs. Z has given birth to twins," with the inducement that Mrs. Z has been married for only a few months. This might defame not only Mrs. Z but also her husband. See Morrison v. Ritchie & Co., (1902) 4 F. 645 (Scot. Ct. Sess.). See generally Fleming, Law of Torts 619–624 (10th ed. 2011); Hanson, Libel and Related Torts ¶¶ 30–31 (1969); Prosser & Keeton, Law of Torts 780–783 (5th ed. 1984).

3. A plaintiff's efforts to draw innuendos from a statement are restrained to some extent by the notion that defamatory meanings are limited to those that could reasonably be inferred by the recipients of the statement. It is for the judge in the first instance to determine whether a defamatory meaning could reasonably have been communicated. If so, it is for the trier of fact to determine whether the statement was so understood. It is necessary that the statement be understood by its recipients in some defamatory sense, but the recipients need not conclude that the statement is literally true or even that its defamatory meaning is true. See Fleming, Law of Torts 619–623 (10th ed. 2011);

Prosser & Keeton, Law of Torts 780–783 (5th ed. 1984). Does plaintiff have an action if the only people who hear a defamatory accusation know that it is false? See Marble v. Chapin, 132 Mass. 225 (1882) (defendant accused listener of sexual intercourse with plaintiff).

4. An analogous principle applies to the "colloquium" element of plaintiff's case. There must be recipients of defendant's statement who reasonably understood it as referring to plaintiff. The judge determines whether the statement could reasonably have been so understood. If so, it is a question of fact whether the statement was so understood. See Davis v. R.K.O. Radio Pictures, Inc., 191 F.2d 901 (8th Cir. 1951); Harper, James & Gray, Law of Torts § 5.7 (3d ed. 2006). It would appear that there has been less judicial restraint of claims that the statement was understood as referring to plaintiff than of claims that the statement was understood in a defamatory sense. See pp. 519–529, infra. But see Rosenblatt v. Baer, 383 U.S. 75 (1966); Sims v. Kiro, Inc., 20 Wash. App. 229, 580 P.2d 642 (1978), cert. denied, 441 U.S. 945 (1979). In some jurisdictions, courts will not receive testimony from recipients of the statement about the meaning they placed on it. But the prevailing rule in the United States permits this testimony as well as testimony concerning whether the recipients understood the statement to refer to plaintiff and whether they were aware of the pertinent extrinsic facts. See Eldredge, Law of Defamation 70–75 (1978); Harper, James & Gray, Law of Torts § 5.4 (3d ed. 2006).

5. Consider whether a cause of action for libel should have been found in the following cases:

(a) A divorced man's application for a marriage license states that the marriage will be his first. Smith v. Smith, 236 N.Y. 581, 142 N.E. 292 (1923). Cf. Barrett v. Barrett, 108 R.I. 15, 271 A.2d 825 (1970) (obituary of married man describing him as bachelor).

(b) A newspaper column implies that a man has just been divorced. In fact, he had long been divorced and had remarried. Pitts v. Spokane Chronicle Co., 63 Wash. 2d 763, 388 P.2d 976 (1964).

(c) A newspaper reports the birth of a child to a man and his wife. The man is actually a bachelor and the "wife" is a "woman of ill repute" with four illegitimate children. Karrigan v. Valentine, 184 Kan. 783, 339 P.2d 52 (1959).

(d) A newspaper announces the engagement of persons who are presently married to other people. Hinsdale v. Orange County Publications, Inc., 17 N.Y.2d 284, 270 N.Y.S.2d 592, 217 N.E.2d 650 (1966).

(e) A single woman is reported to be engaged to a man whose reputation in the community is that of a drunk and degenerate. Orband v. Kalamazoo Telegraph Co., 170 Mich. 387, 136 N.W. 380 (1912). Cf. Sydney v. MacFadden Newspaper Publishing Corp., 242 N.Y. 208, 151 N.E. 209 (1926) (married actress reported to be "lady love" and possible future bride of notorious actor).

(f) Defendant sends plaintiff a post card saying "I'll be in LaGrange next week. Call me at 9693. Love, Mary." The card is read by plaintiff's wife. Freeman v. Busch Jewelry Co., 98 F. Supp. 963 (N.D. Ga. 1951).

(g) An article states that a boxer's "curly headed wife" sees all of his fights. If there is a curly headed woman who sees the boxer's fights, she is not his wife. Hough v. London Express Newspaper, [1940] 2 K.B. 507 (C.A.).

See generally Annot., Libel and Slander: False News Reports as to Births, Betrothals, Marriages, Divorces, or Similar Marital Matters, 9 A.L.R.3d 559 (1966).

6. An author sells his book, with copyright, to the company that publishes it. The company later publishes a revised edition with the author's name on the title page, though the author did not participate in preparing the revision. The revised edition contains errors, discernible to some readers, which allegedly impair the author's reputation. Has the publisher libelled the author? See Clevenger v. Baker Voorhis & Co., 8 N.Y.2d 187, 203 N.Y.S.2d 812, 168 N.E.2d 643 (1960) (yes; publisher had no right to misrepresent author as reviser of inaccurate edition). Compare Shostakovich v. Twentieth Century-Fox Film Corp., 196 Misc. 67, 80 N.Y.S.2d 575 (Sup. Ct. 1948), aff'd, 275 App. Div. 692, 87 N.Y.S.2d 430 (1949), where the works of contemporary U.S.S.R. composers were used as background music in an anti-Soviet motion picture and their names were listed in the film's credits. It was held this was not defamatory of the composers as implying their disloyalty to the Soviet Union, there being no implication they approved of the film.

7. Is there an action if only a small number of people have the specialized knowledge or training necessary to recognize that a statement is defamatory? In Ben-Oliel v. Press Publishing Co., 251 N.Y. 250, 167 N.E. 432 (1929), a newspaper falsely attributed to plaintiff, an expert on Palestinian art and customs, authorship of an article on that subject. The article contained a number of errors and unsound statements, but only persons acquainted with Palestinian life would realize this. It was held that a cause of action for libel was stated. It would also be libellous, the court said, to attribute to a physician a statement regarding an operation or treatment "which shows him to the profession to be an ignoramus and a bungler."

B. Reference to Plaintiff

Giaimo v. Literary Guild

Supreme Court of New York, Appellate Division
79 A.D.2d 917, 434 N.Y.S.2d 419 (1981)

[Plaintiffs (husband and wife) submitted photographs of themselves for an advertisement for a diamond company. Defendant Cochran, a professional photographer, turned the photographs over to an advertising agency which used them, allegedly without plaintiffs' authorization, in advertising for the book *Crazy Love*. One of the photographs was used to illustrate the advertisement for *Crazy Love* in defendant Literary Guild's "Selections for Summer" brochure, distributed to members of the book club. Plaintiffs sued for libel and violation of their right of privacy. The trial court dismissed the libel actions against Literary Guild and another defendant, Doubleday.]

MEMORANDUM DECISION....

... The text was libelous in that it described the book as the story of a marriage in which the husband goes mad and as "[a]n autobiographical account of marriage and madness." Plaintiffs claim that the accompanying photograph, shown in a frame with shattered glass, clearly implies that they are referred to by the text and thus creates an actionable libel.

In order for plaintiff to be entitled to maintain an action for a defamatory statement, it must appear that they are the persons concerning whom it was made. It must be shown that the publication was "of and concerning" them. It is not necessary that they be named in the publication, if the allusion is apparent. "Where the person defamed is not named in a defamatory publication, it is necessary, if it is to be held actionable as to him, that the language used be such that persons reading it will, in the light of the surrounding circumstances, be able to understand that it refers to the person complaining." 34 N.Y. Jr., Libel and Slander Sec. 55. Plaintiffs have been unable to sustain this burden.

The article accompanying the photograph in no way implies it is about the plaintiffs, but prominently displays the author's name and clearly states that the book is an autobiographical account of her marriage. The author's name and picture appear on page two of the brochure, accompanying the report of an interview concerning the book, so that it would be unwarranted for the reader to conclude that the article is about the plaintiffs' marriage.

Since plaintiffs have not established that the article is "of and concerning" them, they have failed to state a cause of action for libel.

[Affirmed. Kupferman, J.P., (with whom Fein, J., joined) delivered a dissenting opinion.]

Helmicks v. Stevlingson

Supreme Court of Wisconsin
212 Wis. 614, 250 N.W. 402 (1933)

FRITZ, Justice.

Appellant, in demurring to the complaint on the ground that it did not state sufficient facts to constitute a cause of action, relies, among other contentions, upon the proposition that the statement complained of is not libelous as to plaintiff because, as there is no reference made therein to an ascertained or ascertainable person, it does not sufficiently identify the plaintiff....

... [T]his court has said: "It is well settled that defamatory words must refer to some ascertained or ascertainable person, and that that person must be the particular plaintiff. Statements are not libelous unless they refer to some ascertained or ascertainable person." Schoenfeld v. Journal Co., 204 Wis. 132, 136, 235 N.W. 442, 444; Williams v. Journal Co. (Wis.) 247 N.W. 435, 439.

In the case at bar the words complained of as published on November 1, 1932, were, "Bank loaned to death by former cashier." Plaintiff alleges that defendant thereby intended "to charge that the Bank of Deerfield had been closed to its death by virtue of the acts of plaintiff, he being the only and former cashier of the Bank of Deerfield since its consolidation," and, in that connection, plaintiff also alleges "that thereafter the said defendant admitted to the said plaintiff that the said words had been by him uttered and that it was the said plaintiff that he, the said defendant, intended to refer to by virtue thereof." However, it also appears from allegations in plaintiff's complaint that the Bank of Deerfield was in existence since 1905; that it was only from October, 1930, when another bank was consolidated with the Bank of Deerfield and the business was continued under the latter name, until that bank closed in January, 1932, that plaintiff was cashier of that bank; and also that in January, 1932, the defendant was employed by that bank and has been cashier thereof.

Manifestly, in view of all of the facts alleged as stated above, the words "former cashier" are applicable to other persons than solely the plaintiff. As far as anything which is stated in the published words is concerned, the words "former cashier" are as applicable to each and every other person, who functioned as cashier of the Bank of Deerfield at any time since it came into existence in 1905, as they are to the plaintiff, who was its cashier for only fifteen months of that period of twenty-seven years. The fact that plaintiff may have been, as is alleged in his complaint, the only and former cashier of that bank since its consolidation, does not confine the application of the published words to him. There is nothing in the words as published that limits their meaning to loans made since the consolidation of the bank, or by its cashier since its consolidation. Neither can the omission of the published words to refer to the plaintiff with the particularity necessary, as a matter of law, to render them libelous as to plaintiff, be supplied by the existence of any unpublished intention on defendant's part to have the words considered applicable to the plaintiff. Consequently, defendant's admission solely to plaintiff that defendant intended by the published words to refer to plaintiff does not constitute a publication to some third party, which must occur before actionable injury to reputation results. As is said in Newell, "Slander and Libel" (4th Ed.) 219: "There is no publication when the words are only communicated to the person defamed, for that can not injure his reputation."

It follows that defendant's demurrer should have been sustained.

[Reversed.]

FOWLER, Justice [with whom Owen and Wickhem, JJ., joined] (dissenting).

The opinion of the court, as far as it goes, correctly states the allegations of the complaint. But the complaint also alleges that the plaintiff was cashier of the bank at the time it closed; that by the statement complained of the defendant intended to designate the plaintiff; and that many persons have been led to believe by the publication that the plaintiff was the cause of the closing of the bank. I think that these averments, giving them reasonable construction and intendment, allege that by the publication the defendant intended to charge that the plaintiff was the cause of the closing of the bank, and that the words were understood by those who read them to refer to the plaintiff and to mean that he was the cause of the bank's closing. I am of opinion that this is a sufficient identification of the plaintiff as the person referred to and understood to be referred to by the use of the words charged....

Notes

1. Consider:

(a) Defendant publishes that an inmate of the county poorhouse died of cold and want of care and attention. Plaintiff is the keeper of the poorhouse. Green v. Telfair, 20 Barb. 11 (N.Y. Sup. Ct. 1854).

(b) Defendant points toward a crowd in plaintiff's direction and says, "There is the man who stole my horse." Bonner v. Boyd, 3 H. & J. 278 (Md. 1811).

(c) The vice president of a company announces to employees that someone lost her job that day because of possession of an unauthorized key. He also states that several items of personal property had been missing. Plaintiff is the only employee discharged that day. Worley v. Oregon Physicians Service, 69 Or. App. 241, 686 P.2d 404 (1984), review denied, 298 Or. 334, 691 P.2d 483 (1984).

(d) Defendant says he saw a man "ravishing a cow" "so early in the morning that a person could not have got far from home." The perpetrator is said to be a young married man with no children. Plaintiff is the only young married man with no children in the neighborhood. Harper v. Delp, 3 Ind. 225 (1851).

(e) Defendant reports the arrest for moonshining of "Wayman Davis … and his brother." Plaintiff is the only one of Wayman Davis' brothers who lives or ever has lived in the county where the newspaper is published and the purported arrest occurred. Three other brothers reside out of state and were there at the time. Davis v. Macon Telegraph Publishing Co., 93 Ga. App. 633, 92 S.E.2d 619 (1956).

(f) Defendant, a newspaper in a small city, publishes an article concerning a "radio racket." Those who conduct this "racket" advertise a free pickup service for the repair of radios. They have no established shop. Contact is by telephone. When a radio is picked up, that is the last the owner sees of it. Plaintiffs (brothers) are the only persons in the city who repair radios, with a free pickup service, and have no shop. Marr v. Putnam, 196 Or. 1, 246 P.2d 509 (1952).

(g) Defendant states that he saw a policeman and a woman he did not recognize having sexual relations in a certain apartment. The apartment is where plaintiff and her husband (who is not the policeman) live. Thiel v. Dove, 229 Ark. 601, 317 S.W.2d 121 (1958). Cf. Hall v. Huffman, 159 Ky. 72, 166 S.W. 770 (1914) (defendant said man had been "cuckolded"; man plaintiff's husband).

(h) Defendant reports that a certain address is the location of a "disorderly house." Plaintiff is one of the residents and the lessee of the house at this address. McClean v. New York Press Co., Ltd., 19 N.Y.S. 262 (Sup. Ct. 1892). See also Fitzpatrick v. Age-Herald Publishing Co., 184 Ala. 510, 63 So. 980 (1913) ("a house which bears a bad reputation with the police"). Cf. Robertson v. Bennett, 12 Jones & Spencer (44 N.Y. Super. Ct.) 66 (1878) (report of "blackmailing crowd" at certain address; plaintiff proprietor of boarding house at that address).

(i) Shortly after plaintiff runs newspaper advertisements offering a free roll of film for every roll brought to plaintiff for developing, a competitor advertises in the same newspaper that it will not inflate developing prices by giving a new roll for free, use inferior materials, or ruin snapshots by hurrying development. Cosgrove Studio and Camera Shop, Inc. v. Pane, 408 Pa. 314, 182 A.2d 751 (1962).

(j) During a special election for a seat in the legislature, defendants, who are in the campaign of one political party, distribute handbills urging votes for the party's candidate. The theme of the handbills is that the opposing political party is favorable to Communism. Plaintiff is the candidate of that party. Vermaas v. Pelser, 1951 (1) S.A. 752 (T).

2. In some cases presenting the question of whether a defamatory statement was "of and concerning" plaintiff, the statement referred to a named individual. For example:

(a) A newspaper states that liens for unpaid taxes have been filed by the government against Harold Michaels of 620 Broadway and the Old Chateau Restaurant. Plaintiff is Harold Michaels, residing at 620 Broadway, who has no restaurant. The newspaper intended to refer to another Harold Michaels—presumably, the one who operated the restaurant. Michaels v. Gannett Co., Inc., 10 A.D.2d 417, 199 N.Y.S.2d 778 (1960).

(b) A Washington, D.C. newspaper reports that "Harry Kennedy, an attorney, 40 years old, was brought back to Washington from Detroit yesterday to face a charge of forgery." Plaintiff is Harry F. Kennedy, an attorney who is about thirty-seven years old—the only attorney in the District named Harry Kennedy. The person arrested was booked under the name "Harry P.L. Kennedy." Washington Post Co. v. Kennedy, 55 App. D.C. 162, 3 F.2d 207 (1925).

(c) A Memphis newspaper carries a wire service report, "datelined" Savannah, of a "mysterious attack upon Mrs. J.C. Johnson found trussed in a coal bin in the basement of her home" after receiving threatening letters that suggested an extramarital affair. This accurately describes an incident in Savannah, Georgia. Plaintiff is Mrs. J.C. Johnson of Savannah, Tennessee. Memphis Commercial Appeal, Inc. v. Johnson, 96 F.2d 672 (6th Cir. 1938).

(d) A newspaper article about a homicide is illustrated by a photograph. The caption under the photograph states the name of the killer, but the photograph is of plaintiff. James v. Ft. Worth Telegram Co., 117 S.W. 1028 (Tex. Civ. App. 1909). Cf. De Sando v. New York Herald Co., 88 App. Div. 492, 85 N.Y.S. 111 (1903) (article on career of Italian bandit, illustrated by photograph of plaintiff, who lived in United States; bandit's name in caption); Peck v. Tribune Co., 214 U.S. 185 (1909) (whiskey advertisement with testimonial by nurse, giving her name and address, and picture of plaintiff, who was not a nurse).

(e) A newspaper publishes a report of the bigamy conviction of "Harold Newstead, thirty-year-old Camberwell man." This is true of a Camberwell barman of that name, but not of a Camberwell hairdresser of the same name and approximate age. Newstead v. London Express Newspaper, Ltd., [1940] 1 K.B. 377 (C.A.).

3. On whether plaintiff was or could be sufficiently "identified" to maintain a defamation action, see generally Annot., Libel and Slander: Sufficiency of Identification of Allegedly Defamed Party, 54 A.L.R.4th 746 (1987); Dobbs, Law of Torts 1134–1137 (2000); Sack, Defamation: Libel, Slander, and Related Problems § 2.9 (4th ed. 2010). This includes consideration of works of fiction, addressed in the next principal case.

—————

Bindrim v. Mitchell

California Court of Appeal
92 Cal. App. 3d 61, 155 Cal. Rptr. 29 (1979),
cert. denied, 444 U.S. 984 (1979)

KINGSLEY, Associate Justice.

This is an appeal taken by Doubleday and Gwen Davis Mitchell from a judgment for damages in favor of plaintiff-respondent Paul Bindrim, Ph.D. The jury returned verdicts on the libel counts against Doubleday and Mitchell....

Plaintiff is a licensed clinical psychologist and defendant is an author. Plaintiff used the so-called "Nude Marathon" in group therapy as a means of helping people to shed their psychological inhibitions with the removal of their clothes.

Defendant Mitchell had written a successful best seller in 1969 and had set out to write a novel about women of the leisure class. Mitchell attempted to register in plaintiff's nude therapy but he told her he would not permit her to do so if she was going to write about it in a novel. Plaintiff said she was attending the marathon solely for therapeutic reasons and had no intention of writing about the nude marathon....

Mitchell entered into a contract with Doubleday two months later and was to receive $150,000 advance royalties for her novel....

Mitchell told Doubleday executive McCormick that she had attended a marathon session and it was quite a psychological jolt. The novel was published under the name "Touching" and it depicted a nude encounter session in Southern California led by "Dr. Simon Herford." ...

The parallel between the actual nude marathon sessions and the sessions in the book "Touching" was shown to the jury by means of the tape recordings Bindrim had taken of the actual sessions. Plaintiff complains in particular about a portrayed session in which he tried to encourage a minister to get his wife to attend the nude marathon....

Plaintiff asserts that he was libeled by the suggestion that he used obscene language which he did not in fact use. Plaintiff also alleges various other libels due to Mitchell's inaccurate portrayal of what actually happened at the marathon. Plaintiff alleges that he was injured in his profession and expert testimony was introduced showing that Mitchell's portrayal of plaintiff was injurious and that plaintiff was identified by certain colleagues as the character in the book, Simon Herford.

... As a public figure, plaintiff is precluded from recovering damages for a defamatory falsehood relating to him, unless he proved that the statement was made with "actual malice," that is, that it was made with knowledge that it is false or with reckless disregard of whether it was false or not.* The cases are clear that reckless conduct is not measured by whether a reasonably prudent man would have investigated before publishing. There must be sufficient evidence to permit the conclusion that the defendant in fact entertained serious doubts as to the truth of his publication....

Mitchell's reckless disregard for the truth was apparent from her knowledge of the truth of what transpired at the encounter, and the literary portrayals of that encounter. Since she attended sessions there can be no suggestion that she did not know the true facts....

However, plaintiff failed to prove by clear and convincing evidence that the original hardback publication by Doubleday was made with knowledge of falsity or in reckless disregard of falsity. McCormick of Doubleday cautioned plaintiff that the characters must be totally fictitious and Mitchell assured McCormick that the characters in "Touching" were incapable of being identified as real persons....

... Doubleday sold the rights [for paperback publication] to the New American Library after receiving a letter from plaintiff's attorney explaining that plaintiff was Herford and the inscription in the paperback said, "This is an authorized edition published by Doubleday and Company." Although, after the receipt of the plaintiff's attorney's letter, Doubleday again inquired of Mitchell as to whether plaintiff was the character in the book, the jury was entitled to find that Mitchell's assurance to Doubleday was not sufficient to insulate Doubleday from liability and that Doubleday had some further duty to investigate. The jury could have inferred that at that point Doubleday either had serious doubts, or should have had serious doubts, as to the possibility that plaintiff was defamed by "Touching"....

Appellants allege that plaintiff failed to show he was identifiable as Simon Herford, relying on the fact that the character in "Touching" was described in the book as a "fat Santa Claus type with long white hair, white sideburns, a cherubic rosy face and rosy forearms" and that Bindrim was clean shaven and had short hair. Defendants rely in part on *Wheeler v. Dell Publishing Co.* (7 Cir. 1962) 300 F.2d 372, which involved an alleged libel caused by a fictional account of an actual murder trial. The *Wheeler* court said (at p.376): "In our opinion, any reasonable person who read the book and was in a position to identify Hazel Wheeler with Janice Quill would more likely conclude that the author created the latter in an ugly way so that none would identify her with Hazel Wheeler. It is important to

---

* This is a rule of constitutional law. See pp. 626–657, infra. [Ed.]

note that while the trial and locale might suggest Hazel Wheeler to those who knew the Chenoweth family, suggestion is not identification. In *Levey [Levey v. Warner Bros. Pictures* (S.D.N.Y. 1944) 57 F. Supp. 40] the court said those who had seen her act may have been reminded of her by songs and scenes, but would not reasonably identify her." However, in *Wheeler* the court found that no one who knew the real widow could possibly identify her with the character in the novel. In the case at bar, the only differences between plaintiff and the Herford character in "Touching" were physical appearance and that Herford was a psychiatrist rather than psychologist. Otherwise, the character Simon Herford was very similar to the actual plaintiff. We cannot say, as did the court in *Wheeler*, that no one who knew plaintiff Bindrim could reasonably identify him with the fictional character. Plaintiff was identified as Herford by several witnesses and plaintiff's own tape recordings of the marathon sessions show that the novel was based substantially on plaintiff's conduct in the nude marathon.

... In the case at bar, apart from some of those episodes allegedly constituting the libelous matter itself, and apart from the physical difference and the fact that plaintiff had a Ph.D., and not an M.D., the similarities between Herford and Bindrim are clear, and the transcripts of the actual encounter weekend show a close parallel between the narrative of plaintiff's novel and the actual real life events....

... It is clear from the transcript of the actual encounter weekend proceeding that some of the incidents portrayed by Mitchell are false: i. e., substantially inaccurate description of what actually happened. It is also clear that some of these portrayals cast plaintiff in a disparaging light since they portray his language and conduct as crude, aggressive, and unprofessional....

... Defendants contend that the fact that the book was labeled as being a "novel" bars any claim that the writer or publisher could be found to have implied that the characters in the book were factual representations not of the fictional characters but of an actual non-fictional person. That contention, thus broadly stated, is unsupported by the cases. The test is whether a reasonable person, reading the book, would understand that the fictional character therein pictured was, in actual fact, the plaintiff acting as described. Each case must stand on its own facts. In some cases, an appellate court can, on examination of the entire work, find that no reasonable person would have regarded the episodes in the book as being other than the fictional imaginings of the author about how the character he had created would have acted.... We cannot make any similar determination here. Whether a reader, identifying plaintiff with the "Dr. Herford" of the book, would regard the passages herein complained of as mere fictional embroidering or as reporting actual language and conduct, was for the jury. Its verdict adverse to the defendants cannot be overturned by this court.

Defendants raise the question of whether there is "publication" for libel where the communication is to only one person or a small group of persons rather than to the public at large. Publication for purposes of defamation is sufficient when the publication is to only one person other than the person defamed. Therefore, [it is] irrelevant whether all readers realized plaintiff and Herford were identical....

[Modified as to damages.]

JEFFERSON, Associate Justice, concurring....

The dissent finds error in the instruction given the jury on the issue of identification. The use of the word "reasonably" in the instruction dissipates the dissent's view that only one person was required to understand the defamatory meaning. If one person "reasonably" understood the defamatory character of the language used, it describes what readers generally would "reasonably" understand....

FILES, Presiding Justice (dissenting).

This novel, which is presented to its readers as a work of fiction, contains a portrayal of nude encounter therapy, and its tragic effect upon an apparently happy and well-adjusted woman who subjected herself to it. Plaintiff is a practitioner of this kind of therapy. His grievance, as described in his testimony and in his briefs on appeal, is provoked by that institutional criticism. Plaintiff's "concession" that he is a public figure appears to be a tactic to enhance his argument that any unflattering portrayal of this kind of therapy defames him.

The decision of the majority upholding a substantial award of damages against the author and publisher poses a grave threat to any future work of fiction which explores the effect of techniques claimed to have curative value....

Defendants' novel describes a fictitious therapist who is conspicuously different from plaintiff in name, physical appearance, age, personality and profession.

Indeed the fictitious Dr. Herford has none of the characteristics of plaintiff except that Dr. Herford practices nude encounter therapy. Only three witnesses, other than plaintiff himself, testified that they "recognized" plaintiff as the fictitious Dr. Herford. All three of those witnesses had participated in or observed one of plaintiff's nude marathons. The only characteristic mentioned by any of the three witnesses as identifying plaintiff was the therapy practiced....

Plaintiff has no monopoly upon the encounter therapy which he calls "nude marathon." Witnesses testified without contradiction that other professionals use something of this kind. There does not appear to be any reason why anyone could not conduct a "marathon" using the style if not the full substance of plaintiff's practices.

Plaintiff's brief discusses the therapeutic practices of the fictitious Dr. Herford in two categories: Those practices which are similar to plaintiff's technique are classified as identifying. Those which are unlike plaintiff's are called libelous because they are false. Plaintiff has thus resurrected the spurious logic which Professor Kalven found in the position of the plaintiff in *New York Times v. Sullivan*, 376 U.S. 254. Kalven wrote: "There is revealed here a new technique by which defamation might be endlessly manufactured. First, it is argued that, contrary to all appearances, a statement referred to the plaintiff; then, that it falsely ascribed to the plaintiff something that he did not do, which should be rather easy to prove about a statement that did not refer to plaintiff in the first place...." Kalven, *The New York Times Case: A Note on "The Central Meaning of the First Amendment,"* 1964 The Supreme Court Review 191, 199....

Whether or not a publication to the general public is defamatory is "whether in the mind of the average reader the publication, considered as a whole, could reasonably be considered as defamatory."

The majority opinion contains this juxtaposition of ideas: "Secondly, the defendants' [proposed] instructions that the jury must find that a substantial segment of the public did, in fact, believe that Dr. Simon Herford was, in fact, Paul Bindrim, was properly refused. For the tort of defamation, publication to one other person is sufficient."

The first sentence refers to the question whether the publication was defamatory of plaintiff. The second refers to whether the defamatory matter was published. The former is an issue in this case. The latter is not. Of course, a publication to one person may constitute actionable libel. But this has no bearing on the principle that the allegedly libelous effect of a publication to the public generally is to be tested by the impression made on the average reader.

The only instruction given the jury on the issue of identification stated that plaintiff had the burden of proving "That a third person read the statement and reasonably understood the defamatory meaning and that the statement applied to plaintiff."

That instruction was erroneous and prejudicial in that it only required proof that one "third person" understood the defamatory meaning....

The majority opinion adopts the position that actual malice may be inferred from the fact that the book was "false." That inference is permissible against a defendant who has purported to state the truth. But when the publication purports to be fiction, it is absurd to infer malice because the fiction is false....

I would reverse the judgment.

Notes

1. The leading case on whether a person may have a defamation action when a fictional character is identified with him is E. Hulton & Co. v. Jones, [1910] A.C. 20 (H.L.), aff'g [1909] 2 K.B. 444 (C.A.). Defendants had published an article saying that Artemus Jones was in France with a woman who was not his wife. They thought Artemus Jones was a name coined by the writer of the article, unlikely to belong to any actual person. It was, however, plaintiff's name and friends of his testified that they had thought the article referred to him. It was held that plaintiff was entitled to recover, despite defendants' lack of intent to refer to him, if reasonable persons would think he was the person referred to. See Smith, Jones v. Hulton: Three Conflicting Judicial Views as to a Question of Defamation, 60 U. Pa. L. Rev. 365, 461 (1912); Mitchell, Artemus Jones and the Press Club, 20 J. Legal Hist. 64 (1999). Compare Clare v. Farrell, 70 F. Supp. 276 (D. Minn. 1947), in which the main character of a novel was "Bernard Clare," an aspiring young writer who led a sordid life. The author testified he used the name because of the character's Irish background. It was also the name of plaintiff, a newspaperman. The court held that the author could not be liable in the absence of a showing that he intended to write of plaintiff, or at least was negligent in using the name.

2. Somewhat closer to the principal case is Corrigan v. Bobbs-Merrill Co., 228 N.Y. 58, 126 N.E. 260 (1920). Defendant published a sensational novel, one of whose chapters brought the hero into New York City's Jefferson Market Court and the courtroom of an unsavory magistrate named Cornigan. Plaintiff was a magistrate who sat in the Jefferson Market Court, named Corrigan. The opinion, which follows the *Jones* case, notes the literary tradition of fictional works depicting as imaginary events "drawn or distorted from real life." See also Smolla, Law of Defamation § 4:46 (2d ed. 1999), which gives the examples of the novel *All the King's Men*, whose principal character resembles Governor Huey Long of Louisiana, and the film *Citizen Kane*, regarded as a thinly disguised portrayal of the newspaper publisher William Randolph Hearst.

3. Other significant libel actions arising from works of fiction include Wheeler v. Dell Publishing Co., quoted in the principal case (novel *Anatomy of a Murder*); Fetler v. Houghton Mifflin Co., 364 F.2d 650 (2d Cir. 1966) (similarities between family in novel and plaintiff's family and events in their lives such that principal character could reasonably be understood as portrayal of plaintiff); Middlebrooks v. Curtis Publishing Co., 413 F.2d 141 (4th Cir. 1969) (character had similar name to plaintiff and story set in his home town; many witnesses testified they believed character was plaintiff; held that in view of differences in age, employment, absence from locale at time of episode and other events in life, character could not reasonably be understood to be plaintiff); Springer v.

Viking Press, 90 A.D.2d 315, 457 N.Y.S.2d 246 (1982), aff'd, 60 N.Y.2d 916, 470 N.Y.S.2d 579, 458 N.E.2d 1256 (1983) (character had same first name as plaintiff, similar physical attributes, graduated from same college and once lived on street where plaintiff lived; plaintiff a college tutor, while character had large income, lived luxuriously and depicted as "whore"; could not reasonably be taken to be plaintiff). If the work includes a statement to the effect that characters should not be taken as portrayals of actual people, this is a factor to be considered but it does not prevent liability. Restatement (Second) of Torts § 564, comment *d* (1977). On the problems of identification of plaintiffs in works of fiction, see Symposium, Defamation in Fiction, 51 Brooklyn L. Rev. 223 (1985).

4. Suppose that a character in a work of fiction can reasonably be identified with plaintiff. Is this sufficient for a cause of action? Restatement (Second) of Torts § 564, comment *d* (1977), requires a showing that it is reasonable for the readers or audience to believe that the character was intended to be a portrayal of plaintiff. Pring v. Penthouse International, Ltd., 695 F.2d 438 (10th Cir. 1982), cert. denied, 462 U.S. 1132 (1983), involved a magazine story, not explicitly labelled as fiction, about the Miss Wyoming at a Miss America pageant. This Miss Wyoming, the story related, believed she could preserve world peace by providing oral sex, in which she was particularly talented, to such national leaders as Fidel Castro, Marshal Tito and the Soviet Central Committee. She displayed this talent with her coach before a national television audience, causing the coach to levitate. The trial court permitted the jury to render a verdict for plaintiff, a former Miss Wyoming, on a finding that readers would understand the character to be plaintiff. The jury awarded one and a half million dollars actual damages and twenty-five million dollars punitive damages. The Court of Appeals ordered the action dismissed, ruling that plaintiff could recover only if the story could reasonably be understood as describing actual facts about her, which it could not. Is this consistent with Burton v. Crowell Publishing Co., p. 501, supra? See also Frank v. National Broadcasting Co., Inc., 119 A.D.2d 252, 506 N.Y.S.2d 869 (1986), appeal withdrawn, 70 N.Y.2d 641, 518 N.Y.S.2d 1032, 512 N.E.2d 558 (1987) (mock commercial on television comedy program for tax consultant with same name as plaintiff; advised ridiculous tax write-offs, such as oil depletion allowance for acne treatment, claiming houseplant as dependent, and treating wife's departure as home improvement).

5. In New Times, Inc. v. Isaacks, 91 S.W.3d 844 (Tex. App. 2002), rev'd, 146 S.W.3d 144 (Tex. 2004), cert. denied, 545 U.S. 1105 (2005), defendants published an article intended to satirize the detention of a thirteen-year-old for five days after he wrote a Halloween story deemed to contain "terroristic threats." The article, which appeared in the "News" section of an "alternative" weekly newspaper that had published other satirical items, recounted the detention of a six-year-old on account of a book report and her appearance in handcuffs and shackles in the court of a juvenile court judge. The judge and the local district attorney sued for libel. Defendants sought summary judgment, contending that reasonable readers would understand the article as satire or parody, not as a report making statements of fact. The Texas Court of Appeals decided that it might be found that the article failed to provide notice to the reader that it was a satire or parody and that a reasonable reader could conclude it made statements of fact. The state supreme court, however, was of the view that even if some actual readers did not "get the joke," the hypothetical reasonable reader could only conclude that this article was satirical and did not state actual facts. Cf. Patrick v. Superior Court (Torres), 22 Cal. App. 4th 814, 27 Cal. Rptr. 2d 883 (1994) (judge not defamed by circulating memo in his name that readers would recognize as parody he did not write).

6. In Vantassell-Matin v. Nelson, 741 F. Supp. 698 (N.D. Ill. 1990), defendant gave reporters a defamatory account of plaintiffs' behavior on an airplane but identified them

only as a "married couple." The reporters obtained their names from other sources and published them with the story. The court held defendant not liable. Is this consistent with the cases on defamatory fiction?

Arcand v. Evening Call Publishing Company
United States Court of Appeals, First Circuit
567 F.2d 1163 (1977)

COFFIN, Chief Judge.

This appeal raises the question whether defendants' allegedly defamatory newspaper column comment made sufficient reference to plaintiffs-appellants to withstand a motion to dismiss the complaint. The case belongs in the ancient but not overpopulated genre of group libel.

Plaintiffs are the twenty-one members of the Bellingham, Massachusetts, Police Department. Defendants are, severally, the Rhode Island writer, editor, and newspaper responsible for the circulation of a column in the Woonsocket Call and Evening Reporter which closed with the provocative question: "Is it true that a Bellingham cop locked himself and a female companion in the back of a cruiser in a town sandpit and had to radio for help?" Each of the plaintiffs claimed grievous professional and personal damage in the sum of $525,000.

The district court, while discounting the defamatory nature of the statement, acknowledged that it was probably libelous if it could be held to refer to a particular individual. But it granted defendants' motion to dismiss on the basis of what it termed "the Prosser principle".[2] It reasoned: "If you say 11 out of 12 people are corrupt, or if you said 20 out of 21 police officers or maybe even 12 out of 21 are corrupt, or even one out of six is corrupt, I think you would have a different situation.... I think it is a combination of the question of numbers and what was said, and I think that as a matter of law, the Court would be obliged to direct an acquittal at the trial of a case of this nature." ...

Over the years several guiding principles have emerged. One is that "Defamation of a large group gives rise to no civil action on the part of an individual member of the group unless he can show special application of the defamatory matter to himself." Tanenhaus, *Group Libel*, 35 Cornell L.Q. 261, 263 (1950); Restatement, Torts, Second, § 564A.

A second principle recognizes a civil action if a defamatory statement applies to all members of a small group. 35 Cornell L.Q. 261, 263, *supra*; Restatement, Torts, Second, § 564A, Comment b.

A third principle is that defamation of part of a group can give rise to a cause of action. As the Restatement puts it, "In general, there can be recovery only if a high degree of suspicion is indicated by the particular statement. Thus the assertion that one man out of a group of 25 has stolen an automobile may not sufficiently defame any member of the group, while the statement that all but one of a group of 25 are thieves may cast a reflection upon each of them." Restatement, Torts, Second, § 564A, Comment c.

---

2. The court had reference to the following comment: "A statement that 'all but one' of twelve are corrupt would seem clearly to affect the entire dozen, where the conclusion scarcely seems justifiable as to one out of twenty." Prosser, Law of Torts, p. 751 (4th ed. 1971).

As might be expected, courts have differed in their allowance of suits involving the defamation of fewer than all members of small groups. Plaintiffs cite *Farrell v. Triangle Publications, Inc.*, 399 Pa. 102, 159 A.2d 734 (1960) (defamation of "a number of township commissioners", of whom there were 13; individual commissioner allowed to sue). On the other hand, as recently as 1950, the catalogue of cases in this category could be reported as follows: "Actions by individuals were unsuccessful against publications alleging that most of the persons at a donation party were there for the liquor, part of a named association consisted of a gang of blackmailers, some members of a particular hose company had committed a theft, one of a man's sons was a thief, and that several of a group of six witnesses would be indicted for perjury. The courts did, on the other hand, find that 'subordinate engineers of a construction company or some of them,' and 'all radio editors save one' were sufficiently narrow categories to permit suits." 35 Cornell L.Q. at 264–65.

Our case would be different if we were confronted with a statement defaming a number of members of a small group. In such an instance, there would seem to be sufficient doubt as to whether the statement could refer to any single member of the group as to justify invoking the aid of a jury. That is, the defamation, encompassing a considerable proportion of the group, can be seen as a blanket slur, reaching all. But here we deal with a defamatory statement aimed at only one unidentified member of a group of 21. By no stretch of imagination can it be thought to suggest that the conduct of the one is typical of all. Noting the individual's membership in the group does not suggest a common determinant of character so much as simply a practical reference point.

This is not to say that each member of a small group does not feel some unease whenever a co-member comes in for criticism, shame, or obloquy. But to predicate liability to all members of a group on such an associational attitude would chill communication to the marrow. Under plaintiffs' theory, statements that a member of the X baseball team was disciplined for brawling, that one of the judges of Y court fell asleep, that a member of the Z band was drunk would be fair game for group libel suits.

We need not decide whether, as appellants argue, the march of law has made obsolete some of the old cases barring suit when fewer than an entire group are defamed. But we have discovered no case where a group libel, justifying suit by all members, was held to arise from a slur against one unidentified member. Particularly where the ratio of the defamed to the total group is 1 to 21, dismissal must be justified.... Were dismissal in such cases not justified, virtually every complaint of group libel would present a jury issue....

Affirmed.

Notes

1. Many cases present problems of "group" or "class" defamation. See Annot., Defamation of Class of Group as Actionable by Individual Member, 52 A.L.R.4th 618 (1987); King, Reference to the Plaintiff Requirement in Defamatory Statements Directed at Groups, 35 Wake Forest L. Rev. 343 (2000); Note, Group Defamation: Five Guiding Factors, 64 Tex. L. Rev. 591 (1985). It is an old problem. See Foxcroft v. Lacy, (1613) Hob. 89, 80 Eng. Rep. 239, Jenk. 297, 145 Eng. Rep. 216 (Ex. Ch.) (during pendency of action by defendant against seventeen people, defendant said they helped to murder person; held that every one of seventeen had action). A logical starting place is the basic requirement that a statement be reasonably interpreted as referring individually to the person bringing suit. Consideration is also due the question of whether the statement had any likelihood of causing harm to persons in the group referred to. Some examples:

(a) Defendant says to a father, "Your boys stole my corn." Maybee v. Fisk, 42 Barb. 326 (N.Y. Sup. Ct. 1864).

(b) Defendant publishes a caricature of a court-martial. Ellis v. Kimball, 16 Pick. (33 Mass.) 132 (1834). Compare Owens v. Clark, 154 Okla. 108, 6 P.2d 755 (1931) (verbal attack on state supreme court); Carter v. King, 174 N.C. 549, 94 S.E. 4 (1917) (trial jury's vote "due entirely to whisky and the appeal made to their prejudice").

(c) A newspaper columnist refers to the "thugs who run Local 299." The leadership of this union local consists of seven men who could be identified from the article. Lins v. Evening News Association, 129 Mich. App. 219, 342 N.W.2d 573 (1983).

(d) A newspaper conveys a police report on the use of drugs by one or more occupants of a car that crashed. Plaintiff is one of the surviving passengers. Sellards v. Express-News Corp., 702 S.W.2d 677 (Tex. App. 1985).

(e) A newspaper states that a suicide victim "might have fared better if his family had not abandoned him." Suit is brought by the victim's mother, sister, two aunts and three uncles. Ogren v. Employers Reinsurance Corp., 119 Wis. 2d 379, 350 N.W.2d 725 (Ct. App. 1984).

(f) A newspaper in a small town attributes a crime problem to "the wine joints that are now in operation here." Plaintiff has a wine-selling establishment in the town. Comes v. Cruce, 85 Ark. 79, 107 S.W. 185 (1908).

(g) An article on the deterioration of a small city asserts that "Arson has become common as people who are unable to sell their devalued buildings burn them for insurance." Plaintiffs own two buildings that burned in the city. The total number of owners of buildings that have burned in the city recently is estimated to be between 204 and 481. Granger v. Time, Inc. 174 Mont. 42, 568 P.2d 535 (1977).

(h) Referring to a city police scandal in which eighteen officers were indicted, an editorial states, "It is inconceivable to us that so much misconduct could have taken place without the guilty knowledge of the unindicted members of the department. If so, they were accessories after the fact, if not before and during." Plaintiffs are twenty-seven of the more than fifty police officers who were not indicted. Brady v. Ottaway Newspapers, 84 A.D.2d 226, 445 N.Y.S.2d 786 (1981).

(i) Defendant makes an accusation of a theft by one of the persons present. Bull v. Collins, 54 S.W.2d 870 (Tex. Civ. App. 1932) (one or other of two employees took money); Wright v. Rosenbaum, 344 S.W.2d 228 (Tex. Civ. App. 1961) (one of four women stole dress from store); Blaser v. Krattiger, 99 Or. 392, 195 P. 359 (1921) (one of twenty to twenty-five persons in hotel lounge stole jewelry); Cohn v. Brecher, 20 Misc. 2d 329, 192 N.Y.S.2d 877 (Sup. Ct. 1959) ("Mr. Cohn, there is a hundred-dollar bill missing and only you three had access to it, Mr. Cohn, and I want that money returned or else I will fire you, you and you."). Compare Albrecht v. Burkholder, (1889) 18 O.R. 287 (Ch. Div.) ("Brayley had got one of the Albrecht girls in trouble"; there were four Albrecht daughters, two of whom were too young to become pregnant).

(j) Defendant states that one member of a township board of supervisors attempted to obtain a bribe in exchange for changing his vote on a question before the board. This would change the result from 3–2 against to 3–2 for. Thompson v. Farley, 14 Bucks Co. L. Rep. 289, 35 Pa. D. & C.2d 157 (C.P. 1964). Compare Farrell v. Triangle Publications, Inc., 399 Pa. 102, 159 A.2d 734 (1960) (statement that investigators from district attorney's office would be questioning township's thirteen commissioners in connection with report that large portion of money for township project "was earmarked for division among a number of township commissioners and others"); McGuire v. Roth, 8 Ohio Misc. 92, 219 N.E.2d 319 (C.P. 1965) ("wondering if the Water Board is getting a 'kick-back'").

2. One of the leading cases is Neiman-Marcus v. Lait, 13 F.R.D. 311 (S.D.N.Y. 1952). The book *U.S.A. Confidential* alleged that some models of the Neiman-Marcus store in Dallas were "call girls." "The salesgirls are good, too … and often much cheaper." Also, "most of the [male] staff are fairies." Actions were brought by all nine of the store's models, fifteen of the twenty-five salesmen, and thirty of the 382 saleswomen. The salesmen and saleswomen sued as representatives of their respective classes as well as on their own behalf. The court held that the salesmen could maintain an action but the saleswomen could not. Suspicion attached to all the salesmen, but the saleswomen constituted too large a group for the public to interpret the book's statement as a reference to any individual. Defendants apparently conceded that the models could maintain suit.

3. Apparently, the American "record" for the largest group ever to be the subject of a successful group defamation claim is held by the University of Oklahoma football team of 1956. Members of the team, which numbered sixty to seventy players, were said to have been given an amphetamine (an illegal drug) in a magazine article on the use of amphetamines by athletes. The Supreme Court of Oklahoma decided that this was a libel of every member of the team and upheld a verdict of $75,000 actual damages in favor of an alternate-squad fullback. Instead of adhering to a flat rule under which members of a "large" group could not recover, the court preferred the criterion of "the intensity of the suspicion cast upon the plaintiff." Fawcett Publications, Inc. v. Morris, 377 P.2d 42 (Okla. 1962), appeal dismissed, 376 U.S. 513 (1964).

4. Members of groups more than twice as large were successful in Pienaar v. Argus Printing and Publishing Co. Ltd., 1956 (4) S.A. 310 (W), and Alberta Union of Provincial Employees v. Edmonton Sun, (1986) 49 Alta. L.R.2d 141 (Q.B.). In the first case, a newspaper editorial had declared that, in order to acquire the position and the salary that went with it, aspirants for a party's nomination to safe legislative seats were prepared to vote for legislation that the newspaper condemned as highly improper. A few days later, the newspaper published a list of the 156 aspirants. Two sued and recovered £100 each. In the second case, columns in a newspaper had made defamatory references to the guards at a jail, who numbered about two hundred. Twenty-five sued and recovered substantial damages.

5. It can be safely predicted that two types of group defamation actions will fail. One is a generalized attack on a professional or occupational group—for example, "all lawyers in _____ are shysters" or "all politicians in _____ take graft." In McCullough v. Cities Service Co., 676 P.2d 833 (Okla. 1984), one of the 19,686 doctors of osteopathy in the United States sued—unsuccessfully—the publisher of a statement that advised people to consult a medical doctor, not an osteopath, the education and training of medical doctors being superior. It should be noted that if the generalized criticism follows a reference to a particular member of the profession or occurs when a member is present, that member has some claim to being defamed individually. See Restatement (Second) of Torts § 564A (1977); Eldredge, Law of Defamation 54–60 (1978).

6. The second type of predictably unsuccessful group defamation action arises from criticism or disparagement of an ethnic or religious group. Attempts by representatives of such groups to maintain defamation actions for this have failed. See Khalid Abdullah Tariq Al Mansour Faissal Fahd Al Talal v. Fanning, 506 F. Supp. 186 (N.D. Cal. 1980)

(action on behalf of world's Moslems for defamation by television program); Pawelek v. Paramount Studios Corp., 571 F. Supp. 1082 (N.D. Ill. 1983) (action against producers of film containing "Polish jokes"); Puerto Rican Legal Defense Fund v. Grace, 9 Media L. Rptr. 1514 (N.Y. Sup. Ct. 1983) (action against businessman who said in speech that 900,000 Puerto Ricans lived in New York and all were "on food stamps"). Should an action be entertained in this type of case? What relief could be given? Beauharnais v. Illinois, 343 U.S. 250 (1952), upholds the constitutionality of criminal sanctions against defamation of ethnic and religious groups. But see Collin v. Smith, 578 F.2d 1197 (7th Cir. 1978), cert. denied, 439 U.S. 916 (1978).

C. Libel and Slander

Matherson v. Marchello

Supreme Court of New York, Appellate Division
100 A.D.2d 233, 473 N.Y.S.2d 998 (1984)

TITONE, Justice Presiding....

On October 28, 1980, radio station WBAB conducted an interview with the members of a singing group called "The Good Rats". Following a commercial which advertised a Halloween party at an establishment known as "OBI", a discussion ensued in which various members of the group explained that they are no longer permitted to play at OBI South because:

> Good Rat #1 Well, you know, we had that law suit with Mr. Matherson.
>
> A Good Rat And we used to fool around with his wife.
>
> Good Rat # 1 And we won.
>
> A Good Rat One of us used to fool around with his wife. He wasn't into that too much.
>
> D.J. Oh yea.
>
> Good Rat #1 (interrupted and joined by another Good Rat) We used to start off our gigs over there with the National Anthem, and he was very upset about that, and now all of a sudden he's very patriotic and he's using it in his commercials.
>
> A Good Rat I don't think it was his wife that he got so upset about, I think it was when somebody started messing around with his boyfriend that he really freaked out. Really.
>
> (Laughter)
>
> That did it man.

[Mr. and Mrs. Matherson] subsequently commenced this action against "The Good Rats" (as individuals and against their record company), alleging that the words "we used to fool around with his wife" and "I don't think it was his wife that he got upset about, I think it was when somebody started messing around with his boyfriend that he really freaked out", were defamatory. They seek compensatory and punitive damages for humiliation, mental anguish, loss of reputation and injury to their marital relationship as well as for the loss of customers, business opportunities and good will allegedly suffered

THE GOOD RATS   Peppi Marchello

by Mr. Matherson. Special Term granted defendants' motion to dismiss, finding that the complaint failed to adequately allege special damages. [Plaintiffs appealed.]

Preliminarily, we observe that if special damages are a necessary ingredient of plaintiffs' cause of action, Special Term properly found the allegations of the complaint to be deficient.

Special damages consist of "the loss of something having economic or pecuniary value" (Restatement, Torts 2d, §575, comment b) which "must flow directly from the injury to reputation caused by the defamation, not from the effects of defamation" (Sack, Libel, Slander and Related Problems, VII 2.2, 345–346) and it is settled law that they must be fully and accurately identified "with sufficient particularity to identify actual losses". When loss of business is claimed, the persons who ceased to be customers must be named and the losses itemized. "Round figures" or a general allegation of a dollar amount as special damages do not suffice. Consequently, plaintiffs' nonspecific conclusory allegations do not meet the stringent requirements imposed for pleading special damages.

We must, therefore, determine whether an allegation of special damages is necessary. In large measure, this turns on which branch of the law of defamation is involved. As a result of historical accident, which, though not sensibly defensible today, is so well settled as to be beyond our ability to uproot it, there is a schism between the law governing slander and the law governing libel.

A plaintiff suing in slander must plead special damages unless the defamation falls into any one of four per se categories. Those categories consist of allegations (1) that the plaintiff committed a crime, (2) that tend to injure the plaintiff in his or her trade, business or profession, (3) that plaintiff has contracted a loathsome disease, and (4) that impute unchastity to a woman.[2] The exceptions were established apparently for no other reason that a recognition that by their nature the accusations encompassed therein would be likely to cause material damage.

---

2. The first three categories were established relatively early. The fourth is of more recent vintage, having first been put into effect in England by the Slander of Women Act of 1891 (54 & 55 Vict., ch. 51); similar statutory additions to the common law were made in this country....

On the other hand, a plaintiff suing in libel need not plead or prove special damages....[3] Thus, unlike the law of slander, in the law of libel the existence of damage is conclusively presumed from the publication itself and a plaintiff may rely on general damages (compare Restatement, Torts 2d, § 569 with § 570; but see Excessiveness or Inadequacy of Damages for Defamation, Ann., 35 A.L.R.2d 218, which suggests, by its scheme of classification, how relatively few cases of libel actually do arise which are not more or less easily referrable to the categories of slander per se)....

Traditionally, the demarcation between libel and slander rested upon whether the words were written or spoken. Written defamations were considered far more serious because, at the time the distinction arose, few persons could read or write and, therefore, anything which was written would carry a louder ring of purported truth. In addition, a written defamation could be disseminated more widely and carried a degree of permanence.

With the advent of mass communication, the differential was blurred. Motion pictures were held to be libel. No set rule developed with respect to radio and television. In some cases, a distinction was drawn between contemporaneous speech, which was classified as slander, and words read from a script, which were classified as libel. This distinction was the subject of considerable criticism and was rejected by later cases which adopted a libel classification irrespective of the use of a script (e.g., *Shor v. Billingsley*, 4 Misc. 2d 857, 158 N.Y.S.2d 476, affd. 4 A.D.2d 1017, 169 N.Y.S.2d 416).

We today hold that defamation which is broadcast by means of radio or television should be classified as libel. As we have noted, one of the primary reasons assigned to justify the imposition of broader liability for libel than for slander has been the greater capacity for harm that a writing is assumed to have because of the wide range of dissemination consequent upon its permanence in form. Given the vast and farflung audiences reached by the broadcasting media today, it is self-evident that the potential harm to a defamed person is far greater than that involved in a single writing. Section 568 A of the Restatement of Torts Second and the more recent decisions in sister states opt for holding such defamation to be libel and we perceive no basis for perpetuating a meaningless, outmoded, distinction....

Taken in the context of a rock and roll station's interview with musicians, and taking note of contemporary usage, we have no difficulty in concluding that the words "fooling around with his wife" could have been interpreted by listeners to mean that Mrs. Matherson was having an affair with one of the defendants. Such charges are clearly libelous on their face, thus obviating any need to allege and prove special damages. While it may be possible to construe the words in an inoffensive manner, since they are susceptible of a defamatory connotation, the cause of action should stand.

[The court accepted plaintiffs' contention that the second comment—"I don't think it was his wife that he got so upset about. I think it was when somebody started messing around with his boyfriend that he really freaked out"—constituted an imputation of homosexuality.] ...

... [D]espite the fact that an increasing number of homosexuals are publicly expressing satisfaction and even pride in their status, the potential and probable harm of a false

3. [The footnote notes the uncertainty concerning whether the "libel per quod" rule was part of New York law. If so, a libel action in which the defamatory import could only be ascertained by reference to "extrinsic facts," i.e. facts not set forth in the publication, would require proof of special damages. A "libel per se," in which "the defamatory import is apparent from the face of the publication itself without resort to any other source," was actionable without proof of special harm.]

charge of homosexuality, in terms of social and economic impact, cannot be ignored. Thus, on the facts of this case, where the plaintiffs are husband and wife, we find, given the narrow scope of review, that the imputation of homosexuality is "reasonably susceptible of a defamatory connotation" and is actionable without proof of special damages.

[Reversed; complaint reinstated.]

Notes

1. *Libel/slander distinction.* One must delve deep into English legal history in order to ascertain why there are two defamation torts rather than one, why the "special damage" requirement was applied to slander but not libel, and why certain types of slander were excepted from the special damage requirement. Some of the history is outlined on pp. 493–494, *supra.* It will suffice here to say that slander developed in the common law courts as an "action on the case for words" and the "gist" of an action on the case was damage. In other words, an action on the case was an action predicated upon suffering damage, so a plaintiff was required to properly plead and prove damage traceable to defendant's wrongful act. Concurrently, libel was a crime within the province of the Court of Star Chamber, which entertained claims for money damages as an adjunct to its criminal law responsibilities. After the Star Chamber was abolished and libel was brought within the jurisdiction of the common law courts, it was held that a civil action for written defamation required no special damage. Damage could be presumed. It became accepted that there was a division between written defamation, called libel, and oral defamation, called slander.

By the early nineteenth century the division was severely criticized, but it had become too well established to be repudiated by the courts and recommendations for the amalgamation of libel and slander by legislation were not implemented. (But see Grein v. La Poma, 54 Wash. 2d 844, 340 P.2d 766 (1959), repudiating the division, apparently in order to abolish the special damage requirement for slander.) The "slander per se" categories other than unchastity developed before libel came into the common law courts, in part because a basis for jurisdiction other than actual damage could be found—most clearly in cases involving accusation of crime, crimes being punishable in common law courts—and in part because these slanders could be regarded as particularly likely to cause damage. Other slanders were actionable "per quod," "per quod" being a term that in common law pleading introduced allegations of damage. See Restatement (Second) of Torts §568, comment *b* (1977); 5 Holdsworth, History of English Law 205–212 (1924); 8 ibid. 333–378 (1926); Ibbetson, A Historical Introduction to the Law of Obligations 112–125 (1999); Donnelly, History of Defamation, 1949 Wis. L. Rev. 99.

2. Libel clearly encompasses handwritten or printed words and other pictorial representations which have a permanent and visible form: signs, drawings, photographs, statues, effigies and the like. It cannot be generalized that libel is addressed to the eye and slander to the ear because defamatory gestures and sign language (formal and informal) are regarded as slander. Thus it would seem that visual communication which has no fixed form is slander. What about oral communication which has been recorded? A.P. Herbert, a determined critic of the libel-slander distinction, satirized it with such examples as defamation by "gramophone" record, by skywriting, by flag signals at sea, and by a parrot taught to repeat defamatory words. Herbert, Bardot M.P.? 38–49 (1965). Whether this conduct is libel or slander remains to be determined. Written matter read aloud and oral communication reduced to writing, perhaps at the direction of the speaker, present further complications. It now appears settled that the sound as well as the image in a film

is libel. See generally Dobbs, Law of Torts 1141 (2000); Prosser & Keeton, Law of Torts 786–787 (5th ed. 1984).

3. As noted in the principal case, no consensus has been reached concerning radio and television broadcasts. The trend in the United States has been toward classifying broadcasts as libel. Outside the United States, the slander classification has prevailed. Through the influence of broadcasters in the United States and politicians (a prominent class of potential defamees) elsewhere, there have been statutory reversals of these positions. See Eldredge, Law of Defamation 81–90 (1978); Fleming, Law of Torts 604 (9th ed. 1998). What is the best approach to defamation by broadcast?

4. A person can be defamed by conduct not intended as a communication at all—for example, putting him in handcuffs or a ward for the insane. A store security guard who searches a person's belongings in view of other customers may convey the meaning that the person being searched is a thief. A dishonored check might imply a credit risk or dishonesty. One case involves conspicuously "shadowing" a person over an extended period. Schultz v. Frankfort Marine Accident & Plate Glass Insurance Co., 151 Wis. 537, 139 N.W. 386 (1913). Another involves an unwanted marriage celebration for a couple married to other persons. Varner v. Morton, (1919) 53 N.S.R. 180, 46 D.L.R. 597 (Full Ct.). The conduct seems closer to the gestures that are treated as slander than the pictorial representations that are treated as libel, but some of the cases lend support to an action for libel. Defamation by taste or smell is possible. Is this libel or slander? See generally Annot., Libel or Slander: Defamation by Gesture or Acts, 46 A.L.R.4th 403 (1986); Prosser & Keeton, Law of Torts 786 (5th ed. 1984).

5. *Libel per quod.* When the division of defamation between libel and slander was established, it became orthodox law that all libel was actionable without pleading and proving special damage. But in the United States there came a change, with many decisions holding that in certain circumstances special damage was required for a libel action. This came to be known as the "libel per quod" doctrine. The origins of the doctrine are unclear. One explanation is that while "slander per se" and "slander per quod" were being used to distinguish slanders that were actionable without special damage from slanders that were not, "libel per se" was being used to distinguish communications that were necessarily libellous from those whose defamatory nature depended upon their interpretation or upon extrinsic facts. Eventually the two usages became confused. Communications which were necessarily libellous were then thought "libel per se" in the sense that they were actionable without special damage, while other libels were "libel per quod" in the sense that liability was conditioned upon special damage.

The principal libel per quod rule was that statements libellous only by reference to extrinsic facts required special damage for liability. (This was not required when extrinsic facts served only to show that a statement was "of and concerning" plaintiff.) Some courts also developed a rule that statements not necessarily defamatory—statements which might be construed in a non-defamatory sense—required special damage. There was division on the question of whether a statement that otherwise would be libel per quod would be libel per se if the defamatory meaning fit one of the per se categories of slander. The libel per quod doctrine once enjoyed a wide, although far short of universal, acceptance in American courts. It has receded to some extent under the weight of criticism (there was a famous debate between Eldredge and Prosser on the subject, culminating in the rejection by the Restatement (Second) of Torts of any special damage requirement for libel) and the belief that Gertz v. Robert Welch, Inc., p. 626, infra, substantially eliminated the advantages of a libel per quod rule. The libel per quod doctrine protects defendants who had no reason to know of a statement's defamatory connotation and prevents liability for substantial amounts when no harm can be proved, but *Gertz* does the same for most libel defendants. Would application of any version of the libel per quod rule have changed the result of Matherson v. Marchello? See generally Eldredge, Law of Defamation 151–192 (1978); Harper, James & Gray, Law of Torts §5.9A (3d ed. 2006).

6. *Special damage.* When special damage must be pleaded and proved, what is required? The definition of special damage is narrow. First, only loss caused by harm to reputation attributable to defendant's defamatory statement qualifies as special damage. Other "actual" damage flowing from the statement does not—for example, emotional stress or illness when plaintiff learns of and worries about the defamation. Second, damage to reputation as such is not special damage, and neither is an adverse change in the attitude of other people toward plaintiff. Special damage is a consequence of damage to reputation: loss of something that plaintiff otherwise would have received or retained. Third, the loss must be of a "pecuniary" or economic nature. See, e.g., Tacket v. Delco Remy Division of General Motors Corp., 937 F.2d 1201 (7th Cir. 1991).

Loss of employment or trade are classic examples of special damage, but courts traditionally have been strict in requirements of pleading and proof. An action may founder on plaintiff's failure to specify how defendant's defamatory falsehood caused, through damage to reputation, pecuniary losses that plaintiff can identify with particularity, excluding other possible causes of these losses. In this respect, defamation actionable with special damage resembles injurious falsehood. See pp. 260–263, supra. It was said in Erick Bowman Remedy Co. v. Jensen Salsbery Laboratories, 17 F.2d 255, 261 (8th Cir. 1926): "It was therefore necessary for the plaintiff to allege either the loss of particular customers by name, or a general diminution in its business, and extrinsic facts showing that such special damages were the natural and direct result of the false publication. If the plaintiff desired to predicate its right to recover damages upon general loss of custom, it should have alleged facts showing an established business, the amount of sales for a substantial period preceding the publication, the amount of sales subsequent to the publication, facts showing that such loss in sales were the natural and probable result of such publication, and facts showing that plaintiff could not allege the names of particular customers who withdrew or withheld their custom." More recent cases take a somewhat more liberal attitude. See Schoen v. Washington Post, 100 U.S. App. D.C. 389, 246 F.2d 670 (1957) (plaintiff pleaded generally damage to business reputation and loss of many customers, plus specified decrease in gross income; showing that decrease in income was consequence of inaccuracies in publication a "matter of proof").

Courts have found pecuniary loss not only in loss of business but also in loss of social hospitality, as food, drink and accommodation have pecuniary value. Also, loss of a gift, inheritance or marriage. Inability to obtain goods or services for which plaintiff would have paid appears to qualify as special damage, as does inability to obtain credit. If special damage is established, plaintiff can recover "general damages" for harm to reputation and for emotional distress and illness. See generally Restatement (Second) of Torts §575, comment *b* (1977); Eldredge, Law of Defamation 193–204 (1977); Prosser & Keeton, Law of Torts 793–795 (5th ed. 1984).

7. Some courts have narrowed the distinction between "per se" and "per quod" defamation by requiring in all cases that there be proof of some actual harm to reputation. United Insurance Co. of America v. Murphy, 331 Ark. 364, 961 S.W.2d 752 (1998); Schlegel v. Ottumwa Courier, 585 N.W.2d 217 (Iowa 1998); Gobin v. Globe Publishing Co., 232 Kan. 1, 649 P.2d 1239 (1982). Or at least that there be proof of actual harm of some type. Walker v. Grand Central Sanitation, Inc., 430 Pa. Super. 236, 634 A.2d 237 (1993), appeal denied, 539 Pa. 652, 651 A.2d 539 (1994); Myers v. Pickering Firm, Inc.,

959 S.W.2d 152 (Tenn. App. 1997). See Annot., Proof of Injury to Reputation as Prerequisite to Recovery of Damages in Defamation—Post-Gertz Cases, 36 A.L.R.4th 807 (1985).

Gunsberg v. Roseland Corporation

Supreme Court of New York
34 Misc. 2d 220, 225 N.Y.S.2d 1020 (1962)

JOHN F. SCILEPPI, Justice....

The plaintiff alleges that at the time of the occurrence complained of he was a duly registered member of the New York State Stock Exchange and a duly registered broker for the purpose of effectuating for the general public the sale and purchase of securities traded upon the said exchange, and was employed as a customer's man. The complaint further alleges that [defendant's employee], in the presence and hearing of numerous, diverse persons gathered in the place of business conducted by the said defendant, known as "Roseland", a public dance ballroom, maliciously, wilfully and wantonly said to the plaintiff, a patron therein, "get out of this place you silly stupid senile bum; you are a trouble maker and should be confined to an asylum."

The defendant moves for the dismissal of the said cause of action on the grounds that the words uttered are not slanderous per se, and therefore, should contain an allegation of special damages. The complaint makes no such allegation....

A slanderous utterance is deemed to be slander per se when its publication (1) charges the commission of a crime, or (2) charges the affliction of a loathsome disease, or (3) charges that a woman is not chaste, or (4) tends to injure the party in his trade, business or profession. Plaintiff contends that the language used by defendant in this case falls within the 4th category, namely: tends to injure the party in his trade, business or profession.

... [In Moore v. Francis, 121 N.Y. 199, 23 N.E. 1127] the Court of Appeals stated, "Words ... are libelous if they affect a person in his profession, trade, or business, 'by imputing to him any kind of fraud, dishonesty, misconduct, incapacity, unfitness, or want of any necessary qualifications in the exercise thereof.'" ... "Words, to be actionable on the ground they affect a man in his trade or occupation, must, as is said touch him in such trade or occupation; that is, they must be shown, directly or by inference, to have been spoken of him in relation thereto, and to be such as would tend to prejudice him therein."

In Shakun v. Sadinoff, 272 App. Div. 721, 74 N.Y.S.2d 556, the Court said, "Words which directly tend to injure or prejudice the reputation of the plaintiff in the way of any office held by him, or in the way of any lawful profession or trade carried on by him, are actionable without proof of special damage. In such cases, the plaintiff must allege in his statement of claim, and prove at the trial, that he held the office, or carried on the profession or trade, at the time when the words complained of were published. He must also allege and prove *that the words were spoken in reference to his character or conduct in such office, profession or trade.* (emphasis supplied) There must be some reference, direct or indirect, in the words or in the circumstances attending their utterance, which connects the slander with such office or profession or trade. If the words merely impute to the plaintiff some misconduct unconnected with his office, profession, or trade, they are not actionable without proof of special damage: it is not sufficient that they are calculated to injure him therein." ...

In this case there is no allegation contained in plaintiff's complaint setting forth that the alleged defamatory matter was stated to the plaintiff with reference to his trade or business, nor that they were spoken in reference to his character or conduct in such office, profession or trade. There is no direct or indirect reference in the words or the circumstances attending their utterance which connects the slander with the plaintiff's position as a stockbroker. Since the words uttered are not slanderous per se, special damages must be pleaded. Motion granted....

Notes

Four categories of slander are actionable without pleading and proving special damage. As with libel, no actual loss need be proved. Harm can be presumed from the fact that the defamation occurred.

1. *Imputation concerning person's business, trade, profession or office.* This category presents substantial problems because it does not include all slanders that harm or are likely to harm a person in a business, trade, profession or office. If one were to accept that the statement in the principal case would cause plaintiff to lose customers or harm his career, it still would not be slander per se. A statement is within this category only if it imputes some unfitness or impropriety "in relation to" plaintiff's business, trade, profession or office. A statement might impute some trait, such as drunkenness, which would be inconsistent with the proper conduct of plaintiff's business; yet, if there is no suggestion that this trait affects the conduct of the business, the statement is probably not a per se slander. However, an imputation of conduct or character believed to be inconsistent with the job or office plaintiff holds might be treated as slanderous per se even when no "on the job" misconduct is implied. Thus, a clergyman may not have to show special damage if it is said that he consorts with prostitutes.

General defamatory comments about a person's conduct in a business, profession or office are slanderous per se—for example, that a contractor is incompetent, a doctor is a "quack," a lawyer is a "shyster." So are statements imputing insolvency, if plaintiff conducts a business. Honorary offices (offices which provide no remuneration) are included, as are offices "for profit." Therefore, a statement that defames the officer of a charitable or civic organization or the holder of a government appointment that carries no salary can be slander per se, provided the statement relates to the office. Plaintiff must, at the time of the slander, be in the business, trade, profession or office concerned, or at least be about to undertake it.

Consider whether and under what circumstances it would be slanderous per se to make the following imputations about the persons holding the positions listed:

bribery	blacksmith
cheating in competition	clergyman
Communism	clerk
contagious disease	government bureaucrat
drug use	judge
foul language	juror
fraud	merchant
gross carelessness	physician
ignorance	politician
mental illness	president of charitable society
passing bad checks	professional sports player

prostitution	store cashier
racial prejudice	teacher
sexual advances	truck driver

See generally Restatement (Second) of Torts § 573 (1977); Eldredge, Law of Defamation 123–150 (1978); Harper, James & Gray, Law of Torts § 5.12 (3d ed. 2006); Prosser & Keeton, Law of Torts 790–792 (5th ed. 1984).

2. *Imputation of crime.* The oldest category of slander per se consists of statements imputing the commission of a crime. It is not the risk of prosecution but the harm to one's relations with the community that is the rationale of this category. Accordingly, it is slander per se to say that a person has committed a crime for which he has already been prosecuted or for which he cannot be prosecuted by reason of a pardon, nonage or the statute of limitations.

Reputation in the community is unlikely to suffer much harm if the crime imputed is regarded as minor or one to which little blame attaches. Courts have attempted to develop requirements concerning the seriousness of the crime. Outside the United States, the standard is that the crime be punishable by death or imprisonment. After a phase in which it was demanded that the imputation be of an indictable crime, American courts moved toward requiring that the crime have an "infamous" or "disgraceful" punishment or that the crime be one of "moral turpitude." In a number of jurisdictions, these are alternatives.

"Infamous" or "disgraceful" punishment apparently means death or a prison sentence, as opposed to a fine or sentence served in the local jail. "Moral turpitude" eludes any precise description. Restatement (Second) of Torts § 571, comment *g* (1977), after noting that moral turpitude has been defined as "inherent baseness or vileness of principle in the human heart," states that it means "shameful wickedness, so extreme a departure from ordinary standards of honesty, good morals, justice or ethics as to be shocking to the moral sense of the community." Perhaps "major social disgrace" is the real test. Consider whether it is slanderous per se to impute the commission of such offenses as assault and battery, being drunk and disorderly, price fixing, child neglect, indecent exposure, uttering a bad check, violations of alcohol or drug prohibition laws, understatement of income on a tax return, conducting business on Sunday, selling adulterated food, dangerous driving.

The crime need not be given its legal description or even specifically identified. It is sufficient that some criminal conduct of the required type is imputed—for example, "He has served time in the penitentiary." But what if defendant said only that plaintiff was a "criminal" or "crook" or "a member of the Mafia"? Or that plaintiff was going to commit a crime? Suppose defendant said that he knew enough to send plaintiff to jail? Is it slanderous per se to allege conduct and describe it as a serious crime when it actually is not a crime? To allege something that is a crime in the place where the words are spoken but not where the conduct supposedly occurred, or vice versa? See generally Restatement (Second) of Torts § 571 (1977); Eldredge, Law of Defamation 99–109 (1978); Harper, James & Gray, Law of Torts § 5.10 (3d ed. 2006); Prosser & Keeton, Law of Torts 788–790 (5th ed. 1984).

3. *Imputation of loathsome disease.* The rationale of this category of slander per se is that a person may be excluded from society if it is thought that he is afflicted by certain types of disease. But the category is limited to a small number of diseases identified several centuries ago: venereal diseases, leprosy and "the plague." Other contagious, much-feared diseases have not been included. Should they be? Would it be right to hold that an imputation of AIDS is slanderous per se? The statement must imply that plaintiff is presently

suffering from the disease, not that he had it in the past. See generally Eldredge, Law of Defamation 109–117 (1978); Harper, James & Gray, Law of Torts § 5.11 (3d ed. 2006).

4. *Imputation of unchastity.* This became a category of slander per se in the nineteenth century through judicial decisions in the United States and statutes elsewhere. Strictly speaking, "unchastity" is to have sexual intercourse outside marriage, but this precise meaning appears not to be demanded. This imputation has been a per se slander only for females, on the premise that unchastity is a social disgrace for a woman but not for a man. What impact will the movement toward sexual equality in the law and greatly altered societal attitudes about extramarital sex have on this element of defamation law? In recent years, some courts have decided that imputations of homosexuality are slanderous per se. See Gallo v. Alitalia-Linee Aeree Italiane-Societa per Azioni, 585 F. Supp. 2d 520 (S.D.N.Y. 2008) (imputation of adultery also slanderous per se); Nazeri v. Missouri Valley College, 860 S.W.2d 303 (Mo. 1993). Contra, Hayes v. Smith, 832 P.2d 1022 (Colo. App. 1991); Yonaty v. Mincolla, 97 A.D.3d 141, 945 N.Y.S.2d 774 (2012). Restatement (Second) of Torts § 574 (1977) would include any "serious sexual misconduct." See generally Eldredge, Law of Defamation 117–123 (1978); Harper, James & Gray, Law of Torts § 5.13 (3d ed. 2006).

D. Publication

Hedgpeth v. Coleman

Supreme Court of North Carolina
183 N.C. 309, 111 S.E. 517 (1922)

The defendant was a merchant, depot and express agent, and postmaster at Lyon. In February, 1918, his storehouse and safe were broken into; and soon thereafter the plaintiff, a boy then between 14 and 15 years of age, found in his individual mail box the following paper writing, sealed in an envelope addressed to him:

Washington, D.C.

Read All This.

We saw you next day after it happened. You showed guilt, but we wanted more evidence. We have plenty of it now, and would come right on and get you, but on account of your age, and for the sake of your relatives, we will give you one chance to make good by taking everything you got, tie it up and throw it into cat hole of shed room door. If he finds it before next Sunday, he will let us know, but unless it is found by Sunday, we will come and get you and there will be no more chance to stop it this side of Atlanta Pen.

If it is found, no one will know that you put it there, and you may not be suspected by everybody, but if we come back, then it matters not who knows it, for we will push it clear through and do it quickly.

Two men, who saw you one Wednesday.

The plaintiff showed this paper to W.T. Hedgpeth, his brother, and to T.M. Parrott, and his brother showed it to the plaintiff's father....

After reading the paper received by plaintiff, W.T. Hedgpeth showed it to the defendant, who denied writing it, but said that "he was knowing to it"; that efforts were being made to locate the person who had broken into the store, and that the matter was in the hands of a detective. Defendant told plaintiff's father that he would be wonderfully surprised when he found out who had broken into the store; that if the person who did so would bring back all he had and put it in the cat hole of the shedroom his name would not be exposed.

The defendant introduced no evidence. At the close of the evidence the defendant moved to dismiss as in case of nonsuit. Motion allowed as to the alleged slander and blackmail, and denied as to the alleged libel. Defendant excepted and appealed.

ADAMS, J....

... [W]hile the defendant does not deny that it is libelous per se, he controverts, chiefly on two grounds, the plaintiff's right to recover damages. These grounds are: (1) That the defendant did not write the paper referred to; and (2) that, even if he did, there has been no publication of it in contemplation of law.

As to the first, the defendant admitted that, while he did not write the communication, "he was knowing to it"; and there was expert evidence tending to show that this paper and a letter, the authenticity of which the defendant did not dispute, were written by the same person on an Oliver typewriter. This ... was evidence of a character sufficiently substantial to warrant the jury in finding as a fact that the defendant was responsible for this typewritten paper of unavowed authorship.

As to the second ground of defense, the general rule unquestionably requires that the defamatory words be communicated to someone other than the person defamed. "The publication of a slander involves only one act by the defendant; he must speak the words, so that some third person hears and understands them. But the publication of a libel is a more composite act. First, the defendant must compose and write the libel; next, he must hand what he has written, or cause it to be delivered, to some third person; then that third person must read and understand its contents; or, it may be that, after composing and writing it, the defendant reads it aloud to some third person, who listens to the words and understands them: in this case the same act may be both the uttering of a slander and the publication of a libel." Odgers on Lib. and Slan. 157.

But it is not necessary that the defamatory words be communicated to the public generally, or even to a considerable number. It is sufficient if they be communicated only to a single person other than the person defamed. For example, it has been held that the publication was sufficient where the defendant had communicated the defamatory matter to the plaintiff's agent, or attorney; or had read it to a friend before posting it to the plaintiff; or had procured it to be copied, or sealed in the form of a letter addressed to the plaintiff and left in the house of a neighbor by whom it was read; or had caused it to be delivered to and read by a member of the plaintiff's family. The fact, therefore, that the paper under consideration may have been seen only by the plaintiff's brother and Parrott cannot exonerate the defendant on the ground that there was no communication to the public.

But the defendant argued that, even if this be granted, still there was no publication by him, because the paper was communicated directly to the plaintiff, and the plaintiff alone divulged its contents. We have stated the general rule to be that the communication of libelous matter to the person defamed does not of itself constitute a publication. The defendant's argument involves the question whether the rule is inflexible or whether it is subject to exception or qualification. The suggestion that as a principle it is immutable cannot be adopted. The ultimate concern is the relation that existed between the writing of the paper and the disclosure of its contents by the plaintiff. For running through the entire law of tort is the principle that a causal relation must exist between the damage complained of and the act which occasions the damage. Unless such relation exists, the damage is held to be remote, and cannot be recovered; but, if such relation does exist, the wrongful act is held to be the cause of the damage. So in this case we cannot disregard the relation of cause and effect. "There is no publication such as to give rise to a civil action where libelous matter is sent to the person libeled, unless the sender intends or has reason to suppose that the matter will reach third persons (which in fact happens) or such result naturally flows from the sending." Street's Found. Leg. Liab. vol. 1, 296.

Under this principle the mailing of a libelous letter to a person whose clerk, in pursuance of a custom known to the sender, opens and first reads the letter constitutes a publication. Whether the principle extends to a disclosure by the person libeled is to be determined by the causal relation existing between the libel and the publication. The sending of libelous matter to a person known by the sender to be blind, or having sight, to be unable to read, and therefore obliged to have it read by another, is, when read, a publication by the sender, because such exposure of the subject-matter is the proximate result of the writing and sending of the communication. These exceptions are based upon the principle that the act of disclosure arises from necessity. But necessity is not predicated exclusively on conditions which are physical. Necessity may be superinduced by a fear which is akin to duress. A threat may operate so powerfully upon the mind of an immature boy as to amount to coercion; and, when an act is done through coercion, it is not voluntary.

In the letter referred to there is a threat of prosecution and imprisonment. When it was received the plaintiff was between 14 and 15 years of age, and his youth was known to the defendant. With knowledge of the plaintiff's immaturity, of the character of the accusation and menace contained in the letter, of the probable emotion of fear, and the impelling desire for advice on the part of the plaintiff, the defendant must have foreseen the plaintiff's necessary exposure of the letter as the natural and probable result of the libel. Indeed, under the charge of his honor the jury found from the evidence that the defendant had reasonable ground to know that the letter would necessarily be seen by third persons. Obviously, then, the act of the defendant was the proximate cause of the publication. This conclusion disallows all the exceptions relating to the motion for nonsuit....

No error.

Notes

1. If the defamatory statement never reaches any person other than the one defamed by it, there is no "publication" and no cause of action for libel or slander. Why is publication required? If defendant deliberately communicates with a person other than the one defamed, there is publication. If defendant places a defamatory statement in records which are usually read by other persons, there is publication. There is also publication when defendant communicates with plaintiff knowing that a third person will receive the communication at the same time, as when defendant speaks to plaintiff with knowledge that third persons can hear and understand the communication, or posts a notice for plaintiff with knowledge that other persons will see it. Publication becomes an issue when a communication addressed only to plaintiff reaches a third person or is transmitted by plaintiff to a third person.

2. In the following situations, it was held that there was no publication. What conclusions should be drawn from these decisions?

   (a) Plaintiff's sons eavesdrop on defendant's telephone call to plaintiff. Smith v. Jones, 335 So. 2d 896 (Miss. 1976).

(b) Defendant mails an envelope to plaintiff, whose wife customarily reads his mail. Weidman v. Ketcham, 278 N.Y. 129, 15 N.E.2d 426 (1938).

(c) A tenant mails a note with a rent check to his landlord, a solicitor with one partner. The envelope arrives at the office on a Saturday morning, when the landlord is absent, and is opened by the partner. Sharp v. Skues, (1909) 25 T.L.R. 336 (C.A.).

(d) A store sends a letter to a seventeen-year-old girl concerning her delinquency in installment payments for a purchase. The letter is opened by her parents. Riley v. Askin & Marine Co., 134 S.C. 198, 132 S.E. 584 (1926).

(e) Defendant mails a note in an unsealed envelope. The note is read by the addressee's curious butler before delivery to the addressee. Huth v. Huth, [1915] 3 K.B. 32 (C.A.).

(f) Defendant mails a post card to plaintiff. Steele v. Williams, 8 Ohio Cir. Dec. 161, 15 Ohio C.C. 52 (1897). Contra, Ostro v. Safir, 165 Misc. 647, 1 N.Y.S.2d 377 (Sup. Ct. 1937) ("publication as a matter of law").

(g) Defendant mails a notice to plaintiff in India, written in Urdu script. Not being conversant with Urdu, plaintiff has the notice translated. Mahender Ram v. Harnandan Prasad, [1958] Patna L.R. 106, [1958] A.I.R. Patna 445.

(h) Defendant sends a letter to plaintiff, who immediately exhibits it to several of his relatives and friends. Sylvis v. Miller, 96 Tenn. 94, 33 S.W. 921 (1896).

(i) Defendants compose a letter, which one writes and mails to plaintiff. Busby v. First Christian Church, 153 La. 377, 95 So. 869 (1923).

(j) Speaking to two plaintiffs, defendant accuses them of a theft. Harbison v. Chicago, Rock Island & Pacific Railway Co., 327 Mo. 440, 37 S.W.2d 609 (1931). But cf. Marble v. Chapin, 132 Mass. 225 (1882) (defendant accused listener of intercourse with plaintiff).

(k) Defendant communicates to plaintiff's attorney concerning a matter in which the attorney represents plaintiff. Freeman v. Dayton Seale Co., 159 Tenn. 413, 19 S.W.2d 255 (1929). Contra, Massee v. Williams, 207 F. 222 (6th Cir. 1913).

3. Can there be publication when defendant speaks to plaintiff without knowing that anyone else can hear what is said or sends a sealed letter to plaintiff, expecting him to read it personally? Publication may well be found if defendant anticipated or reasonably should have anticipated the likelihood of a third person hearing the conversation or opening the letter. (Knowledge that there is some remote possibility of this occurring is not sufficient. Barnes v. Clayton House Motel, 435 S.W.2d 616 (Tex. Civ. App. 1968).) In a number of reported cases, courts have found sufficient evidence to support a conclusion that defendant was responsible for unintended publication to the third person. See Rumney v. Worthley, 186 Mass. 144, 71 N.E. 316 (1904) (business envelope sent to plaintiff's dwelling, adjoining his grocery; opened by daughter, who defendant knew was clerk in grocery); Duckworth v. First National Bank of South Carolina, 254 S.C. 563, 176 S.E.2d 297 (1970) (slander in bank "within earshot" of other persons, although witnesses denied they heard it); Gomersall v. Davies, (1898) 14 T.L.R. 430 (C.A.) (letter sent to plaintiff at address that was both residence and office; opened by clerk); Theaker v. Richardson, [1962] 1 W.L.R. 151 (C.A.) (envelope left at plaintiff's home opened by husband, who took it to be election literature); McNichol v. Grandy, [1931] S.C.R. 696, [1932] 1 D.L.R. 225 (defendant loudly slandered plaintiff in shop; unknown to both, assistant manager listened

to conversation through small hole in wall). Compare Morrow v. II Morrow, Inc., 139 Or. App. 212, 911 P.2d 964 (1996), review denied, 323 Or. 153, 916 P.2d 312 (1996) (defendant deleted computer file, not realizing that it was saved on network; not liable without evidence of negligence). If defendant intended to send the message to plaintiff but erroneously sent it to another person, liability can result, at least if defendant did not exercise due care. See Restatement (Second) of Torts § 577, comment *l* (1977). See generally Annot., Libel and Slander: Publication by Accidental Communication, or Communication Only to Plaintiff, 92 A.L.R.2d 219 (1963).

4. *Liability for communication by plaintiff.* Does the proposition that the sender of a letter to a blind or illiterate person publishes it to the reader of the letter, because the sender can anticipate the addressee's need to have the letter read for him, justify the conclusion that there was publication in the principal case, where the recipient showed the letter to family members after reading its accusation of theft? Recent cases involving discharged employees have taken the notion of publication "by necessity" even further. It has been decided that if an employer makes defamatory explanations for the discharge of an employee, the employee's repetition of the statements when seeking new employment can constitute a publication for which the employer is responsible. See Churchey v. Adolph Coors Co., 759 P.2d 1336 (Colo. 1988); Lewis v. Equitable Life Assurance Society, 389 N.W.2d 876 (Minn. 1986) (defendant subject to liability if it was foreseeable to defendant that plaintiff would be compelled to publish defamatory statement to prospective employer).

5. In Chasewood Construction Co. v. Rico, 696 S.W.2d 439 (Tex. App. 1985), a subcontractor was accused of theft of construction materials by the general contractor and ordered off the job site. It was held that the general contractor knew or should have known that the subcontractor would feel an obligation to explain to his personnel why they were leaving the site; therefore, the general contractor could be liable for the subcontractor's publication of the theft accusation. Cf. Van-Go Transport Co., Inc. v. New York City Board of Education, 971 F. Supp. 90 (E.D.N.Y. 1997) (bidders on city contracts required to provide details of prior contract denials); Belcher v. Little, 315 N.W.2d 734 (Iowa 1982) (defendant's claim to plaintiffs' real property—"slander of title"—communicated by plaintiffs to bank when they applied for mortgage); Bretz v. Mayer, 1 Ohio Misc. 59, 203 N.E.2d 665 (C.P. 1963) (letter to minister threatening legal action over formation of new church, shown by minister to members of group seeking to form church). Is this good law?

6. In Live Oak Publishing Co. v. Cohagan, 234 Cal. App. 3d 1277, 286 Cal. Rptr. 198 (1991), a newspaper, fearing that refusal to publish a letter defaming newspaper publishers and editors would cause more damage than publication, published the letter as a paid advertisement. This was held not to be a situation of compulsion that would allow a libel claim to arise from self-publication. The theory of "compelled self-defamation" liability to former employees is rejected in a number of recent cases. See Cweklinsky v. Mobil Chemical Co., 267 Conn. 210, 837 A.2d 759 (2004); White v. Blue Cross and Blue Shield of Massachusetts, Inc., 442 Mass. 64, 809 N.E.2d 1034 (2004); Sullivan v. Baptist Memorial Hospital, 995 S.W.2d 569 (Tenn. 1999). Policy reasons for these decisions include concerns that liability would produce "employer silence"—employers would not communicate to employees the reasons for termination of employment or what might be constructive criticism of employees' performance—while encouraging employees to repeat the defamatory statements, possibly years after the termination, rather than mitigate the damage. On whether a publication by plaintiff can satisfy the publication requirement, see Annot. Publication of Allegedly Defamatory Matter by Plaintiff ("Self Publication") as Sufficient to Support Defamation Action, 62 A.L.R.4th 616 (1988).

Vermaak v. Van der Merwe

Supreme Court of South Africa, Natal Provincial Division
1981 (3) S.A. 78 (N)

HOWARD *et* THIRION JJ....

The evidence established that during the course of a telephonic conversation in January 1977 Mrs Claassens asked the respondent if she could speak to his wife, and received the reply "Het jy nie gehoor dat sy bly by daardie donderse lesbian nie?" ["Haven't you heard that she is staying with that damned lesbian?"]. The respondent went on to make it clear that he was referring to the appellant. Mrs Claassens explained under cross-examination that at the time of the telephonic conversation she did not know what the word "lesbian" meant and accordingly did not understand it to have any defamatory significance. She later asked her husband what it meant and he told her.

It is common cause that it was defamatory of the appellant to refer to her as a lesbian. The claim failed [in the court below] on the ground that in the circumstances there was no publication of the defamatory statement. Counsel for the appellant, Mr *Harcourt*, contended that there was publication when Mrs Claassens discovered the meaning of the word "lesbian".

... De Villiers *The Roman and Roman-Dutch Law of Injuries*, in annotations to *Voet* 47.10.8 at 90, says: "Defamatory language to be actionable must have been communicated to some other person or persons than the one to whom it relates.... To be defamatory they (ie spoken words) must have been expressed in an intelligible manner so as to be understood by the hearers. For instance, if spoken in a foreign language which no one present understood, the expressions used would be as little injurious in respect of their matter as if they had never been used at all." ...

The view that there is no publication of spoken words unless the hearer understands them ... is expressed in modern South African and English textbooks.

Mr *Harcourt* conceded that there was no publication of the defamatory statement in the course of the telephonic conversation between the respondent and Mrs Claassens....

The question ... is whether there must be contemporaneity between the communication of the defamatory statement and the understanding of its defamatory meaning by the communicatee....

... [T]he one South African decision which appears to be in point is *Ferreira v Sardinha* 1917 TPD 477. The defamatory statement which figured in that case had been written in a complaints book. It was intended to refer to the plaintiff but did not mention his name or otherwise identify him as the person against whom the imputation was made. Those who read the defamatory complaint did not immediately know that it referred to the plaintiff but were informed soon afterwards that it did so. [A judgment for plaintiff was affirmed.] ...

It must happen frequently that the reader or listener does not, on reading or hearing a defamatory statement, immediately grasp its import and appreciate its defamatory meaning. And it is a reasonable assumption that in such cases the reader or listener not infrequently discovers the defamatory significance of the statement later, on further reflection perhaps, or possibly through discussing it with other persons. Particularly must this be so in cases where the statement is only defamatory in some latent or secondary sense. Or it may happen, in a country like ours, where there are many people who, while able to speak a language which is not their mother tongue, are nevertheless not proficient in that language, that the reader or listener may have an imperfect understanding of a word, the true meaning of which would only become apparent on a reference to a dictionary. Thus an Afrikaans-speaking person might not lift an eyebrow when told that his neighbour was "mendacious", but he might well be sufficiently interested in discovering the meaning of the word to look it up in a dictionary. Under these circumstances insistence on strict contemporaneity between the communication of the statement and the understanding of its defamatory meaning by the communicatee would have unsatisfactory results. In our view the law would be deficient in a most material respect if a person who did everything he thought necessary to defame another could escape liability simply because the person to whom he addressed his defamatory statement did not immediately grasp the true significance of what he had been told. If the person addressed discovered the defamatory significance of the statement at a later stage, the defamer should be held liable, regardless of the length of the time lapse between communication and understanding.

It was argued that to hold a defendant liable in the circumstances postulated above would give rise to uncertainty and possibly lead to absurd results, for the reader or hearer might first learn the defamatory meaning of the words quite fortuitously years or even decades after the event. Such cases could occur but they would be rare, and the person defamed would not lightly embark upon litigation after such a long lapse of time, for he would probably have difficulty in proving substantial damages. Although the point was not canvassed specifically it is reasonably clear from the evidence in this case that the communication of the defamatory statement to Mrs Claassens and her discovery of the meaning of the word "lesbian" were substantially contemporaneous. It appears that her husband was sitting on a nearby bench or settee while she was speaking by telephone to the respondent, and that it was after replacing the receiver that she asked her husband what the word meant and he told her. It is unrealistic to hold that under these circumstances the defamatory statement was not published to Mrs Claassens.

The appeal must therefore be allowed. . . .

Notes

1. If defendant speaks defamatory words but there is no evidence that anyone but plaintiff heard them, there is no publication. See Sheffill v. Van Deusen, 13 Gray (79 Mass.) 304 (1859). Does it follow that there is no publication when a third person hears the words but does not understand them? In Economopoulos v. A.G. Pollard Co., 218 Mass. 294, 105 N.E. 896 (1914), it was held that no publication occurred when defendant spoke to plaintiff in Greek, which other persons present apparently did not know. No publication was found in Sullivan v. Sullivan, 48 Ill. App. 435 (1892), in which defendant called plaintiff a "damned old whore" in the presence of plaintiff's children. They did not understand the expression. Suppose the defamatory words are heard and understood, but the reference to plaintiff is not? See Desmond v. Brown, 33 Iowa 13 (1871); Weidman v. Ketcham, 278 N.Y. 129, 15 N.E.2d 426 (1938) (no publication). Since a statement is not actionable as slander or libel unless it conveys a defamatory meaning about plaintiff to another person, does it make any difference whether or not publication occurred?

2. In the principal case, the defamatory meaning of the statement was explained soon after it was heard. Reference is made to a case in which people who read a statement were soon informed of the identity of the person it referred to. Should it be found that defendant published defamatory words when the explanation comes long after defendant made the statement? A more complex situation was presented in Hayward v. Thompson, [1982] Q.B. 47 (C.A.). Defendants published an article concerning an alleged murder

plot. It was said that police had been given the names of two persons "connected with" the matter, one of whom was a wealthy benefactor of the Liberal Party. These persons were not identified. A week later, defendants published an article which said that police wanted to question plaintiff, a wealthy supporter of the Liberal Party, in connection with the murder plot. Plaintiff brought a libel action over the two articles. The first article had been understood by some people to refer to plaintiff. The trial judge told the jury that they could look at the second article to determine whether the first article referred to plaintiff and that damages could be awarded on the basis that the second article identified him as the person referred to in the first. This was upheld on appeal. Cf. WJLA-TV v. Levin, 264 Va. 140, 564 S.E.2d 383 (2002) (news broadcast that named plaintiff and prior promotional advertising that did not considered together for purpose of establishing that plaintiff was person defamed); Baltinos v. Foreign Language Publications Pty. Ltd., (1986) 6 N.S.W.L.R. 85 (Sup. Ct.) (evening television program identified plaintiff; earlier in day, defendant's newspaper published article on unidentified "con-men" which recommended this program).

3. Is there publication when defamatory meaning is given to a statement only by extrinsic facts that are brought to the reader's or hearer's attention some time after the statement is made? In Grappelli v. Derek Block (Holdings) Ltd., [1981] 1 W.L.R. 822 (C.A.), defendants were concert promoters who booked concerts for plaintiffs, a musical group. Defendants, having to cancel some of the concerts because they were unauthorized, gave concert hall managers a false reason for the cancellations: that the principal musician was very ill, so ill he might never tour again. Two months later, advertisements for forthcoming concerts by the musicians were published. Plaintiffs claimed that defendants' statements, in conjunction with the announcements of later concerts, carried the innuendo that plaintiffs pretended the illness as an excuse to cancel concerts. The court held that inferences put on statements by facts learned later could not make the statements defamatory, when not defamatory at the time they were made.

4. Another time problem in the law of defamation is that presented by defamatory wills. If the testator writes a libellous will but shows it to no one before his death, or makes no publication other than a privileged one to his attorney, can his estate be held liable when the will is published after his death? Is the executor, who is obligated to present the will for probate, subject to suit? What about the attorney who drafts a will with libellous statements? Even if in principle there is a cause of action, the privilege for statements made in the course of a judicial proceeding might attach. See Annot., Libel by Will, 21 A.L.R.3d 754 (1968); Eldredge, Law of Defamation 225–230 (1978); Whitcombe, Defamation by Will: Theories and Liabilities, 27 John Marshall L. Rev. 749 (1994).

Vizetelly v. Mudie's Select Library, Ltd.
Court of Appeal
[1900] 2 Q.B. 170

The plaintiff had been employed by Mr. Gordon Bennett of the *New York Herald* to proceed as the head of an expedition to Africa to search for Sir H. Stanley, who was then engaged in an expedition for the rescue of Emin Pasha, and to furnish news to the *New York Herald* on the subject. He met Stanley and Emin Pasha in Africa on their way down to the coast.... Messrs. Archibald Constable & Co., a well-known firm of publishers, in October, 1898, published in this country a book called "Emin Pasha: his Life and Work," [which falsely defamed the plaintiff]. The plaintiff on becoming aware of the libel brought an action for libel against Messrs. Constable & Co., which was settled by their paying 100*l.* damages, apologizing, and undertaking to withdraw the libel from circulation. In the issue of the *Publishers' Circular*, a recognised medium for trade advertisements of the kind, for November 12, 1898, a notice was inserted to the effect that Messrs. Archibald Constable & Co. requested that all copies of vol. i. of "The Life and Work of Emin Pasha" might be returned to them immediately, as they wished to cancel a page, and insert another one in its place, and stating that they would of course defray the carriage both ways, if desired. A similar notice was inserted on the same date in the *Athenaeum* newspaper, a well-known medium of communication among literary people. In March, 1899, it came to the plaintiff's knowledge that the defendants [proprietors of a circulating library with a very extensive business] were lending copies of the work as originally published to subscribers, and also selling surplus copies of the same, and he thereupon commenced the action against them. It appeared that none of those engaged in the conduct of the defendants' business had seen the before-mentioned notices in the *Publishers' Circular* and *Athenaeum*, though the defendants took in those papers. Mr. A. O. Mudie, one of the defendants' two managing directors, who was called as a witness for the defendants, gave evidence to the effect that the defendants did not know when they circulated and sold the book in question that it contained the passage complained of. He stated that the books which they circulated were so numerous that it was impossible in the ordinary course of business to have them all read, and that they were guided in their selection of books by the reputation of the publishers, and the demand for the books. He said in cross-examination that there was no one else in the establishment besides himself and his co-director who exercised any kind of supervision over the books; that they did not keep a reader or anything of that sort; that they had had books on one or two occasions which contained libels; that that would occur from time to time; that they had had no action brought against them for libel before the present action; and that it was cheaper for them to run an occasional risk of an action than to have a reader. The learned judge in summing up in substance directed the jury to consider whether, having regard to the above-mentioned evidence, the defendants had used due care in the management of their business. The jury found a verdict for the plaintiff, damages 100*l.*

The defendants applied for judgment or a new trial....

ROMER L.J. The law of libel is in some respects a very hard one. In the remarks which I am about to make I propose to deal only with communications which are not privileged. For many years it has been well settled law that a man who publishes a libel is liable to an action, although he is really innocent in the matter, and guilty of no negligence. That rule has been so long established as to be incapable of being altered or modified, and the Courts, in endeavouring to mitigate the hardship resulting from it in many cases, have only been able to do so by holding that, under the circumstances of cases before them, there had been no publication of the libel by the defendant. The result, in my opinion, has been that the decisions on the subject have not been altogether logical or satisfactory on principle. The decisions in some of the earlier cases with which the Courts had to deal are easy to understand. Those were cases in which mere carriers of documents containing libels, who had nothing to do with and were ignorant of the contents of what they carried, have been held not to have published libels. Then we have the case of *Emmens v. Pottle* [16 Q.B.D. 354] in which vendors of newspapers in the ordinary course of their business sold a newspaper which contained a libel. It was clear that selling a document which contained a libel was primâ facie a publication of it, but the Court there held that there was no publication of the libel under the circumstances which appeared from the special findings of the jury, those findings being

(1.) that the defendants did not know that the newspapers at the time they sold them contained libels on the plaintiff; (2.) that it was not by negligence on the defendants' part that they did not know that there was any libel in the newspapers; and (3.) that the defendants did not know that the newspaper was of such a character that it was likely to contain libellous matter, nor ought they to have known so. Lord Esher M.R. in this Court was of opinion that, though the vendors of the newspapers, when they sold them, were primâ facie publishers of the libel, yet, when the special findings of the jury were looked at, the result was that there was no publication of the libel by the defendants. Bowen L.J. put his judgment on the ground that the vendors of the newspapers in that case were really only in the same position as an ordinary carrier of a work containing a libel. The decision in that case, in my opinion, worked substantial justice; but, speaking for myself, I cannot say that the way in which that result was arrived at appears to me altogether satisfactory; I do not think that the judgments very clearly indicate on what principle Courts ought to act in dealing with similar cases in future.... The result of the cases is I think that, as regards a person who is not the printer or the first or main publisher of a work which contains a libel, but has only taken, what I may call, a subordinate part in disseminating it, in considering whether there has been publication of it by him, the particular circumstances under which he disseminated the work must be considered. If he did it in the ordinary way of his business, the nature of the business and the way in which it was conducted must be looked at; and, if he succeeds in shewing (1.) that he was innocent of any knowledge of the libel contained in the work disseminated by him, (2.) that there was nothing in the work or the circumstances under which it came to him or was disseminated by him which ought to have led him to suppose that it contained a libel, and (3.) that, when the work was disseminated by him, it was not by any negligence on his part that he did not know that it contained the libel, then, although the dissemination of the work by him was primâ facie publication of it, he may nevertheless, on proof of the before-mentioned facts, be held not to have published it. But the onus of proving such facts lies on him, and the question of publication or non-publication is in such a case one for the jury. Applying this view of the law to the present case, it appears to me that the jury, looking at all the circumstances of the case, have in effect found that the defendants published the libel complained of, and therefore the defendants are liable, unless that verdict is disturbed. Looking at the special circumstances of the case which were brought to the attention of the jury, I cannot say that they could not reasonably find as they did.... For these reasons I think the application must be dismissed.

[A.L. Smith and Vaughan Williams, L.JJ., delivered concurring opinions.]

Notes

1. The *Vizetelly* case is a leading authority on the liability of "secondary publishers"—those who deliver or transmit defamatory material produced by other persons. Should this case be followed in all respects? Secondary publishers are considered not to have published the defamation when they neither knew nor had reason to know of it. "Reason to know" might be found in defendant's knowledge of the source of the material, such as an author or journal with a history of libel. See Dworkin v. Hustler Magazine, Inc., 611 F. Supp. 781 (D. Wyo. 1985); Goldsmith v. Sperrings Ltd., [1977] 1 W.L.R. 478 (C.A.). Typical secondary publishers (or "secondary distributors") are carriers, libraries and vendors of newspapers, magazines, books and films. A printer of matter written by others is a "primary," not secondary, publisher. See generally Restatement (Second) of Torts § 581 (1977);

Harper, James & Gray, Law of Torts § 5.18, at 171–172 (3d ed. 2006); Winfield & Jolowicz, Tort 337–339 (14th ed. 1994).

2. A broadcast station or network can claim the protection accorded a secondary publisher when its facilities are leased to others. See Kelly v. Hoffman, 137 N.J.L. 695, 61 A.2d 143 (1948); Summit Hotel Co. v. National Broadcasting Co., 336 Pa. 182, 8 A.2d 302 (1939). Otherwise, the originator of the broadcast is treated as a primary publisher. Should a station that carries a broadcast coming from a network or another station be regarded as a primary publisher or secondary publisher? Decisions on the question are split. Statutes in numerous states grant stations what is in effect the protection of a secondary publisher: no liability for defamatory statements when the station neither knew of them nor failed to exercise reasonable care to prevent their broadcast. Legislation applies the same rule to statements made during broadcasts originating with the station by persons other than station employees. See Fleming, Law of Torts 542–543 (8th ed. 1992); Harper, James & Gray, Law of Torts § 5.18, at 175–178 (3d ed. 2006); Leflar, Radio and TV Defamation: "Fault" Or Strict Liability?, 15 Ohio St. L.J. 252 (1954).

Lunney v. Prodigy Services Company

Supreme Court of New York, Appellate Division
250 A.D.2d 230, 683 N.Y.S.2d 557 (1998), aff'd,
94 N.Y.2d 242, 701 N.Y.S.2d 684, 723 N.E.2d 539 (1999),
cert. denied, 529 U.S. 1098 (2000)

BRACKEN, J.P.

[An imposter opened a number of accounts with Prodigy, an Internet service provider, under the name of Alexander or Alex Lunney. The imposter then sent, under Lunney's name, a very vulgar and threatening e-mail message to a Boy Scout leader in the area where the real Alexander Lunney—a teenager who was a member of the Boy Scouts—resided. The subject-line of the message was "How I'm Gonna' Kill U." The recipient of the message alerted the police, who commenced an investigation. Prodigy sent Lunney a notice that it was terminating his account because of the transmission of obscene, abusive and threatening material. When Lunney advised Prodigy that he had never subscribed to Prodigy's service and that anyone using his name had done so fraudulently, Prodigy apologized and closed all the Alexander Lunney accounts. Investigation revealed that the imposter had also posted two vulgar messages in Lunney's name on a Prodigy electronic bulletin board. Lunney brought suit against Prodigy, contending that the messages defamed him by portraying him as the author of the offensive contents and that Prodigy was responsible for publication of the messages.*]

The rule of common law, as it originally developed in New York, was that, "[h]e who furnishes the means of convenient circulation, knowing, or having reasonable cause to believe, that it is to be used for that purpose, if it is in fact so used, is guilty of aiding in the publication and becomes the instrument of the libeler" (*Youmans v. Smith*, 153 N.Y. 214, 219, 47 N.E. 265).... Subsequent authority makes it clear beyond dispute, however, that no potential for such liability exists, unless the defendant in question has some "editorial or at least participatory function" in connection with the dissemination of the defamatory material (*Anderson v. New York Tel.*, 35 N.Y.2d 746, 750, 361 N.Y.S.2d 913, 320 N.E.2d 647 [concurring opinion of Gabrielli, J.])....

---

* This statement of facts is taken in part from the Court of Appeals' opinion. [Ed.]

The key case on this point (*Anderson*) was decided well before the advent of personal computers. However, the legal analysis adopted by the Court of Appeals in that case is as persuasive in the case of written text sent over telephone lines, which is the essential nature of "e-mail" and bulletin board postings, as it was in the case of spoken or recorded messages sent over telephone lines, which is the type of communication the *Anderson* case involved.

[*Anderson*] involved the lessee of telephone equipment which enabled him to play, to whomever happened to call either of two telephone numbers, a recorded message containing accusations of misconduct against the plaintiff, the Presiding Bishop of the Church of God in Christ of Western New York. The defendant also had access to a weekly radio program, which he exploited in order to encourage the public to call the two phone numbers containing the scurrilous message.... The Bishop, understandably upset, sued the telephone company. The Court of Appeals, adopting the opinion of the dissenter in the Appellate Division, held that the Bishop had no cause of action.

... [The] telephone company had actually been notified of the improper use to which its equipment was being put. In fact, company employees dialed the numbers and actually listened to the defamatory messages. Nevertheless, the telephone company did nothing to stop the messages, despite the Bishop's repeated requests.

In *Anderson*, the opinion of Justice Witmer, adopted by the Court of Appeals, initially drew a distinction between telegraph companies, which may be considered to have published the messages submitted to them by telegraph senders, on the one hand, and telephone companies, which may not properly be considered publishers, on the other. As stated in Justice Witmer's opinion, a telegraph is sent only "through the direct participation of the agents of the telegraph company" whereas, "[i]n the case of a modern-day *telephone* call ... the caller communicates directly with the listener over the facilities of the telephone company, with no publication by the company itself." The evidence in the present record leads to the conclusion that the role played by Prodigy in connection with the offensive messages sent under the plaintiff's name is, by far, more analogous to that of a telephone company than to that of a telegraph company. Thus, pursuant to the first holding of the Court of Appeals in *Anderson*, we conclude that Prodigy cannot be considered a publisher.

It may be true that Prodigy has devised a method by which certain epithets are automatically excluded from the messages sent via its network. But application of any unintelligent automated word-exclusion program of this type cannot be equated with editorial control. A highly offensive message can be composed in the most impeccable prose, just as the words often thought of as offensive can be used affectionately or humorously in certain contexts. Intelligent editorial control involves the use of judgment, and no computer program has such a capacity. There is certainly no evidence in this record that a human being in the employ of the defendant approved of the transmission of the e-mail or bulletin board messages complained of by the plaintiff. This being the case, Prodigy cannot be considered a publisher of that material.

The *Anderson* case is also authority for the proposition that even if Prodigy could be considered a publisher, it is protected by a qualified privilege.... This statement was based on the qualified immunity which, at common law, had been accorded to telegraph companies which, due to their employees' participation in the transmission of messages, were considered "publishers" with respect to potential liability based on defamation.

The common law has always recognized a qualified privilege for telegraph companies that transmit defamatory messages submitted by their customers pursuant to which the defendant can be held liable only upon a showing of actual malice, that is, knowledge of the falsity of the message, a showing which a plaintiff will rarely if ever be able to make. In *Anderson*, the Court extended that privilege to the telephone company as well.

We are aware, of course, of the decision in *Stratton Oakmont, Inc. v. Prodigy Services Co.* [23 Media L. Rptr. 1794 (N.Y. Sup. Ct. 1995)]. In that case, the Supreme Court held that Prodigy had been shown to have exercised editorial control over a financial bulletin board to the extent that it could be considered the publisher of a defamatory posting, which contained defamatory statements concerning the plaintiff, and which had been placed on the bulletin board by a third party. For several reasons, *Stratton Oakmont* is not controlling here.

First, it is obvious that the *Stratton Oakmont* rationale would apply, if at all, only to the portion of the plaintiff's amended complaint which related to the bulletin board postings. Whatever editorial control over such postings might have been possible, it is clear from the present record that a service provider such as Prodigy cannot screen all of the e-mail sent by its subscribers.

Second, the evidence in the record in *Stratton Oakmont* describes the efforts at editorial control which, according to the evidence in the present record, Prodigy in fact abandoned in January 1994, prior to the events underlying the present complaint. Thus, the decision in *Stratton Oakmont* was made in an entirely different factual context.

Third, the *Anderson* decision, discussed at length above, states that a telecommunications company can be considered a publisher of those messages in whose transmission it actually participates. It does not hold that such a company, if it were to participate in the formulation of the text of one or two messages, would thereupon expose itself to liability based on the text contained in the millions of other messages in whose transmission it did not participate. It is, in other words, irrelevant if Prodigy, in the case at hand, is shown to have exercised the power to exclude certain vulgarities from the text of certain messages. What matters is that there is no proof that any such control was exercised in connection with the transmission of the messages complained of by the plaintiff.

Fourth, as outlined above, the *Anderson* case establishes the rule that even a telecommunications company which in some measure participates in the transmission of a libelous message cannot be held liable unless it knew that the message was in fact libelous, a circumstance which will rarely, if ever, be proved. The common law privilege which benefits telegraph companies must apply to internet service providers as well. E-mail is, in substance, nothing but an updated version of the telegraph.

Our disagreement with the holding in *Stratton Oakmont* is not only compelled by our understanding of the holding of the Court of Appeals in *Anderson*, but is also dictated by at least one simple consideration of fairness. The *Stratton Oakmont* court itself acknowledged that a purely passive on-line service provider would face no liability based on the transmission of defamatory material through its services. Liability was imposed on Prodigy in that case solely because Prodigy had attempted, to some extent, to control the text of the various messages placed on its bulletin boards. The *Stratton Oakmont* holding "appear[s] to encourage systems operators to ignore the content of their bulletin boards in order to attain 'distributor' status" (Sanford, *Libel and Privacy*, 2d ed § 8.4, page 430.19 [1998 Supp.]). Thus, in *Stratton Oakmont* Prodigy was punished for allegedly performing in an inadequate way the very conduct (exercise of editorial control) which, initially, it had no legal duty to perform at all. The rule of law announced in *Stratton Oakmont* discourages the very conduct which the plaintiff in *Stratton Oakmont* argued should be encouraged....

... In *Cubby, Inc. v. CompuServe*, 776 F. Supp. 135 [S.D.N.Y. 1991], the court held that the defendant, another on-line service provider, was not liable for the posting of a defamatory notice on an electronic bulletin board. The court stated, "CompuServe has no more editorial control over such a publication than does a public library, book store, or newsstand, and it would be no more feasible for CompuServe to examine every publication it carries for potentially defamatory statements than it would be for any other distributor to do so."

Our application of the common-law qualified privilege recognized in *Anderson* also renders the outcome in this case in complete harmony with current Federal statutory law contained in the Communications Decency Act (47 USC § 230 *et seq.*). We need not decide what is thus the essentially academic question of whether this Federal statute would apply to all or part of the allegations of the plaintiff's amended complaint....

[Orders denying defendant's motions for summary judgment reversed.]

Notes

1. In affirming the decision, the New York Court of Appeals agreed that Prodigy was not a publisher of the e-mail or bulletin board messages in this case and that it was entitled to the common law qualified privileges accorded to telephone and telegraph companies. However, the court left open the possibility that the role assumed by the operator of an electronic bulletin board in a different case would qualify it as a publisher. See generally Annot., Liability of Internet Service Provider for Internet or E-Mail Defamation, 84 A.L.R.5th 169 (2000). On the liability of telephone and telegraph companies for transmitting defamatory messages, see Annot., Liability of Telegraph or Telephone Company for Transmitting or Permitting Transmission of Libelous or Slanderous Messages, 91 A.L.R.3d 1015 (1979); Eldredge, Law of Defamation 233–236 (1978). One of the rationales for recognizing a privilege for telegraph companies was that without such a privilege, messages would be delayed while they were screened for defamatory meanings and messages that the sender was privileged to send would be refused transmission. See O'Brien v. Western Union Telegraph Co., 113 F.2d 539 (1st Cir. 1940).

2. In Godfrey v. Demon Internet Ltd., [2001] Q.B. 201, someone in the United States had posted an obscene article to an electronic newsgroup, whose contents were available to Internet users throughout the world. The posting purported to come from plaintiff, who was a university lecturer in England, and gave his e-mail address. A few days later, plaintiff notified defendant, an Internet service provider in England, that the posting was a forgery and requested its removal from defendant's news server. Defendant could have removed the posting but no action was taken, so it remained available to be read on the news server for the usual two-week period. The court concluded that whenever a subscriber to defendant's service accessed a newsgroup stored on defendant's news server and saw a defamatory posting in it, there was a publication of the posting by defendant to the subscriber. Defendant was not merely the owner of an electronic device through which postings were transmitted. Discussing the American cases, the court stated that Prodigy would clearly have been the publisher of the messages in the *Lunney* case under English common law. *Anderson* was distinguishable because Demon Internet did not play a merely passive role. It chose to receive, store, make available and obliterate (after a fortnight) postings in the particular newsgroup. The court in a later English case decided that Internet service providers which were a "passive medium of communication" for transmission of defamatory messages from their authors, like the telephone company in *Anderson*, were not publishers. Bunt v. Tilley, [2007] 1 W.L.R. 1243 (Q.B.D.).

3. The Communications Decency Act, mentioned at the end of the principal case, was enacted in 1996. 47 U.S.C. §230(c), headed "Protection for 'good samaritan' blocking and screening of offensive material," provides that "No provider or user of an interactive computer service shall be treated as the publisher or speaker of any information provided by another information content provider." "Information content provider" is defined as "any person or entity that is responsible, in whole or in part, for the creation or development of information provided through the Internet or any other interactive computer service." 47 U.S.C. §230(f)(3). This legislation has been interpreted in a number of cases to immunize computer service providers from tort liability for transmitting or failing to remove or screen material posted by a third party, even when the provider had been notified of the presence of the material and its defamatory nature. See Zeran v. America Online, Inc., 129 F.3d 327 (4th Cir. 1997), cert. denied, 524 U.S. 937 (1998) (offensive messages with plaintiff's name and telephone number, posted on defendant's electronic bulletin board, resulting in numerous abusive and threatening calls to plaintiff); Blumenthal v. Drudge, 992 F. Supp. 44 (D.D.C. 1998) (defamatory material in gossip column available to computer service's subscribers, under contract between service and column's author, as well as e-mail subscribers and web site users; contract gave computer service right to remove or direct author to remove material it determined to be violation of its terms of service); Collins v. Purdue University, 703 F. Supp. 2d 862 (N.D. Ill. 2010) (vitriolic statements in newspaper publisher's web site that allowed posting of readers' comments on newspaper articles). Cf. Doe v. America Online, Inc., 783 So. 2d 1010 (Fla. 2001), cert. denied, 534 U.S. 891 (2001) (use of computer service to sell pornographic photographs and videotapes of minor). Under this interpretation, a computer service does not expose itself to liability by attempting to exercise some control over the content of bulletin board and other messages. This construction of the statute also may be said to promote Internet communication and discourage censorship by protecting computer service providers from tort claims, especially claims alleging publication after the provider was notified that defamatory material was being posted. Barrett v. Rosenthal, 40 Cal. 4th 33, 51 Cal. Rptr. 3d 55, 146 P.3d 510 (2006), extended the statutory immunity for "users" of a computer service to an individual who posted a copy of a defamatory article on an Internet news group web page.

4. A person's repetition of someone else's defamatory statement is a publication of the defamation for which the repeater can be liable. Simply referring to an article in which plaintiff was defamed is not publication of the defamation, at least without calling attention to the defamatory parts. MacFadden v. Anthony, 117 N.Y.S.2d 520 (Sup. Ct. 1952); Carter v. British Columbia Federation of Foster Parents Association, [2005] 10 W.W.R. 427, (2005) 257 D.L.R.4th 133 (B.C.C.A.). What if an article on defamation law cites a defamatory item in a footnote? Does the creator of an Internet web page with hyperlinks to a defamatory article publish the defamation? In Crookes v. Newton, [2011] 3 S.C.R. 269, (2011) 337 D.L.R.4th 1, a majority of the Supreme Court of Canada decided that a hyperlink is not a publication of the material linked to. The decision was influenced by concern that treating a hyperlink as a publication would chill the functioning of the Internet. A concurring opinion would find publication when there was adoption or endorsement of the specific content linked to. Another opinion would apply the test of whether defendant deliberately made the defamatory information readily available in a comprehensible form. Cf. Metropolitan International Schools Ltd. v. Designtechnica Corp., [2011] 1 W.L.R. 1743 (Q.B.D.), holding that the operator of an Internet search engine does not publish the "snippets" of an article appearing with a link to the article when a search is made.

5. Does the proprietor of a business "publish" defamatory graffiti written on the wall of the establishment's building? It has been held that there is publication if the propri-

etor has knowledge of the writing and allows it to remain after a reasonable opportunity to remove it. Hellar v. Bianco, 111 Cal. App. 2d 424, 244 P.2d 757 (1952) (writings implicating plaintiff's chastity on wall of tavern's restroom; knowledge of bartender imputable to tavern operators). See also Byrne v. Deane, [1937] 1 K.B. 818 (C.A.) (proprietors and secretary of golf club were, by allowing anonymous poem to remain on wall of club, taking part in publication of poem). But see Scott v. Hull, 22 Ohio App. 2d 141, 259 N.E.2d 160 (1970) (failure of building owner, or agent who had charge of building maintenance, to remove defamatory graffiti from exterior wall of building after notice and demand for removal not actionable; liability required some positive act). Tacket v. General Motors Corp., 836 F.2d 1042 (7th Cir. 1987), applied the criterion of whether readers would infer from the writing's presence that defendant adopted or acquiesced in it. See generally Annot., Liability for Permitting Walls or Other Portions of Place of Public Resort to Be Occupied with Matter Defamatory of Plaintiff, 28 A.L.R.2d 1454 (1953); Eldredge, Law of Defamation 221–225 (1978).

6. Should the original publisher of defamation be liable for the damage caused by repetition of the defamatory matter by other persons? Formerly, a defendant was held liable only for his own publication and that of his agents. See Maytag v. Cummins, 260 F. 74 (8th Cir. 1919) (presumed that slander will not be repeated; defendant ordinarily not responsible for voluntarily repetition not authorized by defendant); Hastings v. Stetson, 126 Mass. 329 (1879). More recent authority adopts the view that one can be held liable for damage due to repetition that can reasonably be anticipated. See Luster v. Retail Credit Co., 575 F.2d 609 (8th Cir. 1978) (libel); Sawyer v. Gilmer's, Inc., 189 N.C. 7, 126 S.E. 183 (1925) (slander); McManus v. Beckham, [2002] 1 W.L.R. 2982 (C.A.) (harm from extensive media reportage of defamatory statement made by prominent celebrity when in plaintiffs' shop). Note the relationship between this question and the special damage requirement, pp. 536–539, supra. If defendant is not responsible for harm caused by repetition, that harm cannot fulfill the special damage requirement. See generally Annot., Liability of Publisher of Defamatory Statement for Its Repetition or Republication by Others, 96 A.L.R.2d 373 (1964); Eldredge, Law of Defamation 239–242 (1978).

Traditional Cat Association, Inc. v. Gilbreath
California Court of Appeal
118 Cal. App. 4th 392, 13 Cal. Rptr. 3d 353 (2004)

BENKE, Acting P.J....

[Plaintiff Fineran was president of the Traditional Cat Association (TCA). As a result of a dispute with other officers and directors concerning her leadership of the association, Fineran established another organization, The Traditional Cat Association, Inc. (TTCA). On behalf of TTCA, Fineran commenced a series of lawsuits against TCA and its officers. In 1998 one of the TCA officers created a web site on the Internet, which purported to report on the litigation. The web site was highly critical of Fineran and TTCA. On May 22, 2002, Fineran and TTCA commenced this action for defamation. Defendants moved to strike the action on the basis of California's one-year statute of limitations for defamation actions. The web site was still operating when the suit was filed, but it had not been altered within the year prior to the suit. Defendants appealed from the trial court's denial of the motion.]

... Plaintiff's defamation claim is governed by the single-publication rule.

In *Shively v. Bozanich* (2003) 31 Cal. 4th 1230, 7 Cal. Rptr. 3d 576, 80 P.3d 676, the court recently set forth the history and rationale of the single-publication rule. "Under the common law as it existed in the 19th century and early part of the 20th century, the principle that each communication of a defamatory remark to a new audience constitutes a separate 'publication,' giving rise to a separate cause of action, led to the conclusion that each sale or delivery of a copy of a newspaper or book containing a defamation also constitutes a separate publication of the defamation to a new audience, giving rise to a separate cause of action for defamation. This conclusion had the potential to subject the publishers of books and newspapers to lawsuits stating hundreds, thousands, or even millions of causes of action for a single issue of a periodical or edition of a book. This conclusion also had the potential to disturb the repose that the statute of limitations ordinarily would afford, because a new publication of the defamation could occur if a copy of the newspaper or book were preserved for many years and then came into the hands of a new reader who had not discovered it previously. The statute of limitations could be tolled indefinitely, perhaps forever, under this approach.

"The difficulties created by the early common law rule are illustrated in a 19th-century English case that concluded a plaintiff could bring an action seeking redress for libel against a publisher based upon an allegedly defamatory remark contained in a newspaper issued 17 years prior to the plaintiff's discovery of the defamation, on the theory that the sale to the plaintiff of the long-forgotten copy of the newspaper constituted a new publication, starting anew the running of the period of limitations. (*The Duke of Brunswick v. Harmer* (Q.B. 1849) 117 Eng. Rep. 75). Despite the burdens created by the staleness and potential volume of the claims thus permitted, many American courts, and the reporters of the first Restatement of Torts, nonetheless adhered to the rule applied by the English court in the *Duke of Brunswick* case.

"Ultimately, many American courts began to reconsider the common law rule exemplified in the *Duke of Brunswick* case. These courts recognized that the advent of books and newspapers that were circulated among a mass readership threatened unending and potentially ruinous liability as well as overwhelming (and endless) litigation, as long as courts adhered to the rule that each sale of a copy of a newspaper or a book, regardless how long after original publication, constituted a new and separate publication. The early common law rule threatened a volume of litigation and a potential for indefinite tolling of the period of limitations that, these courts realized, would challenge the ability and willingness of publishers to report freely on the news and on matters of public interest....

"Seeking to avoid *both* the multiplicity and the staleness of claims permitted by the rule applied in the *Duke of Brunswick* case, courts fashioned what became known as the single-publication rule, holding that, for any single edition of a newspaper or book, there was but a single potential action for a defamatory statement contained in the newspaper or book, no matter how many copies of the newspaper or the book were distributed. (See, e.g., *Gregoire v. G.P. Putnam's Sons, supra,* 298 N.Y. 119, 81 N.E.2d 45)....

"Under the single-publication rule, with respect to the statute of limitations, publication generally is said to occur on the 'first general distribution of the publication to the public.' Accrual at that point is believed to provide adequate protection to potential plaintiffs, especially in view of the qualification that repetition of the defamatory statement in a *new edition* of a book or newspaper constitutes a new publication of the defamation that may give rise to a new cause of action, with a new accrual date. Under this rule, the cause of action accrues and the period of limitations commences, regardless of when the plaintiff secured a copy or became aware of the publication.

"The single-publication rule largely had been codified in the Uniform Single Publication Act, which has been adopted in many states, including California. (Civ. Code, § 3425.3)[5]...."

In *Shively* the plaintiff argued that notwithstanding the single-publication rule and its premises, the statute of limitations on her claim should have been tolled until she discovered the publication. In rejecting this argument, the court in *Shively* stated: "As is evident, application of the discovery rule to statements contained in books and newspapers would undermine the single-publication rule and reinstate the indefinite tolling of the statute of limitations intended to be cured by the adoption of the single-publication rule. If we were to recognize delayed accrual of a cause of action based upon the allegedly defamatory statement contained in the book, ... on the basis that plaintiff did not happen to come across the statement until some time after the book was first generally distributed to the public, we would be adopting a rule subjecting publishers and authors to potential liability during the entire period in which a single copy of the book or newspaper might exist and fall into the hands of the subject of a defamatory remark...."

The parties have not cited any California authority, and we have found none, which considers whether and how the single-publication rule applies when, as here, an alleged defamatory statement has been made on an Internet Web site. However, the issue was recently discussed by the New York Court of Appeals in *Firth v. State* (Ct. App. 2002) 98 N.Y.2d 365, 747 N.Y.S.2d 69, 775 N.E.2d 463. In *Firth v. State* the court found that the single-publication rule applies to [Internet] publishers. The court stated: "Claimant argues that the single-publication rule should not be applied verbatim to defamatory publications posted on the Internet in light of significant differences between Internet publications and traditional mass media. Instead, claimant maintains that because a Web site may be altered at any time by its publisher or owner and because publications on the Internet are available only to those who seek them, each 'hit' or viewing of the report should be considered a new publication that retriggers the statute of limitations. We disagree.... [¶] The policies impelling the original adoption of the single-publication rule supports its application to the posting of the Inspector General's report regarding claimant on the State's Web site. Communications accessible over a public Web site resemble those contained in traditional mass media, only on a far grander scale. Those policies are even more cogent when considered in connection with the exponential growth of the instantaneous, worldwide ability to communicate through the Internet.... Communications posted on Web sites may be viewed by thousands, if not millions, over an expansive geographic area for an indefinite period of time. Thus, a multiple publication rule would implicate an even greater potential for endless retriggering of the statute of limitations, multiplicity of suits and harassment of defendants. Inevitably, there would be a serious inhibitory effect on the open, pervasive dissemination of information and ideas over the Internet, which is, of course, its greatest beneficial promise."

We find the reasoning of the court in *Firth v. State* persuasive. As the court in *Firth v. State* noted, the need to protect Web publishers from almost perpetual liability for statements they make available to the hundreds of millions of people who have access to the Internet is greater even than the need to protect the publishers of conventional hard copy newspapers, magazines and books. Importantly, the interests in free expression, which the

---

5. That section provides: "No person shall have more than one cause of action for damages for libel or slander or invasion of privacy or any other tort founded upon any single publication or exhibition or utterance, such as any one issue of a newspaper or book or magazine or any one presentation to an audience or any one broadcast over radio or television or any one exhibition of a motion picture. Recovery in any action shall include all damages for any such tort suffered by the plaintiff in all jurisdictions."

court in *Firth v. State* found were worthy of protection by application of the single-publication rule to Web pages, are the very same interests which the court in *Shively v. Bozanich* relied upon in rejecting the notion the single-publication rule should be subject to any discovery exception....

Thus for purposes of determining the motion to strike, plaintiffs' cause of action for defamation arose no later than May 21, 2001, and had expired on May 22, 2002, when plaintiffs filed their complaint. Because the defamation claim was barred as a matter of law, it should have been stricken.

Order reversed with directions that plaintiffs' defamation cause of action be stricken....

Notes

1. In many states, the "single publication" rule has supplanted the common law rule that each delivery of a copy is a publication. A principal function of the single publication rule is that addressed in the principal case: to have the statute of limitations run from defendant's original publication of the defamatory material, not from the latest communication or delivery of a copy. Exactly when does the statutory period begin? See Annot., What Constitutes "Publication" of Libel in Order to Start Running of Period of Limitations, 42 A.L.R.3d 807 (1972). The rule also helps to identify the place where publication occurred, which is important for jurisdiction, venue and choice of law. At a minimum, it implies that publication does not occur in a place simply because a copy or broadcast is received there. Another function of the rule is to require, by providing only one cause of action, that only one suit be brought against a person for publication of the same defamatory material. However, repeated presentations of films, broadcasts and theatrical productions are multiple publications, and the single publication rule does not exclude separate suits against all persons involved in the distribution of copies. See Restatement (Second) of Torts § 577A (1977); Eldredge, Law of Defamation 209–213 (1978); Hanson, Libel and Related Torts ¶¶ 74–76 (1969).

2. The single publication rule limits plaintiff to one action against defendant for each "edition" of a book, newspaper or journal. Is there one edition or two when a libellous article is included in both the morning and afternoon editions of the same newspaper? Both the early and late editions (in which only a few pages are different)? Compare Cox Enterprises, Inc. v. Gilreath, 142 Ga. App. 297, 235 S.E.2d 633 (1977) (multiple publications), with Belli v. Roberts Brothers Furs, 240 Cal. App. 2d 284, 49 Cal. Rptr. 625 (1966) (single publication; statute used "issue" in lieu of "edition"). If a magazine's editorial content is the same everywhere in the United States but the advertising is different in various regions, are there multiple editions? What about a book that is reprinted, perhaps with correction of errors? See Wheeler v. Dell Publishing Co., 300 F.2d 372 (7th Cir. 1962) (reprintings separate editions). A book published in both hardcover and paperback? See Rinaldi v. Viking Penguin, Inc., 52 N.Y.2d 422, 438 N.Y.S.2d 496, 420 N.E.2d 377 (1981) (separate publications). A film released on DVD after it has been shown in theatres? See Nichols v. Moore, 334 F. Supp. 2d 944 (E.D. Mich. 2004) (different publication). There are separate "editions" when the same article is published in clearly different journals or books, even when emanating from the same company. See Graham v. Today's Spirit, 503 Pa. 52, 468 A.2d 454 (1983). See generally Annot., What Constitutes "Single Publication" Within Meaning of Single Publication Rule Affecting Action for Libel and Slander, Violation of Privacy, or Similar Torts, 41 A.L.R.4th 541 (1985).

3. What would have been the outcome of the *Traditional Cat Association* case if the text in defendants' web site had been changed in the year preceding the suit? In Firth v.

State, the court held that modification of a web site by the addition of material, unrelated to the defamation of plaintiff, did not create a separate publication. But it was later decided that moving the statements to a new Internet address was a republication to a new audience that commenced a new period for the statute of limitations to run. Firth v. State, 306 A.D.2d 666, 761 N.Y.S.2d 361 (2003). Compare Canatella v. Van De Kamp, 486 F.3d 1128 (9th Cir. 2007), cert. denied, 552 U.S. 1041 (2007) (putting same material on different page in same web site not a separate publication). Under other decisions, there is a new publication for statute of limitations purposes when there are modifications of or additions to a web site related to the substance of the defamatory material, but the single publication rule applies when the modifications or additions were unrelated to the defamation or did not alter the substance of it. Atkinson v. McLaughlin, 462 F. Supp. 2d 1038 (D.N.D. 2006); Churchill v. State, 378 N.J. Super. 471, 876 A.2d 311 (App. Div. 2005); Woodhull v. Meinel, 145 N.M. 533, 202 P.3d 126 (Ct. App. 2008), cert. denied, 145 N.M. 655, 203 P.3d 870 (2009).

4. In Loutchansky v. Times Newspapers Ltd., [2002] Q.B. 783 (C.A.), defendants argued that the "multiple publication" rule, which had continued to prevail in English law, should be abandoned, especially for publication on the Internet. They contended that liability under the multiple publication rule restricted freedom of expression and inhibited making archives of past publications available to the public; a new cause of action, with its own limitation period, should not arise whenever a web site containing defamatory materials was accessed. The court was not persuaded. Earlier, the multiple publication rule was maintained in a Montana case involving a magazine article. Lewis v. Reader's Digest Association, Inc., 162 Mont. 401, 512 P.2d 702 (1974). The court criticized the single publication rule for leaving the publisher free to "flood" the country with copies after the statute of limitations had run out on an initial distribution of a few copies. This is countered by the decision in Applewhite v. Memphis State University, 495 S.W.2d 190 (Tenn. 1973), that the statutory period begins to run when a copy is distributed in the county where plaintiff brings suit.

5. When a jurisdiction has applied the single publication rule in cases involving mass media, does it also apply to a non-media publication? In Musto v. Bell South Telecommunications Corp., 748 So. 2d 296 (Fla. App. 1999), cert. granted, 741 So. 2d 637 (Fla. App. 1999), review denied, 753 So. 2d 563 (Fla. 2000), a negative credit report concerning plaintiff was communicated by defendant's agent to several parties over a period of some years. Plaintiff did not learn about the report until he was denied credit, three years after the report was first communicated. The court held that the rule of "multiple publication" rather than single publication should be applied. Concern with the possibility of a multiplicity of lawsuits, which was an underlying rationale of applying the single publication rule to mass publications, was thought inapplicable to a credit defamation case, and a plaintiff (as in this case) might not learn of the dissemination of inaccurate credit reports until long after the first issuance. See also Hukic v. Aurora Loan Services, 588 F.3d 420 (7th Cir. 2009) (single publication rule inapplicable to consumer credit reports); Stephan v. Baylor Medical Center at Garland, 20 S.W.3d 880 (Tex. App. 2000) (single publication rule inapplicable to hospital's report on denial of doctor's application for staff privileges). The Supreme Court of California has applied the single publication rule to an item published in only a few copies but publicly available (as in a library), leaving open the possibility that the "discovery rule" would apply to defamatory material "hidden from view." Hebrew Academy of San Francisco v. Goldman, 42 Cal. 4th 883, 70 Cal. Rptr. 3d 178, 173 P.3d 1004 (2007).

6. Through the Internet, a defamatory statement can now be seen anywhere in the world. Whether a single publication rule applies to Internet communications, and whether

computer services are considered publishers of defamatory Internet communications (see pp. 552–557, supra), are two of the many factors bearing on whether a court in one of the nations to which a statement was transmitted will exercise jurisdiction over and sustain a defamation action. American companies and individuals are likely to find themselves defending actions in countries whose defamation laws do not include limitations of liability, especially the substantial limitations derived from constitutional law, that prevail in the United States—a problem highlighted by the High Court's decision in Dow Jones & Co. Inc. v. Gutnick, (2002) 210 C.L.R. 575, that an American media company could be sued in Australia for defamation of an Australian businessman in its web site. Federal legislation enacted in 2010 blocks enforcement in the United States of foreign defamation judgments when the defendant would not have been liable under domestic state defamation law and First Amendment rules. 28 U.S.C. §§ 4101 et seq.

Section 2. Common Law Defenses

A. Truth

Shihab v. Express-News Corporation
Texas Court of Civil Appeals
604 S.W.2d 204 (1980)

CADENA, Chief Justice.

[The magazine *Texas Monthly* published an article highly critical of the two newspapers published by the Express-News Corporation.] A portion of the article charged that "things are made to happen in order to create news" and quoted one reporter as saying that the *Express* and *News* "have both been using fabricated stuff ever since Murdoch took over." The magazine article continued: "The work of now-departed staffer, Aziz Shihab is most often cited in this connection. Shihab authored an expose alleging the Vietnamese refugees were operating a house of prostitution near Lackland Air Force Base. No one else was able to locate the house, and Shihab now describes the story as an exaggeration. He says the *News* sensationalized the story, wrote its own lead, and used his by-line over his protests. Shihab also was responsible for the story that a certain Saudi Arabian sheik wanted to buy the Alamo as a gift for his son. The story was carried worldwide, even drawing a declaration from Governor Dolph Briscoe that the famed landmark was not for sale. A search in Saudi Arabia, however, failed to turn up the sheik, and another search failed to turn up the son. Shihab, now a reporter in Dallas, says he found out about the whole thing from a Houston attorney who cannot be identified. *Express-News* publisher Kilpatrick has steadfastly refused comment."

[Kilpatrick, the publisher of Express-News Corporation's two newspapers, responded to the *Texas Monthly* article by writing a letter to *Texas Monthly* and 31 persons he described as "opinion leaders." It said: "Mr. Smith [author of the magazine article] accused a former reporter for the *News*, Ariz Shihab, of fabricating two stories and he inferred that I participated. Mr. Smith knew when he wrote that allegation that I had fired Mr. Shihab because I had lost confidence in him. This is clearly a distortion and Mr. Smith knew it when he made the charge." Shihab sued Kilpatrick and the Express-News Corporation for libelling him in the letter. The jury's "special issue" findings were that the letter, as it pertained to Shihab, was libellous; the letter was "substantially true"; and when writing the letter Kilpatrick "knew it was false or recklessly disregarded whether it was false or not." The trial court granted judgment for defendants. Shihab appealed.]

There is no evidence in the record suggesting that the two stories mentioned in the magazine article and referred to in the Kilpatrick letter were fabricated by plaintiff. The only evidence of fabrication concerns a third story which appeared in the News on August 1, 1975, with plaintiff's by-line and under the headline, "Gang rips off Lackland." This Lackland gang story was not connected with the story concerning the sale of the Alamo or with the story concerning the Vietnamese brothel.

Plaintiff contends that proof of the fabrication of a story other than the two stories mentioned in the magazine article and the Kilpatrick letter cannot be relied on by defendants as a defense to the libel action.

According to a respected commentator, "[s]pecific charges cannot be justified by showing the plaintiff's general bad character; and if the accusation is one of particular misconduct, such as stealing a watch from A, it is not enough to show a different offense, even though it be a more serious one, such as stealing a clock from A, or six watches from B." W. Prosser, Handbook of the Law of Torts § 116, at 798 (4th ed. 1971).

The American Law Institute, in Restatement (Second) of Torts § 581A, Comment f at 236–37 (1977), deals with the problem as follows: "It is not enough that the accused person is found to have engaged in some other substantially different kind of misconduct even though it is equally or more reprehensible. Thus a charge of burglary against another is not justified by a finding that he has committed a murder. However, many charges are made in terms that are accepted by their recipient in a popular rather than a technical sense. Thus a charge of theft may be reasonably interpreted as charging any form of criminally punishable misappropriation, and in its truth may be established by proving the commission of any act of larceny or embezzlement."

It cannot be said that the Texas cases support Dean Prosser's view....

In *Fort Worth Press Co. v. Davis*, 96 S.W.2d 416 (Tex. Civ. App.-Fort Worth 1936, writ ref'd), the substantial truth of a charge that plaintiff had wasted $80,000.00 of the taxpayers' money on a useless project was considered sufficiently established although the evidence showed that only $17,500.00 had been spent on the project. The Court reasoned that no more opprobrium attached to the waste of $80,000.00 [than] would be attached to the waste of $17,500.00.

Proof that plaintiff had been arrested for illegal possession of beer and wine is sufficient to establish the substantial truth of a statement that plaintiff had been arrested for illicit possession of tequila, whiskey, beer and wine. In reaching this conclusion the Court in *Lundberg v. Brownsville Herald Publishing Co.*, 66 S.W.2d 375 (Tex. Civ. App.-San Antonio 1933, no writ) reasoned that the "gist" of the accusation was that plaintiff had been arrested for illegal possession of intoxicants, and that the truth of that charge was established by proof of arrest for possession of wine and beer, since "it was just as much an offense to have the wine and beer as it would have been to have the tequila and whiskey."

In *Caller Times Publishing Co. v. Chandler*, 122 S.W.2d 249, 252 (Tex. Civ. App.-San Antonio 1938), *aff'd*, 134 Tex. 1, 130 S.W.2d 853 (1939), this Court held that proof that plaintiff had been indicted for conspiracy to burglarize a bank established the substantial truth of a statement that plaintiff had been indicted for conspiracy to rob a bank, because the two offenses, robbery and burglary, were of equal grade and plaintiff had shown no injury resulting from the use of "rob" rather than "burglarize." The result, perhaps, can be explained on the basis of the theory, adopted by the Restatement, that, to the ordinary person, the words "burglary" and "robbery" are synonymous, but neither the court of civil appeals nor the supreme court adopted this rationale....

The rule adopted by Dean Prosser can produce indefensible results. The two statements, "X is a murderer" and "X murdered A" produce the same result in the mind of the reader or listener. According to Prosser, proof that X murdered any person would establish proof of the charge, "X is a murderer." But in order to establish the truth of the statement that X murdered A, proof that X murdered B, or any person other than A, would not relieve the defendant of liability, nor would proof that X had murdered 100 persons benefit defendant if A was not included within the 100. The view of the Restatement is radically different, since it denies the availability of truth as a defense only where the misconduct is of a substantially different kind from the misconduct charged.

The critical test should be whether the defamation, as published, would affect the mind of the reader or listener in a different manner than would the misconduct proved. If the effect on the mind of the recipient would be the same, any variance between the misconduct charged and the misconduct proved should be disregarded. Under such a rule, proof that plaintiff had murdered B would justify the accusation that plaintiff had murdered A, at least in the absence of circumstances establishing a relation between plaintiff and A, which would, in the mind of the average person, brand the murder of A by plaintiff more reprehensible than plaintiff's murder of B. Such a rule would not operate to decrease the protection which the law affords to a person's reputation.

[The court concluded that the "gist" or "sting" of the accusation of fabricating the Vietnamese brothel and sale of the Alamo stories was the charge of fabrication and that these specific accusations were no more damaging to plaintiff's reputation than a simple charge of fabrication or a charge that he fabricated the story of a gang robbery at Lackland Air Force Base. The reference to the two stories did not substantially aggravate or give additional weight to the main charge of fabrication. There was sufficient evidence to support the conclusion that the Lackland gang story had been fabricated. Judgment for defendants was affirmed.]

Notes

1. Truth has long been a complete defense to a civil action for libel or slander, although historically it was not a defense to a prosecution for criminal libel. The defense is known as "justification." A defendant who pleads truth is said to "justify" the defamatory statement. The time seems past when an error in the amount of money plaintiff owed or misappropriated, or the place where plaintiff had illicit intercourse, excluded the defense of truth. Compare Swann v. Rary, 3 Blackf. 298 (Ind. 1833) (statement that plaintiff had stolen hogs not justified by theft of one hog); Green v. Minnes, (1892) 22 O.R. 177 (Q.B. Div.) (statement that plaintiff owed $59.35 not justified by evidence that she owed $24.33); and Sharpe v. Stephenson, 12 Ired. (34 N.C.) 348 (1851) (statement that plaintiff had intercourse with person at particular time and place not justified by proof that plaintiff had intercourse with same person at another time and place); with Putnam v. Browne, 162 Wis. 524, 155 N.W. 910 (1916) (charge of corrupt payment of $385 would be justified if actual amount was $185 or less); Gomba v. McLaughlin, 180 Colo. 232, 504 P.2d 337 (1972) (stated that plaintiff assaulted man at dog show in Cheyenne, Wyoming; in actuality, plaintiff assaulted man from Cheyenne at dog show in Colorado). But a court may still apply strictly the rule, stated in the next principal case, that "A plea of truth as justi-

fication must be as broad as the alleged libel and must establish the truth of the precise charge therein made."

2. The "substantial truth" standard, adopted in the principal case, departs to a limited extent from the rigidity of the older law. See Sack, Defamation: Libel, Slander, and Related Problems § 3.7 (4th ed. 2010); Smolla, Law of Defamation §§ 5:14–5:29 (2d ed. 1999). Consider whether the substantial truth test would change the results in cases where plaintiff was said to have stolen from one person but actually stole from another. Gardner v. Self, 15 Mo. 480 (1852). Where plaintiff was said to have committed adultery with one person but committed it with another, and to have committed rape when actually he attempted rape. Pallet v. Sargent, 36 N.H. 496 (1858). Where plaintiff was described as a convicted criminal when his conviction had been quashed. Howden v. "Truth" and "Sportsman" Ltd., (1937) 58 C.L.R. 416. Where plaintiff was said to be a whore and committed prostitution two months after defendant's statement. Beggarly v. Craft, 31 Ga. 309 (1860).

3. In Hovey v. Iowa State Daily Publication Board, Inc., 372 N.W.2d 253 (Iowa 1985), a newspaper reported that a man was charged with the rape of a bartender. Plaintiff sued on the basis that she was identifiable as the bartender and had not been raped, although she had been forced to perform oral sex. The court held that the newspaper was entitled to judgment because the newspaper article was substantially true regarding plaintiff. Is this correct? Would the result have been the same if the newspaper were sued by the assailant? Cf. Nanji v. National Geographic Society, 403 F. Supp. 2d 425 (D. Md. 2005) (defendant's article said plaintiff was sentenced for raping girl; not convicted for rape or sexual assault but evidence of this was a basis for conviction on different charges). If a libel action is brought because of a report that a person has been charged with a crime, or that a person has been convicted of a crime, what evidence is necessary to prove truth? See Fleming, Law of Torts 636–638 (10th ed. 2011).

4. Does defendant have the defense of truth when:

(a) A newspaper reports that plaintiff, aged fifteen, was charged with possession of marijuana. Under state law, because of plaintiff's age, he could not be charged with commission of a crime, only with delinquency (due to commission of an act that would be a crime if committed by an adult). Piracci v. Hearst Corp., 263 F. Supp. 511 (D. Md. 1966), aff'd, 371 F.2d 1016 (4th Cir. 1967).

(b) A Florida newspaper refers to plaintiff as a "convicted felon." Plaintiff has a misdemeanor conviction in Tennessee for an offense that is a felony in Florida. Bowe v. Palm Beach Newspapers, Inc., 8 Media L. Rptr. 2247 (Fla. Cir. Ct. 1982). What if plaintiff had a felony conviction but it was expunged? Cf. G.D. v. Kenny, 205 N.J. 275, 15 A.3d 300 (2011).

(c) It is reported that "thousands of dollars in jewelry" were found when police raided plaintiff's home and arrested him for burglary and receiving stolen goods. Plaintiff's evidence is that the items found were worth about $500. Turnbull v. Herald Co., 459 S.W.2d 516 (Mo. App. 1970).

(d) A television station reports that plaintiff shot and killed a man outside the victim's home. The shooting actually occurred outside plaintiff's home. Eason v. Federal Broadcasting Co., 697 So. 2d 435 (Miss. 1997).

(e) Plaintiff, a dancer at a lounge, is arrested by a police officer who observed her dancing "topless." A newspaper states that she pled guilty to "nude dancing." In fact, plaintiff was arrested for and pled guilty to dancing without the license required of lounge dancers by a city ordinance. Griffin v. Kentucky Post, 10 Media L. Rptr. 1159 (Ky. Cir. Ct. 1983).

(f) After her insurance company, "Multiplan," refuses to pay a claim for items stolen from her car, defendant paints her car with the legend, "Multiplan won't pay my claim; will they pay yours?" Multiplan Insurance Brokers (Pty.) Ltd. v. Van Blerk, 1985 (3) S.A. 164 (D).

(g) Defendant accuses a public official of squandering a large sum of public money for printing a political slogan on stationery. Defendant cannot prove that charge but may prove that the official, while in the same office, irresponsibly squandered greater sums for different expenditures. Bookbinder v. Tebbit, [1989] 1 W.L.R. 640 (C.A.).

(h) Defendant calls plaintiff a "libellous journalist." Judgment had been given against plaintiff in a libel case. Wakley v. Cooke, (1849) 4 Exch. 511, 154 Eng. Rep. 1316, 13 J.P. 749, 19 L.J. Ex. 91, 14 L.T.O.S. 158 (Ex.). Compare Restatement (Second) § 581A, comment *c* (1977) (person who committed embezzlement called embezzler and person who committed "act of unchastity" called prostitute).

5. What evidence is necessary to "justify" statements that:

(a) Plaintiff is a suspect in a murder or terrorism case. Jewell v. NYP Holdings, Inc., 23 F. Supp. 2d 348 (S.D.N.Y. 1998); Sands v. Channel Seven Adelaide Pty. Ltd., (2009) 104 S.A.S.R. 452 (Sup. Ct.), aff'd, [2010] SASC 202 (Full Ct.)

(b) "Our dad's a pimp." Hughes v. Hughes, 122 Cal. App. 4th 931, 19 Cal. Rptr. 3d 247 (2004).

(c) Embezzlement occurred because plaintiff was either ignorant or in collusion with the embezzler. Bland v. Verser, 299 Ark. 490, 774 S.W.2d 124 (1989).

(d) A union secretary-treasurer misappropriated union funds. Downer v. Amalgamated Meatcutters and Butcher Workmen of North America, 550 S.W.2d 744 (Tex. Civ. App. 1977) (he paid himself advances, intending (he claimed) to repay those which were unauthorized expenses).

(e) Plaintiff has "alleged mob ties" and a relationship to a "Mafia boss." Bufalino v. Associated Press, 692 F.2d 266 (2d Cir. 1982), cert. denied, 462 U.S. 1111 (1983) (official records indicated plaintiff had relationships with participants in organized crime, including family relationship with person identified as leader of Mafia).

(f) As a state legislator, plaintiff has supported decriminalization of marijuana and legalization of homosexuality. Hein v. Lacy, 228 Kan. 249, 616 P.2d 277 (1980) (plaintiff had voted for bills reducing penalty for possession of small amounts of marijuana and decriminalizing consensual homosexual conduct).

(g) Plaintiff has worked in a house of prostitution. Crellin v. Thomas, 122 Utah 122, 247 P.2d 264 (1952) (plaintiff had worked in house of prostitution as one of "dance hall girls," who danced with customers and encouraged them to have drinks but did not work as prostitutes).

(h) "We ... have good reason to believe ... that you are the man that poisoned George West's cattle." Fountain v. West, 23 Iowa 9 (1867). Cf. Shah v. Standard Chartered Bank, [1999] Q.B. 241 (C.A.) (were grounds for suspecting plaintiffs of involvement in fraud).

6. One category of "truth" cases involves true articles with misleading headlines. Should plaintiff have an action because the headline is misleading and a reader may not read through the story that follows? Or should the publication as a whole be regarded as true

because a mistaken impression left by the headline would be corrected by the body of the article? An example is Valella v. Benedetto, 83 A.D.2d 465, 445 N.Y.S.2d 447 (1981), aff'd, 57 N.Y.2d 788, 455 N.Y.S.2d 597, 441 N.E.2d 1115 (1982), in which a campaign leaflet contained the headline "Velella Takes Money from Indicted Landlord." Underneath were copies of a newspaper story reporting the indictment of Velella's landlord and a financial report of Velella's election committee showing a contribution from the landlord several months before the indictment. The opinion in Sprouse v. Clay Communication, Inc., 158 W. Va. 427, 211 S.E.2d 674 (1975), cert. denied, 423 U.S. 882 (1975), states that if a headline is of normal size and does not lead to a conclusion totally unsupported by the body of the story, the headline and story should be considered together; but if an oversized headline leads the average reader to an entirely different conclusion than the facts recited in the body of the story, the headline can be considered separately. See generally Annot., Libel by Newspaper Headlines, 95 A.L.R.3d 660 (1979).

7. It is trite law that such statements as "It has been reported that...," "It is rumored in the community that...," "He told me that...," and "X accused Y of...," cannot be justified by proof that there was such a report, rumor, statement or accusation. The substance of what was reported, rumored, stated or charged must be shown to be true. Otherwise, people could be harmed by the spread of defamatory reports and gossip, with no redress, so long as the speaker did not endorse the truth of what was being repeated. See Stern v. Piper, [1997] Q.B. 123 (C.A.); Fleming, Law of Torts 637 (10th ed. 2011). But how far is this to be carried? If a newspaper reports the existence of rumors concerning a prominent person and his efforts to combat them, must the rumors be proved true? See Cobbs v. Chicago Defender, 308 Ill. App. 55, 31 N.E.2d 323 (1941). If it is reported that the government is investigating whether plaintiff was a source of funding for terrorists, must it be shown that plaintiff did provide such funding? See Global Relief Foundation, Inc. v. New York Times Co., 390 F.3d 973 (7th Cir. 2004). If it is stated that plaintiff has been jailed on a charge of horse stealing, must defendant prove that plaintiff was a horse thief? See Dement v. Houston Printing Co., 14 Tex. Civ. App. 391, 37 S.W. 985 (1896). In Oles v. Pittsburgh Times, 2 Pa. Super. 130 (1896), an ailment suffered by a twelve-year-old boy was attributed by his parents and neighbors to a spell put on him by an old woman living nearby. The boy's parents and neighbors believed that the woman was a witch. Defendant's newspaper published an account of this in an article entitled "Excitement Over Alleged Witchcraft at Washington." The court held that the article imputed witchcraft to the woman named in the article, that this was defamatory—it was injurious due to the belief in witchcraft that some people in the community held—and the accuracy of the report did not establish the defense of truth.

8. The defense of truth requires that the defamatory imputation conveyed by defendant's statement be proved true. It does not suffice that the statement itself is true. When a statement that is true about one person is understood to refer to another person, about whom the statement is false, defendant is considered to have published defamatory falsehood. See pp. 522–523, supra. Putting aside this problem, should defendant be subject to liability because a true statement or combination of true statements can be interpreted to convey some false defamatory meaning? See Spiegel, Defamation by Implication—In the Confidential Manner, 29 S. Cal. L. Rev. 306 (1956). Consider:

(a) A creditor publishes plaintiff's non-payment of a debt. Turner v. Brien, 184 Iowa 320, 167 N.W. 584 (1918).

(b) Defendant says that plaintiff signed someone else's name to checks on that person's account. Love v. Commerce Bank of St. Louis, N.A., 37 F.3d 1295 (8th Cir. 1994) (plaintiff had account holder's permission to draw on account).

(c) Over an innocuous caption, defendant's pornographic magazine publishes a publicity photograph of plaintiff in her amusement park aquatic act with a diving pig. Braun v. Flynt, 726 F.2d 245 (5th Cir. 1984), reh'g denied, 731 F.2d 1205 (5th Cir. 1984), cert. denied sub nom. Chic Magazine, Inc. v. Braun, 469 U.S. 883 (1984).

(d) Plaintiff and defendant have a serious controversy. Defendant tells an audience that shortly after he rejected a settlement offer from plaintiff, his plane was forced to make an emergency landing because of water in the fuel tanks. Church of Scientology of California v. Flynn, 744 F.2d 694 (9th Cir. 1984).

(e) In response to a state senator's speech attacking a newspaper's support for the interests of a large corporation, the newspaper publishes details of the senator's unsuccessful request to the corporation for a large loan shortly after his appointment to a state commission concerned with the corporation's operations. Duncan v. Record Publishing Co., 145 S.C. 196, 143 S.E. 31 (1927).

(f) A newspaper reports that a woman fired a gun at her husband and shot plaintiff after going to plaintiff's house and finding the husband there with plaintiff. Memphis Publishing Co. v. Nichols, 569 S.W.2d 412 (Tenn. 1978) (not reported that at time of shooting, plaintiff's husband and two neighbors had been talking with plaintiff and assailant's husband in living room).

9. In the past, truth was a defense that defendants tried to avoid relying upon. Truth was difficult to prove, and a likely consequence of failure was a higher award of damages to the successful plaintiff. Today, because of the relationship between truth and the constitutional "fault" rules of liability, and a constitutional rule that shifts the burden of proving truth or falsity from defendants to plaintiffs (see pp. 670–674, infra), it may well be profitable for defendants to assert the substantial truth of what was published. See Smolla, Law of Defamation §§ 5:29–5:36 (2d ed. 1999). The constitutional rules require an accurate understanding of what truth is for purposes of the litigation.

10. Should truth be an absolute defense to an action for defamation? Some foreign jurisdictions enacted statutes providing that truth is not a defense unless publication was for the "public benefit." Over a dozen American states imposed such conditions as publication "with good motives and for justifiable ends" or without malice. Supreme Court pronouncements lend support to the view that it is unconstitutional to impose liability for a publication that carries no false defamatory meaning, but whether it is unconstitutional in all circumstances has not been settled. See Harper, James & Gray, Law of Torts § 5.20, at 190–195 (3d ed. 2006); Sack, Defamation: Libel, Slander, and Related Problems § 3.3.2[A] (4th ed. 2010).

Crane v. New York World Telegram Corporation

New York Court of Appeals
308 N.Y. 470, 126 N.E.2d 753 (1955)

FULD, Judge.

On December 6, 1951, there appeared in a column of The *New York World-Telegram and The Sun*, a newspaper of wide daily circulation, this item: "'John Crane, former president of the UFA now under indictment, isn't waiting for his own legal developments. Meanwhile his lawyers are launching a $,$$$,$$$ defamation suit.'" The present action for libel followed....

Defendants ... allege two separate defenses. The first of these purports to establish the truth of the publication. While nowhere stating that plaintiff was indicted by a grand jury—and, concededly, he never was—it asserts, nevertheless, that he was "under indictment" in an alleged nonlegal sense of that term; more specifically, it recites that he had been accused of various crimes by private individuals and was, in fact, guilty of those crimes. In support of the publication's truth under such a construction, it sets forth in considerable detail the substance of the New York City Fire Department scandals and investigations of 1950–1951, in which plaintiff, then president of an association of firemen, and others are depicted as playing a prominent part.

Little purpose would be served by repeating these allegations at any length. It is enough to observe that—while many of them touch on the derelictions of other firemen and relate to matters in which it is not clear that plaintiff was involved—it is recited that plaintiff misappropriated proceeds from the sale of tickets to the annual Firemen's Balls; that he had been accused of criminal activity by fellow firemen and others; and that, in testifying before a New York County grand jury and a committee of the United States Senate, he had admitted, without waiving immunity, facts which established his guilt of larceny and bribery.

The second separate defense, designated "Partial", repeats and makes a part of itself each and every allegation of the first defense. It states that the facts set forth were widely published and commented on by the press of New York City and that "the general reputation of the plaintiff in [that city] and its vicinity was bad" at the time of the publication and for some time before. And, in conclusion, the answer avers that "All of the facts hereinabove ... pleaded" were known to and relied upon by defendants at the time of publication, and induced them to believe in the truth of the alleged libel.

The court at Special Term granted plaintiff's motion, directing that both defenses be stricken as insufficient in law, on the ground that they had no relation to the truth of the publication. [The question of whether this order was correct was certified to the Court of Appeals. It was answered in the affirmative.] ...

In our judgment, the publication complained of, when considered in context as it must be, could reasonably be read and interpreted in only one way, that is, as charging that plaintiff had been indicted by the grand jury for some crime.... There can be no question that the "ordinary meaning" of the term "indictment" is that of the legal process, usually before a grand jury, whereby a person is formally charged with crime and a criminal prosecution begun....

If, as defendants claim, the word permits of a looser, a highly rhetorical, use to signify an accusation by private persons, that sense of the term is so rare, as contrasted with the legal process of indictment, that no reader would so understand or accept it without some qualifying language to indicate that the ordinary meaning was not intended. An example would be a statement that John Doe stands "indicted in the court of public opinion." Absent that sort of indication, or something similar, a newspaper's bald assertion that a person is "under indictment" could only be taken as referring to the legal process, whereby prosecution for crime is begun....

... That being so, it necessarily follows that the first defense is insufficient. That defense is predicated entirely on the assumption that a jury could accept the broader meaning urged by defendants, for it is not even argued that the allegations therein made, of criminal activity and accusation by private persons, establish the truth of the charge that plaintiff had been indicted by a grand jury. A plea of truth as justification must be as broad as the alleged libel and must establish the truth of the precise charge therein made. It is one thing to say that a person has been accused by his colleagues and, without waiving immunity, has testified before a grand jury to criminal activities, and quite another thing to say that an indictment has been brought against him by a grand jury. The former charge may be a serious blot upon reputation, but the latter says, in a practical and amoral sense, much more, for it announces that an actual criminal prosecution has been brought against him, that he must stand trial and may be found guilty and sentenced to a prison term.

Defendants contend, however, that, even though the complete defense be held insufficient, its allegations may properly be repeated in their entirety in the second numbered defense, as a partial defense in mitigation of damages....

The damages recoverable for a defamation consist of two items: (1) compensatory (or actual) damages, of which a major component is the damage to plaintiff's reputation resulting from the libel and (2) punitive (or exemplary) damages, recoverable only if the publication is shown to have been made with "actual malice" — a term taken to include "a libel, recklessly or carelessly published, as well as one induced by personal ill will". Well settled is the basic rule that the amount of plaintiff's recovery may be reduced by proof of facts "tending but failing to prove the truth" of the libel's charge. That proof is relevant in mitigation of punitive damages, for it may negative actual malice by showing that defendant, though mistaken, had reasonable grounds for belief in the truth of the charge contained in the publication. And, turning to compensatory damages, such evidence may serve to reduce them as well, on the theory that, if the actual facts "gave some color of verity to the statements contained in the published article, plaintiff would not be entitled to receive the same damages as if his reputation was beyond unfavorable criticism or comment." Goodrow v. Malone Telegram, 235 App. Div. 3, 5, 255 N.Y.S. 812, 814. But, of necessity, the facts that go to make up a partial defense in mitigation and reduction must *tend to prove the truth of the precise charge* made by the publication....

Defendants advance the additional contention that the pleading should be upheld and sustained, even if it does not tend to prove truth, because *some* of the facts alleged — as to particular acts of misconduct and bad reputation — may, nevertheless, be relevant to negative actual malice or reduce the value of plaintiff's injured reputation....

Considerable doubt exists whether any of the matter pleaded is proper, for the rule is clear that, while defendant may offer proof of plaintiff's bad general reputation prior to the publication, to reduce the value of the injured interest, he may not plead or prove for that purpose "specific acts, or instances, of plaintiff's misconduct" having no connection with the charge of the libel. Such specific misconduct, we have seen, may be admitted only if it also tends but fails to prove the truth of the libel's charge....

The entire thrust and purport of that defense is to establish defendants' belief in the truth of a different charge than the one made by the writing.... [I]t is unthinkable that a defense, otherwise insufficient, should be saved and upheld by the device of simply adding a recital that plaintiff "enjoyed" a bad general reputation.[1] ...

We are not here deciding what facts defendants may adduce and prove in reduction of compensatory damages under the general denial, and nothing that we now say is to be taken as precluding defendants from seeking to amend their answer so as to plead properly matters in reduction of compensatory damages or in mitigation of those that are punitive in character....

[Reversed order of Appellate Division, which had reversed Special Term.]

---

1. Proof of bad reputation is, of course, admissible under the general denial.

Notes

1. *Admissible and inadmissible evidence.* What evidence is admissible in "mitigation" of damages, if truth cannot be established, is one of the more obscure areas of defamation law. Distinctions can be drawn between evidence of plaintiff's conduct, evidence of plaintiff's character, and evidence of plaintiff's reputation. Also between evidence of a trait, or reputation for a trait, of the same type as that imputed in the defamation and evidence concerning a different trait. See generally Annot., Admissibility, for Purpose of Diminishing Damages in an Action for Libel or Slander, of Particular Facts Reflecting Upon Plaintiff's Character or Reputation, 130 A.L.R. 854 (1941); Eldredge, Law of Defamation 563–571, 577–583 (1978); Sack, Defamation: Libel, Slander, and Related Problems § 10.5.5 (4th ed. 2010).

2. In Plato Films Ltd. v. Speidel, [1961] A.C. 1090 (H.L.), the Supreme Commander of Allied (German) Land Forces in Central Europe during World War II alleged libel by a film. The film portrayed him as a spy before the war and a party to atrocities and other "war crimes" during the war, but he sued on the ground that the film depicted him as privy to the assassination of the King of Yugoslavia and the French Foreign Minister in 1934 and as having betrayed Field Marshal Rommel in 1944. Defendants were permitted to introduce evidence of plaintiff's reputation for being a party to war crimes and atrocities, but evidence of his character and of particular war crimes and other misconduct was excluded. See also Sun Printing & Publishing Association v. Schenck, 98 F. 925 (2d Cir. 1900) (irrelevant that plaintiff had been guilty of offenses other than those imputed to him; evidence of this only tended to show that plaintiff's reputation ought to be bad, not that it was bad).

3. Should evidence of prior rumors about the misconduct alleged in the defamation be admissible in mitigation of damages? Compare Sun Printing & Publishing Association v. Schenck, supra (false allegation of indictment for forgery; previous rumors of plaintiff's guilt of that offense inadmissible), with Republican Publishing Co. v. Mosman, 15 Colo. 399, 24 P. 1051 (1890) (evidence of "common report and rumor" at or before publication admissible to show extent of injury to plaintiff's reputation caused by publication). See generally Annot., Common Report as Defense to Action for Libel or Slander, 43 A.L.R. 887 (1926). It has been held that defendants cannot use evidence of other publications containing the same or similar defamatory allegations against plaintiff. See Television New Zealand Ltd. v. Ah Koy, [2002] 2 N.Z.L.R. 616 (C.A.). Why not?

4. *"Libel-proof plaintiffs" and "incremental harm."* A plaintiff alleges errors in a newspaper article which stated that he took part in a stolen car chase and that all victims of a series of slayings in which he participated were raped and strangled. Specifically, he claims that the car involved in the chase was not stolen, not all the murder victims were raped, and not all were strangled. Plaintiff has been convicted of numerous serious crimes, is serving a life sentence for murder, and is under indictment for other murders. If plaintiff's version of the story is correct, can defendant avoid liability? In such a case, the court in Jackson v. Longcope, 394 Mass. 577, 476 N.E.2d 617 (1985), considered plaintiff "libel-proof" — his reputation was so bad at the time of the libellous statement that it could not have been damaged — and held that he should not be able to maintain an action for nominal damages. Summary judgment for defendants was affirmed. Accord, Cardillo v. Doubleday & Co., Inc., 518 F.2d 638 (2d Cir. 1975) (summary judgment against habitual criminal incarcerated in federal penitentiary, regarded as "libel-proof"; if there were some errors in book on organized crime, in which plaintiff was involved, no jury would award him more than few cents). "Libel-proof" plaintiffs were also identified in Davis v.

The Tennessean, 83 S.W.3d 125 (Tenn. App. 2001) (inmate serving ninety-nine-year sentence for aiding and abetting murder sued for newspaper's erroneous statement that plaintiff shot victim); Cerasani v. Sony Corp., 991 F. Supp. 343 (S.D.N.Y. 1998) (plaintiff's well-publicized reputation as criminal and Mafia associate barred action for film depiction of him participating in brutal beatings and murders of organized crime figures); Guccione v. Hustler Magazine, Inc., 800 F.2d 298 (2d Cir. 1986), cert. denied, 479 U.S. 1091 (1987) (prior publicity about plaintiff's living with girlfriend while married to someone else created such notoriety as to preclude libel claim for imputation of adultery); Wynberg v. National Enquirer, Inc., 564 F. Supp. 924 (C.D. Cal. 1982) (in light of plaintiff's general bad reputation and specific reputation for taking advantage of women, including Elizabeth Taylor, he could not recover for article about financial exploitation of his relationship with Taylor). See generally Annot., Construction and Application of Libel-Proof Doctrine, 54 A.L.R.6th 165 (2010). A critical view of the libel-proof plaintiff doctrine is expressed in Note, Libel Proof Plaintiffs—Rabble Without a Cause, 67 Boston U. L. Rev. 993 (1987).

5. A related doctrine is that of "incremental harm." Under the "incremental harm doctrine," defendants are not to be held liable for defamatory material that causes no harm to reputation beyond the harm caused by other material in the same publication. It is applicable when there is some defamatory material in the same publication that the plaintiff has not complained of, or that the defendant could not be held liable for because of its truth, privilege, or the constitutional limitations of defamation liability. The doctrine has received a mixed reception in the courts. See Jewell v. NYP Holdings, Inc., 23 F. Supp. 2d 348 (S.D.N.Y. 1998); Tonnessen v. Denver Publishing Co., 5 P.3d 959 (Colo. App. 2000) (applying doctrine); Masson v. New Yorker Magazine, Inc., 960 F.2d 896 (9th Cir. 1992) (rejected).

6. The libel-proof and incremental harm doctrines were strongly criticized by then-Circuit Judge Scalia in Liberty Lobby, Inc. v. Anderson, 241 U.S. App. D.C. 246, 746 F.2d 1563 (1984), vacated, 477 U.S. 242 (1986): "[W]e cannot envision how a court would go about determining that someone's reputation had already been 'irreparably' damaged.... In any event, the theory must be rejected because it rests upon the assumption that one's reputation is a monolith, which stands or falls in its entirety. The law, however, proceeds upon the optimistic premise that there is a little bit of good in all of us—or perhaps upon the pessimistic assumption that no matter how bad someone is, he can always be worse. It is shameful that Benedict Arnold was a traitor; but he was not a shoplifter to boot, and one should not have been able to make that charge while knowing its falsity with impunity.... Even the public outcast's remaining reputation, limited in scope though it may be, is not inconsequential." The opinion noted that some harmful portions of the publications in issue in the case may have been "unchallenged" only because plaintiffs were unable to assert the wilful falsity required by constitutional law in a public figure case (see pp. 626–657, infra), not because they were true.

7. *Retractions.* If defendant issues a retraction of the defamatory statement, what effect does this have upon plaintiff's recovery of damages? Retraction cannot exonerate the defamer unless it is immediate and in such a form as to negative the imputation created by the original statement. However, evidence of a retraction may serve to show that plaintiff has suffered less damage to reputation than he claims, that defendant did not have the wrongful purpose or disregard for truth that would defeat a claim to qualified privilege, and that defendant did not have the malice or intent to cause harm necessary to justify an award of punitive damages. Evidence of an offer to publish a retraction or apology that plaintiff refused may also be admissible for these purposes. The retraction must be unequivocal. Otherwise, it may be regarded as an aggravation or republication of the

original libel or slander. See Eldredge, Law of Defamation 543–563 (1978); Prosser & Keeton, Law of Torts 845–847 (5th ed. 1984). Does failure to request a retraction have any effect upon the damages recoverable? See Murasky, Avoidable Consequences in Defamation: The Common-Law Duty to Request a Retraction, 40 Rutgers L. Rev. 167 (1987).

8. A majority of the states have statutes concerning retraction. Typically, if defendant has published a timely retraction of the required type, or plaintiff has failed to make a proper demand for retraction, plaintiff's damages are limited—to proved actual or special damages, as opposed to general damages, or at least to compensatory damages. Punitive damages are excluded. The statutes vary considerably in their application. Some apply only to newspapers. Others apply to newspapers and periodicals. Still others encompass radio and television broadcasts. Some apply to any libel action. Under most statutes, only defendants who had a reasonable belief in the truth of the matter published, or at least published it in good faith, are protected. See Sack, Defamation: Libel, Slander, and Related Problems § 11.2 (4th ed. 2010). Defendants in defamation cases are free to refuse to issue a retraction. Courts have no power to order retractions even after a judgment of liability. See Kramer v. Thompson, 947 F.2d 666 (3d Cir. 1991).

B. Absolute Privileges

Mills v. Denny

Supreme Court of Iowa
245 Iowa 584, 63 N.W.2d 222 (1954)

LARSON, Justice.

Plaintiff, an attorney at law practicing in Des Moines, Iowa, brought suit against the defendant, who was the mayor of said city, alleging: "That on July 27, 1953, the defendant, while seated at the council table in the City Council Room ... in the presence and hearing of the other members of the council and the representatives of the press and radio, and a number of citizens ... including ... plaintiff's client, made a statement which was intended to injure the plaintiff and his business, which statement was wrongfully and maliciously spoken, and which was false and defamatory." It was: "Mills, you know that our hands are tied by the courts. You are guilty of dereliction of duty as an attorney towards your client inasmuch as you seemingly advised her that the City Council could take any action which would or could result in the resumption of bus service on the lines abandoned by the Des Moines Railway Company. You have appeared here only as a publicity stunt." A local newspaper printed the story giving it wide publicity. Plaintiff asked damages of defendant in the sum of $4,000.

Defendant's motion to dismiss is urged here solely on the ground that " ... the alleged slander was made by the defendant as Mayor and member of the City Council of the City of Des Moines, Iowa, ... and is therefore a privileged communication and not actionable." ...

Privileged communications are divided into two main general classes, namely: (1) those that are absolutely privileged, and (2) those that are qualifiedly or conditionally privileged.

An absolute privilege affords a complete defense. Even the existence of actual malice will not destroy an absolute privilege when it is applicable.

It may be generally stated that the occasion and the office afford the test as to whether an alleged slanderous or libelous statement may be absolutely privileged, conditionally or qualifiedly privileged, or not at all privileged.

The doctrine of privileged communication is based upon the principle of good public policy. This is especially true with the cases of absolute privilege, where the interests and the necessities of society require that on certain occasions, utterances or publications of individuals, even though they are both false and maliciously made, shall protect the defamer from all liability to prosecution. It rests upon the same basis of necessity that is found in other tort laws. Instances abound where the individual must surrender his personal rights and suffer losses for the benefit of the common welfare. "The right of free speech is in some cases allowed to prevail over the right to reputation, in apparent derogation of the theoretical competence of the law to afford a remedy for every wrong." 9 Columbia Law Review 463.

We do not consider herein the rules applicable to the qualified or conditional privilege, and do not determine whether or not they apply to the case at bar. They will no doubt be considered in the further proceeding below. It is sufficient here that we consider only the absolute privilege. It is generally held that the public welfare alone justifies the privilege on occasions that some persons should be allowed to express their sentiments and speak their minds fully and fearlessly upon all questions and subjects; that all actions for words so spoken are absolutely forbidden, even if it be alleged and proved that the words were spoken falsely, knowingly and with expressed malice. This rule should be and usually is confined strictly to cases in which the public service or the administration of justice require complete immunity, to legislatures in debate, judges and attorneys in the preparation and trial of cases, and in executive and military personnel within the duties of their offices. These classes must of course be limited, and where this limitation is placed there is some split of authority. But most courts as well as textbook writers agree that this class of privilege is and must be restricted to narrow and well-defined limits. The privilege spoken of is in reality an immunity provided, applicable only to recognized positions and occasions.

Absolute immunity, it seems, should be confined to cases where there is supervision and control by other authorities, such as courts of justice, where proceedings are under the able and controlling influence of a learned judge, who may reprimand, fine and punish as well as expunge from records statements of those who exceed proper bounds, and who may themselves be disciplined when necessary. The same is true in federal and state legislatures, and their committees, where the decorum is under the watchful eye of presiding officers and records may be stricken and the offending member punished. If this is not done, the day may come when the courts will no longer recognize and grant absolute immunity even in this field, for then the evil will overshadow the good and will not aid the public welfare. In the case of executive officers, therefore, much narrower limits are necessary, and so only top officers or executives whose acts are of necessity secret or confidential fall within this immunity. Underlying the doctrine of absolute immunity is the concept of an alternate if not adequate remedy. Extension to fields where no such safeguards or remedies are found has been uniformly refused by the courts and justly so, for absolute immunity in defamation matters presents a conflict between two American principles equally regarded in the law, i.e., the right of an individual on one hand to enjoy his reputation unimpaired by defamation attacks, and on the other hand the necessity in the public interest of a free and full disclosure of facts in the conduct of the legislative, executive and judicial departments of government.

Nevertheless the rule is quite well settled in all jurisdictions that the question as to whether or not there is a privilege, absolute or qualified, under the circumstances or occasion involved, is for the court. If found to exist and the court determines the privilege is absolute, the action must be dismissed, and if found to be qualified or conditional, then the question of fact relating to plaintiff's proof of malice is usually for the jury under the usual rules of evidence.

Defendant contends that the occasion presented herein was such that he was entitled to absolute immunity. He contends that the council was in session; that the plaintiff had made a plea for council action by requesting a meeting and an arrangement between the council and the receivers of the bus company to raise fares and restore service on abandoned bus routes within the city; that the mayor, as spokesman for the council, answered the plea in his official capacity and in that answer used the words complained of by plaintiff. Defendant further contends he was acting with the council in a legislative, as well as in a quasi judicial capacity at the time, and that he did not stray or wander from the subject of debate to assail the character of the plaintiff, and should be clothed under these circumstances with absolute immunity from actions on his utterances.

... [C]ouncil action, even under the delegated powers it possesses, does not exercise the legislative or judicial functions intended to merit the privilege of absolute immunity. In Blakeslee & Sons v. Carroll, 64 Conn. 223, 29 A. 473, the court, in a case involving an investigation by a committee of a board of aldermen, said that the legislative delegated power given it cannot be held to confer judicial or quasi judicial power upon the presiding officer, and certainly not upon the committee, though it had the power to issue subpoenas and administer oaths. "A judicial proceeding within the meaning of the rule as to absolute privilege must, we think, be one carried on in a court of justice established or recognized by law, wherein the rights of parties which are recognized and protected by law are involved and may be determined." We believe this to be good logic.

Defendant further contends that the city council of a municipality the size of Des Moines has many vexatious problems similar to the state, and that it has been delegated many legislative and judicial functions by the state legislature, and that it should for the public welfare be extended the privileges and immunities in the performance of its official functions of a legislative or judicial nature. It is obvious that such an extension would of necessity include all such subordinate legislative and quasi judicial bodies, boards and councils, and could not be limited to the size or complexities of a certain few....

In Restatement of the Law of Torts, § 590, we find the statement that a member of Congress or of the state or territory legislatures is absolutely privileged to publish false and defamatory matter of another in the performance of his legislative function. Under Comment (c): "The rule stated in this Section is applicable to members of the Congress of the United States and to members of the highest legislative body of a State or Territory of the United States. It is not applicable to members of subordinate legislative bodies to which the State has delegated legislative power." Under Comment (a), § 599, the conditional privilege which is applicable to such subordinate bodies is also discussed....

In Prosser on Torts, 1941 Ed., p. 828: "It is generally agreed, however, that the proceedings of subordinate bodies performing a legislative function such as municipal councils, or town meetings, are not within the policy underlying such absolute immunity and that members of such bodies are sufficiently protected by exemption from liability in the exercise of good faith."

These authorities announce the majority rule, and we believe the sound rule....

It is true, as defendant here maintains, that some states, principally Michigan, have extended the coverage to municipalities and other subordinate bodies. In Bolton v. Walker, 197 Mich. 699, 164 N.W. 420, the court concluded that a board delegated semi-legislative discretion with power and control in tax matters, by the legislature, was exercising a function of great public concern and should be given legislative or judicial immunity....

It is our feeling that the welfare of society does not require the individual here also to surrender his personal rights absolutely to provide such immunity, though we concede perhaps the cases of abuse would be few. We agree with the majority of the courts in other jurisdictions and textbook writers in holding that the qualified privilege adequately protects such public officials who in good faith make bona fide statements upon any subject matter that are pertinent and relevant to the question on the privileged occasion. Such immunity is sufficient, for of itself it abrogates the rule that every defamatory publication implies malice. There is no necessity, we feel, to go further. Having determined that the utterances or publications of members of a city council are not included in the absolutely privileged communication, we must hold that the action of the trial court in overruling the motion to dismiss was right....

Affirmed.

Notes

1. Most statements to which an absolute privilege attaches are made in connection with the activities of government. There are privileges corresponding to the three branches of government: executive, legislative and judicial. Whether the public good requires an absolute, rather than qualified, privilege is a question that must be addressed in the analysis of each of the privileges.

2. Common law afforded a privilege to members of the national and state legislatures, when they were acting in their capacity as legislators and their statements had some connection to the business of the legislature. Immunity from defamation liability is also provided by the "Speech and Debate Clause" in Article I, section 6, of the United States Constitution: "[F]or any Speech or Debate in either House, [Senators and Representatives] shall not be questioned in any other Place." Parallel provisions are contained in most state constitutions. As the constitutional privilege is broader than the common law privilege, it is constitutional law that is controlling in most cases. Anything said by a legislator on the floor of the chamber or within a committee hearing is privileged, even if it has no pertinence to pending legislative business. Official reports of legislative proceedings, such as the Congressional Record and transcripts of legislative hearings, are within the privilege. What has been contentious is the extent to which privilege attaches to activities that are conducted from a legislator's office, not the legislative chamber or committee room — particularly communications with constituents and with officials of the executive branch. Another issue is the application of absolute privilege to members of legislative staffs. See Eldredge, Law of Defamation 374–388 (1978); Harper, James & Gray, Law of Torts § 5.23, at 229–232 (3d ed. 2006).

3. One of the leading cases is Hutchinson v. Proxmire, 443 U.S. 111 (1979). To publicize what he perceived as waste in government spending, a United States Senator instituted a "Golden Fleece of the Month Award." He and his legislative assistant were sued by a person defamed in a speech in which one of the awards was "presented." The speech was either delivered on the Senate floor or inserted into the Congressional Record as if it had been delivered. An advance press release containing the text of the speech was sent to 275 members of the news media. The essence of the speech was later repeated in a newsletter mailed to 100,000 persons in the senator's state and elsewhere. The senator subsequently referred to the matter in at least one television interview, and his aide

discussed it with a number of federal agencies responsible for the criticized spending. The Supreme Court held that the Speech and Debate Clause did not protect Congressional newsletters, press releases, statements in interviews and the followup telephone calls, even though they republished protected statements made on the Senate floor. Cf. Buchanan v. Jennings, [2005] 1 A.C. 115 (P.C.), holding that privilege did not extend to a member of Parliament telling a reporter that he did not resile from a statement he made in Parliament.

4. Under Gravel v. United States, 408 U.S. 606 (1972), the senator's assistant, acting on behalf of the senator, would have shared whatever privilege the senator, acting personally, would possess. In Chastain v. Sundquist, 266 U.S. App. D.C. 61, 833 F.2d 311 (1987), cert. denied, 487 U.S. 1240 (1988), a Congressman was held to have neither constitutional nor common law privilege for a letter to the Attorney General and the Legal Services Corporation, released to the media, complaining about a Legal Services attorney. Should a member of Congress and Congressional staff have a privilege of the type enjoyed by federal executive officials, see pp. 582–586, infra, which can extend to press releases?

5. As noted in the principal case, there is a split of authority concerning whether absolute privilege applies to local legislative bodies, with some states conferring absolute privilege by statute. Note the problems created if a mayor, supervisor or similar official possessing qualified privilege in his executive capacity is a member of a legislature enjoying absolute privilege. Remarks made during a meeting may be outside any privilege if they are not relevant to the official business of the legislative body. See generally Annot., Libel and Slander: Statements or Utterances by Member of Municipal Council, or of Governing Body of Other Political Subdivision, in Course of Official Proceedings, as Privileged, 40 A.L.R.2d 941 (1955); Eldredge, Law of Defamation 388–392 (1978); Sack, Defamation: Libel, Slander, and Related Problems § 8.2.4[C] (4th ed. 2010).

Adams v. Peck

Maryland Court of Appeals
288 Md. 1, 415 A.2d 292 (1980)

DAVIDSON, Judge....

[A husband/father and wife/mother engaged in a contested divorce proceeding] entered into a separation agreement in which the mother was granted custody of the two minor children and the father was granted visitation rights. In 1977, the mother raised questions concerning the advisability of continuing the father's visitation rights. The mother's attorney referred her and the children to the appellee, Alan H. Peck, M.D. (psychiatrist), for an evaluation. On 17 February 1977, the psychiatrist sent a written report to the attorney in which he expressed the opinion that the father had abused one of the children, and that he was "an ill man and in definite need of psychiatric treatment." Additionally, the psychiatrist urged "that all visitations with the father stop, and the father not be allowed to be around the children." Thereafter, the mother filed a Petition for Modification of Visitation Rights.

[The father sued the psychiatrist, alleging that the psychiatrist had "falsely and maliciously defamed him." The psychiatrist moved for summary judgment on the ground that the report was absolutely privileged because it was made in connection with the pending divorce litigation. The trial court granted summary judgment, from which the father appealed.]

In Maryland, judges, attorneys, parties and witnesses are absolutely privileged[1] to publish defamatory matters during the course of a judicial proceeding. This absolute privilege protects the person publishing the defamatory statement from liability even if his purpose or motive was malicious, he knew that the statement was false, or his conduct was otherwise unreasonable. It extends not only to defamatory statements made in the courtroom during the course of the trial, but also to such statements published in documents which have been filed in a judicial proceeding. *DiBlasio v. Kolodner*, 233 Md. 512, 197 A.2d 245 (1963) (declaration in prior suit); *Bartlett v. Christhilf*, 69 Md. 219, 14 A. 518 (1889) (petition); *Kerpelman v. Bricker*, 23 Md. App. 628, 329 A.2d 423 (1974) (letter of complaint to then Grievance Committee of Maryland State Bar Association initiating a "judicial proceeding"). *See, e.g., Gilpin v. Tack*, 256 F. Supp. 562 (W.D. Ark. 1966) (interrogatories); *O'Barr v. Feist*, 292 Ala. 440, 296 So. 2d 152 (1974) (physician's letter); *Todd v. Cox*, 20 Ariz. App. 347, 512 P.2d 1234 (1973) (affidavit); *Albertson v. Raboff*, 46 Cal. 2d 375, 295 P.2d 405 (1956) (notice of *lis pendens); McDonald v. Lakewood Country Club*, 170 Colo. 355, 461 P.2d 437 (1969) (criminal information); *Zirn v. Cullom*, 187 Misc. 241, 63 N.Y.S.2d 439 (1946) (pleading in prior suit); *Jarman v. Offutt*, 239 N.C. 468, 80 S.E.2d 248 (1954) (affidavit).

This Court has not previously considered whether an absolute privilege applies to defamatory statements published in documents prepared for possible use in connection with a pending judicial proceeding but which have not been filed in that proceeding. However, in [*Kennedy v. Cannon*, 229 Md. 92, 182 A.2d 54 (1962)] we stated in dicta: "[A]bsolute immunity extends ... for defamatory statements uttered in the course of a trial or contained in pleadings, affidavits, depositions, *and other documents directly related to the case.*" (Emphasis added.) We shall here hold that ordinarily an absolute privilege applies to a defamatory statement published in a document which is prepared for possible use in connection with a pending judicial proceeding but which has not been filed in that proceeding. Courts in other jurisdictions which have considered similar questions agree. *E.g., Theiss v. Scherer*, 396 F.2d 646 (6th Cir. 1968) (attorney's letter to another attorney); *McLaughlin v. Copeland*, 455 F. Supp. 749 (D. Del. 1978) (attorney's letter to other attorneys); *Smith v. Hatch*, 271 Cal. App. 2d 39, 76 Cal. Rptr. 350 (1969) (attorney's letter to client); *Anderson v. Matz*, 67 Ill. App. 3d 175, 384 N.E.2d 759 (1978) (physician's report to insurance company); *Middlesex Concrete Products & Excavating Corp. v. Carteret Indus. Ass'n*, 68 N.J. Super. 85, 172 A.2d 22 (1961) (consultant's report to attorney); *Zirn* [supra] (defense attorney's letter to plaintiff); *Vasquez v. Courtney*, 276 Or. 1053, 557 P.2d 672 (1976) (sheriff's letter to parole officer conducting presentence investigation); *Beezley v. Hansen*, 4 Utah 2d 64, 286 P.2d 1057 (1955) (attorney's unfiled deposition).

The question whether a defamatory statement should be absolutely privileged involves a matter of public policy in which the public interest in free disclosure must be weighed against the harm to individuals who may be defamed. The underlying rationale for according an absolute privilege to the defamatory statements made in court by participants in judicial proceedings or to such statements published in documents which have been filed is that such a privilege is necessary to the proper administration of justice. The ultimate purpose of the judicial process is to determine the truth. The investigation, evaluation, presentation and determination of facts are inherent and essential parts of this process. If this process is to function effectively, those who participate must be able to do so without being hampered by the fear of private suits for defamation. As stated by this Court

---

1. Defamatory statements made by judges, parties and witnesses are absolutely privileged even though they have no relation to the judicial proceeding. However, an attorney's defamatory statement is absolutely privileged only if it has some relation to the judicial proceeding.

in *Bartlett*, 69 Md. at 226–27, 14 A. at 520: "… This privilege, protecting against a suit for libel or slander, is founded upon what would seem to be a sound public policy which looks to the free and unfettered administration of justice, though, as an incidental result, it may, in some instances, afford an immunity to the evil-disposed and malignant slanderer…. To allow such suits to prevail, would most effectively deter every one from presenting a well-founded complaint, for fear of being pursued with 'infinite vexation.'"

These public policy reasons are equally applicable to defamatory statements published in documents which are prepared for possible use in connection with a pending judicial proceeding but which have not been filed. In *Watson v. M'Ewan*, (1905) A.C. 480 (HL), … a wife sued her husband for a separation on the ground of cruelty. A physician who had examined her sent a report containing defamatory statements to her husband and his attorney. This document was not filed in the pending litigation for separation. The wife subsequently sued the physician for defamation. There, as here, the question presented was whether an absolute privilege applied to a defamatory statement published in a document which was prepared for use by an attorney in connection with a pending judicial proceeding but which had not been filed in that proceeding. In finding that an absolute privilege applied, the Earl of Halsbury, L.C., speaking for the House of Lords, said: … "It appears to me that the privilege which surrounds the evidence actually given in a Court of justice necessarily involves the same privilege in the case of making a statement to a solicitor and other persons who are engaged in the conduct of proceedings in Courts of justice when what is intended to be stated in a Court of justice is narrated to them…. If it were otherwise … the difficulty in the way of those who were bringing the action would have been removed at once by saying, 'I do not bring the action against you for what you said in the witness-box, but I bring the action against you for what you told the solicitor you were about to say in the witness-box.' If that could be done the object for which the privilege exists is gone, because then no witness could be called; no one would know whether what he was going to say was relevant to the question in the debate between the parties. A witness would only have to say, 'I shall not tell you anything; I may have an action brought against me to-morrow if I do; therefore I shall not give you any information at all.' *It is very obvious that the public policy which renders the protection of witnesses necessary for the administration of justice must as a necessary consequence involve that which is a step towards and is part of the administration of justice—namely, the preliminary examination of witnesses to find out what they can prove. It may be that to some extent it seems to impose a hardship, but after all the hardship is not to be compared with that which would arise if it were impossible to administer justice, because people would be afraid to give their testimony.*" (Emphasis added.)

We agree with the expressed underlying rationale…. The evaluation and investigation of facts and opinions for the purpose of determining what, if anything, is to be raised or used in pending litigation is as integral a part of the search for truth and therefore of the judicial process as is the presentation of such facts and opinions during the course of the trial, either in filed documents or in the courtroom itself. Such evaluation and investigation, and the documents which these activities generate, are directly related to the pending litigation and occur during the course of the judicial proceeding. The people who engage in these activities and who generate such documents must be able to do so without being hampered by the fear of private suits for defamation. Accordingly, any defamatory statement which appears in a document prepared for possible use in connection with a pending judicial proceeding should be accorded an absolute privilege, regardless of whether the document has been filed.

Applying this principle to the instant case produces a clear result. Here, the allegedly defamatory statement was published in a letter from a psychiatrist to an attorney who was then representing the mother in pending divorce litigation. The attorney had solicited the psychiatrist's evaluation of the truthfulness of the child's allegation that his father had abused him, as well as the psychiatrist's opinion as to the advisability of continuing the father's visitation rights. The psychiatrist's evaluation and recommendation were sought for the purpose of determining whether there were probative facts and opinions sufficient to justify raising, in the pending divorce litigation, the issue of a modification of the father's visitation rights. Despite the fact that this document had not been filed in the pending divorce proceeding, it was nonetheless a document prepared for use in connection with the pending divorce proceeding. Under these circumstances, it is manifest that the psychiatrist's letter was directly related to that judicial proceeding, and that the allegedly defamatory statement contained in the letter was published during the course of that judicial proceeding. Accordingly, an absolute privilege applies to the allegedly defamatory statement published in the psychiatrist's letter to the attorney....

JUDGMENT AFFIRMED.

Notes

1. The common law has developed an extensive set of absolute privileges for persons who perform functions within or related to judicial proceedings. The "core" privileges — those which have near-universal recognition and about which few fundamental questions now arise — apply to oral and written statements made within judicial proceedings by the participants: judges, magistrates, counsel, parties, witnesses and jurors. Thus, a judge's statements from the bench or in chambers, when made in a judicial capacity; an attorney's motions, questions to witnesses and arguments to the court; a party's complaint and answer; a witness' testimony; and a juror's statements during jury deliberation are covered by absolute privilege. The privilege extends to statements made before a case reaches open court, as in pleadings, affidavits, depositions, briefs and pre-trial conferences. That the court lacked jurisdiction in the proceedings does not exclude the privilege when there is some "color" of jurisdiction.

Absolute privilege probably applies to court officials in their duties relating to judicial proceedings, such as court clerks, sheriffs and judges' clerks. It definitely applies to grand jurors within their authorized functions, but it is sometimes denied to reports by grand juries that are authorized only to hand down or refuse indictments.

For statements by attorneys, and often for statements of judges and other participants in judicial proceedings, American courts have attached a requirement that the statement have some "connection" or "relationship" or "relevance" to the judicial proceeding at hand. In practice, this requirement is very loose. It bears no resemblance to the relevance rules of the law of evidence. Due allowance is made for latitude in arguments to the court, and witnesses are not denied protection when they misconceive the issues in the case or the questions put to them. The few statements found "unconnected" and thus not entitled to absolute privilege are mainly personal criticisms that could not reasonably be thought to have pertinence to the substance or conduct of the proceeding. For example, in Sussman v. Damian, 355 So. 2d 809 (Fla. App. 1977), during an argument at a deposition about production of documents by a client, one attorney said to another, "You sir, are a damned liar. I gave you everything." Later, during a heated discussion concerning a hearing on this controversy, one attorney accused the other of improprieties in the handling of client funds. The first statement was held absolutely privileged as connected to the pending lawsuit, the second not. See generally Eldredge, Law of Defamation 340–374 (1978); Harper,

James & Gray, Law of Torts § 5.22 (3d ed. 2006); Sack, Defamation: Libel, Slander, and Related Problems § 8.2.1 (4th ed. 2010).

2. Official reports of court proceedings and judicial opinions are absolutely privileged. Murray v. Brancato, 290 N.Y. 52, 48 N.E.2d 257 (1945), denies absolute privilege to a judge who provides an opinion for which there is an official reporter to the publisher of a parallel unofficial reporter. *Murray* has not been applied to opinions published in authoritative reports of courts that have no official reporter, and it may not be followed for parallel unofficial reports, in actions against either the judge or the publisher. See Lowenschuss v. West Publishing Co., 542 F.2d 180 (3d Cir. 1976) (action by attorney criticized in footnote).

3. Absolute privilege usually is extended to proceedings before an administrative tribunal or agency that are judicial or "quasi-judicial" in nature. In a large proportion of the cases in which the question has arisen, the required "quasi-judicial" element has been found. See Annot., Libel and Slander: Privilege Applicable to Judicial Proceedings as Extending to Administrative Proceedings, 45 A.L.R.2d 1296 (1956). Even non-governmental agencies which perform "quasi-judicial" functions that otherwise might be performed by a court or administrative agency can be within absolute privilege. This is particularly true of state bar association grievance and disciplinary proceedings. It may also apply to grievance and disciplinary proceedings of local bars and organizations of professions other than law. See Annot., Libel and Slander: Privilege in Connection with Proceedings to Disbar or Discipline Attorney, 77 A.L.R.2d 493 (1961); Annot., Testimony Before or Communications to Private Professional Society's Judicial Commission, Ethics Committee, or the Like, as Privileged, 9 A.L.R.4th 807 (1981). See generally Eldredge, Law of Defamation 345–352 (1978); Sack, Defamation: Libel, Slander, and Related Problems § 8.2.4[B] (4th ed. 2010). Absolute privilege has also been extended to statements connected to private contractual arbitrations. Yeung v. Maric, 224 Ariz. 499, 232 P.3d 1281 (Ct. App. 2010). Witnesses and other participants in legislative hearings generally enjoy absolute privilege pursuant to the legislative privilege, pp. 573–577, supra. But it might not extend to purely voluntary statements that citizens are permitted to make at hearings. See Dobbs, Law of Torts 1155 (2000); Hanson, Libel and Related Torts ¶ 116 (1969).

4. Should absolute privilege apply to statements made to or by an attorney in connection with pending litigation but not introduced into it, as in the principal case? Should a distinction be drawn between communications with consultants, communications with prospective witnesses, and communications with opposing parties or their attorneys (such as settlement proposals)? Absolute privilege for such statements, when made for purposes of pending litigation or even intended litigation, seems fairly well established. But see Timmis v. Bennett, 352 Mich. 355, 89 N.W.2d 748 (1958) (attorney not absolutely privileged by reason of contemplated litigation). There is less authority on attorney communications that are not made for purposes of litigation and on attorney-client communications — perhaps because of their confidentiality. The authority that exists is in conflict. Compare More v. Weaver, [1928] 2 K.B. 520 (C.A.) (absolute privilege), with Lapetina v. Santangelo, 124 App. Div. 519, 108 N.Y.S. 975 (1908) (qualified privilege). The privilege appears to include an attorney's communications with potential clients to solicit their participation in litigation. See Finkelstein, Thompson & Loughran v. Hemispherx Biopharma, Inc., 774 A.2d 332 (D.C. 2001); Simpson Strong-Tie Co., Inc. v. Stewart, Estes & Donnell, 232 S.W.3d 18 (Tenn. 2007). Is it sound to grant absolute privilege to statements which a court cannot effectively supervise or control? See Annot., Libel and Slander: Out-of-Court Communications Between Attorneys Made Preparatory to, or in the Course or Aftermath of, Civil Judicial Proceedings as Privileged, 36 A.L.R.3d 1328

(1971); Annot., Libel and Slander: Attorneys' Statements, to Parties Other than Alleged Defamed Party or Its Agents, in Course of Extrajudicial Investigation or Preparation Relating to Pending or Anticipated Civil Litigation as Privileged, 23 A.L.R.4th 932 (1983); Eldredge, Law of Defamation 365–369 (1978).

——————

Stukuls v. State

New York Court of Appeals
42 N.Y.2d 272, 397 N.Y.S.2d 740, 366 N.E.2d 829 (1977)

FUCHSBERG, Judge [with whom Cooke, J., joined].

This claim for libel and slander was brought against the State by Dr. Henry I. Stukuls, a former member of the faculty of the State University College at Cortland. The allegedly defamatory matter was uttered and published by Dr. Whitney T. Corey, a vice-president for academic affairs at the college, who, in the absence of Dr. Richard Jones, the college's president, would also act in the latter's stead.[1]

[Plaintiff alleged that Dr. Corey was opposed to plaintiff being granted tenure at the college. With a "malicious and willful design" to have tenure denied, Dr. Corey took advantage of Dr. Jones' absence from the country to take a letter from the president's private file and read it to an *ad hoc* committee charged with passing upon plaintiff's qualifications for tenure. The letter, which plaintiff never had the opportunity to read or hear read, accused plaintiff (a married man) of attempting to seduce a female student in one of his classes. It had arrived at the college months earlier but was never verified. Dr. Corey allegedly knew its accusations had been the subject of a rumor circulated and discredited months earlier. Also, he removed favorable student course evaluations and letters from plaintiff's personnel file before submitting it to the tenure committee. Plaintiff was denied tenure and injured in his personal and professional reputation. His claim was dismissed on the ground that Dr. Corey had absolute privilege. Plaintiff appealed, contending that the applicable privilege was qualified.]

The right of nonjudicial and nonlegislative governmental officials to assert [an absolute privilege] is of relatively recent origin. It had its genesis in England in 1895 (*Chatterton v. Secretary of State of India* [1895], 2 Q.B. 189) and was adopted in this country a year later (*Spalding v. Vilas*, 161 U.S. 483 [postmaster general]). Significantly, both cases involved cabinet officers and were based upon the rationale that such highranking officials, "who speak for the government or as its mouthpiece", formulate and pronounce policy in varying degrees and, therefore, in a broad sense are an embodiment of government itself, should not, while carrying out their official duties,[4] be apprehensive that their motives might become the subject of inquiry in a civil suit.

In England, the doctrine's application for the most part continued to be applied to top-level officials whose conduct constitutes an "act of state", but in the United States it has followed a more checkered jurisprudential course. Our Federal courts, which at first adopted the concept of absolute privilege for the executive branch of Government with

——————

1. The claim is brought against the State alone under the doctrine of *respondeat superior*.
4. Absolute immunity does not apply to a communication outside an official's competence.

great hesitancy, gradually extended the zone of its application to encompass an ever-broadening range of officials....

In the State courts, except for cases against officials of cabinet rank, the decisions have been divided and often inconsistent. This has led to much judicial and other soul-searching, with most of the commentators in the end arriving at the conclusion that absolute privilege for officials of the executive branch of government should be reserved for only those at its highest echelons....

[In New York cases] only a qualified privilege has been extended to the head of a New York State school for deaf mutes, to employees, as distinguished from board members, of a board of education, to a State examiner of accounts, and to a high school principal. It is interesting that, in *Lombardo v. Stoke* [18 N.Y.2d 394, 276 N.Y.S.2d 97, 222 N.E.2d 721], while recognizing an absolute immunity for members of the board of higher education, we would not willy-nilly do so for the president of one of its constituent colleges, but thought it better to save that question for another day. That day is now.

This analysis leads us to conclude that, unless an official is a principal executive of State or local government or is entrusted by law with administrative or executive policy-making responsibilities of considerable dimension, policy considerations do not require that he be given an absolute license to defame. The privilege exists to protect those who bear the greatest burdens of government or those to whose official functioning it is essential that they be insulated from the harassment and financial hazards that may accompany suits for damages by the victims of even malicious libels or slanders. This at least serves a recognized public purpose. But to cloak public officers who do not have such a need with the privilege to wrongfully vilify others with impunity while their critics remain fully liable for their own tortious communications, would tend to squelch criticism of government by its citizens while serving no sufficiently countervailing public purpose. After all, the immunity is intended for the welfare of the public and not for governmental employees. A less discriminating resort to absolute immunity would remove a desirable "check upon calumny" (*Andrews v. Gardiner*, 224 N.Y. 440, 448, 121 N.E.2d 341, 344 [Cardozo, J.]).

Public officials who are not entitled to the immunizing shield of an absolute privilege are not left without the considerable, albeit incomplete, protections from liability for defamation afforded those who communicate orally or in writing in good faith in the course of the performance of their duties of office....

... [W]hile Dr. Corey's role in communicating with the tenure committee no doubt was an important one to the parties involved, and not least of all to himself as acting president and vice-president of the college, neither of his two offices falls within the class of executive positions in our State and local government for whom the extraordinary doctrine of absolute privilege is intended. The State University's decision-making process is vested in its trustees and Chancellor. It is they who administer our system of higher education at its policy-making level, which embraces even the ultimate determination of whether tenure is to be granted. Dr. Corey was not carrying out those functions. His actions under scrutiny here were ones undertaken during the discharge of his own official duties.

Basically, Dr. Corey's functions are akin to those exercised by the heads of the schools in *McAulay v. Maloff*, 82 Misc. 2d 447, 369 N.Y.S.2d 946, and *Hemmens v. Nelson*, 138 N.Y. 517, 34 N.E. 342, to neither of whom the doctrine was found applicable. As Justice Mahoney observed in the course of his dissent at the Appellate Division in the present case, "it is difficult to perceive how the goal of protecting our highest administrative, judicial and legislative officials from undue harassment is advanced by extending the salutary doctrine of absolute privilege to all presidents of public colleges" (53 A.D.2d 368, 373, 385 N.Y.S.2d 852, 855). In fact, one would be hard put to rationalize a recognition of absolute immunity for the president of a public college while limiting the presidents of the many outstanding private colleges in our State, with their often broader, more independent and additional responsibilities in fund-raising and policy-making areas, to the significant safeguards of qualified privilege alone.

Indeed, it seems to us that the proliferation of government into more and more activities which in the past had been confined to the private sector militates against any automatic equating of governmental employment with absolute immunity or its ready extension beyond the areas into which it has heretofore been permitted....

... [G]iven the undisputed responsibilities of the committee, the relationship which Dr. Stukuls and Dr. Corey each bore to its functioning in this instance and the embarrassment which could ensue if, not having been presented to the committee for whatever it was worth, the rumor, if that it was, were to surface later as fact or rumor, it might be well-nigh impossible for Dr. Stukuls to successfully carry the burden of proving that malice was the one and only cause for the publication....

On the other hand, on the basis of the allegations in his claim and his affidavit taken as a whole, it cannot be said in advance of discovery that Dr. Stukuls will not be able to raise an issue of fact. That Dr. Corey uttered the defamatory matter before the committee does not necessarily mean that he was doing so to advance its interests. He may have been acting duplicitiously while motivated solely by his ill will towards Dr. Stukuls....

[Reversed and remanded. Jones, J., (with whom Breitel, C.J., and Gabrielli, J., joined) delivered a concurring opinion. Wachtler, J., (with whom Jansen, J., joined) delivered a dissenting opinion.]

Notes

1. Whether a statement by an officer of the executive branch of government is privileged, and whether the privilege is absolute or qualified, depends primarily upon the office held by the person who issues the statement and the relationship between the issuance of the statement and the duties of the office. The function being performed also plays a role. Officers who generally have only qualified privilege may enjoy absolute privilege when performing certain functions, such as participating in judicial or "quasi-judicial" proceedings, pp. 580–581, supra, or assisting officers who have absolute privilege. See Ward Telecommunications and Computer Services, Inc. v. State, 42 N.Y.2d 289, 397 N.Y.S.2d 751, 366 N.E.2d 840 (1977) (audit report prepared by State Comptroller's staff, issued in his name). In most jurisdictions, absolute privilege has been limited to the principal officers of the government as a whole and the highest-ranking officials of government departments, agencies and diplomatic missions. However, it may not be restricted as tightly as in the principal case. See Lucy v. Muchnok, 36 Pa. Commw. 272, 387 A.2d 945 (1978) (bituminous mine inspectors among "high public officials" enjoying absolute privilege); Lindner v. Mollan, 544 Pa. 487, 677 A.2d 1194 (1996) (borough mayor absolutely privileged); Ranous v. Hughes, 30 Wis. 2d 452, 141 N.W.2d 251 (1966) (director of board of education qualifiedly privileged). See generally Eldredge, Law of Defamation 392–416, 502–505 (1978); Sack, Defamation: Libel, Slander, and Related Problems §§ 8.2.3, 8.2.5

(4th ed. 2010); Becht, The Absolute Privilege of the Executive in Defamation, 15 Vand. L. Rev. 1127 (1962).

2. In Barr v. Matteo, 360 U.S. 564 (1959), the Supreme Court decided that absolute privilege extended into the lower ranks of the federal bureaucracy. It was "not the title of his office but ... the relation of the act complained of to 'matters committed by law to his control or supervision'" that determined the privilege. The privilege applied when "the action ... taken was within the outer perimeter of [defendant's] line of duty." Under the federal rule, absolute privilege has been afforded to a press release in which the Acting Director of the Office of Rent Stabilization announced his intention to suspend two employees for their role in criticized expenditures of agency funds. Barr v. Matteo. A copy to the Massachusetts Congressional delegation of the Boston Naval Shipyard commander's explanation to Navy officials of why he withdrew official recognition of a labor organization. Howard v. Lyons, 360 U.S. 593 (1959). And even a cartoon presented by a Naval Supply Center commander to a departing officer, in keeping with a Navy custom. Frost v. Stern, 298 F. Supp. 778 (D.S.C. 1969). But see Westfall v. Erwin, 484 U.S. 292 (1988) (absolute immunity limited to "discretionary" conduct). The federal position has been adopted in a few states. See McNayr v. Kelly, 184 So. 2d 428 (Fla. 1966); Carradine v. State, 511 N.W.2d 733 (Minn. 1994).

3. Carr v. Watkins, 227 Md. 578, 177 A.2d 841 (1962), involved the federal privilege rule, a state rule, and the question of whether the making of the defamatory statement was sufficiently within the line of duty to come within official privilege. Plaintiff alleged he was fired from his job as a shopping center security guard because a security officer at a Naval Ordinance Laboratory and two county police officers told plaintiff's employer that he had been fired from the laboratory for being drunk and molesting children. Actually, plaintiff had been exonerated and continued in employment until his resignation. The federal rule applied to plaintiff's claim against the laboratory security officer, the state qualified privilege rule to the county policemen; but defendants would not be privileged, the court held, if it were found at trial that their statements were made outside the scope of their duties. Compare Tinkoff v. Campbell, 86 F. Supp. 331 (N.D. Ill. 1949) (Collector of Internal Revenue absolutely privileged in advising plaintiff's clients that he had been disbarred from practicing before Treasury Department, was not reputable and fit person to do business with, and was dishonest); Matson v. Margiotti, 371 Pa. 188, 88 A.2d 892 (1952) (state Attorney General absolutely privileged to write letter to district attorney requesting discharge of assistant district attorney because of her alleged "Communistic associations"). See also Cheatum v. Wehle, 5 N.Y.2d 585, 186 N.Y.S.2d 606, 159 N.E.2d 166 (1959) (Conservation Commissioner not absolutely privileged in after-dinner speech about what was wrong with his department).

4. For persons holding the high rank generally accepted to carry absolute privilege, press releases about matters with their official concern are usually found to be within the scope of their official duties. See Glass v. Ickes, 73 App. D.C. 3, 117 F.2d 273 (1940), cert. denied, 311 U.S. 718 (1941) (Secretary of Interior); Blair v. Walker, 64 Ill. 2d 1, 349 N.E.2d 385 (1976) (governor). Whether statements to the press by lower-ranking officials are within the scope of their duties is debatable. Compare Schlinkert v. Henderson, 331 Mich. 284, 49 N.W.2d 180 (1951) (member of state liquor control commission absolutely privileged to release to press his letter to civil service commission concerning proposed reorganization), with Carradine v. State, supra (state trooper had absolute privilege for statements in arrest report but not statements to press about arrest); Clark v. McGee, 49 N.Y.2d 613, 427 N.Y.S.2d 740, 404 N.E.2d 1283 (1980) (town supervisor absolutely priv-

ileged in statements made during course of duties, but not for statement relating to town government made during radio interview); Oden v. Reader, 935 S.W.2d 470 (Tex. App. 1996) (county attorney's statements to press not absolutely privileged); Smith v. Daniel-czyk, 400 Md. 98, 928 A.2d 795 (2007) (police officers had qualified privilege for statements to media if statements permitted in performance of official duties). In Yoder v. Workman, 224 F. Supp. 2d 1077 (S.D. W. Va. 2002), it was held that a judge could be sued on account of a press release posted on the court's web site that explained the judge's recusal from a case. Cf. Roush v. Hey, 197 W. Va. 207, 475 S.E.2d 299 (1996), in which a judge was sued for statements on a television program about a current case in which he presided. Privilege does not attach simply because a government employee's statement concerns his official duties. To use the Restatement's example, a janitor is not privileged to issue a press release concerning his work and its difficulties. Restatement (Second) of Torts § 591, ill. 2 (1977).

Luttrell v. United Telephone System, Inc.
Kansas Court of Appeals
9 Kan. App. 2d 620, 683 P.2d 1292 (1984),
aff'd, 236 Kan. 710, 695 P.2d 1279 (1985)

PARKS, Judge....

Plaintiff ... alleges that on or about April 6 or 7 of 1982, Mr. R.H. Baranek, an employee of defendant, stated to Mr. R.L. Flint, plaintiff's supervisor, that plaintiff was illegally taping telephone conversations on April 1 and that Baranek had requested him to stop but plaintiff persisted in this illegal activity the rest of the afternoon despite the direct order given him to stop by his supervisor. He further alleged that the communication of the same defamatory information was made by Mr. Flint to Mr. T.V. Tregenza and by Mr. W. Soble, all while acting within the scope of their employment. Defendant filed motion to dismiss ... on the grounds that intracorporate communications did not constitute "publication." ...

In this case, the defendant argued and the district court agreed that there can be no communication to a third person, or "publication," when the defamatory words are exchanged by agents of a single corporate defendant. This issue of first impression is more precisely whether interoffice communications between supervisory employees of a corporation, acting within the scope and course of their employment, regarding the work of another employee of the corporation, constitute publication to a third person sufficient for a defamation action.

There is a considerable division of authority concerning this issue. For example, courts recently considering the laws of Nevada, Missouri, Arkansas, Georgia and Louisiana have all accepted the assertion that intracorporate defamation is simply the corporation talking to itself and not publication. The contrary conclusion has been reached in courts applying the laws of Kentucky, Massachusetts, New York and California.... Prosser also favors the view that such communications are publication and dismisses those cases holding otherwise as confusing publication with privilege. Prosser, Law of Torts § 113, p. 767 n. 70 (4th ed. 1971).

Undeniably, the district court's holding in this case is not without support or technical appeal; however, we believe it ignores the nature of the civil injury sought to be protected in a defamation action.... Certainly, damage to one's reputation within a corporate community may be just as devastating as that effected by defamation spread to the out-side. Thus, the injury caused by intracorporate defamation should not be disregarded simply because the corporation can be sued as an individual entity.

Defendant argues that corporate employers must be free to evaluate and comment on their employees' work performance and that this freedom will be unduly restrained if they are liable for intracorporate defamation. However, the law in this state has already extended protection to comments made within a work situation by means of a qualified privilege. A communication is qualifiedly privileged if it is made in good faith on any subject matter in which the person communicating has an interest, or in reference to which he has a duty, if it is made to a person having a corresponding interest or duty. The essential elements of a qualifiedly privileged communication are good faith, an in-terest to be upheld, a statement limited in its scope to the upholding of such interest and publication in a proper manner only to proper parties. Thus in [*Dobbyn v. Nelson*, 2 Kan. App. 2d 358, 579 P.2d 721, *aff'd*, 225 Kan. 56, 587 P.2d 315 (1978)] the Court held that a letter written by an employee of the Kansas State University library concerning the con-duct of another employee and transmitted to the second employee's superior was quali-fiedly privileged. As a result, the plaintiff was required to prove that the defendants acted with knowledge of falsity or reckless disregard for the truth before the privilege could overcome.

By virtue of the qualified privilege, the employer who is evaluating or investigating an employee in good faith and within the bounds of the employment relationship is pro-tected from the threat of defamation suits by the enhanced burden of proof which the plaintiff would have to bear. We see no reason for greater freedom from liability for defamation to be accorded the corporate employer than that already available to all em-ployers through the qualified privilege.

We conclude that remarks communicated by one corporate employee to another con-cerning the job performance of a third employee are publication for the purposes of a defamation action against the employer. Since the dismissal motion was granted in this case prior to the commencement of any discovery, we make no findings concerning the possible application of qualified privilege to the communication alleged.

[Reversed and remanded.]

Notes

1. *Communications within single business.* Deciding that there is no publication when a business' employee or agent communicates only with another employee or agent of the business in effect creates an absolute privilege. The trend of the more recent decisions, in jurisdictions where the question was not settled by prior rulings, is to hold that there is publication and no absolute privilege. However, as explained in the principal case, qual-ified privilege is likely to apply to internal communications made in supposed furtherance of the employer's business interests. See Popko v. Continental Casualty Co., 355 Ill. App. 3d 257, 823 N.E.2d 184 (2005); Hagebak v. Stone, 133 N.M. 75, 61 P.3d 201 (Ct. App. 2002); Wallulis v. Dymowski, 323 Or. 337, 918 P.2d 755 (1996). Would a court be more willing to accept that there was no publication if the communication was dictation to a typist, or delivery of a document that the recipient put into the business' files (or sent to plain-tiff)? See Annot, Libel and Slander: Dictation to Defendant's Secretary, Typist, or Stenog-rapher as Publication, 62 A.L.R.3d 1207 (1975); Hanson, Libel and Related Torts ¶¶ 66–67 (1969).

2. *Spousal communications.* Some cases find no publication in statements made by one spouse to another spouse. See Sesler v. Montgomery, 78 Cal. 486, 21 P. 185 (1889); Springer v. Swift, 59 S.D. 208, 239 N.W. 171 (1931). A more modern view is that publication occurs but it should be protected by an absolute privilege. See Conrad v. Roberts, 95 Kan. 180, 147 P. 795 (1915) (privileged although spouses living apart); Restatement (Second) of Torts § 592 (1977); Eldredge, Law of Defamation 416–417 (1978). Can the "no publication" position be rationalized with cases that find publication in defamatory communications addressed to *plaintiff's* spouse? See Springer v. Swift, supra. See generally Annot., Communication Between Relatives or Members of a Family as Publication or Subject of Privilege Within Law of Libel and Slander, 78 A.L.R. 1182 (1932) (includes cases of qualified privilege for communications between other family members).

3. *Consent.* Consent by the person defamed is sometimes termed an absolute privilege, as it unconditionally bars an action for libel or slander. In this context, consent means consent to publication of a particular statement, or at least to publication of a certain type of statement. See Lee v. Paulsen, 273 Or. 103, 539 P.2d 1079 (1975) (at public hearing, teacher asked that reason for his dismissal be stated); Borden, Inc. v. Wallace, 570 S.W.2d 445 (Tex. Civ. App. 1978) (by agreeing to polygraph test, employee consented to operator's being told reason for test: suspicion of theft by employee). However, a request for a letter of recommendation is not consent to a defamatory one. Nelson v. Whitten, 272 F. 135 (E.D.N.Y. 1921). Compare Woodfield v. Providence Hospital, 779 A.2d 933 (D.C. 2001) (consent to former employer's furnishing information barred defamation action); Gengler v. Phelps, 92 N.M. 465, 589 P.2d 1056 (Ct. App. 1978), cert. denied, 92 N.M. 353, 588 P.2d 554 (1979) (consent when plaintiff, after notice of discharge by employer, applied for new employment on form which included consent to inquire of employer).

4. If plaintiff procures publication of a document to his agent in order to bring an action, consent will likely be found. See Renfro Drug Co. v. Lawson, 138 Tex. 434, 160 S.W.2d 246 (1942). But a publication procured in order to ascertain whether defendant was making defamatory statements has been distinguished. See Richardson v. Gunby, 88 Kan. 47, 127 P. 533 (1912) (letter, written at plaintiff's behest, requesting credit reference); Smith v. Dunlop Tire & Rubber Co., 186 S.C. 456, 196 S.E. 174 (1938) (statement in response to plaintiff's asking what defendant had said or meant). What if plaintiff challenges defendant to repeat a defamatory statement before witnesses and this is done? See Shinglemeyer v. Wright, 124 Mich. 230, 82 N.W. 887 (1900) (no action for invited publication). Compare Restatement (Second) of Torts § 583, comment *e* (1977) (not consent if intended and understood as request that defendant give plaintiff opportunity to vindicate reputation by lawsuit). If plaintiff can have a defamatory statement deleted, is failure to do this consent? See Carrie v. Tolkien, [2009] E.M.L.R. 164 (Q.B.D.) (plaintiff controlled web site; consent found). See generally Eldredge, Law of Defamation 317–322 (1978); Harper, James & Gray, Law of Torts § 5.17 (3d ed. 2006); Sack, Defamation: Libel, Slander, and Related Problems § 8.2.8 (4th ed. 2010).

5. *Publications required or authorized by law.* There is authority that an absolute privilege applies to publications required by law—for example, a notice or document that an official or private party is legally required to publish. See Weber v. Cueto, 209 Ill. App. 3d 936, 568 N.E.2d 513 (1991), appeal denied, 139 Ill. 2d 605, 575 N.E.2d 925 (1991) (lawyer required by attorney disciplinary rules to report suspected misconduct by another lawyer); Eldredge, Law of Defamation 417–418 (1978). It appears that when a person is privileged to publish a statement, a party that provides appropriate means of publication

shares the privilege, but the provider's privilege may be qualified even if the author's privilege is absolute. See Restatement (Second) of Torts §612 (1977); Eldredge, Law of Defamation 443–446 (1978) (privilege said not to be supported by case law).

C. Qualified Privileges

Flanagan v. McLane

Supreme Court of Errors of Connecticut
87 Conn. 220, 87 A. 727, 88 A. 96 (1913)

… The plaintiff and his helper worked in and about the house of the defendant's husband for some weeks. During this time a sum of money was missed which afterwards reappeared. While the money was missing the defendant wrote the letter set forth in the first count to one Sturtze, a constable of the town of Hamden, informing him of the loss and of her belief that the plaintiff had taken it. She had already written a similar letter, set forth in the fourth count, to the mother of the plaintiff's helper. After the money reappeared the defendant again wrote to Sturtze the letter which is the basis of the second count, saying in effect that the money had been found in a place where she had never put it and that she would do no more about the matter, but was satisfied that the plaintiff had taken it and brought it back again when he found that he was suspected.… The defendant's answer … pleaded privilege and want of malice as to each. [At trial, defendant obtained verdict and judgment.]

BEACH, J. The law implies malice from a libelous publication, except in certain cases of privilege, one of which is "when the author and publisher of the alleged slander acted in the bona fide discharge of a public or private duty or in the prosecution of his own right or interest." "A privileged communication means nothing more than that the occasion of making it rebuts the prima facie inference of malice arising from the publication of matter prejudicial to the character of the plaintiff, and throws upon him the onus of proving malice in fact, but not of proving it by extrinsic evidence only; he still has a right to require that the alleged libel itself shall be submitted to the jury that they may judge whether there is evidence of malice on the face of it." White v. Nicholls, 3 How. 266, 286, 287.

Whether a publication is libelous per se is a question for the court. Whether the occasion is one of privilege is also a question of law for the court.

Whether the defendant in the use of the privileged occasion was or was not actuated by malice in fact is a question for the jury.…

… We think from an examination of the evidence that the jury might properly have come to the conclusion from the defendant's own testimony that she honestly believed that the plaintiff or his helper had taken her money and that the letters in question were written in that belief and without malice in fact.

It is claimed in appellant's brief that the letter set out in the second count, which was written to the officer after the money was found, is beyond the pale of privilege, because the defendant was not then in the discharge of any duty or engaged in an effort to recover her money.…

We think that the letter set forth in the second count, although written after the money was found, must be dealt with as a part of the whole correspondence between the defendant and the officer. It is not very seriously disputed that the first letter to Sturtze, written before the money was found, is, on the facts pleaded, a privileged communication. Sturtze was a constable, and the defendant appealed to him to investigate her loss with a view to get "evidence and threaten them with arrest." She was concerned more with using the law in terrorem than with the punishment of the supposed thief. Then when the money was found she again writes the officer telling him that it is found, but in a place where she never put it; that she will do no more about the matter; and that she is still satisfied that the plaintiff took it and brought it back again. Clearly this second letter would never have been written except for the first. The defendant was in a way bound to let the officer know that the money had been found, and if she said no more her letter would be taken as an admission that her former suspicions were mistaken. We think, under these circumstances, that the defendant in writing to an officer already engaged in investigating the loss was legally entitled, if acting honestly and without malice, to reaffirm her belief in the plaintiff's guilt for the guidance of the officer in case it was or might become his duty to pursue the investigation with a view to criminal proceedings. There is no error.

WHEELER, J. [with whom Roraback, J., joined, dissenting]....

If circumstances came to the knowledge of the defendant which caused her to believe a crime had been committed, it was her civic duty to state to the authorities what she knew and believed; on ground of highest public policy her communication would be a qualified or conditionally privileged one. Moreover, since the defendant had an interest in the recovery of the money, and the person to whom she made the communication had a duty to discharge respecting this she had, so long as she did not act with express malice, the right to communicate to the peace officer the circumstances attending the loss of her money, together with her suspicions and belief and every circumstance relevant to the detection of the theft. She must not make such a charge recklessly or wantonly, or without circumstances reasonably arousing suspicion....

The letter [in the second count] clearly charges the plaintiff with the theft of the defendant's money. It was not written the peace officer for the purpose of having him investigate the theft; nor in furtherance of any feature of the case. It was written primarily to have the peace officer desist from the investigation of the theft of which the defendant had complained to him over three weeks previously. Belief in the charge did not justify her in its reiteration upon withdrawal of it from the officer. She was not engaged in the performance of a public duty, nor in the fair protection of her rights in renewing her charge against the defendant. She had no more right to libel the plaintiff in a communication to the peace officer than in one to any other person. Had her communication been made in furtherance of the detection of the theft or the prosecution of the crime, the occasion might have been a qualifiedly privileged one....

The [majority opinion] holds that the defendant had the right, under the circumstances, "to reaffirm her belief in the plaintiff's guilt, for the guidance of the officer, in case it was or might become his duty to pursue the investigation with a view to criminal proceedings." This conclusion is, we believe, against all authority. The defendant was not engaged in the performance of a public duty, nor in the fair protection of her rights in renewing her libelous charge. She wrote to notify the constable to desist from its continuance. He had then been doing detective work for her in getting evidence, and expected her to pay him for his services. We repeat, her belief in the charge and her freedom from malice did not justify her renewal of the charge of theft to the public officer in discharging him from her service....

Notes

1. "Qualified" or "conditional" privilege is usually distinguished from "absolute" privilege on the ground that an absolute privilege covers statements made with malice but a qualified privilege does not. However, as reflected in the principal cases on qualified privilege and the notes on pp. 609–612, infra, factors other than malice can defeat a defense of qualified privilege that otherwise would be valid. If a defendant publishes a defamatory statement in circumstances of qualified privilege, no liability will result unless plaintiff can prove such "abuse" of the privilege as publication with malice or without belief in the truth of what was communicated. No such proof is necessary when other factors, such as communication beyond the boundaries permitted by the privilege, lead the court to conclude that the statement was not conditionally privileged. In principle, the existence of qualified privilege is a question of law and abuse of the privilege is a question of fact, but case-specific issues bearing upon claims of qualified privilege are often committed to juries. See generally Eldredge, Law of Defamation 448–450, 505–508 (1978).

2. The principal qualified privileges are the privilege to publish statements in furtherance of the "public interest," privileges to publish statements in furtherance of other interests, the privilege to publish reports of public proceedings, the privilege to publish "fair comment," and the privilege of officials of government who do not possess absolute privilege. These privileges have made it possible to act to protect public or private interests or inform the public without the deterrent of strict liability should someone be defamed in error. Absolute privilege—which prevents an inquiry into defendant's motives, grounds and, often, purpose—has been thought unnecessary or inadvisable in these circumstances.

3. Unlike the other "interest" privileges, pp. 593–602, infra, the qualified privilege to publish statements in the "public interest" is quite narrow. It covers statements made to government officials and agencies about problems within their official responsibilities. The public interest privilege serves the public's interest in the proper conduct of government by its officers and in government enforcement of the law against private citizens. Many of the statements within this privilege can be allocated to two categories. One consists of complaints made to a government official about the alleged actions of another official, whose conduct the first official has some power to control. This applies to employees of public school systems as well as to employees performing governmental functions. Usually, the statement is made to a superior of the person about whom the complaint is made, but the privilege may attach when the power of control or influence can be exercised only indirectly—for example, when a citizen complains about bureaucratic action or inaction to a member of Congress or the state legislature. See R. v. Rule, [1937] 2 K.B. 375 (C.C.A.). See generally Eldredge, Law of Defamation 497–502 (1978).

4. The second category consists of communications to law enforcement officials, such as police and prosecuting attorneys, concerning alleged or suspected unlawful activity and communications to agencies responsible for the licensing or discipline of occupational groups about misconduct by a member of an occupation within the agency's jurisdiction. See Eldredge, Law of Defamation 492–497 (1978). Another type of "public interest" statement, which can fall within one of the two categories already mentioned, is a communication concerning a government agency's relations with private citizens, such as recipients and potential recipients of government contracts or benefits, applicants for government employment, and persons whose activities may be

regulated by government. See A & B-Abell Elevator Co., Inc. v. Columbus/Central Ohio Building & Construction Trades Council, 73 Ohio St. 3d 1, 651 N.E.2d 1283 (1995); Annot., Libel and Slander: Privilege of Communications Made by Private Person or Concern to Public Authorities Regarding One Not in Public Employment, 136 A.L.R. 543 (1942).

5. As the principal case indicates, the privilege does not require that defendant's motive in publishing the defamatory statement be disinterested service of the public welfare. A person who identifies to the police a suspected thief in order to recover the missing property, or who complains to a superior about a government official's actions in order to obtain more favorable treatment, is not necessarily outside the privilege. But if defendant's purpose is almost entirely service of a private interest or object, the principles of the "private interest" privileges rather than the public interest privilege should apply. See Restatement (Second) of Torts § 603 (1977).

6. In all of the "interest" privileges, there is an issue of whether the privilege requires merely an actual belief in the truth of what is stated or requires also that defendant have reasonable grounds. See p. 610, infra. Despite the seriously damaging effects of allegations of criminal activity, one can discern a greater tendency to find good faith belief sufficient for the public interest privilege than for the others, lest citizens be deterred by the fear of defamation liability from reporting crime or otherwise assisting law enforcement. See Pecue v. West, 233 N.Y. 316, 135 N.E. 515 (1922); Joseph v. Baars, 142 Wis. 390, 125 N.W. 913 (1910). But see Pierce v. Oard, 23 Neb. 828, 37 N.W. 677 (1888) (probable cause required for accusation of crime). Informal complaints to law enforcement agencies, prosecuting attorneys, grand juries, magistrates, administrative tribunals and professional discipline bodies have sometimes been held to be absolutely, not conditionally, privileged as the initial step in a judicial or quasi-judicial proceeding. Ledvina v. Cerasani, 213 Ariz. 569, 146 P.3d 70 (Ct. App. 2006); Bergman v. Hupy, 64 Wis. 2d 747, 221 N.W.2d 898 (1974). Contra, Fridovich v. Fridovich, 598 So. 2d 65 (Fla. 1992); Caldor, Inc. v. Bowden, 330 Md. 632, 625 A.2d 959 (1993). See Eldredge, Law of Defamation 349–352 (1978); Prosser & Keeton, Law of Torts 819–820 (5th ed. 1984).

7. Should the public interest privilege be extended to communications made not to a government official, but to an organization dedicated to promoting law enforcement, professional ethics or the proper conduct of government? In Dempsky v. Double, 386 Pa. 542, 126 A.2d 915 (1956), defendant wrote a county comptroller to request an investigation into an employee's use of county vehicles for personal purposes. A copy of the letter was sent to the county League of Women Voters. The court held that the copy to the League was privileged because the object of sending it was to have a civic-minded group cooperate in the request for an investigation, thus serving the public welfare. Compare Pecue v. Collins, 204 App. Div. 142, 197 N.Y.S. 835 (1923) (report that plaintiff "keeping girls for immoral purposes" sent to civic league incorporated for purpose of elevating public morals; not privileged because league not part of machinery of government). The privilege might be extended to communications with private security personnel about suspected criminal activity. See Pate v. Service Merchandise Co., Inc., 959 S.W.2d 569 (Tenn. App. 1996), cert. denied, 522 U.S. 821 (1997). A complaint made to a professional body, such as a medical society, about the conduct of one of its members might be accorded the same privilege as a complaint to a professional licensing or disciplinary body established by the state. See Annot., Testimony Before or Communications to Private Professional Society's Judicial Commission, Ethics Committee, or the Like, as Privileged, 9 A.L.R.4th 807 (1981).

Sindorf v. Jacron Sales Company, Inc.
Maryland Court of Special Appeals
27 Md. App. 53, 341 A.2d 856 (1975),
aff'd, 276 Md. 580, 350 A.2d 688 (1976)

ORTH, Chief Judge....

[Sindorf was employed as a salesman by a Pennsylvania corporation, Jacron Sales Company.] He resigned on 23 July 1973 because of a dispute over certain sales made by him and commissions he believed due him. The corporation's president, John Langton, testified that "sales discrepancies" had arisen from Sindorf's selling practices. The discrepancies were not financial but resulted from "selling to people without checking credit ratings...." Sindorf testified that he would not receive his commissions from these credit sales until payment had been received for the goods and that uncollectable debts were shared 50/50 by himself and the corporation. He claimed that he had not been paid his commissions from his charge sales because the corporation said the accounts were not collected. It was these disagreements which culminated in Sindorf's resignation by letter wherein he explained that he was retaining the inventory in his possession "as partial payment of the commissions due me...." Subsequently the corporation initiated criminal proceedings against Sindorf because of his retention of the goods. The disposition of those proceedings is not apparent from the record before us.

A few days after his association with the Pennsylvania corporation terminated, Sindorf was hired by the Tool Box Corporation of Maryland upon an interview with William Brose, president of that company. When Langton learned that Sindorf was working for Tool Box, he called Fridkis, Vice President of [defendant, Jacron Sales Company of Virginia, a subsidiary of the Pennsylvania Jacron]. He asked Fridkis to verify Sindorf's current employment and to ascertain whether Sindorf had been working for Tool Box at the same time he had been working for the Pennsylvania Jacron. Langton told Fridkis why Sindorf left the Pennsylvania corporation: "We had mentioned that we had discrepancies with him, the sales picture, and the policy of how he would sell against company policies and do whatever he pleased, and that he had left us and in his possession he had taken with him his complete inventory and wouldn't return it to us. He claimed that he would return it when he would get his commission money."

Fridkis called Tool Box to talk to Brose, but Brose was not in. Fridkis asked a secretary, Denise Bennett, if Sindorf was then employed by Tool Box. She was not sure. Fridkis said, "Well, have Bill call me, because we have some things missing and I would like to talk to Bill about Jack."

When Brose returned the call, he and Fridkis talked first about routine business matters. Brose testified that he had a "nice" business relationship with Fridkis. Although the Virginia Jacron and Tool Box were competitors, they would, at times, exchange goods and information and buy from and sell to each other. Brose said that if a former employee was employed or was about to be employed by Jacron, he would call Fridkis, discuss the employee and apprise Fridkis of any problems. Eventually the conversation centered on Sindorf. The conversation was recorded by Brose, and a transcript thereof was offered in evidence. We quote that part of the intercourse concerning Sindorf.

Mr. Fridkis: ... I want to talk to you about your new salesman, Jack Sindorf ...

Mr. Brose: he's been working the Ocean City area

Mr. Fridkis: yeh, you know he, he use to work for Jacron

Mr. Brose: understand in Philadelphia

Mr. Fridkis: yeh, Philadelphia and, ah, there was quite a few cash sales and quite a bit of merchandise that was not accounted for ...

Mr. Brose: Oh good heavens

Mr. Fridkis: So I thought I'd better kind of tip you off about it, you know, watch your stock real, real carefully on trucks and things

Mr. Brose: yeh

Mr. Fridkis: when did you hire him, how long

Mr. Brose: I think today, no officially yesterday I guess ...

Mr. Fridkis: Oh, okey cause, ah, ah, someone here says he's been working for you three or four, ah, ah, weeks

Mr. Brose: God, I never met him that long ago

Mr. Fridkis: o. k., o. k.

Mr. Brose: I think, I think the first time I met him was about Thursday or Friday over the phone ... and he was down yesterday morning and we had a chat and decided he's like to represent The Tool Box in that area, he said that he's been working before for Jacron in Philadelphia

Mr. Fridkis: yeh, yeh, well this was what the story was on it and

Mr. Brose: what, did he get fired

Mr. Fridkis: ah, yeh, yeh, they were, ah, ah, noticing things, you know what I mean

Mr. Brose: Oh boy

Mr. Fridkis: ah, noticing things that, ah, ah, were, ah, some checks came in that were made out to him, you know what I mean..., and ah, ah, they were noticing some stuff that was disappearing and he had about $3000 worth of merchandise on the truck and ah, when they turned the things in it just didn't jive ...

Mr. Brose: good heavens

Mr. Fridkis: yeh, and well you know, little things, ah, ah, that he had, you know how guys take stuff out of the place there and he doesn't turn a ticket in on it, you know what I mean

Mr. Brose: oh, oh

Mr. Fridkis: in other words, odd ball stuff, you know, hey he took out three tools there and, ah, that was three weeks ago and we don't have a ticket on it

Mr. Brose: oh, oh

Mr. Fridkis: you know, like what happened to the ticket

Mr. Brose: I think we have pretty good inventory control. I think, well, ah, we can't watch everything, you and I both know that but you just

Mr. Fridkis: yeh, well I just, you know, just tipped you off

Mr. Brose: I appreciate it

Mr. Fridkis: and kind of watch him very, very carefully so far as this is concerned ...

Mr. Brose: yeh, well I sure appreciate your telling me and letting me know about that

Mr. Fridkis: Well I was curious to see when he started working for you. Had he been working for you at the same time he was working for Jacron in Philadelphia.

Mr. Brose: Ah

Mr. Fridkis: got it, got it

Mr. Brose: Unless he's still on their payroll now, I understand that he was

Mr. Fridkis: No, no, he's not on the payroll, he was even fired last week I believe, got it

Mr. Brose: Oh, he told me he was not on their payroll and there was not a written contract or anything so he was open, he was available so

Mr. Fridkis: yeh, yeh

Mr. Brose: He seemed like a real nice guy, real nice fellow

Mr. Fridkis: Well just keep an eye on him that's all and ah, that's all I can say as far as that goes

Mr. Brose: Thanks Bob

Mr. Fridkis: I think I just met the guy personally a few times, I don't really know him. Well I was just talking to Jack and he asked me about it. He was working for you cause he had heard that he had told someone that he had been working for you three or four weeks, you know

Mr. Brose: No, if he had been working for anybody it wasn't The Tool Box

Mr. Fridkis: o. k., that's all

Mr. Brose: If he was, then he and Freddie had something going on the side. I didn't know him that long ago. In fact, it was Thursday or Friday that I talked to him the first time.

Mr. Fridkis: okey Bill

Mr. Brose: Thank you ole buddie....

The conversation returned to other business matters and terminated shortly thereafter.

Brose asked Sindorf to come to the office. Brose told him what Fridkis said. Within two months Sindorf filed the slander action....

[The trial court granted defendant's motion for a directed verdict on the ground that there existed a conditional privilege to defame Sindorf and he had adduced no evidence of malice.]

... In the words of Baron Parke in *Toogood v. Spyring*, 1 C.M. & R. 181, 149 Eng. Rep. 1044 (1834), a publication is conditionally privileged when it is "fairly made by a person in the discharge of some public or private duty, whether legal or moral, or in the conduct of his own affairs, in matters where his interest is concerned." ... [T]he types of interest which are protected by a qualified privilege are classified by Prosser, [*Law of Torts* (4th ed. 1971)] at 786, as interest of the publisher, interest of others, common interest of publisher and recipient, communications made to one who may act in the public interest, and fair comment on matters of public concern....

... [T]he law of this State is that a defamatory publication is conditionally privileged when the occasion shows that the communicating party and the recipient have a mutual interest in the subject matter, or some duty with respect thereto. Over seventy-five years ago the Court of Appeals established that where an employer gives a character of an employee the communication is conditionally privileged under the principle that the party communicating has a duty owed, even though such duty is not a legal one, but only a moral or social duty of imperfect obligation. This is so even though the defamatory information was given voluntarily rather than upon request. *Fresh v. Cutter*, 73 Md. 87, 20 A. 774....

Sindorf argues that because he was never employed by the Virginia Jacron, the privilege recognized in *Fresh* did not arise. We do not read *Fresh* and the authorities so narrowly as to confine the duty as owed only by a former employer. The basis for the privilege depends upon the particular circumstances of the communication. Other persons may have a *bona fide* belief that they owe a moral or social duty to inform a new or prospective employer about an employee. This is not to say that anyone is privileged to communicate adverse information to an employer. In many instances a reasonable man would conclude that to communicate with an employer would be "officious intermeddling", Prosser, at 788, and therefore the communication would not be privileged. The circumstances here, however, were that the defamer was the vice-president of the subsidiary of the corporation which was Sindorf's former employer, and that the communicator and recipient, even though competitors, had a close personal and business relationship. Whether based on a duty owed or a common interest, we think that a qualified privilege arose....

... "[M]alice means 'a reckless disregard of truth, the use of unnecessarily abusive language, or other circumstances which would support a conclusion that the defendant acted in an ill-tempered manner or was motivated by ill-will.'" [*Orrison v. Vance*, 262 Md. 285, 277 A.2d 573.] ...

... "[T]he plaintiff has the right notwithstanding the privileged character of the communication to go to the jury, if there be evidence tending to show actual malice, as when the words unreasonably impute crime, or the occasion of their utterance is such as to indicate, by its unnecessary publicity or otherwise, a purpose wrongfully to defame the plaintiff.... Or, malice may be established by showing that the publication contained matter not relevant to the occasion.... Expressions in excess of what the occasion warrants do not *per se* take away the privilege, but such excess may be evidence of malice." [*Fresh v. Cutter, supra.*] ... We believe that the evidence, when viewed as required by the rule pertaining to the grant *vel non* of a directed verdict, led to conclusions from which reasonable minds could differ. We start with the rule that the publisher's motive will be more carefully scrutinized if his statements are volunteered than if they are in response to an inquiry, in which latter instance, greater latitude is permitted. We observe that Fridkis clearly indicated that Sindorf had been fired, whereas, as far as the record shows, he resigned. It does not appear that Langton told Fridkis that Sindorf was fired, and if Fridkis did not in fact know that Sindorf was not fired, stating that he was fired could be found to be a reckless disregard of truth. Langton, before asking Fridkis to call Brose, told Fridkis that Sindorf claimed he would return the "inventory" Sindorf retained when he received his commission money. This is borne out by a letter, referred to as Sindorf's letter of resignation, sent to Jacron of Pennsylvania under date of 23 July 1973. In that letter, Sindorf enclosed invoices representing material in his possession "which I accept as partial payment of the commissions due me as of July 23, 1973." He added, "At such time as the monies due me are paid, all material will be gladly returned to Jacron Sales Co." None of this was communicated by Fridkis to Brose. According to Langton, Fridkis was to call Brose to verify that Sindorf was working for Tool Box and to ascertain whether he had been working for Tool Box and Jacron at the same time. Fridkis patently went far beyond this in his conversation with Brose. When Fridkis was unable to reach Brose on his first attempt, he spoke to the secretary. What he said to her led her to believe that Sindorf was a thief. The trial judge could not understand how she reached this conclusion, but we cannot say that a reasonable person would be unable to conclude from what Fridkis told her that Sindorf was a thief. We observe that the publisher will be liable if he publishes his statement to accomplish a distinct objective, which may be legitimate enough in itself but is not within the privilege. We think that a reasonable person could conclude from the evidence that Fridkis's communication to Brose was an effort to pressure Sindorf into returning the material he was holding, or, perhaps, simply to ascertain, as Langton requested, the date of employment of Sindorf by Tool Box. Neither would be within the privilege. The short of it is that we cannot find, assuming the truth of all credible evidence on the issue of malice and of all inferences fairly deducible therefrom, and considering them in the light most favorable to Sindorf, that they lead to the conclusions, from which reasonable minds could not differ, that Fridkis, and through him, Jacron, did not abuse the privilege to defame by excessive publication or by use of the occasion for an improper purpose, or by lack of grounds for belief in the truth of what was said. Therefore, the question of malice was properly for the jury and the trial judge erred in granting the motion for a directed verdict. The issue of malice should have gone to the jury with appropriate instructions. We reverse the judgment and remand the case for a new trial....

Notes

1. Claims of qualified privilege resting upon an interest possessed by the maker of a defamatory communication, its intended recipient, or a third party are extremely numerous. No brief statement can explain the law in this area. In addition to the "public interest," pp. 589–592, supra, interests protected by qualified privilege are frequently stated to be (1) an interest of the publisher of the defamatory statement, (2) an interest of a person other than the publisher, and (3) a common interest. See Eldredge, Law of Defamation 452–492 (1978); Prosser & Keeton, Law of Torts 825–830 (5th ed. 1984). How helpful this classification is is debatable. Many defamatory statements fall within at least two of the categories, as in the principal case, and the essential requirement is not that there be an interest of a particular type, but that the maker of the statement reasonably believe that some interest of sufficient importance would be served by the communication. See Restatement (Second) of Torts §§ 594–598 (1977); Harper, James & Gray, Law of Torts § 5.25 (3d ed. 2006).

2. *Interest of the publisher.* An analogy has been drawn between this privilege and the privileges of self-defense and defense of property found in torts to the person and property. Statements made in order to protect oneself from personal injury or misappropriation of property—as when defendant states that plaintiff may steal or otherwise take what rightfully belongs to defendant—or to recover property—as when defendant states that plaintiff may be responsible for the disappearance of goods—are conditionally privileged. So are statements made for the purpose of enforcing a debt or other legal claim, whether against plaintiff or a third person. But the range of interests protected by qualified privilege extends well beyond those which are given specific protection by other branches of law. It may be that a person is privileged to protect any investment sufficiently important and sufficiently threatened to justify making the defamatory statement. But see Shenkman v. O'Malley, p. 602, infra. A distinction has been drawn between "defensive" and "offensive" use of defamatory statements. A business has no privilege to defame competitors in order to acquire customers, although it can protect itself against "unfair" competition. Usually the interest being protected is an economic one, but the privilege can be invoked in aid of such non-economic interests as health and family relationships. It encompasses many communications with employees, agents and professional advisers. Some authority finds no privilege when the recipient of the communication has no interest or duty in the matter. See M. Rosenberg & Sons, Inc. v. Craft, 182 Va. 512, 29 S.E.2d 375 (1944) (de-

fendant wrote letter stating that plaintiff owed long-overdue debt and asking whether plaintiff was employed by recipient, which he was). See generally Eldredge, Law of Defamation 452–461 (1978); Prosser & Keeton, Law of Torts 825–826 (5th ed. 1984); Sack, Defamation: Libel, Slander, and Related Problems § 9.2.1 (4th ed. 2010).

3. There are a number of situations in which defendant can claim to derive some benefit from publishing information but no specific protection of an interest by the recipient of the information. Is there a privilege? Examples:

(a) An employer tells a union's leadership why he did not hire one of the union's members. Hanly v. Pisces Productions Inc., [1981] 1 W.W.R. 369 (B.C. Sup. Ct.) (privileged, in interests of both defendant and union leadership).

(b) A company employing a travelling salesman notifies its customers of the saleman's dismissal on grounds of his dishonesty and endeavors to injure the company's business. Browne v. Prudden-Winslow Co., 195 App. Div. 419, 186 N.Y.S. 350 (1921) (privileged). Compare Shannon v. Taylor AMC/Jeep, Inc., 168 Mich. App. 415, 425 N.W.2d 165 (1988) (vehicle dealer not privileged to tell customers that parts manager fired for dealing in stolen parts).

(c) Plaintiff is defamed in the course of an evaluation of his job performance by a fellow employee or supervisor. McCone v. New England Telephone & Telegraph Co., 393 Mass. 231, 471 N.E.2d 47 (1984) (privileged).

(d) The proprietor of an appliance business approaches his bank for a loan. He is told that if he employs plaintiff as manager the loan will not be made because plaintiff had not remitted the proceeds of appliance sales in accordance with his financial arrangements with the bank. West v. Peoples Banking & Trust Co., 14 Ohio. App. 2d 69, 236 N.E.2d 679 (1967) (privileged in interest of both bank and prospective borrower).

(e) A retail store discharges a service manager on grounds of falsifying records and allowing gambling on company property. The employees whom the fired manager supervised stop work and ask for a meeting with the store manager. At the meeting, they are told the grounds of the service manager's discharge. Haddad v. Sears, Roebuck and Co., 526 F.2d 83 (6th Cir. 1975) (not privileged). Contra, Worley v. Oregon Physicians Service, 69 Or. App. 241, 686 P.2d 404 (1984), review denied, 298 Or. 334, 691 P.2d 483 (1984) (privileged to explain to employees reasons for plaintiff's discharge, which implied theft, in interests of security and employee morale).

(f) A large company issues a news release to regional media stating that management employees have been discharged for improper conduct. Straitwell v. National Steel Corp., 869 F.2d 248 (4th Cir. 1989) (privileged). Cf. Richmond v. Southwire Co., 980 F.2d 518 (8th Cir. 1992) (small-town employer's statement to local newspapers that employees terminated after investigation into possession and use of drugs on company property; privileged). Compare Brown v. First National Bank of Mason City, 193 N.W.2d 547 (Iowa 1982) (bank's press statement about disappearance of small amounts of money, impliedly defaming discharged cashier; not privileged).

Informing persons who demand payment of the reasons for refusal of the demand and "self-defense" against defamatory attack are treated at pp. 602–606, infra.

4. *Interest of another person.* The interest advanced may be the interest of the person to whom the defamatory statement is made or that of a third person. In either case, whether defendant could reasonably believe that making the communication would result in protection of the interest is an important consideration. This privilege is often de-

scribed as the privilege to make a defamatory statement in discharge of a duty owed to another person. In this context, "duty" is not limited to a legal duty to act for the welfare of another, such as that owed by employees to their employers, agents to their principals, trustees to their beneficiaries, professionals to their clients and guardians to their wards. The duty need only be a social or moral one. It exists when "generally accepted standards of decent conduct" direct or at least approve of the making of the communication. See Restatement (Second) of Torts § 595 (1977). Economic, family and social relationships between the parties involved (the parties to the communication and the parties whose interests may be affected) are important factors, and whether the statement was requested or volunteered has frequently played a role. The value of the interest obviously is of great weight. Presumably, the interest of highest value is personal safety, followed by protection of property, but the most typical illustration of this privilege is a reference furnished to someone who will decide whether to employ or extend credit to plaintiff or select plaintiff for some position. This is better explained by society's interest in the provision of candid references than by the existence of any substantial duty to provide a reference. See generally Eldredge, Law of Defamation 461–479, 486–492 (1978); Prosser & Keeton, Law of Torts 826–828 (5th ed. 1984); Sack, Defamation: Libel, Slander, and Related Problems §§ 9.2.2, 9.2.4 (4th ed. 2010).

5. Consider whether the following are "privileged occasions":

(a) A merchant writes a fire insurance company that another merchant's building was, according to neighborhood reports, deliberately burned down by the owner in order to collect insurance. Hubbard v. Rutledge, 57 Miss. 7 (1879) (privileged).

(b) On information from the police, a mayor tells an official guest that the guest's valet is a suspect in the theft of a gold watch in another city. Stuart v. Bell, [1891] 2 Q.B. 341 (C.A.) (privileged).

(c) Parents of a young girl tell neighbors, who are also parents, that they suspect another neighbor had molested the girl. Schmitz v. Aston, 197 Ariz. 264, 3 P.3d 1184 (Ct. App. 2000), review denied, 199 Ariz. 431, 18 P.3d 1230 (2001) (not privileged).

(d) Defendant engages a cook through an employment registry. A few months later, defendant notifies the registry that the cook was discharged, having been "most unsatisfactory." Drunkenness is implied. Farquhar v. Neiss, (1890) 17 R. 716 (Scot. Ct. Sess.) (privileged).

(e) In order to secure accommodation for a new employee, his supervisor asks an acquaintance to provide a room for the employee in his home. Later, the supervisor tells the homeowner that the employee was seen spending the night with plaintiff at a rooming house. Rose v. Tholborn, 153 Mo. App. 408, sub nom. De Van Rose v. Tholborn, 134 S.W. 1093 (1911) (privileged).

(f) A clergyman's sermon criticizes the conduct of a member of the congregation. Hassett v. Carroll, 85 Conn. 23, 81 A. 1013 (1911) (not privileged). See also Adam v. Allan, (1841) 3 D. 1058 (Scot. Ct. Sess.). But see Hester v. Barnett, 723 S.W.2d 544 (Mo. App. 1987) (no liability if plaintiff consented as member of religious body to such discipline).

(g) A neighbor tells plaintiff's brother that plaintiff has been stealing gasoline from the neighbor and others and this "looks bad" for the brother's family. Faber v. Byrle, 171 Kan. 38, 229 P.2d 718 (1951) (privileged).

(h) A man holding hostages at gunpoint indicates that he will surrender peacefully if a newspaper publishes his grievances against plaintiffs. Riches v. News Group Newspapers Ltd., [1986] Q.B. 256 (C.A.)

(i) A friend of the family—the former pastor of the family's church—writes, at the father's request, a letter to the daughter about the unsuitability of a marriage to plaintiff. "Joannes" v. Bennett, 5 Allen (87 Mass.) 169 (1862) (not privileged). Compare Berry v. Moench, 8 Utah 2d 191, 331 P.2d 814 (1958) (in response to request from family physician, psychiatrist supplied information on former patient to parents of someone contemplating marriage to ex-patient; privileged).

(j) A stranger, saying that she would thank anyone who would tell her such things, writes Mrs. Burton: "Dear Madam: Has Mr. Burton not been out of town for the past six months from Wed. to Fridays and has he not told you he was out with his sheep. You may know all about the sheep he is with but if you don't ... this sheep's name is Mrs. Agnes Grim." Burton v. Mattson, 50 Utah 133, 166 P. 979 (1917) (not privileged).

(k) Defendant writes plaintiff to collect on a bill supposedly owed by plaintiff to a doctor's estate. Plaintiff's mother opens the letter while plaintiff is at work. Not knowing why her daughter, who is seventeen, owed money to the doctor, the mother asks defendant what the bill is for. He replies: for performing an abortion. Miller v. Howe, 245 Ky. 568, 53 S.W.2d 938 (1932) (not privileged). Compare Kroger Co. v. Young, 210 Va. 564, 172 S.E.2d 720 (1970) (store privileged to respond to husband's request for reason for wife's discharge from employment: taking money out of till); Chrispen v. Novak, (1995) 132 Sask. R. 11, [1995] 5 W.W.R. 752 (Q.B.) (police officer executing warrant for search of plaintiff's mother's residence privileged to tell mother of suspected criminal acts by plaintiff that led to search).

(l) While staying at a hotel, plaintiff consults a local physician, who provisionally diagnoses a contagious disease and asks plaintiff to leave the hotel for the safety of others, which plaintiff promises to do. The next day, finding that plaintiff has not moved from the hotel, the physician informs the hotel's proprietor that plaintiff has a contagious disease and that certain precautions must be taken in the hotel. Simonsen v. Swenson, 104 Neb. 224, 177 N.W. 831 (1920) (privileged). Cf. Cochran v. Sears, Roebuck & Co., 72 Ga. App. 458, 34 S.E.2d 296 (1945) (department store nurse who concluded employee had syphilis privileged to tell employee's supervisor; store privileged to inform welfare agency looking after employee's children that employee discharged because of syphilis).

6. In some cases involving publication in mass media, defendants have claimed qualified privilege on the basis of their duty to provide information to the public and the public's interest in receiving the information. Courts have usually decided that the media have no common law qualified privilege to publish information of public interest. See Brown v. Kelly Broadcasting Co., 48 Cal. 3d 406, 257 Cal. Rptr. 708, 771 P.2d 406 (1989); Rouch v. Enquirer & News of Battle Creek, 427 Mich. 157, 398 N.W.2d 245 (1986), aff'g 137 Mich. App. 39, 357 N.W.2d 794 (1984); Banks v. Globe and Mail Ltd., [1961] S.C.R. 474, (1961) 28 D.L.R.2d 343. But see Lewis v. Carr, 178 N.C. 578, 101 S.E. 97 (1919) (newspaper privileged to publish for "public good" charge of improper use of public funds by chairman of county board of education). However, the argument that qualified privilege can attach to at least some media communication of information that the public has an interest in receiving has now gained acceptance in England and Canada. Reynolds v. Times Newspapers Ltd., [2001] 2 A.C. 127 (H.L.); Jameel v. Wall Street Journal Europe Sprl, [2007] 1 A.C. 359 (H.L.) (privilege for publication on matter of public interest where there has been "responsible journalism"); Grant v. Torstar Corp., [2009] 3 S.C.R. 640, (2009) 314 D.L.R.4th 1 ("responsible communication on matters of public interest"); Seaga v. Harper, [2009] A.C. 1 (P.C.) (privilege extended to non-media defendant). What effects might such a privilege have?

7. Since a financial institution or creditor is usually privileged to provide information about someone's financial standing or creditworthiness to persons having an apparent need for this information, are companies whose principal business is the provision of such information also privileged? The prevailing view in the United States is that "commercial credit agencies" are conditionally privileged when they limit the information to subscribers who are particularly interested in it. In some states there is no privilege, following Macintosh v. Dun, [1908] A.C. 390 (P.C.). Which is the better position? There is more of a consensus on allowance of a privilege to mutual credit organizations and trade associations in which members exchange credit and debt information, which might be regarded as a situation of "common interest." See generally Eldredge, Law of Defamation 467–473 (1978); Harper, James & Gray, Law of Torts § 5.26, at 270–271 (3d ed. 2006); Sack, Defamation: Libel, Slander, and Related Problems §§ 9.2.2[C]–[D] (4th ed. 2010). Regarding reports furnished by Better Business Bureaus and similar organizations, see Annot., Liability of Better Business Bureau of Similar Organization in Tort, 50 A.L.R.4th 745 (1986).

8. *Common interest.* One person is conditionally privileged to communicate with another on matters of "common interest." The common interest advanced is usually that of the members of a business enterprise, institution or organization to which both the originator of the communication and the intended recipient belong. Thus, employees and investors of a business and members of churches, labor unions, professional associations, non-profit institutions and community associations are privileged to communicate with one another on matters that touch their interests as employees, investors or members. A common interest is also found for co-owners of property and members of a family. The privilege can apply even when the purpose of the communication is to inform persons on a matter relating to their common interest rather than to protect the interest. See Eldredge, Law of Defamation 479–488 (1978); Sack, Defamation: Libel, Slander, and Related Problems § 9.2.3 (4th ed. 2010).

9. Were courts correct to find privilege in the following situations?

(a) At a meeting of an insolvent person's creditors, a creditor's representative states that the insolvent schemed with plaintiffs to defraud the creditors. Smith Bros. & Co. v. W.C. Agee & Co., 178 Ala. 627, 59 So. 647 (1912).

(b) After a cheese factory is destroyed by fire, farmers in the vicinity meet to organize a company that will establish a new factory. One of the farmers tells another that plaintiff should be left out of the new venture because it is suspected that he burned down the old factory. Cook v. Gust, 155 Wis. 594, 145 N.W. 225 (1914).

(c) At a meeting of a town's taxpayers, a complaint is made of extravagant expenses by the town's constable. Spencer v. Amerton, (1835) 1 Mood. & R. 470, 174 Eng. Rep. 162 (Ex.).

(d) After a nightclub and its proprietor fail to pay a group of musicians the sum awarded them by a union arbitration panel, the union includes the nightclub and proprietor in the "defaulters lists" in local and national publications mailed to union members. Zito v. American Federation of Musicians of the United States and Canada, 60 A.D.2d 967, 401 N.Y.S.2d 929 (1978).

(e) After the spread of rumors concerning the reason for the forced retirement of a management-level employee, supervisors and other personnel are told that the reason was the employee's claims of sick leave for periods when she was not ill. Deaille v. General Telephone Co. of California, 40 Cal. App. 3d 841, 115 Cal. Rptr. 582 (1974).

(f) A factory newsletter has a "comings and goings" column which reports grounds for employee terminations. Zinda v. Louisiana Pacific Corp., 149 Wis. 2d 913, 440 N.W.2d 548 (1989).

(g) The official publication of a state federation of labor denounces as "traitors" and "labor spies" three laundry union members who left their employment with a unionized laundry and began work for a non-union laundry, soliciting orders from union members who had patronized the unionized laundry. Bereman v. Power Publishing Co., 93 Colo. 581, 27 P.2d 749 (1933).

(h) Two companies involved in different lawsuits against a salesman who worked for one company and then the other exchange information about his conduct. Spielberg v. A. Kuhn & Brother, 39 Utah 276, 116 P. 1027 (1911).

(i) A religious denomination's regional governing body appoints a committee to investigate the condition of a particular church. The committee's report, which criticizes the pastor, is read to the church's congregation. Bass v. Matthews, 69 Wash. 214, 124 P. 384 (1912). Cf. Slocinski v. Radwan, 83 N.H. 501, 144 A. 787 (1929) (private conversations among parishioners about priest's immoral conduct). Compare Lovejoy v. Whitcomb, 174 Mass. 586, 55 N.E. 322 (1899) (member of church choir not privileged to inform another member of choir director's adultery); Ballew v. Thompson, 259 S.W. 856 (Mo. App. 1924) (member of church's Sunday school and missionary society not privileged to tell another member that third member committed burglary).

Shenkman v. O'Malley

Supreme Court of New York, Appellate Division
2 A.D.2d 567, 157 N.Y.S.2d 290 (1956)

BREITEL, Justice....

Plaintiff is a physician, and defendant is the president of the professional baseball team, best known as the Brooklyn Dodgers. One of the team's starring players, Roy Campanella, suffered a hand injury, which gravely interfered with his playing. An operation was performed by one Dr. Fett to remove a bone chip. Some months later, plaintiff physician recommended and performed a second operation affecting a nerve in the hand. He submitted a bill for his professional services to Mr. Campanella and, later, to defendant O'Malley's corporation in the sum of $9,500. The bill was not paid. Plaintiff physician sued to recover his fee, and through his lawyer, by filing the suit papers and contemporaneous statements, obtained wide publicity, the purport of which was that neither Mr. Campanella nor the Brooklyn Dodgers was paying for an operation which had rehabilitated Mr. Campanella's playing capacity.

The statements of plaintiff Shenkman, through his lawyer, upon which defendant O'Malley relies in asserting his defenses are contained in two newspaper accounts attached as exhibits to the amended answer. The first read as follows:

I sent the $9,500 bill to Mr. Campanella and it was promptly returned with the suggestion that the Brooklyn Dodgers Baseball Club was responsible for the bill.

Then I sent it to the club, and they immediately sent it back, informing me that Campanella alone was responsible for payment.

Between Campanella and the club, I have been paid nothing.

Earlier in the newspaper account plaintiff Shenkman was quoted as having said that Mr. Campanella had "refused to pay one cent." In another newspaper the quoted statement read as follows:

> After it was over, Campy expressed his deep gratitude and told Dr. Shenkman to send the bill to the Brooklyn Ball Club.
>
> He sent the bill there and then the Dodger front office said it wasn't their baby. They disclaimed any responsibility for it. And though Roy was grateful at first, he has apparently forgotten his obligation.

The second newspaper account also contained the general statement that:

> A neuro-surgeon charged today that the Dodgers baseball management has run out on the bill for the operation which brought Roy Campanella's left hand and big bat back into the lineup this year.

Whether these statements are defamatory is not before the court. For the purposes of the second complete defense it will be assumed, as it is alleged by defendant O'Malley, that such statements are defamatory.

Upon release of plaintiff's publicity, defendant O'Malley issued a statement to the press—the subject of this slander action. The statement, as set forth in the answer, reads as follows:

> I am shocked at the self-serving story appearing in evening papers in support of Dr. Shenkman's exorbitant claim of $9,500 for what will probably prove to be an unnecessary second operation on Roy Campanella's hand. The medical profession appreciates that the original operation was successfully performed by a recognized specialist, Dr. Herbert Fett. Dr. Shenkman telephoned me in February and was most anxious to settle his claim, and admitted that he had not fixed a price or advised Roy that he contemplated such a charge. It appears that he thought he was operating on Roy's bankroll. I told him his charge was unconscionable and suggested he sue. He offered to arbitrate before a committee of doctors. I told him I preferred a jury of people who pay doctor's bills not send them. It took Dr. Shenkman a long time to get up courage to sue.
>
> ...

The second complete defense relates to reply to defamatory attack. This defense is available to one who has been defamed in the first instance, and who, in response to the attack, responds in kind. It has been questioned whether it is necessary that the first attacking statement be defamatory. (Seelman, Libel and Slander, § 256.) It would seem that the better rule and the sounder policy is that it should.... The occasion of a non-defamatory attack should not excuse false diatribe in reply. That in its nature would be excessive response. A crude analogy may be drawn from the law of assault where mere words, no matter how provocative, may not justify a battery in response. This defense of reply is material, of course, only where the response in kind is defamatory. The injury, if any, to plaintiff is excused, because it is the plaintiff who started the altercation....

The qualified privilege of reply as a defense to an action for defamation had no substantial recognition in New York before 1910. Where the defense has been allowed, the defamatory nature of the reply bore a pertinency to the content, and was reasonably proportionate to the magnitude of the defamation, in the first attack. Thus, in [Collier v. Postum Cereal Co., Limited, 150 App. Div. 169, 134 N.Y.S. 847], plaintiff had charged defendant with conducting a deliberately false advertising campaign in relation to its food product. To this the defendant replied plaintiff had prostituted truth in its magazine columns to force advertisers, including the defendant, to purchase space in the magazine. Similarly, in Preston v. Hobbs, 161 App. Div. 363, 146 N.Y.S. 419, the initial attack was that defendant's associate had, on the threat of withdrawal of its advertising, bridled the press to suppress unfavorable publicity. The reply was that the plaintiff lied and was a muckraker, with indictments pending against him. In Fowler v. New York Herald, 184 App. Div. 608, 172 N.Y.S. 423, plaintiff had charged that the defendant sponsored an imposter. Defendant thereupon stated that plaintiff, as a result of his physical condition, was incompetent. In Siegel v. Metropolitan Life Ins. Co., 263 App. Div. 299, 32 N.Y.S.2d 658, plaintiff had charged, in a series of radio broadcasts, that defendant insurance company was milking its policy-holders. Thereupon defendant, in a circular letter to its agents, stated that plaintiff was a former agent who had been fired for irregularities in his accounts....

When one examines the allegations of the second complete defense of reply in this case, it cannot be said, as a matter of law, that the counterattack was not pertinent to the initial attack. The initial attack related to the non-payment for medical services rendered. The counterattack, in effect, charged that the services were unnecessary and that the physician believed he was operating on the patient's bankroll, rather than on his hand. Excessiveness of reply aside for the moment, one need not pay for services that are the result of quackery and malpractice. (Of course, once again, if defendant O'Malley's counterattacking statement does not convey as much, in the absence of special damages alleged, it is not slanderous, and there is no office for the defense of reply.) The other test, which the qualified privilege of reply must withstand, is that of excessiveness. Not every counterattack, if defamatory, will be excused, merely because it is in response to defamation. There must be some reasonable proportion between attack and counterattack. Once again, one may draw a crude analogy from the law of assault. If a man, with equal physique, attacks another with his fists it may not justify the use of a firearm in response. But it cannot be said on the pleading alone, as in the law of assault, that defendant O'Malley's response was excessive. That will remain a proper question for the jury to determine....

As noted earlier, the defamatory reply to attack, if it is to be privileged, must, among other things, be a reply to a defamatory attack, not merely to any critical, adverse, unpleasant, or even grossly irritating comment. Of course, the effect of provocation is not ignored by the law but is comprehended under partial defenses in mitigation of damages.

Hence, the second complete defense is sufficient, since there remains to be resolved a question of fact whether the reply to the initial attack was excessive or not, provided, of course, it is found that the initial attack was, as alleged in the amended answer, defamatory.

The third complete defense has been denominated by the defendant as the qualified privilege to protect one's own interest. [The court distinguished cases involving protection of defendant's interest in property.] ...

There just is no general qualified privilege to issue generally a defamatory statement, as distinguished from a reply to defamatory attack, merely because it may serve to "protect a business interest." Not to be confused is the making of a privileged statement to others who share a common interest or duty in the same property, business or relationship, e. g., employer and employees, stockholders and corporation, member and association. Nor should there be such a privilege.

Always to be kept in mind, in considering a defense of privilege, whether qualified or absolute, is that the defendant seeks exculpation for falsely detracting from the plaintiff's reputation to a degree that is slanderous, or, in the appropriate case, libelous. If defendant's assertion is true, there is no need for a defense, and there is no need for a privilege. To say that any protection of a business interest, subjected to criticism, should excuse calumny is foreign to our thinking. Of course, the law of defamation has spelled out privileges to excuse false attack. But the privileges arise only when a supervening public policy dictates the necessity for non-malicious communication in well-defined relationships, where greater harm would be done if persons were permitted to speak only at the peril of complete accuracy. A business interest may be so all-embracive, — and proportionately larger as the business is greater — that the amount of harm that could be done, without remedy, would be incalculable. Indeed, the larger the business the greater would be the scope of immunity from liability for injury. The purposes of the law of defamation would not be served by so untrammeled a privilege as that suggested in the third complete defense.

Hence, the third complete defense is legally insufficient.

Accordingly, the order at Special Term should be modified by reinstatement of the second complete defense....

Notes

1. The privilege to defend one's reputation by reply differs from other applications of the privilege to defend one's interests in that giving widespread publicity to the defamatory statement is permitted, provided the charges replied to received similar publicity. Can self-defense be satisfactorily distinguished from retaliation in this situation? Whether the criticism of defendant must have been defamatory, as held in the principal case, is questionable. What if the criticism was defamatory but true? The reply will not be privileged if the court finds that it concerns a matter unrelated to the charges against defendant, but highly defamatory explanations of why plaintiff made the charges have been found to have sufficient relation to the charges to be privileged. See generally Annot., Libel and Slander: Qualified Privilege of Reply to Defamatory Publication, 41 A.L.R.3d 1083 (1972); Eldredge, Law of Defamation 455–458 (1978); Fleming, Law of Torts 650–652 (10th ed. 2011).

2. Privilege has been found when a government official responded to a press release announcing his dismissal and the grounds for the action with a defense of his record that attacked the official who issued the release. Mencher v. Chesley, 193 Misc. 829, 85 N.Y.S.2d 431 (Sup. Ct. 1948). Also, when defendant referred to plaintiff's "known character as a liar" in a statement responding to plaintiff's statement that defendant's previous statement about plaintiff was a "contemptible, cowardly, malicious lie." Chaffin v. Lynch, 83 Va. 106, 1 S.E. 803 (1887). Cf. Falk v. Smith, [1941] O.R. 17, [1941] 1 D.L.R. 156 (C.A.) (exchange of "stooge" and "liar"). Privilege has been denied when, in response to plaintiff's attacks on the honesty of public officials, defendant has published plaintiff's supposed history of dishonest or immoral conduct. Fish v. St. Louis County Printing & Publishing Co., 102 Mo. App. 6, 74 S.W. 641 (1903) (plaintiff's unethical conduct as attorney); Brewer v. Chase, 121 Mich. 526, 80 N.W. 575 (1899) (plaintiff's embezzlement, arrests for burglary and forgery and mistreatment of women, published to show him unworthy of belief). Borley v. Allison, 181 Mass. 246, 63 N.E. 260 (1902), held that defendant was not privileged to defend himself when, at the time of his statement, he had no knowledge of plaintiff's charges against him.

3. Is there a privilege to defend the reputation of another person? See Ritschy v. Garrels, 195 Mo. App. 670, 187 S.W. 1120 (1916) (son not privileged to make statement in pamphlet published by father that responded to charges against father); Fowler v. New York Herald Co., 184 App. Div. 608, 172 N.Y.S. 423 (1918) (newspaper privileged to respond to plaintiff's denunciation of foreign editor whose appearances in United States were sponsored by newspaper); Krutech v. Schimmel, 50 Misc. 2d 1052, 272 N.Y.S.2d 261 (Sup. Ct. 1966), rev'd, 27 A.D.2d 837, 278 N.Y.S.2d 25 (1967) (no privilege to reply to person who had sent to newspaper letter criticizing public officials); Israel v. Portland News Publishing Co., 152 Or. 225, 53 P.2d 529 (1936) (murder victim's wife and sister privileged to reply to statement that victim had extramarital affair, which wife knew about, with woman who threatened victim's life; reply said that victim had no regard for integrity of person who made statement and therefore would not have confided such matters to him). Kennedy v. Cannon, 229 Md. 92, 182 A.2d 54 (1962), held that an attorney representing a man charged with rape was not privileged to give a newspaper his client's assertion that the complainant had consented to intercourse. The prosecuting attorney's press statement about the case had included the charged man's admission that intercourse occurred. The defense attorney contended that there was some danger of a lynching if the charge of rape was not rebutted.

4. It is likely that if the author of the reply to attack has a privilege, the newspaper, broadcast station or other organ that publishes the reply is also privileged. See Israel v. Portland News Publishing Co., supra; Eldredge, Law of Defamation 443–446 (1978). Contra, Hess v. Gansz, 90 Mo. App. 439 (1895). A number of states have enacted statutes requiring a journal that has published a defamatory statement to publish the defamed person's reply. See Hanson, Libel and Related Torts ¶ 169 (1969). In Miami Herald Publishing Co. v. Tornillo, 418 U.S. 241 (1974), the Supreme Court considered a statute which required a newspaper that attacked a candidate for election to publish a reply by the candidate without charge. Because it overrode editorial judgment on what material should be included in the newspaper, the statute was held to violate the First Amendment. Whether it would be unconstitutional to require publication of a retraction or correction of a false defamatory charge was not addressed. See Smolla, Law of Defamation §§ 9:90–9:92 (2d ed. 1999).

5. Another type of reply is one that explains defendant's refusal to comply with a demand made by plaintiff or on his behalf. In this situation, the rules of the privilege to protect one's own interest apply. See Dano v. Royal Globe Insurance Co., 89 A.D.2d 817, 453 N.Y.S.2d 528 (1982), aff'd, 59 N.Y.2d 827, 464 N.Y.S.2d 741, 451 N.E.2d 488 (1983) (insurance company's attorneys privileged to write plaintiffs' attorneys that plaintiffs' claim on insurance policy rejected because of fraud and misrepresentation); Campbell v. Cochrane, (1905) 8 F. 205 (Scot. Ct. Sess.) (defendant privileged to state when rejecting plaintiff's claim for wrongful dismissal that plaintiff misappropriated to himself what he was bound to deliver to defendant). A refusal of payment that generally traduces plaintiff's character or business conduct is not privileged. See Huntley v. Ward, (1859) 6 C.B.N.S. 514, 141 Eng. Rep. 557, 6 Jur. N.S. 18, 33 L.T.O.S. 137 (C.P.). Is a person who rejects a collection agent's claim for payment of a doctor's bill privileged in accusing the doctor of specific acts of malpractice or in characterizing the doctor's conduct as unprofessional or unethical? See Teichner v. Bellan, 7 A.D.2d 247, 181 N.Y.S.2d 842 (1959) ("highly unprofessional," "unethical," "illegal," "despicable"; privilege not decided); Stevens v. Kitchener, (1887) 4 T.L.R. 159 (Q.B.D.) (carelessness amounting to manslaughter; privileged). See generally Eldredge, Law of Defamation 453–455 (1978).

Benassi v. Georgia-Pacific

Oregon Court of Appeals
62 Or. App. 698, 662 P.2d 760 (1983),
modified, 63 Or. App. 672, 667 P.2d 532 (1983),
review denied, 295 Or. 730, 670 P.2d 1035 (1984)

BUTTLER, Presiding Judge....

... Defendant is a large forest products company with headquarters in Portland at the time here involved. Its operation is organized into divisions, one of which is the machinery construction division, headed by M. Fred Wall, who was also defendant's Director of Purchasing. Plaintiff was hired by Wall as general manager of the division in August, 1977.

Defendant planned to expand its machinery construction division into the southeastern United States, and a business trip was undertaken to Hattiesburg, Mississippi, in July, 1978, by plaintiff, Elmer Arndt, who had been hired as an independent consultant, Richard Galligher and others. While in Hattiesburg an incident occurred at the group's motel in which plaintiff confronted Arndt regarding a telephone call Arndt had made earlier in the evening to Wall. There was testimony, which plaintiff does not dispute, that he used a loud voice and considerable profanity. Plaintiff, Galligher and Arndt had been drinking prior to the incident, although plaintiff states he was "in control of all [his] faculties."

The incident was reported to Wall after the group returned to Oregon, and he called plaintiff into his office, reprimanded him and informed him that he would be terminated immediately if a similar incident occurred again. Plaintiff informed Wall that the incident would not have occurred if liquor had not been involved.

The following May, plaintiff took another business trip to Hattiesburg with a group of defendant's employees. On May 16, following a dinner at which plaintiff consumed wine, he and Galligher went to a cocktail lounge for a "nightcap." While there plaintiff and Galligher discussed a wage dispute brewing at the plant with Richard Miller, an employee of the plant, who was seated farther down the bar; the discussion became heated. Miller was not plaintiff's direct subordinate, but during the argument plaintiff told him that he was fired; his voice was loud and his language was profane. The next morning plaintiff and Miller's plant supervisor agreed that Miller was not fired, and plaintiff and Miller agreed that the incident would not have occurred if liquor had not been involved. Galligher was described by plaintiff as "quite intoxicated." Miller admitted to drinking too much. Plaintiff testified that he was not drunk and was "certainly the most sober" of the participants.

About May 25, Wall received an anonymous letter from Hattiesburg describing that incident. The letter stated that the men were "drunk," that there was an argument between plaintiff and Miller in which plaintiff used profane, loud and nasty language, and that plaintiff made a lot of "nasty" remarks about Wall. Wall phoned Miller and Galligher (and two others who informed him that they did not observe the incident) for confirmation, asking specifically what names he was called. Miller informed Wall that he (Miller) had been drinking, that plaintiff had not called Wall any names and that Galligher was in the worst condition of the three. Neither Miller nor Galligher characterized plaintiff as being drunk. Based on those conversations, and without talking to plaintiff, Wall decided to fire him; he had been "90% sure" he would do so after reading the anonymous letter. Plaintiff sought reinstatement, but admitted that Wall had the right to discharge him.

News of plaintiff's termination began circulating among machinery construction division employees the following weekend, and rumors, including one that the division was going to close, were circulating as well. Morris Rivers, who succeeded plaintiff as general manager of the division, called a general meeting of the employees on June 1 to explain plaintiff's termination, to reassure them and to acquaint them with him. The meeting was attended by most of the 120 employees of the division. Rivers introduced himself, gave some background information on himself and said that he believed it was important to have a candid relationship with division employees. He then made the following statement, which is the subject of plaintiff's defamation claim: "I gathered you all here to tell you why Mr. Benassi is no longer with the company. The man was drunk and misbehaving in a bar. The man had a drinking problem. Georgia-Pacific looks unkindly on this kind of conduct. It was not the first time. He had been warned."

Following his discharge, plaintiff began looking for another job, but had difficulty securing employment.... He contends that his inability to secure a position that paid as well as his former job with defendant was caused by the defamatory statement.

In response to the defamation claim, defendant raised two affirmative defenses: truth and privilege. The trial court ruled that defendant had a qualified privilege to make the statement, but left to the jury whether the statement was true or whether the privilege was lost through abuse. The jury returned a general verdict awarding plaintiff $350,000 damages.

... [D]efendant contends that the trial court erred in denying its motion for a directed verdict on the ground that there was insufficient evidence that defendant abused its qualified privilege....

[The court approved instructions given to the jury by the trial judge: "[A] qualified privilege may be forfeited if it is abused for any one of the four following purposes: (1) a qualified privilege may be forfeited if the Defendants lacked belief or had no reasonable ground for belief in the truth of the complained of statements; (2) a qualified privilege may be forfeited if the complained of statement was published for some purpose other than that for which the particular privilege is given; (3) a qualified privilege may be forfeited if the complained of statement is made to some person not reasonably believed to be necessary for the accomplishment of the purpose of the particular privilege; (4) a qualified privilege may be forfeited if the complained of statement included defamatory matter not reasonably believed to be necessary to accomplish the purpose for which the particular privilege is given. [¶] The Defendant is required to act as a reasonable man under the circumstances with due regard to the strength of his belief, the grounds that he has to support it and the importance of conveying the information."]

Plaintiff contends that there was evidence from which a jury could find that defendant lacked reasonable grounds for belief in the truth of the defamatory matter. We agree. The only "evidence" that plaintiff was drunk at the second incident came from an anonymous letter, but Wall made no attempt to determine who was its author. The employes with whom Wall checked, whom the evidence indicates he trusted, directly contradicted the allegation in the letter that plaintiff said unpleasant things about Wall. A jury could reasonably infer that, given the falsity of that information, a reasonable person would have questioned the accuracy of other statements in the letter. Neither Miller nor Galligher characterized plaintiff as drunk. Moreover, other evidence indicates that Wall had little or no interest in hearing plaintiff's explanation of the incident. In short, in informing its employees that plaintiff was discharged because he was drunk in a bar, defendant chose to rely on an anonymous letter in believing the most unfavorable characterization of plaintiff's condition and conduct, despite contrary evidence from its own officers. A jury could determine that it was unreasonable to do so.

Moreover, we think that a jury could determine that it was unnecessary for Rivers to tell essentially every employe in the machinery construction division that plaintiff was "drunk and misbehaving," that he had a "drinking problem" and that any belief that Rivers may have had as to the necessity of doing so was unreasonable. Although, as the trial court ruled, an employer is privileged to disseminate to its employes a certain amount of information regarding the discharge of another employe in order to protect its interests, Restatement of Torts, §§ 604 and 605, indicate that the amount of defamatory material that it is privileged to publish may depend on the position of the employes to whom the information is given. For example, it may be necessary for the official who makes the decision to terminate to make a full disclosure of all defamatory material to his immediate supervisor, while a simple statement to assembly line workers that a vice president was terminated because of a dispute with higher management over the conduct of his job may be sufficient to protect the legitimate interests of the employer.

Here, Rivers had called a meeting of the supervisory staff prior to the objectionable speech and told them the purported reasons for plaintiff's discharge. The approximately 120 employes gathered for the offending speech, however, included employes two levels below plaintiff. Some of the "rank-and-file" testified that they thought it "strange" that they were informed as to the reasons for plaintiff's discharge, and a supervisor testified that he did not think that it would have caused problems for him if the employes working for him had not been told the reasons. An accountant at the plant testified: "I think it would have sufficed to say that there was disagreements between hiring management and Mr. Benassi rather than saying exactly what the problem was, being a personal problem." We conclude that the question of abuse of the privilege was for the jury....

We conclude that it would be mere speculation to permit the jury to infer that plaintiff was unable to obtain a new job for five months because of the defamation. For that reason, the trial court erred in denying defendant's motion for a directed verdict on plaintiff's claim for special damages in the amount of $16,146. We cannot say with reasonable certainty that submitting the claim for special damages to the jury had no effect on the jury's evaluation of the evidence on liability or on the extent of plaintiff's general damages. Therefore, the case must be reversed and remanded for a new trial....

Notes

1. When a statement is published in circumstances of qualified privilege, the publisher will not be liable unless one of the qualifications upon the privilege comes into play. If the privilege is "exceeded" or "abused" or "forfeited," publication will be regarded as unprivileged and liability can result. The grounds of "forfeiture" are those specified in the instructions given by the trial judge in the principal case and publication with malice. Plaintiff has the burden of proof. If harm resulting from "abuse" cannot be separated from harm that has resulted from proper exercise of the privilege, the privilege is forfeited entirely and the publisher is subject to liability for all harm resulting from publication of the defamatory statement. See generally Restatement (Second) of Torts §§ 599–605A (1977); Eldredge, Law of Defamation 505–535 (1978); Prosser & Keeton, Law of Torts 832–836 (5th ed. 1984); Sack, Defamation: Libel, Slander, and Related Problems § 9.3 (4th ed. 2010).

2. *Lack of belief in or grounds for statement.* Qualified privilege does not protect a defamatory statement published without a good faith belief that it is true. It is often stated that defendant is subject to liability if the statement was published with knowledge of its falsity or reckless disregard of whether it was true or false. Allowance is made for communicating the existence of rumors or suspicions, not believed to be true, when this is reasonable in protection of the interest of a party to the communication. This is unlikely to be found reasonable unless it is made clear that only a rumor or suspicion, not a fact, is stated. It might be thought that knowing falsehood necessarily overlaps the abuses of malice or purpose to cause harm, but this is not always so. See Merriman v. Lewis, 141 Fla. 832, 194 So. 349 (1940) (to recover on indemnity bond for funds actually lost by mistake, employer claimed funds were lost through plaintiff's dishonesty).

3. Whether qualified privilege is abused by publishing a defamatory statement without reasonable ground to believe it is true is the subject of considerable division of authority. The no-liability-without-fault rule of Gertz v. Robert Welch, Inc., p. 626, infra, has caused reconsideration of this question. It is not clear that this rule applies to every defamation case, but in cases governed by the rule a qualified privilege conditioned on reasonable grounds would have no function. When defendant had reasonable grounds, *Gertz* would deny plaintiff a cause of action. For this reason, the drafters of the Restatement (Second) of Torts abandoned the rule, embodied in the first Restatement, that lack of reasonable grounds was an abuse of privilege and limited abuse to knowing falsehood or reckless disregard. Restatement (Second) of Torts §§ 600–601 (1977). Leverman v. Campbell Sharp Ltd., (1987) 12 B.C.L.R.2d 57, 36 D.L.R.4th 401 (C.A.), draws a distinction between carelessness in forming an honest belief, which would not defeat a qualified privilege, and carelessness that caused defendant to state what he did not believe, which would defeat the privilege. (Defendant had published a notice of a partner's bankruptcy which falsely suggested that his firm was in bankruptcy.)

4. One can find in the cases some tendency toward greater generosity (not requiring reasonable grounds) for such favored privileges as public interest, reply in self-defense and statements of public officials, with less generosity (requiring reasonable grounds) for private interest privileges, particularly that granted to credit reporting agencies. Is it consistent to reject the reasonableness standard in favor of reckless disregard when the problem is lack of grounds for defendant's statement, but apply a reasonableness standard when the problem is excessive publication? See Bratt v. International Business Machines Corp., 392 Mass. 508, 467 N.E.2d 126 (1984) (loss of privilege through "unnecessary, unreasonable or excessive publication" requires that defendant act recklessly).

5. *Wrong purpose.* Qualified privileges based upon protection of an interest require that publication have the purpose of serving the interest. If protection of the interest is not the primary purpose, or at least a substantial purpose, of publication, there is an abuse of privilege even if defendant's purpose was not otherwise improper, as when a desire to obtain payment of a debt rather than to assist the employer induces defendant to inform an employer of an employee's misconduct, or when a private business interest or organizational rivalry rather than a desire for law enforcement causes defendant to report plaintiff's alleged misconduct to the police or other public authorities. See Over v. Schiffling, 102 Ind. 191, 26 N.E. 91 (1885); Ramsey v. Cheek, 109 N.C. 270, 13 S.E. 775 (1891); Fleming, Law of Torts 658–661 (10th ed. 2011). So, too, when an improper purpose such as causing injury or embarrassment is the motivation.

6. *Excessive publication.* Qualified privilege does not protect publication of a defamatory statement to more persons than are reasonably believed necessary for the protection of the interest involved. This abuse can occur when defendant deliberately directs publi-

cation to persons whose knowledge of the statement does not advance the interest or when defendant uses a means of communication that will convey the statement to such persons. If it is not practical to limit communication to persons owed a duty or possessing an interest in receiving the statement, it is not abuse to reasonably employ means that enable other persons to learn of the statement. Dictation of defamatory messages for transcription by secretaries appears to be acceptable, but what if the recipient has a secretary and the message is not marked "private" or "confidential"? Speaking defamatory words where they will be overheard by third persons is usually excessive publication, but not when defendant must do so to prevent a possible loss. Sending a telegram message instead of a letter would be an abuse (as would use of a post card instead of a sealed letter) unless urgency justified use of the telegraph. Recognition that communication of a statement to members of a large group served a common interest has led courts to conclude that publication of a defamatory statement in a journal circulated mainly to group members, but also to some non-members, is not excessive publication. Compare Bereman v. Power Publishing Co., 93 Colo. 581, 27 P.2d 749 (1933) (newspaper with circulation confined almost entirely to union members), with Moyle v. Frank, 267 App. Div. 423, 46 N.Y.S.2d 667 (1944), aff'd, 293 N.Y. 842, 59 N.E.2d 437 (1944) (religious organization's publication distributed to non-members willing to pay for it).

7. Is there excessive publication when:

(a) In the presence of store employees and other customers, a customer in a store is stopped at the checkout by a manager and questioned about possessing items not paid for. Kroger Grocery & Baking Co. v. Yount, 66 F.2d 700 (8th Cir. 1933).

(b) After a check with plaintiff's name forged on it is cashed at a retail store, the store places on the cash registers a notice, visible to customers as well as cashiers, that if any check of plaintiff's is presented the person presenting it is to be detained and security personnel called. Pleau v. Simpson-Sears Ltd., (1977) 15 O.R.2d 436, 75 D.L.R.3d 747 (C.A.).

(c) A merchant asks another businessman to witness his questioning and discharge of an employee for stealing. Taylor v. Hawkins, (1851) 15 Jur. 746, 20 L.J.Q.B. 313, 16 L.T.O.S. 409, 16 Q.B. 308, 117 Eng. Rep, 897 (Q.B.).

(d) A company's auditors report to the directors a deficiency of stock, which the auditors attribute to a factory manager's accounts being badly kept and irregularly rendered. The directors order the auditors' report to be printed and sent to the company's stockholders. Lawless v. Anglo-Egyptian Cotton Co., (1869) L.R. 4 Q.B. 262. Compare Parsons v. Surgey, (1864) 4 F. & F. 247, 176 Eng. Rep. 551 (Q.B.N.P.) (matters discussed at shareholders' meeting, to which defendant had invited reporters and other non-shareholders).

(e) The stewards of a race track post on a bulletin board a notice, seen by members of the press and public as well as participants in horse racing, that a veterinarian has been "ruled off" the track for possession of drugs and syringes and unlicensed practice. Porter v. Eyster, 294 F.2d 613 (4th Cir. 1961). Compare Sheftall v. Central of Georgia Railway Co., 123 Ga. 589, 51 S.E. 646 (1905) (dismissed conductor's failure to return tickets in notice circulated to railway employees, including those not handling tickets).

8. *Unprivileged content.* It is an abuse of a qualified privilege to include in a defamatory statement matter unrelated to the purpose for which the privilege is given. This can be seen most clearly in instances where the privilege protects a specific interest and information contained in the statement is irrelevant to the interest, as when a credit reference con-

tains information not bearing upon the subject's credit-worthiness, an employment reference contains details of the subject's personal life not relevant to his suitability for employment, a rejection for a demand for payment attributes to the claimant conduct or character that could not reasonably be regarded as a defense to the claim, or a report to the police about suspected criminal activity extends to matters not connected to the suspect's guilt or apprehension. See also Hines v. Shumaker, 97 Miss. 669, 52 So. 705 (1910) (insurance company's warning to its agents about disparagement by rival company's agent said he lacked honesty and brains); Crawford and Co. v. Graves, 199 Va. 495, 100 S.E.2d 714 (1957) (when advising injured employee to see orthopedic surgeon, defendant's agent said that employee's chiropodist was "not the type of doctor for this kind of work. He is a doctor for ingrowing toenails, flat feet and falling arches."). Authorities state that matter is not privileged when it is not reasonably believed necessary to accomplish the purpose for which the privilege is given. See Restatement (Second) of Torts § 605 (1977). But the operative test may not be necessity but sufficient connection between the subject-matter of the statement and the interest supporting the privilege. See Knapp v. McLeod, (1926) 58 O.L.R. 605, [1926] 2 D.L.R. 1083 (App. Div.) (woman with whom alleged adultery occurred identified when church officeholder informed another officeholder about adultery by minister).

9. *Malice.* Since a qualified privilege is typically defined as a privilege that is overcome by proof of malice, one can expect that a court will find abuse of privilege when defendant's statement was actuated by malice. Many cases in appellate courts address whether plaintiff adduced evidence of malice. Malice might be inferred from disputes between the parties. See Thomas v. Kaufmann's, 436 F. Supp. 293 (W.D. Pa. 1977) (store and employee organizing for union). Or from refusal to retract or correct an erroneous statement. See Vigil v. Rice, 74 N.M. 693, 397 P.2d 719 (1964) (doctor's failure to correct report that plaintiff was pregnant). Cf. Domchick v. Greenbelt Consumer Services, Inc., 200 Md. 36, 87 A.2d 831 (1952) (raising unsubstantiated plea of truth). The primary meaning of malice is spite, ill will or desire to cause harm. But the fact that publication with an improper purpose is also abuse of privilege has led a number of courts to include wrongful purpose, or perhaps any purpose other than the purpose for which the privilege is given, within their definitions of malice. Some courts have used "malice" to signify any state of mind, including knowledge or reckless disregard of falsity, that makes publication an abuse.

Perhaps it would be better to drop malice from the black-letter lists of abuses of qualified privilege and treat publication actuated by spite or ill will as an example of publication with an improper purpose. This is the position of Restatement (Second) of Torts § 603 (1977). It is insufficient that defendant have ill will or a desire to see plaintiff suffer. This must be the principal motive for publication of the statement. What if defendant was so motivated but had good grounds for believing the statement was true? For purposes of the constitutional law of defamation, the Supreme Court has defined "actual malice" as knowledge or reckless disregard of falsity. See pp. 626–645, infra. This definition has had so powerful an influence as to cause a few courts to abandon prior definitions of the malice that defeats common law privilege and substitute knowing falsehood or reckless disregard. See Marchesi v. Franchino, 283 Md. 131, 387 A.2d 1129 (1978); Barreca v. Nickolas, 683 N.W.2d 111 (Iowa 2004). Contra, Great Coastal Express, Inc. v. Ellington, 230 Va. 142, 334 S.E.2d 846 (1985). See generally Dobbs, Law of Torts 1166–1169 (2000); Sack, Defamation: Libel, Slander, and Related Problems §§ 9.3.1–9.3.3 (4th ed. 2010).

Green Acres Trust v. London

Supreme Court of Arizona
141 Ariz. 609, 688 P.2d 617 (1984)

HOLOHAN, Chief Justice.

[Green Acres sued lawyers who brought a class action against Green Acres and the lawyers' clients, who represented the plaintiff class. The trial court entered summary judgment for all defendants. The Court of Appeals affirmed.]

On Friday, March 5, 1976, the lawyer defendants met to review a draft of a class action complaint to be filed against Green Acres which challenged the particular sales technique employed by Green Acres to sell its "pre-paid funerals." … Sometime during the meeting, Edythe Jensen, a reporter for the Phoenix Gazette newspaper, arrived at the law offices where the meeting was held. One of the lawyer defendants had invited Ms. Jensen to the offices to learn about the basis for the class action. Ms. Jensen received a copy of the drafted complaint and discussed the case with at least one of the lawyer defendants.

Based in part on information obtained from a draft of the complaint and conversations held with the lawyer defendants, Ms. Jensen wrote an article describing the grounds of the class action suit. She quoted the clients and lawyer defendants, and unfavorably characterized the manner in which Green Acres marketed their "prepaid funerals." The Gazette published the article on the following Monday, March 8, 1976, the same day the lawyer defendants filed the class action complaint.

In due course, Green Acres sued the class action clients and lawyer defendants for defamation based on communications made by the lawyer defendants to Ms. Jensen. Green Acres did not, however, name Ms. Jensen nor her employer as party defendants. Green Acres' complaint alleged that the clients authorized, and the lawyer defendants published, the following statements by providing a copy of the drafted complaint and through conversations with Ms. Jensen: 1. That the State Attorney General's office had been investigating the Plaintiffs [Green Acres] for the purpose of filing criminal charges against them in the areas of security [sic] violations and fraud. 2. That the Plaintiffs [Green Acres] had "bilked" up to five thousand people. 3. That the Plaintiffs [Green Acres] had deliberately violated state laws. 4. The Plaintiffs [Green Acres] had "intentionally inflicted emotional distress on its victims."

[The court approved the Court of Appeals' decision that in the absence of evidence that they had made or authorized these statements, the clients were not subject to liability. Vicarious liability, under a theory of respondeat superior, was inapplicable because an attorney was an independent contractor, not a servant of the client. See p. 716, infra. The court also held that the attorneys' statements to the reporter were outside the absolute privilege for statements relating to judicial proceedings, pp. 577–582, supra.]

[Restatement (Second) of Torts § 611] provides: "The publication of defamatory matter concerning another in a report of an official action or proceeding or of a meeting open to the public that deals with a matter of public concern is privileged if the report is accurate and complete or a fair abridgement of the occurrence reported." Judicial recognition of this privilege is based on the ambitious goal of informing the public: "Since it is clearly to the interest of the public that information be made available as to what takes place in public affairs, the qualified privilege was recognized, under which a newspaper or anyone else might make such a report to the public. The privilege rests upon the idea that any member of the public, if he were present, might see and hear for himself, so that the reporter is merely a substitute for the public eye—this, together with the obvious public interest in having public affairs made known to all.... An important field for the privilege is the reporting of any judicial proceeding...." Prosser, [*Law of Torts* (4th ed. 1971)] §118 at 830–831.

The privilege to fairly and accurately report about public proceedings differs from other conditional privileges. It is termed a "special" privilege because it does not depend on the occasion giving rise to the publication.... It also differs because the publisher may report statements known to be false so long as the publisher fairly and accurately describes those statements. Ordinarily the privilege would apply to the news media, those in the business of transmitting the news, but the privilege is not limited to the media. Anyone may describe what transpired at a public proceeding so long as the publisher provides a fair and accurate rendition. One exception to this wide application is the speaker who by design uses the privilege to republish defamation he previously made during the public proceeding. The privilege does not sanction self-serving re-publication. [Restatement (Second) of Torts §611, Comments.] ...

In addition to the types of proceedings, the boundaries of the privilege are defined by the manner in which those proceedings are reported. The report must be fair, and it must be accurate. Accuracy means "substantially correct," while fair means balanced. Restatement (Second) of Torts §611, Comment f. In other words, a court must determine whether the report of the public proceeding carries a "greater sting" in defamatory content than the original publication during the proceeding. *Newell v. Field Enterprises, Inc.,* 91 Ill. App. 3d 735, 415 N.E.2d 434 (1980).

The privilege to report about public proceedings has been extended to reports which described the contents of pleadings which have been filed with the court. Two different privileges operate in this context: the absolute privilege protects the lawyer for the contents of the pleading while the category of qualified privilege protects the reporter in reporting the contents of the pleading. "Although it might be thought that the privilege to report should be absolute when the statements reported are themselves absolutely privileged, the policy of encouraging freedom of action by the participants is not applicable to the report, and a qualified privilege is therefore appropriate." *Note, Developments in the Law—Defamation,* 69 Harv. L. Rev. 875, 928 (1956).

The lawyer defendants argue that their "press conference" communications amounted to a fair and accurate report of the contents of the class action complaint. Green Acres counters that the communications went far beyond the borders of the complaint. We do not reach this dispute because we conclude that a pleading must be filed with the court before this privilege may apply to reports which describe the pleading. Though jurisdictions are split over whether filing a complaint is enough in itself, or whether some judicial action must occur before the privilege can attach, no dispute exists over the minimal requirement of filing. Absent filing, the drafted complaint was not a "public" matter.

The "press conference" in the lawyer defendants' office was little more than a private meeting and "the privilege does not extend to a report of a private meeting, not open to the general public...." Restatement (Second) of Torts §611, Comment i. Obviously, there could not be a report of an official or public proceeding absent the existence of that proceeding. The lawyer defendants are not entitled to the qualified privilege to defame under §611....

We conclude that no absolute or qualified privilege to defame protected the lawyer defendants in their communications with the newspaper reporter under the circumstances of this case. [Reversed and remanded.]

Notes

1. The privilege represented by this case is best described as a privilege to report official proceedings, or public proceedings. It is sometimes called a "reporter's privilege" or the privilege of "fair report" or "record libel." The privilege is usually exercised by commercial publishers and broadcasters, but other businesses and individuals are equally entitled to use it. The fundamental requirements of the privilege are that the published matter be an accurate, non-misleading description of a public proceeding or what transpired within it. See generally Eldredge, Law of Defamation 419–420 (1978); Harper, James & Gray, Law of Torts § 5.24 (3d ed. 2006); Sack, Defamation: Libel, Slander, and Related Problems §§ 7.3.5[B]–[C] (4th ed. 2010).

2. Commentary on the proceeding or background information from a source outside the proceeding is not within the privilege because this is not a description of the proceeding. See Geary v. Alger, (1925) 57 O.L.R. 218 (High Ct.), aff'd (1925) 58 O.L.R. 39 (App. Div.) (adding name of person referred to by trial counsel); Horton v. Georgian Co., 175 Ga. 261, 165 S.E. 443 (1932) (narrative of events not in court files); Cass v. New Orleans Times, 27 La. Ann. 214 (1875) (commentary indicating that charge against plaintiff true); Moore v. Dispatch Printing Co., 87 Minn. 450, 92 N.W. 396 (1902) (account of sensational ending to unsuccessful slander action against law student: discovery of pistol with which complainant may have intended to shoot student); Annot., Libel and Slander: Statements in the Nature of Comment upon Judicial, Legislative, or Administrative Proceeding, or the Decision Therein, as Within Privilege Accorded to Proceeding or Report Thereof, 155 A.L.R. 1346 (1945). But see Lal v. CBS, Inc., 726 F.2d 97 (3d Cir. 1984) (television videotape to illustrate case). The privilege does not apply to a story that has its source in a public proceeding or contains the same facts, but is not identified as a description of a public proceeding. See Hughes v. Washington Daily News Co., 90 U.S. App. D.C. 155, 193 F.2d 922 (1952); Lee v. Dong-A Ilbo, 849 F.2d 876 (4th Cir. 1988) (Kaufman, J., dissenting), cert. denied, 489 U.S. 1067 (1989). The privilege does apply to a description of a public proceeding that is based on unofficial sources. See McCracken v. Evening News Association, 3 Mich. App. 32, 151 N.W.2d 694 (1966).

3. To be privileged, the report must be substantially accurate—accurate as an account of the proceedings, not as a description of plaintiff's conduct or character. Examples of reports failing the accuracy requirement can be found in Ballinger v. Democrat Co., 203 Iowa 1095, 212 N.W. 557 (1927) (reported that divorce petition charged respondent with infidelity; actually charged cruelty); Sweet v. Post Publishing Co., 215 Mass. 450, 102 N.E. 660 (1913) (published that plaintiff indicted by grand jury; person indicted was another individual with similar name); Schaffran v. Press Publishing Co., 258 N.Y. 207, 179 N.E. 387 (1932) (reporter assumed truth of evidence presented by petitioner who obtained divorce decree; judge who granted decree did not find evidence true). In applying a test of substantial accuracy, an analogy may be drawn to the "substantial truth" test applied to the defense of truth. Smolla, Law of Defamation § 8:76 (2d ed. 1999). See McCracken v. Evening News Association, supra (reported that plaintiff charged with $100,000 fraud; actually charged with fraud amounting to $50,000); Piracci v. Hearst Corp., 263 F. Supp. 511 (D. Md. 1966), aff'd, 371 F.2d 1016 (4th Cir. 1967) (reported that plaintiff charged with possession of marijuana; actually charged with delinquency on account of possession of marijuana); Nanji v. National Geographic Society, 403 F. Supp. 2d 425 (D. Md. 2005) (reported that plaintiff received prison sentence for rape; actually convicted on very different charges, with evidence of sexual assaults forming part of prosecution's case); Torski v. Mansfield Journal Co., 100 Ohio App. 538, 137 N.E.2d 679 (1956), appeal dismissed, 165 Ohio St. 245, 135 N.E.2d 63 (1956) (reported that plain-

tiff arrested on charge of raping twelve-year-old; victim of rape, which plaintiff did not commit, actually twenty-four). Compare Myers v. The Telegraph, 332 Ill. App. 3d 917, 773 N.E.2d 192 (2002) (report that plaintiff pled guilty to felony possession of marijuana and received probation not privileged when guilty plea was to misdemeanor possession charge and plaintiff received conditional discharge). What if a newspaper reports that "charges of aggravated battery" were filed against a person when the person was sued in a civil action, not prosecuted in a criminal case? See Sivulich v. Howard Publications, Inc., 126 Ill. App. 3d 129, 466 N.E.2d 1218 (1984).

4. Also, the report must not be so selective as to be misleading or decidedly one-sided— hence, the label "fair report." A report may be unfair because of its emphasis or headline. See Lavin v. New York News, Inc., 757 F.2d 1416 (3d Cir. 1985); Schiavone Construction Co. v. Time, Inc., 847 F.2d 1069 (3d Cir. 1988). Fairness does not require that the account be a complete report of the proceedings—if this were required the privilege would be of little value—or a comprehensive summary. The reporter can select the subjects to be addressed. Accuracy and fairness have been triable issues in numerous cases. An amusing instance is Bock v. Plainfield Courier-News, 45 N.J. Super. 320, 132 A.2d 523 (App. Div. 1957).

5. Privilege has long been allowed to descriptions of judicial proceedings. One example of this is Ronwin v. Shapiro, 657 F.2d 1071 (9th Cir. 1981). The subject of suit was a note in the Arizona Law Review on the decision of the Supreme Court of Arizona to deny plaintiff admission to the bar. The ground was that he was not mentally able to practice law. Plaintiff brought an action against the author, the law review editor and the University of Arizona Board of Regents. As the note accurately described the Arizona Supreme Court opinion, plaintiff's action was barred. One limitation on the privilege found in many jurisdictions is that pleadings, affidavits or other papers filed in a case but not yet acted upon by the court are not included. See Sanford v. Boston Herald-Traveler Corp., 318 Mass. 156, 61 N.E.2d 5 (1945); Ilsley v. Sentinel Co., 133 Wis. 20, 113 N.W. 425 (1907); Smith v. Harris, [1996] 2 V.R. 335 (Sup. Ct.). Why is privilege denied to reports of such pleadings or documents? See the dissent in American District Telegraph Co. v. Brink's, Inc., 380 F.2d 131 (7th Cir. 1967). As many states now reject this limitation as adhere to it. See Newell v. Field Enterprises, Inc., 91 Ill. App. 3d 735, 415 N.E.2d 434 (1980); Salzano v. North Jersey Media Group Inc., 201 N.J. 500, 993 A.2d 778 (2010), cert. denied, ___ U.S. ___ (2011); Campbell v. New York Evening Post, Inc., 245 N.Y. 320, 157 N.E. 153 (1927); Annot., Libel and Slander: Reports of Pleadings as Within Privilege for Reports of Judicial Proceedings, 20 A.L.R.4th 576 (1983).

6. Another possible limitation, that can be applied to legislative and administrative proceedings as well as judicial proceedings, is that reports of hearings closed to the public and records not open to public inspection are not privileged. See Shiles v. News Syndicate Co., 27 N.Y.2d 9, 313 N.Y.S.2d 104, 261 N.E.2d 251 (1970), cert. denied, 400 U.S. 999 (1971) (matrimonial case); Ryalls v. Leader, (1866) L.R. 1 Ex. 296. But see Coleman v. Newark Morning Ledger Co., 29 N.J. 357, 149 A.2d 193 (1959) (closed legislative subcommittee hearing). Should privilege apply to publication of material in an investigative report that is not released to the public? See Medico v. Time, Inc., 509 F. Supp. 268 (E.D. Pa. 1980), aff'd, 643 F.2d 134 (3d Cir. 1981), cert. denied, 454 U.S. 836 (1981) (F.B.I. documents on organized crime); Wynn v. Smith, 117 Nev. 6, 16 P.3d 424 (2001) (confidential Scotland Yard report). In Fletcher-Gordon v. Southam Inc., [1997] 6 W.W.R. 155, (1997) 143 D.L.R.4th 560 (B.C. Sup. Ct.), the court decided that qualified privilege applied to publication of government documents obtained under freedom of information legislation.

7. The privilege now applies to accounts of the hearings and meetings of all types of governmental bodies—federal, state and local—and to descriptions of reports made by government officers and commissions. It also applies to reporting of the official acts of government bodies and officers. But not everything a government officer does or says in the line of duty is official action, and it may be desirable to avoid the damage to reputation that could result if an expansive view of what is an official act were adopted in setting the boundaries of the privilege. Thus, a report of an arrest may be accorded privilege on the basis that an arrest is an official act, but not a report of what the police said about the case. See Phillips v. Evening Star Newspaper Co., 424 A.2d 78 (D.C. 1980), cert. denied, 451 U.S. 989 (1981); Billet v. Times-Democrat Publishing Co., 107 La. 751, 32 So. 17 (1902); Jones v. Taibbi, 400 Mass. 786, 512 N.E.2d 260 (1987). But the tendency is to hold that reports repeating statements by police officers and others responsible for criminal investigations are within the privilege. See Whiteside v. Russellville Newspapers, Inc., 295 S.W.3d 798 (Ark. 2009), cert. denied, ___ U.S. ___ (2009); Wright v. Grove Sun Newspaper Co., Inc., 873 P.2d 983 (Okla. 1994). And also statements by a wide range of other government officials. See Brandon v. Gazette Publishing Co., 234 Ark. 332, 352 S.W.2d 92 (1961) (governor's press release about nursing homes); Short v. News-Journal Co., 58 Del. 592, 212 A.2d 718 (1965) (district office of Internal Revenue Service statement about seizure of assets to recover delinquent taxes). What if the media accurately reproduce a statement to the press that inaccurately describes official action? See Short v. News-Journal Co., supra (statement misidentified person whose assets were seized for tax delinquency; privileged); Steer v. Lexleon, Inc., 59 Md. App. 199, 472 A.2d 1021 (1984) (police erroneously stated that plaintiff arrested; privileged).

8. Does the privilege extend to reports of official proceedings in foreign countries? Should this depend upon the extent to which the public in the place of publication have an interest in the foreign government's actions or an ability to influence its actions? See Lee v. Dong-A Ilbo, 849 F.2d 876 (4th Cir. 1988), cert. denied, 489 U.S. 1067 (1989) (press release by South Korean security agency on North Korean spying in United States); Friedman v. Israel Labour Party, 957 F. Supp. 701 (E.D. Pa. 1997) (Israeli government's barring plaintiff from entering country on ground of criminal background or danger to national security); Webb v. Times Publishing Co. Ltd., [1960] 2 Q.B. 235 (Swiss trial of Englishman, with testimony related to English murder case); Benson v. Robinson & Co. (Pty.) Ltd., 1967 (1) S.A. 420 (A.D.) (debate in parliament of neighboring country); Youm, Republication of Foreign Government Statements: The Fair Report Privilege in U.S. Libel Law, 6 Comm. L. & Policy 393 (2001). In a number of states there are statutes establishing a privilege for reports of certain types of official proceedings and actions—in some instances, an absolute privilege. See Sack, Defamation: Libel, Slander, and Related Problems § 7.3.5[B][3] (4th ed. 2010).

9. Reports on non-governmental meetings that are open to the public and address matters of public concern are arguably within the rationale of this privilege because the reporter serves as a substitute for the reader or viewer, who could attend the meeting personally, and the report serves to inform the public on matters of public importance. A few cases have extended the privilege to reports of such meetings. See Borg v. Tribune Publishing Co., 231 F.2d 788 (9th Cir. 1956) (citizens' meeting whose participants urged grand jury investigation of local incident); Phoenix Newspapers, Inc. v. Choisser, 82 Ariz. 271, 312 P.2d 150 (1957) (local candidates' forum). Compare Kimball v. Post Publishing Co., 199 Mass. 248, 85 N.E. 103 (1908) (no privilege to report meeting of corporation stockholders). But the privilege is also premised upon the particular importance of citizens being informed about judicial and legislative proceedings and the official actions of their government. See Note, Privilege to Republish Defamation, 64 Colum. L. Rev. 1102

(1964). Most courts have never specifically addressed the issue of whether reports of open public meetings are entitled to a common law privilege.

10. As conceived by the common law, the privilege to publish reports of official proceedings was a qualified one. Unlike the "interest" privileges, the reporter's privilege could not be abused by excessive publication. The report could be made to anyone the reporter desired. But it was abused by publication actuated by malice (ill will, spite or purpose to cause injury). See Hurley v. Northwest Publications, Inc., 273 F. Supp. 967 (D. Minn. 1967), aff'd, 398 F.2d 346 (8th Cir. 1968); Stevens v. Sampson, (1879) 5 Ex. D. 53. The reporter need not have believed that the statements made in the proceedings were true, but whether the privilege protected reports of statements the reporter knew were false was questionable. It can well be contended that publishers of accurate reports should not be subject to suit and potential liability on grounds of their alleged motives and should not be required to exclude from their reports statements made in the proceedings that are known to be false. See Stover v. Journal Publishing Co., 105 N.M. 291, 731 P.2d 1335 (Ct. App. 1985), cert. quashed, 105 N.M. 290, 731 P.2d 1334 (1987), cert. denied, 484 U.S. 897 (1987). This is the position of Restatement (Second) of Torts §611 (1977). Accord, Moreno v. Crookston Times Printing Co., 610 N.W.2d 321 (Minn. 2000); Salzano v. North Jersey Media Group Inc., 201 N.J. 500, 993 A.2d 778 (2010), cert. denied, ___ U.S. ___ (2011). It in effect makes the privilege an absolute one, conditioned upon accuracy and sufficient "fairness." Contra, Thomas v. Telegraph Publishing Co., 155 N.H. 314, 929 A.2d 993 (2007).

11. The accuracy requirement is now limited by the constitutional rule of no liability without fault, pp. 626–645, infra. See Gobin v. Globe Publishing Co., 216 Kan. 223, 531 P.2d 76 (1975). Fault may be found where a report is inaccurate because of a reporter's or editor's error, but there is a strong argument that fault on the part of the publisher is absent when the inaccuracy stems from misinformation given a journalist by a government official. See Wilson v. Capital City Press, 315 So. 2d 393 (La. App. 1975), review denied, 320 So. 2d 203 (1975).

London Artists Ltd. v. Littler
Court of Appeal
[1969] 2 Q.B. 375

LORD DENNING M.R. In May of 1964 there opened in London a play called The Right Honourable Gentleman. It was staged by Mr. Emile Littler, the defendant, at Her Majesty's Theatre in Haymarket. The three principal actors were Mr. Anthony Quayle, Miss Coral Browne and Miss Anna Massey. Another actor of a well-known family was Mr. Corin Redgrave. The theatre was owned by a subsidiary of Associated Television Ltd., of which the managing director was Mr. Prince Littler, a brother of Mr. Emile Littler. Mr. Emile Littler rented the theatre on the terms that the owner could determine his tenancy if the takings fell below £3,500 a week for two weeks in succession. That is called the "get-out" figure.

Some months later, in September, 1964, there opened in London another play called Robert and Elizabeth. It was staged at the Lyric Theatre in Shaftesbury Avenue. The management of Robert and Elizabeth were very keen to move the play from the Lyric to Her Majesty's Theatre. The Lyric Theatre was controlled by another subsidiary of Associated Television Ltd., of which, as I have said, Mr. Prince Littler was managing director. So Mr. Prince Littler had a considerable voice in the ownership of both theatres.

On June 18, 1965, Mr. Prince Littler wrote to his brother Mr. Emile Littler saying: " … I have had instructions from my board at our meeting yesterday to give you notice to go as soon as you fall below the get-out figure. This is in order to move Robert and Elizabeth which is playing to capacity at the Lyric Theatre to Her Majesty's Theatre … there is an alternative which is—would you be willing to transfer to the Lyric Theatre to enable us to move Robert and Elizabeth in to Her Majesty's…."

Mr. Emile Littler replied the same day saying that "The Right Honourable Gentleman is playing to about the biggest business of any play in London at the present time," and went on to say that he was not prepared to move unless it was made very much worth his while.

A day or two later, on June 22, 1965, Mr. Emile Littler received what to him was a stunning blow. The three top stars in The Right Honourable Gentleman and the satellite all gave four weeks' formal notice in writing to terminate their engagement. Each said that he or she would finish in the play after the evening performance of July 24. The letters were all in the same wording and were all sent by the actors' agents, London Artists Ltd. There had clearly been close collaboration in the sending of them. Such a thing—for all the top performers to remove at once—was almost unprecedented in the theatre world. It was likely to bring The Right Honourable Gentleman to a full stop. Mr. Emile Littler drew the conclusion that it was all a plot to get his play out of Her Majesty's Theatre, so as to get Robert and Elizabeth in. He thought that the owners had got hold of the artists and induced them to give the notices; and that the intermediary between them was Mr. Lew Grade and the Grade Organisation Ltd. So firm was his belief in this plot that the next day, June 23, 1965, Mr. Emile Littler wrote a letter to each of the four artists: and he held a press conference at which he distributed the letter to the press. It was published in the papers the next day. It was in these words. I will read the one to Miss Coral Browne.

> My dear Coral, We have been friends for years and I am hurt that you did not see me before being a party to what, on the face of it, appears to be a plan to close the run of The Right Honourable Gentleman by joining in and sending me a month's formal notice from your agent.
>
> The Right Honourable Gentleman has been one of your greatest hits in London and is still doing better than any play in the West End. In spite of this Her Majesty's Theatre's new directorate are trying to get our play out of the theatre. Fighting for you all, play, artistes, staff and author, I have not acceded to their request to move because we have a valid contract and are paying top rent and faithfully fulfilling all obligations. Until box office takings drop below £3,500 for two consecutive weeks we can contractually continue at Her Majesty's Theatre.
>
> Her Majesty's Theatre, and a great many other theatres in London, are now controlled by Associated Television of which Mr. Lew Grade is the managing director. Mr. Grade's contract for service with Associated Television Ltd. is with the Grade Organisation Ltd. The Grade Organisation Ltd. owns "London Artists Ltd." (and other theatrical agencies) and they manage our stars:—Anthony Quayle, Coral Browne, Anna Massey and Corin Redgrave. London Artists Ltd., on June 22, by identical letters, gave notice to me by hand for each artiste to terminate their services with the play on the same identical date of July 24.
>
> In other words because I do not wish to disturb over a year's established success at Her Majesty's Theatre, I am being put into a position by my landlords, Associated Television Ltd., whereby, by withdrawing all Grade star labour, the play must close down on the date on which these notices expire.

A great part of the success of The Right Honourable Gentleman has been the casting of this show and the combined effort of withdrawing suddenly the three Grade stars and another Grade artiste on a given date must finish our play for everybody at Her Majesty's and give Associated Television Ltd. possession of the theatre. You must all realise this and know that there has never been such a situation in the history of the theatre. I feel this is such a serious matter, affecting all branches of the industry, that I must make this correspondence available to Equity, the Society of West End Theatre Managers and the National Press. Sincerely yours, Emile.

That letter brought a quick retort. On the very next day four writs for libel were issued against Mr. Emile Littler. The plaintiffs were those who were accused of taking part in a plot: London Artists Ltd., who looked after the artistes; Associated Television Ltd., who controlled the theatres; and Mr. Lew Grade, and the Grade Organisation Ltd., who were in between.

Mr. Emile Littler in his defence pleaded justification, privilege and fair comment.... Mr. Emile Littler went to the court hoping to prove the plot. He had no direct evidence of a plot; but hoped to get something in cross-examination out of the mouths of the plaintiffs.

He failed utterly. The stars all gave evidence from which it became apparent that there was no combination between them and the owners at all. Miss Coral Browne earlier in the year had not been in good health. Her husband had recently died. She wished to make arrangements to go to the United States, but when her agent indicated this to Mr. Emile Littler, he made such a fuss that she decided to wait and give formal notice when the time came. Mr. Anthony Quayle decided to leave because he wanted to write a film script and needed a holiday first. When Miss Anna Massey heard that Mr. Anthony Quayle was leaving, she decided to go too. Mr. Corin Redgrave was a young man who wanted to get more experience.

Seeing that there was no evidence of the suggested plot, Mr. Emile Littler on the eighth day of the trial withdrew the plea of justification.... Then the plaintiffs submitted to the judge that there was nothing left in the defence save damages. The judge upheld the submission. He held that the plea of privilege failed because the publication to the Press was not privileged. He held that the plea of fair comment failed because the matter was not one of public interest, and in addition there was no basis of fact to support the plea....

... [The jury] awarded very modest sums. They gave London Artists Ltd. £250; the Grade Organisation Ltd. £500; Associated Television Ltd. £500 and Mr. Lew Grade £1,000. On hearing these figures, Mr. Littler felt that he might have got clear away if the defence of fair comment had been left to the jury. So he appeals to this court on the ground that the judge was wrong in shutting out the defence of fair comment....

The plea of fair comment was in these words: "Further or in the alternative the said words were fair comment made in good faith and without malice upon a matter of public interest namely the fate of the play The Right Honourable Gentleman which was at all material times enjoying a successful run on the public stage at Her Majesty's Theatre, London...."

That plea has been criticised and I think rightly. It refers to "the said words" as if they consisted only of comment. But "the said words" also contained statements of fact. And the plea leaves those statements of fact untouched.... But the plea carries with it an implication that the facts are true on which the comment is based; and the defendant can be ordered to give particulars of those facts. So long as that implication is read into the plea, it is unobjectionable.

Three points arise on the defence of fair comment. First, was the comment made on a matter of public interest? The judge ruled that it was not. I cannot agree with him. There is no definition in the books as to what is a matter of public interest. All we are given is a list of examples, coupled with the statement that it is for the judge and not for the jury. I would not myself confine it within narrow limits. Whenever a matter is such as to affect people at large, so that they may be legitimately interested in, or concerned at, what is going on; or what may happen to them or to others; then it is a matter of public interest on which everyone is entitled to make fair comment. A good example is *South Hetton Coal Co. v. North-Eastern News Association* [1894] 1 Q.B. 133. A colliery company owned most of the cottages in the village. It was held that the sanitary condition of those cottages—or rather their insanitary condition—was a matter of public interest. Lord Esher M.R., said at p. 140, that it was "a matter of public interest that the conduct of the employers should be criticised." There the public were legitimately *concerned*. Here the public are legitimately *interested*. Many people are interested in what happens in the theatre. The stars welcome publicity. They want to be put at the top of the bill. Producers wish it too. They like the house to be full. The comings and going of performers are noticed everywhere. When three top stars and a satellite all give notice to leave at the same time—thus putting a successful play in peril—it is to my mind a matter of public interest in which everyone, Press and all, are entitled to comment freely.

The second point is whether the allegation of a "plot" was a fact which the defendant had to prove to be true, or was it only comment? In order to be fair, the commentator must get his basic facts right. The basic facts are those which go to the pith and substance of the matter. They are the facts on which the comments are based or from which the inferences are drawn—as distinct from the comments or inferences themselves. The commentator need not set out in his original article all the basic facts; but he must get them right and be ready to prove them to be true. He must indeed afterwards in legal proceedings, when asked, give particulars of the basic facts; but he need not give particulars of the comments or the inferences to be drawn from those facts. If in his original article he sets out basic facts which are themselves defamatory of the plaintiff, then he must prove them to be true.... It is indeed the whole difference between a plea of fair comment and a plea of justification. In fair comment he need only prove the basic facts to be true. In justification he must prove also that the comments and inferences are true also.

So I turn to ask what were the basic facts in this case? In the particulars ... Mr. Emile Littler set out very many facts which conveyed no clear picture. But, putting them together, it appears that he was relying on three basic facts. First, that the owners wanted to get The Right Honourable Gentleman out of Her Majesty's Theatre. Second, that the stars and satellite all gave notice by the same agents at the same time in the same form. Third, that there was a plot between the owners and the stars (through the Grade Organisation) to bring to an end the run of The Right Honourable Gentleman. Mr. Emile Littler proved the first two basic facts, but did not prove the third. He failed to prove a plot and had to withdraw the allegation. That put him in a quandary on fair comment. He could not prove one of the basic facts. So he turned right about. He then submitted that the allegation of a "plot" was not a fact at all but only a comment. In my view that submission cannot be sustained.... The first paragraph runs in guarded language, "it appears"; and the fifth paragraph says "in other words"; but the last paragraph speaks of "the combined effort." Reading the letter as a whole, I have no doubt that it stated *as a fact* that there was a plot between the plaintiffs to bring down a chopper on the head of The Right Honourable Gentleman.

Mr. Duncan submitted, however, that the question whether the statement was a statement of fact or comment should have been left to the jury. He would be right if it was reasonably capable of being considered as comment.... But I do not think the statement of a "plot" was reasonably capable of being considered as comment. It was a statement of fact which was itself defamatory of the plaintiffs. The defendant, in order to succeed, had to prove it to be true. He failed to do so, and along with it went the defence of fair comment.

In case, however, I am wrong about this and it could be regarded as comment, then I turn to the third point, which is this: were there any facts on which a fair minded man might honestly make such a comment? I take it to be settled law that, in order for the defence of fair comment to be left to the jury, there must at least be a sufficient basis of fact to warrant the comment, in this sense, that a fair minded man might on those facts honestly hold that opinion. There is no need for the defendant to prove that his opinion was correct or one with which the jury agree. He is entitled to the defence of fair comment unless it can be said: "No fair minded man could honestly hold that opinion".

In this case I am sure that Mr. Emile Littler acted honestly and in good faith. He honestly thought that there was a plot to bring to a stop the run of The Right Honourable Gentleman. He was himself so convinced of it that he took the extreme step of telling it to the world. But I fear that he went beyond the bounds of a fair minded man. He jumped too hastily to his conclusion. He ought not to have been so precipitate. He ought to have made inquiries of the artistes. He ought to have made inquiries of his brother, or wait till he had a letter from him. We know that the brother had on June 23, that very day, written saying "We shall have to continue on the same basis as now." By jumping so quickly to a conclusion Mr. Emile Littler came at odds with the law. He made a public condemnation not only of the artistes themselves but of Associated Television and the agents, London Artists, Mr. Lew Grade and the Grade Organisation. The judge held that in alleging that all those were parties to a plot he was making an imputation without any basis of fact to support it. I think the judge was quite right in so holding and in not leaving it to the jury.

In the upshot it comes to this: the fate of The Right Honourable Gentleman was a matter of public interest. Mr. Emile Littler was fully entitled to comment on it as long as his comment was fair and honest. He was entitled to give his views to the public through the press. But I think he went beyond the bounds of fair comment. He was carried away by his feelings at the moment. He did not wait long enough to check the facts and to get them right. He had no defence except as to damages: and on that he did well. I would dismiss this appeal.

[Edmund Davies and Widgery, L.JJ., delivered concurring opinions.]

Notes

1. The privilege of "fair comment" affords the media and private citizens a large measure of freedom to make defamatory comments on matters of public interest without having to justify them, i.e. prove that the comments were correct, should litigation ensue. The fair comment rule by no means eliminates the problem of justification that a defendant not protected by privilege normally faces, for the comment must be based upon facts "truly stated"—comment based upon a factually erroneous foundation is not privileged—and statements of opinion usually also state or imply facts. But if the facts are correct, defendant's comments or expressions of opinion on the facts are protected by the fair comment doctrine, even if a judge or jury or most people in the community would consider defendant's opinion wrong. See generally Fleming, Law of Torts 668–673

(10th ed. 2011); Harper & James, Law of Torts § 5.28 (1st ed. 1956); Sack, Defamation: Libel, Slander, and Related Problems § 4.4 (4th ed. 2010).

2. One widely recognized qualification upon the "facts truly stated" requirement is that comment can be made upon privileged matter that contains untrue statements, provided the commentator does not endorse the statements as true. Thus, comment can be made upon judicial or legislative proceedings or governmental action within the report of public proceedings privilege, whether or not statements in the proceedings or the action taken falsely defamed plaintiff. See Pauling v. News Syndicate Co., Inc., 335 F.2d 659 (2d Cir. 1964), cert. denied, 379 U.S. 968 (1965); Brent Walker Group Plc. v. Time Out Ltd., [1991] 2 Q.B. 33 (C.A.).

3. The facts upon which defendant's commentary is based must be identified in the statement or generally known to the persons receiving the statement. Otherwise, the statement will be taken to imply the existence of facts, which must be justified, or to be unfair. See A.S. Abell Co. v. Kirby, 227 Md. 267, 176 A.2d 340 (1961); Annot., Reliance on Facts Not Stated or Referred to in Publication, as Support for Defense of Fair Comment in Defamation Cases, 90 A.L.R.2d 1279 (1963). One of the rationales of fair comment is that when the factual basis is known to the recipients, they are in a position to decide for themselves whether defendant's opinion is correct. The recipients really are not in such a position when the comment is on a work of art, literature, drama or science that the recipients have not seen, but in view of the importance of criticism on these subjects and the public's ability to examine the works criticized, identification of the work is generally a sufficient basis for comment on its contents. Joseph v. Spiller, [2011] 1 A.C. 852 (S.C.), held that the basis of the comment does not have to be identified with sufficient particularity to enable a reader to judge whether the comment is well-founded.

4. The expression "fair comment upon a matter of public interest" embodies three major requirements of fair comment: that the matter published be comment, be fair and be on a matter of public interest. All present major problems of definition and application. The least difficult of the three is "matter of public interest." A very broad range of subjects is included. They may be grouped into four categories:

(a) Matters of government and politics: the actions of government bodies and officials, issues that are or may be addressed by them, and the conduct and qualifications of government officers, candidates and political organizations.

(b) The affairs of institutions and organizations whose activities affect the interests of the community at large, such as schools, churches, charities, public utilities, major businesses, and professional and trade associations.

(c) Problems which affect the general interests of the community, such as crime, pollution, unemployment, discrimination, poor housing and fraudulent business practices.

(d) Creative activities, for which public attention and support is usually sought and criticism is usually expected: art, literature, entertainment, sports, speeches, restaurant cuisine, public projects, inventions and achievements in science.

Comment is not on a matter of public interest when it goes to private conduct of no legitimate concern to the community. This may be found when comment on a person whose activities are of public concern extends to matters that do not affect the person's public activities, as when the private life of an artist or actor is discussed. How does one address differences of opinion on what aspects of a person's private life are relevant to his public activities? Restatement of Torts § 606 (1938) applies a reasonableness test to criticism of private conduct or character, although not to criticism on other matters of public concern. See generally Prosser, Law of Torts 812–816 (3d ed. 1964); Sack, Defamation: Libel, Slander, and Related Problems § 4.4.4 (4th ed. 2010).

5. A matter of public interest has been found in comments on delay in a contractor's paving of a city street. Williams v. Daily Review, Inc., 236 Cal. App. 2d 405, 46 Cal. Rptr. 135 (1965). The behavior of a person who attended a political candidate's public meeting. Davis v. Duncan, (1874) L.R. 9 C.P. 396. The presence of a dangerous amount of wood alcohol in vanilla flavoring used by a bakery. Hubbard v. Allyn, 200 Mass. 166, 86 N.E. 856 (1908). A company's claim to a right of way for vehicles over a pedestrian walkway. Slim v. Daily Telegraph Ltd., [1968] 2 Q.B. 157 (C.A.). A physician's failure to provide treatment to a person seeking it in a hospital's emergency room. Alleman v. Vermilion Publishing Corp., 316 So. 2d 837 (La. App. 1975). The selling of books in a church during services and installation of cooking equipment in the church, allegedly causing a fire hazard. Kelly v. Tinling, (1865) L.R. 1 Q.B. 699. An individual's medical quackery. Brinkley v. Fishbein, 110 F.2d 62 (5th Cir. 1940), cert. denied, 311 U.S. 672 (1940). Advertising handbills. Paris v. Levy, (1860) 9 C.B.N.S. 342, 142 Eng. Rep. 135, 7 Jur. N.S. 289, 30 L.J.C.P. 11, 3 L.T.323, 9 W.R. 71 (C.P.). The quality of a device for examining the bore of a gun. Safe Site, Inc. v. National Rifle Association of America, 253 F. Supp. 418 (D.D.C. 1966). The activities, including correspondence with a German national, of a person who made speeches during World War II urging non-payment of federal income taxes to protest government policies. Kellems v. California Congress of Industrial Organization Council, 68 F. Supp. 277 (N.D. Cal. 1946). And the treatment of Roy Campanella's hand in Shenkman v. O'Malley, p. 602, supra.

6. No matter of public interest was found in comments addressed to a successful suit by parents against their son for injuries they sustained in a traffic accident. Kinsley v. Herald & Globe Association, 113 Vt. 272, 34 A.2d 99 (1943) (said to be "legal racket" if insurance company would pay judgment). A civil servant's drawing sick leave pay at a time when he was actively leading a group opposed to a controversial government policy. Russell v. Pawley, [1987] 3 W.W.R. 442, (1987) 36 D.L.R.4th 625 (Man. C.A.) ("strange ... that he couldn't be back working"). And a drug store's ceasing to carry a newspaper because of the store owner's opinion that the newspaper promoted racial animosity. Afro-American Publishing Co. v. Jaffe, 125 U.S. App. D.C. 70, 366 F.2d 649 (1966) (newspaper portrayed owner as bigot).

7. The problem of differentiating comment from fact is central to the law of fair comment. No satisfactory means of resolving it has been devised or is likely to be devised. See Titus, Statement of Fact Versus Statement of Opinion—A Spurious Dispute in Fair Comment, 15 Vand. L. Rev. 1203 (1962), which criticizes the fact-comment distinction. The core idea of "comment" appears to be something that is an observation upon or criticism of or conclusion from facts and is recognizable as opinion by the recipient of the statement. See Mashburn v. Collin, 355 So. 2d 879 (La. 1977); A.S. Abell Co. v. Kirby, 227 Md. 267, 176 A.2d 340 (1961). If defendant set out a fact and then made an observation on it, the latter is likely to be interpreted as comment. A debatable example is found in Davis v. Duncan, supra, in which defendant said that plaintiff and another had "appearances which were certainly consistent with the belief that they had imbibed rather freely of the cup that inebriates." If defendant made a statement not preceded by a reference to facts, it is likely to be taken as implying facts and therefore factual. Statements presented as criticism of art or literature are usually treated as comment, but this is not always the case, as O'Shaughnessy v. Mirror Newspapers Ltd., (1970) 125 C.L.R. 166, illustrates. It was held that a critic's review of a perfor-

mance of *Othello* (entitled "What a Tragedy") could be interpreted as a factual statement that the director dishonestly suppressed the roles of other players in order to highlight his own role.

8. There is considerable authority to the effect that to attribute base motives or character flaws to an author or artist in a criticism of his work goes beyond the bounds of fair comment. See Derounian v. Stokes, 168 F.2d 305 (10th Cir. 1948); Berg v. Printers' Ink Publishing Co., Inc., 54 F. Supp. 795 (S.D.N.Y. 1943), aff'd, 141 F.2d 1022 (2d Cir. 1944); Campbell v. Spottiswoode, (1863) 3 B. & S. 769, 122 Eng. Rep. 288, 9 Jur. N.S. 1069, 27 J.P. 501, 32 L.J.Q.B. 185, 8 L.T. 201, 2 N.R. 20, 11 W.R. 569 (Q.B.). Cf. Sherman v. International Publications, Inc., 214 App. Div. 437, 212 N.Y.S. 478 (1925) (criticism of physician who manufactured and distributed vaccines). What if defendant calls an industrialist's activities "treasonable operations"? See Kellems v. California Congress of Industrial Organization Council, supra (comment). Or says that a television performer's "gags" are "blue" (obscene)? See Bamberger v. Newspapers Ltd., (1969) 43 A.L.J.R. 242 (jury could find it statement of fact).

9. It may be questioned whether the requirement that comment be "fair" adds anything to the requirements already stated and the limitation that fair comment, as a qualified privilege, does not protect statements actuated by malice. If "fairness" has additional content, a court is likely to interpret it in one of two ways: as a requirement that the statement be one that a fair-minded person could honestly hold on the facts stated. See Merivale v. Carson, (1887) 20 Q.B.D. 275 (C.A.). Or as a requirement that the statement express defendant's honestly held opinion. See Dowling v. Livingstone, 108 Mich. 321, 66 N.W. 225 (1896). The first interpretation is appropriate in principle, but it seems to invite a jury decision on whether defendant's comments were unjust or unreasonable. Harsh, extreme and prejudiced comments have been thought well within the fair comment privilege. See Cherry v. Des Moines Leader, 114 Iowa 298, 86 N.W. 323 (1901); Hartmann v. Boston Herald-Traveler Corp., 323 Mass. 56, 80 N.E.2d 16 (1948); McQuire v. Western Morning News Co., Ltd., [1903] 2 K.B. 100 (C.A.). But see England v. Daily Gazette Co., 143 W. Va. 700, 104 S.E.2d 306 (1958) (privilege denied to comments that are unreasonably violent or lack reasonable basis in facts). Telnikoff v. Matusevitch, [1992] 2 A.C. 343 (H.L.), states that the "objective test" of fair comment is "whether any man, however prejudiced and obstinate, could honestly hold the view expressed by the defendant."

10. The second interpretation avoids this problem but presents difficulties for persons who publish material written by others. The statements therein may express the opinion of the author, but not of the publisher sued for defamation. Should a publisher be required to prove that a signed article or letter to the editor expresses the honest opinion of the publisher? Of the author? In Cherneskey v. Armadale Publishers Ltd., [1979] 1 S.C.R. 1067, (1978) 90 D.L.R.3d 321, a newspaper that published a defamatory letter was denied a fair comment defense because the opinions expressed were not the newspaper's opinions and there was no evidence that the letter represented the honest opinions of its authors. In Schomberg v. Walker, 132 Cal. 224, 64 P. 290 (1901), a newspaper's failure to inquire into the truth of charges made in a published letter to the editor, recognized as injurious, was treated as evidence of malice. It is possible that a court will require both that the opinion be honestly held and that it be one that a fair-minded person could form. See Grower v. State, 23 A.D.2d 506, 255 N.Y.S.2d 135 (1965), aff'd, 19 N.Y.2d 625, 278 N.Y.S.2d 408, 224 N.E.2d 899 (1967); Cheng v. Tse Wai Chun, (2000) 3 H.K.C.F.A.R. 339, [2000] 3 H.K.L.R.D. 418 (lack of genuine belief in opinion expressed is malice that defeats fair comment defense). Why did Lord Denning, M.R., conclude in the principal case that defendant "went beyond the bounds of a fair minded man"?

Section 3. Constitutional Law

Gertz v. Robert Welch, Inc.
Supreme Court of the United States
418 U.S. 323 (1974)

Mr. Justice POWELL delivered the opinion of the Court.

This Court has struggled for nearly a decade to define the proper accommodation between the law of defamation and the freedoms of speech and press protected by the First
Amendment. With this decision we return to that effort. We granted certiorari to reconsider the extent of a publisher's constitutional privilege against liability for defamation
of a private citizen.

I

In 1968 a Chicago policeman named Nuccio shot and killed a youth named Nelson.
The state authorities prosecuted Nuccio for the homicide and ultimately obtained a con-
viction for murder in the second degree. The Nelson family retained petitioner Elmer
Gertz, a reputable attorney, to represent them in civil litigation against Nuccio.

ELMER GERTZ   Theodore G. Gertz

Respondent publishes American Opinion, a monthly outlet for the views of the John Birch Society. Early in the 1960's the magazine began to warn of a nationwide conspiracy to discredit local law enforcement agencies and create in their stead a national police force capable of supporting a Communist dictatorship. As part of the continuing effort to alert the public to this assumed danger, the managing editor of American Opinion commissioned an article on the murder trial of Officer Nuccio. For this purpose he engaged a regular contributor to the magazine. In March 1969 respondent published the resulting article under the title "FRAME-UP: Richard Nuccio And The War On Police." The article purports to demonstrate that the testimony against Nuccio at his criminal trial was false and that his prosecution was part of the Communist campaign against the police.

In his capacity as counsel for the Nelson family in the civil litigation, petitioner attended the coroner's inquest into the boy's death and initiated actions for damages, but he neither discussed Officer Nuccio with the press nor played any part in the criminal proceeding. Notwithstanding petitioner's remote connection with the prosecution of Nuccio, respondent's magazine portrayed him as an architect of the "frame-up." According to the article, the police file on petitioner took "a big, Irish cop to lift." The article stated that petitioner had been an official of the "Marxist League for Industrial Democracy, originally known as the Intercollegiate Socialist Society, which has advocated the violent seizure of our government." It labeled Gertz a "Leninist" and a "Communist-fronter." It also stated that Gertz had been an officer of the National Lawyers Guild, described as a Communist organization that "probably did more than any other outfit to plan the Communist attack on the Chicago police during the 1968 Democratic Convention."

These statements contained serious inaccuracies. The implication that petitioner had a criminal record was false. Petitioner had been a member and officer of the National Lawyers Guild some 15 years earlier, but there was no evidence that he or that organization had taken any part in planning the 1968 demonstrations in Chicago. There was also no basis for the charge that petitioner was a "Leninist" or a "Communist-fronter." And he had never been a member of the "Marxist League for Industrial Democracy" or the "Intercollegiate Socialist Society."

The managing editor of American Opinion made no effort to verify or substantiate the charges against petitioner. Instead, he appended an editorial introduction stating that the author had "conducted extensive research into the Richard Nuccio Case." And he included in the article a photograph of petitioner and wrote the caption that appeared under it: "Elmer Gertz of Red Guild harasses Nuccio." Respondent placed the issue of American Opinion containing the article on sale at newsstands throughout the country and distributed reprints of the article on the streets of Chicago.

Petitioner filed a diversity action for libel in the United States District Court for the Northern District of Illinois. He claimed that the falsehoods published by respondent injured his reputation as a lawyer and a citizen. Before filing an answer, respondent moved to dismiss the complaint for failure to state a claim upon which relief could be granted, apparently on the ground that petitioner failed to allege special damages. But the court ruled that statements contained in the article constituted libel *per se* under Illinois law and that consequently petitioner need not plead special damages.

After answering the complaint, respondent filed a pretrial motion for summary judgment, claiming a constitutional privilege against liability for defamation. It asserted that petitioner was a public official or a public figure and that the article concerned an issue of public interest and concern. For these reasons, respondent argued, it was entitled to invoke the privilege enunciated in New York Times Co. v. Sullivan, 376 U.S. 254 (1964). Under this rule respondent would escape liability unless petitioner could prove publication of defamatory falsehood "with 'actual malice' — that is, with knowledge that it was false or with reckless disregard of whether it was false or not." Respondent claimed that petitioner could not make such a showing and submitted a supporting affidavit by the magazine's managing editor. The editor denied any knowledge of the falsity of the statements concerning petitioner and stated that he had relied on the author's reputation and on his prior experience with the accuracy and authenticity of the author's contributions to American Opinion.

The District Court denied respondent's motion for summary judgment.... After all the evidence had been presented but before submission of the case to the jury, the court ruled in effect that petitioner was neither a public official nor a public figure. It added that, if he were, the resulting application of the New York Times standard would require a directed verdict for respondent.... [T]he court submitted the case to the jury under instructions that withdrew from its consideration all issues save the measure of damages. The jury awarded $50,000 to petitioner.

Following the jury verdict and on further reflection, the District Court concluded that the New York Times standard should govern this case even though petitioner was not a public official or public figure. It accepted respondent's contention that that privilege protected discussion of any public issue without regard to the status of a person defamed therein. Accordingly, the court entered judgment for respondent notwithstanding the jury's verdict....

Petitioner appealed to contest the applicability of the New York Times standard to this case. Although the Court of Appeals for the Seventh Circuit doubted the correctness of the District Court's determination that petitioner was not a public figure, it did not overturn that finding. It agreed with the District Court that respondent could assert the constitutional privilege because the article concerned a matter of public interest, citing this Court's intervening decision in Rosenbloom v. Metromedia, Inc. [403 U.S. 29 (1971)]. The Court of Appeals read Rosenbloom to require application of the New York Times standard to any publication or broadcast about an issue of significant public interest, without regard to the position, fame, or anonymity of the person defamed, and it concluded that respondent's statements concerned such an issue. After reviewing the record, the Court of Appeals endorsed the District Court's conclusion that petitioner had failed to show by clear and convincing evidence that respondent had acted with "actual malice" as defined by New York Times. There was no evidence that the managing editor of American Opinion knew of the falsity of the accusations made in the article. In fact, he knew nothing about petitioner except what he learned from the article. The court correctly noted that mere proof of failure to investigate, without more, cannot establish reckless disregard for the truth. Rather, the publisher must act with a "'high degree of awareness of ... probable falsity.'" St. Amant v. Thompson, 390 U.S. 727, 731 (1968). The evidence in this case did not reveal that respondent had cause for such an awareness. The Court of Appeals therefore affirmed, 471 F.2d 801 (1972). For the reasons stated below, we reverse.

II

The principal issue in this case is whether a newspaper or broadcaster that publishes defamatory falsehoods about an individual who is neither a public official nor a public figure may claim a constitutional privilege against liability for the injury inflicted by those statements. The Court considered this question on the rather different set of facts presented in Rosenbloom v. Metromedia, Inc. Rosenbloom, a distributor of nudist magazines, was arrested for selling allegedly obscene material while making a delivery to a retail dealer. The police obtained a warrant and seized his entire inventory of 3,000 books and magazines. He sought and obtained an injunction prohibiting further police interference with his business. He then sued a local radio station for failing to note in two of its newscasts that the 3,000 items seized were only "reportedly" or "allegedly" obscene and for broadcasting references to "the smut literature racket" and to "girlie-book peddlers" in its coverage of the court proceeding for injunctive relief. He obtained a judgment against the radio station, but the Court of Appeals for the Third Circuit held the *New York Times* privilege applicable to the broadcast and reversed.

This Court affirmed the decision below, but no majority could agree on a controlling rationale. The eight Justices who participated in *Rosenbloom* announced their views in five separate opinions, none of which commanded more than three votes. The several statements not only reveal disagreement about the appropriate result in that case, they also reflect divergent traditions of thought about the general problem of reconciling the law of defamation with the First Amendment. One approach has been to extend the *New York Times* test to an expanding variety of situations. Another has been to vary the level of constitutional privilege for defamatory falsehood with the status of the person defamed. And a third view would grant to the press and broadcast media absolute immunity from liability for defamation. To place our holding in the proper context, we preface our discussion of this case with a review of the several *Rosenbloom* opinions and their antecedents.

In affirming the trial court's judgment in the instant case, the Court of Appeals relied on Mr. Justice Brennan's conclusion for the *Rosenbloom* plurality that "all discussion and communication involving matters of public or general concern" warrant the protection from liability for defamation accorded by the rule originally enunciated in New York Times Co. v. Sullivan. There this Court defined a constitutional privilege intended to free criticism of public officials from the restraints imposed by the common law of defamation. The Times ran a political advertisement endorsing civil rights demonstrations by black students in Alabama and impliedly condemning the performance of local law-enforcement officials. A police commissioner established in state court that certain misstatements in the advertisement referred to him and that they constituted libel *per se* under Alabama law. This showing left the Times with the single defense of truth, for under Alabama law neither good faith nor reasonable care would protect the newspaper from liability. This Court concluded that a "rule compelling the critic of official conduct to guarantee the truth of all his factual assertions" would deter protected speech and announced the constitutional privilege designed to counter that effect: "The constitutional guarantees require, we think, a federal rule that prohibits a public official from recovering damages for a defamatory falsehood relating to his official conduct unless he proves that the statement was made with 'actual malice'—that is, with knowledge that it was false or with reckless disregard of whether it was false or not."

Three years after *New York Times*, a majority of the Court agreed to extend the constitutional privilege to defamatory criticism of "public figures." This extension was announced in Curtis Publishing Co. v. Butts and its companion, Associated Press v. Walker, 388 U.S. 130, 162 (1967). The first case involved the Saturday Evening Post's charge that Coach Wally Butts of the University of Georgia had conspired with Coach "Bear" Bryant of the University of Alabama to fix a football game between their respective schools. *Walker* involved an erroneous Associated Press account of former Major General Edwin Walker's participation in a University of Mississippi campus riot. Because Butts was paid by a private alumni association and Walker had resigned from the Army, neither could be classified as a "public official" under *New York Times*.... [A] majority of the Court agreed with Mr. Chief Justice Warren's conclusion that the *New York Times* test should apply to criticism of "public figures" as well as "public officials." The Court extended the constitutional privilege announced in that case to protect defamatory criticism of nonpublic persons who "are nevertheless intimately involved in the resolution of important public questions or, by reason of their fame, shape events in areas of concern to society at large."

In his opinion for the plurality in Rosenbloom v. Metromedia, Inc., 403 U.S. 29 (1971), Mr. Justice Brennan took the *New York Times* privilege one step further. He concluded that its protection should extend to defamatory falsehoods relating to private persons if the statements concerned matters of general or public interest. He abjured the suggested distinction between public officials and public figures on the one hand and private individuals on the other. He focused instead on society's interest in learning about certain issues: "If a matter is a subject of public or general interest, it cannot suddenly become less so merely because a private individual is involved, or because in some sense the individual did not 'voluntarily' choose to become involved." Thus, under the plurality opinion, a private citizen involuntarily associated with a matter of general interest has no recourse for injury to his reputation unless he can satisfy the demanding requirements of the *New York Times* test.

Two Members of the Court concurred in the result in *Rosenbloom* but departed from the reasoning of the plurality. Mr. Justice Black restated his view, long shared by Mr. Justice Douglas, that the First Amendment cloaks the news media with an absolute and indefeasible immunity from liability for defamation. Mr. Justice White concurred on a narrower ground. He concluded that "the First Amendment gives the press and the broadcast media a privilege to report and comment upon the official actions of public servants in full detail, with no requirement that the reputation or the privacy of an individual involved in or affected by the official action be spared from public view." ...

In *Rosenbloom* Mr. Justice Harlan ... acquiesced in the application of the privilege to defamation of public figures but argued that a different rule should obtain where defamatory falsehood harmed a private individual. He noted that a private person has less likelihood "of securing access to channels of communication sufficient to rebut falsehoods concerning him" than do public officials and public figures and has not voluntarily placed himself in the public spotlight. Mr. Justice Harlan concluded that the States could constitutionally allow private individuals to recover damages for defamation on the basis of any standard of care except liability without fault.

Mr. Justice Marshall dissented in *Rosenbloom* in an opinion joined by Mr. Justice Stewart. He thought that the plurality's "public or general interest" test for determining the applicability of the *New York Times* privilege would involve the courts in the dangerous business of deciding "what information is relevant to self-government." He also contended that the plurality's position inadequately served "society's interest in protecting private individuals from being thrust into the public eye by the distorting light of defamation." Mr. Justice Marshall therefore reached the conclusion, also reached by Mr. Justice Harlan, that the States should be "essentially free to continue the evolution of the common law of defamation and to articulate whatever fault standard best suits the State's need," so long as the States did not impose liability without fault. The principal point of disagreement among the three dissenters concerned punitive damages. Whereas Mr. Justice Harlan thought that the States could allow punitive damages in amounts bearing "a reasonable and purposeful relationship to the actual harm done," Mr. Justice Marshall concluded that the size and unpredictability of jury awards of exemplary damages unnecessarily exacerbated the problems of media self-censorship and that such damages should therefore be forbidden.

III

We begin with the common ground. Under the First Amendment there is no such thing as a false idea. However pernicious an opinion may seem, we depend for its correction not on the conscience of judges and juries but on the competition of other ideas. But there is no constitutional value in false statements of fact. Neither the intentional lie nor the careless error materially advances society's interest in "uninhibited, robust, and wide-open" debate on public issues. New York Times Co. v. Sullivan, 376 U.S., at 270. They belong to that category of utterances which "are no essential part of any exposition of ideas, and are of such slight social value as a step to truth that any benefit that may be derived from them is clearly outweighed by the social interest in order and morality." Chaplinsky v. New Hampshire, 315 U.S. 568 (1942).

Although the erroneous statement of fact is not worthy of constitutional protection, it is nevertheless inevitable in free debate. As James Madison pointed out in the Report on the Virginia Resolutions of 1798: "Some degree of abuse is inseparable from the proper use of every thing; and in no instance is this more true than in that of the press." 4 J. Elliot, Debates on the Federal Constitution of 1787, p. 571 (1876). And punishment of error runs the risk of inducing a cautious and restrictive exercise of the constitutionally guaranteed freedoms of speech and press. Our decisions recognize that a rule of strict liability that compels a publisher or broadcaster to guarantee the accuracy of his factual assertions may lead to intolerable self-censorship. Allowing the media to avoid liability only by proving the truth of all injurious statements does not accord adequate protection to First Amendment liberties. As the Court stated in New York Times Co. v. Sullivan, "Allowance of the defense of truth, with the burden of proving it on the defendant, does not mean that only false speech will be deterred." The First Amendment requires that we protect some falsehood in order to protect speech that matters.

The need to avoid self-censorship by the news media is, however, not the only societal value at issue. If it were, this Court would have embraced long ago the view that publishers and broadcasters enjoy an unconditional and indefeasible immunity from liability for defamation. Such a rule would, indeed, obviate the fear that the prospect of civil liability for injurious falsehood might dissuade a timorous press from the effective exercise of First Amendment freedoms. Yet absolute protection for the communications media requires a total sacrifice of the competing value served by the law of defamation.

The legitimate state interest underlying the law of libel is the compensation of individuals for the harm inflicted on them by defamatory falsehood. We would not lightly require the State to abandon this purpose, for, as Mr. Justice Stewart has reminded us, the individual's right to the protection of his own good name "reflects no more than our basic concept of the essential dignity and worth of every human being—a concept at the root of any decent system of ordered liberty. The protection of private personality, like the protection of life itself, is left primarily to the individual States under the Ninth and Tenth Amendments. But this does not mean that the right is entitled to any less recognition by this Court as a basic of our constitutional system." Rosenblatt v. Baer, 383 U.S. 75, 92 (1966) (concurring opinion).

Some tension necessarily exists between the need for a vigorous and uninhibited press and the legitimate interest in redressing wrongful injury. As Mr. Justice Harlan stated, "some antithesis between freedom of speech and press and libel actions persists, for libel remains premised on the content of speech and limits the freedom of the publisher to express certain sentiments, at least without guaranteeing legal proof of their substantial accuracy." Curtis Publishing Co. v. Butts, 388 U.S., at 152. In our continuing effort to define the proper accommodation between these competing concerns, we have been especially anxious to assure to the freedoms of speech and press that "breathing space" essential to their fruitful exercise. To that end this Court has extended a measure of strategic protection to defamatory falsehood.

The *New York Times* standard defines the level of constitutional protection appropriate to the context of defamation of a public person. Those who, by reason of the notoriety of their achievements or the vigor and success with which they seek the public's attention, are properly classed as public figures and those who hold governmental office may recover for injury to reputation only on clear and convincing proof that the defamatory falsehood was made with knowledge of its falsity or with reckless disregard for the truth. This standard administers an extremely powerful antidote to the inducement to media self-censorship of the common-law rule of strict liability for libel and slander. And it exacts a correspondingly high price from the victims of defamatory falsehood. Plainly many deserving plaintiffs, including some intentionally subjected to injury, will be unable to surmount the barrier of the *New York Times* test. Despite this substantial abridgment of the state law right to compensation for wrongful hurt to one's reputation, the Court has concluded that the protection of the *New York Times* privilege should be available to publishers and broadcasters of defamatory falsehood concerning public officials and public figures. New York Times Co. v. Sullivan; Curtis Publishing Co. v. Butts. We think that these decisions are correct, but we do not find their holdings justified solely by reference to the interest of the press and broadcast media in immunity from liability. Rather, we believe that the *New York Times* rule states an accommodation between this concern and the limited state interest present in the context of libel actions brought by public persons. For the reasons stated below, we conclude that the state interest in compensating injury to the reputation of private individuals requires that a different rule should obtain with respect to them.

Theoretically, of course, the balance between the needs of the press and the individual's claim to compensation for wrongful injury might be struck on a case-by-case basis. As Mr. Justice Harlan hypothesized, "it might seem, purely as an abstract matter, that the most utilitarian approach would be to scrutinize carefully every jury verdict in every libel case, in order to ascertain whether the final judgment leaves fully protected whatever First Amendment values transcend the legitimate state interest in protecting the particular plaintiff who prevailed." Rosenbloom v. Metromedia, Inc., 403 U.S. at 63. But this approach would lead to unpredictable results and uncertain expectations, and it could render our duty to supervise the lower courts unmanageable. Because an *ad hoc* resolution of the competing interests at stake in each particular case is not feasible, we must lay down broad rules of general application. Such rules necessarily treat alike various cases involving differences as well as similarities. Thus it is often true that not all of the considerations which justify adoption of a given rule will obtain in each particular case decided under its authority.

With that caveat we have no difficulty in distinguishing among defamation plaintiffs. The first remedy of any victim of defamation is self-help—using available opportunities to contradict the lie or correct the error and thereby to minimize its adverse impact on reputation. Public officials and public figures usually enjoy significantly greater access to the channels of effective communication and hence have a more realistic opportunity to counteract false statements then private individuals normally enjoy. Private individuals are therefore more vulnerable to injury, and the state interest in protecting them is correspondingly greater.

More important than the likelihood that private individuals will lack effective opportunities for rebuttal, there is a compelling normative consideration underlying the distinction between public and private defamation plaintiffs. An individual who decides to seek governmental office must accept certain necessary consequences of that involvement in public affairs. He runs the risk of closer public scrutiny than might otherwise be the case. And society's interest in the officers of government is not strictly limited to the formal discharge of official duties. As the Court pointed out in Garrison v. Louisiana, 379 U.S., at 77, the public's interest extends to "anything which might touch on an official's fitness for office.... Few personal attributes are more germane to fitness for office than dishonesty, malfeasance, or improper motivation, even though these characteristics may also affect the official's private character."

Those classed as public figures stand in a similar position. Hypothetically, it may be possible for someone to become a public figure through no purposeful action of his own, but the instances of truly involuntary public figures must be exceedingly rare. For the most part those who attain this status have assumed rules of especial prominence in the affairs of society. Some occupy positions of such persuasive power and influence that they are deemed public figures for all purposes. More commonly, those classed as public figures have thrust themselves to the forefront of particular public controversies in order to influence the resolution of the issues involved. In either event, they invite attention and comment.

Even if the foregoing generalities do not obtain in every instance, the communications media are entitled to act on the assumption that public officials and public figures have voluntarily exposed themselves to increased risk of injury from defamatory falsehood concerning them. No such assumption is justified with respect to a private individual. He has not accepted public office or assumed an "influential role in ordering society." Curtis Publishing Co. v. Butts, 388 U.S., at 164 (Warren, C.J., concurring in result). He has relinquished no part of his interest in the protection of his own good name, and consequently he has a more compelling call on the courts for redress of injury inflicted by defamatory falsehood. Thus, private individuals are not only more vulnerable to injury than public officials and public figures; they are also more deserving of recovery.

For these reasons we conclude that the States should retain substantial latitude in their efforts to enforce a legal remedy for defamatory falsehood injurious to the reputation of a private individual. The extension of the New York Times test proposed by the Rosenbloom plurality would abridge this legitimate state interest to a degree that we find unacceptable. And it would occasion the additional difficulty of forcing state and federal judges to decide on an ad hoc basis which publications address issues of "general or public interest" and which do not—to determine, in the words of Mr. Justice Marshall, "what information is relevant to self-government." Rosenbloom v. Metromedia, Inc., 403 U.S., at 79. We doubt the wisdom of committing this task to the conscience of judges. Nor does the Constitution require us to draw so thin a line between the drastic alternatives of the New York Times privilege and the common law of strict liability for defamatory error. The "public or general interest" test for determining the applicability of the New York Times standard to private defamation actions inadequately serves both of the competing values at stake. On the one hand, a private individual whose reputation is injured by defamatory falsehood that does concern an issue of public or general interest has no recourse unless he can meet the rigorous requirements of New York Times. This is true despite the factors that distinguish the state interest in compensating private individuals from the analogous interest involved in the context of public persons. On the other hand, a publisher or broadcaster of a defamatory error which a court deems unrelated to an issue of public or general interest may be held liable in damages even if it took every reasonable precaution to ensure the accuracy of its assertions. And liability may far exceed compensation for any actual injury to the plaintiff, for the jury may be permitted to presume damages without proof of loss and even to award punitive damages.

We hold that, so long as they do not impose liability without fault, the States may define for themselves the appropriate standard of liability for a publisher or broadcaster of defamatory falsehood injurious to a private individual. This approach provides a more equitable boundary between the competing concerns involved here. It recognizes the strength of the legitimate state interest in compensating private individuals for wrongful injury to reputation, yet shields the press and broadcast media from the rigors of strict liability for defamation. At least this conclusion obtains where, as here, the substance of the defamatory statement "makes substantial danger to reputation apparent." This phrase places in perspective the conclusion we announce today. Our inquiry would involve considerations somewhat different from those discussed above if a State purported to condition civil liability on a factual misstatement whose content did not warn a reasonably prudent editor or broadcaster of its defamatory potential. Such a case is not now before us, and we intimate no view as to its proper resolution.

IV

Our accommodation of the competing values at stake in defamation suits by private individuals allows the States to impose liability on the publisher or broadcaster of defamatory falsehood on a less demanding showing than that required by *New York Times*. This conclusion is not based on a belief that the considerations which prompted the adoption of the *New York Times* privilege for defamation of public officials and its extension to public figures are wholly inapplicable to the context of private individuals. Rather, we endorse this approach in recognition of the strong and legitimate state interest in compensating private individuals for injury to reputation. But this countervailing state interest extends no further than compensation for actual injury. For the reasons stated below, we hold that the States may not permit recovery of presumed or punitive damages, at least when liability is not based on a showing of knowledge of falsity or reckless disregard for the truth.

The common law of defamation is an oddity of tort law, for it allows recovery of purportedly compensatory damages without evidence of actual loss. Under the traditional rules pertaining to actions for libel, the existence of injury is presumed from the fact of publication. Juries may award substantial sums as compensation for supposed damage to reputation without any proof that such harm actually occurred. The largely uncontrolled discretion of juries to award damages where there is no loss unnecessarily compounds the potential of any system of liability for defamatory falsehood to inhibit the vigorous exercise of First Amendment freedoms. Additionally, the doctrine of presumed damages invites juries to punish unpopular opinion rather than to compensate individuals for injury sustained by the publication of a false fact. More to the point, the States have no substantial interest in securing for plaintiffs such as this petitioner gratuitous awards of money damages far in excess of any actual injury.

We would not, of course, invalidate state law simply because we doubt its wisdom, but here we are attempting to reconcile state law with a competing interest grounded in the constitutional command of the First Amendment. It is therefore appropriate to require that state remedies for defamatory falsehood reach no farther than is necessary to protect the legitimate interest involved. It is necessary to restrict defamation plaintiffs who do not prove knowledge of falsity or reckless disregard for the truth to compensation for actual injury. We need not define "actual injury," as trial courts have wide experience in framing appropriate jury instructions in tort actions. Suffice it to say that actual injury is not limited to out-of-pocket loss. Indeed, the more customary types of actual harm inflicted by defamatory falsehood include impairment of reputation and standing in the community, personal humiliation, and mental anguish and suffering. Of course, juries must be limited by appropriate instructions, and all awards must be supported by competent evidence concerning the injury, although there need be no evidence which assigns an actual dollar value to the injury.

We also find no justification for allowing awards of punitive damages against publishers and broadcasters held liable under state-defined standards of liability for defamation. In most jurisdictions jury discretion over the amounts awarded is limited only by the gentle rule that they not be excessive. Consequently, juries assess punitive damages in wholly unpredictable amounts bearing no necessary relation to the actual harm caused. And they remain free to use their discretion selectively to punish expressions of unpopular views. Like the doctrine of presumed damages, jury discretion to award punitive damages unnecessarily exacerbates the danger of media self-censorship, but, unlike the former rule, punitive damages are wholly irrelevant to the state interest that justifies a negligence standard for private defamation actions. They are not compensation for injury. Instead, they are private fines levied by civil juries to punish reprehensible conduct and to deter its future occurrence. In short, the private defamation plaintiff who establishes liability under a less demanding standard than that stated by *New York Times* may recover only such damages as are sufficient to compensate him for actual injury.

V

Notwithstanding our refusal to extend the *New York Times* privilege to defamation of private individuals, respondent contends that we should affirm the judgment below on the ground that petitioner is either a public official or a public figure. There is little basis for the former assertion. Several years prior to the present incident, petitioner had served briefly on housing committees appointed by the mayor of Chicago, but at the time of publication he had never held any remunerative governmental position. Respondent admits this but argues that petitioner's appearance at the coroner's inquest rendered him a "de facto public official." Our cases recognized no such concept. Respondent's suggestion would sweep all lawyers under the *New York Times* rule as officers of the court and distort the plain meaning of the "public official" category beyond all recognition. We decline to follow it.

Respondent's characterization of petitioner as a public figure raises a different question. That designation may rest on either of two alternative bases. In some instances an individual may achieve such pervasive fame or notoriety that he becomes a public figure for all purposes and in all contexts. More commonly, an individual voluntarily injects himself or is drawn into a particular public controversy and thereby becomes a public figure for a limited range of issues. In either case such persons assume special prominence in the resolution of public questions.

Petitioner has long been active in community and professional affairs. He has served as an officer of local civic groups and of various professional organizations, and he has published several books and articles on legal subjects. Although petitioner was consequently well known in some circles, he had achieved no general fame or notoriety in the community. None of the prospective jurors called at the trial had ever heard of petitioner prior to this litigation, and respondent offered no proof that this response was atypical of the local population. We would not lightly assume that a citizen's participation in community and professional affairs rendered him a public figure for all purposes. Absent clear evidence of general fame or notoriety in the community, and pervasive involvement in the affairs of society, an individual should not be deemed a public personality for all aspects of his life. It is preferable to reduce the public-figure question to a more meaningful context by looking to the nature and extent of an individual's participation in the particular controversy giving rise to the defamation.

In this context it is plain that petitioner was not a public figure. He played a minimal role at the coroner's inquest, and his participation related solely to his representation of a private client. He took no part in the criminal prosecution of Officer Nuccio. Moreover, he never discussed either the criminal or civil litigation with the press and was never quoted as having done so. He plainly did not thrust himself into the vortex of this public issue, nor did he engage the public's attention in an attempt to influence its outcome. We are persuaded that the trial court did not err in refusing to characterize petitioner as a public figure for the purpose of this litigation.

We therefore conclude that the *New York Times* standard is inapplicable to this case and that the trial court erred in entering judgment for respondent. Because the jury was allowed to impose liability without fault and was permitted to presume damages without proof of injury, a new trial is necessary. We reverse and remand for further proceedings in accord with this opinion....

[Blackmun, J., delivered a concurring opinion. Douglas, J., delivered a dissenting opinion expressing his position that the First Amendment prohibits the imposition of damages for "discussion of public affairs." White, J., delivered a dissenting opinion which contended that the First Amendment should not be held to affect state law in defamation actions by persons who are neither "public officials" nor "public figures." The same position appears to be taken in a dissenting opinion by Burger, C.J.]

Mr. Justice BRENNAN, dissenting.

... I adhere to my view expressed in Rosenbloom v. Metromedia, Inc. that we strike the proper accommodation between avoidance of media self-censorship and protection of individual reputations only when we require States to apply the New York Times Co. v. Sullivan knowing-or-reckless-falsity standard in civil libel actions concerning media reports of the involvement of private individuals in events of public or general interest....

... I stated in *Rosenbloom*: "The *New York Times* standard was applied to libel of a public official or public figure to give effect to the [First] Amendment's function to encourage ventilation of public issues, not because the public official has any less interest in protecting his reputation than an individual in private life. While the argument that public figures need less protection because they can command media attention to counter criticism may be true for some very prominent people, even then it is the rare case where the denial overtakes the original charge. Denials, retractions, and corrections are not 'hot' news, and rarely receive the prominence of the original story. When the public official or public figure is a minor functionary, or has left the position that put him in the public eye..., the argument loses all of its force. In the vast majority of libels involving public officials or public figures, the ability to respond through the media will depend on the same complex factor on which the ability of a private individual depends: the unpredictable event of the media's continuing interest in the story...." 403 U.S., at 46–47....

The Court does not discount altogether the danger that jurors will punish for the expression of unpopular opinions. This probability accounts for the Court's limitation that "the States may not permit recovery of presumed or punitive damages, at least when liability is not based on a showing of knowledge of falsity or reckless disregard for the truth." But plainly a jury's latitude to impose liability for want of due care poses a far greater threat of suppressing unpopular views than does a possible recovery of presumed or punitive damages. Moreover, the Court's broad-ranging examples of "actual injury," including impairment of reputation and standing in the community, as well as personal humiliation, and mental anguish and suffering, inevitably allow a jury bent on punishing expression of unpopular views a formidable weapon for doing so. Finally, even a limitation of recovery to "actual injury"—however much it reduces the size or frequency of recoveries—will not provide the necessary elbowroom for First Amendment expression. "It is not simply the possibility of a judgment for damages that results in self-censorship. The very possibility of having to engage in litigation, an expensive and protracted process, is threat enough to cause discussion and debate to 'steer far wider of the unlawful zone' thereby keeping protected discussion from public cognizance.... Too, a small newspaper suffers equally from a substantial damage award, whether the label of the award be 'actual' or 'punitive.'" *Rosenbloom*, 403 U.S., at 52–53.

On the other hand, the uncertainties which the media face under today's decision are largely avoided by the *New York Times* standard....

Stone v. Essex County Newspapers, Inc.

Supreme Judicial Court of Massachusetts
367 Mass. 849, 330 N.E.2d 161 (1975)

HENNESSEY, Justice....

... On November 4, 1969, Jeffrey C. Stone, the then twenty year old son of the plaintiff, appeared in District Court charged with being present where narcotic drugs were illegally kept and with illegal possession of narcotics. A tablet alleged to be a "harmful drug" was introduced in evidence. The city marshal, Robert F. Jones, testified that the other defendants in the District Court case had indicated to him that the defendant Stone was the owner of the harmful drug....

Anthony Pearson, a reporter for the defendant's newspaper, the Newburyport Daily News, was in court covering the proceedings. Pearson had been at work just four months as a reporter and had received only several hours of instruction in the work. Unaware that there was a reporter's table near the witness stand, Pearson sat in the back of the court room. So positioned, he had trouble hearing some of the witnesses, including Jones.

Pearson interpreted Stone's testimony to be that "Mr. Stone" was the owner of the "harmful drug," and inferred that the title "Mister" was used to distinguish the father, who was in the court room, from the son.

That evening, Pearson wrote his story on the trial, translating the "Mr. Stone" of his notes to "John J. Stone," which he had discovered the father's name to be. He submitted it to William Coltin, the editor who ordinarily checked over and edited his copy. Coltin testified that he read it about midnight and was "surprised" at the information about the plaintiff (whom he had known for twenty years and whom he considered an "excellent citizen"), but accepted it as the testimony of a reliable public official under oath. He "may have" been surprised enough to question Pearson but did not see the reporter's notes on the story; he very rarely went back to check a reporter's notes. The article, which had been written for inclusion on November 5, 1969, the day following the trial, was crowded out and its publication postponed for twenty-four hours. During that time Coltin did not communicate any concern about the story to his superiors.

There also was evidence from which the jury could infer that police testimony was produced in the District Court proceeding to show that the substance in question was not a harmful drug or narcotic, and that Pearson's notes and the news story did not include an account of that testimony.

The article was published on November 6, 1969. Shortly after it reached the public, the plaintiff called Coltin to complain of its inaccuracy. Coltin discussed the matter with John J. O'Neil, the managing editor, and then checked with Jones and discovered the plaintiff had had nothing to do with the case. [O'Neil discussed a retraction with plaintiff, who "said it was fine but the damage had already been done."] ...

[Plaintiff sued for libel. The trial judge in substance charged the jury that defendant could be found liable without fault for having published a falsehood defamatory of plaintiff. Plaintiff obtained verdict and judgment, from which defendant appealed. The Supreme Judicial Court, applying the opinion of Brennan, J., in Rosenbloom v. Metromedia, Inc., 403 U.S. 29 (1971), held that the event reported was a matter of public interest and consequently the standard of New York Times Co. v. Sullivan, 376 U.S. 254 (1964), applied. To recover, plaintiff was required to show that defendant published the libel with "actual malice," i.e. knowledge or reckless disregard of falsity. Plaintiff's petition for rehearing was granted because of the United States Supreme Court's decision in Gertz v. Robert Welch, Inc., p. 626, supra.]

... [I]n this case we must define as matter of State Law the standards by which a publisher or broadcaster is to be adjudged liable for the publication of falsehoods, to wit, we must decide whether such publication need simply be proved negligent or whether a heavier burden such as publication with reckless or intentional disregard of the truth is required....

... [T]he *Gertz* case held, inter alia, that (1) the First Amendment protection afforded to defendants against defamation suits by public persons is not to be extended to defamation suits by private individuals even though the defamatory statements concern an issue of public or general interest, (2) so long as they do not impose liability without fault, the States may define for themselves the appropriate standard of liability for a publisher or broadcaster of defamatory falsehood injurious to a private individual, and (3) the States may not permit recovery of presumed or punitive damages, at least when liability is not based on a showing of knowledge of falsity or reckless disregard for the truth.

Accordingly, we hold that private persons, as distinguished from public officials and public figures, may recover compensation on proof of *negligent* publication of a defamatory falsehood....

In considering whether private individuals should be governed by a different rule from that governing public persons, we find the *Gertz* case convincing in its reasoning that public officials and public figures usually enjoy greater access to the channels of effective communication and hence have a more realistic opportunity to counteract false statements than private individuals normally enjoy, and that public persons have thrust themselves forward, have invited attention and comment, and thus (unlike private persons) have voluntarily exposed themselves to increased risk of injury from defamatory falsehoods. Thus, private individuals are not only more vulnerable to injury than public officials and public figures—they are also more deserving of recovery.

We turn now to a consideration of the principles which we hold shall control the assessment of damages in defamation actions in this Commonwealth. The rule defining the limits of damages, like the rules defining liability, must take cognizance of the need to reconcile the State interest in permitting defamation actions against the competing values of the First Amendment. The *Gertz* case so requires: "[T]he States have no substantial interest in securing for plaintiffs such as this petitioner gratuitous awards of money damages far in excess of any actual injury." However, the *Gertz* opinion also apparently provides that a State may constitutionally permit the award of punitive damages to a plaintiff who proves under the *New York Times* Co. standard, wilful or reckless defamation by a publisher or broadcaster. Presumably in such aggravated cases, the damages may be permitted as private fines levied by civil juries to punish reprehensible conduct and to deter its future occurrence.

We reject the allowance of punitive damages in this Commonwealth in any defamation action, on any state of proof, whether based in negligence, or reckless or wilful conduct. We so hold in recognition that the possibility of excessive and unbridled jury verdicts, grounded on punitive assessments, may impermissibly chill the exercise of First Amendment rights by promoting apprehensive self-censorship....

[Plaintiff owned a catering business and was employed by the city of Newburyport school department as "food service director." His duties involved the purchasing of food and equipment for two school cafeterias, preparation of menus, and hiring and firing employees. In addition, from 1963 to 1972, plaintiff was a member of the Newburyport Redevelopment Authority. At the time the newspaper article was published, he was treasurer of the authority. He was authorized to co-sign checks and thus had a degree of management of the authority's funds, which exceeded $1,000,000.]

... [T]he question whether the plaintiff is a public official or a public figure is one for the court to answer whenever (a) all of the facts bearing thereon are uncontested or agreed by the parties (b) the case is tried before a judge without a jury, or (c) all of the facts bearing thereon are specially found and reported by the jury by way of answers to special questions submitted to them; ... otherwise, in a case tried to a jury, it is a question for the jury to answer after instructions by the judge on the applicable law and on what facts must be found to constitute the plaintiff a public official or a public figure.

It is not crucial that the newspaper article did not refer to the plaintiff's public capacity. It is clear that the defendant did not criticize the plaintiff's official conduct per se.... To a large extent his public position seems irrelevant to the defendant's article. Yet that is not controlling, for "a charge of criminal conduct against an official or a candidate, no matter how remote in time or place, is always 'relevant to his fitness for office' for purposes of applying the *New York Times* rule of knowing falsehood or reckless disregard of the truth." Ocala Star-Banner Co. v. Damron, 401 U.S. 295, 300 (1971)....

The mere fact that a plaintiff was a government employee is also not determinative, for such employees in the lower ranks are clearly not public officials for purposes of the rule, but the designation of public official applies at least to government employees who have, or publicly appear to have, substantial responsibility for control of public affairs. [The court quoted from Rosenblatt v. Baer, 383 U.S. 75 (1966), discussed in Kahn v. Bower, p. 657, infra.] ...

Since the inquiry into relevant facts such as remuneration, duties, and participation in decisions on public issues was limited at the prior trial, we express no opinion or prediction whether the plaintiff here was a public official at the time of the publication. We leave that ruling for development at a new trial....

... [T]he plaintiff clearly was not shown to be a public figure. Although he was, aside from his official duties, an active participant in community affairs and a member of certain fraternal organizations, he had not "thrust himself into the vortex of ... public issue[s], nor did he engage the public's attention in an attempt to influence ... [the] outcome [thereof]." Gertz v. Robert Welch, Inc., 418 U.S. at 352.

We turn next to a consideration of the meaning of "actual malice." This concept becomes relevant, of course, if the plaintiff is shown to be a public official or a public figure....

Actual malice is not necessarily proved in terms of ill will or hatred, but is proved rather by a showing that the defamatory falsehood was published with knowledge that it was false or reckless disregard of whether it was false.... "'Reckless disregard,' it is true, cannot be fully encompassed in one infallible definition.... [H]owever ... [t]here must be sufficient evidence to permit the conclusion that the defendant in fact entertained serious doubts as to the truth of his publication. Publishing with such doubts shows reckless disregard for truth or falsity and demonstrates actual malice." St. Amant v. Thompson, 390 U.S. 727, 730–731 (1968). Thus, the test is entirely a subjective one. That information was available which would cause a reasonably prudent man to entertain serious doubts is not sufficient. In order to negate the privilege, the jury must find that such doubts were in fact entertained by the defendant, or by the defendant's servant or agent acting within the scope of his employment. The jury may, of course, reach this conclusion on the basis of an inference drawn from objective evidence, since it would perhaps be rare for a defendant in such a circumstance to admit to having had serious, unresolved doubts....

... Despite evidence of what the jury could find to be gross carelessness on the part of Pearson, it does not appear that the evidence would have been sufficient to warrant a conclusion of recklessness on his part. Of course, we have no way of knowing what the evidence at a new trial may show as to his state of mind.

However, the evidence concerning the defendant's news editor Coltin was sufficient to warrant submission of the case to the jury. Coltin allowed the story to be printed despite serious doubts as to its accuracy with respect to the plaintiff. Coltin admitted he was "surprised" by the report of the plaintiff's involvement. He denied that this term was an understatement and stated that he accepted the reported testimony of the city marshal. Nevertheless, combining this admission with his testimony that he considered the plaintiff, whom he knew well, to be an "excellent citizen," and the fact that the article was written by an inexperienced reporter, of whose minimal training Coltin was fully aware, a jury might draw the inference that the news editor had in fact entertained doubts as to the story's accuracy. The detailed evidence of Coltin's knowledge of the plaintiff's reputation and character, all of which evidence could be found to be inconsistent with the nature of the crime charged, might well support such a finding.

Assuming a jury so found, the amount of time necessary and available for checking the accuracy of the story might be considered relevant to determine whether pushing aside or disregarding those doubts rose to the level of recklessness. In this regard, there was evidence of a delay of a full day in the publication of the story....

In any case where the plaintiff is required to prove actual malice he must do so, not merely by the fair preponderance of the evidence, but by "clear and convincing proof." See Gertz v. Robert Welch, Inc., 418 U.S. 323, 342; New York Times Co. v. Sullivan, 376 U.S. 254, 285–286.... In ruling on a defendant's motion for a directed verdict in a defamation case, the judge certainly must apply the "clear and convincing proof" standard. That is to say, the judge must determine whether the jury would be warranted in concluding that malice was proved by clear and convincing evidence. Further, at least until the Supreme

Court makes additional comment on the issue, if it does, the jury should be charged according to that standard.

The *New York Times* and the *Gertz* cases offer no definition of the meaning of "clear and convincing proof," to assist in formulating jury instructions. However, from other sources we find the phrase defined. Clear and convincing proof involves a degree of belief greater than the usually imposed burden of proof by a fair preponderance of the evidence, but less than the burden of proof beyond a reasonable doubt imposed in criminal cases. It has been said that the proof must be "strong, positive and free from doubt" and "full, clear and decisive" [citing Massachusetts cases predating *New York Times*].

The defendant's exceptions are sustained and the case is remanded to the Superior Court for a new trial on all issues.

[Quirico, J., delivered a concurring opinion.]

Notes

1. With the exceptions of the right to trial by jury and the rule of "no prior restraint," discussed below, constitutional law played no significant role in the tort law of defamation until 1964. Then, in the landmark case of New York Times Co. v. Sullivan, 376 U.S. 254 (1964), the Supreme Court held that the First Amendment's provisions for freedom of speech and freedom of press, as applied to the states by the Fourteenth Amendment, required limitation of liability for defamatory statements. The court held that a public official could recover damages for a defamatory falsehood relating to his official conduct only if it was proved that defendant made the statement with "actual malice," specially defined as "knowledge that [the statement] was false or ... reckless disregard of whether it was false or not." The court also held that an otherwise impersonal criticism of government operations could not be found to be "of and concerning" the official bringing suit simply because he had official responsibility for the operations being criticized (in this case, actions of the police force).

2. In the companion cases of Curtis Publishing Co. v. Butts and Associated Press v. Walker, 388 U.S. 130 (1967), the requirement that "actual malice" be proved, now known as the "*New York Times* rule," was extended to actions for defamation of a "public figure." The court's opinion in *Gertz* traces the development of the constitutional doctrine, including the extension by the plurality in Rosenbloom v. Metromedia, Inc., 403 U.S. 29 (1971), of the *New York Times* rule to defamation of private individuals in publications on matters of "public or general interest." The limitations of defamation liability established through interpretation of the Constitution in effect create "constitutional privileges" for false defamatory publications, additional to the privileges of the common law. Has the Supreme Court struck the right balance between freedom of expression and redress of harm to personal reputation?

3. One important constitutional rule for defamation long predates *New York Times*. Under Near v. Minnesota ex rel. Olson, 283 U.S. 697 (1931), there can be no prior restraint of defamatory speech. Much American authority flatly rejects issuance of injunctions against repetition or dissemination of defamatory statements. E.g. Murphy v. Daytona Beach Humane Society, Inc., 176 So. 2d 922 (Fla. App. 1965). See Annot., Injunction as Remedy Against Defamation of Person, 47 A.L.R.2d 715 (1956); Dobbs, Law of Remedies §7.2(14) (2d ed. 1993). However, the "no prior restraint" rule and the right to trial of defamation cases by a jury do not necessarily bar injunctions after a final determination that the statements are defamatory and false. See Kramer v. Thompson, 947 F.2d 666 (3d

Cir. 1991); Balboa Island Village Inn, Inc. v. Lemen, 40 Cal. 4th 1141, 57 Cal. Rptr. 3d 320, 156 P.3d 339 (2007); Hill v. Petrotech Resources Corp., 325 S.W.3d 302 (Ky. 2010); Smolla, Law of Defamation §§ 9:85–9:89 (2d ed. 1999); Gold, Does Equity Still Lack Jurisdiction to Enjoin A Libel or Slander?, 48 Brooklyn L. Rev. 231 (1982).

4. Although called "actual malice," what *New York Times* requires is quite different from the common law concept of malice as ill will, spite or desire to cause harm. The Supreme Court has equated reckless disregard for truth with "high degree of awareness of … probable falsity." Garrison v. Louisiana, 379 U.S. 64 (1964). And with defendant's "entertain[ing] serious doubts as to the truth of his publication." St. Amant v. Thompson, 390 U.S. 727 (1968). The Times' failure to check the accuracy of the advertisement complained of against news stories in its files was held not to be reckless disregard. Courts are required to determine whether there is "clear and convincing" evidence of actual malice. If not, defendant is entitled to judgment, even summary judgment. See Anderson v. Liberty Lobby, Inc., 477 U.S. 242 (1986). On the independent review of the evidence that must be made by a court if a jury finds "actual malice," see Harte-Hanks Communications, Inc. v. Connaughton, 491 U.S. 657 (1989). In that case the court, accepting the evident jury decisions on witnesses' credibility, concluded that the record supported a finding of malice — specifically, a finding that in the face of obvious reasons to doubt the credibility of its principal informant, defendant made a deliberate decision not to acquire knowledge of facts that might confirm the falsity of the informant's charges. The improbability of the statements may be some evidence of "actual malice," but it is not sufficient on its own to prove malice. See Revell v. Hoffman, 309 F.3d 1228 (10th Cir. 2002), cert. denied, 540 U.S. 818 (2003).

5. One Supreme Court decision on the malice requirement, Masson v. New Yorker Magazine, Inc., 501 U.S. 496 (1991), holds that malice can be found when defendant, knowing what plaintiff actually said, published as quotations of plaintiff's remarks statements that differed materially in meaning from plaintiff's actual words. Alteration of a speaker's words would not show malice when there was no material change in meaning. Otherwise, to publish with knowledge or reckless disregard of the differences between what was said and what was quoted was publication with malice. There was no license to present as quotations "rational interpretations" of actual statements. A public official or public figure cannot avoid the actual malice requirement by suing for infliction of emotional distress instead of defamation. Hustler Magazine, Inc. v. Falwell, 485 U.S. 46 (1988). When the publication is presented as a parody, as in the *Falwell* case, or as a work of fiction, as in Bindrim v. Mitchell, p. 523, supra, what is the meaning of "actual malice"? In New Times, Inc. v. Isaacks, p. 528, supra, where plaintiffs contended that a satirical "news" story could be taken by readers to be factual, the Texas Court of Appeals decided that the dispositive issue was whether defendants either knew or strongly suspected that the article was misleading or created a substantially false impression.

6. Many cases in state and federal courts involve the question of whether sufficient evidence of knowledge or reckless disregard of falsity was presented. See Annot., Libel and Slander: What Constitutes Actual Malice, Within Federal Constitutional Rule Requiring Officials and Public Figures to Show Actual Malice, 20 A.L.R.3d 988 (1968); Smolla, Law of Defamation §§ 3:37–3:87 (2d ed. 1999). Federal cases include Goldwater v. Ginzburg, 414 F.2d 324 (2d Cir. 1969), cert. denied, 369 U.S. 1049 (1970) (magazine's psychological profile of Republican nominee for president; judgment for nominee affirmed); McFarlane v. Sheridan Square Press, Inc., 320 U.S. App. D.C. 40, 91 F.3d 1501 (1996) (book on alleged conspiracy to delay release of American hostages in Iran until after 1980 presidential election so that Ronald Reagan would win; summary judgment for publisher

affirmed); McManus v. Doubleday & Co., Inc., 513 F. Supp. 1383 (S.D.N.Y. 1981) (book stated that Irish Embassy file on priest supporting nationalists in Northern Ireland mentioned "homicidal tendencies"; questions concerning credibility of author and source precluded summary judgment for author, but judgment granted to co-author and publisher, who relied upon author); Howard v. Antilla, 294 F.3d 244 (1st Cir. 2002) (article on whether company chairman was really person with different name who had been convicted of securities fraud and other offenses and reporter's investigation of this; plaintiff had unequivocally denied it and tenor of article was "agnostic" on whether rumor about plaintiff's identity was true or false; judgment for plaintiff reversed). On the retrial of the *Gertz* case, the jury found actual malice and awarded $400,000 in compensatory and punitive damages. Gertz v. Robert Welch, Inc., 680 F.2d 527 (7th Cir. 1982), cert. denied, 459 U.S. 1226 (1983).

7. Cases in state courts include Hansen v. Stoll, 130 Ariz. 454, 636 P.2d 1236 (Ct. App. 1981) (defendant believed accusations but "close[d] his eyes to the obvious truth," established through investigation and litigation; judgment for plaintiffs affirmed); Khawar v. Globe International, Inc., 19 Cal. 4th 254, 79 Cal. Rptr. 2d 178, 965 P.2d 696 (1998), cert. denied, 526 U.S. 1114 (1999) (tabloid newspaper repeated allegations in book that Robert Kennedy had been assassinated by plaintiff rather than person convicted of crime; malice could be found because newspaper had obvious reasons to doubt book's claim and made no effort to verify claim by inspecting documents on assassination or contacting witnesses); Pacella v. Milford Radio Corp., 18 Mass. App. Ct. 6, 462 N.E.2d 355 (1984), aff'd, 394 Mass. 1051, 476 N.E.2d 595 (1985), cert. denied, 474 U.S. 844 (1985) (host of radio program did not use seven-second delay device to delete anonymous caller's defamatory question from broadcast; judgment for defendants notwithstanding verdict for plaintiff); Chase v. Daily Record, Inc., 83 Wash. 2d 37, 515 P.2d 154 (1973) (newspaper report implied that port commissioner repaid public funds he had improperly received, when commissioner had notified newspaper that he had not received public funds; summary judgment for newspaper reversed); Sprouse v. Clay Communication, Inc., 158 W. Va. 427, 211 S.E.2d 674 (1975), cert. denied, 423 U.S. 882 (1975) (malice found in headlines that intentionally misled readers to conclusion different from that of stories beneath headlines). Cf. Carter v. Willett Home Products, Inc., 714 S.W.2d 506 (Mo. 1986) (in denying she made statements about judgments, garnishments and credit complaints against plaintiff, defendant's employee testified she had no knowledge of these things; testimony considered evidence of reckless disregard for truth in making statements).

8. The question of who is a "public official" or "public figure" is treated in pp. 646–662, infra. Should such a person be denied an action for publication resulting from failure to verify a defamatory statement or from a stupid mistake, such as reporting that plaintiff committed a crime because his name was the same as the person charged? Lewis v. Coursolle Broadcasting of Wisconsin, Inc., 127 Wis. 2d 105, 377 N.W.2d 166 (1985). Or changing a report that plaintiff was raising funds to help solve the drug addiction problem to a report that plaintiff was raising funds to help solve *his* drug addiction problem? Rood v. Finney, 418 So. 2d 1 (La. App. 1982), cert. denied, 420 So. 2d 979 (La. 1982), cert. denied, 460 U.S. 1013 (1983). Could redress for this be devised without denying necessary "breathing space" for publications on public figures and officials?

9. Gertz v. Robert Welch, Inc., with its rule of no liability without fault, limitation of presumed and punitive damages, and repudiation of what had been taken to be the rule of Rosenbloom v. Metromedia, Inc., dramatically altered the body of constitutional law pertaining to defamation. The *Gertz* opinion did not define "fault," but it is generally thought, as in the *Stone* case, that the Supreme Court established negligence as the thresh-

old requirement of liability. Fault can be found through vicarious liability as well as personal responsibility. See Cantrell v. Forest City Publishing Co., 419 U.S. 245 (1974); Embrey v. Holly, 293 Md. 128, 442 A.2d 966 (1982). The court undoubtedly had in mind failure to exercise sufficient care to ensure that what was published was accurate. Would fault based on factors other than accuracy, such as wrongful purpose, excessive or accidental publication, or presence of another tort, qualify? What if defendant's statement was accurate, but could be interpreted to have a meaning that defendant did not intend or apply to a person to whom defendant did not intend to refer? See New England Tractor-Trailer Training of Connecticut, Inc. v. Globe Newspaper Co., 395 Mass. 471, 480 N.E.2d 1005 (1985).

10. When the issue is reasonable care with respect to accurate publication, on what basis can the standard of care be ascertained? Is there any model of the reasonably prudent broadcaster or print journalist? See Annot., Libel and Slander: Necessity of Expert Testimony to Establish Negligence of Media Defendant in Defamation Action by Private Individual, 37 A.L.R.4th 987 (1985), noting that some cases draw an analogy to professional malpractice, even to the extent of requiring expert testimony, while a greater number adopt a generalized negligence test. In Appleby v. Daily Hampshire Gazette, 395 Mass. 32, 478 N.E.2d 721 (1985), summary judgment against plaintiff was approved where newspapers had published, without verification, Associated Press and United Press International reports originating not far from the newspapers' offices. Is this sound? With the exception of cases in which reports from news services were published without material change, how often will a falsely defamed plaintiff fail to establish a jury-submissible issue of negligence? On fault generally, see Dobbs, Law of Torts 1179–1183 (2000); Smolla, Law of Defamation §§ 3:88–3:93 (2d ed. 1999).

11. *Gertz* is the first of the defamation cases in the Supreme Court to establish constitutional rules for the assessment of damages. In *New York Times, Butts, Walker* and *Rosenbloom*, juries had awarded huge sums ($500,000 in *New York Times*; $60,000 compensatory damages and $3,000,000 punitive damages in *Butts*, with punitive damages reduced to $400,000 by the trial court; $500,000 compensatory damages and $300,000 punitive damages in *Walker*, the trial court rejecting the award of punitive damages; $25,000 compensatory damages and $725,000 punitive damages in *Rosenbloom*, with punitive damages reduced to $250,000 by the trial court). Undoubtedly this was a major factor in the Supreme Court's decision to hear these cases and its determination that liability under common law rules was inconsistent with the First Amendment. But the court's response was to impose a requirement of knowing or reckless falsehood in order for defendant to be held liable, not to require that defendant's liability be limited to a reasonable compensatory amount supported by evidence. Might the latter have served the need to control the "chilling" effects of potential defamation liability as well as the actual malice requirement? See Justice White's concurring opinion in Dun & Bradstreet, Inc. v. Greenmoss Builders, Inc., 472 U.S. 749 (1985).

12. There are numerous pre-*Gertz* cases in which appellate courts upheld awards of compensatory damages far exceeding any amount of harm plaintiff could possibly have suffered. An outstanding example is Fawcett Publications, Inc. v. Morris, 377 P.2d 42 (Okla. 1962), appeal dismissed, 376 U.S. 513 (1964), in which a member of the alternate squad of a college football team recovered $75,000 for an article that said team members were given amphetamines. How effective is the *Gertz* "actual injury" rule? Six-figure judgments are not rare in the post-*Gertz* era. See Annot., Excessiveness or Inadequacy of Compensatory Damages for Defamation, 49 A.L.R.4th 1158 (1986), which lists a number of

awards, held not to be excessive, for more than half a million dollars. An award of almost two hundred million dollars was confirmed in Cantu v. Flanagan, 705 F. Supp. 2d 220 (E.D.N.Y. 2010). The prohibition of presumed damages does not prevent a jury or trial judge from making a rough estimate of the harm to plaintiff's reputation that has been caused or will be caused by the defamatory publication. Also, as specified in *Gertz*, "actual injury" includes personal humiliation and emotional distress, for which substantial damages may be given even if there is no proven harm to reputation. See Time, Inc. v. Firestone, 424 U.S. 448 (1976). Some state courts condition liability on proof of some harm to reputation. See pp. 538–539, supra.

13. The *Gertz* opinion states, "[W]e hold that the States may not permit recovery of presumed or punitive damages, at least when liability is not based on a showing of knowledge of falsity or reckless disregard for the truth." This is interpreted, as in the *Stone* case, to mean that punitive damages are constitutionally permissible when knowing or reckless falsity is proved. Do punitive damages for defamation have any constitutional justification? See Comment, The Constitutionality of Punitive Damages in Libel Actions, 45 Ford. L. Rev. 1382 (1977). A private citizen, not required to prove "actual malice" for liability, may attempt to prove it in order to recover punitive or presumed damages. The constitutional requirement may be applied in conjunction with a state rule that recovery of punitive damages requires proof of common law malice. This occurred in an action brought by the entertainer Carol Burnett against *The National Enquirer*. Punitive damages were approved but the jury's award of $1,300,000 was reduced to $150,000. Burnett v. National Enquirer, Inc., 144 Cal. App. 3d 991, 193 Cal. Rptr. 206 (1983), appeal dismissed, 465 U.S. 1014 (1984).

14. The rejection in *Gertz* of the plurality opinion in Rosenbloom v. Metromedia, Inc. induced defendants to argue that as a matter of *state* constitutional or common law, there should be no liability for defamatory publication on a matter of "public or general interest" or of "public concern" without proof of defendant's knowledge or reckless disregard of falsity. This argument has failed in most of the appellate courts in which it has been presented. See Miami Herald Publishing Co. v. Ane, 423 So. 2d 376 (Fla. App. 1982), aff'd, 458 So. 2d 239 (Fla. 1984); Troman v. Wood, 62 Ill. 2d 184, 340 N.E.2d 292 (1975); Kennedy v. Sheriff of East Baton Rouge, 935 So. 2d 669 (La. 2006). But there have been a few exceptions. See Walker v. Colorado Springs Sun, Inc., 188 Colo. 86, 538 P.2d 450 (1975), cert. denied sub nom. Woestendiek v. Walker, 423 U.S. 1025 (1975); Journal-Gazette Co., Inc. v. Bandido's, Inc., 712 N.E.2d 446 (Ind. 1999), cert. denied, 528 U.S. 1005 (1999); Senna v. Florimont, 196 N.J. 469, 958 A.2d 427 (2008). New York has adopted a requirement of proof that the publisher "acted in a grossly irresponsible manner without due consideration for the standards of information gathering and dissemination ordinarily followed by responsible parties." Chapadeau v. Utica Observer-Dispatch, Inc., 38 N.Y.2d 196, 379 N.Y.S.2d 61, 341 N.E.2d 569 (1975). A state may also protect defendants by disallowing punitive or presumed damages in situations where the Supreme Court has not done so. In Wheeler v. Green, 286 Or. 99, 593 P.2d 777 (1979), as in the *Stone* case, awards of punitive damages in defamation cases were prohibited without exception. See generally Annot., State Constitutional Protection of Allegedly Defamatory Statements Regarding Private Individual, 33 A.L.R.4th 212 (1984); Smolla, Law of Defamation §§ 3:27–3:36 (2d ed. 1999).

Wolston v. Reader's Digest Association, Inc.

Supreme Court of the United States
443 U.S. 157 (1979)

Mr. Justice REHNQUIST delivered the opinion of the Court.

In 1974, respondent Reader's Digest Association, Inc., published a book entitled KGB, the Secret Work of Soviet Agents (KGB), written by respondent John Barron. The book describes the Soviet Union's espionage organization and chronicles its activities since World War II. In a passage referring to disclosures by "royal commissions in Canada and Australia, and official investigations in Great Britain and the United States," the book contains the following statements relating to petitioner Ilya Wolston:

> Among Soviet agents identified in the United States were Elizabeth T. Bentley, Edward Joseph Fitzgerald, William Ludwig Ullmann, William Walter Remington, Franklin Victor Reno, Judith Coplon, Harry Gold, David Greenglass, Julius and Ethel Rosenberg, Morton Sobell, William Perl, Alfred Dean Slack, Jack Soble, *Ilya Wolston*, Alfred and Martha Stern.*
>
> * No claim is made that this list is complete. It consists of Soviet agents who were convicted of espionage or falsifying information or perjury and/or contempt charges following espionage indictments, or who fled to the Soviet bloc to avoid prosecution....

(emphasis supplied). In addition, the index to KGB lists petitioner as follows: "Wolston, Ilya, Soviet agent in U.S."

Petitioner sued the author and publishers of KGB in the United States District Court for the District of Columbia, claiming that the passages in KGB stating that he had been indicted for espionage and had been a Soviet agent were false and defamatory. The District Court granted respondents' motion for summary judgment. 429 F. Supp. 167 (1977). The court held that petitioner was a "public figure" and that the First Amendment therefore precluded recovery unless petitioner proved that respondents had published a defamatory falsehood with "'actual malice'—that is, with knowledge that it was false or with reckless disregard of whether it was false or not," *New York Times Co. v. Sullivan*, 376 U.S. 254, 280 (1964). While the District Court agreed that the above-quoted portions of KGB appeared to state falsely that petitioner had been indicted for espionage, it ruled, on the basis of affidavits and deposition testimony, that the evidence raised no genuine issue with respect to the existence of "actual malice" on the part of respondents. The Court of Appeals for the District of Columbia Circuit affirmed. 188 U.S. App. D.C. 185, 578 F.2d 427 (1978)....

During 1957 and 1958, a special federal grand jury sitting in New York City conducted a major investigation into the activities of Soviet intelligence agents in the United States. As a result of this investigation, petitioner's aunt and uncle, Myra and Jack Soble, were arrested in January 1957 on charges of spying. The Sobles later pleaded guilty to espionage charges, and in the ensuing months, the grand jury's investigation focused on other participants in a suspected Soviet espionage ring, resulting in further arrests, convictions, and guilty pleas. On the same day the Sobles were arrested, petitioner was interviewed by agents of the Federal Bureau of Investigation at his home in the District of Columbia. Petitioner was interviewed several more times during the following months in both Washington and in New York City and traveled to New York on various occasions pursuant to grand jury subpoenas.

On July 1, 1958, however, petitioner failed to respond to a grand jury subpoena directing him to appear on that date. Petitioner previously had attempted to persuade law enforcement authorities not to require him to travel to New York for interrogation because of his state of mental depression. On July 14, a Federal District Judge issued an order to show cause why petitioner should not be held in criminal contempt of court. These events immediately attracted the interest of the news media, and on July 15 and 16, at least seven news stories focusing on petitioner's failure to respond to the grand jury subpoena appeared in New York and Washington newspapers.

Petitioner appeared in court on the return date of the show-cause order and offered to testify before the grand jury, but the offer was refused. A hearing then commenced on the contempt charges. Petitioner's wife, who then was pregnant, was called to testify as to petitioner's mental condition at the time of the return date of the subpoena, but after she became hysterical on the witness stand, petitioner agreed to plead guilty to the contempt charge. He received a 1-year suspended sentence and was placed on probation for three years, conditioned on his cooperation with the grand jury in any further inquiries regarding Soviet espionage. Newspapers also reported the details of the contempt proceedings and petitioner's guilty plea and sentencing. In all, during the 6-week period between petitioner's failure to appear before the grand jury and his sentencing, 15 stories in newspapers in Washington and New York mentioned or discussed these events. This flurry of publicity subsided following petitioner's sentencing, however, and, thereafter, he succeeded for the most part in returning to the private life he had led prior to issuance of the grand jury subpoena. At no time was petitioner indicted for espionage....

... [In *Gertz v. Robert Welch, Inc.*, 418 U.S. 323 (1974), we] identified two ways in which a person may become a public figure for purposes of the First Amendment: "For the most part those who attain this status have assumed roles of especial prominence in the affairs of society. Some occupy positions of such persuasive power and influence that they are deemed public figures for all purposes. More commonly, those classed as public figures have thrust themselves to the forefront of particular public controversies in order to influence the resolution of the issues involved."

Neither respondents nor the lower courts relied on any claim that petitioner occupied a position of such "persuasive power and influence" that he could be deemed one of that small group of individuals who are public figures for all purposes. Petitioner led a thoroughly private existence prior to the grand jury inquiry and returned to a position of relative obscurity after his sentencing. He achieved no general fame or notoriety and assumed no role of special prominence in the affairs of society as a result of his contempt citation or because of his involvement in the investigation of Soviet espionage in 1958.

Instead, respondents argue, and the lower courts held, that petitioner falls within the second category of public figures — those who have "thrust themselves to the forefront of particular public controversies in order to influence the resolution of the issues involved" — and that, therefore, petitioner is a public figure for the limited purpose of comment on his connection with, or involvement in, Soviet espionage in the 1940's and 1950's. Both lower courts found petitioner's failure to appear before the grand jury and citation for contempt determinative of the public-figure issue. The District Court concluded that by failing to appear before the grand jury and subjecting himself to a citation for contempt, petitioner "became involved in a controversy of a decidedly public nature in a way that invited attention and comment, and thereby created in the public an interest in knowing about his connection with espionage...." Similarly, the Court of Appeals stated that by refusing to comply with the subpoena, petitioner "stepped center front into the spotlight focused on the investigation of Soviet espionage. In short, by his voluntary action he invited attention and comment in connection with the public questions involved in the investigation of espionage."

We do not agree with respondents and the lower courts that petitioner can be classed as such a limited-purpose public figure.[7] First, the undisputed facts do not justify the conclusion of the District Court and Court of Appeals that petitioner "voluntarily thrust" or "injected" himself into the forefront of the public controversy surrounding the investigation of Soviet espionage in the United States. It would be more accurate to say that petitioner was dragged unwillingly into the controversy. The Government pursued him in its investigation. Petitioner did fail to respond to a grand jury subpoena, and this failure, as well as his subsequent citation for contempt, did attract media attention. But the mere fact that petitioner voluntarily chose not to appear before the grand jury, knowing that his action might be attended by publicity, is not decisive on the question of public-figure status. In *Gertz*, we held that an attorney was not a public figure even though he voluntarily associated himself with a case that was certain to receive extensive media exposure. We emphasized that a court must focus on the "nature and extent of an individual's participation in the particular controversy giving rise to the defamation." In *Gertz*, the attorney took no part in the criminal prosecution, never discussed the litigation with the press, and limited his participation in the civil litigation solely to his representation of a private client. Similarly, petitioner never discussed this matter with the press and limited his involvement to that necessary to defend himself against the contempt charge. It is clear that petitioner played only a minor role in whatever public controversy there may have been concerning the investigation of Soviet espionage. We decline to hold that his mere citation for contempt rendered him a public figure for purposes of comment on the investigation of Soviet espionage.

Petitioner's failure to appear before the grand jury and citation for contempt no doubt were "newsworthy," but the simple fact that these events attracted media attention also is not conclusive of the public-figure issue. A private individual is not automatically transformed into a public figure just by becoming involved in or associated with a matter that attracts public attention. To accept such reasoning would in effect re-establish the doctrine advanced by the plurality opinion in *Rosenbloom v. Metromedia, Inc.*, 403 U.S. 29 (1971), which concluded that the *New York Times* standard should extend to defamatory falsehoods relating to private persons if the statements involved matters of public or general concern. We repudiated this proposition in *Gertz* ... and we reject it again today. A libel defendant must show more than mere newsworthiness to justify application of the demanding burden of *New York Times*.

Nor do we think that petitioner engaged the attention of the public in an attempt to influence the resolution of the issues involved. Petitioner assumed no "special prominence in the resolution of public questions." His failure to respond to the grand jury's subpoena was in no way calculated to draw attention to himself in order to invite public comment or influence the public with respect to any issue. He did not in any way seek to arouse public sentiment in his favor and against the investigation. We find no basis whatsoever for concluding that petitioner relinquished, to any degree, his interest in the protection of his own name.

This reasoning leads us to reject the further contention of respondents that any person who engages in criminal conduct automatically becomes a public figure for purposes of comment on a limited range of issues relating to his conviction. We declined to accept

---

7. Both lower courts found that petitioner became a public figure at the time of his contempt citation in 1958. Petitioner argued below that even if he was once a public figure, the passage of time has restored him to the status of a private figure for purposes of the First Amendment. Both the District Court and the Court of Appeals rejected this argument. And petitioner has abandoned the argument in this Court. Because petitioner does not press the issue in this Court and because we conclude that petitioner was not a public figure in 1958, we need not and do not decide whether or when an individual who was once a public figure may lose that status by the passage of time.

a similar argument in *Time, Inc. v. Firestone* [424 U.S. 448 (1976)], where we said: "[W]hile participants in some litigation may be legitimate 'public figures,' either generally or for the limited purpose of that litigation, the majority will more likely resemble respondent, drawn into a public forum largely against their will in order to attempt to obtain the only redress available to them or to defend themselves against actions brought by the State or by others. There appears little reason why these individuals should substantially forfeit that degree of protection which the law of defamation would otherwise afford them simply by virtue of their being drawn into a courtroom. The public interest in accurate reports of judicial proceedings is substantially protected by *Cox Broadcasting Co.* [*v. Cohn*, 420 U.S. 469 (1975)]. As to inaccurate and defamatory reports of facts, matters deserving no First Amendment protection…, we think *Gertz* provides an adequate safeguard for the constitutionally protected interests of the press and affords it a tolerable margin for error by requiring some type of fault." We think that these observations remain sound, and that they control the disposition of this case. To hold otherwise would create an "open season" for all who sought to defame persons convicted of a crime.

Accordingly, the judgment of the Court of Appeals is

Reversed.

Mr. Justice BLACKMUN, with whom Mr. Justice MARSHALL joins, concurring in the result.

I agree that petitioner is not a "public figure" for the purposes of this case.…

In *Gertz v. Robert Welch, Inc.*, this Court held that a person may become a public figure for a limited range of issues if he "voluntarily injects himself or is drawn into a particular public controversy." Such a person, the Court reasoned, resembles a public official in that he typically enjoys "significantly greater access to the channels of effective communication" and knowingly "runs the risk of closer public scrutiny" than would have been true had he remained in private life. The passage of time, I believe, often will be relevant in deciding whether a person possesses these two public-figure characteristics. First, a lapse of years between a controversial event and a libelous utterance may diminish the defamed party's access to the means of counterargument. At the height of the publicity surrounding the espionage controversy here, petitioner may well have had sufficient access to the media effectively to rebut a charge that he was a Soviet spy. It would strain credulity to suggest that petitioner could have commanded such media interest when respondents published their book in 1974. Second, the passage of time may diminish the "risk of public scrutiny" that a putative public figure may fairly be said to have assumed. In ignoring the grand jury subpoena in 1958, petitioner may have anticipated that his conduct would invite critical commentary from the press. Following the contempt citation, however, petitioner "succeeded for the most part in returning to … private life." Any inference that petitioner "assumed the risk" of public scrutiny in 1958 assuredly is negated by his conscious efforts to regain anonymity during the succeeding 16 years.

This analysis implies, of course, that one may be a public figure for purposes of contemporaneous reporting of a controversial event, yet not be a public figure for purposes of historical commentary on the same occurrence. Historians, consequently, may well run a greater risk of liability for defamation. Yet this result, in my view, does no violence to First Amendment values. While historical analysis is no less vital to the marketplace of ideas than reporting current events, historians work under different conditions than do their media counterparts. A reporter trying to meet a deadline may find it totally impossible to check thoroughly the accuracy of his sources. A historian writing *sub specie aeternitatis* has both the time for reflection and the opportunity to investigate the veracity of the pronouncements he makes.

For these reasons, I conclude that the lapse of 16 years between petitioner's participation in the espionage controversy and respondents' defamatory reference to it was sufficient to erase whatever public-figure attributes petitioner once may have possessed. Because petitioner clearly was a private individual in 1974, I see no need to decide the more difficult question whether he was a public figure in 1958.

Mr. Justice BRENNAN, dissenting.

... I agree with the holding of the District Court, affirmed by the Court of Appeals, that petitioner qualified "as a public figure for the limited purpose of comment on his connection with, or involvement in, espionage in the 1940's and '50's." I further agree ... that petitioner also qualified as a public figure in 1974. That conclusion follows, in my view, for the reasons stated by the Court of Appeals: "The issue of Soviet espionage in 1958 and of Wolston's involvement in that operation continues to be a legitimate topic of debate today, for that matter concerns the security of the United States. The mere lapse of time is not decisive."

I disagree, however, with the holding of the District Court, affirmed by the Court of Appeals, that respondent Barron was entitled to summary judgment. In my view the evidence raised a genuine issue of fact respecting the existence of actual malice on his part. I would therefore reverse the judgment of the Court of Appeals and remand to the District Court for trial of that issue.

―――――――

Clyburn v. New World Communications, Inc.

United States Court of Appeals, District of Columbia Circuit
284 U.S. App. D.C. 212, 903 F.2d 29 (1990)

STEPHEN F. WILLIAMS, Circuit Judge:

In a series of articles and editorials in 1986 the Washington Times described Joann Medina's collapse from a drug overdose and her death four days later. The paper depicted Medina's boyfriend, plaintiff John Clyburn, as waiting "several critical hours" after Medina's collapse to call for help, in order to allow other partygoers to leave the scene. Clyburn sued ... for libel....

Joann Medina collapsed at an apartment on North Capitol Street in Washington, D.C. sometime in the early morning hours of December 10, 1983. Clyburn was one of those with her at the time. Someone called 911, and paramedics came and attempted unsuccessfully to revive her; she lapsed into a coma and died four days later. The barbiturates, cocaine, and alcohol found in her body led the coroner initially to call her death a suicide; he later changed it to "undetermined."

In 1984 agents from the Drug Enforcement Administration interviewed Clyburn on the subject. In particular, they asked whether Medina had obtained the drugs from Karen Johnson, a friend of Mayor Barry's who had been convicted of possession and conspiracy to distribute cocaine, and whether any highranking city officials had been at the apartment with Medina and Clyburn that night.[1] Clyburn also spoke to a reporter from the Washington Post about the circumstances surrounding Ms. Medina's collapse. At both in-

―――――――

1. The record does not reveal why the DEA investigation sought links to Ms. Johnson or high-ranking officials of the Barry administration. Possible reasons were Clyburn's presence at the scene of her collapse, his longtime association with Mayor Barry, and the presence of members of the Barry administration at Medina's funeral.

terviews, Clyburn said that he had called 911 and that he was alone with Ms. Medina at the time. He admitted later that he was not alone and that a woman called the paramedics.

Washington newspapers covered the event in some detail in 1984. The Washington Post ran a story in August discussing the medical examiner's claim that political pressure had been exerted to make him change Medina's death certificate. The article also noted that "[t]he U.S. Attorney's office is trying to determine how Medina died and how she obtained the cocaine found in her blood." The Washington Times published six articles describing the ongoing investigation by the D.C. Police Department, the DEA, and the U.S. Attorney's office, especially their inquiry into whether any highranking Barry administration officials had been at the party. Four of the six articles mentioned Clyburn, including his consulting firm's contracts with the D.C. government and his presence at the scene of Medina's collapse.

In 1986 the Times published the articles that are the subject of this lawsuit. Aside from rehashing what had appeared previously, they stated that those at the party, including Clyburn, waited "several critical hours" after Medina's collapse before calling an ambulance so that those present could clear out before the police arrived. This assertion formed the basis of Clyburn's libel suit.

[The district court granted the Times' motion for summary judgment on the ground that Clyburn was a public figure for purposes of this case and he failed to introduce enough evidence of actual malice.]

Under *Gertz v. Robert Welch, Inc.*, 418 U.S. 323, 351 (1974), a person may "inject[] himself or [be] drawn into a particular public controversy" sufficiently to become "a public figure for a limited range of issues." On those issues, such a person can prevail in a defamation suit only by proving the defendant's "actual malice".... In *Waldbaum v. Fairchild Publications, Inc.*, 627 F.2d 1287, 1296–98 (D.C. Cir. 1980), we formulated a three-part test for identifying a limited-purpose public figure, requiring (1) that there have been a public controversy; (2) that the plaintiff have played a sufficiently central role in the controversy; and (3) that the alleged defamatory statement have been germane to the plaintiff's participation in the controversy. In fact the third component plainly goes not to identifying the plaintiff as a public figure, but to whether the defamatory statement is adequately linked to the issues for which he is a public figure.

People's interest in a story purely as voyeurs is not enough to make it a public controversy for these purposes. There must be "foreseeable and substantial ramifications for nonparticipants." Here, the DEA, the U.S. Attorney's office, and the D.C. Police Department investigated Medina's death to see whether there was any connection between her drug abuse and the Barry administration—particularly whether a Barry associate was a source of her drugs or a member of his administration attended the party at which she collapsed. These issues were a subject of DEA and Washington Post interviews. The 1984 newspaper coverage—which Clyburn does not claim libelled him—made the inquires public. Possible drug dealing and drug use by public officials and their friends obviously have ramifications for others, and thus the controversy satisfies *Waldbaum*.

In discussing whether a plaintiff's role in a controversy was central enough to justify imposing the actual malice burden, the Supreme Court has explained that a private individual typically lacks the public figure's ability to use the media for rebuttal, and "[m]ore important," has not run "the risk of closer public scrutiny" that falls on those who, for example, seek public office. *Gertz*, 418 U.S. at 344. Clearly concerned lest the *New York Times* standard be thrust on individuals who chose not to run such risks, the Court declared that though it "may be possible for someone to become a public figure through no purposeful action of his own, ... the instances of truly involuntary public figures must be exceedingly rare." Typically, the Court suggested, limited-purpose public figures will be persons who "have thrust themselves to the front of particular public controversies in order to influence the resolution of the issues involved."[2] Clyburn denies that he injected himself into the public controversy at all.

Courts have placed weight on a plaintiff's "trying to influence the outcome" of a controversy. Of course, this can not include statements that merely answer the alleged libel itself; if it did, libellers could "create their own defense by making the claimant a public figure." *Hutchinson v. Proxmire*, 443 U.S. 111, 135 (1979). Similarly, we have doubts about placing much weight on purely defensive, truthful statements made when an individual finds himself at the center of a public controversy but before any libel occurs; it is not clear why someone dragged into a controversy should be able to speak publicly only at the expense of foregoing a private person's protection from defamation. Indeed, the cases have suggested that ordinarily something more than a plaintiff's short simple statement of his view of the story is required; he renders himself a public figure only if he voluntarily "draw[s] attention to himself" or uses his position in the controversy "as a fulcrum to create public discussion." *Wolston*, 443 U.S. at 168. See also *Time, Inc. v. Firestone*, 424 U.S. 448, 454 n. 3 (1976) (plaintiff not limited public figure because she confined her press conferences to issues of no legitimate public concern). Here, Clyburn *falsely* told the Washington Post that he had been alone with Medina and had called 911. We view this cover-up attempt as going beyond an ordinary citizen's response to the eruption of a public fray around him.

More important, Clyburn's acts *before* any controversy arose put him at its center. His consulting firm had numerous contracts with the District government, he had many social contacts with administration officials, and Medina, at least as one may judge from attendance at her funeral, also enjoyed such ties. Clyburn also spent the night of Medina's collapse in her company. One may hobnob with high officials without becoming a public figure, but one who does so runs the risk that personal tragedies that for less well-connected people would pass unnoticed may place him at the heart of a public controversy. Clyburn engaged in conduct that he knew markedly raised the chances that he would become embroiled in a public controversy. This conduct, together with his false statements at the controversy's outset, disable him from claiming the protections of a purely "private" person. See, e.g., *Marcone v. Penthouse International Magazine for Men*, 754 F.2d 1072, 1086 (3rd Cir. 1985) (plaintiff's "voluntary connection" with widely publicized motorcycle gangs contributed to his public figure status); *Rosanova v. Playboy Enterprises, Inc.*, 580 F.2d 859, 861 (5th Cir. 1978) (plaintiff held to be limited-purpose public figure because he "voluntarily engaged in a course that was bound to invite attention and comment"); see also *Jensen v. Times Mirror Co.*, 634 F. Supp. 304, 310–13 (D. Conn. 1986) (plaintiff held to be limited public figure because she roomed with (and moved in social circles that included) a well-known public figure who was "underground" but whose true identity was known to plaintiff).

Finally, the alleged defamatory statement — that Clyburn and his friends delayed calling for help so that other party-goers could first leave — relates directly to Clyburn's role in the controversy with respect to which he became a limited-purpose public figure....

Affirmed.

---

2. Almost anyone who finds himself in the middle of a controversy will likely have enough access to the press to rebut any allegedly libelous statements, thus satisfying the Supreme Court's first concern. It is perhaps because of this that the Court has regarded the second justification as more important.

Notes

1. Compare the D.C. Circuit's three-part test for identifying a limited-purpose public figure with the five requirements used in Fitzgerald v. Penthouse International, Ltd., 691 F.2d 666 (4th Cir. 1982), cert. denied, 460 U.S. 1024 (1983): "(1) the plaintiff had access to channels of effective communication; (2) the plaintiff voluntarily assumed a role of special prominence in a public controversy; (3) the plaintiff sought to influence the resolution or outcome of the controversy; (4) the controversy existed prior to the publication of the defamatory statements; and (5) the plaintiff retained public figure status at the time of the alleged defamation." See also Dalton, Defining the Limited Purpose Public Figure, 70 U. Det. Mercy L. Rev. 47 (1992).

2. *Gertz, Wolston* and Time, Inc. v. Firestone, 424 U.S. 448 (1976), are the Supreme Court's most important pronouncements on the question of who is a "public figure." The essence of *Firestone* is recapitulated in the *Wolston* opinion. The *Firestone* case arose from a news magazine's report of the decree in a much-publicized divorce case. The parties were prominent members of Palm Beach, Florida society and the husband was an heir to the Firestone tire fortune. The Supreme Court held that the wife was not a public figure. She did not "freely choose to publicize issues as to the propriety of her married life." Her institution of matrimonial litigation was not such a choice. Also, dissolution of marriage through judicial proceedings, while of interest to some portion of the public in this case, was not "the sort of 'public controversy' referred to in *Gertz.*" Hutchinson v. Proxmire, 443 U.S. 111 (1979), specifies that defamers cannot create a defense for themselves by initiating a controversy that makes plaintiff a public figure.

3. Whether a defamed plaintiff has the status of public figure is addressed in many cases in other courts. See Annot., Who is "Public Figure" for Purposes of Defamation Action, 19 A.L.R.5th 1 (1994); Smolla, Law of Defamation §§ 2:4–2:98 (2d ed. 1999). One might find no overall pattern in the cases beyond the one established in the *Gertz* case. Much is made of the proposition that an individual who does not have "such pervasive fame or notoriety [to become] a public figure for all purposes and in all contexts" can become "a public figure for a limited range of issues" by injecting himself or being drawn into a particular public controversy. This holds out the possibility that a person well-known in connection with a certain range of issues or activities will avoid the "actual malice" requirement on the ground that the defamation was unrelated to those issues or activities. See Ryder v. Time, Inc., 181 U.S. App. D.C. 201, 557 F.2d 824 (1976) (plaintiff had retired from politics after brief period in legislature; allegedly defamed in relation to his conduct as attorney); Durham v. Cannan Communications, Inc., 645 S.W.2d 845 (Tex. App. 1982) (plaintiff well-known locally for legal activities, including appointment as special counsel for investigation of county funds; defamed by reported connection to house of prostitution). But see Bell v. Associated Press, 584 F. Supp. 128 (D.D.C. 1984) (professional football player public figure for purpose of charge of criminal misconduct—here, "lewdness"—because of public interest in and concern about off-field misconduct of professional athletes).

4. It is more likely that emphasis on the issues to which the defamatory publication is related will lead to the conclusion that plaintiff is a "limited issue" or "limited purpose" public figure because there is public recognition of plaintiff's connection to these issues. In Dameron v. Washington Magazine, Inc., 250 U.S. App. D.C. 346, 779 F.2d 736 (1985), cert. denied, 476 U.S. 1141 (1986), it was held that plaintiff had involuntarily become a limited purpose public figure as to publication about a major airplane crash that occurred while he was sole air traffic controller on duty at an airport. Is this substantially differ-

ent from the approach of Rosenbloom v. Metromedia, Inc., which was rejected in *Gertz* and *Wolston*? More supportable is the decision in Dombey v. Phoenix Newspapers, Inc., 150 Ariz. 476, 724 P.2d 562 (1986), that plaintiff was a public figure for purposes of articles on his conduct as a large county's "agent of record" for employee insurance programs. He had not inserted himself or his views into any public controversy (there was no controversy until publication of the articles) and plaintiff did not have the regular and continuing access to the media characteristic of a public figure. Being the subject of media attention in itself did not make plaintiff a public figure. However, by voluntarily assuming the position he held, plaintiff invited public scrutiny and should have expected that the manner in which he performed his duties would be a legitimate matter of public concern, exposing him to public and media attention.

5. Since Greenbelt Cooperative Publishing Association, Inc. v. Bresler, 398 U.S. 6 (1970), it has been clear that local prominence makes one a public figure for purposes of a locally disseminated publication. See Lewis v. Coursolle Broadcasting of Wisconsin, Inc., 127 Wis. 2d 105, 377 N.W.2d 166 (1985). Does it follow that prominence in a profession or trade or large company makes one a public figure for purposes of publication directed to persons within that profession, trade or company? See Lawlor v. Gallagher Presidents' Report, Inc., 394 F. Supp. 721 (S.D.N.Y. 1975), remanded, 538 F.2d 311 (2d Cir. 1976) (plaintiff defamed in publication directed to high executives of nation's "top 100 corporations," of which plaintiff was one; not public figure); Korbar v. Hite, 43 Ill. App. 3d 636, 357 N.E.2d 135 (1976), cert. denied, 434 U.S. 837 (1977) (employees credit union president public figure as to article in labor union newsletter); Materia v. Huff, 394 Mass. 328, 475 N.E.2d 1212 (1985) (union local's secretary-treasurer, running for re-election, public figure as to defamatory letter sent to local's members by opposition candidates).

6. Entertainers, sports personalities, and others who make public appearances (in person or in the mass media) are usually considered public figures. They either have such celebrity status as to be general purpose public figures. See Carafano v. Metrosplash.com, Inc., 207 F. Supp. 2d 1055 (C.D. Cal. 2002), aff'd, 339 F.3d 1119 (9th Cir. 2003), and Carson v. Allied News Co., 529 F.2d 206 (7th Cir. 1976), where not only Johnny Carson but also his wife-to-be were so treated. Or they are public figures for purposes of defamatory publication on the particular activities in which they are engaged. See James v. Gannett Co., Inc. 40 N.Y.2d 415, 386 N.Y.S.2d 871, 353 N.E.2d 834 (1976) (article on belly dancer who performed in cabarets); Vitale v. National Lampoon, Inc., 449 F. Supp. 442 (E.D. Pa. 1978) (plaintiff had posed for photographs in *Playboy*, including magazine's nude centerfold feature; centerfold photograph used for mock advertisement in parody of *Playboy*). However, in Braun v. Flynt, p. 478, supra, the court held that plaintiff was not a public figure by virtue of her performances at the amusement park. "She was involved in no public controversy and had no hand in determining the outcome of any important public issues. She certainly cannot be said to have relinquished interest in protecting her name and reputation by force of her limited role as an entertainer. A private individual is not automatically transformed into a public figure just by becoming involved in or associated with a matter that attracts public attention." See also Wayment v. Clear Channel Broadcasting, Inc., 116 P.3d 271 (Utah 2005), holding that a local television reporter was not a public figure because she had not become involved in a public controversy.

7. Among the persons held to be a public figure for purposes of defendant's publications are an investigative reporter for a newspaper, who revealed to her employer that her roommate was a notorious fugitive. Jensen v. Times Mirror Co., 634 F. Supp. 304 (D. Conn. 1986), on reconsideration, 647 F. Supp. 1525 (D. Conn. 1986). A janitor suspected of involvement in a $1,500,000 mail robbery, who had given several interviews and held

a press conference on the investigation of the case and alleged harassment by postal inspectors. Tripoli v. Boston Herald-Traveler Corp., 359 Mass. 150, 268 N.E.2d 350 (1971). The holder of a city's exclusive contract for vehicle towing and wrecker services. (Publicity had previously been given to criticism of his performance and plaintiff's responses to the criticism.) Vandertoon v. Bonner, 129 Mich. App. 198, 342 N.W.2d 297 (1983). And an attorney who had well-publicized professional and non-professional ties to two motorcycle gangs and had been indicted in a large marijuana trafficking conspiracy case. (The charges against him were dropped. Defendants subsequently reported that the attorney had financed marijuana transactions.) Marcone v. Penthouse International Magazine for Men, 754 F.2d 1072 (3d Cir. 1985), cert. denied, 474 U.S. 864 (1985).

8. In Gannett Co., Inc. v. Re, 496 A.2d 553 (Del. 1985), an inventor was held not to be a public figure for purposes of an article about him that referred to one of his inventions: a car powered by compressed air, which he had demonstrated to the press. (The article was about plaintiff's indictment on charges related to another automotive fuel-saving invention.) In Greenberg v. CBS Inc., 69 A.D.2d 693, 419 N.Y.S.2d 988 (1979), a physician who had published fifty articles in medical journals and scientific books was held not to be a public figure for purposes of a *60 Minutes* broadcast. (His articles apparently were on subjects different from the medical subject addressed in the broadcast.) Why would these plaintiffs not be classified as public figures? In Sellars v. Stauffer Communications, Inc., 9 Kan. App. 2d 573, 684 P.2d 450 (1984), aff'd, 236 Kan. 697, 695 P.2d 812 (1985), two closely divided courts held that the wife of a county sheriff in the midst of a campaign for re-election was not a public figure. Before her marriage, she was an inmate of the county jail and then a clerk-typist in the sheriff's office. Defendant published articles addressing whether she was paid salary during the time, shortly before the marriage, when she spent two weeks in an out-of-state jail.

9. *"Involuntary" public figures.* Under what circumstances does a person become an "involuntary public figure" for purposes of a defamation claim? In Wells v. Liddy, 186 F.3d 505 (4th Cir. 1999), cert. denied, 528 U.S. 1118 (2000), the court decided that it must be demonstrated that plaintiff had become a central figure in a significant public controversy and assumed the risk of publicity by taking action, or failing to act when action was required, in circumstances in which a reasonable person would understand that "publicity would likely inhere." Also, the defamatory statement must be related to that controversy. Applying this test, a secretary at the Democratic National Committee headquarters at the time of the Watergate break-in, which led to the resignation of President Nixon, was not an involuntary public figure because she was not a central figure in the Watergate controversy. Furthermore, she had not become a public figure by making limited responses to reporters and a historian years after the break-in or writing a letter-to-the-editor to *The New York Times* denying an allegation about her, as she had not attempted to influence the merits of the Watergate controversy or draw attention to herself in order to invite public comment.

See also Khawar v. Globe International, Inc., p. 643, supra (tabloid repeated false claim in book that plaintiff assassinated Robert Kennedy; book had sold few copies and plaintiff was never a suspect in investigation of assassination; person who had neither engaged in purposeful activity inviting criticism nor acquired substantial media access in relation to controversy not public figure); Atlanta Journal-Constitution v. Jewell, 251 Ga. App. 808, 555 S.E.2d 175 (2001), cert. denied sub nom. Jewell v. Cox Enterprises, Inc. 537 U.S. 814 (2002) (security guard who found bomb at locale of Olympics and assisted in evacuation of public an involuntary public figure; played central role in controversy over Olympic Park safety and was well-known to public when defendant published story that he was suspected of planting bomb); Bay View Packing Co. v. Taff, 198 Wis. 2d 653, 543 N.W.2d 522 (Ct. App. 1995) (packing company and its president had become involuntary limited purpose public figures by failure to promptly recall products containing city water when large city's water supply contaminated; contamination had caused illness to hundreds of city residents and there was public controversy concerning distribution of contaminated food products); Erdmann v. SF Broadcasting of Green Bay, Inc., 229 Wis. 2d 156, 599 N.W.2d 1 (Ct. App. 1999), review denied, 230 Wis. 2d 274, 604 N.W.2d 572 (1999) (plaintiff became limited public figure when family's suspicion that plaintiff shot sixteen-year-old boy resulted in warning to public that he was dangerous and police search that led to his arrest; boy had actually shot himself in stomach and fabricated story of being shot by intruder).

10. *Corporations and other entities.* As corporations and associations can maintain actions for defamation, courts have been required to decide whether they are public figures. Not surprisingly, churches, extensively advertised retail businesses, and foundations engaged in large scale public fund-raising have been found to be public figures. See Gospel Spreading Church v. Johnson Publishing Co., 147 U.S. App. D.C. 207, 454 F.2d 1050 (1971); Steaks Unlimited, Inc. v. Deaner, 623 F.2d 264 (3d Cir. 1980); National Foundation for Cancer Research, Inc. v. Council of Better Business Bureaus, Inc., 705 F.2d 98 (4th Cir. 1983), cert. denied, 464 U.S. 830 (1983); Izuzu Motors Ltd. v. Consumers Union of United States, Inc., 66 F. Supp. 2d 1117 (C.D. Cal. 1999). But a number of opinions deny that corporations that sell to the public are public figures in relation to statements about their products or services, in the absence of a pre-existing controversy or an attempt by the corporation to influence public opinion. See Bruno & Stillman, Inc. v. Globe Newspaper Co., 633 F.2d 583 (1st Cir. 1980); Blue Ridge Bank v. Veribanc, Inc., 866 F.2d 681 (4th Cir. 1989); Computer Aid, Inc. v. Hewlett-Packard Co., 56 F. Supp. 2d 526 (E.D. Pa. 1999); Rancho La Costa, Inc., v. Superior Court, 106 Cal. App. 3d 646, 165 Cal. Rptr. 347 (1980), appeal dismissed, 450 U.S. 902 (1981). It is understandable that a company would not be found a public figure when it conducts a specialized non-retail business. See Kroll Associates v. City and County of Honolulu, 833 F. Supp. 802 (D. Hawaii 1993) (business investigation firm); Varian Medical Systems, Inc. v. Delfino, 113 Cal. App. 4th 273, 6 Cal. Rptr. 3d 325 (2003), rev'd, 35 Cal. 4th 180, 25 Cal. Rptr. 3d 298, 106 P.3d 958 (2005) (technological equipment manufacturer). Or conducts a retail business that does not use the corporate name. See Vegod Corp. v. American Broadcasting Companies, Inc., 25 Cal. 3d 763, 160 Cal. Rptr. 97, 603 P.2d 14 (1979), cert. denied, 449 U.S. 886 (1980) (corporations conducting "closing out sale" for department store). But is it sound to hold that the proprietor of a business that uses the name of the proprietor and that depends upon the custom of the general public is not a public figure for purposes of criticism of its products or services?

11. *Former public figures.* Should a person be treated as a public figure when a defamatory statement concerns his role as a public figure but is published after he has become an obscure private citizen? Most cases on the subject treat the defamed person as a public figure in these circumstances, although the concurring opinion in the *Wolston* case takes an opposing view. See Holt v. Cox Enterprises, 590 F. Supp. 408 (N.D. Ga. 1984) (plaintiff public figure for purpose of 1979 article on 1961 college football team incident in which he was involved, quoting defamatory statements made in 1961); Newson v. Henry, 443 So. 2d 817 (Miss. 1983) (former sheriff public figure for purpose of 1980 accusation about his last, unsuccessful election campaign in 1967); Smolla, Law of Defamation §§ 2:44–2:49 (2d ed. 1999). The leading case is Street v. National Broadcasting Co., 645 F.2d 1227 (6th Cir. 1981), cert. dismissed, 454 U.S. 1095 (1981). Plaintiff had been

a central figure in one of the most publicized and controversial court cases in American history: the "Scottsboro" case, in which nine black men were accused in Alabama of raping two white women. One of the two women retracted the accusation. Plaintiff was the other. The prosecution's case depended upon her and she insisted, both in and out of court, that the rape occurred. After the trials, in which juries found the accused guilty, plaintiff married and lived a life of total obscurity. In holding (2–1) that she was a public figure for the purpose of a television broadcast more than forty years after the Scottsboro trials, the court rejected the arguments that the passage of time diminished the public's need for information and that the absence of reporters' deadlines allowed for more verification and accuracy. "Although information may come to light over the course of time, the distance of years does not necessarily make more data available ... : memories fade; witnesses forget; sources disappear." Also, past public figures had access to channels of communication if they chose to comment on their role in controversial events.

Kahn v. Bower

California Court of Appeal
232 Cal. App. 3d 1599, 284 Cal. Rptr. 244 (1991)

KLINE, Presiding Justice.

[Plaintiff was employed by the Alameda County Social Services Agency as a child welfare worker. She brought a libel action for a letter sent to her supervisor by the director of a facility providing psychological testing and counselling for children. The letter complained of experiences in the facility's dealings with plaintiff and charged her with "incompetence."]

Defendants have consistently asserted that plaintiff is a public official required to plead and prove that defendants published a knowing or reckless falsehood....

In *Rosenblatt v. Baer* [(1966) 383 U.S. 75] the court considered whether the former operator of a publicly owned resort area was a "public official." The court noted that the constitutional privilege announced in *New York Times Co. v. Sullivan* rested on two vital constitutional interests: "There is, first, a strong interest in debate on public issues, and, second, a strong interest in debate about those persons who are in a position significantly to influence the resolution of those issues.... It is clear, therefore, that the 'public official' designation applies at the very least to those among the hierarchy of government employees who have, or appear to the public to have, substantial responsibility for or control over the conduct of governmental affairs.... Where a position in government has such apparent importance that the public has an independent interest in the qualifications and performance of the person who holds it, beyond the general public interest in the qualifications and performance of all government employees, both elements we identified in *New York Times* are present and the *New York Times* malice standards apply.... The employee's position must be one which would invite public scrutiny and discussion of the person holding it, entirely apart from the scrutiny and discussion occasioned by the particular charges in controversy."

Thus the touchstone for public official status is the extent to which the plaintiff's position is likely to attract or warrant scrutiny by members of the public. Such scrutiny may follow either because of the prominence of the position in the official hierarchy, or because the duties of the position tend naturally to have a relatively large or dramatic impact on members of the public. Illustrative of the latter situation are the many cases holding that lower echelon law enforcement officers are public officials for purposes of the federal constitutional privilege. On the other hand, where the plaintiff has no policy making authority, where her "control … over the conduct of government is at most remote and philosophical," she will not be held a public official. (*Franklin v. Benevolent etc. Order of Elks* (1979) 97 Cal. App. 3d 915, 924, 159 Cal. Rptr. 131 [high school teacher not a public official]).

Nothing in the record before us indicates plaintiff had any significant control over governmental *policy*. The same may be said, however, of a patrolman. Nonetheless, the power exercised by police officers, and their public visibility, naturally subject them to public scrutiny and make them public officials for purposes of defamation law. Plaintiff too possessed considerable power over the lives affected by her work as a child welfare worker. Her assessments and decisions directly and often immediately determined whether the educational, social, medical and economic needs of developmentally disabled children in her care would adequately be met. She exercised far more control over the lives she touched than does a classroom teacher.

Plaintiff's power is illustrated by events described by defendant Bower in the allegedly defamatory letter. According to Bower, plaintiff asked defendants to evaluate the case of a teenage girl, originally from Alaska, now in the foster care of a military family stationed in Alameda. The family was about to be transferred to Germany, and this called for an updated evaluation to determine whether the child should go with the family to Germany. According to the letter, defendants performed the evaluation, concluding that the parents and the child loved each other, that "the parents were quite suitable … and that the child should stay with them." After submitting a report to that effect, however, defendants learned that plaintiff had "t[aken] it upon herself to go and pick up the girl from the foster parents and send the girl back to Alaska." According to the letter, plaintiff justified this action by falsely stating defendants had recommended removing the child from the foster parents' custody.…

[In] *Villarreal v. Harte-Hanks Communications* (Tex. Civ. App. 1990) 787 S.W.2d 131, cert. den. (1991) [499 U.S. 923], the court observed that the plaintiff, a child protective services specialist, "exercised authority on the State's behalf. She served as an investigator, she had authority to recommend whether children could be removed from their homes, she could physically remove children from their environments and place them in foster care, she could establish conditions governing the circumstances by which parents could regain custody of their children, and she provided services to abused and neglected children. She also had substantial public contact relating to her official duties. Appellant certainly had greater control over governmental affairs than a court reporter, school teacher, attorney or justice of the peace."

We hold that a social worker exercising this kind of power is more closely akin to a prosecutor or police officer than to a classroom teacher, and that plaintiff should be deemed a public official.…

[W]hile every public employee has not assumed the risk of being defamed in every aspect of his or her life, all public employment is a matter of profound, abiding, and legitimate public interest, and everyone entering it invites public attention to the quality and efficiency of his or her work. The very term "public servant" reflects the concept that the public is, in a sense, the employer. The public pays directly for inefficiency, incompetence, and unfitness. There is no market mechanism to automatically correct for inefficiency; the "customer" of a public agency cannot choose to patronize a competing "business." A citizen aggrieved by a public servant's misfeasance, malfeasance, or nonfeasance often has no recourse but to complain to those in charge. If the complaint is justified it serves a public benefit. Its communication should not be discouraged by a rule which holds the complainant liable for negligently misperceiving the facts, overlooking something, or being swept away by the strong feelings which often accompany encounters with the agents of government.

Accordingly we believe plaintiff was required to plead a knowing or reckless falsehood in order to state a cause of action for defamation. She did not do so, and has never requested leave to do so. Therefore the trial court did not err by granting the motion for judgment on the pleadings....

The judgment is affirmed.

Notes

1. Who is a "public official" for purposes of the *New York Times* rule? Review Stone v. Essex County Newspapers, Inc., p. 637, supra. It was assumed that the Supreme Court intended to include candidates for elective office as well as holders of elective office, a view confirmed by Monitor Patriot Co. v. Roy, 401 U.S. 265 (1971). Many non-elected officials are also included, but Rosenblatt v. Baer, 383 U.S. 75 (1966), and Kahn v. Bower make clear that there are some appointed officials and public employees who are not to be classified as public officials and required to prove actual malice in order to recover for defamation. The many cases addressing whether particular officeholders are public officials are collected in Annot., Who is "Public Official" for Purposes of Defamation Action, 44 A.L.R.5th 193 (1996). See also Smolla, Law of Defamation §§ 2:99–2:111 (2d ed. 1999); Elder, Defamation, Public Officialdom and the *Rosenblatt v. Baer* Criteria—A Proposal for Revivification: Two Decades after *New York Times Co. v. Sullivan*, 33 Buffalo L. Rev. 579 (1984).

2. Persons held to be public officials include the chief deputy clerk of a circuit court. Cooper v. Rockford Newspapers, Inc., 50 Ill. App. 3d 247, 365 N.E.2d 744 (1977). A member of a city board of tax assessors. Eadie v. Pole, 91 N.J. Super. 504, 221 A.2d 547 (App. Div. 1966). A village building inspector. Dattner v. Pokoik, 81 A.D.2d 572, 437 N.Y.S.2d 425 (1981), appeal dismissed, 54 N.Y.2d 750, 442 N.Y.S.2d 996, 426 N.E.2d 491 (1991). The administrator of a county motor pool. Clawson v. Longview Publishing Co., 91 Wash. 2d 408, 589 P.2d 1223 (1979). An Internal Revenue Service agent. Angel v. Ward, 43 N.C. App. 288, 258 S.E.2d 788 (1979). A naval officer on a ship that came under enemy attack. Spitler v. Young, 25 Media L. Rptr. 1243 (Mass. Super. Ct. 1996), appeal denied, 25 Media L. Rptr. 1254 (Mass. App. 1996). Members of a grand jury. Standke v. B.E. Darby & Sons, Inc., 291 Minn. 468, 193 N.W.2d 139 (1971), cert. dismissed, 406 U.S. 902 (1972). And a parish (county) director of public welfare, defamed after her selection but before the commencement of her employment. Bienvenu v. Angelle, 254 La. 182, 233 So. 2d 140 (La. 1969).

3. With few exceptions, police officers and law enforcement personnel, of whatever rank, have been treated as public officials. See Meiners v. Moriarity, 563 F.2d 343 (7th Cir. 1977) (agents of federal drug law enforcement office); Ethridge v. North Mississippi Communications, Inc., 460 F. Supp. 347 (N.D. Miss. 1978) (police investigator and undercover agent); Coursey v. Greater Niles Township Publishing Corp., 40 Ill. 2d 257, 239 N.E.2d 837 (1968) (police patrolman); Rotkiewicz v. Sadowsky, 431 Mass. 748, 730 N.E.2d 282 (2000) (state trooper); Beeton v. District of Columbia, 779 A.2d 918 (D.C. 2001) (officer of corrections facility). But see Kiesau v. Bantz, 686 N.W.2d 164 (Iowa 2004) (deputy sheriff not public official); Himango v. Prime Time Broadcasting, Inc., 37 Wash. App. 259, 680 P.2d

432 (1984), review denied, 102 Wash. 2d 1004 (1984) (police officer on vice squad not public official, even for purpose of statement that he had been observed in "compromising position"); Smith v. Copley Press, Inc., 140 Ill, App. 3d 613, 488 N.E.2d 1032 (1986), cert. denied, 479 U.S. 916 (1986) (police department jailer not public official). What about a fire-fighter? See Jones v. Palmer Communications, Inc., 440 N.W.2d 884 (Iowa 1989). Should a government lawyer who is not in a supervisory position be classified as a public official? See Mandel v. The Boston Phoenix Inc., 322 F. Supp. 2d 39 (D. Mass. 2004), vacated, 456 F.3d 198 (1st Cir. 2006), subsequent proceedings, 492 F. Supp. 2d 26 (D. Mass. 2007) (assistant state's attorney); Porcari v. Gannett Satellite Information Network, Inc., 50 A.D.3d 993, 856 N.Y.S.2d 217 (2008) (associate corporation counsel of city).

4. Should teachers and other employees of public school systems be classified as public officials? See Kelley v. Bonney, 221 Conn. 549, 606 A.2d 693 (1992) (junior high school teacher; public official); True v. Ladner, 513 A.2d 257 (Me. 1986) (high school teacher; not public official); Johnson v. Robbinsdale Independent School District No. 281, 827 F. Supp. 1439 (D. Minn. 1993) (elementary school principal; public official); Beeching v. Levee, 764 N.E.2d 669 (Ind. App. 2002) (elementary school principal; not public official); Johnston v. Corinthian Television Corp., 583 P.2d 1101 (Okla. 1978) (grade school wrestling coach; public official); O'Connor v. Burningham, 165 P.3d 1214 (Utah 2007) (high school basketball coach; not public official); Van Dyke v. KUTV, 663 P.2d 52 (Utah 1983) (college director of financial aids; public official); Grossman v. Smart, 807 F. Supp. 1404 (C.D. Ill. 1992) (assistant professor not public official but professor who chaired search committee was). A student elected to a university senate was treated as a public official in Klahr v. Winterble, 4 Ariz. App. 158, 418 P.2d 404 (1968).

5. Some persons and businesses performing services under contracts with governmental agencies have been held to be public officials. See Green v. Northern Publishing Co., Inc., 655 P.2d 736 (Alaska 1982), cert. denied, 463 U.S. 1208 (1983) (physician providing medical services for area jails, while also in private practice); Turley v. W.T.A.X., Inc., 94 Ill. App. 2d 377, 236 N.E.2d 778 (1968) (practicing architect supervising design, construction and furnishing of county office building); Doctors Convalescent Center, Inc. v. East Shore Newspapers, Inc., 104 Ill. App. 2d 271, 244 N.E.2d 373 (1968) (nursing home in which state placed retarded children who were wards of state). Such plaintiffs were found not to be public officials in Arctic Co., Ltd. v. Loudoun Times Mirror, 624 F.2d 518 (4th Cir. 1980), cert. denied, 449 U.S. 1102 (1981) (archaeological consultant to county water authority); Dombey v. Phoenix Newspapers, Inc., 147 Ariz. 61, 708 P.2d 742 (Ct. App. 1985), vacated, 150 Ariz. 476, 724 P.2d 562 (1986) ("agent of record" for employee insurance programs of county government, compensated by commissions); and Zeck v. Spiro, 52 Misc. 2d 629, 276 N.Y.S.2d 395 (Sup. Ct. 1965) (members of county sewer district's law firm). Should an attorney employed in a public defender's office be considered a public official? See James v. San Jose Mercury News, Inc., 17 Cal. App. 4th 1, 20 Cal. Rptr. 2d 890 (1993).

6. To what extent can the *New York Times* rule be avoided by the argument that the defamatory statement did not relate to plaintiff's official conduct or fitness for office? In Monitor Patriot Co. v. Roy, 401 U.S. 265 (1971), a newspaper column had referred to a senatorial candidate as a "former small-time bootlegger." This apparently stemmed from rumors about the candidate's activities during Prohibition, which had ended a quarter-century earlier. The trial judge had the jury decide whether this was "relevant to his fitness for the office for which he was a candidate" or was "a bringing forward of the plaintiff's long forgotten misconduct in which the public had no interest." The Supreme Court held this erroneous. As a matter of constitutional law, a charge of criminal conduct, no mat-

ter how remote in time or place, could never be irrelevant to a candidate's or official's fitness for office. Plaintiff could only recover upon a showing of knowledge or reckless disregard of falsehood. This was applied to an action brought by a public school teacher in Luper v. Black Dispatch Publishing Co., 675 P.2d 1028 (Okla. App. 1983), and also to the *Stone* case.

7. In contrast to *Stone* and Goodrick v. Gannett Co., Inc., 500 F. Supp. 125 (D. Del. 1980), where an assistant public defender's photograph was mistakenly used to illustrate an article about a jail inmate, Bufalino v. Associated Press, 692 F.2d 266 (2d Cir. 1982), cert. denied, 462 U.S. 1111 (1983), holds that the public official rule does not apply when the defamatory publication did not identify plaintiff as a public official and he was not recognized in the community as a public official. See also Foster v. Laredo Newspapers, Inc., 541 S.W.2d 809 (Tex. 1976), cert. denied, 429 U.S. 1123 (1977), in which the article complained of apparently referred to plaintiff in his capacity as a private consulting engineer rather than his capacity as elected county surveyor, and Tucker v. Kilgore, 388 S.W.2d 112 (Ky. 1964), in which *New York Times* was held inapplicable because the attack was directed not at plaintiff's conduct as a policeman, but at his "fitness and character as a man," exemplifying the low quality of a fraternity that was the real object of defendant's tirade.

8. It has been assumed in some cases that holders of public office in foreign countries are to be treated as public officials. E.g., Coliniatis v. Dimas, 965 F. Supp. 511 (S.D.N.Y. 1997). But this is questioned in Lopez v. Univision Communications Inc., 45 F. Supp. 2d 348 (S.D.N.Y. 1999). The *New York Times* rule is usually applied to statements about former public officials, when related to their conduct in office. See Zerangue v. TSP Newspapers, Inc., 814 F.2d 1066 (5th Cir. 1987); Peterson v. New York Times Co., 106 F. Supp. 2d 1227 (D. Utah 2000); Stripling v. Literary Guild, 5 Media L. Rptr. 1958 (W.D. Tex. 1979), aff'd, 636 F.2d 312 (5th Cir. 1981) (former chief investigator of House of Representatives Committee on Un-American Activities defamed decades later). Compare Durham v. Cannan Communications, Inc., 645 S.W.2d 845 (Tex. App. 1982) (rule not applied to report connecting former special counsel for inquiry into management of county funds with house of prostitution). In Rosenblatt v. Baer, 383 U.S. 75 (1966), the Supreme Court considered of no "decisional significance" that plaintiff had left his position as supervisor of a county recreation area when the column complained of appeared. "To be sure, there may be cases where a person is so far removed from a former position of authority that comment on the manner in which he performed his responsibilities no longer has the interest necessary to justify the *New York Times* rule. But here the management of the area was still a matter of lively public interest...." A defeated candidate for public office can be treated as a public figure. See Redmond v. Sun Publishing Co., Inc., 239 Kan. 30, 716 P.2d 168 (1986).

9. Is plaintiff's status as public official or public figure to be decided by a jury (under appropriate instructions), as held in the *Stone* case? Or is it to be decided by the judges? In Harris v. Tomczak, 94 F.R.D. 687 (E.D. Cal. 1982), the court believed the sound position was to have the jury resolve contested facts bearing on the public official or public figure question but that Supreme Court and lower court opinions directed otherwise — among them, the Court of Appeals' opinion in the *Wolston* case. In its reversal of the judgment, the Supreme Court had not suggested that the Court of Appeals was wrong to conclude that it was for the court, not the jury, to decide whether Wolston was a public figure. See also Brewer v. Memphis Publishing Co., Inc., 626 F.2d 1238 (5th Cir. 1980), cert. denied, 452 U.S. 962 (1981); Mandel v. The Boston Herald Phoenix, Inc., 456 F.3d 198 (1st Cir. 2006); Lewis v. Coursolle Broadcasting of Wisconsin, Inc., 127 Wis. 2d 105,

377 N.W.2d 166 (1985). Contra, Nash v. Keene Publishing Co., 127 N.H. 214, 498 A.2d 348 (1985). Should a jury be excluded from the decision in a case like Cerrito v. Time, Inc., 302 F. Supp. 1071 (N.D. Cal. 1969), aff'd, 449 F.2d 306 (9th Cir. 1971), in which defendant's magazine reported—and plaintiff denied—that plaintiff was the head of a Cosa Nostra family? Or a case like Bolam v. McGraw-Hill, Inc., 52 A.D.2d 762, 382 N.Y.S.2d 772 (1976), in which defendant's publication claimed that plaintiff was really Amelia Earhart, the famous aviator who disappeared while flying over the Pacific Ocean in 1937?

Dun & Bradstreet, Inc. v. Greenmoss Builders, Inc.

Supreme Court of the United States

472 U.S. 749 (1985)

Justice POWELL announced the judgment of the Court and delivered an opinion, in which Justice REHNQUIST and Justice O'CONNOR joined....

Petitioner Dun & Bradstreet, a credit reporting agency, provides subscribers with financial and related information about businesses. All the information is confidential; under the terms of the subscription agreement the subscribers may not reveal it to anyone else. On July 26, 1976, petitioner sent a report to five subscribers indicating that respondent, a construction contractor, had filed a voluntary petition for bankruptcy. This report was false and grossly misrepresented respondent's assets and liabilities. That same day, while discussing the possibility of future financing with its bank, respondent's president was told that the bank had received the defamatory report. He immediately called petitioner's regional office, explained the error, and asked for a correction. In addition, he requested the names of the firms that had received the false report in order to assure them that the company was solvent. Petitioner promised to look into the matter but refused to divulge the names of those who had received the report.

After determining that its report was indeed false, petitioner issued a corrective notice on or about August 3, 1976 to the five subscribers who had received the initial report. The notice stated that one of respondent's former employees, not respondent itself, had filed for bankruptcy and that respondent "continued in business as usual." Respondent told petitioner that it was dissatisfied with the notice and it again asked for a list of subscribers who had seen the initial report. Again petitioner refused to divulge their names.

Respondent then brought this defamation action in Vermont state court. It alleged that the false report had injured its reputation and sought both compensatory and punitive damages. The trial established that the error in petitioner's report had been caused when one of its employees, a seventeen year old high school student paid to review Vermont bankruptcy pleadings, had inadvertently attributed to respondent a bankruptcy petition filed by one of respondent's former employees. Although petitioner's representative testified that it was routine practice to check the accuracy of such reports with the businesses themselves, it did not try to verify the information about respondent before reporting it.

After trial, the jury returned a verdict in favor of respondent and awarded $50,000 in compensatory or presumed damages and $300,000 in punitive damages. Petitioner moved for a new trial. It argued that in *Gertz v. Robert Welch, Inc.* [p. 626, supra], this Court had ruled broadly "that the States may not permit recovery of presumed or punitive damages, at least when liability is not based on a showing of knowledge of falsity or reckless disregard for the truth," and it argued that the judge's instructions in this case permitted the jury to award such damages on a lesser showing. The trial court indicated some doubt as to whether *Gertz* applied to "non-media cases," but granted a new trial "[b]ecause of ... dissatisfaction with its charge and ... conviction that the interests of justice require[d]" it. [The court had instructed the jury that because the report was libellous *per se*, plaintiff was not required "to prove actual damages ... since damage and loss [are] conclusively presumed." The court also instructed that the jury could award punitive damages only if it found "actual malice" but defined malice to include bad faith, intent to injure plaintiff and reckless disregard of the consequences as well as the *New York Times Co. v. Sullivan* formulation of knowing falsehood or reckless disregard for truth.]

The Vermont Supreme Court reversed. 143 Vt. 66, 461 A.2d 414 (1983). Although recognizing that "in certain instances the distinction between media and nonmedia defendants may be difficult to draw," the court stated that "no such difficulty is presented with credit reporting agencies, which are in the business of selling financial information to a limited number of subscribers who have paid substantial fees for their services." Relying on this distinguishing characteristic of credit reporting firms, the court concluded that such firms are not "the type of media worthy of First Amendment protection as contemplated by *New York Times* and its progeny." It held that the balance between a private plaintiff's right to recover presumed and punitive damages without a showing of special fault and the First Amendment rights of "nonmedia" speakers "must be struck in favor of the private plaintiff defamed by a nonmedia defendant." Accordingly, the court held "that as matter of federal constitutional law, the media protections outlined in *Gertz* are inapplicable to nonmedia defamation actions."

Recognizing disagreement among the lower courts about when the protections of *Gertz* apply, we granted certiorari....

In *Gertz*, we held that the fact that expression concerned a public issue did not by itself entitle the libel defendant to the constitutional protections of *New York Times*. These protections, we found, were not "justified solely by reference to the interest of the press and broadcast media in immunity from liability." Rather, they represented "an accommodation between [First Amendment] concern[s] and the limited state interest present in the context of libel actions brought by public persons." In libel actions brought by private persons we found the competing interests different. Largely because private persons have not voluntarily exposed themselves to increased risk of injury from defamatory statements and because they generally lack effective opportunities for rebutting such statements, we found that the State possessed a "strong and legitimate ... interest in compensating private individuals for injury to reputation." Balancing this stronger state interest against the same First Amendment interest at stake in *New York Times*, we held that a State could not allow recovery of presumed and punitive damages absent a showing of "actual malice." Nothing in our opinion, however, indicated that this same balance would be struck regardless of the type of speech involved.[4]

---

4. The dissent states that "[a]t several points the Court in *Gertz* makes perfectly clear [that] the restrictions of presumed and punitive damages were to apply in all cases." Given the context of *Gertz*, however, the Court could have made "perfectly clear" only that these restrictions applied in cases involving *public speech*. In fact, the dissent itself concedes that "*Gertz* ... focused largely on defining the circumstances under which protection of the central First Amendment value of robust debate of *public issues* should mandate plaintiffs to show actual malice to obtain a judgment and actual damages...."

The dissent also incorrectly states that *Gertz* "specifically held" both "that the award of presumed and punitive damages on less than a showing of actual malice is not a narrowly tailored means to

We have never considered whether the *Gertz* balance obtains when the defamatory statements involve no issue of public concern. To make this determination, we must employ the approach approved in *Gertz* and balance the State's interest in compensating private individuals for injury to their reputation against the First Amendment interest in protecting this type of expression. This state interest is identical to the one weighed in *Gertz*....

The First Amendment interest, on the other hand, is less important than the one weighed in *Gertz*. We have long recognized that not all speech is of equal First Amendment importance. It is speech on "'matters of public concern'" that is "at the heart of the First Amendment's protection." *First National Bank of Boston v. Bellotti*, 435 U.S. 765, 776 (1978). As we stated in *Connick v. Myers*, 461 U.S. 138, 145 (1983), this "special concern [for speech on public issues] ... is no mystery": "The First Amendment 'was fashioned to assure unfettered interchange of ideas for the bringing about of political and social changes desired by the people.' '[S]peech concerning public affairs is more than self-expression; it is the essence of self-government.' Accordingly, the Court has frequently reaffirmed that speech on public issues occupies the '"highest rung of the hierarchy of First Amendment values,"' and is entitled to special protection." In contrast, speech on matters of purely private concern is of less First Amendment concern. In such a case, "[t]here is no threat to the free and robust debate of public issues; there is no potential interference with a meaningful dialogue of ideas concerning self-government; and there is no threat of liability causing a reaction of self-censorship by the press...." *Harley-Davidson Motorsports, Inc. v. Markley*, 279 Or. 361, 366, 568 P.2d 1359, 1363 (1977).

While such speech is not totally unprotected by the First Amendment, its protections are less stringent. In *Gertz*, we found that the state interest in awarding presumed and punitive damages was not "substantial" in view of their effect on speech at the core of First Amendment concern. This interest, however, is "substantial" relative to the incidental effect these remedies may have on speech of significantly less constitutional interest. The rationale of the common law rules has been the experience and judgment of history that "proof of actual damage will be impossible in a great many cases where, from the character of the defamatory words and the circumstances of publication, it is all but certain that serious harm has resulted in fact." W. Prosser, Law of Torts § 112, p. 765 (4th ed. 1971). As a result, courts for centuries have allowed juries to presume that some damage occurred from many defamatory utterances and publications. This rule furthers the state interest in providing remedies for defamation by ensuring that those remedies are effective. In light of the reduced constitutional value of speech involving no matters of public concern, we hold that the state interest adequately supports awards of presumed and punitive damages—even absent a showing of "actual malice."

The only remaining issue is whether petitioner's credit report involved a matter of public concern. In a related context, we have held that "[w]hether ... speech addresses a matter of public concern must be determined by [the expression's] content, form, and context ... as revealed by the whole record." *Connick v. Myers*, 461 U.S., at 147–148. These

---

achieve the legitimate state purpose of protecting the reputation of private persons...," and that "unrestrained presumed and punitive damages were 'unnecessarily' broad ... in relation to the legitimate state interests." Although the Court made both statements, it did so only within the context of public speech. Neither statement controls here. What was "not ... narrowly tailored" or was "'unnecessarily' broad" with respect to public speech is not necessarily so with respect to the speech now at issue. Properly understood, *Gertz* is consistent with the result we reach today.

factors indicate that petitioner's credit report concerns no public issue. It was speech solely in the individual interest of the speaker and its specific business audience. This particular interest warrants no special protection when — as in this case — the speech is wholly false and clearly damaging to the victim's business reputation. Moreover, since the credit report was made available to only five subscribers, who, under the terms of the subscription agreement, could not disseminate it further, it cannot be said that the report involves any "strong interest in the free flow of commercial information." [*Virginia Pharmacy Board v. Virginia Consumer Council*, 425 U.S. 748, 764 (1976).] There is simply no credible argument that this type of credit reporting requires special protection to ensure that "debate on public issues [will] be uninhibited, robust, and wide-open." *New York Times Co. v. Sullivan*, 376 U.S., at 270.

In addition, the speech here, like advertising, is hardy and unlikely to be deterred by incidental state regulation. It is solely motivated by the desire for profit, which, we have noted, is a force less likely to be deterred than others. Arguably, the reporting here was also more objectively verifiable than speech deserving of greater protection. In any case, the market provides a powerful incentive to a credit reporting agency to be accurate, since false credit reporting is of no use to creditors. Thus, any incremental "chilling" effect of libel suits would be of decreased significance.[9]

We conclude that permitting recovery of presumed and punitive damages in defamation cases absent a showing of "actual malice" does not violate the First Amendment when the defamatory statements do not involve matters of public concern. Accordingly, we affirm the judgment of the Vermont Supreme Court.

[Burger, C.J., and White, J., delivered concurring opinions.]

Justice BRENNAN, with whom Justice MARSHALL, Justice BLACKMUN and Justice STEVENS join, dissenting....

Relying on the analysis of the Vermont Supreme Court, Respondent urged that ... the applicability of *Gertz* [be restricted] to cases in which the defendant is a "media" entity. Such a distinction is irreconcilable with the fundamental First Amendment principle that "[t]he inherent worth of ... speech in terms of its capacity for informing the public does not depend upon the identity of its source, whether corporation, association, union, or individual." *First National Bank of Boston v. Bellotti*, 435 U.S. 765, 777 (1978). First Amendment difficulties lurk in the definitional questions such an approach would generate.[6]

---

9. The Court of Appeals for the Fifth Circuit has noted that, while most States provide a qualified privilege against libel suits for commercial credit reporting agencies, in those States that do not there is a thriving credit reporting business and commercial credit transactions are not inhibited. *Hood v. Dun & Bradstreet, Inc.*, 486 F.2d 25, 32 (1973), cert. denied, 415 U.S. 985 (1974)....

6. An attempt to characterize petitioner Dun & Bradstreet illustrates the point. Like an account of judicial proceedings in a newspaper, magazine or news broadcast, a statement in petitioner's reports that a particular company has filed for bankrupt is a report of a timely news event conveyed to members of the public by a business organized to collect and disseminate such information. Thus it is not obvious why petitioner should find less protection in the First Amendment than do established print or electronic media. The Vermont Supreme Court nonetheless characterized petitioner as a nonmedia defendant entitled to less protection because it is "in the business of selling financial information to a limited number of subscribers who have paid substantial fees for [its] services." The court added that "[t]here is a clear distinction between a publication which disseminates news for public consumption and one which provides specialized information to a selective, finite audience."

No clear line consistent with First Amendment principles can be drawn on the basis of these criteria. That petitioner's information is "specialized" or that its subscribers pay "substantial fees" hardly

And the distinction would likely be born an anachronism. Perhaps most importantly, the argument that *Gertz* should be limited to the media misapprehends our cases. We protect the press to ensure the vitality of First Amendment guarantees. This solicitude implies no endorsement of the principle that speakers other than the press deserve lesser First Amendment protection. "In the realm of protected speech, the legislature is constitutionally disqualified from dictating ... the speakers who may address a public issue." [*Id.*], at 784–785.

The free speech guarantee gives each citizen an equal right to self-expression and to participation in self-government. This guarantee also protects the rights of listeners to "the widest possible dissemination of information from diverse and antagonistic sources." *Associated Press v. United States*, 326 U.S. 1, 20 (1945). Accordingly, at least six Members of this Court (the four who join this opinion and Justice WHITE and THE CHIEF JUSTICE) agree today that, in the context of defamation law, the rights of the institutional media are no greater and no less than those enjoyed by other individuals or organizations engaged in the same activities....

The credit reporting of Dun & Bradstreet falls within any reasonable definition of "public concern" consistent with our precedents.... [A]n announcement of the bankruptcy of a local company is information of potentially great concern to residents of the community where the company is located.... And knowledge about solvency and the effect and prevalence of bankruptcy certainly would inform citizen opinions about questions of economic regulation. It is difficult to suggest that a bankruptcy is not a subject matter of public concern when federal law requires invocation of judicial mechanisms to effectuate it and makes the fact of the bankruptcy a matter of public record....

Even if Justice POWELL's characterization of the credit reporting at issue here were accepted in its entirety, his opinion would have done no more than demonstrate that this speech is the equivalent of commercial speech. The opinion, after all, relies on analogy to advertising. Credit reporting is said to be hardy, motivated by desire for profit, and relatively verifiable. But this does not justify the elimination of restrictions on presumed and punitive damages. State efforts to regulate commercial speech in the form of advertising must abide by the requirement that the regulatory means chosen be narrowly tailored so as to avoid any unnecessary chilling of protected expression.

The Court in *Gertz* specifically held that unrestrained presumed and punitive damages were "unnecessarily" broad, in relation to the legitimate state interests. Indeed, *Gertz* held that in a defamation action punitive damages, designed to chill and not to compensate, were "*wholly irrelevant*" to furtherance of any valid state interest. The Court did not reach these conclusions by weighing the strength of the state interest against strength of the First Amendment interest. Rather, the Court recognized and applied the principle that regulatory measures that chill protected speech be no broader than necessary to serve the legitimate state interest asserted. The plurality opinion today recognizes, as it must, that the state interest at issue here is identical to that at issue in *Gertz*. What was "irrele-

---

distinguishes these reports from articles in many publications that would surely fall on the "media" side of the line the Vermont Supreme Court seeks to draw. Few published statements are of universal interest and few publications are distributed without charge. Much fare of any metropolitan daily is specialized information for which a selective finite audience pays a fee. Nor is there any reason to treat petitioner differently than a more widely circulated publication because it has "a limited number of subscribers." Indeed, it would be paradoxical to increase protection to statements injurious to reputation as the size of their audience, and hence their potential to injure, grows.

vant" in *Gertz* must still be irrelevant and the requirement that the regulatory means be no broader than necessary is no less applicable even if the speech is simply the equivalent of commercial speech. Thus, unrestrained presumed and punitive damages for this type of speech must run afoul of First Amendment guarantees.[11]

... [T]he states' regulatory interest in protecting reputation is served by rules permitting recovery for actual compensatory damages upon a showing of fault. Any further interest in deterring potential defamation through case-by-case judicial imposition of presumed and punitive damage awards on less than a showing of actual malice simply exacts too high a toll on First Amendment values. Accordingly, Greenmoss Builders should be permitted to recover for any actual damage it can show resulted from Dun & Bradstreet's negligently false credit report, but should be required to show actual malice to receive presumed or punitive damages. Because the jury was not instructed in accordance with these principles, we would reverse and remand....

Notes

1. The *Dun & Bradstreet* case requires that a distinction be drawn between defamatory statements that "involve matters of public concern" and statements that do not. This is almost identical to the Rosenbloom v. Metromedia, Inc. formulation of "matter of public or general concern," which was used interchangeably with "matter of public or general interest." Why would the author of the court's opinion in *Gertz* give new life to *Rosenbloom*? Will the "matter of public concern" criterion be applied when the defamed person is a public official or public figure?

2. Which matters are "of public concern"? See Stern, Private Concerns of Private Plaintiffs: Revisiting a Problematic Defamation Category, 65 Mo. L. Rev. 597 (2000). Precedent may be found in cases applying *Rosenbloom* and perhaps in cases applying the fair comment criterion of "matter of public interest," pp. 623–624, supra, as well as in cases interpreting *Dun & Bradstreet*. In most defamation cases arising from media publication and statements to the press, it is clear that a matter of public concern was addressed. See, e.g., Time, Inc. v. McLaney, 406 F.2d 565 (5th Cir. 1969), cert. denied, 395 U.S. 922 (1969) (influx of American gangsters in Bahamas and its role in Bahamas election campaign); Alpine Construction Co. v. Demaris, 358 F. Supp. 422 (N.D. Ill. 1973) (involvement of organized crime in legitimate businesses); Trails West, Inc. v. Wolff, 32 N.Y.2d 207, 344 N.Y.S.2d 863, 298 N.E.2d 52 (1973) (safety of buses transporting children on tour); Mellor v. Scott Publishing Co., Inc., 10 Wash. App. 645, 519 P.2d 1010 (1974) (controversial appraisal of farm land for tax purposes). Such non-media statements as a complaint about the handling of a business transaction or a supervisor's criticism of an employee's job performance, as well as purely personal remarks, are likely to be found to involve no matter of public concern. See Hirsch v. Cooper, 153 Ariz. 454, 737 P.2d 1092 (Ct. App.

---

11. One searches *Gertz* in vain for a single word to support the proposition that limits on presumed and punitive damages obtained only when speech involved matters of public concern. *Gertz* could not have been grounded in such a premise. Distrust of placing in the courts the power to decide what speech was of public concern was precisely the rationale *Gertz* offered for rejecting the *Rosenbloom* plurality approach. It would have been incongruous for the Court to go on to circumscribe the protection against presumed and punitive damages by reference to a judicial judgment as to whether the speech at issue involved matters of public concern. At several points the Court in *Gertz* makes perfectly clear the restrictions of presumed and punitive damages were to apply in all cases.... [footnote to omitted text].

1986); Cooper v. Portland General Electric Corp., 110 Or. App. 581, 824 P.2d 1152 (1992), review denied, 313 Or. 209, 830 P.2d 595 (1992); Great Coastal Express, Inc. v. Ellington, 230 Va. 142, 334 S.E.2d 846 (1985). The court in Sunward Corp. v. Dun & Bradstreet, Inc. 811 F.2d 511 (10th Cir. 1987), found no matter of public concern in a Dun & Bradstreet financial report even though at least 340 copies were sent, in contrast to the five sent in the principal case.

3. Is a matter "of public concern" addressed when the subject of defendant's statement is the quality of food in a take-out restaurant? Steak Bit of Westbury, Inc. v. Newsday, Inc., 70 Misc. 2d 437, 334 N.Y.S.2d 325 (Sup. Ct. 1972). The conditions in which birds at a pet shop are kept? Safarets, Inc. v. Gannett Co., Inc., 80 Misc. 2d 109, 361 N.Y.S.2d 276 (Sup. Ct. 1974), aff'd, 49 A.D.2d 666, 373 N.Y.S.2d 858 (1975). A person's alleged commission of a sexual assault (for which no charges were brought)? Carney v. Santa Cruz Women Against Rape, 221 Cal. App. 3d 1009, 271 Cal. Rptr. 30 (1990). A snowplow operator's excessive charge for clearing a driveway after a heavy snowstorm? Matus v. Triangle Publications, Inc., 445 Pa. 384, 286 A.2d 357 (1971), cert. denied, 408 U.S. 930 (1972). Loan transactions between a bank and its chairman? Sisler v. Gannett Co., Inc., 104 N.J. 256, 516 A.2d 1083 (1986). A court case in which a golfer sued his partner for hitting him in the eye with a ball? Sellers v. Time Inc. 299 F. Supp. 582 (E.D. Pa. 1969), aff'd, 423 F.2d 887 (3d Cir. 1970), cert. denied, 400 U.S. 830 (1970). The installation of a furnace in a house shortly before a fatal fire? AAFCO Heating and Air Conditioning Co. v. Northwest Publications, Inc., 162 Ind. App. 671, 321 N.E.2d 580 (1974), cert. denied, 424 U.S. 913 (1976). An owner's difficulty in recovering stolen antiques from a shop that (in good faith) purchased them? Walker v. Colorado Springs Sun, Inc., 188 Colo. 86, 538 P.2d 450 (1975), cert. denied sub nom. Woestendiek v. Walker, 423 U.S. 1025 (1975). The "undesirables" whose association with a nightclub in which a football player had an interest led to the player's departure from professional football? Schwartz v. Time, Inc., 71 Misc. 2d 769, 337 N.Y.S.2d 125 (Sup. Ct. 1972). The competency of a person performing psychological testing of a child? Saunders v. Van Pelt, 497 A.2d 1121 (Me. 1985). A bishop's attendance at a nightclub performance by a member of the church choir? Washington v. New York News Inc., 37 A.D.2d 557, 322 N.Y.S.2d 896 (1971). Family problems which led to the nervous breakdown of a mental patient, selected to illustrate the fifty thousand patients being transferred from mental hospitals to nursing homes? Gaeta v. New York News Inc., 62 N.Y.2d 340, 477 N.Y.S.2d 82, 465 N.E.2d 802 (1984). Of these cases, the only ones in which no matter of public concern or public interest was found are Saunders v. Van Pelt, the only case involving non-media publication, and Matus v. Triangle Publications, Inc., in which the person allegedly overcharged was the radio announcer's wife.

4. A media publication was found not to involve a matter of public concern in one of the most extensive judicial analyses of the subject: Firestone v. Time, Inc., 271 So. 2d 745 (Fla. 1972). (The U.S. Supreme Court's later opinion in this case is noted p. 653, supra.) *Time* had reported in its "Milestones" column the divorce of the Firestones. It was said that the divorce was granted to Mr. Firestone on grounds of extreme cruelty and adultery and that the seventeen-month intermittent trial had produced, in the words of the judge, enough testimony of extra-marital adventures on both sides "to make Dr. Freud's hair curl." Because of the sensational testimony at the trial and prominence of the couple — they were among the "400" of Palm Beach society and the husband was an heir to the Firestone tire fortune — the divorce trial had been the object of national news coverage. The court drew a distinction between matters which were "newsworthy," in the sense that the public was interested in them, and matters of "real public or general concern." Matters of real public or general concern were "those which invoke common and pre-

dominant public activity, participation or indulgence, and cogitation, study and debate," including government, the arts, sciences, religion, morality and "matters relating generally to the health, well-being and general comfort of the public *as a whole*." Only if there was a "logical relationship" between what was reported and one of these matters was the report on a subject of public concern. The court found no "logical relationship" between the *Time* report and a subject of public concern. The report served "prurient curiosity." Marital infidelity involved morality, but infidelity in a particular marriage was not of public importance. The result would be different if the alleged infidelity had been linked to some subject that was of public concern, such as professional marriage counselling by one of the spouses, or the electronic eavesdropping that was exposed in another article about the Firestones. Interviews given by plaintiff (Mrs. Firestone) to the press did not "raise the untidy affair to the dignity of true public concern." She was not seeking public patronage, but "merely satiating the appetites of a curious press."

5. Does *Dun & Bradstreet* settle the question of whether "media defendants" enjoy a protection from defamation liability that is not also extended to "non-media defendants"? Does a distinction between media and non-media defendants have merit? Can it survive in an era when anyone can communicate through the Internet to a potentially vast, but in reality often very small, readership? Prior to *Dun & Bradstreet*, there was a large measure of agreement that in actions for defamation of public officials and public figures, the "actual malice" requirement applied to claims against any defendant. See Rodriguez v. Nishiki, 65 Hawaii 430, 653 P.2d 1145 (1982); Wattigny v. Lambert, 453 So. 2d 1272 (La. App. 1984); Wheeler v. Green, 286 Or. 99, 593 P.2d 777 (1979). Cf. Trails West, Inc. v. Wolff, 32 N.Y.2d 207, 344 N.Y.S.2d 863, 298 N.E.2d 52 (1973) (*Rosenbloom* applied to non-media defendants). But courts were quite divided on whether *Gertz*, with its requirement of fault and "actual injury" rule, applied or should apply to non-media defendants. See Annot., Defamation: Application of New York Times and Related Standards to Nonmedia Defendants, 38 A.L.R.4th 1114 (1985). A leading case applying the *Gertz* rules to non-media defendants is Jacron Sales Co., Inc. v. Sindorf, 276 Md. 580, 350 A.2d 688 (1976), on appeal from the case at p. 593, supra. One reason was the extent to which there was non-media discussion of matters of public interest. Another was the court's belief that it would be strange as a matter of tort law for individuals, even in a casual conversation with one person, to be strictly liable while the press, composed of professionals and causing much greater damage because of the wider distribution of its communications, was being held liable only for negligence. Also, most non-media defamation cases involved common law privileges, so liability without fault was unusual, and applying *Gertz* to both types of defendants would promote consistency and simplicity.

6. Does *Dun & Bradstreet* permit states to impose liability without fault when defamation is not on a subject of public concern? Justice White, concurring, believed this followed from the plurality opinion and agreed. Accord, Snead v. Redland Aggregates Ltd., 998 F.2d 1325 (5th Cir. 1993), cert. dismissed, 511 U.S. 1050 (1994). Cf. the decision in Roffman v. Trump, 754 F. Supp. 411 (E.D. Pa. 1990), that only state law applied to a private figure's action for statements on a matter of private concern. The court in New England Tractor-Trailer Training of Connecticut, Inc. v. Globe Newspaper Co., 395 Mass. 471, 480 N.E.2d 1005 (1985), however, considered the *Gertz* fault requirement to be intact. In U.S. Healthcare, Inc. v. Blue Cross of Greater Philadelphia, p. 259, supra, the Third Circuit decided that "commercial speech" was not entitled to the same protection as non-commercial speech and therefore was not protected by "actual malice" liability requirements. A defendant could be held liable for defamatory commercial speech without proof of knowing falsehood or reckless disregard of truth. The court relied in part on the *Dun & Bradstreet* premise that different categories of speech were of different "First Amend-

ment importance" and attracted different levels of First Amendment protection. It applied the reasoning that potential defamation liability was unlikely to "chill" publications motivated by economic self-interest. See also Procter & Gamble Co. v. Amway Corp., p. 260, supra.

7. To the extent that *Dun & Bradstreet* permits liability without fault, or recovery of presumed or punitive damages, will states return to the pre-*Gertz* common law? The court in *New England Tractor-Trailer* refused to bring liability without fault back into the state's common law. In Great Coastal Express, Inc. v. Ellington, 230 Va. 142, 334 S.E.2d 846 (1985), the court permitted recovery of presumed damages but required proof of fault and, for punitive damages, knowing or reckless falsehood.

Philadelphia Newspapers, Inc. v. Hepps
Supreme Court of the United States
475 U.S. 767 (1986)

Justice O'CONNOR delivered the opinion of the Court....

Maurice S. Hepps is the principal stockholder of General Programming, Inc. (GPI), a corporation that franchises a chain of stores—known at the relevant time as "Thrifty" stores—selling beer, soft drinks, and snacks. Mr. Hepps, GPI, and a number of its franchisees are the appellees here. Appellant Philadelphia Newspapers, Inc. [published in its newspaper a series of five articles, the general theme of which] was that appellees had links to organized crime and used some of those links to influence the State's governmental processes, both legislative and administrative.... A grand jury was said to be investigating the "alleged relationship between the Thrifty chain and known Mafia figures," and "[w]hether the chain received special treatment from the [state governor's] administration and the Liquor Control Board."

Appellees brought suit for defamation against appellants in a Pennsylvania state court. Consistent with *Gertz*, Pennsylvania requires a private figure who brings a suit for defamation to bear the burden of proving negligence or malice by the defendant in publishing the statements at issue. As to falsity, Pennsylvania follows the common law's presumption that an individual's reputation is a good one. Statements defaming that person are therefore presumptively false, although a publisher who bears the burden of proving the truth of the statements has an absolute defense.

... [T]he trial court concluded that Pennsylvania's statute giving the defendant the burden of proving the truth of the statements violated the Federal Constitution. The trial court therefore instructed the jury that the plaintiffs bore the burden of proving falsity....

[The jury found for defendants. Plaintiffs appealed to the Supreme Court of Pennsylvania, which remanded the case for a new trial, having concluded that a showing of fault did not require a showing of falsity and that placing upon defendants the burden of showing truth was not unconstitutional.] ...

Our opinions to date have chiefly treated the necessary showings of fault rather than of falsity. Nonetheless, as one might expect given the language of the Court in *New York Times*, a public-figure plaintiff must show the falsity of the statements at issue in order to prevail on a suit for defamation. See *Garrison v. Louisiana*, 379 U.S. 64, 74 (1964).

Here, as in *Gertz*, the plaintiff is a private figure and the newspaper articles are of public concern. In *Gertz*, as in *New York Times*, the common-law rule was superseded by a constitutional rule. We believe that the common law's rule on falsity—that the defendant must bear the burden of proving truth—must similarly fall here to a constitutional requirement that the plaintiff bear the burden of showing falsity, as well as fault, before recovering damages.

There will always be instances when the factfinding process will be unable to resolve conclusively whether the speech is true or false; it is in those cases that the burden of proof is dispositive. Under a rule forcing the plaintiff to bear the burden of showing falsity, there will be some cases in which plaintiffs cannot meet their burden despite the fact that the speech is in fact false. The plaintiff's suit will fail despite the fact that, in some abstract sense, the suit is meritorious. Similarly, under an alternative rule placing the burden of showing truth on defendants, there would be some cases in which defendants could not bear their burden despite the fact that the speech is in fact true. Those suits would succeed despite the fact that, in some abstract sense, those suits are unmeritorious. Under either rule, then, the outcome of the suit will sometimes be at variance with the outcome that we would desire if all speech were either demonstrably true or demonstrably false.

This dilemma stems from the fact that the allocation of the burden of proof will determine liability for some speech that is true and some that is false, but *all* of such speech is *unknowably* true or false. Because the burden of proof is the deciding factor only when the evidence is ambiguous, we cannot know how much of the speech affected by the allocation of the burden of proof is true and how much is false. In a case presenting a configuration of speech and plaintiff like the one we face here, and where the scales are in such an uncertain balance, we believe that the Constitution requires us to tip them in favor of protecting true speech. To ensure that true speech on matters of public concern is not deterred, we hold that the common-law presumption that defamatory speech is false cannot stand when a plaintiff seeks damages against a media defendant for speech of public concern.

In the context of governmental restriction of speech, it has long been established that the government cannot limit speech protected by the First Amendment without bearing the burden of showing that its restriction is justified. It is not immediately apparent from the text of the First Amendment, which by its terms applies only to governmental action, that a similar result should obtain here: a suit by a private party is obviously quite different from the government's direct enforcement of its own laws. Nonetheless, the need to encourage debate on public issues that concerned the Court in the governmental-restriction cases is of concern in a similar manner in this case involving a private suit for damages: placement by state law of the burden of proving truth upon media defendants who publish speech of public concern deters such speech because of the fear that liability will unjustifiably result. Because such a "chilling" effect would be antithetical to the First Amendment's protection of true speech on matters of public concern, we believe that a private-figure plaintiff must bear the burden of showing that the speech at issue is false before recovering damages for defamation from a media defendant.

We recognize that requiring the plaintiff to show falsity will insulate from liability some speech that is false, but unprovably so. Nonetheless, the Court's previous decisions on the restrictions that the First Amendment places upon the common law of defamation firmly support our conclusion here with respect to the allocation of the burden of proof. In attempting to resolve related issues in the defamation context, the Court has affirmed that "[t]he First Amendment requires that we protect some falsehood in order to protect speech that matters." *Gertz*, 418 U.S., at 341. Here the speech concerns the legitimacy of the political process, and therefore clearly "matters." To provide "'breathing space,'" for true speech on matters of public concern, the Court has been willing to insulate even *demonstrably* false speech from liability, and has imposed additional requirements of fault upon the plaintiff in a suit for defamation. We therefore do not break new ground here in insulating speech that is not even demonstrably false.

We note that our decision adds only marginally to the burdens that the plaintiff must already bear as a result of our earlier decisions in the law of defamation. The plaintiff must show fault. A jury is obviously more likely to accept a plaintiff's contention that the defendant was at fault in publishing the statements at issue if convinced that the relevant statements were false. As a practical matter, then, evidence offered by plaintiffs on the publisher's fault in adequately investigating the truth of the published statements will generally encompass evidence of the falsity of the matters asserted....[4]

[Reversed and remanded. Brennan, J., (with whom Blackmun, J., joined) delivered a concurring opinion.]

Justice STEVENS, with whom THE CHIEF JUSTICE, Justice WHITE, and Justice REHNQUIST join, dissenting.

[Because of the *Gertz* fault requirement] the only litigants—and the only publishers—who will benefit from today's decision are those who act negligently or maliciously....

... I simply do not understand ... why a character assassin should be given an absolute license to defame by means of statements that can be neither verified nor disproven. The danger of deliberate defamation by reference to unprovable facts is not a merely speculative or hypothetical concern. Lack of knowledge about third parties, the loss of critical records, an uncertain recollection about events that occurred long ago, perhaps during a period of special stress, the absence of eyewitnesses—a host of factors—may make it impossible for an honorable person to disprove malicious gossip about his past conduct, his relatives, his friends, or his business associates....

The Court's result is plausible ... only because it grossly undervalues the strong state interest in redressing injuries to private reputations. The error lies in its initial premise, with its mistaken belief that doubt regarding the veracity of a defamatory statement must invariably be resolved in favor of constitutional protection of the statement and against vindication of the reputation of the private individual....

In my view, as long as publishers are protected by the requirement that the plaintiff has the burden of proving fault, there can be little, if any, basis for a concern that a significant amount of true speech will be deterred unless the private person victimized by a malicious libel can also carry the burden of proving falsity. The Court's decision trades on the good names of private individuals with little First Amendment coin to show for it....

Notes

1. The burden of proof on the issue of truth is to be distinguished from the burden of proof on the issue of fault. *New York Times* requires proof of defendant's knowledge or reckless disregard of falsity—not just by the preponderance of evidence, but with "convincing clarity." There never has been doubt that the burden of proving this rests upon plaintiffs subject to the *New York Times* rule: public officials and public figures. *Gertz*, on

---

4. We ... have no occasion to consider the quantity of proof of falsity that a private-figure plaintiff must present to recover damages. Nor need we consider what standards would apply if the plaintiff sues a nonmedia defendant, or if a State were to provide a plaintiff with the opportunity to obtain a judgment that declared the speech at issue to be false but did not give rise to liability for damages.

the other hand, neither imposes a heightened standard of proof nor states that plaintiffs must bear the burden of proving fault. It merely directs that defendants not be liable without fault. Defendants could be required to prove freedom from fault. Nevertheless, it has generally been assumed that plaintiffs are required to prove fault in cases governed by *Gertz*. See Jacron Sales Co., Inc. v. Sindorf, 276 Md. 580, 350 A.2d 688 (1976); Gazette, Inc. v. Harris, 229 Va. 1, 325 S.E.2d 713 (1985), cert. denied sub nom. Fleming v. Moore, 472 U.S. 1032 (1985), cert. denied sub nom. Port Packet Corp. v. Lewis, 473 U.S. 905 (1985); Restatement (Second) of Torts § 580B, comment *j* (1977).

2. There is no theoretical inconsistency in requiring plaintiff to prove defendant's reckless disregard of falsity and requiring defendant to prove the truth of the defamatory statement, but it is not likely that the justices who decided *New York Times* would have found this constitutional. Also, as a practical matter, it is very unlikely that a plaintiff could prove with "convincing clarity" defendant's reckless disregard of the truth without proof of falsity. Consequently, the usual position before *Hepps* was to allocate the burden on truth or falsity to plaintiffs in public official and public figure cases. See Cianci v. New Times Publishing Co., 639 F.2d 54 (2d Cir. 1980); Farnsworth v. Tribune Co., 43 Ill. 2d 286, 253 N.E.2d 408 (1969); Harper, James & Gray, Law of Torts § 5.20, at 172–176 (2d ed. 1986).

3. It was different in private figure cases, in which defendants could be liable on a showing of negligence. In many jurisdictions, truth continued to be treated as a defense, as under the common law. See Rogozinski v. Airstream by Angell, 152 N.J. Super. 133, 377 A.2d 807 (Law Div. 1977), modified, 164 N.J. Super. 465, 397 A.2d 334 (App. Div. 1979); Memphis Publishing Co. v. Nichols, 569 S.W.2d 412 (Tenn. 1978). However, there were a number of decisions foreshadowing *Hepps*. See Dunlap v. Philadelphia Newspapers, Inc., 301 Pa. Super. 475, 448 A.2d 6 (1982); Gazette, Inc. v. Harris, supra; Betancourt v. Whittle, 659 S.W.2d 895 (Tex. App. 1983). Will states retain the common law rule for cases not within the mandate of *Hepps*? In Wilson v. Scripps-Howard Broadcasting Co., 642 F.2d 371 (6th Cir. 1981), cert. dismissed, 454 U.S. 1130 (1981), the court reasoned that the elements of carelessness and falsity were inevitably linked. Ordinarily, it would be impossible to determine whether defendant exercised reasonable care in checking on the truth or falsity of a statement without first determining whether the statement was false. Also, a rule placing upon defendant the burden of proving truth would permit in certain situations the imposition of liability without fault. Is this correct?

4. Does the principal case have implications for subjects other than the burden of proof? Does it affect the issue of when there can be tort liability for a true statement? Is the meaning of truth for purposes of constitutional law the same as the meaning of truth in the common law of defamation? In Schaefer v. Lynch, 406 So. 2d 185 (La. 1981), concurring opinion, 483 So. 2d 607 (La. 1986), and Mihalik v. Duprey, 11 Mass. App. Ct. 602, 417 N.E.2d 1238 (1981), courts held that articles containing a series of accurate facts which conveyed a false defamatory insinuation about a public official were not actionable. Cf. Pietrafeso v. D.P.I., Inc., 757 P.2d 1113 (Colo. App. 1988), holding that if the statements in defendant's publication are true or substantially true, a public figure cannot sue for defamation "by innuendo." In Diesen v. Hessburg, 455 N.W.2d 446 (Minn. 1990), cert. denied, 498 U.S. 1119 (1991), a plurality held that a public official cannot recover on the basis of false implications arising from true statements even when defendants published in reckless disregard of the falsity of the implication. This was rejected in Turner v. KTRK Television, Inc., 38 S.W.3d 103 (Tex. 2000), which held that a public figure could maintain an action when the individual statements were literally or substantially true but the publication as a whole conveyed a false defamatory meaning through juxtaposition

or omission. Masson v. New Yorker Magazine, Inc., p. 642, supra, can be read to adopt for constitutional purposes the rule of "substantial truth," discussed pp. 562–568, supra. See also the next principal case.

Barry v. Time, Inc.
United States District Court, Northern District of California
584 F. Supp. 1110 (1984)

PATEL, District Judge.

[*Sports Illustrated*, a magazine published by Time, Inc., published two articles focusing on the University of San Francisco's investigation of allegations that Quintin Dailey, a star player on the USF basketball team who went on to play professional basketball, received improper payments, in violation of the rules of the National Collegiate Athletic Association, from a company owned by a USF supporter. Controversy surrounding allegations of illegal recruiting methods ultimately led to cancellation of the men's basketball program by USF's president in the month the *Sports Illustrated* articles appeared. The articles reported accusations by Dailey that USF's head basketball coach at the time, Pete Barry, was involved in the payments and had personally transmitted money to Dailey in violation of NCAA rules. The articles also contained denials from Barry that he had ever been involved in any illegal or questionable payments to Dailey or any other player while he was coach.]

[Barry brought a slander action against Dailey and a libel action against Time, alleging that the articles were understood by some readers to imply that Barry had transferred money improperly to USF basketball players and that readers were led to accept this as true by *Sports Illustrated*'s report of a "scandal" and "shocking conditions" in the USF basketball program. Time moved for dismissal. The court held that Barry was a "public figure" for purposes of the case and that he had failed to plead "actual malice" with sufficient specificity to survive a motion to dismiss.]

American courts have traditionally refused to distinguish between publishers and republishers of defamatory statements, on the theory that "tale bearers are as bad as tale makers."

In *Edwards v. National Audubon Society, Inc.*, 556 F.2d 113 (2d Cir.), *cert. denied sub nom. Edwards v. New York Times Co.*, 434 U.S. 1002 (1977), the Second Circuit elucidated for the first time a constitutional privilege of neutral reportage, under which a republisher who accurately and disinterestedly reports certain defamatory statements made against public figures is shielded from liability, regardless of the republisher's subjective awareness of the truth or falsity of the accusation.

Edwards considered whether liability could be imposed upon the *New York Times* for publishing an article which accurately reported an accusation of the National Audubon Society that certain scientists were "being paid to lie, or ... parroting something [they] knew] little about." The newspaper account quoted Audubon Society officials who identified five prominent scientists as the persons attacked, and also contained denials from the three defamed scientists who could be reached for comment. These accusations were reported in the context of an already acrimonious public controversy over the use of DDT.

Both sides conceded that the *Times* had accurately reported both the substance of the Audubon Society publication and the names of the five scientists accused of being "paid liars." Under these circumstances, the Second Circuit found that a libel judgment against the *Times* was constitutionally impermissible: "Succinctly stated, when a responsible, prominent organization like the National Audubon Society makes serious charges against a public figure, the First Amendment protects the accurate and disinterested reporting of those charges, regardless of the reporter's private views regarding their validity. What is newsworthy about such accusations is that they were made. We do not believe that the press may be required under the First Amendment to suppress newsworthy statements because it has serious doubts regarding their truth. Nor must the press take up cudgels against dubious charges in order to publish them without fear of liability for defamation. The public interest in being fully informed about controversies that often rage around sensitive issues demands that the press be afforded the freedom to report such charges without assuming responsibility for them." The court emphasized the requirements of neutrality, noting that "a publisher who in fact espouses or concurs in the charges made by others, or who deliberately distorts these statements to launch a personal attack of his own on a public figure, cannot rely on a privilege of neutral reportage. In such instances he assumes responsibility for the underlying accusations." ...

... Neither the Ninth Circuit nor any of the district courts in the circuit appears to have either adopted or rejected the privilege of neutral reportage. ...

Having carefully reviewed the arguments touching on all aspects of the issue as expressed by judges and commentators, this court finds itself in agreement with Judge Kaufman that "[t]he public interest in being fully informed about controversies that rage around sensitive issues demands that the press be afforded the freedom to report such charges without assuming responsibility for them." *Edwards*, 556 F.2d at 120.

Recognition of the public's "right to know" that serious charges have been made against a public figure is an important application of the Supreme Court's concern that "debate on public issues be uninhibited, robust, and wide-open." *New York Times Co. v. Sullivan*, 376 U.S. 254, 270 (1964). If a republisher may be held liable for passing on newsworthy but defamatory information to the public, it is likely that he will decline to publish this information for fear that his doubts will later be characterized as "serious" and therefore actionable. Even if he does not fear ultimate liability, the mere threat of costly and time-consuming inquiry into his state of mind may cast a chilling effect on publication. In this way, the public will be deprived of the opportunity to make informed judgments with respect to public controversies.

Contrary to the conclusions of some courts the privilege, as defined, does not call into play the kind of *ad hoc* determinations of "newsworthiness" that concerned the *Gertz* court. Under *Gertz* and its progeny, the court must already engage in the evaluation of whether the plaintiff is a public figure and what constitutes a public controversy. In order to apply the neutral reportage doctrine the court in addition need only assess whether the defamer is a party to the controversy and whether the report is accurate and neutral.

Plaintiff argues that the *Edwards* privilege does not apply to the facts of this case, since Dailey is not a "responsible, prominent organization [or individual]," but rather is a convicted felon who has failed a lie detector test. In other words, plaintiff contends that the neutral reportage privilege requires an assessment by the press of the credibility of an alleged defamer.

Very few courts have addressed the issue of whether the neutral reportage privilege applies when the underlying defamation was not made by a "responsible and prominent" organization or individual.[18] ... This Court does not read [*Fogus v. Capital Cities Media, Inc.*, 111 Ill. App. 3d 1060, 444 N.E.2d 1100 (1982)] as denying the privilege because the

---

18. Although *Edwards* spoke only of "organizations," there is no logical or constitutional basis for differentiating between organizations and individuals in this context. ...

defamers were not "trustworthy," but rather because they were "unnamed" and there was thus no means by which readers of the article could discern the veracity of the allegations. In [*Krauss v. Champaign News Gazette*, 59 Ill. App. 3d 745, 375 N.E.2d 1362 (1978)], by contrast, the privilege applied not because the State's Attorney was inherently more believable than the defamers in *Fogus*, but rather because the State's Attorney, being a public figure, was well-known in the community and the members of the public could therefore judge for themselves whether or not to believe his accusations. *Fogus* and *Krauss* thus do not stand for the proposition that a defamer must be "trustworthy" in order for the privilege to apply, but rather that the defamer must be "prominent."

More on point than *Fogus* is *Oliver v. Village Voice, Inc.*, 417 F. Supp. 235 (S.D.N.Y. 1976), decided before *Edwards*. In *Oliver*, the court considered defendant newspaper's liability for quoting an identified "Watergate investigator" to the effect that plaintiff was involved with the CIA. It appeared through deposition testimony that, while the article attributed the statements to a Watergate investigator, Rosenbaum, the real source of the information was Howard Hunt. Plaintiff argued that defendant was reckless to rely upon anything known to have emanated from Hunt, "give his dubious reputation for reliability." The court ... found that Hunt's reliability was irrelevant, since the mere fact of his having made the statement was newsworthy....

This court is of the opinion that the neutral reportage privilege does not depend solely upon the "trustworthiness" of the individual or organization making the allegedly defamatory statements. Neither *Edwards* nor *Fogus*, nor any other case, advance a cogent policy reason for differentiating among defamers on the basis of their trustworthiness or credibility. Indeed, the primary rationale of *Edwards*—the public interest in being fully informed about public controversies—is inconsistent with such a differentiation. Moreover, it could create a chilling effect on the members of the press if they were required to be the arbiters of how "trustworthy" a source is. A much more sensible approach is to extend the neutral reportage privilege to *all* republications of serious charges made by one participant in an existing public controversy against another participant in that controversy, regardless of the "trustworthiness" of the original defamer....

... *[I]t is the neutrality of the report* which is critical. So long as the publisher does not "espouse or concur in the charges" or "deliberately distort" the charges, protection against defamation claims should be afforded. *Edwards*, 556 F.2d at 120. In this way, the public, not the press, is the ultimate arbiter of the truth of accusations made during the course of a public controversy.

The neutral reportage privilege, so construed, is not without limitations. It cannot be used as an absolute privilege to republish defamatory statements about purely private persons not already caught up in a public controversy. The privilege applies where the defamed person is a public figure, whether general or limited purpose, who is involved in an existing controversy, and the defamatory statement is made by a party to that controversy. The republication must be accurate and neutral. While the rationale justifying the neutral reportage privilege may apply equally to non-public plaintiffs involved in an existing controversy, the court need not reach that issue here.

It is clear from the foregoing that Time's republication of Dailey's accusations against Barry is constitutionally protected by the privilege of neutral reportage. Plaintiff concedes that the articles in question accurately report the accusations made by Dailey against Barry. Furthermore, plaintiff does not and could not assert that the articles present an unbalanced or one-sided picture of the public controversy over alleged recruiting violations at USF. As in *Edwards*, Time elicited and published a denial from Barry that he had ever been involved in any illegal or questionable payments to Barry or any other USF basketball player.... Time responsibly did not conceal from its readers facts about Dailey which tended to impugn his credibility, such as his guilty plea to aggravated assault charges and his failure to pass a lie detector test regarding the assault. Under the circumstances, this court finds that the public's interest in knowing that Dailey, a central actor in the public controversy concerning alleged recruiting violations at USF, made such serious accusations against Barry, another key participant in the controversy, outweighs Barry's interest in preventing the incremental diminution of his reputation which may have occurred following republication of Dailey's allegedly defamatory remarks.

Independent of the ... complaint's failure to plead actual malice with sufficient specificity, therefore, this court concludes that summary judgment in favor of Time must be granted.

Notes

1. The neutral reportage doctrine enunciated by the Second Circuit in Edwards v. National Audubon Society, Inc. has received a mixed reception in other courts. A number have rejected it completely. One rationale for rejection is that the doctrine's element of newsworthiness conflicts with the disapproval of Rosenbloom v. Metromedia, Inc. in the *Gertz* case. *Gertz* is read to require that constitutional protection (beyond protection from liability without fault) depend upon plaintiff's status as a public official or public figure, not the subject-matter of the defamatory statement. See Newell v. Field Enterprises, Inc., 91 Ill. App. 3d 735, 415 N.E.2d 434 (1980); Hogan v. Herald Co., 84 A.D.2d 470, 446 N.Y.S.2d 836 (1982), aff'd, 58 N.Y.2d 630, 458 N.Y.S.2d 538, 444 N.E.2d 1002 (1982). Has this been overtaken by subsequent decisions of the Supreme Court? Another rationale for rejecting a constitutional argument for neutral reportage is inconsistency with the Supreme Court's definition of "reckless disregard" in St. Amant v. Thompson, 390 U.S. 727 (1968). The definition includes publication of a defamatory statement when the publisher has serious doubts about its truth. See Dickey v. CBS Inc., 583 F.2d 1221 (3d Cir. 1978). It also has been thought that the Supreme Court would not limit defamatory liability further than the "actual malice" requirement. Norton v. Glenn, 580 Pa. 212, 860 A.2d 48 (2004), cert. denied sub nom. Troy Publishing Co., Inc. v. Norton, 544 U.S. 956 (2005).

2. Almost all the litigated issues concerning the scope of the neutral reportage privilege are touched upon in the principal case. Courts that do not categorically reject the neutral reportage doctrine have used the language of the *Edwards* opinion to limit its application. In Cianci v. New Times Publishing Co., 639 F.2d 54 (2d Cir. 1980), the court emphasized the *Edwards* elements of a responsible organization making serious charges, newsworthy because they were made, against public figures, where there was a public interest in being fully informed about a controversy, with the reporter publishing a fair and dispassionate account that included the accused persons' responses. In McManus v. Doubleday & Co., Inc., 513 F. Supp. 1383 (S.D.N.Y. 1981), the court denied that the privilege applied to reporting a statement made by a representative of an organization to an investigative reporter. The reporter was not covering an "autonomous news event," and there was no prior controversy about the statement.

3. In Fogus v. Capital Cities Media, Inc., 111 Ill. App. 3d 1060, 444 N.E.2d 1100 (1982), where a newspaper had reported accusations by youths arrested in a drug raid of abusive treatment by the police, the court said that if the neutral reportage doctrine survived as a constitutional or common law privilege, it would be narrowly limited to situations in which a responsible prominent person or organization made serious charges against a public figure. (This, not the anonymity of the persons making the charges, was the ra-

tionale of the court's decision that the *Fogus* defendants were not protected by the doctrine.) DiSalle v. P.G. Publishing Co., 375 Pa. Super. 510, 544 A.2d 1345 (1988), allocatur denied, 521 Pa. 620, 557 A.2d 724 (1989), cert. denied, 492 U.S. 906 (1989), requires that the accusation be made by a public figure or official. In Orr v. Lynch, 60 A.D.2d 949, 401 N.Y.S.2d 897 (1978), aff'd, 45 N.Y.2d 903, 411 N.Y.S.2d 10, 383 N.E.2d 562 (1978), however, the court held that a radio station was not liable for reporting accusations against the police by a man wounded in an exchange of gunfire with police officers. The station had previously reported the police version of the incident. Should the privilege apply to accusations by unnamed persons? To reports of rumors circulating in the community? See Martin v. Wilson Publishing Co., 497 A.2d 322 (R.I. 1985); Burns v. Times Argus Association, Inc., 139 Vt. 381, 430 A.2d 773 (1981).

4. Should a neutral reportage privilege be confined to reports of charges against public officials or public figures? The court in April v. Reflector-Herald, Inc., 46 Ohio App. 3d 95, 546 N.E.2d 466 (1988), decided that no distinction should be made between reporting of newsworthy accusations against private figures and reporting of accusations against public figures. But it was held in Khawar v. Globe International, Inc., p. 643, supra, that the neutral reportage privilege did not extend to statements about a person who was not a public official or public figure. The court accepted an argument that to hold otherwise would be inconsistent with the U.S. Supreme Court's balancing of the First Amendment interest in dissemination of information against private figures' reputation interests. It reasoned that a report of defamatory accusations against a private figure could have a devastating effect on the individual's reputation but would rarely provide information of value in the resolution of a controversy over a matter of public concern.

5. If the media accurately report that the government is investigating plaintiff as a suspect in serious criminal activity, should the accuracy of the report be held to bar defamation liability (if the report is not protected by the common law privilege to report governmental proceedings)? If so, is this because the neutral reportage doctrine or something analogous to it should apply? Should news media in these circumstances be found not at fault, for purpose of the *Gertz* no-liability-without-fault rule, or to have published without reckless disregard for truth, when plaintiff is a public figure or public official? See Donnellan & Peacock, Truth and Consequences: First Amendment Protection for Accurate Reporting on Government Investigations, 50 N.Y. L. Sch. L. Rev. 237 (2005).

6. Has the absence of a recognized neutral reportage privilege substantially hindered the reporting of newsworthy accusations? Would its acceptance undermine the common law maxim that "tale bearers are as bad as tale makers"? Should such a privilege extend to reports by individuals who are outside the news media? See generally Annot., Libel and Slander: Construction and Application of the Neutral Reportage Privilege, 13 A.L.R.6th 111 (2006); Smolla, Law of Defamation §§ 4:96–4:101 (2d ed. 1999); McCraw, The Right To Republish Libel: Neutral Reportage and the Reasonable Reader, 25 Akron L. Rev. 335 (1991).

Milkovich v. Lorain Journal Company

Supreme Court of the United States
497 U.S. 1 (1990)

Chief Justice REHNQUIST delivered the opinion of the Court.

[Milkovich was the wrestling coach at Maple Heights High School. The Ohio High School Athletic Association, following a hearing on an altercation between Milkovich's team and a visiting team, placed the Maple Heights team on probation. This action was challenged in a lawsuit. Milkovich and the local superintendent of schools testified in both the OHSAA hearing and the lawsuit. Milkovich's libel action concerned a newspaper column published on the day after the court issued its decision overturning the OHSAA sanctions. The column, which appeared on the sports page and bore the author's name and photograph, carried the headline "Maple beat the law with the 'big lie.'" It included the passage: "Anyone who attended the [wrestling] meet … knows in his heart that Milkovich and [the superintendent of schools] lied at the hearing after each having given his solemn oath to tell the truth. [¶] But they got away with it."]

[The Ohio courts, in common with numerous other courts, interpreted a passage in *Gertz v. Robert Welch, Inc.* to establish that the First Amendment forbids the imposition of defamation liability for expressions of opinion. This passage, which opens Part III of the Supreme Court's opinion in *Gertz*, states: "We begin with the common ground. Under the First Amendment there is no such thing as a false idea. However pernicious an opinion may seem, we depend for its correction not on the conscience of judges and juries but on the competition of other ideas. But there is no constitutional value in false statements of fact." The Ohio Court of Appeals affirmed the grant of summary judgment to the defendants in Milkovich's action on the ground that the newspaper column was opinion and therefore constitutionally protected from liability.]

… As the common law developed in this country, apart from the issue of damages, one usually needed only allege an unprivileged publication of false and defamatory matter to state a cause of action for defamation. The common law generally did not place any additional restrictions on the type of statement that could be actionable. Indeed, defamatory communications were deemed actionable regardless of whether they were deemed to be statements of fact or opinion. As noted in the 1977 Restatement (Second) of Torts § 566, Comment *a*: "Under the law of defamation, an expression of opinion could be defamatory if the expression was sufficiently derogatory of another as to cause harm to his reputation, so as to lower him in the estimation of the community or to deter third persons from associating or dealing with him.… This position was maintained even though the truth or falsity of an opinion—as distinguished from a statement of fact— is not a matter that can be objectively determined and truth is a complete defense to a suit for defamation."

However, due to concerns that unduly burdensome defamation laws could stifle valuable public debate, the privilege of "fair comment" was incorporated into the common law as an affirmative defense to an action for defamation. "The principle of 'fair comment' afford[ed] legal immunity for the honest expression of opinion on matters of legitimate public interest when based upon a true or privileged statement of fact." 1 F. Harper & F. James, Law of Torts § 5.28, p. 456 (1956).…

Respondents would have us recognize, in addition to the [previously established constitutional safeguards], another First Amendment-based protection for defamatory statements which are categorized as "opinion" as opposed to "fact." For this proposition they rely principally on the … dictum from our opinion in *Gertz* … Judge Friendly appropriately observed that this passage "has become the opening salvo in all arguments for protection from defamation actions on the ground of opinion, even though the case did not remotely concern the question." *Cianci v. New Times Publishing Co.*, 639 F.2d 54, 61 (CA2 1980). Read in context, though, the fair meaning of the passage is to equate the word "opinion" in the second sentence with the word "idea" in the first sentence. Under this view, the language was merely a reiteration of Justice Holmes' classic "marketplace of ideas" concept. See *Abrams v. United States*, 250 U.S. 616, 630 (1919) (Holmes, J., dissenting)

("[T]he ultimate good desired is better reached by free trade in ideas … the best test of truth is the power of the thought to get itself accepted in the competition of the market").

Thus we do not think this passage from *Gertz* was intended to create a wholesale defamation exemption for anything that might be labeled "opinion." See *Cianci, supra*, at 62, n. 10 (The "marketplace of ideas" origin of this passage "points strongly to the view that the 'opinions' held to be constitutionally protected were the sort of thing that could be corrected by discussion"). Not only would such an interpretation be contrary to the tenor and context of the passage, but it would also ignore the fact that expressions of "opinion" may often imply an assertion of objective fact.

If a speaker says, "In my opinion John Jones is a liar," he implies a knowledge of facts which lead to the conclusion that Jones told an untruth. Even if the speaker states the facts upon which he bases his opinion, if those facts are either incorrect or incomplete, or if his assessment of them is erroneous, the statement may still imply a false assertion of fact. Simply couching such statements in terms of opinion does not dispel these implications; and the statement, "In my opinion Jones is a liar," can cause as much damage to reputation as the statement, "Jones is a liar." As Judge Friendly aptly stated: "[I]t would be destructive of the law of libel if a writer could escape liability for accusations of [defamatory conduct] simply by using, explicitly or implicitly, the words 'I think.'" See *Cianci, supra*, at 64. It is worthy of note that at common law, even the privilege of fair comment did not extend to "a false statement of fact, whether it was expressly stated or implied from an expression of opinion." Restatement (Second) of Torts, *supra*, § 566 Comment *a*.

Apart from their reliance on the *Gertz* dictum, respondents do not really contend that a statement such as, "In my opinion John Jones is a liar," should be protected by a separate privilege for "opinion" under the First Amendment. But they do contend that in every defamation case the First Amendment mandates an inquiry into whether a statement is "opinion" or "fact," and that only the latter statements may be actionable. They propose that a number of factors developed by the lower courts (in what we hold was a mistaken reliance on the *Gertz* dictum) be considered in deciding which is which. But we think the "'breathing space'" which "'freedoms of expression require in order to survive,'" [*Philadelphia Newspapers, Inc. v. Hepps*, 475 U.S. 767, 772, quoting *New York Times Co. v. Sullivan*] is adequately secured by existing constitutional doctrine without the creation of an artificial dichotomy between "opinion" and fact.

Foremost, we think *Hepps* stands for the proposition that a statement on matters of public concern must be provable as false before there can be liability under state defamation law, at least in situations, like the present, where a media defendant is involved. Thus, unlike the statement, "In my opinion Mayor Jones is a liar," the statement, "In my opinion Mayor Jones shows his abysmal ignorance by accepting the teachings of Marx and Lenin," would not be actionable. *Hepps* ensures that a statement of opinion relating to matters of public concern which does not contain a provably false factual connotation will receive full constitutional protection.

Next, the *Bresler-Letter Carriers-Falwell* line of cases provide protection for statements that cannot "reasonably[be] interpreted as stating actual facts" about an individual. [*Hustler Magazine, Inc. v. Falwell*, 485 U.S. 46, 50 (1988).] This provides assurance that public debate will not suffer for lack of "imaginative expression" or the "rhetorical hyperbole" which has traditionally added much to the discourse of our Nation.

The *New York Times-Butts* and *Gertz* culpability requirements further ensure that debate on public issues remains "uninhibited, robust, and wide-open." Thus, where a statement of "opinion" on a matter of public concern reasonably implies false and defamatory facts regarding public figures or officials, those individuals must show that such statements were made with knowledge of their false implications or with reckless disregard of their truth. Similarly, where such a statement involves a private figure on a matter of public concern, a plaintiff must show that the false connotations were made with some level of fault as required by *Gertz*. Finally, the enhanced appellate review required by [*Bose Corp. v. Consumers Union of United States, Inc.*, 466 U.S. 485 (1984)] provides assurance that the foregoing determinations will be made in a manner so as not to "constitute a forbidden intrusion of the field of free expression."

We are not persuaded that, in addition to these protections, an additional separate constitutional privilege for "opinion" is required to ensure the freedom of expression guaranteed by the First Amendment. The dispositive question in the present case then becomes whether or not a reasonable factfinder could conclude that the statements in the Diadiun column imply an assertion that petitioner Milkovich perjured himself in a judicial proceeding. We think this question must be answered in the affirmative. As the Ohio Supreme Court itself observed, "the clear impact in some nine sentences and a caption is that [Milkovich] 'lied at the hearing after ... having given his solemn oath to tell the truth.'" This is not the sort of loose, figurative or hyperbolic language which would negate the impression that the writer was seriously maintaining petitioner committed the crime of perjury. Nor does the general tenor of the article negate this impression.

We also think the connotation that petitioner committed perjury is sufficiently factual to be susceptible of being proved true or false. A determination of whether petitioner lied in this instance can be made on a core of objective evidence by comparing, *inter alia*, petitioner's testimony before the OHSAA board with his subsequent testimony before the trial court. [As the Ohio Supreme Court noted in addressing the companion case brought by the school superintendent named in defendants' column] "[w]hether or not H. Don Scott did indeed perjure himself is certainly verifiable by a perjury action with evidence adduced from the transcripts and witnesses present at the hearing. Unlike a subjective assertion the averred defamatory language is an articulation of an objectively verifiable event." ...

[Reversed and remanded. Brennan, J., (with whom Marshall, J., joined) delivered a dissenting opinion. Brennan, J., concluded that the statements in the column could not reasonably be interpreted as stating or implying defamatory facts about Milkovich. The basis of this conclusion was Brennan, J.'s belief that the only reasonable interpretation of the column was that the columnist was engaging in conjecture and speculation, not offering factual information. Therefore, under the principles stated in the majority opinion, the statements in the column were constitutionally protected from liability. Brennan, J., wrote of the importance of conjecture as a means of fueling discourse on matters of public concern and stimulating public pressure for answers from those who have more knowledge. He agreed with the majority's decision that there is no privilege for opinion additional to the First Amendment protections previously established.]

Notes

1. Is the position adopted in *Milkovich* preferable to the proposition that the First Amendment precludes defamation actions for expressions of opinion? Does the Supreme Court's resolution of the issue make much difference to the scope of defamation liability? See McLean, Determining What Constitutes Opinion, 25 Comm. & L. No. 3, 33 (2003); Sowle, A Matter of Opinion: *Milkovich* Four Years Later, 3 Wm. & Mary Bill of Rts. J. 467 (1994). "*Milkovich* issues" are now found in numerous defamation cases. Examples:

(a) A newspaper editorial, endorsing plaintiff's opponent in an election for the state Public Service Commission, states that plaintiff changed his name to a name resembling the governor's, believing he might fool voters into electing him. Collins v. Cox Enterprises, Inc., 215 Ga. App. 679, 452 S.E.2d 226 (1994).

(b) A property appraiser concludes his analysis of another appraiser's report by saying that the data in the report combined to present such a misleading indication of the property's value as to be considered fraudulent. Beattie v. Fleet National Bank, 746 A.2d 717 (R.I. 2000).

(c) Speaking to a reporter about the mother of his child, defendant says that "She's unfit to have a kid." Webster v. Wilkins, 217 Ga. App. 194, 456 S.E.2d 699 (1995).

(d) Defendant says that he suspects a theft was committed by plaintiff. Garrett v. Tandy Corp., 295 F.3d 94 (1st Cir. 2002).

(e) In a telephone conversation, an anesthesiologist states to another physician that plaintiff, also an anesthesiologist, "seemed to set himself up as an expert in pediatric anesthesia," "did not have the full support of the men in the anesthesia group," had a poor reputation as an anesthesiologist, and "didn't meet the standard ... that he should have." Leyba v. Renger, 874 F. Supp. 1218 (D.N.M. 1994).

(f) In a television report on plaintiff's marketing of a $29.95 packet of information and forms for implementing a "living will," it is said that forms needed to implement an effective living will are available free of charge from hospitals and libraries. A medical ethicist states: "I think it's a scam.... [T]hey will send in $29.95 and [be] totally taken." NBC Subsidiary (KCNC-TV), Inc. v. Living Will Center, 879 P.2d 6 (Colo. 1994), cert. denied, 514 U.S. 1051 (1995).

(g) Columns by a newspaper's theatre critic assert that plaintiff's musical production of *Phantom of the Opera* thrived on confusion with the successful Andrew Lloyd Webber production. It is insinuated that the confusion is intentional. One column quotes another critic's description of plaintiff's show as "a rip-off, a fraud, a scandal, a snake-oil job." Phantom Touring, Inc. v. Affiliated Publications, 953 F.2d 724 (1st Cir. 1992), cert. denied, 504 U.S. 974 (1992).

(h) A brokerage firm analyst who follows a drug company's stock reports that the Church of Scientology "and other related special interest groups have, in our opinion been on a vendetta to discredit" a product of the drug company. Church of Scientology International v. Eli Lilly & Co., 778 F. Supp. 661 (S.D.N.Y. 1991).

(i) A directory of attorneys states of one: "At least one plaintiff has described [him] as an 'ambulance chaser' with interest only in 'slam dunk cases.'" Flamm v. American Association of University Women, 201 F.3d 144 (2d Cir. 2000), rev'g 28 F. Supp. 2d 185 (S.D.N.Y. 1998). Compare Sullivan v. Conway, 157 F.3d 1092 (7th Cir. 1998) ("a very poor lawyer").

2. Pre-*Milkovich* cases raising "opinion" issues include:

(a) An employer writes of an employee's discharge: "This termination is for unsatisfactory performance." Adler v. American Standard Corp., 538 F. Supp. 572 (D. Md. 1982). Cf. Hopewell v. Vitullo, 299 Ill. App. 3d 513, 701 N.E.2d 99 (1998), appeal denied, 181 Ill. 2d 571, 706 N.E.2d 496 (1998) ("fired because of incompetence").

(b) A newspaper editorial states that a police sergeant, "who makes Jackie Gleason look diminutive," "carries too much mass to be ... an effective cop on the beat." Caron v. Bangor Publishing Co., 470 A.2d 782 (Me. 1984), cert. denied, 467 U.S. 1241 (1984).

(c) A columnist states that a publisher "runs a newspaper by paranoids for paranoids." Loeb v. Globe Newspaper Co., 489 F. Supp. 481 (D. Mass. 1980).

(d) A newsletter sent by a manufacturer to its distributors states, in reference to a product performance test commissioned by a competitor, "This was a (purposely) very poor test designed to snow the customer." Potomac Valve & Fitting Inc. v. Crawford Fitting Co., 829 F.2d 1280 (4th Cir. 1987).

(e) A magazine article entitled "Best & Worst: Sports" names a television station announcer as the "worst" sports announcer in the city, saying that he is not knowledgeable or serious about coverage and that he is the only newscaster in town "enrolled in a course for remedial speaking." Myers v. Boston Magazine Co., Inc., 380 Mass. 336, 403 N.E.2d 376 (1980).

(f) A newspaper reports an acquaintance's statement that plaintiff "was a smooth talker. He was a con artist. I would never lend him money." Yancey v. Hamilton, 786 S.W.2d 854 (Ky. 1989).

(g) A magazine article states that the founder of a right-wing political group seeks to "destabilize society" and create a climate of fear in order to "seize real political power," and that he exhibits characteristics of "inherent or incipient fascism," including "virulent anti-Semitism," "incessant Red-baiting," "superpatriotism," "a perverted brand of nationalism," "the use of lies and half-truths," "denigration of democracy," and "adulation of Adolf Hitler." Liberty Lobby, Inc. v. Anderson, 241 U.S. App. D.C. 246, 746 F.2d 1563 (1984), rev'd, 477 U.S. 242 (1986).

Would *Milkovich* prevent liability in the cases, pp. 501–504, supra, finding defamation in publications that caused plaintiffs to be ridiculed?

3. Under *Milkovich*, is a person subject to defamation liability when he makes what is clearly a deduction from or speculation about a true fact and the deduction or speculation is provably false? Consider:

(a) Defendant explains plaintiff's intemperate statements by saying "Maybe she has a mental illness." Cf. Capan v. Daugherty, 402 N.W.2d 561 (Minn. App. 1987).

(b) A letter to the editor of a community newspaper states that the town mayor and tax collector, who had repeatedly refused to reveal the names of delinquent property taxpayers, might be engaged in a "huge coverup" or "conspiracy." Kotlikoff v. Community News, 89 N.J. 62, 444 A.2d 1086 (1982).

(c) After a Medical Board employee embezzles a large amount of board funds by cashing checks payable to the board at the Bank of Harrisburg, the board's secretary says, "I'm telling you, the head teller in the Bank of Harrisburg has to be the dumbest, most stupid, ignorant person; or second, there is collusion." Bland v. Verser, 299 Ark. 490, 774 S.W.2d 124 (1989).

(d) Defendant says of plaintiff, "He only got into the fire department because the court made them hire more minorities, so he has to be below their standards." Cf. Jones v. Palmer Communications, Inc., 440 N.W.2d 884 (Iowa 1989).

(e) During the bench trial of a physician for sexual assault, a city councilman says, "That's the best judge money can buy." When the physician is acquitted, the councilman says of the judge, "Do you think he was paid off in cash or cocaine?" The trial was preceded by widespread allegations of misconduct and corruption in the local legal and medical professions. Keohane v. Stewart, 882 P.2d 1293 (Colo. 1994), cert. denied, 513 U.S. 1127 (1995).

4. On the constitutional framework of the law of defamation and some proposed reforms, see LeBel, Reforming the Tort of Defamation: An Accommodation of the Competing Interests Within the Current Constitutional Framework, 66 Neb. L. Rev. 249 (1987). What will be the impact of constitutional developments on common law rules of defamation that have not been explicitly addressed by the Supreme Court? Will courts reformulate common law on such subjects as "unintentional" defamation, slander per se and libel per quod (if not the entire libel/slander distinction), secondary publishers, truth, qualified privileges and damages? Or will courts adhere to traditional law except to the extent that constitutional doctrine requires otherwise?

5. The constitutional law, like the common law, is not without a multitude of critics and proposals for reform. One frequently-made observation is that under the law that now prevails, both sides lose. Although their success with juries is high, plaintiffs ultimately win a very small proportion of defamation suits, and defendants must incur large expenses to avoid falling within that small proportion—even larger than under the common law because of the expenses of an "absence of malice" or "not at fault" defense. Two reforms now prominent in academic circles are provision for recovery of legal fees by successful parties, which would promote settlements as well as protect defendants from the costs of defending suits that have little chance of success, and the establishment of a declaratory judgment procedure, in which persons could clear their names through a judgment that they were defamed falsely, without recovering damages. Consider the constitutional questions that would be presented if these proposals were adopted. See generally Franklin, Good Names and Bad Law: A Critique of Libel Law and a Proposal, 18 U.S.F. L. Rev. 1 (1983); Symposium: New Perspectives in the Law of Defamation, 74 Calif. L. Rev. 677 (1986); Symposium: Libel, 38 Mercer L. Rev. 767 (1987).

Chapter 7

Judicial Process and Civil Rights

Section 1. Malicious Prosecution

Halberstadt v. New York Life Insurance Company

New York Court of Appeals
194 N.Y. 1, 86 N.E. 801 (1909)

The action is brought to recover damages for an alleged malicious prosecution claimed to have been instituted by the respondent against the appellant in Mexico. It is in the complaint, amongst other things, alleged that the respondent through its agent in the criminal court of the city of Mexico charged the appellant with the crime of embezzlement, "and thereupon and in and by virtue of said charge and the institution of said criminal proceedings a warrant was issued by said court for the arrest of the plaintiff (in this action)," and that thereafter "the said criminal proceedings for the punishment of said plaintiff were dismissed and extinguished and the said prosecution was thereby wholly determined ... in favor of the plaintiff." ...

HISCOCK, J....

The respondent's first ... contention is based upon the fact that the complaint does not allege any act subsequent or in addition to the mere issuance of a warrant in the criminal proceeding complained of, does not allege that the warrant was ever executed in any way whatever, or that the appellant was ever actually brought into said proceedings either by force of process or voluntary appearance. Therefore the question is presented whether the mere application for and issuance to a proper officer for execution of a warrant on a criminal charge may institute and constitute such a prosecution as may be made the basis of a subsequent civil action by the party claimed to have been injured. In considering this question, we must keep in mind that the facts alleged in the complaint and in the light of which it is to be determined do not show, as the answer does, that the defendant in those proceedings was beyond the jurisdiction of the court....

... In opposition to what was said in [Heyward v. Cuthbert, 4 McCord (S.C.) 354], the sole foundation for an action of malicious prosecution is not "the wrong to the plaintiff by the direct detention or imprisonment of his person." In an action for false imprisonment that would be so. But in an action of the present type the substantial injury for which damages are recovered and which serves as a basis for the action may be that inflicted upon the feelings, reputation and character by a false accusation as well as that caused by arrest and imprisonment. This element "indeed is in many cases the gravamen of the action." But, no matter how false and damaging the charge may be in a criminal proceeding upon which a warrant may be issued, damages for the injury caused thereby cannot under any ordinary circumstances be recovered in an action for libel or slander. Therefore it follows that a person who has most grievously injured another by falsely making a serious criminal accusation against him whereon a warrant has been actually issued may escape all liability by procuring the warrant at that point to be withheld unless an action for malicious prosecution will lie. It seems to me that under such circumstances we should hold that such action will lie, if for no other reason than to satisfy that principle of law which demands an adequate remedy for every legal wrong.

Deciding, therefore, that the appellant's complaint does state a cause of action, we are brought to the direct consideration of the respondent's answer ... : That the appellant fled from Mexico before the warrant could be served on him for the purpose of avoiding service, and remained out of the country and beyond the jurisdiction of the court for such a length of time that the criminal proceeding was finally dismissed, presumably because prosecution was not and could not be carried on. The question is whether a dismissal or discontinuance of a criminal proceeding under such circumstances is that kind of a termination which will support an action for malicious prosecution. If it is, the answers are bad; otherwise, not. While it is elementary that a criminal proceeding must be terminated before an action for malicious prosecution can be begun, there has been much discussion of the nature of this necessary termination....

... I think two rules fairly may be deduced. The first one is that, where a criminal proceeding has been terminated in favor of the accused by judicial action of the proper court or official in any way involving the merits or propriety of the proceeding or by a dismissal or discontinuance based on some act chargeable to the complainant as his consent or his withdrawal or abandonment of his prosecution, a foundation in this respect has been laid for an action of malicious prosecution. The other and reverse rule is that, where the proceeding has been terminated without regard to its merits or propriety by agreement or settlement of the parties, or solely by the procurement of the accused as a matter of favor or as the result of some act, trick, or device preventing action and consideration by the court, there is no such termination as may be availed of for the purpose of such an action. The underlying distinction which leads to these different rules is apparent. In one case the termination of the proceeding is of such a character as establishes or fairly implies lack of a reasonable ground for his prosecution. In the other case no such implication reasonably follows. When we apply these rules to the defenses which have been pleaded, it is evident that they sufficiently allege a termination of the Mexican proceeding which is not of a character to sustain this action, and ought not to be. That proceeding came to a dismissal and end, not because of any judicial action in favor of the accused for lack of merits or because of a withdrawal or abandonment of it by the prosecuting party, but simply because the defendant therein succeeded in escaping from the country and eluding the jurisdiction of the court and thereby preventing a prosecution. He by his flight, as in other cases the accused had done by agreement, settlement, or trick, prevented a consideration of the merits, and he ought not now to be allowed to claim that there were no merits. In some of the cases refusing to allow the maintenance of such an action as this by a party who had procured a discontinuance of criminal proceedings by settlement, it has been said that the reason for such rule is that such settlement was so far a recognition of the propriety of the proceeding that a party making it is subsequently estopped from questioning them. It may be that the conduct of the present appellant in fleeing from Mexico was discreet or even justifiable by virtue of facts which do not appear to us. At the present time, however, it does not to my mind carry any such presumption of innocence in connection with the termination of the proceedings in that country as impliedly condemns them for having been instituted maliciously and without ground....

[Order overruling plaintiff's demurrer to defendant's answer affirmed.]

VANN, J. [with whom Cullen, C.J., and Willard Bartlett, J., joined]. I concur in the result because there was merely an attempt to prosecute with no actual prosecution. The Mexican court did not acquire jurisdiction of the person of the plaintiff for he was not arrested, nor was process or notice of any kind served upon him. He was not brought into court and the prosecution could not end because it was never begun. He could not be a party defendant until he was notified or voluntarily appeared. He was threatened with prosecution, but neither his person nor his property was touched. There can be no prosecution unless knowledge thereof is brought home to the alleged defendant in some way. If there had been a prosecution commenced, the crime could not have outlawed during the defendant's absence, as is admitted of record....

Notes

1. What must transpire in the criminal proceeding in order for the accused person to have an action for malicious prosecution? The prevailing view is that arrest or imprisonment is not essential to the action. The proceeding need not have advanced to the stage of issuing process to compel the accused's attendance. Injury is found in the charge itself. See Casey v. Automobile Renault Canada, Ltd., [1965] S.C.R. 607, (1965) 54 D.L.R.2d 600, rev'g (1964) 49 M.P.R. 154, 46 D.L.R.2d 665 (N.S. Full Ct.) (for purposes of malicious prosecution action, criminal prosecution considered commenced when information laid before magistrate alleging matters within magistrate's jurisdiction); Restatement (Second) of Torts § 654 (1977); Harper, James & Gray, Law of Torts § 4.3 (3d ed. 1996).

2. Malicious prosecution must be distinguished from false imprisonment (or "false arrest"). The action for malicious prosecution protects the interest in freedom from unjustifiable legal process rather than the interest in freedom from confinement. A false imprisonment action will not lie when there is a valid warrant or other legal authority for the accused's arrest. See Broughton v. State, 37 N.Y.2d 451, 373 N.Y.S.2d 87, 335 N.E.2d 310 (1975), cert. denied sub nom. Schanbarger v. Kellogg, 423 U.S. 929 (1975); Prosser & Keeton, Law of Torts 53–54 (5th ed. 1984). Arrest or imprisonment procured for improper purposes may give rise to liability for abuse of process. See pp. 718–725, infra.

3. Can proceedings for any offense for which there is a penalty be the subject of a malicious prosecution action, or must the charge and potential punishment be of some real seriousness? In Wiffen v. Bailey, [1915] 1 K.B. 600 (C.A.), defendants preferred a complaint against plaintiff for non-compliance with a direction to abate a nuisance. The court rejected plaintiff's malicious prosecution action, reasoning that while a fine might have been imposed, plaintiff had not been put in peril of losing his liberty and had not suffered harm to his reputation ("fair fame"). Compare Restatement (Second) of Torts § 654, comment *a* (1977) (proceeding for any offense involving "penalty of a criminal character," including minor traffic violation, qualifies). A proceeding that does not threaten plaintiff's reputation or liberty might be actionable on the same basis as malicious civil prosecution if the required damage is shown. See Berry v. British Transport Commission, [1962] 1 Q.B. 306 (C.A.), rev'g [1961] 1 Q.B. 149 (prosecution for pulling communication cord on passenger train without reasonable cause).

4. To maintain a malicious prosecution action, plaintiff must show that the underlying criminal action terminated in his favor. An unreversed conviction will preclude recovery for malicious prosecution. Impeachment of such a conviction, as by showing fraud or perjury, is not allowed. See Turbessi v. Oliver Iron Mining Co., 250 Mich. 110, 229 N.W. 454 (1930); Annot., Unreversed Conviction as Conclusive in Action for Malicious Prosecution, 69 A.L.R. 1062 (1930). When the accused was convicted but the conviction was reversed or set aside, the conviction is usually held to establish that there was probable cause for the prosecution, which defeats the tort claim. See p. 697, infra. If plaintiff was charged with more than one offense, arising from the same incident, and a conviction was obtained only for one charge, may plaintiff sue for malicious prosecution of the other charge(s)? See Janetka v. Dabe, 892 F.2d 187 (2d Cir. 1989); Cuthrell v. Zayre of Virginia, Inc., 214 Va. 427, 201 S.E.2d 779 (1974) (conviction for disorderly conduct not bar to action for malicious prosecution of more serious charge); Kossler v. Crisanti, 564 F.3d 181 (3d Cir. 2009) (acquittal on felony assault charge not favorable termination when accused convicted for disorderly conduct on account of "same course of conduct"); Pugach v. Borja, 175 Misc. 2d 683, 670 N.Y.S.2d 718 (Sup. Ct. 1998) (conviction on one harassment count barred action for malicious prosecution of other charges of harassment and abuse of same person).

5. Dismissal of charges by a magistrate for inadequacy or lack of evidence is usually held to satisfy the termination requirement, at least when new proceedings for the same offense are not pending. See Jaffe v. Stone, 18 Cal. 2d 121, 114 P.2d 335 (1941) (dismissal at preliminary hearing); Waldron v. Sperry, 53 W. Va. 116, 44 S.E. 283 (1903) (state's witness did not appear); Annot., Dismissal by Magistrate or Other Inferior Court for Lack or Insufficiency of Evidence as a Final Termination of Prosecution as Regards Action for Malicious Prosecution, 135 A.L.R. 784 (1941). Dismissal because a district attorney did not proceed with a prosecution may leave the private citizen who initiated the charges open to a malicious prosecution suit. See Wynne v. Rosen, 391 Mass. 797, 464 N.E.2d 1348 (1984); Loeb v. Teitelbaum, 77 A.D.2d 92, 432 N.Y.S.2d 487 (1980), amended, 80 A.D.2d 838, 439 N.Y.S.2d 300 (1981).

6. Is discharge of the accused by writ of habeas corpus a termination that supports a malicious prosecution action? Some cases hold that it is, reasoning that the discharge effectively puts an end to the prosecution and that action by a judge should not be given less effect than discharge by a magistrate. See Millar v. Sollitt, 131 Ill. App. 196 (1907); Zebley v. Storey, 117 Pa. 478, 12 A. 569 (1888). Cf. Nzekwu v. Onowu, (1928) 9 Nig. L. Rep. 70 (Div. Ct.) (native court tried accused for one offense, convicted him of another; released by Supreme Court on habeas corpus; native court said to have exceeded jurisdiction). A larger number of cases hold that it is not, especially when subsequent action on the criminal charge, such as consideration by a grand jury, is possible. See Walker v. Martin, 43 Ill. 508 (1867); Hinds v. Parker, 11 App. Div. 327, 42 N.Y.S. 955 (1896). Cf. Cowan v. Gamble, 247 S.W.2d 779 (Mo. 1952) (discharge of person held for prosecution in another state). See generally Annot., Discharge in Habeas Corpus Proceedings as Constituting Favorable Termination of Criminal Proceedings Requisite to Maintenance of Malicious Prosecution Action, 30 A.L.R.2d 1128 (1953).

7. If criminal charges against the accused are dismissed as a result of a compromise by the parties, does this constitute a "termination in favor of the accused"? It is generally held that such a settlement, often not based on the merits of the prosecution, does not fulfill the termination requirement. See Leonard v. George, 178 F.2d 312 (4th Cir. 1949), cert. denied, 339 U.S. 965 (1950); Joiner v. Benton Community Bank, 82 Ill. 2d 40, 411 N.E.2d 229 (1980); Annot., Termination of Criminal Proceedings as Result of Compro-

mise or Settlement of Accused's Civil Liability as Precluding Malicious Prosecution Action, 26 A.L.R.4th 565 (1983); Restatement (Second) of Torts § 660 (1977). This assumes that the settlement was voluntarily and understandingly made. See Gowin v. Heider, 237 Or. 266, 386 P.2d 1 (1963), modified on reh'g, 237 Or. 306, 391 P.2d 630 (1964) (dismissal pursuant to agreement made under duress—detention in jail—not bar to action). Should an agreed disposition of criminal charges bar a malicious prosecution action? Van Heeren v. Cooper, [1999] 1 N.Z.L.R. 731 (C.A.), decided that a malicious prosecution action could be brought following dismissal or withdrawal of the charge as a result of compromise, unless there had been a finding of guilt.

8. Is it an element of the favorable termination requirement that the termination be for reasons having an implication that plaintiff was not guilty of the criminal charge? This is required by some decisions. See Swick v. Liautaud, 169 Ill. 2d 504, 662 N.E.2d 1238 (1996) (abandonment of prosecution not favorable termination when reason not "indicative of the innocence of the accused"); Bearden v. BellSouth Telecommunications, Inc., 29 So. 3d 761 (Miss. 2010) (dismissal of criminal case for lack of jurisdiction not favorable termination). Other decisions require only that the termination be consistent with plaintiff's being innocent. See Smith-Hunter v. Harvey, 95 N.Y.2d 191, 712 N.Y.S.2d 438, 734 N.E.2d 750 (2000), holding that dismissal of criminal proceedings because of statutory speedy trial requirements was a favorable termination. It was noted that a contrary decision would require a person who was improperly charged to waive speedy trial rights and go to trial in order to have a civil remedy. Compare Martinez v. City of Schenectady, 97 N.Y.2d 78, 735 N.Y.S.2d 868, 761 N.E.2d 560 (2001), in which plaintiff's conviction was reversed because evidence had been obtained under a faulty search warrant. Holding that there was no favorable termination, the court reasoned that plaintiff's conviction was not reversed because of a lack of culpability.

9. Defendant obtains a warrant for the search of plaintiff's premises, alleging that contraband or stolen property is concealed there. Can this be a basis for a malicious prosecution action? Cases indicate that it can be, but how is the requirement of favorable termination to be applied? See Carey v. Sheets, 67 Ind. 375 (1879); Spangler v. Booze, 103 Va. 276, 49 S.E. 42 (1904); Gibbs v. Rea, [1998] A.C. 786 (P.C.), recognizing malicious prosecution of a search warrant as a distinct tort. The favorable termination rule is not applied when the prosecution took the form of ex parte proceedings, since the accused normally had no opportunity to contest the truth of the complaint. See Lanterman v. Delaware, Lackawanna & Western Railroad Co., 229 F. 770 (D.N.J. 1916) (plaintiff, permitted to contest sufficiency but not truth of complaint, required to give bail); Fleming, Law of Torts 700 (10th ed. 2011).

Fusario v. Cavallaro

Supreme Court of Errors of Connecticut
108 Conn. 40, 142 A. 391 (1928)

HINMAN, J.

[Cavallaro was assaulted by Frank Fusario. Frank's brother, Joseph, was not present at the time, and shortly after the assault Cavallaro told a policeman that Frank, not Joseph, committed it. Later, however, as a result of statements made to the police by a Mrs. De Felice, Joseph was arrested on a charge of breach of the peace. Subsequently, a charge of assault with intent to disfigure was added. Cavallaro was present in court during the several continuances of the case. At Joseph's trial, Cavallaro falsely testified that Joseph held him while Frank bit off Cavallaro's nose. Joseph was acquitted. On the day the criminal case first came up in the city court, Cavallaro commenced suit against Joseph and Frank for assault and battery (arising out of the same facts). At the trial of the civil action, Cavallaro testified substantially as he had in the criminal case. Judgment was rendered against Frank but for Joseph. Joseph sued Cavallaro for malicious prosecution of the criminal case and was given judgment, from which Cavallaro appealed.]

The three essential elements of an action for malicious prosecution, the discharge of the plaintiff, want of probable cause, and malice, are unmistakably present upon the facts found. The general inquiry presented by the appeal is whether the defendant's connection with, and conduct pertaining to, the prosecution were such as to render him liable.

The defendant claimed, upon the trial, that, since he did not prefer the charge against the plaintiff, or cause or bring about the prosecution, he could not be held liable. This contention is disposed of by our recent holding that not only one who actually procures or causes such a prosecution, but all who knowingly aid, abet, assist in, or adopt, the same, are liable, as joint tort-feasors, for the damage done. McGann v. Allen [105 Conn. 177, 185, 134 A. 810]....

The further contention of the appellant is that the acts and conduct of the defendant, as revealed by the finding, are insufficient to support the trial court's conclusions that he knowingly aided, abetted, and assisted in the prosecution of false charges against the [plaintiff] and adopted them as his own. The finding indicates that the defendant's presence in the city court as a witness was under subpoena, so that, technically, his appearance may be said not to have been voluntary. It is found, however, that he knew that the plaintiff did not participate in the assault, nor was he present at the time. Therefore his testimony to the contrary was voluntarily false. His prompt utilization of the charge embraced in the criminal prosecution as the basis for a civil action was likewise voluntary.

The proposition chiefly relied on is that the giving of false testimony in the criminal case does not constitute an aiding and abetting in causing or procuring the prosecution; but liability is not confined to so narrow a ground. If, after proceedings have been commenced, parties voluntarily conspire and maliciously join in the prosecution without probable cause, they may be held liable. Voluntary and active "countenance and approbation" of the maintenance of a malicious prosecution involves liability.

This case is not within the scope or reason of the general rule that an action will not lie in favor of a party, against whom a judgment is rendered in a case, against one who gave false testimony on the trial. In McClarty v. Bickel, 155 Ky. 254, 159 S.W. 783, the case primarily relied upon by the appellant, it was held that a civil suit for malicious prosecution will not lie for the giving of false testimony to aid in securing the conviction of the accused, on the ground that it must appear that the party sought to be charged was the proximate cause of putting the law in motion, and there is no analogy between the making of false statements causing a party to be arrested and false testimony in court against a party already arrested and on trial. This appears to ignore the element of subsequent adoption or ratification which characterizes the general rule. However, liability in the present case is not dependent upon the element of perjured testimony alone. Combined with and characterizing this is the course of conduct of the defendant in seizing upon the criminal charge against the plaintiff, which he, above all others, knew to be groundless, as the basis of a civil suit. The trial court was justified in its finding that the defendant so aided, abetted, and adopted the prosecution as to render him liable.

There is no error.

Notes

1. In general, passive conduct is not a sufficient basis for a malicious prosecution action. The defendant must have been active in the initiation or continuance of the criminal proceeding. See McNamara v. Pabst, 137 Md. 468, 112 A. 812 (1921); Annot., Defendant's Acquiescence in, Approval of, or Silence Regarding, Acts of Another for Which He Was Not Otherwise Responsible as Ground of Liability in Action for Malicious Prosecution or False Arrest, 120 A.L.R. 1322 (1939). On potential liability when a police officer or public prosecutor initiates prosecution in response to a complaint by defendant, see the next principal case. Malicious prosecution is an intentional tort. If a person has negligently caused another to be prosecuted, the proper action, if any, is one for negligence. See Collins v. City National Bank & Trust Co. of Danbury, 131 Conn. 167, 38 A.2d 582 (1944) (bank erroneously returned check cashed by plaintiff with notation "no account," causing arrest for obtaining money by false pretenses); Firstley v. Bill Watson Ford, Inc., 268 So. 2d 314 (La. App. 1972) (automobile dealer had plaintiff use demonstrator car which dealer had reported stolen and never reported recovered). Some courts have rejected the proposition that there is an action for negligently causing prosecution. Wilson v. O'Neal, 118 So. 2d 101 (Fla. App. 1960), appeal dismissed, 123 So. 2d 677 (Fla. 1960), cert. denied, 365 U.S. 850 (1961); Bromond v. Holt, 24 Wis. 2d 336, 129 N.W.2d 149 (1964). What if defendant caused prosecution by committing the crime of which plaintiff was suspected? Compare Diminnie v. United States, 522 F. Supp. 1192 (E.D. Mich. 1981), aff'd, 728 F.2d 301 (6th Cir. 1984), cert. denied, 469 U.S. 842 (1984) (defendant confessed to writing extortion letters after plaintiff's conviction; no action), with Seidel v. Greenberg, 108 N.J. Super. 248, 260 A.2d 863 (Law Div. 1969) (persons who intentionally caused fire on company's property could be liable to company's key employee, prosecuted for fire). Under Restatement (Second) of Torts § 871A (1979), it can be a tort to intentionally create criminal liability.

2. Various theories of liability might be raised by a person claiming to have suffered damage as a result of the presentation of false evidence—not only malicious prosecution, but also defamation, injurious falsehood, deceit, invasion of privacy and interference with contractual or business relations. Almost all authority agrees that there is no cause of action in tort for harm caused by perjury or other false testimony, either in open court or in depositions or affidavits. Testimony is absolutely privileged as to liability for defamation. See pp. 577–582, supra. Given that a witness is not liable for harm caused by false testimony as such, under what circumstances can a witness be held liable for malicious prosecution? Persons making affidavits of criminal complaint have been considered sufficiently active in instigation of the prosecution to incur liability. Otherwise, witnesses are not held liable unless they testified on their own initiative rather than in response to the prosecution's request. The testimony is admissible and may constitute a basis of liability if, taken with other circumstances, it shows that defendant instituted or continued an action against plaintiff maliciously and without probable cause. See Hall v. Adams, 128 Ark. 116, 193 S.W. 520 (1917); Fitzjohn v. Mackinder, (1861) 9 C.B.N.S. 505, 142 Eng. Rep. 199, 7 Jur. N.S. 1283, 25 J.P. 244, 30 L.J.C.P. 257, 4 L.T. 149, 9 W.R. 477 (Ex. Ch.). See generally Annots., Testimony of Witness as Basis of Civil Action for Damages, 12 A.L.R. 1247 (1921); 54 A.L.R.2d 1298 (1957).

3. In order to ensure independence of action and freedom from fear of liability, judges have been held immune from liability for malicious prosecution (or abuse of process), so long as they act within their jurisdiction. A few cases have held liable judges acting from corrupt motives. See Annot., Civil Liability of Judicial Officer for Malicious Prosecution or Abuse of Process, 64 A.L.R.3d 1251 (1975). In most of the United States, prosecuting attorneys have an absolute immunity from liability for initiation and participating in judicial proceedings. See Buckley v. Fitzsimmons, 509 U.S. 259 (1993); Brown v. Dayton Hudson Corp., 314 N.W.2d 210 (Minn. 1981). Contra, Nelles v. The Queen in Right of Ontario, [1989] 2 S.C.R. 170, (1989) 60 D.L.R.4th 609. A more qualified immunity is usually accorded such law enforcement officers as policemen, marshals, sheriffs and F.B.I. agents acting within the scope of their employment. See Annot., Civil Liability of Law Enforcement Officers for Malicious Prosecution, 28 A.L.R.2d 646 (1953). Apart from possible immunity, it has been found that a local government cannot be liable for malicious prosecution because it cannot entertain the requisite malicious intent, or because its officers and employees cannot be regarded as its agents in performing the acts in question. See Neighbors v. City of Birmingham, 384 So. 2d 113 (Ala. 1980); McIntosh v. City and County of Denver, 98 Colo. 403, 55 P.2d 1337 (1936); Annot., Liability of Municipality or Other Political Unit for Malicious Prosecution, 103 A.L.R. 1512 (1936).

Gustafson v. Payless Drug Stores Northwest, Inc.

Supreme Court of Oregon
269 Or. 354, 525 P.2d 118 (1974)

DENECKE, Justice.

The plaintiff was acquitted of a criminal charge of shoplifting. She brought this malicious prosecution action, the jury awarded her damages and the defendant, Payless Drug Stores, appeals.

The principal assignment of error is that the trial court erred in denying the defendant's motion for directed verdict. Payless urges that the trial court erred in this regard because Payless had probable cause to prosecute plaintiff. Proof of probable cause is a complete defense to the action. [The court had adopted Restatement, Torts § 662:] "One who initiates criminal proceedings against another has probable cause for so doing if he (a) reasonably believes that the person accused has acted or failed to act in a particular manner, and (b)(i) correctly believes that such acts or omissions constitute at common law or under an existing statute the offense charged against the accused, or (ii) mistakenly so believes in reliance on the advice of counsel...."

For the defendant to have probable cause it must have both a reasonable belief in the guilt of the accused as well as a subjective belief.

Whether the defendant had probable cause to institute the criminal proceeding is a matter for the court to decide and not the jury.... "If the facts or inferences are in dispute the jury must decide the facts and the court must instruct the jury what facts constitute probable cause." [Varner v. Hoffer, 267 Or. 175, 515 P.2d 920 (1973).] ... [I]nstructing on the issue of probable cause is very difficult when the jury can find a number of different fact combinations. Another possible procedure is to settle the factual disputes by having the jury answer special interrogatories....

The evidence is as follows:

The plaintiff and her husband live in California and were visiting relatives in Salem. Plaintiff and her elderly mother-in-law went to the defendant's store to shop. They purchased a bulky swing set and then separated. The mother-in-law looked in one part of the store for a gift and the plaintiff went to another area of the store to pick up film. After plaintiff picked up her film she could not find her mother-in-law so she went up and down several aisles in search of her. While so doing, plaintiff came under the scrutiny of Mrs. Yaw, defendant's security officer, although plaintiff did nothing to excite Mrs. Yaw's suspicion. Mrs. Yaw stayed at a distance and followed plaintiff.

Plaintiff came to a counter containing cartons of cigarettes for sale. She picked up a carton in the manner of an ordinary shopper without putting it in her purse or in another bag she was carrying. At all times thereafter, she carried it so that it was visible. She found her mother-in-law who had selected a pants suit for purchase. The mother-in-law paid for the clothing and the plaintiff attempted to pay for the cigarettes; however, the cashier-checker told her she would have to go to a cash register in another part of the store to pay. Mrs. Yaw witnessed all of this and knew what transpired.

Plaintiff and her mother-in-law went back to the variety section passing the wrong way through a line of check-out counters. The mother-in-law could not find what she was looking for. As they shopped the two had an intense discussion over who should pay for the item previously purchased. Plaintiff became aware that the time had arrived when her husband was to meet them in the parking lot with his pickup. Plaintiff and her mother-in-law walked toward the door of the store by a normal route. They were not required to pass through any check-out counters to get to the store exit.

Plaintiff and her mother-in-law remained right outside the door for about five minutes continuing their conversation. Plaintiff's husband drove up, parked nearby and opened the tailgate of his pickup in order to load the swing set. Plaintiff hurried to the truck, dumped all of her packages, including the carton of cigarettes, in the truck bed and turned to go back toward the store to help load the swing set. At this point Mrs. Yaw stepped up to her and said, "There's something there that you forgot to pay for." Plaintiff exclaimed, "Oh my God, the cigarettes," and apologized profusely and told Mrs. Yaw she and her mother-in-law were talking so much she forgot about the cigarettes. Mrs. Yaw said that she should come back in and pay for them. When she got into the store Mrs. Yaw ordered plaintiff to go upstairs into a small room where she told plaintiff she was being arrested for shoplifting. Mrs. Yaw called a police officer who took plaintiff to the police station.

Defendant contradicted this evidence in three particulars. Mrs. Yaw testified that before plaintiff went out of the store she passed through a manned check-stand by walking around the people in line. Mrs. Yaw also testified that Mrs. Gustafson placed the cigarettes on the extreme left side of the bed of the pickup away from her other packages. She also testified that when she accosted Mrs. Gustafson, the plaintiff casually said, "I must have forgotten" and plaintiff did not appear flustered and apologetic.

As to Mrs. Yaw's conclusion that plaintiff attempted to hide the cigarettes when plaintiff put them in the bed of the pickup, we find such a conclusion unreasonable and not warranted by what Mrs. Yaw testified she saw. The evidence is uncontradicted that the tailgate of the pickup was down, the objects on the bed of the pickup were plainly visible and the cigarettes were lying not more than a foot from the other objects plaintiff placed in the pickup.

Assuming that the defendant's version of what occurred is correct on the other two disputed issues, we, nevertheless, hold that the plaintiff proved lack of probable cause....

"'Probable cause,' of course, is not grounds that carry conviction of guilt beyond a reasonable doubt, but they must do more than to create a mere suspicion or suggestion of guilt." 1 Harper and James, Law of Torts, 311, §4.5.

Ordinarily, a storekeeper will have probable cause to believe a customer is shoplifting if the essential facts are that the customer took merchandise and walked out of the store without paying for the merchandise.... We find, however, that in the present case there are significant additional details. After the plaintiff picked up the cigarettes she never concealed or attempted to conceal them. Plaintiff tendered payment to an employee at a check-stand. Plaintiff had an almost constant conversation with her mother-in-law as she walked through various parts of the store. Plaintiff waited immediately outside the store for five minutes engaging in further conversation. Mrs. Yaw was aware of this conduct.

We admit that a subtle shoplifter could dispel suspicion by offering to pay at a check-stand where she knew her offer would not be accepted and by walking around a store carrying the merchandise she intended to steal in plain view. We are of the opinion, however, that the odds that a person so conducting herself is a shoplifter are so slight that this conduct, plus the other circumstances here present, does not amount to probable cause.

Admittedly, this evidence presents a close question, as the presence of the dissenting opinion indicates. With the choice of deciding either that there was or there was not probable cause, we find the evidence preponderates to a decision that there was not probable cause.

Payless also contends it had probable cause because it acted upon the advice of the deputy district attorney.

The evidence was that Mrs. Yaw and plaintiff and her husband talked to the police officer summoned by Mrs. Yaw. The officer wrote down a summary report of what he had been told. A deputy district attorney read the officer's report and signed a shoplifting complaint against plaintiff.

From these facts it is evident that Payless did nothing upon the advice of the deputy district attorney. However, the action of the deputy district attorney is relevant upon another contention of Payless; that is, that Payless did not cause the prosecution of plaintiff, rather, the prosecution was instituted as a result of the investigation of the police officer and the decision of the deputy district attorney.

We have frequently said that the test of whether the defendant instigated the prosecution is, "'was defendant actively instrumental in putting the law in force?.... To impose liability there must be some affirmative action by way of advice, encouragement, etc.'" [Meyer v. Nedry, 159 Or. 62, 68, 78 P.2d 339, 341 (1938).] ...

[Humbert v. Knutson, 224 Or. 133, 354 P.2d 826 (1960)] held as a matter of law that the defendant did not institute the criminal proceeding. We based our decision upon the ground that the defendant accurately gave all the necessary information to the police who, in turn, made an independent investigation. The defendant left the decision whether to prosecute entirely to the law enforcement officers.

In the present case, Mrs. Yaw arrested plaintiff and called for a police officer to take plaintiff to be booked. Mrs. Yaw signed a form and gave it to the officer "demanding" that the officer "conduct this person whom I have arrested to the nearest magistrate to be dealt with according to law" and further stating, "I will then and there sign, under oath, the appropriate complaint against this person for the offense which this person has committed...." This must be coupled with the fact that the jury could have found that Mrs. Yaw did not supply the deputy district attorney, through the police officer, with all the material facts. Comment g. to § 653, Restatement, Torts, states: " ... In order to charge a private person with responsibility for the initiation of proceedings by a public official, it must therefore appear that his desire to have the proceedings initiated expressed by direction, request, or pressure of any kind was the determining factor in the official's decision to commence the prosecution or that the information furnished by him upon which the official acted was known to be false."

The same rule applies if the private person knowingly fails to furnish information which the jury could find the private person knew was material to action by the official.

In the present case the jury could find that Mrs. Yaw did not inform the officer that plaintiff attempted to pay for the cigarettes but the defendant's cashier would not accept the tender; that plaintiff at all times carried the cigarettes throughout the store so that they were visible; or that plaintiff stood outside the store with the cigarettes for five minutes. The deputy district attorney was not aware of these facts when he signed the complaint.

With this evidence it was for the jury to decide whether defendant caused the prosecution.

Defendant also contends it was entitled to a directed verdict because there was no evidence of malice. Malice is an essential ingredient of the action of malicious prosecution.

Malice, unlike probable cause, is a question for the jury....

We consistently have held that the jury may make a finding of malice based upon lack of probable cause....

In the present case we hold the lack of probable cause was sufficient evidence of malice upon the part of the defendant to enable the jury to find for plaintiff.

Defendant also contends that the trial court erred in denying its motion for a new trial upon the ground that the damages awarded, approximately $36,000, including $25,000 punitive, were excessive and were given under the influence of passion, sympathy and prejudice. The trial court did not err in this regard.

[Affirmed. Holman, J., (with whom Bryson and Langtry, JJ., joined) delivered a dissenting opinion.]

Notes

1. When a private citizen causes the initiation of criminal proceedings by giving information about alleged criminal activity to a law enforcement officer or other public official, is the citizen considered to have caused the proceedings? Usually not, when a public official makes an independent decision to initiate the proceedings, even though the decision is based on the information. An exception is made when the source of the information knew it was false, on the rationale that the source procured the prosecution by means of the false information and there was no independent exercise of discretion by the official who initiated the proceedings. See Browning-Ferris Industries, Inc. v. Lieck, 881 S.W.2d 288 (Tex. 1994); Martin v. Watson, [1996] A.C. 74 (H.L.); Restatement (Second) of Torts § 653, comments *d–g* (1977).

2. Lack of probable cause is often regarded as the key element of the malicious prosecution action. The existence of probable cause depends not on the accused's guilt or innocence, but on the belief of the person prosecuting and the reasonableness of that belief. Opinion is divided on whether the prosecutor must actually and reasonably believe that the accused is guilty, or whether the standard is reasonable belief in probable guilt (or strong suspicion of guilt), sufficient to warrant institution of criminal proceedings. See

Prosser & Keeton, Law of Torts 876–877 (5th ed. 1984); A v. New South Wales, (2007) 230 C.L.R. 500. Failure to exercise due care in investigating a charge is not equivalent to lack of probable cause, for the prosecutor may nonetheless have reasonably believed, on the basis of the evidence before him, in the accused's guilt. See Singh v. MacDonald, 55 Utah 541, 188 P. 631 (1920). What if it appears at the time the prosecution was launched that the accused had committed a crime, but information obtained subsequently makes this doubtful? See Blunk v. Atchison, Topeka & Santa Fe Railroad Co., 38 F. 311 (C.C.W.D. Mo. 1889); Restatement (Second) of Torts § 662, comment *f* (1977). See generally Annot., Necessity and Sufficiency of Allegations in Complaint for Malicious Prosecution or Tort Action Analogous Thereto That Defendant or Defendants Acted Without Probable Cause, 14 A.L.R.2d 264 (1950).

3. Is there probable cause for prosecution if the prosecutor's belief about what the accused did was correct or reasonable, but the prosecutor's belief that this constituted the crime charged was erroneous? One position is that the prosecutor lacks probable cause if the prosecution is based upon an erroneous belief about the law, however reasonable, unless the prosecutor is acting on the advice of legal counsel. Another position is that a reasonable but mistaken belief about the law stands on the same footing as a reasonable but mistaken belief about the facts. See Harper, James & Gray, Law of Torts § 4.5, at 4:27–4:28 (3d ed. 1996); Prosser & Keeton, Law of Torts 877–878 (5th ed. 1984). If the latter view is adopted, in what circumstances would a non-lawyer have probable cause for instituting a prosecution without first obtaining legal advice? See Restatement (Second) of Torts § 662, comment *i* (1977).

4. If a person relies on the advice of a public prosecutor in instigating a criminal action, is there necessarily probable cause? See South Arkansas Petroleum Co. v. Schiesser, 343 Ark. 492, 36 S.W.3d 317 (2001); Carbaugh v. Peat, 40 Ill. App. 2d 37, 189 N.E.2d 14 (1963) (liability where it could be found that defendant did not fully and fairly state relevant facts to prosecuting attorney); Annot., Reliance on Advice of Prosecuting Attorney as Defense to Malicious Prosecution Action, 10 A.L.R.2d 1215 (1950) (usually probable cause if full and fair disclosure made to prosecuting officer, who then advised prosecution, and acted on officer's advice in good faith). Reliance upon a private attorney's advice is similarly treated. The weight of authority is that reliance upon the advice of other persons who might be thought to know the law, such as magistrates, court clerks and police officers, does not exclude liability. See Annot., Malicious Prosecution: Defense of Acting on Advice of Justice of the Peace, Magistrate, or Lay Person, 48 A.L.R.4th 250 (1986).

5. The jury's function in malicious prosecution actions is more limited than in most civil actions. It is believed that juries may not be able to divorce the question of the plaintiff's innocence from the question of the defendant's fault. Consequently, the issue of probable cause in most jurisdictions is decided by the court, not the jury. However, questions concerning specific elements of probable cause, such as defendant's knowledge of the facts and actual belief in the accused person's guilt, are submissible to the jury. Thus, probable cause is sometimes said to be a mixed question of law and fact. See Palmer Ford, Inc. v. Wood, 298 Md. 484, 471 A.2d 297 (1984); Staley v. Rife, 109 W. Va. 701, 156 S.E. 113 (1930); Annot., Probable Cause or Want Thereof, in Malicious Prosecution Action, As Question of Law for Court or of Fact for Jury, 87 A.L.R.2d 183 (1963).

6. It often has been held that the accused's possession of recently stolen property is probable cause for regarding him as the thief. See Annot., Malicious Prosecution: Possession of Stolen Property as Probable Cause, 172 A.L.R. 1340 (1948). In Richey v. Brookshire Grocery Co., 952 S.W.2d 515 (Tex. 1997), plaintiff had been charged with theft of a pack

of cigarettes from a grocery store. He had put the cigarettes in his pocket and walked out of the store without paying for them—inadvertently he claimed—while paying for a large amount of groceries and making a sizeable donation to the store's charity bin. The jury found him not guilty after deliberating only a few minutes. On appeal from a judgment in his favor against the store for malicious prosecution, the majority of a closely-divided court concluded that plaintiff's taking concealed merchandise out of the store without payment made it reasonable to believe that plaintiff was guilty of theft, without more investigation of whether he had an intent to steal the cigarettes, and therefore established probable cause for the prosecution. Probable cause may be absent if a reasonable explanation is given by the possessor or if a substantial time has passed since the theft. See Grimes v. Greenblatt, 47 Colo. 495, 107 P. 1111 (1910) (accused was junk dealer); Dorsey v. Winters, 143 Md. 399, 122 A. 257 (1923) (two weeks had elapsed and accused promptly explained possession). On whether delivery of an insufficient-funds check constitutes probable cause for a "bad check" charge, see Dunn v. Alabama Oil & Gas Co., 42 Tenn. App. 108, 299 S.W.2d 25 (1956).

7. An unreversed conviction not only shows no termination of the proceedings in favor of the accused but also conclusively establishes probable cause. See Annot., Unreversed Conviction as Conclusive in Action for Malicious Prosecution, 69 A.L.R. 1062 (1930). Even when the conviction has been reversed, it is often treated as establishing probable cause. This might be rebutted by evidence that the conviction was obtained by fraud, perjury or other corrupt means. See Desmond v. Fawcett, 226 Mass. 100, 115 N.E. 280 (1917); Hanson v. City of Snohomish, 121 Wash. 2d 552, 852 P.2d 295 (1993); Annot., Right of Plaintiff in Malicious Prosecution to Impeach for Fraud or Unfair Means Conviction in Lower Court Which Was Reversed or Dismissed on Appeal, 97 A.L.R. 1022 (1935); Annot., Conclusiveness, as Evidence of Probable Cause in Malicious Prosecution Action, of Conviction as Affected by the Fact That It Was Reversed or Set Aside, 86 A.L.R.2d 1090 (1962). What if conviction by a municipal court is reversed after trial de novo by a superior court? See Wisniski v. Ong, 94 Ariz. 123, 382 P.2d 233 (1953) (petty theft conviction in city court established probable cause despite acquittal upon trial de novo); Sundeen v. Kroger, 355 Ark. 138, 133 S.W.3d 393 (2003) (municipal court conviction conclusive of probable cause despite entitlement to trial de novo). But see Lind v. Schmid, 67 N.J. 255, 337 A.2d 365 (1975) (restaurant patrons prosecuted for obtaining food with intent to defraud; municipal magistrate decided case on irrelevant findings, with no finding of intent to defraud; conviction held not to show probable cause).

8. When the accused is committed or held to bail by a magistrate, this usually constitutes evidence (not conclusive) of probable cause. See Gallucci v. Milavic, 100 So. 2d 375 (Fla. 1958); Penton v. Canning, 57 Wyo. 390, 118 P.2d 1002 (1941); Annot., Malicious Prosecution: Commitment, Binding Over, or Holding for Trial by Examining Magistrate or Commissioner as Evidence of Probable Cause, 68 A.L.R.2d 1168 (1959). Indictment of the accused by a grand jury is also evidence of probable cause. See Wilkinson v. McGhee, 265 Mo. 574, 178 S.W. 471 (1915); Hill v. Rhode Island State Employees' Retirement Board, 935 A.2d 608 (R.I. 2007); Annot., Malicious Prosecution: Effect of Grand Jury Indictment on Issue of Probable Cause, 28 A.L.R.3d 748 (1969). Such evidence can be rebutted by a showing of fraud or perjury. See Freides v. Sani-Mode Manufacturing Co., 33 Ill. 2d 291, 211 N.E.2d 286 (1965); Jones v. Jenkins, 3 Wash. 17, 27 P. 1022 (1891).

9. Does acquittal of the accused establish that there was no cause for instigation of the proceedings? Generally, acquittal is not considered even prima face evidence of a lack of probable cause. See Randleman v. Boeres, 93 Cal. App. 745, 270 P. 374 (1928). On the other hand, discharge by a magistrate, or refusal of a grand jury to indict, usually is ad-

missible. See Stouts Mountain Coal Co. v. Grubb, 217 Ala. 274, 116 So. 156 (1928); Lowther v. Metzker, 69 Idaho 115, 203 P.2d 604 (1949). It is thought that abandonment of the prosecution at the instance of the prosecuting attorney or complaining witness is no evidence of lack of probable cause. See Norvell v. Safeway Stores, Inc., 212 Md. 14, 128 A.2d 591 (1957). Contrary decisions on all these points can be found. See generally Annots., Acquittal, Discharge, or Discontinuance of Criminal Charge as Evidence of Want of Probable Cause in Malicious Prosecution Action, 24 A.L.R. 261 (1923); 59 A.L.R.2d 1413 (1958); Restatement (Second) of Torts §§ 663–665, 667 (1977).

10. Can defendant avoid liability by showing that plaintiff, though found innocent, was in fact guilty? In Mooney v. Mull, 216 N.C. 410, 5 S.E.2d 122 (1939), it was held that the accused's guilt is to be determined as of the date of the malicious prosecution trial and that defendant may introduce evidence of plaintiff's guilt even though defendant did not know of the evidence when initiating the criminal prosecution. Why should a person who has been acquitted be subject to retrial of the issue of his guilt or innocence? See Threefoot v. Nuckols, 68 Miss. 116, 8 So. 335 (1890); Van Heeren v. Cooper, [1999] 1 N.Z.L.R. 731 (C.A.); Annot., Right, in Civil Action for Malicious Prosecution, to Prove or Rely on Facts Not Known to Defendant When He Began Prosecution or Action Which Show or Tend to Show Guilt or Liability of Plaintiff, 125 A.L.R. 897 (1940); Harper, James & Gray, Law of Torts § 4.4, at 4:20–4:21 (3d ed. 1996).

Royal Oil Company, Inc. v. Wells

Supreme Court of Mississippi
500 So. 2d 439 (1986)

ROBERTSON, Justice....

[Wells worked as a waitress and cashier in The Dodge Store, a convenience store owned by Royal Oil Company. The Dodge Store was managed by April Miller. April's husband Curtis was an employee in the store.]

According to Wells, her relationship with the Millers was a good one until they found out that her husband was a black man, at which time they began harassing her and criticizing her work. She thereafter received two warning slips concerning her job performance. One warning slip indicated that Wells had failed to clean off the shelves in the store and the other indicated a $40.00 shortage occurring during her shift.

Ricky Carter worked at the club located next door to The Dodge Store. On the morning of January 12, 1982, Carter came into the store and purchased three or four cups of coffee from Pamela Wells. Carter gave Wells a ten dollar bill and Wells gave him his change. According to Carter, Wells rang up a "no sale" on the register and placed the $1.53 on top of the register. Carter telephoned Curtis Miller and told him that Wells had not rung up the sale. Curtis discussed the situation with Thomas F. Barnes, a Jackson County deputy sheriff, and then proceeded to the office of Jackson County Justice Court Judge Carroll Clifford. There Miller initiated a criminal charge of embezzlement against Pamela Ann Wells by executing and filing an affidavit charging Wells with the embezzlement of the $1.53. Judge Clifford then issued a warrant for Wells' arrest. All of this was done before Wells was given an opportunity to explain her side of the story.

Shortly thereafter, on the morning in question, Wells was summoned to the store office whereupon April and Curtis Miller accused her of the Ricky Carter incident. A few minutes later, Deputy Sheriff Barnes arrived with the warrant for Wells' arrest. Wells was taken into custody and in due course released on $1,000.00 bond.

A preliminary hearing was held in Justice Court before Judge Carroll Clifford at the conclusion of which Pamela was bound over to await the action of the April 1982 Jackson County Grand Jury. A transcript of the testimony of Curtis Miller and Ricky Carter from the Justice Court proceeding was prepared and sent to the Circuit Court to be presented to the grand jury. On April 14, 1982, the grand jury "no billed" the complaint.

[Wells sued Curtis Miller and Royal Oil Company, d/b/a The Dodge Store, for malicious prosecution. Defendants appealed from a jury verdict and judgment for $9600 compensatory damages. The court rejected defendants' argument that the action must fail because the Justice Court judge found probable cause to bind Wells to await the action of the grand jury.]

Here, the jury *could* reasonably have believed that Pamela Wells had done no wrong and that there was no reasonable basis for a belief of the contrary. Wells testified that April Miller called her back to her office on the day that she was arrested and asked her about the coffee sales that she was accused of not ringing up. The officer arrived with a warrant for her arrest at this time and the document bore Curtis Miller's signature. Obviously, the warrant was sworn out and the officer on his way to arrest Wells before she was confronted with the charge of not ringing up the coffee sale. Wells attempted to explain that it was not uncommon for her to put change on top of the register because she periodically used the coins to fill up the machine that gave change to the customers automatically. After her arrest the drawer was checked, which she had been in charge of that day, and a $6.00 overage found. Testimony was that there was no consecutive coffee sale rung up on the detail tape which would indicate that Pamela Wells did not ring up the three or four coffee sales made to her customer. However, this tape was lost and not in evidence at trial.

The verdict makes clear that the jury resolved conflicts in the testimony in the favor of Wells. When the testimony of the witnesses is looked at in the light most favorable to the verdict, the jury finding of no probable cause is not an unreasonable one.

"Malice" in the law of malicious prosecution is used in an artificial and legal sense and applied to a prosecution instituted primarily for purpose other than that of bringing an offender to justice. In cases such as this, malice is most often proved by circumstantial evidence. Absence of probable cause for the prosecution is circumstantial evidence of malice, although the converse is not necessarily so.

... [W]e find Wells' proof legally adequate. The "other purpose" suggested here was that Pamela Wells was the target of the Millers' anger because of her marriage to a black man. Wells testified that relations between her and her employers cooled perceptibly once they knew of this marriage. In spite of her claim that she remained conscientious about her work, she began to receive warning slips. Wells testified that hints and smart remarks concerning her marriage were made at work and that someone wrote the word "nigger" on the side of her car about one week before the incident occurred. The record reflects that April's brother, Darrell Ladner, also an employee of The Dodge Store, hated black people because he had been beaten up by a black prisoner when he was in prison and had a permanent scar from the incident.

This "other purpose" evidence when coupled with the inferential evidence emanating from want of probable cause, are ... sufficient to insulate from our authority to reverse the jury's malice finding....

[The court sustained Wells' contention that the trial judge erred in refusing to submit to the jury the question of whether punitive damages should be assessed, stating that factual evidence sufficient for a jury finding of malice should suffice to submit the question of a punitive damages assessment to a jury.]

[Affirmed as to liability and compensatory damages; remanded for a trial limited to whether punitive damages should be assessed. Hawkins, P.J., (with whom Lee, J., joined) dissented from the decision on punitive damages.]

Notes

1. "Malice" is an essential element of a malice prosecution action. Why is it required? How is it to be defined? The typical common law concept of malice as a motivation of ill will, spite or purpose to harm is expressed in many malicious prosecution cases, but it does not supply the definition of malice for this tort. A person is treated as having commenced or continued a prosecution maliciously if his principal purpose was something other than bringing an offender against the criminal law to justice. See Glenn v. Lawrence, 280 Ill. 581, 117 N.E. 757 (1917); Johns v. Marsh, 52 Md. 323 (1879); Sanders v. Daniel International Corp., 682 S.W.2d 803 (Mo. 1984); Restatement (Second) of Torts §§ 653, 668 (1977) ("primarily for a purpose other than that of bringing an offender to justice" substituted for malice as element of tort). It follows that if defendant's primary motive in prosecuting plaintiff was ill will or a desire to harm plaintiff, malice is present. See Meyer v. Ewald, 66 Wis. 2d 168, 224 N.W.2d 419 (1974); Restatement (Second) of Torts § 668, comment *f* (1977).

2. Separate from the definition of malice is the question of what evidence permits the trier of fact to find that malice existed. Evidence of defendant's ill will toward plaintiff or a dispute between the parties is admissible for this purpose. See Sims v. Kent, 221 Ala. 589, 130 So. 213 (1930). So is a considerable variety of other circumstantial evidence. E.g., Stubbs v. Mulholland, 168 Mo. 47, 67 S.W. 650 (1902) (failure to make inquiries when they could easily be made); Glinski v. McIver, [1962] A.C. 726 (H.L.) (possible retaliation by police for giving testimony for defense in criminal case). It is often said that malice may be inferred from lack of probable cause but lack of probable cause cannot be inferred from malice (nor the presence of probable cause inferred from lack of malice). See Bailey v. Century Finance Co., 119 Ga. App. 845, 169 S.E.2d 173 (1969); Restatement (Second) of Torts §§ 669, 669A (1977). Absence of probable cause usually is a sufficient basis for a finding of malice, but occasionally it will be found insufficient, as in Barker v. Waltz, 40 Wash. 2d 866, 246 P.2d 846 (1952).

3. Because the only proper purpose for the initiation of criminal proceedings is enforcement of the criminal law against offenders, a person who caused a prosecution for some other purpose is considered to have acted with malice, even if the purpose could lawfully be achieved and no motivation of spite or desire to cause harm is proved. Thus, if a person initiates a prosecution primarily to achieve recovery of property or the enforcement of a debt or other claim, a malicious prosecution action can lie. Restatement (Second) of Torts § 668, comment *g* (1977). See Suchey v. Stiles, 155 Colo. 363, 394 P.2d 739 (1964) (defendant made larceny complaint to obtain property he thought belonged to him); Robinson v. Econ-O-Corporation, Inc., 62 Ill. App. 3d 958, 379 N.E.2d 923 (1978) (store manager had customer arrested on bad check charge in order to collect debt evidenced by check); Hall v. American Investment Co., 241 Mich. 349, 217 N.W. 18 (1928) (conditional seller charged purchaser with fraudulent disposition of car in order to repossess it); Creelman v. Svenning, 1 Wash. App. 402, 461 P.2d 557 (1969) (defendant charged neighbor with criminal trespass because of dispute about use of road near property line).

4. Should obtaining restitution of property be considered an improper purpose for making a charge of larceny? See Gann v. Varnado, 51 La. Ann. 370, 25 So. 79 (1899); Perreault v. Lyons, 99 N.H. 169, 106 A.2d 380 (1954) (yes). Contra, Bolster v. Cleland, [1919] 1 W.W.R. 1020, (1919) 45 D.L.R. 574 (Alta. App. Div.) (motive to recover property not improper if there is honest belief that theft was committed). If enforcement of the criminal law is the primary motive for the prosecution, the presence of private motives or ill will does not constitute malice. See Thompson v. Beacon Valley Rubber Co., 56 Conn. 493, 16 A. 554 (1888); Kelsea v. Swett, 234 Mass. 79, 125 N.E. 143 (1919) (not malice if defendant actuated by desire to recover property but also by purpose to vindicate justice and protect community from crime).

5. Consider whether malice can be found in the following cases:

(a) Learning that Johnson has a promissory note forged in Ebberts' name, Ebberts has Johnson arrested for forgery. In the malicious prosecution action that follows, Ebberts testifies that Johnson "had my note and I wanted to know how he got it." Johnson v. Ebberts, 11 F. 129 (C.C.D. Or. 1880). Cf. Glover v. Fleming, 36 Md. App. 381, 373 A.2d 981 (1977) (complaint filed against suspect because "we wanted to find out who the guilty party was").

(b) Rowley has Hammond arrested on a charge of unlawfully taking away oysters from grounds leased for the cultivation of oysters, in order to deter entries onto the leased oyster beds. Hammond v. Rowley, 86 Conn. 6, 84 A. 94 (1912). Cf. Stevens v. Midland Counties Railway Co., (1854) 2 C.L.R. 1300, 10 Exch. 352, 156 Eng. Rep. 480, 18 Jur. 932, 18 J.P. 713, 23 L.J. Ex. 328, 23 L.T.O.S. 70 (Ex.) (prosecution for purpose of deterring others).

(c) The police take into custody a man whose behavior is quite violent. Two physicians who examine the man at the police station say he is mentally ill and requires early attention in a mental hospital. In order to get the man into a mental hospital quickly, the police sergeant lays a charge of vagrancy against him. Williams v. Webb, [1961] O.R. 353, (1961) 27 D.L.R.2d 465 (C.A.). Cf. Rapley v. Rapley, (1930) 30 S.R. (N.S.W.) 94 (Full Ct.) (defendant charged mother with being insane person wandering at large in order to prevent her unwisely disposing of her property).

On the malice requirement of malicious prosecution generally, see Harper, James & Gray, Law of Torts § 4.6 (3d ed. 1996); Prosser & Keeton, Law of Torts 882–885 (5th ed. 1984). Authority on improper purpose for use of the criminal law is also found in cases on abuse of process. See pp. 718–725, infra.

6. Actual damage is required for a malicious prosecution action but, in effect, is presumed from the malicious institution of criminal proceedings. The jury has considerable discretion in assessing damages, which can include compensation for injury to reputation and emotional distress as well as economic loss and harm caused by arrest or confinement. See Restatement (Second) of Torts §§ 670–671 (1977); Harper, James & Gray, Law of Torts § 4.7 (3d ed. 1996). Punitive damages are usually permitted, though of course not required. See Annot., Defendant's State of Mind Necessary or Sufficient to Warrant Award of Punitive Damages in Action for Malicious Prosecution, 94 A.L.R.3d 791 (1979).

7. Malicious prosecution is usually not a viable cause of action for people who are exonerated after years of imprisonment for a crime they did not commit. The difficulty of establishing that the persons responsible for prosecution acted without probable cause, for a purpose other than bringing a supposed offender to justice, the tendency to treat a conviction as establishing probable cause even if it was later set aside, and the immunities of prosecutors and police make it very unlikely that a malicious prosecution action

could succeed. The federal government and a majority of states have now enacted statutes for compensation of people who were wrongfully convicted and imprisoned. However, the statutes' eligibility requirements, burden of proof requirements and caps on damages substantially limit the relief that is available. See Bernhard, A Short Overview of the Statutory Remedies for the Wrongfully Convicted: What Works, What Doesn't and Why, 18 Boston U. Public Interest L.J. 403 (2009); Kahn, Presumed Guilty Until Proven Innocent: The Burden of Proof in Wrongful Conviction Claims Under State Compensation Statutes, 44 U. Mich. J. L. Reform 123 (2010).

8. In the law of malicious prosecution one finds a conflict between interests of major social importance: the interests served by protecting citizens who assist law enforcement by initiating criminal proceedings and the interests served by deterring and providing a remedy for unjustified use of legal process. See Fleming, Law of Torts 693 (10th ed. 2011). Does contemporary law reflect an appropriate balance between these interests?

Section 2. Wrongful Civil Proceedings

Myhre v. Hessey

Supreme Court of Wisconsin
242 Wis. 638, 9 N.W.2d 106 (1943)

FOWLER, Justice....

[Plaintiff's second cause of action was for malicious prosecution of a series of civil actions. The trial court dismissed this action because there was no evidence of interference with plaintiff's person or property. In Luby v. Bennett, 111 Wis. 613, 87 N.W. 804 (1901), paragraph 6 of the syllabus of the court ("Syl. 6") had stated: "The general rule which prevails in England, and has the greater support of judicial and elementary authority in this country, is that a civil action, maliciously prosecuted, where neither the person nor the property of the defendant is interfered with, inflicting special damages to him, will not sustain an action for malicious prosecution."]

... [In Luby v. Bennett] Cooley on Torts, 2d Ed., 219, is quoted: "He [Judge Cooley] confines the civil actions that may support one for damages for malicious prosecution by the settled law, to maliciously instituting and prosecuting proceedings in bankruptcy, suits in which the defendant is arrested, suits in which the property of the defendant is attached, and proceedings to have a party declared insane and placed under guardianship. He says, as to other civil actions: 'In some cases it has been held that an action may be maintained for the malicious institution without probable cause of any civil suit which has terminated in favor of the defendant; but the English authorities do not justify this statement, and there is much good reason in what has been said in a Pennsylvania case (Mayer v. Walter, 64 Pa. 283), that "if the person be not arrested or his property seized, it is unimportant how futile and unfounded the action might be; as the plaintiff, in consideration of law, is punished by the payment of costs." If every suit may be retried on an allegation of malice, the evils would be intolerable, and the malice in each subsequent suit would be likely to be greater than in the first.'"

In addition to the basic actions specifically mentioned in the above quotation from Cooley on Torts, supra, should be added equity cases wherein plaintiff is excluded from possession of his property through its being turned over to a receiver, as in the Luby case; and perhaps juvenile court proceedings wherein a child is charged with being a "delinquent child" and "incorrigible." The opinion seems to imply that preferring such a charge maliciously and without probable cause, would of itself constitute basis for a malicious prosecution action....

It should be noted that the rule of Syl. 6 has not yet been adopted in this state. This appears from the statement in the Luby case that the proposition stated in Syl. 6 "ought not to receive approval as the law of this state without the most careful consideration of the subject in a case necessarily depending upon a correct solution of it."... [T]he Restatement of the Law, Torts, is apparently contrary to it. [§ 674] states the rule to be that instituting a civil proceeding creates liability for harm done if (a) instituted (1) without probable cause and (2) primarily for purpose other than securing adjudication on the claim involved, and (b) (except where ex parte) the proceedings have terminated in favor of the person against whom they are brought. Comment Fourth states that the plaintiff under this section must show either material harm or violation of a legal right in itself sufficient to support an action for damages.

[§ 681] states the damages that are recoverable ... : [a] harm by interference with personal property; (b) harm to reputation by reason of defamatory matter alleged as basis of the suit; (c) expense reasonably incurred in defending; (d) specific pecuniary loss; (e) distress caused by the proceedings.

It appears that under the rules as stated in the Restatement no damage resulted to the plaintiff from prosecutions of the civil actions unless the cost of defending them be considered an item of such damage....

... The matter seems to depend on which the court considers the less evil: subjecting individuals to the expense of defending groundless civil actions prosecuted maliciously and without probable cause, or subjecting individuals who lose lawsuits which they institute to the possibility of malicious prosecution actions because they lost them, and subjecting the courts and the public to a possible flood of such actions that may follow adoption of the Restatement rule.... It is pointed out in [34 Am. Jur. 707, § 9] that prior to the enactment of the statute of Marlbridge, 52 Henry III, enacted in 1267, an action lay for malicious prosecution of a civil action without probable cause; that that statute gave costs to the successful defendant, not as a general statute regulating costs, but "to afford a summary remedy to the successful defendant in place of the existing right of action to recover his damages on account of the malicious prosecution of a civil action against him" and that after the passage of that statute the rule of Syl. 6 was generally applied by the English courts because the costs recovered were considered adequate compensation for the damages suffered.... Some [American] cases apply the Restatement rule on the express ground that the costs imposed under the English practice include attorney fees both for preparing the basic case for trial and for trying it, while in this country generally no attorney fees are included in the costs and where they are, as in Wisconsin, they are so small as to bear no relation to the expense of the plaintiff in defending as costs under the English practice....

We conclude that as a matter of public policy the rule of Syl. 6 is the sounder, and we therefore adopt it....

[Shedd v. Patterson, 1922, 302 Ill. 355, 134 N.E. 705] holds that although a single civil action maliciously prosecuted will not support an action for malicious prosecution unless there is interference with the person or property of the plaintiff, the rule does not apply where there are several such prosecutions. We do not perceive that a different rule should apply in case of a series of civil actions than in the case of one. The inference of malice, under all the facts, may be stronger in a case of a half dozen actions all resulting in favor of the plaintiff than in a single case. But malice has no causal relation to interference with plaintiff's person or property. The reason for the fundamental proposition that the action does not lie except there be interference with property or person applies just the same whether one basic action is involved or more than one. In none of the civil actions here involved was plaintiff's person or property interfered with.... The judgment dismissing the second cause of action is affirmed....

Notes

1. *Malicious prosecution of civil proceedings.* Do the reasons supporting a tort action for malicious prosecution of criminal proceedings justify an action for malicious prosecution of civil proceedings? Should the elements of liability be the same for both actions? Stating that a malicious prosecution action requires that defendant have initiated or continued criminal proceedings against plaintiff, the court in LaMantia v. Redisi, 118 Nev. 27, 38 P.3d 877 (2002), rejected an action for malicious prosecution of civil claims. The House of Lords has ruled decisively against any liability for malicious prosecution of civil proceedings, other than in some special cases supported by English precedent such as bankruptcy proceedings and executions against property. Gregory v. Portsmouth City Council, [2000] 1 A.C. 419 (H.L.). A malicious prosecution action was thought unnecessary. Injustices resulting from groundless and damaging civil proceedings could, it was thought, be addressed by application or extension of other torts, including defamation, injurious falsehood and conspiracy. In England, unlike the United States, groundless civil actions were deterred by awards of legal costs to defendants in unsuccessful civil actions. The House of Lords noted the role the absence of such cost awards had played in the extension of malicious prosecution to civil proceedings in the United States.

2. In the United States, the majority view now is to permit an action for malicious prosecution of a civil case, i.e. wrongful commencement or continuation of civil proceedings, even if there was no interference with plaintiff's person or property. See Nelson v. Miller, 227 Kan. 271, 607 P.2d 438 (1980); Annot., Prosecution of Civil Suit, Without Arrest of Person or Seizure of Property, as Ground of Action for Malicious Prosecution, 150 A.L.R. 897 (1944); Restatement (Second) of Torts § 674 (1977). A substantial minority of jurisdictions require plaintiff to establish "special injury" or "special damages" in order to recover. See Melvin v. Pence, p. 707, infra; Berlin v. Nathan, p. 710, infra; Harper, James & Gray; Law of Torts § 4.8 (3d ed. 1996). In some states, the action has acquired the label "malicious use of process," not to be confused with "abuse of process." See LoBiondo v. Schwartz, 199 N.J. 62, 970 A.2d 1007 (2009).

3. Because of the harm to business credit caused by the institution of bankruptcy and other insolvency proceedings, it has long been established that these can be the basis of an action for malicious prosecution, and some courts which generally adhere to the "special injury" rule do not apply it to such proceedings. See Balsiger v. American Steel & Supply Co., 254 Or. 204, 451 P.2d 868 (1969), reh'g denied, 254 Or. 210, 458 P.2d 932 (1969); Annot., Action for Malicious Prosecution Based on Institution of Involuntary Bankruptcy, Insolvency, or Receivership Proceedings, 40 A.L.R.3d 296 (1971). Some jurisdictions follow Shedd v. Patterson, discussed in the principal case, in not applying requirements of "special injury" or interference with person or property when defendant has instituted

more than one wrongful suit against plaintiff. See Soffos v. Eaton, 80 U.S. App. D.C. 306, 152 F.2d 682 (1945) (landlord sued tenant four times for possession of premises). But see Pye v. Cardwell, 110 Tex. 572, 222 S.W. 153 (1920) (seven successive suits instituted against plaintiff, who had them dismissed as fast as counsel employed).

4. Jurisdictions which require "special injury" in an action for malicious civil prosecution often define it as injury which is not a necessary result in such a case, or injury beyond the usual expense, annoyance and inconvenience of defending a lawsuit of the type brought against plaintiff. How "special" an effect must the lawsuit have had upon plaintiff? See Petrich v. McDonald, 44 Wash. 2d 211, 266 P.2d 1047 (1954) (attachment of vessel necessary to in rem foreclosure action; no special damage); Schier v. Denny, 12 Wis. 2d 544, 107 N.W.2d 611 (1961) (complaint against real estate broker, filed with state administrative agency, caused some of broker's employees to quit; advertising expenses in connection with seeking new employees and loss of income because of employees' departure not special damage); Berlin v. Nathan, p. 710, infra. Compare Bank of Lyons v. Schultz, 78 Ill. 2d 235, 399 N.E.2d 1286 (1980) (injunctions restraining distribution of life insurance proceeds to beneficiary constituted seizure of property or other special injury). In Engel v. CBS, Inc., 93 N.Y.2d 195, 689 N.Y.S.2d 411, 711 N.E.2d 626 (1999), the New York special inquiry requirement was liberalized to include "highly substantial and identifiable interference with person, property or business" beyond the "physical, psychological or financial demands of defending a lawsuit."

5. May a malicious civil prosecution action arise from a counterclaim? A baseless defense? It appears that a counterclaim may give rise to a malicious prosecution action because a counterclaim asserts a claim for affirmative relief distinct from the original action. See Bertero v. National General Corp., 13 Cal. 3d 43, 118 Cal. Rptr. 184, 529 P.2d 608 (1974); Slee v. Simpson, 91 Colo. 461, 15 P.2d 1084 (1932). The prevailing view is that there is no action for a malicious defense. See Forberg v. Stumbos & Mason, 217 Cal. App. 3d 1171, 266 Cal. Rptr. 436 (1990); Young v. Allstate Insurance Co., 119 Hawaii 403, 198 P.3d 666 (2008); Baxter v. Brown, 83 Kan. 302, 111 P. 430 (1910). Why not? In Aranson v. Schroeder, 140 N.H. 359, 671 A.2d 1023 (1995), the court created a cause of action for malicious defense, with requirements parallel to those of the action for malicious prosecution of civil proceedings. See generally Annot., May Action for Malicious Prosecution Be Predicated on Defense or Counterclaim in Civil Suit, 65 A.L.R.3d 901 (1975); Van Patten & Willard, The Limits of Advocacy: A Proposal for the Tort of Malicious Defense in Civil Litigation, 35 Hastings L.J. 891 (1984). Should there be an action for prosecution of a meritless appeal? See Coleman v. Gulf Insurance Group, 41 Cal. 3d 782, 226 Cal. Rptr. 90, 718 P.2d 77 (1986) (no). What about an action for malicious prosecution of a malicious prosecution suit? This was permitted in Hopke v. O'Bryne, 148 So. 2d 755 (Fla. App. 1963). One possibility for relitigation of issues raised in the former action is foreclosed. In an action for malicious prosecution of criminal proceedings, defendant can use as a defense proof that plaintiff really was guilty of the offense charged, but in an action for malicious prosecution of civil proceedings, defendant cannot use as a defense that he actually had a cause of action against plaintiff. Restatement (Second) of Torts § 674, comment *e* (1977).

6. *Absence of probable cause.* There is no cause of action when there was probable cause to institute the earlier proceeding. Probable cause to institute a civil proceeding has been defined as a reasonable belief that the claim may be valid under the applicable law and that the facts on which the claim is based exist. Restatement (Second) of Torts § 675 (1977). Bradshaw v. State Farm Mutual Insurance Co., 157 Ariz. 411, 758 P.2d 1313 (1988), uses, perhaps inconsistently, the tests of whether the suit's initiator reasonably believed he had a good chance of establishing the case in court and whether the initiator

reasonably believed there was a possibility that a court would find the claim valid. Under these standards, when does an attorney have probable cause to initiate suit for a client? See pp. 715–716, infra.

7. Dismissal of a lawsuit, or other termination unfavorable to the person bringing the suit, is generally regarded as no evidence of lack of probable cause. See Barton v. Woodward, 32 Idaho 375, 182 P. 916 (1919); Novick v. Becker, 4 Wis. 2d 432, 90 N.W.2d 620 (1958). A voluntary dismissal or discontinuance usually is treated similarly. See Asevado v. Orr, 100 Cal. 293, 34 P. 777 (1893); Cohn v. Saidel, 71 N.H. 558, 53 A. 800 (1902). Contra, Kolka v. Jones, 6 N.D. 461, 71 N.W. 558 (1897). Could want of probable cause be found if the initiator of the prior civil action had a foundation for stating the elements of a prima facie case but knew that a complete defense to the action was available to all defendants? See Empiregas, Inc. of Elberta v. Feely, 524 So. 2d 626 (Ala. 1988) (attorney knew action brought after statute of limitations expired and dismissed action when it was contested; judgment for plaintiffs in malicious prosecution action affirmed). In Robinson v. Goudchaux's, 307 So. 2d 287 (La. 1975), a store referred an unpaid bill to its attorneys for collection. After a demand for payment, the attorneys commenced suit against the debtor. Before the suit was filed, the debtor paid the store in full, but the store did not notify the attorneys. Was there a want of probable cause on the part of the store or the attorneys? Would there be liability for continuing a lawsuit after discovering a lack of probable cause for it? See Zamos v. Stroud, 32 Cal. 4th 958, 12 Cal. Rptr. 3d 54, 87 P.3d 802 (2004) (yes).

8. *Malice.* What constitutes the malice element of an action for malicious prosecution of a civil proceeding? If in actions for malicious prosecution of a criminal case malice is defined as prosecution for a purpose other than bringing an offender against the criminal law to justice, what should be the definition of malice in a suit arising from a civil case? If it is "improper purpose," what is an improper purpose for the initiation or continuation of a civil case, and who decides whether a purpose is improper? For civil process, unlike criminal process, a purpose to secure a private advantage is not necessarily improper. A private advantage that would be secured by the proper adjudication of the claim on which the action is based is a proper purpose for the action. A different ("collateral") advantage is not. Thus, if an action is brought not to secure the resolution of the claim or the relief demanded but to delay or prevent an opposing party from entering a transaction or using property or pursuing a claim of his own, there is an improper purpose. See Restatement (Second) of Torts § 676 (1977); Dobbs, Law of Torts 1230–1231 (2000).

9. Would an allegation that defendant commenced an unmeritorious action in order to extract an undeserved settlement payment meet the malice requirement of a malicious prosecution action? See Shaffer v. Stewart, 326 Pa. Super. 135, 473 A.2d 1017 (1984). What if it is alleged that an attorney brought an action in order to obtain a contingency-fee payment? See Miskew v. Hess, 21 Kan. App. 2d 927, 910 P.2d 223 (1996). Cf. Cole v. Neaf, 334 F.2d 326 (8th Cir. 1964) (malice not inferred from fact that estate administrator would gain fee if his claim against plaintiff for proceeds of life insurance succeeded).

10. Johnson v. Mount Ogden Enterprises, Inc., 23 Utah 2d 169, 460 P.2d 333 (1969), is an example of malice being found because of defendant's improper purpose in bringing the prior action. Defendant had applied for and obtained a temporary injunction restraining plaintiffs from cutting off a supply of water to defendant. At a hearing a few days later, defendant elected to dismiss the case. The court found that defendant instituted suit solely for the purpose of using plaintiff's water supply without right until a separate water system could be installed. It is more typical for the malice requirement to be satisfied by use of the rule that malice can be inferred from lack of probable cause. See Robin-

son v. Goudchaux's, supra; Kryszke v. Kamin, 163 Mich. 290, 128 N.W. 190 (1910). In Cole v. Neaf, supra, the rule was acknowledged but the court rejected plaintiff's contention that the inference of malice was mandatory. Malice can be established by evidence that the action was brought primarily to vex or harass or from motives of ill will or spite, and bringing an action known to be groundless is treated as malicious. See Pangburn v. Bull, 1 Wend. 345 (N.Y. Sup. Ct. 1828); Restatement (Second) of Torts §676, comment *c* (1977).

Melvin v. Pence

United States Court of Appeals for the District of Columbia
76 U.S. App. D.C. 154, 130 F.2d 423 (1942)

RUTLEDGE, Associate Justice.

The suit is in the nature of an action for malicious prosecution. The defendants appeal from a judgment for plaintiff for $1250, rendered after trial before a jury. Plaintiff is a duly licensed private detective. The gist of his complaint is that defendants instituted proceedings before the licensing authorities of the District of Columbia which resulted in their refusal to renew his license, but terminated in his favor on appeal....

The case is an outgrowth of the marital troubles of defendant Melvin and his former wife.... Early in August, 1937, she employed plaintiff to follow the movements of her husband. On the morning of August 18, that year, plaintiff accosted the defendants as they came out of an apartment. Defendant Elna N. Smith asked his identity. He replied by showing her his badge. It contained his name, "F.G. Pence," at the top. In a circular portion was an eagle surrounded by the words "Washington Detective Agency." This was his trade name. Plaintiff testified that Elna Smith read the badge; he said nothing to her, but she later asked to see the badge again. He denied telling her who he was or stating he was from the Washington Detective Bureau (a branch of the Metropolitan Police Department) or from the Washington Detective Agency.

On October 26 plaintiff received a letter from the secretary of the Commissioners of the District saying that, upon the recommendation of the Superintendent of Police, his license would not be renewed. The basis for this was two affidavits filed by defendants. They are not in the record, but it discloses they set forth that plaintiff had interviewed defendants on August 18 on a domestic matter and had stated he was from the Washington Detective Bureau.

Plaintiff's license expired November 1. He appealed to the Commissioners from the refusal to renew it. A hearing was arranged before the License Denial and Revocation Board for December 15. Defendants testified at the hearing. It resulted favorably to plaintiff, and a license was issued January 5, 1938. Near the end of November, 1937, he received permission to operate pending the disposition of his appeal....

... [N]o issue is before us concerning the existence of malice and probable cause. It must be taken as established that the defendants without probable cause charged plaintiff with impersonating a police officer, a criminal offense; made the charge for the purpose of having his license revoked, to the only authority having power to do this, and did so as an immediate consequence of his surveillance of their movements. It must be accepted also as proven that their action caused the administrative proceedings which resulted in the refusal to renew plaintiff's license, but terminated on appeal in his favor....

The facts therefore follow the usual pattern of suits for malicious prosecution, successfully maintained, except that the proceedings were administrative, not judicial in character. Defendants make this the principal, in fact the only, issue on the appeal, except for their contentions in respect to the disputed items of damage. In this respect they rely upon the common statement that the tort of malicious prosecution requires the institution of judicial proceedings as an essential element in the wrong....

... [U]nsuccessful efforts to secure the institution of proceedings, however malicious or unfounded, are not actionable as malicious prosecution. In Peckham v. Union Finance Co. [60 App. D.C. 104, 48 F.2d 1017], a civil action was begun and terminated favorably to the defendant. But the court held this would not sustain a suit for malicious prosecution, notwithstanding malice and want of probable cause, "when there has been no arrest of the person or seizure of the property of the defendant, and no special injuries sustained, which would not necessarily result in all suits prosecuted to recover for like causes of action." ...

... This limitation, and the broader English one, are thought necessary to maintain free access to the courts by persons with grievances, who otherwise might be restrained from seeking redress through fear of liability in the event of failure. Consequently, by the more general rule, special injury must be shown when the suit relied upon is a civil cause.

The limitation is sound. When disputes reach the litigious stage, usually some malice is present on both sides. Friendly tort suits are not common. Nor is existence or want of probable cause always easy to determine until the event of the litigation is known. Some margin of safety in asserting rights, though they turn out to be groundless and their assertion accompanied by some degree of ill-will, must be maintained. Otherwise litigation would lead, not to an end of disputing, but to its beginning, and rights violated would go unredressed for fear of the danger of asserting them.

Access to the courts and other tribunals, however, should not be abused. The freedom to use their processes is not absolute. When malice motivates a groundless claim and results in special injury beyond what assertion of rights ordinarily entails, remedy is afforded. The right to litigate is not the right to become a nuisance. When the proceeding has no relation to protection of any right of the suitor or any public right which he reasonably may have a hand in vindicating, the reason for his protection fails and he must respond.

We agree with plaintiff that these principles are clearly applicable to administrative proceedings. Much of the jurisdiction formerly residing in the courts has been transferred to administrative tribunals, and much new jurisdiction involving private rights and penal consequences has been vested in them. In a broad sense their creation involves the emergence of a new system of courts, not less significant than the evolution of chancery. The same harmful consequences may flow from the groundless and malicious institution of proceedings in them as does from judicial proceedings similarly begun. When one's livelihood depends upon a public license, it makes little difference to him whether it is taken away by a court or by an administrative body or official. Nor should his right to redress the injury depend upon the technical form of the proceeding by which it is inflicted. The administrative process is also a legal process, and its abuse in the same way with the same injury should receive the same penalty....

... [T]he absence of a right to appeal to the courts is immaterial. If it has any effect, it would seem to make application of the principle to administrative proceedings all the more necessary. Second, if some judicial element were regarded as essential, it would be supplied by the fact that the Commissioners' action in arbitrarily refusing or revoking a license would be reviewable, if in no other way, by independent suit in equity....

The limitations upon the rule should follow it in the new application. The same reasons which require them when the proceeding is judicial do so when it is administrative. There can be no doubt that institution of these proceedings resulted in special injury to the plaintiff sufficient to sustain the action. His license was, in effect, revoked. His livelihood depended upon it. For nearly a month he was disabled to carry on his work. It is immaterial that he kept open his office for collection of money previously earned or that he later secured permission to operate pending disposition of the appeal. The latter factor went only to reduce his damages. The lapse in the license not only interrupted his business, but very probably caused harm in other respects. The injury was not slight. Nor was it one essential or conducive to protection of any right of defendants or its assertion. The proceeding in no way involved protection of their interests. It was directed solely to the detriment of plaintiff's right to work. The proceeding therefore falls squarely within the limitations upon the institution of other than criminal prosecutions.

There is some attempt to argue that the defendants did not institute or instigate the proceedings. They do not deny making the charge or its character, or that it was made to the licensing officials or with intent to secure revocation or refusal to renew plaintiff's license. The argument apparently is that all this did not amount to institution or instigation. Clearly it amounted to instigation, as appears from the reason assigned for the refusal and the absence of other cause. Their complaint was the moving force in bringing about the official action and all that followed. Instigation is sufficient, when institution actually follows from it.

We do not agree with defendants that injury to reputation and mental suffering were not proper elements of damage or that there was error in the instructions permitting them to be taken into account. These items are commonly allowable in suits of this character. Injury to reputation is a usual result of groundless charges publicized by litigation. The wrong is closely akin to defamation. The nature of the charge and of the resulting proceedings in this case was such that the good name and fame of the plaintiff were bound to suffer. Necessarily also he must have experienced mental and emotional stress, uncertainty and worry while the proceedings were undetermined, as he testified he did....

As the case has been presented to us, perhaps the weakest features are in the elements of malice and want of probable cause, though as has been said these issues are not properly before us. The similarity of plaintiff's trade name, Washington Detective Agency, and the official designation of the detective division of the Police Department, Washington Detective Bureau, coupled with plaintiff's admitted failure to make the difference clear when he was asked by defendants to identify himself, may have led them unwittingly and not unreasonably to conclude that he was a police officer and possibly also, when they discovered he was not, to infer that he was impersonating one. Not all citizens are so acute that they would readily distinguish a private badge and name, such as these, from official ones....

The judgment is affirmed.

Notes

1. There has been considerable litigation over what kinds of legal proceedings can, if maliciously maintained, give rise to an action for malicious prosecution. See Chauncey v. Niems, 182 Cal. App. 3d 967, 227 Cal. Rptr. 718 (1986). Most authority agrees with the principal case that administrative action, such as a proceeding to revoke a business license, can provide a basis for a malicious prosecution claim. See Hardy v. Vial, 48 Cal.

2d 577, 311 P.2d 494 (1957) (affidavits accusing college professor of base and depraved conduct filed with college and State Personnel Board); Dixie Broadcasting Corp. v. Rivers, 209 Ga. 98, 70 S.E.2d 734 (1952) (petition to Federal Communications Commission to revoke plaintiff's radio station permit); Kauffman v. A.H. Robins Co., 223 Tenn. 515, 448 S.W.2d 400 (1969) (complaint filed with state Board of Pharmacy alleging misconduct by pharmacist). But cf. Stanwyck v. Horne, 146 Cal. App. 3d 450, 194 Cal. Rptr. 228 (1983) (attorney disciplinary proceeding considered initiated by state bar, not person who made accusation to bar about attorney). Is there an action for a malicious will contest? See MacDonald v. Joslyn, 275 Cal. App. 2d 282, 79 Cal. Rptr. 707 (1969); Annot., Liability for Malicious Prosecution Based on Contest or Caveat to Will, 35 A.L.R.3d 651 (1971). Should supposed malicious prosecution of an adoption proceeding be grounds for liability? See Rushing v. Bosse, 652 So. 2d 869 (Fla. App. 1995). What chances of success do such actions have if special injury is required? See Schier v. Denny, 12 Wis. 2d 544, 107 N.W.2d 611 (1961).

2. A maliciously instituted insanity proceeding is actionable, Annot., Liability for Malicious Prosecution Predicated Upon Institution of, or Conduct in Connection With, Insanity Proceedings, 30 A.L.R.3d 455 (1970), as is a disciplinary proceeding against a professional. See Annot., Malicious Prosecution or Similar Tort Action Predicated Upon Disciplinary Proceedings Against an Attorney, 52 A.L.R.2d 1217 (1957); Annot., Malicious Prosecution Predicated Upon Prosecution, Institution, or Instigation of Disciplinary Proceeding Against Member of Medical or Allied Profession, 39 A.L.R.3d 473 (1971). Some cases have held that public policy requires that filing an action or complaint against an attorney be privileged. See Toft v. Ketchum, 18 N.J. 280, 113 A.2d 671 (1955), aff'd on reh'g, 18 N.J. 611, 114 A.2d 863 (1955), cert. denied, 350 U.S. 887 (1955), which observes that the state Supreme Court has inherent power to punish for contempt a person who files a baseless complaint. Some of the above-mentioned proceedings might be classified as criminal or quasi-criminal and treated as malicious criminal prosecution, with no special injury requirement.

3. Suppose a baseless action is brought *against* a government agency or entity. Should it be able to use a malicious prosecution action to recover the costs of defending the earlier proceeding? In City of Long Beach v. Bozek, 31 Cal. 3d 527, 183 Cal. Rptr. 86, 645 P.2d 137 (1982), vacated, 459 U.S. 1095 (1983), on remand, 33 Cal. 3d 727, 190 Cal. Rptr. 918, 661 P.2d 1072 (1983), it was held that the constitutional right to petition government for redress of grievances barred malicious prosecution actions by governmental entities. The court in Cate v. Oldham, 450 So. 2d 224 (Fla. 1984), after considering the right to petition, held that the common law did not allow a state official sued in his official capacity to maintain a malicious prosecution action.

Berlin v. Nathan

Appellate Court of Illinois
64 Ill. App. 3d 940, 381 N.E.2d 1367 (1978),
cert. denied, 444 U.S. 828 (1979)

ROMITI, Justice....

The pleadings reveal that on October 1, 1973 Harriet Nathan entered the Skokie Valley Community Hospital complaining of an injury to the little finger of her right hand. An x-ray was taken under the supervision of Dr. Berlin, a radiologist on the staff of the hospital. Dr. Berlin read the film as revealing a dislocation of the finger. Dr. Meltzer then applied treatment appropriate for a dislocation. In November, another x-ray was taken. This x-ray disclosed that there had been a chip fracture of that finger.

On September 11, 1975, about two weeks before the statute of limitations would have run, Harriet Nathan, through her attorneys, Benjamin and Shapiro, filed suit against Dr. Berlin, Dr. Meltzer and the hospital alleging various acts of malpractice in the taking of the x-rays and the making of the diagnosis. Dr. Berlin thereupon filed a suit against Mr. Nathan (at whose specific instance and request, he alleged, the malpractice suit was specifically brought), Mrs. Nathan and her attorneys Benjamin and Shapiro. In Count I of that suit he alleged that all four defendants owed him a duty to refrain from willfully and wantonly bringing suit against him without having reasonable cause to believe that he had been guilty of malpractice; that the defendants instead, although having no cause whatsoever to believe he had been guilty of malpractice, had instituted suit with reckless disregard as to the truth or falsity of the allegations. Specifically, Dr. Berlin in Count I complained that Benjamin and Shapiro had acted willfully and wantonly and without probable cause since they had not, before filing suit, obtained an opinion from another physician as to the quality of the x-rays and the correctness of their interpretation thereof; and moreover, that the ad damnum ($125,000), which bore no reasonable relationship to the injuries allegedly sustained, was devised to intimidate Dr. Berlin and might affect his ability to procure malpractice insurance at reasonable rates. Dr. Berlin in Count I specifically alleged that Harriet Nathan brought suit willfully and wantonly and without probable cause in that she at no time prior to suit obtained from another physician an opinion as to the quality of the x-rays, the correctness of their interpretation or an opinion whether the condition of which she complained resulted from malpractice by either Dr. Berlin or Dr. Meltzer. Dr. Berlin further alleged that the Nathans had been told by another orthopedic surgeon, prior to the institution of the suit, that no malpractice had occurred but that they willfully and wantonly incited and instituted the suit in retribution for real or imagined discourtesies to them by Dr. Meltzer. . . .

In Count III, Dr. Berlin alleged that the attorneys, Benjamin and Shapiro, had a duty to the plaintiff not to file the malpractice lawsuit without reasonable evidence to support the allegations therein since, as attorneys, they were particularly aware of the time and expense that litigation causes and could foresee the harm an unfounded lawsuit could cause to the reputation and mental well-being of a physician; that by filing the complaint without reasonable cause, the attorneys fell below the standard of care required of attorneys in the performance of their professional duties in good faith and in a legal manner and were negligent towards Dr. Berlin. . . .

On May 27, 1976 the original malpractice suit was voluntarily dismissed, with prejudice, on the motion of Harriet Nathan. The action on the countersuit then proceeded to trial. . . .

The jury found all four defendants guilty of willful and wanton misconduct proximately causing injury to Dr. Berlin and awarded Dr. Berlin $2,000 in compensatory damages and $6,000 in punitive damages. . . .

The *amicus curiae* has argued that the jury verdict should be upheld since the jury properly found defendant guilty of malicious prosecution. We disagree since we find that the plaintiff's complaint was not sufficient to state a claim for malicious prosecution against any of the defendants, and the instructions to the jury certainly did not submit a claim for malicious prosecution.

Tort litigants, such as the Nathans, may be held liable for malicious prosecution. However, since the law does not look with favor on such suits, there are strict limitations on the availability of such suits. Suits for malicious prosecution cannot be maintained in Illinois unless the plaintiff alleges and proves that the plaintiff in the original tort action acted maliciously and without probable cause; that the prior cause terminated in the plaintiff's favor; and that some special injury not necessarily resulting in any and all suits prosecuted to recover for like causes of action was suffered. It is clear that in this case neither of the last two elements was pleaded and, even if we liberally construe the complaint to allege that the suit was brought maliciously and without probable cause by the Nathans, that issue was not submitted to the jury.

Special damages ... are those not necessarily resulting in any and all suits prosecuted to recover for like causes of action. The only damages that Dr. Berlin claimed he suffered are (1) his reputation in his profession has been attacked; (2) he has suffered mental anguish; (3) he has been forced to spend time on the defense; (4) he will be required to pay increased insurance premiums. The first three items of damage claimed are so patently common to all litigation that no discussion is warranted.... [A]n increase in insurance premiums, while perhaps not a necessary result of the litigation, is, assuming the allegation is anything more than pure speculation, an item necessarily incident to all malpractice cases and not therefore amounting to damages suffered specially by Dr. Berlin as distinct from other physicians who have been defendants in malpractice suits.

The defendant and *amicus curiae* both, however, contend that the requirement of special damages is unreasonable and should be abolished. First of all, we have no authority to overrule the Illinois Supreme Court. But in any event, we agree with ... *Ammerman v. Newman* (D.C. App. 1978), 384 A.2d 637 which rejected precisely the same argument.... "Appellant seeks to avoid the application of the rule by arguing that it is inequitable in the context of medical malpractice actions. He contends that the fact that such actions are particularly harmful to the reputations and livelihood of physicians calls for a modification of the rule with respect to them. The purpose of the special injury rule, however, is to strike a balance between allowing free access to the courts for the vindication of rights without fear of a resulting suit, and the undue exercise of such right. Appellant's argument, if accepted, would upset that delicate balance. The nature of his profession, given its profound impact on the lives of those with whom he deals, cannot be allowed to insulate him from potential liability. In order to maintain a free access to the courts by persons with grievances who might otherwise be restrained from seeking redress because of their fear of liability should they fail, the special injury rule has consistently been upheld." ...

Basically, the complaint against the Nathans merely alleges that their conduct was willful and wanton. Willful and wanton conduct does not amount to malice. However, a suit brought for an improper motive may be malicious, and Dr. Berlin did allege that the Nathans brought suit solely in retribution for the real or imagined discourtesies of Dr. Meltzer. But, the plaintiff clearly abandoned any attempt at trial to prove a cause of action against the Nathans for malicious prosecution since in the instructions submitted to the jury, the jury was solely instructed as to willful and wanton misconduct....

A suit for malicious prosecution can be brought against an attorney since an attorney cannot always justify himself merely by showing he followed his client's instructions. If an attorney, acknowledging there is no cause of action, and knowing this dishonestly and for some improper purpose files suit, or even if an attorney merely acts knowing that his client has no just claim and that his client is actuated by illegal or malicious motives, the attorney may be held liable for malicious prosecution.

However the plaintiff's complaint was totally insufficient to support a claim against the attorneys for malicious prosecution. First, there is no allegation that the attorneys acted maliciously or knew that their client did so. As we noted previously, willful and wanton conduct does not constitute malicious conduct, particularly where, as here, no improper motive of any kind on the part of the attorneys is suggested. Basically, the plaintiff simply complains that the defendants did not get another doctor's opinion before filing suit. But the undisputed facts are that the finger was fractured and that this fracture was not discovered for several weeks. Perhaps more investigation before filing suit would have been prudent, but as the Louisiana court remarked in *Spencer v. Burglass* (La. App. 1976), 337 So. 2d 596 at 599, 600: "There are no factual allegations to suggest that when defendant filed his client's suit he knew the allegations were false or that he had a reckless disregard as to whether the allegations were false or not. On the contrary, plaintiff's allegations are to the effect that defendant simply did not know enough about the case at the time he filed it and now in retrospect plaintiff would say this was malice on defendant's part. If that be so many a successful lawsuit would never have been or never would be filed because oftentimes the case comes to the attorney just prior to prescription date and the evidence is not discovered and developed until after the suit is filed. We therefore conclude that the allegation of 'frivolously filing suits' cannot be construed as an allegation of malice.... Finally, there is the allegation that defendant failed to obtain 'competent medical advice,' etc. Does this constitute an allegation of malice? It would seem that an affirmative answer to this query would mean that before the attorney brings a malpractice case to trial he must find a medical person who supports the attorney's theory or that of his client, who is willing to testify favorably and who is 'competent' by someone's (plaintiff's?) standards. If he finds no such person but he nevertheless, places whatever evidence he can before the court perhaps relying on circumstantial evidence, reasonable inferences and common sense and perhaps realizing that he will probably lose, he runs the risk of having his conduct branded as malicious. When the bald allegation in question is considered in this light it can hardly be construed as one alleging malice. At worst, the allegation is that defendant went to trial with a poor case and got his just desserts, to wit, he lost. If that constitutes malice, the courtrooms are full of malicious attorneys. This we cannot accept."

... [F]inally, there is no allegation that the malpractice case was terminated favorably to the present plaintiff before the complaint was filed. In fact it is conceded that at the time of filing, the original tort action was still pending. As the court observed in *Lyddon v. Shaw* (1978), 56 Ill. App. 3d 815, 820, 372 N.E.2d 685, 688, to permit the filing of such an action against the attorney prior to the termination of the initial malpractice action "would tend to drive a wedge between the malpractice plaintiff and his attorney; the attorney may be diverted from properly preparing the client's malpractice case by the necessity for readying his own defense to the physician's countersuit, and may, in some cases, even be forced to withdraw from the malpractice action." This we cannot permit.

It is clear, therefore, that Dr. Berlin's complaint is insufficient to allege a cause of action for malicious prosecution. Indeed, he has not on appeal contended that it is. What he does claim, contrary to the well-established law in Illinois that "a person is not liable for bringing any suit, criminal or civil, ... if the court had jurisdiction of the subject-matter and the parties, unless he acts maliciously and without probable cause" (*Hill Co. v. Contractors' Supply Co.* (1911), 249 Ill. 304, at 310, 94 N.E. 544, at 546), is that he should be able to recover against all of the defendants for the willful and wanton filing of a frivolous lawsuit. But *Hill* still represents the state of the law in Illinois. Furthermore, since "it takes a 'special injury' to recover for the malicious pursuit of an unfounded civil action, it would be incongruous to base a recovery on mere carelessness without the same requirement." (*O'Toole v. Franklin* (1977), 279 Or. 513, 569 P.2d 561, at 566.) Likewise ... failure to plead the outcome of the malpractice action would constitute a fatal defect to Dr. Berlin's complaint, even if he were correct in his contention that malicious prosecution is not the sole course of action available to a party who is put to the expense and vexation of defending a baseless lawsuit. The considerations underlying the requirement that a complaint for malicious prosecution plead the favorable outcome of the prior cause are, in effect, broader than the rule itself. Indeed, we hold that permitting the filing of such a complaint against the attorney before the termination of the original suit would be against public policy since it would tend, as we pointed out earlier, to create a conflict of interest between attorney and client....

We are not persuaded by the plaintiff's argument that in light of the recent rise in the volume of malpractice litigation, including the filing of frivolous malpractice suits purely for their settlement value, public policy demands the creation of a cause of action to protect the courts from their misuse and the physician from the resulting harm.

... [I]t is doubtful that the creation of this new remedy would reduce the amount of litigation; it is far more likely that litigation would be increased since each successful defendant would bring suit against the original plaintiff. But even if the creation of this new remedy would reduce congestion in the courts, the price the public would have to pay for the benefit is too great. It is the overriding public policy of Illinois that potential suitors must have free and unfettered access to the courts. The Illinois courts have consistently adhered to the established policy "that the courts should be open to litigants for settlement of their rights without fear of prosecution for calling upon the courts to determine such rights" (*Franklin v. Grossinger Motor Sales, Inc.* (1970), 122 Ill. App. 2d 391, at 396, 259 N.E.2d 307, at 309, *leave to appeal denied, cert. denied*, 403 U.S. 911 (1971)....

... Since ... the very purpose of a court of law is to determine whether an action filed by a party has merit, it would be incongruous to hold a party liable in tort for negligently or even wantonly failing to determine in advance that which ultimately only the court can determine.

And as pointed out in *Lyddon v. Shaw*: "These considerations apply with equal force, not only to a party litigant, but to his counsel, since a litigant's free access to the courts would frequently be of little value to him if he were denied counsel of his choice by a rule which rendered attorneys fearful of being held liable as insurers of the merits of their client's case, and therefore unwilling to undertake representation in close or difficult matters."

Indeed, we believe it would be contrary to public policy for us to hold that an attorney has a duty to an intended defendant not to file a weak or perhaps "frivolous" lawsuit since we would be creating an insurmountable conflict of interest between the attorney and the client. The attorney owes a duty to his or her client to present the client's case vigorously in a manner as favorable to the client as the rules of law and professional ethics demand. When a tort action is brought he has but one intended beneficiary, his client; the adverse party is certainly not an intended beneficiary of the adverse counsel's client. Thus, even in states extending the attorney's responsibility and liability to intended beneficiaries of the client's conduct, such as intended legatees under a will, no liability to the adverse party sued by the client has been found absent malicious prosecution.

Furthermore, we are not convinced by Dr. Berlin's argument that since the defendant attorneys are officers of the court and can be disciplined by the court, they should be held liable in tort for breach of ... the Illinois Code of Professional Responsibility (1970).

First of all, the Code is not "designed solely to prevent the risk of the plaintiff's being piqued at being sued. That would be an oversimplification of the ethical complexities which govern the lawyer's conduct to his client, the court and the public." (*Spencer v. Burglass* (La. App. 1976), 337 So. 2d 596 at 601). Secondly, we see no violation of the Code. The provisions relied on by Dr. Berlin read as follows: Illinois Code of Professional Responsibility, D.R. 7-102(A)(1) (1970): "... a lawyer shall not: (1) File a suit ... when he knows or when it is obvious that such action would serve merely to harass or maliciously injure another." Illinois Code of Professional Responsibility, E.C. 7-10 (1970): "The duty of a lawyer to represent his client with zeal does not militate against his concurrent obligation to treat with consideration all persons involved in the legal process and to avoid the infliction of needless harm." As we have already noted, plaintiff in his complaint at no time alleged that the defendant attorneys filed the action knowing it would serve merely to harass or maliciously injure another. All he alleged was that they failed to make the investigation he, Dr. Berlin, felt was proper instead of relying on their client's statement. But, to reiterate, "if that constitutes malice, the courtrooms are full of malicious attorneys." And the injunction to avoid infliction of needless harm can hardly be interpreted as an injunction against the filing of weak lawsuits. The attorney is liable if he is guilty of malicious prosecution, that is enough. To create liability only for negligence, for the bringing of a weak case, would be to destroy his efficacy as advocate of his client and his value to the court, since only the rare attorney would have the courage to take other than the "easy" case....

... [T]he judgment of the trial court in favor of Dr. Berlin is reversed and the case is remanded for the entry of an order dismissing the plaintiff's complaint....

Notes

1. *Liability of attorneys.* An attorney can be held liable for malicious civil prosecution if the attorney initiates or continues an action without probable cause and primarily for a purpose other than securing proper adjudication of a claim. See Restatement (Third) of the Law Governing Lawyers § 57, comment *d* (2000); Annot., Liability of Attorney, Acting for Client, for Malicious Prosecution, 46 A.L.R.4th 249 (1986). An attorney's failure to adequately investigate a client's claim might bear upon the probable cause issue in a malicious prosecution action. See Nelson v. Miller, 227 Kan. 271, 607 P.2d 438 (1980) (facts that attorney could have learned by diligent effort to be considered). But some courts have declared that lack of probable cause is not to be found in a failure to investigate thoroughly. Wong v. Tabor, 422 N.E.2d 1279 (Ind. App. 1981); Friedman v. Dozorc, 412 Mich. 1, 312 N.W.2d 585 (1981) (no obligation to investigate if attorney could reasonably believe facts to be as client alleged). Courts have been unwilling to permit negligence actions against attorneys by opposing parties. See pp. 230–233, supra. Note the problems of attorney-client privilege that can arise if an attorney is sued.

2. In Sheldon Appel Co. v. Albert & Oliker, 47 Cal. 3d 863, 254 Cal. Rptr. 336, 765 P.2d 498 (1989), the Supreme Court of California decided that in a malicious prosecution action against an attorney, probable cause was established upon a finding that the prior action was "objectively tenable" on the facts known to the attorney. When there was no dispute as to the facts on which an attorney acted in commencing the action, the probable cause issue was "purely a legal question, to be determined by the trial court on the basis of whether, as an objective matter, the prior action was legally tenable." A claim would be legally tenable unless any reasonable attorney would think it was untenable. The court criticized Tool Research and Engineering Corp. v. Henigson, 46 Cal. App. 3d

675, 120 Cal. Rptr. 291 (1975), for bringing into the probable cause determination the questions of whether the attorney had a subjective belief that the client's action was tenable and whether the attorney performed adequate legal research before filing or continuing the action. These questions were relevant to the issue of the whether the attorney acted with malice but not, the court thought, to probable cause. If the action was legally tenable on an objective standard, commencing it was objectively reasonable and the opposing party was not subjected to unjustifiable litigation. Is this sound? See the opinions in Dutt v. Kremp, 111 Nev. 567, 894 P.2d 354 (1995). Does it mean that an attorney is to be found to have probable cause when the sole factual basis for litigation is what the client tells the attorney, without any further investigation of relevant facts? See Lucero v. Stewart, 892 F.2d 52 (9th Cir. 1989).

3. Is the attorney subject to liability if a lawsuit is initiated for a client who has malice and lacks probable cause? Is the client who believes he has a bona fide claim liable when the attorney knows or should know the claim lacks merit? The *Tool Research* case, supra, rejects an argument that attorney and client are legally responsible for each other's conduct, but it states that for some purposes the attorney is treated as the client's agent. See Restatement (Second) of Agency § 253 (1958) (principal's liability for tortious legal proceedings brought to accomplish principal's purposes). Horwitz v. Holabird & Root, 212 Ill. 2d 1, 816 N.E.2d 272 (2004), holds, contrary to some other authority, that a lawyer's client is not vicariously liable for an act committed by the lawyer in the exercise of independent professional judgement. In these circumstances, the lawyer was to be regarded as an independent contractor, not the agent of the client. Liability would attach only when it was proved that the client either specifically directed, controlled or authorized the lawyer's "precise method of performing the work" or subsequently ratified the lawyer's tortious conduct. See also Green Acres Trust v. London, p. 613, supra. A client could claim probable cause in reliance on the attorney's advice, but it is required that the client make full disclosure to the attorney of all facts that should be recognized as material. See National Surety Co. v. Page, 58 F.2d 145 (4th Cir. 1932), reh'g denied, 59 F.2d 370 (4th Cir. 1932); Bertero v. National General Corp., 13 Cal. 3d 43, 118 Cal. Rptr. 184, 529 P.2d 608 (1974); Restatement (Second) of Torts § 675, comment *g* (1977).

4. Should attorneys be subject to tort liability if they violate a code of professional responsibility? Courts have found no action for damages arising from violations of court rules or statutory provisions for the conduct of attorneys. See Baxt v. Liloia, 155 N.J. 190, 714 A.2d 271 (1998); Bob Godfrey Pontiac, Inc., v. Roloff, 291 Or. 318, 630 P.2d 840 (1981). However, under Rule 11 of the Federal Rules of Civil Procedure and its state counterparts, sanctions, including an order to pay legal expenses, incurred as a result of the rule's violation, can be imposed upon an attorney who makes claims or defenses that lack evidentiary support, that are not warranted by existing law or a nonfrivolous argument for change in the law, or that are "presented for any improper purpose, such as to harass, cause unnecessary delay, or needlessly increase the cost of litigation." Numerous states now have statutes providing for the award of attorneys' fees or costs generally to persons against whom groundless, frivolous, vexatious or harassing litigation has been brought. E.g., Cal. Civ. Proc. Code § 128.5; Colo. Rev. Stat. § 13-17-102; Ga. Code § 9-15-14; N.H. Rev. Stat. Ann. § 507:15; N.J. Stat. Ann. § 2A:15-59.1. See Wade, On Frivolous Litigation: A Study of Tort Liability and Procedural Sanctions, 14 Hofstra L. Rev. 433 (1986). Do such measures provide an adequate alternative to tort liability?

5. *Barratry, maintenance and champerty.* The common law recognized the crime of barratry: the offense of frequently exciting or stirring up suits and quarrels between others. Usually at least three such acts were required for liability. Can a tort action be based

on barratrous conduct? The principal case, in a portion of the opinion not reproduced here, held that a tort action might lie against a "common barrator" but the stirring up of a single suit was insufficient. Two related common law crimes, also concerned with the promotion of unnecessary litigation, were maintenance and champerty. Maintenance existed when a non-party bore all or part of a person's litigation expenses. It may have extended to other forms of support of litigation. Champerty was a species of maintenance in which a non-litigant acquired an interest in a suit's outcome, bearing a party's legal expenses in exchange for a portion of the matter involved in the suit, should the party be successful. Maintenance and champerty are now recognized in the United States only in modified form and limited circumstances, as when a person supports litigation without a legitimate interest in its subject-matter or an attorney acquires a financial interest in an action in violation of a statute or ethical rule. Causes of action are generally assignable. At common law, a tort action could be brought for any form of maintenance, but there are few modern cases. See Schnabel v. Taft Broadcasting Co., Inc., 525 S.W.2d 819 (Mo. App. 1975); American Home Assurance Co. v. Brett Pontiac Buick GMC Ltd., (1992) 116 N.S.R.2d 319, 96 D.L.R.4th 485 (App. Div.); Annot., Validity and Propriety of Arrangement by Which Attorney Pays or Advances Expenses of Client, 8 A.L.R.3d 1155 (1966); 4 Blackstone, Commentaries 134–136 (9th ed. 1783).

6. *Favorable termination.* The requirement of malicious prosecution that the underlying action terminate in favor of the present plaintiff precludes suit when proceedings are pending at the trial level, as in the principal case, and also, according to most authority, during the pendency of an appeal. See Moran v. Klatzke, 140 Ariz. 489, 682 P.2d 1156 (Ct. App. 1984); Annot., Pending Appeal in Civil Action as Precluding Malicious Prosecution Action Based on Successful Termination in Trial Court, 41 A.L.R.2d 863 (1955). A favorable final judgment does not always satisfy the termination requirement. In Lackner v. LaCroix, 25 Cal. 3d 747, 159 Cal. Rptr. 693, 602 P.2d 393 (1979), the underlying suit had been dismissed because of the statute of limitations. The court declared, "If the termination does not relate to the merits—reflecting on neither innocence of nor responsibility for the alleged misconduct—the termination is not favorable in the sense it would support a subsequent action for malicious prosecution." Accord, Palmer Development Corp. v. Gordon, 723 A.2d 881 (Me. 1999), with the court declaring that "Society does not want litigants who committed the acts of which they are accused, but who were able to escape liability on a 'technicality' or procedural device, to turn around and collect damages against their accuser." But see Lumpkin v. Friedman, 131 Cal. App. 3d 450, 182 Cal. Rptr. 378 (1982) (dismissal as sanction for failure to comply with discovery requirement is favorable termination). The proposition that plaintiff must have prevailed on the merits is rejected in Hammond Lead Products, Inc. v. American Cyanamid Co., 570 F.2d 668 (7th Cir. 1977) (dismissal for lack of venue), and Cult Awareness Network v. Church of Scientology International, 177 Ill. 2d 267, 685 N.E.2d 1347 (1997), cert. denied, 523 U.S. 1020 (1998) (actions terminated by summary judgment and voluntary and involuntary dismissals). Should voluntary dismissal be treated as favorable termination? The prevailing view is that this depends on whether the circumstances of the dismissal indicate that the action lacked merit. See Abbott v. United Venture Capital, Inc., 718 F. Supp. 828 (D. Nev. 1989); Siliski v. Allstate Insurance Co., 174 Vt. 200, 811 A.2d 148 (2002). See generally Annot., Nature of Termination of Civil Action Required to Satisfy Element of Favorable Termination to Support Action of Malicious Prosecution, 30 A.L.R.4th 572 (1984).

7. When plaintiff's victory was obtained on appeal, after an adverse judgment below, it has been held that the adverse judgment conclusively establishes probable cause for the underlying action and thereby prevents malicious prosecution liability. This is subject to

exceptions for judgments shown to have been obtained by fraud, perjury, withholding of evidence or other improper means; judgments granted by a court without jurisdiction; judgments that are void (not merely erroneous); and judgments granted without affording a chance to controvert the alleged facts. See Annot., Judgment in Prior Civil Proceedings Adverse to Instant Plaintiff in Malicious Prosecution as Evidence of Probable Cause, 58 A.L.R.2d 1422 (1958).

8. Favorable termination is not required if the maliciously prosecuted proceeding was ex parte. See Zinn v. Rice, 154 Mass. 1, 27 N.E. 772 (1891) (action for maliciously making excessive attachment may be brought before termination of underlying suit, in which validity of debt not disputed); Kryszke v. Kamin, 163 Mich. 290, 128 N.W. 190 (1910) (injunction granted, subsequently dissolved); Prosser & Keeton, Law of Torts 892 (5th ed. 1984). Cf. Blankenship v. Staton, 348 S.W.2d 925 (Ky. 1961) (action based on wrongful attachment would lie even though suit on notes had resulted in judgment against plaintiff). What if judgment was confessed by power of attorney? See Annot., Institution of Confessed Judgment Proceedings as Ground of Action for Abuse of Process or Malicious Prosecution, 87 A.L.R.3d 554 (1978) (must be vacated or voided). Termination by compromise does not qualify. See Wong v. Tabor, 422 N.E.2d 1279 (Ind. App. 1981); Tower Special Facilities, Inc. v. Investment Club, Inc., 104 Wis. 2d 221, 311 N.W.2d 225 (Ct. App. 1981).

Section 3. Abuse of Process

Ellis v. Wellons
Supreme Court of North Carolina
224 N.C. 269, 29 S.E.2d 884 (1944)

SCHENCK, Justice....

"Abuse of legal process consists in the malicious misuse or misapplication of that process to accomplish some purpose not warranted or commanded by the writ. In brief, it is the malicious perversion of a regularly issued process whereby a result not lawfully or properly attainable under it is secured.... The abuse may be of civil or criminal process." 1 Am. Jur., Abuse of Process, par. 2, p. 176. The distinctive nature of an action for abuse of process is the improper use of process after it has been issued, and not for maliciously causing it to issue. Where the process has been lawfully issued and has subsequently wilfully been perverted so as to accomplish a result not commanded by it or lawfully obtainable under it the action for abuse of process lies. There are two essential elements for an action for abuse of process, (1) the existence of an ulterior motive, and (2) an act in the use of the process not proper in the regular prosecution of the proceeding. Measured by this standard there was sufficient evidence in the case at bar to be submitted to the jury and to sustain the verdict rendered [for plaintiff].

It was admitted that the defendant procured the arrest and prosecution of the plaintiff. The plaintiff testified that he did not owe the defendant any amount and that when he (plaintiff) refused to pay him (defendant) the amount claimed, the defendant procured the warrant from the clerk of the recorder's court charging the plaintiff with having disposed of a crop of tobacco, after executing an agricultural lien thereon without applying the proceeds in payment of such lien, with intent to defeat the rights of the defendant, lienee, and had the plaintiff arrested and incarcerated thereunder; that after such warrant was issued the defendant told plaintiff he would not have it served if plaintiff would pay the defendant what he claimed was due to him by plaintiff; and after plaintiff had been arrested and lodged in jail upon said warrant, and while he was in jail, the defendant came to him and told plaintiff that he, defendant, would procure his release if he, plaintiff, would agree to pay him, defendant, the amount he claimed, and further, he, defendant, would procure plaintiff's release if he would agree to go to Fayetteville and work in defendant's guano plant and there work out the amount claimed. This was evidence that the motive of the defendant was to collect what he claimed was due him from the plaintiff, which was an ulterior motive, a motive foreign to the only legitimate purpose for which the warrant could have issued, namely, to punish the person charged for the commission of the offense against which the law inveighs. This was not only evidence of an ulterior motive, bad intent or wicked purpose, but also evidence of such motive, intent or purpose finally culminating in an abuse, which is the gist of the action....

The defendant advances the argument that since the jury failed to find the absence of probable cause for the prosecution of the plaintiff by the defendant upon the charge of disposing of crops upon which a lien existed without settling with the lienee, and thereby denied the plaintiff's alleged cause of action for malicious prosecution, the plaintiff was thereby also denied the right to recover on his alleged cause of action for abuse of process, and for that reason the court erred in failing to instruct the jury not to consider the evidence applicable to the first cause of action in considering the issues as to the second cause of action. This argument is untenable for the reason that while there is a definite distinction between an action for malicious prosecution and an action for abuse of process in that, among other things, in the former want of probable cause is a requisite and not in the latter, the same evidence may be competent on both causes of action....

[Affirmed.]

STACY, Chief Justice [with whom Winborne and Denny, JJ., joined] (dissenting).

An offer to alleviate a writ is not to abuse the process, and that's all that is left on this record after eliminating the first cause of action which was resolved in favor of the defendant and from which neither side has appealed.... Speaking to a similar situation in Stanford v. Grocery Co., 143 N.C. 419, 55 S.E. 815, 816, it was said: "While the complaint endeavors to set up two causes of action, as a matter of fact the testimony only discloses one — that for malicious prosecution — and the allegations purporting to be a second cause of action amount to nothing more than the assertion of a bad motive prompting the first."

Conceding the defendant's purpose was to collect a debt, this goes only to the motive which is not enough in an action for abuse. To make out his case, the plaintiff must aver and prove irregular steps taken under cover of the process after its issuance, and injury resulting therefrom.... "The bad intent must finally culminate in the abuse; for it is only the latter which is the gist of the action." Walker, J., in Carpenter, Baggott & Co. v. Hanes, 167 N.C. 551, 83 S.E. 577, 580. "An abuse of process consists in its employment or use for some unlawful purpose, which it was not intended by the law to effect, and amounts to a perversion of it." Wright v. Harris [160 N.C. 542, 76 S.E. 490]....

... The issue of abuse of process was answered against the defendants on the theory that if the defendant's purpose was to collect a debt, rather than to prosecute the plaintiff for a violation of the criminal law, "that would amount to an abuse of process". Led-ford v. Smith, 212 N.C. 447, 193 S.E. 722. The law is otherwise when probable cause exists for issuing the writ, and no perversion is shown....

The essentials of an action for abuse of process, as distinguished from one for malicious prosecution, are purposely left indefinite by the courts. Perhaps the main reason for this is to afford a remedy in cases of actionable injury resulting from the improper use of judicial process which may not come within the narrow confines of an action for malicious prosecution. Thus an action for abuse of process has been held to lie for an excessive levy or needlessly harsh execution; greatly disproportionate attachment; seizure of exempt property; injury to property attached or improper eviction; oppressive treatment of one in custody; extortion by means of arrest; and one may be held liable for making an arrest in an unauthorized manner. In a number of cases, it is said that two elements must concur in order to give rise to an action for abuse of process: First, an ulterior purpose; and, second, an act in the use of the process not proper in the regular prosecution of the proceeding. In addition, the plaintiff must show damage from the irregular act.

The present case, stripped of any malicious prosecution, falls in none of the foregoing categories. My vote is for a reversal.

Notes

1. Abuse of process differs from malicious prosecution in that the latter involves the wrongful commencement of an action or legal process while the former involves the use of process for an improper purpose once it has been issued. See Tappen v. Ager, 599 F.2d 376 (10th Cir. 1979); C. C. & J., Inc. v. Hagood, 711 So. 2d 947 (Ala. 1998); Harper, James & Gray, Law of Torts § 4.9 (3d ed. 1996). Both malicious prosecution and abuse of process may arise from the same proceedings, as when abuse occurs in the course of proceedings that were malicious and groundless from the start. See Ash v. Cohn, 119 N.J.L. 54, 194 A. 174 (1937). It is generally agreed that use of the criminal law to collect a civil debt amounts to abuse of process, provided criminal process is so used after its issuance. See C. C. & J., Inc. v. Hagood, supra; Wood v. Graves, 144 Mass. 365, sub nom. Wood v. Bailey, 11 N.E. 567 (1887); Annot., Use of Criminal Process To Collect Debt as Abuse of Process, 27 A.L.R.3d 1202 (1969). But see Vasseur v. Eunice Superette, Inc., 386 So. 2d 692 (La. App. 1980), review denied, 393 So. 2d 747 (La. 1980) (no abuse found in filing bad check charges to obtain payment and dropping charges when payment made).

2. The abuse of process theory may be advantageous to plaintiff, as he need not establish that the underlying proceedings were brought without probable cause and terminated in his favor, but plaintiff may have difficulty in establishing that process was improperly used. See, e.g., Union National Bank of Little Rock v. Kutait, 312 Ark. 14, 846 S.W.2d 652 (1993); Peisner v. Detroit Free Press, 68 Mich. App. 360, 242 N.W.2d 775 (1976) (commencement of lawsuit for improper purpose insufficient). If defendant causes seizure of plaintiff's property by attachment, garnishment or other ancillary process, knowing that the process is groundless or excessive, is this abuse of process, "malicious prosecution" of the process, or both? See Morfessis v. Baum, 108 U.S. App. D.C. 303, 281 F.2d 938 (1960) (defendant obtained writ of attachment and garnishment of plaintiff's funds in execution of judgment which already had been satisfied); Annot., Liability of Creditor for Excessive Attachment or Garnishment, 56 A.L.R.3d 493 (1974). Recall that it is not necessary in malicious prosecution to establish favorable termination of the underlying proceedings in plaintiff's favor when they were ex parte. See p. 718, supra.

3. Plaintiff and defendant are opponents in domestic relations litigation. Their respective rights to property are in issue. Plaintiff commences a "claim and delivery" action against defendant to recover possession of a Cadillac, which is part of the disputed property, and has issued a writ directing the sheriff to take possession of the car. The sheriff goes to defendant's house and places a seal on the car. Plaintiff arrives and says he will drop his proceeding for recovery of the car if defendant will abandon her domestic relations action. Defendant notifies her attorney, who promptly obtains an order enjoining the sheriff from seizing the Cadillac. In her answer to the claim and delivery action, defendant counterclaims for abuse of process. Is this claim valid? See Spellens v. Spellens, 49 Cal. 2d 210, 317 P.2d 613 (1957), vacating 305 P.2d 628 (Cal. App. 1956). If so, is the tort dangerous to settlement of civil cases, as well as criminal cases?

4. A controversial satirical magazine repeatedly publishes defamatory references to a prominent businessman. Claiming to have been libelled in three successive issues of the magazine, the businessman brings suit against the magazine's editor, publisher and primary distributors, and also many proprietors of stores which sell the magazine. His legal representatives enter settlement negotiations with the representatives of the retail outlets. He agrees to drop the libel actions against retail outlets which undertake not to sell any issues of the magazine in the future, but rejects offers not to sell future issues which contain defamatory statements about him. Is there an abuse of process? Would there be an abuse if the businessman were satisfied with an undertaking not to sell issues of the magazine that defame him? Would it be an abuse to use suit against the magazine's principals to obtain a withdrawal of the charges and a commitment not to libel the businessman in future issues? See Goldsmith v. Sperrings Ltd., [1977] 1 W.L.R. 478 (C.A.).

5. Use of a threat to bring legal proceedings is not an abuse of process. However, lawyers must be attentive to criminal law and ethical considerations in suggesting criminal or administrative prosecution during communications with opponents in civil matters. Obtaining a financial or property settlement by threatening to report an alleged offense to the authorities may constitute extortion. Belief that the accusation is true or that the client is entitled to what is received is not necessarily a defense. However, threatening to file a charge for a criminal act if an honest civil claim for harm allegedly caused thereby is not resolved by negotiation may be lawful. See Model Penal Code § 223.4, comment 2(f). A.B.A. Model Code of Professional Responsibility DR 7-105(A) declares: "A lawyer shall not present, participate in presenting, or threaten to present criminal charges solely to obtain an advantage in a civil matter." An allusion to the criminal nature of the opposing party's conduct may be regarded as a "threat." The A.B.A. Model Rules of Professional Conduct contain no corresponding provision. Does this mean that there is to be no ethical restraint of threats of prosecution other than the law of extortion? See Richmond, Sabre-Rattling and the Sound of Professional Responsibility, 34 Am. J. Trial Adv. 27 (2010).

Hauser v. Bartow

New York Court of Appeals
273 N.Y. 370, 7 N.E.2d 268 (1937)

HUBBS, Judge.

This is an action to recover damages for malicious abuse of process. The lower courts have dismissed the complaint on the ground that it fails to state a cause of action. The complaint alleges that respondent conspired with others "maliciously and willfully, and without legal cause or warrant," to have appellant declared incompetent so that she might control his property and prevent his executing a new will; that without the knowledge of appellant, respondent commenced a proceeding in the Supreme Court to have herself appointed committee of his person and property, and falsely and maliciously represented in that proceeding that he was violent and that it would endanger his life to appear in court and thereby induced the court to issue its process; that she was thereafter appointed committee of his person and property; that she caused him to be removed as an officer and director of a company in which they were each stockholders, sold certain securities, and otherwise managed his property; that appellant was unaware of these proceedings until some time thereafter when respondent threatened to deprive him of his liberty; that he then applied to the Supreme Court, a jury trial was had on the issue of his competency, resulting in a verdict to the effect that appellant was then competent and an order was entered discharging respondent as committee and ordering her to account; and that she accounted and allowances were made to her for commissions, attorneys' fees, and other expenses....

The legal purpose of appointing a committee of one's person and property is to conserve the property of the incompetent and to look after, care for, and protect the person.

The complaint in effect alleges that such was not the purpose of the respondent, but that knowing that he was not incompetent, she conspired with others to have him wrongfully declared to be incompetent for a wrongful and ulterior purpose; that the apparently lawful act was unlawful because done untruthfully and maliciously with the sole purpose of injuring and damaging the appellant in order to bring about a financial benefit to herself....

It is not enough that the actor have an ulterior motive in using the process of the court. It must further appear that he did something in the use of the process outside of the purpose for which it was intended. Every one has a right to use the machinery of the law, and bad motive does not defeat that right. There must be a further act done outside the use of the process—a perversion of the process. If he uses the process of the court for its proper purpose, though there is malice in his heart, there is no abuse of the process. He may be liable for malicious prosecution, but the distinction between these two wrongs must be kept in mind. As soon as the actor uses the process of the court, not to effect its proper function, but to accomplish through it some collateral object, he commits this tort. A concrete example may make this more intelligible. If one resorts to legal process to have another declared incompetent, and uses it for that purpose, he does not commit the wrong, though he may be guilty of another wrong, no matter what his motives, hopes or expectations may be. But if he makes use of that process not for the purpose of attaining its proper end, but to extort money, or to coerce action, that is a perversion of process.

In this case, whatever may have been respondent's motives, she used the process of the court for the purpose for which the law created it. She used it, she did not abuse it. Nowhere in the complaint can there be found any allegation that respondent did any act by virtue of the order adjudging the appellant incompetent and appointing her as committee of his person and property which was not within the scope of her duties as such committee or was in excess of the powers granted to her as such committee. The complaint, therefore, fails to state a cause of action for abuse of process....

... [T]here has been a conclusive adjudication that the original order was valid; that is, issued upon sufficient cause.... [This] bars an action for malicious prosecution....

[Affirmed. Crane, C.J., (with whom O'Brien, J., joined) delivered a dissenting opinion which concluded that plaintiff pleaded an action for malicious prosecution. The Supreme Court's original decision to declare plaintiff incompetent and appoint a committee did not bar the action because plaintiff had not been given a hearing or notice prior to the decision.]

Notes

1. It is often said that the gist of the abuse of process action is the use of process to accomplish an unlawful purpose. However, it is sufficient that the process be used to accomplish what the court in the principal case termed a "collateral object"—a purpose for which such process is not legally intended—even if the object might be obtained lawfully by other means. See Annot., Action for Abuse of Process, 80 A.L.R. 580 (1932); Restatement (Second) of Torts § 682 (1977). This was established in Grainger v. Hill, (1838) 1 Arn. 42, 3 Bing. N.C. 212, 132 Eng. Rep. 769, 2 Jur. 235, 7 L.J.C.P. 85, 5 Scott 561 (C.P.). Defendants were creditors of plaintiff, a ship's master. Concerned about the security for repayment of the debt, defendants resolved to obtain the ship's register, without which plaintiff could not go to sea. Defendants had plaintiff arrested for nonpayment of the debt and then required him to give up the register in order to secure his release. The court rejected defendants' arguments that the action could not be maintained without proof of termination of the process in plaintiff's favor and want of probable cause.

2. Another case of this type is White v. Apsley Rubber Co., 181 Mass. 339, 63 N.E. 885 (1902), in which a landlord, in order to induce a tenant to abandon a claim of right to occupy a house and to vacate the premises, had the tenant arrested for malicious injury to the landlord's property. See also Flynn v. Songer, 399 S.W.2d 491 (Ky. 1966), in which a retailer's credit manager was arrested for practicing law without a license to induce him to release garnishment of the defendant's wages for a $34.53 account balance. Closer to the principal case is Sarvold v. Dodson, 237 N.W.2d 447 (Iowa 1976), in which a police officer allegedly had plaintiff committed to a mental institution in order to thwart plaintiff's efforts to have the officer disciplined or discharged from his position. Cf. Maniaci v. Marquette University, 50 Wis. 2d 287, 184 N.W.2d 168 (1971), in which a university had a student committed temporarily to prevent her leaving the university without parental consent. Abuse of process was also found in Williams v. Spautz, (1992) 174 C.L.R. 509, reh'g denied, (1993) 67 A.L.J.R. 388. A lecturer dismissed from his employment with a university instituted criminal defamation proceedings against several university officials. The lecturer had a purpose to vindicate his reputation, but his predominant purpose was found to be securing reinstatement or a favorable settlement of his wrongful dismissal action against the university.

3. Abuse of process exists if property is attached in order to prevent its lawful transfer to another person. See Malone v. Belcher, 216 Mass. 209, 103 N.E. 637 (1913). Or if an action is used to deter potential customers or buyers from dealing with the party sued. See Speed Seal Products Ltd. v. Paddington, [1985] 1 W.L.R. 1327 (C.A.). Cf. Vittands v. Sudduth, 49 Mass. App. Ct. 401, 730 N.E.2d 325 (2000) (litigation involving plaintiff's vacant lot, allegedly used to prevent development so defendants could continue to use lot as "park"). If a creditor to which an insufficient funds check is given has the debtor arrested on a bad check charge, with the object of recovering the debt, and then accepts payment, is there abuse of process? The court which decided Ellis v. Wellons, p. 718, supra, found no abuse in this situation. Neither issuance of process nor evil purpose es-

tablished liability; the purpose must have led to abuse after the writ was issued. Melton v. Rickman, 225 N.C. 700, 36 S.E.2d 276 (1945).

4. Plaintiff leases land from defendant for use as a golf course. The lease provides that the lessee will pay the taxes on the property. If the lessee fails to pay the taxes or otherwise fails to comply with the terms of the lease, the lease becomes void at the lessor's option. After a dispute about defendant's laying a sewer line across the golf course, plaintiff sues defendant for trespass and breach of the lease agreement. Subsequently, a $33.68 real estate tax notice is sent to defendant. Defendant does not forward the notice to plaintiff or pay the taxes due. The property is sold to the state on account of the taxes owed. Defendant then redeems the property, notifies plaintiff that it has failed to comply with the lease, declares the lease void and orders plaintiff to vacate the property. Following the eviction notice, defendant counterclaims in plaintiff's suit, claiming unlawful detainer and demanding possession of the premises. Plaintiff amends its complaint to demand damages on the ground that defendant's counterclaim is an abuse of process. Should the demand succeed? In Warwick Development Co., Inc. v. GV Corp., 469 So. 2d 1270 (Ala. 1985), a 5–4 majority found a basis for the abuse of process claim in plaintiff's contentions that defendant's only purpose in filing the counterclaim was retribution for being sued and that the nonpayment of taxes was orchestrated in order to set up the unlawful detainer action. The dissent found no improper use of the process, only the use of a process to contest the survival of the lease and obtain plaintiff's eviction on grounds of the non-payment of the taxes. Cf. Tranchina v. Arcinas, 78 Cal. App. 2d 522, 178 P.2d 65 (1947) (landlords permitted to commence eviction proceedings during World War II only by obtaining certificate from Office of Price Administration, which they did by representing they desired to occupy premises themselves; they actually intended to sell premises).

5. In principle, any type of judicial process may be the subject of an abuse of process claim, but with some types it may be quite difficult to prove an irregular act or improper purpose. See Coleman v. Gulf Insurance Group, 41 Cal. 3d 782, 226 Cal. Rptr. 90, 718 P.2d 77 (1986) (appeal, allegedly meritless and taken solely to gain benefit of delay and induce plaintiffs to settle; no wrongful act found in defendant's settlement offer); Miller v. Stern, 262 App. Div. 5, 27 N.Y.S.2d 374 (1941) (order for deposition of attorney for opponent in litigation); Tsiopoulos v. Commercial Union Assurance Co., (1986) 57 O.R.2d 117, 32 D.L.R.4th 614 (High Ct.) (demand for punitive damages, allegedly intended to induce opponent to settle); Young v. Allstate Insurance Co., 119 Hawaii 403, 198 P.3d 666 (2008) (insurance company's alleged "scorched earth litigation tactics" designed to deter claims and punish plaintiff for litigating claim). Compare Crackel v. Allstate Insurance Co., 208 Ariz. 252, 92 P.3d 882 (Ct. App. 2004) (insurance company's alleged strategy of making litigation so expensive for claimants that they would surrender claims); Younger v. Solomon, 38 Cal. App. 3d 289, 113 Cal. Rptr. 113 (1974) (interrogatories, apparently relevant to main action, addressed to defendant in action; claimed that plaintiff's attorney had purpose of damaging defendant's reputation and eliminating him as competitor). See Annot., Civil Liability of Attorney for Abuse of Process, 97 A.L.R.3d 688 (1980). In addition, some jurisdictions require for abuse of process liability that there be interference with plaintiff's person or property. See Hoppe v. Klapperich, 224 Minn. 224, 28 N.W.2d 780 (1947) (indirect injury to person's good name or business not sufficient); Williams v. Williams, 23 N.Y.2d 592, 298 N.Y.S.2d 473, 246 N.E.2d 333 (1969) (alleged that plaintiff sued to ruin his reputation by publication of complaint). Contra, Neinstedt v. Wetzel, supra.

6. Can an abuse of process action lie for raising an invalid defense or adducing false evidence for the purpose of defeating a valid claim made by plaintiff? Metall und Rohstoff

A.G. v. Donaldson Lufkin & Jenrette Inc., [1990] 1 Q.B. 391, 467–473 (C.A.), holds there is no abuse of process action for defendant's presentation of a false case to defeat plaintiff's action. Having the purpose of defeating plaintiff's claim, defendant did not use legal process for a purpose other than that for which it was designed. The court believed that if an abuse of process action were allowed, honest litigants might be deterred from pursuing honest defenses. It suggested that such an action would conflict with the established immunity from civil liability for harm caused by giving or presenting false evidence (see pp. 689–691, supra). Cf. the cases on whether there is an action for "malicious defense," p. 705, supra.

7. Can a person other than the party against whom the process was issued have an action for abuse of process? In Board of Education v. Farmingdale Classroom Teachers' Association, 38 N.Y.2d 397, 380 N.Y.S.2d 635, 343 N.E.2d 278 (1975), a board of education sued a teachers' association whose attorney had subpoenaed eighty-seven of the board's teachers to appear in a proceeding. The board was required to hire seventy-seven substitute teachers. It was held that the board could maintain an action for abuse of process because it allegedly was the target and victim of a perversion of legal process.

8. For an innovative decision that surmounts the barriers in the law of abuse of process and malicious prosecution in order to provide an effective remedy for wrongful use of actions, defenses and litigation procedures, see Yost v. Torok, 256 Ga. 92, 344 S.E.2d 414 (1986). One feature of the remedy created by the court is a requirement that it be claimed as a counterclaim or additional claim in the action in which defendant's wrongful conduct took place, not as an independent action. The grounds of the claim are similar to those specified in statutes on groundless and vexatious litigation (see p. 716, supra), but damages are not limited to litigation costs. See also DeVaney v. Thriftway Marketing Corp., 124 N.M. 512, 953 P.2d 277 (1997), cert. denied, 524 U.S. 915 (1998), replacing malicious prosecution and abuse of process with a new tort of "malicious abuse of process" that combines elements of the two common law torts. On counterclaims alleging abuse of process in the opponent's action, see Annot., Necessity and Permissibility of Raising Claims for Abuse of Process by Reply or Counterclaim in Same Proceeding in Which Abuse Occurred—State Cases, 82 A.L.R.4th 1115 (1990).

Section 4. Interference with Civil Rights

Ashby v. White

Court of Queen's Bench
(1703) Holt K.B. 524, 90 Eng. Rep. 1188,
2 Ld. Raym. 938, 92 Eng. Rep. 126, 3 Ld. Raym. 320,
92 Eng. Rep. 710, 6 Mod. 45, 87 Eng. Rep. 808,
1 Salk. 19, 91 Eng. Rep. 19, 3 Salk. 17, 91 Eng. Rep. 665,
rev'd, (1704) 1 Bro. Parl. Cas. 62, 1 Eng. Rep. 417,
2 Ld. Raym. 958, 92 Eng. Rep. 138 (H.L.)

[Plaintiff brought an action on the case, declaring that he was qualified to vote in an election for members of Parliament, and defendants, borough constables conducting the election, "well knowing the premises, but contriving and fraudulently and maliciously intending to damnify him … in this behalf, and wholly to hinder and disappoint him of his privilege," prevented plaintiff from voting. Two candidates were elected without his vote. Plaintiff claimed £200 damages and obtained a verdict in his behalf.]

POWYS Justice … [N]o action lies against the defendant,

1. Because the defendant as bailiff is quasi a judge, and has a distinguishing power either to receive or refuse the votes of such as come to vote, and does preside in this affair at the time of election: though his determination be not conclusive, but subject to the judgment of the Parliament, where the plaintiff must take his remedy.

2. … [I]f you allow the plaintiff to maintain an action for this matter, then every elector may bring his action, and so the officer shall be loaded with a number of actions, that may ruin him; and … A. B. C. D. E. and a hundred more, may at this rate bring actions.

3. … [I]t is objected, that by the law of England every one who suffers a wrong has a remedy; and here is a privilege lost, and shall not the plaintiff have a remedy? To that I answer, first, it is not an injury, properly speaking; it is not damnum, for the plaintiff does not lose his privilege by this refusal, for when the matter comes before the committee of elections, the plaintiff's vote will be allowed as a good vote; and so in an action upon the case by one of the candidates for a false return, this tender of his vote by the plaintiff shall be allowed as much as if it had been given actually and received. And if this refusal of the plaintiff's vote be an injury, it is of so small and little consideration in the law, that no action will lie for it; it is one of those things within the maxim, de minimis non curat lex. … The late statute 7 & 8 W. 3, c. 7, gives an action against the officer for a misfeasance to the party grieved, i.e. to the candidate, who is to give his vote; so that by the judgment of the Parliament he cannot have any action. Before the Statute of 23 H. 6, no action lay for the candidate, who was the party aggrieved, against the officer, for a false return, because it related to Parliamentary matters, and yet he had an injury. …

4. This action is not maintainable for another reason, which I think is a weighty one, viz. this action is primae impressionis; never the like action was brought before, for if it had lain, it would have sometimes been put in use. …

5. Another reason against the action is, that the determination of this matter is particularly reserved to the Parliament, as a matter properly conusable by them, and to them it belongs to determine the fundamental rights of their House, and of the constituent parts of it, the members; and the Courts of Westminister shall not tell them who shall sit there. Besides, we are not acquainted with the learning of elections, and there is a particular cunning in it not known to us, nor do we go by the same rules, and they often determine contrary to our opinion without doors. … Suppose in this action we should adjudge one way, and after in Parliament it should be determined another way; or suppose a Judge of Nisi Prius, before whom the cause comes to be tried, should say, I am not bound by the rule of the last determination in Parliament in this action, for this is another sort of action, not within the meaning of the statute; these things would be of ill consequence.

6. Another reason against this action is, that if we should allow this action to lie for the plaintiff, a fortiori we must allow an action to be maintainable for the candidates against the defendant for the same refusal; for the candidates have both damnum et injuriam, and are the parties aggrieved; and if we should allow that, we shall multiply actions upon the officers at the suit of the candidates, and every particular elector too; so that men will be thereby deterred from venturing to act in such offices, when the acting therein becomes so perilous to them and their families. … [T]he Courts at Westminister must not inlarge their jurisdiction in these matters, farther than the statute gives them;

and indeed it is a happiness to us, that we are so far disengaged from the heats, which attend elections. Our business is to determine of meum and tuum, where the heats do not run so high, as in things belonging to the Legislature....

[Gould and Powell, JJ., delivered concurring opinions.]

HOLT Chief Justice [dissenting]. The single question in this case is, whether, if a free burgess of a corporation, who has an undoubted right to give his vote in the election of a burgess to serve in Parliament, be refused and hindered to give it by the officer, if an action on the case will lie against such officer.

I am of opinion that judgment ought to be given in this case for the plaintiff.... [T]he defendant neither is a judge, nor any thing like a judge, ... for the defendant is only an officer to execute the precept, i.e. only to give notice to the electors of the time and place of election, and to assemble them together in order to elect, and upon the conclusion to cast up the poll, and declare which candidate has the majority.

... [E]very man, that is to give his vote on the election of members to serve in Parliament, has a several and particular right in his private capacity, as a citizen or burgess. And surely it cannot be said, that this is so inconsiderable a right, as to apply that maxim to it, de minimis non curat lex. A right that a man has to give his vote at the election of a person to represent him in Parliament, there to concur to the making of laws, which are to bind his liberty and property, is a most transcendant thing ... and so great a privilege, that it is a great injury to deprive the plaintiff of it....

If the plaintiff has a right, he must of necessity have a means to vindicate and maintain it, and a remedy if he is injured in the exercise or enjoyment of it; and indeed it is a vain thing to imagine a right without a remedy; for want of right and want of remedy are reciprocal.... Where a man has but one remedy to come at his right, if he loses that he loses his right. It would look very strange, when the commons of England are so fond of their right of sending representatives to Parliament, that it should be in the power of a sheriff, or other officer, to deprive them of that right, and yet that they should have no remedy; it is a thing to be admired at by all mankind. Supposing then that the plaintiff had a right of voting, and so it appears on the record, and the defendant has excluded him from it, no body can say, that the defendant has done well; then he must have done ill, for he has deprived the plaintiff of his right; so that the plaintiff having a right to vote, and the defendant having hindered him of it, it is an injury to the plaintiff. Where a new Act of Parliament is made for the benefit of the subject, if a man be hindered from the enjoyment of it, he shall have an action against such person who so obstructed him.... This right of voting is a right in the plaintiff by the common law, and consequently he shall maintain an action for the obstruction of it. But there wants not a statute too in this case, for by West. 1, 3 Ed. 1, c. 5, it is enacted, that forasmuch as elections ought to be free, the King forbids, upon grievous forfeiture, that any great man, or other, by power of arms, or by malice or menaces, shall disturb to make free election. And this statute, as my Lord Coke observes, is only an inforcement of the common law; and if the Parliament thought the freedom of elections to be a matter of that consequence, as to give their sanction to it, and to enact that they should be free; it is a violation of that statute, to disturb the plaintiff in this case in giving his vote at an election, and consequently actionable.

And I am of opinion, that this action on the case is a proper action. My brother Powell indeed thinks, that an action upon the case is not maintainable, because here is no hurt or damage to the plaintiff; but surely every injury imports a damage, though it does not cost the party one farthing, and it is impossible to prove the contrary; for a damage is not merely pecuniary, but an injury imports a damage, when a man is thereby hindred of his right.... And it is no objection to say, that it will occasion multiplicity of actions; for if men will multiply injuries, actions must be multiplied too; for every man that is injured ought to have his recompence. Suppose the defendant had beat forty or fifty men, the damage done to each one is peculiar to himself, and he shall have his action. So if many persons receive a private injury by a publick nusance, every one shall have his action....

But in the principal case my brother says, we cannot judge of this matter, because it is a Parliamentary thing. O! by all means be very tender of that. Besides it is intricate, and there may be contrariety of opinions. But this matter can never come in question in Parliament; for it is agreed that the persons for whom the plaintiff voted were elected; so that the action is brought for being deprived of his vote: and if it were carried for the other candidates against whom he voted, his damage would be less. To allow this action will make publick officers more careful to observe the constitution of cities and boroughs, and not to be so partial as they commonly are in all elections, which is indeed a great and growing mischief, and tends to the prejudice of the peace of the nation. But they say, that this is a matter out of our jurisdiction, and we ought not to inlarge it. I agree we ought not to incroach or inlarge our jurisdiction; by so doing we usurp both on the right of the Queen and the people: but sure we may determine on a charter granted by the King, or on a matter of custom or prescription, when it comes before us without incroaching on the Parliament. And if it be a matter within our jurisdiction, we are bound by our oaths to judge of it. This is a matter of property determinable before us. Was ever such a petition heard of in Parliament, as that a man was hindred of giving his vote, and praying them to give him remedy? The Parliament undoubtedly would say, take your remedy at law. It is not like the case of determining the right of election between the candidates.

... My brother Powys has cited the opinion ... that no action lay ... because none had ever been brought, yet he cannot depend upon it. Indeed that is an argument, when it is founded upon reason, but it is none, when it is against reason.... Let us consider wherein the law consists, and we shall find it to be, not in particular instances and precedents; but on the reason of the law, and ubi eadem ratio, ubi idem jus. This privilege of voting does not differ from any other franchise whatsoever....

[The court's] judgment was reversed in the House of Lords, and judgment given for the plaintiff by fifty Lords against sixteen. Trevor Chief Justice and Baron Price were of opinion with the three Judges of the King's Bench. Ward C. B. and Bury and Smith Barons were of opinion with the Lord Chief Justice Holt, Tracy dubitante....

Notes

1. The decision of Holt, C.J., ultimately prevailed in Ashby v. White, and numerous later cases have recognized the existence of a common law action in favor of a person improperly deprived of political rights. But in the context of the particular case are the arguments of Holt, C.J., more persuasive than those of Powys, J.? A number of cases have found liable an official who, with improper motive or in bad faith, refused to allow a qualified citizen to register or vote. There is some early authority favoring liability regardless of motive. Hill v. Carr, 186 Ill. App. 515 (1914), held that a primary election candidate stated a cause of action by alleging that election judges wilfully neglected and refused to count all the votes cast for him, thus depriving plaintiff of the nomination and a position on the general election ballot. See Annot., Personal Liability of Public Officer for Breach of Duty in Respect of Election or Primary Election Laws, 153 A.L.R. 109 (1944); Restatement (Second) of Torts § 865 (1979) (liability for consciously wrongful depriva-

tion of right to vote or hold office). Cf. Tozer v. Child, (1857) 7 E. & B. 377, 119 Eng. Rep. 1286, 3 Jur. N.S. 774, 26 L.J.Q.B. 151, 5 W.R. 287 (Ex. Ch.) (if malice shown, action lies against churchwarden presiding at church election for refusing vote or candidacy of qualified person). See also Socialist Workers Party v. Attorney General of United States, 463 F. Supp. 515 (S.D.N.Y. 1978) (action allowed for illegal wiretaps, break-ins, opening of mail and other activities designed to disrupt efforts of political association). If a candidate for office alleges he lost the election because of bribery, is there an action for damages against the persons engaged in the bribery? Shields v. Booles, 238 Ky. 673, 38 S.W.2d 677 (1931), decided that there was no cause of action. Claims by persons denied the right to vote were distinguished. See also Nichols v. Kansas Political Action Committee, 270 Kan. 37, 11 P.3d 1134 (2000), rejecting a defeated candidate's action alleging that defendants made illegal campaign contributions to the successful candidate.

2. Does Ashby v. White support tort liability for interference with civil rights when no election or political activity is involved? For example, would there be an action against a court clerk who refused to accept plaintiff's filing of a lawsuit? Would there be a tort action against a private citizen who compelled plaintiff under duress to abandon a lawsuit, or who retaliated against plaintiff for instituting or participating in legal proceedings? De-Marco v. Publix Super Markets, Inc., 384 So. 2d 1253 (Fla. 1980), aff'g 360 So. 2d 134 (Fla. App. 1978), holds that there is no liability for firing an employee because he refused to withdraw a personal injury action against the employer, as an employer was free to terminate employment at will for any reason, but Smith v. Atlas Off-Shore Boat Service, Inc., 653 F.2d 1057 (5th Cir. 1981), holds that this is a tort under maritime law. Cf. Groce v. Foster, 880 P.2d 902 (Okla. 1994), holding (5–4) that discharge of an employee for refusal to dismiss a negligence action against a customer of the employer is actionable. In deciding that an employer did not violate public policy in discharging an employee because the employee had sued the employer, the court in Watson v. Peoples Security Life Insurance Co., 322 Md. 467, 588 A.2d 760 (1991), reasoned that an employer was not required to retain a discontented employee. Suppose an employee is discharged for seeking legal advice in a matter involving the employer? See Porterfield v. Mascari II, Inc., 374 Md. 402, 823 A.2d 590 (2003) (no liability because no "clear mandate of public policy" violated); Simonelli v. Anderson Concrete Co., 99 Ohio App. 3d 254, 650 N.E.2d 488 (1994), appeal denied, 72 Ohio St. 3d 1422, 648 N.E.2d 514 (1995) (employer may be liable).

3. In McPherson v. McCarrick, 22 Utah 232, 61 P. 1004 (1900), plaintiff sued for deprivation of jury service and juror's fees. He was discharged from a venire when another juror refused to serve with plaintiff because of his race. Attorneys in the case were afraid that their clients' interests would be jeopardized if they resisted the objection. This was held not to form the basis of an action for damages against the objecting juror, even though the objection to plaintiff was "frivolous ... and unworthy." Compare Nees v. Hocks, 272 Or. 210, 536 P.2d 512 (1975). When a clerical employee was summoned for jury duty, her employers gave her a letter asking that she be excused because they could not spare her for a month. The employee gave this letter to the court clerk but said that she would like to serve on jury duty. She was not excused. When the employers learned that the employee had said she wanted to serve, they fired her. She sued the employers for damages. The court held that there should be a cause of action in tort, notwithstanding the general principle that an employer can discharge an employee for any reason, because of the employer's "socially undesirable motive" and interference with the important community interest in having citizens available for jury duty.

4. Cases in the preceding two notes are part of a rapidly expanding body of law on damages claims for wrongful discharge from employment. There is now wide (although

not unanimous) acceptance of the principle that it is wrongful under tort law or the employment contract for an employer to discharge an employee for a reason that contravenes public policy. Violation of public policy might be found when an employer fires an employee for having filed a workers' compensation claim. See Annot., Recovery for Discharge from Employment in Retaliation for Filing Workers' Compensation Claim, 32 A.L.R.4th 1221 (1984). Or because of the employee's refusal to participate in unlawful conduct, or reporting unlawful conduct to the authorities. See Annot., Common-Law Retaliatory Discharge of Employee for Refusing to Perform or Participate in Unlawful or Wrongful Acts, 104 A.L.R.5th 1 (2002); Annot., Common-Law Retaliatory Discharge of Employee for Disclosing Unlawful Acts or Other Misconduct of Employer or Fellow Employees, 105 A.L.R.5th 531 (2003). What if an employee is discharged for refusing to engage in such lawful conduct as participation in the employer's legislative lobbying or other political efforts? See Novosel v. Nationwide Insurance Co., 721 F.2d 894 (3d Cir. 1983). Borse v. Piece Goods Shop, Inc., 963 F.2d 611 (3d Cir. 1992), holds that an employee who was discharged for refusal to submit to drug testing and property searches would have an action if the testing and searches were wrongful invasions of privacy under standards established in tort actions for intrusion upon seclusion.

5. When a cause of action is asserted by a person whose employment has been or is about to be terminated, interference with civil rights might be utilized as a basis of plaintiff's action. So might tortious interference with plaintiff's employment contract, which is addressed in Chapter 2, supra. Other possible theories, which may be considered in a course on Labor Law or Remedies, include a tort action for interference with statutory rights, such as the right to worker's compensation for employment-related injuries or the right to redress for discriminatory practices; an action implied in statute for violating a statutory prohibition against interference with the exercise of statutory rights; breach of contract, the employment contract being found to contain an implied condition of good faith; breach of contract, the employment contract (construed according to the dictates of public policy) not permitting discharge for the exercise of civil or statutory rights or the performance of such civic duties as jury duty, providing law-enforcement authorities or a court with evidence of illegal activities, or refraining from illegal conduct desired by the employer; a tort of "wrongful discharge" when an employee is discharged for such reasons; and tortious ("bad faith") breach of contract when an employee is discharged for such reasons. On possible tort claims for discharge of employees generally, see Annot., Modern Status of Rule that Employer May Discharge At-will Employee for Any Reason, 12 A.L.R.4th 544 (1982).

Nevin v. Pullman Palace Car Company

Supreme Court of Illinois
106 Ill. 222 (1883)

Mr. Justice MULKEY delivered the opinion of the Court:

[Action on the case. The trial court sustained a demurrer to plaintiff's declaration. He alleged that while a passenger on an Illinois Central train, he entered a sleeping car operated by defendant and reserved sleeping berths for himself, his wife and niece, the conductor] promising to have them made up a little later in the night; that he and his wife took the seats in the berth assigned to them, and remained sitting up, in an orderly manner, until about twelve o'clock, frequently, in the meantime, requesting the conductor to have the berths made up, so they could retire to rest, and at the same time tendering to him the price agreed to be paid therefor; that on the arrival of the train at Lena ... plaintiff temporarily left his seat, and stepped out on the platform of the sleeper, intending to return immediately to his berth, when the conductor instantly closed and secured the outer doors of said sleeper, and thereby prevented him from again entering the same; that plaintiff endeavored to open said doors and reenter said car, and frequently requested the conductor to permit him to do so, but that said conductor, instead of complying with his request, removed his satchel, coats and shoes from the berth so assigned to him and his wife, to another car, and ejected the latter from said sleeper, by means of which plaintiff was compelled to take and occupy a seat in a common passenger car on said train till its arrival in Chicago, by reason of which plaintiff was deprived of his rest and sleep, in consequence of which "he became exceedingly weary and sick, and was greatly humiliated," etc.; that his expulsion from his berth in the manner stated was done willfully and maliciously, and that the only reason assigned by the conductor for refusing the price of the berths was, "that they were not made up." ...

... [T]he contention is, that all the defendant did on the occasion was a mere breach of the special contract between the parties, and that the remedy therefore is on the contract, and not in tort. ...

It is a familiar doctrine that case will lie for a mere non-feasance against persons exercising certain public trades or employments, where no contractual relation exists between them and the plaintiff, as, where a common carrier, having the requisite means of transportation, refuses to carry goods or passengers. Chitty, in discussing this matter, in his work on Pleadings, says: "There are, however, some particular instances of persons exercising certain public trades or employments, who are bound by law to do what is required of them in the course of their employments without aid of express contract, and are in return entitled to a recompense, and may, therefore, be sued in case, as for a breach of duty in refusing to exercise their callings, — as, where a common carrier, having convenience, refuses to carry goods, being tendered satisfaction for the carriage; or an innkeeper to receive a guest, having room for him; or a smith, having materials for the purpose, to shoe a horse for a traveler; or a ferryman to convey one over a common ferry, and the like." (Vol. 1, 136.) It is clear, from the language of this author, the classes of persons enumerated are intended as mere examples of the application of the general principle stated, and not as a limitation of the rule itself, and by a well recognized rule of the common law the same principle should be extended to all other trades and callings that bear the same relation to the public as those just enumerated. ...

... In what respect, then, does this company differ in its relation to the public, so far as the present inquiry is concerned, from an ordinary railway company? No difference has been pointed out by counsel, and we are confident none can be. Why, then, should not the same principles be held to apply to it that apply to common carriers, and others in like employments, in so far as their relation to the public is the same? ...

If then, this company owes any duties to the community by reason of its relation to the public, as we hold it does, manifestly one of them is, that it shall treat all persons whose patronage it has solicited with fairness, and without unjust discrimination. When, therefore, a passenger, who, under the rules of the company, is entitled to a berth upon payment of the usual fare, and to whom no personal objection attaches, enters the company's sleeping car at a proper time for the purpose of procuring accommodations, and in an orderly and respectful manner applies for a berth, offering or tendering the customary price therefor, the company is bound to furnish it, provided it has a vacant one at its disposal. ... Holding then, as we do, where there are sleeping berths not engaged, it is the duty of the company, upon the payment or tender of the customary price, to furnish them to applicants when properly called for by unobjectionable persons, it follows the defendant was not justifiable in refusing to let the plaintiff have one for himself and wife, and it is well settled the fact there was a special contract between the company and the plaintiff, upon which an action of assumpsit might have been maintained, does not at all affect the right to recover in the present form of action, which is founded upon the defendant's common law liability....

[The court also held that an action on the case would lie for breach of duty arising from the contract between the parties. Reversed.]

Bhadauria v. Board of Governors of Seneca College of Applied Arts and Technology

Ontario Court of Appeal
(1979) 27 O.R.2d 142, 105 D.L.R.3d 707,
rev'd, [1981] 2 S.C.R. 181, (1981) 124 D.L.R.3d 193

WILSON, J.A. [Plaintiff held a Ph.D. in mathematics and qualifications to teach in Ontario, with seven years' teaching experience. Over a four-year period she applied for ten openings on the teaching staff of defendant's college. All of the openings were advertised in the Toronto press. Plaintiff was not granted an interview for any of them although she had the required qualifications. She alleged that this was because of her East Indian ethnic origin. The *Ontario Human Rights Code*, R.S.O. 1970, c. 318, s. 4, provided: "No person shall, (*a*) refuse to refer or to recruit any person for employment; (*b*) dismiss or refuse to employ or to continue to employ any person ... because of race, creed, colour, age, sex, marital status, nationality, ancestry, or place of origin of such person or employee." Instead of filing a complaint pursuant to the provisions of the Code, plaintiff commenced an action for damages, alleging deprivation of the opportunity to join defendant's teaching staff and earn her livelihood as a teacher and the suffering of mental distress, frustration and loss of dignity and self-esteem. The trial court held that she stated no cause of action.]

... [Plaintiff] alleged two separate causes of action arising from the same set of facts. She alleged first that the respondent was in breach of its common law duty not to discriminate against her and secondly that the respondent was also in breach of its statutory duty not to discriminate against her. Only the second raises the question whether a violation of s. 4 of the *Ontario Human Rights Code* gives rise to a civil cause of action....

A convenient starting point for a consideration of [the common law claim] is the decision of the Supreme Court of Canada in *Christie v. York Corp.*, [1940] S.C.R. 139, [1940] 1 D.L.R. 81, an appeal from the Quebec Court of King's Bench, Appeal Side, in which the defendant's employees refused to serve a glass of beer to the plaintiff because they were under instructions from their employer not to serve coloured persons. The plaintiff sued for damages for humiliation. Mr. Justice Rinfret, speaking for the majority, said: "In considering this case, we ought to start from the proposition that the general principle of the law of Quebec is that of complete freedom of commerce. Any merchant is free to deal as he may choose with any individual member of the public. It is not a question of motives or reasons for deciding to deal or not to deal; he is free to do either. The only restriction to this general principle would be the existence of a specific law, or, in the carrying out of the principle, the adoption of a rule contrary to good morals or public order." He found neither in this case....

A similar situation arose in *Rogers v. Clarence Hotel et al.*, [1940] 3 D.L.R. 583, [1940] 2 W.W.R. 545, 55 B.C.R. 214. The proprietor of a beer parlour in Vancouver refused to serve a Negro and the *Christie* case was applied by the majority of the British Columbia Court of Appeal. Freedom of commerce was held to be just as paramount in British Columbia as in the Province of Quebec. However, O'Halloran, J.A., delivered a strong dissent. He pointed out that the appeal involved questions of fundamental importance. One of them was whether a judgment of the Supreme Court of Canada based on the civil law of Quebec was binding on the Courts of the common law Provinces. He held that it was not. Another important question raised on the appeal was whether it was contrary to the common law for the defendant to refuse to serve a customer solely because of his colour or race. He concluded that it was. He said:

> The first ground, that refusal to serve the respondent solely because of his colour and race is contrary to the common law, is founded upon the equality of all British subjects before the law. The respondent is a British subject. All British subjects have the same rights and privileges under the common law—it makes no difference whether white or coloured; or of what class, race or religion. This elementary principle of the common law seems to have been overlooked entirely in the restaurant decision, *Franklin v. Evans* (1924), 55 O.L.R. 349 [in which it was held that a restaurant proprietor, unlike an innkeeper or hotel-keeper, was not under a common law duty to provide service to all who sought it and, therefore, was not liable for refusal to serve a customer because of his race.] ... In *Rothfield v. North British Ry. Co.*, [1920] S.C. 805, the railway company sought to exclude Rothfield from its Edinburgh hotel during the last Great War. Lord Anderson, the Lord Ordinary said: " ... *It is obvious that the defenders are not entitled to exclude the pursuer from their hotel because he is a Jew; and it would have made no difference, in my opinion, had it been proved that he is a Jew of German origin. An individual is not responsible, and ought not to be made responsible, for his ancestry....* Nor is it a sufficient ground of exclusion that the pursuer is a money-lender. That is a lawful occupation, and therefore money-lenders are entitled to all privileges enjoyed by other members of the State, including the right to be entertained in the common inns of the country." (The italics are mine).
>
> On the appeal in that case, while it was held there was evidence justifying the pursuer's exclusion for reasonable cause, yet the Lord Ordinary was upheld on the question of law that race or lawful occupation as such do not constitute reasonable cause....

[*Constantine v. Imperial London Hotels, Ltd.*, [1944] 2 All E.R. 171, in which the defendant hotel had refused the plaintiff a room because of his colour] applied the celebrated principle of *Ashby v. White et al.* (1703), 2 Ld. Raym. 938, 92 E.R. 126, enunciated by Chief Justice Holt: "If the plaintiff has a right, he must of necessity have a means to vindicate and maintain it, and a remedy if he is injured in the exercise or enjoyment of it; and indeed it is a vain thing to imagine a right without a remedy; for want of right and want of remedy are reciprocal." Mr. Justice Birkett found that a common law right of the plaintiff was violated in this case. The defendant was an innkeeper under a duty to receive and house the plaintiff. The action was maintainable without proof of special damage because, as Chief Justice Holt had made plain, the injury itself imported damage. He awarded the plaintiff nominal damages in the amount of five guineas.

Because of the fact that the foregoing cases and others of similar import which pre-date them all involved hotels, theatres or restaurants, it was submitted by counsel for the defendant that they afford no assistance to the plaintiff in attempting to establish a cause of action in the circumstances of this case. The plaintiffs in those cases, it is argued, had some basis for asserting a common law right to the service being provided to other members of the public and it was the violation of that right that afforded them a cause of action and not any right not to be discriminated against *per se*. I think this is probably a reasonable perspective from which to view those authorities. Only Mr. Justice O'Halloran in his dissenting judgment in *Rogers v. Clarence Hotel et al., supra*, appears to have based his decision squarely on the fact that the plaintiff was being refused accommodation on racial grounds, something which he found to be totally repugnant to the principle of equality before the law which he described as "elementary" and "deeply rooted" in the British system of justice. He would have imposed a duty on the Clarence Hotel not to discriminate against the plaintiff....

Prosser in his text, *Handbook of the Law of Torts*, 4th ed. (1971), at pp. 3–4, states: "The law of torts is anything but static, and the limits of its development are never set. When it becomes clear that the plaintiff's interests are entitled to legal protection against the conduct of the defendant, the mere fact that the claim is novel will not of itself operate as a bar to the remedy." I think there can be no doubt that the interests of persons of different ethnic origins are entitled to the protection of the law. The preamble to the *Ontario Human Rights Code* reads as follows:

> WHEREAS recognition of the inherent dignity and the equal and inalienable rights of all members of the human family is the foundation of freedom, justice and peace in the world and is in accord with the Universal Declaration of Human Rights as proclaimed by the United Nations;
>
> AND WHEREAS it is public policy in Ontario that every person is free and equal in dignity and rights without regard to race, creed, colour, sex, marital status, nationality, ancestry or place of origin;
>
> AND WHEREAS these principles have been confirmed in Ontario by a number of enactments of the Legislature;
>
> AND WHEREAS it is desirable to enact a measure to codify and extend such enactments and to simplify their administration....

I regard the preamble to the Code as evidencing what is now, and probably has been for some considerable time, the public policy of this Province respecting fundamental human rights. If we accept that "every person is free and equal in dignity and rights without regard to race, creed, colour, sex, marital status, nationality, ancestry or place of origin", as we do, then it is appropriate that these rights receive the full protection of the common law. The plaintiff has a right not to be discriminated against because of her ethnic origin and alleges that she has been injured in the exercise or enjoyment of it. If she can establish that, then the common law must, on the principle of *Ashby v. White et al., supra*, afford her a remedy.

I do not regard the Code as in any way impeding the appropriate development of the common law in this important area. While the fundamental human right we are concerned with is recognized by the Code, it was not created by it. Nor does the Code, in my view, contain any expression of legislative intention to exclude the common law remedy. Rather the reverse since s. 14*a* appears to make the appointment of a board of inquiry to look into a complaint made under the Code a matter of ministerial discretion.

It is unnecessary, in view of the finding that a cause of action exists at common law, to determine whether or not the Code gives rise to a civil cause of action....

Appeal allowed.

Notes

1. On further appeal, the Supreme Court of Canada ordered that plaintiff's action be dismissed. [1981] 2 S.C.R. 181, (1981) 124 D.L.R.3d 193. It held that the comprehensive provisions of the Ontario Human Rights Code for enforcement of the Code and hearing of discrimination complaints (including judicial review) foreclosed any common law action for discrimination or civil action for violation of the Code. Ashby v. White and the innkeeper cases were distinguished on the ground that plaintiffs there had a legally protected interest, whereas refusal to enter into contractual relations such as employment (or to consider contractual relations) gave rise to no tort liability at common law. What are the prospects of a common law action for discrimination being established in American law? Should it be?

2. As stated in the *Nevin* case, a common carrier is required to provide transportation to members of the public requesting it, when space is available. See Hannibal Railroad v. Swift, 12 Wall. (79 U.S.) 262 (1871). A number of cases concern discrimination by railroad sleeping car companies. The companies usually were held liable to ticketholders for refusal of accommodation. See Speaks v. Southern Railway Co., Carolina Division, 90 S.C. 358, 73 S.E. 625 (1912); Pullman Palace-Car Co. v. Cain, 15 Tex. Civ. App. 503, 40 S.W. 220 (1897) (sleeping car company liable for railroad's ejection of black passenger from berth when train entered state whose law required segregation); Annot., Liability of Sleeping Car Company for Refusal to Furnish Accommodations, 23 A.L.R. 1302 (1923). A public utility offering essential services to the general public is not free to discriminate on the basis of some "collateral matter" unrelated to its service. See Vanderberg v. Kansas City, Mo., Gas Co., 126 Mo. App. 600, 105 S.W. 17 (1907) (gas company could not refuse service to married woman in her own name); Annot., Right of Public Utility Corporation to Refuse Its Service Because of Collateral Matter Not Related to That Service, 55 A.L.R. 771 (1928). See also Annot., Civil Rights: Racial or Religious Discrimination in Furnishing of Public Utilities Services or Facilities, 53 A.L.R.3d 1027 (1973). If a municipality or other governmental unit discriminates unreasonably in provision of public services, an injunction may be obtained. See Annot., Discrimination in Provision of Municipal Services or Facilities as Civil Rights Violation, 51 A.L.R.3d 950 (1973).

3. At common law persons engaged in certain "public callings," such as innkeepers, were under an obligation to provide service to all who sought it, without discrimination. See Rothfield v. North British Railway Co., discussed in the *Bhadauria* case; Prosser & Keeton, Law of Torts 662–663 (5th ed. 1984). Proprietors of other privately owned businesses and places of entertainment were under no such duty and could deny admission to whomever they pleased. Sometimes a breach of contract action would arise—if, for instance, a person purchased a ticket and then was denied the service to which the ticket entitled him. See Annot., Exclusion of Person (for Reason Other Than Color or Race) from Place of Public Entertainment or Amusement, 1 A.L.R.2d 1165 (1948). Should courts adhere to the old law on this subject?

4. Many state statutes now prohibit discrimination by businesses. Should a court accept a claim for damages allegedly caused by prohibited discrimination in the provision of services? An early case so holding is Ferguson v. Gies, 82 Mich. 358, 46 N.W. 718 (1890), involving a restaurant manager who refused to serve black patrons in the better part of the establishment. What if the statute provides a remedy to the victims of the discrimination? In Odom v. East Avenue Corp., 178 Misc. 363, 34 N.Y.S.2d 312 (Sup. Ct. 1942), plaintiffs were entitled by a civil rights statute to recover a penalty for being denied service by a restaurant because of their race. The innkeeper's special common law duty was

found to apply because the restaurant was within a hotel. The court reasoned that when there was a pre-existing right and a common law cause of action for its violation, a statutory remedy was an additional means of relief. It was not the exclusive remedy. Therefore, common law liability could still be imposed.

5. Many modern statutes limit the factors that an employer may include in decisions on hiring and continuation of employment. In the absence of an express provision for liability, should violation of such a statute give rise to a cause of action? In Perks v. Firestone Tire & Rubber Co., 611 F.2d 1363 (3d Cir. 1979), employers had been prohibited from requiring a polygraph test as a condition of initial or continued employment. It was held that plaintiff would have a cause of action if he was discharged for refusal to submit to a polygraph examination. Tate v. Browning-Ferris, Inc., 833 P.2d 1218 (Okla. 1992), applied the theory of tort liability for discharge of an employee in contravention of public policy, discussed on pp. 729–730, supra, to conduct that violated statutes prohibiting employment discrimination. The court held that an employee terminated in violation of state and federal employment discrimination statutes could maintain a tort action against the employer. The statutory remedies were not exclusive of others. In Williams v. Dub Ross Co., 895 P.2d 1344 (Okla. App. 1995), it was decided that this theory did not extend to discriminatory refusal to hire. Should a court entertain a common law action for a type of discrimination prohibited by statute if defendant is not one of the employers to which the statute applies? See Jennings v. Marralle, 8 Cal. 4th 121, 32 Cal. Rptr. 2d 275, 876 P.2d 1074 (1994) (age discrimination by employer of less than five persons; no action); Thibodeau v. Design Group One Architects, LLC., 260 Conn. 691, 802 A.2d 731 (2002) (pregnancy discrimination by employer of less than three persons; no action); Roberts v. Dudley, 140 Wash. 2d 58, 993 P.2d 901 (2000) (gender discrimination by employer of fewer than eight persons; actionable as discharge contrary to public policy).

Davis v. Passman

Supreme Court of the United States
442 U.S. 228 (1979)

Mr. Justice BRENNAN delivered the opinion of the Court....

[Congressman Otto Passman of Louisiana hired Shirley Davis as a deputy administrative assistant in 1974. A few months later he terminated her employment, writing her a letter which stated that she was "able, energetic and a very hard worker," but the diversity of the job and heavy work load made it "essential that the understudy to my Administrative Assistant be a man." Davis brought suit in federal court, alleging that Passman's conduct discriminated against her on the basis of sex in violation of the Due Process Clause of the Fifth Amendment to the Constitution. She sought damages in the form of backpay. She also sought equitable relief (reinstatement, promotion and increase of salary), but this became unavailable when Passman was defeated for re-election. The Court of Appeals held that "no right of action may be implied from the Due Process Clause of the fifth amendment."]

In *Bivens v. Six Unknown Named Agents of the Federal Bureau of Narcotics* [403 U.S. 388 (1971)] federal agents had allegedly arrested and searched Bivens without probable cause, thereby subjecting him to great humiliation, embarrassment, and mental suffering. *Bivens* held that the Fourth Amendment guarantee against "unreasonable searches and seizures" was a constitutional right which Bivens could enforce through a private

CONGRESSMAN OTTO PASSMAN AND PRESIDENT RICHARD NIXON
University of Louisiana at Monroe Library, Special Collections/Archives

cause of action, and that a damages remedy was an appropriate form of redress. Last Term, *Butz v. Economou*, 438 U.S. 478 (1978), reaffirmed this holding, stating that "the decision in *Bivens* established that a citizen suffering a compensable injury to a constitutionally protected interest could invoke the general federal-question jurisdiction of the district courts to obtain an award of monetary damages against the responsible federal official."

Today we hold that *Bivens* and *Butz* require reversal of the holding of the en banc Court of Appeals....

The Fifth Amendment provides that "[n]o person shall be ... deprived of life, liberty, or property, without due process of law...." In numerous decisions, this Court "has held that the Due Process Clause of the Fifth Amendment forbids the Federal Government from denying equal protection of the laws." *Vance v. Bradley*, 440 U.S. 93, 95 n. 1 (1979). "To withstand scrutiny under the equal protection component of the Fifth Amendment's Due Process Clause, 'classifications by gender must serve important governmental objectives and must be substantially related to achievement of those objectives.'" *Califano v. Webster*, 430 U.S. 313, 316–317 (1977). The equal protection component of the Due Process Clause thus confers on petitioner a federal constitutional right to be free from gender discrimination which cannot meet these requirements.[11] ...

---

11. Respondent argues that the subject matter of petitioner's suit is nonjusticiable because judicial review of congressional employment decisions would necessarily involve a "lack of the respect due coordinate branches of government." We disagree. While we acknowledge the gravity of respondent's concerns, we hold that judicial review of congressional employment decisions is constitutionally limited only by the reach of the Speech or Debate Clause of the Constitution, Art. I, §6, cl. 1. The Clause provides that Senators and Representatives, "for any Speech or Debate in either House, ... shall not be questioned in any other Place." It protects Congressmen for conduct necessary to perform their duties "within the 'sphere of legitimate legislative activity.'" The purpose of the Clause is "to protect the integrity of the legislative process by insuring the independence of individual legislators." Thus "[i]n the American governmental structure the clause serves the ... function of reinforcing the separation of powers so deliberately established by the Founders." ...

… [T]he Court of Appeals concluded that petitioner lacked a cause of action … through the application of the criteria set out in *Cort v. Ash*, 422 U.S. 66 (1975), for ascertaining whether a private cause of action may be implied from "a statute not expressly providing one."[19] … This was error, for the question of who may enforce a *statutory* right is fundamentally different than the question of who may enforce a right that is protected by the Constitution.

Statutory rights and obligations are established by Congress, and it is entirely appropriate for Congress, in creating these rights and obligations, to determine in addition, who may enforce them and in what manner. For example, statutory rights and obligations are often embedded in complex regulatory schemes, so that if they are not enforced through private causes of action, they may nevertheless be enforced through alternative mechanisms, such as criminal prosecutions or other public causes of actions. In each case, however, the question is the nature of the legislative intent informing a specific statute, and *Cort* set out the criteria through which this intent could be discerned.

The Constitution, on the other hand, does not "partake of the prolixity of a legal code." *M'Culloch v. Maryland*, 17 U.S. (4 Wheat.) 316, 407 (1819). It speaks instead with a majestic simplicity. One of "its important objects" is the designation of rights. And in "its great outlines" the judiciary is clearly discernible as the primary means through which these rights may be enforced. …

At least in the absence of "a textually demonstrable constitutional commitment of [an] issue to a coordinate political department," *Baker v. Carr*, 369 U.S. at 217, we presume that justiciable constitutional rights are to be enforced through the courts. And unless such rights are to become merely precatory, the class of those litigants who allege that their own constitutional rights have been violated, and who at the same time have no effective means other than the judiciary to enforce these rights, must be able to invoke the existing jurisdiction of the courts for the protection of their justiciable constitutional rights. … Traditionally, therefore, "it is established practice for this Court to sustain the jurisdiction of federal courts to issue injunctions to protect rights safeguarded by the Constitution and to restrain individual state officers from doing what the 14th Amendment forbids the State to do." *Bell v. Hood*, 327 U.S., at 684. Indeed, this Court has already settled that a cause of action may be implied directly under the equal protection component of the Due Process Clause of the Fifth Amendment in favor of those who seek to

---

19. See n. 8, supra [stating:]

The criteria set out in *Cort v. Ash* are: "First, is the plaintiff 'one of the class for whose especial benefit the statute was enacted.' — that is, does the statute create a federal right in favor of the plaintiff? Second, is there any indication of legislative intent, explicit or implicit, either to create such a remedy or to deny one? Third, is it consistent with the underlying purposes of the legislative scheme to imply such a remedy for the plaintiff? And finally, is the cause of action one traditionally relegated to state law, in an area basically the concern of the States, so that it would be inappropriate to infer a cause of action based solely on federal law?"

The Court of Appeals had some difficulty applying these criteria to determine whether a cause of action should be implied under the Constitution. It eventually concluded, however, (1) that although "the fifth amendment right to due process certainly confers a right upon Davis, the injury alleged here does not infringe this right as directly as" the violation of the Fourth Amendment rights alleged in *Bivens*; (2) that "[c]ongressional remedial legislation for employment discrimination has carefully avoided creating a cause of action for money damages for one in Davis' position;" (3) that, unlike violations of the Fourth Amendment, "the breadth of the concept of due process indicates that the damage remedy sought will not be judicially manageable;" and (4) that implying a cause of action under the Due Process Clause would create "the danger of deluging federal courts with claims otherwise redressable in state courts or administrative proceedings. …"

enforce this constitutional right.[20] The plaintiffs in *Bolling v. Sharpe*, 347 U.S. 497 (1954), for example, claimed that they had been refused admission into certain public schools in the District of Columbia solely on account of their race.... [T]his Court held that equitable relief should be made available.

Like the plaintiffs in *Bolling v. Sharpe*, petitioner rests her claim directly on the Due Process Clause of the Fifth Amendment. She claims that her rights under the Amendment have been violated, and that she has no effective means other than the judiciary to vindicate these rights.[21]

We conclude, therefore, that she is an appropriate party to invoke the general federal question jurisdiction of the District Court to seek relief. She has a cause of action under the Fifth Amendment.

Although petitioner has a cause of action, her complaint might nevertheless be dismissed under Rule 12(b)(6) unless it can be determined that judicial relief is available. We therefore proceed to consider whether a damages remedy is an appropriate form of relief.

... "[I]t is ... well settled that where legal rights have been invaded, and a federal statute provides for a general right to sue for such invasion, federal courts may use any available remedy to make good the wrong done." *Bell v. Hood*, 327 U.S., at 684. *Bivens* holds that in appropriate circumstances a federal district court may provide relief in damages for the violation of constitutional rights if there are "no special factors counselling hesitation in the absence of affirmative action by Congress."

First, a damages remedy is surely appropriate in this case. "Historically, damages have been regarded as the ordinary remedy for an invasion of personal interests in liberty." *Bivens, supra*, at 395. Relief in damages would be judicially manageable, for the case presents a focused remedial issue without difficult questions of valuation or causation. Litigation under Title VII of the Civil Rights Act of 1964 has given federal courts great experience evaluating claims for backpay due to illegal sex discrimination. Moreover since respondent is no longer a Congressman, equitable relief in the form of reinstatement would be unavailing. And there are available no other alternative forms of judicial relief. For Davis, as for Bivens, "it is damages or nothing."[23]

Second, although a suit against a Congressman for putatively unconstitutional actions taken in the course of his official conduct does raise special concerns counselling hesitation, we hold that these concerns are coextensive with the protections afforded

---

20. *Jacobs v. United States*, 290 U.S. 13 (1933), held that a plaintiff who alleged that his property had been taken by the United States for public use without just compensation could bring suit directly under the Fifth Amendment.

21. Clause 9 of Rule XLIII of the House of Representatives [provides]: "A Member, officer, or employee of the House of Representatives shall not discharge or refuse to hire any individual, or otherwise discriminate against any individual with respect to compensation, terms, conditions, or privileges of employment, because of such individual's race, color, religion, sex, or national origin." Clause 9 was adopted ... approximately six months after petitioner's discharge. In 1977 the House Commission on Administrative Review (the "Obey Commission") termed "the anti-discrimination provisions of Rule XLIII ... all but unenforceable." ...

23. Respondent does not dispute petitioner's claim that she "has no cause of action under Louisiana law." And it is far from clear that a state court would have authority to effect a damages remedy against a United States Congressman for illegal actions in the course of his official conduct, even if a plaintiff's claim were grounded in the United States Constitution. Deference to state court adjudication in a case such as this would in any event not serve the purposes of federalism, since it involves the application of the Fifth Amendment to a federal officer in the course of his federal duties. It is therefore particularly appropriate that a federal court be the forum in which a damages remedy be awarded.

by the Speech or Debate Clause. See n. 11, *supra.* If respondent's actions are not shielded by the Clause, we apply the principle that "legislators ought ... generally to be bound by [the law] as are ordinary persons." *Gravel v. United States,* 408 U.S. 606, 615 (1972)....

Third, there is in this case "no *explicit* congressional declaration that persons" in petitioner's position injured by unconstitutional federal employment discrimination "may not recover money damages from" those responsible for the injury. The Court of Appeals apparently interpreted § 717 of Title VII of the Civil Rights Act of 1964 as an explicit congressional prohibition against judicial remedies for those in petitioner's position. When § 717 was added to Title VII to protect federal employees from discrimination, it failed to extend this protection to congressional employees such as petitioner who are not in the competitive service.[26] There is no evidence, however, that Congress meant § 717 to foreclose alternative remedies available to those not covered by the statute. Such silence is far from "the clearly discernible will of Congress" perceived by the Court of Appeals....

We hold today that the Court of Appeals for the Fifth Circuit, en banc, must be reversed because petitioner has a cause of action under the Fifth Amendment, and because her injury may be redressed by a damages remedy. The Court of Appeals did not consider, however, whether respondent's conduct was shielded by the Speech or Debate Clause of the Constitution. Accordingly, we do not reach this question. And, of course, we express no opinion as to the merits of petitioner's complaint.

[Reversed and remanded. Burger, C.J., (with whom Powell and Rehnquist, JJ., joined) and Stewart, J., (with whom Rehnquist, J., joined) delivered dissenting opinions.]

Mr. Justice POWELL, with whom THE CHIEF JUSTICE and Mr. Justice REHNQUIST join, dissenting....

The Court's analysis starts with the general proposition that "the judiciary is clearly discernible as the primary means through which [constitutional] rights may be enforced." It leaps from this generalization, unexceptional itself, to the conclusion that individuals who have suffered an injury to a constitutionally protected interest, and who lack an "effective" alternative, "*must* be able to invoke the existing jurisdiction of the courts for the protection of their justiciable constitutional rights." (emphasis supplied). Apart from the dubious logic of this reasoning, I know of no precedent of this Court that supports such an absolute statement of the federal judiciary's obligation to entertain private suits that Congress has not authorized. On the contrary, I have thought it clear that federal courts must exercise a principled discretion when called upon to infer a private cause of action directly from the language of the Constitution. In the present case ... principles of comity and separation of powers should require a federal court to stay its hand....

Whether or not the employment decisions of a Member of Congress falls within the scope of the Speech or Debate Clause of the Constitution, a question the Court does not reach today, it is clear that these decisions are bound up with the conduct of his duties.... Because of the nature of his office, he must rely to an extraordinary extent on the loyalty and compatibility of everyone who works for him. A Congressman simply cannot perform his constitutional duties effectively, or serve his constituents properly, unless he is supported by a staff in which he has total confidence.

---

26. .... In *Brown v. General Services Administration,* 425 U.S. 820 (1976), we held that the remedies provided by § 717 are exclusive when those federal employees covered by the statute seek to redress the violation of rights guaranteed by the statute.

The foregoing would seem self-evident even if Congress had not indicated an intention to reserve to its Members the right to select, employ and discharge staff personnel without judicial interference. But Congress unmistakably has made clear its view on this subject. It took pains to exempt itself from the coverage of Title VII....

Notes

1. There has developed a body of authority accepting a cause of action against government officials based directly on violation of federal constitutional rights. This supplements the remedies for deprivation of constitutional rights provided by 42 U.S.C. § 1983 and other statutes. The leading case is Bivens v. Six Unknown Named Agents, discussed in the principal case. The provisions of the Constitution whose violation has been found to be a basis for an action for damages include the First Amendment, Dellums v. Powell, 184 U.S. App. D.C. 275, 566 F.2d 167 (1977), cert. denied, 438 U.S. 916 (1978) (arrests of demonstrators, infringing their rights and rights of congressman who was to address them); Fourth Amendment (*Bivens*); Fifth Amendment (*Davis*); Sixth Amendment, Berlin Democratic Club v. Rumsfeld, 410 F. Supp. 144 (D.D.C. 1976) (electronic surveillance of attorney-consultant communications); Eighth Amendment, Carlson v. Green, 446 U.S. 14 (1980) (alleged deliberate indifference to federal prisoner's needs for medical treatment, resulting in death); and Fourteenth Amendment, Gentile v. Wallen, 562 F.2d 193 (2d Cir. 1977) (denial of due process to teacher by school board).

2. An action also may arise from violations of a state constitution. See Binette v. Sabo, 244 Conn. 23, 710 A.2d 688 (1998) (action against police officers for violations of Connecticut constitution); Widgeon v. Eastern Shore Hospital Center, 300 Md. 520, 479 A.2d 921 (1984) (action against state hospital and individuals for violations of Maryland constitution); Dorwart v. Caraway, 312 Mont. 1, 58 P.3d 128 (2002) (action for search and seizure by deputy sheriffs violating Montana constitution); Brown v. State, 89 N.Y.2d 172, 652 N.Y.S.2d 223, 674 N.E.2d 1129 (1996) (action for violations of equal protection and search and seizure provisions of New York constitution); Annot., Implied Cause of Action for Damages for Violation of Provisions of State Constitutions, 75 A.L.R.5th 619 (2000). Compare Martinez v. City of Schenectady, 97 N.Y.2d 78, 735 N.Y.S.2d 868, 761 N.E.2d 560 (2001), which rejects an action by a person who had been convicted and imprisoned because of evidence obtained by an invalid search warrant. A damages remedy was thought unnecessary. Vindication of plaintiff's rights and deterrence of constitutional violations could be achieved by exclusion of evidence in the criminal case. Also, plaintiff had not "distinguished her case from that of any criminal defendant who has been granted suppression, or reversal of a conviction, based on technical error at the trial level."

3. The constitutional tort theory of liability is subject to substantial limitations. It was held in Carlson v. Green, supra, that a "*Bivens*-type" action could be brought against prison officials even though plaintiff's allegations would support an action against the government under the Federal Tort Claims Act. But usually no constitutional tort action will be accepted when there is some statutory remedy. See Bush v. Lucas, 462 U.S. 367 (1983) (demotion of federal employee, who had statutory right of appeal and remedies of reinstatement and back pay); Schweiker v. Chilicky, 487 U.S. 412 (1988) (denial of Social Security disability benefits). It is held that an action lies only against the individuals responsible for the constitutional violations. Federal agencies, municipalities and other governmental bodies do not incur respondeat superior liability. Federal Deposit Insurance Corp. v. Meyer, 510 U.S. 471 (1994); Dean v. Gladney, 621 F.2d 1331 (5th Cir. 1980), cert. de-

nied sub nom. Dean v. County of Brazoria, Texas, 450 U.S. 983 (1981). Ashcroft v. Iqbal, 556 U.S. 662 (2009), excludes "supervisory liability" for officials who know of and acquiesce in subordinates' unconstitutional conduct. Government officers enjoy a qualified immunity, which shields them from liability when they reasonably believed their actions consistent with the rights allegedly violated. See Harlow v. Fitzgerald, 457 U.S. 800 (1982) (presidential aides); Anderson v. Creighton, 483 U.S. 635 (1987) (F.B.I. agent); Ashcroft v. al-Kidd, ___ U.S. ___ (2011) (Attorney General). Some officers enjoy absolute immunity. See Butz v. Economou, 438 U.S. 478 (1978) (persons, such as hearing examiners, performing adjudicatory functions; persons performing functions analogous to those of prosecutor, such as initiation of administrative enforcement proceedings); Nixon v. Fitzgerald, 457 U.S. 731 (1982) (President of United States). Finding "special factors counselling hesitation," the Supreme Court has held that military personnel may not sue superior officers for alleged constitutional violations, Chappell v. Wallace, 462 U.S. 296 (1983), and may not claim damages for injuries that "arise out of or are in the course of activity incident to service," United States v. Stanley, 483 U.S. 669 (1987).

4. In Correctional Services Corp. v. Malesko, 534 U.S. 61 (2001), the Supreme Court held (5–4) that *Bivens* constitutional tort liability would not be extended to a private corporation acting under federal law — in this case, a company operating correctional facilities for prisoners and other detainees under a contract with the Bureau of Prisons. Its reasons included the availability of other tort remedies and the decision in Federal Deposit Insurance Corp. v. Meyer, supra, that federal agencies, as distinct from the individuals in the agencies, were not liable for constitutional violations. The dissent would have found a cause of action on the basis that the corporation was a federal agent. See also Minneci v. Pollard, ___ U.S. ___ (2012). It still may be possible to sue individuals not employed by the federal government who acted as agents of the government. See Vector Research, Inc. v. Howard & Howard Attorneys, P.C., 76 F.3d 692 (6th Cir. 1996) (private attorneys participating in search by United States marshals).

5. Is constitutional tort liability much of a deterrent to violations of the Constitution? Does it fulfill an otherwise-unmet need for compensation? See generally Note, Two Approaches to Determine Whether an Implied Cause of Action Under the Constitution is Necessary: The Changing Scope of the *Bivens* Action, 19 Ga. L. Rev. 683 (1985); Student Project, Constitutional Torts Ten Years After *Bivens*, 9 Hofstra L. Rev. 943 (1981).

Index